CYBERSOURCE

CyberSource

CyberSourceCyberSourceCyberSourceCyberSc

CYBERSOURCE

erSourceCyberSourceCyberSourceCyberSour

FREDERIC E. DAVIS, Editor

ZIFF-DAVIS PRESS

Emeryville, California

Development Editor	Stephanie Raney
Copy Editors	Stephanie Raney, Nicole Clausing
Assistant Editor	Karen Wickre
Editorial Assistant	Michael DeLacy
Proofreaders	Carol Burbo, Vanessa Miller
Cover Design	Regan Honda
Book Design	Peter Tucker
Screen Graphics Editors	Joe Schneider, Sarah Ishida
Word Processing	Howard Blechman
Page Layout	Tony Jonick, Kelly Jonick, M.D. Barrera

Ziff-Davis Press books are produced on a Macintosh computer system with the following applications: FrameMaker®, Microsoft® Word, QuarkXPress®, Adobe Illustrator®, Adobe Photoshop®, Adobe Streamline™, MacLink®*Plus*, Aldus® FreeHand™, Collage Plus™.

If you have comments or questions or would like to receive a free catalog, call or write:
Ziff-Davis Press
5903 Christie Avenue
Emeryville, CA 94608
1-800-688-0448

ISBN 1-56276-284-2

Manufactured in the United States of America
10 9 8 7 6 5 4 3 2 1

CONTENTS

fun

Self

Community

WELCOME TO *CYBERSOURCE!*

This is a new kind of computer book.

Using this familiar analog medium, we've assembled a paper database of all sorts of cool stuff related to the wide world of computers. The way most people find out about computer products is to take a trip to the local store or scan the pages of their favorite computer magazine. But neither of these methods really shows you the full spectrum of what's possible with today's powerful, personal computers. Instead, you only get a glimpse at a small portion of the personal computer world. Well, lucky you—it's *CyberSource* to the rescue.

The basic idea for *CyberSource* was simple. A bunch of us were sitting around and someone said, "I wish there were a big book, sort of like the *Whole Earth Catalog,* but just about computers." Well, luckily, the bunch of us sitting around the room happened to be computer journalists, so we charged up our word processors and cranked out a proposal that led to this book. Then we got together all the coolest reviews and essays about nifty and neat computer stuff written by the best and brightest computer journalists, tossed in some computer trivia and humor, and voilà, here it is!

We've organized the book in a very informal manner. There are five sections, each dealing with a broad area of the cyberworld. There's Learning, because we all know that computers are good for your brain (there may be some dissension about this in your family, as there is in mine, but then again, if you really felt that way, you probably wouldn't be reading this book). The Real World covers all sorts of software and hardware that you need in order to get things done with your computer. Fun is a section devoted to the principle that computers are more effective at destroying personal productivity than any force to ever sweep the planet.

Self is for you, whether you're getting fit or working on a hobby—this covers the most personal part of personal computing. And last, but certainly not least, is Community, about that great, online universe that us Netheads fondly call cyberspace.

CyberSource is a work in progress. In other words, yes, Virginia, there will be new editions of *CyberSource*, and we'd like to ask you to help write them. *CyberSource* is meant to be a collaborative effort that shows a wide array of personal viewpoints about computer products. If you've discovered a useful—or delightfully time-wasting—piece of hardware or software, let us know and we'll beg and plead with you to write up your thoughts for the next edition of *CyberSource*.

On a final practical note, please remember that the computer industry is constantly reinventing itself. Companies are bought and sold, they rename themselves and their products, and they are forever changing and upgrading software and hardware. We've done our best to make sure that the information included here, such as addresses, phone numbers, and names is correct, but you may find that a new version of the software has been released, a phone number has changed, or a company has moved. The prices given with the reviews should be used only as ballpark amounts. If you shop around, you will almost certainly be able to find better prices in discount club stores, catalogs, or computer stores.

Hope you enjoy this book. Let us know what you think, so we can make it even better next time around. Happy computing and may your hard disk never crash!

Learning

Learning

Learning

Learning. It's not just for kids anymore. In today's fast-paced ever-changing world, the only way to survive is to make sure you're learning all the time. I'm telling you, computers got here just in time. It used to be that discoveries were few and far between, so that anyone with a college degree or a solid high-school education would pretty much know almost everything there was to know. Now, thanks to the technology and information explosion, the entire body of human knowledge doubles every few years. Your brain would explode if you tried to keep pace, so computers arrived just in the nick of time. Now you can use your computer as a friendly personal tutor and trainer, who can guide you through the rapidly expanding information universe.

Here in CyberSource: Learning, we'll show you the tip of the computer education iceberg. Some of the software we describe actually makes it fun for your kids to learn, so they'll take on extra homework without even knowing it. Luckily, you too can have a little fun while sharpening your mind and keeping abreast with the world of knowledge with programs that are designed to stimulate your senses as well as your brain. To get you started, we've selected some of the best products and programs for learners of all ages, running the gamut from history, science, and natural history, to more practical concerns, such as learning how to type or helping a high-school student hunker down for the S.A.T.

REFERENCE

Compton's Interactive Encyclopedia 1995

You want facts and polish? Use Compton's Interactive Encyclopedia 1995. Its Idea Search scours the disc's 35,000 articles for variations on a theme. If that doesn't appeal to you, the Info Pilot leads you serendipitously from Margaret Bourke-White to transcendentalism. With interface choices like newsrooms or spaceships, you can click on objects to get to the facts—or have Patrick Stewart beam in for a guided tour. And in the Editing Room, students can piece together multimedia show-and-tells.

However, its MIDI tracks sound like a wind-up toy on many sound cards, and the slow-drawing maps lack detail. Otherwise, it's a pleasure.—Ron White

> *Compton's Interactive Encyclopedia 1995*
> *Compton's NewMedia*
> (800) 862-2206
> $80

Compton's Interactive Encyclopedia

If you think the best CD-ROM encyclopedia is the one that's best for kids, get Compton's Interactive Encyclopedia. It's easy to use, and its content—5,200 feature articles and 28,000 shorter articles—is designed to be understood by children as young as six.

A unique feature in Compton's Interactive Encyclopedia is an integrated dictionary: When young readers don't understand a word, they can simply double-click on it for a definition. This product's multimedia amenities include over 7,000 pictures, 800 maps, 50 minutes of audio, and 12 animations on topics such as the amoeba, how birds fly, asexual reproduction, chemical reactions, wind carrying pollen, and nuclear fission. It also includes 60 entertaining and informative video clips on subjects as wide-ranging as cell division and the civil rights movement.

Though it doesn't support Boolean searches, Compton's Interactive Encyclopedia has nine entry paths to help you find out-of-the-way information. For example, initiating a search for the word design using the InfoPilot retrieval utility gives references to articles on industrial design and fashion design, along with the names of famous designers and architects.

> *Compton's Interactive Encyclopedia*
> *Compton's NewMedia*
> (800) 862-2206
> $149.95

The 1995 Grolier Multimedia Encyclopedia

This version of the Grolier Multimedia Encyclopedia has more videos and animation than ever before, as well as clever touches such as Pathmakers—grainy video interviews with people like Buzz Aldrin discussing exploration and Kurt Vonnegut, Jr. discussing the novel. They join the Knowledge Explorers, which are multimedia essays on broad topics such as architecture, world history, the human body, and technology.

For those who read, Grolier's information is substantial. However, it has some dubious access routes. The time line and toolbar are great for photos, videos, or maps. But within the text you can't use the keys to scroll; you have to use the mouse. More curious is "related concept searching," which adds irrelevancies to a normal topic search. For example, a simple search of the Beatles gets Buddy Holly and Joe Cocker, which makes sense. But Walter Matthau (from his role in Buddy, Buddy, as in Buddy Holly), cocker spaniels (because of Joe Cocker), and management science and animal experimentation? Why? Search me. In an age of information overload, this just adds more superfluous facts to the heap.—Ron White

Grolier Multimedia Encyclopedia

Looking for the best electronic encyclopedia? If best means the most accurate and comprehensive, choose New Grolier Multimedia Encyclopedia. This disk is based on the 21-volume Academic American Encyclopedia, many of whose 2,300 contributors are authorities in their fields.

This disk boasts 10 million words of text—more than any other electronic encyclopedia—along with comprehensive bibliographies, discographies, fact boxes, and tables. Some 7,000 of its 33,000 articles are

new or have been updated for the 1994 edition.

Grolier supplements its text with 4,000 photos and illustrations; 1,000 are new, and most of these are in color. This package also includes 53 video sequences, over 300 maps, 4 hours of multimedia features, and a good search engine. The 5,000-entry time line is linked to the encyclopedia's text, so that clicking on a time-line item will take you to a relevant article.

The latest edition offers 15 animated Multimedia Maps on such topics as the growth of American railroads, the development of the women's suffrage movement, and the progress of the Gulf War. Microsoft Encarta Multimedia Encyclopedia may offer more dazzle, but this encyclopedia provides

the most information.—Rubin Rabinovitz

New Grolier Multimedia Encyclopedia 6.0

There's a lot to see, hear, and do in the New Grolier Multimedia Encyclopedia (NGME) Release 6. But unlike its competitors, this CD-ROM is less a multimedia experience than an old-fashioned encyclopedia with some multimedia thrown in.

The completeness and scholarship of NGME's articles equals and often surpasses that of Microsoft's Encarta and Compton's Interactive Encyclopedia. Grolier has added four hours of multimedia items to this release, which opens with a graphical menu containing icons leading to key features. But NGME's timeline tells the tale: It's a thorough text list of 5,000 historical events, compared to Encarta's and Compton's more visually engaging graphical timelines with links to articles and multimedia items.

On the other hand, Grolier's searching capabilities excel, letting you use a simple dialog box and Boolean (and/or/not) operators to fine-tune information searches. Text articles appear in windows, with icons leading to related multimedia items. Double-clicking on any

word in an article leads to an index of related articles.

However, NGME's navigation tools, while easy to use, are neither as robust nor as fun as its competitors'. You can't jump directly from one article to another without first going through an index, and because the program doesn't track your path, it's difficult to backtrack to previously viewed items. This lack of basic capabilities makes NGME less suitable for casually jumping from topic to topic.

The New Grolier Multimedia Encyclopedia is a much better encyclopedia than "edutainment" vehicle. And that's not bad, especially if you believe that the function of an encyclopedia should be education, not entertainment.

Britannica CD

Back in my college days, there was only one encyclopedia you'd dare to cite in your reports—the Encyclopedia Britannica. To this day it remains the most authoritative and respected printed encyclopedia. Now the complete text—82,000 articles and 16 million references, plus the complete Merriam-Webster's Collegiate Dictionary of 70,000 definitions—is available on one

CD-ROM as Britannica CD. You won't find a more thorough reference on disc.

The Windows version is as unfrilly as the printed version. In fact, the early version I reviewed didn't have even the relatively few illustrations of the hard-copy edition. (By the time you read this, however, a new illustrated and speed-enhanced CD version will be available.) But searches are fast and the list of articles that match a search item are scored for relevance.

One source of real irritation accompanies the Britannica CD—a copy protection dongle that plugs into a parallel port, without which you can't spin the disc. But when a CD-ROM costs nearly $1,000, you can expect a publisher to get a bit paranoid.—Ron White

The World Book New Illustrated Information Finder

Just when you thought you had only three CD-ROM encyclopedia choices— Compton's Interactive Encyclopedia, Microsoft's Encarta, and the New Grolier Multimedia Encyclopedia—a fourth contender has entered the ring. The World Book New Illustrated Information Finder has emerged from its pictureless DOS cocoon, with

toward it, too. Whatever the case, the conclusion is the same: It's possible that we can no longer keep up with the

LearningLearningLea

a Windows interface providing push-button access to articles, tables, maps, historical events, and research topics. The visual redesign transforms this research tool, making it much more appealing, but unfortunately still short on multimedia pizzazz.

Information Finder has been around since 1988, but previous releases were all text. The new release still offers speedy access to the complete text of both The World Book Encyclopedia and The World Book Dictionary, but it also boasts more than 3,000 captioned illustrations and 260 maps. Articles frequently contain one or more pictures that you can view in a small window while you read, or in a larger window over the text. A Gallery button in the top-of-screen control bar browses pictures without text, organized by topic.

Like other online encyclopedias, World Book's lets you search for information by topic or keyword. Type in a term, and Information Finder swiftly shows an appropriate article, highlighting each instance of the search word. Clicking on the Results button displays a list of other related articles and resources, ranked by the number of search hits or alphabetically. You can perform Boolean searches, too.

Once you've got the article you want on screen, you can double-click on any word therein to get a dictionary definition, or click on specially marked text to jump to a cross-reference or related arti-

cle. A notepad holds your personal comments and article excerpts. This is useful if you're using the disc as a research tool; you can also save its contents to disc as a text file for use with other applications.

The disc's bookmark function lets you mark up to 25 passages for later reference. Additional options let you browse topics and articles organized by subject area; scroll quickly through articles by viewing their outlines; and print articles and maps.

Unlike Compton's, Microsoft's, and Grolier's encyclopedias, Information Finder lacks animated graphics, motion-video clips, sound, and music, so if multimedia entertainment is your first criterion, World Book's disc will disappoint you. On the other hand, if you want a powerful, user-friendly general research tool, Information Finder's comprehensive, accurate content is a fact-finder's dream come true.—Carol S. Holzberg

The World Book New Illustrated Information Finder
World Book Educational Products
101 Northwest Point Blvd.
Elk Grove Village, IL 60007
(800) 433-6580; (708) 290-5300
$389

🖐 71 percent of America's 97 million households have children under 18. That's why, according to the International Workstation Group, today's $500 million entertainment software market will blossom into a $9.1 billion multimedia market by 1998.

Microsoft Bookshelf 1994 Edition

Microsoft Bookshelf has plenty of savvy no matter what your business, thanks to the wide spectrum covered by its seven reference books: The Columbia Dictionary of Quotations, The American Heritage Dictionary of the English Language, The Original Roget's Thesaurus, The People's Chronology, The Concise Columbia Encyclopedia, The Hammond World Atlas, and The World Almanac and Book of Facts 1994. Animation, video, and sound clips have spiced up the books, but the emphasis here is still on that common currency of communication: words.

If the fact, word, map, or inspiration you want can't be found in either Bookshelf or Business Library, you aren't looking hard enough. And in Bookshelf, that's difficult to

imagine. A revamped Windows interface makes searches a snap and integrates Bookshelf with your other applications. A separate program, QuickShelf, creates a Windows toolbar that stays on top of your other applications so you can activate the Bookshelf reference materials from within any Windows application.—Ron White

Microsoft Bookshelf
Microsoft Corp.
One Microsoft Way
Redmond, WA 98052-6399
(800) 426-9400; (206) 882-8080
$79.95

Microsoft Bookshelf

Connect a search engine to a bunch of reference works and let users retrieve data from a number of these works in a single pass: That's the inspired idea that made Microsoft Bookshelf a CD-ROM hit back in 1987. The

same idea is at the heart of Microsoft Bookshelf 1994 Edition, along with some of the original reference works: The Concise Columbia Encyclopedia (15,000 entries and 1,300 images), the Hammond Intermediate World Atlas (more than 100 political and topographic maps), and the World Almanac and Book of Facts (recently updated for 1994).

New to Bookshelf is The People's Chronology, a year-by-year survey of historical, cultural, and scientific events. One somewhat questionable enhancement is the substitution of the 18,000-entry Concise Columbia Dictionary of Quotations for the classic Bartlett's Familiar Quotations, with its 22,500 entries.

The American Heritage Dictionary now has many more entries, but its operation has become more cumbersome. Roget's Thesaurus is also bigger, with 250,000 synonyms, though many terms are not exact synonyms. Based on the sheer wealth of reference material included, Microsoft Bookshelf 1994 Edition is very much a program worth getting.

Microsoft Bookshelf
Microsoft Corp.
(800) 426-9400
$99

THE PERFECT READ

The Standard Periodical Directory on CD-ROM

Whether you're looking to equip a library or tracking

taskmaster we've created. In short, computers are killing us. 🖳 They're taking away our time and damaging us phys-

ningLearningLearning

down a niche publication, Oxbridge Communications's CD-ROM version of its Standard Periodical Directory (SPD) offers data you won't find on any newsstand. The SPD is a regularly updated reference classic that provides details such as circulation, key personnel, and synopses for over 85,000 North American periodicals.

The disc's $695 price tag weeds out casual users. More serious researchers will find the CD-ROM a valuable tool; they'll also find the Folio Views 3.0 interface rough around the edges.

Search filters let you select publications by format, frequency of publication, whether the mailing list is for sale, and so on. You can also scroll through the full listing or a hot-linked title index, or build Boolean query searches. The latter can be complex or simple, but are limited to "and" and "or" combinations—the search engine lacks a "not" function. Nor does the disc support proximity searching, which is the ability to search for two words near each other.

Still, the SPD's searches are adequate for simple hunts. The program offers words from its list as you type.

Wild cards broaden requests, and extensive hypertext links make exploring easy. Double-clicking on green text leads to pop-up windows; on red text, to another place in the database. And double-clicking on any valid word or selected text range uses it as the basis for a query. Besides navigational buttons, the program offers bookmarks, highlighters, and pop-up notes. You can also gather selected records and print lists.

While the database remains on CD-ROM, the software can maintain separate hard-disk files for different users. These work like different versions of the program, with personal notes attached to records, modifications of existing entries, and additions to the database. A Windows-based setup program, a comprehensive but obtuse 200-page user's manual, a 10-page quick-reference booklet, and an online hypertext manual all help you make the most of the SPD's features.

Unless you're the next J. Pierpont Morgan, this disc is too costly to make it to the CD-ROM rack of your home PC. But for those involved with print media, it's a perfect match.—Philip F.H. Rose

The Standard Periodical Directory on CD-ROM Oxbridge Communications Inc. 150 Fifth Ave. Suite 302 New York, NY 10011 (800) 955-0231; (212) 741-0231 $695

MULTIMEDIA CUTS BOTH WAYS

Microsoft Encarta

We love new technology. We also hate new technology.

The reason for the paradox is simple: When you work with something on the cut-

ting edge, you never know which way it's going to cut. If you're fortunate, it slices through your work, saving time and sometimes even improving the quality of what you do. If you're unlucky, new technology can cut you, leaving you angry, frustrated, and disappointed. Some technologies do both, delivering incredible benefits one minute and inducing furious frustration the next.

Take, for example, multimedia software. Everybody's talking about multimedia, and the talk sounds pretty good. You know the spiel: Soon, all our desktop computers will bristle with huge monitors, CD-ROM drives, and crystal-clear speakers. At the office, we'll participate in video conferences while

working on 3-D spreadsheets, with CNN rolling in a corner of the screen and Beatles Muzak playing softly in the background. At home, we'll gather around our electronic hearths and watch in delight as our children learn from computerized tutors—programs so friendly and informative that we'll shake our heads and wonder how we ever survived the days of merely human teachers.

Never mind for now that, to us, this dream is partly exciting and partly horrifying. Those who promote it point to the rapid increase in power and decrease in price of multimedia hardware as proof that these days are not far away.

What they miss is a simple fact of the computer era:

Software almost always lags behind hardware. Whenever any type of hot new hardware appears, the first programs to run on that hardware are typically tired translations of existing programs, plus some early experiments that are at best unsatisfying and at worst downright annoying.

Consider Encarta, Microsoft's encyclopedia on CD-ROM. We recently bought CD-ROM drives for the PCs our kids use, so we naturally ended up with copies of Encarta. After using it for a while and watching the kids play with it, we've found Encarta to be a useful but often frustrating tool. It makes a great demo; it's basically as good as any other CD encyclopedia. But it leaves you wanting much more than it delivers.

The basic mechanisms of Encarta are usable enough: a few cute icons, a few menus, and the dreaded but possibly unavoidable giant scrolling table of contents. The trouble starts when you find something you want to investigate.

Look up elephants, for instance, and you'll see still photos that are bearable but frankly worse than those in a real encyclopedia. Full-motion video clips, the much-anticipated step up from photos, are rare and short. Check out Martin Luther King, Jr., and you get a black-and-white photo and a sound bite of the line, "I have a dream," but no more.

Why not let you play the whole speech, or at least read

ically as well as emotionally. The most obvious example of injury is carpal tunnel syndrome. This is where my wife comes

LearningLearningLearningLea

the text of the rest? Print encyclopedias typically offer more detail and are ultimately more satisfying.

On the other hand, Encarta also offers occasional glimpses of the kinds of information that multimedia presentations can convey much more effectively than books. One of the best entries is an animated explanation of the way bees signal to their hive the location of newly found flowers. Just a couple of minutes' animation communicates this information more clearly than pages of text in a printed encyclopedia.

So why doesn't Encarta do more of the same? Why don't more of its entries offer us the chance to watch and even play in ways not possible otherwise?

Imagine an entry on basic physical mechanics that includes an online experiment table where you can dial the force of gravity, the slope of a ramp, and the coefficient of friction to see just how each can affect a ball rolling down the ramp. Imagine exploring harmonic motion with different springs and weights, or showing and hearing Doppler phase shifts.

No printed encyclopedia can do that. Unfortunately, at the moment, neither can one on CD-ROM.

Encarta is a piece of first-generation software, a product designed more to plant a stake in fertile marketing territory than to realize the full potential of the medium. Microsoft predictably and understandably wants a big

piece of the multimedia pie, and it can't afford to wait to enter the market until it has something truly exciting to offer.

To be fair, Encarta is hardly the only multimedia product with these deficiencies. Pretty much all the CD-ROMs we've seen suffer from these or similar problems. This whole technology is still cutting us more than helping us.

Despite that, we did buy our kids those CD-ROM drives, and we are hopeful. We're eagerly awaiting a wave of second-generation CDs that take full advantage of the potential of multimedia. If you see any, let us know. If you're a vendor with a product you think makes this step forward, drop us a copy and we'll check it out.

And then we'll report back and let you know which way it really cuts.—Mark L. Van Name and Bill Catchings

Microsoft Encarta
Microsoft Corp.
One Microsoft Way
Redmond, WA 98052-6399
(800) 426-9400

Microsoft Encarta '95

Microsoft Encarta '95 has an interface as slick as anything this side of a St. Louis card shark—and at times just as bewildering. Oh, it's pretty, all right. There's hardly a page of text that isn't accompanied by exemplary multimedia: 6,500 photos, 100 videos, 83 animations, and hundreds of maps, graphs, and sound bites. It's fun to

browse through, but if you're looking for something specific for that term paper due tomorrow, the ride is rough. So many menus and icons pop out from every direction that Encarta seems to be saying it has nothing to match what you're looking for even though you know it damn well does—you saw it just three program crashes ago. (I should point out that Encarta freezes up frequently and gobbles system resources. If Microsoft ever faces an antitrust suit alleging its application group gets secret help from the OS programmers, the company lawyers can use this disc as proof positive that it doesn't.)

Sometimes it's possible to be too pretty. Microsoft Encarta '95 needs more information and less interface.

Microsoft Encarta
Microsoft Home
(800) 426-9400; (206) 882-8080
$99.95

Microsoft Encarta

Searching for a CD-ROM encyclopedia with killer multimedia features? Look no further: Microsoft Encarta Multimedia Encyclopedia is tops in this category. No CD-ROM encyclopedia can match its numbers: over 7,300 images, 8 hours of audio, and 100 video clips and narrated animations—plus numerous photographs, maps, charts, foreign-language samples, instrument sounds, animal cries, and a time line. You can watch demonstrations of how

an internal combustion engine works and how bees use dance to communicate. You can also enjoy the works of Leonardo daVinci, Picasso, and Rembrandt, or listen to excerpts from Bach, Beethoven, and Mozart.

Encarta's 26,000-article text never reaches the high standard set by its multimedia features, but no other encyclopedia provides the full CD-ROM experience offered by this disc.

Microsoft Encarta
Microsoft Corp.
(800) 426-9400
$139

CD-ROM is going to make a lot of word lovers happy. Though no multimedia extravaganza—it omits all illustrations and supplements—this text-based disc has all the meat of the book version, containing a full 315,000 entries. The dictionary's search engine (provided in DOS, Windows, and Macintosh versions, all with modest hardware requirements) makes looking up words a breeze. In addition to typing in a word, you can look up any part of its definition by selecting it and clicking on the Lookup button. Other useful options include the ability to browse forward through the dictionary, to

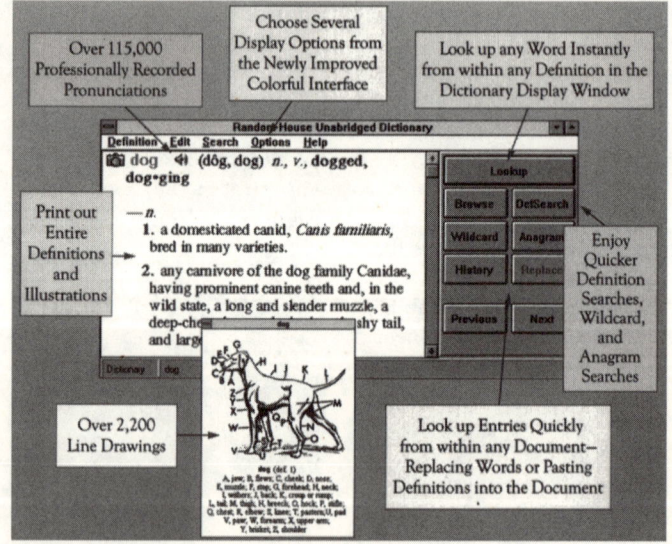

AN UNABRIDGED DELIGHT
Random House Unabridged Dictionary

The Random House Unabridged Dictionary on

review the last 20 words looked up, and (in the Windows version) to set the type size of the definitions displayed. There's even an anagram function that constructs all possible words

ningLearningLearningLearning

from the letters that make up the word in question.

You can also perform wildcard searches or construct complicated Boolean searches that find all words whose definitions meet your requirements. Best of all, you can define a hotkey that lets you access the dictionary while editing documents in your word processor. While it cannot compare to the magisterial Oxford English Dictionary on CD-ROM, this costs a tenth as much and is just as much fun to use. If you love words, this is a must-buy.—John Gliedman

Random House Unabridged Dictionary
Random House Reference and Electronic Publishing
201 E. 50th St.
New York, NY 10022
(800) 726-0600
$100 (CD-ROM only); $200 (bundled with book)

Jargon: An Informal Dictionary of Computer Terms

Jargon is a rather unconventional dictionary that goes above and beyond most dictionaries, certainly those specific to computers. Perhaps the most useful aspect of the book is the inclusion of an index. If you don't know much about a topic, how else are you expected to find all the relevant cross-references? The index is a great way to discover all there is to know about any given term.

Best of all, once your students get to the right location, they're not confounded by cryptic definitions. Williams takes confusing technical concepts and brings them to a comprehensible level without sounding condescending.

Wherever relevant, graphic images are included to help explain a term. For instance, the textual description of *palette* is followed by a drawing of the type of palette—complete with 10 tools and a close box—that you would find when using SuperPaint.

Be forewarned: Give your students lots of time. They—and you—are going to be tempted to read this dictionary cover to cover. The book goes beyond being informative—it's an absolute treat. You're sure to be smiling after you've encountered the cartoon that shows two men standing beside a Rolodex three times their height with the caption "…And this was our first mainframe." The book covers more than just the serious terms—you'll find the definition of *propeller head* nestled between *prompt* and *proportional spacing*, illustrated with a photo of Williams's brother, Jeffrey, wearing the classic propellered beanie.

For those who want to test their degree of computer knowledge, there's a crossword puzzle at the end of the book. And direct shoppers will treasure the 15-page appendix entitled, "How to Read a Computer Ad." This section includes an extremely

Bridging Language Gaps in Cyberspace

While 1995 may turn out to be the year of the family PC, the United Nations's Year of the Family has already begun. In recognition, teenagers from Canada, France, Germany, Italy, Mexico, Spain, and the U.S. are participating in a cross-cultural technology project sponsored by the Global SchoolNet Foundation. The Family Write project connects kids around the world via e-mail. They'll use translation software to bridge the communication gap.

The assignment is to take oral histories of family members, write reports in their native languages, and exchange findings with pen pals around the world. To help get the project off the ground, Globalink, of Fairfax, Virginia, donated its expertise in language translation software and its Language Assistant software series.

The project represents a new direction for translation software at a time when it's simple to fetch online information from around the world via the Internet. Translation software is reaching beyond its roots in documentation to the localization of the sea of online information. Michael Tacelosky, CEO of Globalink, which bought out competitor Microtac last year, is now working to set a standard for language translation much as Creative Labs set the Sound Blaster standard for PC-based audio.

If Globalink succeeds, you'll be able to buy an e-mail package or word processor that's translation-enabled and then plug in a translator. The two will be integrated much as spell-checkers and word processors are today. Globalink is taking integration a step further by saving you the trouble of having to import and export a file from and to the translation program. Instead, if you receive an e-mail message in Russian, you can translate it from within the e-mail program.

While there's no questioning the need for improvements in translation algorithms, the technology continues to evolve. Developers are adding vocabulary, understanding collocation of words, and writing sophisticated rules that recognize the difference between "fired a clay pot" and "fired an employee."

Developers at Globalink have already defined the applications programming interface and expect to have a development kit ready for software vendors when Windows 95 ships. Companies interested in helping build the Global SchoolNet can contact Yvonne Andres at (619) 931-5934.■

useful chart of terms, along with their aliases. For instance, the chart shows that *CPU* could also be listed as *Central Processing Unit*, *Microprocessor*, or *Processor*.— Mindy Basser

Jargon: An Informal Dictionary of Computer Terms
By Robin Williams with Steve Cummings
Peachpit Press Inc.
2414 Sixth St. Berkeley, CA 94710
(510) 548-4393
$22

Webster's Interactive Encyclopedia

The best thing about this British import Windows CD is that the audio help is spoken by an Englishwoman, which makes you feel cultured even when you aren't learning a thing. Webster's Interactive Encyclopedia would make great reading for a multimedia PC in your bathroom. Every item in this *USA Today* of encyclopedias is short. And the multimedia, while copious, is hard to find. The best thing about the interface is its clear, logical Boolean search window. But that nice touch is canceled out because the disc tells you how many articles matched the search but doesn't display them. You have to then ask it to display the list—handy if you just want to count articles without going to the trouble of actually learning anything.

Webster's Interactive Encyclopedia
Cambrix Publishing
(800) 992-8781; (818) 992-8484
$39

McGraw-Hill Encyclopedia of World Economies on CD-ROM

It used to be that the McGraw-Hill Multimedia Encyclopedia of Science and Technology was my favorite dweeb's CD. But this CD-ROM is even dweebier. It's only in DOS; there's no multimedia; it uses color so sparingly that it might as well be monochrome; it barely knows how to use a mouse; and it's nothing but statistics, statistics, statistics. Don't get me wrong. I know there are people for whom it's very important to find out that the 1993 monthly wage in Albania was $83 (up from a low of $39 in 1991). The CD is chock full of economics info, and for people who live on that type of data, this disc is surely a godsend. I just don't want any of them to corner me at a party.

McGraw-Hill Encyclopedia of World Economies on CD-ROM
McGraw-Hill
(800) 262-4729
$345

Oxford English Dictionary

The 20-volume *Oxford English Dictionary, Second Edition*, is the second-best dictionary ever compiled. The best is the Oxford English Dictionary, Second Edition, on CD-ROM.

This disc contains the full text of the printed version: 616,500 words, 137,000 pronunciations, 249,000 etymologies, 2.4 million illustrative quotations, and 577,000 cross-references. Data access is provided by a powerful search engine and a query-language retrieval program that let you gather data in ways you can't with printed dictionaries.

You can conduct wildcard searches, jump to cross-references, filter search results by date or part of speech, and conduct Boolean searches. For more complex searches, however, you'll need to invest some time in learning the program's query language.

This product is a word lover's dream, but in view of the $895 price, many word lovers won't see that dream become a reality.

Oxford English Dictionary
Oxford University Press
(800) 334-4249 ext. 7390
$895

Library of the Future

You'd need an 18-foot floor-to-ceiling bookcase for printed editions of the 1,750 volumes in the Library of the Future, Third Edition. What makes the program doubly useful is a search engine that lets you sift through its many works of fiction, poetry, history, politics, science, religion, and ethics.

Library of the Future,
Third Edition
World Library Inc.
(800) 443-0238
$149.95

The Deluxe American Heritage Dictionary The Random House Unabridged Dictionary The Oxford English Dictionary

Searching an online dictionary sure beats thumbing through the pages of a conventional reference book, especially when you're not quite sure what word you're looking for. Mac users now have a trio of such online works to choose from—the Deluxe American Heritage Dictionary comes on 18 floppy disks, and the Random House Unabridged Dictionary and the Oxford English Dictionary (OED) each come on CD-ROM.

Although all three online dictionaries share the advantage of hypertext searches, each has distinctive strengths and weaknesses. The $895 Oxford English Dictionary on CD-ROM is clearly the odd man out. Tailor-made for academics, the scholarly work contains half a million words and more than two million quotations, making it ideal

of carpal tunnel syndrome until a few years back when it started to crop up all over the place. Most news organizations

ningLearningLearning

for distribution on CD-ROM. By purchasing the OED on CD-ROM, you save considerable money and shelf space over the $2,750, 20-volume printed edition.

The $129 Deluxe American Heritage Dictionary and the $79 Random House Unabridged Dictionary are fairly inexpensive, but their content differs. The more comprehensive Random House contains about 315,000 entries, and the American Heritage contains about 200,000. Each work has a distinct editorial bias. The Random House aims to be the most complete and up-to-date compendium of American English. The American Heritage trades completeness for usefulness—it's easier to read, offering a more lively and less lexicological style than the Random House. Its interface is also better designed, allowing you to access features by using fewer steps.

All three dictionaries support wildcard searches, which come in handy when you're not sure how to spell a word. A ? substitutes for a single letter (bl?ck finds black and block, for example); you can broaden the search with an asterisk, which substitutes any number of letters. In the American Heritage, for example, comput* yields 41 possibilities, ranging from computability to computerizing. The American Heritage allows wildcard searches from its standard entry box, but the other two require you

to enter a command that brings up a dialog box.

All three dictionaries also let you search the entire contents of the dictionary, using keywords. The American Heritage and Random House let you build simple queries (the American Heritage also includes a scrolling list of categories you can use to narrow the search), and the OED comes with a full-blown query language.

Keyword searches can be time-consuming. A simple search to locate words with definitions containing computer and person took close to a minute and resulted in 34 entries with the American Heritage. The Random House found 73 entries but took more than four minutes. The OED retrieved 27 words in a blazing 15 seconds but required a formal query.

In fact, the OED's search capabilities are stunning in their speed and thoroughness but, like much of this lofty work, beyond the needs of most users. You can search the entire text of the dictionary or single out definitions, etymologies, or quotations. You can search by date, author, title, or parts of speech. You can even do proximity searches that retrieve all entries with definitions containing a specific word that occurs within 32 words of another. However, you can't do a comparative search without building a query—a time-consuming process.

Most features of the American Heritage and

Random House dictionaries are self-explanatory. The Random House package doesn't even provide a manual, although its online help and Balloon Help is complete. The American Heritage teams online help and Balloon Help with a small but helpful 32-page manual. The OED comes with online help, a 100-page manual, and a 70-page guide to the dictionary.

Of the three online dictionaries reviewed here, the OED is the most remarkable and monumental, but its high price and unattractive interface limit its appeal.

For those who haven't purchased a CD-ROM drive, the floppy-disk-based Deluxe American Heritage Dictionary is a solid work that's extremely simple to use. It is also an ideal tool for PowerBook users. The CD-ROM-based Random House Unabridged Dictionary is more complete than the American Heritage, but its interface isn't as well designed.—Clay Andres

American Heritage Dictionary Deluxe Third Edition
Softkey International, Inc.
Cambridge, MA
(617) 494-1200
$129

Oxford English Dictionary (Second Edition) on CD-ROM
Oxford University Press
New York, NY
(800) 451-7556; (212) 679-7300
$895

Random House Unabridged Dictionary, Second Edition
Random House Reference and

Electronic Publishing
New York, NY
(800) 733-3000; (410) 848-1900
$79

FUN-FILLED FACTS

Merriam-Webster's Dictionary for Kids

There's something about Merriam-Webster's Dictionary for Kids that tells you right away it isn't designed with adult users in mind. It may be the bold, brightly colored graphics, or it may be something in the program's brash attitude. The Search icon, for instance, initiates its surprisingly fast lookup procedures with a loud quack. Other features allow you to click on a Mouth icon to hear a word pronounced or on a Part of Speech icon to learn the difference between an adverb and a verb. While there are over 32,000 entries, only about 500 are enhanced with photographs, drawings, or animations.

The five games included on this CD-ROM are all attractive, slightly unhinged variations on popular themes. Alphabet Soup, for example, is a word search game in which the host (and hint-giver) is a cockroach. Other games include variations on Concentration, Hangman, Cryptograms, and Laddergrams.

Unfortunately, there are no links between the dictionary and the games, so you can't

click on a word to bring up its definition while playing. Further, the exaggerated laughter you hear if you give up in a game hardly constitutes positive reinforcement. —Barry Brenesal, Charles Taft, and J.W. Olsen

Merriam-Webster's Dictionary for Kids
Mindscape Inc.
(415) 883-3000
$49.95

Morgan's Trivia Machine

Morgan is a chimp with class. He and his friends—Bernaardvark, Skatergator, Kangaruth, Alicat, and Hip-Hop Hippo—invite you into Morgan's tree house, where you'll learn about science, geography, and other topics in a humorous environment.

Once you're in the tree house, you can play a variety of trivia-based games. Morgan's Trivia Machine, the HAM 9000, offers some important choices for game setup, including the number of characters who will play, the identities of the characters who will be playing on-screen for you, the skill level of each player, the subject covered, and your choice of three games to play.

The first game, Score More, challenges you to answer more questions correctly than your opponent to earn more points; the second, Mountain Climbing on Mars, challenges you to ascend the slopes by answering questions correctly. The third game, Quizzy Wig, is a game

now have committees to deal with the problem because it has become a plague in the newsroom. People have been pound-

LearningLearningLea

show in which answering correctly wins you a zany wig and the chance to see your character wear it.

The games are fun for both kids and adults, thanks to adjustable difficulty levels for each player. Questions range from simple to challenging to somewhat bizarre. In addition to more than 1,000 questions, there are photographs, videos, and animations that all add to the fun. Climb on up into Morgan's tree house, meet his friends, play the games, and enjoy!—Barry Brenesal, Charles Taft, and J.W. Olsen

Morgan's Trivia Machine
Morgan Interactive Inc.
(800) 245-4525
$34.95

Rescue the Scientists

Once you've coaxed it to run on your computer, both you and your kids will love Rescue the Scientists. Your kids will delight at the impressive graphics, the scrolling arcade action, and the special guest appearance by actor Christopher Lloyd. You'll be happy knowing that they're learning science and history while having fun.

The story is simple. Aliens have traveled through time and space to capture Earth's foremost scientists and give them amnesia. Your young hero or heroine must find the scientists and help return their memory. To succeed, your child must work through level after level of challenges, along the way

solving entertaining and informative puzzles—from jigsaws to phrase scrambles, word searches, and more— and collecting scientific artifacts that will jog the victims' memories.

The graphics and sound are top-notch, as is the educational content. The program also earns an A for its political correctness; kids can choose to play either a male or female character, and the scientists are of varied ethnicities. But we wish we had found Einstein ourselves before trying to install this memory-intensive and at times temperamental game. Luckily, the installation effort pays off: Rescue the Scientists will please your kids as much as you. Just don't tell them it's so educational!—Barry Brenesal, Charles Taft, and J.W. Olsen

Rescue the Scientists
Compton's NewMedia
(619) 929-2500
$49.95

Kids who use computers, reports Opinion Research Corp., watch less TV. Even more important, this survey found that 90 percent of parents are satisfied that computers help improve reading, writing, and math skills.

Reader Rabbit's Interactive Journey

Think of Reader Rabbit's Interactive Reading Journey as the Swiss Army knife of reading programs; it combines phonics and sight-reading and includes animation, music, and spoken words—all of which will keep your child amused while she learns to read. In this program, children travel with Reader Rabbit, his friend Mat the Mouse, and Sam the Lion through 20 Letter Lands. Each Letter Land has a Skill House, where children learn phonics and words through games and activities, and two Storybooks, which introduce new words and offer simple sentences. When kids click on hot spots in each Letter Land, they discover sounds and animations that begin with the letter being learned.

The curriculum for Reader Rabbit's Interactive Reading Journey is based on the highly successful Southwest Regional Laboratory for Educational Research and Development Beginning Reading program and gives children a whole year's worth of reading activity. The program allows parents to tailor lessons to their children's needs by determining the percentage of correct answers required to advance to the next level, how many Letter Lands are available at one time, and whether the Interactive Journey characters or the child reads the Storybooks.

The program presents new material and reinforces what has already been learned in a supportive, nonthreatening manner that encourages children to discover and learn while they journey down the road that will lead to a lifetime of reading pleasure.— Charles Taft

Reader Rabbit's Interactive
Reading Journey
The Learning Company
(800) 852-2255.
$99

Same & Different

Just because they can't yet read doesn't mean your little ones can't use the computer. With spoken help, colorful animations, and some very recognizable characters, Same & Different is one package that can turn your computer into a preschool classroom.

The first title in the Jim Henson's Muppets/Brighter Child Software series, Same & Different offers pre-readers 20 activities to help them master object recognition and differentiation skills. The focus of each of these tasks is either to identify objects that are the same or to single out the one object in a group that is different. While they're matching similar objects, kids also learn important skills such as letter and word recognition and street safety.

All of the lessons are taught by some very familiar faces: the Muppets. Kermit is looking for teammates to play baseball; Miss Piggy

needs help sorting through a closet of mismatched shoes, and Rowlff has to match up letters and signs.

Add a sound card to your PC and pre-readers can use this program by themselves. The directions for each activity are read aloud when a new screen appears, and sound effects indicate whether the child has chosen correctly or incorrectly. If they've forgotten what the goal of the exercise is, kids can click in the direction box at any time to hear the instructions again. Each correct response triggers an amusing animation sequence; incorrect responses trigger a sound effect and a prompt either to try again or to have the program display the correct answer.

The vivid illustrations, entertaining animations, and familiar Muppet characters in Same & Different will keep kids amused for hours. And while they are playing with their animated friends, they'll be learning some valuable skills.—Gayle C. Ehrenman

Same & Different
American Education Publishing
(614) 848-8866
$19.99

ing on keyboards for years, but never before was this weird problem an epidemic. Years ago, a reporter would slowly

ingLearningLearningLearning

Lenny's MusicToons

Lenny may seem like just another penguin to you, but to your kids, he'll seem like a musical genius. After all, Lenny is no ordinary penguin; he's the bird who can take kids aged 4 and up through the land of MusicToons, where just about anything can happen.

This musical cartoon adventure helps children learn musical skills and concepts through exciting animations, interactive exercises, and fun arcade games. The graphics are vivid, the music pulsing, and the learning deftly hidden beneath the fun.

But your kids won't care about any of that. All they'll care about is staging their own concerts to debut in Lenny's Theatre and producing their own music videos for PTV (Penguin Television). While they're choosing the stars, and types of music for their videos, kids will also be learning about tempo and composing. They can even record their video produc-

tions and play them back for their adoring parents.

For more musical fun, kids can try their hands at Pitch Attack—a shoot-'em-up game in which hitting the right key on the keyboard saves the world—or Lenny's Puzzle Book—where unscrambling a musical puzzle saves Lenny's cat from Gonzo Gorilla, a simian gone wrong.

After Lenny, your kids may even want to practice the piano.—Gayle C. Ehrenman

Lenny's MusicToons
Paramount Interactive
(415) 813-8040
$49.95

Bug Adventure

You knew they were creepy and disgusting, but did you also know that aphids are the sweetest-tasting bugs and cockroaches the fastest? You would if you spent some time

with Bug Adventure. This latest offering in the Knowledge Adventure line takes kids aged 3 through 8 into the flitting, flying world of bugs—without bringing the critters into your world.

Kids have six multimedia activities to choose from: the Bug Storybook, where they can read along with a bug tale; the Honeycomb Theatre, where they can watch bug movies with an animated insect audience; the Bug Reference, the heart of the program and where the study material is housed; the identification games Can You Find Me? and Who Am I?; and the 3-D Bug Basement, where they can don silly glasses to view full-screen bug images.

Each of these areas is just a mouse click away, thanks to an amusing and intuitive graphical interface. (One of the highlights is a flyswatter used for returning to the main menu.) There's lots of learning to be had here, but kids will just think they're having fun.

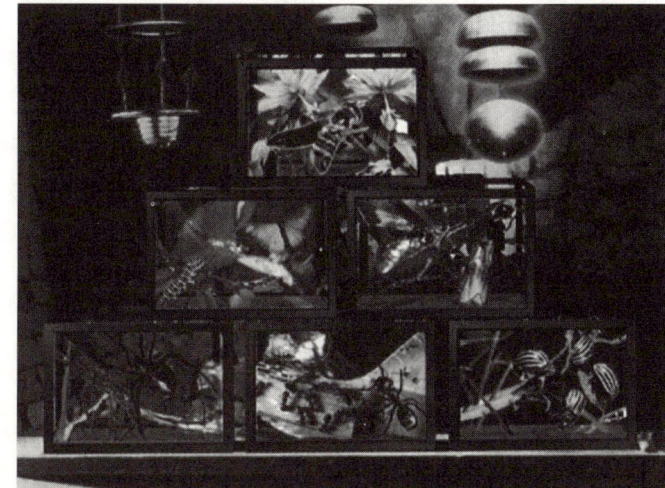

You may be repulsed by the videos and 3-D pictures, but chances are good that there's a budding entomologist in your midst who would really benefit from a Bug Adventure.

Bug Adventure
Knowledge Adventure Inc.
(818) 542-4200
$69.95

Putt-Putt Goes to the Moon

Sometimes sequels are every bit as good as the originals. Such is the case with this latest adventure for Putt-Putt, the talking purple car who made his debut in Putt-Putt Joins the Parade.

As the latest title suggests, our pal Putt-Putt winds up on the moon—thanks to a freak accident at a fireworks factory. His little friend, Rover (an abandoned lunar-terrain vehicle), and their adventures together will keep kids aged 3 through 8 clicking and laughing from start to finish.

Like the first package in the series, this is an animated adventure game that encour-

ages kids to click every object they come across. Some clicks will activate witty animations, such as a rocket launching, while others will help kids acquire the pieces they need to build the rocket that will transport Putt-Putt and Rover back to Earth. Along the way, your kids will be treated to beautiful anima-

tions, fun sound effects, and talking characters—including some two-headed ice cream peddlers and assorted other Moon People.

This may seem like just a game, but while kids are pointing and clicking, they are developing motor skills, as well as problem-solving abilities. They're also learning about tolerance and cooperation, but you don't have to tell them that.

Putt-Putt Goes to the Moon
Humongous Entertainment Inc.
(206) 485-1212
$49.95

crank out a story. It would be edited with a pencil and sent to a copy boy who would take it to an editor or to someone

LearningLearningLea

Wavetable Promises and Pitfalls

All wavetable sound sets are not created equal. Because Yamaha first decided to allocate only 2MB of ROM for wavetable samples in the specification for its OPL-4 wavetable chip, 2MB quickly became the de facto standard size for storing General MIDI's 128 instrument and 51 drum patches. The problem is that it's difficult to cram this many samples into 2MB of ROM without compromising the samples' sonic fidelity.

As a result, several ad hoc methods are now used to pack samples into limited ROM. And some net better sound quality than others. A brute-force way for sound-card manufacturers to solve the space problem is simply to cut down the number of sample bits used for each patch.

Consequently, some sound cards sample sounds at 12 bits and add four "dummy" bits to each sample cycle. Although 16-bit data is ultimately passed on to the digital-to-analog converter, the resulting sound could hardly be called CD-quality.

Another workaround of the 2MB ROM barrier is to compress the samples. Many sound cards, including Turtle Beach's, utilize mu-law or A-law compression algorithms. However, these are better suited for compressing voice, not music data. The preferred compression method is to use Adaptive Pulse Code Modulation (ADPCM). ADPCM is used in the Sierra chip set aboard the Diamond Sonic Sound,

though other factors kept this card's MIDI performance from being up to par in our evaluations here.

A third method is to divide the complex waveform envelope of a sample into its component parts (Attack, Sustain, Decay, Release), and to loop, or repeat, the sample to simulate a naturally sustaining and decaying sound. Sound cards using the ICS chip sets often employ this method. The output can sound realistic, as was the case with Turtle Beach's ICS-based Monterey, which also incorporates a mu-law compression algorithm. However, the resulting sound is never as convincing as a sample of the entire wave envelope.

Until sound-card manufacturers choose to break through Yamaha's arbitrary 2MB ROM barrier,

compromises like these will continue to detract from the quality promised by MIDI wavetable synthesis.

This was supposed to be the year wavetable synthesis replaced the toy-like sounds of FM synthesis on most mainstream sound cards. But while wavetable synthesis is a quantum leap above FM, its current implementation on PC sound cards suffers from a number of limitations, chief among them being that with a ROM-based wavetable card, you aren't free to assemble your own sample library as you can with a professional studio-quality sampler.

It won't be long, however, before programmable-RAM wavetable cards give you this ability. Relatively simple versions of this feature

are already available on the Turtle Beach Monterey and Sound Blaster AWE32, and Ensoniq plans to ship a programmable-RAM card in early 1995.

Over the next year, you'll begin to see much more sophisticated implementations of programmable RAM. New features will include multisampled patches that dedicate different samples to specific pitch ranges, and the ability to use each note's volume level to determine which sample to play. The latter is especially useful for instruments like pianos and brass, which change timbre at different volumes.

Along with programmable RAM, 1995's sound cards will increasingly feature digital effects like reverb, chorus, and echo, which make MIDI patches

to retype it. It was a convoluted process, and a silly one in light of the editing revolution that computers have ushered

ningLearningLearningLearning

sound more natural. And these next-generation cards will certainly begin to expand the number of MIDI voices beyond the 32 available on most sound cards today.

Further into the future, physical-modeling synthesis promises to vastly increase the quality of MIDI reproduction on the PC. Unlike wavetable synths, which play back static recordings that can be modified only after the fact with MIDI controllers like modulation wheels and foot pedals, physical-modeling synths store complex mathematical models of physical instruments. They create sounds on the fly by exciting a model—the equivalent of blowing into a mouthpiece or plucking a string—and then calculating how the instrument's physical properties would shape the resulting sound. Such virtual instruments can be

controlled in the same ways as their physical counterparts; specifying that a pizzicato note be plucked near the bridge of a virtual cello would produce exactly the same effect you'd expect from a physical instrument.

While the mathematics of physical modeling require so much CPU power that it will be a while before you'll find a physical-modeling synth on a Sound Blaster, it's a powerful technology that will certainly be a standard feature on the budget sound card of 2001.

The ability to unlock people's untapped creative abilities is one of the great potential benefits of multimedia technology. Given the breadth of personal tastes, it's both fun and awesome to be able to create something that actually manages to satisfy your personal tastes. Along this line comes The Key from

Lonestar Technologies, a new instrument that could become one of the most promising developments in interactive music. The Key looks somewhat like a guitar but instead of strings, it features a group of strange plastic ridges that you strum, and instead of frets, the neck is made up of keys. The product is still under development at the time of this writing, but Lonestar promises you'll be able to use the Key with specially encoded video or multimedia CD-ROMs and your jamming will sound great even if you don't know how to play. That's what the multimedia revolution is all about: products that help empower people's creativity and provide entertainment as well, not just weak rehashes of previously released material.—Fred Davis ∎

Kid Works 2

Buy your children Kid Works 2 and they'll have no excuse for not being creative. Combining a paint package with a word processor and text-to-speech capabilities, Kid Works provides the perfect environment for kids aged 3 and up to try their hands at writing and illustrating their own stories.

Kids compose text in Story Writer, a simple word processor with a couple of unique capabilities: It uses a simple kiddie font for display, and it can substitute icons for many words. Story Illustrator is the next stop on the creativity train; it's here that kids create the pictures to accompany their words, or they can use the paint tools to color in an electronic book. When they're done creating, Story Player will read the masterpiece aloud.

Kids will love the power this package provides, but they may need a little help figuring out how everything works.

Kid Works 2
Davidson & Associates Inc.
(800) 545-7677
$59.95

Macmillan Dictionary for Children

This dictionary is a study in simplicity; scroll through the word list or click on "Go To" to find what you need quickly. Each of the 12,000 words has a definition and an audio pronunciation, and each is hot-linked to other words. Kids can make up their own word lists, too, and then print them or use them to play one of three games. There's not much multimedia glitz, but kids aged 7 through 12 will find this indispensable at homework time.

Macmillan Dictionary for Children
Simon & Schuster Interactive
(800) 983-5333
$29.95

in. Today's writer is a machine that often pushes the limit of human capability. ▢ It turns out that the frenetic work

LearningLearningLea

The Berenstain Bears Learning at Home, Volume 2

These favorite bears are back in a fully interactive journey through their tree house. Here, kids aged 2 through 7 can learn life lessons in home safety, manners, and skills such as reading and number recognition. They may need help navigating through the colorful animations and games, though; guide the youngest to keep them from becoming frustrated.

The Berenstain Bears Learning at Home, Volume 2
Compton's NewMedia
(619) 929-2500
$39.95

Operation Neptune

If you can decipher the percentage of unhealthy barnacles in a given area, you may

be able to save the world's oceans. This underwater adventure builds pre-algebra math skills as it transports you 20,000 leagues under the sea in a challenging and

engaging search-and-rescue mission. There is also some arcade action, so while the going may be tough, it's never boring.

Operation Neptune
The Learning Co.
(800) 852-2255
$59.95

MULTILINGUAL FUN ON THE FARM
Sitting on the Farm

Not every picnic is ruined by ants. In Sitting on the Farm, a parade of unexpected guests turns a little girl's picnic into a multimedia adventure that educates while it entertains.

As with many products for young readers, the core of Sitting on the Farm is an animated storybook with text, sound, and pages to turn. The difference here is that kids can read along by themselves or choose a male or female reading partner to read the story aloud in English, French, or Spanish. In addition, they can click on individual words to hear them pronounced or click on the movie camera to watch an animation. And there are hot spots on every page that launch animated events and sound effects when clicked.

Kids can also create a story of their own in the Write-Along module. Here, young readers can write a new story to accompany the original illustrations or fill in

the blanks to create a story with a different setting. All of these stories can be saved and printed.

Besides helping with reading and vocabulary, Sitting on the Farm teaches kids about music through its Sing-Along mode. This karaoke option lets kids record themselves singing the story's song and then play the sample back with musical accompaniment. Budding mixmasters will enjoy choosing from the many playback options.

The combination of language, music exploration, and vividly drawn scenes makes the Sitting on the Farm program a real picnic.—Gayle C. Ehrenman

Sitting on the Farm
Sanctuary Woods Multimedia Corp.
(415) 578-6340
$39.95

SPREADSHEET FOR THE ENTIRE FAMILY
The Cruncher

If someone had to make a spreadsheet program that would be fun for the whole family (and it was perhaps inevitable that someone would), it's a good thing that educational-software developer Davidson & Associates did it first. With earlier programs such as KidCAD, Davidson has shown its ability to bring grown-up software concepts to kids in a fun way.

The Cruncher ($59.95), a Windows-based starter spreadsheet, teaches math concepts to kids by supplying hours of real-world projects. And since its underlying spreadsheet has all the features and formulas needed for adult-level calculations, The Cruncher is a program kids can grow with.

Kids can dive right into one of ten projects from the main screen, including Can

We Get a Pet?, Baseball Statistics, Recipe Converter, Party Planner, and Put Your Money to Work. These are actually spreadsheet templates accompanied by simple instructions. Kids can follow along and plug in their own numbers. After mastering the six tutorials and the projects, a young entrepreneur can make a painless transition to working with a basic spreadsheet for recording allowance payments or tracking babysitting profits.

For advanced users—both young and adult—there are 23 complex cell calculations and advanced trigonometry functions, as well as a basic charting function for bar, line, scatter, and pie graphs. It isn't Microsoft Excel or Lotus 1-2-3, but it is a functional spreadsheet.—Carol Levin

The Cruncher
Davidson & Associates Inc.
19840 Pioneer Ave.
Torrance, CA 90503
(800) 545-7677; (310) 793-0600
Fax: (310) 793-0601
$59.95; teacher edition, $99.95;
site license for schools, $899.95.

pace forced on writers is not an isolated trend. I was at the IBM research labs in the United Kingdom and saw an amaz-

ningLearningLearning

Microsoft Creative Writer and Microsoft Fine Artist

Microsoft threw out the rules when it developed Creative Writer and Fine Artist, two neat applications for kids.

Forget the stuffy screens with ambiguous icons and confusing commands. Climb on board a shopping cart and ride into the world of McZee, a goofy nerd with polka-dot underwear and a schnozz the size of Tennessee who guides you through the programs. These applications share the most understandable user interface Microsoft has ever produced, not to say the funniest. How many programs go "Splorp!" when you click on Okay? How many programs let you erase things with a noisy vacuum cleaner?

They're designed for kids, but who cares? Creative Writer has basic word processing and desktop publishing tools to create stories, cards and newsletters. Fine Artist has standard drawing tools like fill patterns, paintbrush styles, and animation.

They also have a handful of other creativity tools. Learn how to draw on a 3-D grid. Create banners with clip art. Play with the Splot Machine to generate random one-sentence story ideas: The 300-year-old rock star /dropped the treasure/inches from a tough and troubled part of town. The tiny wrestler/languished for years/in a pitch-black elevator. You get the idea. Oh, and Elvis is hiding in the basement.—Norvin Leach

Microsoft CreativeWriter and Microsoft FineArtist
Microsoft Corp.
One Microsoft Way
Redmond; WA 98052-6399
(800) 426-9400; (206) 882-8080

☞ Corporate members of the Software

Publishing Association say that the fastest-

moving CD-ROMs programs are reference

guides, like encyclopedias and dictionaries,

games, and education titles.

MAKE MAC-BASED
MULTIMEDIA CHILD'S PLAY

**MAKE MAC-BASED
MULTIMEDIA CHILD'S PLAY**

HyperStudio

HyperStudio, Roger Wagner Publishing's popular low-end multimedia authoring system for the Apple IIgs, is now available for the Macintosh. Aimed primarily at schoolchildren, the program mixes full-color painting; animation; sound recording and playback; scrollable text; and support for CD-ROM, laserdisc, and QuickTime movies within the confines of an easy-to-use interface that shouldn't intimidate kids or adults. It's reasonably powerful in some ways, frustratingly simplistic in others.

HyperStudio Mac lists for $179.95, with multiple-copy lab packs and licenses available for teachers. It is based entirely on the HyperCard metaphor, with cards, stacks, objects, and buttons. You create multimedia effects by attaching events such as movie clips or sound files to buttons on a card. The program comes with some background graphics, clip art, and sound files, so you can create your first multimedia effects within minutes. The program will work on any Mac, but you'll probably want to use it on a newer model since HyperStudio can take advantage of built-in

sound input. Color doesn't hurt, either.

You won't be able to create stunning graphics or special effects with the simple tools such as the program's paint module. Also, HyperStudio's presentations are limited to a 512×384-pixel on-screen box, though you can use the full screen as workspace for tear-off menus while developing presentations.

Still, the program delivers on its promise—it's a fun and simple place to make multimedia. Children in school or at home can use HyperStudio

to create their own multimedia presentations, either as class projects or just for fun, and include the HyperStudio Player runtime module with their stacks for royalty-free (non-profit) distribution. The program also includes a version of Logo, the classic educational graphics language, which provides a familiar

means for kids to add programming to their stacks.

Another plus for the educational market is HyperStudio's support of several Pioneer laserdisc players; while most home users don't own one of these units, they are fairly common in schools. HyperStudio can control a laserdisc player attached to the computer to play a video segment in an on-screen window. It can also control CD-ROM players to play a track or segment as an event when a button is pressed, or at other times.

HyperStudio's home-grown flavor is obvious throughout, from its nonslick graphics to its spiral-bound manual. The latter is two manuals in one, reference and tutorial, starting from opposite ends of the book—you flip it over to read each section. The manual was obviously translated from the IIgs version, and includes Apple

ing product that presages the future. I was shown a software package that controls large-scale PBX switching gear for

LearningLearningLea

II-style file names in several places, as well as a few incorrect statements about the files and documents included in the package.

HyperStudio's biggest asset may be the classroom acceptance of its earlier IIgs version, along with its ability to read IIgs stacks. Teachers will find forums with sample files on services such as America Online. The HyperStudio Network ($29 for one year, $55 for two) provides users with a shareware disk, a quarterly newsletter, and discounts on other related products.

If you're worried that multimedia for kids means they'll be sitting watching a screen, don't. HyperStudio gets children involved with the tools they need to create their own multimedia, rather than staring at someone else's.—Philip F.H. Roth

HyperStudio for Macintosh
Roger Wagner Publishing Inc.
1050 Pioneer Way
Suite P
El Cajon, CA 92020
(800) 421-6526; (619) 442-0522
$179.95, single copy, $479 for
5-copy lab pack, $1,195 for
30-user network version, $1,595
for 50-user site license

Thinkin' Things

Children may not think the words thinking and fun have much to do with each other—until they discover Thinkin' Things, from Edmark. The six learning activities in this program give 4-to-8-year-olds a head start with memory, critical thinking, problem solving, and creativity. They are also way more fun than you'd expect.

In Oranga Banga, a friendly orangutan with a drum set helps children develop auditory and visual discrimination and memory. Fripple Shop asks children to help a series of comical customers select specific Fripples according to such attributes as curly hair and purple stripes; in the process, players learn to recognize AND, OR, and NOT (Boolean logic) relationships. Feathered Friends asks children to create birds

with the right characteristics to complete a series. In Toony Loon, children improvise or match musical patterns on some very unusual xylophones to increase memory and musical skills.

Each of these four activities has a Create mode as well as a more directed Question & Answer mode, in which the program adjusts the difficulty of the questions automatically. (An adult section lets you set the initial difficulty level.) Used with Edmark's KidDesk, the program can track levels for more than one child at a time.

Two more activities, Flying Spheres and Flying Shapes, help children develop spatial awareness as they select shapes and set them into motion—creating colorful, sound-enhanced kinetic art. Our student testers liked these activities best of all, and even adults find them hard to

resist. Thinkin' Things epitomizes our definition of the ideal toy: While promoting thinking skills, it entertains the child in all of us.—Denise Green and Doug Green

Thinkin' Things
Edmark Corp.
Redmond, WA
(206) 556-8484
$59.95; school version, $69.95
(includes lesson plans)

Bailey's Book House

Preschoolers can explore reading with Bailey the cat in Bailey's Book House. Clicking on an object in Bailey's room takes children on a journey of reading, spelling, and other literacy skills. This colorful, musical program also provides options for parents to guide their children's learning.

Bailey's Book House
Edmark
$49.95

Stickybear's Early Learning Activities

Stickybear's Early Learning Activities provides six activities to help preschoolers learn basic skills such as recognizing letters, shapes, opposites, groups, and colors and counting. Parents choose a Structured or Free Play format: Structured asks them to identify objects; Free Play tells kids the answers. Available in either English or Spanish text and voice.

Stickybear's Early Learning
Activities
Optimum Resource
$59.95

Yearn 2 Learn Peanuts

With the help of the Peanuts gang in Yearn 2 Learn Peanuts, kids aged 3 through 10 can learn everything from reading to counting. They can choose learning levels and read along with the narrator. They can also color pictures, solve geography puzzles, and count Woodstocks. The sound and music are great.

Yearn 2 Learn Peanuts
Image Smith
$64.95

Al Gore UNIX Virus—Whenever you inquire about one of your environment variables, it shows you the current setting, but then tacks on an alarmist message concerning the future of the variable.

telemarketing. It was designed to let the computer dial phone numbers concurrently and direct calls so that the caller

ningLearningLearning

Parents, Kids and Computers

If you'd like to be more involved in your kids' computer use, pick up a copy of *Parents, Kids and Computers*. This book contains information on selecting the right equipment for your youngsters (it covers PCs as well as Macs) and instructions on how to make the best use of the myriad of kids' educational and entertainment products.

Parents, Kids and Computers
Random House Electronic Publishing
$20

Word Tales

New readers (from 4 to 7 years old) will love Word Tales, a collection of games featuring an animated character called Milo, who teaches children the sounds of letters and how they combine to form words. In the first part of the game, children match the correct initial letter to a word; when that's done, an animated scene appears containing several items that begin with that letter. But it's not all work—there's also an arcade game kids can play as a reward as they successfully complete each Word Tale.

Word Tales
Time-Warner Interactive Group
2210 W. Olive Ave.
Burbank, CA 91506
$59.99

Peter's Adventures

In the past, kids have played games, music, and movies to distraction; modern children are expected to go through software routines repeatedly. As a result, they will learn many of their basic language and math skills from the PC. To this end, this software puts kids through a series of drills that don't always come out the same way, teaching them to stay on their toes.

Peter—our hero—takes kids through a series of adventures having to do with animals, geography, words,

colors, and numbers. Each screen contains several hot spots that prompt activities for the various characters and things. For instance, the Numbers Adventure takes kids to a series of 10 islands, each shaped like a number. Each has a theme and a purpose: On one island, when you drop a rock into a pond it traces concentric eights.

There's a bonus—each of Peter's Adventures is in four languages: English, French, Spanish, and German. This makes it versatile, and marketable in a range of locales. Moreover, it allows kids to learn to count in another tongue, once they've learned the fundamentals of their native language. This is also a boon for parents, who may get tired hearing the same stuff over and over and will find solace in the repetition of a more romantic language.—Charles Bermant

Peter's Adventures
IMSI
(415) 454-7101
$49.95

NATURAL HISTORY

MICROSOFT SURVEYS DANGEROUS (AND ENDANGERED) CREATURES

Microsoft Dangerous Creatures

Microsoft Dangerous Creatures is the title, but that's an exaggeration used to pull in the *Jurassic Park* crowd. (Unless, of course, you're timid enough to think of the platypus and sloth as fearsome.) The CD-ROM's subtitle "Explore the Endangered World of Wildlife," is more to the point. The disc provides entertaining information about more than 60 of the world's most interesting animals.

Each creature's information screen shows several highlighted features you can click on for additional data. Choose the "petite but powerful" label beside the wolverine, for instance, and you get a second screen about the animal's defensive behavior, along with a photograph and illustrative video.

To make learning about animals more fun, Dangerous Creatures includes three online guides—a naturalist, photographer,

was talking continuously. Instead of waiting for a phone to ring, the caller always had a recipient on the line. It was amaz-

LearningLearningLea

and storyteller. All sound like actors, an exceptionally poor one in the naturalist's case, but the material they read is worthwhile. The naturalist takes you on an African safari, an Australian walkabout, a North American trek, and an Amazon adventure. The photographer dives near a coral reef, tells you how difficult shots are taken, and discusses male/female roles among different animal species. The storyteller offers a series of animal tales from aboriginal, African, Asian, and Native American legends.

Microsoft could have increased the disc's value by offering suggestions of books, videos, and wildlife sanctuaries for further exploration. Even so, Dangerous Creatures remains an excellent introduction to our world and the animals that inhabit it—sometimes precariously.—Barry Brenesal

Microsoft Dangerous Creatures
Microsoft Corp.
One Microsoft Way
Redmond, WA 98052-6399
(800) 426-9400; (206) 882-8080
$59.95

TRAVEL BACK IN TIME WITH PREHISTORIA
Prehistoria

Dinosaurs may get all the glory, but they weren't the only creatures roaming prehistoric Earth. This disc, devoted to all forms of early life, provides a multimedia look at everything from flying lizards with wing spans

wider than World War II fighter planes to dinosaurs no larger than chickens.

The package provides more than 60 minutes of multimedia content spanning 500 million years of natural history. The material is arranged in five easy-to-access areas: the Gallery, the Creature Show, the Time Tracker, Classifications, and the Grolier Museum. The Gallery offers groupings of similar prehistoric creatures, while the Creature Show lets you zero in on your favorites through full-color illustrations and detailed text describing the characteristics of each animal. The Time Tracker allows you to search for particular types of creatures in any of 11 geological eras, while the Grolier Museum is where you'll find narrated videos and audiovisual essays on paleontology, prehistoric life, and more. To make it even easier to find that certain Diprotodon (a rhinoceros-size marsupial resembling a wombat), there's also a classification list.

Kids aged 10 and up will find that researching has never been easier—or more attractive.

Prehistoria
Grolier Electronic
Publishing Inc.
(800) 285-4534; (203) 797-3530
$69.95

Microsoft Dinosaurs

It seems as though everywhere you look there's a dinosaur CD, but few are as attractive as this one. Behind Microsoft Dinosaurs's stone-carved interface is some of the best-organized, most accessible prehistoric trivia around.

The disc is arranged into four main areas: Atlas, Families, Timeline, and Index, any of which can be used for tracking down the dinosaur of your dreams. In addition, you can take a guided tour or watch a dinosaur movie; both provide a good means of getting your feet wet.

What makes this disc such a winner, though, is its extensive use of hypertext linking. Almost everything you click

on is a hot spot; some clicks will take you to related topics, while others will launch spoken pronunciations of tricky names. And for the trading-card fanatics, there are Fact Cards that present statistics on dinosaurs instead of designated hitters. About the only thing missing is a full-text search engine.

Microsoft Dinosaurs
Microsoft Corp.
(800) 426-9400; (206) 882-8080
$79.95

3-D Dinosaur Adventure

Another dino disc—but with a 3-D twist. Don your cardboard glasses and you'll feel as though you're a tyrannosaurus tidbit. The multimedia special effects are sparkling but sparingly used. The Dino Encyclopedia is a good reference tool, and the theme-park atmosphere is easy to settle into. Kids aged 3 and up will love the 3-D Museum, where they can roam among the Deinonychus and Apatosaurus, and the Create-A-Saurus module, which lets them create wild new creatures.

3-D Dinosaur Adventure
Knowledge Adventure Inc.
(800) 542-4240
$79.95

ing. If two lines were ringing at the same time and both were answered simultaneously—just as the telemarketer went

ringLearningLearningLearning

The San Diego Zoo Presents . . . the Animals!

You may not be able to smell the animals, but you'll be able to learn far more about them from this disc than you would on a trip to the zoo. Text, photos, and videos combine to present a wealth of information on animals and their habits and habitats. The videos are not of the highest

Dictionary of the Living World

From abaxial to zygotene— with 2,600 stops in between— the Dictionary of the Living World defines, explains, and illustrates life on earth. Movies, animations, and photos combine with narration and text to explore biological processes, habitats, and animal life—the QuickTime

Whales and Dolphins

Whales and Dolphins is the second in a series of beautiful interactive zoo discs from REMedia (the first one was about butterflies). Simple animations and QuickTime movies supplement chapters on the creatures' life cycle, body plan, and ecology.

Whales and Dolphins
REMedia
7430 Trade St.
San Diego, CA 92121
$59.95

LINKING EXPLORERS PAST AND PRESENT

The Discoverers

It may be a cliché, but few places are as exciting to explore as the human mind.

The Discoverers, a new disc from Knowledge Adventure, traces a Möbius strip of exploration that moves seamlessly from ancient history to contemporary hypothesis. The origin of this CD-ROM can be traced to Daniel Boorstin's popular book of

the same name, while much of its presentation comes from the film produced and directed by Greg MacGillvray. The movie was designed for the huge IMAX format, which surrounds viewers with sights and sounds.

quality, but the interface is fairly intuitive, and there's a spoken help section.

The San Diego Zoo
Presents…the Animals!
Mindscape
(415) 883-3000
$59.95

movie of two adorable baby emperor penguins is alone worth the price of admission.

Dictionary of the Living World
Compton's NewMedia
2320 Camino Vida Roble
Carlsbad, CA 92009
(800) 862-2206
$149.95

"Some people will always be content to merely listen to music. But if you like the cutting edge, you want more. Very soon, thanks to the latest wave of advances in digital technology, you'll be able to reach far beyond the ordinary listening experience. You'll be able to conduct or arrange recorded music to perfectly match your momentary mood or yen. Or, you'll be able to jam along with famous musicians even if you're a tone-deaf klutz. And for total immersion, you'll have the chance to create your own music videos, play with a virtual band, or even explore virtual musical worlds. If this sounds like a far-out fantasy, it isn't. In fact, the interactive entertainment revolution is already underway. The major players in the music industry are jockeying for position, even while they are still trying to identify and understand the new array of multimedia opportunities. Some of the players are truly interested in the new, creative options, whereas others are just lured by the latest technocraze. And some are even on a mission—Peter Gabriel, for one, thinks that new multimedia technologies can help him better promote world peace and understanding."

—FRED DAVIS

LearningLearningLea

What the CD-ROM version brings to the mix is interactivity. As you play the film, you can click on the screen to learn more about the subject on display. Further, the program uses the familiar Knowledge Adventure interface, which combines a timeline, a map for searching by geography, and a picture window that users can click to examine further details or uncover related topics.

By highlighting the links between ancient and contemporary explorers, The Discoverers illuminates a path through the database of human knowledge. Users might sail with Ferdinand Magellan as his ships round Tierra Del Fuego and reach the Pacific Ocean in 1521, then find an echo of that explorer's journey in the Magellan spacecraft that mapped Venus.

The Discoverers is more than a hyperlinked audio-visual reference, however. You can explore some of humankind's great discoveries right on your PC's screen—manipulating two prisms, for instance, to simulate Newton's experiments. For an experience no historical explorer has shared, you can watch lunar and solar eclipses from a viewpoint outside the solar system. Additional features include a set of games and a description of easy science experiments you can perform on your own. Clearly, this disc captures the discoverer's spirit.—Peter Scisco

The Discoverers
Knowledge Adventure
4502 Dyer St.
La Crescenta, CA 91214
(800) 542-4240; (818) 542-4200
$39.95

UFO

Still waiting for aliens from Alpha Centauri to beam you up to their mothership? Maybe you've been trying to get picked up in the wrong places. You need UFO, a Windows CD that contains a complete database of UFO encounters organized by place, date, number of flying saucers, and whether or not anyone was abducted. Based on the criteria you choose, a map pinpoints popular spots for the vacationing extraterrestrial. You can click on any of these spots to get details of past encounters, and many of the summaries include video or still photos. UFO: Don't leave Earth without it.—Ron White

UFO
Software Marketing Corp.
(800) 545-6626; (602) 893-3377
$59.95

Distant Suns

As I'm writing this, the comet Shoemaker-Levy 9 is crashing into Jupiter. The collision didn't start a cataclysmic chain reaction and destroy the entire solar system—which nixes my best excuse for missing deadlines.

A new version of Distant Suns cunningly plays on the astronomical event of a lifetime. But don't buy the CD just for the Shoemaker-Levy animations. Get it if you have any interest in astronomy. Distant Suns is a terrific and imaginative way to explore the heavens. Position yourself anywhere in the solar system and observe the planets and stars, using the disc as your guide. The program gives you complete control over the amount of detail you want to include. It's endlessly fascinating.—Ron White

Distant Suns
Virtual Reality Laboratories
(805) 545-8515
$149.95

A CD-ROM FOR SERIOUS SCIENTIFIC EXPLORATION

McGraw-Hill Multimedia Encyclopedia of Science & Technology

Most multimedia encyclopedias are intended as learning experiences first and reference guides second. This is not the case, however, with the McGraw-Hill Multimedia Encyclopedia of Science &

Technology. The $1,300 package is a sober, rich guide for serious research and exploration.

easy it would be to sell this to an organization: All you'd have to do is demonstrate how the telemarketers could double

ningLearningLearning

This CD-ROM encyclopedia really comes into its own when the information you need is specialized in nature. Abscisic acid, for instance, rates an article of more than 1,400 words. That's 1,400 words more than any of the general-interest CD-ROM encyclopedias devote to the subject. A large percentage of McGraw-Hill's 7,300 articles and 122,600 definitions are devoted to similarly recondite scientific themes; you'll also find information here on more general scientific concepts.

While the information may be esoteric, accessing it couldn't be easier. The program quickly processes keyword, Boolean, and hypertext searches; buttons on the toolbar let you call up a list of articles related to the topic you're currently viewing, or examine a series of related article subheadings. You can simultaneously peruse and print as many of the encyclopedia's articles and illustrations as your Windows memory permits. Science & Technology is also very application-cooperative. It has no objections to being shunted aside while you examine a spreadsheet, fix an advertising layout, or e-mail messages.

When it comes to multimedia effects, however, the current crop of general-interest encyclopedias win hands down. Science & Technology's brief animated sequences are generally poor and don't portray any additional information. For the most part,

they're too short to make any point and too small to show any detail. The visually crude illustrations encounter the opposite shortcoming. They're drawn full-screen, and won't shrink-to-fit. Voiceovers are muffled, noisy, and hard to understand. And although McGraw-Hill permits you to set a default font and size, it does not use scalable fonts, so on-screen reading can be difficult at times.

While it's only adequate for recreational use, the McGraw-Hill Multimedia Encyclopedia of Science & Technology really shines when the questions you're asking can't be answered by a multimedia Mr. Wizard CD. As a computerized reference tool for in-depth scientific knowledge, it is unsurpassed.—Barry Brenesal

McGraw-Hill Multimedia Encyclopedia of Science & Technology.
McGraw-Hill Inc.
New York, NY
(800) 722-4726
$1,300

Isaac Asimov Science Adventure II

Isaac Asimov Science Adventure II is noteworthy for its spectacular computer graphics and the high quality of its articles, which are based on Isaac Asimov's Chronology of Science and Discovery. Although coverage of the material is not very deep, the disk embraces a

wide range of topics and includes a myriad of slick animation demos, from roller-coaster acceleration to planetary orbits to a pulley demonstration. It also features several games.

The central mode of the program is its reference screen, where text panels, pictures, a time line, and a globe are displayed. With a click of a button, you can switch the text panel from adult to child mode, which contains less information and an easier vocabulary. All areas are hyperlinked to other topics.

Isaac Asimov Science Adventure II has a highly graphical interface, which actually is often counterproductive. The icons are very cryptic, making user navigation difficult. The initial area, for example, is a 3-D lobby in which all the icons are pictures hanging on the walls. It's attractive but not very intuitive. Nevertheless, this is a wonderful program for introducing children to the

world of science. Their parents can learn a lot as well.—Barry Simon

Isaac Asimov Science Adventure II
Knowledge Adventure Inc.
(800) 542-4240; (818) 542-4200
$69.95

Beyond Planet Earth

As its name implies, Beyond Planet Earth focuses on astronomy and, more specifically, the solar system. The opening screen branches to four areas: The Planetary Theatre, The Solar Gallery, Space Experts, and Mission to Mars.

The first area has five short videos culled from The Discovery Channel on fascinating topics such as "what

happened to the dinosaurs," which explains the currently fashionable theory that their extinction was due to a cosmic collision. The most extensive and impressive component of the disc is The Solar Gallery, which includes a very educational series of stills from space shuttle flights and snapshots of the solar system.

One of the best features of the Gallery is a series of slide shows about each of the planets using photographs taken by NASA. Also included here is a discussion of moons and an introduction to astronomy beyond the solar system. There's even a discussion with four astronomers about a possible mission to Mars in the next century.

As reference material, Beyond Planet Earth is not the best CD-ROM you can find. But if you and your children want to learn about the solar system in a most engrossing way, then Beyond

Planet Earth is certainly worth your while.

Beyond Planet Earth
The Discovery Channel
(301) 986-0444 ext. 5880
$49.95

or triple their productivity as the computer cranked through the work of contacting the suckers. Talk about speed up!

LearningLearningLea

Simple Machines

Simple Machines's subject matter—the inclined plane, lever, screw, pulley, and wheel—is rather prosaic compared with many other discs, but it conveys a real understanding of the material rather than the trivia-contest information so common in many educational titles.

Unlike the material, the presentation is anything but dry. Simple Machines's underlying metaphor is of children traveling across the globe to learn about machinery, and it features colorful animations, enlightening demos, and insightful quizzes.

It's hard to imagine making a discussion of how machines work fun and fascinating, but Science for Kids pulls it off.

Simple Machines
Science for Kids
(800) 572-4362
$199 (teacher's edition, $289)

Expert Astronomer

Expert Astronomer is a cornucopia of delights for the astronomy fan. It includes a planetarium that lets you see how any part of the night sky looks and over 500MB of stunning pictures and

engrossing information, with 40 minutes of entertaining videos. For astronomy buffs, this is the CD to buy.

Expert Astronomer
Expert Software Inc.
(800) 759-2562
$49.95

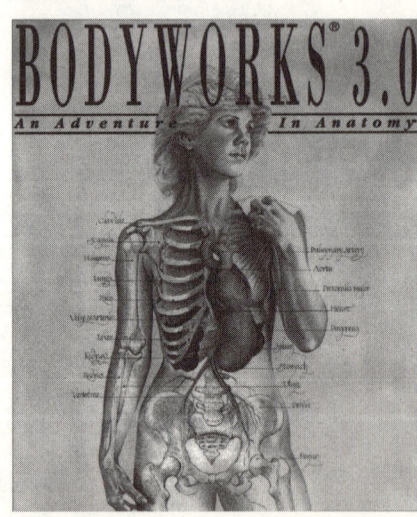

Bodyworks

The Windows-based Bodyworks, Version 3.0, is a superbly designed, comprehensive anatomy reference

with wonderful supporting multimedia. From a button bar or menu you choose one of the top-level body systems: skeletal, muscular, nervous, cardiovascular, respiratory, digestive, sensory, lymphatic, endocrine, or genitourinary. The window then shows the appropriate diagram; you can focus on individual organs by clicking either on the diagram or on an adjacent scrolling list.

Click on the mouth in the skeleton, for example, and a close-up view of an open mouth appears, complete with teeth, tongue, and epiglottis. There is a text description with hyperlinks to other articles and a glossary. The clear color diagrams (over 140) are supplemented by 14 3-D models and 37 videos and animations.

The 3-D area has a couple of nice surprises. The models can be shown as wireframe, smooth, or angular. All can be rotated, even the simple 3-D models, which are redrawn in real time as you move them. Among the multimedia movies included on the CD-ROM are the brief "A Firing Synapse," the mildly disgusting "Chewing and Swallowing," and the inspiring and surprisingly complete "Childbirth."

Lessons and tests are also included. This is an ideal program for high-school stu-

dents and others who are interested in anatomy.

Bodyworks, Version 3.0
Software Marketing Corp.
(800) 364-5451
$69.95

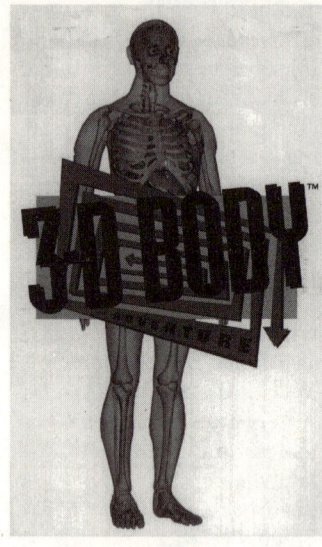

3-D Body Adventure

3-D Body Adventure is intended to provide an entertaining way to turn young students on to anatomy. Its spectacular multimedia demos include 3-D wireframe views and fly-throughs of the heart and other body parts. Two pairs of 3-D glasses that bring the animations to life are included. This is an ideal program for kids of 7 to 12.

3-D Body Adventure
Knowledge Adventure Inc.
(800) 542-4240; (818) 542-4200
$69.95

RedShift Multimedia Astronomy

How would you like to take off for 10 minutes and view a spectacular solar eclipse from the surface of the moon? Check out RedShift Multimedia Astronomy. It's the first CD-ROM-based planetarium program and the only one in any format that combines ease of use, accuracy, and enormous visual flare.

RedShift is really three programs in one. The first employs a proprietary celestial-mechanics engine to plot and track the position of 250,000 stars and 40,000 deep-space objects. The second is a very precise orbital-mechanics

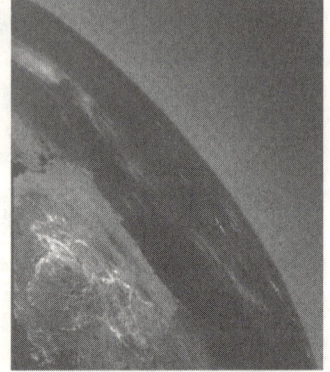

engine that positions objects in our solar system at any moment in time between 4,000 B.C. and 11,000 A.D.

The most spectacular program element for the non-astronomy buff, however, is a virtual-reality module, which wraps bitmapped images of photographed planetary surfaces around scalable, rotating 3-D spheres. RedShift can

⊡ I think of products like this and I'm sure that the rest of the world laughs at Americans and our productivity fanati-

ningLearningLearningLearning

manipulate several of these objects simultaneously, taking into account your vantage point and sun-derived shadow effects. The results are breathtakingly cinematic—and appropriately enough, you can record sequences for later review using the included QuickTime Movie Player. The program also includes topological maps with thousands of named locations and an online version of Jacqueline Mitton's the Penguin Dictionary of Astronomy.

RedShift is the only computerized planetarium that conveys the silent majesty that lies behind astronomy's dry precision. It reaches far into the night skies of the past and future and turns your workstation into an ultramodern observatory. Expect to spend many hours of glorious nighttime stargazing—in the middle of the day—with RedShift.—Barry Brenesal

RedShift Multimedia Astronomy
Maris Multimedia
(510) 652-4746
$99

🖐 Worldwide PC sales will increase to

$94 billion in 1995—up from $74 billion in 1993,

according to an estimate from Dataquest.

In the U.S. alone, almost 19 million PCs were

sold in 1994.

TRAVELING THE ANCIENT AND MODERN WORLDS

TOOLS FOR TRAVELING
AAA Trip Planner

Here's a brand-new offering from Compton's NewMedia: AAA Trip Planner. This $59.95 disc should help make any trip easier.

The key to Trip Planner is its Directions function. Type in your departure and destination points, selected from a database of more than 125,000 locations, and the program will produce a set of detailed directions. These include mileage and driving times, in addition to the roads and directions of travel. You'll probably want to double-check the results against a current road atlas, however—Trip Planner once routed me through a non-existent interstate exchange. You can also

view your route on-screen with a series of state and city maps.

Another handy feature, Travel Tools, will help you find places to stay and things to do at your destination. You can search for hotels and restaurants using quality and price ratings; the resulting lists include prices, addresses, phone numbers, directions, and maps showing the general location of each establishment.

The Travel Tools feature can also search for nearby attractions arranged by dozens of categories, including museums, recreational sites, zoos, and children's attractions. The listings aren't comprehensive, but they do an excellent job of hitting the high points.

The disc also provides state profiles, with a narrated

slide show for each, as well as lists of all the AAA offices in the U.S. and Canada. This is an excellent resource, whether your trip is for business or pleasure.—Alfred Poor

AAA Trip Planner
Compton's NewMedia Inc.
2320 Camino Vida Roble
Carlsbad, CA 92009-1504
(800) 862-2206; (619) 929-2500
$59.95

Everywhere USA Travel Guide

If you already know where you're going and how to get there and are looking for something to do once you arrive, try the Everywhere USA Travel Guide. Deep River Publishing's two-disc set covering the Eastern and Western halves of the country lists for $59.95.

You can search for attractions by state, or within a 25-, 50-, 100-, or 250-mile radius of a specific point. You can search within individual categories, like museums, parks, science and nature, or sports and amusements. You can also limit your search to locations with specific features, such as guided tours, activities for children, or free admission, or even find attractions open during certain hours or months.

Once you've set your search parameters, click on the Go button, and the program provides a listing of attractions. You'll see one or more slides of the location on

the left of the screen, with a text window on the right that describes the attraction and lists icons for the different facilities and features it offers. A Locator button displays a regional map, with a dot showing the attraction.

Some of the locations also include video clips, and you can put together a slide show for all the selected locations. You can display slides as thumbnail images, which you click to display full information. Everywhere USA Travel Guide is colorful and packed with useful information. It's best for recreational trips, though business users will find it handy when trying to find something to do on a free weekend away from home.—Alfred Poor

Everywhere USA Travel Guide
Deep River Publishing Inc.
P.O. Box 9715-975
565 Congress St.
Portland, ME 04104
(800) 643-5630; (207) 871-1684
$59.95

Expert Travel Planner CD-ROM

Expert Software's multimedia trip-planning title, Expert Travel Planner CD-ROM, provides routing, information on sites and attractions, and a customizable database. The central feature of the $49.95 program is the Quick Planner. Enter a departure and destination point, and up to three intermediate points, and the program generates a route for you. You need enter only part

LearningLearningLea

of a city name; the program will display all the matching cities it finds in its database, and you can pick the correct one. You can ask the program to create up to three routes, finding the shortest, quickest, or preferred route for your trip. The last option lets you provide weighted preferences for highways, toll roads, and primary and secondary roads.

You can view or print the results as an itinerary that shows route, mileage on various roads, and estimated driving time. Adjustable levels of map detail let you include major cities, road numbers, airports, parks, and points of interest. Double-click on a location icon to open a window of information about the site, with a slide show, video clip, or both for some locations. Finally, the disc also offers useful lists of things like hotel reservation numbers, emergency numbers, and maps of area codes and time zones.

Expert Travel Planner could stand some improvements, however. Map redrawing is fairly slow, especially if you have primary and secondary roads displayed. The routing feature is of limited use, particularly around major cities where you can probably do better

with an atlas. Some of the chosen routes through Philadelphia and New York were a bit bizarre. Fortunately, a booklet with city maps is included with the package. Finally, the database recognizes a relatively small number of locations, and while you can add your own locations, it would be helpful if there were more cities and towns in the system from the start.

In spite of its flaws, the program works well and provides useful information about hundreds of locations around the country. You'll probably still need to turn to other references, but the Expert Travel Planner CD-ROM is a good place to start.—Alfred Poor

Expert Travel Planner CD-ROM
CD-ROM Expert Software
800 Douglas Rd.
Executive Tower
Coral Gables, FL 33134
(800) 759-2562; (305) 567-9990
$49.95

Scientific American Exploring Ancient Cities

Stodginess and eggheadedness are not what archeology is about, but you would never know that from this disc. The romance of digging lives and whole societies out of the ashes of a buried past are reduced here to the dryness of a late-afternoon classroom lecture.

Certainly, the grand tours of the ancient cities of Crete, Petra, Pompeii, and Teotihuacan are a nice cross-cultural mixture. The architecture, sculpture, and paintings are immensely appealing, but the folks who put this CD together are much better at words than visuals. The slide shows are indifferent, and the few videos are so hidden beneath an awkward interface that you could easily miss them. The narration that accompanies grand tours is interesting, but the visuals don't match the language. But the maps are great, espe-

cially because you can click on specific objects to bring up photos of them. If Scientific American tries this again, they should remember that it's not required viewing. It needs to be exciting.—Ron White

Scientific American Exploring
Ancient Cities
Sumeria
(415) 904-0800
$59.95

TOUR LONG-LOST REAL ESTATE

Exploring Ancient Architecture

Medio's Exploring Ancient Architecture CD-ROM turns its audience into electronic pilgrims. It guides them through a multimedia tour of historic architectural sites, going back in time to examine the building styles of the late Stone Age (Neolithic), Egyptian, Greek, and Roman cultures. An in-depth

overview introduces the features of each period through descriptive narrations, colorful slides, and text.

You can inspect seven magnificent buildings in detail, each one a realistic 3-D re-creation. Decide where to walk by selecting arrow buttons on the screen's navigation panel. The sites include a Neolithic Dolman tomb in France; Stonehenge in England; the ancient Egyptian temples of Mentuhotep and Khons; Greece's gorgeous Parthenon and Ecclesiasterion; and the Basilica of Maxentius in Rome. With a personal tour guide providing detailed explanations, you never have to worry about getting lost.

The program presents an amazing collection of multimedia sights and sounds. Operating instructions are provided online and operation is very easy—you simply click on-screen buttons to select a period, overview, or building tour.—Carol S. Holzberg

Exploring Ancient Architecture
Medio Multimedia Inc.
2703 152nd Ave. NE
Redmond, WA 98052
(800) 788-3866
$59.95

TRAVEL TO THE PAST

Microsoft Ancient Lands

Don't come to Ancient Lands expecting Encarta, much less the British Museum. The emphasis here is on building a youngster's interest in the distant past. As such, Ancient

Lands doesn't provide long articles, but it does offer a large number of interesting historical subjects accompanied by narration, animation, photographs, and video clips.

You can access all this information from a map or an index or by choosing major subject categories. The most exciting way for kids to use

Lands shouldn't be purchased as a substitute for that trip to the museum, but as a way of getting kids primed to go there.—Barry Brenesal

Microsoft Ancient Lands
Microsoft Corp.
(800) 426-9400
$59.95

"I think computers change our lives in ways we don't anticipate. They change our lives in ways that perhaps only the Ted Nelsons or Doug Engelbarts or a few anticipate it, and when they anticipate it, nobody takes them seriously. Ted Nelson would say on this line, 'Many people find it very difficult to imagine how something would feel without tangibly seeing it and feeling it.' The example he gave was that a large percentage of people would be able to understand why a Walkman would be a good idea. But if there's one sitting in the middle of the table, they'd say, 'Wait a minute! I can listen to music while I'm jogging.' "

—JOHN WALKER, FOUNDER OF AUTODESK, 1994

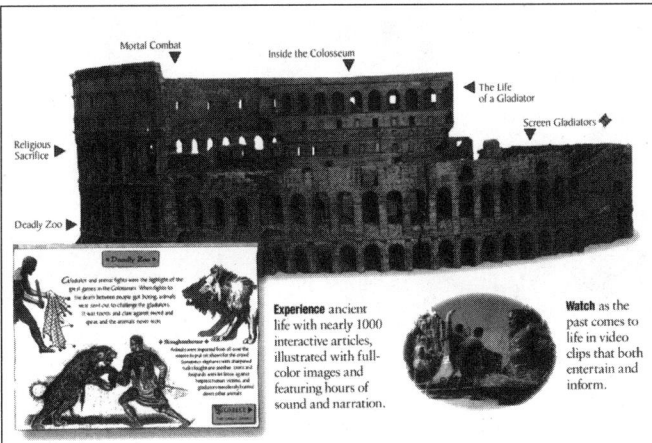

Mortal Combat   Inside the Colosseum   ◄ The Life of a Gladiator

Religious Sacrifice   Screen Gladiators ◄

Deadly Zoo

Experience ancient life with nearly 1000 interactive articles, illustrated with full-color images and featuring hours of sound and narration.

Watch as the past comes to life in video clips that both entertain and inform.

Ancient Lands, though, is through the Guides. These are 18 "people" from different walks of life in Egypt, Greece, and other ancient lands. The Egyptian guides include a craftsman, a priestess, and an embalmer's daughter; the Greeks supply, among others, a bard, an actor, and a goddess from the Greek pantheon. These narrators provide an entertaining dose of conversation as they move through a variety of subjects.

Short shrift is paid to other cultures, however; some receive only a single screen, while others are totally omitted. For this reason, Ancient

Global Explorer

Global Explorer covers the world from all angles. From the broadest perspective, you see the world; at the most microscopic, you see streets in major cities. In between, you get the best-looking, most detailed online maps of the world. Global Explorer includes descriptions of 20,000 historical and geographical features, and street maps for 100 cities.

Global Explorer
DeLorme Mapping
(800) 452-5931
$99

The Software Toolworks World Atlas

The maps in The Software Toolworks World Atlas, Version 4.0, aren't as detailed as Global Explorer's, but this program does include over 1,000 color photos, 270 film

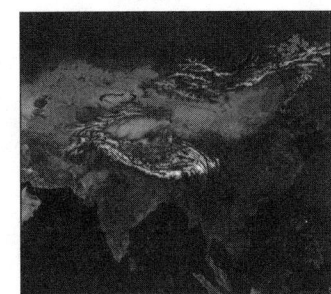

clips, and audio clips with country-name pronunciations. And if all this data overwhelms you, you can look at the flags of 200 countries while listening to each country's national anthem.

The Software Toolworks
World Atlas
Mindscape
(415) 883-3000
$59.95

Journey to the Source

Journey to the Source: An Expedition Along the Yangtze River allows you to follow along with acclaimed explorer How Man Wong as he searches for the source of the renowned river. With this interactive coffee-table book, you can explore China through photos, video clips, and maps, as well as through the text of the explorer's book. You can listen as the explorer narrates the tale or explore a particular region. Like the best paper-based coffee-table books, Journey to the Source is entertaining, educational, and beautiful.—Gayle C. Ehrenman

Journey to the Source
Grid Media Ltd.
011-852-591-0730 (Hong Kong)
$59.95

Adventures

Adventures will help you plan a vacation even if you initially don't know what you want to do or where you want to do it. Search its data-

base of 1,160 activities until you find something exciting. Pick a state, province, or country and use the pull-down list to scan the attractions. You can also query by activity, selecting from 30 categories—which include aerial sports, biking, economy vacations, and snow sports. Or you can use the custom-search feature to find some of the activities, festivals, and events occurring in a particular month.

You can also use the search feature to generate a list of specialized activities. Select those adventures classified as "difficult" and you'll get a list of nine excruciating

Connect. Their pitch: It's within the office environment itself that most pagers are needed. People need pagers when

LearningLearningLea

vacations, including climbing Mount McKinley, trekking at nosebleed altitudes in Nepal, and rafting the Futaleuf River in Patagonia. If those are too tame, touring Hungary on horseback might get your blood flowing.

The disc contains about 2,500 color photographs and 40 minutes of video supplied by state travel departments. For each adventure, there's a written description along with dates, cost, and contact information. About 60 percent of the adventures are outside of the U.S., so this is an ideal CD if you plan on traveling abroad.—Donald B. Trivette

Adventures
Deep River Publishing Inc.
(207) 871-1684
$49.95

Astonishing Asia

Astonishing Asia is part documentary, part travel guide, and part Ripley's Believe It or Not. This is not a guidebook; it is, rather, a strange trip for the armchair traveler.

You access the adventures by country or by any of nine themes. Some of the themes—death rites, stimulants, rituals, and medicine—conjure up images of the mysterious East, while others—such as sports, religion, and festivals—are more conventional fare. Lengthy video clips of the Monkey God Festival in Hong Kong and the cremation ritual in Nepal are two of the more offbeat attractions.

Astonishing Asia has 30 minutes of digital video and 600 color photos set to appropriate music. Some of the topics use slide-show presentations instead of video. Astonishing Asia may not be for everyone, but those interested in Asia with a taste for the occult will be quite—well, astonished.

Astonishing Asia
InterOptica Publishing
(800) 708-7827
$49.95

From Alice to Ocean

From Alice to Ocean documents Robyn Davidson's extraordinary camel journey from Alice Springs, Australia, across the expanse of the outback to the Indian Ocean. Directly addressing the viewer, Davidson describes the hardships and dangers of her yearlong journey. The armchair traveler can interrupt at any time to view maps or photographs, or to select questions from an interactive menu.

Although the trip took place 15 years ago, the chronicle CD of Davidson's journey first appeared two years ago when it was bundled with 500,000 Apple CD-ROM computers and became a bestseller; the multiplatform disc was released last November.

The CD-ROM is bundled with a beautiful 200-page book filled with color photographs. The disc, however, contains many more photos than the book, all of which are of great quality. This is a fascinating chronicle of a remarkable journey.

From Alice to Ocean
Claris Clear Choice
(800) 325-2747
$69

Asia Alive

Asia Alive is a multimedia guide to Australia, China, Hong Kong, Indonesia, Japan, Laos, Malaysia, New Zealand, the Philippines, Singapore, South Korea, Taiwan, Thailand, and Vietnam. The disc includes 37 maps, 30 videos with regional music, and 500 color photos that cover countries, cities, sights, activities, and customs. It's the content—not the multmedia—that makes this disc worthwhile.

Asia Alive
MediAlive
(408) 752-8500
$49

Europe Alive

Europe Alive, the European travel-guide companion to Asia Alive, covers Austria, Belgium, France, Germany, Great Britain, Ireland, Italy, the Netherlands, Portugal, Spain, Switzerland, and Scandinavia. Though there are plenty of video clips of these locales, you'll get much more satisfaction from the information provided.

Europe Alive
MediAlive
(408) 752-8500
$49

 Guess what's the fastest growing category

for software sales? Education, followed

by entertainment, databases, and paint or

drawing programs.

they're away from their desks, roaming the halls, or hanging around the water cooler. Pagers free people from feeling

ningLearningLearningLearning

New York, NY

This is an entertaining collection of 100 color photographs—each with a short caption—that can be displayed on-screen in either large or small formats. In addition, there are 25 10-second video clips of landmarks like the Statue of Liberty, the Brooklyn Bridge, and Rockefeller Center. It's a video picture book, ideal for those who prefer to experience New York from the safety of their own homes.

New York, NY
Aris Entertainment Inc.
(310) 821-0234
$29.95

FINDING THE PERFECT PLACE

InfoNation—Rating the U.S.A. to Z

Looking for a warm-weather vacation spot heavy on wax museums and top-rated restaurants? How about a new place to live that has real seasons, a diverse culture, and plenty of bookstores? Whatever your reasons, concerns, and interests, if you're looking for a place, InfoNation—Rating the U.S.A. to Z stands a good chance of helping you find it.

This reference tool lets you rank states and 300 or so metropolitan areas based on any combination of 1,200 criteria. Much of the supporting data, which was culled from publications of the U.S. Census Bureau and 36 other sources, constitutes the sort of mundane though helpful informa-

tion you might expect—including population by age, sex, race, marital status, and education level.

The real charm of the package, though, lies in the addition of the stuff fun and fulfillment are made of, such as arts and sports, and the control the software provides in determining the weight of any given factor. Most of us will find at least a few topics we care about, but few of us will demand that our own little Eden rank high in everything: InfoNation lets you set the weight to be given to each topic across any or all of the software's ten data categories.

InfoNation also provides detailed, multilayered graphics of the United States, can generate graphs and map overlays to illustrate rankings, and supports map export.—Mitt Jones

InfoNation—Rating the
U.S.A. to Z
Software Marketing Corp.
(602) 893-3377
$49.95

Small Blue Planet

Map lovers and would-be astronauts will thrill to the wealth of maps and satellite images in Small Blue Planet, an interactive electronic atlas. Navigate among a world political map (complete with statistics and historical information for each country), global and U.S. relief maps, and a gallery of breathtaking satellite images ranging from major cities to glaciers and canyons. You also get The Chronosphere, which correlates times and dates with the patterns of night and day across the globe.

Small Blue Planet
Now What Software
203 Sacramento St.
San Francisco, CA 94115
$159

Exotic Japan

If you want to learn about Japanese culture, traditions, and language but can't swing the plane fare just yet, pick up a copy of Exotic Japan. This disc is more than just a

travel guide or language program; it helps you understand Japanese society.

Exotic Japan
The Voyager Company
$99.95

MUSIC

STRIKING A CHORD WITH NOVICES

Personal Piano Learning System

If you can't tell a quarter note from a Quarter Pounder, can't stand the embarrassment of taking piano lessons with little kids, and have $600 burning a hole in your pocket, you're a prime candidate for the Advanced Gravis Personal Piano Learning System, a hardware/software bundle that will have you playing tunes like the "Five-Finger Rag" in less time than

it takes Van Cliburn to toss up the tails of his tuxedo.

Like the long-available (and lower-priced) Miracle Piano Tutor from Software Toolworks, the Advanced Gravis package presents you with a pint-sized keyboard and some software. After that, you're on your own, setting your own pace through a series of lessons.

The Personal Piano Learning System throws more than just a keyboard and a few disks at you, though. The set also includes a hybrid 8- and 16-bit sound card (Gravis's low-end UltraSound), a pair of powered speakers, and a MIDI adapter, though it lacks any foot-pedal control.

Although this glut of stuff looks daunting—like a plastic model with a million pieces—installation is straightforward. A handy Quick Start card walks you through the process, though you should figure on a solid couple of hours to get everything up and running, with the bulk of the time spent installing the UltraSound card and software, and the MIDI piano patches.

Once everything's working, and you've added Musicware's Piano program to your hard drive, you can start to play. This Windows application presents a variety of exercises, flash-card drills, and pop quizzes in a series of over 200 lessons. You'll learn—and then be tested—on such skills as note recognition and playing rhythm. Feedback is immediate, and

guilty about roaming. Consequently, they'll roam more freely. ⌨ That's the argument, anyway. Motorola's product is

LearningLearningLearningLea

you can always retake a lesson. The program also tracks multiple learners, so the family can take turns.

The Personal Piano Learning System includes Musicware's Course One, whose 50 songs and 2,500 exercises take you through the equivalent of a year of traditional piano instruction. Courses Two and Three, which provide second- and third-year lessons respectively, can be ordered directly from Musicware for $60 each.

The Personal Piano Learning System's half-length, four-octave MIDI keyboard looks and feels a bit on the cheap side, but it sounds surprisingly good, thanks in part to its 192 MIDI instruments. Although it's a velocity-sensitive keyboard, you won't mistake its touch for a real piano, but its sound was close to the upright in our house. And the lessons and songs in Course One, while no challenge to an eight-year-old girl with a year of piano lessons under her belt, were more than enough for her tone-deaf dad.

The best thing about the Gravis package, of course, is that it lets you learn on your own time, in privacy. If you heard me play Beethoven's "Ode to Joy," you'd want me playing in private, too.—Gregg Keizer

The Personal Piano Learning System
Advanced Gravis Computer Technology Ltd.
1790 Midway Ln.
Bellingham, WA 98226
(800) 663-8558; (604) 431-5020
$599.95

C O M P O S E R
QUEST
AN EXPLORATION OF MUSIC, HISTORY AND THE ARTS

Composer Quest

Unfortunately, Composer Quest is an example of how not to combine music and CD-ROM. The obvious problem: Opcode Interactive doesn't own the rights to the music it wants to cover. The result is that its survey of music ends with early swing, about the time copyrights for later works start clicking in. So you can hear Scott Joplin's "The Entertainer" (yet again), but no Louis Armstrong (for shame).

The sections about classical music are more satisfying—several long selections that give you an idea of a composer's work. And with all the sections, there are good written materials. But—oh, dear—the disc is held together by an ill-conceived game. You have to answer questions about who wrote what piece, and if you answer correctly, you save a vanishing composition to a Digital Gizmotron. We know a pop quiz when we see one, and Composer Quest isn't fooling us a bit.—Ron White

Composer Quest
Opcode Interactive
(800) 557-2633; (415) 494-1112
$69.95

G-Vox

If you've ever looked on in awe as leather-clad rockers perform complex riffs at finger-blurring speeds, you know that it takes more than practice to mimic the masters. Rather than staying stuck in the doldrums of the pentatonic blues scale, take a lesson with Lyrrus's G-Vox. It's a hardware/software combination that links your guitar with your PC or Mac and interactively guides you through challenging musical phrases, chords, and exercises. And while this product is definitely not for beginners, it could certainly supplement a teacher's lessons.

Setup involves attaching G-Vox's scratch-proof pickup to virtually any acoustic or electric guitar; connecting the belt pack (which converts notes you play into electronic signals) to the computer's serial port; and loading the utilities software. Lyrrus also offers a number of complementary software titles, ranging from Riffs and Chords to Tour and MIDI disks, plus an

ever-expanding set of riff libraries.

After this relatively simple setup, you'll be tuning your guitar via the computer and then watching what you play appear on the on-screen fretboard in real time. Listen to the software's version of a riff or chord and then try it yourself, making sure that you hit the right notes on the fretboard in time with the computer. The demo riffs are played by an internal guitar waveform, but you can also listen to a sample of the lick as played by a real guitarist.

Unlike practice tapes that can only play at two speeds (fast and slow), G-Vox can play at any speed from 30 to 240 beats per minute. It will even play one note at a time, waiting for you to join in before jumping to the next note, so you can work and learn at your own pace.

Lyrrus's Artist Library series contains useful and practical samples. Some of the samples stretch the boundaries of classic rock/blues licks by incorporating jazz and atonal concepts as well. Remarkably, G-Vox's Chords software actually understands the chords you play and translates them for you—A7#9b11 means A7 sharp 9 flat 11, for example.

The MIDI software allows you to record, edit, and save what you play as a MIDI file, while the Tour disc contains two exercises that can set you up as a street musician in front of an audience. Play the correct notes, or they'll throw fruit at you.

It would be nice if G-Vox were able to transpose the riffs, or include a function to make your own riffs, but as long as Lyrrus continues to develop more library discs, this innovative product will push guitar study to the next level.—Chris Phillips

G-Vox
Lyrrus Inc.
35 North 3rd St.
Philadelphia, PA 19106
(215) 922-0880
$399; additional titles: $79-$149

Coda Vivace Personal Accompanist

Until now, if you wanted to rehearse an orchestral piece, you had to either use recorded music, which doesn't make allowances for tempo changes or creative improvisation, or do without accompaniment altogether. Since you can't hire an entire symphony orchestra to practice with you, Coda Music Technology has put one in its outstanding intelligent autoaccompaniment system, Vivace.

Unlike accompaniment software such as PG Music's Band-in-a-Box, which forces you to play with the accompaniment rather than lead it, Vivace actually "listens" to what you play and adjusts the tempo of the accompanying music accordingly.

You install the Vivace software on your Mac, connect a cable between one of the Mac's serial ports and the serial port on the back of the

Vivace box, attach speakers or headphones to the box to hear Vivace's accompaniment, and clip the included microphone to your brass or woodwind instrument. Slide one of the Vivace music cartridges into the box, and as soon as you start playing, Vivace starts playing with you. As you change tempo, Vivace does too.

The Vivace box contains a 32-voice synthesizer, based on E-mu Systems's Proteus modules, that accompanies you with full orchestral, continuo, piano, or jazz-trio arrangements. You're limited to the musical pieces available on the Vivace cartridges, which cost $30 to $80 each and contain a single piece or a few dozen, depending on the music's density and length.

Vivace can also play great jazz accompaniments to the Jamey Aebersold jazz-improvisation library. But when in Jazz mode, the system works like any other music-minus-one system—it does not support intelligent tempo changes.

Vivace currently supports over 1,100 solo accompaniments for brass and wind instruments. In Coda's current catalog, the classical selections are particularly strong and range from Baroque to contemporary. The selections include everything from pieces easy enough for junior-high-school musicians to compositions that will challenge professionals.

In the Vivace package, you also get a software strobe tuner that works both visually and aurally; an online dictionary of musical terms; and features that let you add and subtract instruments from the jazz-band accompaniment, transpose a piece while a tune is playing, and loop particular sections of a piece so you can practice difficult passages.

An incredible tool for beginning and advanced musicians, Vivace is an ideal addition to school music programs. It should be in every music classroom, from junior high to college.—Christopher Breen

Vivace
Coda Music Technology
Eden Prairie, MN
(612) 937-9611
$2,295

MUSIC SOFTWARE TO SOOTHE THE SAVAGE PC

Midisoft Music Mentor Midisoft Multimedia Songbook

Long known for its advanced PC music software, Midisoft Corp. enters the music edutainment field with two strong products. Midisoft Music Mentor covers a lot of ground in the music edutainment field, from fun tutorials that guide you through a variety of musical topics such as notation and harmony, to biographical sketches of figures in the music world.

The many lessons and guided practice sessions

encourage you to develop basic skills in music theory and musicianship. There's also a mixer for rearranging the MIDI selections and an instrument gallery, both of which are also in Midisoft Multimedia Songbook. An automated historical time line allows you to trace the history of music and understand it in the context of the events and society around it. The section on contemporary performers, profiling such figures as Chuck Berry and Stevie Wonder, lets you listen to selections in their styles, although not to samples of the artists' own work. The brief dictionary of musical terms can pronounce each word and use it in a sentence.

Even more along the lines of an electronic music-appreciation class is Midisoft Multimedia Songbook. This CD-ROM features a collection of over 190 songs that you can play on your PC using a MIDI sound board. The seven categories include Holiday Favorites, Kids' Songs, Classics, Jazz Hits, Pop Tunes, International, and Inspirational. Older tunes are better represented than modern ones. The piano arrangements are warm and musical, while the more fully orchestrated pieces suffer from the limitations of MIDI. You can also read quick bits of background information about many of these songs.

You can find more information about the instruments used to record these songs in the Instrument Gallery; here there are entertaining and

"Musicians have been traditionally anal about the way they present the musical ideas, which they stole anyway. Interactivity involves the whole concept of giving people the option of experiencing your music in a way that might reveal details that you used to gloss over before. Now the audience has the opportunity to dwell on some particular piece of the music that might reveal your worst possible moments in the entire musical performance."

—TODD RUNDGREN, MULTIMEDIA COMPOSER/ SINGER, 1994

informative summaries of the best-known instruments and their histories and characteristics, and a few random attempts at humor that aren't terribly funny and dilute the authority of the information.

Since Midisoft makes the notation and sequencing programs that are included with many popular sound cards, it's not surprising that Multimedia Songbook includes limited notation and mixing components. Perhaps

employers to keep office workers at their virtual desks all day long! Can workers really maintain such an attachment?

LearningLearningLea

the highlight of this package is the Midisoft Noodler, which allows you to perform inspired improvisations of the songs in the collection (if you have a MIDI keyboard). You can also watch the music scroll by in real time on the notation screen and can rearrange or reorchestrate any of the songs by using Multimedia Songbook's mixer.

Midisoft Music Mentor
Midisoft Corp.
(206) 881-7176
$29.95

Midisoft Multimedia Songbook
$39.95

Music Time

MusicTime is a low-cost, junior version of Encore, the popular professional notation package from Passport Designs. Though not as powerful as its older sibling, it has a personality all its own and a few unique features that make it a bit more useful to the casual, nonprofessional user.

This package is intended as a recreational music tool, and though some study is required to get to know it, the documentation makes using MusicTime as easy as can be for MIDI under Windows. You can use your QWERTY keyboard to input music and hear it play, although it's easier to work with a MIDI instrument. You can also use your mouse to click notes onto the standard musical staff and play them back,

then select, copy, and paste to rearrange your opus.

MusicTime also serves as a rudimentary sequencer and MIDI editor, which makes it useful as a good, basic MIDI music utility. You can load a MIDI file from any source, let MusicTime notate it, then edit it yourself to reassign instrumental parts and perform simple balancing and mixing using the usual Windows cut-and-paste methods. Of course, there are other products available to fill these functions at a much more sophisticated level (many also sold by Passport), but if you need a Swiss Army knife for MIDI files, MusicTime will fill the bill.

Don't be misled by the goofy beatniks on the splash screen; though MusicTime is meant for fun, it's entirely suitable for producing professional printed scores as long as they're not too ambitious. With a maximum of four voices on up to eight staves, it can handle most standard piano-vocal or quartet music. You wouldn't want to tackle Beethoven's *Ninth Symphony* with MusicTime, but for $99 it's hard to beat.

MusicTime
Passport Designs Inc.
(800) 443-3210
$99

Soloist

There's very little software on the market that can recognize pitch from a microphone, and what exists is very limited in ability. Soloist, from Ibis

Software, is one of the few music education games that uses a microphone for input rather than a keyboard or other MIDI device.

The purpose of the game is to read the notes presented on the screen and sing or play their pitches accurately into the microphone. Soloist doesn't really recognize absolute pitch; it can distinguish C from D, but it can't always distinguish middle C from high C because of the acoustical phenomenon known as the overtone series. Overtones allow your ear to tell the difference between a piano and a trumpet, even when they play the same note, but they make it very difficult for a PC to determine the fundamental pitch of a note accurately. Given the difficulty, Soloist is a primitive but useful tool for teaching beginning sight singing.

The best thing about Soloist is that it doesn't require you to use a MIDI instrument; in fact, only a normal acoustic instrument will work. There are some drawbacks to the program, however: It will not save your input in MIDI format, the games are limited to three keys (C, F, and G), and rhythm is not considered at all.—Bill Dyszel

Soloist
Ibis Software
(415) 546-1917
$59.95

Microsoft Musical Instruments

Of the handful of electronic music guides available on CD-ROM, few compare with Microsoft Musical Instruments. It takes you on tour of a wide musical world with over 200 instruments from alto sax to zither, indexed and cataloged for your listening pleasure. The program includes Families of Instruments, which classifies instruments by the method they use to make music; the Musical Ensembles section, which tells you how instruments make music together; and Instruments of the World, which explains the origin and heritage of the instruments. You simply click an icon to hear each instrument playing.—Bill Dyszel

Microsoft Musical Instruments
Microsoft Corp.
(800) 426-9400; (206) 882-8080
$59.95

PUTTING THE FUN IN MUSIC FUNDAMENTALS

MusicAce

MusicAce is an educational game designed to teach beginners the most rudimentary elements of pitch matching and key signatures. It's recommended for ages eight and up, but it's really most suitable for the preadolescent set.

The package as a whole is lively, colorful, and inviting, and the graphics and musical samples are unusually well done for a DOS game. At the core of the program lie a series of lessons designed to teach beginners fundamental music skills such as scales, key signatures, and keyboard basics. After each of the self-paced lesson, young musicians can test their newly acquired knowledge by playing arcade-like music games MusicAce also includes a jukebox for playing the included song files, and a Music Doodle Pad for creating and playing users' simple compositions with a variety of different instrument sounds.

Parents and educators should take note that MusicAce focuses entirely on

It's possible that the psyche of the individual requires getting away in some sneaky way to maintain mental stability. Has

ringLearningLearningLearning

pitch, not rhythm, and when rhythm gets involved, MusicAce does not use standard musical notation with note stems and tails; it relies on its own system of variously shaped note blobs to express rhythmic value. That may not fit everyone's teaching philosophy, but the fact that it's fun to use, runs under DOS, and doesn't require a MIDI device to use may outweigh any reservations.

If you're not interested in learning to read music, MusicAce is captivating because it's so much fun to watch. The program opens by showing you a grand staff accompanied by a catchy, boogie-woogie tune. As the tune plays, cartoon notes jump around the staff. It's a merry musical animation that makes learning fun.
—Bill Dyszel

MusicAce
Harmonic Vision
(708) 467-2395
$59.95

The Viking Opera Guide on CD-ROM

Bravo! The inclusion of color pictures, music excerpts, and an audio introduction turns a great print reference into an even better tool. The best part is that the package includes both book and disc.

The Viking Opera Guide on
CD-ROM
Penguin Books USA
(800) 253-6476
$99.95

MUSIC: LEARNING TO PLAY PIANO

Musicware Piano for Windows

Sure, when you were a kid piano lessons were a loathsome thing, but now you wish you knew how to play. Those who played second base instead of Chopin can now take advantage of Musicware Piano, a self-pacing instructional system that makes it possible to learn to play piano while sitting at your PC.

While other systems stress the fun or performance aspects of playing, Musicware Piano takes a more structured approach. It starts with the basics and builds skills from there. Here, the basics means learning the keyboard, the positioning of the hands, and the concept of rhythm. The software also provides instruction in music theory, notation, ear training, and sight reading.

What makes Musicware Piano such a good teacher is the on-screen, immediate feedback it provides. For example, when you're trying to play a piece of music in rhythm, you follow the rhythm line, matching the length of your notes to that of the ideal line displayed on-screen.

Course One of the Musicware Piano system covers the entire first year of piano instruction, with more than 200 lessons in all. When you're ready to move on, you can purchase more advanced

courses for $99.99 each; song packs are also available.

If you have a multimedia PC and a MIDI keyboard, you have no excuse for not learning how to play. Musicware Piano won't have you playing Beethoven the first time you load up the software, but it will teach you the skills you need to make music for a lifetime.
—Gayle C. Ehrenman

Musicware Piano for
Windows, Course One
$129.95

The Miracle Piano Teaching System

Remember when you were young and your mother made you practice the piano for hours on end? Today's kids have The Miracle Piano Teaching System. This interactive teaching system uses a Mac, a piano keyboard, and software to teach piano fundamentals. Click on a room in the Conservatory, and choose the lesson you want to practice.

The Miracle Piano
Teaching System
The Software Toolworks
$499.95

So I've Heard

If you don't know a lot about "highbrow" music, the So I've Heard series of CD-ROMs written by music critic Alan Rich will painlessly educate you both to the joys of the classics and to which

versions of classic works you should buy when you hit the CD store.

So I've Heard
The Voyager Company
$24.95 per volume.

The Orchestra: The Instruments Revealed

Featuring Benjamin Britten's *The Young Person's Guide to the Orchestra* (in a performance conducted by the composer), The Orchestra: The Instruments Revealed is a wonderful introduction to the instruments of the symphony orchestra. Audio examples, exercises, and analyses are entertainingly presented.

The Orchestra:
The
Instruments
Revealed
Time-Warner
Interactive
Group
$79.98

anyone studied the psychology of all this? Nope. 💻 Too many computer products do nothing more than squeeze more

LearningLearningLearningLea

Microsoft Multimedia Stravinsky

Not all symphonic music has a calming effect. Stravinsky's

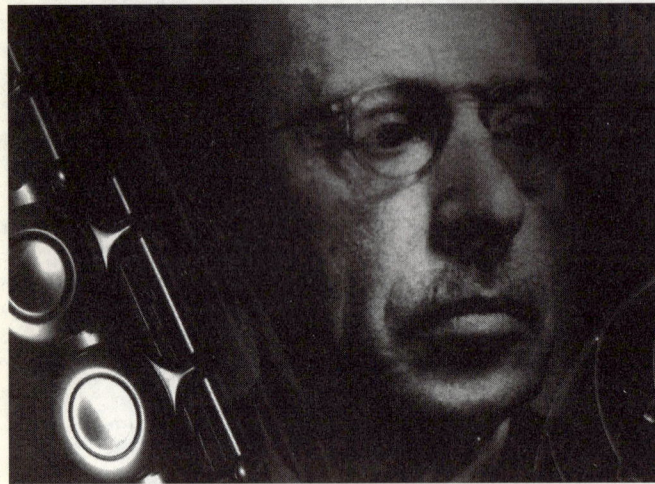

The Rite of Spring, for example, caused a riot when it was first performed in 1913. Ever since then, audiences have found this seminal composition interesting but often difficult. On Microsoft Multimedia Stravinsky: The Rite of Spring, UCLA music professor Robert Winter manages to make *The Rite of Spring* much more accessible.

Employing an array of multimedia techniques, Winter offers insights and brings a cohesion to Stravinsky's famous work that listeners might not otherwise discover. There's an aural tour of the orchestra, notes on Nijinsky's ballet, a biographical sketch of the composer, and even a game.

Relatively sophisticated classical music buffs will

appreciate Winter's close analysis, which takes you through Charles Dutoit's Montreal Symphony Orchestra performance note by note and instrument by instrument.

Microsoft Multimedia Stravinsky
Microsoft Corp.
(800) 426-9400; (206) 882-8080
$79.95

Beethoven's 5th

Perhaps no music is more recognizable than the opening strains of Beethoven's *Fifth Symphony*, but this exploration will enhance your appreciation of its grandeur. Beethoven's 5th: The Multimedia Symphony includes video clips of musicians, a section on the instruments, and the entire score, with a performance by the Zagreb Philharmonic under Richard Erdlinger. This well-

rounded disk should pique your interest in the Fifth beyond *da-da-da-dum*.

Beethoven's 5th:
The Multimedia Symphony
Interactive Publishing Corp.
(800) 472-8777
$59.95

ROLL OVER, BEETHOVEN

Multimedia Mozart Multimedia Stravinsky

Microsoft has added two more titles to the interactive CD-ROM series that began with Multimedia Beethoven. Mozart's *Dissonant* quartet and Stravinsky's *The Rite of Spring* may never share a concert bill, but together they illustrate the series's diversity. The discs, compiled by UCLA professor Robert Winter, teem with information.

The *Dissonant* quartet was written in 1785 as part of a set of six string quartets dedicated to Haydn, who pretty much formalized that instru-

mental structure. While it's impossible for us to listen to the piece with 1785-era ears, Multimedia Mozart does its best to re-create the period. An interactive tour of Mozart's life includes 66 screens of photos and information that expand into hypertext definitions, bibliographical citations, and musical examples. A section titled Quartet Listening does an excellent job of explaining the whys and wherefores of the format, and why the quartet has been so attractive to composers—and listeners—for so long.

By contrast, the Multimedia Stravinsky disc focuses on the orchestra and the dance. *The Rite of Spring* was written for Sergei Diaghilev's dance company, Ballets Russes, and choreographed by the legendary Vaslav Nijinsky. The pounding, manic rhythms of the work alternate with music of such sensuous languor that many in the original 1913 audience were outraged.

That's not likely to be the reaction today, which is why the 157-screen Rite Listening section is essential to develop a sense of musical and historical context. Breaking the

work down into its components of theme, harmony, rhythm, and cadence, the section and its many musical examples remind us how powerful a piece *The Rite of Spring* remains. There's also an engaging look at the original choreography, long lost but recently reconstructed.

Each disc finishes with a quiz in the form of an interactive game. At the heart of both discs is the music itself, which plays continuously in the Close Listening section to a succession of informative screens. Along the way you can stop, examine musical scores, and listen to component themes. What's most valuable about the CD-ROMs' interactive, multimedia approach to music is that they provide an active listening experience for aculture that has grown accustomed to music as background noise.—B.A. Nilsson

Multimedia Mozart
Multimedia Stravinsky
Microsoft Inc.
One Microsoft Way
Redmond, WA 98052
(800) 323-3577; (206) 882-8080
$79.95

What's the Macintosh versus IBM-PC breakdown? Surveys show it's 22 percent Macintosh owners and 72 percent PCs.

ningLearningLearningLearning

Microsoft Multimedia Schubert

Voyager wrote the CD-ROM on how to create top-notch multimedia titles. The company is responsible for an entire line of superlative classical CD-ROMs (sold through Microsoft), including Multimedia Schubert: The Trout Quintet, a disk that represents the pinnacle of Voyager's series so far.

Schubert's lyrical quintet is a masterpiece that requires no introduction, but this disk manages to illuminate the music without stepping on it or boring the user. Most of the credit goes to music critic Alan Rich, who does an excellent job bringing Schubert's music to life.

Though other classical music CD-ROM titles often come off as dry or disorganized, Rich's homespun eloquence strikes the right chord, conveying his obvious enthusiasm for the quintet and instilling in the listener a new appreciation for this subtle piece of music. The material is well written and interspersed with lively quotes

and anecdotes that prevent it from slipping into mere pedantry.

Highlights of the disk include articles and slides that take us through 1819 Vienna and Schubert's short life. It also has an intriguing close reading of the work, complete with a performance by Elisabeth Leonskaya and the Alan Berg Quartet.

*Microsoft Multimedia Schubert
Microsoft Corp.
(800) 426-9400; (206) 882-8080
$79.95*

Mozart String Quartet

Can CD-ROMs provide an experience equivalent to chamber music? The best way to find out may be to try Mozart String Quartet, Voyager's treatment of one of Amadeus's most sublime works (K. 145). For serious

multimedia mavens, this one is also available with an accompanying laser disc performance.

*Mozart String Quartet
The Voyager Company
$59.95*

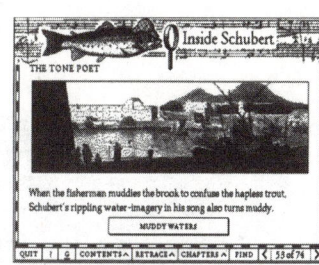

Schubert Trout Quintet

The CD-ROM format often seems to best lend itself to program music such as the famous *Trout Quintet*. The disc Schubert Trout Quintet offers a fascinating analysis of the structure of the quintet as well as information about Schubert the man and the composer.

*Schubert Trout Quintet
The Voyager Company
$59.95*

Beethoven: Symphony No. 9

Beethoven: Symphony No. 9 was the first CD-ROM Guide to the Classics, and it still holds up well, largely because of the contagious enthusiasm of its author, Robert Winter. No wonder

Microsoft licensed this program as a show-piece for Windows.

*Beethoven: Symphony No. 9
The Voyager Company; $79.95.*

Strauss: Three Tone Poems

Strauss: Three Tone Poems takes three of Richard Strauss's tone poems—*Don Juan, Till Eulenspiegel*, and *Death and Transfiguration*—and gives them Voyager's usual high-class(ical) treatment. It's in black-and-white

only, but its beautiful art-nouveau graphics put many color programs to shame.

*Strauss: Three Tone Poems
The Voyager Company
$59.95*

via the network. Most machines with built-in microphones let you turn on the microphones remotely, allowing employers

LearningLearningLea

HISTORY

ON THE BEACH AT NORMANDY

The Simon & Schuster D-Day Encyclopedia

Until last spring, if you asked a person on the street about Omaha, the answer probably had to do with Nebraska. But the media's 50th-anniversary blitz has brought Omaha Beach and the rest of the D-Day invasion back into the limelight. Now students and history buffs can share in the sights and sounds of June 6, 1944 with Context Systems's CD-ROM edition of The Simon & Schuster D-Day Encyclopedia.

Context Systems has given the printed encyclopedia the full Windows multimedia treatment. Along with some 400 articles and photos describing the events of and around D-Day, the disc includes animated graphics, archival video clips, and voiceover commentary.

Take the Media Tour to start your D-Day experience, and you'll come face to face with newsreel footage of the armada assembled to carry the invasion forces across the Channel. As a narrator talks, barges slide from their moorings and smash into the Channel waters. Or for an overview, the annotated Timeline Tour presents a historical perspective.

To review what came before Operation Overlord, you can run for shelter during the Blitz, as waves of V-2 flying bombs, fighter planes,

and bombers carve the reality of war into the London skyline. The sound of a V-2's buzz overhead is as unmistakable as the whistle of falling bombs. Once the Allies have arrived on the continent, news footage takes you into the middle of tank and artillery duels in the cornfields of western France.

Text descriptions of the events leading up to D-Day, the invasion itself, and its aftermath form the foundation for more spectacular videos. Still photos detail places, events, and people— both major players and the more numerous, anonymous soldiers and civilians.

The D-Day Encyclopedia is also filled with full-color maps; some are static re-creations of their paper counterparts, while others are interactive. They feature landmark and participant labels that you can click on to reveal more details about mission objectives and the forces involved. D-Day represents a portion of history we can't afford to forget. And the D-Day Encyclopedia is an excellent reference to this event.—Bill O'Brien

*The Simon & Schuster
D-Day Encyclopedia
Context Systems Inc.
2935 Byberry Rd.
Hatboro, PA 19040
(215) 675-5000
$79.95*

🐍 David Duke Virus—Makes your screen go completely white.

"I'm a '60s historian—I've studied the sixties, and my background is in the computer industry. This (the CD-ROM, "Haight-Ashbury in the Sixties") is my artistic statement. The '60s gave me a context to live in: John Lennon, a lot of musicians, Allen Ginsberg, Tim Leary, a lot of people who really pushed the boundaries of thought and who were involved in a cultural renaissance. I have the same kind of enthusiasm that a scholar would have for any period of history he was studying."

—TONY BOVE, MULTIMEDIA HISTORIAN, 1994

Time Almanac of the 20th Century

Ever doubted that this is one of the most exciting centuries in history? If so, get Time Almanac of the 20th Century. Through sound clips, video, photography, and text, this Windows program covers the aging century in a mixture of politics, war, technology, and people. Getting to the presentations and media clips from various approaches lets you

amble through the century wherever your interests take you. The CD-ROM includes a game called NewsQuest that looks like some dork educator's idea of how to trick pupils into learning history. It's nowhere near as interesting as the rest of the disc—or the last 90 years.—Ron White

*Time Almanac of the
20th Century
Compact Publishing
(800) 964-1518
$69.95*

Time Almanac of the 20th Century

There's no time like the present. Time Almanac of the 20th Century's 2,000 articles, 500 photos, and 40 minutes of video—all of good quality— provide a colorful decade-by-decade introduction to recent history. Narrated photo essays such as "Russia, the Death of the Dream" compare the U.S.S.R. of the 1930s to the disintegrating Soviet Union of the 1990s.

Time Almanac of the 20th century also contains maps, graphs, a time line, statistical tables, 12 photo essays on key 20th-century figures, and extensive coverage of all presidential elections since 1924. Additional material includes *Time* "Man of the Year" stories and original cover art since 1927, and Newsquest—a game to test your knowledge of 20th-century history. There's a great deal of essential information here for those interested in recent history.

*Time Almanac of the 20th
Century
Compact Publishing Inc.
(800) 964-1518; (202) 244-4770
$69.95*

to eavesdrop on the employees in their cubicles. TV cameras are the next tool in that game. Numerous programs count

ningLearningLearning

Gettysburg Multimedia Battle Simulation

For any Civil War buff, this CD is worth your PC's weight in gold. The Gettysburg Multimedia Battle Simulation will keep the war alive as long as there's a CD-ROM drive still standing. The disc is half history and half game. If you just want to learn how the battle was fought, sit back and watch the troops' movements on a map, read a written log, and listen to the narration by Shelby Foote, whose stellar PBS documentary on the Civil War won ratings by the million; you can even watch scenes from the movie Gettysburg. But if you think you can top the generals of the North or South, take command yourself—direct troops, try out tactics, and see if you can change the course of history.

Gettysburg Multimedia Battle Simulation
Swfte Intl.
(800) 237-9383
$69.95

Normandy: The Great Crusade

Oh, why couldn't history have been like this when I was in school? With its newsreels, radio recordings, and photographs, Normandy: The Great Crusade proves that learning history can be more interesting and immediate than a prime-time eyewitness news report.

This disc does an excellent job of bringing the Discovery Channel's documentary to your PC. Explore D-Day through maps or on-the-scenes newsreels, read soldiers' letters, and listen to narration that brings it all together. Immerse yourself in the mood of the home front, too—right down to the latest swing tune. For people who know of Omaha Beach only as a textbook reference, this is a great CD.

Normandy: The Great Crusade
Discovery Communications
(301) 986-0444
$49.95

The Constitution Papers

No multimedia frills here. This CD is a text-only, DOS-based collection of 44 key historical documents, including the U.S. Constitution, the Declaration of Independence,

the Federalist Papers, and the constitutions of the original 13 colonies. These texts have been analyzed by WordCruncher, a concordance program that lists all the significant words in its database. This is an invaluable research tool for students and historians.

The Constitution Papers
Johnston & Co.
(801) 756-1111
$99

The Haldeman Diaries

Okay, H.R. Haldeman may not be at the top of your most-admired list. Nevertheless, The Haldeman Diaries: Inside the Nixon White House gives a compelling, behind-the-scenes view of the Nixon administration from its times of triumph through the Watergate events.

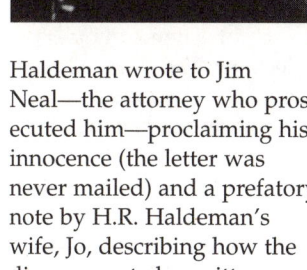

As White House chief of staff, Haldeman was in a position to record numerous historical and personal details that are essential reading for anyone studying the Nixon presidency. Along with the full text of Haldeman's 1,521-entry, 2,200-page diary, the disk includes Richard Nixon's presidential logbook and 2,000 pages of related documents. Other items of interest are a 120-page letter

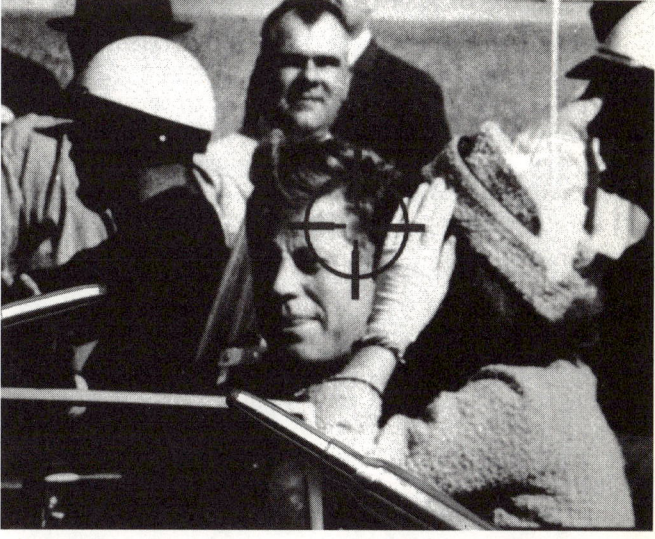

Haldeman wrote to Jim Neal—the attorney who prosecuted him—proclaiming his innocence (the letter was never mailed) and a prefatory note by H.R. Haldeman's wife, Jo, describing how the diary came to be written.

The program's textual material, accessible through a search engine and hyperlinks, is supplemented by 850 photographs and more than an hour of Haldeman's own White House home movies, edited down from more than 27 hours of footage. This program is a great example of how a CD-ROM can be more fun and more useful than a book.—Rubin Rabinovitz

The Haldeman Diaries
Sony Imagesoft
(800) 922-7669
$69.95

JFK Assassination

JFK Assassination: A Visual Investigation is more than a good history program; it's a model for how such programs should be put together. The written material includes the full text of two books on the Kennedy assassination—Crossfire, by Jim Marrs (the basis of Oliver Stone's film JFK), and The John F. Kennedy Assassination: A Complete Book of Facts—as well as the Warren Commission Report.

All of the text is easily accessible: You can use an index, a retrieval engine, or a copious array of hyperlinks to find material on the events of November 22, 1963. There's a lot of material here; for example, a search on Parkland leads to 137 references to Parkland Memorial Hospital.

JFK Assassination comes with 30 minutes of full-motion, full-screen video clips documenting the assassination, including the Zapruder film and other assassination eyewitness films. There are 22 computer-animated depictions of key events, showing such details as bullet angles, and an indexed photo library. Different portions of the program present biographical facts about President Kennedy, the events in Dallas, conspiracy theories, and the aftermath of the assassination. Regardless of your theories about the Kennedy assassination, this disc will inform and entertain you.

JFK Assassination:
A Visual Investigation
Medio Multimedia Inc.
(800) 788-3866
$59.95

The Anglo-Saxons

Recent discoveries have helped us learn more about life in early Britain. The Anglo-Saxons, developed in cooperation with the British Museum, conveys this information in a most attractive way. You can listen to Anglo-Saxon music, tackle Anglo-Saxon riddles, look at pictures of imaginary beasts, learn about the lives of British kings, find out about life in the monasteries, and get suggestions for places to visit if you're planning a trip to England.

You'll find fascinating illustrations of relevant artifacts, weapons, and manuscripts from the British Museum's extensive Anglo-Saxon Collection and other collections. The Anglo-Saxons also features quizzes based on the included material. Anyone studying medieval history, art, and architecture will not only learn a great deal from this program but will enjoy using it.

The Anglo-Saxons
Cambrix Publishing
(800) 992-8781
$59.95

Who Built America?

Every student of American history will probably be enthralled with Who Built America?, a multimedia CD-ROM featuring the complete text of a two-volume history book, hundreds of pictures, 45 minutes of QuickTime video, and loads of recorded voices and music. (There's even a copy of the world's first crossword puzzle!) The subject? America from 1876 to 1914, the period that saw the growth of the United States from a rural backwater into the beginnings of a world superpower.

Who Built America?
The Voyager Company
$99.95

samples from historic speeches, QuickTime movies of historical events, and extensive original source documents.

The Enduring Vision
D.C. Heath and Co.
125 Spring St.
Lexington, MA 02173
(509) 468-0807
$44.95

The Oregon Trail

The Oregon Trail puts you into the shoes of a pioneer traveling from Missouri to the Willamette Valley. You have to decide what to pack, when to go, the pace of your journey, and what to do in an emergency. Each decision

The Enduring Vision

An interactive textbook covering American history from the 1700s to the mid-1900s, The Enduring Vision contains the same information you'd find in a conventional textbook but also includes sound

affects the outcome of your journey, so be careful!

The Oregon Trail
MECC
6160 Summit Dr. N.
Minneapolis, MN 55430
(612) 686-0779
$69.95

The Anglo-Saxons

An Exploration of their Art, Literature and Way of Life

LITERATURE

SIX LITERARY GREATS STAR ON AFTER THE FIRE CD-ROM

After the Fire

Using After the Fire from the BookWorm Student Library line is like having a topnotch professor sitting beside you as you read the classics— well, many of the classics—of late 19th-century American

literature. Like a good professor, Communication and Information Technology's Macintosh CD-ROM (a Windows version is due presently) not only provides scholarly details, but makes its subject fascinating.

The disc includes selected works of Kate Chopin, Stephen Crane, Emily Dickinson, Frederick Douglass, Henry James, and

Mark Twain. Besides providing complete texts, After the Fire also provides an array of tools to help you analyze the authors' works.

Most notably, the books in After the Fire are extensively annotated; you access the annotations simply by clicking on highlighted text. Depending on the importance and complexity of a passage, there may be several different annotations from which to choose. Many include still images or audio, and the Twain works have dramatic videos.

You can also create your own annotations, which can include your own text notes or pictures, movies, sounds, or hyperlinks to other elements in the work. Other tools include a dictionary for defining any word in the text,

the ability to search for specific text, and options to create bookmarks and marginal notes. A button click accesses tools.

One weakness of After the Fire is that it doesn't contain the complete works of some of its authors. For example, Stephen Crane's *The Red Badge of Courage* is missing. Nor does After the Fire have room for some of the other literary giants of the past century, such as Hawthorne, Melville, or Thoreau. Other discs in the BookWorm catalog make up for that shortcoming, but After the Fire would still benefit from a general overview of this fascinating era in America's literary history.

Overall, After the Fire's limitations make it best suited as an introduction to the authors, not as a complete guide to their best works or to their lives and times. Still, if you're interested in the literature of the late nineteenth century, After the Fire is an excellent teacher. It's also an excellent example of how multimedia can enhance great literature, but not replace it.—David Haskin, Preston Gralla

After the Fire
Communication and
Information Technology
11020 Solway School Rd.
Suite 103
Knoxville, TN 37931
(800) 845-1755; (615) 927-4601
$59.95

THE LIFE AND TIMES OF SAMUEL CLEMENS COME TO DISC

Twain's World

Twain's World is a happy departure from the literary CD-ROM tedium of the past. There's much more to Bureau Development's new disc than just a catchy title. It's a well-thought-out tribute to Samuel Clemens (aka Mark Twain), who not only serves as the role model for most of today's gadflies in print, but is generally acknowledged as this country's greatest humorist—not to mention, at least in Hemingway's opinion, author of its greatest novel.

In addition to the expected collection of Clemens's written works, Twain's World brings the temper of the author's times and the little-known tragedies of his life into sharp focus with a

wealth of photos and narration artfully integrated into the fabric of the written materials. Dozens of clever animation sequences are embedded into the written text. For example, as you read about Huck Finn rafting down the river, a brief part of the scene is played out in motion and sound.

The written compendium is scholarly and complete. Unabashed fans of Clemens will be delighted to find that the disc includes both versions of The Celebrated Jumping Frog of Calaveras County, for instance. The original holds its own as an example of overstated American folklore; Twain's later rewrite, occasioned by an unflattering translation of the original tale by an unmitigated Gaul, is a satiric gem. Augmenting the hilarious text of The Re-Translation, Clawed Back From the

modem jack and a power cord. But apparently this trend is too healthy! It seems that now we expect people to work like

LearningLearningLea

French, Into a Civilized Language Once More is a wealth of satisfying critical, historical, and biographical background material.

A logically organized graphic menu makes getting into Twain's World easy even for total novices. Terms with which the reader may not be familiar are highlighted and hotlinked to descriptive passages available at the click of a mouse. For the adventurous, a flexible search engine, plenty of navigation buttons, and a solid bookmark facility make a detailed exploration of the disc an easy task. Twain's World has written a new chapter in the evolution of literary MPC titles. In comparison, previous CD-ROMs of the same ilk are little more than rough drafts.—Arlan Levitan

Twain's World
Bureau Development Inc.
141 New Rd.
Parsippany, NJ 07054
(201) 808-2700
$39.95

Twain's World

Buy this one for the text—not the multimedia effects. Twain's World contains the complete works of Mark Twain, including his essays, speeches, and letters, all of which are indexed for searching. The Timeline is a powerful tool for tracking the author's life, and the quizzes are good study tools. There are few video clips, though, and some of the cartoonish

animations are downright offensive.

Twain's World
Bureau of Electronic
Publishing Inc.
(201) 808-2700
$79.95

Poetry in Motion

If you think contemporary poetry is a rather dull business, this unique multimedia anthology may change your mind. It includes the full text of poems from 23 poets, but that's just the start. Poetry in Motion also gives you QuickTime videos of the authors reciting, ranting, or otherwise performing their works, often with musical backup. The writers—among them Allen Ginsberg, Robert Creeley, John Cage, and Ntozake Shange—were chosen as much for their striking reading styles as for the significance of their work. This means there's rarely a slow moment, even when the poetry itself isn't of the highest literary quality. Video interviews with many of the poets provide some intriguing insights into their writing. English Lit 101 was never like this.—Robert Kendall

Poetry in Motion
Voyager
(800) 446-2001; (914) 591-5500
$29.99

Poetry in Motion

"Poetry's always been said to be a private hidden art, not appreciated," said Charles

Bukowski. Poetry in Motion successfully dispels this myth by turning poetry from something read alone at home or in a library into something heard and seen on a PC.

Filmed by Ron Mann, Poetry in Motion contains 24 contemporary poets reading from their work. Additional interviews are included for most of the authors. Although the video plays in tiny windows, the readings bring the works alive, revealing intonations a solitary reader might not otherwise notice. The poets range from the famous (Allen Ginsberg) to the relatively unknown (Chris Dewdney) to those more widely known for their music (Tom Waits and the late John Cage).

Voyager has made the user controls on this disk as unobtrusive and flexible as possible, with sound-level and playback buttons neatly hidden behind the words and images.

Poetry in Motion
The Voyager Co.
(800) 446-2001
$29.95

The Columbia Granger's World of Poetry

For general use, The Columbia Granger's World of Poetry is hard to beat. It offers a good, representative collection of the best-known poems in English, a well-designed interface, and a powerful search engine. Though it's available only in

a DOS version, it can run in a Microsoft Windows DOS box.

Granger's gives the full texts of 8,500 poems—more than any rival program—and this is one of its most impressive features. It includes 3,000 quotations from 1,500 other works, along with title and first-line information for 100,000 poems. These works encompass the text of Granger's Index to Poetry, Eighth Addition; The Columbia Granger's Index to Poetry, Ninth Edition; The

Columbia Dictionary of Poetry Quotations; and The Columbia Granger's Guide to Poetry Anthologies. In all, the database covers 15,000 poets, 550 poetry anthologies, and 4,000 subject headings, including Aardvarks, Abandonment, Abbeys, and much more.

You can search through the ample database by title, first line, author, and key word or phrase. Search strings are limited to 40 characters, though, and search

"I actually think that although we've been talking about multimedia for about five years, I believe over the next three years we'll actually see customer adoption of real products.

It also means being able to create products that incorporate a much greater level of intelligence for customers. For example, in the graphics area, we have a lot of customers who really are not artists, who need a significant level of intelligence built into their applications. In the database arena, they need this intelligence in the area of searching and the ability to do pattern recognition on a level we've never seen before.

Within three years, we'll see significant breakthroughs in greater intelligence in applications, greater support among multimedia types, and greater support of new forms of pattern recognition—whether handwriting or voice. All of the things we have been dreaming about for the last decade will become real at what we think of as mainstream application price points of $1,000, $2,000, and $3,000."

—DAN EILERS, VICE PRESIDENT, APPLE COMPUTER, 1994

Some industry analysts predict the home market will become the biggest PC market by the year 2000.

routines can be quite slow. These are just minor drawbacks of an otherwise commendable product. The main drawback is Granger's steep $699 price tag; for occasional use, a different package might be in order. Serious poetry scholars, however, can do no better.—Rubin Rabinovitz

The Columbia Granger's World of Poetry Columbia University Press (800) 944-8648; (212) 666-1000 $699

Great Poetry Classics

For the casual poetry fan, or someone just looking for on-screen versions of old favorites, World Library's Great Poetry Classics is the disc to choose. Though this $49.95 bargain is available in both DOS and Windows editions, the outstanding interface of the Windows version makes it the preferred choice. With the Windows version, you can use the Clipboard to move text into your own files and work with as many as eight different poems at once. You can select the size and style of the screen fonts and, if you'd like, display stanza and line numbers for the poems. Great Poetry Classics offers another valuable feature, Autoscroll, which continuously moves the text of a poem up the screen at the speed you choose (it looks something like movie credits rolling).

The drawback of this disc is that it includes only 1,150

poems, versus Granger's 8,500. There are no poems by Swift, Hopkins, Auden, or Stevens; Marlowe, Marvell, Dryden, Pope, and Eliot are represented by only one selection each. And though the disc does credit the translators of foreign-language poems, the translations are not always the versions favored by poetry scholars.

Even so, Great Poetry Classics does include the full texts of some important long works, among them Homer's *Iliad*, Beowulf, Dante's *Inferno*, Chaucer's *Canterbury Tales*, and Byron's *Don Juan*. Having these texts available in searchable electronic form opens up interesting possibilities for analysis. For example, you could compile comprehensive lists of color images in *The Canterbury Tales*, of references to the gods in *The Iliad*, or—by searching for like and as—of similes in *Don Juan*. This capability alone is worth the price of the program.—Rubin Rabinovitz

Great Poetry Classics World Library Inc. (800) 443-0238; (714) 756-9500 $49.95

Poem Finder 94

Unlike Granger's and Great Poetry Classics, Roth Publishing's $295 Poem Finder 94 doesn't provide the texts of the poems it indexes: It's restricted to titles, first lines, and (for some entries) last lines. Thus you'll need to look in an anthology to follow up on the program's refer-

ences, and key-word searches won't work if you remember only a random line of a poem. These limitations make the DOS-only Poem Finder more suitable for scholarly research than for casual perusal.

Poem Finder's strength is its gargantuan database, which indexes 360,000 poems and 44,000 authors. The package draws data from 1,600 anthologies, 2,100 single-author collections, and 109 periodicals. Unlike Granger's and Great Poetry Classics, Poem Finder includes many contemporary poems and foreign poems in translation.

Along with titles and first lines, Poem Finder can locate verse by subject, author, or translator—even by author's nationality, religion, or profession. For example, the "Actresses" heading will help you discover that Katherine Hepburn once published a poem called "Thank You, Gorbachev!"

Poem Finder is unrivaled when it comes to tracking down poems on unusual topics. Granger's and Great Poetry Classics have no listings for poems about com-

puters; Poem Finder has 10. The program can refer you to 271 poems about death and 1,760 about love. It can help you find poems about Cleopatra, Beethoven, Lenin, Elvis Presley, and Muhammad Ali. In short: If poem finding's the racket, Poem Finder can hack it.—Rubin Rabinovitz

Poem Finder 94 Roth Publishing Inc. (800) 899-7684; (516) 466-3676 $295

All My Hummingbirds Have Alibis

Inspired by Max Ernst's collage novels, All My Hummingbirds Have Alibis provides a taste of how multimedia will change and challenge artistic expression in the future. With its combination of Ernst's mystical artwork, Morton Subotnick's music, and informative commentaries, this is a fascinating disc to explore.

All My Hummingbirds Have Alibis The Voyager Company $39.95

A Zillion Kajillion Rhymes

If you are a frustrated garage-band songwriter or a tender-hearted poet, check out A Zillion Kajillion Rhymes. Now if you really need to figure out what rhymes with

banana for your groundbreaking "Ode to Fruit," you can list all your options in no time—bandanna, hosanna, and vox humana—to name just a few.

A Zillion Kajillion Rhymes Eccentric Software $49.95

and employers. You can't push a "fast" button on employees. They start to fall apart. Or they rebel and wreck the place.

LearningLearningLea

Expanded Books

Voyager's line of Expanded Books keep getting better and better. New books on-disc include Randy Shilts's *Conduct Unbecoming* and Scott Turow's *Pleading Guilty*—perfect for reading online on your PowerBook. Macmillan New Media has jumped on the bandwagon, releasing its own Expanded Books: the I Love series of travel guides for Boston, New York, and Washington as well as other titles such as an on-disc version of Peter Gammons's book *Coming Apart at the Seams.*

Expanded Books
The Voyager Company and Macmillan New Media
$19.95 to $29.95

BOOK TO THE FUTURE

Electric Science Fiction: Hugo and Nebula Anthology

Books on disc have been around a while, but Electric Science Fiction: Hugo and Nebula Anthology goes worlds beyond the usual. This CD-ROM from ClariNet Communications contains five complete novels as well as numerous short stories and art that were nominated for either Hugo or Nebula awards. At $29.95, it's the best deal in electronic books. Because the anthology was assembled in short order so that SF fans could read nominated works before casting award ballots, some manuscripts went directly from their authors' computers to

the CD-ROM. So download a novel to your laptop and find out just how good your favorite author's spelling actually is.—James Bradbury

Electric Science Fiction: Hugo and Nebula Anthology
ClariNet Communications
(408) 296-0366

LANGUAGE LEARNING/ SPEAKING IN TONGUES

Power Japanese 1.1

To most Americans, the prospect of learning to speak Japanese seems about as likely as climbing Mt. Fuji. But a remarkable audio-enhanced program called Power Japanese brings the language of the world's second-largest economic power within reach.

Power Japanese does not make learning Japanese fast or easy—that's simply not possible. Japanese is a dizzyingly difficult language by Western standards. However, Power Japanese does manage to parcel the language into digestible portions. More important, the Windows program enlivens its lessons with sound, graphics, and simple animations that hold your interest even if you're not a dedicated student.

The package includes a tiny sound adapter that plugs into a parallel port, headphones, the software (on 16 disks), an exercise book, a stack of flash cards, and a translation dictionary. The sound adapter and headphones make it an ideal product for portable PCs, though the software also

works with desktop PC sound boards and speakers.

The software is divided into four "books." The first two cover the phonetic symbols used for writing native Japanese and foreign words; the last two cover key grammatical concepts. Installing all four books (and their 2,000-plus sound files) consumes a whopping 34MB of disk space, so BayWare advises installing the 5MB to 8MB books one at a time.

Using the program, you page through screens of liberally illustrated, colorful instructions and drills. Power Japanese also does something that makes perfect sense for a language learning tool: It talks. Point and click on a word or phrase, and you hear the correct pronunciation by a Japanese speaker. In addition, the software gives you the opportunity to practice drawing the symbols of Japanese by following animated writing sequences— though the mouse is a poor substitute for the pen.

BayWare claims that you can learn to speak, read, and write basic Japanese in less than 10 weeks. I've been using the program for less than half that, but having learned a foreign language before (and having been to Japan), it's clear that "basic" is the key word here. Fluency would take much longer— and likely require either a fluent colleague for conversation or an extended stay in Japan.

Version 2.0 of Power Japanese, which should be available now, adds more advanced tutoring, a built-in Japanese word processor, an online dictionary, more digitized pronunciations, and a voice record-and-compare feature so you can better measure your progress in speaking the language. The new version will also be available on CD-ROM.

If you're feeling ambitious, you can hone your skills with Kanji Moments, a series of supplementary programs that list for $89 apiece. Kanji is the traditional set of Japanese

characters, each representing a word or idea, derived from Chinese. There are thousands of Kanji characters; the six volumes of Kanji Moments cover the mere hundreds you need to get by in everyday life.

Power Japanese is not magic; it still requires time and practice to see results. But it may be the closest thing to magic ever put into a language learning course.— Christopher O'Malley

Power Japanese 1.1
BayWare Inc.
1720 S. Amphlett Blvd.
Suite 205
San Mateo, CA 94402
(800) 538-8867; (415) 312-0980
$389

Berlitz Live!

Business travelers don't need large vocabularies or a knowledge of complex grammar rules. Simple stock phrases for everyday situations will suffice, along with enough advice to avoid making major cross-cultural gaffes. Berlitz Live! Spanish meets these conditions in a colorful and entertaining way.

Live! Spanish covers the grammatical essentials but spends most of its time teaching conversational specifics on subjects such as eating out and going through customs. Each of these sections contains dozens of useful phrases ("We have 80 percent of the U.S. market"). There are hotkey screens where you can click objects to find out their names and chapter-end quizzes to test how much you've learned. Live! Spanish also

ningLearningLearning

supplies cultural tips. Everything here you'll find in a decent travel book, such as visa requirements and advice on how to greet new contacts, but Live! Spanish accompanies it all with folk melodies.

Stunning artwork, interactive dialogues, well-chosen phrases, quizzes, and folk songs make Live! Spanish an entertaining and useful tool for business travelers.—Barry Brenesal

Berlitz Live! Spanish
Sierra On-Line Inc.
(206) 649-9800
$134.95

Learn to Speak Spanish

With Learn to Speak Spanish, you'll not only understand the language, you'll speak it fluently. This program uses an all-inclusive approach in its 30 chapters. You hear a word in context in one of 60 staged conversations. Then you read the word in written transcripts of dialogue, see it represented as an object, say it using an optional microphone to record your voice, and write it in a series of sentence-based drills. The program also offers easy-to-access hints and translations.

This program is definitely not for the person who just wants to learn the basics. But given time, patience, and dedication, its approach will pay off handsomely.—Barry Brenesal

Learn to Speak Spanish
Hyperglot Software Co.
(800) 726-5087; (615) 558-8270
$179.95

Power Spanish

Instilling you with linguistic confidence rather than expertise is the main goal of Power Spanish. The focus isn't on teaching grammatical rules. The package instead sets out to bring students quickly up to the level of simple conversation.

The methods used toward achieving this make Power Spanish a maverick among Spanish tutorials. It avoids cultural discussions; there are, for example, no references to Latin America or Spain. Visual associations between words and objects are eschewed, and new words aren't usually introduced within vocabulary lessons; they occur in sentences beside already familiar terms. It's up to you to click on any word you don't know if you want to hear its translation and pronunciation. Expect very little grammar instruction from Power Spanish. You will, however, find a set of lessons—which you may explore in or out of sequence—and a series of games, drills, and exercises that encourage you to start using the language as quickly as possible. Power Spanish also includes a 10,000-word dictionary, grammatical reference tables, and a bundled copy of Microtac Software's Spanish Assistant for Windows.

If you come to Power Spanish expecting a traditional language course, you'll be disappointed. But if you're prepared to adapt to its appearance and teaching methods,

you'll find yourself on an effective path to beginning-Spanish mastery.—Barry Brenesal

Power Spanish
BayWare Inc.
(800) 538-8867; (415) 286-4480
$149

Triple Play Plus Spanish

Triple Play Plus Spanish teaches object names and modifiers via 20 colorful games including bingo, Concentration, jigsaw puzzles, and map activities. Just choose your subject category—Home and Office, Transportation, People, Food, Numbers, or Activities—and prepare to be entertained. There are multiple levels of difficulty and practice modes. An additional 12 games, which take the form of talking comic strips, highlight commonplace situations such as visiting a restaurant. The games involve matching spoken passages to the correct visual frames. It's not as hard as it sounds, since you can hear dialogue at a slow speed, repeat isolated words and phrases, and access online help.

Some of the program's games integrate speech recognition. Using the included microphone, you can, for example, supply a requested object name instead of clicking on the answer. In sum, no Spanish tutorial is easier to use than Triple Play Plus Spanish.—Barry Brenesal

Triple Play Plus Spanish
Syracuse Language Systems
(315) 478-6729
$99.95

> "The real difference is that the multimedia experience is a creative experience and the user is not simply under a lot of rocks and discovering more information, which can be interesting but is cerebral. You have to be able to take possession of it."
>
> —ANN GREENBERG, VICE PRESIDENT, ION

Video Linguist Spanish

Video Linguist Spanish takes a very different approach to teaching Spanish. It offers no games, word lists, or grammar lessons—just 44 videos taken straight from Spanish television. And they aren't simply reruns of Robin Hood crying "Buenos noches, Sheriff de Nottingham" as he escapes out a window, either. These video clips concentrate on a range of typical Spanish television programming; you'll hear a running commentary on a basketball game and explore several of Spain's most famous art museums, for example.

You can switch between English and Spanish subtitles, or turn them off altogether. Highlight a word or phrase and the cinematics stop; you'll receive an instantaneous translation from the 3,000-word dictionary. Once you've got it down pat, you can record and play back your own pronunciation. An absence of hand-holding might make the program a bit daunting for the beginner, but Video Linguist is a perfect follow-up to Triple Play

Plus Spanish or Live! Spanish.—Barry Brenesal

Video Linguist Spanish
Cubic Media
(800) 232-8242; (215) 576-1200
$99

Word Torture

Learning a foreign language—especially building your vocabulary in that language—can be tough. Painful as it sounds, using Word Torture is a relatively easy way to learn words in whatever foreign language you're studying. And if you miss a word, Word Torture doesn't let you off easy—it repeats it again later, to see if you've learned your lesson.

Word Torture
HyperGlot
$49.95

Think and Talk

Each Think and Talk package is a seven-CD-ROM set that promises to teach you to speak and write Spanish, French, German, or Italian. Complete vocabulary lists,

will not contribute in any significant way to the welfare of the company. Too many employers don't seem to care about

LearningLearningLea...

conjugation tables, and pronunciation are included.

Think and Talk
HyperGlot Software
$199

MISCELLANEOUS

USING YOUR COMPUTER AS A TYPING TUTOR

Expert Typing for Windows

If cost is your primary consideration, take a look at Expert Typing for Windows. This low-cost program will teach you typing while offering a few niceties and extras.

Among other things, Expert Typing for Windows allows you to change screen colors, change the size of on-screen type, and set your own frustration level, which determines the number of characters you must type incorrectly before the program asks if you want to take a break. One of the extras is the Typing Gallery, a shooting gallery-type game in which you must type words as they appear on the screen. This may sound easy, but try it when there are three word bands on the screen and additional words popping up at random!

This one may not offer many bells and whistles, but it's a good low-price choice for older beginning typists.

Expert Typing for Windows
Expert Software
(800) 759-2562
$14.95

Kid Keys

Young children can be intimidated easily by the prospect of typing on a keyboard. To help them overcome this fear, Kid Keys uses animations, digitized speech, and sound to make keyboarding a fun, nonthreatening experience.

The secret is Keystone the Dragon, who guides youngsters through three activities: The Magic Keyboard, Dragon Tunes, and Monster Rescue. In the Magic Keyboard, children can choose to explore the keyboard on their own, or

they can choose to find letters and words as prompted by the program. At the toughest level, they're asked to find the first letter of the word whose picture appears on the screen. The Dragon Tunes exercise enables children to

play popular songs by typing letters on the keyboard. The Monster Rescue activity invites children to help free four monsters from the castle and send them home before dark.

As kids play the tunes and free the monsters, they grow more comfortable with the keyboard and learn how to use it. But don't tell them that; they'll just think they're having fun.

Kid Keys
Davidson & Associates
(800) 556-6141;
$49.95

Kid's Typing

Your host, tour guide, and playmate for Kid's Typing is Spooky, a friendly ghost who lives in the attic of a suburban home. Spooky teaches you the keys and has you type exercises. When you complete a lesson, he'll take you to another room in the house to practice what you've learned. Type Spooky's assignment and you'll haunt the room and cause strange things to happen. In the child's room, for example, you'll make the xylophone play as you type.

After each exercise, Spooky gives you spoken and on-screen feedback on your typing successes; he'll also adapt the lessons to your individual needs. If you want a change of pace, you can go to the Library and practice typing sections from classic stories, such as *The Emperor's New Clothes* and *Cinderella*. To practice typing a particular letter, choose a book on the encyclopedia shelf in the Library: Choose the letter A and you'll have to type things such as "Al, an anteater from Arkansas…." The program gives you two on-screen gauges: one for speed, the other for accuracy.

Spooky's encouragement and sense of humor make typing fun; and his tips on typing (such as keep your feet flat on the floor) will teach good habits, too.

Kid's Typing
Bright Star
(800) 757-7707
$49.95

Mario Teaches Typing

Your child says he's practicing his typing, but when you go near the computer, you hear the familiar sound of music from Mario games. Not to worry! Mario Teaches Typing is an ideal way to keep your young gamer interested in learning to touch-type; it teaches keyboarding while offering the excitement and familiarity of the Mario arcade games.

Sign in to Mario Teaches Typing and choose your alter ego: Mario, Luigi, or The Princess. Next, choose one of the three levels.

In Mario's Smash and Dash, you type the letters that appear on-screen to make your character run and jump, bust bricks, and kick turtle butt. Mario's Wet World Challenge takes you

underwater, where you type whole words while trying to avoid the marine creatures. Mario's Tunnel of Doom has you typing full sentences as you navigate a dangerous underground tunnel filled with falling bricks and quicksand. When you've built your

ningLearningLearningLearning

typing speed up to 50 words per minute, you've completed the program.

A DOS-based CD-ROM version features more lessons, as well as a talking Mario who introduces the lessons. And yes, he does speak with an Italian accent.

Mario Teaches Typing
Interplay Productions
(714) 553-6655
$39.95

Mavis Beacon Teaches Typing, Version 3.0

Mavis Beacon is the Cadillac of typing programs for older students. It contains all the features you could ever need—and some you may never have thought of but will be happy to have.

Mavis Beacon interweaves skill practice with a variety of games. To improve your skills, Mavis puts you in the

classroom, where she gives instruction and helps you develop your typing expertise. Mavis wouldn't want you to become dull or bored, so she'll sometimes invite you to join the Traveling Circus and play the Card Flip game (type the right letters, and the people holding cards will turn them over and create a picture that animates), use your keypad to pop balloons, help a clown win the Clown race (the faster you type—accurately—the faster he runs), or practice your rhythm with RoboMan by typing letters as he methodically walks along the track.

As you use the package, you're given your scores and error rates. If you do well, Mavis congratulates you; if you make too many mistakes, she lets you know and helps you improve. The program is even able to tailor instruction to your individual needs, allowing you to create your own lessons. The 79-page user manual alone is worth the price of the software; it includes a history of the typewriter, an overview of the skills Mavis will teach you, practice exercises, and a section dealing with the proper style and formatting of business letters, as well as a description of the artificial intelligence system the soft-

ware uses to diagnose your individual problems and needs. If you only buy one typing program, it should be Mavis Beacon.

Mavis Beacon Teaches Typing,
Version 3.0
Mindscape
(800) 234-3088
$49.95

Capitol Hill

In Capitol Hill, you assume the role of a newly elected representative. With your personal digital assistant (PDA) in hand and helpful

commentary from both the narrator and Representative Lynn Woolsey (D) of California, you navigate the maze known as federal government.

If it's been a while since high-school civics class, you can take a freshman orientation on our government's history and operation. There's even an interactive tour.

Video clips from C-SPAN's Mike Michaelson add depth to the narrator's remarks.

Of course, most of your time in office will be spent, well, in office. You take calls, read mail, and vote on various pieces of legislation. You explore your new digs, review your weekly agenda, check out your office budget, and hire staff.

Finally, when you think you've got the experience, you can make a "Power Play" and try to become Speaker of the House. Power Play is the electronic equivalent of a board game. In order to win,

you answer multiple-choice questions. If you're right, you move forward. If you're wrong, you move back. If you answer too many questions incorrectly, someone else is elected instead. This hardly seems worthy of an interactive multimedia title. Other aspects detract from the experience. Phone calls

don't sound like phone calls. The PDA is just a table of contents. You don't really meet the key players in Washington, you read their personnel files.

The most frustrating aspect of Capitol Hill is a sense of futility. None of the things you do really affect anything that happens. Everything boils down to gathering answers for the Power Play questions.

In today's world of gaming, especially with CD-ROMs, there's got to be a better, more imaginative way of playing the political game.—Bruce Onder

Capitol Hill
Mindscape
60 Leveroni Ct.
Novato, CA 94949
(800) 283-8499; (415) 883-3000
$49.95

Capitol Hill

Don't just write your congressman; be him with this political simulation game. Video, animations, and illustrations help users play congressperson while they choose a staff and learn everything from how a bill becomes a law to how to balance a budget.

Capitol Hill
Mindscape
(8000 234-3088; (415) 883-3000
$49.95

MAVIS BEACON
TEACHES TYPING!
THE WORLD'S BEST-SELLING TYPING PROGRAM

NEW!

♦ IMPROVE PRODUCTIVITY
♦ ELIMINATE TYPING MISTAKES
♦ QUICK TO LEARN, FUN TO USE!

people to death. Who cares? Computers can help us make sure people do their jobs!" ▢ Congratulations to the com-

LearningLearningLea

The Gospels, A Multimedia Guide to the Bible

The best-selling book of all time goes high-tech on a CD-ROM that adds video and narration to the greatest stories ever told. You can search through the full King James text of the Old and New Testaments, but not the Apocrypha.

The Gospels, A Multimedia Guide to the Bible
Cinerom Inc.
(714) 660-7111
$49.95

Cliffs StudyWare for the SAT I

All students recognize the familiar yellow covers of the Cliffs Notes study guides. Now, they'll want to become familiar with Cliffs StudyWare for the SAT I, an electronic SAT-prep package that combines a software component, called the Computerized Tutor, with a comprehensive test-preparation guidebook. The software itself includes

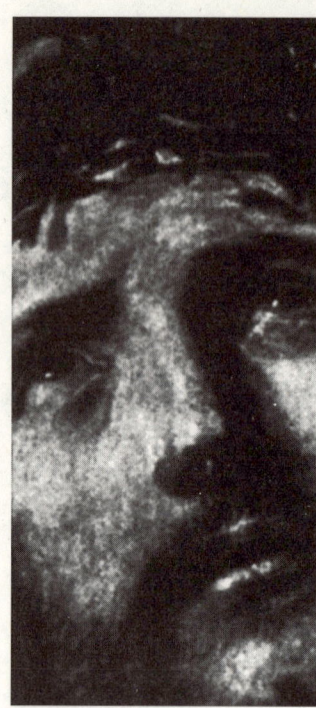

two complete online exams modeled after the new SAT and answer sheets for the three additional Cliffs Notes tests included in the guide book.

Students can take the online StudyWare Exams in either Test or Tutor mode. Tutor mode, which explains why an answer is correct or incorrect, is especially useful in the early stages of study. The Test mode, which offers no explanations, simulates the actual test. It's possible to switch modes at any time. Cliffs StudyWare for the SAT I won't guarantee a perfect score. But it will help students make smart use of their study time.—Peter Scisco

Cliffs StudyWare for the SAT I
Cliffs Notes Inc.
(800) 228-4078; (402) 423-5050
$49.95

Your Personal Trainer for the SAT

Your Personal Trainer for the SAT does the best job among our tested products of capturing the feel of taking an SAT exam. Using test booklets that look exactly like the real thing, students move through a series of preliminary tests to determine where they need the most work. All tests are timed and the program displays a countdown clock.

Having completed a preliminary test, students can get an instant assessment of

their skills. The answers to all questions in the preliminary test are displayed, along with the student's choices. Totals for the number of correct, incorrect, and omitted questions are also displayed, as is the percentage of correct and incorrect answers.

Once a student sees where work is needed, he or she can turn to the program's Training Schedule. Options

for a quick course or a more thorough review benefit students who only need to brush up, as well as those who need more extensive work.

After taking a practice exam, students are ready to perform post-test analysis, where their scores indicate how far they have progressed. They can then graph their scores to show their percentage of correct responses, as well as how their performance stacks up against their peers. One particularly fascinating (or fearsome) graph shows how the student's score compares with scores from students at more than 325 colleges and universities. A student intent on getting into Wake Forest University, for example, can see his or her score compared against the average scores posted by incoming freshman at that school. Your Personal Trainer for the SAT strikes a good balance between bells and whistles and solid review. The design makes it easy to use, and the content of the material is first-rate.—Peter Scisco

Your Personal Trainer for the SAT
Davidson & Associates Inc.
(800) 545-7677; (310) 793-0600
$49.95

The New Family Bible

The New Family Bible is a fascinating historical reference on CD-ROM for anyone interested in reading the best-selling book of all time. The New Family Bible features the Old Testament, and forty stories—including the Creation, Noah and the Flood, and Daniel in the Lions' Den—are also told in slide-show format. An audio overview gives you the historical context.

The New Family Bible
Time Warner Interactive Group
$49.99

Performa Made Easy

Know someone new to the Mac? In the Performa Made Easy tape series, friendly voices walk new users through the process of learning how to use a Mac at their own pace—without the cost of hiring a local whiz kid to spend hours tutoring them.

Performa Made Easy
Personal Training Systems
$59.95

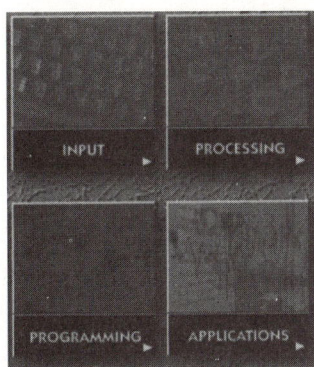

How Computers Work

Based on the Time-Life books *How Things Work* and *Understanding Computers*, How Computers Work is an easy-to-follow interactive guide to what's under your computer's hood. With its online textbook, a time line showing high points in the development of the computer, a peek at future trends, and activities ranging from knowledge tests to a programming exercise, this is an entertaining and educational tool for curious adults and teenagers.

How Computers Work
Time-Warner Interactive Group
2210 W. Olive Ave.
Burbank, CA 91506
$79.99

DOS upon a Midnight Dreary

Once upon a midnight dreary,
fingers cramped and vision bleary,
System manuals piled high and wasted paper on the floor.
Longing for the warmth of bedsheets,
Still I sat there, doing spreadsheets;
Having reached the bottom line, I took a floppy
from the drawer.

Typing with a steady hand,
Then invoked the Save command,
But I got a reprimand: it read "Abort, Retry, Ignore."
Was this some occult illusion?
Some maniacal intrusion?
These were choices Solomon himself had never faced before.
Carefully, I weighed my options.
These three seemed to be the top ones.
Clearly I must now adopt one:
Choose "Abort, Retry, Ignore."

With my fingers pale and trembling,
Slowly toward the keyboard bending,
Longing for a happy ending, hoping all would be restored,
Praying for some guarantee
Finally I pressed a key—
But on the screen what did I see?
Again: "Abort, Retry, Ignore."

I tried to catch the chips off-guard—
I pressed again, but twice as hard.
Luck was just not in the cards.
I saw what I had seen before.
Now I typed in desperation
Trying random combinations.
Still there came the incantation:
Choose: "Abort, Retry, Ignore."

There I sat, distraught, exhausted,
by my own machine accosted.
Getting up I turned away and paced across the office floor.
And then I saw an awful sight:
A bold and blinding flash of light—
A lightning bolt had cut the night and shook me to my very core.
I saw the screen collapse and die.
Oh no—my database, I cried!
I thought I heard a voice reply,
"You'll see your data Nevermore!"

To this day I do not know
The place to which lost data goes.
I bet it goes to heaven where the angels have it stored.
But as for productivity, well
I fear that IT goes straight to hell.
And that's the tale I have to tell.
Your choice: "Abort, Retry, Ignore."

—ANONYMOUS

SECTIONS

ESSAYS

RealWorld

The Real World

t he real world. That's why computers were originally designed—to help us deal with reality. The nitty-gritty of number-crunching, word processing, and the like propelled computers into a multibillion dollar business long before anyone had ever heard of multimedia. Luckily for us, those useful computer tools that have done so much to help big businesses are now inexpensive and easy enough for everyone. Armed with our personal computers, we can whip up a publication with professional polish, even if we only print a personal résumé or a flyer for a garage sale. Now it's no problem to crunch numbers that are just as crunchy as you'll find in any corporation—you can even make your own financial predictions or business projections that might put you ahead of the professional analysts.

In CyberSource: Real World, we'll review some of the better tools on the market today for doing business, starting with hardware for the modern office such as monitors and printers, to the variety of portable computing products such as powerbooks and PDAs. On the software front, we'll describe some of the best work programs, which include everything from accounting, database, and reference tools to desktop video and multimedia packages, which enable you to add a creative touch to your presentations.

Computers really are the ultimate tool for modern times. And now your personal tool can be just as good as any big corporation's.

HARDWARE

KEEPING TRACK: POWERSYNC UPDATES LOCAL, REMOTE FILES

PowerSync 1.1

The problem is nearly as old as the PC itself: How do you keep the files on your laptop or home computer in sync with the files on your office PC? Now Linkpro Inc. of Irvine, California, offers a new solution to an old problem with PowerSync 1.1.

PowerSync provides a wide range of options for synchronizing files. This easy-to-use package works hand in hand with your direct-connection (serial- or parallel-port link), communications, and network software. You can even synchronize hard-drive files with those on a floppy disk or synchronize files located in different directories on the same computer. By default, PowerSync makes sure that both machines possess the latest versions of all files in selected directories. Transfer times are held to a minimum because PowerSync only copies those files whose versions differ on the local and remote machines.

You can also perform one-way updates from the remote to your machine or vice versa. Other options include unattended operation and directory displays that only show different versions of the same file on the local and the remote. When files have been erased on one machine but not the other, you can control which erased files are restored. The Synch History log makes it easy to keep track of all your changes.

Users of client/server applications will love Power-Sync because they can run their applications in the usual way even when PowerSync is running. In contrast to other file-synchronization software, PowerSync runs on the local computer, not on the computer you want to access. Power-Sync is an intelligent choice for users who like to work while away from their desks. For those who need to, it's a lifesaver.—John Gliedman

PowerSync for Windows 1.1
Linkpro Inc.
P.O. Box 6044
Irvine, CA 92716-6044
(800) 449-7962; (714) 854-3322
$89.95

BOOST YOUR SOUND

Sony CSS-B100

With the advent of the multimedia revolution, there are a good number of "computer-ready" mini-speaker systems, but there hasn't been a well-designed single-module sound-delivery system made specifically for computers. Until now.

Sony Electronics Inc. has created a true computer-oriented speaker system. The CSS-B100, part of a new family of multimedia products, is a combination monitor stand, speaker system, and input-cable conduit. Fashioned of high-impact plastic in a platinum color that'll fit into any Mac owner's color scheme, the CSS-B100 is 14.6 ¥ 15.9 inches, and 3.7 inches tall at its highest (which is the front-panel speaker housing).

The speakers, a pair of 3-inch drivers with a 70Hz to 25KHz frequency response, are mounted on the front of the unit. A sound cavity inside the unit provides surprisingly strong bass response for so small a set of speakers; Sony also includes a "Bass Boost" control to further enhance the boom in this box. Naturally, the Sony speakers are magnetically shielded to reduce interference with computer monitors.

Your monitor sits right on top of the CSS-B100. A special pedestal passes through the speaker-housing unit of the CSS-B100, but is physically isolated from it to reduce interference from speaker vibrations. The unit supports

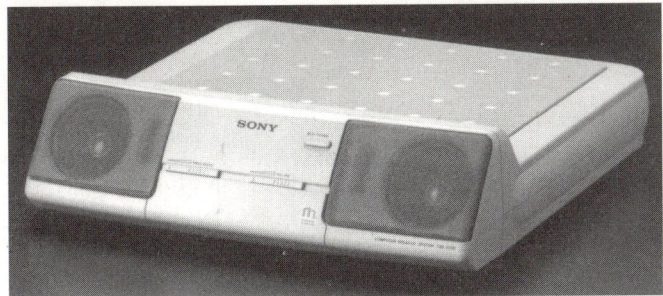

most 17-inch monitors with weights up to 55 pounds.

The most impressive feature is a pass-through system that lets you connect computer audio and video ports to connectors on the rear of the CSS-B100 and access them from ports on the front panel. Sony provides three RCA jacks for video and stereo sound in, mono and stereo mini-jack microphone ports, and a headphone mini-jack that cuts off sound through the speakers when in use. However, AV and Power Mac microphones are not compatible with standard mini-jacks.

The CSS-B100 is a solidly built addition to any multimedia system. The smart design, integrating a monitor stand with the speakers, as well as video and stereo jacks, offers the best use of limited desktop space we've seen, and the sound of the system is superior to the plethora of computer mini-speakers on the market.—Jeffrey Sullivan

Sony CSS-B100
Sony Electronics Inc.
Component and Computer
Products Group
3300 Zanker Rd.
San Jose, CA 95134
(800) 352-7669
$129.95

A SMALL-FOOTPRINT DIGITIZING TABLET
Kurta XGT68

If you need a digitizing tablet for graphics, CAD, or CAM applications, take a look at Kurta's XGT 6" x 8". As the name implies, the tablet offers an active digitizing area of 6 × 8 inches. More importantly, the footprint is an impressively tiny 11.2 inches wide by 8.7 inches high—barely larger than a letter-size piece of paper.

As tested, the package included a pressure-sensitive pen and drivers for DOS, Windows, and ADI (for AutoCAD and other Autodesk products). For testing purposes, Kurta provided a demonstration version of Fractal Design Painter 2.0a, a pressure-sensitive-aware program that lets you change line width or some other variable as you draw by changing pressure on the pen. Other third-party pressure-sensitive applications include Adobe Photoshop and Fauve Matisse.

Installing the package consists of little more than plugging the tablet's cable into a serial port, plugging the power cord into the tablet's connector at the serial port, and installing the drivers you need. As with most tablets,

you can also use the pen as a mouse. Unlike many, you can also have a mouse active in Windows, but not DOS. This gives you the luxury of being able to use either the mouse or the tablet, depending only on which is more convenient for any given program. This last feature is a compelling one for users of word processing and spreadsheet applications.

By the time you read this, Kurta should be offering a CAD package for the tablet at the same price. This version will have a four-button, mouse-like cursor instead of the pressure-sensitive pen, and an AutoCAD on-screen template. Kurta also plans to sell the cursor alone for $70, and both pen and cursor are cordless. The package includes a lifetime warranty for all parts.—M. David Stone

Kurta XGT68
Kurta Corp.
3007 E. Chambers St.
Phoenix, AZ 85040
(800) 445-8782; (602) 276-5533
$395

THREE OFFICE MACHINES IN ONE
OfficeJet

Hewlett-Packard combines an inkjet printer, plain-paper fax machine, and copier into one handy unit. If you work at home, your computer is probably the nerve center of your setup. However, to make your home office as complete as a corporate office, you need to add a printer, a fax

machine, and a copier. Enter Hewlett-Packard with the bright idea of combining these three add-ons into one unit: the OfficeJet.

At the heart of the OfficeJet resides a thermal inkjet printer, which uses the same print engine found in the reliable HP DeskJet 520. Resolution is 600 × 300 dpi with 256 gray-scale levels, and includes HP's Resolution Enhancement Technology, which varies the size and placement of the dots produced by the printer to smooth curves and edges of individual characters.

Although rated at 3 pages per minute (ppm), actual throughput is less than 2 ppm. In informal tests, an eight-page text document from a DOS word processor took a shade under five minutes to print out. Switch to Windows, and throughput drops to about 1 ppm.

Print quality is roughly equivalent to a 300-dpi laser printer, although you can see a marked image diffusion when you compare it to a 600-dpi laser printer. A half-dozen buttons help you select from portrait or landscape mode; draft- or letter-quality output; fonts; paper eject; and other printer functions.

Any decision to purchase the OfficeJet rests on what equipment you already own and how often you use fax machines and copiers. If you already own a laser printer, fax machine, and personal copier, there's little reason to even look at the OfficeJet. If you lack only the fax machine, you might consider a $100 to $200 fax/modem instead of a fax machine. If, however, you are just starting out in a home office, or upgrading from a dot matrix printer, this $959 (list price) combination printer, fax

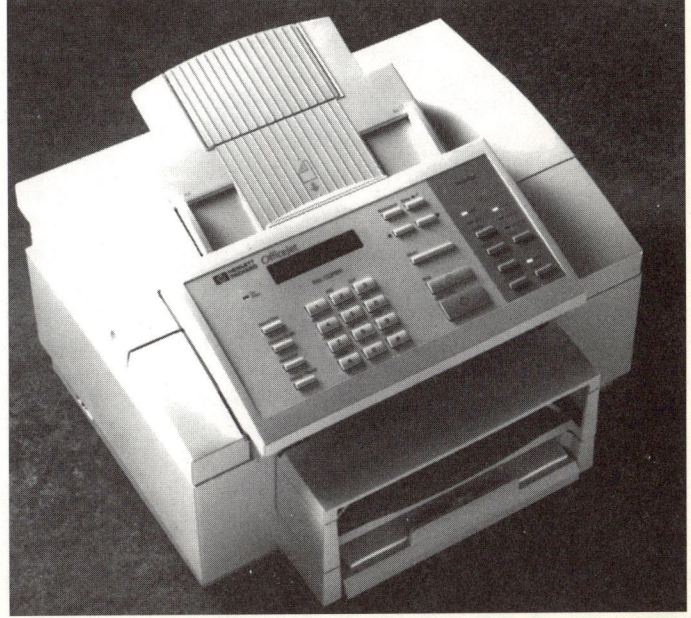

was written by someone who works in an office, and it showed. The telecommuting issue popped up again when one of my editors at a sister magazine expressed concern about how horrible it would be if a bunch of his

RealWorldRealWorld

machine, and copier provides a simple way to get everything you need in one package.—Russ Lockwood

HP OfficeJet
Hewlett-Packard Co.
P.O. Box 58059, MS 511-SJ
Santa Clara, CA 95051
(800) 752-0900
$959

OfficeJet

When it comes to saving space on that cluttered desk in your crowded office, nothing makes more sense than Hewlett-Packard's versatile OfficeJet. The OfficeJet rolls three requisite office technologies—an ink-jet printer, fax machine, and copier—into one great product with a pleasingly small footprint. It plugs into your PC's parallel port like an ordinary printer, while allowing you to print a file and send or receive a fax simultaneously—for a street price of less than $800.

The OfficeJet isn't the first multifunction printer we've seen, but it is the least expensive. High-end offerings such as Canon's Fax B340 cost more than twice as much ($1,795) and contain items that most offices already have, such as a telephone and answering machine. But one advantage of the high-priced products is that you get a laser printer rather than an ink jet, which means faster printing and better output.

The OfficeJet prints on plain paper, but it's functional with glossy paper and transparencies as well (watch out for streaking and smudg-

ing on these other media types). You can also quickly and easily adjust the paper tray to legal- or letter-sized envelopes, and A4 and legal-sized paper. The OfficeJet includes 14 scalable TrueType fonts for Windows (6 for DOS) and connects through a high-speed parallel interface.

As for performance, if you print a lot of standard business letters (text only), the OfficeJet screams: It beat HP's DeskJet 520 by more than 90 percent. And if you spend much of your business day sending and receiving faxes, the OfficeJet can help automate and ease your work. You can preprogram up to 65 frequently faxed numbers into memory, and the OfficeJet automatically redials busy signals up to five times.

If you need to distribute the same information to multiple locations, the OfficeJet lets you fax a document to up to 10 different numbers—ideal for marketing announcements and sales materials.

One of the drawbacks of this printer is its lack of a fax modem: Every fax you send must come from a printed copy. If you don't have a fax modem, this means wasting paper to print those business letters so you can send them from your OfficeJet.

While you wouldn't want to tackle a large copying job with the OfficeJet, its copier function certainly is handy if you need a few extra copies and don't want to spend the time and hassle driving to your local copy shop (or

walking down the hall to wait in line at the main copier).

Setup of the unit is easy—we had it working in less than an hour. The OfficeJet's front-panel LED includes an easy-to-use Option menu that lets you access everything from resolution control to speed dialing—without having to look up confusing function codes. If you're trying to find an integrated office solution for faxing, printing, and copying at a reasonable price, you simply can't go wrong with HP's OfficeJet.—Richard Schwerin

OfficeJet
Hewlett-Packard Co.
(800) 752-0900; (415) 857-1501
$799

LOOK AND LISTEN: TATUNG'S AUDIO 15 MULTIMEDIA MONITOR IS A WINNER

Tatung Audio 15

Tatung's new CM15VBE Audio 15 multimedia monitor sounds as good as it looks. A pair of side-mounted built-in speakers and a .28mm dot pitch, flat-square 15-inch screen give you everything you need to view and hear multimedia CD-ROMs or desktop presentations in a single box. Unless you require audiophile resonance or a viewing area larger than its 13.8-inch diagonal, this sub-$500 monitor offers a combination of sound/image convenience and quality that's tough to beat.

Tatung mounts the Audio 15's speakers flush with the

flanks of the monitor, rather than in front-facing "wings." There seems to be little sound quality lost from this configuration. Tatung claims a frequency response of 100Hz to 20KHz.

Plug in the power, connect the VGA cord to your video card, mate the supplied audio cable to the output jack of your sound card and the input jack on the rear of the monitor, and you're ready to crank up your applications, CD-ROM, or audio CD. A convenient headphone connection can be used when you want some privacy.

The Audio 15's Hitachi CRT displayed crisp text and graphics with no discernible misconvergence, moire patterns, flicker, or distortion at noninterlaced resolutions up to 1,024 × 768 (using a 75Hz vertical refresh rate). Most

users will prefer the easier-to-view 800 × 600 mode. The factory screen settings can be changed or restored using five front-mounted digital controls. A "zoom" button lets you expand an image for presentations.

Mounted on a sturdy tilt/swivel stand, the 27.3-pound monitor can be adjusted 45 degrees right or left, tilted down five degrees or up 15. It's furnished with a permanently attached VGA cable and a removable power cord. The Audio 15 meets MPR II emission standards and is Environmental Protection Agency Energy Star-compliant, drawing fewer than 30 watts of power during standby mode. It's backed with a one-year limited warranty. After using the multimedia Tatung for a few moments, you'll wonder why

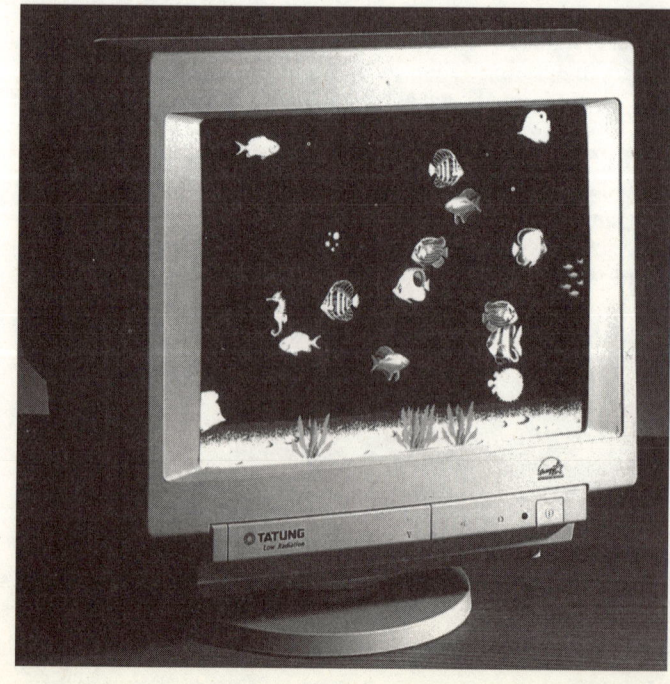

staffers started to telecommute. ☐ I got into a minidebate about this, but to no avail. I'm a big advocate of telecommuting and wish the whole country would do it. I've telecommuted myself for over 12 continuous years. If

all VGA displays don't come with built-in speakers in this sound-filled age of computing.—David D. Busch

Tatung Audio 15
Tatung Company of America Inc.
2850 El Presidio St.
Long Beach, CA 90810
(213) 979-7055
$499

HANDHELD PRESENTATION PIZZAZZ

Remote Control IR50 F/X

Mind Path's $229 Remote Control IR50 F/X may be the most useful presentation tool since the extendible pointer. This handheld infrared device, which is about the size of a TV remote control, provides as much control over Windows programs as a mouse—but without the cord. Indeed, you can manipulate programs and presentations on the fly from up to 45 feet away.

The IR50 F/X comes with a receiver that plugs into a nine-pin serial port and shows a red light when active. An automated install utility loads the Windows-based Presentation F/X software. Total installation time is under five minutes, and the device does not affect keyboard or mouse use. A TSR is provided for use with DOS applications.

The key to control is the mousedisc: a circular button about an inch in diameter that you operate with your thumb. If you press the edge of the mousedisc, the cursor moves whichever way you tilt the disc. The center of the disc is the same as a mouse button,

I Spy

In the late 1980s, Aldrich "Rick" Ames, the infamous CIA agent who sold out to the Russkies, starts arriving at work in clothes more appropriate for a banker than a bureaucrat, and nobody cares. He flies to Switzerland to stash a million bucks, and nobody notices. He plunks down cash for a new Jaguar, new teeth, and a new house, and nobody raises a fuss. So what finally trips him up? His root directory.

In 1993, Ames and his CIA boss attend a conference in Turkey. Ames brings along a notebook PC packed with computer games…and megabytes of purloined government secrets. His boss asks to play one of the games, and when he looks to see what's on the hard disk, just happens to notice a file named for Rick's Russian contact along with tons of classified info. Ames is nabbed.

(Funny thing—if Ames had known how to use certain features in DOS a little better, the guy could be dining tonight on paté à choux rather than prison chow.)

Nobody's going to grieve for Ames, who deserves what he gets. But every day, naive business people end up getting grief they don't deserve. Their PCs may not contain official secrets, but somewhere on their hard disks are sensitive files like business plans, personnel records, résumés, and personal letters or financial information they'd rather not share. And if they're as lax about locking it all up as Ames was, they're asking for trouble.

Trouble is, we all have too many bank and online passwords and PIN numbers already. We don't want more. And yet we lock our desks and file cabinets but think PC passwords are a nuisance and don't use them. Or pick obvious ones like our first names or phone extensions. We casually reveal them when coworkers need to retrieve files. Or write them down on Rolodexes or yellow Post-it notes stuck to our monitors. Or leave our systems wide open when we walk away.

And we almost never modify them. Quick test—if you use a password, when's the last time you changed it? If it's more than a month or two, you're hosed. Worse, users can easily be lulled into a false sense of security because of these flimsy passwords, and use dopey easy-to-spot filenames like SALARY.DOC or BUDGET95.WK4. And they never conceal or encrypt anything—no matter how sensitive. All Ames had to do was hide the dangerous data and subdirectories with the DOS ATTRIB +H command, which, like a cheap lock, will keep the honest people out.

Users sometimes think it's so hard to locate files on their own hard disk that they figure a snooper will be even more confused. Wrong. You don't have to be a CIA agent to bust into most systems and walk off with megabytes of vital data. Hey—how do you know it hasn't happened to you already?—Paul Somerson ■

so you can single- and double-click in application programs. To drag and drop, you press and hold the disc down (which changes the cursor from white to black), release the disc, and thumb the cursor to where you want, then press the disc again to drop.

This sounds complicated, but a few games of solitaire will improve your proficiency. However, the IR50 F/X is more than just a long-range mouse. Bundled with Presentation F/X software, it lets you annotate and accentuate your Windows applica-

tions with 21 special effects. Five buttons act as function keys to invoke these effects.

The IR50 F/X may not help the content of your presentation, but this handy accessory will help with style—and a little pizazz can go a long way.—Russ Lockwood

Remote Control IR50 F/X
Mind Path Technologies Inc.
12700 Park Central Dr.
Suite 1707
Dallas, TX 75251
(214) 233-9296
$229

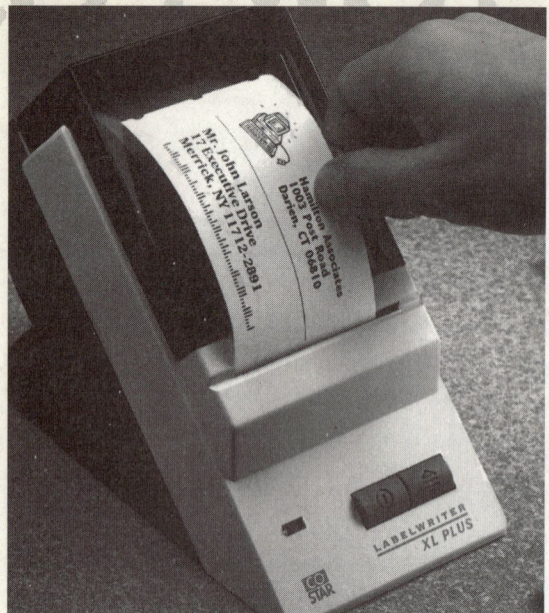

A DESKTOP LABEL SPECIALIST

LabelWriter XL Plus

If you subscribe to Augustus Caesar's maxim that "well done is quickly done," you'll love CoStar Corp.'s LabelWriter XL Plus. While this new label printer has its weak points, it is one of the easiest ways to produce labels. The $6.5 \times 4.5 \times 7$-inch XL Plus and its narrower companion product, the XL, replace the LabelWriter II line. The new models double the print resolution to 203 dpi and come with new software that provides LAN support.

The key to this product is convenience. It connects to your computer's serial port (25- or 9-pin, using an included cable), so it can be used in addition to your full-sized printer on a parallel port. A parallel-port adapter also is available for a list price of $99.95, and there is a version for Mac users.

The included DOS and Windows programs let you print labels individually or by merging data from a list (you can import dBASE or comma-delimited files). Under Windows, the program can automatically load any data in the Clipboard into the current label format. There are also macros for Windows word processing applications (Microsoft Word 2 and 6, Ami Pro, and WordPerfect) so that you can print a label from within the program or choose to automatically print a label whenever you print a letter. The LabelWriter XL Plus can also extract ZIP code information and add PostNet bar codes to address labels.

You can create custom label layouts using PCX, BMP, or TIFF formatted images. The Windows program will use any Windows font, including any TrueType fonts you have installed. One flaw in the program is the lack of drawing tools; to add a line or box, you must import a picture of the object.

The thermal print head produces sharp images, though the output is coarser than an inkjet or laser printer.

It does demand special label stock, but you are not limited to plain white address labels; CoStar sells labels for everything from VCR cassettes to 3.5-inch disks. Depending on size and style, labels cost between 2 cents and 7 cents apiece.—Alfred Poor

LabelWriter XL Plus
CoStar Corp.
100 Field Point Rd.
Greenwich, CT 06830-6406
(800) 426-7827; (203) 661-9700
$299.95

MIDI MASTERS: SONIC REALISM FOR INEXPENSIVE SOUND CARD

Creative Labs Sound Blaster AWE32

With an average mail-order price of $265, Creative Labs's Sound Blaster AWE32 is a bit pricier than other mid-range sound boards. The added expense is justified, however, by Creative Labs's inclusion of an impressive assortment of application software, as well as a good quality microphone and stand. More important, the AWE32 delivers sparkling clean MIDI output just a hair behind the top-rated mid-range board, the Ensoniq Soundscape.

Most of the Sound Blaster's audio measurements were no better than average. On the 44.1KHz 16-bit audio digitization tests, the Sound Blaster exhibited a fairly quiet –61dB signal/noise ratio. It earned a respectable 0.0939 percent THD score on the distortion test. Frequency response on the digital-audio tests suffered from rolloffs at the high end of the audio spectrum.

But the Sound Blaster's EMU8000 synthesizer was another story, producing strikingly realistic MIDI brass, woodwind, and piano sounds. The only factors that prevented it from giving the best-sounding wavetable cards more competition were a few synthetic-sounding patches that also suffer from boosted high-frequency response—particularly annoying on instruments like harpsichord and clarinet. These deficiencies make the board's MIDI patches better suited for desktop multimedia than serious recording projects.

The AWE32's extensive selection of bundled software includes CD, MIDI, and WAV players; mixer and waveform-editing programs; and a variety of speech-synthesis applications that include a talking dictionary, a text-to-speech converter, and singing demos. Also included are "lite" versions of Cakewalk for Windows and HSC's sophisticated Interactive multimedia-presentation program.

Rounding out the software bundle are utilities exploiting the AWE32's onboard reverb and chorus features, and its QSound Virtual Sound capabilities, which let the card generate sounds that seem to appear from points not between the speakers. The AWE32's one significant drawback is the 87K it requires for memory-resident DOS drivers, which can easily cause problems for memory-hungry DOS programs like the popular shareware game Doom.

The AWE32 is a comprehensive product that covers most of the required features in a good sound card. It may not satisfy serious musicians looking for the sonic excellence of a Monterey or RAP-10. Still, its great sounding synth and huge software bundle make it a good option for just about everybody else.—Don Labriola

Sound Blaster AWE32
Creative Labs Inc.
1901 McCarthy Blvd.
Milpitas, CA 95035
(800) 998-1000; (408) 428-6600
$399.95

Ensoniq Soundscape

Ensoniq's Soundscape doesn't quite match the sound of the best wavetable boards, but it holds its own against any product in its price class: about $220 by mail. The Soundscape's OTTO synthesizer chip sounds great and earned a third-place finish in most of our audio tests.

Like all the synthesizers we tested, the OTTO chip's wavetable set is a mixture of the good and the bad. Its keyboard, percussion, and ethnic instruments are outstanding, but a few other patches aren't as impressive. The guitars, for example, are buzzy and the solo strings sound a bit synthetic. Overall, though, our panel agreed that the OTTO's MIDI performance was clearly outclassed only by the RAP-10 and the MultiSound Monterey.

In terms of its general audio performance, the Soundscape turned in overall good test results. Its analog section was the second-quietest of the test group—a very respectable –76.5dB, and its distortion level was a mere 0.0354 percent. Unfortunately, its performance during recording and playback of 44.1KHz WAV files wasn't as good—in these tests, the Soundscape's low frequency response, especially below 100Hz, showed noticeable attenuation.

The Soundscape's excellent documentation and auto-mated utilities made installation relatively painless, despite the presence of a fair number of jumpers. Adding a CD-ROM, though, isn't as easy, requiring users to manually add lines to AUTOEXEC.BAT and CONFIG.SYS.

The Soundscape is bundled with a generous collection of software that includes media players, a waveform editor, and a 16-track graphical MIDI mixer. There are also an OLE text-to-speech applet and an introductory version of Blue Ribbon Software's SuperJAM, an accompaniment program that can be programmed to play MIDI arrangements in a variety of styles.

Although the differences between cards in the test group were sometimes minute, we judged the Soundscape to be the best-sounding of the general-purpose boards in our roundup, a group that includes products from Advanced Gravis, Creative Labs, and Logitech. Its closest competitor is the Sound Blaster AWE32, which includes a microphone and an even larger collection of software, but has a mail-order price about $40 higher and requires nearly 90K of memory for DOS drivers.—Don Labriola

Soundscape
Ensoniq Corp.
155 Great Valley Pkwy.
Malvern, PA 19355
(800) 776-8637; (215) 647-3930
$279

SoundMan Wave

Despite a $299 list price, Logitech's SoundMan Wave can be acquired by mail for only about $180. Its audio quality and Yamaha OPL-4 synthesizer aren't quite on a par with those of heavyweights like the Monterey or RAP-10, but they're competitive with those of most of the other boards tested. These factors, along with its SCSI interface, excellent installation tools, and built-in ADPCM compression, make the SoundMan Wave one of the best values we found among general-purpose wavetable sound boards.

Installing the SoundMan Wave is a pleasure. There are no jumpers to set, and the installation program plays sounds along the way to verify that you've picked workable settings. Even the often-daunting task of installing a CD-ROM is relatively painless.

The SoundMan's audio section is also impressive, producing results that were consistently good. Its analog section was a very quiet –74.6dB, accompanied by a low 0.0250 percent THD score—the second-best in the group.

Our listening panel placed the OPL-4's MIDI output in the same class as that of the Advanced Gravis Ultrasound MAX—slightly below that of the Sound Blaster AWE32 and Ensoniq Soundscape. The OPL-4's basses, leads, pads, and percussion patches all sound great, although its solo brass and woodwind patches sound a bit synthetic.

The SoundMan Wave offers excellent game compatibility. Its onboard synthesizer contains a complete Sound Blaster-style OPL-2 FM synth, and the board also comes with a MIDI interpreter that lets it play wavetable sounds when used with programs that are designed for FM synthesizers.

The SoundMan Wave is bundled with the usual suite of mixer and CD/MIDI/WAV-player utilities, as well as several speech-synthesis applets; Midisoft Recording Session; and Moon Valley's Icon Hear-It, a program that enhances Windows's sound capabilities. The net result is a package that provides all-around good performance at a terrific price.—Don Labriola

SoundMan Wave
Logitech Inc.
6505 Kaiser Dr.
Fremont, CA 94555
(800) 231-7717; (510) 795-8500
$299

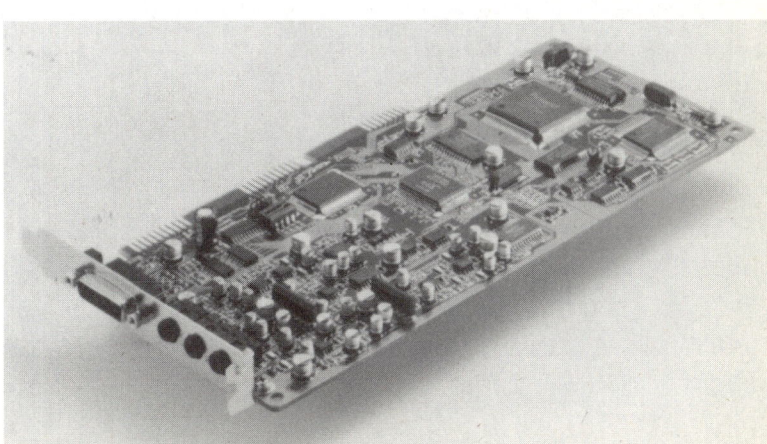

ers are alone all the time. This means there is a wife, husband, girlfriend, boyfriend, roommate, or children to worry about. As annoying as interruptions are, my advice is to live with them. It's not much different from

Whiteboard Software:
Remote Conferencing Made Simple

Workgroups trying to collaborate remotely on important documents or presentations have historically had two choices: Use the markup tools and embedded notes in Windows-based spreadsheets and word processors to share ideas, or buy videoconferencing technology.

The rapidly growing category of whiteboard software offers a third option. Far cheaper than videoconferencing (prices start at $99, compared to $1,600 per seat), and more interactive and less confusing than passing around edited versions of a document, whiteboard software allows users to work together in real time over LAN or modem links, viewing the same file and exchanging comments.

Whiteboard software is also designed to facilitate remote presentations and conferencing, so it's often capable of accommodating long-distance slide shows, presentations, and training sessions, with chat boxes for user comments and questions.

Products like Intel's ProShare Personal Conferencing Software, Future Labs's TalkShow, and IBM's Person to Person for Windows range in price from $100 to $300 and accommodate varying numbers of users. These packages work on both LANs and modems, but some whiteboard programs, like Modus Software's Syconference, are limited to modem communications only.

The features of modem- and LAN-based document-conferencing packages are often the same, but ones that support both kinds of connections are more popular. Surprisingly, you don't get a break in price for most modem-only programs.

Obviously, compared to modem links, LAN communications are faster and don't involve the cost of a phone call. But synching speeds on a LAN also can be difficult, so documents don't always transmit quickly, says Becky Taylor of Moonbeam Corp., makers of FarSite for Windows.

There are other pitfalls to be wary of: Simple factors like different modems, even running at the same speed, can cause problems. Display resolutions also can be a snag: If one conference participant has a 1,024x768 screen and another is plain VGA, they'll get the same information, but the latter will see only part of it at a time; the sender legislates the resolution.

Second-generation software is expected to compensate for these shortcomings. But while you can encounter compatibility and display problems with today's products, they're already proving a worthy solution for many small-business users who don't need talking heads in their remote-conference sessions.—Kathy Yakal ■

Roland RAP-10/ATB

At $349, Roland's RAP-10/ATB is one of the more expensive sound boards available today—but it's also one of the best. Although it lacks features like a SCSI interface, Sound Blaster compatibility, CD audio connector, and mic input, its combination of superb MIDI output and low-noise operation earned it first place in our listening evaluations.

Strangely enough, the RAP-10 rarely led the pack in our audio measurements. While its analog section was the third quietest in the group, with a S/N ratio of −75.1dB, its 0.0430 percent analog THD score was only the fourth best. In the 44.1KHz sampling tests, the RAP-10's THD jumped to 0.2882 percent, and its frequency response rolled off noticeably below 100Hz.

The RAP-10's Sound Canvas synthesizer, on the other hand, was judged consistently excellent. Although some MIDI patches sounded better on other cards, none could equal the Sound Canvas's overall quality. Even its weakest sounds were superior to most, and the best, like the keyboards and basses, were absolutely stunning. With the addition of the RAP-10's built-in chorus and reverb, this board sounds great.

But despite all its strengths, the RAP-10 has one serious flaw: an incompatibility with certain motherboards that interferes with its ability to record 16-bit 44.1KHz stereo. We don't expect this problem to be resolved by the time you read this, so check with Roland before buying to verify that the RAP-10 is compatible with your machine.

The RAP-10 is bundled with a good selection of software aimed primarily at music and recording applications. In addition to the same Asystem suite that comes with Orchid's SoundWave 32, the bundle includes an innovative WaMI Mixer, which lets you combine WAV and MIDI files into a single synchronized song file.

The RAP-10 isn't perfect—its average mail-order price of around $250 is expensive, it doesn't make a very good game card, and it may not work with certain motherboards. But it's the best-sounding MIDI board we've ever heard.—Don Labriola

RAP-10/ATB
Roland Corp. U.S.
7200 Dominion Circle
Los Angeles, CA 90040-3696
(213) 685-5141
$349

Turtle Beach MultiSound Monterey

Because of its solid reputation, Turtle Beach's follow-up to the original MultiSound card (now out of production and called the MultiSound Classic) has been long-awaited by sound enthusiasts. A truly revolutionary 16-bit card in its prime, the MultiSound card set the standard for high-quality recording and state-of-

the-art wavetable patches when it was released several years ago. Despite a few early glitches, the Turtle Beach MultiSound Monterey is shaping up to be a worthy successor.

Like its predecessor, the Monterey features superlative audio specs: low noise levels, low THD figures, and ruler-flat frequency-response curves that are all in a class with the MultiSound Classic. Unfortunately, the Monterey also has many of the MultiSound's deficiencies, including its lack of a SCSI interface, mic input, and Sound Blaster compatibility.

Instead of the impressive E-mu Proteus synthesizer used in the MultiSound Classic, the Monterey uses ICS's WaveFront General MIDI synth, which although good, sounds different. The WaveFront excels, for example, in areas like solo strings, drum sounds, and special effects, but can't compete with the Proteus's guitar or organ sounds. Nonetheless, the WaveFront is a terrific sound-board synth, approaching the overall quality of our personal favorite, the Roland RAP-10's Sound Canvas.

The Monterey also offers the best sound-card reverb and echo we've ever heard, providing 16 preset effects, and the ability to control parameters like decay time and room size, as well as a SampleStore feature that lets you load any WAV file into onboard memory and use it as a new synthesizer sound. The Monterey's bundled soft-

ware includes mixer, MIDI, and CD-player utilities; a calibrated VU meter that lets you set accurate gain levels; outstanding automated diagnostics; and Turtle Beach's excellent Wave SE digital-recording package.

The Monterey is fairly expensive, especially when you take into account the fact that you must add up to 4MB of memory in order to use its SampleStore feature. Nonetheless, with its impressive sound quality, the board is an outstanding performer.—Don Labriola

MultiSound Monterey
Turtle Beach Systems Inc.
52 Grumbacher Rd.
Suite 6
York, PA 17402
(800) 645-5640; (717) 767-0200
$399

OCR BECOMES EASIER YET
WordScan Plus 3.0

With scanner prices plummeting, a growing number of everyday business users are adding full-fledged OCR capabilities to their systems. Calera Recognition Systems's WordScan Plus 3.0 will appeal to these users as well as to old hands. The latest version of this highly regarded OCR package combines the accuracy and productivity tools of last year's release with a much easier interface and a dramatically improved online help system.

If you are already familiar with such Microsoft Office applications as Word for Windows or Excel, you will

be instantly at home with WordScan Plus 3.0. Its commands, menu structures, and dialog boxes now closely follow Microsoft Office conventions. When you select the Acquire Image option from the main File menu and choose the type of input to convert (for example, scanner input or a disk file), WordScan Plus displays the document in the zoomable and scrollable Preview area. You can convert the document to text by clicking the main toolbar's OCR button; other options let you perform OCR as you scan in a document or receive a fax.

Since even the best OCR program makes mistakes, proofing tools are essential. WordScan Plus shines here as well. As soon as OCR processing is complete, WordScan Plus displays the converted text in its Proofing Editor. Simple keystroke commands, like Shift-Tab, make it easy to review the highlight-

ed words and the characters that were flagged as uncertain during processing. The pop-up display of each item's magnified bitmapped image makes it easy to confirm or correct WordScan Plus's interpretation.

Zoning—choosing which parts of the page to process—speeds processing and improves accuracy. However, unless you are using an HP scanner that supports Hewlett-Packard's AccuPage technology, all zones must be defined manually. You do this by using the mouse to draw up to 100 rectangles (zones) around those parts of the page you want WordScan to process; everything outside a zone is ignored during OCR processing.

While zoning is not strictly required, it is the only way to get WordScan to place OCR text and graphics from a scanned document into separate files. Otherwise, WordScan performs OCR on

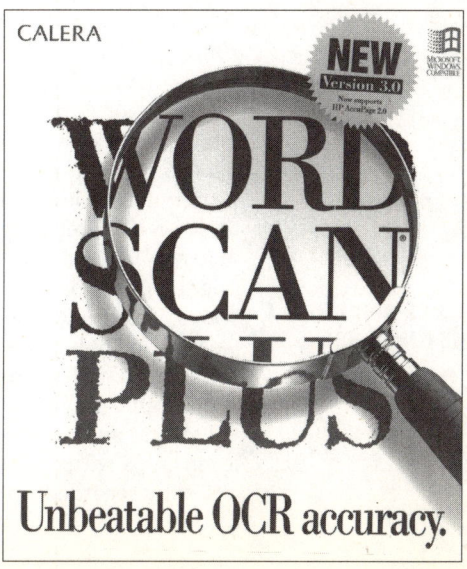

And if you keep the door open, you invite interruption. 3. Do only a day's work. Avoid guilt tripping yourself about not putting in enough hours. It's hard to judge how much work you are doing when you are out of the office.

RealWorldRealWorld

text and ignores the graphics; you end up with an OCR-generated text file and a TIFF file containing the original mixture of text and graphics.

You can improve performance still more by specifying whether the type in a text zone is variable pitch, fixed pitch, dot matrix, numeric, small type (six points or less), or some appropriate combination of the above. You can tell WordScan to save graphic zones in a host of different graphics formats, including PCX and four different versions of TIFF. Text can be saved in more than 40 different word processor and spreadsheet file formats.

When you need to process a large number of similar documents, such as forms, you can save your zone information as a reusable template. You can also define custom font, point size, line spacing, and margins for converted documents. These custom formats can be saved as stylesheets for future use.— John Gliedman

WordScan Plus 3.0
Calera Recognition Systems Inc.
475 Potrero Ave.
Sunnyvale, CA 94086
(800) 422-5372, ext. 22
(408) 720-8300
$595

DATA/FAX/VOICE MODEM IS A RECEPTIONIST-IN-A-BOX

FASTalk 3.0

Adding high-speed data/fax/voice mail to your system with extras like fax-on-demand can easily cost up to

$2,000 or more. But Orion Telecom's FASTalk 3.0 can do it all for $299. It features a V.32bis high-speed modem with 14,400-bps fax capabilities on an internal card that detects whether an incoming call is fax or voice, and switches modes automatically.

The modem comes bundled with SoftKlone's Mirror-Fax with Voice. This DOS-based software includes separate data and fax modules for general communications purposes, but the program's power lies in its seamless integration of all three functions: data, fax, and voice. FASTalk answers calls; directs them to the appropriate extension or mailbox; switches to a different line with a Centrex-type phone system; receives and stores data or faxes; and sends prestored faxes automatically. The modem can forward a message, alert a pager, and even accept a voice message along with a fax.

Setup is painless. The hardest part is deciding which functions to choose. Once you plan a multilevel tree structure of messages and functions, the program presents a telephone-keypad interface with pop-up menus to define each level. You'll need an extra telephone or microphone to record messages, but the package provides high-fidelity stereo speakers for playback. The software is multilingual as well, supporting up to 10 languages simultaneously. It even ships with a standard set of prerecorded English

messages and lets you record their foreign-language counterparts.

Fax-on-demand is delivered by immediate fax-back on the same line (the caller pays for the call), or by a two-line system that hangs up and redials. An intuitive interface helps organize faxes into an unlimited number of catalog groups. You create fax files simply by faxing a document from your stand-alone fax machine to FASTalk; or a conversion utility creates fax files from ASCII text, PCX, TIF and other standard file formats.

The voice and fax-on-demand features of FASTalk must run in the foreground. A large hard drive is also a good idea since a three-minute message, even with compression, could eat up nearly a megabyte. Therefore, you'll need a dedicated PC with a hefty hard drive to take full advantage of this fast-talking receptionist-in-a-box.—Kathryn Alesandrini

FASTalk 3.0
Orion Telecom Inc.
1925 E. Beltline
Suite 405
Carrollton, TX 75006
(800) 669-8088; (214) 416-3720
$299

SIX SOFT PORTS AND LOTS OF HARD DATA

Soft I/O Card

While modems keep getting faster, serial ports and their underachieving 8250 UARTs continue to lag behind. Rather than throw out the

high-tech baby simply because of its backwater communications ability, the sensible solution is to consider an I/O upgrade. Which is precisely why Axxon's Soft I/O Card is worth a look. This $199 board features four serial ports and two parallel ports. Its serial ports are driven by Startech 16552 UARTs. The parallel ports are bidirectional, not only for the myriad disk and tape drives that lately seem to require them, but also because they offer an alternate communications port. Even 16550-based serial ports have a practical limit of 115.2K/sec, and several of the newer V.FC modems use the parallel port to circumvent that particular boundary.

The Soft I/O Card doesn't require you to play with jumpers or DIP switches. Instead, Axxon includes a configuration program that sets the addresses and IRQs. It's not a TSR and only needs to be run if the configuration changes; once it's done, it's gone from memory.

The board uses an address that can't be altered. Other than that, however, you can play musical IRQs and addresses for each of the six ports. The only thing the Soft I/O doesn't do is share them with another device, but that shouldn't be a problem—with the exception of 6, 8, 13, and 14, IRQs 3 through 15 are assignable to any ports on the card. The four typical serial-port addresses and two parallel-port addresses are interchangeable.

While the technical content of the Soft I/O's manual is considerable, helpful explanations are limited. Axxon's toll-free tech support should provide a good balance between the two. And the five-year warranty ensures that the Soft I/O will solve your I/O needs for years to come.—Bill O'Brien

Soft I/O Card
Axxon Computer Corp.
3979 Tecumseh Rd.
E. Windsor, ON N8W 1J5
Canada
(800) 361-1913; (519) 974-0163
$199

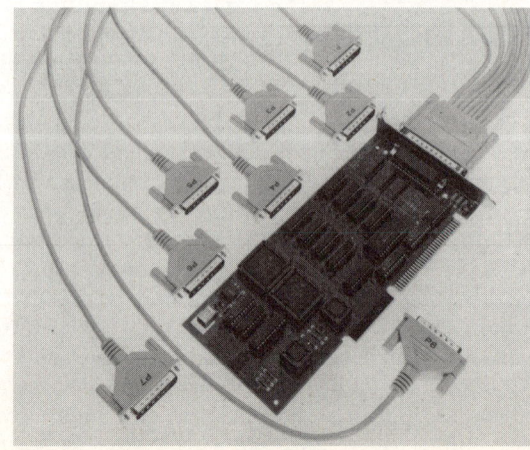

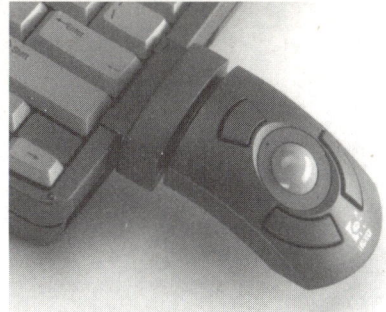

LOGITECH'S VOYAGER TRAVELS WELL

TrackMan Voyager

Logitech has a knack for creating impressive pointing devices. Its newest addition to the field, the TrackMan Voyager, is a fully programmable, fully portable trackball with features not seen in other similar devices. The TrackMan Voyager is aptly named: It was designed to be used with laptops and functions best in their company. It is small—only about 3×2 inches—but its clever design can make it seem much bigger. Its cover, which protects the device during transit, attaches to one end and acts as a wrist support if desired.

The Voyager has a standard center-mounted trackball with a forward "primary" button and two side "secondary" buttons. All of the buttons are fully programmable, and any of the three can be awarded primary status.

Additionally, the Voyager has a clip that enables it to attach to the front, right, or left side of the keyboard. The included software allows the user to easily reconfigure the direction in which the trackball moves the cursor.

Despite initial installation trouble, solved painlessly by a quick call to technical support and a bit of system reconfiguration, the Voyager performed expertly. Even with a notebook on your lap and the Voyager clipped to the side, pointing and clicking are effortless, and the programmable double-click function was a treat.

While the TrackMan Voyager was designed for the road, the folks at Logitech know that laptops don't always sit on your lap. For this reason, they designed the Voyager to be able to mimic a desktop trackball, which it does successfully.—Joshua Piven

TrackMan Voyager
Logitech Inc.
6505 Kaiser Dr.
Fremont, CA 94555
(800) 231-7717
$89.95

Mac Power On/Off+ Aux Port

If you're computing on the road, but the file you need is on your office or home Mac, remote-control software is the right answer—but what if you forgot to leave your computer on?

Mac Power On/Off+Aux Port turns on a remote Macintosh and peripherals in response to a telephone call. When the call is completed, it shuts down the system. It works on any Mac running System 7 or higher, and requires only 20K of memory.

The Power On/Off hardware consists of a box about the size of a modem, and an Intelligent Power Module (IPM) that plugs into a wall outlet. The Mac and its peripherals plug into the IPM. Meanwhile, one end of a supplied Y-cable plugs into an RJ-11 jack on the IPM. A second leg of the cable goes to an Apple Desktop Bus (ADB) port on the Mac. The third leg plugs into the back of the Power On/Off box. There are other connections for the telephone line, a modem, the power supply, and a fax. By the time you're finished setting up, all those cables can make your unit resemble an octopus. Fortunately, the documentation is well-written, and if all the steps are taken in sequence, everything falls into place.

The default setup calls for the Power On/Off module to respond to the first ring. The unit first turns on the peripherals, then a signal is sent to

the Mac's ADB port to power it up. If you have a Mac that does not have an ADB port, it will simply power up at the same time as the peripherals.

When the call ends, the software waits a set interval, then performs a software shutdown of the Mac. The Power On/Off hardware monitors the phone line and waits until after the caller has hung up, then signals the IPM to turn off the power. Both these intervals and the ring count are user-configurable.

Mac Power On/Off is a valuable accessory for anyone regularly accessing an unattended remote Mac.

Mac Power On/Off+ Aux Port
Server Technology Inc.
1288 Hammerwood Ave.
Sunnyvale, CA 94089
(800) 835-1515; (408) 745-0300
Fax: (408) 745-0392
$199.95; bundled with
Timbuktu: $219.95

DragonDictate for Windows 1.0 DragonDictate Power Edition 3.0 Microsoft Windows Sound System 2.0 Voice for Windows

I found the DOS-based DragonDictate fastest in recognizing words and responding to corrections. The Windows products were a bit slower, and occasionally had to repeat a word that was ignored while the software looked up the preceding statement. All three products took about the same amount of time to set up and produced acceptable results, once they were trained. The Windows products had a definite advantage, since it was easy to move data between applications. The common command set used by most Windows programs reduced the effort in setting up command and control functions, too.

Both DragonDictate and Voice can switch between dictation mode and command-and-control functions. Properly trained systems can provide hands-free operation for most users. This is a real advantage for people with disabilities or those working in harsh industrial environments. During the training process, users repeat common operating-system or environment commands as well as navigational phrases in addition to words used to train the general recognition engine.

Commands are generally compound words that the software will recognize and interpret as an instruction, rather than a word to be placed in a file. Some commands are internal; for example, "Scratch that" is used by DragonDictate to erase the previous word, and "Oops" is used to correct the preceding word. Saying it brings up a window with a series of words the system feels might be the logical alternative.

You can verbally confirm a listing by saying, "Choose n," with the number of the option replacing the letter n. To actually enter "Oops" in this paragraph, I spelled it out using the International alphabet: "Oscar-Oscar-Papa-Sierra." Speaking the phrase resulted in the command function being activated. The same technique can be used to add new words to the active dictionary via the microphone.

Mouse- and cursor-movement commands are handled

> "I have this hairball theory of computing: if you have a mainframe, you create hairball database and application environments. Big huge, messy, slimy, fuzzy, ugly hairballs. What the world needs to do is what I call kiss-cubed: keep it small, simple, and separate. Object-oriented programming is decomposing the the BWOS—the big wad of software, the hairball. Pizza-box computing, distributed computing, peer computing, client server computing, rightsizing, whatever you call it, is decomposing the mainframe hairball, database and applications. There's going to be hundreds of billions of dollars worth of business over the next 20 years decomposing all the hairballs that have been built over the past 20 years."
>
> **—SCOTT MCNEALY, PRESIDENT, SUN MICROSYSTEMS, 1994**

the same way. You can say phrases like "Move up two" or "Double-click" to operate the program. DragonDictate for Windows has a slick feature that automatically creates a command vocabulary for Windows applications by reading the menus for the program. Users can still access the keyboard to enter commands or data.

Installing a voice-recognition system will take at least an hour—more if you run into hardware conflicts. First you have to install the sound card, then feed a stream of anywhere from 10 to 20 floppy disks. Some systems can use regular off-the-shelf sound cards, but many require proprietary boards specially designed to work with a given software package. Virtually all these products currently require some form of digital signal processor (DSP) from the sound card. Fortunately, as SRT vendors move to the Windows environment, they're starting to support popular boards like Creative Labs's Sound

Blaster, and the Microsoft Windows Sound System.

During informal testing, we found that some compatible cards were often not compatible enough. A genuine Microsoft Sound System card worked fine, but two Sound Blaster clones gave less than stellar performances. If you're hoping to use an off-the-shelf sound card with these products, it's wise to check with the vendor before making a purchase. The same holds true for the microphone. Right now, I'm using DragonDictate for Windows with the supplied IBM M-APC sound card and speaking into a Shure SM10A headset. According to Dragon Systems, the card and mic must match. I'd have to switch mics if the card was switched.

To make matters worse, the special drivers used to control voice-recognition functions on the sound card are generally incompatible with regular multimedia applications. If you need both speech-recognition and multimedia operations, you may have to go through the arduous task

of switching drivers or even resort to using two computers.

Once everything is running properly, it's time to experiment with performance. Most vendors offer significant tuning resources that can dramatically alter how fast or accurately the program performs recognition. Usually, there is a trade-off between the two. Just before writing this paragraph, I adjusted the number of words held in the RAM-based cache. Small variations in this value can alternately cut or increase processing time by as much as 30 percent.

Also, don't forget to examine your startup files, both at the DOS level and in Windows for Windows-based SRT. Re-adjusting the memory management and system resources can improve performance and make the installation more stable. Remember that voice recognition is resource-intensive; if your system isn't configured properly, the application may hang and data will be lost.

Those warnings aside, dictation software is addictive. Once you get used to talking

to your computer, it's difficult to go back to punching keys. In the early 1980s, using a mouse was uncommon. Few applications supported the new pointing device. Today, virtually all new computer systems are sold with mice. As mainstream vendors add voice SRT capability, the microphone also may become an ubiquitous component of entry-level systems. That day may be sooner than many of us expect.

Prices are down dramatically on discrete speech-recognition products. High-end editions dropped from about $4,000 down to $1,700 this year. Entry-level programs with 5,000-word active vocabularies are selling for under $400. Since they can be used with regular sound cards, the only other expense you'll incur (provided you've already got a multimedia PC) is the purchase of a compatible microphone.—James Karney

DragonDictate for Windows 1.0
Dragon Systems Inc.
320 Nevada St.
Newton, MA 02160
(800) 825-5897; (617) 965-5200
$395, Starter Edition; $695,
Classic Edition; $1,695, Power
Edition Avg

DragonDictate Power Edition
3.0
Dragon Systems Inc.
320 Nevada St.
Newton, MA 02160
(800) 825-5897; (617) 965-5200
$1,995

16-hour day they're putting in. Get real. Don't fret over the hours. Pace yourself by projects. Make sure you get the job done. Supervisors are convinced that work-at-home telecommuters are goofing off all the time. Make

Microsoft Windows Sound
System 2.0
Microsoft Corp.
One Microsoft Way
Redmond, WA 98052
(800) 426-9400; (206) 882-8080
$59, software only; $149, soft-
ware with sound

Voice for Windows
Kurzweil Applied Intelligence
Inc.
411 Waverly Oaks Rd.
Waltham, MA 02154
(800) 380-1234; (617) 893-5151
$995

FAX, COPY, AND FILE

PaperMaster 1.0 for Windows
E-Quip+

DocuMagix's PaperMaster 1.0 for Windows and Alacrity's E-Quip+ turn your computer and peripherals into a full-featured faxing, copying, and filing system. In our tests, both products filed documents after receiving them via fax or scanner or by copying them from another Windows application. You can use a scanner with either package to fax documents directly; add a printer, and you can copy documents easily. Both packages let you annotate filed documents, but neither allows you to edit those documents.

PaperMaster runs background OCR to identify filed faxes and scans during keyword searches, but it doesn't create editable files with the OCR. E-Quip+ does create

editable files, but it can't use OCR for searches. Instead, you can tag each document with a title the program can use when searching. PaperMaster stores all documents using a filing-cabinet and file-folder metaphor. E-Quip+ lacks a central filing system.

E-Quip+ offers more features than PaperMaster: It requires no supporting fax software, for instance, and offers a sophisticated form fill-in function and fancier annotation. In every other way, though, we found PaperMaster vastly more elegant and easier to use.— Edward Mendelson

PaperMaster 1.0 for Windows
DocuMagix
(800) 362-8624
$169

E-Quip+
Alacrity Systems
(800) 252-2748
$159

A COLOR WORKHORSE FOR THE OFFICE

Kodak XLS 8600 PS Printer

Kodak gives its competition something to worry about with its latest entry in the increasingly crowded dye sublimation printer field. The Kodak XLS 8600 PS produces such superb prints that its only real competitor is Kodak's own top-of-the-line $20,000 XL 7720 printer— which offers one-third higher resolution and slightly more

dynamic range. In addition, the prints from Kodak's new XtraLife ribbons are nearly indistinguishable from photographic enlargements and have a new coating that resists fading.

The XLS 8600 PS—as well as the non-PostScript XLS 8600 version—incorporates an impressive lineup of enhancements and new features. The 300-dpi printer comes with 32MB RAM (upgradable to 64MB). With additional memory added, we were able to print multiple files in sequence and process larger image files at higher speeds. Together, these enhancements mean higher throughput for this workhorse of a printer. The XLS 8600 PS has a rated monthly duty cycle of 12,000 prints— higher than most other dye sublimation printers, though considerably less than Kodak's XL 7720.

Most users will immediately notice the XLS 8600's exceptional printing speed: It is up to three times faster than its predecessor, Kodak's XLS 8300. This is due to hardware refinements as well as significant improvements to Kodak's printer drivers, especially the driver for Photoshop Export mode.

Another speed enhancer is the XLS 8600 PS's SCSI-2 port, which, unlike most other printers with a built-in SCSI interface, can be used for transferring print data— and not just as an auxiliary storage option for fonts. For example, we printed a 27.5MB PostScript file in 1

minute 15 seconds via the SCSI/Export mode. The same file took 4 minutes 30 seconds in parallel/export mode, and 24 minutes in parallel mode using Kodak's Windows PostScript driver. Because the XLS 8600 PS can crank out multiple prints directly from memory—at a speed of about 1 page per minute—the printer can improve the productivity of a busy service bureau or corporate graphics department.

An important innovation is UltraColor, an advanced color management system compatible with the new ColorSync Consortium standards. UltraColor produced realistic skin tones and other hard-to-render hues.

The printer connects to your PC in several different ways: through built-in parallel, SCSI, and LocalTalk interfaces, or via an optional $995 network card that supports NetWare, EtherTalk, and TCP/IP. During testing, the printer was able to correctly sense which interface was being used, and all ports can be active simultaneously.

Setting up and installing the printer and drivers was painless and trouble-free. The only problem we encountered was having to manually tape the ribbon to the take-up spool—a minor hassle at worst. The XLS 8600 PS doesn't use a ribbon carrier, either, so switching between 8.5 × 11-inch ribbons and 9.5 × 14-inch ribbons is a slight inconvenience.

Our biggest configuration problem occured when we attached the unit to a 486 PC via the computer's parallel port and to a Macintosh Quadra 950 via the Ethernet module. The printer initially failed to print from the PC, producing one short and cryptic error message after another on full-size paper—at a cost of $2.60 per page. Rather than see our paper, ribbon, and money wasted, we would have preferred if the error codes were displayed on the printer's front panel or the PC's screen.

Unable to decipher the printer's error messages, we contacted Kodak's technical support staff, who diagnosed the problem as a conflict between the PC's parallel port and the Lantastic network it was connected to. Once we severed the PC from the network, the printer worked perfectly. We were able to alternate between printing from the PC and the Mac without changing any settings, since the printer determines priority by chronological order, regardless of the port.

Kodak has greatly improved the printer's ribbon. The dyes in the three-color (CMY) ribbon are able to deliver blacks that are as dark as those produced by a conventional 4-ribbon CMYK color printer. Regardless of image content, the prints created by the XLS 8600 PS were generally brilliant and deeply saturated with sharp and well-defined lines and edges.

Instead of a black ribbon, Kodak has substituted a clear

🐝 Robert Frankston and Dan Bricklin created Visicalc, the original spreadsheet, from which Lotus 1-2-3, Excel, and all the others have emanated. Visicalc was originally sold on a cassette tape for the Apple II in 1977 before floppy-disk drives had been introduced.

sure to get some goofing-off time in to suit them. 4. Focus on work, not housework. Do not be cowed into doing the dishes during working hours. My first stint at telecommuting was during a time when my wife worked.

RealWorldRealWorld

laminate coating, called XtraLife, that protects the print against environmental ravages. Because XtraLife filters out ultraviolet light, Kodak guarantees that the prints produced by the XLS 8600 PS will last as long as conventional color prints—about 10 years. Unfortunately, the XtraLife ribbon is available only for 8.5 × 12-inch output at this time.

The bottom line is that the XLS 8600 PS produces the best pictures we have yet to see from a desktop printer.—Daniel Grotta; Sally Wiener Grotta

Kodak XLS 8600 PS Printer
Eastman Kodak Co.
Rochester, NY
(800) 235-6325.
$9,995

THE POSITIVE SIDE TO SCANNING SLIDES

Coolscan
SprintScan 35

With all the talk about video on PCs these days, it's easy to forget that many of the images we'd like to funnel into our computers are static ones. But getting pictures from film to file requires a slide scanner, traditionally a tool reserved for graphics professionals. Nikon changed the rules with its Coolscan slide scanner, a compact, easy-to-use, and relatively affordable model that yields high-quality digitized images from 35mm film. Now Coolscan has company in the form of a slide scanner from

another big name in photography: Polaroid. And true to its instant-picture heritage, Polaroid's new SprintScan 35 does what the Coolscan does, only much faster.

At first glance, the SprintScan 35 has much in common with the Coolscan. Both are optical scanners that can digitize 35mm slides in a single pass (compared to earlier scanners that used three passes, which is generally slower and less accurate). Both units cost about $2,500 and can scan almost any type of 35mm image—monochrome or color, positive or negative. And both make stunning 24-bit color copies at resolutions of up to 2,700 dots per inch.

The Coolscan and SprintScan 35 each scan in images using a film-strip holder. The scanning software resembles what's included with color flatbed and document scanners, with a prescan procedure and controls for brightness, contrast, color, focus, cropping, film type, and so on. Both models come with software that can act as a "plug-in" to Adobe's Photoshop (or compatible applications), but you needn't have a copy of Photoshop in order to scan.

As for results, the Coolscan seems to do a slightly better job of getting the scan right on the first take, though both units are prone to mild distortions, color variations, and unwanted shadows. Such problems are usually easy to correct via software.

The SprintScan 35, on the other hand, sprints past its competitor when it comes to scanning speed. capturing a color slide at maximum resolution takes a mere 40 seconds or so with this unit. Capturing the same image at the same resolution with the Coolscan takes much longer—about 10 minutes is required.

Neither slide scanner is for the faint of hardware: Images scanned at full resolution can occupy 28MB of disk space each. A 24-bit video setup is also advised. The SprintScan 35 comes with a SCSI-2 interface board, while the Coolscan includes a standard SCSI card.

Nikon's Coolscan and Polaroid's SprintScan 35 both do an exceptional job of getting 35mm film images into your PC at a justifiable price. The SprintScan 35 simply does the job a lot faster.—Chris O'Malley

Coolscan
Nikon Electronic Imaging
(800) 526-4566
$2,600 for external ($2,300 internal)

SprintScan 35
Polaroid Corp.
(800) 816-2611
$2,495

EASY-AS-PIE COLOR PRINTING

DeskJet 540

If you've been waiting for that perfect moment to buy a low-cost ink-jet printer, now is the time to take out your wallet. For a combined list

price of just over $400, HP's new DeskJet 540 and its color upgrade kit can give you 600 × 300-dpi black output and 300 × 300-dpi color output to spice up any document.

The DeskJet 540 replaces HP's DeskJet 520, a low-end monochrome ink-jet printer. Snap in the color upgrade kit, and the DeskJet 540 is also a replacement for HP's DeskJet 500C, an all-in-one printer with a sleek, new design.

There's a new trend in low-end ink-jet printers: simplicity. But we've never seen an ink-jet printer as easy to set up as the DeskJet 540. Just plug it in, snap in a cartridge, and install a driver; HP takes care of the rest. If you switch your black printing cartridge to the color cartridge, the printer is one step ahead of you and will configure the software accordingly. And if you go to print an all-black document using your color cartridge, the software will suggest that you switch cartridges—no need to tell this printer anything.

The DeskJet 540 ships with easy-to-use Windows software (DOS users must follow the conventions set forth by the applications they use). If you want to get fancy and fiddle with your color options, the included ColorSmart software lets you specify the type of document you're printing (graphics or photographs, for example), the quality you want (best, normal, or economy), and the material you're printing on (such as transparencies or glossy paper). The software

takes care of the rest. The software even contains an animated online tutorial to help you with common questions.

When compared to the older DeskJet 500C, the DeskJet 540's output appears richer and its colors truer. In a head-to-head comparison with Texas Instruments' microMarc Color Inkjet, the DeskJet 540's colors are smoother and more consistent.

If you use its color cartridge to print plain text, your blacks will have a greenish tint. This is because the DeskJet 540 (like other low-end color printers) uses a composite black—a combination of cyan, magenta, and yellow—instead of true black. For plain text, it's better to swap the color cartridge out for the all-black unit. This will make your text output better, though not quite up to the level of Canon's BJC-4000

The DeskJet 540 isn't a speed demon, but it is competitive with other printers in its class. In our tests, it was 21 percent faster than the DeskJet 500C for a business report containing both text and graphics, but about 7 percent slower for a color presentation. All in all, the speed is nothing to shout about. However, if you plan your printing ahead of time, the DeskJet 540 won't keep you waiting long.

It's hard to go wrong with the rock-bottom price of this printer. Without the $49 color option, it will set you back only $365 (less than $300 on the street). And although there are other printers in this price range—even some that are less expensive—when you consider the easy-to-use features of the DeskJet 540 and output quality that surpasses its closest competitors, those few extra dollars won't mean a thing.

Sleek and Simple: HP's DeskJet 540 sports a new design that's as functional as it is attractive. Gone are the days of front-panel controls—with the DeskJet 540 and its user-friendly software, you drive the printer from the keyboard of your computer.—Kyla K. Carlson

DeskJet 540
Hewlett-Packard
(800) 752-0900
$365

TAKE IT WITH YOU
Plug-and-Scan 256

Mustek's recent release of a PC Card Type II grayscale hand scanner seems like nothing new, but it is: The Plug-and-Scan 256 is a 5-volt "green" scanner that uses less than half the juice of a regular device. The result? It works off your subnote's batteries. TWAIN support and bundled Perceive Personal software provide the fax front end. For even less space, try a pen-shaped parallel scanner from I.R.I.S. or Primax.

Plug-and-Scan 256
Mustek
(800) 468-7835
$249

PocketJet

Output? Try the one-pound Pentax PocketJet, a 3-ppm, 300-dpi serial or parallel printer. Its direct thermal printing needs no supplies except coated paper. And on a 70-minute charge, it prints dozens of pages. The as-yet-unannounced Citizen AmericaPN60 promises to weigh in about the same, but that's all we know.

PocketJet
Pentax
(800) 543-6144
$499

SONY WAVES A MAGIC MESSAGE WAND
Magic Link 1000

You say you have faxes to receive, e-mail to send, meetings to schedule, and phone calls to return—and you're in the middle of a three-week, 14-city marketing tour? Good luck. Take some No Doz and pick up a Magic Link Personal Intelligent Communicator 1000, Sony's first entry into the PDA arena.

The Magic Link comes with a wealth of messaging features courtesy of AT&T's PersonaLink Services. The services run on the Magic Link using General Magic's Magic Cap object-oriented operating system.

One notable omission from this PDA is two-way wireless communication—the Magic Link communicates via built-in RJ-11 phone jack. Its steep price tag is also a disappointment: At $800 on the street, the Magic Link is certainly

not for everyone. But if you're the Mad Max of mobile professionals, you should give it serious consideration.

The heart of the PersonaLink Services are the intelligent agents that can be incorporated into your messages. In standard e-mails, these agents can carry voice recordings, animated icons, and instructions for forwarding and filing messages. On a grander scale, the agents, using General Magic's Telescript technology, can carry billing information, instructions, and procedural data to commercial services.

Through a special gateway to AT&T's EasyLink Services, you can send and receive e-mail from the Internet, MCI Mail, CompuServe, Prodigy, PersonaLink Services, AT&T Mail, and X.400-based mail services. You can also send faxes to just about anyone, and with an optional PC Card pager from SkyTel, you can even receive pages.

The 1.2-pound Magic Link also maintains your schedule and to-do list, and keeps your contact list current—though its 1MB of RAM fills up pretty quickly.

Although the Magic Link doesn't currently support handwriting recognition, a version of Palm's Graffiti should soon be available for Magic Cap. An innovative handwriting recognition engine, Graffiti relies on a specialized alphabet. You can also plug in an optional external keyboard for more serious data entry. (The other must-have option is a flyweight telephone headset that turns

the Magic Link into the world's most expensive telephone—albeit one that has its own built-in address book.)

Connectivity between the Magic Link and a desktop PC or Macintosh is accomplished through IntelliLink's Magic Xchange. This program supports data transfer, translation, and backup for many file formats and applications, including Lotus's Organizer and Microsoft's Schedule +. And by the time you read this, the program should also support Act, Calandar, Commence, Ecco Professional, Sidekick, Excel, dBase, and Paradox.

The Magic Link includes a number of useful applications on its 4MB of ROM. Chief among them is Intuit's Pocket Quicken, an outstanding financial manager that links into Quicken on your desktop PC. And if you absolutely must use a spreadsheet on the Magic Link's tiny screen, Pen-Ware's PenCell is included.

The Magic Link is leaps and bounds beyond other PDAs. The big price tag and lack of wireless capabilities are hard pills for most casual users to swallow, but for mobile e-mail mavens, the Magic Link provides communications links of a kind you can't find anywhere else.—Richard Schwerin

Magic Link 1000
Sony
(800) 556-2442; (201) 930-1000
$800

TURN YOUR MODEM AND PRINTER INTO A FAX COPIER
ScanMan PowerPage

More than three million Americans work the same way I do. We're employed by a corporation, but we do a lot of work at home. The problem: We can't justify the purchase of photocopiers, fax machines, and other work necessities for our home offices—nor can we afford the space. So we get by with a PC, a fax modem, a printer…and that's about it.

At least that's how I struggled before I got my anxious hands on Logitech's ScanMan PowerPage. This foot-long grayscale scanner and its simple software expanded my printer and fax modem into a photocopier and an honest-to-goodness fax machine. All I had to do was plug it into my spare parallel port (luckily, I had one left over after hooking up my printer) and install the software (which included yet another copy of Delrina's WinFax 3.0 for my private collection).

Now, whenever I need to send a fax or make a photocopy, I slip paper into the scanner. It detects the paper and kicks up a control-panel button bar that has four buttons: Picture, Text, Copy, and Fax. If I want a TIFF file or text recognition, I click on one of the first two buttons. More often I want to run off a convenience copy or need to send out a fax.

Actually, ScanMan PowerPage doesn't just replace a fax and photocopier. It's better than any fax machine and

Real World Real World Real World

the mess in your office and do housework only with your partner, not for your partner when you should be working. 5. Be as mobile as you can. Have a laptop and a desktop or some sort of combination machine. If you

North Carolina Info Highway Open for Business Next Summer: Educational, Legal, Medical Videoconferencing Also Planned

high-speed cruisers, at least state-affiliated ones, recently entered the North Carolina Information Highway (NCIH), signaling one of the first of many AT&T-connected, full-scale state systems to come in the next year or so. NCIH's estimated $160 million infrastructure is provided by a collaboration of local exchange carriers, including BellSouth, Carolina Telephone and Telegraph, and GTE.

But the highway's ribbon-cutting doesn't yet mean a green light for state businesses. Private industry in North Carolina will have to wait for access until next summer, when usage rates are approved by the public utility commission. Expect a similar lag time with other implementations as they emerge.

The first state applications to go online are distance-learning programs that connect college and high-school classrooms with videoconferencing—one of the state's first widespread, mainstream applications of videoconferencing in its own right. The same technology is also being used to arraign criminal suspects on a video link between courthouses and jails.

Next to link up will be health-care providers, so rural doctors can send diagnostic images such as X-rays and CAT scans to city hospitals. Later, multimedia kiosks around the state will dispense an array of government services, such as driver's-license renewals.

State users pay a basic monthly service charge of $4,000, which buys them 44 hours of video. Additional video time costs $75 per hour. Data use counts against those hours, but at a much reduced rate.

Asynchronous transfer mode (ATM) and synchronous optical network (SONET) lines won out over ISDN as the network option, because ISDN lacks the bandwidth to support multilocation video. In addition to their technical credentials, ATM and SONET have the advantage of being at the beginning of their life cycle. "They won't have to be replaced in three to five years," says Glen James, partner of the firm Deloitte and Touche, which reviewed the state project.

One drawback of ATM, however, is that its newness means near-term users will have to convert to another technology, such as SMDS, to connect to smaller locations in other states. James says businesses are showing a lot of interest in the service. Other states actively pursuing information-highway projects include Arizona, Iowa, Kentucky, Maryland, New York, and South Carolina.—John Zyskowski ■

photocopier that sells for $449. I hate shiny fax paper, and I have no patience for the fiddly control panels those machines have. And no copier I could afford reproduces graphics as well as ScanMan PowerPage and my laser printer.

Logbook Entries:

August 22, 1994: It's 8 a.m. and I have a meeting downtown. But I still have a "How It Works" sketch due for a 9 a.m. meeting at the office.

OK, I'll fax it. The office fax machine doesn't respond, so I scan it and e-mail it.

September 15, 1994: Did my quarterly expenses. Total line items for photocopies and faxes: zero. I'm happy; the local copy shop isn't.

October 2, 1994 (Sunday): Windows 95 ate my homework! And there are no undelete tools in my beta. But I have draft printouts—

ScanMan PowerPage's OCR module saves the day.

November 13, 1994: At Comdex I'm faced with a sheaf of articles to edit and two choices: pay $2 a page for the hotel fax service or leverage my fax modem with ScanMan PowerPage.— Matthew Lake

ScanMan PowerPage
Logitech
(800) 231-7717
$449

HOT NEWS: A PAGING PC CARD

SkyCard

Stay in touch wherever you roam with SkyTel's SkyCard PC Card pager. It takes messages when your notebook is turned off—even when it's unplugged. This $249 Type II card manages messages with Windows software or uses DDE links to Microsoft Mail or Lotus's cc:Mail. The same

DDE support can also deliver news briefs or stock quotes into a spreadsheet.—Richard Schwerin

SkyCard
SkyTel Corp.
(800) 759-9779
$249

IBM Simon

Everyone has a cellular phone. Many people have little electronic organizers, too. But what else do you need on the road? Fax? Pager? E-mail? If you were to add up everything, you'd be left with two options: a carry-on bag full of gadgets and batteries, or BellSouth's handful of digital tricks, Simon.

Describing Simon isn't simple. It's a large cellular phone with a backlit LCD touch-screen. But it's also a send-and-receive fax machine. It's an electronic organizer with calendar, clock, to-do lists, address books, scheduler, and alarms. But it's also a stylus-based sketch pad. It looks pretty cute, too, until you check out the sticker: $899 list, plus monthly service and usage charges.

To read a fax on Simon's oddly shaped 6 × 2-inch screen, you turn the device sideways and hit a button to scroll the fax. This works fine for short faxes, but it becomes laborious by the third page of longer ones. To type in your own message, Simon displays an on-screen keypad.

Except for somewhat inconvenient typing and a high price, Simon's biggest drawback is that it's simply too appealing. We wanted to rely on it all the time, but we got only 8 hours of juice before needing another

recharge—and that was from modest use and 20 minutes on the phone. By four o'clock, we were unable to receive faxes, phone calls, or reminders. But if you want to impress people at any cost— or you need to receive and send faxes anytime, anywhere—Simon is the gadget for you.—Matthew Lake

IBM Simon
BellSouth Cellular Corp.
(800) 746-6672
$899–$1,099

SCAN, READ, RECOGNIZE, REMEMBER

RollandRead Professional

You say you need document management but can't justify the desk space? Recognita's RollandRead Professional, a TWAIN-compliant sheet-feed scanner, is less obtrusive than a phone-and-modem tag team and provides all that a small department needs to manage incoming paper.

Slide in an interface card, snap on the paper guides, and the RollandRead is ready to pump six pages per minute from its 10-page feeder. The RollandRead scans in up to 256 levels of gray, and its Recognita Plus 1.2 OCR software is a healthy performer that recognizes 80 languages—better than your average businessperson. For tracking what you scan, the

included document manager, Watermark 1.04, incorporates workgroup-oriented OLE technology.

Drawbacks? The graphics software, Photo Plus, is only for quick-and-dirty use. The OCR software doesn't handle multicolumn text formatting well, and it falters on narrow line spacing. And unlike the nearest competitor, Visioneer's $499 PaperMax, it requires you to insert an interface card. The RollandRead costs $695, which is as much as a color flatbed scanner. But for a cramped desk with stacks of paper, it's a standout.—James Oliver Cury

RollandRead Professional
Recognita Corp.
(800) 255-4627; (408) 241-5772
$695

TD-3 Personal Work Station ViewSonic 17 and 21

Monitor the Facts: Crunch data and graphics faster with Intergraph's CAD-blasting TD-3 90MHz Pentium. And use a big-screen SVGA ViewSonic monitor to view them.

TD-3 Personal Work Station
Intergraph Corp
(800) 345-4856
$7,300

ViewSonic 17 and 21
ViewSonic Corp
(800) 888-8583
$1,045 and $1,995

Mirage CompuPhone

This Keyboard Speaks! With the CompuPhone keyboard, just plug in a headset—such as the Plantronics's Mirage— and you have a zero-footprint phone. Dial out from the keypad or with its software.

Mirage
Plantronics
(800) 544-4660
$88

CompuPhone
Integrated Technology
(800) 393-8889
$159

HOW TO ESCAPE THE MOUSE TRAP

Expert Mouse 4.0 and WinTrac

It takes over your desk, demands that you keep a clean space for it, and then rewards you by knocking over your coffee cup with its tail. A mouse can be so inconsiderate. But it doesn't have to be this way. Enter two new trackballs: Kensington's Expert Mouse 4.0 and MicroSpeed's WinTrac.

Both Expert Mouse and WinTrac are well-designed and comfortable to use, for righties and southpaws alike. Expert Mouse 4.0 looks slick-

er, but WinTrac has a smoother feel. The WinTrac's clean, three-button layout is enhanced by the best feature ever put on a trackball: the TrackWheel, a one-axis roller above the main trackball that lets you page down or cursor down with the slightest gesture. The Expert Mouse's two-button design is adequate, but limited without something like the TrackWheel.

Which one is best for you? Expert Mouse is built better, with superior documentation and cable adapters. But WinTrac, with its clever and incredibly useful TrackWheel, rolls away with our recommendation.—John Taschek

Expert Mouse 4.0
Kensington
(800) 535-4242; (415) 572-2700
$149

WinTrac
MicroSpeed
(800) 438-7733; (510) 490-1665
$149.95; $179.95 for bus version

PUTTING THE SQUEEZE ON VOICE

TrueSpeech

DSP Group's TrueSpeech compression technology is the leading compression choice for voice. DSP Group engineers, working in labs in Silicon Valley and Israel, are improving voice-compression algorithms so that sound can be stored more efficiently. The advances are opening new frontiers in real-time voice compression and digital voice mail.

Based on mathematical algorithms derived from the way airflow from your lungs is shaped by the throat, mouth, and tongue when you speak, TrueSpeech can compress a 900K file—a minute of voice data—to a 60K file by throwing out redundant and unnecessary information about the sound.

TrueSpeech is off to a good start: It is already embedded in Microsoft Windows Sound System, and Microsoft has adopted it as the speech-compression tool in Windows 95. It has also been adopted by semiconductor makers Analog Devices, Intel, and Motorola, and DSP Group is actively participating in U.S. and international standards groups.—Carol Levin

TrueSpeech
DSP Group

...AND ONE FOR YOUR POCKET
Sharp OZ-9520 Wizard

A handy little companion turns the Sharp OZ-9520 Wizard into a very convenient pocket communicator. The CE-FM4 Fax/Modem is a compact (0.7 by 1.7 by 3.5

inches, HWD) unit that attaches neatly onto the side of the Wizard. Once in place, the modem lets you take advantage of the Wizard's built-in fax software—which includes an automatic cover sheet builder—to send faxes at 9,600 bps. If you're adventurous, you might also try to send and receive e-mail at a slower 2,400 bps through the Wizard's terminal emulator. Although the terminal emulator works, it's arcane. —T. Albano

OZ-9520 Wizard
Sharp
(800) 237-2800
$149

FINGER NAVIGATION
GlidePoint Portable

Traveler's nightmare number 37: While you're using your laptop at 30,000 feet, your pointer locks in place, and no amount of playing with the trackball frees it. After you open the trackball to clean

the actuator wheels, the ball slips out of your fingers and rolls down the aisle. Suddenly, you're flying in coach and your ball is riding in first class. Cirque Corp.'s GlidePoint Portable, a unique nonmechanical pointing device, rules out such airline ball games and lets you sleep easy.

The flat GlidePoint Portable (3.4 × 2.7 × 0.5 inches) represents the latest thinking in pointing devices. To control the pointer, just run your finger across or just above the unit's motion-sensitive surface. Clicking is accomplished by tapping one of the two mechanical buttons at the bottom of the unit or by tapping the GlidePoint's surface. Long, slow movements across the screen may require you to lift and reposition your finger. It takes a few minutes to become familiar with the GlidePoint and just a day or so to become truly comfortable.—Ben Gottesman

GlidePoint Portable
Cirque Corp.
2850 East 3300 South
Salt Lake City, UT 84109
(800) 454-3375; (801) 467-1100
$99

DELTEC UPS PROTECTS YOUR PC WITHOUT HURTING YOUR POCKETBOOK
PowerRite Plus

The advantage of an off-line UPS system is low cost, but the trade-off is that battery rundown and recharge may leave a system exposed to power failures. The PowerRite Plus series of off-line UPS systems include Deltec's battery management feature, which provides adequate protection for a stand-alone PC or network node without requiring you to spend a lot of money. Best of all, if the battery management system detects any problems, you can call Deltec and they'll ship you another unit so you don't have to deal with the battery disposal. The Plus family line is available for 250VA, 400VA, or 600VA power ratings in either 50- or 60-Hz models. The units come with a five year warranty.—Adam A. Hicks

PowerRite Plus
Deltec Electronics Corp.,
2727 Kurtz St.
San Diego, CA 92110
(800) 854-2658; (619) 291-4211
Fax: (619) 291-2973
Starts at $139 for a 250VA unit

GET YOUR MESSAGE ACROSS WITH DESKTOP BANNERS AND POSTERS
ProImage PosterPrinter

It's the amazing poster machine! Varitronic Systems's ProImage PosterPrinter is a

stand-alone device that combines a 400-dot-per-inch scanner and poster-sized printer that automatically enlarges images to poster- and banner-size printouts. The new ProLynx Interface links the ProImage to your PC via the parallel port so you can do the same enlarging for files sent from DOS and Windows applications. The package gives people who need to create posters and banners a professional look with little effort. The unit stores a single 23-inch-wide, 100-foot paper roll that can produce posters in four different sizes: 23 × 31 inches, 17 × 22 inches, 33 × 44 inches, and 45 × 59 inches, or banners up to 23 inches wide and 100 feet long. The thermal transfer paper rolls are available in different colors and textures for prices that range from $79.95 to $199.95. The printer outputs single-color printing at 300 dpi and also does reverse printing.— Adam A. Hicks

ProImage PosterPrinter with
ProLynx Interface
Varitronic Systems Inc.
Minneapolis, MN
(800) 637-5461; (612) 542-1500
Fax: (612) 541-1503
$3,995

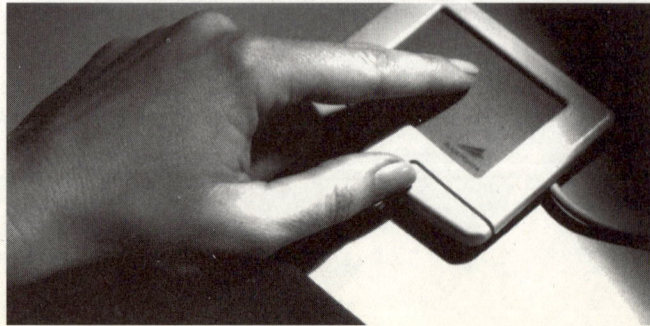

Take a Letter, Hal;
Speech-Recognition Technology Doesn't Wait for the Future

i t seems a bit like science fiction, watching these words appear on the monitor without my touching the keyboard. You see, instead of typing, I'm wearing a headset and speaking fluidly, albeit distinctly, into its microphone, making sure to leave a slight pause between each word. This essay is being created on a Micronics 60MHz Pentium PC using speech-recognition technology (SRT).

Until recently, it would have been virtually impossible to use voice-recognition technology for any practical task, let alone a large-scale project such as writing a book, which I recently did using SRT. While SRT isn't perfect, at least I can say from solid experience that with a modest investment in time and your average power-user's hardware setup, SRT is a twentieth-century reality. While our PCs may not be a match for Arthur C. Clarke's HAL, today's SRT applications are more than just a hint of things to come. They've arrived and are gaining not just in popularity but in functionality.

People with disabilities who can't use their hands can still operate a computer with the aid of an SRT system. Doctors and lawyers can use it to dictate case and patient records. Laboratory workers can enter data or fill out reports without stopping their work. Voice recognition is being used to teach foreign languages using an interactive system that can speak a phrase, then listen to you repeat it and evaluate your performance. Syracuse Language Systems offers CD-ROM-based language programs in French, German, and Spanish. The voice-recognition component makes it easy to pick up the nuances of a dialect, making near-native fluency much more attainable.

Throughout 1995, expect to see voice recognition become more common on our desktops. In a report available from Sage Research of Natick, Mass., the PC SRT market is set for dramatic expansion. IBM has indicated that it may include some form of speech capability on its PowerPC laptop, and Lotus is rumored to be adding it to future releases of Notes. Apple added SRT to its Power Mac line at introduction. Several airlines and many banks are exploring ways to improve customer service by offering interactive voice services to provide flight and account information.

Simple SRT applications are widely in use today, as near as your own telephone. If you have made a collect call recently, odds are an automated system was used to identify you to the recipient and verify the charges. This is called "command and control," and involves a limited vocabulary. Rudimentary command-and-control devices can be used by almost anyone without requiring training. The collect-call example merely requires capturing and playing back the caller's name and recognizing the difference between the words "yes" and "no." The sounds of those two words are not similar, and so are easy to identify if they are the only accepted answers.

Such applications are speaker-independent. The user does not have to train the system to recognize his or her voice. While speaker-independent products are not as reliable as those that can be tuned to an individual user, they manage to overcome difficulties with dialect and accents within their limited scope.

Data-entry SRT applications and advanced command-and-control systems are more complicated. The more sophisticated data-entry SRT programs are often tuned to a specific task, like filling in a database or electronic forms. They work with a larger vocabulary of 100 to 1,000 words, generally require little training, and often don't have to be tuned to a specific user. Perhaps the best-known example is Voice Pilot, which Microsoft introduced with its Windows Sound System.

as much as you think it should, go ahead and spend your own money for high-quality ancillary gear such as V.34 (28.8Kbps) modems and maybe a good PostScript printer or two (color and speed). Most telecommuters have

RealWorldRealWorld

With a little effort and maybe some luck, you can use this software to execute routine Windows commands like opening files, cutting, copying, and pasting. Voice Pilot has one major advantage: It's basically free with the purchase of the sound card. The downside is the difficulty you'll have getting the system to recognize words, the amount of disk space required, and the system resources demanded by the sound card.

Grumman Data Systems has created a custom workstation-based application for military use that lets aircraft mechanics enter reports on a plane's maintenance. Compaq and many other companies are turning to SRT for order entry and similar services. Users can perform various tasks like inspecting returned merchandise, and enter data at the same time. SRT offers great potential for reducing turnaround time on reports that used to require dictation or laborious manual entry.

Of course, expanding the vocabulary increases the complexity of managing voice recognition. Making a product that can actually perform dictation in real time is a true engineering challenge.

Products that let users handle routine data entry or command tasks do increase productivity, but the real goal of current development by vendors is a product that can handle continuous speech in real time. While current speech-recognition applications that can perform dictation are workable—and even useful—don't expect to walk into a room and say, "Computer, take down this letter." The popular image of a person simply talking into a computer that easily converts spoken words into a digital format is still a bit naive.

However, we are getting close. The current top-of-the-line PC-based SRT packages are collectively known as discrete speech systems. These programs have large dictionaries, up to about 200,000 words. Most of them let you actually dictate directly into a word processor or other application, while a few, like IBM's Personal Dictation System, make you work with their own editor. All this sounds pretty good, but it's not that simple for the developer or the user. While there are commonalities to each approach, each vendor uses its own technology and proprietary algorithms to process speech into computer data.

Anyone who has ever recorded sound onto a PC's hard drive knows how much memory even a short sound clip can consume. A single second captured for recognition can produce a scratch file containing 10,000 or so bits of data that all need to be processed. That kind of data flow would choke a PC, so the process has to be streamlined. It's not just the amount of data, it's that speech conversion is one of the most processor-intensive operations you can design.

First, you'll run into the human-to-machine barrier. To turn analog human speech into digital signals, you've got to break down that speech into acoustic elements known as phonemes and sub-phonemes. It is these elements (converted into digital form), rather than the actual words, that are used to form the words' characters.

Naturally, SRT products use a sound card to handle digital-to-analog conversions. This part of the process identifies variations in speech content and discards redundant portions. During this phase, about 90 percent of the data is removed, leaving only key markers that are used during the actual voice-recognition process.

As you can guess, the second hurdle is making sense of all this phonemic information. The software engine reduces the possible number of word matches by identifying the first part of the sound with models in the active dictionary. Then the phonemes are analyzed, and a hit list gets prepared. Statistical analysis and language models are then used to rank the possible words, output the most likely word, and usually offer a pop-up list of alternatives.

At this point, control of the input is passed to the user. Spoken language contains many words that either sound alike (e.g., "four," "fore," and "for") or are composed of similar phoneme structures. Watching the pop-up selection menu can be educational. For example, speaking the word "speaking" produced the options of "sticking," "seeking," and "speeding."

much better equipment at home than they do at the office. Better equipment means more efficiency, and efficiency is what telecommuting is all about. 8. Stay in touch with gurus. Stay tight with the network administrator

Real World Real Worl

The difference in the optional words points out the importance of paying careful attention to what the program places in your document. When I spoke the word "places," DragonDictate (my present SRT program of choice) offered "game" as the most likely word. All the other words in the preceding two paragraphs were correctly identified. If I did not correct the "game" error, the correct hit ratio would deteriorate. If I continually ignored errors like this, the software would soon require another training cycle.

Microphone technique can be tricky, too. Properly adjusted ones can improve recognition by providing uniform input levels and reducing extraneous noise. If you position the mouthpiece wrongly, distortion and random sounds can alter recognition or produce spurious output. Early in testing, I answered the phone thinking I had turned off the mic. It was still on, and several paragraphs of strange sentences had appeared on the page by the time the conversation ended. Recognition dropped to below 30 percent, and the system had to be retrained.

Generally, most of us don't use anywhere near the active vocabulary included with these programs—let alone their total. The active vocabulary contains your most frequently used words, and the words your vendor considered most likely to be used in standard communications. As you use words that aren't currently in the active vocabulary, they replace the least-used words to improve processing time. The better SRT products are adaptive, and will improve their recognition if you're conscientious in correcting their errors.

And speaking of using words, don't expect to be able to use your normal speaking rhythm with these programs, either. Discrete speech means that you must clearly pause for about one-tenth of a second between each word. People who think verbally, like most professional writers, will have problems with that delay at first. The slow speech will seem frustrating and the measured pace will be a distraction. After a few days, most users will adapt and speed will improve. Even so, you'll still have to pay close attention. Leaving a mistake in a sentence can train your software to adapt to your speech improperly. The result will be more missed words.

Some psychologists say that people tend to think in one of two ways: visually or verbally. People who think in words may take a bit of time to become comfortable with speech recognition as a "writing" tool. At first, I found listening to my own voice a distraction. Early efforts produced a typing speed between three to seven words per minute. Taking the time to correct words that the system identified incorrectly often brought the effective speed to a standstill—or even worse. With practice, I was able to slightly exceed my average typing skills, and my spell checks ended up going more quickly as well, since the program didn't produce my usual typos.

Continuous speech systems on PCs are still two or three years away, and even the current high-end offerings only get the job done adequately. They offer real benefits to those willing to take the time to learn and teach them, but the time when we really can speak into our computers and watch the words fly onto virtual pages is still just one more computer era away.—James Karney ■

DICTATE TO YOUR PC WITH KURZWEIL VOICE

Voice for Windows, Release 1.0

With the power to turn an office full of keyboard clatter into one full of the chatter of voices, Kurzweil Voice for Windows, Release 1.0, is a good first attempt at voice-recognition technology. This first dictation-capable voice-recognition product for Microsoft Windows is a complete hardware-software package and is generally about as fast and accurate as an average typist.

Besides issuing voice commands for navigating through the Windows environment—an already common voice-recognition practice—Kurzweil's Voice lets you dictate directly into applications. When installing the software, you must select between two vocabularies: one with 20,000 words that requires 8MB of system memory, or the other with 40,000 words that requires 16MB of RAM. In addition, Voice needs an 8-bit ISA slot for its proprietary coprocessing board.

Voice is extremely resource-hungry. For instance, if you use the larger vocabulary, Voice will need 20MB of system memory when you take the needs of Windows into account. Even with sufficient RAM, Voice refuses to load when available Windows resources fall below 50 percent. You also must devote about 30MB of your hard disk to Voice.

Kurzweil's Voice is impressive if you consider it as start of the art. But talking to your PC as naturally as if you were aboard the Starship Enterprise is still in the future. Even with its limitations, though, Voice is a solid if sometimes frustrating input solution.—David Haskin

Kurzweil Voice for Windows, Release 1.0
Kurzweil Applied Intelligence Inc.
411 Waverley Oaks Rd.
Waltham, MA 02154
(800) 380-1234
Fax: (617) 893-6525
$995

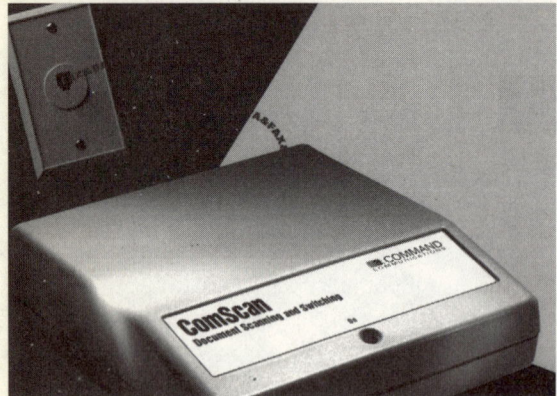

TURN YOUR FAX MACHINE INTO A SCANNER

ComScan

If you occasionally needed to turn paper documents into digital form, you had two expensive alternatives: Either buy a dedicated scanner or use a service bureau. You now have a third choice: Command Communication's $139 ComScan, a device that turns your fax machine into a scanner. ComScan is convenient and easy to use, but its scans are limited by the resolution of your fax machine.

Setup is deceptively simple: Just plug the small ComScan box (5.25 × 4.75 × 1.75 inches) into the incoming phone line, the fax machine, and your PC's fax modem; there's no software to worry about. When you're ready to scan a document, your fax machine acts as a scanner and ComScan, which connects directly to your fax modem, simulates the phone ring needed to start your PC's fax receive program. The resolution of a typical Group 3 fax machine—200 × 200 dots per inch—is adequate for text.

ComScan can sense whether an incoming call is a fax or data transmission. It can also let you use your fax machine as a printer. But even though ComScan is an adequate and inexpensive scanning solution for casual use, it's no match for a true scanner if you plan to do a lot of scanning.—Brian Nadel

ComScan
Command Communications Inc.
10800 E. Bethany Dr.
Aurora, CO 80014
(800) 288-6794: (303) 751-7000
Fax: (303) 750-6437
$139

HP DeskJet 310

At 5.6 pounds with battery and AC adapter, Hewlett-Packard's color-capable DeskJet 310 printer is a little heavier than most of its competitors, but it's also relatively fast and produces gorgeous output. HP sells the DeskJet 310 as a portable printer that can also do low-volume duty on the desktop, a dual role that the DeskJet 310 fills adeptly. You can even print in color (including a composite black) by replacing the black ink cartridge with a three-color version. The DeskJet 310 doesn't offer four-color printing, however, so it may not be ideal for reports combining black text and color graphics.

The DeskJet 310 folds shut for travel into a 2.5 × 12.1 × 5.7-inch brick. Unfolded and with the sheet feeder attached, the printer occupies a surface area of about a foot square. The sheet feeder is available either as a $99 option or bundled with the printer for a total price of $455. If you don't use the sheet feeder you have to feed paper one sheet at a time, a slow but smooth operation that caused no paper jams or twisting on our tests.

The package includes a Windows printer driver disk with HP's SmartColor, which analyzes each print job and prompts you to insert the black or color ink cartridge as required. HP estimates that one black ink cartridge will last for 1,000 text pages; color ink, for 676 pages. Per-page cost for black text works out to a low 2.2 cents; color at 30 percent page coverage is estimated at 23 cents. The DeskJet 310's battery is rated for 100 pages.

If you can put up with its slightly higher bulk and weight, the DeskJet 310's speed and extremely high print quality will pay you back richly.—Bruce Brown

HP DeskJet 310
Hewlett-Packard Co.
P.O. Box 58059
Santa Clara, CA 95051
(800) 752-0900
Fax: (800) 333-1917
$379; with sheet feeder, $455

DRAW CONCLUSIONS ABOUT TABLETS WITH KURTA'S XGT

Kurta XGT

Digitizing tablets may never become mainstream computing peripherals, but as more users experiment with graphics on the PC, the usefulness of having a pen rather than a mouse as an input device becomes obvious. Kurta's $399 XGT tablet is feature-rich enough to attract the attention of artists, but its small size—6 × 8 inches of active drawing area in an 8.5 × 11-inch package—makes it destined for the average

desktop, too. With 256 levels of pressure sensitivity (when you push down harder you draw a thicker line), the XGT is twice as sensitive as its closest competitor. What mouse users will notice first about using the XGT (or any tablet) is its concept of absolute positioning. Where the pen lands is where the cursor lands. You don't have to push the cursor around as you do with a mouse. The XGT's cordless pen is somewhat chunky because it is battery-powered. So what's the advantage? You can use it up to almost an inch above the tablet, and that means you can trace drawings out of thick documents with little difficulty.—Don Willmott

Kurta XGT
Kurta Corp.
3007 E. Chambers
Phoenix, AZ 85040
(602) 276-5533
Fax: (602) 276-9007
$399

KONEXX KEEPS THE ACOUSTIC COUPLER CONCEPT ALIVE

Konexx Koupler Model 204 Konnex Modem Koupler Model 305

Instead of searching for the right phone to connect your notebook to, you may want to try a connector that will work with any phone. Unlimited Systems Corp. has released a portable device that can make your notebook talk to any type of phone,

including cellular and airplane phones. The Konexx Koupler Model 204 cradles the phone's receiver and transmits analog signals from your modem or portable fax machine via an RJ-11 connection. The device weighs only 9 ounces and transmits at a slow 2,400 bps on standard pay phone lines. Unlimited Systems also sells the Konexx Modem Koupler Model 305, which has a built-in 2,400/9,600-bps data fax modem. The 305 connects directly to your notebook with either a 9-pin or 25-pin serial connector and ships with Windows and DOS communications software.—Adam A. Hicks

Konexx Koupler Model 204
Konnex Modem Koupler
Model 305
Unlimited Systems Corp., Inc.
8586 Miramar Pl.
San Diego, CA 92121
(800) 275-6354; (619) 622-1400
Fax: (619) 550-7330
$149 (Model 204);
$299 (Model 305)

PaperMax

Before your computer can do the amazing things it does, it needs your input—your text, numbers, thoughts, and ideas. You spend a lot of time entering characters, one at a time, into your PC. For entering data already stored on temporary cellulose transmission matter (paper), look into a scanner. The best scanners are fast, support OCR, and are easy to use. Visioneer's PaperMax scanner, in fact, is so easy that we wonder how we ever managed without it.

Think the paperless office is just a pipe dream? Not so anymore—Visioneer's PaperMax hardware-and-software package will get rid of your piles of pages in no time. Simply take your faxes, memos, and expense reports,

and scan them in. And talk about usability—the PaperMax doesn't even have a power switch. You just feed a sheet in, and it nabs the paper from your hand like a soda machine taking your dollar (it handles everything from legal-sized paper down to business cards). Then the MaxMate software pops up and lets you file your document, run OCR on it (sorry, OCR software not included), or send it via e-mail or fax. MaxMate lets you pile your documents on-screen the way you lump them on your desk, but with the addition of a suite of search tools to find what you're looking for. Installation is quick. Unlike some scanners, there's no need for a proprietary board connector—it plugs right in to your serial port.

PaperMax
Visioneer Communications
(800) 787-7007
$499

ONE PHONE LINE, TWO SIGNALS

DataPort 2001

To most people, AT&T's DataPort 2001 may look, sound, and act like any other standard modem. But this is no ordinary bit blaster: The DataPort 2001 can use the same analog phone line to transmit voice and data simultaneously.

Why should you care? If you're in a large office with a PBX, the VoiceSpan technology that multiplexes voice and data over a single line

The Modern Mailbox

before the PC, offices had assistants. Now we have high technology—and the avalanche of e-mail, voice messages, and incoming faxes. Who has the time to dig out from under all that fax paper and to argue with Jane Voicemail?

There is a solution. It's called the universal mailbox, and it's the holy grail of the e-mail industry. Whether it's a software/service combo (from Delrina), a solution that works with an officewide PBX (from WordPerfect), or a new computer that comes with voice-mail and fax capabilities out of the box (from Compaq, AST Research, or Hewlett-Packard), there are now ways to consolidate your mail traffic into one handy PC-based front end.

Delrina recently announced its Fax Mailbox service for WinFax Pro 4.0 users: For $9.95 a month (plus a per-page fax charge), users can get their faxes, e-mail, and even voice messages delivered directly to their WinFax Pro mailbox. ConnectSoft, makers of E-Mail Connection, plans to offer a similar service in the future. Modem manufacturers—including Intel and Motorola—are following the trend by embedding voice multiplexing into their modems.

Offices that already have a PBX-based voice-mail system and an e-mail infrastructure need more advanced products, like WordPerfect's Telephone Access Server for Office (Office is now called Symmetry), which uses text-to-speech conversion to let users dial in for their e-mail and schedule information. And just wait for Microsoft Mail, Lotus Notes, and cc:Mail to transform into universal inbox products. But OCR and voice technology are letting us down: We want the option of reading our voice mail and listening to our faxes. And that still seems to be a long way off. ■

probably isn't worth the extra $50 to $150 it will cost you compared to a data-only 14.4-Kbps modem. But this poor-man's ISDN could make multimedia applications like desktop conferencing a reality for smaller offices.

The DataPort 2001 isn't the first modem available that shares a single line for voice and data transmission. But unlike one competitor, Multi-Tech's MultiModem, it doesn't require a proprietary telephone. You install the DataPort 2001 just like any other modem, then simply plug a standard analog phone into the back of it.

The bad news is that in order to transmit voice and data at the same time, the modem needs to talk to a device that supports the VoiceSpan protocol. The good news is that AT&T has licensed this protocol to other vendors (SpectraFax, for example, which provides network-based fax-on-demand systems). In addition, the modem will work with VoiceView, a similar protocol that will be included with Windows 95.

Once the hardware is set up, you can use the DataPort 2001 in conjunction with any communications package. You'll have to modify the AT command string if you want to use VoiceSpan, but after initiating a regular data call, you can add voice to the mix simply by picking up the telephone and dialing—a usability gem.

Unlike the MultiModem, AT&T's DataPort 2001 doesn't digitize the voice portion of a call, so there's no noticeable voice degradation. Instead, it establishes two different virtual transmission channels: an analog channel for voice and a digital channel for data. While that means that the voice quality stays high throughout a call, you can expect the data rate to drop to 4.8 Kbps when you add voice to the mix. It's not a staggering performance hit for most applications, but expect to bog down if you're trying to share huge graphics files.

The DataPort 2001 would be the ideal modem for a small office if, like the MultiModem, it included features for voice mail, as well as fax-on-demand. Although it does come bundled with DataBeam's nifty desktop conferencing software, FarSite, this is not the most robust package of its kind we've seen. Still, FarSite lets you and a remote user collaborate on a shared electronic whiteboard, which works well for desktop conferencing on a limited budget.

Before you rush out and buy a DataPort 2001, stop and consider that it's about $100 more expensive than other 14.4-Kbps modems and that for now you need one on both ends of a line to use VoiceSpan. In some cases, it might be cheaper for you to simply install a second analog phone line and do simultaneous voice and data the old way.—Shyamala Reddy

A SMALL PRICE TO PAY FOR VALUABLE CONNECTIVITY
One-Man-LAN Version 1.5

Following the maxim, You're never too well-connected, PC InterConnect introduces an inexpensive PC-connectivity product that allows you to share data, printers, and CD-ROMs between two PCs.

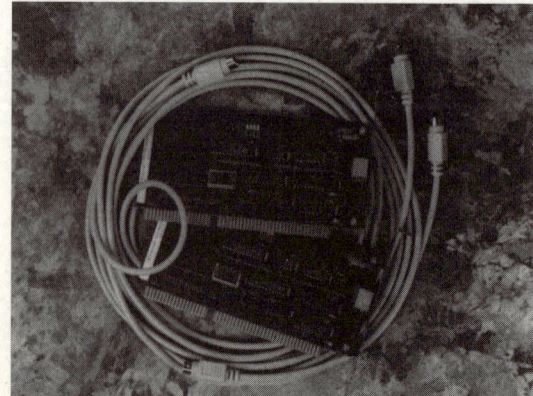

One-Man-LAN version 1.5 is a single-user network for sharing data and peripherals, but it is not a peer-to-peer network—it lacks the necessary throughput. Priced at $129, the product includes two 8-bit adapters, 12 feet of cable, and software for two PCs.

You can use One-Man-LAN as a file-transfer program like Traveling Software's LapLink, a docking station like Xircom's Pocket Ethernet adapter, or as a remote-access program like Norton's pcAnywhere. At this writing, the product requires an adapter card in each PC, but PC InterConnect plans to release an external parallel-port version.

One-Man-LAN requires a dedicated PC, called the secondary PC, and a client PC, called the primary PC. You can use the primary PC to access the disk drives, printers, and CD-ROMs located on the secondary PC. (for example, you can assign your drive F: to the host's floppy drive).

If the secondary PC is attached to a larger network, you can access all of the network drives from your PC. One-Man-LAN thus spares you the high cost ($300 or more) of a pocket Ethernet adapter or docking station.

The One-Man-LAN system operates over a proprietary cable that is limited to 120 feet and offers a throughput rate of 130 Kbps. While this speed is slow compared to a normal Ethernet or Token-Ring network, it is acceptable for accessing data files from the host PC. After you are connected to the dedicated secondary PC, you can execute any program located on that PC. Unlike a remote-control program, the application executes on your PC using your computer's RAM.

If you need to share data and printers between two PCs but don't want to spend the money on a network or remote-access program, One-Man-LAN is one solution worth exploring.—Steve Rigney

UPTOWN VALUE AT A BARGAIN-BASEMENT PRICE
Nova 9200

If footprint size and your wallet affect your decision to buy a keyboard, the Nova 9200 from Maxi Switch will get your attention. Maxi Switch has built a reputation by offering top-flight keyboards

at outstanding prices. The $29, 18 × 7-inch Nova 9200 is smaller and less expensive than many of its competitors, but it still offers a lot.

The 101-key keyboard senses whether it's connected to an AT or PS/2 system, providing real plug-and-play usability. The board is easy on the eyes, with rounded corners and a matte finish that lets it nearly disappear on most desktops. Alphanumeric keys—laid out in familiar fashion—are colored to contrast with the Ctrl, Alt, Shift, and other specialty keys. There are also 12 function keys across the top, a numeric keypad on the right, and a trio of green lights that indicates when the Caps, Num, and Scroll keys are locked.

If this board's fit, finish, and price don't win you over, the Nova 9200 has an added hook—a touch and feel that's better than a cotton T-shirt. Key travel is medium in length, and its click is firm, with just enough resistance to take the drudgery from data entry. If you thought you couldn't buy a fine keyboard on a pauper's budget, think again.—Chuck Miller

Nova 9200
Maxi Switch Inc.
2901 E. Elvira Rd.
Tucson, AZ 85706
(602) 294-5450
$29

Listen for Windows

It'll be a few years before your computer can read your mind, but you needn't wait for it to read your lips. If you think a spoken interface is strictly for Jean-Luc Picard, try Verbex Voice Systems's Listen for Windows. As its name implies, this combined hardware and software package brings voice recognition to Windows. Unlike some other products, however, the $495 Listen for Windows supports continuous speech, which means you can run words together while speaking, just as you would when talking to a person. Other voice-recognition systems require you to speak each word separately and distinctly in order to work.

This continuous-speech feature isn't just a matter of learning complete phrases, either. The Listen software understands individual words, which it can then recognize when they are strung together to create certain phrases. The hardware card's onboard coprocessor, a digital signal processor (DSP) by Texas Instruments is a new image-editing program that combines image-enhancement features with a vast array of artistic tools such as multi-tipped brushes and user-definable paper textures. Although the new user might be overwhelmed with the multitude of tools, the well-crafted interface takes some of the sting out of the learning curve. The main toolbox holds tools for entering text, creating shapes, selecting objects, creating marquees, panning, and zooming. Other boxes, such as the Brush box, Brush Options, and color palements, is one reason for its sophisticated recognition capabilities.

Like all voice-control systems, Listen for Windows requires training. It takes about five minutes to teach the system to recognize your voice for the demonstration files, which include a simple poker game. Training the system for general Windows commands (such as using Program Manager and accessories like Calculator and Write) takes about 15 minutes. The training module provides good prompts, runs quickly, and mixes up words and phrases to make a potentially boring step as short and as interesting as possible.

Once you've taught the system to recognize your voice, you can really take Listen for Windows to town. The program emits a discreet beep signal to indicate when it has recognized a command—which it does extremely accurately, even with fairly loud music playing in the room. Before you begin training, Listen for Windows performs a background noise check so that it knows how much ambient noise to block out. You need to train it in as quiet a surrounding as you can, however.

Available phrases change with the context of the work you're doing; if you can't remember which ones are available at a given time, just say, Show phrases window, and the list will appear. If you want Listen for Windows to take a break, tell it to stop listening, and it does until you order it to activate listening again.

The hardware includes a 16-bit ISA expansion card, which will work in an 8-bit slot if necessary, and an over-the-ear earpiece with a boom noise-canceling microphone with a quick-disconnect plug on its cord. Installation is a breeze, and the default switch settings worked right from the start. On the software side, you get various command files for many popular programs, including WordPerfect for Windows, Word for Windows, Excel, and CorelDraw. Additional files are available from Verbex. Unfortunately, the basic Listen package (as opposed to the developer's kit) offers no way to create command files of your own, so you're limited to generic Windows commands for any program not supported directly.

While the lightweight headset is comfortable to wear, some users may prefer to use a stand-alone microphone and separate speakers.

According to a Verbex representative, you'll need to use a high-quality microphone in order to get accurate results. The company offers an optional microphone you can mount on your monitor. No PC-based voice-control system is perfect yet, but the Listen for Windows package provides excellent recognition at a reasonable price. Captain Picard would be proud.— Alfred Poor

Listen for Windows
Verbex Voice Systems Inc.
1090 King Georges Post Rd.
Bldg.107
Edison, NJ 08837-3701
(800) 275-8729; (908) 225-5225
$495

EYEING THE WORLD FROM YOUR DESKTOP
FlexCam

When Jerry from Accounting sees FlexCam's long, flexible neck and unblinking eye, he'll say it looks like an alien. Go ahead and switch it on— when he sees his surprised face on your monitor, he'll think FlexCam is a cross between E.T. and Big Brother.

FlexCam is actually a color desktop video camera clothed in off-white molded plastic— with the profile of an alien mechanoid. Bend its 18-inch neck over a pile of books like a goosenecked lamp, and no one will notice it. But FlexCam's eye, with its adjustable focus ring, will notice you the moment you raise its head and switch on its power.

Two pinhole directional microphones lie discreetly under the lens for monitoring earthly voices. FlexCam's lamp-style cord contains three male plugs, one for video and two for left/right audio output, as well as a female jack for its power cord.

Instead of a charge-and-go snapshot camera like Logitech's FotoMan Plus, FlexCam is a permanent resident of the desktop. While the gray-scale FotoMan Plus requires no capture board to take crisp, sharp pictures, it captures only still images. FlexCam funnels into your video-capture board (not included) color NTSC video signals, which you can view live on your PC's monitor. Using your capture board and software, you can save motion video or stills to disk.

While FlexCam's video played through a Creative Labs Video Blaster rather well, its captured images are subject to the limitations of any video board. Depending on your board, stills may look fuzzy or grainy. VideoLabs suggests using a high-quality TV set to see FlexCam at its best, but cautions that connecting to a TV may create audio feedback. Adjusting the viewing angle of the camera brought only momentary interference to the monitor.

With proper hardware, though, FlexCam's all-seeing eye can pipe out live head-and-shoulders shots for videoconferencing, close-ups of small items such as photos and documents, or continu-

ous surveillance of what's going on behind you in your workroom. Its range of focus is from 0.25 inches to infinity.

The Video Blaster used for testing restricted colors to 256, but FlexCam supports true color as well. The unit, including its AC adapter, weighs 3.5 pounds. With its electrical gear stowed in its small-footprint base, FlexCam is weighted for stability on the bottom and flexibility on top.

My solitary complaint is that VideoLabs doesn't include an adapter to change FlexCam's two male audio plugs to a single male plug for use with my Sound Blaster Pro. Otherwise, FlexCam takes the job of camera jockey seriously, leaving hands free and desktops tidy. If you need live color video, give FlexCam an audition.— Rebecca Rohan

VideoLabs FlexCam
VideoLabs Inc.
5270 W. 84th St.
Minneapolis, MN 55437
(612) 897-3597
$595

BUILDING A BETTER TRACKBALL
Logitech TrackMan

Tired of mousing around, but conventional trackballs give you a pain in the neck—and wrist? Logitech's new TrackMan trackball for the Macintosh combines an ergonomic design and high-resolution optics for greater ease in navigating your desktop.

Resembling the Philadelphia Phillies's logo turned on its head, the TrackMan boasts a slick design that lets you rest your palm on the case while using your thumb on the trackball and other fingers on three mouse buttons. The TrackMan ships with Logitech's MouseKey software, which allows you to customize button functions. Southpaws are currently out of luck: The TrackMan is designed exclusively for right-handed users.—Jason Snell

TrackMan
Logitech
(800) 889-0063; (510) 795-8500
$139

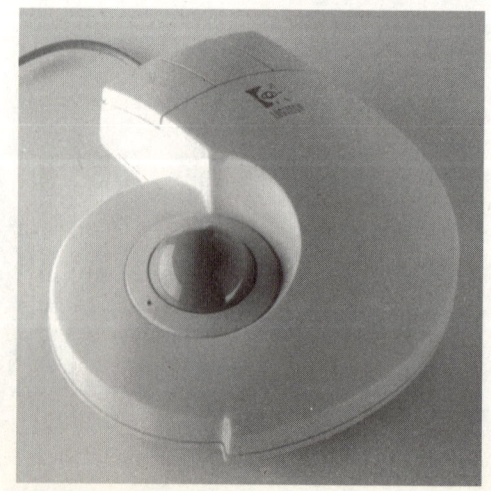

MONITORING ENERGY WASTE
MonitorMiser

Makers of Macintosh monitors are sinking a lot of energy into saving energy: Power-management schemes that put watt-hungry displays into low-consumption "sleep" mode are becoming standard features on new hardware. If you want to do your part to reduce global energy use (and save some cash in the process) but you're not in the market for a new monitor, Inversion Development's MonitorMiser may be for you. This simple hardware box, just a bit larger than a pack of cigarettes, enables your energy-hungry monitor to nap after a specified duration of inactivity.

To configure the MonitorMiser, hook up the included cables and set DIP switches on the bottom of the box to a delay of 10, 18, 26, or 42 minutes. If your Mac is idle for the specified duration, your monitor's power will be reduced. Moving the mouse or touching a key wakes it up. No software is required.

The MonitorMiser carries the U.S. Environmental Protection Agency's Energy Star designation for saving power, and Inversion Development claims that the MonitorMiser can save you as much as $130 per monitor each year.—Jim Shatz-Akin

MonitorMiser
Inversion Development
(415) 940-7805
$79.95

On Personal Information Management

W hat kind of calendar do you keep—last year's Christmas gift, a more functional, less picturesque one, a Day Timer, or one that's computerized? How about all those phone numbers—what if you misplaced the listing of names and numbers; would you be lost? (Everyone backs up copies of disk files; how many make photocopies of their paper based personal address book?)

Generic software products, including word processing, spreadsheet, and database software can all be used to create your own information manager. Type the information into your word processor or spreadsheet and let the system retain that information for you. If your lists are of reasonable length, say 2–4 pages or under 200 names, it is very workable. Information can be edited and changed, Items can be sorted, and you can search for specific names or numbers. It is a small improvement over the range of paper only documents.

Simple calendar and address book list software can also be used. More sophisticated is the wide range of software products that fall within the category of PIMs. These products vary in functionality and features and are intended to bring some order to the morass of information that is flowing across your desk. Just as a good accounts receivable system can provide quick retrieval of old invoices or all billings to a single customer, PIMs have the facility to group information in lots of different forms and enable retention of information that your personal memory can no longer easily store. It is a way of electronically remembering Aunt Mildred's birthday—you can even track what presents you have given, and received.

Your information, after it is collected, sorted, and classified, has to be constantly tended, just like a garden of vegetables. Information changes continuously; some becomes stale and can be archived. The key to any good information system, paper or electronic, is that the information is valuable and, when found, is accurate. If you are going to rely on this information, it has to be correct. Therefore, just like the vegetables, work with the data and the program, daily, weekly, monthly, whatever it takes to keep it growing.

Assessment of any product that provides personal productivity has to consider the return on your time and dollar investment. If you have no time, no typing skills, and are away from your desk a lot, picking a PIM should be delegated to your assistant as you will not have time to learn or use the product. However, if you are part of the growing number that rely on some or all of their information being computer based, then these products will clearly help you.

The idea behind a contact manager is to maintain some order for the wide range of promises and commitments that have been made by you and to you. If this is a large part of your work then stay within the contact manager category—ACT, Commence, Ecco, GoldMine, InfoCentral. These products each have a slightly different interface. If you have unique sets of data then the customization of Commence may prove best. If your work tends towards entering lots of information in a series of outlines, then Ecco has an edge. If your work emphasizes contacts and follow up requirements, then GoldMine and ACT should have principal consideration. If there are lots of cross referrals and interlinking of companies and people, check out InfoCentral.

Other programs indicated should be considered if there is no need for the features that have been presented. If all your needs will be met by maintaining a calendar and a "ToDo" list then do not spend hundreds of dollars. Buy one of the inexpensive, yet useful calendaring programs. For other productivity information programs like maps and business card maintenance, the choices are yours if they can make your work time more effective.

So how do you go about automating your personal information? The first thing to do is decide what and how you will automate. Assume that you want to give it a try and the information to be captured is some combination of telephone numbers, addresses, a calendar, and specific information about individuals, such as when phone calls were made and future dates for follow up events. The next decision you must consider is where this is going to be done; in the office, on the road with a portable, at home, or all of the above.Part of the problem of using the information is having the data in one place and you somewhere else. You know what it is like to go into a meeting with one folder of papers left back in your office. Do you go back to the office or proceed without it?

A key to success with a PIM is matching your needs with your working habits to develop a comfort level between usability and use.
—Richard K. Oppenheim ■

INSTANT, INEXPENSIVE TEXT RECOGNITION

TextBridge for Macintosh 2.0

OCR (optical character recognition) software, which translates hard copy into editable text, often straddles the line between being a handy utility and a full-featured—and accordingly priced—application. With TextBridge 2.0, Xerox offers users a rich OCR application at the cost of a utility.

TextBridge includes several features that speed recognition and increase accuracy. Like a spelling checker, Lexifier identifies word and numerical patterns as it goes along. When it encounters a Social Security number, for example, Lexifier knows to use the number 0 instead of the letter O. Word Verifier lets you view and correct words during recognition. The software learns from common mistakes and detects recurring errors. TextBridge also retains text formatting, columns, and graphics. When it runs into a low-resolution or degraded document, it automatically switches to the more sensitive Fax mode.

The program supports System 7 and TWAIN. It ships with dictionaries for five foreign languages, with others sold separately, and has Export options for popular Mac and PC word processors and other applications.—Pamela Pfiffner

TextBridge for Macintosh 2.0
Xerox
(800) 248-6550; (508) 977-2000
$99

PHOTO-REALISTIC COLOR PRINTING THAT'S EASY ON THE BUDGET

Fargo Primera

Until recently, if you wanted a photo-realistic printer for color proofing, your choices were few and expensive. High-end dye-sublimation printers offer superior image quality, but their prices typically start at about $10,000. A newly introduced upgrade for the $995 Fargo Primera thermal-wax printer changes all that. For a list price of less than $1,500, Mac users can now dabble in the world of continuous-tone color.

Measuring 14 × 6 × 10 inches and weighing just less than 16 pounds, the Primera is small enough to fit easily on the corner of your desktop. Portability and size are important, because the only way you can connect the Primera to your Mac is via the Mac's serial port—network printing is not an option.

Priced at just short of $1,000, the original release of the Primera thermal-wax printer gained wide acclaim in the Windows market but went largely unnoticed in the Mac community until the release of a QuickDraw driver in the middle of last year. The Mac interface kit—priced at about $200—includes a QuickDraw driver, Apple's ColorSync software, and an interface cable that connects the parallel port of the printer to the serial port of the Mac.

But the big news is that Fargo now sells a $250 photo-realistic-dye-sublimation upgrade kit for the Primera that contains drivers for Macs as well as Windows machines, a small sample (ten pages) of dye-sub paper and ink ribbon, and a spare ribbon-cartridge holder. Refills of the dye-sub materials cost about $3 per page, and the thermal-wax media cost less than 50 cents per page.

The dye-sub upgrade that makes the Primera such a deal is accomplished exclusively in software. Once it's been upgraded, the Primera becomes quite versatile—to save time and expense when you're proofing, you can opt for a down-and-dirty preproof in thermal-wax mode and then switch to dye-sub mode for the final proof. To switch between modes, you simply swap ink cartridges and paper and select the appropriate setting in the Page Setup dialog box of your application.

Although you won't mistake the Primera's photo-realistic output for that of its higher-priced competitors, the printer's low price makes the Primera well worth considering. More important, at less than one-fifth the cost of most other dye-sublimation printers, the Primera's pricing heralds some exciting changes to come in the affordable low end of the color-imaging market.—Anita Epler

Primera
Fargo Electronics
Eden Prairie, MN
(800) 327-4622; (612) 941-9470
$995

A BARGAIN-PRICED ALL-IN-ONE SCANNING PACKAGE

Caere OmniScan

The caere omniscan lets you do virtually anything you can think of with the humble bitmap, including faxing, scanning, manipulating images, and doing OCR (optical character recognition).

The OmniScan package includes a standard handheld scanner, a SCSI- interface box (which must be the first or only device on your SCSI chain), and three programs: OmniPage Direct, for scanning and recognizing text via OCR; FaxMaster, for sending, receiving, and recognizing the text in faxes; and Image Assistant GS, for scanning and editing gray-scale images.

You can use OmniPage Direct to scan text directly into any application that

Gary Kildall created CP/M, the operating system that DOS was based on. Originally, IBM wanted Kildall's company, Digital Research (originally, Intergalactic Digital Research) to create DOS, but Kildall got greedy and asked for a king's ransom. A young fellow in Seattle named Bill Gates offered IBM a clone of CP/M at a much cheaper price and landed the deal of the century that got Microsoft where it is today. Gates could afford to undercut Kildall because he bought the rights to DOS from a company called Seattle Computer Products for a mere $50,000.

allows text entry; for images, you need to scan into Image Assistant GS. You scan by drawing the handheld scanner across or down the page. If the text block or image is narrow enough (about 4 inches or less), you can scan in one pass; otherwise, the OmniScan scanner can stitch your multiple passes into a seamless whole by eliminating overlapping areas.

As with other handheld scanners, you need the hand/eye coordination of a fighter pilot if you want accurate character recognition. Spines of books and magazines can cause troublesome wavy-edged scans, and the bump from the scanner falling off the bottom of a book or magazine page often prompts OmniPage Direct to complain that you're pulling the scanner too fast and make you start all over again. In addition, OmniPage Direct's OCR facility is sensitive to off-kilter scans—the kind that Light Source's Ofoto image-scanning program has no problem reorienting automatically. In our tests, incorrect or unrecognized characters appeared in about one word in six.

Taken individually, none of the OmniScan package's components offers the best available approach to carrying out its function. The scanner is comparable to other handheld scanners—that is, it's less accurate and trickier to use than a flatbed scanner. OmniPage Direct lets you scan text into any application that can handle text input, but it's not adept at deciphering

off-kilter scans. FaxMaster can recognize characters in an incoming fax, but expect a long wait. The also-slow Image Assistant GS meets its modest image-manipulation goals, but it's no Photoshop. Still, you do get all these elements for just $595. If you have less money than time, the OmniScan package might be just the ticket.—Joe Clark

OmniScan for Macintosh
Caere Corp.
Los Gatos, CA
(800) 535-7226; (408) 395-7000
$595

EtherWave

These days Ethernet has become a necessity rather than a luxury. As more and more data gets pushed across networks, LocalTalk just can't cut it anymore. That's why Apple has put Ethernet on most of its motherboards, and that's why easy connection to Ethernet is in great demand. But why can't setting up an Ethernet network be as easy as stringing a bunch of Macs together with phone wire and PhoneNET connectors? Now it is: Farallon Computing's EtherWave brings the simplicity of PhoneNET's plug-and-play networking to Ethernet.

EtherWave lets you daisy-chain as many as eight Ethernet devices, using standard 10BASE-T wiring—you can even connect an EtherWave daisy chain to an existing 10BASE-T network without mishap. Plug-and-play twisted-pair Ethernet and compliance with the

10BASE-T standard were oxymorons until now, but EtherWave changes that. EtherWave's ease of setup is perfect for small, independent networks; small workgroups connecting to an existing larger net; or impromptu stand-alone meeting-room networks.

The EtherWave product line has something for everyone: NuBus cards for the Mac; ISA cards for PCs; and adapters for Apple's AAUI Ethernet port, traditional AUI ports, and LocalTalk printers, as well as a high-speed non-SCSI adapter for PowerBooks that, according to Farallon, consistently outperforms SCSI Ethernet adapters. This broad support for all types of Ethernet-able devices makes EtherWave attractive for any 10BASE-T network.

The price of Ethernet is constantly falling, and the amount of data that needs to be transported over networks is constantly growing—just look at QuickTime files and large color images—so an easy- to-install high-speed

network is a must. EtherWave delivers.

EtherWave
Farallon Computing
(510) 814-5100

FARALLON BEEFS UP TIMBUKTU

Timbuktu Pro for Macintosh

Easy remote control of networked Macs and PCs has long been the forte of Farallon's Timbuktu. The newly released Timbuktu Pro for Macintosh ($199) adds

increased speed, industrial-strength security, and support for System 7 Pro's PowerTalk.

If you're making your Macintosh a host for others to log on to, Timbuktu Pro lets you create your own user accounts with passwords and privileges similar to those used by AppleShare. Network administrators have even more control over security and can set such criteria as minimum password requirements for users.

Timbuktu Pro clients and hosts are listed in PowerTalk's desktop Catalogs directory-services feature. You can also use Timbuktu Pro from the System 7 Pro desktop, using Timbuktu's PowerTalk Business Cards, which are similar to System 7 Pro's information cards and contain Control, Observe, Send, and Exchange buttons.

Timbuktu Pro uses compression to reduce network traffic, which Farallon says can result in as much as a 400-percent speed improvement when running over

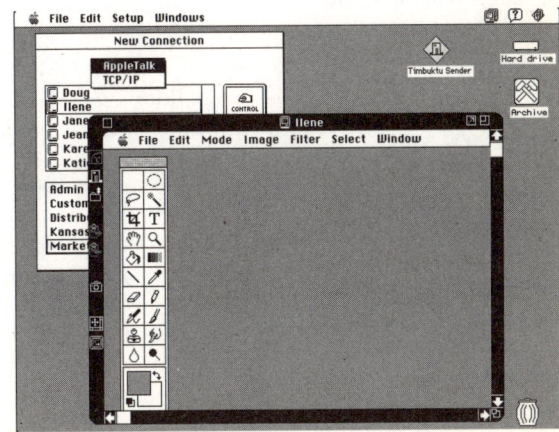

professional gear), but get ready to make a change. What triggered my forecast? A killer product: the Kodak digital camera system (DCS), which the company loaned to me for a month. As an amateur photographer, I've

Apple Remote Access. Timbuktu Pro also provides remote control of and file transfer over TCP/IP networks, including the Internet. Unfortunately, however, AppleTalk is still the only network option for PCs running Timbuktu for Windows, and there is as yet no support for Novell's IPX protocol.

Farallon has also released a minor upgrade for Timbuktu for Windows: Version 1.1 improves printing and adds support for more network-interface cards as well as for Farallon's revolutionary EtherWave, a daisy-chainable Ethernet system.

Timbuktu Pro for Macintosh
Farallon Computing
(510) 814-5100

MOUNT DAT ON YOUR DESKTOP

DeskTape

Drawn to DAT (digital audiotape) for portable gigastorage but apprehensive about inconvenient data access? Here's good news: Optima's DeskTape, which lets you mount a DAT cartridge directly on your Mac's desktop, is now available as a stand-alone product that works with any DDS/SCSI-2-compatible DAT drive (versions for Exabyte tapes, quarter-inch cartridges, and Teac drives are also available). You can browse the contents of a tape, drag and copy files, and even play QuickTime movies—operations unheard of before DeskTape.

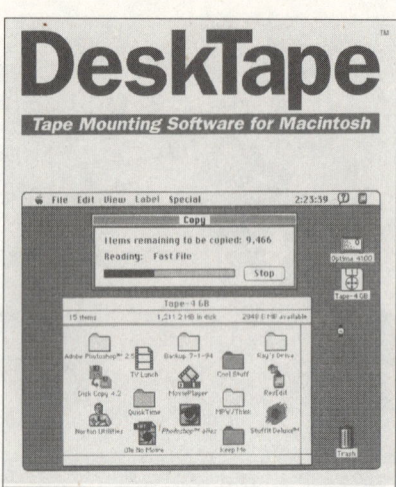

DeskTape also lets you write to tapes, providing a useful format for transporting large files; for read access, the recipient need install only the DeskTape control panel, rather than the entire DeskTape application.

DeskTape provides its illusion of immediate file access by keeping a copy of the tape's directory on your startup drive (where it uses 2.5MB or more of contiguous space), but it can't provide the quick access times you get with a hard drive, because tape doesn't allow random information access. You can browse the contents of the tape, but opening subsubfolders can take several seconds. Running an application from the tape is painfully slow, as is editing a tape-based document—you're better off editing it on your hard disk. And if your tape contains many files, mounting a DeskTape cartridge isn't as fast as mounting a removable cartridge.

Although it carries limitations intrinsic to streaming-tape technology, DeskTape makes those gigabytes of DAT storage much easier to access. If you regularly lug stacks of SyQuest cartridges to a service bureau, you're a DeskTape candidate.—Jeffrey Milstead

DeskTape
Optima Technology Corp.
Irvine, CA
(714) 476-0515
$299

Sony SRSPC Series

To take full advantage of your Mac's sound capabilities, you need external speakers. The Sony SRSPC series of personal-computer speakers are some of the best we've

seen, and they're less expensive than most. If you have a CD-ROM drive, external speakers are a must.

Sony SRSPC Series
Sony Computer Peripherals
$79.95 to $199.95

Translation

ranslation is a difficult art, whether it's between French and Chinese, between PCs and Macs, or even between two Macintosh applications. Mac users have had to wrestle with this problem ever since the first Macintosh systems hit the shelves; recently, it's become a lot easier.

You would think that cross-platform translation would be more complex than cross-application translation within the same system. As far as the Mac is concerned, the two operations are very similar.

Apple's PC Exchange, an optional extension to System 7, makes moving files between Macs and PCs as painless as possible. With PC Exchange, your Mac will automatically recognize a DOS disk and display its contents on the Mac desktop like any other Mac floppy. It allows users to open, save, rename, copy, delete, or import DOS and Windows files into Mac-based applications. For example, if you inserted an MS-DOS disk containing a Word for Windows file into your Mac, PC Exchange would allow you to see the Word for Windows file icon on your desktop. However, you can't actually open the file without the proper translators.

General Applications

Probably the easiest way to handle file conversions is to let your existing applications do it. The simplest way to share text is to use ASCII, a format common to virtually all platforms. However, if you save a word processing file in ASCII, you lose all the nice formatting you've done in your word processor.

Fortunately, many word processing programs come equipped with conversion filters. For example, WordPerfect 3.0 for the Mac can import and export WordPerfect 4.2 and 5.x DOS files using its own translator. It also comes with import-only conversion filters for Rich Text, MacWrite and MacWrite II, Microsoft Word (Mac) through version 5.1, and WriteNow 2.2.

As for graphics applications, there are a number of file formats common to both Mac and PC platforms. Adobe Photoshop, for example, can import and export Amiga IFF, BMP, GIF, EPS, JPEG, MacPaint, PCX, Photo CD, Scitex, Targa, and TIFF files. Odds are good that anyone you'll be swapping files with will be able to give you a file saved in one of those formats.

But what if your current applications don't have the necessary translation filters? Claris has pioneered a technology called XTNDs: plug-in filters you place in a folder on your Mac's hard disk. When you're importing or exporting a file from within an application, you can use any of the XTND filters you've installed.

XTND filters are always included with Claris applications, and they can sometimes be found on online services or packed in with other programs such as WordPerfect 3.0. There's also a host of applications that do nothing but file translation, both PC to Mac and Mac to Mac.

Specialized Tools

To smooth the translation process, Apple uses a technology that it developed—Easy Open. It associates DOS and Windows files with their correct Macintosh applications. However, Easy Open can't do the translation job by itself; it merely provides the path, and relies upon translation filters to do the job.

In order to fill this gap, several third-party file-conversion products are available that offer various translation filters. For example, Word For Word from Mastersoft, which can translate compound documents (that is, documents that combine text and graphics), also provides System 6 users with an independent interface for Easy Open, which normally requires System 7 to operate. Word For Word has over 100 filters for graphics,

concept. Now all we have to do is wait for the price to drop by $9,000 or so—as it inevitably will. ⌨ Let me run down a few details on the Kodak DCS. It's a special camera back attached to a Nikon 8008. Inside, you can

spreadsheet, word processing, and other data formats. AccessPC from Insignia Solutions includes both Easy Open and Word For Word, while DataViz sells MacLinkPlus/Easy Open, which offers Easy Open with additional translators.

Besides MacLinkPlus/Easy Open, DataViz also sells MacLinkPlus/Translators Pro, which includes the translators and a separate stand-alone application. The application senses the format of the source file, and tries to guess—based on either explicit instructions or past actions—what format you want to wind up in. The application is fast, and the translator documents are always up to date and complete.

If you own an older Mac without a SuperDrive, or if shuffling floppies from machine to machine morally offends you, DataViz sells a package called MacLinkPlus/PC Connect that includes the translators, the PC Exchange software, and a cable that runs from your Mac to your PC. You can perform all file conversions and pipe files from one machine to another. The $199 package can be handy if you're doing lots of conversions at the same time. Choosing between these packages is a matter of making sure that the one you pick has the translation filters you need.

And in the Future?

At this writing, the first Power Macintoshes are coming off the line. Some of them will, by virtue of the PowerPC 601 chip and SoftWindows emulation, run Windows software, but only in Standard mode. Insignia Solutions, maker of SoftWindows, has promised a 486 emulator by this fall, which should both be faster and be able to run Windows in Enhanced mode. However, file conversion between applications will still be an issue.

You can cut and paste between Windows and Mac documents with Apple's new Quadra 610 DOS-compatible system. The Quadra comes with a PDS slot emulation board that runs on its own 486SX/25 chip. The board lets you run Windows (or DOS) and Mac operating systems concurrently. As a result, you can cut and paste between Mac and Windows applications.

File translation is an issue that all computer users have to face, but things are much better today than they have been.—Daniel J. Rosenbaum ■

store 50 photos compressed onto an 80MB hard drive. You offload through a SCSI port using an Adobe Photoshop plug-in that comes with the camera.  If you've toyed with Logitech's Fotoman digital camera or any of the

POWERBOOKS, OTHER PORTABLES, AND HANDHELD SYSTEMS

Apple Newton

Apple has done a lousy job of explaining and promoting its personal digital assistant, Newton. Three quarters of the people I meet have never heard of it and the rest have heard mostly bad things about it. Whenever I reach into my coat pocket for my paperback-sized Newton MessagePad 110, though, people cluster around and start oohing and aahing. They're amazed, even though they see only a fraction of the stuff inside. When I tell them I use Newton to send faxes, receive long text messages wirelessly, send and receive e-mail, download data from my desktop spreadsheet, record and organize all kinds of ideas and information as they come to me wherever I am, or even to locate a moderately priced Nepalese restaurant in London, they want to know more. There's a lot more to know.

Apple's first Newton model, introduced in August 1993, was panned by much of the business and technology press because it was over-hyped and its handwriting recognition was lousy. But Newton is not a single product, it's a platform, and like all healthy platforms it is growing in many directions. With the addition of a little utility program called Graffiti, handwriting recognition is not an issue. There are now hundreds of shareware and commercial applications available. Emerging wireless connections and new Newton models from Apple and other companies promise more amazements to come. Don't look for Newton to replace your desktop computer or even your laptop, but it will definitely extend your computing and communications range in ways that may surprise and delight you.
—Barry Owen

Apple Newton
Apple Computer
(800) 538-9696; (408) 996-1010

HELP FOR YOUR PDA IS AT YOUR FINGERTIPS

PalmConnect

The small size of a PDA is impressive only until you're faced with actually entering considerable amounts of data. Ever attempt serious data input using a pen stylus? And if you do indeed manage to enter all the data, the next question becomes how to actually back it up. If you happen to use Casio's Z-7000 or Tandy's Z-PDA, or the Zoomer, Palm Connect is a software solution to these problems that just may get your hands clapping.

A serial cable connects your PDA to your PC. This allows for two-way transfer of files, enabling backup of information in the PDA to the PC.

Given the state of handwriting recognition, data entry on PDAs is often done with the aid of the on-screen keyboard, by selecting characters with the stylus. While this is satisfactory for entering a few addresses, it isn't practical for a large group of them. With Palm Connect installed, you can enter data for Address, Note, and Scheduling files on your PC, and then download them in the exact format used on the Zoomer and Z-7000. The icons and forms displayed on your PC are identical to those used on the PDA.

Data must first be entered on the PC and then transferred to the Z-PDA, or entered into the Z-PDA and uploaded to your PC. Palm Connect will also not operate on a doubled hard disk under such programs as Stacker or DoubleDisk.

If you need input and backup assistance for your Z-7000 or Zoomer PDA, PalmConnect is worth getting your hands on.—Stan Veit

PalmConnect
Palm Computing Inc.
4410 El Camino Real
Suite 108
Los Altos, CA 94022
(800) 881-7256; (415) 949-9560
$129

PowerBook File Assistant

One of first forays into the software-utilities market, PowerBook File Assistant is a low-end file synchronizer accompanied by a few extra utilities from System SoftwareLand. "Low end" is not a put-down here; it merely means you won't have a lot of choices when you're setting up links between folders and files on your PowerBook and their counterparts on your desktop machine. A full-fledged file-syncing program such as PowerMerge or FileRunner lets you work with sets of files specified by sophisticated rules—for example, "Everything in this folder except for files whose names include Copy." In contrast, low-end utilities match up

specific files or entire folders unconditionally.

File Assistant has an impressively neat interface for performing all the basic file-synching tasks. You indicate which folder on one disk should be matched with which folder on the other disk, set the link for either or for both directions, and let it go. If you install File Assistant's Finder replacement (version 7.1.1), you can set up links just by dragging the appropriate folders into the File Assistant window.

While synching files, the program notifies you if a file has been modified on both disks since the last synch; it also asks whether you want files deleted from one folder if they've been deleted from the other. File Assistant is also smarter than the Finder

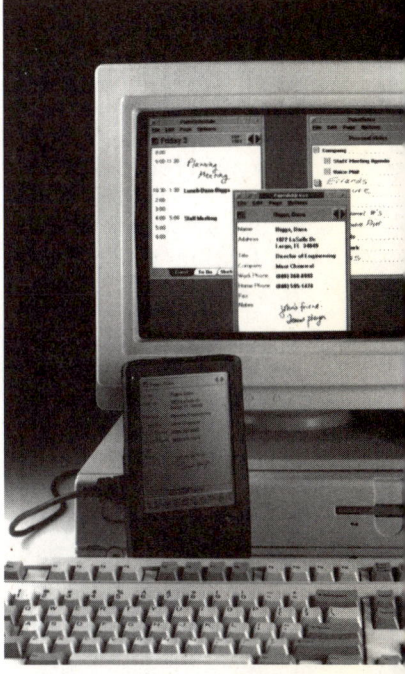

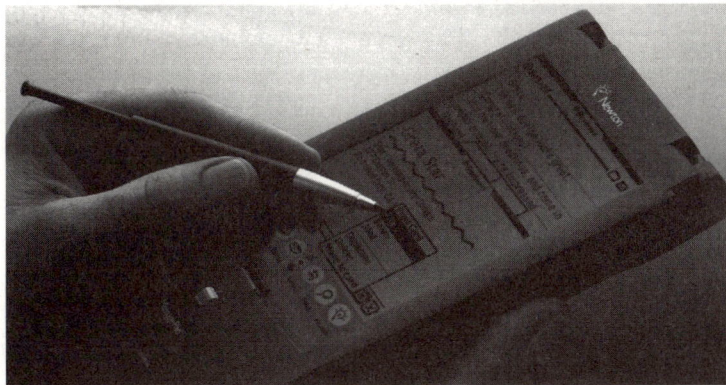

other low-resolution devices out there, believe me you're living in the past. The DCS takes a tremendous picture and leverages Photoshop, one of the greatest software packages I've ever used. Most cool graphics tools

RealWorldRealWorld

about replacing a file with one of the same name if they have different creation dates—it doesn't do it, on the assumption that they're not the same file. File Assistant's one minor flaw is that it's too easy to set the synching process in motion; you just click on the arrow between two files you've linked—right near where you click to select the linked pair for editing.

For those who don't need sophisticated controls over file synching, File Assistant is the best low-end option around. And it's obviously an Apple product—not because you get system software but because the multilanguage licensing agreement is longer than the documentation.—Sharon Zardetto Aker

PowerBook File Assistant
Apple Computer
Cupertino, CA
(800) 538-9696; (408) 996-1010
$79

GREEN LIGHT
Keep It Simple Software
SunPack PB

Like four-wheel trucks, PowerBooks in magazine advertisements are often pictured outdoors—preferably in the lap of someone perched high on a ledge in Yosemite or against some other scenic backdrop. If that's how you use your PowerBook—rather than on airplanes like the rest of us—then Keep It Simple Software (KISS), of Helena, Montana, has an accessory you'll want

to strap to your backpack. The SunPack PB is a $229 pair of folding solar panels that its maker says can supply enough power—given direct sunlight—to keep an all-in-one PowerBook running indefinitely. This assumes that you're practicing every other conceivable power-saving measure at the same time, however (turning down the CPU speed and using a RAM disk, for example), and that you don't have an energy-hungry color screen. But even if you can't toss out your AC adapter, the SunPack PB will make it possible to work longer on one battery.

As if being able to spend all afternoon out on the deck with your PowerBook weren't enough, KISS also makes two single-panel products for the Newton. The SunPack ($199) doubles as a carrying case for the Newton and accessories; the SunPack Jr. ($159) has a simpler design with a single outside pocket.

Solar panels might seem like a fringe technology, but they're a great deal lighter than conventional auxiliary

batteries and the extra energy is free of charge—to you and to the environment.—James Bradbury

SunPack PB
Keep It Simple
Software
Helena, MT
(800) 327-6882;
(406) 442-3559
$299

DiskLock PB

Storing confidential information on a PowerBook can be riskier than storing it on your desktop Mac. The password protection provided by most PowerBook utilities is pretty simple to bypass: All anyone has to do to get to your files is start up your PowerBook with a floppy disk. DiskLock PB supplies a deeper level of protection: You can password-protect your hard disk so that others will always need a password before the disk will mount.

You can set DiskLock to lock your disk under various conditions: sleep, restart, shutdown, and even after a crash. When you shut down the PowerBook or put it to sleep, a notice that the disk is being locked appears in the menu bar. The locking doesn't take long, but sometimes the delay between issuing the Shut Down or Sleep command and receiving the notice is long enough to make you think your system has frozen. When the PowerBook wakes or starts

up again, it asks for a password. Three wrong passwords in a row shuts down the PowerBook, although you can restart it immediately and try again. DiskLock PB keeps track of incorrect passwords and the time they were tried, so you'll know if someone's been trying to get to your data.—Sharon Zardetto Aker

DiskLock PB 1.0
Symantec Corp.
Cupertino, CA
(800) 441-7234; (503) 334-6054
$59

On The Road

On The Road lets you queue all of your print jobs while you're traveling, just as you would if you were actually attached to a printer. Then, when your PowerBook is reconnected to a network, On The Road seeks out the printer of your choice and prints the lot. It also defers your faxes until you've attached your fax modem to a phone line.

On The Road
Palomar Software
$99.99

PB Tools
CPU 2.0

Every PowerBook user should have a set of PowerBook utilities to do such things as extend battery life and make cursors more easily visible on the LCD screen. One favorite is Inline Software's PB Tools, which

stores information about your PowerBook's power consumption over time. Another option is Connectix's CPU 2.0, the granddaddy of PowerBook utilities.

PB Tools
Inline Software
$99.55

CPU 2.0
Connectix
$99

The PowerBook Companion
The Digital Nomad's Guide

Using a PowerBook creates a whole set of concerns that don't arise when you're using a desktop Mac, so it's a good idea for first-time PowerBook owners—whether they're jaded Mac experts or not—to read up on their new machines. *The PowerBook Companion* gives you the skinny on maximizing your battery life and even shows you how to open up your PowerBook to install RAM or an internal modem. PowerBook: *The Digital Nomad's Guide* is an entertaining look at the needs of PowerBooks and the people

Bobbit Virus—It turns a 7.5MB hard drive to a 3.5-inch floppy drive.

Thoughts on Electronic Commerce
(or Electronic Data Interchange)

first, it was barter. Then, soft (sometimes precious) metal was used as coin of the realm. Then, paper currency, checks, and finally electronic funds transfer. These payment mechanisms are the end of the transaction, a process that started when people obtained goods for goods, or for services, or for currency. The process usually was initiated by a request: "Gimme that or I'll bash your dog." As civilization advanced, commerce became more civil: "I'll swap you an apple for your orange." Then, "Shave and a haircut, two bits," that is, payment for services.

Various trauma or milestones marked changes. The advance to electronic commerce can be traced to the Berlin Airlift, when for the first time goods could be shipped as fast as the traditional means of conveying the paperwork. In order for the airlift to work properly, the paperwork needed to *precede* the goods, so the logistics people at the destination could know what was coming, and where it needed to go. Hence, the teletype for transmittal, and forms and standards called Electronic Data Interchange, to make it work. Now, tens of thousands of worldwide businesses use EDI to order everything from pens to penicillin, aspirin to zoology texts, fish tanks to fishing lures.

At the other side of electronic purchasing is electronic payment, best exemplified by the CheckFree service that accompanies Intuit/Microsoft's bookkeeping software. We're not yet at a paperless office, but less paper? Definitely.

1994 was a year of two ground-breaking electronic commerce applications, pioneered in two industries: healthcare and transportation. In the first example, and despite the disappointing (to some) failure of the Clinton Administration's healthcare initiative, several companies banded together to launch an initiative to drive some of the administrative costs from hospital procurement. Regardless of what happens to the legislation, this system for electronic commerce will save overhead costs, drive errors from the former manual process, and save time and inventory costs for its users.

Four separate vendors to the healthcare community—Baxter Healthcare, Eastman Kodak, Boise Cascade, and Bergen Brunswig—sponsored development of a new system to automate procurement from a single, standards-based PC. The revolutionary idea here is that Baxter agreed to abandon its ASAP proprietary terminal and embrace a vendor-neutral system into which even its competitors would be welcome. The system rolled out to hospitals in the third quarter, and additional vendors signed on with the software developer, TSI International, of Wilton, Connecticut. The software is a composite of Microsoft's Access database, plus TSI's Trading Partner PC package.

The transportation industry development was called OCEAN, for Ocean Carriers' Electronic Access Network. Using this system, which went into advanced customer test in the third quarter of 1994, any shipper could call the ocean carrier and find out the status of its goods, estimated time of arrival, and so on. Instead of having a truck sitting at the docks, waiting for the ship to come in, shippers and customers would be totally up-to-date in a computer-based system, obviating the myriad telephone calls and manual lookups which characterized the industry.

The world's seven largest container-ship lines received permission from the Maritime Commission to put aside competitive issues and collaborate, again with TSI International as the software developer, to produce a database-oriented system that would provide immediate access to information. These included SeaLand, American President Lines, [want them all?]

TV advertisements proclaim the customer response that the computer brings to Federal Express, which derives competitive advantage from such service. In the case of OCEAN, these seven competitors banded together for the benefit of their common customers, to provide the same type of information, all from the same database. The healthcare and transportation examples have one element in common, representing a trend into the next century: competitors cooperating for customer benefit. In the case of ocean carriers, it's booking shipments and inquiry. In healthcare, it's doing away with a single-vendor system.

It's only a matter of time before electronic payment is integrated into the process, bringing the entire transaction into the realm of electronic commerce. People who are, say, in their 50s have been alive for the entire transition from totally paperbound to totally electronic commerce.
—Edward J. Bride ■

who use them. Each book includes a disk of shareware PowerBook utilities.

The PowerBook Companion
Addison-Wesley Publishing
$24.95

Digital Nomad's Guide
Random House Electronic
Publishing
$24

PowerPrint

The PowerPrint software/cable combination lets PowerBook users print their files to just about any PC-compatible printer, including dot-matrix printers.

PowerPrint
GDT Softworks
$149

SCSI Doc!

Use the SCSI Doc! connector to attach your PowerBook to any regular Mac SCSI device or to attach your PowerBook to a desktop Mac as if it were a SCSI device itself.

SCSI Doc!
APS Technologies
$49

Phone Kit

Just because your PowerBook can travel with you around the world doesn't mean your modem will be able to speak the language when you get to a foreign land. But the adapters in the Teledapt Phone Kit can convert any country's phone jack into a

standard American plug. You can buy individual plugs, packages for regions or a catch-all package that covers pretty much every phone jack in the world.

Phone Kit
Teledapt
individual connector, $22.50;
region pack, $149.99; world
pack, $899.99

ThinPack

The 1.5-pound ThinPack battery is small enough not to be a burden but powerful enough to slake your PowerBook's thirst for energy for five to seven hours when you use it in combination with a PowerBook's internal battery. It's perfect for people who are tired of swapping batteries in the middle of a long flight.

ThinPack
VST Power Systems
$179.99

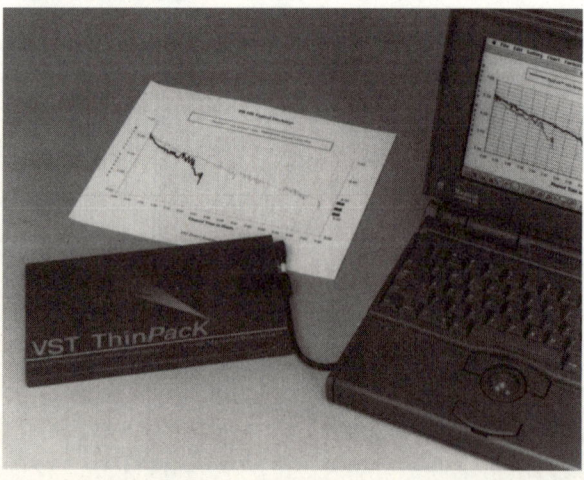

WRAP CARRYING CASES

Notecover
Saddlebag

If you want a case that fits your PowerBook like a glove, check out the WraP Notecover. It's made of neoprene—the same material wet suits are made of. Zippers on the back allow full access to the back panel, and an extra pocket gives you enough room to keep papers and spare disks. If you need even more carrying room, just sling the WraP Saddlebag over the Notecover.

WraP Saddlebag
$95

WraP Notecover
$69

Computers as Appliances

t is already difficult to tell the difference between a PC Expo or a Comdex and a three-ring circus. It won't be long before you can sit down on your couch, in front of your PC, yell channel 54, and start shouting your bids in a live auction of a five-foot tall, genuine-plastic, glow-in-the-dark religious statue.

That's the future the computer and entertainment industries have planned for you. It's America's ultimate dumbing-down. Like it? If you do, be sure you own a Pentium-powered, GUI-operated, multimedia computer with 32MB of RAM, a 4G hard drive and a 21-inch monitor.

For those unlobotomized users who still enjoy computing the old fashioned way—without the noise, the graphics, the video, and all the rest of the contemporary crap—I suggest, that as a matter of principle, you refuse to buy any machine with more power than a 386 can provide. If you don't already own a computer, run out and buy a copy of my book, *Computing for Cheapskates*. It will show you that any 286 will, eventually, do everything you may ever want to. And, best of all, you can get one for next to nothing.

To appreciate what dumbing-down can do, you need only look at how 35mm SLR cameras were "improved" into irrelevance. Sorry to have rained on this parade. It's just that I love computing as it is and truly hate what it is becoming.—Bob

POWERTUNING AND CUSTOMIZING

SPEEDING YOUR MAC TO THE MAX

Maxima 3.0

If you are an experienced Mac user, then you've probably heard about using a RAM disk. It's not hard to do, but there are some details you should know. Many Mac users, especially PowerBook users, set up a portion of system RAM as a temporary disk that functions as a floppy or hard drive, only faster. This technique also saves precious battery power. However, information stored on a RAM disk is volatile. When you turn off your computer or your system crashes, all RAM disk contents vanish. Maxima 3.0 partially remedies the volatile RAM situation while adding some benefits of its own.

Maxima 3.0 creates a "permanent" RAM disk that preserves contents during restarts, shutdowns, or system crashes. When you turn off your Macintosh, Maxima automatically backs up RAM disk contents to a hard disk folder. You can have it back up RAM disk contents on demand as well. It restores all this information to the RAM disk at startup. If power cuts out unexpectedly (brownouts, blackouts, electrical storms, accidentally yanking the plug, and so on), Maxima will restore the RAM disk to its last saved state at startup.

Maxima has some other useful features. It works with machines that do not support Apple's built-in RAM disk, such as the IIsi and IIcx. It safeguards disk contents by preventing other applications from writing to the RAM disk memory allocation. A "remember" mode directs it not to back up files that have not changed. Also, unlike Apple's own RAM disk, Maxima can create a double-capacity RAM disk. If you reserve 8MB of physical RAM, Maxima can set up a 16MB RAM disk using data compression. To speed up performance, data on the disk is not compressed until the RAM disk is more than 50 percent full.

Improvements come with "age" because Maxima tracks memory-usage history, adjusting what is compressed and left uncompressed over time. Checks revealed that initially MacWrite Pro took longer to launch from RAM than from the hard disk. Yet the more the same files were used, the less time Maxima required to open these files. Maxima eventually shaved more than six seconds off the time it took to launch a 300K FileMaker Pro file.

PowerBook and Duo users can expect Maxima to extend their battery life. With files in RAM rather than on the hard disk, the computer won't have to access the hard drive as frequently. Spinning the hard disk drive on your portable is one of the biggest battery-draining culprits.

Like other RAM disk utilities, Maxima's one big disadvantage is that the memory it allocates to the RAM disk becomes unavailable to other programs. Moreover, you'll only notice a real performance boost with often-used software applications and data files. Otherwise, speed improvements are negligible. Unless you're concerned about extending PowerBook/Duo battery life, your computer system may run more quickly if you configure the extra memory as a disk cache.—Carol S. Holzberg

Maxima 3.0
Connectix
2600 Campus Dr.
San Mateo, CA 94403
(800) 950-5880
$99

MOVE WINDOWS TO THE FAST LANE

Power Pak for Windows

This well-known utility optimizes Windows for maximum speed, including a replacement print driver and cache. Although Windows had its advantages, it sometimes seems to slow your system down to a crawl. PC-Kwik's new Power Pak for Windows offers three modules—Super PC-Kwik, KwikPrint, and KwikScreen—that can help put the gusto back inside your GUI.

Power Pak for Windows, like its DOS-based predecessor, centers around Super PC-Kwik, the award-winning cache. It's extremely fast and configurable, with a variety of options that let you control everything from track-buffer size to the respective priorities of read and write caching. If cache micro-management isn't your style, however, Super PC-Kwik comes with sample initialization files, suggested optimal settings for systems with 2MB, 4MB, 8MB, and 16MB of RAM.

Super PC-Kwik 6.0 supplies a solid foundation to Power Pak for Windows. It's a major upgrade, with improvements to CD-ROM caching at the top of the list. Installation is much easier: You no longer have to place PCKCDROM.SYS, the CD-ROM caching device driver, within 64K of the CD-ROM driver itself. (Rearranging these drivers in memory with a clumsy memory manager like MS-DOS's Memmaker was akin to skeet-shooting blindfolded.) You also have access to Windows-based configuration menus in lieu of noninformative command-line switches in DOS-based Power Pak, and excellent, context-sensitive online help.

CD-ROM caching is faster, too. The type of disk activity determines how much improvement you'll observe, but we measured a 40 percent speed increase over Super PC-Kwik 5.1 on repeated searches, using an NEC MultiSpin 3X.

Even Windows itself will load much more quickly from DOS, thanks to KwikLoad Optimizer. KwikLoad maintains in cache memory all those programming files your SYSTEM.INI and WIN.INI require when you run Windows. As a result, Windows loads in less than half the time. (Make that one-quarter the time, if you have a very large cache buffer.)

Most spoolers place their buffers on your hard disk. KwikPrint establishes its print buffer in RAM. RAM is much faster, by a factor of 10 to 1—roughly the same ratio that exists between hard drive and floppy disk access. In addition, other spoolers generate their buffers after processing your data through the Windows print driver, one of the worst bottlenecks in the environment. You don't regain control of operations until the driver finishes its preparations. KwikPrint, though, creates its buffer first and returns control to you, before sending on information to the print driver.

KwikPrint's graphical interface is very easy to use (and it's a genuine interface, not a group of commands that are "downloaded" to a DOS-based spooler, as in PrintQueue). You can choose which printers to spool, how much RAM to allocate, and whether to display spooling progress reports.

Power Pak's cache and KwikPrint are excellent, but KwikScreen, the program's Windows display driver, is problematic. Compatibility is the issue. Some video chip sets respond to KwikScreen's Windows display driver with relish. Others turn into molasses.

But on the whole, no other utility package concentrates so singlemindedly—and in general, successfully—on speeding up the Windows environment as Power Pak for Windows. Even if you don't own a chip set that will

benefit from KwikScreen, that still leaves KwikPrint, Super PC-Kwik, and KwikLoad to achieve some striking results. There's no better software-based remedy than Power Pak for Windows to pump some adrenaline into those tired pixels.— Barry Brenesal

Power Pak for Windows
PC-Kwik Corp.
15100 S.W. Koll Pkwy.
Beaverton, OR 97006-6026
(800) 284-5945; (503) 644-5644
$99.95

CRASH TEST: DATASAFE DOCUMENTS SYSTEM CRASHES, RECOVERS YOUR WORK

DataSafe 1.0

We all know that system crashes only occur when you haven't been saving your work frequently. Landmark's DataSafe 1.0 not only gives you the opportunity to recover and save your work after a crash, but it also lets you document each crash—and what you were doing before it happened. Further, it helps you troubleshoot five kinds of system errors to minimize their continuing occurrence and gives you instant access to information about your system and applications.

Though DataSafe must be constantly resident to function, as a background application it uses less than 2 percent of system resources, no screen space, and less than 20K of memory. Five different types of Windows system errors can be detected:

General Protection Faults (GPFs), Stack Faults, Floating Point Faults, Integer Divide By Zero Faults, and Bad Page Faults. When an error occurs, a dialog box indicates which one it is; at that point, you click the Record button and document the error, then click Recover. DataSafe lets you go back into your application and save your work before shutting down and restarting.

DataSafe's troubleshooting tutorial (both on-screen and in the manual) explains what may have caused your crash, and documents system information in its error log that may be helpful if you need to call technical support. Beyond simple system parameters, the log also contains your CPU register values at the time of the crash, which can be very helpful to a professional troubleshooter.

Two other utilities round out DataSafe's main functions: The System Information tool displays current parameters of your Windows environment and applications (such as version, free memory, and number of data objects), and Crash-O-Matic lets you test DataSafe's capabilities by simulating a crash and giving you a

chance to recover. Of course, the thought of actually causing a system crash may seem distasteful—a bit like intentionally initiating a car wreck. However, Crash-O-Matic can be helpful in preparing you for errors when they really do occur.—Kathy Yakal

DataSafe 1.0
Landmark
703 Grand Central St.
Clearwater, FL 34616
(800) 683-6696; (813) 443-1331
$49

SLICES, DICES, AND TAKES OUT THE TRASH

Open Sesame 1.1

Open Sesame automates your Macintosh work environment by observing what you do and when you do it (using Apple Events to track your actions). Open Sesame has a learning curve, and it asks a lot of questions. However, the longer you use it, the more it will have learned and the less intrusive it becomes. If you prefer, Open Sesame can give you its observations at a particular time, or notify you by an icon in your screen's corner. Then it gives you the option of performing those

tasks with one simple keystroke. You decide when (specific day or time) and how often (that is, "at," "after," or "every") to take action, and whether it should warn you before it carries out the task. The program can display observation dialogs with your name, or alert you by voice or with a flashing icon. Open Sesame supports the voice-recognition and speech synthesis in AV Macintoshes. If you install Apple's Speech Manager software, Open Sesame talks to you when it makes an observation.

Open Sesame can automate Finder operations such as opening and closing files; shutting down; rebuilding the desktop; and moving items into or out of the Apple and Startup Items folders.

For example, if Open Sesame notices that you regularly drag unwanted files and folders to the trash, it asks if it can schedule this event, and, if so, automatically empties the trash for you. Similarly, if you regularly use certain programs, it inquires if it can place aliases of these applications in the Apple menu for easy access.

But it goes beyond simple tasks. Open Sesame also monitors a variety of time-based events. It notices when you open or close an application or document, and when you shut down your system. In fact, you can direct it to shut down your Macintosh at a specific time each day. In addition, when you regularly work with files contained in a single folder such as a report,

RealWorldRealWorl

you usually toss into the trash—and enhance it to the extreme. If you want to, you can take thousands of shots, look at them, erase the hard disk, and then start all over, keeping what few you desire. No film! 🖥 As far as

chart, and table, you can create an Open Sesame instruction to open all these documents automatically whenever you open the folder.

Open Sesame installs both as a System extension and as a 68K application, which runs automatically at Startup. If you turn it off, it neither observes how you work nor follows instructions it has created for automating tasks.

If your work habits are such that you would like to be reminded when it's time to perform a certain task, or if you want a program to do routine tasks for you automatically, give Open Sesame a try. This intelligent assistant can handle recurring tasks without a complaint.
—Carol S. Holzberg

Open Sesame
Charles River Analytics
55 Wheeler St.
Cambridge, MA 02138
(800) 913-3535
$59

MULTIMEDIA STACKER FREES PRECIOUS MEMORY
Multimedia Stacker

What could be better than turning a 500MB hard disk into a 1G hard disk through disk compression? Regaining the memory used by the compression software's driver.

Stac Electronics's Multimedia Stacker uses Helix Software's Multimedia Cloaking to produce nearly invisible drivers for software caching, mouse control, and CD-ROM extensions. Together, these cloaked drivers take up only 10K of memory—one-eighth as much as the MS-DOS drivers—freeing up space for multimedia or other purposes.

These drivers are fully functional—they just have a smaller footprint. We found the menu-based installation was simple and straightforward, but the command-line-

based configuration was awkward at times.

Also included is Helix Software's Discover memory analysis utility, which provides a good level of memory allocation information. Stacker itself can now handle 32-bit file access under Windows for WorkGroups, producing a boost to disk speed.

Starting with the assumption that you can never have enough hard-disk space and memory, MultiMedia Stacker succeeds on both counts.—Barry Brenesal

Multimedia Stacker
Stac Electronics
San Diego, CA
(800) 522-7822; (619) 794-4317
$99

REMOVE-IT ONCE AND FOR ALL
Remove-IT

Vertisoft Systems's Remove-IT is one of those gotta-have utilities that can safely and conveniently purge the leftovers of old programs. Remove-IT cleans up Program Manager groups, Windows .INI files, and hard-disk directories of unwanted applications, making this program the most complete Windows uninstaller available.

In addition to searching program headers for associations to .DLL files and .INI files (as well as auxiliary programs), Remove-IT includes a pair of watchdog TSR programs: Log-IT keeps track of new applications, while Watch-IT measures DOS and Windows usage frequency.

The Watch-IT utility displays a pie-chart graph of application and driver usage, letting you single out dead-weight files from your disk. On the downside, we found that Watch-IT is incompatible with Windows for WorkGroups' 32-bit file-access feature.

Once you know what to throw away, Remove-IT's deletion module can erase, compress, or archive any application to a backup directory. We found that the program did a splendid job of deleting programs, but archiving Microsoft Access, which comprised 8MB of files, took about 45 minutes.

We found that Remove-IT could tell the difference between different versions of the same program and deleted only those files linked to the version being removed. Shared .DLLs and WIN.INI-associated documents are recognized and assigned a yellow warning flag; those elements used by other applications get a red flag. To help you make a decision about the yellow-flagged files, the link button displays all the .DLLs and programs in the search path that refer to or are referenced by the file you want to purge.

As thorough as it is, we found that when we removed PageMaker 4.0, Remove-IT missed the Table Editor icon, although everything in the PM4 directory was removed from the disk. When purging Corel Ventura 4.2, we found that the corresponding entry in WIN.INI remained. On the

plus side, Remove-IT's emergency recovery disk can help you get back on your computing feet again should disaster ever strike. Like the Norton Utilities, it preserves partition information and DOS and Windows system files.

If programs come and go on your system and you're looking for more hard-disk space, Remove-IT can recover what previous applications took away.—Lenny Bailes

Remove-IT
Vertisoft Systems Inc.
San Francisco, CA
(800) 466-5875; (415) 956-5999
$69.95

JUST BUTTONS MAKES YOUR MOUSE ROAR
just Buttons 1.03h

By supercharging your mouse, Chrisalan Designs's just Buttons can transform the way you use your PC. This $39 program allows you to assign a range of tasks to your mouse buttons, which can save time and keystrokes.

In order to edit or create a just Buttons script, all you do is choose which mouse button you wish to enhance, and click on Button Setup. The dialog box that appears takes you step-by-step through the process; there are 17 different types of actions from which to choose. You can also customize each action in a script.

just Buttons can handle everything from the trivial to the complex. Actions such as launching File Manager or a Control Panel are easy to set up; you can even get fancy if you want, launching File Manager with specific directories opened. But when you need the functions that are associated with programming languages, just Buttons presents a huge leap forward.

just Buttons also includes a variety of functions to manipulate text and variables. Unfortunately, the dialog boxes tend to be nothing more than multiline edit windows where you type in code with minimal assistance from the program. And some actions—such as choosing a menu item in another application—are only accessible via commands that you must manually type into a Control Script edit box.

Included in the just Buttons program is a powerful scheduler that can automatically start scripts. Because a scheduled item can run a script, it can test the many system variables that just Buttons tracks and react accordingly. For example, when the program senses low system resources, it closes nonessential applications.

A first effort, just Buttons is missing many of the elements that you might expect to find in such a scripting product. There is no DDE support or ability to drive other programs via OLE automation. Moreover, there is no dialog box editor, so data can only be input via specific kinds of dialog boxes.

The product is very much one that is rapidly evolving. The documentation for just Buttons looks like an online help section. A powerful

Command Line Plus item was recently added in the version that we reviewed (allowing you to search for a running application). It worked quite well, but was not covered in the program's documentation. Fortunately, the new function's dialog box structure was coherent enough to guide the curious user. On the other hand, the online help function list includes many items with blank sections—indicating that the developers are planning greater support in future versions of the program.

Overall, just Buttons is currently in a form that requires a sophisticated user—and one who is willing to invest a little time to get the most out of this unique product. The program represents an exciting peek into the future of Windows application automation.—Barry Simon

just Buttons 1.03h
Chrisalan Designs Inc.
Wenatchee, WA
(509) 663-7770
$39

MANAGES FILES AS GOOD AS GOLD

XTreeGold 4.0 for Windows

If the built-in File Manager in Windows suits all of your needs, then you're in the minority. File Manager doesn't compress, encrypt, or preview files, and it wouldn't earn two stars for usability. But people still struggle with it

because the alternatives usually come in big utilities collections with big price tags and big learning curves.

Not so when it comes to XTreeGold 4.0 for Windows. It creates, expands, and even password-protects PKzip-compressed files. You can configure its file windows into various looks (including a Windows 95-like tree of all your system's drives). And once you've created a custom view, you can assign that view its own tab, and click to change between views.

But perhaps the biggest bonus is that XTreeGold expands Windows's common dialog-box engine to copy, delete, compress, expand, and view from every Windows app's File Open dialog box. XTreeGold's file management isn't for everyone, but its dialog-box enhancements are addicting.—Matthew Lake

XTreeGold 4.0 for Windows
Central Point Software
(800) 445-4208
$99

OS/2: THIS TIME, IT'S PERSONAL

OS/2 Warp, Version 3

Of course you want a fast, low-maintenance, 32-bit preemptive multitasking operating system. You also want strong applications to run on it. But what's this? You say you want all of this now? In that case, OS/2 Warp, Version 3, is just the thing you're looking for—an industrial-strength operating system

and integrated suite of personal applications together in the same box.

The new OS/2 has a slim, speedier kernel, more usable interface features, better handling of Windows applications, and low system requirements—it will actually work on a 4MB 386SX. It's doubtful Windows 95 will ever make that claim.

OS/2 Warp, Version 3, does Windows better than ever. Over any Windows 3.1 installation, OS/2 supports all Windows modes, including those that require Microsoft's 32-bit API Win32s. Our testing found that even graphic-intensive applications ran without problems, and at normal speeds. In addition, this operating system enables Windows and OS/2 applications to run on the same desktop side by side. The only drawback is with applications that require VxDs, which OS/2 does not support.

The new OS/2 is also better with hardware than before. It has more video- and sound-card drivers, and there's a point-and-click configuration tool that uses OS/2's new Play at Will interface to provide easy card setup. With this Plug-and-Play look-alike, simply slip in a fax modem and you'll be ready to receive incoming faxes right away.

With OS/2 Warp, Version 3, the operating system is just the beginning. It comes with a suite of applications called IBM Works, which includes a word processor, spreadsheet, database, PIM, and

scheduler—all drag-and-drop enabled. Need to schedule an appointment? Drag your client's information from the phone book into the scheduler and you're set.

There's also a built-in set of Internet access utilities: a native TCP/IP stack, gopher, ftp, newsreader, and mail utilities. An OS/2 version of the popular Mosaic browsing utility is planned, and to round out the I-Way offerings, IBM doubles as an Internet service provider with an access point through its Advantis service.

Other native 32-bit Presentation Manager applications included are Faxworks fax software, Person to Person (a multi-participant whiteboard application), an OS/2 version of the CompuServe Information Manager, and a system interrogator utility that checks on the status of resources.

So whether you look at the new OS/2 as a Works program with the bonus of an operating system or as an operating system with free utilities that outshine Windows 3.x's applets, it's a good deal. If you can't wait for Windows 95, this system offers some of the high points in advance.—Scott Naylor

OS/2 Warp, Version 3
IBM Corp.
(800) 426-7695

for all practical purposes, film photography will eventually be as dead as the daguerreotype. Imagine an all-digital world where everyone can make—instead of just shoot—great photographs. Or should I say "images?"

Always by Your Side

I t used to be easy, even on the road. A notebook PC and a modem were all you needed: Dial in, read, and answer e-mail. That was it. But now there's much more: You need to be out there continually, keeping the customer satisfied in a highly competitive environment. You need full access to the main office's network and all its tools. Groupware, presentations, updated quotes, and new features documents—you name it, you have to have it. And you shouldn't have to go home again to get it.

The Problem

You're ready for remote access but the process of connecting to the office and downloading files is too slow to be useful.

The Solution

Make sure everyone has a high-speed modem. Anything less than 14.4kbps is unacceptable, especially if you're after remote control as well as remote access. You can pick these up for $120 to $150 apiece. Here's an even more cost-effective solution: Get 28.8kbps modems ($280 to $400 each) on both the host and the remote machines. Until the V.34 standard shakes itself out, however, stick with like machines, rather than risking incompatibility between competing brands. Springing for 28.8kbps may seem expensive at first glance, but it's much cheaper than being late for an appointment on the other side of the country. You may be surprised by how fast remote access equipment will pay for itself. Being able to work from anywhere on the road increases productivity enormously, which in turn earns back the cost of access in little time.

The Problem

Basic e-mail access is fine, but what your remote users really need is complete access to their desktop computers.

The Solution

Consider using a remote-control package. These do far more than just file transfers. They let remote users dial in and use the software on their desktop machines as if they were sitting in the office. By using remote-control software, especially with a high-speed modem, you can keep your road warriors in the collaboration loop at all times, providing them access to groupware and other networking features. Symantec's Norton pcAnywhere is strong, as are Stac Electronics' ReachOut Remote Control and Norton-Lambert's Close-Up. Each costs less than $200.

Remote-control software can be paired with fax software to integrate fax management into e-mail management. This makes managing and sharing data easier and reduces the response lag-time that workers may incur while on the road.

The Problem

How do you make sure that your remote users—who are now so well-equipped that they can remain on the road for extended periods—stay in the loop on the kinds of decisions that get influenced by conversations at the office water fountain? And how do you manage them?

Furthermore, as the word processor defined the modern writer and opened the door to a new wave of scribes who could do better work on the computer than on the mistake-prone typewriter, so too will digital photography

RealWorldRealWorld

The Solution

Set up your own bulletin board. A good BBS, such as PCBoard, Galacticomm's The Major BBS, and Wildcat (from Mustang Software), or a discussion database such as those found in Lotus Notes or OpenMind, can stock all the files, documents, and discussions a dial-in employee needs, and as a bonus it can keep excellent track of who's been accessing it, when, and what they've done with it. A BBS costs around $150 a month for a commercial service—less for shareware—and it can be a superb secret weapon, but only if it's maintained and updated continually.

The beauty of a flexible system for discussion becomes clear when remote users get involved. It is precisely those folks who aren't around for casual idea-sharing who profit most from such channels as a BBS or discussion database. You may well find that your investment in a vehicle for disseminating information will pay you back by providing ideas. Reticent staffers may speak up more on a bulletin board.

The Problem:

You've now got a dozen or more remote users and they're tying up your lines. How can they connect without crippling the main office?

The Solution

If you have a large number of users who travel constantly and need full access to your LAN, try a remote-node package. For $2,500 to $6,000, products such as Shiva's LanRover/E for NetWare and Microcom's LANexpress (which includes four 28.8kbps modems) establish the remote computers as full nodes on the network, with full capabilities. The price tag may look high, but think about it—your remote users are getting the best of both worlds: The ability to get their work done on the road without sacrificing their commitments at headquarters. For extra cost-effectiveness, it's even possible to combine remote-node and remote-control access using two separate products, all over the same modem.—Neil Randall ■

SideBar 2.01 for Windows

Killing time until Windows 95 arrives? You could play a few hands of solitaire—or you could rearrange your desktop with Quarterdeck's SideBar 2.01 for Windows, the latest minimalist Program Manager replacement. SideBar provides a sneak peek at elements you'll see in the Windows 95 shell. You can drag program items, folders, and data files onto the desktop. A customizable icon bar with a clock and Run button can be anchored on either side of the screen. A fast File Manager replacement displays Program Manager groups as folders in the same treelike display. And yes, you can nest folders within folders.

The interface's otherwise elegant appearance is marred by a few downright ugly sections. The File Manager's use of drag and drop isn't consistent with the rest of the program or the rest of the industry. Clunky confirmation dialog boxes are filled with empty space and ungrammatical messages. Some menu choices are head-scratchers as well: Want to create a new folder? Look for Make, Hidden under the View menu. Fortunately, there are numerous right-mouse-button shortcuts.

We found a few minor display bugs along with missed opportunities. The drag-and-drop Recycler, for example, is welcome, though it would be better if it could link to an Undelete program. And why doesn't SideBar's clock let you reset the system date and time if you double-click on it?

Despite these flaws, SideBar 2.01 is a capable Program Manager replacement that's especially stingy with system resources. And its modern interface suggests it has a promising future, even after Windows 95 arrives.—Ed Bott

SideBar 2.01 for Windows
Quarterdeck Office Systems
(800) 354-3222; (310) 392-9851
$59.95

Multimedia Cloaking

As memory managers have improved, RAM cram has given way to another memory lapse—upper-memory cram. Helix Software has come to the rescue of your beleaguered upper memory with a set of three utilities geared to revving up multimedia systems. Multimedia Cloaking consists of a CD-ROM driver to replace Microsoft's MSCDEX, a disk cache like DOS's SmartDrive that also handles CD-ROM caching, and a small-footprint mouse driver. What's the big deal about a bunch of tools you got for free when you bought MS-DOS? All three of Multimedia Cloaking's tools take up only 8K of conventional memory and no upper memory at all. Apart from the tiny 8K rub, the rest of the utilities run under 32-bit protected mode in extended RAM.

In our tests of Multimedia Cloaking, we won back 22K more RAM under 640K and 50K more RAM in upper memory—more than 70K that DOS-based apps could use for themselves. And our informal tests of the disk cache support Helix's claims that its CD-ROM caching is faster than DOS 6.2's SmartDrive.

Best of all, the cloaking system isn't tied to any specific memory manager. The utilities worked with DOS's EMM386, QEMM-386, 386Max, and, of course, Helix's own Netroom. On any system suffering from bloated CD-ROM drivers, the utilities in Multimedia Cloaking are keepers—until Windows 95 ships, anyway. And even then, there could still be a place for smart system management like this.—Ron White

Multimedia Cloaking
Helix Software
(800) 451-0551; (718) 392-3100
$39.95

POWERHOUSE TOOLKIT OFFERS NEAR-FOOLPROOF DISK REPAIR

MacTools Pro

MacTools Pro offers a great deal of hand-holding when it comes to identifying and fixing disk problems, which makes it an excellent choice for less experienced users. MacTools Pro 4.0 combines disk-repair and optimization tools, antivirus functions, diagnostic facilities, and file-recovery tools into one main window, called the MacTools Clinic.

By default, the first thing you see when you launch MacTools Clinic is the QuickAssist dialog box, which is where you indicate the symptoms you're experiencing (such as crashes, sluggishness, and lost files). MacTools then uses your choices to direct its disk-checking and -fixing operations. The Custom QuickAssist dialog box, which has a more detailed list of problems, is also available, but most expert users will

probably find even Custom QuickAssist too elementary to be useful.

The best enhancement in this version of MacTools Pro is the speed of DiskFix, which performs disk checks and repairs. DiskFix's disk scans are much faster than in previous versions and finally rival the speed of Norton Utilities's scans.

A new feature is RAMboot, which saves time by letting you repair your startup disk from a RAM disk rather than from a floppy disk. However, you still need to keep an emergency disk on hand, in case your Mac won't start at all.

A welcome enhancement to MacTools's handy TrashBack feature, which lets you quickly and easily recover any files you've inadvertently deleted in the Trash, is a viewer for deleted files. MacTools's security features have been beefed up as well—a new DOD Wipe option permanently erases files according to U.S. Department of Defense specifications.

MacTools Pro is clearly based on the belief that an ounce of prevention is worth a pound of cure. The program's AutoCheck feature runs in the background and checks disk structure while your system is idle, allowing MacTools Pro to identify problems before they become serious. You can choose to have AutoCheck run at specified intervals or continuously. It fixes minor problems automatically, without requiring

you to run DiskFix, and creates weekly or monthly reports on any problems it finds. Network administrators can use AutoCheck to compile reports on any networked Mac. One caveat: AutoCheck requires 500k of memory, and it can slow down your system.

MacTools Pro is the most comprehensive disk-utility package you can buy. Like Norton Utilities, it provides disk-repair, disk-optimization, and file-recovery facilities in addition to backup and disk-copy utilities. However, unlike Norton Utilities, it also provides networkable diagnostic reporting and antivirus capabilities. If disk problems strike terror into your heart, you'll probably be happy with MacTools Pro, which offers automated repair; user assistance; and convenient tools, such as AutoCheck and RAMboot.—Susan Janus and John Mitchell

MacTools Pro 4.0
Symantec
Central Point Division
Beaverton, OR
(800) 964-6896; (503) 690-8088
$149.95

Norton Utilities for Macintosh

Norton Utilities is easy enough for novices to use, but if you consider yourself a disk jockey—a hard-disk jockey, that is—then you'll feel especially at home with Norton Utilities. It fixes and optimizes disks, recovers

files, and provides a backup utility (FastBack, formerly a Fifth Generation product), but unlike MacTools Pro, it offers less in the way of automated disk repair and assistance for basic tasks. On the other hand, it provides more control over advanced disk-repair functions than MacTools Pro does, making it the best choice for knowledgeable users.

For example, a newly added component in the latest release is Norton Disk Editor, which lets you examine and edit data anywhere on a disk. Experienced users can use Disk Editor to manually repair and recover low-level file-system data. You can access the bits and bytes of a file and view file contents in either hexadecimal or ASCII format. A search facility lets you search disks for phrases or sentences, and you can view the contents of documents without opening them. Disk Editor is an invaluable tool for sophisticated users but an extremely dangerous tool in the hands of novices. If you don't know what you're doing, steer clear of Disk Editor—you can potentially damage files and disks beyond repair.

FileSaver, Norton Utilities's facility for tracking deleted files, has been enhanced in the latest release to perform background disk scans at startup, shutdown, or idle time. It lets you know if it detects a problem, it does not automatically repair the problem—you must do so manually, using Norton Disk

Doctor. However, FileSaver requires only 80K of memory. It also lets you know when you need to optimize your disk or perform a backup.

Also new in Version 3.0 is System Info, a benchmarking utility that tests the speed of your CPU, floating-point unit, video monitor, and any writable-disk systems. The utility subsequently compiles a report and compares its findings with reference benchmarks for the Mac model you're testing. For disk-savvy users, Norton Utilities provides more bells and whistles and gives expert users more control over the disk-repair and file-recovery process.—Susan Janus and John Mitchell

Norton Utilities for Macintosh 3.1.1
Symantec
Cupertino, CA
(800) 441-7234; (503) 334-6054
$149

CREATE SCREEN-SAVER SLIDE SHOWS

PhotoGenix

Why settle for flying toasters, fighting Klingons, or the indignity of a blank screen when you can create a customized screen saver with photographs, drawings, or images of any kind? That's the idea behind PhotoGenix, a $149 program that not only allows users to produce their own Windows-based screen-saver slide shows but comes with a license that permits unlimited royalty-free distrib-

Fax to the Max

obody can doubt that faxing is central to business. But there's faxing and then there's power faxing, which can be among your most important business weapons. Information management can't be overused, and power faxing is all about managing your information. The standard fax machine is useful, but a network of PCs stocked with fax boards, OCR software, and fax-management software is a juggernaut.

Once everything's in place, information can emerge as the real secret weapon.

The Problem

Faxing can expedite your work, but if you have limited line space, voice telephone calls have to take priority.

The Solution

There's nothing more annoying than calling a telephone number and hearing that screeching fax noise. So do your clients a favor: Get a fax board that distinguishes between incoming data and voice calls, or invest in a separate phone line for each if it's important that faxes don't cut into telephone time. Furthermore, consider fax boards that offer you complete background faxing (the $199 Intel SatisFaxion is one of the best of these). If you don't have background faxing, the PC slows to a crawl every time a fax is being received, which results in lost productivity.

You might also consider a software solution that features both fax/voice detection and background faxing. GFI Fax & Voice's FaxMaker can handle this task for less than $300.

The Problem

You've got a lot of purchases clamoring for your budget. How do you deploy power faxing without breaking the bank?

The Solution

You don't need a fax board for every computer. PCs on a LAN can share fax boards, and most networking software makes this possible. Shared fax boards are better than shared fax machines, because networked fax boards can queue faxes automatically for transmission as soon as the line is free, and nobody has to stand around waiting. Many fax software programs offer scheduling as well. Some good contenders include Delrina's WinFax Pro and Global Village Communication's Faxworks Pro. Using one of these products, faxes can be scheduled to be sent from PCs at convenient or less expensive times. For large numbers of users, consider a fax server, which tracks all activity for costs and use. You might also want to consider using a network printer with fax capabilities such as Digital Equipment's DEClaser 3500 fax card, which lets the laser printer receive and print out high-quality faxes on plain paper. Also, Toshiba's TF505 is a full-featured laser-quality fax machine that can double as a regular laser printer for a PC or small LAN.

The Problem

Training users to fax directly from their computers is time-consuming. And the time they spend sending faxes from within various Windows applications costs money.

The Solution

Buy fax software that automatically installs a fax command in your most important applications, or at the very least have fax commands custom-

end up with some unusual newspaper photographs, that's for sure. Instead of using a 6-to-8 frame-per-second camera with a limited number of shots before you run out of film, you can shoot 30 frames per second for two

programmed. Here's an added bonus: You avoid the possibility of an employee forgetting to select the laser printer for the next real print job, and faxing a sensitive document to someone who shouldn't see it. Choosing fax software that has a truly usable interface makes a difference, especially when you need to fax information from a variety of source applications. With Watermark from Watermark Software, you can send faxes from within any application by linking them as OLE objects. DCA's CrossFax will append faxes to each other, to save time.

The Problem

What about all your remote users? Can they be power faxers?

The Solution

Fax management is difficult enough in the office, but from the road it's a nightmare. Fortunately, Delrina's WinFax Pro offers remote fax retrieval and, at the same time, remote e-mail management. The product, available on the street for $120, also offers rental fax mailboxes and other extremely useful features, and is a must for power faxers until the other packages catch up. Remote users can also set up their own fax-on-demand systems to handle fax requests while they're out of the office. Products such as FaxMaker from GFI Fax & Voice can streamline call-in fax responses, and permit fax requests to be forwarded or fielded from a remote location.—Neil Randall ■

ution of runtime modules for advertising or promotional purposes.

PhotoGenix is so simple that a first-time user can create a screen-saver show in minutes. The first step is to select a previously created image file—in Targa,

TIFF, .BMP, .GIF, or JPEG format—or use one of 200 royalty-free photos included on the CD-ROM. Next, use a mouse to select how long the image will stay on the screen, as well as one of 15 incoming and outgoing transition effects. Photo Genix will run through a slide show of up to 200 images, displaying each image for a duration ranging from 1 second to 10 minutes. When you're satisfied with the selection and transitions, clicking on the Make button automatically generates a slide-show screen saver on your hard disk or a runtime module on floppy disks. The images are compressed and saved in .BMP format; you can save to multiple floppy disks if necessary.—Daniel Grotta and Sally Wiener Grotta

PhotoGenix
Firefly Software Corp.
P.O. Box 756
Jericho, NY 11753
(800) 224-2778; (516) 935-7060
Fax: (516) 932-7905
$149

A WINDOWS SHELL FOR DOS USERS

FrontRunner

If you're a fan of DOS apps and you use Windows mainly for task switching, FrontRunner may give your work more of a multitasking feel. When you use FrontRunner, you can launch DOS sessions as part of your Windows startup, from a File Run dialog box, from a pull-down menu off a Program Manager group, or from Front-Runner's own Launch toolbar. These DOS sessions can run full-screen, but FrontRunner really shines when you run them as MDI

child windows inside the FrontRunner window. FrontRunner windows have scroll-back memory so you can view what has scrolled off the screen.

You can configure FrontRunner's status bar to show free disk space, free memory, the time (but not date), and the first part of any text in the Clipboard. The Launch toolbar lets you place quick launch buttons at the top of the FrontRunner window. There's also a File Find

dialog box that searches for filenames or text within files.—Barry Simon

Front Runner, Version 1.0.
Phar Lap Software Inc.
60 Aberdeen Ave.
Cambridge, MA 02138
(800) 292-9622; (617) 661-1510
Fax: (617) 876-2972
$139

LOW-IMPACT APPROACH TO ORGANIZATION

WindowMagic

WindowMagic desktop organizer is from a company that hasn't forgotten the programmer's golden rule: Write tight code. There are four new productivity applets—Get-It, Disk-It, Print-It, and X-It—plus enhancements to the program's ToolBars, QuickAccess, and FastLaunch. The cost in hard disk space for all these improvements? A mere 500K.

WindowMagic's winning characteristic is its ability to

Real World Real World

organize Program Manager without changing it. Your SHELL= statement still points to Program Manager, and there's very little new to learn. You organize Program Manager by assigning customized WindowMagic icons to minimized groups. WindowMagic makes these groups accessible via a neat little Get-It applet. Clicking on the Get-It hand brings up a menu that allows you to switch to any application that is currently running. Print-It lets you drag your documents onto an icon for printing; Disk-It puts disk-drive icons on your desktop (including a CD-ROM drive); Run-It saves File Run commands for faster program access; and X-It, for a fast Windows exit. Many other Windows utilities do some of what the WindowMagic program does (and WindowMagic doesn't do everything), but as a low-impact tool for making some sense out of Windows, WindowMagic achieves its goal.—Carole Patton

WindowMagic, Version 3.0
WinWear Inc.
14150 NE 20th, #346
Bellevue, WA 98007
(800) 803-9358; (206) 635-0856
Fax: (206) 635-0823
$89.95

CacheAll 1.2

Two things make C&D Programming's CacheAll special: It can cache virtually anything, including CD-ROMs and network drives, and it uses a hard-disk swap file to cache slow devices. At $79, CacheAll stands out in the crowded software-cache market.

CacheAll's network support means you can cache repetitive network accesses. This both improves workstation performance and relieves the network of some load. With its swap-file feature, CacheAll maintains a modifiable list of "slow" devices, and caches them to the swap file if cache memory runs out. The result is performance that approaches memory-caching levels. For some applications, such as those with heavy network-drive access and plenty of local hard-disk space, this option is promising.

Still, CacheAll is a bit rough around the edges. Information provided in CacheAll's usage report is short, though adequate. In addition, while the package comes with a Windows utility, Windows installation is not fully automated. And while the Windows utility lets you change the lists of cached devices, it doesn't let you alter the cache's size or other basic attributes. For these, you must enter DOS commands or modify the startup command in AUTOEXEC.BAT. Also, documentation was con-

siderably out of sync with the program's revisions.

In our benchmark tests, CacheAll performed well in specific areas—for instance, in the controlled environment where the file being cached was bigger than the cache but smaller than the swap file. CacheAll excels here because of its unique swap-file feature. But other benchmark performance ran a bit behind the competition.

CacheAll also lacks delayed write-caching, which normally would seriously hamper write performance. However, unlike most cache utilities, you can run CacheAll with SmartDrive, which fully supports write-caching. This means you can use SmartDrive to cache your hard disk and CacheAll to handle your CD-ROM or network drive. Yet CacheAll lacks the ability to adjust its size to share memory, which is bad news if your RAM is limited—and whose isn't?

But if you have plenty of RAM, own SmartDrive, and can

use the unique features, CacheAll is a suitable caching solution.—Philip F.H. Rose

CacheAll
C & D Programming Corp.
P.O. Box 581012
Salt Lake City, UT 84158
(800) 847-5676
$79

STRETCHING YOUR MAC'S RAM

OptiMem

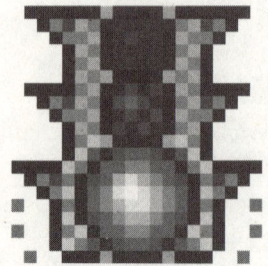

OptiMem can make a little RAM go a long way. If three or four of your favorite programs take up all your available RAM, or you inexplicably run out of memory during a lengthy session—even though the About This Macintosh box shows plenty available—OptiMem may help.

This System 7 extension takes control of application memory at startup, allocating it in the minimum size needed to launch each program. OptiMem doles out additional RAM as needed, so multiple programs can share memory efficiently. However, if you want to edit a 6MB TIFF file on an 8MB machine, you're out of luck. OptiMem isn't a virtual memory manager; it can't create something from nothing.

We loaded a suite of programs that included Photoshop, Aldus FreeHand 3.1, Microsoft Word 5.1, Canvas 3.5, HyperCard, and ZTerm on a 24MB Quadra 650. These and the System file consumed a total of 16,780K, leaving 7,796K for files. One or two 24-bit TIFF

files could eat that up in a hurry. With OptiMem, those same applications loaded into 11,969K of RAM, a 5MB bonus. Photoshop loaded in 3,099K (instead of 5,120K), while Word and FreeHand each used over a megabyte less RAM.

Besides letting you run programs on less memory, OptiMem prevents memory "loss." Normally, you lose memory in one of three ways. First, newly opened applications grab the full amount indicated under Preferred Size in their Get Info box, hanging onto that much or more until closed. Also, released memory blocks may be too small or scattered through your Mac's available RAM to be usable by applications needing certain amounts of contiguous memory. OptiMem uses smaller, relocatable blocks of RAM, so free memory is always maintained in larger chunks. Finally, if a program crashes or is forced to quit, its blocks of RAM may never be released for use by other applications. While OptiMem can't recapture memory lost to ungraceful program exits, it reduces the number of crashes caused by low memory.

OptiMem does clash with programs that use their own memory-management routines. We were unable to load Pixar Typestry 2.0 and a few other programs until we checked the OptiMem Off button for those applications in the program's Control Panel. OptiMem maintains a list of your programs and you can exclude those which conflict.

You can set the Suggested Memory Size and Minimum Memory Size settings in your applications's Get Info boxes yourself. But if you want an easier way to run more programs on a memory-starved machine, OptiMem is a reasonable way to stretch the RAM you have.—David D. Busch

OptiMem
Jump Development Group
1228 Malvern Ave.
Pittsburgh, PA 15217
(412) 681-2692
$129

OPEN A NEW WINDOW ON YOUR DOS COMMAND PROMPT

Landmark DOS

Many longtime PC users have never given up on that old reliable DOS command prompt. Yet when you use DOS from Windows, you lose all the advantages of the Windows interface. Now there's an alternative for DOS-addicts. DOS for Windows, a sophisticated upgrade of a popular free-

ware program called Impostor, puts the DOS command prompt in the Windows environment, letting you do all your traditional DOS operations from a window. As with the regular DOS prompt, you can use the DOS for Windows prompt to launch programs and issue virtually all DOS commands, such as Copy, Delete, and Rename.

While it works like the regular DOS prompt, DOS for Windows is more powerful since it adds the convenience of Windows to your old DOS commands. For example, if you double-click on a program file listed by the Dir command, DOS for Windows automatically launches it. DOS for Windows also has commands that DOS doesn't. One of the most useful is the CDD command, which changes drives and directories with one step. You can also take advantage of aliases: mini-macros that let you abbreviate complex commands with a few characters.

While DOS for Windows operated flawlessly, there are some features that could have been added. For example, Hewlett-Packard's Dashboard

2.0 lets you drag items from a Dir listing and drop them on your Windows desktop as icons. Nevertheless, DOS for Windows's enhanced set of commands provides more power and flexibility than DOS while letting you stay in Windows. If you still have a taste for DOS, Landmark DOS for Windows is a surprisingly handy tool for simplifying many file-management tasks.—David Haskin

DOS for Windows
Landmark Research
International Corp.
703 Grand Central St.
Clearwater, FL 34616
(800) 683-6696; (813) 443-1331
$49

ALLright Enhancements

When a new System 7 utilities package arrives on the scene, the obvious question is, Do we really need another one? MSA obviously thinks so, judging by its recent release of ALLright Enhancements. A package of nine modules and a management application, ALLright Enhancements claims to improve your productivity by making your Mac easier to use.

The most instantly useful module for anyone on a large network is Printers, which lets you switch printers without going to the Chooser. You can add keyboard command equivalents so you can switch printers just by pressing a couple of keys.

The also-helpful Copies module, based on MSA's popular CopyRight extension, lets you copy in the background, copy multiple items to multiple destinations, and schedule copies for simple backups. Don't expect faster copying, though. You get the perception of speed, because copies happen in the background, but our informal tests showed that Copies's copies can actually be slower than the Finder's.

The Extensions module is also useful. Like other extensions managers, it lets you turn extensions and control panels on and off as well as save sets for different computing needs—a particularly helpful feature lets you toggle "families" of related extensions on and off with one master control.

A fourth intriguing module is Notes, which adds a digital Post-it notepad to your desktop. Beyond the usual uses for such a notepad—saving phone numbers and jotting down sudden inspirations—you can also attach a note to a folder so it opens automatically (in Notes or TeachText format) when the folder is opened.

MSA has clearly tried to make ALLright Enhancements fit everyone's work style. You

Quick Takes: Leveraging Your Fax Power

1. Don't waste time standing by a fax machine—rig one inside your PC and let 'er rip. With background faxing, you can do other things while your fax is being sent. The time you save will pay for the fax board faster than you can hit the Send button.

2. You can set up fax-on-demand telephone systems, forward faxes to be received in remote locations, and send them to one or many recipients from on the road just as easily as you can from your home.

3. Tired of deciphering low-quality fax printouts? Consider employing a hybrid fax device as part of your office technology. Fax machines that double as printers—and printers with fax cards built in—can now spit out laser-quality faxes on plain paper. ∎

can access the modules from the menu bar, the Apple menu, or a tool bar; you can also turn off any modules you don't want. If you share your Mac with others, you can each save your preferences individually—and PowerBook users can save different settings for different locations.—Victoria von Biel

ALLright Enhancements
MSA, Inc.
Pittsburgh, PA
(800) 366-4622; (412) 471-7170
$129

RAM Doubler

When A Claim Seems too good to be true, it probably isn't. Or so we thought before we tried RAM Doubler, an inexpensive software utility that claimed it would double our RAM with no significant loss in performance—and actually did so.

Run RAM Doubler's one-step Installer and restart, and—presto—your RAM is exactly doubled. If you don't believe it, check out the Finder's About This Macintosh window. Even better, start launching applications and discover how many more you can now keep open simultaneously. Only two caveats apply to the RAM doubling: You must have 32-bit addressing turned on for your doubled RAM to exceed 16MB, and RAM Doubler can't increase your doubled RAM beyond 256MB.

RAM Doubler is compatible with all 68030 and 68040 Macs—including Power-

Books—that have at least 4MB of RAM originally. And more important, it probably won't cause conflicts with your other software. True, it does have some problems with Photoshop and a few other programs that use nonstandard methods of memory management. We know of a few control panels that don't work with RAM Doubler. And we (as well as some other users we contacted) had occasional system crashes that were apparently related to using the program. Still, such problems are definitely rare. Usually RAM Doubler works wonderfully; many users have reported no problems at all. In terms of both compatibility and simplicity, RAM Doubler far outdistances OptiMem, a competing memory-enhancing utility.

Overall, RAM Doubler is a spectacular success. If you need more RAM (and who doesn't?), RAM Doubler may well be the best investment you'll make this year.—Ted Landau

RAM Doubler for Macintosh
Connectix Corp.
San Mateo, CA
(800) 950-5880; (415) 571-5100
$99

Conflict Catcher for Macintosh 2.0.1

In the Old Days, diagnosing a startup conflict—generally a recurring crash, freeze, or bomb duplicable upon or after startup—was a major pain. It usually meant taking all of your extensions and control panels out of the System Folder and then putting them back one at a time, restarting after each addition. But now there's Conflict Catcher, a uniquely helpful program that automates most of this tedious process, quickly determining which control panel, extension, or combination of the two is to blame.

When you tell it to perform a conflict test, Conflict Catcher systematically disables combinations of extensions and control panels and asks you to determine whether the problem is still occurring. If it is, you go through another restart and respond to the dialog box again. After the minimum necessary number of restarts, Conflict Catcher tells you what it's identified as the problem. In several months of heavy use, Conflict Catcher correctly identified the conflicting extension or control panel every time we used it and successfully diagnosed at

least one tricky three-way conflict.

Conflict Catcher is also an excellent start-up manager. Like other startup managers, it lets you create sets (combinations of fonts, extensions, and control panels that load when you press particular keys during startup) and links (startup files that must or shouldn't run together or that need to load in a particular order). Unlike the others, however, Conflict Catcher recognizes aliases of extensions, control panels, and fonts—a feature RAM-disk users will love. Conflict Catcher's ability to enable and disable files in your Startup Items and Fonts folders is also unique.—Bob LeVitus

Conflict Catcher 2.0.1
Casady & Greene, Inc.
Salinas, CA
(800) 359-4920; (408) 484-9228
$79.95

TASK-AUTOMATION UTILITY JUST KEEPS GETTING EASIER

QuicKeys 3.0

Few programs have done as much to make Macintosh users' lives easier as CE Software's QuicKeys, now faster and easier to learn in version 3.0. QuicKeys automates repetitive tasks on your Mac, letting you execute almost any task or sequence of tasks with a single key-

board shortcut. If you perform an operation more than once a day, it's a good candidate for a QuicKeys shortcut.

QuicKeys is based on the concept of shortcuts. A shortcut consists of a task or series of tasks and a trigger that executes the task sequence. Usually triggered by a keystroke, QuicKeys shortcuts can also be triggered from a menu, a pop-up palette, a quick-reference window, or a timer. A shortcut can also be saved as a QK Icon, a self-contained program you trigger by double-clicking. If you have one of the new av Macs, you can use Apple's PlainTalk speech recognition to trigger a shortcut with your voice.

You can create a shortcut either by definition or by

their camcorders for photography, and fewer still can afford the $10,000 DCS camera, we will start to see other alternatives emerging. Canon, Yashica, and others have nifty digital cameras that store images on little

example. To create a shortcut by definition, you choose a shortcut category from the Define menu and then use a dialog box to specify shortcut options and assign a trigger. Creating a shortcut by example is even easier—just turn on QuicKeys' built-in sequence recorder and perform a task or series of tasks. The recorder doesn't always interpret your actions exactly as you intend it to—for example, it might interpret your pause as a timed wait or a conditional wait. However, you can fine-tune your shortcut with the easy-to-use sequence editor after you've recorded it.

Another powerful feature is QuicKeys's seamless integration with System 7 (required for this version). You can easily set up shortcuts involving Chooser and control-panel actions—for example, a shortcut that selects a printer without your having to open the Chooser.

QuicKeys may be the most useful third-party utility ever made. If you've never used it, you owe it to yourself to check out its time-saving wonders; if you're already a

QuicKeys user, you'll find version 3.0 is well worth the upgrade cost.—Bob LeVitus

QuicKeys 3.0
CE Software
West Des
Moines, IA
(515) 221-1801
$169; upgrade, $49.95

At Ease

Apple's customizable interface At Ease makes the Mac even easier to use than it already is. If you share your computer with others, think about getting this software. It'll save a lot of worry about important files or applications being deleted by other people. You select the applications and files you want accessible, and they appear on the At Ease desktop.

At Ease
Apple Computer; version 2.0
$79

eDisk and Stacker for Macintosh

Two new driver-level compression utilities aim to double the size of your hard disk automatically. Stacker for Macintosh, from the veteran PC-compression-software company Stac Electronics, and eDisk, from Alysis Software, each offer a more feature-rich route to expand-

ed disk space than the first driver-level compressor for the Mac, Golden Triangle's TimesTwo. Of the three, Stacker gains the edge with its simplicity and ease of use.

Unlike TimesTwo—a stand-alone disk formatter that installs its own custom driver on your hard disk— eDisk and Stacker each patch your existing disk's driver with compression routines. That means if your existing driver features partitioning and universal support for a full range of media, you'll get the same functionality with your expanded disk (one exception is driver-level password security).

If you have a temporary need for more disk space or if you simply can't afford a higher-capacity hard drive, a driver-level compression utility is a worthy solution. However, none of the three packages currently available—eDisk, Stacker for Macintosh, and TimesTwo— is completely flawless. Hard-drive speed is somewhat compromised, and there's a slight risk of losing low-level data that may be crucial to some disk-recovery operations.

Of the three products, Stacker wins for the present. It's quick and simple. With a

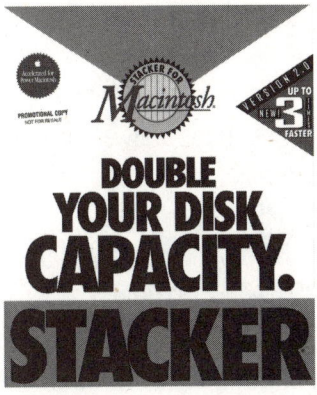

couple of interface improvements and a less cumbersome installation process, eDisk could be in the same class. And for those who consider the highest compression ratio to be their most important criterion, eDisk has the advantage.—Andy Ihnatko

eDisk
Alysis Software Corp.
1231 31st Ave.
San Francisco, CA 94122
(415) 566-2263
$149.95.

Stacker for Macintosh 1.0
Stac
5993 Avenida Encinas
Carlsbad, CA 92008
(619) 431-7474
$149

CLImate

If the Mac's friendly desktop can't keep you from sometimes longing for the efficiency of a CLI (command-line interface) such as that of DOS or UNIX, Orchard Software's CLImate might be just the utility for you. Then again, it might not. Although CLImate offers a CLI and a scripting

language, there are many things it can't do or doesn't do well.

CLImate provides a CLI that works alongside the Finder's graphical user interface. You use an English-like language to list directories, copy and delete files, run applications, format floppy disks, and so on. In addition to a basic set of commands that parallel Finder operations, CLImate includes a scripting language that's a subset of the venerable programming language BASIC. CLImate's BASIC dialect supports moderately advanced features such as loops, conditionals, and subroutines, but it requires line numbers—a clunky approach.

CLImate can be useful if you want a CLI to facilitate or automate simple file-manipulation tasks such as copying groups of files. For more-complex system scripting, though, you'll have more success with Frontier or AppleScript.—Jeffrey Sullivan

CLImate
Orchard Software, Inc.
P.O. Box 380814
Cambridge, MA 02238
(617) 876-4608
$59.95

Endangered Software

you've probably never heard of endangered software. Wildlife and the environment, yes, but software? Nonetheless, thousands of software systems and programs have been lost forever, and thousands more are threatened with extinction every time we upgrade our systems or when an entire computer architecture becomes obsolete. The disappearances of some of them are scarcely noticed because they never became popular enough to affect a large number of users, but others constitute a major loss of sorts.

It's important to preserve software developed for older or obsolete systems, since it's essentially a record of computing history. Studying the programs of the past will help us develop the software of the future. The philosopher George Santayana once said, "Those who cannot remember the past are condemned to repeat it." The software created for today's computers are memory hogs; they include all kinds of bells and whistles that boost the required disk and RAM space to multiple megabytes.

For instance, I recently loaded WordPerfect for Windows 6.0. It took 16MB of hard disk space for the complete program. WordPerfect used to be a word processor that ran on IBM PCs with a maximum of two 360K floppies and 640K of RAM. I wrote books and articles in WordStar on a CP/M machine that had 64K of RAM and two 180K floppies. I also built fairly complex spreadsheets in VisiCalc on an Apple II with 48K of RAM and two floppies.

To make this possible, the programmers who created applications wrote in assembly language, and they were clever in coding their programs. This kind of knowledge is almost a lost art now, but it's again becoming necessary. People who program PCMCIA cards are working with a small amount of ROM (Read-Only Memory) and, like the old-time programmers, they must be clever and learn to make every byte count.

Texas Instruments and Apple

Software becomes endangered when the computers it runs on go out of production and the owners move to more modern machines. When this happens, the user groups, online libraries, and collectors of public-domain and user-supported software become the suppliers to the remaining community of users. The software, though now endangered, continues to live as long as there are machines to run it. Several systems have lingered for years because of the persistence of some hobbyists. Typical of this is the Texas Instruments 99/4A, which has been out of production for over 10 years, but still has many devoted users.

Introduced in 1977, the Apple II was often called the Volkswagen of computers. It has now passed out of production, even though millions of Apple II computers are still operating and are supported by one of the largest collections of software in history. Despite this, it's only a matter of time before the Apple II and its related software fade into oblivion. The ill-fated Apple III is already far down that road with its never-popular SOS operating system. Even the older 68000-based Macs are becoming rarer, and with each passing update to the Mac system, more software becomes obsolete and disappears.

Tyrannosaurus Tandy and Antiquated Atari

The TRS-80 machines from Tandy/Radio Shack also were introduced in 1977 and became another popular family of 8-bit computers. Nicknamed Trash-80 by some of its detractors, this family might be called the Model-T of computers. Starting with the Z-80-based Model 1, Level 1, 4K RAM, cassette-operated machine and ending in 1990 with the Z-80A-based, 128K RAM, double-density disk-operated Model 4, the TRS-80 computers brought more people into computing than any other machine. It has a library of software as large as the Apple II, but as its models advanced, some of the older software became obsolete and unusable. For most of the life of the TRS-80, Tandy deliberately made its TRSDOS operating system incompatible with the CP/M OS most used with 8080 and Z80 computers, thus cutting it off from the mainstream of software development.

However, the TRS-80 was sold in such quantities that it engendered a huge library of applications, yet these would run only on this machine. When the TRS-80 Model III passed on, Tandy finally gave up its path of incompatibility and adopted CP/M as one of the available operating systems for the TRS-80 Model IV. However, by this time, the IBM PC had appeared upon the scene, and although the TRS-80 continued to be sold, mostly as replacements for school systems, Tandy soon moved to MS-DOS systems.

The Tandy Color Computer (commonly called the CoCo) was a 6809-based home computer that lasted through several models. Popular with hobbyists, the Color Computer used an operating system called OS/9 and accumulated a large collection of software. Today, this software is supported by user groups, but is fast disappearing as users move to MS-DOS systems.

The Atari 8-bit machines used a unique software system that ran excellent graphics for its time. These machines have just about disappeared from the scene, and only a handful of hobbyists continue to run the software. It will shortly disappear, as the last of the 8-bit computers go out of service. The successor to this 8-bit family was the Atari ST line; with its TOS operating system, this generation was designed to rival the Macintosh environment at a much lower price.

The system gained much favor for a while, but Atari never really supported it in the United States. Although it still has a dedicated group of supporters in the U.S., it has mainly been sold outside the country. Yet with the worldwide spread of low-cost MS-DOS computers, the Atari ST and its software definitely are high on the endangered list.

Cold Commodore

Commodore has probably built and sold more computers than any other company. Its original PET and CBM computers were very popular in homes, schools, and small businesses. They used a unique operating system that was built into the disk subsystem and was incompatible with all other machines, including those later built by Commodore. This family of software was one of the first to disappear because there are almost no operating computers that can run it.

The computers we now identify with Commodore are the C-64 and C-128. These were sold by the millions and have a vast library of software. Although they are on the endangered list in this country, developers outside the U.S. are still writing software for them, and many user groups here continue to support them. These systems will be around for a few more years, yet most of the hobbyists are moving over to the MS-DOS or Macintosh platforms.

The Commodore Amiga computers have carved a niche in the video and graphics industry and will still occupy this position for a year or so. The advent of advanced MS-DOS and Macintosh computers with fast CPUs and extended memory may ultimately endanger the Amiga as well.

Old-Time CPM

The largest body of endangered software is the vast collection of CP/M software. It began in, again, 1977 with the first disk-based Imsai and Altair systems. The very first microcomputers used paper-tape data storage, then audio-cassette-based software. This category must be considered completely dead—there simply are no machines left to run it on. I have in my collection a paper tape of the first Altair BASIC by Microsoft. However, all I can do is look at it. To run it, I would need an ASR-33 Teletype hooked up to an Altair 8800.

The first disk systems were 8-inch, single-sided 120K floppies. They ran CP/M, and the first commercial microcomputer applications were written for them. Today, though, almost none of these single-density floppies exist. The 8-inch floppy-disk systems were very expensive, and few hobbyists could afford them.

The 5.25-inch mini-floppies began to appear in 1977, but they couldn't run CP/M, and their 80K capacity was hardly sufficient for anything but a mini-operating system. Each of the major manufacturers—Percon, North Star, and Micropolis—had its own operating system and version of BASIC. A lot of software was written for these systems, but all of it can be considered lost. As the technology advanced, the mini-floppies evolved to support double-sided, double-density data storage.

Finally, Larry Alcoff developed CP/M for North Star 5.25-inch disks; this was soon followed by an explosion of CP/M software. However, one problem would still exist if we tried to run this software today. The original and still-used IBM disk format (called soft-sectored) has one index hole in the disk, but most of the mini-floppy manufacturers did not use this scheme in order to avoid paying royalties to IBM. They used an index hole for each sector, a scheme called hard-sectored. North Star disks had ten holes and Micropolis disks had 16. When Steve Wozniak designed the Apple II Disk System, he used an index system that was based completely upon software control. That's why the Apple II disk drives can use any type of disk and format it correctly.

Other large software families on the endangered list or already extinct include software by or for Ohio Scientific's OS65U; the Digital Group; Processor Technology's PTDOS; and Southwest Technical Products' FLEX. Early versions of MS-DOS and non-IBM-compatible MS-DOS are also nearly extinct.

As we advance and develop new operating systems, much of the software we use today will become endangered. If we do not wish it to become extinct because machines to run it on no longer exist, someone must establish a software library equipped with the required computers. In fact, it is still not too late to recover much of the lost software of the past. If you know of a person or organization that is addressing this need, please write to me, c/o *Computer Shopper*, Editorial Dept., One Park Ave., 11th Fl., New York, NY 10016.—Stan Veit ■

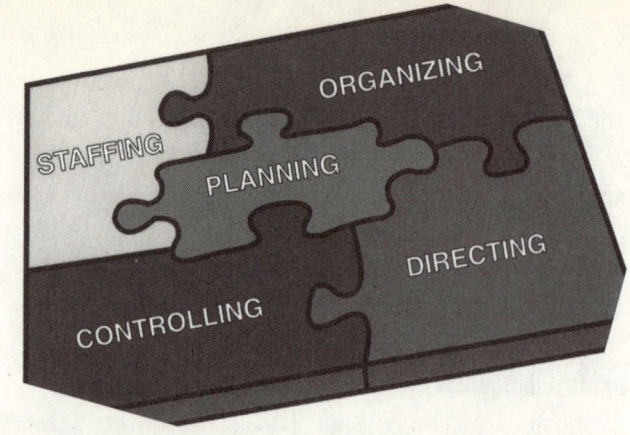

BUSINESS

Employee Appraiser

Austin-Hayne's Employee Appraiser writes first-rate reviews and offers the most control over the tone and language a reviewer uses. Unlike other products, which use numerical ratings systems, Employee Appraiser uses language only.

To create reviews, you choose the appropriate review topics for the employee (such as leadership or communication) and select performance levels from a list under each topic. Under "leadership," for example, the choices may range from "establishes a clear focus and direction" on the high side, to "establishes unclear focus" on the low. In between are three steps: "usually" and "sometimes develops clear focus," and "develops unclear focus." Select the appropriate performance level, and Employee Appraiser suggests applicable paragraphs.

The writing tuner, a computerized attitude adjuster, lets you fine-tune the text's tone by clicking on positive and negative arrows that make the text more affirmative or pessimistic. This works, but the resulting changes are virtually imperceptible to all but the most sensitive wordsmiths.

Traditionally, reviews provide summaries, and that's where Employee Appraiser falls short. While other programs provide summary suggestions, Employee Appraiser asks you to search the document and copy statements. You essentially write summaries yourself, with little help from the program.

In all, Employee Appraiser does the job. Its nonratings approach will make it stronger for some users, but less intuitive and slower for others.—Wayne Kawamoto

Employee Appraiser 2.0
Austin-Hayne Corp.
3 Lagoon Dr.
Suite 340
Redwood City, CA 94065
(415) 610-6800
$129

One Click Manager 1.0

Austinsoft's One Click Manager offers a wide array of modules, including a review writer. This all-for-one approach provides useful, but limited, capability in all areas of business planning. However, the review module falls far short of the other programs we have seen.

The review module lets you rate an employee's strengths, accomplishments, and problem areas on a scale of 1 through 5 (5 being best) on a customizable list of topics. Simply check off ratings in each category and then write the review in each program section. One Click Manager doesn't suggest text as the others do—it only provides a place to organize the review and rate employees. The writing, language, and tone are all up to you. Of course, this isn't necessarily a drawback, especially for managers who have good writing skills. But in comparison to the suggested text included in other packages, the program comes up short here.

An ambitious package, One Click Manager covers lots of topics. The planning module lets you work budgets and sales plans and perform break-even analysis. For strategic planning, another module records customer requirements and records your marketing plans to sell more. An organizing/managing module tracks contacts, along with their responsibilities and deadlines.

One Click Manager strives to be everything to every manager. It is useful, but only offers the basic structure to organize your information and comes with little expertise. As an organizer, it succeeds as a database for storing management-related information. However, as an employee reviewer, it's not quite in the same league as others.—Wayne Kawamoto

One Click Manager 1.0
Austinsoft Corp.
9600 Great Hills Trail
Suite 150-W
Austin, TX 78759
(800) 501-1333; (512) 502-1333
Fax: (512) 502-1233
$69

Performance Now for Windows 1.0

KnowledgePoint's Performance Now is a strong product that offers a straightforward, step-by-step ratings process to build employee reviews. To write reviews, you enter the employee information, select the appropriate performance factors (such as teamwork or initiative), and, in each category, rate the employee on a scale of 1 through 5 (5 being best). For example, under "initiative," topics include aspects like "volunteers readily" and "seeks increased responsibilities."

Based on your ratings, Performance Now generates text, calculates the average rating, and suggests possible summaries and plans for improvement—the only program to offer such plans. You also can edit the text with the limited built-in word processor. Like the others, Performance Now scans the review for inappropriate language. If you like, you can use one of the program's five templates: management, clerical, production, sales/service positions, or general reviews. A form designer lets you easily create custom templates.

The well-written manual provides a discussion of performance reviews, along with how-to steps. The intuitive interface displays all program functions on a handy toolbar. To start, an excellent tutorial takes you through the program's features, and helpful online information and advice is a button press away.

Performance Now for Windows is an excellent choice to do the job. Using numerical ratings is easier than selecting text, and it's one of the few packages that offers a framework to create summaries and plans for improvement—a real plus.— Wayne Kawamoto

Performance Now for
Windows 1.0
KnowledgePoint
1129 Industrial Ave.
Petaluma, CA 94952-1141
(707) 762-0333;
Fax: (707) 762-0802
$129

wants to watch their pictures on TV? People like putting photos in albums. A cheap color printer for digital photographs should be the next step in this evolution. ▢ Of course that leaves Kodak out in the cold, doesn't it?

Avantos Review Writer 1.0

Offering an easy, straightforward method, Avantos Review Writer leads you, step-by-step, through review writing. Its comprehensive approach evaluates employee goals as well as performance factors. Review Writer uses a rating system and adds an excellent multiple-choice approach to generate review text.

Review Writer's helpful QuickBuild mode directs you through the evaluation process from start to finish. Under each topic presented, you use a five-point scale to agree or disagree with statements. For example, under "planning," there are statements like "plans and develops effective strategies" and "effectively documents progress of plans and strategies." With each statement, you decide whether you agree or disagree using the five-point scale. If you want more flexibility with less hand-holding, you can use the program's Document Mode, which gives you more control over the process with a minimum of prompting.

If you like, you can adjust the ratings scale, or work from one of 15 predefined templates for salespeople, project leaders, department managers, and other positions. You also can create your own. In addition, the program can weight certain factors to set performance priorities.

After writing the review, you can edit the document, and then the program checks for spelling and inappropriate use of language, and looks to see that all areas of the review are complete. Review Writer also helps to write the summary, but other programs do a much better job.

The interface is excellent, with tabbed cards and clear step-by-step-instructions. Review Writer can import employee information, goals, and performance from Avantos' sister program, ManagePro. Even if you don't use ManagePro, Review Writer can track employee events through the year. Although the edge is slight, Avantos Review Writer offers the easiest and most straightforward way to create reviews.—Wayne Kawamoto

Avantos Review Writer 1.0
Avantos Performance Systems Inc.
5900 Hollis St.
Emeryville, CA 94608
(800) 282-6867; (510) 654-4600
$129

AVANTOS
REVIEW Writer™
* Writes custom text for you
* Evaluates factors and goals
* Helps avoid costly legal problems
* Leads you from start to finish

Write High Quality Reviews. Fast! Easy! Done!

FIRST STEP FOR START-UPS
Business Plan Pro

Business-plan software is a potentially good source for management advice and guidance when one is running or starting a business, but efforts so far have been disappointing. Palo Alto Software takes a step forward with its all-in-one Business Plan Pro, which walks you through the process of designing a credible and workable business plan. Its integration, flexibility, and navigational ease set new standards for this genre.

A realistic business plan requires numerous pages of text outlining such details as your firm's services or products, market and competition analysis, and sales strategies. A good plan must also incorporate financial statements and projections. Business Plan Pro covers these bases well. Its outline format walks you through what's needed at each step and comes with five pre-set business types built in: service, retail, distribution, manufacture, and a combination of the above. There's also a home-office option. Each business type has a different sequence of statements and questions designed to stimulate your thinking and help you focus your plan. We were pleased to discover we could toggle between an explanation and an example upon entering specific information about our company. Depending on your style, you can tackle the topics sequentially or jump around.

Three icons in the upper-right-hand corner let you toggle among text, chart, and table modes. Pull-down menus can also be used for navigation and must be used on some screens to grab charts. You can replace boilerplate data in table templates to reflect your company's own financial aspirations. These tables translate into colorful charts, which can be exported in .BMP and .WMF formats for the final report.

Because most business-plan programs lack smooth integration, printing a finished plan with tables and graphs automatically inserted in the right place can be difficult. We were impressed with Business Plan Pro's abilities to print text, numbers, and graphics in logical order. You can also print only selected elements.

The program's written documentation fleshes out the guidance offered on-line, but it would be nice to see more background information and advice that would make the program a general business resource. More page-formatting commands would be welcome as well, though the default printed output looks very professional.

Nevertheless, no business-plan software can match Business Plan Pro for its navigational ease, customizability, and superb integration.—Kathy Yakal

Business Plan Pro
Palo Alto Software
(800) 229-7526; (503) 683-6162
$149.95

CLARIS PUTS IT ALL TOGETHER
ClarisWorks 3.0 for Windows

Elements of integrated software should (as the name implies) work well together and form a program that is above all easy to use. Claris-Works 3.0 for Windows—which contains a word processor, a spreadsheet, a database, and an illustration program—meets these goals. And at $99, ClarisWorks is a bargain of a program that includes a lot for a little.

Most of the work that went into ClarisWorks 3.0 was aimed at making the whole greater than the sum of the individual parts. Many integrated programs use object linking and embedding (OLE) to bring disparate parts of the package into a cohesive whole—so that a portion of a spreadsheet or graphics image can liven up a document. The downside is the increased memory requirements and slow response that OLE brings to the party.

Claris forged its own path with a proprietary—and much simpler—integration method. With ClarisWorks, you can add text, a spreadsheet, or a drawing to a document by clicking on an icon for that type of object and then drawing a frame that defines the added element's size and shape directly in your document. When you select the frame, the menus and toolbars change to reflect the contents of the frame.

The result is a more straightforward approach to integration than OLE 2.0's edit-in-place capabilities. But you can't create a "live" link between a spreadsheet and a word processing document that automatically updates the document when you alter the spreadsheet's contents. The ClarisWorks way is to create a series of linked frames throughout the document. For example, we created one frame in our test sales report document showing budget projections for each quarter of the year and added a linked frame later in the document showing only the budget totals. When we changed a quarterly figure, the total was updated.

In the word processing module, a notable addition is the ability to wrap text around frames. All you have to do is select a frame and choose how the text would wrap from the dialog box. After that, you can move the frame anywhere in the document and text continues to wrap around it.

The word processor's new outliner is helpful for organizing your thoughts. Unfortunately, it was our experience that using the outliner was clumsy for creating a consistently formatted structure of headings and subheadings. Though you can create custom text attributes for each level of outline headings, those attributes disappear when you return to normal word processing mode to flesh the document out. To create an outline with, say, an underlined and boldfaced top-level heading, you must create a separate text style in normal word processing mode and apply it manually to each top-level outline heading.

The spreadsheet module is reasonably powerful (it supports about 100 functions), but the charting capabilities offer just 12 styles and only limited control over the final product. By contrast, we found the database to be a powerful tool that was relatively easy to use. It includes a dialog box that walked us through the process of creating queries—including queries based on spreadsheet functions and automatic field validation.

At the other extreme, the mail merge capabilities in ClarisWorks are simple to use but not very powerful. Merge fields can be added to a word processing document from a simple dialog box, but you can't select database records to include in the merge from that dialog box. Rather, you must sort the database before the merge—an awkward process that puts the cart before the horse. The resulting merge file can't be saved as a new document.

The ClarisWorks illustration modules are composed of drawing and painting programs and now include a palette from which you can select color or black-and-white gradient fills. ClarisWorks' greatest strength in this area is a wide variety of drawing tools for such tasks as creating complex polygons and Bézier curves.

Impressively, it also allows you to select a portion of a raster image and, by dragging handles, apply effects like perspective distortion.

ClarisWorks goes further than the competition by allowing you to create on-screen slide shows composed of any combination of document pages. Though you can't add flourishes like background sound or transitions, ClarisWorks's slide shows will be all you need to create basic presentations.

Besides adding power, Claris made this program simpler to use by incorporating Assistants that, like Microsoft's Wizards, walk you through basic tasks. The Assistants work well, but Claris only includes seven of them. Missing are Assistants for such elementary tasks as creating labels and database queries.

Paradoxically, ClarisWorks is now both easier to use and more powerful—but it will likely appeal to a more sophisticated user.—David Haskin

ClarisWorks 3.0 for Windows
Claris Corp.
Santa Clara, CA
(800) 325-2747; (408) 987-8227
$99

How to Really Start Your Own Business

Starting your own business can be one of the most exciting experiences of your life. It

Telecommuting Takes Hold

isasters both natural (California earthquakes) and man-made (corporate downsizing) are helping to speed the acceptance of telecommuting. Link Resources, a market-research firm, estimates that in two years, over 2.5 million employees will be working at least part-time at home.

IBM, for example, recently set up a work-at-home program for 175 Milwaukee-based sales, marketing, and tech-support employees, each of whom got a ThinkPad notebook for communicating with the office. Three-fifths of the IBM personnel in six Indiana cities who began telecommuting late last year claim their productivity has improved as a result.

Several other firms including Hewlett-Packard and 3Com Corp. are part of a telecommuting pilot project called Smart Valley. Participants recently issued guidelines to help businesses determine which employees are best suited to telecommuting. The obvious answer: Well-motivated self-starters with home workspaces conducive to concentration.—Anthony Strattner ■

can also be one of the most terrifying. No matter how much you may know about balancing profits and losses, you're bound to have nagging doubts and questions. *Inc.* magazine's How to Really Start Your Own Business tackles these tough questions.

This interactive CD-ROM, which is adapted from an *Inc.* book and video series, offers business advice from nine people who started small and hit it big. Among the mentors who share their theories and experiences are David Liederman of David's Cookies, Gordon Segal of Crate & Barrel, and Mo Siegel of Celestial Seasonings.

What sets this multimedia learning tool apart from most how-to guides is the way it tailors the presentation of its information to the user's needs. When you launch the program, you're asked a few brief questions about what you hope your business will accomplish five years from now. Your answers will determine which Mentor Panel of three online entrepreneurs can best help you achieve your goals. These mentors share their theories and experiences through brief video clips.

The program's 11 chapters cover everything you need to know, from developing an initial idea, to structuring your business, to managing your cash flow. For those who don't want to learn chapter by chapter, there's an Info Map that shows the entire branching structure of the program. Here, impatient entrepreneurs can pick and choose the topics they're interested in. Those who need more detailed information about a subject can turn to the Resource Guide, which provides valuable contact information.

How to Really Start Your Own Business presents a wealth of useful information in an attractive, concise, and easy-to-understand manner. It can't guarantee that your business will be as profitable as those highlighted on the

disk, but it can ensure that you get off on the right foot.—Gayle C. Ehrenman

How to Really Start Your Own Business
Zelos Digital Learning
San Francisco, CA
(800) 345-6777; (415) 788-0566
$49.95

A SOLID FRAMEWORK FOR BUSINESS
BizPlanBuilder 5.0

Expertly designed sample templates let you use your own word processor and spreadsheet to build a business plan. Creating a credible business plan that you can take to your bank's loan officer or show to potential investors requires two distinct sets of tools: state-of-the-art word processing and spreadsheet software, and an expertly designed framework that advises you on the text and financials required. No software package wraps that all up neatly and thoroughly in one stand-alone product, but Jian offers a logical, usable alternative.

BizPlanBuilder 5.0 consists of two sets of templates—one for your current word processor and another for your spreadsheet—that guide you through the process of designing, formatting, and printing a business plan. BizPlanBuilder's meticulous outline is one of the best available, and its use of your own familiar word processor and spreadsheet minimizes your learning time. If you're already using state-of-the-art

Windows applications for text and financials, your finished business plan can embody the best of both worlds: content backed by expert tutelage, combined with the most professional-looking output laser printers can offer.

BizPlanBuilder's templates can be dropped into all major DOS, Windows, and Mac word processors and spreadsheets. When you install, you select your preference from the list provided. BizPlanBuilder adds a directory to each of your applications and adds all its files to those directories.

The text portion of your business plan is divided into six separate topics with numerous subtopics. In the Vision and Mission section, you lay out your present situation, express vision and mission statements, and outline strategic goals. Next, your Company Overview explores specifics related to your management team and contains a legal business description. Product Strategy discusses your proposed products, and research and development efforts. Important external factors like market definition, competition, potential-customer profiles, and risk factors are reviewed in the Market Analysis section. And your Marketing Plan deals with your blueprint for sales, distribution, advertising, promotion, and publicity. Finally, the Executive Summary always appears first in a business plan, though it's often written after the rest of the plan is mapped out.

The outlines for each chapter consist primarily of three types of guidance: questions, lists of issues to consider, and boilerplate text that serves as a model for paragraphs you might write. These can be modified or completely rewritten, since the templates are simply word processing documents. You probably won't deal with absolutely every element of every template or even with every template, necessarily, so you'll have to go in and clean up all the text you haven't used as you're finishing each section. This is an inconvenience at best, and a real pain at worst, depending on how much tweaking you've done.

If you've created business plans before, or at least know what's important to include, you may be able to work only with the online sample text. If not, you'll find BizPlanBuilder's written documentation helpful. You're directed at the top of each sample template to read a portion of the manual before starting in, to understand why that particular element is important, and get some guidance on how you might make each section as concise and compelling as possible.

Three additional templates are available for use in your completed business plan: a sample title page, cover letter, and nondisclosure agreement. If you're comfortable using your word processor's charting capabilities, you may find it helpful to drop a few charts here and there throughout your documents.

The second element of your business plan, specific financial information and projections, is completed in much the same way, though with less onscreen guidance. Twelve sample templates are included, with figures from a sample plan filled in as a model. In some worksheets, you'll get online directions, but it's highly advisable to read the manual's informative text before you get started here.

There are two options for preparing financials. You can enter data in each of the 11 basic worksheets, standard files like Balance Sheet, Break-Even Analysis, Gross Profit Analysis, and Income and Cash Flow Statements. Or you can use BizPlanBuilder's single Integrated Financials spreadsheet, which requires less data entry and less accounting knowledge, and integrates all your numbers to reduce the chance of making transposition errors when you have to carry figures over from one spreadsheet to another manually. Not all spreadsheet processors are capable of handling the complex formulas and large data files required by the Integrated Financials format, so check with Jian before buying if you know you'd prefer this option.

Once you've combed all your text files and worksheets to make sure you've covered all the bases and deleted unnecessary boilerplate information, you simply print the completed files in the order you want them to appear.

Version 5.0 of BizPlanBuilder includes several enhancements over the previous version. Installation has been streamlined, and a new Getting Started Guide offers specific startup instructions for individual applications. The User Guide offers more thorough explanations and examples, and a Personal Financial Statement has been added to the list of spreadsheet templates. Existing spreadsheets offer more flexible calculating capabilities.

The ideal business-plan program would guide you through the process of creating a business plan similar to the way today's best income tax preparation programs walk you through your 1040 and its supporting forms, spitting out a perfectly formatted set of documents.

Competing business-plan programs attempt that by offering an online navigator, but some of those lack BizPlanBuilder's depth, and others, its potential for easy, polished final output. If you don't mind foregoing the cohesiveness of a stand-alone product, BizPlanBuilder's strategy of using the best tools for the job—backed up by sound expert advice—may be just right for you.—Kathy Yakal

BizPlanBuilder 5.0
Jian
1975 W. El Camino Real
Mountain View, CA 94040-2218
(800) 346-5426; (415) 254-5600
$129

QUICKXPENSE DOES THE EXPENSE ACCOUNT DIRTY WORK

QuickXpense

Portable Software's QuickXpense is a one-trick pony: All it does is automate the preparation of expense reports. Yet it does this onerous task so well, it should appeal to anyone who travels for a living. The $99.95 program handles an impressive variety of expense recording and reporting needs, and hides its complexity behind one of the best user interfaces around.

QuickXpense offers a choice of 15 expense report forms, including standard weekly, biweekly, semimonthly, and monthly forms, as well as those tailored for the needs of consultants, lawyers, realtors, and salespeople. In addition, for $49.95, Portable Software will create an electronic version of your company's form for use with QuickXpense (Fortune 1000 companies can get their custom forms created for free).

QuickXpense works well on the road because entering data is easy. Like Microsoft Money and Quicken, QuickXpense anticipates your data entry needs. Out of the box it knows the names of the principal car rental firms and hotel chains—so with a click of a mouse button, you can pick Hertz or Hilton from a drop-down list. When you enter a new name, QuickXpense adds it as a menu pick. We found that as we used the program, it learned our favorite watering holes.

The program handles such details as cash advances, company cars, and company credit cards. QuickXpense can also generate detailed breakdowns of meetings and events, listing attendees, the purpose of the meeting, and so on. Expense reports that include currency conversions detail the reimbursable amounts in the home currency, but also generate an itemized listing of your foreign-currency transactions. There's even a reminder that appears around the time you should expect a reimbursement check. All expense reports are stored in a database, and the program provides reporting tools for analyzing spending patterns.

If you use ACT! or WinFax PRO, QuickXPense can read your contact lists. You can also create links to files in .DBF databases or delimited formats. All in all, this is one smart and useful piece of software.—Craig Stinson

QuickXpense
Portable Software Corp
Bellevue, WA
(800) 626-8620; (206) 637-8808
$99.95

WHICH & WHY ASKS ALL THE RIGHT QUESTIONS

Which & Why for Windows

Which & Why for Windows is a decision-support package that helps you compare alternatives, quantify decisions, and back up conclusions. The software analyzes both hard and soft data, which you input and organize into groups containing similar factors. Which & Why evaluates the decision model you have constructed and recommends the alternative that addresses your specific needs most closely. If cost is at stake, for example, Which & Why determines the price discount that must be applied to make all options equally attractive. The product contains over 100 decision models, including car selection and personnel hiring.—Asa Somers

Which & Why for Windows
Arlington Software Corp.
Baie D'Urfe
Quebec, Canada
(613) 746-1140
$349

YOUR PC CAN HELP MARKET YOUR PRODUCT

Plan Write for Marketing.

Business Resource Software has announced Plan Write for Marketing, a new product that includes all the tools necessary to generate a comprehensive marketing plan. The program presents you with a step-by-step outline that leads you through the planning process, taking into consideration such issues as market segmentation, evaluation of the competition, sales and distribution plans, and financial projections. Plan Write includes a glossary of marketing terms, its own word processor and integrated spreadsheet, and a chart generator that uses supplied data to create any of 14 different chart types.—Asa Somers

Plan Write for Marketing
Business Resource Software Inc.
Austin, TX
(800) 423-1228; (512) 251-7541
$129.95

GO WITH THE FLOW
CorelFlow 2.0

CorelFlow 2.0 gives you the benefits of a rich feature set and ease of use. This CD-ROM-based package includes gads of tools and image libraries, with more than 2,000 predesigned shapes, photos, and clip-art images, and more than 100 TrueType fonts.

To help you get started quickly and easily, CorelFlow displays ten types of sample diagrams. Each of these diagrams is linked to the appropriate Smart Library, which saves you from having to navigate through menus for the right objects. For example, if you're working on a network diagram, CorelFlow opens four LAN Smart Libraries with network-oriented objects and symbols.

All Smart Libraries roll up into one-line floating toolbars, and they're fully configurable, just like the program's other toolbars and palettes. You can also make your own objects and add them to the Smart Library of your choice. For only $99, you'll be hard-pressed to find a more feature-rich package. For a wealth of images and powerful features, go for CorelFlow 2.0.—James Oliver Cury

CorelFlow 2.0
Corel Corp.
(800) 836-3729; (613) 728-8200
$99

LEARNING YOUR ABCS
ABC SnapGraphics 2.0

ABC SnapGraphics 2.0 is great for the notoriously impatient nonartist. It's designed to be fast and easy with few extraneous frills. Getting started is a one-minute process: Choose a chart template from the Template Gallery and away you go.

As with CorelFlow, once you open a new template, corresponding palettes appear as floating toolbars. In addition, SnapGraphics automatically opens Quick Tips, which will hold your hand through the diagramming process. Other useful features in SnapGraphics include SnapShapes, SnapSteps, SnapText, and SnapLines—each of which makes using SnapGraphics, well, a snap. Objects and shapes can be edited, added, or deleted quickly. The program even includes presentation features such as a slide show, chart sorter, and drawing tools.

It's hard to find feature-packed applications like these at such low prices. Competitors start at $100 and work their way up to four digits—and they often don't include clip art, photos, or multiple fonts. For pure ease of use and speed, consider ABC SnapGraphics 2.0.—James Oliver Cury

ABC SnapGraphics 2.0
Micrografx Inc.
(800) 733-3729; (214) 234-1769

FINANCIAL FORECASTING FOR THE REST OF US
Forecast Pro for Windows

OK, so you made the mistake of mentioning that you once pulled a median on a spreadsheet range, and now everyone at the meeting has voted you Most Likely to Forecast First-Quarter Sales. The problem: How do you complete this assignment and still have a life? The solution: Forecast Pro for Windows.

Forecast Pro is much more than a spreadsheet. Its best feature is that you don't have to guess which of its forecasting models to use. A rules-based expert system takes care of that for you, and an excellent tutorial walks you through the brief, icon-driven process of building a forecast. And you can depend on the program's full index and glossary for definitions of all those two-dollar stat terms.

Forecast Pro and its bigger brother, Forecast Pro XE, include several variations on the most popular statistical forecast methodologies, including single- and multi-variable time series (stat-speak for examining, say, last year's electricity costs, usage, or both). You'll also find moving averages, dynamic regression for including multiple variables, Box-Jenkins for long data sets, and several methods of exponential

smoothing. Its modeling tools will satisfy the most persnickety stat freak, but the program is really meant for the average businessperson who just wants to do the job—and get to the gym early.

The functionally identical Forecast Pro XE adds a few higher-level models that adjust for things like special events in conjunction with seasonal changes in data. But either product will find patterns in historical data that suggest the way the numbers will fall in the future.

The toughest part of using Forecast Pro is making sure the format of your historical data is consistent before you import it (the program works with spreadsheets, databases, and ASCII text, as well as via DDE links). Once your data is imported, it takes just a few quick clicks to build a forecast. Your data is then represented by a nice trend line, and the forecast is a line heading off into the future.

Under the hood, Forecast Pro's expert system crunches your data 50 to 100 different ways to find the model that best fits. You can go with Forecast Pro's suggestion or you can override it in the event that you want to take another method for a walk and compare the results. For example, you might use moving averages to take a rolling 30- or 120-day slice of a stock price line in order to predict whether that line will go up or down over the next month. In addition to the quick way of comparing outcomes, Forecast Pro lets you withhold the most recent period of known results from the data set to check the accuracy of its prediction.

There are no dense data tables to pore over. Instead, use Peek and Poke to examine data points once they're graphed, to smooth lines by dragging points, and to have a Forecast Pro dialog box give you the date and value of a new point.

There are more elaborate (and more expensive) forecasting packages than Forecast Pro, and there are cheaper and less powerful alternatives. But for the occasional statistician, there's a 95 percent probability that Forecast Pro is your best choice.—Mike Hogan

Forecast Pro for Windows
Business Forecast Systems
(617) 484-5050
$595, $995 for Forecast Pro XE

Platform Choices

y wife—a Mac devotee—needs a new computer. During our discussion of what Mac might be best for her, I suggested she use a Windows machine. I've come to the conclusion that Windows has become an acceptable alternative, if only because Microsoft's Word for Windows is pretty much the same as Microsoft Word on the Mac. If you know how to use one, you can use the other, so why not use it on a Windows machine?

She then burst into a diatribe about how Windows is to a Mac what a transvestite is to a real woman. She uses this analogy whenever she can, to imply that Windows users are somehow easily fooled.

Maybe this was true years ago, but things have changed. Let's compare a Windows machine with a Mac and try to see what lies in the future.

Here's How the Mac Is Better

1. Robustness. The Mac crashes less than any Windows machine I've ever used. From my experience, I'd say that Windows crashes the whole system (requiring a reset of the machine) two to three times as often as the Mac does. Crashes really annoy people.
2. True drag and drop. To install a new feature in your Mac, you just drop an icon into a folder. With Windows, you run a complex install program that sometimes requires tweaking or editing of system files.
3. SCSI support. Apple's implementation of the SCSI interface is a dream come true for people who want to add peripherals to their machine. It's true plug and run.
4. Mouse feel. If you're going to use a mouse, don't you think the mouse should have a good feel to it? Apple has all sorts of amazing algorithms to make the mouse easy to use. With Windows, the mouse is jumpy and hard to control. Whatever algorithms Windows is using to control the arrow aren't doing the job.
5. Better-looking output. Fonts on the Mac have more hinting, and Mac documents look better, however subtly.

Now, all five of these reasons can be disputed. Many Windows users have few crash problems. The install programs are a pain, but how many do you have to run in a lifetime? SCSI support in Windows machines is improving. The mouse feel is a nonissue as long as the mouse actually works. Who cares if it's not perfect in Windows? Ever used a mouse with a Sun workstation? The better-looking output is especially debatable.

Okay, Does a Windows Machine Have Any Advantages?

1. Cheapness. It costs less to buy a Windows machine, MIPS for MIPS, but the machines are much shoddier than the Mac.
2. Newer software. Most development is being done for the Windows machines. This may be negated by some outstanding Mac-oriented software in the development labs. We'll see.
3. Greater variety of machines. Gee, people moaned and groaned when Apple broadened its line of computers. Now there aren't enough of them, if we are to believe this argument.
4. Cheaper, faster IDE hard drives. You can now get a 1.2-gigabyte hard drive with 8-millisecond access time for $850. Tough to argue against this factor.
5. Upgradability. Most of the newer Windows systems have provisions for newer chips and higher speeds. This means a machine can have a much longer useful life.

I make a list like this every few years to see which platform is gaining the advantage. As of today, I'd say it's a wash. The Mac still seems like the better machine overall, with clear advantages. But the other platform may be turning into the VHS of computers while the Mac becomes the Betamax.

let you plug into his BBS. I imagine that someone with addressable cameras located all over his house and reachable via a BBS would provide hours of entertainment for anyone who simply wants to watch how others live.

Remember how, during that battle between VCR standards, the defenders of Beta howled about superior quality? Today's Mac users make the same appeal, but the offices of America aren't flocking to the Mac in droves, are they? Only graphic artists and other sensitive people are addicted to the Mac. This artsy market, although large, won't stay viable if the same software packages can be shown to run on a PC under Windows. The word-processing and spreadsheet markets are what drive the business buyers.

Although the parallel between the Mac and Sony's Betamax is apt, it doesn't indicate a completely bleak future. Sony ended up producing VHS machines and made Hi-8 a fantastic alternative, especially for camcorders. And Sony took much of its Betamax technology and turned it into a broadcasting standard format called Betacam. If Apple follows the same path, the Mac will turn into a specialized, professional graphics workstation (a la Betacam) and Apple will roll out the PowerPC Mac (Hi-8) and sell a PC clone (VHS)! It's this last action that will forever gall the Mac diehards. —John C. Dvorak ■

DRAG, DRAW, AND YOU'RE DONE

FORECASTING YOUR BUSINESS'S FUTURE

Forecast Pro for Windows 2.0

Most of us are more likely to rely on hunches, intuition, and a horoscope than a statistical model for predicting a future event. Forecast Pro for Windows 2.0 from Business Forecast Systems (BFS) would like to change that. According to BFS, no background in statistics is necessary to use Forecast Pro. What you do need is the willingness to read the manual and go through the tutorial. To its credit, Forecast Pro has a well-written manual, interactive tutorial, extensive index, glossary, and on-screen help that explains every statistical buzzword you encounter and offers detailed procedural help. The product is sold in two configurations, Forecast Pro 2.0 and Forecast Pro Extended Edition (XE). Both are nearly identical in appearance and operation, but XE

includes additional forecasting tools.

The basic version of Forecast Pro offers four statistical methodologies. These include moving average, an ongoing average in which, for example, a 30-day moving average would add day 31 and drop day 1 as the days go by, and exponential smoothing with nine different models, which compares historical and forecast values with ongoing adjustments for forecasting errors. The other two are dynamic regression (generalized trends) with up to 50 independent variables, and Box-Jenkins, combining dynamic regression with moving average. The XE version adds detailed event models; multiple-level and cumulative forecasting; and Census X-11, which factors an additional time series into major components.

Both versions open on a blank screen called the "audit trail," which keeps a running on-screen explanatory log of the forecasting process and the logic Forecast Pro is using to make its suggestions. The

audit trail can be edited and saved to an ASCII file.

Making a forecast begins with data entry, giving Forecast Pro the real-world history of your situation, upon which it bases its prognostications. If, for instance, you want to get a forecast of your airline's ticket sales for each of the next 12 months, you need to tell Forecast Pro how many tickets you sold each month in the past, for as far back as possible. You must have at least 24 months of history, because there must be at least two historical variables for each month being projected. The more historical data you have, the more accurate your forecast.

Forecast Pro can import from WK1 and XLS formats, as well as MLT ASCII files, in which records are delineated by a semicolon, and fields by a space or carriage return. It also fully supports DDE. As with most import situations, the format of your data is critical. That's not particularly difficult, but you will probably have to adjust your spreadsheet format a bit before importing.

The Options icon opens a dialog box for selecting the file format when you're importing, or setting up a DDE. In the same box, you select the upper and lower confidence limits (defaults are 97.5 and 2.5) and the forecast horizon (the number of time periods) the forecast is to cover.

The File Tableau Current icon lets you select the file from which to import, or you can enter data directly, one item at a time. The Expert icon, a little brain in a box, then takes over, analyzes your data, and selects your forecast method: exponential smoothing, dynamic regression, or Box-Jenkins for Forecast Pro basic—another three options for XE. You can take the Expert's advice or use a method of your own choosing.

The Graph icon shows the entire time line for which you have input data values, followed by the time periods for which you requested a forecast. You can make changes to the historical data directly on the graph. For instance, if you know that the historic data (ticket sales) for March 1974 were mis-entered by a

keypunch operator, you can make the correction by clicking on the graph line over March 1974 and dragging to the appropriate point on the y-axis (number of seats sold).

If you're a statistician by trade, you should be impressed by the features of Forecast Pro. The multiple methodologies give you the versatility to handle many different types of forecasting situations. If you're a rank statistical greenhorn, you will spend some time wading through the unavoidable jargon, and may make a few calls to the patient tech-support people. But it will be worth it.—Steve Gilliland

Forecast Pro for Windows 2.0
Business Forecast Systems
68 Leonard St.
Belmont, MA 02178
(617) 484-5050
$595

THE EASIEST SPREADSHEET EVER?

Quattro Pro 6.0 for Windows

Any spreadsheet can crunch numbers. But making sure that your data looks good—without you having to spend hours tweaking colors and charts—well, that's a different story. Quattro Pro 6.0 for Windows makes you look good. And best of all, it's easier to use than ever. Version 6.0 is virtually oozing with improvements. And it's undergone radical menu surgery (part of a larger effort to streamline the applications in WordPerfect's PerfectOffice 3.0 suite): The new menus are better organized, and there are fewer toolbars to contend with.

Quattro Pro now has a draw layer on each worksheet, which makes it a breeze to add annotations and diagrams to your work. And you'll find a lot of other new knockout features in Quattro Pro: In-cell editing, word wrap within cells, vertical text alignment, and an improved method of generating range names are just some of the additions. And while all spreadsheets have some kind of automatic table formatting, Quattro Pro lets you create and save your own autoformat options.

Quattro Pro's consistent and intuitive interface makes learning the basics a snap. Beginners will find several new Coaches that offer helpful information, and advanced users will appreciate time-saving Experts like the Budget Expert, which helps you create an entire customized budget model complete with formulas and formatting.

Version 6.0 adds ease of use to the program's already powerful graphics capabilities. In-place graph editing means that you can just click on a graph to make all of the changes you want. You'll also find lots of enhancements to Quattro Pro's impressive presentation slide-show feature, as well as several attractive new charting aids.

The new Formula Composer makes building and debugging formulas a snap. It offers an easy-to-interpret expandable outline format and uses more or less plain English. It gives you quick access to Quattro Pro's nearly 400 @functions.

On a network? Quattro Pro lets you send and receive files and messages directly from your spreadsheet environment. It supports the usual VIM and MAPI or Groupwise e-mail standards, as well as Borland's OBEX (Object Exchange) workgroup technology that uses VIM, MAPI, or MCI mail as a transport for data to another OBEX-supported user. And Quattro Pro now supports OLE 2 as both a client and a server, making interapplication projects easier.

As good as this new version is, a few areas are still lagging. For example, both Excel and 1-2-3 for Windows provide better methods for manipulating worksheet databases, and Quattro Pro has no equivalent of Excel's built-in outlining and automatic subtotal feature.

With a list price of $395, Quattro Pro 6.0 is not the low-priced bargain of earlier versions. However, advanced users will find little lacking in terms of analytical power and development capabilities, and new users can get productive quickly.—John Walkenbach

Quattro Pro 6.0 for Windows
WordPerfect/Novell Applications Group
(800) 321-4566; (801) 225-5000
$395

CLICK, DRAG, DRAW, AND YOU'RE DONE

Visio 3.0

Graphically disinclined but need pictures to explain your point? Visio has been a salvation to many users since its first release, and the new Visio 3.0 is even better.

The basics of the program haven't changed much. It still comes with 22 stencils of commonly used business shapes, including flow charts, organization charts, and network diagrams. Simply drag shapes to the work area, and when you've put enough of them together, you have a business drawing.

Visio 3.0 further simplifies matters by automatically connecting shapes such as the boxes in organization charts: Click on a toolbar button, highlight a shape, drag another shape, and Visio connects them.

Besides being easier to use, Visio 3.0 feels more familiar. Its toolbar can be configured to mimic the look of either Microsoft Office or Lotus's SmartSuite. If you have one of those suites, Visio even installs its own button in your suite's toolbars to launch Visio's OLE 2.0 edit-in-place capabilities.

Visio 3.0 has more graphical power than any of its competitors, and its new suite-integration features make it a natural add-on for anyone who needs to illustrate a point.—David Haskin

Visio 3.0
Shapeware Corp.
(206) 521-4500
$199

SEIZING THE DAY, HOUR, AND MINUTE

Timeslips 5.1 for Windows

Whether you charge by the hour or by the project, you need an accurate and easy way to track time, record costs, and bill clients. Of course, you don't want this to cut into your billable hours. Timeslips, which includes multiple-project tracking for individual clients, is a smart solution for single users and small companies.

Timeslips features a variety of user-configurable reports (including billing, receiving, and payment reports) and can track separate projects for the same client. For first-time users, Timeslips's Navigator (a series of PERT charts) guides you through basic procedures. Using the Navigator is like having your own personal time tutor. Select a procedure from a row of icons—Bill Cycle, for example—and the Navigator switches you to the appropriate procedural chart. Click on the area you want to access—Aged A/R Balances under Transactions, for example—and the Client Reports dialog box pops up. The Navigator makes time accounting a breeze. Single users and small companies without separate "front" and "back" offices will find Timeslips' complete time tracking and billing indispensable.—Barry Brenesal; James Oliver Cury

Timeslips 5.1 for Windows
Timeslips Corp.
(800) 285-0999; (508) 768-6100
$299.95 for single station (up to 8 users), $79.95 upgrade
$599.95 for two-station network version (up to 250 users)

Carpe Diem

Carpe Diem is a groupware time solution that focuses on automation and ease of use. It can be customized to reflect specific corporate billing procedures, and is an excellent choice for large companies with extensive billing and time-management needs. If you need to track time among diverse networked users in a large corporation, this is your answer. You create the prototype, adhering to your company's billing conventions, while Carpe Diem tracks time and updates bills. The program is also an excellent time-management tool for tracking exactly how much time was spent on any specific task.

If your business juggles clients and billing plans, you'll benefit from Carpe Diem's SmarTimer. This is a configurable floating time palette that lets you create as many separate stopwatch

timers for various projects as needed. Each tracks time in any Windows application, and each timer can represent a different client or individual projects for the same client. For instant time tallies, you can drag and drop SmarTimer results to a timesheet to update your billable hours. Also, Carpe Diem's central database runs on any network and works with any billing system that imports and exports ASCII files.

Larger companies should consider the high-end Carpe Diem, with its extensive billing system compatibility. If you bill by the minute or by the project, this solution is worth your time.—Barry Brenesal; James Oliver Cury

Carpe Diem for Windows
ProSoft Corp.
(800) 477-6763; (214) 386-7769
$3,000 (up to ten users)

CHARTING A BUSINESS COURSE
MapInfo 3.0 for Windows

Not long ago, analyzing business data meant delving into miles of dot matrix printouts—with a bottle of aspirin nearby. Then spreadsheets became powerful visual tools featuring 3-D graphics and made your data a little more accessible. But something was still missing. If only you could view your business geographically, then you'd be able to answer the really important questions: Which state buys the most widgets? What's the median

age and income for customers in the northern district? If this is the information you're looking for, consider a geographic information system (GIS) like MapInfo 3.0 for Windows.

MapInfo 3.0 is a relational database tool with a twist: a map-based front end that incorporates data from your database, spreadsheet, or remote SQL databases, in addition to CAD packages and ASCII files.

There are several ways to view your chart data. The first is called Thematic Mapping, which color-codes map elements (like states) based on your data. You can also place charts with more detailed data (like ethnic demographics) over each state. Once the data is displayed, you can double-click on a region to see a row-and-column display of the data for that area. MapInfo can also correlate its own geographical datapoints (cities and other elements) with your database. You can choose to display only cities with total sales over a certain amount, for example.

In addition to the mapping regions supplied, you can add your own maps. These extra maps can be used either as primary backgrounds for your data or as overlays for the included maps. Of course, any data to which you can assign geographical coordinates can be mapped and correlated with other data. For example, if you have a collection of business locations and want to

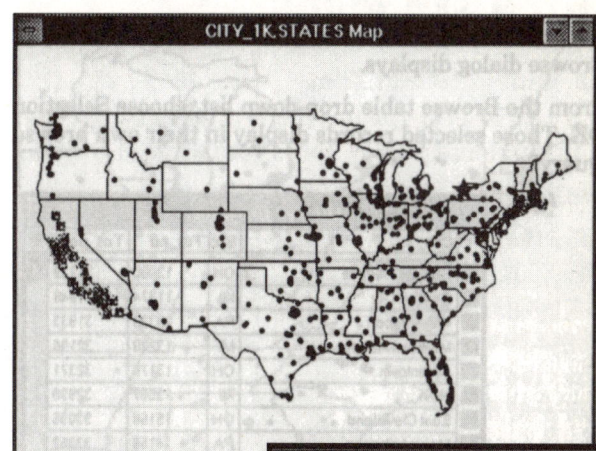

show which are generating the most sales, it's as simple as correlating two databases to create an easy-to-visualize depiction of the successful regions.

MapInfo also offers MapBasic, a scripting language sold separately for in-house application development. For easy distribution, applications written in MapBasic can be compiled into executable files.

Several spreadsheet applications have added limited mapping functions, yet none offers the GIS power of MapInfo. Lotus 1-2-3 Release 5, for example, has a built-in mapping module that can automatically display a map with color coding based on data ranges, but only if country or state codes are included in a range of data. MapInfo can use other types of geographical coordinates, such as geocodes or latitude and longitude, to generate similar maps.

MapInfo is not a program you can learn by simply clicking on things to see what happens. It's intuitive to a point—and then you run into new concepts like geocodes, which will send you running to the manual for explanation. But it's worth the steep learning curve. MapInfo 3.0 is a powerful geographical analysis tool that lets you look at your business from an entirely new perspective.—Yael Li-Ron

MapInfo 3.0 for Windows
MapInfo Corp
(518) 285-6000
$1,295

Move Your Data: Modems That Run at True V.Fast Speeds, Network, and Go Wireless

a decade or so ago, a typical modem was Anderson-Jacobson's acoustic model—a $300 breadbox-sized device that moved data at 300 bits per second (bps) and could barely communicate outside the U.S. because it didn't follow international standards. Today's modems are far smaller and faster, but just as dependent on telecommunications standards.

Specifically, after years of waiting for committees and playing with makeshift proprietary protocols, modem makers are finally poised to take the next step in modem speed—to the 28,800-bps V.34 or V.Fast standard. Yet even as the industry has traversed generations of compression and data-correction standards to reach this latest milestone, modem buyers' two imperatives have remained the same—speed and compatibility.

Speed is paramount in data communications. Users connecting to online services today want to download and view large graphics files in real time. Technical-support personnel want to troubleshoot remote installations without being slowed to a crawl by the overhead of modern operating systems and graphical user interfaces. Even simple e-mail these days can bring older modems to their knees, as users attach ever larger documents or multimedia files to their messages.

But opting for speed without compatibility is a risky gamble. If you're buying a modem today, you should either play it safe with a modem meeting the previous international standard—V.32bis or 14,400 bps—or hold out for one of the genuine V.34 28.8-Kbps models that should have reached dealers by the time you read this. (By that time, in fact, modems based on AT&T's unprecedented new V.34 33.6-kbps chip set may be available).

Anything in between, such as modems based on US Robotics' 16.8-kbps HST chip set, AT&T's 19.2-kbps V.32terbo chip set, or Rockwell International's V.Fast Class (V.FC) 28.8-kbps chip set, is a proprietary solution. Such a modem may or may not be easily upgradable to the recently ratified V.Fast standard, and hence may not be able to guarantee V.Fast compatibility. The result can actually be decreased performance, as dissimilar modems trying to find a common protocol sometimes drop all the way back to 9,600 bps to establish a connection.

Real Protocols and Pretenders

Worldwide modem standards are set by a committee called the International Telecommunications Union (ITU), formerly known by the French initials CCITT (see the "V.Glossary"). When the committee ratified the V.32bis (14.4 kbps) protocol in 1991, discussion of higher data-transfer rates had already been underway for some time, because new applications such as videoconferencing and software-based whiteboard presentations are nearly useless at 9,600 bps and slower speeds.

One proposal, dubbed V.32terbo, promised a slightly faster rate of 19.2 kbps, but the committee rejected it on the grounds that it was too incremental an upgrade—especially because, then as now, industry analysts predicted that super-fast, fiber-optic Integrated Services Digital Network (ISDN) installations would soon replace today's general switched telephone network (GSTN) wiring. With digital instead of analog phone lines, users wouldn't need modems at all. Some committee wits had already joked that any additional analog standards should be called not "V.Fast," but "V.Last."

As months and years passed, however, ISDN installations continued to fall behind schedule, while the V.Fast—formally V.34—talks bogged down. Several large modem-chip vendors grew impatient and introduced faster-than-V.32bis products using proprietary data-transmission algorithms, preliminary sketches of the V.34 spec, or both.

These modems include such contenders as AT&T Paradyne's Comsphere 3830, a V.32terbo unit; Motorola's Codex 3261Fast, which delivers 24.4 kbps using some aspects of V.34 encoding; and a slew of products based on Rockwell's 28.8-kbps V.FC chip set, adopted by vendors ranging from Hayes and Microcom to Boca Research and Zoom Telephonics.

The good news about these interim modems is that they've flooded the market, helping drive V.32bis modem prices below $200. The bad news is that they've caused a great deal of market confusion. Used in pairs (for transmitting and receiving), they can indeed deliver better-than-14,400-bps performance. But they generally fail to reach top speed when the receiving modem is based on a different technology than the sending unit. In some cases, modems based on the same chip set (such as Rockwell's V.FC set), but implemented by different manufacturers, fare no better than modems with different chip sets.

Fortunately, the ITU approved a genuine V.34 specification in early June and met to ratify it in September, so as you read this, modems with official V.34 chip sets should be just weeks away. These modems will send data over ordinary phone lines twice as fast as a V.32bis unit. Quadruple that throughput, thanks to V.42bis data compression, and the new V.34 models will, under ideal conditions, pump upwards of 115,200 bits of data through your serial port every second. That's 400 times the throughput of that old acoustic model, for about the same initial cost ($300).

As a bonus, fully V.34-compatible modems promise to deliver more reliable high-speed performance than any of their predecessors. Depending on line conditions, which the modems can actively assess during their initial handshake and monitor during data transmission, the new modems will be able to choose from among several techniques to achieve their 28.8-kbps transfer rate. Should connection at that rate be unsuccessful, V.34 modems will have a wide range of fallback rates—descending in 2,400-bps increments—-to try, and their active monitoring will let them crank the rate back up if line conditions improve.

Upgradability

With so many modems introduced ahead of the official V.34 standard, it's become important to consider a modem's upgrade path. This makes sense for the first generation of V.34 products, too—previous experience has shown that early implementations of new standards are sometimes less than perfect.

The easiest modems to upgrade are the few entirely programmable software-based units (more on them in a moment). Next are those that, like some modern PC-system BIOSs, use software-upgradable flash ROM. Most vendors offering these products provide their latest ROM code as an executable program file available on a BBS or online-service forum. Once you've downloaded the program, simply turn on your modem and run the program to update its firmware.

This works well when all you need to do is swat a bug or enhance an existing feature, but things can be a bit more complicated if your unit is based on an older or proprietary standard. Depending on the individual modem, you may need to replace the main chip or a daughtercard containing the chip, or even trade in the whole modem. Many vendors urge you to send the modem back to the factory rather than perform such upgrades yourself, and despite pledges of speedy turnaround or even loaner units, you should be prepared to suffer some downtime during service.

The announced cost of a V.34 upgrade, for instance, ranges from free to $70 in the case of many modems based on Rockwell's V.FC chip set (such as US Robotics' Courier V.34 Ready, Hayes' Optima 288 V.FC, and Supra's SupraFax 288). Rockwell, by the way, promises V.34-to-V.FC compatibility, so users who don't upgrade will be able to make 28.8-kbps connections with those who do.

The upgrade may cost more, or mean less, in the case of some other modems. Motorola's Codex 3261-Fast, for example, can be upgraded to V.34 compliance at no charge, but will only connect with V.34 modems at its pre-upgrade peak of 24.4 kbps—the upgrade to 28.8 kbps requires a complete and relatively costly design change. Most V.32terbo units will also require a major upgrade.

If you anticipate such serious upgrades, the use of flash ROM doesn't make much difference—if you've got to perform modem surgery and swap other chips, it's no big deal to swap a ROM chip as well. The value of flash ROM, which does add roughly $50 to a modem's cost, is its convenience in the likelihood of a minor code revision that doesn't require any hardware changes. Several vendors give you a choice, offering two product lines with and without flash ROM at slightly higher and lower respective costs.

The DSP Advantage

Advances in equalization techniques have been instrumental in squeezing more performance out of outmoded GSTN lines, but the key to reaching V.34 speeds has been the increased power and reduced cost of digital signal processor (DSP) chips. The advent of versatile, inexpensive DSPs has benefited many branches of the computer industry—they're key parts of high-quality multimedia sound cards and voice-mail boards, for example. But DSPs are absolutely essential to rapid data transfers over noisy analog phone lines. The DSPs in V.34 modems will execute between 30 and 40 million instructions per second.

Most high-speed modem vendors rely on what is essentially a two-chip modem package—a traditional hard-coded processor chip, or data pump, which contains the algorithms necessary to utilize the bandwidth of the telephone lines, and a DSP programmed to perform the computations required by the data pump. But some modems, notably AT&T Paradyne's Comsphere series and the SoftModem line from Digicom Systems Inc., do away with hardwired processor chips altogether.

Digicom's single-chip solution combines a general-purpose programmable DSP from Analog Devices with 32K of RAM to perform all of the functions necessary for high-speed data transfer. The modulation and controller algorithms for a particular implementation are stored on your PC's hard disk and uploaded into the modem's memory during system startup. Thus the modem can accept new algorithms or instructions on the fly, and upgrades are a simple matter of installing some new software on your hard drive, rather than swapping ROM chips or daughtercards. (That's true as long as the new instructions aren't too much for the DSP to execute. You can expect a DSP-based modem to be easily upgradable, but don't expect it to obviate the need for any future sound or video cards, any more than you'd expect your old 286 to run Windows NT.)

Correction and Compression

With the flood of fast new modems turning their V.32bis predecessors into bargains, you might be tempted to save money and stick with 14,400 bps. That's not a bad idea if your communications mostly involve online services such as ZiffNet and CompuServe, where 14.4-kbps access is still relatively new and 28.8-kbps support will be scarce for some time.

On the other hand, if you regularly connect with other PCs—exchanging files with a branch office, say—it makes sense to get all the speed you can, with V.34 modems on both ends of the line. As mentioned above, the V.34 standard also goes a long way toward reducing transmission errors due to noise and varying line conditions.

Nevertheless, existing error-correction protocols—principally V.42—remain important, especially for connection to 9.6-kbps or 14.4-kbps modems. All V.34 modems will incorporate V.42 correction, plus Microcom's MNP Classes 2-4 for further backward compatibility.

Similarly, look for V.42bis data compression, which can increase effective modem speed fourfold, and MNP 5 software-based compression. The latter is important primarily for compatibility with older communications software that doesn't support V.42bis.

Another Microcom error-correction protocol, MNP 10, has become a minimum requirement for modems offering cellular connectivity.

Surpassing the Serial Port

Sometimes, even with V.42bis compression, clean phone lines, and matching 28.8-kbps modems, you might see transmission rates stuck at a snail's pace. What's going on? The answer could lie in an inexpensive but often overlooked component—your PC's serial port, whose limitations are compounded by communications under Windows or other multitasking environments.

For your CPU to process data received from a serial port (or any other input/output device, such as a disk drive), it must receive an interrupt from the device. A serial port generates an interrupt when its port buffer is full.

Older PCs, and a surprising number of newer ones, have serial ports based on 8250 or 16450 UARTs (universal asynchronous receiver/transmitters), which contain a 1-byte buffer. Back in the days of 300-bps modems, that was more than sufficient; a modem could fill that buffer—and hence generate an interrupt—about 30 times per second, which left plenty of time for the PC's processor to service the requests. Increase speed to 28,800 bps, and nearly 3,000 interrupts occur each second.

Under Windows, the situation is even worse, because Windows is frequently off doing something else, such as writing data to the swap file on your hard drive, while the serial port is crying for service. By the time your CPU responds to the interrupt, another character has moved into the buffer, and the first character has been lost. At best, the entire data packet must be retransmitted, causing a drop in performance; at worst, your communications software allows the modem to continue transmitting, with possible data loss.

The first step out of this morass is to make sure that your serial port uses a 16550A UART, which has a larger 16-byte buffer. Buying an internal modem can help you avoid the confusing business of determining whether or not you need to upgrade your serial port, since today's internal modems come with 16550A UARTs (or emulators). Several, such as Hayes' Optima 288 series and Supra's SupraFax 288, provide enhancements in the form of larger buffers or better flow control than the UART can provide alone. External modem buyers should either check their PCs' serial circuitry, or invest in a plug-in serial-port card that uses the 16550A.

Even that, however, may not be enough once you throw data compression into the mix. Using V.42bis compression effectively multiplies a 28,800-bps V.34 link by four, which means even a 16550A UART generates over 1,400 interrupts per second—right at the fringe of a manageable number of requests under Windows 3.1, as long as other applications aren't hogging the CPU.

One solution is a "smart" serial-port card such as Hayes' ESP-2 Communications Accelerator (also marketed by Practical Peripherals as the ProClass High-Speed Serial Port) or Telcor Systems' T/Port. For around $100 (with one serial port) or $140 (with two ports), such a card combines a larger serial-port buffer—1K in the case of the Hayes card, 14K for sending and 16K for receiving in the case of the Telcor—with a coprocessor to provide intelligent flow control. Higher-priced boards, such as Digiboard's PC/Xe ($299) or Metacomp's ATcomm/XL ($700 and up), add still larger buffers—up to 2MB for the Metacomp card—plus additional coprocessing and compression power.

Microcom's DeskPorte Fast and TravelPorte Fast modems get around serial-port limitations entirely by redirecting serial-port traffic to your PC's parallel port. Since it transmits 4 bits at a time (8 bits in some newer PCs), a parallel port is inherently faster than any serial port; Microcom claims throughput of up to 250 kbps. The drawback is that the Microcom modems lack a pass-through connector for a parallel printer. That's no problem if you're connected to a network printer, but if you're not, you may need to provide another LPT port to accommodate your printing needs—not an option for most portable machines.

There are also software solutions. Windows' standard communications driver gets the shakes at speeds over 19,200 bps; many of today's "intelligent" or "enhanced" serial-port options replace it with a proprietary driver for better performance. However, such a step may cause compatibility problems with some communications-software packages. While these problems are the exceptions, rather than the rule, check with the vendor about specific program suitability before you buy.

Portable and PCMCIA Modems

While some notebook PC makers offer proprietary internal modems, most portable modems are either external, pocket-sized units that plug into serial ports or, increasingly, PCMCIA cards.

The latter are more compact and don't protrude from the back of your notebook, but oblige you to check for compatibility problems. See if the modem lists your exact make and model among the portable PCs supported, and whether it works with your notebook's PCMCIA Card Services and Socket Services software drivers or comes with its own. Note, too, that PCMCIA modems get their power from your portable's battery pack, rather than their own AC adapters, or 9-volt or AA batteries as pocket modems do. Be prepared to recharge your notebook more frequently with a PCMCIA modem installed.

A distinguishing factor among PCMCIA modems is their implementation of the Data Access Arrangement (DAA) —an often cumbersome connector that dangles from the card to provide an RJ-11 jack for the phone line, or a line that you plug into an RJ-11 wall socket. (You may have to carry an adapter to be prepared for either type of hotel or pay-phone connection.)

Megahertz Corp.'s popular XJack PCMCIA modems put the DAA into the card—you simply press a button and a miniature tray with the RJ-11 connector pops out. Even this design has proved problematic, however, with some users finding the tray too fragile or having the entire notebook dragged to the floor when someone trips over the cord. Angia Communications' rebuttal, called SafeJack, is an edge connector that plugs into Angia's PCMCIA cards but releases from the card with a slight tug. The Angia SafeJack modems also have a second RJ-11 jack so that you can hook up the modem and a telephone at the same time.

Dozens of manufacturers offer 14.4-kbps PCMCIA and pocket modems. At this writing, both Microcom and US Robotics have announced V.34 pocket modems, but only Microcom has announced its V.34 PCMCIA upgrade policy. Not surprisingly, upgrading a pocket or PCMCIA modem is more expensive than upgrading one of its deskbound cousins—swapping chips at home is an unlikely proposition, so your best bet is to settle for a V.32bis offering if you can't afford to wait for V.34. For much the same reason, buying a flash ROM- or DSP-based, software-upgradable modem makes even more sense for portable users than it does for desktop models.

Faxes, Bells, and Whistles

With the global acceptance of the Group 3 (9,600-bps) fax standard, it's increasingly hard to find a data modem that isn't also a fax modem. Adding send-and-receive fax capability typically adds less than $50 to the price of a data modem, and nearly all of the major modem-chip vendors—such as

Rockwell, whose chips claim 70 to 80 percent of the market—have integrated Group 3 compatibility into their chip sets. New V.34 modems will detect and respond to Group 3 fax signals during the initial handshake.

In fact, 9,600 bps should be considered a fax minimum—the 14,400-bps V.17 fax standard is becoming common among fax modems, if not yet among dedicated fax machines. Steer clear of some older portable modems that may send faxes at 9,600 bps but receive at only 4,800 bps, or handle 9,600-bps fax but are limited to a prehistoric 2,400 bps for data communications.

Internal and PCMCIA modems have speakers that let you listen for a ringing phone, a busy signal, or the sounds of a connection being made. External modems go further, with diagnostic LED lights—or, better yet, LCDs with words and numbers—to give feedback on the status of your connection. (If you use an internal modem but crave this data, some software utilities, such as Microcom's ModemWatch, can display simulated status panels on your PC's screen.) The beeps and squawks of a modem can be a nuisance in a crowded office, so an external volume control is a plus.

Most modems ship with data and (if appropriate) fax software, but don't expect too much—a bundled data-communications program may not support all the terminal emulations and file-transfer protocols you need, and a free fax package may lack OCR-file import, TWAIN compatibility, or a broad set of file-import/export formats. If you're serious about communications, you'll probably spring for separate software, especially for a specialized modem such as a network, cellular, or voice-aware device.

Ready, Set, Connect

If you had doubts about buying a new modem based on a proprietary standard, your time has finally come. Both in speed and accuracy, V.34 is a vast improvement over V.32bis and interim pseudo-standards. If you can't wait the few weeks for a genuine V.34 modem, check out the vendor's "V.34-ready" or "V.Fast Class" upgrade offering carefully, especially if you can't afford the downtime of returning a modem to the factory for an upgrade.

If you're unsure about whether your PC's serial port uses an up-to-date 16550A UART, choose an internal modem if you have a free expansion slot (or, in the case of a portable, a PCMCIA slot). If you don't have an empty slot, or want top-flight performance, invest in a smart serial-port card and external modem, or perhaps a parallel-port modem.

And if V.34 is beyond your reach, don't be ashamed—economical 14,400-bps modems have a lot of life left. The important thing is to get connected and start enjoying the rewards of putting your PC online.

V.Glossary: Making Sense of Modem Standards

International modem standards, such as the new 28,800-bps V.34 protocol, are set by the Technical Standards Section of the International Telecommunications Union (ITU), formerly known as the Comité Consultatif Internationale de Télégraphique et Téléphonique, or CCITT. (The suffix "bis" appended to some protocol names is French for "second" or "version 2.0.")

The ITU standards enjoy the most worldwide acceptance, but haven't stopped various modem and chip-set manufacturers from creating their own. The most prominent examples are AT&T's V.32terbo, US Robotics' HST, and Rockwell International's V.Fast Class.

ITU protocols specify reverse compatibility, so a modem that adheres to the V.34 standard should be able to communicate with earlier modems that support earlier, slower protocols such as V.32, albeit at the slower modem's speed. In practice, it's sometimes necessary to use communications software to force the faster modem to negotiate the connection at the lower speed.

The high-speed protocols also specify both fallback and fall-forward capability. This means that a pair of modems can automatically decrease transmission speed if line quality deteriorates, and speed up again if line quality improves.

In addition to speed protocols, there are the error-correction and data-compression protocols known respectively as V.42 and V.42bis. Error correction is more accurately known as Automatic Repeat Request (ARQ), involving detection and automatic retransmission of defective blocks of data. Some older correction protocols, which are included in V.42, are known as MNP (Microcom Networking Protocol) Classes 2, 3, and 4, and LAPM (Link Access Procedure for Modems).

V.42bis data compression, which works only between modems using V.42 error correction, can cut connect time by squeezing data files by as much as a 4-to-1 ratio, depending on the type of file. Text and graphics files are most compressible; executable programs are less so. Archive files that have already been compressed using a utility such as PKware's PKZIP can't be compressed further; in fact, there may be a slight transmission-time penalty as the modem wastes time trying to do so.

Shopping Tips

Buy a modem that's based on one of the official ITU standards, either V.32bis (14,400 bps) or the new, soon-to-be-widely-available V.34 (28,800 bps). In-between or proprietary protocols can mean compatibility hassles, and such modems may be tough to upgrade to genuine V.34 status.

If you are going to be upgrading your unit, the best modems are those that use flash ROM or software-programmable DSPs. They make upgrades as simple as downloading and running a software utility, rather than pulling chips or—worst of all—mailing the modem back to the factory.

Besides V.34 or V.32bis, other initials to look for include V.42 and MNP 2-4 error correction, which help when communicating with older modems (though the new V.34 standard includes sophisticated error-correction and line-noise-fighting features of its own).

To lower your phone bill, insist on V.42bis and MNP 5 data compression. Fax users can cut connect time by specifying V.17 (14,400-bps) as well as Group 3 (9,600-bps) fax compatibility.

External modems offer more convenient status displays, but work best if your PC's serial port uses an up-to-date 16550A UART. Internal modems generally come with a 16550A UART or emulator built in; some add extra data buffering or flow control as well.

Serial-port cards with larger buffers or coprocessors can make high-speed communications more successful, particularly under Windows. So can a modem that uses a parallel instead of serial port.

Portable modems are available in pocket-size external and PCMCIA internal models; the latter draw power from a notebook PC's battery, while pocket modems rely on their own batteries or an AC adapter. Hardware and software compatibility for PCMCIA modems is less erratic today than it was a year or two ago, but it is still worth double-checking, as is your preference in built-in or plug-in RJ-11 jack connectors.—John Hill ■

Astound for Windows

When it's time to give an electronic presentation, Astound outshines the rest in terms of pizzazz and performance. This package lets novice users create simple stand-alone or interactive presentations, and at the same time offers a powerful set of tools for the more advanced presentation developer. The product's approach to traditional hard-copy-based presentations is less automated and robust than much of the competitions's, but it does the job.

The key to Astound's strength as a multimedia presentation tool is its exceptionally intelligent media handling and easy-to-understand animation and synchronization tools. When you add external elements, such as sounds, animations, and videos, Astound loads the elements and makes them accessible for all slides. Astound's chart animation is especially powerful: You can control the movement of any chart element, right down to the individual faces of a 3-D graph. A built-in sound editor also lets you edit .WAV files; looping and fading controls are also provided.—Lori Grunin

> *Astound for Windows,*
> *Version 1.5*
> *Gold Disk Inc.*
> *3350 Scott Blvd.*
> *Building 14*
> *Santa Clara, CA 95054*
> *(800) 982-9888; (408) 982-0200*
> *Fax (408) 982-0298*
> *$399*

ManagePro for Windows and Macintosh

In today's intense world of "rightsizing," managers are being assigned more and more people to keep track of. That means more people to track for reviews and goals. In the past composing a review used to mean going through your notes and files, e-mail and yellow Post-it notes, then trying to remember what those items didn't cover. And goals? Usually a combination of corporate-speak and pie in the sky-ism. Now, there is ManagePro from Avantos Software, which was designed by management consultants for overburdened managers.

ManagePro is designed to simplify the job of managing people and goals, and it does very well. It establishes and monitors the goals of your people, tracks workloads and generates periodic reports and reviews for you. It even includes an electronic "assistant" to let you know of upcoming critical events (reviews, coaching, and so forth) as well as an "advisor" to counsel on thorny managing issues.

ManagePro has the ability to export your data files so you can take them with you on a laptop or to your home (when you're not playing Doom or Myst) and it will

even prompt you for updates when you return. ManagePro is designed to work in the real multiplatform world, with Windows, Macintosh, and UNIX versions available.—Randy Dugger

ManagePro
Avantos Performance Systems, Inc.
5900 Hollis St.
Emeryville, CA 94608
(800) AVANTOS (282-6867);
(510) 654-4600
$395

EASY ENTRY-LEVEL ACCOUNTING

M.Y.O.B. 4.0

Though double-entry accounting hasn't changed much in its 500-year history, double-entry-accounting software changes as frequently as the weather, if not as predictably. M.Y.O.B. 4.0 now adds an interactive tutorial, an introductory video tape, and expanded context-sensitive help, along with a revamped Payroll module that's the smartest we've ever seen. Enter the name and address of an employee—M.Y.O.B. checks through its 200 tax tables and automatically figures federal, state, and local taxes, writes the check, and creates a payroll check stub. These and other new features build on the solid foundation of earlier editions of M.Y.O.B.

As in earlier versions, M.Y.O.B. 4.0 has six integrated modules for General Ledger, Accounts Payable, Accounts Receivable, Inventory, Checkbook, and (optionally) Payroll. Screens are uncluttered and easily read, opening on the "Command Center," where eight icons—General Ledger, Checkbook, Sales, Purchases, Payroll, Inventory, Card File, and Administration—each lead to a screen resembling a flowchart, with each element representing an M.Y.O.B. command. The Checkbook icon, for instance, opens flow-chart (command) boxes for a paper look-alike check, a deposit slip, or checkbook reconciliation, as well as the Cash Disbursements/Receipts Journals and a cashflow worksheet. Pull-down text menus duplicate all Command Center options. The Command Center is always available, regardless of where in M.Y.O.B. you happen to be.

An on-screen checklist guides you through, with detailed online help always available—as it is everywhere in M.Y.O.B. Setting up the Chart of Accounts, the first and usually most difficult step in double-entry accounting, is a breeze. Thirty sample Starter Charts (up from five in 3.0) provide charts for a variety of small businesses, from a day-care center to a dance studio. Setting initial balances and creating linked accounts is also a simplified process, assuming your old bookkeeping system is up to date.

M.Y.O.B., in common with many other entry-level accounting programs on the market, hides the double-entry details, using data derived from everyday tasks—writing a check, preparing an invoice, receiving a payment—to automatically debit and credit the proper accounts. In M.Y.O.B., you pay your bills and collect receivables with as many checking accounts as you need. Oft-repeated transactions—checks, deposits, sales, purchase orders, and journal entries—can be made recurring, and there is help with checkbook reconciliation.

The program provides sales invoices for both services and inventoried items. Each customer can have his or her own credit limit, item and volume discount, discount for payment in less than a defined time, and late-payment interest charge. There are a couple of unfortunate omissions: There is only one ship-to address, and sales-tax percentages are entered on customer invoices, not in the customer data file.

Inventory items can be individually priced, and you can set an on-hand minimum, with a purchase order automatically created when the items on hand reach the minimum. If you attempt to sell more items than inventoried, you can back-order the entire amount or only the number of items needed to fill the invoice.

More than 80 customizable reports include management aids not often found in programs of this price, including 10 sales-analysis reports for a comparison of sales (this year vs. last year) by inventory item, customer, or salesperson. Furthermore, you can quickly backtrack from any item on an analysis report or journal entry, "drilling down" through the pertinent entries until you come to the original transaction. Clicking on Analyze Payables, for example, takes you to a summary of all unpaid purchases.

M.Y.O.B. also features a constantly updated cash-flow report that tracks recurring transactions, receivables, payables, and past-due invoices and bills. A To Do list—also maintained as you create invoices and purchase orders—reminds you of receivables, payables, recurring transactions, expiring discounts, and inventory reorder. New with version 4.0 is batch processing of To Do items. If you have several pending payables on which the discount is about to expire, one command processes and prints checks.

A "Card File" keeps customer, vendor, employee, and personal databases, and provides two features not often found in accounting programs. If you have a modem, M.Y.O.B. will dial a customer's number and keep a simple log of customer contacts. The program also uses Card File information to create mailing labels or tab-delimited ASCII data files for your word processor to use in mail-merge letters.

Another welcome feature: You can configure the program as Changeable or Unchangeable during setup. Changeable allows editing or deletion of any transaction at any time, but no audit trail is kept and no reversing or adjusting entries are necessary. Selecting Unchangeable provides a complete audit trail, which requires adjusting entries for error correction (reversing debits and credits to negate the erroneous transaction). However, M.Y.O.B. makes these adjusting entries automatically. Other programs—Microsoft Profit, for example—require the user to enter adjustments manually, an error-prone task even if you have an understanding of debits and credits.

Documentation and on-screen help are understandable and thorough. Multilevel password protection provides security. Technical support is provided free for 30 days, $79 per year thereafter. You pay for the call. M.Y.O.B. needs individually customized sales-tax amounts, and could use more than one ship-to address, but most businesses won't find these faults fatal. Otherwise, this program is as complete, powerful, and easy to use as any entry-level accounting program on the market.—Steve Gilliland

M.Y.O.B. 4.0 for Windows
Best!Ware Inc.
300 Roundhill Dr.
Rockaway, NJ 07866
(800) 322-6962
$99.95 (with Payroll, $199.95)

PREPARE YOURSELF FOR BUSINESS
Plan Write for Windows 3.0

Be prepared should be the slogan for business, not just the Boy Scouts. Business Resource Software's Plan Write for Windows 3.0 helps you assemble a solid business plan before you open your doors. This simple integrated package—word processor, spreadsheet, and charting module—hands you a ready-to-go plan outline and the tools necessary to flesh out a blueprint specific to your business.

Plan Write's business-plan outline alone makes it worthwhile for budding entrepreneurs. The outline is augmented with numerous spreadsheet templates (including Profit & Loss, Cash Flow, and Balance Sheets) and detailed documentation. You simply step through the outline, expanding on each item by typing detailed notes and explanations, fiddling with numbers, and producing illustrative charts from spreadsheets. By the time you've gone through the entire outline, you have a polished plan.

Plan Write's tool set is simple stuff, nothing that you wouldn't find in a basic integrated package. The word processor includes stock editing and formatting features, plus some intriguing extras like a one-button tool that miniaturizes the text to fit

inside any window. Its outliner, however, is far from flexible—it won't let you move or rank items by dragging them on the screen. The spreadsheet, on the other hand, offers 32 functions, named ranges, and cell protection, and should be solid enough for the planning work you'll do. But because Plan Write's chart maker—the weakest of the three tools—can't be called directly from within the spreadsheet, you must manually copy and paste data between the two.

If you've built a business plan before, Plan Write doesn't have much to offer. But for those who haven't, Plan Write is an affordable teacher with an adequate set of tools.—Gregg Keizer

Plan Write for Windows 3.0
Business Resource Software Inc.
2013 Wells Branch Pkwy.
Suite 305
Austin, TX 78728
(800) 423-1228; (512) 251-7541
$129.95

POWER, SIMPLICITY, AND FLEXIBILITY FLOW IN ABC
FlowCharter 3.0

If you really want to go with the flow(chart), ABC FlowCharter 3.0 is the way to do it. This superb upgrade combines simplicity with power to make flowchart creation easy and flexible. ABC Flow-Charter comes with palettes containing generally accepted shapes for use in process and workflow charts. It also includes a generous supply of shapes for other types of charts like organization charts and network diagrams.

To create a chart, you click on a shape and then click where you want to place it. ABC FlowCharter will automatically add connecting lines, or you can draw your own with your mouse. You click on icons to select characteristics like line thickness and colors, and add text by clicking on the shape and typing.

This upgrade is OLE 2.0 compliant, meaning you can now drag items from other applications directly to the ABC FlowCharter work area. You can load other charts or even other applications by clicking on shapes within a chart; and you can make shapes "smart" so they automatically position themselves in relation to each other.

While ABC FlowCharter is for serious flowcharters, it doesn't have error-checking capabilities like the competing allClear flowcharting program.

This means that FlowCharter won't prevent you from starting a process and inadvertently failing to conclude it, a danger with complicated charts. However, the price you pay for allClear's error checking is that you end up needing to learn its programming language as well.

ABC FlowCharter's lack of complexity and generous supply of shapes make it a good choice not only for the creators of flowcharts, but also for the unartistic who must produce organization charts and other simple business graphics. While at $495, ABC FlowCharter is a bit expensive, it is a well-designed product.—David Haskin

ABC FlowCharter 3.0
Micrografx Inc.
1303 E. Arapaho Rd.
Richardson, TX 75081
(800) 676-3110; (214) 234-1769
$495

ACCOUNTING WITH UNDERSTANDING
DacEasy Accounting for Windows

It's one of the best marriages yet of sound low-end accounting and a sensible interface.

DacEasy has traditionally delivered accounting products that were heavy on functionality, but sometimes left users scratching their heads in confusion. DacEasy Accounting for Windows may change that. The program's financial processing power rivals the best low-end accounting products, surpassing some of them in areas like inventory. And its new Windows interface clears an accessible path to understanding the arduous task of double-entry bookkeeping.

DacEasy Accounting for Windows offers a sturdy set of integrated modules: General Ledger, Accounts Receivable, Accounts Payable, Inventory, Purchase Order, Fixed Assets, and Payroll. You can establish and track budgets; print checks and invoices; and define and print all the necessary reports. Beyond processing financial transactions with customers and vendors, you can communicate with them easily, sending faxes and doing mail merges. You can't export data except to files from a report, but can import in Quicken format.

Like other Windows accounting programs, DacEasy groups toolbar icons around familiar concepts such as Customers, Vendors, Products, and Purchases, rather than module names such as Accounts Receivable. Click on one, and a window pops up with appropriate sub-icons. Select the activity you want, and fill in the blanks, pressing F5 or clicking on the lookup button whenever there's a list available. Radio buttons, dialog boxes, and command buttons and bars further simplify data entry.

DacEasy does what it can to ease the laborious setup process by providing four sample Charts of Accounts and letting you set up customers, vendors, and inventory products on the fly. You can establish periods by fiscal or calendar year, and leave up to 12 periods open at once. Ten-digit account numbers are permitted, and two levels of password security—one for the main program and one for payroll—are available.

The program also offers impressive flexibility in processing customer transactions. You can set up departments; assign tax codes individually for each customer; establish credit terms by number of days; print invoices and credit memos for either products or services; and generate packing slips. Using DacEasy Accounting's built-in template, you can

attach notes to customer records and generate past-due letters.

Unlike some of its rivals, DacEasy lets you create and print purchase orders as part of its Vendor/Accounts Payable capabilities. You can attach notes and enter credit limits here, too. And you can get a quick look at the essen-

tials in a customer or vendor's records by clicking on the Activity button—you'll see year-to-date sales, credit limit, and balance. Click on the Aged button to see how old the totals are, and the History button to display a transaction history. A special Criteria button—available on selected screens here and elsewhere in the program—lets you do simple and Boolean searches to pull together related groups of people and transactions.

DacEasy's inventory capabilities are more far-reaching than those of many competitors. You can choose between average costing and FIFO, and assemble items. If you're entering an invoice and the number of items requested exceeds what's in inventory, you won't be allowed to go into a negative quantity.

Product screens also track the on-hand amount, on-hand value, and on-order and committed amounts. Click on Sales in a product screen, and you'll see a 12-month chart of the quantity sold and sales value; clicking a button brings up a colorful graph.

Like the inventory module, the payroll module is unusually full-featured and flexible. You can process withholdings, standard taxes like SUTA and FUTA, overtime, sick time, vacation time, and multiple local tables for an unlimited number of employees. You can print paychecks, W-2s, and 941 worksheets. If you have random data about an employee, you can pull up a notes

screen, or use the more structured personnel-management features to track hire dates or pay increases.

Though DacEasy's list of standard reports isn't as long as some products's, you can easily create your own, or modify the layouts and contents of the prefab reports offered. You can define parameters (accounts and date ranges) on some; designate which fields to include on others; and print reports to the screen, printer, or a file. Reports range from the basic Chart of Accounts, Trial Balance, Balance Sheet, and Income Statement to more specific choices like Vendor Discounts, Product History, and Customer Balances.

DacEasy Accounting for Windows also offers some extras, like boilerplate letters dealing with a variety of situations. Click on the Fax icon while a company's record is highlighted, and up pops Delrina's WinFax Pro if you have it installed. You can also auto-dial any phone number in your files, or run a batch print of labels when you have bills or checks to go out.

There are several error-correction options available. You can void a check, delete a transaction, or reverse a transaction, either by entering a matching transaction that undoes its effect or entering one that would make up the difference. Reversed transactions appear in the Audit Trail report, as do deleted and voided ones.

We ran into some rough edges while testing DacEasy

Accounting—most notably, some system error messages, one of which shut down the program. Overall, though, DacEasy acted reliably. The documentation could be a bit more verbose in places, especially to help novice accounting-software users. We encountered an annoying number of busy signals when trying to call technical support, but when we got through, the staff at DacEasy's 900 line answered promptly.

There are several strong competitors among today's Windows accounting packages, but DacEasy is catching up fast. It has produced a low-end accounting program that meets solid standards for functionality, yet is accessible enough for novices.—Kathy Yakal

DacEasy Accounting for Windows 1.0
DacEasy Inc.
17950 Preston Rd.
Dallas, TX 75252
(800) 322-3279; (214) 248-0305
$149.95

EASY APPS FOR OS/2
Footprint Works 1.0
This inexpensive integrated package offers several easy-to-use applications for OS/2 systems.

Many PC users have modest needs and limited resources. For these folks, an integrated application that includes basic features can handle many of their computing tasks. A new integrated package for OS/2,

Footprint Works 1.0, provides a word processor, spreadsheet, database, charting module, and report writer. At its low price ($149), it's an incredibly good value.

The integration between Footprint Works's modules is well executed. The word processor works smoothly in tandem with the database, and the database is logically connected to the report writer. You can access the chart features directly from within the spreadsheet, and hot-link spreadsheet data and graphics to the word processor. Best of all, the features really work as advertised, in a real-world fashion. We easily created an integrated application for a hypothetical musical-instrument builder.

It's easy to learn the program, with the help of the adequate (though not stellar) tutorial. In fact, a novice user of our acquaintance was able to give a demonstration with less than an hour of preparation. He put together a well-laid-out letter with a database, simple spreadsheet, and mail merge.

Footprint Works includes an impressive number of features for a product this inexpensive. For instance, the word processor includes a thesaurus, stylesheets, and tables; database field types include multiline text and pictures; and the report writer supports up to three levels of grouping. There are several nice touches: You can list files either alphabetically or by date, and add descrip-

tions to files. Print preview is only one mouse click away. While these aren't remarkable features in a stand-alone application, it's great to find them in a package whose street price is under $100.

Everything seems to be designed for straightforwardness and simplicity. Every module uses the same ribbon bar, with font and document formatting shortcuts. It's a cinch to create a database, and even easier to put together a columnar report. Not once did we find the program frustrating; instead, we were repeatedly astonished by how much fun it was to use. Its consistency makes it an excellent program for PC novices.

Footprint Works communicates effectively with the outside world, importing and exporting most standard file formats. For example, the word processor can import and export data from eight other packages, including WordPerfect and Word for Windows. Surprisingly, it does not read DeScribe for OS/2 documents. The database reads xBase files as well as comma- and tab-separated variables. Four spreadsheet

formats are supported, as are 22 graphic formats.

The program's integration with the OS/2's Workplace Shell is a little short of ideal; Footprint Works co-exists with, rather than exploits, the OS/2 environment. Unlike most native OS/2 applica-

tions, you can't drag and drop a background or text color to the Footprint Works screen; your only choices are a visually attractive though sometimes hard-to-read etched gray background, and a plain white screen. Nor can you drag and drop a document icon to the printer. The program's support of long file names (one of the advantages of OS/2's HPFS) is patchy,

too—you can use a long file name as long as it doesn't have too many spaces in it.

However, Footprint Works makes excellent use of multithreading, which is arguably more important. You can drag and drop text and graphics between modules, though not within a module. And the product is CID-enabled, which makes it easy to install and maintain across an OS/2-aware network. Installation is straightforward and trouble-free. The program uses about 8MB of hard-disk space. You do have to install the entire pack-

age; if you want to use just the word processor and the spreadsheet, and ignore the database and other modules, you are out of luck.

Some of Footprint Works's limitations are a result of its nature as a low-end product. The database is flat-file only, for instance, and you can't attach different stylesheets to separate documents.

The program also exhibits a few teething problems that remind you this is Version 1.0. It will occasionally fold up and disappear—without even the grace of crashing. We quickly learned to save often. The program doesn't remember which directory you accessed last, so it can be time-consuming to retrieve several files from a non-default directory. However, Footprint Works's rough edges feel like imperfections in its polish, not structural flaws. Its problems are minor irritations, rather than major annoyances.

Footprint Works is smooth and refined, despite an occasional snag. It's worth recommending if your OS/2 application needs are simple, or if you want an application that will fit on your laptop computer. Even if you already own a high-end OS/2 word processor and a serious database, but you need a simple spreadsheet, Footprint Works is worth the price.

Footprint Works for OS/2 1.0
Footprint Software Inc.
53 Yonge St.
4th Floor
Toronto, ON M5E 1J3 Canada
(800) 465-8470; (416) 943-4652
$149

The Future of the Office

digital Convergence. Ubiquitous Computing. Call it what you like, big things are happening. Really big. Technologies are colliding. Computing now encompasses everything from futuristic set-top cable boxes to pocket-sized PDAs. And new products and technologies are arriving almost as fast as businesses can deploy them.

This mind-bending pace of change shows no sign of slowing either. Two years ago the cement for the information superhighway wasn't even mixed; today, any company not writing I-Way access into its business plan is on a dead-end dirt road. Products that were cutting edge when we began planning this story—portables equipped with speakerphones and CD-ROM drives, for example—are already yesterday's news. Meanwhile, seductive new next-generation technologies such as voice recognition, real-time 3-D interfaces, and smart peripherals are vying for mindshare.

Change brings excitement, but it brings uncertainty as well. To stay ahead, companies have to plan ahead, and that often means writing twenty-first century technologies into a five-year business plan—no easy task when even the view out over 12 months is hazy. Prognosticators are certain to make embarrassing mistakes.

If the digital future is a bit murky, one trend is crystal clear: The technology juggernaut will dramatically (and quickly) change the way you work. The office of tomorrow will look different: Those big desk-hogging computers and peripherals will shrink until they become invisible. It will also move around—like the Filofaxes of today, Office 2000 may not even be a place you go to, but an accessory you carry with you everywhere. And it will function differently—workgroup tools and wireless connections will become a seismic force that will collapse convoluted org charts and let the best ideas bubble to the surface.

Other trends are also emerging. We talked to hundreds of R&D experts and other future-watchers to get a clearer picture of what lies ahead. Here's a brief tour of some of the products available today (or very soon) that are changing the office and workflow as we know it. To peer even further into the future, we also visited some of the most prestigious research and development labs around the country, including MIT's Media Lab, and Xerox's Palo Alto Research Center (PARC), birthplace of the graphical user interface and the mouse.

Not all of the products covered on these pages are ready for prime time—many cost a small ransom. But all speak volumes about the shape of things to come.

Universal Mailbox

If there's any consensus among the future-watchers we talked to, it's that the Internet fever we've seen in the last year is not just a fluke. Not only will online destinations continue to proliferate—Apple, AT&T, Microsoft, and Sony are just a few of the companies offering new commercial services—the types of information we receive and the ways in which we get it will change as well. Microsoft will include Radish Communications's VoiceView voice protocol in the next version of Windows, along with other communications plumbing. The idea? Create a universal mailbox to which all fax, voice, and data messages are routed. Likewise, the VoiceView protocol will let PC users send data and voice information across a single phone line—ideal for document conferencing software, which lets two or more users simultaneously view, annotate, and edit live computer documents. U.S. Robotics and Hayes Microcomputer Products are already at work on modems that support VoiceView. AT&T has announced its own simultaneous voice/data (SVD) modem called DataPort 2001. It uses AT&T's VoiceSpan voice/data protocol. Both protocols breathe new life into the aging analog telephone network.

Conferencing-Enabled

Sharing this data is getting easier as well, thanks to new applications for videoconferencing and document conferencing. Creative Labs's Sharevision PC3000, for example, is the first videoconferencing product that lets callers simultaneously send voice, video, and data information across analog phone lines. Digital connections like integrated services digital network (ISDN) and asynchronous transfer mode (ATM) will likely replace or complement analog phone connections in most offices, making full-blown videoconferencing systems such as Intel's ProShare Personal Conferencing Video System 200 standard fare on corporate desktops. Just as applications have become e-mail-enabled over the past few years, they're soon likely to become conference-enabled as well.

Wireless

Elsewhere, the cord has been cut: Printing, copying files, and connecting to other hardware in your arsenal will become ever more accessible. Infrared technology is already standard in portables like IBM's ThinkPad 755 series, Hewlett-Packard's OmniBook 600, and Sharp's PC-8700. Infrared-equipped printers from HP and IBM are also in the pipeline now that standards are being forged. The payoff? Your portable and desktop PC will synchronize files the minute you walk into your office. You'll also be able to queue jobs to the printer or fax machine so that they're processed as soon as your portable is within range.

Infrared isn't the only wireless technology to watch for. Radio and Cellular Digital Packet Data (CDPD) devices are also stretching the power of the ubiquitous cellular phone network for transferring data on the road. Sierra Wireless has developed a CDPD modem that allows high-speed, wireless transmission of packetized data over the cellular network used by portable phones. And Traveling Software offers LapLink Wireless, a hardware-software combination that retrofits any system and portable to sync files via tiny radio modules that attach to serial ports.

Smart Software

Feel like you're drowning in information? As the connections from our PCs to the outside world become more complex, we'll need smarter software to manage the information coming at us. Sony's new Magic Link personal digital assistant, for example, is the first device to use both the Magic Cap operating system from General Magic and AT&T's PersonaLink Services e-mail and information service. Together these technologies let computer users easily program electronic agents, autonomous software routines that let you start a transaction on your computer, then seamlessly pass off the request to one or more other computers running different operating systems. For example, you could tell your PDA that you want to book travel reservations. It could then send an agent to find the database for the airline that it knows you prefer, find the best prices and times for your schedule, and record the results in your expense report and schedule—all while you're doing something else with your time. Motorola has already announced (but not shipped) Envoy, its own PDA that will support these services; other companies are expected to announce products later this year. Although Magic Cap currently works only on PDAs, General Magic is working on a desktop version that should be ready sometime this year. Other applications to employ agents, butlers, and information editors are not far off.

There will be other software refinements as well: 3-D and natural-language interfaces will also have us working smarter. Using technology born out of its PARC labs, Xerox's XSoft division developed Visual Recall—a document management/information visualizer that uses 3-D to convey relationships between files. This makes it easy to spot related documents or anomalies, or to view the hierarchical relationships between files. The program uses linguistic techniques (also developed at PARC) to perform more sophisticated queries. Search for the word mouse, for example, and it will also pull documents that contain derivatives of the word, such as mice.

Intelligent Peripherals

Still haven't mastered the advanced features of the fax machine? Expect to see peripherals gaining smarts as well. Hybrid devices such as Okidata's Doc-It 3000 scanner/printer/fax machine have been around for years, but entirely new devices are also appearing. HP's OmniShare, for example, is an odd-looking gadget that combines a tablet-based computer with a fax machine and voice/data modem so that two people can simultaneously view, annotate, and talk about an electronic document. HP plans to eventually create a version for desktop PCs as well. Another device called a SoftBoard from Microfield Graphics is akin to a giant electronic chalkboard that connects to a PC (or Macintosh): Anything written on the whiteboard also displays on the PC's screen.

Zenith, meanwhile, recently announced a device called a CruisePad, an LCD tablet that wirelessly connects to your main system so you can interact with it while you roam around the office. Nothing is stored or processed on the tablet—it's merely a viewport to your PC's display through which you can open and edit files, check your e-mail, or search a database. It's a harbinger of the pad-style computers at Xerox PARC.

Other peripheral makers are working with Microsoft on its At Work software to let you control office devices via an LCD panel with a familiar Windows interface (instead of cryptic analog buttons). Ricoh's IFS66 is one of the first of these At Work devices. Unlike conventional fax machines, Ricoh's can double as a document scanner or printer, and more importantly, it can manage the faxes it receives by routing them to e-mail boxes on the network. It can even pull client lists from the network for broadcast faxing. Microsoft showed us a prototype of an At Work telephone; look for copiers and other devices with Windows-like interfaces to appear soon.

Novel Input

Finally, over the next few years you can expect your computer to gain sight, sound, and other senses. Digital cameras like Apple's QuickTake 100 give your PC eyes; snap a photo of an object and you can develop the image and e-mail it around the globe in seconds. For voice, you can buy products such as Verbex Voice Systems's Listen for Windows and Kurzweil's Voice for Windows, which let you command your PC to open files or highlight paragraphs. Many of these programs can also read text aloud and proofread spreadsheet numbers. They can't replace your keyboard, and true, continuous text-to-speech (and the other way around) is still years away. But even this rudimentary voice recognition can be harnessed to read your e-mail. MIT's Media Lab, meanwhile, is taking this natural interaction one step further: Its technicians are working on teaching computers to respond to human gestures, eye contact, and hand movements.

Until now, one of the main obstacles to this kind of natural interaction has been the lack of processor bandwidth. But with CPU speeds soon hitting near-gigahertz levels, that limitation will vanish as well. When it does, the workplace will never be the same.—Wendy Taylor ■

COMPLEX MATH FOR BUSINESS

Mathcad for Windows

Over the years, Mathcad for Windows has carved out a well-deserved reputation as the best general-purpose science and engineering math program on the market. But until now, Mathcad's inability to manipulate large data sets limited its value for business and financial power users. The latest version of the $495 package corrects this problem. Mathcad 4.0 can manipulate larger data sets than spreadsheet programs like Excel 4.0, and supports a much wider range of row and column combinations.

In addition, the Windows interface is easier to use, partial OLE 2.0 and DDE support has been added, and the product's already formidable equation-solving capabilities have been greatly strengthened. While Mathcad's graphing capabilities remain limited relative to a spreadsheet's, support for polar plots has been added. Mathcad 4.0 is, on average, twice as fast as Version 3.1 because it runs in Windows 32-bit Protected mode.

Using Mathcad is a lot like using a spreadsheet—except that Mathcad is often easier. As soon as you type in a formula and supply values for its variables, Mathcad displays the results. Just as in a spreadsheet, Mathcad supports user-defined functions. You can assign a name to a complicated formula and use that name as shorthand for the formula in subsequent calculations. The well-written manual and excellent context-sensitive help make Mathcad as easy to learn for newcomers as any spreadsheet.

The spreadsheet similarities end there, however. Mathcad-created documents lack the spreadsheet's familiar grid of cells; instead, text, numbers, and math symbols display the way they do in a WYSIWYG word processor or

rest on our laurels. It's going to take powerful machines and processors. It's also going to require us to get more involved with our local phone-service providers and to get them on the ISDN bandwagon. This means per-

a book. Gone are the fixed-font ASCII codes that make equation editing on a spreadsheet's tiny formula bar so hard on the eyes. Mathcad's equations and math symbols adjust their size to match the font size you choose for displaying variables and constants. You can enter common math symbols by clicking on their icons in a scrollable toolbox. These and many other symbols can also be entered from the keyboard with shortcut keys.

Dedicated number crunchers will love SmartMath, Mathcad's new expert system module. When you toggle on SmartMath, it automatically translates an equation into its simplest and easiest-to-calculate form before Mathcad evaluates the equation numerically. This results in a significant improvement in speed and accuracy.

If you're a power user, you'll like the new OLE 2.0 support. You can embed any Mathcad document into a spreadsheet application, or create OLE links between text in Mathcad and your favorite Windows word processor. Unfortunately, you still can't link data stored in Mathcad and a spreadsheet—linked programs always treat each other's embedded equations and data as bitmapped graphics.

However, since Mathcad can save and read data in ASCII delimited format, it's easy to move data between Mathcad and a spreadsheet application. In addition, you can now paste the first 200 items in a vector or the first 200 rows and columns of a matrix from Mathcad into your spreadsheet from the Windows Clipboard. (There's no limit to the size of Clipboard transfers from a spreadsheet to Mathcad.) Thanks to new support for DDE links between single-value variables, you can even turn Mathcad into a spreadsheet add-in when working with small data sets. For example, you can link two arrays, one in Mathcad and the other in Excel, by using DDE's POKE command to establish a separate link between each of the arrays's components.

While the base package lets you define most types of specialized financial and statistics equations from scratch, two add-ins make Mathcad even better at creating models and searching for patterns in data. The $129 Differential Equations Function Pack gives Mathcad the ability to solve systems of first-order differential equations. The $249 Signal Processing Function Pack supplements Mathcad's powerful Fourier analysis functions with sophisticated data-analysis tools.

Mathcad's growing library of $69–$149 hypertext handbooks make Mathcad even more powerful and versatile. Handbook topics range from the technically arcane to statistics, personal finance, and refresher courses in basic math. Each handbook is a fully functional Mathcad doc-

ument; you can edit all its equations, type in new variables and function definitions, modify font size and typeface to enhance readability, and paste any part (including formulas) into your own Mathcad documents. The $99 Treasury of Methods and Formulas is a must—its in-depth discussions of Mathcad's built-in functions and features carry online help to new heights.

Though designed with the needs of scientists and engineers in mind, Mathcad 4.0 marks a milestone in its evolution into a powerful tool for prototyping, documenting, and augmenting complex spreadsheet applications. The future is even brighter. When Mathcad provides full DDE and OLE 2.0 support, it will be the ultimate spreadsheet add-in.—John Gliedman

Mathcad 4.0
MathSoft
101 Main St.
Cambridge, MA 02142
(800) 628-4223
$495

ClarisImpact

Easy-to-use, versatile software takes you over the hurdles of creating polished business graphics. If daunting best describes your experience with creating sophisticated business graphics, then ClarisImpact may be for you. Until now, if you wanted to combine several types of elements—a spreadsheet chart, a timeline, and an organization chart, for example—in a sin-

gle report, you were probably forced to juggle several graphics applications plus a word processor to piece together a document. Add a presentation-software package if you created slides or an on-screen presentation.

Enter ClarisImpact, which rolls the major features of several specialized business-graphics applications into one software package. By design, ClarisImpact won't give you the high-end features of the more powerful specialized applications. Instead, it focuses on accessibility and versatility, enabling you to quickly and easily create polished business graphics to communicate your plans and ideas.

The well-designed ClarisImpact interface makes learning the program a snap. A tool panel houses basic drawing and text tools as well as tools for creating the program's seven basic chart types (called models): calendars, data charts, flowcharts, organization charts, outlines, tables, and timelines. A style bar under the main menu bar provides handy access to

styling tools for specifying fill colors and patterns, line widths, text formatting, and drop shadows.

To create a model, you simply select the correct model tool and click in the drawing area. A dialog box appears with a variety of model-specific options. Once you've made your selection, ClarisImpact draws the model, complete with placeholders you replace with your own information.

The package comes with a healthy assortment of clip art and supports the following formats for placing data, text, graphics, and movies created with other programs: BMP, CGM, DRW, DXF, EPS, IGES, MacDraw II, MacDraw Pro, MacPaint, MacWrite II, Microsoft Excel, Microsoft Word, PCX, PIC, PICT, PICT2, QuickTime, TIFF, and WMF.—Shelley Cryan

ClarisImpact
Claris Corp.
Santa Clara, CA
(800) 544-8554; (408) 727-8227
$399

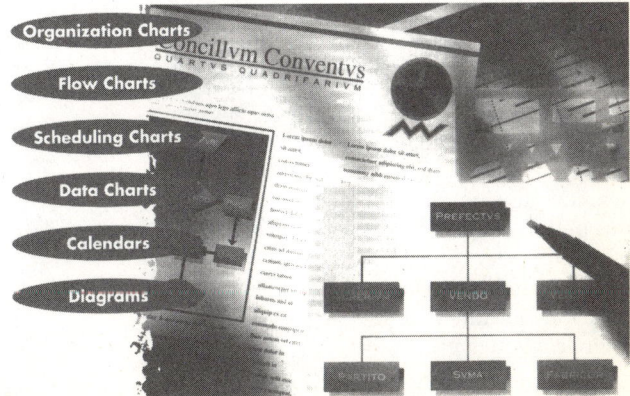

sonal activisim. ☐ At first, there will be plenty of confusing and incompatible standards for personal conferencing, but these things usually shake out faster than you'd expect.

THE SMART WAY TO SOLVE DIFFERENTIAL EQUATIONS ON YOUR DESKTOP

HiQ 2.0

The next time someone tells you Macs can't do real math, reach for a copy of HiQ. HiQ not only solves applied-math and engineering problems easily but it also does so with a friendly interface and a speed that beats all competitors's—plus version 2.0 has many handy new features.

With version 2.0, HiQ's developers have revamped the program's interface to improve adherence to Mac conventions (adding a Find command, for example). They've also added a graphical function browser, making it easier to build custom mathematical worksheets, models, and equations.

New features include built-in solvers (HiQ parlance for symbols) that let you approximate or calculate integrals and derivatives and handle ordinary differential equations (ODEs). There's also a new function that performs partial-derivative meshes, important in many engineering and modeling contexts. In addition, the new version lets you overlay plot

graphs and animate graphs to show changes over time.

HiQ 2.0 handily disproves the big lie that Macs can't do math well. Although it doesn't handle symbolic algebra, it's great at numerical math, easily handling matrix problems and boundary-value problems for differential equations that other math programs find difficult or impossible. Although most Mac users don't have to build and run an ODE model in their work, those who do will appreciate HiQ's combination of number-crunching power, easy scripting, and user-friendly interface. For engineers and scientists, HiQ is a must-buy.—Don Crabb

HiQ 2.0.2
National Instruments
Austin, TX
(800) 433-3488;
(512) 794-0100
$695

PublicityBuilder

If you need to let the public know what you've got, PublicityBuilder, from Jian, lets you create a PR strategy on your Mac. It contains templates that let you write pitch letters, contracts, and press releases and plan objectives. The manual explains how to develop a PR message and deal with the media.

Jian Tools for Sales
$129

REVIEW COPY
NOT FOR RESALE OR REPRODUCTION

Gain Media Coverage for Your Business

JIAN
Publicity Builder.
Proven Public Relations Campaign Software

ORGANIZATION

InfoRecall 4.1

If the basis of your business life is free-form computer notes and snippets of information, you may be interested in Phantech Software's InfoRecall 4.1. This PIM manages unstructured text (like customer contact notes and collections of background information) and adds an extensive search mechanism that makes putting these bits and pieces together easy.

Each record in InfoRecall can consist of as much as 32K of free-form text, which translates into about 25 pages. InfoRecall includes a built-in text editor and an entry template for adding basic contact information such as a customer's name, address, and company. We found that the template was a handy way to record basic information, but you can't modify it or create additional templates.

Once a record is named, InfoRecall's extensive text-searching capabilities can scan an on-screen record or the entire database. Unfortunately, InfoRecall's searches within a single record are far more limited than universal searches. With a universal search, you can use Boolean AND, OR, and NOT operators; search for records containing a range of numbers; and even conduct fuzzy searches for phonetically similar words.

Rudimentary hypertext links between records can be established, and InfoRecall uses DDE (Dynamic Data Exchange) to transfer selected text or an entire record directly to word processors such as Lotus's Ami Pro or Microsoft Word for Windows. On the other hand, InfoRecall has weak import capabilities and was unable to filter out extraneous characters when importing some older word processor files. InfoRecall can import only one file at a time and can't use text strings to chop up large incoming files into a series of records. This makes it cumbersome, for example, to add the contents of a large ASCII file containing multiple messages from an online forum to your InfoRecall database.

Despite this shortcoming, InfoRecall is an inexpensive and easy-to-use PIM for collections of text information. For heavy-duty text management tasks, however, products like askSam for Windows offer a more complete set of tools.—David Haskin

InfoRecall 4.1
Phantech Software Inc.
Toronto, Ontario
Canada

(800) 208-1311; (416) 502-1311
$99.95

Ecco Professional 2.0

This year's new and improved Ecco Professional 2.0 is a PIM for the power user. Once you grasp the basics, you'll be hooked and join the ranks of Ecco groupies who refuse to use anything else. Version 2.0 offers workgroup features such as shared calendars, phone books, and outlines. And Ecco now handles enterprise-wide scheduling through e-mail standards such as MAPI and VIM. Group scheduling is a breeze because Ecco alerts you to conflicts in users's schedules and identifies alternative times when everyone is available. Ecco's DDE-based program interface lets you exchange information with your other applications. Integration with WinFax Pro is also new to Version 2.0. Finally, an impressive synchronization feature makes it possible to keep multiple copies of your database current without having to transfer megabytes of data every time you want to do an update. This is an awesome personal information manager—for the whole workgroup.

Ecco Professional 2.0
Arabesque
(800) 457-4243
$200

Sidekick for Windows

This PIM is not feature-rich, far from it—Sidekick is a non-networkable, bare-bones information manager. But what it does, it does well—and quickly. Sidekick also offers useful features: drag and drop for moving information, and printing to DayTimer and other popular formats. It also has knockout searching and sorting features.

Sidekick for Windows
Borland Intl.
(800) 331-0877
$35

SCANCARD FOR WINDOWS 1.0 KEEPS IT SIMPLE

ScanCard

While there are an endless number of PIMs useful for organizing highly structured information, the ways to organize unstructured and semi-structured information effectively are few and far between. One answer has been to eschew the computer for The Executive Gallery's ScanCard,

which consists of a series of folders, each of which houses columns of staggered cards. Since these color-coded cards reveal their titles at the top, the system is ideal for scanning through to jog your memory about some neglected task or needed follow-up call. Now The Executive Gallery has released the $149 ScanCard for Windows 1.0, which uses the same metaphor and retains the product's simplicity.

In the program's main window, you can open one or more folders of cards. Each folder holds a pair of columns with pockets for eight cards each; of course, you can add additional pages to the folders. The card titles stick out of the pockets, so you can scan through them just as easily as in the non-PC version. Click on any card and the contents are revealed, enabling you to check details or update information.

For users with lots of disparate, free-form data to organize and those with lots of tasks to track, ScanCard is an attractive first offering that complements The Executive Gallery's non-PC system. Requires 2MB RAM, 1.5MB hard-disk space, Windows 3.1 or later.—Barry Simon

ScanCard for Windows 1.0
The Executive Gallery Inc.
814 W. Third Ave.
Columbus, OH 43212
(800) 848-2618; (614) 421-3400
fax: (614) 421-3422
$149

PERSONAL SECRETARY

GoldMine 2.5A for Windows

In these days of continued company downsizing, few of us have the luxury of a personal secretary. Enter GoldMine. GoldMine is a contact manager for the network that tracks of all your customers, schedules group meetings, does merge letters/faxes, prints labels/envelopes, and lets you delegate to others with RSVP. You can even analyze all of these activities with bar chart and statistical output (for the anal-ly inclined).

And just like any good secretary who covers for you while you're out of the office, GoldMine helps you keep track of the hubbub back at headquarters via its unique remote data synchronization. For instance, if Colleen in collections sends you an e-mail that your customer, Wizard Wickets, isn't paying up, you can be sure to delicately mention that at your next meeting. Best of all, you got the dirt on your notebook minutes before the meeting on the cab ride over. GoldMine even has connections to beepers, palmtops, and wireless modems—pretty neat.

GoldMine's new Automated Processes feature makes you even more productive by automatically scheduling events and activities based on a customer or prospect "track." Just sign up one of your prospects to a predefined track and

GoldMine automatically schedules all of your calls and next actions, prints out and faxes letters, and more. This is whiz-bang stuff, kids.

GoldMine, however, has a few drawbacks; it won't babysit for you or wash your car—yet. On the upside, forgetting flowers on Secretary's Day won't be as catastrophic.—Brenda Christensen

GoldMine
ELAN Software Corp.
17383 Sunset Blvd., Ste. 101
Pacific Palisades, CA 90272
(800) 654-3526 x1505
fax: (310) 454-4848
BBS: (310) 459-3443
CompuServe: 74431,1624
CompuServe Forum:
GO:GOLDMINE
MCI: 516-3182
CIS: 73053,2571
AOL: BrendaELAN

THE JAWS OF CONTACT MANAGEMENT

Sharkware Professional 2.0

Like its predatory namesake, CogniTech's Sharkware Professional 2.0 powerfully

focuses on a single task—in this case, managing business contacts. It also incorporates strategic advice for business success from expert Harvey Mackay. And Version 2.0 has grown some new competitive teeth, including OLE 2.0, better printing capabilities, and limited e-mail support.

Sharkware's straightforward interface presents basic contact information at the top of each contact record and tabs at the bottom that reveal pending activities, contact history, and a free-form notes field.

As for most of the other basic contact-management features, they work well here but don't stand out from the crowd. Fortunately, the program has thorough personal scheduling capabilities and connects tightly to your word processor.

CogniTech has added limited e-mail support to Sharkware. But it can't serve as an e-mail front end. Instead, it launches your regular MAPI e-mail front end, passing to it the names and e-mail addresses of selected contacts.

Sharkware Professional 2.0 offers desktop power and simplicity over

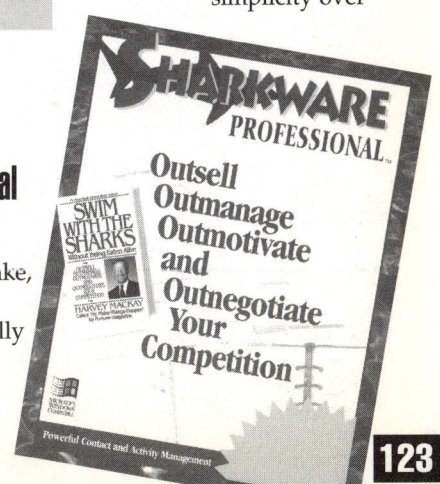

finesse. When it comes to more advanced features and workgroup capabilities, the competition still has the upper fin.—David Haskin

Sharkware Professional for
Windows 2.0
CogniTech Corp.
(404) 518-4577
$109 est. street price

AN INNOVATIVE PIM LINKS UP YOUR DATA
CrossTies

CrossTies is a cutting-edge product that replaces your current personal information manager (PIM) and creates a unique Windows environment in which you can develop powerful—and easily accessible—webs of related information. It seamlessly integrates all your data, no matter what the source, into its innovative Windows interface, making it a powerful tool for controlling and accessing information.

CrossTies's environment is object-oriented, meaning that it blends information and the application that created it into a single object. The practical advantage of turning information into objects is that you don't have to worry about which application created the information and where you stored it. Also, you can give these information objects long names without worrying about shorter DOS filenames, and link the objects together into webs.

You start the process of creating objects using a sim-

ple dialog box. First, you determine the type of object you want to create. Then CrossTies displays a second dialog start with a complete set of related information, but you can follow a trail of objects as well, which can lead to information you never expected to find.

These innovative capabilities allow CrossTies to serve as an object-oriented Windows shell that's more like the Macintosh environment or Hewlett-Packard's NewWave than Windows' Program Manager. Because CrossTies also lets you optionally maintain your old program groups, however, this environment will remain familiar even to new Windows users. Yet it's also more powerful—and more futuristic—than environments like NewWave, because CrossTies' webs of interrelated objects help you feel unusually connected to all your information.

If all you need is a simple PIM, CrossTies is hard to recommend. But if you need a system for controlling torrents of information—and can live with its shortcomings as a PIM—CrossTies' Windows environment is an innovative and powerful tool.—David Haskin

CrossTies 1.0
CrossTies Software Corp.
2445 Midway Rd.
Suite 200
Carrollton, TX 75006
(800) 955-8437; (214) 407-9996
$149

A PROFESSIONAL AMONG WINDOWS PIMS
Winfo Pro

For many, the answer to getting organized is getting a personal information manager (PIM). If you're ready to trash the Post-it Notes and toss the Rolodex, then Winfo

Pro is a Windows-based PIM with a lot to offer. Its modules include a cardfile, autodialer, and integrated to-do list/calendar with year, week, two-day, and one-day views. It supports recurrent-events scheduling, and it color-codes late, delayed, and completed to-do items for easy reference.

Some of Winfo Pro's additional features aren't to be found in heavy-duty contact managers, much less other PIMs. For example, a quick card-search feature lets you type the first few letters of a last name in your cardfile—for instance, "JAC" for "Jackson, Mary"—and Winfo

Xerox PARC: In the Office of the Future, Computers Are Ubiquitous

ask the folks at Xerox's Palo Alto Research Center about computers of the future, and they'll tell you that they're nonintrusive—and they're everywhere. As part of its Ubiquitous Computing study, Xerox has outfitted its lab with hundreds of wirelessly interconnected computers. The goal is to make computers so readily available that they are invisible.

Chalk Board
A wall-sized interactive surface, the LiveWorks division's LiveBoard is the digital equivalent of an office whiteboard.

Wall Computers
Scattered throughout the building are wall-mounted touch-pad displays that help you locate anyone in the building, schedule conference rooms…or check the last time someone brewed fresh coffee.

Tab
The smallest of these wireless devices is the pocket-sized Tab. An information doorway, a Tab is a cross between a PDA and a pager. It can deliver messages, check e-mail, and hold a small number of data files.

Pad
Notebook-sized Pads are the equivalent of electronic scratch pads. Instead of bringing pen and paper to a meeting, use a Pad to take notes. ∎

Pro will highlight the name for easy review.

Winfo Pro also prints popular label and envelope forms, including many Day-Timer, DayRunner, and Franklin styles. Further, you can create and save your own.

Predefined databases and forms include phone books, mail lists, and video/music/software collections. You can design or customize your own Winfo Pro database, creating fields, screens, views (re-sorted and re-indexed fields on identical screens), and reports. The design procedure itself is relatively painless, employing a series of easy-to-use dialog boxes to guide you.

There are 20 buttons on Winfo Pro's screen-design button bar, and 19 on the main button bar—too many images in a small space. The result is poor object definition and low resolution. Winfo Pro's menu selections come off better, with the most commonly accessed selections tied to function keys.

On the whole, fully customizable screens, extensive print options, and numerous predefined databases for quick entry make Winfo Pro an impressive PIM.—Barry Brenesal

Winfo Pro 2.0
WinWare Inc.
4665 Lower Roswell Rd.
Suite 9
Marietta, GA 30068
(404) 612-0806
fax:(404) 993-2351
$49.95

Q&A for Windows

Living up to a sibling's lofty reputation is difficult, but Q&A for Windows succeeds. By adding a creditable word processor and automation for several common procedures, this flat-file database for Windows easily matches its popular older DOS version's reputation for power and simplicity. Symantec has aimed the Windows version at individuals and small workgroups, not at database-application developers, just as the company targeted Q&A for DOS. Databases for end users had better be simple, and Q&A for Windows is.

Its simplicity becomes evident when you create your first database. You create fields, name them, and select field types from a single dialog box. Then you refine those fields in a spreadsheet-like view in which row headings are the field names and column headings list customization options such as default field values. Clicking on the cell in which a field name and customization option intersect displays a dialog box that sets specific options for the field.

You enter and examine data either in a spreadsheet view or in forms you select from a drop-down list in the toolbar. Like high-end databases, you can customize both the formatting and behavior of data-entry forms. For example, you can apply different colors and fonts to forms, and include fields that

automatically calculate the contents of other fields.

Q&A's signature feature is its natural-language querying capabilities. This lets you locate information by typing requests like Find the records where the city is Chicago, rather than learning complex query languages or wrestling with query-by-example tables. A new feature in Q&A for Windows called Do Anything Very Easily (DAVE) walks you through the query-creation process, much like the Query Guide in the DOS version. Unlike the DOS version, though, DAVE also automates creating simple reports and reusable scripts.

DAVE breaks down jobs into a series of small steps, each of which contains several choices. You highlight a choice, click on a button, and DAVE displays the next series of choices. If, for example, you select Find, the next set of choices includes All Records and The Records Where. Subsequent steps further refine the query.

Task automators like DAVE and Microsoft's Wizards are the rage now, and although

each has a slightly different focus, DAVE compares well. At this writing, Microsoft's database applications had no Wizards for creating queries as DAVE does. For creating reports, DAVE's step-by-step approach takes a bit more time than the more automated Wizards, but DAVE gives you more precise control over report contents. However, while DAVE focuses on the contents of queries, reports and scripts, it doesn't help with formatting. You still must use Q&A's ample design tools to create fancy-looking reports.

You can't use DAVE for everything. For example, DAVE doesn't help much with complex script-language syntax. Even database beginners sometimes need fields that automatically calculate numbers from other fields, for example. DAVE takes you further than Wizards—right to the point at which you create an expression—but you're on your own when it comes to using the correct syntax.

DAVE doesn't do mail merges, either. To help with that task, Symantec includes

its Q&A Write for Windows, an easy-to-use word processor that has ample power to satisfy most users. It is, however, missing high-end features such as a grammar checker, field commands, and automatic table of contents and index creation.

The database and word processor are well-integrated; you can launch each program from the File menu of the other. Because you can manipulate Q&A databases—and dBASE, Paradox, and comma-delimited files—from within the word processor, this bundle is a mail-merge maven's delight.

A dialog box in Q&A Write lets you select the databases you want to merge. You then choose the specific fields for merging; you also can run a query or apply a formula to database fields. This lets you customize your merge letters and add conditional statements. For example, you can send collection letters only to those whose payments are more than 60 days late, and also insert in the letter the amount they owe. Furthermore, Q&A Write can simultaneously create envelopes to match merged letters.

There are opportunities for trouble here, however. For example, Q&A Write lets you create a merge document with names from one database and unrelated addresses from another, which would create unpredictable results. When you try to merge the document, Q&A Write tells you there is an error in a merge field, but doesn't divulge what the error is. This is a competitive shortcoming for Q&A; high-end word processors like Word for Windows 6.0 now use task automators like DAVE both to connect to external databases and to check for merge errors.

Still, Q&A for Windows succeeds because it craftily balances power with ease of use. Its database capabilities should suffice for all but the most demanding users, and its self-evident interface and DAVE make it easy, almost pleasant, to learn. And because it is file- and keystroke-compatible with the DOS version, it works well in mixed environments.—David Haskin

Q&A 4.0 for Windows
Symantec Corp.
10201 Torre Ave.
Cupertino, CA 95014-2132
(800) 441-7234; (408) 253-9600
$249.95

FREE-FORM DATABASE
askSam for Windows

askSam for Windows, from askSam Systems, is a freeform database that doesn't require you to fit your data to a structure before you import it. Instead, with askSam you can first dump files with different formats and then create your structure, making it a tool of choice for coordinating searches of information with different structures (such as joining up all those ftp downloads you've culled from the Internet). askSam lets you import data from

new filters including comma and tab delimited, fixed position, CompuServe, the Internet, Lexis, and Nexis. You can also customize toolbars, perform mail-merges, lay out reports by dragging and dropping fields, search multiple databases for text strings, and place bookmarks within documents that act like hypertext links to other points in the database.— Adam A. Hicks

askSam for Windows 2.0
askSam Systems
P.O. Box 1428
Perry, FL 32347
(800) 800-199; (904) 584-6590
fax:(904) 584-7481
$149.95

FoxPro for Macintosh 2.5

Leapfrogging several version numbers to reach parity with DOS and Windows versions, FoxPro 2.5 for Macintosh is a relational-database-management system that's packed with features and honed for speed. It's also a professional development environment, with all the power and complexity such an environment requires.

FoxPro's programming language is tremendously rich. It incorporates all the constructs found in structured programming languages such as C and Pascal, including loops, conditionals, subroutines, arrays, local and global variables, and parameter passing by value or reference. FoxPro also supports the use of HyperCard-style XFCNs and XCMDs.

Speed is one of FoxPro's major selling points. FoxPro uses a proprietary query-optimization technology called Rushmore to provide blazing speed on sorts, queries, and indexing. The DOS and Windows versions are consistently ranked faster than all competitors, and FoxPro for Macintosh looks to continue that trend—even before the native PowerPC version becomes available, with the 2.6 release.

FoxPro's on-line help system, which is context-sensitive, provides a thorough and handy reference to FoxPro's environment and programming language. The help application—based heavily on the help system for the Windows version—runs separately from FoxPro, communicating with FoxPro via Apple events. FoxPro also provides Balloon Help for most parts of the development environment and lets you create Balloon Help for your applications.

Another useful component of FoxPro is Wizards, which,

as in other Microsoft products, automate complex tasks. FoxPro includes Wizards for creating reports, display and entry screens, and graphs (Graph Wizard is similar to the graphing Wizards offered in other Microsoft products, such as Excel and Word). Version 2.6 of FoxPro will add Wizards for queries, tables, and mail-merge.—Jeffrey Sullivan

FoxPro for Macintosh 2.5
Microsoft Corp.

SPEED PLUS FLEXIBILITY ADD UP TO A WINNING CONTACT MANAGER
Now Contact

If you use Now Software's elegant workgroup calendar program, Now Up-to-Date, you'll welcome the latest addition to the company's PIM line. As you can guess from its moniker, Now

Contact is a full-featured contact manager. Even for those who don't use Now Up-to-Date, Now Contact does a good job of simply managing contacts; if you combine it with the calendar features of Now Up- to-Date, the program truly shines.

Now Contact presents two main views of your contact information—a List view and Detail view. The Detail view resembles a standard Rolodex-style card. You have a variety of options for modifying the way the program presents contact data in its views, or you create your own view. The program allows as many as 250 views—you control font, style, size, color, the fields displayed, and the location of each field.

As good as Now Contact is on its own, it's most useful when teamed with Now Up-to-Date 2.1. Using Apple events under System 7 (which Now Contact requires), you can link events in Now Up-to-Date with specific contacts in Now Contact. The links enable you to view the Now Up-to-Date appointments, notes, and to-do items relating to the linked contacts from within Now Contact.

Conversely, while you're working in Now Up-to-Date, you can view all the contacts associated with an event.

Now Contact provides all the essential contact-management features that businesspeople and home users could ask for. Among noteworthy strengths are the program's brisk performance, flexible views, and outstanding documentation. Last but not least, Now Contact's tight integration with the Now Up-to-Date calendar program provides you with a complete personal organizer.—Jeffrey Sullivan

Now Contact
Now Software, Inc.
Portland, OR
(800) 237-3611; (503) 274-2800
$99; bundled with
Now Up-to-Date, $179

Seize the Day

If you're going to be organized, you might as well make the process pleasant. Seize the Day is a personal scheduler and organizer that opens each day with an inspirational quote. To dress it up, you can choose Living Scenes artwork or add a plug-in module. Shadowcatcher, a collection of Edward Curtis photographs of Native Americans, is the only plug-in module now available, but more should be coming soon.

Seize the Day
$59.95

PLUG-IN PATTERN POWER

Terrazzo

Terrazzo is a powerful image-enhancing filter and pattern factory, disguised as a mild-mannered Adobe Photoshop-compatible plug-in filter. As with most Adobe-standard plug-ins, Terrazzo works with any compatible program, including Photoshop, Fractal Design Painter, PixelPaint Pro 3, and Deneba Canvas. Terrazzo can quickly generate a never-ending array of kaleidoscopic patterns from an image, while allowing the digital artist to accurately control opacity, transitions, saturation, and dozens of other parameters.

Terrazzo builds pattern tiles by applying effects such as mirroring, rotating, and repeating to an entire image or part of an image. The filter's dialog box allows you to choose which portion of the image you want Terrazzo to reflect and twist based on one of 17 different kaleidoscopic symmetrical patterns. Warping an existing image is a sophisticated way to generate patterns that are automatically color-coordinated.

You can choose from effects such as Pinwheel, Whirlpool, or Sunflower, then play with Terrazzo's controls in real time to preview thousands of effects in minutes. Xaos warns that this "continuous preview" can slow down some color Macs, but on our Quadra 650 test system, the display was updated instantaneously.

Once you have rendered your pattern, the Mode menu—which operates similarly to the Mode menu in Photoshop—lets you control how the pattern is applied to another image. The pattern that you've rendered in Terrazzo can modify another image through parameters such as Lighten, Darken, Hue, Saturation, Color, and Luminosity.

The boundaries between portions of the pattern can be feathered to produce a smooth transition, and you can adjust opacity so that the underlying image shows through to varying degrees. Terrazzo can save patterns as

Sony: A World of Information Appliances for the Office and Home

 lat-panel displays are coming, but conventional cathode-ray tubes aren't likely to disappear anytime soon. Sony's vision of the future includes offices and homes filled with smart monitors: display-based devices with built-in peripherals tailored to handle special tasks such as video-conferencing, faxing, and other communications.

Think Big

Until now, the largest high-resolution desktop monitors maxed out at 21 inches. Sony's taken that one step further to create a mammoth 28-inch display, the biggest Trinitron you can buy. Unlike current grainy TV-sized presentation monitors, this one displays images at a supersharp 1,920 × 1,080-pixel resolution.

Better than Paper

Other things you can expect to see in the future: superhigh resolutions and enhanced display clarity. Sony already has the technology to create CRTs that offer more precision and detail than paper.

Smart Monitors

What will these smart monitors look like? Much like the one that sits on your PC today—except that they'll also be outfitted with a CPU, speakers, a printer, a camera, or a microphone. ■

PICT files that can be tiled seamlessly for use as desktop wallpaper or presentation backgrounds. Programs like Photoshop and Fractal Design Painter can use these PICT files as instant textures.

Terrazzo is an extremely useful tool for graphic artists, and for the budding computer artist it's also a lot of fun. Its interface is relatively simple, and the effects one can create are both elegant and limitless. If you want to generate patterns that tile, spice up your images with wondrous textures, create imaginative textile designs, or just play with abstract geometry, you should add Terrazzo to your plug-in library.—David D. Busch

Terrazzo 1.0
Xaos Tools Inc.
600 Townsend St.
Suite 270 E
San Francisco, CA 94103
(415) 487-7000
$199

GRAPHICS GADGETS: IMAGE-CAPTURE, CONVERSION, CATALOGING, AND EDITING TOOLS

Collage Complete

Collage Complete is a fairly lean collection of DOS and Windows programs priced at $149. The Windows side includes a screen-capture utility and a second program that doubles as an image manager and editor.

The capture module is the most robust aspect of the package. You can save screens to a file, printer, or the Windows Clipboard. Collage can automatically increment numbered file names when taking a sequence of shots, and is one of only a few capture utilities with a countdown feature, which lets you initiate some action before the screenshot shutter clicks.

Collage is especially adept at partial screen captures. Unlike other programs, which require you to define an area on-screen before you capture it, Collage always grabs the entire screen and places it in a preview window. You can then crop the image, using a zoom feature to place the crop lines precisely.

The package's Image Manager has some special features of its own. You can use it to add text to images, and it is one of the few programs to include paint features. It also supports TWAIN-compatible scanners. The DOS utilities, including a capture utility and a file-

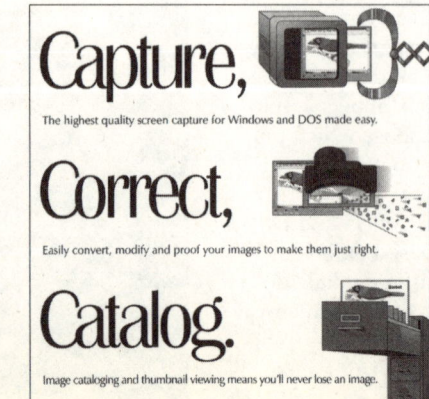

preview/slide-show module, are an added bonus.

The package does have its shortcomings, however. It works only with bitmap images, not vector, and while it does support Kodak PhotoCD files, otherwise it has a very limited set of supported image formats. And though you're not likely to buy a utility package based on its bundled clip art, it's still disappointing that Collage is one of the few packages that doesn't include a single sample image. If you need a strong screen-capture program that handles the most common bitmap file formats, Collage Complete delivers for both DOS and Windows. There are other choices, however, that deliver broader file-format support.—Alfred Poor

Collage Complete
Inner Media Inc.
60 Plain Rd.
Hollis, NH 03049
(800) 962-2949; (603) 465-3216
$149

Conversion Artist 2.0

Conversion Artist 2.0's list price of $99.95 is toward the low-end of the price range for similar products. Unfortunately, North Coast Software's package fits near the bottom in terms of features as well. Conversion Artist integrates all functions under a single set of menus, a more convenient approach than the traditional method of providing separate modules for each task. Its screen-

capture function works well, copying captured images to files, Windows's Clipboard, or the Conversion Artist editing window. The capture feature's only shortcoming is that it doesn't capture the mouse pointer as part of the image; other packages give the option of either including it or leaving it out.

In addition to its paint features, Conversion Artist's image-editing functions are more complete than most of the other programs's. You get a wide range of effects and filters, as well as a mask feature that comes with 17 predefined shapes. Conversion Artist can handle 32-bit color images and create automatic color separations.

The program doesn't work with vector-based images except Windows meta-files (WMF), but it can read 31 different bitmap formats and write 19. One unique output

format is an executable JPEG format, which creates an .EXE file you can run within Windows to view the JPEG-compressed image. Conversion Artist supports batch conversions, but it doesn't handle batch print jobs, nor does it offer any catalog feature for image files.—Alfred Poor

Conversion Artist 2.0
North Coast Software Inc.
P.O. Box 459
265 Scruton Pond Rd.
Barrington, NH 03825
(800) 274-9674; (603) 664-7871
$99.95

DoDot 4.0

Halcyon Software's DoDot 4.0 is actually a collection of five separate Windows programs. DoDot acts as the command center for the other five modules. While its editing tools are fairly typical, DoDot is one of the few programs that is capable of raster-to-vector conversion—it includes a trace feature that can be used to convert bitmap images to vector formats.

The screen-capture module, DoSnap, has all the standard features, including the ability to save the captured image to the Clipboard, a file, printer, or any combination of the three. DoView provides an easy way to view the contents of a graphics file. DoThumbnail is an image-cataloging utility, which also lets you append descriptions to an image for easy searches. DoConvert lets you convert a file or group of files in a single pass.

DoDot supports one of the largest ranges of graphics-file formats around, including 11 fax formats. It is one of the few that can read and write HPGL plotter-command language files, as well as write HPPCL laser-printer-control language files. It provides support for TWAIN scanners and can create automatic color separations from images.

There are a few drawbacks to DoDot, including its lack of support for compressed JPEG images (although you can download a filter from the company BBS) and the fact that it comes with only four sample images. Its inter-face has a few rough edges as well, such as its inability to list all the files in a directory—you must first specify the file format. Still, if you don't need paint or image-filter functions, DoDot will probably serve you well. It's not quite as feature-rich or easy to use as some other programs, but it gets the job done.—Alfred Poor

DoDot 4.0
Halcyon Software
1590 La Pradera Dr.
Campbell, CA 95008
(408) 378-9898
$189

HiJaak Pro 2.0

Inset Systems's HiJaak is a graybeard in this field; the DOS version was one of the earliest screen-capture utilities for PCs. HiJaak Pro 2.0 includes a copy of the DOS screen-capture utility, a Windows image-editing and conversion program, and a Windows image-catalog pro-gram, all for a list price of $169.

HiJaak's screen-capture features are on a par with the competition, including the ability to send the image to any combination of four different destinations: the HiJaak window, the Windows Clipboard, a printer, or file, in your choice of formats.

The image-editing functions do not include any paint features or special filters, but the program does offer the unusual option of letting you change the colors in an image. These color changes are stored by the program so you can apply the same changes to subsequent images. In another interesting feature, HiJaak lets you substitute any TrueType font installed on your system for text in some vector-based images. You cannot change the actual characters (to correct a spelling error, for example), only the appearance of the text.

Except for its lack of a trace feature, HiJaak is the file-conversion ruler. It supports a large number of formats—including faxes and PhotoCD—and includes the ability to write EPS and read and write PCL 4 files.

The thumbnail Browser makes it easy to organize your images, and you'll need to be organized since HiJaak comes with 300 WMF clip-art images, and Inset sends you another 200 when you register. The images have no keywords or descriptions, but you can place images in dif-ferent folders, making it easy to scan pictures arranged by subject.

HiJaak Pro is an excellent program, and it should be even better by the time you read this. Inset is replacing its Windows package with HiJaak Graphics Suite, which will add raster-to-vector con-versions and more image-editing functions, including various special effects for bitmaps and a copy of Micrografx Windows Draw for creating vector images. The program will also be able to extract text from vector images and search it using the Browser.—Alfred Poor

HiJaak Pro 2.0
Inset Systems
71 Commerce Dr.
Brookfield, CT 06804
(800) 374-6738; (203) 740-2400
$169

ImagePals 2.0

At $199 list, ImagePals 2.0 from Ulead Systems is priced about the same as other pack-ages, but it delivers more functionality than the rest of the pack in nearly every cate-gory. Like many of the others, ImagePals is a collection of separate Windows programs that work together. In fact, each program has a special Pals menu you can use to call the others.

ImagePals's capture mod-ule has a full set of features, including a countdown delay and the unique ability to take successive screenshot images automatically at timed inter-vals. Another clever detail comes to light when you choose to capture just a por-tion of the screen: A small window opens to reveal a magnified view, making it easier to crop the image more precisely.

The Viewer module lets you open any of the wide range of image files support-ed by the program. You can also use the Viewer to con-vert files by saving them in a new format. The CD-Browser lets you view thumbnail images of PhotoCD files from a CD-ROM, while the Album feature lets you create collec-tions of files, and then use keywords and other attribut-es to search for the files you want. Album works with more than just still images, too—you can use it to orga-nize anything from word pro-cessing documents to anima-tions to sound clips.

The power of ImagePals lies in the image editor. You'll find simple draw and paint features, including the ability to add text to an image. There is also a sophisticated cloning tool, which lets you duplicate one item in an image at another point in the image. Special effects such as sharp-en, blur, emboss, mosaic, and fisheye filters are also includ-ed. There's even a wonderful warp tool, which lets you

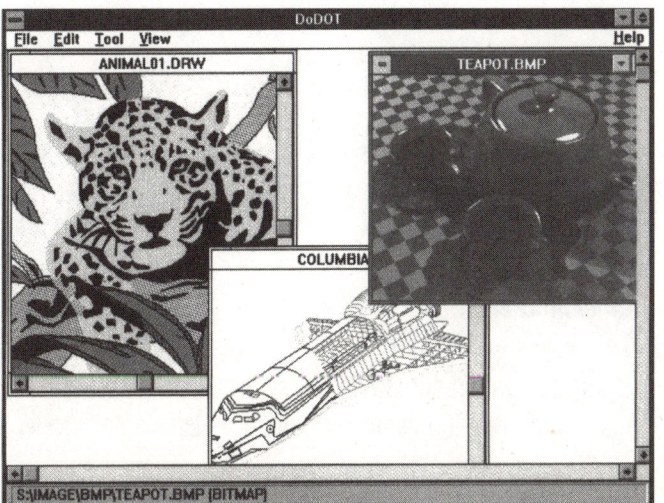

deform the shape of an image as if it were mapped onto a 3-D surface. The editor also lets you control color settings, adjust brightness and contrast, and perform dozens of other transformations on your images.

To make sure you have plenty of images with which to practice, Ulead includes a handful of images on floppy disks, plus a CD-ROM with 2,000 JPEG-compressed photos and another 47 PhotoCD images, all organized by subject into ImagePals's albums. A slide-show feature is also provided, complete with optional MIDI soundtrack.

ImagePals's few weaknesses, like its lack of support for fax formats, do not detract from its overall excellence. If you're looking for one program to do it all, look no further.—Alfred Poor

ImagePals 2.0
Ulead Systems
970 W. 190th St.
Suite 520
Torrance, CA 90502
(800) 858-5323; (310) 523-9393
$199

Pizazz Plus 4.0

Applications Techniques's Pizazz has long had a reputation for being able to grab even the most recalcitrant of DOS-application screens. The $149 Pizazz Plus 4.0 for Windows package bundles the company's collection of DOS utilities with a pair of Windows programs. While the combination isn't flashy, it's a reliable performer.

The CaptureEze screen-capture module has essentially the same set of features as most of the other programs. One handy feature is that you can define two different areas to capture and choose a separate hotkey for each. If you're taking a series of screenshots, for example, some of which are full screens while others require cropping, this feature will prevent you from having to reset capture parameters between shots.

The Pizazz Plus for Windows module provides limited image-editing features. You can crop images, change their orientation, and change the scale, but there are no paint features, filters, or special effects. The package does not have a catalog or album feature, nor does it support JPEG or PhotoCD image formats. It only works with bitmap formats, though it does support a wide range of these. The Windows utilities don't support batch processing, either, though you can do batch conversions and printing using DOS commands.

The features offered in Pizazz Plus for Windows are fine as far as they go, but they simply don't go far enough. For capturing DOS screens that resist other products, Pizazz Plus is an excellent choice; otherwise, you should explore other options.—Alfred Poor

Pizazz Plus 4.0
Applications Techniques Inc.
10 Lomar Park Dr.
Pepperell, MA 01463
(800) 433-5201; (508) 433-5201
$149

SnapPro 3.0

SnapPro is another Windows bundle, originally developed by Window Painters and now published by C-Star Technology. Rather than sharing a standard Windows menu bar, the different programs have button toolbars. Except for the main SnapPro module, these buttons are not labeled, and the only way to divine their function is to press the right mouse button. The mouse is certainly handy, but the program would be stronger if it supported the

FROGDESIGN: Visual and Functional: The Shape of Things to Come

Strategic-design firm frogdesign, architect of the distinctive Next computer and several of Logitech's ergonomic mice, is preparing for another kind of convergence: the merging of furniture and electronics. "In the future, we'll see microprocessors embedded in walls, tables, and chairs," says Strategic Design Manager Steven Holt.

Sleek

Change and opportunity will drive future technologies, such as video phones, digital cameras, and new wireless devices that are yet to be imagined.

Touch Me

The design of a product should be a celebration of content, part of the entire experience. Motorola's Magic-Cap PDA, Envoy, invites your hands to pick it up and hold it.

Fashion Statement

As markets mature, design becomes a differentiator. Frogdesign also crafted Packard-Bell's systems, which come with color panels for personalizing (and accessorizing) your PC.

Building Blocks

The pieces to Media Vision's Memphis Multimedia Upgrade System slide together so you can add, subtract, upgrade, and customize the look. ■

key-
board as well.

SnapPro itself is responsible for doing the bulk of the image-capture and conversion work. You can define a hotkey for capture, file destination, format, and area to be captured. You can also open and preview images and save them in different formats or with different color depths. SnapPro can quickly capture a portion of a screen.

If you want to make changes to an image or combine images, you need to use the Builder module. Builder can apply relatively few transformations to an image, but it does let you change orientation and duplicate the image.

SnapShow, the slide-show utility, lets you select a batch of BMP images to show in sequence. You can also specify a digitized sound or MIDI file to accompany your slide show.

Finally, SnapPro Gallery lets you view thumbnails of graphics files. The program does not support keywords or searching and can only view files from a single directory. On the positive side, a gallery can include motion video and sound as well as image files; a special viewer program lets you view motion-video clips. Overall, SnapPro is neither as easy nor as versatile as some of its

rivals. It may, however, be a good choice on a tight budget.—Alfred Poor

SnapPro 3.0
C-Star Technology
10250 Valley View Rd.
Suite 137
Eden Prairie, MN 55344
(612) 943-1565
$99.95

CUSTOM FONT CREATION MADE EASY
Adobe Type Manager 3.0

Adobe Systems Inc.'s new Adobe Type Manager 3.0 for Windows now gives PC users the same built-in tools for modifying Adobe's special multiple-master typefaces that Macintosh users have grown to love. These tools make it easy to create countless variations of each typeface by modifying its default weight, width, and size.

Each custom font takes up a mere 3K of hard-disk space and functions just like a standard Type 1 font. Documents containing custom fonts can be exchanged: They print and display normally on any machine where ATM is running and where the multiple-

master typeface or typefaces upon which they are based have been installed.

ATM 3.0 comes with one multiple-master typeface that can be customized (Tektron) and 29 standard Type 1 typefaces that cannot. Besides the 13 typefaces usually found in PostScript printers (such as Times Roman and Courier), there are 16 Type 1 typefaces new to release 3.0. These newcomers are a nice mixture of the serious and the whimsical, ranging from Baskerville and Berthold to Giddyup, a western-style font with characters that look like braided rope.

Network support is enhanced in release 3.0. You now can install ATM on a shared version of Windows running on virtually any network that supports Windows.

Unfortunately, most users will find the customizable Tektron, an informal handwriting style with limited applications, something of a disappointment. However, 13 other customizable multiple-master typeface packages are available from Adobe for $75 to $205 each. These include such styles as ITC Garamond and ITC Avant Garde Gothic. PC users are sure to love the customizable functionality that ATM 3.0 provides.—John Gliedman

Adobe Type Manager 3.0
Adobe Systems Inc.
1585 Charleston Rd.
P.O. Box 7900
Mountain View, CA
94039-7900
(800) 833-6687;
(415) 961-4400
$60

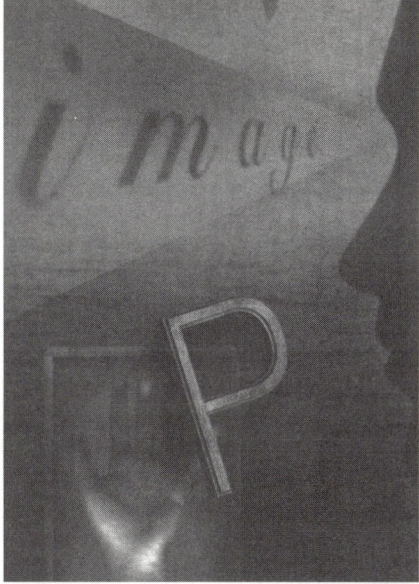

A NEW GRAPHICS POWERHOUSE
Photoshop 3.0

While yielding major increases in productivity, computer graphics tools also have had a limiting effect on design creativity. With the introduction of Photoshop 3.0, Adobe Systems Inc.'s latest upgrade to its paint and photo retouching software, a new age is dawning in the computer graphics and design world. Rather than limiting creativity, Adobe Photoshop 3.0 actually provides a working environment where artists can let their imaginations roam free.

As should be expected, Photoshop 3.0 code has been optimized to run native on the Power Mac. A smart installer determines whether a PowerPC chip is present and installs the appropriate version of the software automatically. You can also choose to install a "universal" fatbinary version that runs in native mode on both Power

Macs and 68K machines. But interface innovations and new functionality are what really make this the most significant upgrade since the introduction of the program.

The major new feature addition to Photoshop 3.0 is multiple image layers. Although previous versions of Photoshop allowed for the creation of files with a full-color composite image and separate 8-bit channels, these channels had limited editing capabilities and were intended for use in color separation or the creation of masks. While this capability still remains, the Layers feature provides fully editable, full-color layers that can be included in a single file. With Layers, elements of an image can be manipulated individually on separate layers and viewed as a single composite image. Now changes can be made to elements on individual layers, modified and viewed without destroying any image data. For example, you can render type on one layer and a background on another. If the type must be changed, the type layer can be modified, leaving the background layer untouched. Rerendering a complete file from scratch is no longer required—and you save a lot of time.

A customizable function palette similar to the one

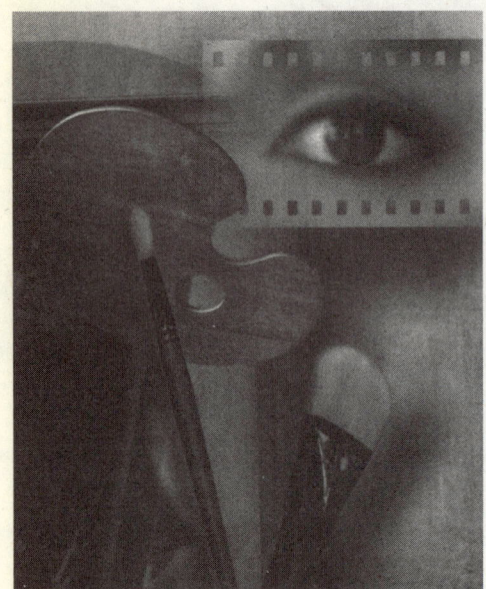

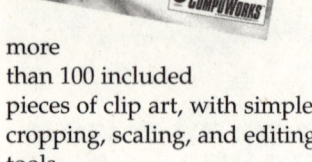

found in Adobe Premiere 4.0 has made its debut in Photoshop 3.0. Often-used menu commands can be linked to on-screen buttons found in a floating palette, and keyboard equivalent function keys can be assigned to them as well. Other palettes, like the brushes, magic-wand settings, layers, and pen tool, can be grouped in floating palettes as well, and little folder-like tabs allow users to switch from one to another.

With Photoshop 3.0, Adobe has implemented drag-and-drop throughout the application. Objects from an image, including selections, layers, channels, and paths, can be dragged from one window and dropped into another, instantly creating a new layered composite. In addition, tool palettes can be dragged from one floating window to another, allowing users to combine the tools they most often use into one handy tool palette. While the net result of this technique is similar to Microsoft's customizable tool ribbons, Adobe's interface innovations are clearly the model to follow. Two new tools have also made their debut in version 3.0. The move tool can reposition selections, while the sponge tool is for increasing or decreasing the color saturation in an image.

Whether you are a first-time Photoshop user or a pre-press professional, you will surely find Photoshop 3.0's interface, features, and efficiency a pleasure to work with.—Ben Goodman

Photoshop 3.0
Adobe Systems Inc.
1585 Charleston Rd.
P.O. Box 7900
Mountain View, CA 94039-7900
(800) 833-6687
$895; $149 upgrade

PRESS FOR LESS
CompuWorks Publisher 1.0

CompuWorks Publisher 1.0 is a minimalist DTP product. For $49.95, WizardWorks's bundle gives you GST Software's 1st Press, which is also included in Delta Point's Freeze Frame bundle, plus some fleshed-out documentation. Elementary graphics and text-editing tools reside in a simple, understandable interface, and ten templates further simplify your design process. CompuWorks Publisher does little in the way of taking new users by the hand and walking them through the job of document creation, but its low price and sparse feature set may make it attractive to users who want the basics at a rock-bottom price.

CompuWorks's templates, including flyer, letter, memo, and newsletter, are geared toward both small-business and personal applications. Like other low-end DTP programs, CompuWorks lets you define styles or use the ready-made styles included (like bulleted list, caption, footer, and subhead). By building master pages for documents, you can create your own templates to augment the built-in collection. You can use the template as design guidelines; simply replace what's there with your own text and graphics, and modify styles or other attributes to create and save your own templates. If you start from scratch, you're confined to six page formats including a small organizer-type as well as letter- and legal-sized pages.

The program can import text and clip art in many popular formats; you can touch up imported images, or the more than 100 included pieces of clip art, with simple cropping, scaling, and editing tools.

CompuWorks Publisher has two selling points: It's inexpensive, and it offers the most commonly used DTP tools without overwhelming less-experienced users with unnecessary features, power, or control. None of its features particularly stands out, and it offers less functionality than most other programs, especially in terms of guiding the design-impaired through the surprisingly frustrating process of making a simple card or brochure—after all, even low-end desktop publishing tasks are difficult if you don't understand the basics and can't get a helping hand. If, however, you don't need the horsepower of a pricier program or the assistance offered by the likes of other programs, Compu-Works will get the job done.—Kathy Yakal

CompuWorks Publisher 1.0
WizardWorks Inc.
3850 Annapolis Ln.
Suite 100
Minneapolis, MN 55447
(800) 229-2714; (612) 559-5140
$49.95

Easy Working Desktop Publisher 1.1

Easy Working Desktop Publisher looks and works like a state-of-the-art, entry-level DTP program—from three years ago. Nevertheless, this $59.95 package is extraordinarily easy to learn and use, letting novices turn out simple documents in minutes. The limited range of documents supported, though, and the paucity of samples, walk-throughs, and design tips, make it suitable only for users whose needs fall within its narrow range of templates, or who are willing to work on a blank canvas with a limited number of tools.

Originally produced by Spinnaker Software, Easy Working Desktop Publisher was acquired along with the rest of the Spinnaker line by SoftKey International and has gone for two years without an upgrade. While it works fine under Windows 3.1, it was built for Windows 3.0. In fact, it comes with the Publisher's PowerPak collection of 50 scalable fonts for Windows 3.0, which is likely to crash your system if you try installing it under Windows 3.1. SoftKey support staff indicated that this is a common problem, and that crash victims must rerun Windows Setup from DOS to get things working again. In other words, stick with your existing Windows 3.1 fonts.

Easy Working Desktop Publisher consists of two separate but integrated elements:

a main document-production screen and a tables editor. The latter provides tools for building simple calculating worksheets for your documents. You can import and export tabular data in popular spreadsheet and text formats including WKS and CSV.

If you know the basics of working with frames, typing in or importing text, and assigning fonts, sizes, and attributes, working with the text portion of your Easy Working documents will be a snap. You can adjust margins, view your work at several zoom levels, and wrap text around graphic objects. The program automatically generates indexes and tables of contents, and includes a spell checker and thesaurus to check your work, but no auditor to pinpoint layout problems.

Easy Working Desktop Publisher's simplicity is admirable, but obviously limiting. Novices may be frustrated by the program's lack of guidance, and both beginners and experienced users will find more and better graphics and text tools in several other products.—Kathy Yakal

Easy Working Desktop Publisher 1.1
SoftKey International Inc.
201 Broadway
Cambridge, MA 02139
(800) 227-5609; (617) 494-1200
$59.95

Microsoft Publisher 2.0

No one has done more to accommodate the needs of amateur designers than Microsoft. Publisher 2.0 offers the best of both worlds: enough design tools to build professional-looking documents, plus multiple layers of step-by-step guidance that will satisfy even the most timid beginner. Other similar products offer only pieces of the puzzle that Publisher has capably solved.

Publisher's graphics tools don't approach the level of their high-end professional relatives's but are more than adequate for everyday publishing. Besides the artistic tools of Microsoft Draw, the program offers 20 TrueType fonts, over 100 predesigned borders, 135 clip-art images (along with a gallery to view and organize all of your clip-art images), a shape tool, irregular text wrap, and 256-color support.

Support for OLE 2.0 data exchange, TWAIN image scanning, and Kodak PhotoCD images provides generous connections to the outside world. Publisher's text-handling tools include rotation, kerning, justification, automatic bulleted and numbered lists, and drag-and-drop editing. You can create or import styles, and import text from most word processors.

When developing a design, you can choose from three different approaches. Publisher's 17 PageWizard assistants offer the most prolific help. They run the gamut from business (brochures and newsletters) to personal (invitations and greeting cards) to whimsical (paper airplanes and origami). PageWizards lock you into their own prefab designs, asking you for text to pour into designated spaces. You simply choose an overall design and answer on-screen questions, and Publisher does the rest.

If you want a bit more control over your design but don't want to start from

square one, you can use one of Publisher's 35 templates. These, too, range from personal to professional applications, accommodating documents ranging from manuals and menus to resumes and jar labels. You work directly on each template page, replacing text and changing fonts and attributes, and using supplied clip art or choosing your own.

Finally, for free-form design, you can select from eight different document formats, including full-page, book, tent-fold card, business card, and banner, and use the same tools available within the templates to create on a blank page.

When you think you're done, Publisher's Layout Checker and Print Troubleshooter combs your design, alerting you to potential problems. While this auditor isn't as thorough a check as you'd get from a professional standing over your shoulder, it will point out obvious problems such as text running over an edge.

About the only negative is that Publisher can be a bit of a system-resource hog. If you're running another large application in the background, or if you've interacted with other applications extensively, you may lose access to some parts of the program. Quitting and restarting Publisher should fix the problem. Still, that's a small complaint. When it comes to a combination of tools, templates, and multilevel assistance, no other

entry-level DTP program can match Microsoft Publisher.— Kathy Yakal

Microsoft Publisher 2.0
Microsoft Corp.
One Microsoft Way
Redmond, WA 98052
(800) 426-9400; (206) 882-8080
$99; $39.95

PFS:Publisher 1.1

PFS:Publisher, another of SoftKey's acquisitions from the late Spinnaker Software Corp., is more competent and better geared to novice DTP users than its sister product, Easy Working Desktop Publisher. Though the program hasn't been upgraded for over a year and is overpriced at $79.95, PFS: Publisher implements at least some of the tools found in today's best Windows 3.1 programs, such as OLE and right-mouse-button support and a configurable tool palette. Had Spinnaker survived long enough to improve on these fine beginnings with the kind of step-by-step navigation found in Microsoft Publisher, there'd be a closer race today for low-end DTP dominance.

Though it lacks Publisher-like assistants, PFS:Publisher does provide a variety of ease-of-use features. Starting your own publication from scratch, if you don't understand the basics of desktop publishing, is difficult no matter what DTP program you use. PFS: Publisher simplifies the process in many ways. Its written user's guide

MIT Media Lab: Computers Comfortable Enough to Wear

To visit MIT Media Lab is to wish yourself five years or more into the future, where computers are so friendly and easy to use that they actually see, hear, and talk.

Imagine technology comfortable enough to wear—like an old sweater. Computers will dissolve into the walls and background; when you step into a room, it will know something about you.

Omni Sensorium

As part of its Living Room of the Future project, MIT envisions the I-Way and its contents coming at you on a large-screen TV/projector from the comfort of your couch.

Universal Remote

A wireless, modular, PDA-sized remote controls the sound, lights, and content.

BodyNet

Why carry a computer when you can wear it? One group at MIT is working on embroidering cellular phones or wireless computers into fabric and furniture.

The Walls Electric

Wireless positioning sensors in the walls and furniture will be able to detect and respond to your location in a room. ■

and reference guide comprise probably the best off-screen assistance available among similar products. An online help system covers concepts, commands, and terms; and a customizable QuickButtons palette can hold up to 24 of your most often-used icons.—Kathy Yakal

PFS:Publisher 1.1
SoftKey International Inc.
201 Broadway
Cambridge, MA 02139
(800) 227-5609; (617) 494-1200
$79.95

Pressworks 1.03

Long-time low-priced software vendor Timeworks recently closed its doors, and with it went the well-known entry-level DTP package Publish It. But Britain's GST Software, the original designers of Publish It, as well as the ubiquitous 1st Press, will continue to support Publish It, and will offer users of that program the option to upgrade to their new product, Pressworks. The program doesn't come close to Microsoft Publisher's help system or PagePlus's powerful design features, but it remains a good option for faithful Publish It fans.

Pressworks's strengths include a generous stable of templates, an adequate set of tools encased in an easy-to-understand interface, and OLE support. The 47 previewable templates range from business forms and newsletters to invitations and manuals. The program's main toolbar toggles between draw, text, paragraph, and frame modes.

On the text side, five ready-made paragraph styles (bullet, caption, heading, subhead, and body text) get you started, and you can easily define and add others using Pressworks's icon-driven style-definition process. You can import text from major word processors, then add formatting and other attributes, or enter your own using Pressworks's basic text tools. PowerText functions let you jazz up your text by placing it along circles, lines, or arches.

Graphically speaking, Pressworks offers hundreds of clip-art images plus drawing tools including lines, line segments, circles, rectangles, and freehand sketching. You can use a wide variety of color fills and patterns to dress up backgrounds, text, and hand-drawn objects or open spaces, and scale or crop images to fit your page frames.

Pressworks includes a spell checker and thesaurus, but no auditor-type tool for checking your layout. An online how-to section, glossary, and searchable help files supplement the program's clear, complete documentation and quick-start guide.

If your budget will not permit more than $50 for a DTP package, Pressworks will do the job. It doesn't coddle novices, but once you get the hang of working with its text and graphics functions, Pressworks allows you to create documents with as much structure or creative freedom as you like.—Kathy Yakal

Pressworks 1.03
GST Software
Meadow Ln.
St. Ives Huntindon
Cambridgeshire PE17 4LG UK
(800) 236-1062

GET QUICKER, SHARPER PAGES

SuperPrint 3.1

Tired of playing tug-of-war with your printer for control of your PC during long print jobs? Even the relatively simple documents we produced while testing entry-level DTP programs took as long as three minutes to print, due to a Windows Print Manager spooler weighed down by complex graphics and lengthy documents. If you're repeatedly tinkering with a document and printing it to check your results, three minutes of downtime per draft can add a lot of wasted time to your design process.

Zenographics offers a clever solution to this problem with its SuperPrint 3.1—a software package that you install as a Windows printer driver, defining it as your default printer for all applications or switching to it only for printing-intensive workdays. SuperPrint's 32-bit drivers replace those supplied with Windows's 16-bit Print Manager, formatting and generating your print job in the background while you continue to work. The package supports both single and networked printing, and most

popular laser, inkjet, dot-matrix, and thermal printer models.

If you're working with very large applications or have limited RAM, you can tell SuperPrint to delay printing—storing documents in a queue, rather than printing them in the background. Once you've set up delayed print jobs, you'll need to open the SuperPrint application to "release" them, printing them one at a time or as a batch. You also can cancel print jobs, or rearrange them to print in a different order.

Whether in background, delayed, or batch mode, SuperPrint works by building what Zenographics calls SuperMetafiles every time you invoke the print command. These object-based files take up far less memory than Print Manager files, so you get your cursor—and control of your PC—back in seconds, rather than minutes. In our tests, a document that took Print Manager three minutes took SuperPrint about six seconds.

Moreover, SuperPrint's SuperDrivers improve not only print speed but the quality of the completed document, by offering finer controls than traditional Windows printer drivers. The program's 256 shades of gray and 16.7 million colors, as well as a variety of halftone options, make for crisper, more colorful and detailed graphics and text.

There's only one caveat: Documents previously created in some DTP applications, such as Microsoft Publisher, may need some reformatting before you can print them correctly with the SuperPrint driver. If you can't find a solution to this or other printing problems, you can consult SuperPrint's thorough help system or get support via phone, fax, or CompuServe.—Kathy Yakal

SuperPrint
Zenographics
(714) 851-6352
$99.95

CorelDraw 5

Version 5 of Corel's well-known suite of graphics programs is a let's-get-it-all-together upgrade. The components—some of which originated in very different forms—now look much more alike. And where CorelDraw once flouted its own common

interface, it now sports button-laden ribbons, Microsoft-ish dialog boxes with tabbed headers for easy switching among component screens, and help boxes that pop up beside your cursor if you linger near a button or toolbar tool.

Drawing and editing in Draw, the centerpiece of the suite, is still as comfortably quirky as ever, carrying on such traditions as a single click to move an object and a second click to rotate it. It's a program for the artistically minded, but it's no longer just for the artist. The new release has improvements that makes this program—

and this package—a complete design and publishing utility.

All the programs in the suite share OLE 2.0 functions (for example, drag and drop)

and a new color-management system licensed from Candela. This allows you to create a system profile of your hardware by selecting its components from a prede-fined list and allowing the individual programs to per-form automatic color match-ing, optimizing that matching for bitmaps or vector draw-ings. Tools are also available for manually creating a sys-tem profile. FOCOLTONE and Dainippon color models have been added, CMYK val-ues can be individually cali-brated, and separations can be previewed on-screen.

Draw and PhotoPaint, the vector- and bitmap-editing

programs, make extensive use of roll-up menus—floating dialog boxes that can be reduced to a single bar (like rolling up a window shade) to

give you quick access to the options while reducing on-screen clutter. These programs have undergone many other changes and improvements. For example, Draw has added tools to ease technical draw-ing requirements such as the Transform roll-up menu, which boasts new placement and measurement features for precise object positioning, using absolute or relative scales and working to within a thousandth of an inch.

Intricate masking and pasting is available with the PowerClip tool, which lets you place one object inside another to create a mask, and even nest one PowerClip inside another. Better 3-D extrusion lets objects share vanishing points and achieve shading from up to three light sources; settings can be customized and saved. Thanks to the increased num-ber of detailed roll-up menus and good context-sensitive help, all of the new features (and most of the old ones) are easier to use.

Draw now creates a CMX (Corel Presentation Exchange) file format as part of the tradi-tional CDR file, allowing such files to be imported into other Corel applications, a capabili-ty that did not exist with the CDR format alone. Although Draw and PhotoPaint are still very much stand-alone appli-cations, they can work more easily with one another's files. And to assist in finding those files, CorelMosaic, a graphics-image file manager, can be called from within any of the component programs.

PhotoPaint has evolved into a high-end bitmap-editing tool that shows the influence of Fractal Design Painter and Fauve Matisse. Its new painting and retouching tools and filters allow you to add all those quasi-Impressionist effects that have become so popular. In fact, it will work with any Adobe-compliant plug-in, such as Kai's Power Tools, adding to an already impressive collection of filters.

PhotoPaint works with images as complex as 32-bit CMYK files; the maddening process of editing a large image is eased by the ability to partially load a file and to crop it on import. The program now has its own native TIFF format that allows pasted objects to float, and therefore remain editable, until specifically merged. Vector-based files are converted to bitmaps when imported; the results are impressive, provided the curves in the original aren't too complicated.

CorelTrace, an included utility, works the other way, converting bitmaps into vector files. By default, it aims for simple, quick conversions; with some tinkering, it will try to distinguish among the more subtle color and shading differences, but you're still left with a fairly Impressionistic rendering if the original is very detailed.

As if that weren't enough, there's even a spreadsheet program, CorelChart, which renders information in any of over 90 chart types, including new Gantt, polar, radar, and bubble styles. On the spread-sheet side, 250 new functions have been added, and cells can be edited and formatted using Draw tools.

Many of the processes in Draw can now be recorded as a macro, and most user-definable effects in any of the programs can be saved and re-used. In fact, whenever something is automatic or definable, such as brush shapes or canvas styles, chances are that the program includes a library of samples somewhere. The clip-art and typeface collections alone are worth the cost of this program.

The CorelDraw package is also drifting more and more into multimedia. There's now a CD-ROM-based QuickTour with selectable on-screen instructions about the various applications. The animation application, CorelMove, adds a morphing feature to a collection of tools for combining animation and sound. And CorelShow, the slide-show module, adds on-screen text editing and a notes-for-speakers facility; it also works with output from the other Corel applications.

Someday, there probably will be one big Corel program that incorporates all of these many features. In the meantime, this set of talented siblings is getting along much better now, looking more alike, and giving terrific value for the money.—B. A. Nilsson

CorelDraw 5
Corel Corp.
P.O. Box 3595
Salinas, CA 93912-3595
(800) 778-3332

Freeze Frame 2.0

Once merely a collection of graphics utilities, Delta Point's Freeze Frame has evolved into a low-end DTP package with the addition of GST Software's 1st Press and 1st Design. In trying to do two things well, however, Freeze Frame does both poorly: It may be helpful to users who need a suite of graphics tools, but Freeze Frame does not work well as an integrated DTP title. Furthermore, you'll find no context-sensitive guidance, no walk-throughs of the design process, few templates, and little clip art.

Freeze Frame installs as five separate icons in two program groups. 1st Press is the same stand-alone DTP program found in CompuWorks Publisher, while 1st Design is a separate drawing package. A Media Manager, which also includes limited image-editing tools, lets you view and manage collections of graphics and multimedia files as thumbnail sketches, and convert them to any of 44 bitmap, fax, and vector-graphics formats. Finally, a screen-capture utility snaps screen shots, and an icon editor lets you create custom icons.

You'll do the lion's share of page makeup in 1st Press, but you can also create your whole document in 1st Design, using one of 10 templates for documents such as charts, invitations, or posters. You also can use the more artistic capabilities of 1st Design to create an image, then export your finished picture into 1st Press. The former includes drawing tools such as shapes, Bézier curves, blends, and autotrace to enhance your creations, and lets you enter or import text (42 TrueType fonts are provided) before fine-tuning it with kerning, leading, and spacing tools. Local menus simplify navigation when you're working with objects.

While there's no step-by-step guidance or context-sensitive help, Freeze Frame does offer some step-by-step instructions, and you can hit F3 to perform up to 50 levels of undo. Still, Freeze Frame's mishmash of tools and applications makes for a disjointed DTP solution. It offers a few utilities that other titles in this price range don't. 1st Design is not a bad little design package (though less muscular than the likes of PagePlus). But Freeze Frame gives little help to users unaccustomed to manipulating text and graphics into a finished document.—Kathy Yakal

Freeze Frame 2.0
Delta Point Inc.
2 Harris Ct.
Suite B-1
Monterey, CA 93940
(800) 446-6955; (408) 648-4000
$49.90

FREEZE FRAME 2.0 CAPTURES THE BEST OF LOW-END DESKTOP PUBLISHING

Freeze Frame 2.0

Delta Point's Freeze Frame 1.0, a popular low-end graphics utility, has evolved into a true low-end desktop-publishing program. For $89.95, version 2.0 offers the earlier product's graphics-conversion and screen-capture utilities, while also incorporating GST Software's 1st Design drawing program and 1st Press desktop-publishing software. An icon editor and media manager round out Freeze Frame's impressive array of applications. Delta Point has combined some of the best features of competing graphics utilities, drawing programs, and DTP products at a price that's lower than most of them sold individually.

Freeze Frame's Media Manager catalogs your graphics files in any of the bitmap, fax, and vector file formats that are supported by the program's graphics-conversion utility. These include BMP, CGM, CLP, DRW, EPS, FAX, GIF, PCD, PCX, and WMF. You can display images as on-screen thumbnails, define the size and sort order, and print them.

1st Press is best suited for nonprofessionals who want to create documents such as newsletters and brochures. It can't compete with Microsoft Publisher in terms of help for novices, but it does offer templates and an understandable interface. Several page sizes and views are supported, as are both ATM and TrueType fonts (42 are included). Standard graphics and editing tools are built in, and you can fill text and shapes with 36 different patterns or choose from 150 clip-art images.

1st Design imports and exports in several formats, including BMP, GEM, PCX, TIF, and WMF. Drawing tools include shapes and Bézier lines and curves; power tools let you autotrace, and blend shapes, lines, and colors.

Two other extras round out Freeze Frame's tool palette. The screen-capture program grabs screens in any of several formats, such as PCX, TIF, and WPG. Color comes in 16-color, 256-color, 16-bit, or 24-bit varieties with monochrome screens also supported. You can also create icons from scratch or modify existing ones.

Freeze Frame 2.0 has taken a giant step since its earlier version, from a grab bag of utilities into a worthy competitor of low-end graphics and DTP products. While more automated design processes, more thorough documentation, and a better melding of the many applications within Freeze Frame would be welcome, it certainly has the raw materials to be a winner.—Kathy Yakal

Freeze Frame 2.0
Delta Point Inc.
2 Harris Ct.
Suite B-1
Monterey, CA 93940
(800) 446-6955; (408) 648-4000
$89.95

OOGLER GOADS GRAPHICS VIEWING BACK TO BASIC

OOgler

If you are looking for a very simple, low-cost graphic viewer, OOgler from Inset

Systems may be worth an ogle. For a mere $37.50, you might, as the brochure trumpets, see OOdles of pictures and have OOdles of fun. But the program's limitations make it a questionable investment for all but the most rudimentary systems.

Once installed, OOgler allows you to view a file in several different ways: by using OOgler directly, by double-clicking on an image file in the File Manager, or by dragging an image file name in the File Manager onto the OOgler icon.

Inset has tailored the interface to meet the needs of novice Windows users, with large, legible buttons and an uncomplicated menu bar. The buttons let you open and close files, zoom in and out, and get image information as well as general help. But that's it. There's no provision for file conversion or rudimentary image management, which, the brochure explains, prevents anyone from tampering with disk files.

The documentation is tailored to the program's sim-

plistic outlook, consisting of a glossy card with information about installation, how to view images, and how to use OOgler in the File Manager. The online help contains very good basic information about graphic files in general and a comprehensive explanation of the program's features.

OOgler provides viewers for 24 raster and 11 vector formats, but the program can't handle popular formats such as EPS or CDR, and has an intrinsic limit on JPEG files of 1,500 × 1,500 pixels. And although it claims to support JPEG and PCD files, attempting to view them crashed the program with a message regarding the current video mode and instructions to see TroubleShooting Help. There wasn't any. A call to Inset's tech support revealed that OOgler isn't comfortable with ATI video cards, the ATI Ultra Pro in particular. Changing the settings in OOgler's configuration file fixed the problem, but screen updates were painfully slow.

OOgler ships with 200 pieces of clip art in CGM and JPEG format, a valuable example of getting what you pay for. In sum, OOgler may fill the bill if you need an inexpensive, general-purpose image viewer without any additional frills.—Susan Glinert

OOgler
Inset Systems
71 Commerce Dr.
Brookfield, CT 06804
(800) 374-6738; (203) 740-2400
$37.50

Altamira Composer 1.01

An image-editing program in name only, Composer uses a different metaphor and language to perform its bitmap magic. Other image editors like PhotoPaint and Picture Publisher have implemented the bitmap-as-object concept by placing each object on its own layer. Composer was designed from the ground up as an object-oriented application. Thus, you can't just open a bitmap file and start painting. You have to create objects before you can do any work, either by importing them or creating them from scratch with Composer's high-powered toolbox.

The learning process is complicated by the 180 icons used to access common Composer functions, including non-standard representations for many frequently used features such as copy and paste. You won't see any familiar selection handles around the current object, either, but must hold down a shift key to see which object is active.

The terminology is also new—Composer refers to points as "ducks," the background as "the void," and a gradient as a "ramp." You'll also need to read the manual for the meaning of terms unique to Composer such as "color lift." But you'll have a great deal of fun experimenting, and you can customize or

turn off the toolbars to lessen the on-screen confusion.

Once you get used to its new concepts, you'll find Composer an amazing creative tool for producing unusual photo compositions. Rather than paintbrushes and spray cans, Composer's toolbox offers functions usually found in vector-based applications. For example, you can stack and group objects; apply permutations, textures, transforms, and warps; and adjust color with the Touchup and Enhance tools. No matter which transformation you apply, separate objects remain independently editable—and also maintain their image quality, thanks to the program's inherent intelligence and excellent anti-aliasing.

The Texture function, which copies pixels of an underlying object into those of an object floating above it, is one of Composer's most powerful tools. Because objects can contain partially transparent areas, you can easily configure the Texture tool to cut out an arbitrarily shaped portion of an image, then apply that texture to another object. For example, you can map a semi-transparent texture onto the surface of a glass-shaped object, making it appear realistically clear.

Another basic utensil, the Duff Spline tool, passes a smooth curve through user-defined points. Since you don't have any traditional Bézier handles to worry about, the curve is easy to edit. Working together, the

Spline and Texture tools let you accurately cut out shaped objects from a background.

Composer supplies a good set of filters for softening, sharpening, embossing, and adjusting colors (and works with Photoshop plug-ins, too, if you prefer). You also get a set of warps that distort the alpha and color channels—causing a selected area of an image to warp around a protruding, truncated cone, for example, or inverting spokes of an imaginary disk within a selected area.

Composer supports all of the popular bitmap formats, and implements an alpha-channel extension to them so that they can be used as library images. The program is also Kodak PhotoCD-enabled for any of that standard's five resolutions. If you want to use a Composer image with another program, you can export it as an EPS, PostScript, or TIFF file. Because Composer lacks prepress tools, you'll need another image editor to perform various functions such as dot-gain adjustment, separations, and undercolor removal.

Considering the product's complexity, Composer's documentation is pretty good, though it's sparse on pictures of effects you can obtain with the toolbox. Once you work through the tutorial and learn your way around the toolbars, the program will seem a little less intimidating. At any rate, if you're tired of applying the same old whirlpools and camera filters, Composer

will broaden your creative horizons.—Susan Glinert

Altamira Composer 1.01
Microsoft Corp.
$795

Corel PhotoPaint 5

Corel's PhotoPaint has evolved from a pleasant, low-level bitmap manipulator to a top-quality image-editing program. Version 5 is full of sophisticated new features, as well as a wonderful interface, tight integration with the rest of the Corel suite of products, and OLE 2.0 support—you can drag and drop information from the company's Draw and Mosaic, for instance, giving you access to an enormous library of clip art and vector graphics, which PhotoPaint automatically converts to bitmaps when you open them. If that's not enough, PhotoPaint offers over 40 import filters.

The Corel products all use roll-ups—scrollable floating palettes from which you select and adjust options. Not only are roll-ups a convenient way to access commands, but they take up little room on-screen. A new context-sensitive button bar changes depending on what tool is selected.

Other productivity enhancements include the ability to open sections of a file to crop and resample before opening the entire file. You can also load, save, node edit, and resize masks, and save the alpha channel in PhotoPaint's CPT format.

Masks can be easily added or subtracted, and the Color Mask roll-up lets you protect or select specific colors.

The interface, familiar to CorelDraw users, lets you double-click on an object to bring up rotation handles, and click and drag to resize an object while keeping its proportions intact. The Checkpoint command, which saves the current version of an image, is a real time-saver. A Restore Checkpoint command can undo all changes made after you set the Checkpoint.

PhotoPaint lets you define selected bitmaps as independent objects; a set of object-selection buttons makes it as easy to clip and build objects as it is to create masks. Each object resides on a separate layer, which can be turned on or off at will. Any manipulation that can be applied to an image—fills, transformations, and so on—can be applied to an object.

While this feature is great, there isn't much flexibility in merge control. Unlike Picture Publisher, which lets you merge objects by color, luminosity, and so on, PhotoPaint only lets you control the degree of an object's transparency and feathering, making complex compositing difficult. Corel does promise another upgrade soon.

PhotoPaint's strengths lie in the ease with which you can edit objects and the special effects with which you can perform transformations. The program lets you use CorelDraw's famous fractal fills, natural-appearing bitmap textures such as clouds and minerals, as well as a raft of filters and third-party plug-ins. A new Mesh Warp feature lays a grid over a selected area, helping create customized warping effects, while the Perspective filter lets you transform an object to produce a quasi-3-D effect.

PhotoPaint 5's new professional-level color-management system creates a System Color Profile tailored to your monitor, scanner, and printer. The package has powerful color-separation tools, and the ability to accurately convert and edit in

CMYK mode. You have precise control over screening and output resolution, and automatic trapping is built in.—Susan Glinert

Corel PhotoPaint 5
Corel Corp.
1600 Carling Ave.
Ottawa, ON K1Z 8R7
(800) 772-6735; (613) 728-8200
$249

Picture Publisher 4.0

For heavy-duty, repetitive production tasks, no program outguns Picture Publisher. Its simple interface and breadth of tools make it appealing to the occasional user as well. And at $595, Picture Publisher costs hundreds of dollars less than the competition.

Powerful features like layered objects, keystroke macro recording, multiple file selection from an array of thumbnails, and the ability to load and edit image sections set Micrografx's program apart from the competition. As an extra convenience, you can open an image at a lower resolution, decide what editing needs to be done, record a macro with those changes, open the original file, and let Picture Publisher execute the macro. Opening files is quick, too—Picture Publisher loaded a 5MB image in 9 seconds, compared to 45 seconds for Photoshop.

Picture Publisher offers a context-sensitive toolbar for each basic function—masking, painting, and so on. For example, when you click on the Paint icon, you get drop-down

selectors for setting brush size, shape, and style, and a feathering adjustment. Toggle buttons on the lower right of the display let you instantly access color shields, a ruby-mask overlay, the mask channel, the color palette, and image information. The PgUp and PgDn keys quickly zoom in and out of an image.

Like PhotoPaint, Picture Publisher lets you create independent objects, but its implementation of this feature is considerably more powerful. Picture Publisher treats each object as a separate layer—the objects float over the base image and are independently editable. This capability lets you create and maneuver grouped objects, and change the front-to-back order of the layers. A floating Object List window displays thumbnails of each object in the current image; to switch among them, just click on the thumbnail.

The flexible Merge mode lets objects overlap in 16 different ways, by color channel, hue, or luminosity, for example. Objects remain layered as long as you save files in Picture Publisher's proprietary format; exporting the file to a standard format automatically creates a merged image.

Picture Publisher's mask editing is the best of many programs we've seen. In addition to geometric, adjustable Bézier, and free-form masks, version 4.0 adds an alpha channel and a flexible snap-to auto-mask feature that lets you edit as you travel along the edge of an object. You can also specify whether feathering should occur inside or outside the mask, and use color shields to protect certain colors from editing.

Picture Publisher is one of the few programs that will create a palette from an image; others make you laboriously add each color to a palette with an eyedropper tool. Unfortunately, Picture Publisher does not support spot color-matching standards such as Pantone and TruMatch.

A wide range of filter effects are provided; an Effects Browser lets you select, configure, and preview such filters as emboss, facet, metal, ripple, twirl, and wind. The program also supports third-party plug-in filters for either Photoshop or PhotoStyler, but doesn't support Kai's Power Tools's Path Gradients.

The program comes with a handy image browser that lets you organize your files into collections called albums, and view them as either file names or thumbnails. Albums are useful for performing searches and other housekeeping chores such as copying and renaming. As an additional bonus, Micrografx is one of the few companies to provide 24-hour weekday technical support; hours are 8 a.m. to 5 p.m. on weekends.—Susan Glinert

Picture Publisher 4.0
Micrografx
1303 Arapaho Rd.
Richardson, TX 75081
(800) 676-3110; (214) 234-1769
$595

Kai's Power Tools 2.0

If you can afford only one plug-in, make it Kai's Power Tools. You won't find these spectacular effects anywhere else. HSC Software's package offers a set of fancy filter effects like Page Curl, Pixel Storm, and Stereo Noise, but its best features are its user-interface effects, which let

you design and save your own filters.

For starters, there's the Gradient Designer, which lets you create complex fountain fills, including frames and transparencies that can be used as masks in an alpha channel. For programs that support paths, the Gradients on Paths effect smoothly wraps a blend around any user-defined free-form path. With this tool, you can create interesting effects like glows, halos, metallic tubes, rainbows, and complex type outlines.

Kai's Power Tools also offers four filters for exploring Julia and Mandelbrot Set fractals. The filters wrap gradients around the sets and give you control over looping, repeat count, and spiral-angle settings. Finally, the Texture Explorer lets you generate random textural effects that simulate natural entities such as clouds, marble, and wood.

Kai's Power Tools 2.0
HSC Software
1661 Lincoln Blvd.
Suite 101
Santa Monica, CA 90404
(800) 472-9025; (310) 392-8441
$199

Aldus Gallery Effects

Not as glitzy as Kai's Power Tools, Aldus's filter sets nonetheless provide a wide range of interesting effects you can layer onto your image. These packages are a good investment; they can save you hours of time if you need to create a certain look from a scanned and canned photo.

The filters are arranged in three volumes of 16 effects each. Volume 1, which includes Chrome, Fresco, Spatter, and Watercolor filters, is only compatible with PhotoStyler. The other two volumes work with any program compatible with PhotoStyler or Photoshop plug-ins. Volume 2 includes Colored Pencil, Palette Knife, Rough Pastel, and Stamp, while Volume 3 features Crosshatch, Neon Glow, Plastic Wrap, and Sponge.

Aldus Gallery Effects
Aldus Corp.
411 First Ave. S.
Seattle, WA 98104
(800) 628-2320; (206) 622-5500
$199 for Volumes 1 and 3;
$149 for Volume 2

I Love My Platform

bow to no man or woman in my regard for John C. Dvorak. When I was a tiny little zygote swimming in the early protean waters of 8088-based cyberspace, there was the monolithic Rock of Dvorak poking its huge mass above the seas of confusion. He kicked butt and mentioned names. He was fun. Even when he wandered off into the land of goo-goo Mac worship, he was still right there on the edge, showing us a good time.

Until now.

Now he's got me mad, thanks to this stupid, dangerous thing he wrote not long ago. Get this: Dvorak has suggested that a platform shift away from Windows/Intel is not unthinkable. He mentions the fact that the CD replaced the vinyl record album almost overnight. He notes the slam-bam transition from CP/M to DOS in 1981. "Today there's pent-up demand for a new PC architecture," he writes, and goes on to lather, "The platform shift of 1981 is an act that can be repeated. Don't let them kid you into thinking otherwise."

Now hear this, folks. Hear it loud and clear. I am not about to change my platform. I don't want to. And it's not just that I can't afford to, because in truth I probably can. It's that, deep in my heart, I don't believe I should have to. As Nixon told Haldeman, it would be wrong. Basically, I feel the same way about people who suggest otherwise as I would about those who want to move my corporation to New Jersey, who want to take away my frequent flier miles and give them to the company for ethical reasons, who believe taverns should be smoke-free. I want to kill them.

Reasons? Sure, I've got some. But the bottom line is this: I work on this freaking machine, see? I make spreadsheets on it, and charts and reports, and I communicate with other electronic citizens. I make my living on it. Improve it, yes. Juice it up, certainly. Blow me completely off the planet, make me discard my entire universe so that a couple of high-end geeks with an infinite thirst for the squeakiest bell/whistle combination can ooh and ahh over the shock of the new? Bag it, dudes. Just get out of here and take your apologists with you.

How about some rational reasons:

1. I don't need it. I don't want it. It's too fast for me. I don't know about you, but I'm still reeling from the way my 50MHz 486 rips through the 18th level of Doom. I've got 850 True Type fonts on my system. About 80 applications. A dual-speed CD-ROM drive patched up to a SCSI card. After thousands of hours of cursing, praying, tinkering, ratcheting, tweaking—it all works! So don't tell me I can't use it anymore!

2. I'm still having fun at a price that makes me, not my reseller, happy. Have you noticed how amazingly cheap it is to get a 90MHz Pentium? And 1-gig hard drives are under $750! There are so many vendors that everybody loves you! Why in the world would we want to kiss off this entirely enthusiastic, competitive, responsive marketplace? These guys remind me of the people who said we'd all be using Unix by now. Why? Because it's better, you know. Elitism! Feh!

3. The forces of darkness lie. Well, maybe that's a little harsh. They tell semitruths, like…the Power PC runs Windows, for instance. Does it? Does it really? Or does it run Windows only in…Standard Mode? Hah! That's like giving somebody a Porsche and then telling them they can only drive it in first gear. "Native applications!" they scream. Show me some! I am not a 3-D modeler! I reserve the right to be not interested—a right I couldn't exercise if you went and changed my platform, Sparky!

4. I don't want Big Brother (or Sister) to determine my future. I hate to have things done to me. I don't mind participating if invited, of course. But I hate the idea of troopers with big helmets and sticks coming into my house and yelling, "You will use Herculon furniture from now on!" Even if, you know, it's great furniture.

No, gang. The paradigm we should be investigating here is not the customer-hostile mutation of vinyl into CD. It's the changeover from leaded to unleaded fuel, which took a gradual process of decades to accomplish. It's high definition TV, which the Feds have decreed must take place in such a way as to make sure that nobody is forced to trade in a perfectly good old TV for a high-def new one they don't really want. It's the story of digital audio tape, which was greeted by consumers across the world with the message: "No more new formats! Stick it in your ear!" and sent back to Japan on the first boat out.

If you agree with me, vote with your voices, your modems, your feet. Open your windows (the real ones) and scream so that the world may hear: Evolution, yes! Revolution, no!

If you build it, we will not come!—Gil Schwartz ■

STATE OF THE ART
America Remembered

America Remembered, from Boraventures Publishing, contains reproductions of 500 penny postcards from the early 1900s. The 300-dpi PICT images retain the sepia tones and hand-colored pastels of the originals—as well as their blurry, blotchy appearance. Subjects include scenic wonders, cowboys on the range, urban architecture, and the Pan-Pacific World's Fair.—Aileen Abernathy

America Remembered
Boraventures Publishing
(800) 648-9009; (203) 254-2959
$70

Retro Americana

PhotoDisc's $299 Retro Americana covers the era of "Father Knows Best" and "Ozzie and Harriet." The 336 black-and-white stock photos, taken from the 1920s to the 1960s, feature wholesome housewives, clean-cut businessmen, dreamy teens, cuddly couples, and oh-so-precious kids. As in all of PhotoDisc's other superb titles, the full-page images are saved in both 72-dpi TIFF and 300-dpi JPEG formats. For those who are more interested in Renaissance-era masterpieces than American kitsch, PhotoDisc also offers Italian Fine Art, Prints and Photographs (also $299), a lovely collection of antique maps, historical photographs, botanical and zoological prints, and trade illustrations that spans the 14th to the 20th century.—Aileen Abernathy

Retro Americana
PhotoDisc
(800) 528-3472; (206) 441-9355
$299

Classic Graphics

Planet Art casts a wider net, bringing the world's art treasures to your desktop. Each CD-ROM in its Classic Graphics series has 100 images from a specific artist, period, or style—such as Michelangelo, Albrecht Durer, William Morris, French Posters (featuring Toulouse-Lautrec), Navoi's Arabic Tiles, Medieval Alphabets, Japanese Art, Architecture, and Icons. There are loads of images that also make wonderful backgrounds and textures. The images do tend to be muddy, requiring color and contrast tweaks—but then so are their physical counterparts, after a few hundred years.—Aileen Abernathy

Classic Graphics
Planet Art
(800) 200-3405; (213) 651-3405
$90

OBJECT-ORIENTED
Visual Symbols Library

Need a picture of just a piggy bank? Full-screen photographs require editing expertise (and Adobe Photoshop) to separate a desired item from its surroundings. Now several companies have taken the next logical step: photographed objects, isolated against white backgrounds (often with naturally cast shadows) for easy selection.

CMCD, a branch of designer Clement Mok's company, offers the Visual Symbols library: seven business-oriented collections on CD-ROM that include Everyday Objects, Just Tools, Just Documents, Just Hands, and Metaphorically Speaking (a black sheep, golden handcuffs, a broken record). Each disc contains more than 100 good-looking, well-chosen images in Photo CD format. Although Photo CD gives you five resolutions to work with, it unfortunately doesn't support clipping paths—carefully drawn outlines you can use as selection areas when copying or manipulating an object. As a result, you must spend time carefully separating objects from their backgrounds, which (in case you're thinking of using them) are occasionally marred by dirt specks.—Aileen Abernathy

Visual Symbols library
CMCD
(800) 664-2623; (415) 703-9907
$129 each

CLIPPING PATHS
Sports Equipment; Food & Grocery Items; Business & Medical Items; Toys, Models & Game Pieces

Three companies offer images that include clipping paths; outlines you can use as selection areas when copying or manipulating an object. Digital Media has four Stock Options titles: Sports Equipment; Food & Grocery Items; Business & Medical Items; and Toys, Models & Game Pieces. The 75 to 100 images on each CD-ROM are saved as high-resolution CMYK TIFF files and include such hard-to-find items as fishing lures, stuffed olives, and trademarked items such as Tinker Toys, so read the licensing agreement carefully.—Aileen Abernathy

Sports Equipment; Food &
Grocery Items; Business &
Medical Items; and Toys,
Models & Game Pieces
Digital Media
(800) 786-2512; (714) 362-5103
$99 each

The Classic Photographic Image Objects (PIO) Library

The Classic Photographic Image Objects (PIO) Library, from Ridgley Curry & Associates, supplies vintage props and memorabilia from the storehouses of Hollywood's 20th Century Props. The ten volumes include classic Telephones, Radios, Cameras, Kitchen Appliances, Business Equipment, and Fashion Accessories. Each CD-ROM has two views each of 20 objects. The TIFF images are saved in low and high resolutions and contain alpha-channel masks for each object, making it easy to add transparency to a blender's glass, for example.—Aileen Abernathy

The Classic Photographic Image
Objects (PIO) Library
Ridgley Curry & Associates
(818) 564-1215
$70

ObjectGear Collection

Image Club Graphics's ObjectGear collection falters in terms of image selection, but it is easy to use. Its 85 photographs are saved in two resolutions as CMYK EPS files with embedded clipping paths, allowing you to import a cropped object directly into a page layout without first visiting Photoshop. The disc also supplies separate TIFF files containing two types of shadows (drop and cast) for each object.—Aileen Abernathy

ObjectGear collection
Image Club Graphics
(800) 387-9193; (403) 262-8008
$99

Virus, They Wrote

they lurk in the dark alleys off the Infobahn, these perps who live to hit and run. They do their dirty work, jump the curb, and disappear from the scene of the digital grime. They're virogens, the writers of perverted little programs that seduce data and corrupt programs on your computer. In many ways these virogens are as remorseless as the evil software they create, with no compassion for their victims, whether human or hardware.

Like a jack-in-the-box, the virus writer will hide in the dark and wait until someone turns the handle. Then…pop! There he is, a harlequin with an evil grin, unexpected, unwelcome, unforgiving, vomiting bits of code and staining everything in sight. An ugly picture.

These technotaggers are your worst enemies. They're random beyond reason. They don't care how much cache you have on you. They don't hear when your processor screams.

They don't twitch if your company's financial data rots just because you recalculated some spreadsheets at home one night, and it turned out that your kid had just played some games from a friend's disk on your PC. The virus slinked from your home PC hard disk back to the hard disk on your PC at work. And suddenly it's over the network and you're over at the unemployment office.

Virogens don't need passports because they don't respect borders. They don't use names, just aliases—monikers like Dark Avenger. The Unforgiven. Hellraiser.

If you want to find them, a few simple queries on a handful of bulletin boards can smoke them out. They love publicity. They communicate via anonymous Internet messages with bizarre routing addresses. They call over untraceable phone lines. They're careful not to leave tracks, because they are pursued by their own personal sleuths—virus researchers and security specialists from around the world.

They're part of a weird little symbiotic world full of intrigue, where even the good guys use online aliases. The virus researchers think the antivirus software developers inspire the virogens with financial rewards. The software developers accuse the researchers of building viruses on the side. The virogens suck up the resulting fame and infamy like oxygen. It's hard to separate truth from innuendo. Who are these virogens? And why would they intentionally murder an innocent passerbyte?

The Criminals: Baudfellas

"If someone gets a virus, it's their own f—-ing fault," growls The Unforgiven from Sweden.

The 19-year-old virogen called one Saturday night on somebody else's krona, certainly not his own. With him on the weak telephone link was his 18-year-old pal Metal Militia. The line cracked like knuckles, but the voices were those of teenagers at a loss for weekend entertainment. Their outlook is simple: They're not responsible for what happens when, for fun, they create a virus that takes up residence in a computer's memory and gloms onto every disk that comes near as easy as drive A:, B:, C:.

If you're looking for the bad guys, insists Metal Militia, they're the users. "If they don't back up, it's their own fault. They're the ones using pirated software. They're the ones not using antivirus programs."

The boys from Sweden are part of a busy group of college students that has written more than 30 viruses. They publish them in a newsletter aptly called Insane Reality. They take a detached, bloodless view of their antics. "We don't harm people. We harm data," The Unforgiven says sharply, to which his partner adds coldly, "We're not affecting people's lives." Hey, they're not throwing bombs—they're just building them. In their eyes, there's a difference.

Are these two antisocial baudfellas typical technotaggers? Even the folks who track virogens can't be sure. Security specialist Pam Kane, president of Panda Systems in Wilmington, Delaware, says, "I don't think there is ever going to be a virus-writer profile, like there is for the airline hijacker." As with any other tagger, by the time their work is discovered they're long gone. Staying invisible at the end of an untraceable phone line, they prevent the authorities from building accurate psychological sketches.

Maybe. But stitch together a picture of young, disaffected rebels, vicious and without remorse, describe them to a Harvard headshrinker, and you get a different opinion. Professor W. Lawrence Hartmann, a psychiatrist specializing in adolescent behavior, diagnoses the virogens thus: "It sounds like an adolescent joy in a newfound kind of potency. Writing a virus gives the author a sense of power and an exaggeration of one's own presence, like writing graffiti on a much larger scale."

And once past adolescence, the virogens seem to be infected by what passes for maturity. One Chicago-area virus writer, no older than 25, has already checked out of the virus-writing game. Going by the name Nowhere Man, he got into it "to see if it could be done. Once you've done it, it's not worth doing again," he says. He does, however, pass out software that helps other aspiring virogens build their own viruses. He describes his "virus creation library" (VCL) utility like a developer selling an application's ease of use. "You don't have to have a programming background to use VCL," he says.

Another virus writer in his 20s, going by the alias Hellraiser, acknowledges over the telephone, "I was always the rebellious type, so as soon as I got into computers I had to go to the rebellious part of the computer world—the underground hacking, phreaking, viruses. When you are a kid with a computer, what are you going to do? Do you want to go on public domain boards and download shareware and write messages on Fidonet? No, you want to do something cool."

Kane, however, doubts that many of the current, sophisticated viruses are the work of kids. "It takes a very talented programmer with a lot of experience," she says.

That would describe one of the most famous players on the virus stage, Dark Avenger. No one seems to know what he's avenging, but it's believed he started out as a computer science student at the University of Sofia in Bulgaria.

To Dark Avenger, his viruses are his passport. "The American government can stop me from going to the U.S., but they can't stop my virus," he boasted to one virus researcher. "The idea of making a program that would travel on its own and go to places its creator could never go was the most interesting thing for me."

His darkest contribution isn't a virus at all—it's a toolkit he calls the "Mutation Engine." It lets viruses change their appearance and internal structure as they spread, making them difficult to find. He's also written a kind of schizoid virus. The fast-acting version actively searches for targets, spreading and replicating itself on the host system and any other system connected to it. A timed-release variant slowly and almost invisibly eats away at data on a disk so it's unlikely you'll notice until it's time to kiss your data good-bye.

He may be prolific, but he's also uncharacteristically shy. One person who's smoked him out is an American virus researcher named Sara Gordon. Asking to keep her employers anonymous, Gordon says she is an "independent researcher" at a Midwestern university who works under contract to several corporations as a security specialist.

She first came across Dark Avenger's name during an online virus conference. Participants lambasted his work. That intrigued her. She in turn managed to intrigue Dark Avenger, first by posting questions about him on several bulletin boards, and finally by challenging him to write a virus for her. Sure enough, early in 1992, a new virus called Dedicated appeared. In it, an internal string read, "We dedicate this little virus to Sara Gordon." Eventually, using a Bulgarian dictionary and a British BBS, she posted a message to him. He replied with a modern pen-pal request: to scan her photo into a graphics file and send it to him. She did.

In the atmosphere of paranoia in the virus underground, some don't believe that Gordon and the Dark Avenger have actually spoken. But if you ask her, she'll hand over transcripts of conversations she had with him to reveal what makes him tick.

He told her that he never imagined the viruses would hurt people, just data. In Bulgaria, he said, "PCs were just very expensive toys which nobody could afford and nobody knew how to use. They were only used by some hotshots or their children who had nothing else to play with. I was not aware that there could be any consequences. [My first] virus was so badly written that I never imagined it would leave the town. I only imagined it could leave the neighborhood."

Dark Avenger shrugged off any responsibility as neatly as an operator dropping a caller into voice mail. Like most of the virus writers, he separated his work from its effect. No system would become infected, he said, if people avoided pirated software. "It all depends on human stupidity, you know. It's not the computers' fault that viruses spread."

The Gumshoes: Choose Your Alias

Tracking virus writers and their antagonists is like walking into a convention of JFK assassination-conspiracy buffs. All the players—the authors, the security specialists, and the antivirus software developers—know each others' identities or at least aliases. They have their own unshakable beliefs about who's really responsible for the problem of spreading viruses.

Want wild theories? Some folks who claim to write viruses are actually cops trying to entrap the real criminals.

Want cynical motives? Ask yourself who benefits more from the spreading of viruses than the developers of antivirus software and security consultants. Some virus authors claim that antivirus software developers are responsible for spreading many infections just to boost software sales. Why would they say such a thing? Maybe it's because in the past at least one major antivirus maker has offered cash bounties to individuals or companies supplying examples of new viruses. That way, they can figure out a method to inoculate against it and sell updates. Are virus writers surviving and thriving because they have a ready market for their work?

That's ridiculous, counter the antivirus developers. Like police, lawyers, and judges, they wouldn't have anything to do unless some jokers were operating outside the bounds of ordinary society; in most cases, though, the antivirus software developers haven't caused the problems they're out to solve. Their intentions may be pure. (That didn't stop some of them from exploiting the Michelangelo scare to the hilt, even if they had nothing to do with encouraging the virogen who wrote it.)

Some of those same developers whisper that some academic virus "researchers" are actually creating the strains they claim to study. Other denizens of this world claim that Vesselin Vladimirov Bontchev, currently a member of the University of Hamburg's Virus Test Center, is none other than the Dark Avenger himself; he denies the charge, insisting he's hot on the trail of his fellow Bulgarian.

Bontchev started following Dark Avenger's trail when he was director of the Laboratory of Computer Virology at the Bulgarian Academy of Sciences in Sofia. Bontchev believes there are currently about 4,100 known PC viruses in the world, with less than 10 percent—about 300—originating in Bulgaria. But he admits that's still a disproportionately large number of viruses for such a small group of users. He cites Russia, The Netherlands, Italy, and the United States as the major virus-producing countries.

Bontchev describes Dark Avenger as "sick enough to enjoy causing trouble to other people. Most of his viruses are maliciously destructive, slightly and slowly corrupting your data, so that you do not notice it for a long time. When you eventually notice it, it is too late because the corrupted data is already on your backups and there is no way to determine which part of it is corrupted and which is not."

Dark Avenger is such a creep that the one piece of antivirus software he wrote snuffs two of his viruses but silently unleashes a third one at the same time.

Sadly, all Bontchev has to show for five years of study are some clues about Dark Avenger's style. He writes his viruses so that they have a round number of bytes, and he frequently refers to heavy metal groups such as Iron Maiden in his virus code. It's not clear what's going to happen if Bontchev collars Dark Avenger—Bulgarian law being vague on the subject of hacking—but he does say that he knows some folks who'd like to rough him up for the data he's destroyed.

Back here in the States, another cynical detective in the virus underworld is Joe Piazza, president of the Institute of Data Security and Integrity, a computer security firm in Wilmington, Delaware. He blames the antivirus software developers for priming the market with cash bounties. "It is absolutely in their best interests to keep the viruses flowing," he says, accusing them of significantly contributing to the nasties' numbers.

Of course, viruses also help keep Piazza and other security professionals in business, because they assess companies' exposure to security lapses. He believes companies will thrive or die based on the safety of their data. And in this oddly symbiotic world, he needs the virus writers, too. "The hackers and crackers are serving a good function—they are letting us know what the loopholes are so that we can fix them."

The Hideouts: Where Taggers Dare

In this rats' nest of intrigue, where do the rodents hang out? Same place any group of technothusiasts hangs out—electronic bulletin board systems. On these BBSs, virus authors spew their nastiest bugs in hopes of getting not only the plaudits of fellow outlaws but also widespread distribution. People like Dark Avenger, Hellraiser, and Nowhere Man are heroes sanctified in great awe. Other authors—those stupid or unfortunate enough to be caught (like Internet worm creator Robert Morris, Jr.)—are categorized as either martyrs to the cause or cautionary examples of poor procedure. Not surprisingly, the antivirus makers also frequent these bulletin boards in search of the latest viruses.

A man who goes by the alias Aristotle is the system operator of one of these bulletin boards. At age 34, he's an old man among the virus kids. "People in the underground think because I'm 34, I'm some kind of fed," he says. Married and the father of two, he recently went back to school to complete his college degree and now does computer consulting work for a government contractor.

He is also a self-proclaimed expert on the way antivirus makers purposely or accidentally move viruses around the world. He says that on many virus BBSs, the system operators require users to upload contributions in exchange for downloads of the latest files. He accuses antivirus makers of often adding a new infectious agent for each one they retrieve.

Aristotle tracks viruses the way some folks track carrier pigeons. "I'd create a virus and give it out to somebody, then delete it from my system, and see what happens. The first one I gave somebody showed up three days later on a bulletin board in Switzerland."

Aristotle's no anomaly. A 20-year-old computer store employee who goes only by the initials TL is already a retired virus BBS sysop. He's moved on to phone phreaking—using long-distance lines without paying—and was, naturally, calling on what he said was a temporary and untraceable line.

TL insists that anyone outside the virus clique couldn't possibly understand the kick somebody gets out of having the power to destroy an entire computer system. "When you hack a system, it takes no brain at all to come in and nuke everything, but it takes one hell of a brain to remain on the system. It is a lot more challenging to avoid antiviral software than it is to nuke a drive."

As for the idea of an online community of taggers, TL compares it to a literary roundtable. Writing viruses shouldn't be illegal—it should be thought of as a creative process like writing a book. "Some people write books about suicide. That's a lot more destructive," TL insists. "I don't think it should be illegal to write viruses, but it should be to spread them."

But where's the glory in being the author of a work you dare not acknowledge publicly? Panda Systems's Pam Kane has an interesting analogy for the sort of fame that "successful" virus authors might achieve. They're like some wealthy crazy who hires a thief to steal a famous work of art. "The person who now owns it cannot [display it]. It hangs in a very small room of a very large house."

She insists that we're still not safe from really nasty viruses. They're not likely to be posted on BBSs frequented by The Unforgiven and his ilk, because that gives the antivirus developers an immediate heads-up that a new strain is a potential threat. "If there is a seriously malevolent virus writer out there," says Kane, "he will not put it up on a BBS."

It's the same old story: When you're walking in a bad neighborhood, you've gotta watch your back. But now that your PC makes the entire world your neighborhood, you've gotta watch your disk. They'll find you if you let them.—Corey Sandler ∎

MAPPING THE TERRAIN

MapArt CD-ROM series

If you chart the modern-day world, you may be familiar with Cartesia Software's MapArt CD-ROM series ($60 to $200) of excellent EPS (or PICT) two-dimensional maps.—Aileen Abernathy

MapArt
Cartesia Software
(800) 334-4291; (609) 397-1611
$60-$200

Mountain High Maps

Non-members of the Flat Earth Society will appreciate Digital Wisdom's Mountain High Maps CD-ROM. This unique collection of relief maps duplicates the land and ocean-floor contours of the world, providing a better sense of natural terrain than do satellite images. The 74 gray-scale projections of continents and countries and 39 globe views are based on a set of carefully constructed scale models used in atlases. Each TIFF file comes in two resolutions. To get the most out of the maps, you'll need a program such as Photoshop, because they look better in color and you'll want to add details such as text, borders, or roads. Mountain High Maps gives you a head start, with its precreated masks and helpful hints on modifying the maps, but Digital Wisdom can also sell you Frontiers, a $120 CD-ROM of editable map outlines that can be overlaid on the topological maps.—Aileen Abernathy

Mountain High Maps
Digital Wisdom
(800) 800-8560; (804) 758-0670
$995

INSTANT BROCHURES, NEWSLETTERS, FLIERS

Page Magic, Version 1.01

Page Magic is a low-priced desktop publishing program designed for people who aren't interested in learning about design or about the intricacies of complicated layout software. The $69.95 Page Magic 1.01 package, from NEBS, a large paper manufacturer, comes with a wide variety of preformatted templates and the unique ability to match the paper to the task.

If Page Magic looks familiar, that's because it's an enhanced version of the package formerly marketed by Timeworks as Publish It for Windows and by GST Software (the author of the program) as PressWorks. NEBS now has exclusive rights to this hybrid program, which mixes many of the features of a desktop publishing package with some of the features of a word processor, along with the ability to import clip art, screen captures, and images from Photo CDs.

The program comes with 104 preset templates, including those for fliers, business cards, newsletters, brochures, and envelopes. Almost all of these instant designs come in blank versions, where you fill in the text, as well as versions filled with dummy text that

you replace. You're likely to be impressed with Page Magic's flexibility and solidity but a little disappointed by the excessive number of mouse clicks that it requires before you can get any work done.

Page Magic uses frames as containers for adding text, graphics, and OLE objects to a document. Unfortunately, the program isn't smart enough to understand that you want to put text in a frame if you start typing while the frame is selected. Instead, you have to click on toolbar buttons to switch among four modes: frame, text formatting, paragraph formatting, and drawing. As you switch modes, the toolbar changes to match the kind of work you're doing. A more convenient feature is a horizontal color palette, which is permanently displayed at the foot of the screen and allows quick color changes for whatever object you're working on. It does have one caveat: You can't view more than one page at a time.

Text features include automated bullets and a convenient bullet-selection menu. We found that Page Magic can alter word spacing, but only by adjusting the spacing between letters. For the most part, the formatting menu is overly complex. Text can flow around graphics, but only if you draw the outline of the graphics by hand.

When you import text or graphics, Page Magic lists the file names in a Ventura-style list of stories, bitmaps, line art, and OLE objects.

Smoothly implemented OLE 2.0 support lets you use the toolbars and menus of OLE servers such as Visio or WordPerfect Draw while you edit an imported object directly on the Page Magic page. Graphics imports include most major formats, and we had no problem importing files that some other programs can't handle. Text imported from major word processors comes with much of the document's original formatting intact. The program doesn't recognize Microsoft Word for Windows 6.0 or WordPerfect 6.x files. Using imported text, we were able to create a document of over 400 pages, but the program crashed after we moved a few times from the beginning to the end.

A suite of add-in programs, which are accessible from the toolbar, includes a clip-art browser that displays only the line art supplied with the program (you can't add your own). A "keypad" program, similar to Windows's own Charmap, lets you select special characters.

Page Magic lacks the formatting flexibility of Serif's PagePlus and the stunning automation of Microsoft Publisher, but it's a highly effective package for anyone who wants to use standard templates for creating competent (though unspectacular) documents.

For more colorful documents, NEBS offers something that other software of this type doesn't: the ability to choose from a variety of

specialized papers that work with the Page Magic templates. Using the Company Colors stock, we were able to create professional-looking designs that had a banner here or a ribbon there with minimal input. And after all, that's the purpose of Page Magic—quick and easy business forms and brochures.— Edward Mendelson

Page Magic, Version 1.01
NEBS Inc.
Groton, MA
(800) 822-5254; (508) 448-6111
$69.95

WORD PROCESSING FOR SCIENTIFIC MINDS

Scientific WorkPlace 2.0 for Windows

When TCI Software Research brought out Scientific Word a few years back, you could almost hear the collective sigh of relief in the academic world. Here at last was a Windows technical word processor that not only made it easy to create documents mixing text and math, but provided a front end to the LaTeX computer typesetting system that most people consider the leader in scientific publishing.

Scientific WorkPlace 2.0 builds on these achievements. Like Scientific Word, it displays formulas and functions as they appear in books, and it spares users the need to insert hellishly complex LaTeX formatting codes into their documents manually. But the package does much more: It provides a fairly complete implementation of Waterloo Maple Software's highly regarded symbolic and numerical mathematics program Maple V release 3.

If you are familiar with Scientific Word, you will be right at home with Scientific WorkPlace. The two products offer the same word processing features. However, newcomers have a surprise in store for them. Although Scientific WorkPlace has the overall look and feel of a standard Windows word processor, it purposely has not been designed to be WYSIWYG. You can change the onscreen appearance of your documents to your heart's content—these changes just don't affect the appearance of the printed text. But what if you really need to modify an existing style or create a new one from scratch? You can—by running a separate Style Editor, which, however, does not let you interactively preview your changes. Whether or not TCI Software Research is right in claiming that this approach makes it easier to concentrate on content will be a matter of personal taste.

In any event, it's impossible not to be impressed by Scientific WorkPlace's splendid array of easy-to-use tools for entering mathematical expressions into documents. Nearly a score of icons on the main toolbar provides access to different palettes and pick lists of mathematical symbols, functions, operators, and the like. In addition, the

program provides a Find and Replace function that works as well with mathematics as with text. There's also a convenient table editor for placing tables in your documents. And more than 100 predefined styles make it easy to create documents that conform to the style requirements of a host of technical publishing houses and scores of academic journals.

Unfortunately, despite its many innovations and general ease of use, Scientific WorkPlace still suffers from some of the traditional aggravations of LaTeX and TeX systems. LaTeX is a dialect of TeX that adds support for such things as automatic table-of-content generation and cross-references. Like virtually every other TeX system, Scientific WorkPlace

lacks any file-export function. The reason: Translating TeX codes for mathematics into anyone else's codes poses daunting technical challenges. You can import ANSI, ASCII, RTF, and WordPerfect text files into Scientific WorkPlace, but any mathematics in these files are stripped out. At least one oversight can't be blamed on LaTeX and TeX's intrinsic

complexity: The program lacks a macro function that would let users create their own keystroke shortcuts for common editing commands.

On the other hand, TCI Software Research has done a superb job of integrating the Maple kernel into the Scientific WorkPlace interface. Scientific WorkPlace provides a generous sampling of the heavy-duty

Tips from the Virogens for Avoiding Their Work

Virus writers enjoy their work too much to give it up—and even if they mend their ways, there will always be newly adventurous technotaggers to take their place. So how do you avoid becoming one of their victims? Here, in their words, are what the virogens advise you to do.

Aristotle: [Virus writers] are going to write something that is totally undetectable. That means that virus scanners are essentially useless. They act as coroners to tell you what it was that ate you. There is no education in the system to teach people how to use the computer so that they don't bring things [like viruses] in. They don't establish rules where if somebody brings in something from home and puts it on a company computer, they get fired. These are million-dollar investments we're talking about; they are not toys.

Dark Avenger: Antivirus products are as useless as viruses. The users spend much more money on buying such products and their updates than they would lose on data damage because of viruses. Viruses would spread much less if "innocent" users did not steal software and if they worked a bit more at their workplace, instead of playing games.

Hellraiser: Get a good scanner first thing. And [develop] a good eye to notice when something is wrong—files running slower than they should, weird error messages. If you turn on your computer and it says, "Mr. Virus has destroyed your hard drive," that's a clue.

Nowhere Man: The fact is that 99 percent of all viruses are not much of a threat if you have any kind of a clue. I'm not saying viruses don't hurt people, but usually when they affect people, it's almost always the person's fault.

TL: On my drive, I have 2,000 viruses just laying around and never in many years has one gotten loose. I don't run scanners. I just categorize what I take from people. I don't run things on my good machines. I don't understand why people actually get infected. ■

graphic, numeric, and symbolic computational functions provided in the package. Many types of computations are easier to perform in Scientific WorkPlace than in the full version of Maple. One reason is that while Scientific WorkPlace displays mathematics the way you learned it, Maple V 3.0 for Windows still displays unsolved equations as complicated ASCII mnemonics and codes. Also, a single Scientific WorkPlace menu option, such as Factor, performs the same functions as several Maple commands (Factor, used with numbers, and Ifactor, used with equations). And Scientific WorkPlace is less picky about mathematical syntax than Maple is.

Still, there's no free lunch, even at the digital deli. For one thing, Scientific WorkPlace's generally excellent online help system provides not a whisper of assistance for Maple. Fortunately, TCI Software Research supplies a well-written manual that puts most of the documentation provided with the full version of Maple to shame. And Maple's programming function and its file input/output functions are disabled in the Scientific WorkPlace version. This means that you can't, for example, write a short Maple program that reads data into a large matrix from a disk file, perform some calculations on the matrix, and then store the results in a new disk file.

A number of important Maple graphics capabilities are missing. Scientific WorkPlace lacks the marvelous interactive tools that let you instantly modify your view of a 3-D graph. In addition, you cannot create animations or manipulate the position of highlights and shadows in 3-D graphs. Nor can you place text anywhere you wish on a graph or use different types of lines (solid, dashed, and so on) when displaying more than one data set on a graph. But these caveats are relatively minor. Scientific WorkPlace will not be for everyone—but then, neither is number theory, matrix algebra, or calculus. For technical users who need to move their ideas to paper in the shortest possible time, Scientific WorkPlace's seamless integration of mathematics with word processing makes it a pearl beyond price.—John Gliedman

Scientific WorkPlace 2.0
for Windows
TCI Software Research
1190 Foster Rd.
Las Cruces, NM
(800) 874-2383; (505) 522-4600
$595

MacDraft 4.0

A database with a report generator plus new floating palettes and additional tools for drawing and editing mark the latest release of Innovative Data Design's accessible drawing and drafting program. With its well-designed interface and easy-to-use tools, MacDraft 4.0 is tailor-made for users who have little or no drafting experience.

MacDraft 4.0's new floating palettes let you complete drawings faster and more easily than before. In place of the previous version's single tool palette, version 4.0 displays several well-organized smaller palettes that expand and enhance the program's functionality.

The main tool palette contains several new tools, including ones for drawing parallel offsets for lines, circles, and arcs. Missing, however, is a tool for creating general offsets. Additionally, to help you navigate within your drawings, the palette includes a new 1:1 button that gives you a nonmagnified view of the area you're working on.

Other palettes include one for dimension tools and one that groups general tools, such as the fillet and the chamfer, with MacDraft's new Boolean tools. The Boolean tools let you either add two objects together to form a new polygon or subtract one object from another to form a new shape. Although these tools are useful, they have several limitations that make them unsuitable for creating complex shapes. Once you've used them to create an object, you lose the ability to edit it—you can only resize it. In addition, the subtract tool doesn't work with objects that have holes.

A big plus with MacDraft 4.0 is that it overcomes the limitations on object scaling and duplication that existed in the previous version. Resizing objects is a snap with the new Resize palette, which lets you enter numeric values for object dimensions. MacDraft displays the correct measurement parameters in the palette, based on the type of object you have selected—width and height for rectangles, for example, and percentages for object groups.

Another welcome new feature is MacDraft's sophisticated duplication tool. Using the Linear Duplication option, you can duplicate objects linearly in rows and columns. The Circular Duplication option creates an array of shapes around a specific point.

MacDraft 4.0 also adds DXF (Document Exchange Format) import and export for users who need to exchange drawings with other CAD programs. This feature is useful for those who are not CAD professionals but need to use technical drawings. Space planners, for example, may want to use DXF building layouts as a starting point for facilities management. In our tests, MacDraft was able to import our DXF test files, although we did have to remove some elements from the original drawing, because MacDraft doesn't support all DXF object types.

IDD has done a good job of refining MacDraft's basic functionality, but the most significant enhancement in version 4.0 is the addition of a database with a report generator. You can now assign information to objects in a drawing and extract it in report format, so, for example, you can determine the cost of a project or how many items of a specific kind are in a drawing.

MacDraft's database provides five user-definable fields, including name, type, and manufacturer, for attaching information to objects. The Find/Replace function lets you reassign information if you decide you want to make global changes to a drawing, such as changing the manufacturer for a group of objects. However, if you want to change the attributes for some, but not all, of a group of objects by using Find/Replace, MacDraft doesn't make it as easy as it could be. First, it would be helpful to be able to view the objects you want to edit, so you can determine exactly which ones you want to change and exactly how you want to change them. In addition, the Edit Object Info command works with only a single object at a time, which makes the process of reassigning information to multiple objects tedious.

MacDraft's report generator uses a spreadsheetlike window. You can create multiple reports from a single drawing and extract object information such as area, height, length, perimeter, width, x dimension, and y dimension. If you need report functions that are more powerful than those provided by MacDraft, you can replicate a report as an Excel worksheet by simply clicking on

MacDraft's Apple events-driven cloning button. You can even create live links between your drawing and the Excel worksheet so that when you make changes to your drawings, the corresponding object information also will be updated in the worksheet.

MacDraft is an excellent tool for creating floor plans and technical drawings and is the best program we've seen for users with little or no drafting experience. It's also the only program in its class that incorporates a database and report generator—both of which are extremely useful tools for doing cost estimation.—Sean J. Safreed

MacDraft 4.0
Innovative Data Design
Concord, CA 94520
(510) 680-6818
$449

DRAG-AND-DROP IMAGE CATALOGING
Cumulus PowerPro 2.1

System 7.5 integrates numerous prior enhancements to the system, such as AppleScript and Macintosh Drag and Drop, into one unified release. Cumulus PowerPro 2.1, from Canto Software, exploits both of these technologies to make image cataloging easier.

AppleScript, Apple's scripting language, automates tasks within an application and across applications that support it. Cumulus ships with a variety of sample scripts that show you how to integrate images from

any catalog into your page-layout program automatically. For instance, with a sample script included with Cumulus, you can use your photos to produce a contact sheet in PageMaker.

Cumulus also allows you to import images into QuarkXPress through Drag and Drop. For example, dragging a picture from the Cumulus window to an open layout in QuarkXPress automatically creates a picture box and drops in a photo. Cumulus extends the drag-and-drop metaphor a step further by turning any picture or piece of text into a drag-and-drop element. So the tedious chore of assigning keywords can become a one-step operation; all you have to do is drag keywords from a list into any database field.

Besides running native on the Power Mac, this version has an improved client/server architecture that speeds searches.—Sean J. Safreed

Cumulus PowerPro 2.1
Canto Software
(415) 431-6871
Cumulus PowerLite
(single-user version), $199;
Five-user client/server PowerPro
version, $1,495

IMAGE EDITING WITHOUT PHOTOSHOP
PhotoFlash 2.0

Not an image-editing application *per se*, PhotoFlash makes it simple to put pictures into any document. The new version allows multiple open catalogs and drag-and-drop

among catalogs, and it offers more AppleScript features than its predecessor did. It additionally has a nice search feature that looks at a picture and identifies matches by appearance, so, for instance, you can locate all the pictures in a catalog that look like a sunset.

PhotoFlash now offers rudimentary color correction through a new color-correction filter, although it doesn't let you edit CMYK images. It also comes with new scripts for placing photos in FileMaker Pro and Word 6.0 and a CD-ROM of images from Clement Mok Designs.—Jason Snell

PhotoFlash 2.0
Apple Computer
(408) 996-1010
$129

PhotoFix

This new $250 program offers image cataloging, via Kudo's Image Browser. It also includes multicolor gradients, filters for blur and sharpen, and advanced color-correction capabilities. PhotoFix enables you to use Photoshop plug-in filters and switch among folders instantly.

The program includes a High Quality Printing feature, which allows you to get a better color match between your printer and your monitor. In addition, an extended color picker lets you create your own color picker by selecting a range of colors from an open image. You can't work in CMYK mode,

although you can export images as CMYK files.—Jason Snell

PhotoFix
Microspot
(800) 622-7568; (408) 253-2000
$250

POLISH UP YOUR GRANITE
Adobe Texture Maker

Wood and marble backgrounds make an elegant statement in any presentation. Rather than purchase a CD-ROM of static textures, you can use texture-making software to create your own. There's been a slew of texture generators recently, including this new program from Adobe.

Adobe TextureMaker 1.0 focuses on unique natural textures. It ships with more than 100 templates in categories such as marble, wood, granite, and fabric. All the textures use a layering method that uses prebuilt texture generators and filters to achieve a natural look. For instance, you can use a granite generator in combination with a noise filter in order to create stone. When you apply the custom lighting controls and engraving effects of TextureMaker, you can render a professional-looking texture. You can use Photoshop-compatible filters with TextureMaker too, to provide an endless variety of looks.

Adobe Texture Maker
Adobe
(919) 832-4124
$89

Alien Skin

Alien Skin, from Virtus, lacks the easy customization of a program like TextureMaker, but it produces otherworldly textures with one-button simplicity. A click of the texture-generator button produces several variations on the currently selected texture. Drag-and-drop swatches allow you to save textures in custom libraries. Alien Skin offers hundreds of textures and is available as either a standalone application or as a Photoshop plug-in ($99, 919 467-9700).

You might recognize Alien Skin as the name of a company. Alien Skin Software wrote Virtus's Alien Skin application, and the company additionally publishes a set of Photoshop filters called The Black Box. The filters are Power Mac-native and include such operations as automatic creation of drop shadows and instantaneous text embossing.—Sean J. Safreed

Alien Skin
Virtus
(919) 467-9700
$189

TYPESTRY'S NEW TRICKS
Pixar Typestry

Those of us who are easily distracted by bright and shiny objects—or who like to create them—will find Pixar's Typestry hard to pass up. The new version of this $299 3-D type-effects product adds a variety of nifty tricks, though

Digital Trip Wires for Safety

b
elieving that a virus won't attack you is a common mistake. Protect yourself. Whatever some denizens of the virus world think about antivirus software developers, we recommend you take precautions. Symantec (through the Peter Norton Group and the recently acquired Central Point), McAfee, and Reflex all make products that can keep a network or desktop PC safer by preventing, detecting, and helping to repair or recover from a virus attack.

Antivirus software works by scanning for known virus signatures. Every virus has a unique signature or fingerprint to identify itself. The software is also on the alert behind the scenes, looking for virus-like activity such as corrupted file or code trying to write to the boot sector. With a method called checksumming, it creates a numeric representation of the file, takes snapshots of the checksum, and compares it to the original file. A red flag goes up if something looks suspicious. To be effective, a virus must attach itself to an executable or load itself into memory and replicate. Antivirus software commonly isolates the virus and stops the replication, in effect, crippling the virus. If the files are infected, the damaged code is deleted and the proper data pieced back together and, in a sense, "cleaned."

Look for alarm and report features in today's antivirus software products. Schedulers for routine scanning, configurable reporting features, and alarms are important, but these should be considered secondary factors. When selecting a package, make sure the one you choose has the following basic features: scanning capabilities for detection of known viruses; a TSR or some sort of resident program that continuously monitors not only for known virus signatures but also for virus-like activity; and the ability to remove a virus and then help to repair or recover from an attack.

Is your network environment compatible with the antivirus software package? Look at what kind of interaction you and your users have with the outside world (via notebooks, modems, and so on). Do you need to support multiple platforms? Be sure to check that the product's site license lets you install it on home computers or networks, as well as on all of your workplace desktops. Bringing infected floppies or files from home to the office is one of the easiest and most common ways to spread viruses.

Software is only as good as the user. You must always scan incoming floppies and files before you introduce them to your PC—even those from shrink-wrapped packages. Antivirus software experts recommend quarantining a dedicated PC to scan all foreign floppies before they are introduced to your system. Most of the top products automatically scan for viruses and virus-like activity, and won't let you install something that is infected. However, reckless users can turn this feature off or choose not to install that portion of the program.

Keep current with regular updates of virus signature files, since 40 to 50 new viruses are discovered each month. Updates are usually available quarterly and are mailed to users directly, or they can be downloaded from a bulletin board system, CompuServe, or America Online.

Back up data religiously. In the event that you are unable to clean up after a virus attack and your only option is to delete the infected files, you risk losing all your data and applications unless you have a clean backup copy of data and programs. Be sure to rotate the disks that you use for backups.

Educate your fellow users about the ramifications of viruses and the vital importance of scanning, updates, and backing up data. There's no worse killer of productivity than the wrenching cry of "virus!" Otherwise, using antivirus software is similar to flossing your teeth just before you go to the dentist—it's worthless. Unless you follow the regimen at all times, you're still at risk.—Liesl La Grange ■

not quite as many as we would have liked.

The new version lets you wrap text around a sphere or tube, map it onto a wavy sheet, and Bézier-edit bevels. It now imports .EPS files to add simple nontext objects. A new constructive solid geometry-based engine lets Typestry combine or subtract objects. Pixar also gives you greater access to the formidable RenderMan engine and to such characteristics as the shininess and glow of Looks (Pixar's term for materials).

Of the new effects, we liked particle spray best, though it sprays particles only in every direction. Being able to specify trajectory to create a drip effect would be an improvement.

Despite beefed-up tools for its keyframe animation and a redesigned interface that adheres more to Windows conventions, Typestry still requires a little too much jumping around. Thankfully, the beta version we tested performed relatively nimbly on a Gateway 2000 66-MHz 486 with 28MB of RAM and a 64-bit ATI Mach 64 graphics accelerator.—Lori Grunin

Pixar Typestry
Pixar
1001 W. Cutting
Richmond, CA 94804
(800) 888-9856
$299

SMARTSKETCH TURNS IDEAS INTO DRAWINGS

SmartSketch

Attention, graphics users frustrated by the current crop of illustration software: FutureWave Software's $99 SmartSketch may be the drawing program that best fulfills the needs of the business user, while giving more than a nod toward an artist's sensibility. Installation is simple and fast. An interactive tour through the product launches immediately after installation, allowing you to play around with some of SmartSketch's more advanced features.

The help menu provides access to EasyArt, over 600 pieces of standard-fare clip art, which can be accessed by subject. EasyArt lives up to its name: It features drag-and-drop positioning, and its keyword indexing is simple to understand. Another useful feature, the Assistant dialog box, lets you customize automated features such as straight line, curved line, and shape recognition depending on the precision of your drawing skill. We found the basic tools easy to use; the best way to get to know SmartSketch is to experiment with features like the brush size and shape options.

The addition of object-oriented editing lets your creativity expand with your level of sophistication, although there are limits. We found selecting pieces of an ungrouped object for editing to be difficult at times. Still,

the program's 20 levels of undo provided enough peace of mind to promote exploration, and if you have the hardware to support it, the package offers a 16.7-million-color picker as well as compatibility with digitizing tablets—although it does not support pressure sensitivity. The program is an OLE 2.0 client and server, and you can opt to install the SmartSketch icon in Microsoft Word or Microsoft Excel; SmartSketch supports .DXF, .WMF, and EPS file formats.

For business users, and especially those who want to stretch their drawing horizons, SmartSketch does the trick.—Eryn Brown

SmartSketch
FutureWave Software Inc.
San Diego, CA
(800) 619-6193; (619) 637-6190
$99

PAINTER 3 AIMS HIGH AND LOW

Painter 3.0

Seeking to appeal to a broader audience, Fractal Design is pushing its Painter 3 illustration program into new territory. With added image-editing capabilities and a plethora of new features, Painter remains a high-end professional illustration tool that artists can't live without. At the same time, Painter 3 borrows a lot from Fractal Design's entry-level Dabbler program.

The big changes in the $499 Painter package include a new interface, innovative

tools, and a laundry list of enhancements. But two things haven't changed: a deep-seated respect for the nuances of traditional art media and methods, and an infectious enthusiasm for eye-popping image-editing effects.

Painter 3 is more intuitive than ever because several of the program's new functions mimic conventional art processes. One of the most intriguing new features, the Frame Stack, is based on old-fashioned animation techniques. It allows you to overlay up to five layers of transparent sheets and trace images from one frame to the next, altering each slightly. By employing Painter's other tools in combination with Frame Stacks, you can recreate the nostalgic look and feel of a pencil test animation.

The downside is that Painter 3's fidelity to traditional frame-by-frame methods can be time-consuming and arduous work. We found that the only way to automate this process was to apply a previously recorded work session to all of the frames in a new movie.

Experienced textile designers will feel immediately at home with Painter's virtual loom—a module that allows you to weave fill patterns resembling fabric. We created a complex pattern by choosing a weft and warp combination, and by adjusting the thickness and color of the fibers. Unfortunately, inventing your own weaving patterns requires you to

learn the loom's programming language.

In contrast, the new Image Hose tool has absolutely no conventional counterpart in the art world. Instead of using brush strokes, we were able to paint an image directly onto the program's canvas. It is as easy as choosing a series of images—which Painter calls a nozzle—and swabbing the page with the image. Generating your own nozzles can be either complicated or straightforward, depending upon the creation method you choose. You can arrange a series of pictures in a grid, group several different floating selections together, or convert a digital video clip into Publisher's native .RIF format.

If you find inspiration in new tools and techniques, you'll love Painter, because it can now reproduce the striations and color variations of bristle brushes much more realistically. Several new brush variants—like Big Loaded Oils—take advantage of this technology to produce startlingly naturalistic brush strokes. The new gradient fill options, which include unusual "ramps" (which look like a spiral) and the ability to map a gradient to a picture's luminence values, promise to produce a whole new generation of Peter Max wannabes.

The most impressive new painting mode is called—rather confusingly—Capture Pattern. It intricately wraps color to the opposite side of the picture whenever you paint off the edge of the canvas—creating a seamless repeating pattern. And the new Image Warp filter lets you push or pull the surface of a picture to create funhouse mirror effects.

The smallest enhancements ultimately deliver the biggest productivity gains. For example, adjusting brush size while you paint by using a keyboard shortcut is an enormous time-saver. The ability to draw selection areas using editable Bézier curves or to adjust the feathered edge of a mask using the HSV slider bring Painter's selection tools up to par with dedicated image-editing products like Adobe PhotoShop.

The program's revamped interface arranges all of the painting tools and art materials into drawers—an organizational metaphor borrowed from Fractal Design's Dabbler. Because Painter is a more complex program than Dabbler, the result is a sometimes confusing collection of drawers that open and close, palettes that expand and contract, and brush configuration options that are split across several different control palettes.

Painter's $499 price tag is justified by the inclusion of object layering functions that were previously available only in Painter X2—a $149 add-on. One of the most elegant implementations of object layering around, it provides robust object-management functions (such as grouping), sophisticated compositing options (such as gel or colorize) and

automated effects (such as the new drop shadow effect). As a bonus, Painter 3 includes a CD-ROM filled with stock photographs, sample movie clips, paper textures, Image Hose nozzles, and brush looks.

Ironically, several useful features present in Painter 2—including the ability to export .EPS files with a clipping path and the ability to tear off a single brush variant from the brushes palette—have been dropped from Painter 3; hopefully, they'll reappear in the next version. In the meantime, no one will be disappointed with Painter 3—this is a program for anyone who is interested in making serious art or having serious fun.—Luisa Simone

Fractal Design Painter
Fractal Design Corp.
Aptos, CA
(800) 297-2665; (408) 688-5300
$499

BRINGING GRAPHICS IMAGES TO LIFE

HiJaak Graphics Suite

HiJaak Graphics Suite does for graphics-image mavens what products like PC Tools did for DOS users: It provides a solid, low-cost, everything-but-the-kitchen-sink collection of utilities. The five interconnected programs in HiJaak Graphics Suite make up a comprehensive toolbox for managing and editing images, and converting them from one format to another.

The focal point of the suite is the Browser, which

lets you find and catalog images, and gain access to the suite's other capabilities. Browser's File Manager-like interface displays three types of information.

The most basic information consists of the familiar listing of your drives and directories in the left window and specific files in the right window. Initially, Browser represents individual files with generic icons. Clicking on the Update toolbar button tells Browser to replace the icon with either a thumbnail image if it's a graphics file, or the Windows icon for applications and nonimage data files. This process must be repeated for each new file you add.

The update process also creates a database-like index containing information such as the file name and location so you can search on those elements quickly. Impressively, Browser indexes text that is part of vector image files. This will particularly benefit CAD users, who can search on text in their drawings.

Collections make up the second type of information Browser displays in its tree structure. A collection could be any files related to a specific project, or could consist of groups of similar files, like images of company officers. Typically, these are graphics files, but you can store any type of file in a collection.

You can gather collections by using the third type of information Browser manages: searches. A search begins when you click on a

toolbar button and fill in the search dialog box. You can search on the basis of attributes, such as file names, or on keywords, including text associated with indexed vector files. However, Browser doesn't support Boolean AND/OR/NOT operators.

When the search is completed, Browser displays the results in the right window. You can save the search to use again or as a new collection. Accessing saved collections and searches is simple: Browser's left window lists Searches and Collections as directories, and displays specific saved searches and collections as subdirectories. You can also add to a collection by dragging files from the right window and dropping them in a collection listed in the left window.

Browser also serves as a gateway, with buttons for launching the suite's other programs. Dragging an image from the right window and dropping it on an application's icon loads both the application and the specific file.

Browser incorporates most of the capabilities of another suite member, HiJaak Pro. This veteran format-conversion program can now convert raster images to vector images. Inset Systems also added support for several additional image formats, bringing the total of supported formats in HiJaak Pro to 75.

To convert the image from within Browser, you select it in Browser's right window, then choose the Convert option in the File menu. From

the dialog box, you pick a destination format. You can also click the Options button for another dialog box that fine-tunes the image's appearance after you convert it. For example, the options for fine-tuning conversions to the Windows BMP format include control over scaling, color, and brightness.

Loading HiJaak Pro separately provides more controls over raster-to-vector conversions than you'll get from within Browser. It also provides other fine-tuning capabilities, like the ability to crop and resize images before conversion.

The third star of this suite is Smuggler, which inserts Browser's image-management feature into Windows applications, thus letting you drop images in various formats into applications that do not support those formats. Smuggler automatically adds itself to the Edit menu of many Windows applications, but for some applications, such as Word for Windows, you access the Smuggler window with the Control-Shift-S key combination. To add an image to a document, you select it in the right window, and either click OK or drag it to your application. Smuggler also includes the Options button for fine-tuning images before insertion.

The other two elements of this suite, HiJaak TouchUp and HiJaak Draw, help you edit your images. Unfortunately, these programs have very different interfaces, which increases the learning curve.

TouchUp, the raster image editing program, has some nice touches. Specifically, TouchUp's "test strips" show variations of an image on-screen, each with different brightness, contrast, and gamma settings. Rather than forcing you to make those adjustments manually and to repeatedly test-print the image until you get the one you want, the test-strips feature lets you pick the right image and print it once. However, beyond basics like posterization and embossing, TouchUp offers few special effects.

Draw, however, is impressive. It includes a thorough set of drawing tools for creating vector images, and has capabilities like masking and the ability to fit text around curves. Its scissors tool, which lets you easily crop vector images and cut out specific parts, is also fine. While art professionals still need an advanced drawing program like CorelDraw, HiJaak Draw provides plenty of power for most nonprofessional users.

Inset Systems has done an excellent job of assembling a group of essential utilities that provide a thorough solution for managing, converting, and editing images.—David Haskin

HiJaak Graphics Suite
Inset Systems Inc.
71 Commerce Dr.
Brookfield, CT 06804
(800) 374-6738; (203) 740-2400
$99

VENTURA ADVANCES UNDER WINDOWS

Ventura 5

If you've been publishing documents on a PC since the DOS days, chances are you've used Ventura Publisher. But if you left Ventura behind when you moved to Windows, prepare to welcome it back onto your hard disk. The new Windows version, published by Corel, has enough muscle to challenge heavyweights like PageMaker, including improved color printing, typography control, and database publishing features.

The older Windows version of Ventura was a DOS/GEM program at the core, with a thin veneer of Windows slapped on. Not so with Corel's Ventura 5. The vestiges of its GEM past—WID font width files and the time-wasting and disk-hogging graphics conversions have been removed. Instead, Ventura now taps into Windows's PFM files and imports graphic file formats directly—including JPEG and Photo CD.

A new CorelDraw-style interface makes using Ventura easier than before—especially if you get it as part of the $899 CorelDraw 5 megabundle. Graphics handling has been improved with a new irregular text-wrap feature that lets you choose from a variety of wraps and modify them with Bézier tools. You can also rotate frames of graphics or text in 0.1-degree increments, though rotation of text within a frame is limited to 90-degree increments. For layout protection you can lock a frame's size and position, and under Corel's guidance, Ventura has acquired a pasteboard similar to PageMaker's.

But judging from our tests of a still-buggy final release candidate, Ventura has a way to go. You still can't open more than one document at a time, nor can you use tabs in justified text. And to compete with FrameMaker for producing long documents, Corel will need to provide other missing features: character tags, multiple indexes and tables of contents, a choice of footnotes or endnotes, and a built-in macro language, not to mention Macintosh and Unix versions.

Still, FrameMaker, QuarkXPress, and PageMaker can't beat the level of formatting and typographical control offered by Ventura's paragraph-based style sheets—a boon when your document requires a complex, structured format. FrameMaker may be more capable for technical documentation—where you need elaborate cross indexing, multilevel paragraph and illustration numbering, indexes, and tables of contents—but Ventura is certainly no slouch here either. QuarkXPress and PageMaker, however, have Ventura beat when it comes to mixing type and graphics in documents and doing freestyle design.

For projects that occupy the middle ground between graphically intense ad work and technical documentation, Ventura 5 is definitely worthy of consideration.—Bob Weibel

Ventura 5
Corel Corp.
(800) 772-6735
$495 for CD-ROM
($595 with floppies)

FILL YOUR BOILERPLATES

HotDocs

"Stop spending money on printing forms," insists the head of your accounting department. The alternative? Harness the power in your computer.

We challenged our testers to come up with templates for a power-of-attorney form and a fax cover sheet, and as a result, we found one tool—Capsoft's HotDocs—that made a significant difference to them.

Using only their word processors, our testers were routinely frustrated by the perceived complexity of the task and the lack of adequate documentation (users accessed help more for this task than any other). Given the need to learn complex macro languages like WordBasic in order to automate templates like the ones we asked for, this was hardly surprising.

In the process of doing the power-of-attorney boilerplate, our testers often found themselves lost and frustrated with inadequate documentation in the manuals and the online help. Some couldn't complete the task within the time allotted for this test.

With HotDocs, our testers no longer needed to learn about fields and macro languages. They liked the way HotDocs integrated itself into their word processors and walked them through the process. As a result, it won almost unanimous praise.—Gordon Meyer

HotDocs
Capsoft
(801) 763-3900
$60

QuarkXPress 3.3

When you need professional-strength page layout, you need a program that gives you tight control over typography and color, cross-platform compatibility, and enough flexibility to mold the program to work the way you do. QuarkXPress 3.3, designed for magazine and advertising work, is your choice. Few programs can match its on-the-fly page layout and graphic design features, precision typography, and superb color control. Better yet are the myriad QuarkXTensions—add-ons that let you select your own tools for custom solutions. QuarkXPress isn't the easiest program to learn, but once learned, it's easy to use. It has superior graphical control and can handle formatted text with WYSIWYG ease. Its full array of color models and matching systems is equaled only by those in PageMaker.

Despite the great strengths of its close competitors, Quark-XPress is still the best choice for well-integrated and customizable page layout for precision design-driven publishing.

QuarkXPress 3.3
Quark
(800) 788-7835
$799

Publisher 2.0

So you say you don't know your x-height from a hole in the ground? Fire up Microsoft Publisher 2.0, go through its lineup of publication-building PageWizards, pick the one you like, and follow the instructions. This isn't something you'd use for creating technical documentation, but for quick and easy one-off documents, it's tough to top.

Publisher 2.0
Microsoft
(800) 426-9400
$99

Ten Tips from the Virus Trackers

hat the experts advise:

1. Use antivirus software that combines scanning, checksum, and monitoring facilities.

2. Update your scanning software regularly to make sure it can find newly unleashed viruses.

3. Don't use pirated software—you don't know where it's been.

4. Don't move copies of executable files from one computer to another; always install from the distribution disk.

5. Don't boot from a floppy disk of unknown origin; perform a virus scan before using files from such a disk.

6. Treat executable files downloaded from BBSs with suspicion; scan the programs before use.

7. If your system is part of a network, use passwords and other security measures to block unauthorized access.

8. Don't use an obvious password for your account, and don't use the same password on multiple systems.

9. Back up your data files regularly, and rotate the backup disks so that you have copies of files on different disks going back several weeks. Keep backups of your applications' disks, too.

10. If your system begins to act strangely, if program files behave in an unexpected way, or if a file's length or "last saved" date changes unexpectedly, assume you have a virus and perform an aggressive scan. Have a plan in place for notifying users of a possible virus attack. ■

MORE FEATURES AND YOU MIGHT GET HURT

WordPerfect 6.1

For any business that produces large volumes of complex documents, there's no such thing as a minor upgrade to a word processor. Every improvement that lets users work in new ways can be a revolution—and every new bug a catastrophe. By those standards, WordPerfect 6.1 is a coup d'état over Microsoft's Word and Lotus's Ami Pro.

WordPerfect is always one step behind you as you write, sweeping up your little blunders. QuickCorrect—first seen in Word 6.0 as AutoCorrect, the feature that corrects frequent typos as soon as you make them—will now capitalize the first letter of a sentence, change two spaces to one, and give you more options for handling quotation marks.

Furthermore, you'll find many improvements in WordPerfect 6.1 that probably you didn't think were possible. Take tables, for example. A Table Expert now lets you apply any of 40 predefined styles for appearance. Another new feature automatically changes the width of a column to fit the widest text in any of its cells.

With WordPerfect 6.1, working with documents has never been easier. Quick-Format, the feature that lets you apply the style of selected text to other text in your document, has been revamped to include AutoUpdate—if you make a formatting change, WordPerfect will automatically update all sections that share that formatting. And while the spelling checker and writing tools in WordPerfect 6.0 were never broken, WordPerfect fixed them anyway. The spelling checker, thesaurus, and find-and-replace capabilities now correct or replace entire word forms. For example, perform a find-and-replace on the word fly, and the program will catch flew, flown, and flying. Want to replace fly with drive? No problem. All forms will match the original version of the word, including drove, driven, and driving.

WordPerfect has overcome some technical glitches that plagued earlier versions. For example, Version 6.1 supports up to 300 levels of undo. And drag-and-drop finally lets you move or copy text between two on-screen documents. You'll also find that WordPerfect 6.1 is OLE 2.0-compliant, making it cooperate nicely with other OLE 2.0-supported applications such as Excel or Quattro Pro 6.0.

Some annoying quirks are fixed, such as the inability of 6.0 to make Zoom to Margins the default display. And there are several other changes, including some designed to make WordPerfect consistent with other members of the new PerfectOffice.

So is WordPerfect 6.1 a flawless gem? No. WordPerfect still doesn't have the equivalent of AutoFormat, the automatic formatting feature found in Microsoft Word. Some of the dialog boxes, particularly the one for spelling correction, could use some streamlining.

But is WordPerfect 6.1 a treasure? You bet. This version broadens those areas in which WordPerfect has led Word and closes the gap on nearly all of the Word features that WordPerfect lacked.—Ron White

WordPerfect 6.1
The Novell Applications Group
(800) 321-4566; (801) 225-5000
$495

WORKING-CLASS WINDOWS FONTS

FontWorks 1.0 for Windows

Fonts are cheap to buy and easy to use, but managing fonts in a workgroup environment is both daunting and expensive. Documents move from computer to computer, and fonts don't. If the appearance of your documents is important, standardize on Elseware's FontWorks to remove your workgroup font worries.

For as little as $30 per PC, FontWorks installs 153 typefaces in about 3MB (less than half the disk space you'd expect) and provides tight font management and accurate substitutes when documents arrive with fonts you don't have.

Instead of relying on Windows's TrueType rasterizer or Adobe's Type Manager, FontWorks quickly creates TrueType fonts on demand from compact 4k Infinifont

files. Only a type expert could spot the difference in printed quality.

FontWorks also stores a database of font metrics for more than 500 other fonts. If it recognizes a font name, FontWorks makes a forgery of it from some matching font. This font substitution ability differs from Ares's Font Chameleon, which creates new fonts by redesigning or morphing two fonts into one. Better yet, FontWorks provides font group management—including TrueType, Type 1, and FontWorks Terafonts—and a Font Advisor tutorial created by type specialist Daniel Will-Harris, which helps you make appropriate font choices for most types of documents.

For handling the myriad of fonts in your workgroup and learning how to use them better, FontWorks is your best option.—Bob Weibel

FontWorks 1.0 for Windows
Elseware Corp.
(800) 357-3927
$129.95 for single user,
$600 for 10 users,
$1,525 for 50 users

Masterclips: The Art of Business

There are many collections of clip art on CD-ROM, but the majority of them don't contain images suitable for business use. Masterclips: The Art of Business, on the other hand, is a collection of 6,000 images, any one of which could be used to doctor a marketing

plan, spruce up a direct-mail campaign, or add a little extra oomph to an overhead.

The illustrations aren't fancy, which is exactly what's good about them. They can fit tastefully into any business setting and not draw unnecessary attention to themselves. You won't find any cute cartoons of birds or hearts on this disc.

The images are designed to work with all presentation, word processing, and desktop publishing programs, and best of all, the manual contains hard copy of all the images so you don't have to waste time displaying them on-screen. But if you swore off manuals years ago, there's also an impressive Windows search engine to help you find an image online. It's all designed for the businessperson who needs functional illustrations but wants to think about them as little as possible.—Ron White

Masterclips: The Art of Business
IMSI
(800) 833-8082; (415) 454-7101
$149.95

DAD, CAN I BORROW THE DTP?

PagePlus 3.0

When Serif's PagePlus grows up, it wants to be a high-end desktop publisher. With Version 3.0, it's stuck in that awkward teen stage—way too powerful to fit in the low-end market, and not seasoned enough to go to bat against the mature Aldus PageMaker or QuarkXPress.

But PagePlus 3.0 is a sleek, sharp, hormone-ridden powerhouse of a teenager that is perfect for those who lust after some of those grown-up DTP features, but find the price and complexity of PageMaker or QuarkXPress daunting. PagePlus, the $59.95 wonder, gives you the power to create stunning documents using text rotation, irregular text wraps, and color separation—all complex features that nearly put PagePlus in the league of much more expensive products.

With Version 3.0, you'll find some welcome enhancements, including automatic page numbering, an integrated word processor, automatic hyphenation, running headers and footers, tabs and tab leaders, and master pages.

PagePlus even includes some indispensable features that, unbelievably, you won't find in the higher-priced PageMaker, including a thesaurus, a JPEG import filter, a word and character counter, and a print preview window. (You can also find these features in QuarkXPress.) The table editor also works better than PageMaker's. In addition, Serif has added enough ease-of-use enhancements to make learning the program a snap—without ever having to crack open a manual.

While PagePlus really packs in the goodies, it has only about half the features and controls of PageMaker or QuarkXPress. Most notably, PagePlus lacks long-document features such as indexing, table of

contents generation, and multifile book-building. This program is not designed for those kinds of tasks. Also missing is the capability to open more than one document at a time without running multiple versions of the application. You won't find a multiple paste feature, for example, which in PageMaker lets you place multiple copies of an object at defined offsets. Other high-end options and refinements are either watered down or missing.

PagePlus still has its Change Bar floating palette, Serif's version of PageMaker's Control palette and QuarkXPress's Measurements palette. All of these let you format text or modify objects without opening menus, but the PagePlus version is clunkier and less comprehensive than those of the bigger programs.

The WritePlus text editor, like PageMaker's story editor, lets you apply paragraph styles and font characteristics (such as boldface or italics), but you can't change fonts without applying styles, a real usability blunder. PagePlus also lacks PageMaker's automatic baseline leading option, which

precisely controls where the first baseline of text falls, something professional designers need.

Nonetheless, PagePlus 3.0 is an awesome deal for the money. When it comes to price, its competitor is the $139 Microsoft Publisher, which has a Page Wizard that beats PagePlus in the ease-of-use category, but PagePlus is much more powerful. For the price, it is a truly excellent program.—Bob Weibel

PagePlus 3.0
Serif
(800) 697-3743; (603) 889-8650
$59.95; $99.95 for the
Publishing Suite

VERSATILE AND SIMPLE, CLARIS'S NEW DRAW PROGRAM SCRAMBLES TO CATCH UP WITH THE COMPETITION

ClarisDraw

The latest incarnation of Claris's venerable MacDraw draw program, ClarisDraw, keeps the easy-to-use, stylish design we've come to expect from Claris products and has a bevy of well-implemented new features, many clearly culled from its rivals's feature lists. Streamlined and simple, it's tolerably fast on 680x0 Macs and downright zippy on Power Macs, on which it can run in native mode. But for the same price or less, Deneba's Canvas and Aldus's IntelliDraw have more features geared toward more-sophisticated illustration work.

Many of ClarisDraw's new features have Smart in their names—appropriate, because many of them emulate similar features in IntelliDraw, the first draw program that let you create links between objects to automatically keep alignment, proportioning, and other relationships in effect. But whereas IntelliDraw's brainy links can be bewilderingly complex, ClarisDraw's are simple and spare. For example, to use SmartAlign, you select two or more objects in your illustration and use the Alignment palette to choose the way you want them to be aligned with each other. As you move one object, the other objects remain aligned to it, according to the relationship you've set up between them.

SmartAlign isn't the only smart feature. Smart-Connectors are lines that remain attached to objects—if you want to use ClarisDraw to create flowcharts, for instance, lines can remain connected between boxes no matter where you move the boxes on your chart. And if you need precise measurements, you can create AutoSize lines, which tell you how long they are. (We were disappointed, however, that you can't turn the SmartConnector lines into AutoSize lines.) Smart-Embossing and SmartShadow, just as their names imply, let you create rudimentary 3-D effects and drop shadows.

The PointGuide cursor, which changes its appearance when it's over an object's center or corners, and Guide-liner, which provides guide-lines that show you how objects align with other objects, are handy features for positioning items. Claris-Draw's Object Info palette lets you precisely reposition, rotate, and resize objects, using numerical values.

ClarisDraw ships with 2,400 pieces of clip art, called SmartSymbols. You can drag a SmartSymbol out of a library palette and drop it right into your document—repeatedly if you wish. You can replace any SmartSymbol with any other by using the Replace Clones command. It's somewhat like a Find/Replace command in a word processor, and although it's not as fast and elegant as IntelliDraw's method of automatically updating your documents, the Replace Clones command does get the job done.

ClarisDraw has drastically improved text-handling tools compared with MacDraw's. You can bind text to a path on the inside or the outside of a closed shape and convert type into outlines, which you can reshape by using Bézier points and fill with gradients or patterns. You can link text boxes to each other and wrap text around objects, both of which can be useful for simple, artistic desktop-publishing tasks, even though you can't kern or track type at all.

Although it's no substitute for Microsoft PowerPoint or Aldus Persuasion, you can also use ClarisDraw to prepare simple business presentations and slide shows. The program lets you use as many as ten different on-

screen pointers and create fades between slides.

When it comes to color control, ClarisDraw will disappoint more-demanding users. It can import and export 24-bit-color images, which MacDraw never could, but it still has the 256-color palette that dates back to the days when most Macs had only 8-bit color, if any. It still doesn't support CMYK mode or popular color systems such as Pantone. Not surprisingly, ClarisDraw can't output color separations, although you can save documents in EPS for placement in, and printing from, more color-savvy applications.

Besides providing the basic manipulation tools we've mentioned, ClarisDraw can lighten and darken images, distort them vertically or horizontally with a new shearing feature, and scale them by percentage. But unlike its competitors, it doesn't have envelope warping, shape extrusion, or cropping.

ClarisDraw is a versatile and easy-to-use draw program, but we found ourselves wishing it had more of the tools its rivals have. If you need to create basic graphics quickly and don't have the time to learn to use new tools, invest in ClarisDraw. But if you want more-sophisticated tools, other draw programs will give you more to work with for a similar price.—Eric Taub

ClarisDraw
Claris
(408) 727-8227
$399

CANVAS 3.5: THE SWISS ARMY KNIFE OF ILLUSTRATION

Canvas 3.5

A full-featured paint/draw program, Deneba Software's Canvas 3.5 tries to be all things to all people—and often succeeds. Like Illustrator and FreeHand, Canvas includes PostScript drawing capabilities. But in addition, Canvas offers bit-map-editing tools, and the program handles output to QuickDraw printers better than FreeHand or Illustrator. Straddling another line, Canvas comes in identical Mac and Windows versions; files are fully interchangeable between the two. Canvas can also create decent four-color separations.

The drawing portion of Canvas contains features that are useful for drafting. For example, an autodimensioning feature lets you create numerically accurate floor plans and industrial designs. Powerful layer-management tools (similar to those in Illustrator and FreeHand) help in creating and editing complex, multilayer drawings such as technical illustrations.

Convenience is a key concept in Canvas. You can search for specific fill properties and objects within a drawing. The Smart Mouse feature—unique to Canvas—helps automate many alignment and constraint tasks. For instance, if you specify that all angles be drawn in increments of 30 degrees, the Smart Mouse feature will automatically adjust angles as you draw them.

When it comes to text handling, Canvas's features rival those of Illustrator. Canvas includes full kerning and tracking features, and it can wrap text around or flow it within any shape. A built-in spelling checker rounds out Canvas's text toolbox.

What you don't get with Canvas, however, is extrafine control over illustrations. For example, although Canvas' curve- and path-editing tools work well, they don't include as many options as those in Illustrator 5.0. Nor does Canvas include all the features FreeHand includes for producing page layouts. In addition, with Canvas, you're limited to one level of undo—not only a scary proposition when you're creating complex images but also a damper on what-if experimentation.

If you're looking for a bargain, Canvas is an excellent choice. For a low street price of $265, you get one program that lets you produce both bit-mapped and PostScript drawings, and the company offers free, unlimited technical support. Canvas is an especially good choice for students and for users who need to create basic CAD diagrams or technical illustrations.

Canvas 3.5
Deneba Software
Miami, FL
(800) 622-6827
$265

CyberMesh

Developed by John Knoll, one of Photoshop's inventors, CyberMesh lets you create 3-D images from any 2-D gray-scale images in Photoshop and save them as DXF files. This export plug-in sports an intuitive, Photoshop-like interface. Controls for creating meshes from simple geometric shapes are neatly displayed, with sliding controls that automatically update your model in a preview window. In addition to icons that let you zoom into a model, rotate it, and view it in wireframe or shaded modes, CyberMesh gives you everything you need to create landscapes, asteroids, and more. Objects can then be rendered in any 3-D package that accepts DXF files.—Sean Safreed, Jason Snell

CyberMesh
Knoll Software
(415) 453-2471
$49

FotoMagic Series 1

Ring of Fire, a Japanese start-up, has erupted into the U.S. market with FotoMagic Series 1, a package of eight Photoshop filters exclusively for working with an image's colors. Other plug-ins alter individual pixel positions to produce unusual effects, but these filters extend Photoshop's native color-correction tools by letting you manipulate just the image colors. Highlights of FotoMagic Series 1 include ColorRanger, which divides an image into color ranges, so you can create pop-art effects; Color-Filters, which work like negative and positive color filters on a camera, for selectively changing the lightness of a color or range of colors; and ColorShifter, which changes an image's tint or cast. Two more sets of FotoMagic filters should be ready by the time you read this.—Sean Safreed, Jason Snell

FotoMagic Series 1
Ring of Fire
(800) 990-0990; (408) 992-0400
$199

Pattern WORKSHOP

MicroFrontier has taken a kernel from its image editor, Color It!, and turned it into a Photoshop filter that lets you create and edit patterns and organize them for later use. You can choose from 160 patterns—from textiles to patriotic symbols—or use Pattern WORKSHOP's built-in pattern editor to make your own. You can pick pattern dimen-

sions and then grab patterns right out of Photoshop files. And if the patterns you make still aren't enough, you can buy a volume containing 160 more patterns.—Sean Safreed, Jason Snell

Pattern WORKSHOP
MicroFrontier
(515) 270-8109
$49.95; additional pattern library, $24.95

STARTLING, BRUSH-BASED SPECIAL EFFECTS

Paint Alchemy

Paint Alchemy gives your Photoshop-filter-compatible applications the power to transmute any RGB image into a stunning array of brush strokes. Paint Alchemy-filtered images have a distinctive, organic look you can't create any other way—not on a Mac, at least. Xaos (pronounced "chaos") has used this algorithmic paintbrush technology for years in its high-end animation production work as well as in a pricey special-effects animation package called Pandemonium, which runs on Silicon Graphics machines. Now, by putting the technology into a plug-in filter, Xaos has made it accessible to mainstream Mac applications such as Adobe's Photoshop and Premiere, Fractal Design's Painter, VideoFusion's VideoFusion, and CoSA's AfterEffects.

Paint Alchemy's power lies in the sophisticated control it gives you over five basic brush attributes (color, size, angle, transparency, and brush shape) and in its ability to alter these attributes based on the values of pixels in the image—for example, using larger brush strokes for cool hues than for warm hues. You specify combinations of brush controls in five simple screens called Control Cards; when you create a combination that you particularly like, you can save it for subsequent use. The standard package includes 75 preset styles (such as Vortex, Threads, and Spatula); a floppy disk called Floppy Full of Brushes, which contains 50 additional brush shapes, costs $19.95. You can also use any gray-scale image as a basic brush shape.

Animated Brushwork. Video and animation fans, take note: Paint Alchemy's most dazzling effects result from using it with QuickTime movies (or other types of animation files). When you type 13 into the randomization-seed setting on the Brush Control Card, Paint Alchemy randomizes the brush seed applied to multiple animation or QuickTime frames, yielding incredible animated brush effects—you get brush strokes wriggling with life.

Regardless of its less-than-blinding speed, Paint Alchemy is a dazzling addition to any image-processing toolbox. If you're looking for delicious eye candy, look no further.—David Biedny

Paint Alchemy
Xaos Tools
San Francisco, CA
(415) 487-7000
$99; 50 add-on brushes, $19.95

SHED THE JAGGED EDGES FROM YOUR IMAGES

JAG II

We've all seen those telltale jaggies in an image—the stairstep edges that scream "computer generated!" JAG II not only eliminates the jaggies (as its predecessor, JAG, did) but it also adds new capabilities for boosting the resolution of black-and-white images and includes new filtering capabilities for color images.

JAG II uses a technique called resolution boosting, which lets it take a MacPaint-style black-and-white 72-dpi image and enlarge it to 300 dpi. Although they aren't perfect, the results are surprisingly good. On complex images, such as black-and-white woodcuts, this technique provides better results than any auto-tracing program could, and in less time: The process takes only a couple of minutes.

JAG II remains a good value for animators and 3-D artists wanting to save time—especially now that the program can process QuickTime files. With its new resolution boosting for black-and-white images, JAG II is also a good choice for those who want better laser-printer output.—Sean Safreed

JAG II
Ray Dream, Inc.
Mountain View, CA
(800) 846-0111; (415) 960-0768
$129

CATALOG IMAGES FOR EASY RETRIEVAL

Shoebox

The name of the latest entry in the image-database market may evoke closets full of unmounted photo collections, but Eastman Kodak's Shoebox is a far more efficient storage mechanism than its real-world namesake. Shoebox provides a one-stop catalog of your visual media, letting you sort, search, retrieve, copy, and print as many as 30,000 images per catalog. Each cataloged image is represented by a thumbnail image and data values you enter.

As you might suspect, Shoebox is optimized for images in the Kodak Photo CD format. You can retrieve a Photo CD image in any of the five available resolutions and view it in various color depths, including gray-scale and 24-bit color. Shoebox supports other file types, including EPS, PICT, TIFF,

QuickTime, and AIFF sound files, but the support is only minimal. For example, CMYK TIFF files invariably become garbled images.

Shoebox shines in its handling of data entry. In addition to providing fields for keywords and captions, the program lets you define as many as 100 additional data fields. To make data entry easier and more accurate, you can use the Entry Helper to create pop-up lists of often-used values. During data entry, you can select multiple thumbnails and then simultaneously enter shared data values for them—a real time-saver. Shoebox also lets you customize several aspects of the layout, such as thumbnail size, but there's no Undo command for restoring default settings.

If you deal mainly with Photo CD images or need lots of user-definable fields, Shoebox may be a good fit. Otherwise, you're better off with a program such as Aldus Fetch that's easier to use and supports more file types.—Aileen Abernathy

Shoebox
Eastman Kodak
Rochester, NY
(800) 242-2424; (716) 724-4000
$245

DTP Reference Kit

Neophyte desktop designers can't ask for more than the DTP Reference Kit, a bag containing five rulers, a screen-percentage table, keyboard command shortcuts for Aldus PageMaker and QuarkXPress, a guide to Zapf Dingbats, and printers' and proofreaders' marks.

DTP Reference Kit
The Communications Shop
$29.95

PaperTemplates

If you don't have an artistic bone in your body but have to design things on your Mac, PaperTemplates, from PaperDirect, is the answer. With it, you can create brochures, mailers, business cards, and other business forms from within Microsoft Word, PageMaker, or QuarkXPress. Designed to be used with PaperDirect's wide selection of papers, Paper-Templates contains more than 130 designs.

PaperTemplates
PaperDirect
$39.95

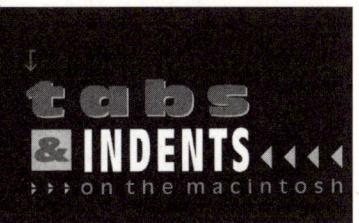

Tabs and Indents

You need to know a few tricks in order to turn out polished and professional-looking documents with your Mac. *Tabs and Indents*, by Robin Williams (author of the best-selling *The Mac Is Not a Typewriter*), gives you a grounding in how to format word-processing documents. The enclosed disk contains skill exercises and a couple of useful freeware programs.

Tabs and Indents
Peachpit Press
$12

AgfaType CD-ROM 4.0

Unlockable CD-ROMs have been slow to take off, but the AgfaType CD-ROM 4.0 font collection may convert skeptics. Not only does it give you instant phone access to high-quality fonts from Agfa, Adobe, and the Font Bureau but you also get an interactive type tutorial, an extensive glossary, and 12MB of graphics-related shareware.

AgfaType CD-ROM 4.0
Agfa Division, Miles, Inc.
200 Ballardvale Street
Wilmington, MA 01887
(617) 944-3700; (800) 424-8973
$99 (starter set)

Silent Partners

Soon to be your sidekicks, smart software agents will do much more than offer jazzy help. They may even take over the whole job.

It's 3:00 p.m. and you have to get your hands on the 1994 budget numbers. Oh, and you need them in time for tomorrow morning's management meeting. Are you sweating it? No way: You have the world's most reliable assistant, who will relentlessly scour the network for the spreadsheet you need. You won't even have to pay overtime. It's all in the line of duty for your average software agent.

Just turn to your PC and instruct your agent what to search for and where by setting parameters with a click or two of the mouse. While you finish up the day's business, your agent will scour online databases, gathering the information you need and returning it to your PC.

Welcome to the new PC software order. After nearly a decade of nonstop feature wars—the escalation of ever-mightier program functions for ever-more-rarefied tasks—software developers are getting back to the original vision of personal computing. What most PC users have always wanted is a way to turn their PCs into electronic brains that can take over tedious business procedures and simplify their complex tasks. So it should come as no surprise that in place of yesterday's buzzwords—power and productivity—today's software vocabulary is brimming with the likes of intelligence and smarts.

Mainstream business applications now offer incarnations of intellect with names like Assistants, Coaches, Experts, and Wizards. The major vendors are already devising next-generation solutions that move core applications closer to anticipating users' needs. In the pages that follow, we'll look first at the current approaches to software automation from companies like Borland International, Lotus Development, Microsoft, and WordPerfect. Then we'll focus on what these vendors, and other major players, have in store for years to come.

While your word processor and spreadsheet get smart, scripting languages such as General Magic's Telescript will soon cull information from corporate databases and screen your e-mail. It's only the tip of the iceberg. Programs with embedded intelligence will make suggestions to improve your productivity. At the same time, a secret agent may be telling your supervisor when you play Solitaire. It's a brave new world, filled with problems as well as promise.

"I wanted an agent to be responsible for getting something done while I was busy with a research problem," says Oliver Selfridge. It was this vision that prompted the former Massachusetts Institute of Technology researcher to dream up software agents. For Selfridge, an agent should resemble a valued assistant with which one can communicate in a kind of shorthand and rely on its sense of responsibility to get the job done.

So far, Selfridge's dream hasn't been fully realized. The virtues that Selfridge thought an agent should have—super intelligence, self-motivation, and loyalty—are not yet found in software agents. Nonetheless, through a combination of wishful thinking and marketing cunning, the term agent is being applied to a broad range of manifestations: from simple adaptable interfaces to sophisticated self-modifying program objects that can do your shopping.

"Lately, the word agent is used any time PC users think some personality in their computer is doing something for them," explains Ted Selker, a lecturer at Stanford University who teaches the course "Proactive and Reactive Agents in User Interfaces."

Selker's interest in agents dates back to graduate school when he created his first agent—Coach, shorthand for cognitive adaptive help—for his PhD thesis. In the mid-1980s, he contributed to Atari's research effort into intelligent encyclopedias and video games, the precursors of today's multimedia software.

How smart are these so-called agents? Selker rates agent intelligence on a continuum from preprogrammed macros to human-faced personalities on screen. You'll find clever programming and lots of human ingenuity in each agent, but currently

there isn't enough problem-solving intelligence. A truly intelligent agent should be capable of original thinking, giving it the ability to solve problems independently. For example, it should adapt to changing circumstances by coming up with an alternate plan of attack.

The leading software vendors boast of "artificial intelligence" for largely cosmetic features, like menu bars, icons, smart help, and even tutorial videos. Still, when learning to use a program costs more in lost productivity than the software price itself, it's hard to resist even the illusory promise of PC intelligence.

Is Today's Software Smart?

Consider this: Lotus successfully packages its combined applications (1-2-3 for Windows, Ami Pro, Freelance Graphics, Lotus Organizer, and Approach) as its SmartSuite. But don't look

for breakthrough artificial intelligence here. All of the programs include SmartIcons, which are really no more intelligent than icons that launch Windows applications via macros. Their smartness refers to the fact that they are consistent across Lotus applications.

By the next version of SmartSuite, each program will include the ScreenCam screen-recorder utility, which debuted last November in Lotus 1-2-3 Release 4 for Windows. About as smart as a camcorder, ScreenCam records program screens, mouse and cursor movements, menu selections, and audio. These live-action screen captures can be used to create quick custom tutorials to train users how to do something correctly— how to generate an invoice in Approach, for example. In the absence of built-in or third-party tutorials, ScreenCam is a savvy feature only if a systems manager or net-

work administrator has the smarts to create onscreen lessons.

While ScreenCam sounds like something TV's David Letterman would skewer, it does demonstrate the need for more imaginative ways to teach people how to master their software. "Anything that makes computers less forbidding involves intelligence," insists Alex Morrow, general manager of systems architecture at Lotus. By accelerating the learning curve, even the dumbest tutorial can boost human intelligence. "Showing things as animated examples reassures new users that tasks can be accomplished," Morrow adds.

Another example of simple tutorials that save time, Coaches were introduced in WordPerfect 6.0 for DOS and Windows. "The idea is not to ask the computer to do things for you, but just to show you how," says Dave LeFevre, product manager for WordPerfect. Coaches are

canned walk-throughs of multistep tasks such as mail merges. Although they don't adapt to the individual user's work habits or situation, Coaches provide an interactive experience that prompts users to input data, acts on the input, and walks the user to the next step.

To call up a Coach in WordPerfect, you click on an icon with a cartoon profile of a football coach, then select from among 12 esoteric tasks, such as creating labels or footnotes. While LeFevre admits that today's Coaches are little more than well-designed macros, they won't always be this limited. "Within a year or two, you'll see active agents in Word-Perfect, so tasks in software will be simplified."

The next version of WordPerfect will have what LeFevre refers to as morphological capabilities. This means it will be able to break down sentences and search for syntactical elements as you input text. For example, future agents will recognize incorrect verb forms and correct them in real time. "Your software will show you what you're doing that is grammatically incorrect and suggest corrections or automatically do them for you," says LeFevre. After this technology was in development for more than three years at WordPerfect, efforts were accelerated by the purchase of Reference Software International, a leader in dictionary and lexical software.

If LeFevre is right, by 1996 your word processor will be able to diagram a sentence about as well as any substitute teacher can, totally recasting the sentence order if necessary. Maybe substitute teachers won't diagram sentences anymore, since PCs will do it for them. Still, syntactical understanding doesn't include the common sense needed to properly interpret the various meanings words convey. Efforts are under way to impart common sense to PC software, but intelligence on a par with a human personal assistant will probably have to wait until the next generation of PCs arrives.

Help! Smart Help!

A peek into the future of automated help came last October at a big bash in New York, when Microsoft Chairman and CEO Bill Gates unveiled Microsoft Office Version 4 for Windows, an application suite that includes Excel 5.0, Power Point 4.0, and Word 6.0. Gates also announced Microsoft's new IntelliSense technology. IntelliSense is a grab bag of Microsoft's automated tutorials (Wizards), context-sensitive help, automated formatting, and spelling correction. But with agents sure to become a major battleground for competing software developers, Microsoft is giving itself a migration path from Wizards to more powerful agents.

Chris Peters, vice president of Microsoft's Office Business Unit, is credited with coining the term IntelliSense. He explains, "IntelliSense is everything from simple artificial intelligence [AI] to powerful AI that delegates tasks to your computer. It can turn 100 steps into 5 steps." Or automatically correct errors.

In its product launch for Office Version 4, Microsoft stressed that each of the 100 most common tasks users perform with Office can now be accomplished in a single step. In some cases, IntelliSense means automatic execution of common correction and formatting functions, while in others, IntelliSense guides the user though complicated tasks such as programming with macro languages.

More often than not, Office's IntelliSense involves a Wizard. "A Wizard actually does a task for the user," says Peters. Wizards first appeared in Excel 4.0 as dialog boxes that walked you through the steps required to perform a task, much like WordPerfect's Coaches. In Excel 5.0, the FunctionWizard alone provides help for 200 worksheet functions. Activated whenever you load a text file, the Text Import Wizard offers counsel on formatting. Most of these Wizards are easily summoned by clicking on an icon bearing a Wizard's wand.

"You have a sense of accomplishment when you get a Wizard to complete a task by pushing its Finish button," Peters points out. In Excel 5.0, that might be the new PivotTable Wizard, walking you through the steps for pivoting chart data to create alternate data. In Word 6.0, the AutoFormat Wizard scans a document and makes it look nicer by automatically replacing common eyesores. For example, asterisks used for bullet points are replaced by dingbats, and straight quotation marks are replaced by curly ones. PowerPoint's AutoContent Wizard prompts you through your choice of six generic business presentation types, which are meant to inspire creativity while you're producing your own presentation.

Microsoft has taken Wizards a step further with IntelliSense Wizards. Lurking in the background of your Office Version 4 applications, TipWizards are activated when they notice a task that could be performed more efficiently. When this happens, the lightbulb on the TipWizard icon bar turns yellow. Click on the icon and the shortcut comes up. As intelligent as they sound, TipWizards are essentially just clever built-in macro commands. With more than 1,000 of these in Excel 5.0 alone, you get a feeling of security from being watched over by an army of software magicians.

Since Microsoft is the industry leader in suites and office applications, its commitment to IntelliSense provides a big target for competing software publishers. "Our spreadsheet is smarter," Daniel Rosenberg, user interface architect for Borland, says about Quattro Pro 5.0 for Windows. "We have simple learning algorithms built into the program, like the Intelligent Graph feature." Depending on the amount of data to be displayed, this subroutine tries to pick out an appropriate chart style for you without requiring your input.

Quattro Pro 5.0 also features Borland's answer to Microsoft Wizards: Experts. Like Wizards, Experts guide you through complex tasks. For example, the Analysis Expert offers you lists of spreadsheet analysis choices,

then follows through with the analysis once you have entered the selected data. The term Experts brings to mind the expert systems in artificial intelligence research, such as sophisticated programs that consistently provide medical diagnoses—based on interviews with medical experts—that are better than the diagnoses by attending physicians. But Borland's Experts are far less intelligent. Rosenberg admits that "Experts and Wizards don't do real, intelligent processing. Neither really works for you or advises you on better results."

In the pending release of Lotus Approach 3.0 for Windows, Lotus also responds to Microsoft's Wizards with its own software helpers, called Assistants. These will eventually show up in all Lotus SmartSuite programs. A Lotus product manager explains, "With our Assistants, you can go back and change para-

meters if you're not happy with the results. With Wizards, once you push the Finish button, you can't backtrack."

With the availability of adaptable scripting languages, we can begin to create "the electronic assistant for the rest of us." Smart software can be programmed to incorporate truly autonomous agents to interact with data and events on other systems—to access external databases, exchange correspondence, and route documents for review.

The Butler Did It

"To have software agents, at the very least you need the ability to schedule events, either by time or by a triggering action, and to script actions for the agent," explains Leon Navickas, general manager for the Lotus Notes research and development effort. "It's no secret that Lotus is working on this

for the next version of Lotus Notes, Release 4."

For anyone who has ever dabbled with a macro language to access and search a remote information service or to monitor e-mail, the prospect of using a scripting language shouldn't be daunting. "We'll make things a lot easier for end users," Navickas says. For starters, Notes will finally support the full functionality of the rules in Lotus's own e-mail package, cc:Mail. "There's little opportunity for mistakes because the scripting is very context-driven. It's very easy to write a script to filter out junk e-mail messages."

The e-mail or fax butler—hip to the difference between junk communications and career-essential data, fastidious about cleaning out your telecommunications files without being asked—is today's recurring office fantasy for smart software. Is it just a dream? Or is

e-mail screening the killer app that will make smart PC software a necessity?

In the wake of software giants Microsoft and Lotus, which combined sell the vast majority of e-mail software, at least one company has staked its future on claims of a smarter scripting language. Beyond Inc., a firm specializing in e-mail software, is tied to the success of its core product, BeyondMail—which it calls "a next-generation rule-based electronic mail system." More than a clever hack, BeyondMail was inspired by research at the M.I.T. Sloan School of Management on the Information Lens, a way of sorting online data so managers won't be flooded by an information glut. According to Eugene Lee, Beyond's vice president for product planning, BeyondMail offers custom forms and a rule engine so that you can write applications relating the real world to a script.

BeyondMail is not quite an e-mail butler, but its sophisticated scripting language gives you the tools you need to create the butler. Users can program agents to perform desired actions in background mode. With add-on products like the Beyond Notes Connection for enhanced access to Lotus Notes, WinRules for links to Microsoft Mail, and PowerRules for Macintosh applications, Beyond has a window of opportunity to convince users that e-mail is more than just messaging.

Other companies have also settled on the Notes desktop as the platform from which to launch agents with more than their share of smarts. SandPoint's Hoover is one example. Says Mike Kinkead, SandPoint president and CEO, "A software agent retrieving information on the Internet for you can already act as intelligently as an office clerk, although certainly a lot less intelligently than a good executive secretary."

By many accounts, Hoover is the best agent-based software to be offered commercially for PCs. SandPoint describes its leading-edge product as an active information agent that can search, retrieve, and integrate information from multiple external sources. Hoover, like the vacuum cleaner or the FBI's J. Edgar, knows how to dig out dirt. Hoover queries online data services, parses the information it finds there, and delivers it in a neatly formatted briefing document to the Notes desktop.

SandPoint's stock-in-trade, it turns out, isn't its impressive software, but an information republishing business. "Hoover redistributes data from 40 online publishers," says Kinkead. Among its popular real-time computerized publishing services: NewsAlert, which moni-tors trends and topics on the leading news wires, and *The Wall Street Journal*, which provides full-text electronic delivery of the daily national business newspaper into a Notes database which Hoover then parses.

At a monthly fee of $233 per user, Hoover can be a high-priced luxury for enterprises trying to scale down expenses. SandPoint's Kinkead argues that the service pays for itself by saving time and effort in gathering current information for business planning. Still, he warns, "Agents are at a new, very early stage of development." As with other burgeoning institutions on the Information Superhighway, let the user beware.

While Hoover concentrates on gathering data from external sources, Trinzic's Forest & Trees software for Lotus Notes specializes in agent-based gathering of information from internal company databases. Product Manager Brad Haigis calls Forest & Trees "desktop decision support or executive system-analysis software." Among its powers, Forest & Trees can gather information from 25 main-frame and PC database formats on a regular basis, applying alarms and triggers if the data falls outside a preprogrammed range.

According to Haigis, a major Midwestern manufacturing company monitors its parts inventory with Forest & Trees, automatically placing reorders whenever inventory falls below preassigned limits: "We've shortened the reaction time for companies in fast-changing industries," asserts Haigis. The usefulness of this kind of data pump is limited only by the ease of its user interface.

The pedigree of two of General Magic's founders, Bill Atkinson and Andy Hertzfeld—who helped design the first Macintosh computer more than ten years ago—assured the company's January announcement of agent-based technology the widest press coverage to date of a still-esoteric area of computer science. The emphasis on agents that shop for your Mother's Day flowers via an AT&T network called PersonaLink made for jovial copy in the pages of *The Wall Street Journal* and *Business Week*, but General Magic is seeking a serious role as the standard programming medium for agents on the Internet.

"Our agents are not intelligent, but they are programmable," says George Fan, product manager for the Telescript language. Telescript is at the heart of General Magic's Magic Cap interface for "the handheld desktop of tomorrow"—a technology that could turn out to be less important than Telescript itself. According to Fan, "One definition of an agent is a remote mobile program helping manage flow and routing of messages. Telescript provides the remote programming architecture to make this possible." Among the functions it defines for an agent: a unique security code used for authentication, authority to charge items to your account up to a specified amount, and even specification of an agent's life span and date of demise, so cyberspace won't become overpopulated with out-of-date agents.

"One person can have several agents, and an agent can create other agents," Fan observes. Telescript's authentication and life span limits for agents are essential to avoid the kind of mutation that could turn into a disastrous virus on the interlinked world of the Internet—a concern that's been raised by many critics.

The new scripting languages are enhanced versions of communications software and database scripts that automate recurring tasks. The future of agents really lies along the lines of software that learns from observing a user's patterns. By developing a user profile, an agent can learn to anticipate the user's needs.

It's easy to get paranoid about smart PC software that can learn about a user, discern patterns and tasks amidst the keystrokes, anticipate needs, and offer advice for productivity gains. Stanford's Ted Selker calls these entities proactive agents because they decide to do something without your asking for it. "Before you press a mouse button, proactive agents will tell you what you need by virtue of the relationship between user and agent."

One such proactive agent is Computer Associates' personal finance program, Kiplinger's CA-Simply Money for Windows. The software includes a background Advisor that monitors personal financial transactions and offers pointers when it discerns patterns in your bill paying and other fiscal activities.

Another proactive agent, Open Sesame from Charles River Analytics, is a more general-purpose program. Currently available for Macintosh computers only, it uses a neural network (a pattern of logic connections inspired by the structure of brain cells), and expert systems techniques from artificial intelligence. Open Sesame compares high-level events, like opening a file folder, with low-level events, like the keystrokes typical of the user's tasks. If it finds a pattern, it automatically proposes a way to automate the recurring series of keystrokes without the user having to create a

macro manually. It will save time because users will be able to launch an elaborate string of actions with a simple command.

Central Intelligence Agents?

Agents are here to stay. Even if Assistants, Coaches, Experts, and Wizards don't catch on with current PC users, IBM is staking the future of its next-generation Power PC systems on "The Art of Intelligence" and "Technologies with a Human Touch." These strategies were announced in a November 1993 position paper by the IBM Power Personal Systems Division. Among its declarations, Big Blue is aligning its fate with software agents, 3-D sense-based user interfaces, and artificial intelligence that will go beyond today's most sophisticated macros and enable the computer to understand natural language commands.

How smart will your PC software get? With all of this ongoing development activity, need anyone ask?—Steve Ditlea ■

DESKTOP VIDEO/ MULTIMEDIA

CONTROL SIGHTS AND SOUNDS WITH MULTIMEDIA TOOLBOOK 3.0

Multimedia ToolBook 3.0

Multimedia ToolBook provides the necessary additions to let ToolBook users create applications—database, training, interactive-kiosk, game, and other programs—that incorporate images, video, and sound. The program supports a wide range of formats, ranging from MIDI and WAV sound files to AVI, MPEG, and QuickTime digital video clips, along with most popular still-image and PhotoCD formats, and FLC, FLI, and Macromedia Director movies. Moreover, with the right hardware, Multimedia ToolBook can also control devices ranging from CD audio players to VCRs and laserdisc players.

Adding multimedia to a ToolBook book (Asymetrix's

name for an application) requires opening the clip editor, selecting a clip, and—if you like—picking a start and end point to excerpt from a long clip. An array of script commands controls opening, playing, rewinding, or otherwise manipulating the sound or video file. Playing a video clip on Multimedia Tool-Book's resizable on-screen "stage" is a simple process, often requiring as few as two lines of script code.

The package also includes Asymetrix's Digital Video Producer, a timeline-based application that can be used to produce video files combining frames from multiple video sources. If you have a video-capture card and the ability to control video sources, you can capture and edit videos on the fly. Digital Video Producer worked well with the AVI files we used in testing, making smooth transitions from one video source to another.

Multimedia ToolBook can help make adding multimedia to your applications relatively easy, especially with the aid of its interactive tutorials and extensive documentation. For experienced ToolBook develop-

ers, Release 3.0's improved performance and support for new media types are welcome additions, as are special optimization and caching options, which should yield fewer playback delays for "books" to be produced on CD-ROM. With powerful tools backed by a free run-time module, Multimedia ToolBook 3.0 is an attractive environment for serious multimedia developers.—Mark Brownstein

Multimedia ToolBook 3.0
Asymetrix Corp.
110 110th Ave. N.E.
Suite 700
Bellevue, WA 98004
(800) 448-6543; (206) 462-0501
$895

MORPHING AND SPECIAL EFFECTS 101

RomeBlack xTransit

Beyond the novelty of transforming Uncle Ed into the family dog, morphing programs have become accepted as mainstream multimedia graphics tools. A newcomer to the field, xTransit competently performs the requisite morphing maneuvers and special effects and readily blends effects within sequences, but it lacks the video-editing capability and higher-end features of competing products.

RomeBlack's package is one of the easiest to use when assigning the points that relate the first image of a morph to the last one. It marks active points by color

for easy identification and adjustment, and also lets you perform warping, a related technique that distorts an object's or person's features. However, xTransit neglects to show the image itself while you adjust the points.

In addition to morphing and warping, xTransit offers 27 transitions and effects, including various fades, wipes, and color changes, plus radical distortions such as wave, ripple, vortex, bubble, and fisheye views. It gives you excellent control options, letting you adjust these distortions and apply more than one effect in a sequence. For analyzing and fine-tuning your clips, xTransit displays transitions on storyboards and lets you preview a single intermediate frame before committing to the time-consuming process of constructing all in-between frames.

If you work with images from different sources, xTransit supports a number of graphics formats, including PCX, TIFF, Macintosh PICT, GIF, and JPEG. It also supports different codecs and lets you adjust frame speed, dithering, and pixel depth (up to 24 bits), but lacks video

compression. xTransit's interface is logical and easy to use when creating morphs and applying effects, but could be better when working with video.

The procedure for opening and viewing video clips within the program is particularly confusing. When you're scrolling individual video frames, it's annoying to have to incessantly click the mouse to sequence them. Also, from a technical standpoint, xTransit lacks rudimentary video-editing capability beyond simple sequence-ordering. Worse, scrolling through individual images sometimes left annoying on-screen lines, a phenomenon that RomeBlack's support staff couldn't explain.

The program's documentation takes you step-by-step through the basics, but doesn't discuss video in detail or offer advice on creating morph sequences. In fact, xTransit's morphing examples are poor—portions of the first image fade out with no link to the final image. Finally, some commands listed in the manual differ from those on the software menu.—Wayne Kawamoto

xTransit
RomeBlack Inc.
180 Varick St.
Suite #12A
New York, NY 10014
(212) 727-9735
$79.99

THE REVOLUTION WILL BE DIGITIZED

Adobe Premiere 4.0

Computer-based video-editing tools are revolutionizing video production as we know it. New tools like Adobe Premiere 4.0 and QuickTime 2.0, along with relatively inexpensive video-digitizing hardware, are leveling the video-production playing field. In the same vein, Adobe Premiere is a "scalable" digital video-editing tool that succeeds in both high- and low-end environments. It allows anyone with a Mac to edit QuickTime video clips and output QuickTime movies to tape or generate edit-decision lists. In addition, Adobe has published its plug-in filter specification and provided the tools for users to build their own plug-ins, inviting a broad range of new, third-party features. In short, Adobe Premiere is expanding the digital video frontier, providing access to a much broader range of computer consumers.

The current upgrade from 3.1 to 4.0 offers a product optimized for PowerPC performance. It also includes several new features and enhancements that

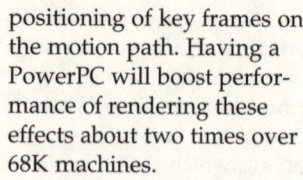

make it more than just a compatibility upgrade. The interface has been made simpler and more flexible, while the tools are more accessible. The editing process also is faster, easier, and more precise. Now packaged with both disks and a two-CD-ROM set, the upgrade contains a wealth of new features.

The most significant new feature is the Project Controller, which lets you control the entire program from the Preview Window without having to exit. Instant previews of edits are now available, requiring no rendering. Needless to say, this is a huge time saver. Effects and transitions still require rendering, but straight-cut edits can be previewed without any waiting. Filters and transitions can be animated, while the Filter and Transition Factories allow you to build and save custom effects. A new Trim Window has been added as well, so both your in and out points can be viewed and adjusted with frame-accurate precision, much the way traditional analog systems work. An improved Motion Control Window provides for frame-accurate

positioning of key frames on the motion path. Having a PowerPC will boost performance of rendering these effects about two times over 68K machines.

Premiere 4.0 also includes the capability to read time code from videotape. This useful feature allows for accurate time-code capture without requiring expensive tape decks and video-capture equipment. For those users who have machine-control capability, 4.0 includes shuttle control during capture (which lets you go forward and back, frame by frame), as well as stop-motion and batch-mode capture.

Like the video filters and transitions, audio filters can be previewed and animated over time. Stereo audio can now be panned, and a new Downsample Filter provides a quick way of reducing the sampling rate (and thus the size) of audio clips while maintaining high-quality sound. This feature should prove especially useful in CD-ROM authoring.

With Premiere 4.0, Adobe has made a solid product even better. It runs in native mode on Power Macs, and it adds considerable new features that make the editing tools more precise and the program's interface much less cumbersome.—Ben Goodman

Adobe Premiere 4.0
Adobe Systems Inc.
1585 Charleston Rd.
P.O. Box 7900
Mountain View, CA 94039
(800) 833-6687
$695

NOT JUST ANOTHER PAGE TURNER

Lotus SmarText 3.0

While there is some controversy over electronic publications vs. traditional hard copy, the former certainly holds many advantages: color, animation, interaction, and the ability to find that needle-in-a-haystack detail buried in a mass of information instantly. SmarText is an electronic-publishing program suitable for publishing large documents online, including policy and procedure guides, technical handbooks, and training manuals. The package comes with two applications: a Builder for creating the documents, and a Reader for using them.

Based on an intuitive book metaphor, SmarText provides an electronic table of contents, embedded illustrations, an index, bookmarks, and even sticky notes for online documents. Electronic books can be arranged on—what else?—electronic bookcases, with separate bookshelves dedicated to a particular subject, server location, or type of user. Each section of an electronic document (the illustrations, outline, index, text of the document) corresponds to a book on the bookshelf and, ultimately, a separate window on the display screen using the familiar Windows interface.

The program accommodates up to 3,500 text and 3,500 graphics source files. It supports all of the popular word processors, including Ami Pro, Lotus Write, Microsoft Word, WordPerfect,

and others. You also can include ASCII files from non-supported word processors or other applications. Graphics source files may include Windows bitmap (BMP) and metafiles (WMF), Paintbrush (PCX), Computer Graphics Metafile (CGM), Freelance (DRW), Lotus (PIC), Ami Pro Draw (SDW), and others.

The Builder program analyzes the text of target word processing files and stores information about their structure and relatedness in control files. It begins by creating an outline based on one of five characteristics: paragraph styles, table of contents entries, numbered headings, unnumbered headings, or specified text. The method you choose for creating an outline depends on how the text files were created and how the document is organized.

SmarText Builder is easier to use than an authoring system such as Toolbook or Director by several orders of magnitude (at least). For those facing too much paperwork, too much to read, or too much to know, SmarText is an effective way to conquer information overload.—Kathryn Alesandrini

Lotus SmarText 3.0
Lotus Development Corp.
1000 Abernathy Rd.
Suite 1700
Atlanta, GA 30328
(800) 831-9679; (404) 399-0011
$495 (Builder); $99 (Reader)

The Business Week Guide to Multimedia Presentations

Because it imbues multimedia with a specific purpose right at the outset, *The Business Week Guide to Multimedia Presentations* is both a more sharply focused and deeper volume than similar references. It's also easily the best-written book, mixing a conversational style with a level of nontechnical intelligence that's rare in computer tomes (perhaps because the author is an expert in business presentations, not just technology).

For those who are eager to jump into the technical whizbangs of an audio/video presentation, the book starts a bit slowly by talking about such things as the rationale for multimedia and the art of communication and persuasion. But it sets a precedent that the rest of the book largely follows: Multimedia is viewed as a means to an end (in this case, presentations), not as a hazy fog of colors and sound. Even once you're entrenched in later chapters about planning and authoring multimedia presentations, there are insightful chapters about understanding electronic "conversations" and aesthetics.

In fact, while it covers the technical bases in a reasonable amount of depth, the real strength of *The Business Week Guide to Multimedia Presentations* is its ability to keep technology in perspective. Rather than breathlessly extolling the virtues of video, for example, the book takes note of its tremendous demands and points out specific areas in which video is worth the effort. While hardly a producer's bible, this book is a savvy aid for businesspeople seeking to put multimedia to work.— Christopher O'Malley

> The Business Week Guide to Multimedia Presentations
> *By Robert Lindstrom*
> *Osborne/McGraw-Hill*
> *2600 Tenth St.*
> *Berkeley, CA 94710*
> *(800) 227-0900; (510) 549-6600*
> *$39.95*

SUPERNATURAL 3-D TERRAINS MADE EASY

KPT Bryce

KPT Bryce, a new tool for designing realistic landscapes, is the 3-D modeling equivalent of a paint-by-number set. Even if you have no artistic skills or 3-D modeling experience, you can create breathtaking landscapes on your Mac.

Unlike professional 3-D modeling programs, you can express your own vision easily with KPT Bryce. Using an interface that's reminiscent of Kai's Power Tools, a Photoshop plug-in, KPT Bryce quickly leads you through all the steps needed to generate your own scene. You can create a ready-to-render scene in less than five minutes, or fiddle with the controls to more precisely dictate the rendered outcome to your liking.

To create a basic scene, you first choose sky and terrain types from a library of preset textures. After a skeleton-like wireframe prepresentation of your scene appears, you click on "render" and watch your Mac do the rest of the work. Bryce starts by painting a preview window with an extremely coarse rendition, then gradually brings the image into sharper focus as it calculates texture, lighting, and shading over the course of many minutes.

Though un-Mac-like, the tools are powerful and easy to use. For instance, to rotate an object along its x-, y-, or z-axis, you select and drag it to one of the rotate icons. The adjustments

KPT Bryce.

you make are updated almost instantly in the wireframe preview model or in a special preview window. You can also populate your world with a variety of objects, either with those supplied or those you design. Cloud frequency, fog, lighting, and your viewpoint are all fully editable. Texture editing is also possible. Particularly useful terrain effects include clipping, erosion, noise, and smoothness controls designed so you can make your mountains look rugged like the Rockies or smooth and ancient like the Appalachians. Since a Power Mac native version isn't available yet, a bare-bones mountain scene measuring a mere 520x354 pixels took 62 minutes to render on a Quadra 650. More ambitious terrain designers can set up the program to render batches of images.

Aside from illustrators or animators looking for realistic backgrounds, most Mac users will want this $199 utility just for the fun of it. To enjoy your work, there's a slide-show utility, and a 360-degree panoramic After Dark screen saver plug-in. Paint-by-numbers never gave results that are this good.—David D. Busch

> KPT Bryce
> *HSC Software Corp.*
> *Santa Barbara, CA*

ADD MUSIC TO PRESENTATIONS WITH SOUND CHOICE

Sound Choice Volumes I and II

Let's face it: Clip-media discs are a dime a dozen. With the huge number of clip art, PhotoCD, video, sound, and MIDI collections on the market, it takes something special to distinguish a new offering from the legions of lookalikes. One bundle that does manage to stand out is Cambium Development's $69 Sound Choice CD-ROM. This disc is expressly designed to complement multimedia presentation and authoring packages by combining royalty-free CD audio, WAV, and MIDI music files with an innovative Windows-based sound-management system.

Each Sound Choice volume contains approximately 30 one-minute-long selections that span musical genres from rock to world music. You also get several shorter versions of each selection intended for functions such as slide transitions. All are designed to work with multimedia programs that loop sounds to create repeating "grooves."

Each piece is provided in nine formats: CD audio, Device-Independent MIDI, Extended General MIDI, and six WAV formats ranging from 8-bit, 11KHz mono to 16-bit, 22KHz stereo. Unique to Sound Choice is that it stores half its WAV files using ADPCM compression, which lowers disk-space require-

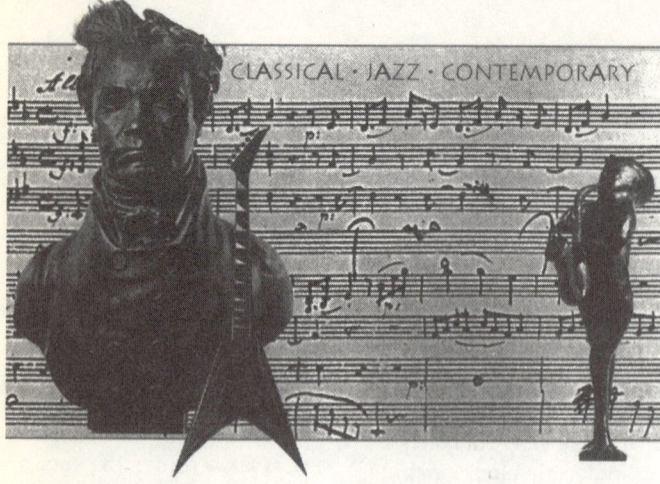

ments and lets DSP-equipped sound cards load the files more quickly.

The supplied application software provides a variety of file-management functions and Media Player-style playback controls. It also gives the ability to generate excerpts of longer selections; define custom fades; and locate clips by genre, mood, tempo, or user-defined keywords or comments. We found the software easy to learn and use, but were disappointed by Sound Choice's lack of 44.1KHz WAV files. The only way to generate high-quality WAV audio is to manually record the CD-audio tracks.

The music itself is better than you'd expect, although it's hardly perfect—the original compositions sound like good-quality trade-show music, while the classical pieces suffer from being played on electronic instruments. Nevertheless, most users will find the music—and Sound Choice itself—a useful resource for adding soundtracks to multimedia applications.—Don Labriola and Preston Gralla

> Sound Choice Volumes I and II
> Cambium Development Inc.
> Box 296-H
> Scarsdale, NY 10583-8796
> (800) 231-1779; (914) 472-6246
> $69 per disc

MAKE MULTIMEDIA GROOVY WITH MCS SOUNDTRAK
MCS SoundTrak

Where was MCS SoundTrak when we really needed it? Back in the 1970s, when everyone was looking for secret messages recorded backward on the Beatles's White Album, people were taping the tracks and playing them back in reverse. With Animotion Development Corp.'s $59.95 utility, they easily could have recorded the album (assuming it was on CD, and they had CD-ROM drives and sound cards), highlighted the suspect tracks, and reversed the sound. They would then have known in minutes whether "Number Nine" spoken in reverse really said, "Turn me on, dead man."

For a low-cost sound capture, modification, and edit-

ing package, MCS SoundTrak packs some punch. Running under Windows on any MPC-compatible system, it's the only sound editor in its class that comes with QSound, a technology that enhances the sound separation of stereo audio tracks.

QSound also lets you adjust the apparent location of sounds anywhere along a 180-degree range—from far left to far right. A utility called QBit enhances the separation, reducing the volume of center-channel sources and boosting the differences between left and right sound channels. The result is striking. On one stereo track captured from a movie, the original sample sounded like a center-channel voice. After a few passes through QBit, the voice dropped out, leaving an underlying (previously undiscovered) music channel.

MCS SoundTrak's user interface is intuitive: Two rows of button bars let you click on available editing options. A wide range of special effects—echoes, amplification, channel-switching, reversing, and more—lets you modify existing WAV files, while recording controls let you capture sounds from outside sources.

When editing, you can define the start and end spots for a clip to within 1/1000 of a second. Extracting choice sound bites from bulky sound files is a cinch, and you can create a playlist of sound files that you want to work with or play back. Perhaps SoundTrak's biggest weakness is that it does so much—the documentation can't keep up.

MCS SoundTrak is a bargain for would-be audio sleuths and a useful tool for

serious sound capture and editing.—Mark Brownstein

> MCS SoundTrak
> Animotion Development Corp.
> 3720 4th Ave. S.
> Suite 205
> Birmingham, AL 35222
> (800) 536-4175; (205) 591-5715
> $59.95

MOTION JPEG GIVES MIROVIDEO DC1 TV A SPEED ADVANTAGE
miroVIDEO DC1 tv

Now that CD-ROM drives and sound cards are commonplace, motion-video cards may be the Next Big Thing. Miro Computer Products's new miroVIDEO DC1 tv ($899) gives PCs the ability to record and play full-screen video at speeds up to 30 frames per second (fps). Although not intended for professional broadcast video, the card's output quality is first-class—easily good enough for work with applications such as multimedia presentations and computer-based training.

The DC1 works its magic by using Motion JPEG, a new hardware-assisted video-compression standard that produces exceptional speed and good picture quality. The board squeezes out further gains by recording only one video field per frame—North American broadcast-TV standards call for two. This compromises resolution and smoothness a bit, but shouldn't cause significant problems if you stick to higher frame rates.

All you need is...

miro

MTD 1/94

The Miro card also accepts both composite and S-video signals, and supports a variety of industry standards including QuickTime for Windows; Video for Windows; and the NTSC, PAL, and SECAM video formats.

Installing the DC1 tv in a heavily loaded multimedia PC was painless, thanks to the board's excellent documentation and jumperless hardware design. Unlike with some products, installation doesn't require touching your graphics adapter or sound board. The DC1 has no VGA or audio capabilities of its own, but works seamlessly with your existing boards without video pass-through connectors or other add-ons.

With every machine we tried, the miroVIDEO gave surprisingly good results—even a 40MHz 386 system produced credible 15-fps full-screen video, though it took a little tweaking. With our 50MHz 486, the quality wasn't quite up to MTV standards, but it was more than sufficient for most multimedia applications. In every case, color accuracy was exception-

al and jitter was minimal.

The miroVIDEO DC1 tv is bundled with U-Lead's VideoStudio suite, which performs tasks such as video capture and storage and provides still-image and video-clip editors. For an extra $100, Miro throws in the Windows version of Adobe Premiere, a more ambitious program that lets you assemble movies by dragging icons onto a time-line. Both packages are easy to learn and use, but neither provides the functionality of the best Macintosh video editors, much less that of high-end video workstations.

In fact, the miroVIDEO DC1 tv is a terrific piece of hardware, hampered mostly by the lack of topnotch Windows video-editing software. Once such applications hit the market—which should happen soon—the DC1 tv will be an outstanding solution for developers who want the ease, flexibility, and affordability of personal desktop video production.— Don Labriola

miroVIDEO DC1 tv
Miro Computer Products Inc.
955 Commercial St.
Palo Alto, CA 94303
(800) 249-6476; (415) 855-0940
$899;
with Adobe Premiere, $999

Cakewalk Professional for Windows 3.0

Twelve Tone Systems's Cakewalk line of MIDI sequencers has long been the best-selling in the PC market, boasting quick performance and a host of sophisticated features for playing, recording, viewing, and editing MIDI files. The company's latest top-of-the-line product, the $349 Cakewalk Professional for Windows 3.0, adds support for new types of MIDI devices, a smoother interface, and innovative quantization functions that can make sterile MIDI sequences sound more natural.

One of Cakewalk 3.0's most interesting new features is a Groove Quantization function that copies a track's feel—the subtle variations in note duration, timing, and volume that differentiate musical styles—onto another piece of music. Cakewalk ships with a dozen prede-fined feel templates that can turn mechanical-sounding sequences into swinging shuffles or driving hard rock. You can create more templates yourself, or buy inex-pensive feel collections from Twelve Tone.

Other new features include the ability to operate MIDI-controlled tape decks, a graphical drum mode specifi-cally for editing percussion tracks, and an expanded Faders view that lets you mix up to 96 MIDI channels as if they were tracks on an analog

tape. The program also cor-rects most of the minor user-interface inconsistencies that plagued earlier versions; its enhanced usability features include multilevel undo and redo functions, right-button-click pop-up menus, a macro recorder, and a LISP-like MIDI programming language called CAL for power users.

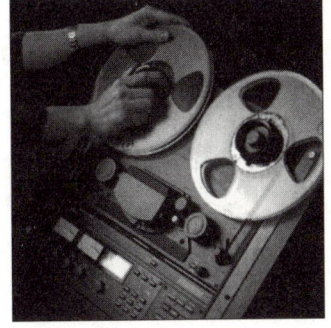

Like earlier versions, Cakewalk 3.0 offers a multiple-view interface that provides five ways to display and edit MIDI data. You can manually type MIDI events into an Event List; drag, cut, and paste measures of music in a Track/Measure View; manipulate individual notes in a graphical Piano Roll View; control the values sent to MIDI controllers, such as sustain pedals and pitch-bend wheels, by drawing curves in a Controller View; and invoke a Staff View to perform basic score editing in standard musical notation.

Cakewalk can record up to 256 tracks in one MIDI file, allocating them across as many as 16 MIDI interfaces and sound boards. It sup-ports all four SMPTE time-code formats and can embed

WAV files into MIDI sequences, making it a good tool for soundtrack work. All this adds up to a winning combination of flexible func-tions and ease of use. If you're looking for a more powerful MIDI solution than the "lite" sequencers bundled with most sound boards, you'll have a hard time find-ing anything better.—Don Labriola

Cakewalk Professional
for Windows 3.0
Twelve Tone Systems Inc.
P.O. Box 760
Watertown, MA 02272
(800) 234-1171; (617) 926-2480
$349

Quad Studio

If you plan on using your PC to record, edit, and manipu-late CD-quality 16-bit, 44.1KHz audio files, Turtle Beach's innovative Quad Studio digital audio system belongs on your shopping list. This top-quality card puts a multichannel digital audio-mastering studio at your fingertips for about the price you'd pay for a less-capable analog four-track recording deck.

The $499-list-price Quad Studio package consists of Turtle Beach's Tahiti sound card and two Windows-based audio applications: Wave SE, for recording, edit-ing, and signal-processing stereo WAV files; and Quad Studio itself, which simulates a four-track player/recorder. If you already own a Turtle Beach Monterey or MultiSound board, you can buy the Quad Studio software alone for $199.

The Tahiti board is a superb Windows sound card, based on the same speedy Motorola 56001 digital signal processor as the Monterey and the MultiSound. The board boasts Turtle Beach's Hurricane architecture for optimum recording to and playback from hard drives. We digitized a seven-minute stereo audio sample into a 70MB WAV file with nary a stutter—it sounded as good as the original RDAT source.

The main Quad Studio screen resembles the front panel of a typical portable four-track cassette recorder, with pushbuttons for all transport functions, a timer display, and the familiar linear faders representing volume and pan settings. Each channel module also contains solo, mute, and edit buttons; group level controls (Quad gives you three grouping levels); and an LED-like visual audio-level indicator. Recording is simply a matter of assigning a new WAV file name to a channel and clicking the record button. If you make an error, you can punch in and out to fix your mistakes.

Although Quad Studio bills itself as a four-track recorder, the number of digital audio tracks it's capable of recording is really limited only by the size of your hard drive. In theory, Quad can mix or "bounce" a limitless

number of overdubs onto a single digital track, with no generation loss. The downside of this process is that any independent channel-level changes are lost once the original source tracks are erased. Fortunately, Quad Studio makes complex pre-mixing tasks easy with a mixing-automation tool called Turtle Recall, which memorizes fader, mute, and pan control changes for each channel.

Once you've finished your multitrack master, it's easy to save it as a Quad "project," which stores mix, channel, and other information about the WAV files used. You can also remix files to a stereo WAV file for additional editing and signal processing using the Wave SE editor, or simply record the output onto an external RDAT, which will free up some much-needed disk space. A five-minute, four-track recording sampled at 44.1KHz consumes approximately 100MB.

Rich in depth and simple to use, Quad Studio turns a desktop PC into a professional-quality recording studio. It's a great tool for Windows musicians.—Steve Baldwin

Quad Studio
Turtle Beach Systems
52 Grumbacher Rd.
York, PA 17402
(800) 645-5640; (717) 767-0200
$499

TRULY SPECTACULAR 3-D ILLUSTRATIONS

trueSpace 1.01 for Windows

This impressive program combines professional-quality 3-D illustration features with a dynamite interface. Caligari's press release for trueSpace confidently claimed that with trueSpace and a few miscellaneous pieces of computer hardware, you can create photorealistic images suitable for the cover of *Time*. This assessment is absolutely accurate. Caligari's trueSpace brings easy 3-D modeling to the desktop at a very affordable price.

For such a complex program, trueSpace has an amazingly simple interface—one of the best we've ever seen. For starters, tight integration of features means you don't need to switch to separate modules to perform rendering (showing finished surfaces) or animation. The uncluttered desktop consists of a 3-D space and a toolbar with icons arranged in logical groups—Animation, Edit, Libraries, Model, Navigation, Render, and Window.

Many tools have variants accessible from a pop-up window. For example, the Point Edit tool can be set to Pick Face, Pick Edge, Pick Vertex, and Pick All. Many tools also have control panels that open automatically when the tool is selected with the right mouse button. And there's a dynamic prompt line that informs you of what each tool does when the cursor passes over

it. There are no hidden layers and no confusing menus—everything is easily accessed from the toolbar or the modeless dialog boxes.

It's easy to navigate around the trueSpace world using the different views and coordinate systems. By clicking on Eye Move and moving the mouse, the view shifts depending on which axes are currently selected. The left button controls the X and Y direction; the right the Z direction. You can also add different views as inset windows so you can look at your object from several different directions at the same time. Caligari's trueSpace automatically switches coordinates, depending on the context. For example, if you are rotating an object, the program defaults to object axes; but if you are moving the object, the program uses world coordinates instead.

Objects are the fundamental building blocks in trueSpace. You can create objects using the Primitives panel, which contains basic 3-D shapes like cubes and spheres. Or you can draw spline curves, and extrude or sweep them to generate 3-D projections. You can move and rotate points, vertices, and faces individually. The Deform tool sets up a deformation matrix that lets you mold an object like clay. These

matrices can also be detached and used in an animation.

Objects can be static or animated, depending on whether your final application is an illustration or movie. A few complex objects are supplied with the program (cars, a plane, a teapot), and when you send in your registration card, you'll receive a CD-ROM with loads of samples.

Caligari's trueSpace supplies an enormous range of tools for adding color and texture to objects. Material libraries hold texture maps of all descriptions: ceramic, metals, organic surfaces, stone, textiles, and water. The program will use BMP or TGA files as textures, so if you have a program like Kai's Power Tools, you can generate an unlimited range of spectacular surfaces to use as paint.

All materials have adjustable attributes for faceting, shading, and smoothness. You can also apply materials as bumps, textures, and transparencies, as well as environment maps that make shiny objects appear to reflect their surroundings.

It's easy to animate objects, thanks to trueSpace's ability to switch transparently between keyframe and path-based animation. Caligari's trueSpace imports BMP, TGA, and TIFF files directly, and supports 3-D formats such as DFX, LightWave, 3D Studio, and WaveFront. The program can export 24-bit broadcast-quality output with maximum resolutions of up to 8,000 × 8,000 pixels. If you need to transfer animations to videotape, you can do so, or save the scene in AVI format. Also supported are scalable TrueType fonts, which can be manipulated as objects to produce spectacular type effects.

Engineering types might not be swayed from other modeling programs, as trueSpace lacks dimensioning tools and accurate alignment functions. And at $795, trueSpace isn't exactly an impulse buy. But considering that it has the power of similar programs costing thousands of dollars more, any users who want to add 3-D modeling to their professional graphic toolboxes should consider buying it. They'll be dazzled with the breadth of special effects and ease of use provided in this superlative, tightly integrated package.—Susan Glinert

trueSpace 1.01 for Windows
Caligari Corp.
1955 Landings Dr.
Mountain View, CA 94043
(800) 351-7620; (415) 390-9600
$795

FROM 2-D TO 3-D IN A SNAP
Dimensions 2.0

When Adobe released Dimensions 1.0, artists rejoiced in its ability to create 3-D PostScript objects quickly and easily. Yet when creating original shapes and text to make into 3-D objects, they

were frustrated by the constant need to toggle between Dimensions and PostScript illustration programs such as Adobe's Illustrator.

Dimensions 2.0 maintains the ease of use of 1.0, but now includes an illustration module. The latter uses basic tools from Adobe Illustrator, allowing you to create your outline profiles or text in Dimensions. The 2-D edit tools include single-object and group selection, type creation, scissors, pen, scale, and rotate, as well as circle and rectangle creators.

The 2-D module also lets you create outlines of type; edit type (as to its vertical and horizontal positioning); and join, average, and compound your paths (lines or curves that make up objects). You can also import outlines or text created in another pro-

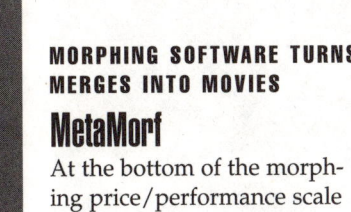

gram for rendering into 3-D. With further additions such as multiple undos, send to back/front, hide/preview selections, editable bevels, extrusion, revolving, and exporting with previews, this new upgrade virtually eliminates the need to switch back to an illustration program at all.

After you have created a 2-D object, such as a circle, you drag it onto the 3-D window, apply lighting and surface texture (smooth, matte, glossy), then finally render it. Rendering can be quite fast, since Dimensions 2.0 is a native PowerPC product (68K and PowerPC versions come in the same box). Guide creation lets you define the axis around which the artwork

can revolve into a 3-D shape. In addition, you're not locked into viewing objects from a few fixed perspectives. You can adjust perspective from 0 degrees (no perspective) to 160 degrees (very wide angle), as well as use the fixed wide-angle, normal, or telephoto views.

Dimensions 2.0 also supports custom colors. You can assign any color to an object, its frame, and even its shadow. Blending has been enhanced with a built-in calculation control that optimizes the number of blends for the output device.

Dimensions 2.0 has many new and welcome features, and it also removes many extraneous steps in creating 3-D objects from 2-D. Now artists can focus on being creative, instead of having to deal with awkward interfaces.—Chris Phillips

Dimensions 2.0
Adobe Systems Inc.
1585 Charleston Rd.
P.O. Box 7900
Mountain View, CA 94039-7900
(800) 833-6687; (415) 961-4400
$199

MORPHING SOFTWARE TURNS MERGES INTO MOVIES
MetaMorf

At the bottom of the morphing price/performance scale is MetaMorf, a rare DOS-based morphing package. The program guides you through loading the starting and ending pictures, and then adding a matrix grid to set the corresponding points.

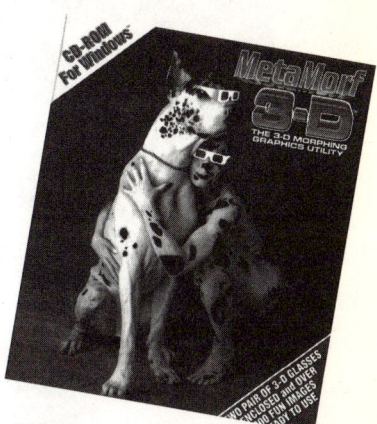

When you've edited the grid lines as desired, you select the number of intermediate frames, then click on either Warp or Morph. MetaMorf generates only FLI movies, but it's uncomplicated and inexpensive—a good starting point in the morph arena.

MetaMorf
Villa Crespo Software
1725 McGovern St.
Highland Park, IL 60035
(800) 521-3963; (708) 433-0500
$29.95

Digital Morph

We like the uncomplicated approach of HSC's Digital Morph. The program's tutorial is simplicity itself: Open two images, enter field lines to outline the common areas, and then animate the result. The lines need not be connected, and you can easily copy field lines from the source to the destination. However, the program had difficulty correctly importing most of the JPEG and TIFF images we tried—some gave an error message, while others came in as gray-scale

rather than color. HSC says that version 2.0, which should be available by the time you read this, will include full-motion morphing, masking, filled-line previews, special effects, and a CD-ROM full of royalty-free video clips.

Digital Morph
HSC Software
1661 Lincoln Blvd.
Suite 101
Santa Monica, CA 90404
(800) 472-9025; (310) 392-8441
$149

Morph for Windows

Gryphon Software's Morph, Windows version, is simple and intuitive, with a great tutorial. After opening the source and destination images, setting key points, and generating a movie, you can easily access each frame to get an intermediate morph image, or send output to videotape. Morph also offers some advanced film-editing features. You can replace backgrounds via chromakeying; attach different attributes such as color shift, rota-

tion, and tension to key points; and rearrange frames within the movie sequence.

Morph, Windows Version
Gryphon Software Corp.
7220 Trade St.
Suite 120
San Diego, CA 92121
(800) 795-0981; (619) 536-8815
$169

VideoShop

With an aggressive $395 price, new features, and bundled sound and royalty-free movie files, VideoShop 3.0 could rank with Adobe Premiere 4.0 in the field of top video-editing tools, especially for desktop-video hobbyists, who don't require high-quality output to video. But, unfortunately, this latest release suffers from inconsistent performance and some buggy behavior. And contrary to Avid's claim that VideoShop is "the video software anyone can use," learning how to use it is not exactly an easy process.

If you're using a specific folder to store all your QuickTime-media files, you can see and sort all the files in that folder in VideoShop's Desktop window. In addition to being able to sort your folders and files by type, size, date, and other criteria, you can double-click on items in the Desktop window to have VideoShop open them in a QuickTime player window. What makes the Desktop window more practical than a Finder-within-a-program is its ability to show VideoShop's unique moving icons, called Micons. Other programs show the first frame of a QuickTime movie as a static thumbnail picture, but VideoShop's Micons are anything but static. By default, 60 frames of a movie loop when you select a Micon.

To begin editing a movie, you can either drag the file from VideoShop's Desktop window into the Sequencer window or use the Open com-

mand to show a QuickTime clip in its player window and then drag the clip to the Sequencer window. Although Avid's internal drag and drop works well, we would like to have seen support for Apple's drag-and-drop architecture from the Finder.

You do most of your work in the Sequencer window, where you splice clips together and add effects. VideoShop plays the results of your edits in the Canvas window. The program has an excellent collection of filters and transitions, and it supports a wide variety of file formats, including AIFF, PICS, Audio CD and MIDI for sound, and PICT and PhotoCD for graphics. For those who do rotoscoping, VideoShop comes with excellent QuickTime import/export plug-ins that let Adobe Photoshop and Fractal Design's Painter import and export QuickTime movies. It even has a special Titling window you can use for adding fixed and scrolling titles to your movies.

Instead of piecing together a QuickTime movie with transitions and filters in one window and then spending several minutes—or hours—rendering your final construction, VideoShop breaks the time-consuming process into bite-sized pieces, rendering just the current selection as you apply an effect to it.

We found the Sequencer window to be the source of most of VideoShop's shortcomings. When you drag a clip to it, the program doesn't give you any visual feedback or control over where the clip

is placed; in contrast, Premiere highlights the frames in its construction window to show you exactly where your clip goes. The Sequencer window has 17 icons around it for video-editing features such as Apply Filter and Jump to Next Clip and includes two new icons for Quick Fade-in and Quick Fade-out. As you move the cursor over the icons, their names show up in the new Info palette. At first we found the icons a bit confusing; some hot tips or Balloon Help would be very welcome here.

VideoShop's PowerPC plug-in speeds up the time it takes the program to apply filters and transitions from 100 to 150 percent, according to Avid, and in this aspect, VideoShop was fairly quick with simple movie constructions on our Power Macintosh 8100/80.

Version 3.0 is considerably more stable than version 2.0, but it still isn't as robust as it should be. Large audio clips and complicated film constructions severely degraded VideoShop's speed and caused our machine to crash when we applied transitions, using the high-quality setting. Avid says using QuickTime 1.6.2 or earlier corrects these problems, even though VideoShop 3.0 supports only QuickTime 2.0. VideoShop 3.0.2, due out by the time you read this, will also support QuickTime 1.6.1. Additionally, we experienced intermittent screen problems: VideoShop sometimes lagged in its on-screen response when we

Did I Disable Five Security Measures or Six?

Y ou better ask yourself, punk, Do I feel lucky?' Well, punk, do you?

"Three strikes you're out." This was a damn president talking and it's seductive. Three violent felony convictions and you leave jail only in a coffin. Get it? Well, if you don't get it, it don't matter because ignorance of the law is no excuse and that's another good rule.

Let's hope if the federal "three strikes" rule goes through it doesn't affect any of us except to make us a tad safer. (Why should I hope it doesn't put any of you in the joint? If there are murderers and rapists reading my column, they should be stopped. Well, maybe if they really like my column and write kind letters to my editor—four strikes.)

It's hard for government to deliver real tough justice. We want the benefit of the doubt. We all read Kafka—what if it's Penn K. who's being framed for the third time? But we want justice—on the mean streets and on our computer cybergeek streets. (AI calls this the "mean superhighway.")

I went to a survivalist convention, a trade show for Yosemite Sam—guns, dried food, and stickers for your back door that say, "There's nothing in here worth your life." I loved the entire booth with crudely illustrated books on home booby traps.

Booby traps are justice. In Texas (or someplace that to my New York tunnel-visioned ignorance seems like Texas), a guy with a shotgun popped a stranger through his back door and walked! (I sure hope the Watchtower had a stringer on that case.) It must be hard to pull that trigger—but booby traps make that tough decision for you. They are mechanical judge, jury, and executioner. A piece of twine connecting a trigger to a door knob is very sophisticated A.I. "The sign said, Keep Out!'"

You're supposed to keep your house safe for burglars or you get sued. I guess that's okay, and if I were a meter reader or a B&E guy, I'd think that was a great idea. All the same, I can't forget this diagram for making a toaster blow up if a "safe switch" isn't touched first. (I don't know how many criminals break in and prepare a Thomas's, but if they do…) It was ingenious and goofy—a toaster not to be messed with. (I'll beg PC/C to print the maiming toaster diagram. They'll crybaby that it's irresponsible and doesn't have enough to do with computers. But, hey, if you installed OS/2, you don't need my help blowing up a toaster.)

What about booby traps, Trojan horses, bombs, and even viruses in our geek world? Say the client doesn't pay the bill—the programmer either does something to start, or does nothing to stop, some hidden bugger. Once activated, the evil thurman goes to work, putting up annoying messages or erasing the "stolen" code. It can even crash the machine or erase data. I have friends good enough to write code that will blow up your toaster. Is it okay to shut down Revlon in Toronto because you know in your heart that they owe you money?

Shutting down a computer is not blowing off someone's good toast-making hand, but it still bothers me. I love the elegance of "instant justice" written into the product itself, and I dig picturing software developers starring in Death Wish VII. But when I watch a vigilante flick, I'm secretly identifying with the bleeding heart idealist who says, "You can't take the law into your own hands!"

And then the wimp gets punched in the face and his toaster blows up.—Penn Jillette ∎

[Editor's Note: This essay originally appeared as a column in *PC/Computing*.]

selected information in the Sequencer window.

VideoShop works with any QuickTime-video card, and if you use a top-of-the-line card, such as the Radius VideoVision Studio, it can turn your QuickTime movies into 640 × 480-dpi, 60-fps videotape. But because VideoShop does not support subpixel interpolation, some finished movies don't play smoothly. Applications, such as Premiere and CoSA's After Effects, that support subpixel interpolation produce higher-quality movies, because they break each pixel down into tiny pieces, allowing much more accurate blends, colors, and movement.

VideoShop's Logging window lets you catalog and select clips from a videotape for batch digitization—in the order and with the effects you denote—into a VideoShop QuickTime file. Although the scripts in the Logging window are now analogous to EDLs (Edit Decision Lists), Video-Shop's Logging scripts support only VISCA (Video System Control Architecture) devices and Sony serial-protocol devices. You can't create EDLs that would let you use professional video-production systems such as those from Grass Valley Group or even those from Avid.

VideoShop's documentation is fairly comprehensive. The user guide appears to cover all of VideoShop's features, but some of the feature explanations are incomplete. The slim tutorial is also unnecessarily vague, and its explanations are not always clear. Avid's technical support, however, is superb—we spoke to a real person and received thorough answers to every one of our questions.

VideoShop could truly be great if the company solved some interface problems, making it not only more responsive but also more intuitive. There are some problems with inconsistent performance, and the program could be more robust. Still, if you're only dabbling in QuickTime moviemaking, using short clips and few transitions, and you don't foresee a need for commercial-quality video, VideoShop 3.0 is a cost-effective alternative to Adobe's Premiere or CoSA's After Effects.—Blake Roberts

VideoShop 3.0
Avid Technology
Tewksbury, MA
(800) 949-2843; (508) 640-6789
$39

Scenery Animator

Slightly easier to use than Vistapro but lacking the realistic scenery of KPT Bryce, Scenery Animatorm is an acceptable, but not outstanding, tool for creating virtual landscapes.

To create 3-D terrains, you use U.S. Geological Survey Digital Elevation Mapping (DEM) data, gray-scale PICT files in which the brightest parts are the highest, or the built-in fractal generator. You then add oaks, redwoods, clouds, and water to your scene. You can also specify tree- and snow-altitude lines

for your world. But the program restricts you to choosing from existing elements; Scenery Animator has little in the way of useful or creative customization tools. As a result, the trees look unnaturally similar and rendered water looks unusably unrealistic. Scenery Animator has some great sample terrains, and you can render your scene at three levels of detail or export it as a DXF file for rendering in another 3-D program.

You can create still images as well as animated flying sequences you save as QuickTime movies. Setting up keyframes for your animation is easy, especially compared to doing so in Vistapro, and Scenery Animator does a good job of creating in-between frames, complete with camera moves such as autobanking. The program also has good camera-positioning controls. And for speed mavens who have Power Macs, the package includes a native version.—David Biedny

Scenery Animator
Natural Graphics
Rocklin, CA
(916) 624-1436
$149

A 3-D BARGAIN
Simply 3D

Think of Visual Software's $59 Simply 3D as a low-cost version of Visual Reality, the company's $595 high-end 3-D package. Simply 3D uses the same complex, ornery interface as Visual Reality and in

our tests proved every bit as difficult to use; it simply lacks some key features—most notably, a modeler—of the bigger product.

Simply 3D offers one of the most powerful feature sets you can find in a Windows rendering package. The product provides separate resource designer dialog boxes for views, objects, lights, materials, and images, allowing delicate fine-tuning. Effects include reflection mapping, transparency, bump mapping, and other high-end features.

Of course, without a modeler, you won't be able to create your own objects. Instead, you'll have to use the 100 wireframe objects that come with the package on CD-ROM or limit yourself to text effects; the CD-ROM also includes Visual Font, which extrudes TrueType fonts to create 3-D text. You'll also find 70 JPEG texture maps.

Those intimidated by the difficult task of modeling should find enough options here to create stunning graphics at a great price.

Simply 3D
Visual Software, Inc.
21731 Ventura Blvd
#310
Woodland Hills, CA 91364
(800) 699-7318
$59

YOUR LOW-PRICE TICKET TO THE THIRD DIMENSION
Simply 3D

Now that high-powered PCs have brought real-time 3-D modeling to the desktop, there will likely be a flood of inexpensive software that can turn run-of-the-mill 2-D drawings and text into elaborate eye-popping 3-D graphics. Visual Software's $59 Simply 3D is aimed at 3-D amateurs who want to add special effects and depth to illustrations and presentations.

While it doesn't pack as many features as the company's $595 Visual Reality or AutoDesk's $3,000 3D Studio, many graphics professionals will still be impressed by Simply 3D. The downside is that the program offers so many modeling possibilities, many newcomers to the third dimension may get lost.

Simply 3D is composed of several connected programs that form a full 3-D toolbox. Renderize Live EZ does the actual 3-D rendering from a 2-D image or text file, while Visual Font can bevel, skew, and extrude TrueType characters. Visual Software also provides Autodesk's Animator, Microsoft's Media Player, and its own Visual Player, as well as a half-hour multimedia presentation and an 80MB

collection of 70 textures and 100 3-D objects.

Program installation from the CD-ROM is simple and foolproof. We found that for maximum performance, we had to set up a 25MB permanent swap file and that nothing but DOS could be loaded into high memory. These parameters are outlined in the documentation.

Building 3-D effects starts with importing a 2-D file. The file can then be viewed as a wireframe model, and the user can select the details for the image: depth, camera angle, and lighting, to name a few. Actual 3-D rendering is relatively fast; performance depends on your PC's processor and the amount of system memory, and there's a faster low-resolution preview option. The 3-D images Simply 3D creates are as good as those produced by more expensive programs. Renderize Live EZ builds animation projects by assigning keyframes and selecting beginning and ending ranges. It then saves the file in .AVI, .FLC, or .FLI format.

Unfortunately, Simply 3D isn't very easy or intuitive to use, primarily because it suffers from an overabundance of tools and effects available to users. There are literally dozens of commands accessible from button bars, pull-down menus, and toolboxes that may delight the pro but will likely intimidate the 3-D novice. The documentation is comprehensive but not particularly easy to follow, and includes only a handful of illustrated examples. Overall, however, Simply 3D is a powerful program that's certainly worth its $59 price tag.—Daniel Grotta and Sally Wiener Grotta

Simply 3D
Visual Software Inc.
Woodland Hills, CA
(800) 881-4108; (818) 883-7900
$59

JASC MEDIA CENTER ORGANIZES MULTIMEDIA

Jasc Media Center 2.0

JASC, best known for its Paint Shop Pro image capture and conversion utility, is putting the emphasis on the multi in multimedia with its Jasc Media Center, Version 2.0 (formerly called Image-Commander). This $39 program lets you catalog the sights and sounds of multimedia while organizing all the related files into logical albums.

After opening an album, you add files either by specifying them by name or by telling Media Center to catalog the material based on the file type. We were able to catalog an entire hard disk with just a few mouse clicks. And with support for more than 30 image formats, as well as .WAV and MIDI sound files and .AVI and .FLC/.FLI video files, versatility is Media Center's strength.

We found that reordering the thumbnail placeholders for images and sounds by dragging them to new positions was easy and intuitive. You

I May Not Know C++, but I Know Great Art When I See It

talented artists have always toiled in obscurity.

In the Middle Ages, artisans served lengthy apprenticeships to earn the privilege of serving at the pleasure of a prince or a king. They created works of exquisite beauty that are preserved in museums and cathedrals to this day. But with rare exceptions, none were allowed to sign their names to their work. For every Michelangelo there were a hundred anonymous artists whose names aren't known to historians today.

In this postindustrial era, the Age of Information, there's a new class of artisans whose works we see, use, and admire every day. Some work in sheet metal and plastic. Others mold silicon into microscopic patterns of unbelievable complexity. Still others organize collections of electrons into elegant dances that unfold on our CRTs.

A few of these geniuses work alone. Most work in teams. And virtually all of them labor in obscurity, revered only by a handful of their peers. If you don't believe we're surrounded by works of art disguised as computer hardware and software, just consider these examples:

Dream Dialogs

Just for fun, see if you can find a copy of Windows from 1989 or earlier. Check out the crude, blocky, one-dimensional dialog boxes. They're the software equivalent of the 10,000-year-old cave paintings at Altamira in northern Spain—a fascinating but primitive piece of art history. Who first devised the gray-on-gray, three-dimensional dialogs we take for granted today? Who knows? But he or she ought to get a federal grant to do a makeover of something really hideous, like Tammy Faye Bakker.

Creative Construction

IBM was doing plug and play long before the marketing hotshots at Microsoft and Compaq coined the term. It's hard to believe that the PS/2, with its clean lines and easy-open case, first appeared seven years ago. Dell's new desktops use the same thumbscrew design that the PS/2 pioneered, and the world would be a better place if more PC makers followed their lead. Does anyone know who's responsible for this artistry? If that genius had a penny for every time we've cursed at the back of a PC chassis, he or she could buy one wing of the Louvre.

can also sort album contents automatically by any of ten useful criteria, including filename, date, disk on which the files reside, image resolution, and size. As with most image-cataloging products, you can copy, delete, print, and rename the thumbnails. But because Media Center incorporates Paint Shop Pro's conversion engine, you can convert image file formats on the fly without switching applications.

Actually displaying a file's contents is also easy. Double-clicking your left mouse button on a thumbnail displays the image or plays the sound file. Double-clicking the right button calls up the default image or sound editor you've assigned to the thumbnail's file type. At this point, we found we could add comments and keywords to thumbnails for later retrieval. You can also run slide shows, complete with background music and transition effects.

Media Center automatically keeps track of file locations on removable disks such as floppy disks and CD-ROMs—a definite plus. When you click on a thumbnail to view or play its file, you're prompted to insert the correct disk. The product ships with 100 rather pedestrian clip-art images and, more important, with an exceptionally detailed and well-written 100-page manual.

If you've been looking for one tool to manage diverse types of multimedia files, Jasc Media Center may end your search.—J.W. Olsen

Jasc Media Center 2.0
JASC Inc.
Minnetonka, MN
(800) 622-2793; (612) 930-9171
$39

Miniature Masterpieces

Four hundred years after Leonardo da Vinci's death, we still marvel at the scientific breakthroughs foreshadowed in his notebooks. If Leonardo were around today, he'd probably be working to get a bigger hard drive and a brighter color screen into a featherweight 486 notebook. And he'd probably be doing it for Toshiba instead of the Borgias. He'd have had a hard time, though, improving on probably the greatest notebook ever designed, Toshiba's T2200SX. While others were struggling to get their laptops under 8 pounds, some genius at Toshiba created this 5.5-pound classic, the first portable PC that deserved to be called a notebook. It belongs in a permanent collection somewhere with appropriate credit given to its creator.

The Keys to the Kingdom

We're not accustomed to pounding on works of art, so it's easy to ignore the aesthetic achievements of the computer keyboard. And frankly, the flimsy $10 keyboards that plug in to most of today's PCs are to great art what Bart Simpson is to a Botticelli. But just look at the keyboards that are coming out of Lexmark International these days. Better yet, pick one up. It has heft. It has clean, classic lines. It is a piece of art, not a peripheral. Many talented hands sculpted the mold that made this keyboard. But they don't get credit. Is that fair?

Perfect Packaging

In the Dark Ages, giant computer companies three-hole-punched their manuals and threw them into cardboard boxes alongside matching binders. Styrofoam was everywhere. The self-canceling phrase, "This page intentionally left blank," actually appeared on paper. In a cleaner, greener age, there has to be a less wasteful alternative. And there is. Second Nature, a tiny company in Portland, Oregon, produces screen savers and wallpaper for Windows that put great art—from Audubon engravings to Impressionist masterpieces—on your screen. But the packaging of these single-floppy collections is a work of art as well. Each comes in a CD-style jewel box with a slim manual. There's nothing to discard, and all profits go to the Nature Conservancy (call 800-782-7000 if you are interested). It's a creative concept that deserves to be copied. And whoever dreamed it up deserves a medal.

Pursuit of Perfection

In ancient China, artists who wove tapestries for the emperor would deliberately weave a subtle flaw into their work. It would be presumptuous of mere mortals to achieve true perfection, they believed. Presumably, the artists who create classic code at Borland International follow the same principle and cleverly misspell a word somewhere in a help screen. Otherwise, their work might be too perfect. The Philistines of Wall Street may not appreciate Borland's bug-free software, but the rest of us get a graduate seminar in art appreciation every time we start a Borland application. And none of its creators gets public credit in the finished work.—Ed Bott ■

RAY DREAM DESIGNER CAN DRAW WHAT YOU DREAM UP

Ray Dream Designer 3.0

Originally developed for the Macintosh, Ray Dream Designer now moves to the Windows platform, bringing with it the program's renowned power, ease of use, and intuitive interface. Ray Dream Designer 3.0 is an economical path to professional-looking, three-dimensional still images.

Although installation was simple and trouble-free, producing 3-D images is a complex business. Even a rudimentary understanding of the program should consume from a few hours to a few days. Luckily, Ray Dream's tutorial does a good job of covering all the basics of the program, as well as its 3-D nomenclature (which may be unfamiliar to new users).

The first problem is to capture and represent three dimensions on a two-dimensional monitor. Traditionally, this has been done with odd-looking and hard-to-understand wireframe representations. Ray Dream does away with wireframes (though they are a preview option) by using realistic-looking objects with color and shading, which can be sized, aligned, rotated, and otherwise manipulated. We found the result to be a more intuitive feel for the drawing we were creating.

Ray Dream makes full use of drag-and-drop technology, an open plug-in architecture, and highly customizable tools. Together, these give the pro-

gram a wide array of options and features. The program's key windows are Perspective, Hierarchy, Modeling, Object Browser, and Shaders Browser.

Perspective is where the 3-D scene starts. The Hierarchy window keeps track of the objects placed in the scene, while the Modeling Window is where shapes are molded. We found it remarkably simple to customize 3-D objects, create others from scratch, or base new ones on vector shapes imported from other programs. The Object Browser stores basic 3-D shapes (cone, sphere, text, cube, cylinder, free form, or icosahedron), as well as libraries of 3-D clip art. The Shaders Browser holds colors and textures and contains one of the best and most powerful shading editors we've seen.

Since even a complex 3-D scene is really just a compilation of simple geometric objects that are covered with textures, colors, and shading, Ray Dream provides all the elements for building entire three-dimensional worlds. For instance, we modeled a snowman by combining three spheres (for the head and body), a cone (the carrot nose), and a tall and a flat cylinder sitting atop each other (the top hat), then covered it with a rough, white coat to represent snow.

Among Ray Dream's more innovative features are its 3-D brushes, which allow the painting of a surface with either rectangular, elliptical, polygonal, or free brush strokes. On the other hand,

Ray Dream's Fog Atmosphere effect was extremely difficult to master. Its use requires some sophisticated mathematics, but can add a needed sense of distance and photo-realism to 3-D scenes.

Lights and cameras are necessary in any 3-D program to establish illumination and perspective. Ray Dream's highly customizable lights (Ambient, Distant, Spot or Bulb) and cameras provide a wide range of features that lend a professional level of finesse and control. Once an illustration is defined, all we had to do was render it to create a usable and realistic looking scene.

It took us about a half-hour on a 486DX2/66 PC with 64MB of RAM to render a 4 × 3-inch, 72 dpi resolution scene consisting of two lights and six groupings of objects. More complicated scenes can take hours.

To eliminate mistakes before rendering, Ray Dream has several preview modes: Basic Preview gives shape and coarse color information; the appropriately named (but slower) Better Preview shows bumps, highlights, surface shading, and color variations. Render Preview includes reflections, refractions, and shadows.

The only major drawback to the program was that it produces only still images. To create eye-popping animated 3-D work requires a more sophisticated and expensive product along the lines of AutoDesk's 3D Studio. Ray Dream delivers with a pow-

erful, feature-rich 3-D modeling program that raises the bar on software targeted to the professional and amateur artist.—Daniel Grotta and Sally Wiener Grotta

Ray Dream Designer 3.0
Ray Dream Inc.
Mountain View, CA
(800) 846-0111; (415) 960-0768
$349

MOVING SCREEN SHOTS THAT TALK

ScreenCam 1.1 for Windows

Here's how not to create in-house software training or demos: Hire a $50-an-hour programmer, put up with weeks of revisions, then trash the whole project when it turns out wrong. Instead, we recommend you invest in Lotus Development's ScreenCam 1.1 for Windows and do the whole thing yourself in less time than it takes to sign a programmer's contract.

ScreenCam records movies of screen activities, along with a soundtrack so you can explain what you're doing. The process is simple: Click on the Record button, start operating the software you want to demo, and record your voice-over at the same time. Then save the file in Lotus's proprietary ScreenCam Movie format and distribute it with the free run-time ScreenCam player. Alternatively, you can combine the player with the SCM

movie to make a one-off, self-running executable file.

ScreenCam movies require lots of storage—up to 1.5MB per three minutes—and there's no way to compress a movie's soundtrack to shrink its file. In fact, about the only way to save disk space is to record at low VGA resolution and low color depth. Apart from ScreenCam's lack of file compression, its most significant drawback is that its SCM files cannot be edited. Future releases will probably address this problem, but for now it's like this: Make a mistake, start over. If the ability to edit your movies or record just part of the screen is important to you, try ScreenCam's competitor, Motion Works International's CameraMan 2.0 for Windows ($149). It creates Video for Windows AVI files that you can edit by using Adobe Premiere or another video editing program.

ScreenCam's appeal to technical support staff and computer instructors is clear. It doesn't get any easier than this—mainly because tricky movie editing isn't possible.—Yael Li-Ron

ScreenCam 1.1 for Windows
Lotus Development Corp
(800) 343-5414
$79

YOUR DAILY DOSE OF MULTIMEDIA

Wired for Sound Pro 3.0

So you've finally invested in multimedia trappings for your PC, but when you're not

using your favorite games or edutainment discs, it feels like the same old Windows? If you want total multimedia immersion, check out Aristosoft's Wired for Sound Pro 3.0. It brings sound and video elements from the sidelines and puts them smack in the middle of your daily computing routine.

You don't have to install the program's full 68MB—just the media files and applications you need. Choose from 2,000 sounds, 200 video clips, 250 MIDI files, and 200 pictures, plus some so-so icons and truly awesome cursors. Wired for Sound installs tiny "virtual files" on your hard drive to represent files you haven't installed, so if you try to use a file that's not available, the PC will skip instead of trip over it.

The Wired for Sound applications start with a group of chatterboxes: Talking Calculator, Calendar, Clock, and System Monitor tell the facts, while Talking Minesweeper and Solitaire open their virtual mouths to help you cheat at Windows' popular games. The program lineup also includes Multimedia Jukebox, Screen Saver, Wallpaper Changer, Sound Editor, CD Browser, and Mediascape Changer.

The last lets you choose an animated face and voice to front for your system; you can choose from normal-sounding folks or lame impressions of VIPs from Clinton to Schwarzenegger. Still more programs include Cursor Changer, Icon Changer, and Groupie, the last of which lets you change Program Manager group icons and nest groups within groups.

Intruder Alert, a password-protected screen saver with a realistic car-alarm sound, protects your data. Post This!, a "sticky note" utility, is also useful. And there are lots of great sounds in Wired for Sound's repertoire, organized into categories like Funny, Human, Destructive, Cartoon, Equipment, Illness, Impact, Musical, Sports, and Job Saver. Music tracks and minimovies are similarly arranged.

Wired for Sound Pro is almost mandatory if you want to maximize your PC's multimedia capabilities.—Rebecca Rohan

Wired for Sound Pro 3.0
Aristosoft Inc.
7041 Koll Center Pkwy.
Pleasanton, CA 94566
(800) 338-2629
$79.95

RECORD AND MIX WAV FILES
Sound Impression 3.5

Midisoft's Sound Impression 3.5 provides an inexpensive way for novices and professionals alike to mix and record digital audio. Its slick graphical interface mimics a set of rack-mount components, turning your desktop into an easy-to use mixer, MIDI and CD audio player, and WAV file recorder and player. In addition to these basics, Sound Impression provides outstanding OLE support. You can transfer any supported sound data (MIDI, CD, or WAV) to an OLE client application with a few keystrokes, or even link your current Mixing Panel settings to a Windows client.

Three powerful tools augment the main program module: Wave Composer, Session Manager, and Wave Editor. Wave Composer lets you mix up to 16 separate WAV files into a composition. Special tools make it easy to precisely control the onset of any track and to change its position relative to other tracks. Session Manager lets you assign one-

line descriptions to each currently open file. The fairly powerful Wave Editor lets you clean up a sound segment with a noise filter, remove or add silence, or cut, crop, and apply other editing tools. You can add special effects such as echo, chorus, flange, fade, crossfade, and pan to parts or all of a session. Other controls let you speed up or slow down speech and music segments, and set sampling rates for recording (you can record sound in 8- or 16-bit mono or stereo at 11, 22, or 44KHz). Insert up to 16 placemarkers into a waveform or form a stereo track by mixing two mono tracks.

Sound Impression is an easy and cost-effective way to create and edit sound for multimedia applications. Its interface is easy to navigate, and its WAV editor and composer are ideal for generating smaller sound files.—John Gleidman

Sound Impression 3.5
Midisoft Corp.
P.O. Box 1000
Bellevue, WA 98009
(800) 776-6434; (206) 881-7176
$79.95

STUDIO USES CLASSICAL NOTATION TO COMPOSE MODERN MIDI FILES
Studio 3.1

Midisoft released its first MIDI sequencer for Windows, Studio 3.0, at the end of 1991—somewhat prematurely, thanks to pressure from the MPC Council, which

wanted to get a crop of multimedia applications to market in a hurry. Now Midisoft has released Studio 3.1, which implements features that were promised but not delivered in version 3.0. Registered users of Studio 3.0 are eligible for free upgrades.

Studio 3.1 differentiates itself from rival sequencing packages by displaying song information in standard music notation, rather than in unfamiliar piano-roll symbols. The Windows interface splits the screen into two parts. The score view shows each track of the current file in standard music notation; as Studio plays your song, each note on the score is highlighted in turn. The mixer view offers dials for volume, chorus, reverb, and panning, and buttons for solo playing, muting, and recording for each track. The mixer also has master controls for volume, tempo, and effects, as well as tape player-like controls.

Input music with a MIDI instrument or with the mouse. The latter is a tedious process; you select a note duration (whole note, quarter note, and the like) and place the note on the score. Depending on the note's duration, the cursor automatically snaps to the most appropriate position for the next note. For example, if you select a half note, when you attempt to place the next note, the mouse cursor snaps halfway across the measure.

For music editors, Studio has important features such as transpose and quantize, which respectively allow you to change key or improve rhythmic precision. Unfortunately, the program's editing tools are not very intuitive. You can drag, insert, or delete notes with the mouse, but it's hard to tell which note is highlighted by the pointer and far too easy to select or delete the wrong note—and there's no undo option for such mistakes.

When you're finished spicing up your song, you can save it as a MIDI file or as a proprietary song (SNG) file. Studio also offers rudimentary printing capabilities, but it lacks powerful scoring functions. For a one-on-one music lesson, input a song (or download a MIDI file from a bulletin board), then mute a track so you can play along.

Midisoft Studio is a musical tool with great potential for both composing and learning about music. With another revision to boost Studio's editing capabilities, the program could become an indispensible composition partner for PC musicians.—David S. Levy

> *Midisoft Studio 3.1*
> *Midisoft Corp.*
> *P.O. Box 1000 Bellevue, WA*
> *98009*
> *(800) 776-6434; (206) 881-7176*
> *$249.95*

SCAN SCORES INTO MIDI FILES

MIDIScan for Windows

Musitek has woven another product category—scanning—into the tapestry of multimedia. The California firm's MIDIScan for Windows employs music reading software (MRS) technology—the musical equivalent of optical character recognition for text—to convert scanned TIFF files into playable, editable MIDI music files.

MIDIScan provides no scanning software, so you'll have to rely on a scanning service or the software bundled with your scanner. After scanning a 1-bit line-art file at 300-dpi resolution, you save it as a TIFF file and import it into MIDIScan. You can use the program's primitive TIFF editing tools, such as the pixel editor or rotation option, but any major changes will call for more advanced image-editing software.

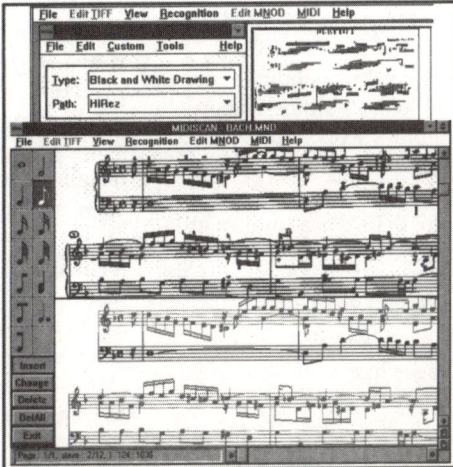

When you're ready to begin recognition, MIDIScan examines the graphic file and decides what the notes, key signatures, and other symbols mean, ignoring extraneous information such as lyrics and guitar chords. The program then asks if its assumptions are correct and allows you to make adjustments. When this process is complete (it takes about two minutes per page), MIDIScan saves the information as a Music Notation Object Description (MNOD) file.

The MNOD file, an intermediate, proprietary format, is MIDIScan's interpretation of the scanned file. You can use the MNOD toolbox to add, delete, or change notes, rests, and time/key signatures. Unfortunately, the editing tools are poorly implemented. Further, there is no undo function, and the awkward editing process alone causes many mistakes. After you're satisfied with the edited MNOD file, MIDIScan writes a true MIDI file.

The program does not always recognize time signatures and will create a MIDI file without one. If you try to play such a file with Windows' Media Player, you'll get a divide by zero error. Moreover, MIDIScan's accuracy is not yet up to par. Hand-scanned scores typically result in error-ridden files. A flatbed scanner improves accuracy significantly, but the resulting MNOD files are still far from perfect.

Still, Musitek deserves credit for pioneering this technology and will hopefully continue to improve the product. Music-reading software has enormous potential as a teaching tool—scanning scores with parts for multiple instruments, for example, then programming the sequencer to silence your own instrument, so you can play with full band or orchestral accompaniment. Another valuable use would be to scan unfamiliar music, then listen to what it's supposed to sound like before you attempt the piece. MIDIScan still has some rough edges, but it—and MRS technology in general—have the potential to ignite a mini-revolution in the multimedia industry. Stay tuned.—David S. Levy

> *MIDIScan for Windows*
> *Musitek*
> *410 Bryant Circle, Suite K*
> *Ojai, CA 93023*
> *(805) 646-8051*
> *$379*

FIGHT DISTORTION TWO WAYS

YST-M10 Powered Monitor Speakers

Yamaha Corp.'s pair of YST-M10 Powered Monitor Speakers squeeze high-quality sound into a tiny space ($3.8 \times 8.75 \times 6.4$ inches each). Unlike most speakers in this price or size range, the YST-M10s boast a 10-watt-per-channel stereo amplifier. This extra power means the Yamaha speakers produce less distortion at high sound levels than systems using 3- to 5-watt amplifiers.

But that's not the only reason the YST-M10s sound so good. Thanks to Yamaha's active servo technology, the 3.5-inch speakers deliver an unusually crisp bass response. This isn't your usual bass boost, either: The amplifier contains special circuitry that changes the way the speakers produce low-frequency sounds. The result is a pleasing and relatively flat frequency response across the 80Hz to 20KHz range.

The speakers fight visual as well as audio distortion because—unlike your hi-fi system's speakers—they're magnetically shielded, so you can place them next to your monitor without worrying about interference from the fields produced by the system amplifier and the magnets surrounding each speaker cone. The YST-M10s' shielding worked well—no color or image skewing was visible, even when the speakers were placed right up against a monitor during testing. Still, Yamaha advises against storing floppy disks or tapes next to the speakers, and you may want to keep them away from hard drives as well.

An easy-to use control panel, located on the front of the right speaker cabinet, provides volume and presence controls as well as a power switch. The presence control is an especially nice touch, allowing you to produce a warmer, more intimate sound with speech and lyrics. However, the panel has no controls for speaker balance or tone.

The YST-M10s delivered first-rate sound when plugged into the headphone jack of a Microsoft Sound System card, or into the sound card's separate stereo outputs. However, when the speakers were attached to an NEC CD-ROM headphone jack, it was necessary to keep the headphone volume control on low to avoid serious sound distortion.

If you need to connect the speakers to several outputs, a low-cost audio switching box from Radio Shack or some other source is a must, since the system provides a single 3.5 mm jack for all stereo inputs. (Adapters are provided for use with 6.25 mm phone jacks or phono/RCA-type connections.) The lack of a separate headphone jack will be a drawback if your sound board provides only a single stereo output.

Nonetheless, these are small complaints—perhaps fitting for small speakers with a small price tag of $149.95. If you're looking for attractive, affordable audio—available in either light gray or black, yet—the YST-M10s are a sound choice.—John Gliedman

YST-M10 Monitor Speakers
Yamaha Corp. of America
Consumer Products Division
6600 Orangethorpe Ave.
Buena Park, CA 90620
(714) 522-9240
$149.95

PhotoMorph for Windows

North Coast Software's PhotoMorph is an intriguing set of tools that lets you morph one graphic image into another and perform some rudimentary video editing. The morphing capabilities are useful, but the other tools fall short of professional quality.

Morphing is the technique by which a computer dissolves one image into another. Dissolves have long been used in movies as transitions from one scene to another. Dissolving one PC graphics file into another, however, is a much newer trick.

At a suggested retail price below $150, PhotoMorph costs far less—about 99 percent less—than the Silicon Graphics workstations used in the movies. It shouldn't come as a great surprise, then, that its capabilities are somewhat limited, but still fine for casual uses.

PhotoMorph lets you select "start" and "end" images in any of eight formats: Amiga IFF, BMP, GIF, JPEG, PCX, PICT, Targa, and TIFF. You then point and click to specify which points on the start image should get mapped to the end image. If you're morphing from one face to another, for instance, you'd pick several points around the eyes, lips, ears, and chin to make the first image change gradually into the other. The more accurately you can map the points, the smoother the morph will be. Once you've mapped the points to your satisfaction, click on a button to generate an AVI-format video. PhotoMorph includes a run-time version of Microsoft Video for Windows (VFW).

PhotoMorph also lets you warp an image, changing the shape of a graphic. For example, you can map Arnold Schwarzenegger's face to the shape of a block of wood. The technique is essentially the same as that for a morph, except that you wind up with a changed original image instead of a new end image.

You also get a rudimentary video editor, letting you chain, cut, and paste AVI files to create a longer video. Like PhotoMorph's graphic manipulations, the video editor is simple but effective. It is dependent on VFW, however, so don't expect cinema-quality clips or playback.

PhotoMorph's interface is clean and simple, ably supported by help screens and printed documentation. The software's manual, while clear, could use a redesign—its index is placed up front, instead of in the back where an index belongs.

The recommended system requirements, a 386SX with 4MB of RAM and 4Mb of hard disk space, should be regarded as the barest of a minimum. As video clips, PhotoMorph's files will tax even speedy systems during playback; they'll also gobble up storage space, so 4MB won't last long if you want to collect your creations.—Daniel J. Rosenbaum

North Coast Software Inc.
P.O. Box 459
265 Scruton Pond Rd.
Barrington, NH 03825
(603) 664-6000
$149.95

Virtus WalkThrough Pro

The creation of easy-to-navigate 3-D worlds of virtual buildings and spaces has long been the forte of Virtus WalkThrough, which has gained a strong following with architects and filmmakers. Now, with Virtus WalkThrough Pro, you can add static as well as dynamic texture maps to those 3-D worlds. Plus, thanks to WalkThrough Pro's impres-

sively fast rendering, you can explore these texture-enhanced worlds at a reasonable pace—and you'll be able to do so at real-time speed when Virtus releases the recently announced PowerPC version of the program.

WalkThrough Pro's working environment is fairly intuitive, even for users who aren't accustomed to working in a 3-D program (although basic 3-D skills help you get the most from the program). WalkThrough Pro's learning curve is relatively short compared to that of more-traditional 3-D tools, and the clear and informative documentation makes the process as painless as possible.

In WalkThrough Pro, you create virtual spaces consisting of objects—walls, floors, windows, furniture, and more. You can assign textures to objects and place lights in and around them. When you're done, it's easy to take a 3-D walk through the design.

The program presents an uncluttered interface to help you perform these tasks, complete with clearly arranged menus and tool palettes. The main tool palette changes options intelligently as you select windows. When you're in an object-editing window, you get tools for creating, editing, and adding textures to objects; when you're in the rendered Walk View window, the palette includes position and focal-length controls for the virtual camera.

Architects and others who want to create easily tourable 3-D environments will find no competition for Virtus WalkThrough Pro. Decent performance, easy-to-use tools, and good support from a company committed to extending the usefulness and flexibility of its products make WalkThrough Pro a hands-down winner.—David Biedny

Virtus WalkThrough Pro
Virtus Corp.
Cary, NC
(800) 847-8871; (919) 467-9700
$395

After Effects 1.1

Digital-video technology is sweeping through Hollywood and corporate video-production facilities nationwide, promising leaps in productivity in both video and film editing as well as hot new special effects—at a fraction of the cost of existing systems. One product that delivers all these benefits is After Effects, from the Company of Science & Art (CoSA).

After Effects is a digital-video special-effects application designed for professional videographers. Whether it's compositing, morphing, warping, or any other special effect you're looking for, After Effects offers the most control of any product available today. It comes with its own set of plug-in effects, but the application also accepts your favorite third-party plug-ins, such as Kai's Power Tools, Xaos Tools's Paint Alchemy, or other Photoshop modules, which you can apply over time.

Because After Effects offers the power of a complex, professional special-effects suite, it can take some time to master—its interface is not for the fainthearted. That said, it's one of the few products capable of generating true broadcast-quality special effects on the Mac today.

Above all, for just about $1,300, After Effects can replace hundreds of thousands of dollars' worth of older, analog special-effects equipment. As a result, a whole new group of Mac users has developed. Videographers who might otherwise be interested only in Silicon Graphics machines for producing computerized special effects now have a

Satisfaction——One Foot in the Grave

It's been over a year since I got a new computer. That's just not healthy.

I've had a slew of computers since my first Kaypro in 1985: Zeniths I loved, Grids I kissed, and brands I've forgotten because they blew. No matter what was on my desk, one thing was constant: Within a few months I wanted something faster, smaller, harder, stronger, sexier—less and more.

Among my many stereotypical high-school girl attributes is keeping a journal. Bubble baths, manicures, big hair, malls, giggling, sports ignorance, and Madonna identification are also on the list, and you can bet a few meg that I'll get to all those subjects in future columns. (It amuses me that some people reading this page for the first time and seeing the sexually ambiguous name, "Penn," might say, "Isn't that wonderful? A nerd column written by a high-school-aged woman—what a positive role model!")

Every day I write a "Dear Diary." A WordPerfect macro pulls up my entry from last year, and, after I read it, dumps me, all time and date stamped, into the current file. It's great for self-examination. I start every morning by considering my lot in light of what was happening to me a year ago. (Next year I'll read how Details magazine interviewed me about Uma Thurman because I have mentioned her—and will continue to mention her—more than any other writer in the world.)

In last year's entry I was setting up a new computer. So what? I do that every couple of months. The man-bites-pit-bull part is that it's the same computer I'm typing on right now! What the hell is going on? I've never been content!

viable alternative and a fresh reason to consider the Mac. And as the power of high-end video systems becomes more accessible, After Effects could move into the mainstream as well. Perhaps that's why Aldus, the company that pioneered desktop publishing nearly a decade ago, purchased CoSA last year.

After Effects
The Company of Science & Art
(CoSA)

UTILITIES

CONVERSIONS PLUS 2.5 EXTENDS ITS PC-TO-MAC LEAD

Conversions Plus 2.5

In the past, if you wanted to cross the border between PCs and Macintoshes, you had two choices: a DOS product with device drivers that treat PC floppy disk drives as virtual Macintosh drives or a Microsoft Windows application that also reads Mac disks. Conversions Plus 2.5, from DataViz, combines both capabilities to translate files accurately between the two worlds.

What sets Conversions Plus apart from competitors is its excellent and complete file-format translation. Where other products essentially transfer only files, ignoring format incompatibilities, Conversions Plus maintains file formatting. Version 2.5 supports the latest releases of popular word processors and spreadsheet and database formats, and offers some degree of support for graphics embedded within word processor documents, including .BMP, .WMF, and .WPG formats for PCs, plus Pict and Pict2 for Macs. It also supports OLE objects within Excel, Microsoft Word, and Works for Windows documents.

MacAccess, a DOS device driver that creates virtual Mac drives, lets your 1.44MB drive takes on a split personality, acting as either a PC drive or a Mac drive. On the downside, it supports only 1.44MB PC drives and high-density Mac disks but not lower-density Mac disks.

Conversions Plus now translates between popular PC formats as well. You can, for example, convert a file from WordPerfect to Word for Windows or from Excel to Quattro Pro. Powerfully expanded translating powers keep Conversions Plus comfortably ahead of the pack. Requires: 3MB RAM, 6MB hard-disk space, Microsoft Windows 3.1 or later — J.W. Olsen

Conversions Plus
DataViz
55 Corporate Dr.
Trumbull, CT 06611
(800) 733-0030; (203) 268-0030
fax: (203) 268-4345
$149; upgrade, $39.95

CLEAR OUT OLD FILES WITH DISK HISTORIAN

Disk Historian 2.1

When trimming old, unused files from your PC, you want to cut enough to free up valuable disk space; but if you slice too deeply, you might regret your actions. Disk Historian 2.1 is a powerful tool that keeps track of how often files are used to help you prune your hard disk. The program creates a database of files that is updated with usage information every time you close Microsoft Windows. The

"Clean up your hard disk safely"

Get rid of unused files & recover up to 70% of your valuable hard disk space

DISK HISTORIAN

You don't get a new computer because it wears out, you get a new one because there's cooler stuff that you need. But I'm happy with this computer. It's covered with filthy London Velvet Underground backstage stickers (man, those were great shows).

I've had this machine so long even the beige is stained; the keyboard is even starting to smell like me for chrissakes.

I don't want to be coy about mentioning this computer's name—that would be tight-assed and cheesy. Yet to drop it's brand name might sully a pristine back page with an unpleasant whorishness.

Yeah, sure. It's a Toshiba T4400-SXC. Toshiba didn't even exactly give it to me (although now, they sure as hell better give me a second one free—it's so humiliating to be unpleasantly whorish gratis).

It's possible that any computer I bought last year would still please me. A Toshiba can't be that much better than everything else on the market—it just can't be.

Is the future finally here? Or is it the poverty of my imagination that stops me from filling the giant hard disk with my ramblings? Don't I think and type fast enough to see the irritating delays that must be there? Do I lack the eye to perceive the shades of color that this baby can't display?

Will evil worldly contentment begin to spread? Will my stereo seem loud enough? Movies scary enough? Popcorn salty enough? Will I start thinking that I've seen enough attractive people naked?

I'm begging—will someone please come out with a smaller, faster, sexier machine before I start digging VH-1? Hey, maybe it's good enough.—Penn Jillette ■

database is excellent for clearing out old files: You can use either Disk Historian's default criteria or your own parameters for determining which files are current. Disk Historian is a valuable tool for reducing the information age's flotsam and jetsam. Requires: 4MB hard-disk space, DOS 5.0 or later, Microsoft Windows 3.1 or later. —Brian Nadel

Disk Historian 2.1
Solid Oak Software Inc.
P.O. Box 6826
Santa Barbara, CA 93160
(805) 967-9853
fax: (805) 967-1614
$79.95

VoiceLock Seals Off Your PC

VoiceLock is an innovative program that limits user access to a PC by requiring not a password, but a voice match. VoiceLock works with

any sound card and limits access in two ways. The program can automatically encrypt directories when exiting Microsoft Windows and decrypt them to an authorized user's voice when entering again. When encrypted, the files are hidden from the Windows File Manager and the DOS DIR command. The program also locks the system when the PC's screen-saver program kicks in; only the specified voice will open it.

To get it to work, you'll have to train VoiceLock. This is as simple as reading a few sentences into a microphone. When you've finished training it, the program will produce a voiceprint. VoiceLock then displays a special security screen and plays a .WAV file instructing you to proceed by speaking into the microphone. Authentication takes just a few seconds. If your voice is verified, you're in; if not, the screen saver stays on. Requires: 30K RAM, 2MB hard-disk space, math coprocessor, sound board, microphone, Microsoft Windows 3.1 or later. —Lee Schlesinger

VoiceLock 1.04
QVoice Inc.
P.O. Box 645
Andover, NJ 07821
(201) 786-6878
fax: (201) 786-5868
$79.95

Norton pcAnywhere for DOS
Norton pcAnywhere for Windows

Think of them as Range Rovers of the PC remote-control software world. Symantec's Norton pcAnywhere for DOS, Version 5.0, and pcAnywhere for Windows, Version 1.0, can comfortably cruise the streets and highways of online communications, but these packages are built to handle a range of exotic terrains where family sedans cannot hope to operate. They can tackle remote control and file transfers not only over dial-up connections but also with other kinds of hosts (mainframes, BBSs, and online services). Also, both can do over a network or direct serial link just about anything they can do via modem.

Once you've completed the no-sweat installation process, you'll be struck by the products' simple and unusual look. The main screen of pcAnywhere for Windows has three big icons that give you one-click access to the product's most common tasks: Be a Host PC, Call a Host, and Call an Online Service. Each icon provides access to tools related to the task at hand, including hardware and software setup. Less-standard operations—setting up gateways and accessing utilities—are controlled via pull-down menus. In the DOS product,

Gateways and Utilities join the three primary tasks as entries on the main menu. In both packages, though, you may find some of the more advanced settings, such as limiting the number of log-on attempts allowed, difficult to locate.—Ted Stevenson

Norton pcAnywhere for DOS
Norton pcAnywhere for Windows
Symantec Corp.
10201 Torre Ave.
Cupertino, CA 95014-2132
(800) 441-7234; (408) 253-9600
fax, (800) 441-7234
$179

THE PREMIER PHONE DIALER COMES TO WINDOWS

HotLine

For years, HotLine was the best phone-dialing utility for DOS users. Now Smith Micro Software has brought the $99.95 program to Windows, and the result establishes a new standard for phone dialers.

To get started, you can enter or import your own phone list and/or use the 2,400-item American Business sampler that ships with the product. Additionally, you can purchase the $149.95,

130,000-entry National Business Phone Directory—Electronic Edition.

HotLine has everything you could expect from a phone dialer: up to ten speed-dialing entries that you access with a hotkey, automatic sensing and redialing of busy numbers, and the ability to dial any number placed in the Clipboard. It also has special support for Mwave modems and their speakerphone capabilities.

HotLine has a window that displays area codes, zip codes, and time zones for a huge number of U.S. and international cities (there are over 300 Californian cities listed, for example). It also includes little extras such as a quick-launch icon bar you can add to the HotLine window, a call timer, and a phone log.—Barry Simon

HotLine for Windows
Smith Micro Software Inc.
51 Columbia, #200
Aliso Viejo, CA 92656
(800) 964-7674; (714) 362-5800
fax: (714) 362-2300
$99.95; upgrade, $59.95

FAST AND FRIENDLY REMOTE COMPUTING

Carbon Copy for Windows 2.5

When there's some distance between you and your main PC, remote-computing software can supply the missing link to run applications, access data, and view e-mail back at your office. Carbon Copy for Windows 2.5 is the latest in Microcom's well-known line of remote-computing packages. This program offers fast performance; is particularly easy to use; and comes with built-in communications features, LAN support, and a software gateway.

During remote-computing sessions, Carbon Copy shows the host display (the distant PC that you're controlling) in a fixed full screen on the remote (the computer you're using to control the host). This full-screen approach is usable, but other programs that more closely follow Windows conventions are easier and more convenient to use. For example, Symantec's Norton pcAnywhere for Windows displays a host screen in a discrete window that can be resized, and makes it easy to access other applications running on the remote desktop.

Carbon Copy's interface is friendly and easy to use. Large buttons represent each of the program's main functions. A remote clipboard lets you cut and paste text or graphics between applica-

tions running on the remote and the host. However, Carbon Copy's full-screen approach makes this less intuitive than in pcAnywhere, which lets you cut and paste between windows on the desktop.

Carbon Copy comes equipped with the requisite basics. Security features include password protection, the ability to blank the host screen, and the ability to reboot after a session. But Carbon Copy can't limit user access to specific directories. The chat mode is well done, and both sides can simultaneously type messages in their own windows. If you want to bill the other party for the price of the phone call, you can connect to a remote or host computer, and Carbon Copy will call you back.

The easy-to-use file transfer feature works much like a combination XTREE and Windows File Manager utility. You can graphically select files to copy between the host and remote, and even drag and drop them.

All in all, Carbon Copy for Windows is easy to install and run, a remote-computing speedster, and among the most stable in its connections. If your computer beckons you from afar, you won't go wrong with Carbon Copy for Windows.—Wayne Kawamoto

Carbon Copy for Windows 2.5
Microcom Inc.
500 River Ridge Dr.
Norwood, MA 02062-5028
(800) 822-8224; (617) 551-1000
$199

SAVE YOURSELF TIME AND ENERGY

Quick Restart

Say Word for Windows is running, with three unsaved documents still waiting to be named. Say you've been working on a complex CorelDraw graphic for hours and haven't saved it either. Say the security guard downstairs has just called to inform you that your car is being towed away. Say you don't function too well under that kind of pressure.

For laptop owners, this scenario is all in a day's work. Just press the Autoresume button and run. Your work, though not yet saved, is intact. Next time you turn the machine on, the entire configuration is there, right where you left off. No need to reboot or reload Windows, Word, Corel, and all your files,

because they've been frozen in time.

Alas, most desktop computers are still a long way from this convenience. PowerPro Software's Quick Restart is a solution. It's a software-based panic button, and once you see it, you may wonder how you ever managed without it.

Quick Restart offers fast and safe power-down at the press of a predefined hotkey. It's that easy. But the program also serves an important role beyond moments of terror. Press the hotkey at the end of the day, and you won't have to repeat that tedious startup procedure tomorrow morning.

This little gem has a RAM footprint of only 15K of conventional memory and 6K of high memory. There's a DOS interface as well as a Windows module, and both install during the simple setup procedure. Now, isn't that a better alternative?— Yael Li-Ron

Quick Restart for Windows and DOS
PowerPro Software Inc.
$59.95
(415) 345-9278

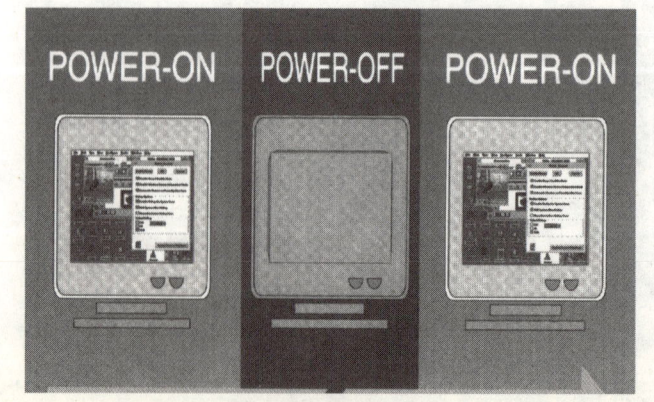

KEEP YOUR WINDOWS DIRECTORIES SPICK-AND-SPAN

UnInstaller 2

It was all so much simpler in DOS: You installed a program in its own directory, and when you didn't want it any more, you deleted everything in the directory. That was that. In Windows, however, nothing is simple. A new program can plant its own INI and DLL files in various parts of your hard drive, not to mention the additions it makes to Windows' main WIN.INI file. The result— especially if you like to experiment with shareware, or have changed applications recently—can be a hard drive crammed with unused and unusable files.

MicroHelp's UnInstaller 2 can be the perfect answer for people who want a clean, efficient hard drive. The first version of this Windows-based utility neatly and quickly searched out all the places where an application had left its marks and then deleted them, including the icon on Program Manager.

This second version vastly increases UnInstaller's capabilities. The main Uninstall function has been fine-tuned so that now you can both search for applications from a file listing, or simply choose them from existing Program

Manager groups. Whereas previously you could view all the elements you were about to delete (and choose among them if you wished), now you can do a "trial run," generating a report that tells you exactly what was deleted and how much room you saved.

There are also several new features, some equally as valuable as the uninstall function. System Cleanup will look for display drivers, system-support files, Windows fonts, and non-Windows application-support files, then give you the chance to get rid of any that aren't being used. IniClean (also available in the previous version) lets you scan through your WIN.INI, SYS.INI, and other INI files, ridding them of unnecessary references. Orphan Finder searches out applications and DLLs that aren't referenced in your Windows shell (UnInstaller works with most popular shells) and gives you the opportunity to clean them out. Finally, the DupeFinder finds duplicate files, and lets you view and/or delete them. Between outdated README.TXT files and copies of old files that were accidentally saved to the wrong subdirectory, at least 5MB to 10MB of free hard drive space was returned to our test system.—Barbara Krasnoff

UnInstaller 2
MicroHelp Inc.
4359 Shallowford Industrial Pkwy.
Marietta, GA 30066
(800) 922-3383; (404) 516-0899
$69.95

DISTRIBUTING DIGITAL DOCUMENTS

Common Ground

Common Ground is an efficient and inexpensive way to distribute digital documents from system to system.

As more companies and individuals turn to e-mail, packaging tools to handle the gigabytes of data soon to be cruising the information highway are vitally needed.

Baby Steps toward Ubiquitous Computing; Your PC Should Know You on Sight

t he most common mistake the computer industry makes is selling perfectly good technologies before their time. In fits of money-fueled mass hysteria, every fool out there takes a developing technology and sells it as if that technology were ready to save the world today. Networking went through this evolution; the 1980s gave us multiple "years of the LAN." Multimedia, already far enough along that the very term has become passe, is just now entering the truly useful stage of its life. This pattern is so common that it's shocking to find a technology the industry is, for the most part, actually underselling. But we have.

We're talking about ubiquitous computing. To be precise, we're talking about certain aspects of ubiquitous computing that could deliver real value in the near future. Ubiquitous computing is a perfect candidate for premature selling. Fortunately, the technology's roots are in Xerox's Palo Alto Research Center (PARC), so we're probably safe. PARC is the home of a zillion great ideas, including the workstation, the mouse, the laser printer, and icons. PARC is also the property of Xerox, a company that couldn't market water in the desert.

The dream of ubiquitous computing is computer power wherever you are, whenever you want it, tailored to the way you work and live. At PARC, for example, you wear a badge that contains a small computer and wireless transmitter. Every phone, computer, and even whiteboard in the place is computerized and linked to a blend of traditional wired and wireless networks.

When you enter a room, your badge announces your presence to the many computers in the room. If someone calls you, the computer that manages the phones routes the call to the phone nearest you. If you sit down at a computer, it's your computer, ready to work. Pushed to its limit, ubiquitous computing means that every computer you would encounter, whether in your phone, TV, or toaster, would know it was you and act appropriately.

The phone would know all your speed-dial numbers; the TV, your favorite shows; and the toaster, how dark you like your toast. All this is way cool, but it will be a long time before our toasters know who we are. What's exciting, and what the industry is not pursuing aggressively enough, is the subset of ubiquitous computing that could make us more productive now—well, in late 1995 or early 1996, anyway.

Common Ground from No Hands Software is just such a paving tool, and joins Adobe's Acrobat and Farallon's Replica in the young crop of cross-platform digital-document distribution programs.

At $189.85, Common Ground is a good value. It is also well-positioned for users wishing to distribute small to medium-sized documents across Windows and Mac systems while maintaining all the formatting, fonts, and graphics found in the original documents. No Hands plans to release future versions for DOS, OS/2, Unix, and PenPoint. With the last, Common Ground's viewer will be included in the operating system.

Common Ground installs as two major components: a Common Ground printer driver with full viewer and miniviewer programs, and Zenographics' ZScript PostScript driver and applications. The product's PostScript half is geared primarily toward users working with PostScript-intensive documents—such as Adobe Illustrator, Aldus PageMaker, and QuarkXPress files—that include Encapsulated PostScript (EPS) graphics. If you don't need the added PostScript power (the standard Common Ground driver handles TrueType and Type 1 PostScript fonts), you can save disk space and not install the components during setup. A full installation snags about 3.9MB of disk space, including OLE 2.0 server components that allow drag-and-drop embedding into other documents.

Creating a DigitalPaper document, as No Hands dubs its cross-platform file format, is as simple as printing. After installation, simply select Common Ground or the Common Ground ZScript driver as your printer, open a document, and print. A dialog box offers you the opportunity to choose where to save the file, whether to view the DigitalPaper file after printing, and whether to include the miniviewer—which adds about 100K to the total file size and transforms a DigitalPaper (DP) document

Your PCs and You

The key is to concentrate on the desktop and notebook PCs we use today at work and at home. These computers could and should know who we are and how we work. Getting these systems to know who we are is simple: We just tell them by logging in.

The next step is the one that requires work, but it's also the one that can deliver real value now. Once we've logged in, the system should retrieve our working preferences and obey them. The number of preferences we all end up teaching each computer we use is staggering.

First, the list of applications we use is itself a personal preference. Then there are all the little ways we customize our operating environments, from the order in which we place program groups on our desktops to our wallpaper, mouse-speed settings, and so on and so on. We also shape each application to our particular needs and working styles, setting everything from custom dictionaries and default fonts to margins and compatibility modes.

All this information should be in an identity database that the operating system(s) and applications should share. This identity database should, of course, live on a server when possible, so you could easily change physical computers and keep on working. For those walking through the implementation details, yes, this means all the applications would either have to live on a server or get installed locally after login to be available. Even if we require every system to have all the applications installed locally, this would still be a big win.

Each system should also have a local copy of the identity database for those times when the network is down, or in the case of a notebook, if the system is away from the network. Notes-style replication should reconcile the local and server copies of the identity database the next time you connect to the LAN.

This identity database is completely achievable. It needs only a major backer, an API specification, and the cooperation of other vendors. In this case, however, "only" is clearly a lot to ask. Apple, IBM, Microsoft, and Novell are the only players with even a prayer of making the OS side of the identity server happen, and you could make a good case for Microsoft being the only real hope.

Still, it is possible. The rest of ubiquitous computing could evolve at a natural, slower pace. It could grow from your local network to WANs to wireless links, and maybe even one day to phones and TV sets. The identity server, though, is possible in the next 12 to 18 months, and we want it. Our toasters can wait.—Mark L. Van Name and Bill Catchings ■

THE SIMPLE WAY TO SHARE YOUR DOCUMENTS ELECTRONICALLY!

into a stand-alone, double-clickable EXE file. Once generated, the DP or EXE files can be sent to anyone.

Common Ground's printer-setup dialog offers options including high-resolution information, which is required for recipients to print at high quality; JPEG graphics compression, which dramatically reduces the size of documents with color or gray-scale images; whether to save bitmap graphics at screen resolution, which saves space, but significantly lowers print quality; and optional disabling of copying and printing for view-only documents.

Unfortunately, there's no provision within the Common Ground full viewer for transforming regular DigitalPaper files into EXE files at a later time. Reprinting the document from the original application and opting to include the miniviewer at that point is the only recourse.

The miniviewer can be distributed free of royalties for non-commercial purposes; commercial-distribution licenses are available for $500. However, it's limited to simple viewing and printing of DigitalPaper documents. The full Common Ground viewer provides thumbnail views of each page, plus a toolbar with zooming from 100 to 400 percent, navigation, and marquee-selection tools. With the full viewer on hand, you can search the document and save selected text to disk in a variety of formats. Unfortunately, multicolumn

documents save to disk in a jumble of text fragments, as Common Ground saves text by processing across the page rather than down columns in sequence. To save columns, you need to painstakingly select each column with the marquee tool and then save it. Neither viewer lets you annotate documents or create hyperlinks as you can with Adobe's Acrobat.

Selected text can be copied and pasted into other documents, and complete Common Ground files can be embedded elsewhere via OLE 2.0. Saved text uses the built-in Panose Typeface Matching System to map the DigitalPaper fonts to the closest available font on your system.

Where Common Ground falters a bit next to Acrobat is in easy cross-platform capability, since DigitalPaper documents created in Windows require a small additional processing step when brought to the Mac. The newly released Common Ground 1.1 Mac version can embed a Windows miniviewer into DigitalPaper files, but

the current Windows 1.0 version can't correspondingly embed a Mac viewer. Another sticking point in the digital-document equation is fonts. Opening a word processing file created by another system using fonts not present in the destination system often results in bizarre font mappings. Adobe's PostScript-based Acrobat and Farallon's Replica take different strategies. Acrobat uses multiple-master PostScript technology, while Replica offers a number of options centered around font embedding.

By contrast, Common Ground tackles the tricky What Font You Used Is What I See (WFYUIWIS) issue by capturing font information for all the characters in a document at 72 dots per inch, the Mac's screen resolution; 96 dpi, Windows' screen resolution; 200 dpi for faxing; and 300 dpi for printing, rastering the document once for each resolution. Font information isn't stored as bitmaps or outlines, but in a proprietary compressed database. The outcome is that original files are precisely preserved—like a fly in digital amber—without the overhead of font embedding. The catch is that while both Replica and Acrobat are resolution-

independent and can print at an output device's highest resolution, Common Ground's output is limited to a maximum of 300 dpi.

The end result is Common Ground files that are typically smaller than Replica's and comparable to Acrobat's—an important characteristic in documents destined to head across networks or down modems.

Despite its drawbacks, Common Ground 1.0 is currently the best value for creating cross-platform digital documents from small to medium-sized original files. Common Ground's overhead is low, its portable files are relatively small, and it supports full PostScript files, a feature that costs extra in Acrobat and is currently unavailable in Replica. With additional tweaking, added hyperlinks, and higher-resolution printing support, it could give the higher-end Acrobat a run for its money as well.—Rich Santalesa

Common Ground for
Windows 1.0
No Hands Software Inc.
1301 Shoreway Rd. #220
Belmont, CA 94002
(800) 598-3821; (415) 802-5800
Internet: nohands@netcom.com;
CompuServe: 74740,2142
$189.95

MULTIPLATFORM COMPUTING JUST GOT EASIER WITH MACDISK FOR THE PC

MacDisk

With Insignia Solutions' MacDisk for the PC, Macintosh integration is at last made easier. Requiring only a high-density floppy drive, MacDisk for the PC gives your PC the ability to format, write to, and read Macintosh disks. The program consists of a TSR, a DOS utility, a Windows utility, and help files for each. Once installed, it lets you insert any high-density Macintosh disk, and retrieve a DOS directory or view the disk in a Windows 3.1 File Manager directory.

MacDisk automatically remaps file and directory names to conform with DOS standards. To avoid confusion, the MacDisk utility provides a directory view of the original Macintosh names alongside their remapped DOS equivalents. There are options for sorting by DOS or Mac filename, showing or hiding resource forks, and applying search filters to locate a specific file. Since Mac disks behave just like normal PC disks, however, you will find the Windows File Manager more adept at performing most of your file-maintenance tasks. The MacDisk utility includes a Macintosh disk-format capability that worked remarkably well. In fact, MacDisk successfully formatted a disk that was formatted for the PC.

PC files can be saved directly onto a Mac disk, and directories can be added to or removed from a Mac disk using DOS or Windows 3.1 commands. These directories appear as folders when viewed on the Macintosh Desktop and retain the hierarchy assigned them when viewed on either platform. Because PC applications don't generate a Mac resource fork, a file saved to a Mac disk from the PC does not appear with an application-specific file icon on the Mac. Though MacDisk for the PC doesn't handle file translation, for mixed computing environments, MacDisk flawlessly performs a much-needed task and is well worth the price.—Ben Goodman

MacDisk for the PC
Insignia Solutions Inc.
1300 Charleston Rd.
Mountain View, CA 94043
(800) 848-7677; (415) 694-7600
$99.95

AccessPC 3.0

Insignia Solutions has been a pioneer in the art of getting the Macintosh to talk to other computers. AccessPC 3.0 is another winner: a set of utilities you should seriously consider if your work involves getting documents from one platform to another.

AccessPC is, at its heart, a file-conversion program. It will translate files from one word processing or spreadsheet program to another— either DOS or Mac. More than that, it uses Apple's new Macintosh Easy Open translation system and Masterwork's Word for Word translators to open files for which you do not have the creating application. You can, for instance, double-click on a WriteNow file, and have the document open in WordPerfect. There is also Multi-Driver, a caching software driver that lets your Mac handle DOS-formatted removable hard drives, and Media Formatter, which enables Multi-Driver to see Macintosh removable drives.

AccessPC is comprised of several parts. The AccessPC Control Panel lets a SuperDrive-equipped Macintosh read and write to DOS- format disks. The Control Panel also enables you to assign Macintosh applications to DOS file system extensions; for example, telling the Mac to always use Excel to open files whose names end in WKS. By assigning new extensions, you also can keep the utility up to date with new file formats such as Lotus 1-2-3 version 4 or WordPerfect 6.0.

The EasyOpen translation system is represented by a Control Panel and an Easy Open document called a droplet. Dragging documents and dropping them on the droplet causes the document to be acted on. It works the same way as printing a document by dragging and dropping its icon onto a printer icon. By double-clicking on the droplet, you can select which document format the file is converted to. You can create droplets to convert files to obscure formats as Lotus Manuscript or Legacy, MultiMate Advantage, or Signature, or more common but specialized ones such as FrameMaker MIF, Interleaf Publisher 5.2, or PostScript.

AccessPC can be fooled a little by file extensions, but EasyOpen can't. If you rename a TeachText document with a DOC extension, AccessPC will cause the Mac to give that document the appropriate icon for a DOC-formatted file. However, if you try to drag that document to a droplet, the droplet won't accept it if it can't handle TeachText; it recognizes the true format of the file, not the icon.

While AccessPC lets you import foreign files on the fly, EasyOpen droplets are the only way you can export files; you can't save files in a foreign format during the conventional save process. And although several tools are available to bring foreign-format files into Mac applica-

tions, there are few for translating existing files into non-Mac formats.

The package also contains a set of disk-formatting tools. Aside from the ability to format Mac and PC floppies, AccessPC can read and initialize a great range of removable media. The world of PC removable-drive formats is much larger than that for the Macintosh. AccessPC's Multi-Driver can format and partition drives using formats supported by SCSI adapters from Always, Control Concepts, Corel, Format Three, Future Domain, Iomega, PLI, SCSI Master, SyQuest, and Trantor. Each partition can be mounted (or not) through the AccessPC Control Panel.

Insignia includes a disk initializer called Media Formatter, and the Multi-Driver software caching controller. Multi-Driver, which requires you to initialize your hard drive using Media Formatter, supports one of five types of disk cache. The documentation includes English-language directions for selecting one type of cache over another. While Multi-Driver includes the option of queued writes, the documentation clearly recommends using against it, in case of system crashes. The utility also allows use of any installed FPU.

In addition, Multi-Driver mea-

sures and displays the performance increase using your current caching setup; you can pick from among several choices depending on the speed gain the utility measures. With its droplets, file translation, and caching drivers, AccessPC is a tool that is not duplicated in the Macintosh market.—Daniel J. Rosenbaum

AccessPC 3.0
Insignia Solutions
1300 Charleston Rd.
Mountain View, CA 94043
(800) 848-7677; (415) 694-7600
$129.95

DOCUMENT SHARING MADE EASY

Face to Face

Desktop-conferencing software is currently a hot product category, and Face to Face is an impressive entry from Crosswise Corporation. In this, its first version, Face to Face lets two Mac users collaborate on a multipage document over a network, modem connection, or ISDN line. Future releases will

increase the number of users it can serve, and a Windows version, for cross-platform conferencing, should be available by the time this book sees print.

When a meeting begins, Face to Face synchronizes the participants' documents by checking file names and content. (Because Face to Face is designed to work cross-platform, and since all participants may not use the same applications, all documents are first converted to Face to Face's ImageDocument format.) If two different documents share the same name, the Caller is asked to rename his or her files. If either machine does not already have the requested document, it is transferred via a quick, bidirectional file-transport capability.

Once the file lists are synchronized, the caller is "in control" of the meeting. Double-clicking on a document brings it up on both screens, where the Caller can make notations. The other participants can take control at any time by making a menu choice. A new document can be opened and used as a whiteboard so attendees can "chat" with one another.

Like MacDraw, Face to Face uses a layer system, so notations can be made without touching the original. Layers can be added and named, or deleted, by whoever is in control. When it's time to incorporate the changes back to the original source document, notes can be transferred as editable

text. Everything else is treated as an individual image that can be cut and pasted. The resulting Image Document, and all its layers and notes, can be saved or printed out at any time either as separate documents or as one compound document.

Face to Face is fast because it stores full copies of files on both machines and keeps them synchronized. Therefore, it can share multipage documents easily, without long waits for scrolling. Instead of sending time-consuming screen refreshes over the connection, the program sends only commands, such as "scroll," thus minimizing transmissions. As a result, even a 2,400-bps modem link is a practical connection.

At $295, Face to Face is a deceptively simple, quick, and powerful addition to the desktop-conferencing market.—Dennis Fowler

Face to Face for Macintosh 1.0
Crosswise Corp.
105 Locust St., Suite 301
Santa Cruz, CA 95060
(800) 747-9060; (408) 459-9060
$295

SAFEGUARD YOUR MAC
Safety Suite

Safety Suite, from Claris' Clear Choice division, cobbles together a dozen utilities into a single package. Safety Suite's security functions include password-protected file encryption; "document shredding," which triple-erases trashed files perma-

nently; and a chime that alerts you when someone has connected to your Mac via System 7's file sharing.

Safety Suite also protects you from your own mistakes—it backs up documents when your Mac is idle, autosaves files every few minutes, records your keystrokes in case there's a system crash, and lets you "undelete" documents you've recently trashed (but not shredded).—Jason Snell

Safety Suite
Claris
(408) 727-8227
$99

Norton DiskLock 3.0

The Norton DiskLock 3.0 is a new version of Symantec's venerable password-based security program. DiskLock requires users to enter a password before being given access to a Mac's hard disk. Because the program uses

driver-level security, nobody can get to your hard disk by booting your system from a floppy. DiskLock doesn't work with driver-level compression programs, however.

DiskLock 3.0 also comes with two drag-and-drop applications that allow users to automatically encrypt and decrypt files and folders, keeping them secure even when the disk isn't locked.

Norton DiskLock 3.0
Symantec
(503) 334-6054
$129

EASY FILE ENCRYPTION
CryptoMatic 1.01

What do love letters, tax records, and new business proposals have in common? They're all too sensitive to leave lying around unprotected on your hard disk. CryptoMactic, from KentMarsh, offers five levels of encryption for documents and applications and also lets you "incinerate" files, using similar schemes. A replacement for MacSafe II in the KentMarsh line of security software products, Crypto-Mactic is well designed and extremely easy to use.

CryptoMactic consists of an extension and an application called CryptoMactic Administrator. Installing the CryptoMactic extension places a new menu in the Finder's menu bar. To encrypt a selected file or group of files, you simply choose Encrypt from this new menu (or you can press Command-1) and then select the method of encryption you want from a dialog box and enter a key-combination code as many as 16 characters long. To decrypt a file, you double-click on it and enter the code in the resulting dialog box.

Two of the five encryption methods, LightningCrypt and QuickCrypt, are proprietary algorithms developed by KentMarsh. Each provides a fast way to encrypt your files securely enough for most purposes. The other three—DES, DES-CBC, and Triple-DES—are based on the Department of Defense-approved Data Encryption Standard ANSI X3.92-1981 specification; they're slower but more secure. DES is the plain vanilla version, which even the best hacker would have only a 1-in-70-quadrillion chance of cracking. DES-CBC adds a "cipher block chaining" rou-

tine, and Triple-DES adds a second code-key layer. Bottom line: No one gets in without the key.

With CryptoMactic, you can create self-decrypting files similar to the self-extracting archive files (SEAs) most compression software creates. Using this option, you can securely encrypt a file and send it to others who don't own CryptoMactic—all they need is the code key. CryptoMactic also offers a secure file-trashing option as well as easy file trashing from the keyboard. If you need to protect sensitive information from possible snoopers, CryptoMactic should be your first choice. There's nothing easier to use or harder to defeat.—Tom Petaccia

CryptoMatic 1.01
KentMarsh Ltd.
Houston, TX
(800) 325-3587; (713) 522-5625
$99

Lockette

The Lockette is for the security-conscious. It lets you lock your computer to your desk, your car, or even your leg. It also enables you to lock your floppy drive.

Lockette
Z-Lock Manufacturing
$19.95

3M Privacy Filter

Anyone whose family room doubles as an office will love the 3M Privacy Filter, a polarizing filter that fits over the front of your display and makes it impossible to see what's on the screen unless you're directly in front of it. Several models are available, some of which also cut out glare and radiation.

3M Privacy Filter
3M Optical Systems
$189.95 to $329.95

PKZIP MAC UNLOCKS YOUR DOS-BASED ZIPPED FILES

PKZIP

The barriers between the DOS and Mac worlds keep falling. Files compressed with PKZIP are now accessible by Macintosh users, thanks to PKZIP Mac from Ascent Solutions Inc. Not only can DOS files be decompressed on a Mac, but this $54.95 utility enables you to compress files on a Mac and later UNZIP those same files on DOS machines. For users of online services (such as ZiffNet) that specify PKZIP as the compression standard for all the files in their download libraries, this cross-platform capability is indispensable.

The key behind PKZIP Mac is the PKZIP technology that Ascent Solutions licensed from PKWARE Inc. PKZIP Mac has all the features of DOS PKZIP v2.04g, including 32-bit CRC error checking; user-selectable high-speed or high-compression operations; data encryption; and the ability to add, freshen, move, and update files in an archive. Only the ability to create a self-extracting archive is lacking. By saving Macintosh

To Whom It May Concern: Help!

there you sit, stalled by a software problem. You don't just want answers, you want answers fast. Who're you gonna call? These days, you're likely to call for support from an unaffiliated third party rather than the software publisher. According to a recent Dataquest survey of 221 corporations in several industries, 40 percent of a company's budget for employees' software support goes to third parties.

Is third-party support a perfect solution? Definitely not. Certain kinds of software don't even make the list. Software Support (Heathrow, Florida; 800-756-4463), a leading third-party provider, supports more than 150 titles but not a single accounting package, CAD program, or programming tool. The company's fees are very reasonable, though, and you call one number to get answers on any supported title. Corporations pay Software Support $170 per user for one year of 24-hour, 7-day-a-week support. A noncorporate user buying the same level of support pays $199.95. Corporate Software (Norwood, Massachusetts, 800-677-4000) provides third-party support for far more titles—over 800—and charges different prices for various levels of support. The company's Silver support plan, for example, costs $15,000 for one year of 24-hour, 7-day-a-week support for five users.

Third-party support won't entirely supplant in-house help desks. Dataquest's survey respondents are less willing to outsource certain kinds of problems than others. Which type of support is least likely to be sought out-of-house? Disaster recovery. Over 45 percent of respondents said they're not willing to outsource such support.

Meanwhile, third-party tech-support companies are increasing the sophistication of their support with remote-diagnostics software. Staffers at Software Support field about 15,000 calls a day and can access system inventories remotely by modem and avoid lengthy interviews with callers. Many PCs already come preloaded with remote-diagnostics software, and Traveling Software plans to announce that a major PC maker will preload LapLink for Windows on its systems, which will link users directly to the manufacturer for support.

Whether the support staffer you call accesses your system from afar or resorts to old-fashioned Q&A, it's less and less likely that you'll be talking to a software publisher.—Sebastian Rupley ■

resource fork information separately from general information, PKZIP Mac allows for full PKZIP compatibility while retaining all the Macintosh attributes.

To create a new ZIP file, you type a name for the file and highlight the files that you want compressed. You UNZIP a file following a similar method, with the option of extracting all the files contained in the ZIPped file or selectively choosing those to be extracted.

Documentation is the only weak aspect of this otherwise solid utility. Unfortunately, online help is missing, and the manual fails to cover the product's greatest strength: cross-platform compression. Omitted from the manual is any discussion of Macintosh and DOS considerations that must be taken into account when compressing files for use on the two different operating systems.

PKZIP Mac's ease of use and functionality more than compensate for the weak documenta-

tion. If you work with both Macs and PCs, and you have to deal with file-compression-compatibility issues, PKZIP Mac is the tool you have been looking for.—Paul Gudelis

PKZIP Mac
Mac Ascent Solutions Inc.
10460 Miamisburg-Springboro Pike
Dayton, OH 45342
(513) 885-2031
$54.95

SECURITY FOR MODERN TIMES
NightWatch II

If virus-protection programs are the equivalent of safe sex for computers, then security programs like NightWatch II are the modern chastity belt. NightWatch II provides several levels of security that allow users to protect sensitive data from unauthorized use.

Installation is quick and simple. The NightWatch Administrator main screen contains options that determine what disks are affected and the level of protection. The program comes with three types of locking arrangement: Standard, Token Disk, and Key Disk. Standard-level security automatically requests a valid user name and password combination when the Mac is turned on or the screen saver is disengaged. The next level, Token Disk, works like the old master-disk copy-protection scheme. In addition to

typing the name and password combination, a user must insert a floppy disk containing a database of valid user names and a password for that particular Mac.

The final level, Key Disk, is a variation on Token Disk protection. A user is required to have a properly authorized floppy disk, in this instance called a key disk, but is not required to supply a user name/password combination. Key Disk protection will also

prohibit the use of recovery-software tools to recover files on a disk protected by NightWatch II.

Other protection options common to all three locking methods include minimum password length; password expiration dates; a limit on the days and/or times the disk may be unlocked by a user; write-protecting the hard disk after it's unlocked; a limit on whether or not the user can insert floppy disks (to preclude the introduction of a virus); at what point NightWatch II locks the screen; and when or if the token or key disk expires.

Once a user is admitted, NightWatch II is unobtrusive.

Its screen saver isn't an aesthetic replacement for After Dark, but it is serviceable and has a random feature that selects a different graphics module each time the saver is engaged.

NightWatch proved to be a very stable product. There were no crashes or freezes on the test Quadra 650, running System 7.1 and a double handful of INITs and extensions.

A poorly designed security program has the potential to be more of a headache than a help. NightWatch II easily qualifies as a help, providing a level of hard disk security that will meet or exceed any degree of paranoia on the part of the owner or security administrator. If you're feeling less than secure about your data, NightWatch II can restore your peace of mind.—Michael R. Shannon

NightWatch II
Kent Marsh Ltd.
3260 Sul Ross
Houston, TX 77098
(800) 325-3587; (713) 522-5625
$160

CAN OPEN AND SALVAGE ANY FILE
CanOpener 2.5

Nothing can be more frustrating than a file that has become damaged or unreadable. One solution could be Abbott Systems's CanOpener. CanOpener opens any damaged or undamaged file on your desktop. It allows you to snoop inside damaged

files, displaying and saving any text or graphics stored there. You can recover text, graphic, or sound information from a damaged hard disk when its data has been jumbled by a disk-recovery utility.

CanOpener examines an opened file and presents you with a list of recognizable pictures, text, and sounds. Any of these can be displayed in a viewer window, copied to the Clipboard, or saved in a separate file. The program can detect data in a number of formats: FSSD and SND sound files, MacDraw, MacPaint, PICT, TIFF, Quick-Time movies, MacWrite, and ASCII text.

Text, pictures, and sounds embedded in a file can be saved to individual files or pasted into a CanOpener library file. A library feature can be used to store data during a salvage operation for later cutting and pasting into individual files or applications.

When salvaged files are no longer readable by their application, CanOpener lets you perform searches for text within a file. The program allows you to specify the types of searches conducted. For example, you can specify a minimum and maximum ASCII string length to recognize and cut. If you know that there aren't any words in your text document shorter than ten characters, you can set the minimum ASCII length to ten, and CanOpener will cut any text over ten unspaced characters in length. It can also search and cut strings of a single repeated text character. CanOpener can search both the data and resource forks of Mac files.—Lenny Bailes

CanOpener 2.5
Abbott Systems Inc.
62 Mountain Rd.
Pleasantville, NY 10570
(800) 552-9157
$125

WHAT'S IN A NAME? HIGH-TECH SECURITY, THAT'S WHAT

Cadix ID-007

Cadix International has announced the new Cadix ID-007 security system, which controls virtual access to data or physical entry into facilities by verifying a hand-written signature. Using a pressure-sensitive pen and tablet, the Microsoft Windows-based ID-007 software checks three different criteria—the shape of the signature, the speed at which it is written, and the pressure of the pen stroke—in order to detect and reject unauthorized signatures, including forgeries. Signature verification typically takes less than one second.

The ID-007 security system learns individual signatures based on several samples, and can adapt to normal variations in a signature over time. It can even generate a report alerting the system administrator to changes in an individual's signature pattern.—Asa Somers

Cadix ID-007
Cadix International Inc.
Atlanta, GA
(404) 804-9951
$2,500; pressure-sensitive tablet,
$200 to $2,000, depending on
model

INFOBASE PRODUCTION KIT FOR WINDOWS

Folio Views 3.1

Folio Views 3.1 Infobase Production Kit for Windows towers over its competitors. The "infobases" created by this hypertext authoring program convey the greatest variety of information in the most efficient ways and provide the most flexibility in exchanging updated data between a central office and multiple sites elsewhere.

Folio Corp.'s software comes in three varieties. The $295 Infobase Manager lets end users view, annotate, edit, and update existing infobases but only allows creation of the simplest new infobases. (A similar product that reads the same infobases is available for DOS, and a Macintosh version is due soon.) The $895 Infobase Production Kit includes the Infobase Manager and adds both simple and advanced tools for creating and modifying infobases using files imported from all standard word processor, spreadsheet, and database formats. A $3,995 Professional Infobase Development Kit (not tested by PC Labs) adds runtime infobases for corporate or commercial distribution on disk or CD-ROM. A separate $1,995 Software Developers Kit lets C programmers use Folio's application program interface (API) to customize toolbars, OLE objects, or help systems, or to integrate Folio Views into complex applications.

A Folio Views infobase is basically a continuous text stream divided into records in the same file with a full-text index and a hierarchical table of contents. Records can be paragraphs, rows of data, embedded bitmap graphics or spreadsheets, or links to external objects such as video clips. Objects can be positioned anywhere in the text.

Hypertext links can be displayed as colored, underlined text as in the Windows help system, or as graphic buttons. Each outline level has its own text formatting, and the author has complete control over format and background color, using either character or paragraph styles or direct formatting of selected text. Formats can be set in both Folio Views and the original word processor documents. The author can't lock the display to a specified width or height, so the text width changes when the window is resized. Easy customization menus let the author select icons that appear on a toolbar in the final product, but without the SDK the author can't change the program's menus or create new icons.

Infobases open by default in the text window, but it takes only two keystrokes to display text and outline windows simultaneously. An optional reference window at the top of the text window displays all the headings and subheads that identify the current position. A click on any line in the outline or reference window moves the text window to the matching position, and all moves are nearly instantaneous. For moving through an infobase, an icon offers a backtrack feature, and a menu displays a history of the reader's moves. A "group" feature—not as intuitive as it should be—lets authors and readers combine widely scattered records into named groups that can be searched as a unit.

Security and password options let the author of an Infobase permit or prevent a variety of types of editing, linking, and annotations. If the author permits, a reader can modify text, attach sticky notes, or (by using multiple, customizable highlighters) alter the color, size, and font of any text. A unique and powerful feature lets all changes be stored optionally in a reader's private "shadow" file, for selective incorporation into the original infobase by the reader or author. Multiple users can read and modify the same infobase simultaneously. Changes made using a shadow file can be noted to provide a simple audit trail.

Searches are startlingly fast. They can include Boolean operators and after readers learn some mildly complex procedures, they can use the menus to limit searches to outline levels, groups, notes, highlighted text, or other subcategories of an infobase. By opening more than one infobase in the manager, readers can search multiple infobases with one command. A template editor lets authors build graphical fill-in menus for complex queries.

Folio Views's import filters outclassed everything else in this survey; they even allow export if you prefer to edit in your word processor. The Infobase Production Kit comes with filters for the most common formats, and the superb Microsoft Word 6.0 and WordPerfect for Windows 6.0 filters support advanced layout features such as borders. These high-speed filters convert paragraph styles into outline levels so the author can transform a well-designed word processing document into a complete infobase with a simple import command. A separate $195 filter pack supports 50 less common formats. Once the author imports the files, he or she can discard the originals and use the infobase manager for editing and spell-checking. A complete infobase, with index, can run half the size of the original files.

Authors and readers can export infobases to an ASCII flat-file format and manipulate links, styles, outline levels, and other features using a text editor or a DOS-based search-and-replace engine in the Infobase Production Kit.

In our testing, Folio Views was fast, flexible, and rock-solid. It imported files that made other programs crash, and made virtually every step of creating and using an Infobase simple and enjoyable. You'll need very convincing reasons for choosing anything else.—Edward Mendelson

Folio Views 3.1 Infobase Production Kit for Windows
Folio Corp.
5072 North 300 West
Provo, UT 84604
(800) 543-6546; (801) 229-6700
$295; Infobase Production Kit, $895

LOCK DOWN THAT HARD DRIVE

DiskGuard 1.0

ASD Software's disk-security package works on all SCSI disks, including removable media, and can protect disks at startup, at PowerBook wake-up, or after a user-defined period of inactivity. Users can even be limited to access only during certain hours or days of the week.—Jason Snell

DiskGuard 1.0
ASD Software
(909) 624-2594
$60

FolderBolt Pro 1.0.1

This new version of Kent Marsh's FolderBolt allows users to password-protect folders and make them read- or write-only. Among the enhancements in FolderBolt Pro are improved network-administration abilities and

Power Mac-native encryption modules for ensuring file security.—Jason Snell

FolderBolt Pro 1.0.1
Kent Marsh
(714) 522-5625
$129

Mac Control 1.8

This utility from BDW Software protects files and folders from alteration while allowing users to move them around in the Finder. It

restores files to their original locations at restart.—Jason Snell

Mac Control 1.8
BDW Software
(612) 686-5462
$59

Hi Resolution

Also Power Mac-native, Hi Resolution's folder-management utility MacPrefect now lets administrators choose what windows

will open at startup, determine what Chooser devices are accessible, and limit how many copies of a document a user can print. As always, it restricts the moving and editing of files and folders.— Jason Snell

MacPrefect 2.4
Hi Resolution
(508) 463-6956
$61

On Guard 1.1

This utility from Power On Software controls where users can open, save, or view files and folders and launch applications. Setting up individual accounts and passwords is optional.—Jason Snell

On Guard 1.1
Power On Software
(612) 946-1272
$57

Batteries That Think

just how far are you willing to go for an extra four hours of battery life? Would you schlepp an extra pound or shell out an extra hundred dollars? Most people would accept an extra 12 ounces, a smaller keyboard, and a quarter-inch in size, and would pay an extra $100 for a notebook that delivered an extra four hours of juice, according to a survey of mobile computer users by H&M Consulting.

Momentum is building now for a "smart battery" standard designed to improve runtimes. Unlike conventional batteries, an intelligent battery is equipped with a chip that issues accurate reports on battery conditions. IBM has developed its own solution for its ThinkPad notebooks, and over a dozen manufacturers, including Canon, Citizen, and Compaq, have signed on to the Intel/Duracell Smart Battery Data Specification, a fledgling standard that defines the pathway for communication among the smart battery, the notebook, and the charger.

Today, most notebooks come with a battery indicator that estimates remaining time. According to Duracell, inaccurate estimates can result in up to 20 percent of the battery's overall life not being used. A smart battery collects and communicates a range of statistics such as capacity, chemistry, remaining battery time, temperature, and voltage. According to SystemSoft, which has written a smart battery interface, a notebook with a smart battery lasts longer because users are given accurate battery status and can budget battery life with power management tools.

Smart batteries that are based on the Intel/Duracell specification have two basic components: the System Management Bus (SMBus), which is an extension of a notebook's BIOS, and a microcontroller located on the battery that stores data about the battery and monitors its status. Information such as remaining battery time is transferred over the SMBus to the system and displayed on-screen. Since the standard is chemistry-independent, it supports nickel hydride, nickel cadmium, and lithium ion batteries.—Carol Levin ∎

INTEXT PUTS A FINGER ON INFORMATION

InTEXT

Information may be power, but unless you know where each piece of data lurks, that power may be only so much unused potential. Island Software's $399 InTEXT for Windows is a network-capable text- and document-management package that uses simple English requests to retreive documents.

Based on a hierarchical file cabinet/folder metaphor, InTEXT uses SmartFolders to organize documents that originated in Microsoft Word for Windows, WordPerfect for Windows, Lotus Ami Pro, Microsoft Write, or any ASCII-based application. Rather than force you to manually deposit documents in folders, InTEXT automatically fills folders based on filters that you set. Though not foolproof, we found this to be a quick way to categorize information.

Before documents are available for search and retrieval, they must be indexed. A 5,000-word document took a minute and a half to index over a Windows for Workgroups network. Once indexed, documents can be retrieved with simple English requests—such as "Show me all documents that deal with personal finance and mention Lire"—rather than cryptic keywords and complex logical separators.

When the program locates the files, they can be viewed without launching the native application. InTEXT's links to

the supported word processors are excellent. Within Microsoft Word, for instance, toolbar buttons and macros let you file, index, or summarize the active document without having to leave the application.

Summarizing documents is a good way to highlight the salient portions. You can set the length of the summary, view the highlights in context, search on and display any of its keywords, and print or copy the results to the Clipboard—although you can't save these summaries as separate documents.

InTEXT's biggest shortcoming is its prodigious space demands. Because it creates copies of the filed documents, our evaluation cabinet of 25 documents took up nearly 4MB of disk space—to store and index what had originally been just 200K of files. And InTEXT limits its searches to a maximum of ten cabinets. As a document-management system, InTEXT lacks some crucial components, such as OCR input, automated person-to-person routing, and integrated links to e-mail packages.

Overall, however, we found that InTEXT, with its SmartFolders and summary skills, is a credible text-retrieval application for both workgroups and single users.—Gregg Keizer

InTEXT
Island Software
Novato, CA
(800) 255-4499; (415) 884-4400
$399

ACROBAT JUMPS THROUGH HOOPS

Adobe Acrobat

At one time, sharing a document meant reaching for a piece of carbon paper and pressing harder on the keys as you typed. Over the years, the technology of producing and distributing documents has advanced radically. Most documents now begin their lives electronically. Yet, as inexorably as salmon swimming upstream, those documents still manage to make their way to paper.

The most compelling reason may be appearance; increasingly, a document's format—its layout, fonts, graphics, and color—is as much a part of the information to be conveyed as the words themselves.

But while printing preserves a document's appearance, it also compromises the accessibility of the information it contains: No matter how powerful your desktop computer, it can't search for keywords through a stack of printed documents.

Of course, electronic document exchange is no walk in the park, either, thanks to differences between types of computers such as PCs and Macs, operating systems, applications software, printers, and installed fonts.

The problem of exchanging documents among different types of computers, or brands of software on the same computer, is not new. The traditional low-tech approach—converting it to an

ASCII text file—gains you accessibility, but at the cost of appearance. A scanner and an optical character recognition (OCR) program turns hard copy into an electronic text file that can be searched and edited, but you lose all graphics and other formatting.

A better solution lets users distribute fully-formatted documents across different platforms for their colleagues to view and annotate. Several such products have recently surfaced, including No Hands Software's Common Ground, WordPerfect Envoy, and Farallon's Replica. The leading example of this electronic document publishing technology is Adobe Acrobat.

Adobe Acrobat is a group of applications that segments the publishing process into two discrete steps: creation and viewing. It allows published documents to be distributed, viewed, and printed without requiring the recipient to have the applications or hardware with which the document was created. The recipient sees an on-screen representation of the document, including the text, fonts, page layout, and graphics, exactly as it will appear on paper—kind of like an electronic photocopy.

The basic Adobe Acrobat package contains everything you'll need to create, use, and distribute documents. The process it uses is simple. To bridge the gap between incompatible systems, Acrobat defines an intermediate file format called the portable document format

(PDF), which can be written or read by any type of computer. Document creation begins with the Acrobat PDF Writer, a device driver that your application uses to print your documents to disk as PDFs. PDF Writer is available for Windows and Macintosh systems.

The Acrobat Reader program, in DOS, Macintosh, Unix, and Windows versions, lets you view and print PDF documents. The Reader program may be distributed free with PDF documents and lets users read all annotations, bookmarks, and links that are part of the PDF file. However, the Reader doesn't let you alter the document. To do that, you would use the Acrobat Exchange program. Exchange isn't an editor, but it does let you annotate a document with pop-up notes. You can also build in bookmarks for quick navigation through the document. The PDF Writer system works for most business applications, with limitations.

Documents that contain high-resolution scanned images, encapsulated PostScript (EPS) images, blends, gradient fills, or other PostScript-specific features are normally sent to PostScript printers, and don't survive well in the translation through PDF Writer.

Acrobat Pro includes everything in Acrobat, plus the Acrobat Distiller program, designed specifically to convert PostScript language files into PDFs. Distiller is run on the same system that creates the document, where it accesses all the fonts and resources used by the document to successfully create the PDF file. Distiller offers a lossless compression option for text and outline graphics. To reduce storage requirements, complex graphics such as scanned images can be compressed further by using one of several techniques, including a procedure called downsampling, as well as JPEG (for 16-and 24-bit color images) and LZW (for low-resolution color and grayscale images).

Acrobat for Workgroups includes Distiller, a ten-user license for Acrobat, and the Acrobat Catalog software. The Acrobat Catalog program creates live full-text indexes for groups of PDF documents. When combined with Acrobat Search (distributed in all variations of Acrobat), hundreds or thousands of documents can be searched with a single command.

All Acrobat versions include Adobe's Type Manager software, Multiple Master font technology, and 14 Adobe Type 1 fonts. Although documentation is included in each package, the manuals are provided as PDF files, not hard copy.

Of course, Acrobat hasn't conquered every potential document problem you'll encounter. An 8.5 × 11-inch page, for example, simply can't be displayed legibly on a standard 14-inch monitor. Complete document portability is a myth. But in many cases it's also unnecessary.

Acrobat's platform-independence makes it easy and inexpensive to create and broadcast complex documents. It also opens the way for on-demand publishing, warehoused document banks, and archival storage. PDF files maintain a document's appearance without compromising its value as pure information. PDF files are easy to annotate and search, and provide a good basis for work-in-progress editing.

Acrobat seems to have struck that tenuous balance between power and ease-of-use.—Robert L. Hummel

Adobe Acrobat
Adobe

ProComm Plus 2.0

This old standby continues to set the standard for communications software. There's a new, completely standard Windows interface, a more powerful scripting language, and new usability features like drop-down dialing lists and programmable button bars. But what really sets ProComm Plus 2.0 for Windows apart are its fax features—the best of any communications program. In addition to the expected send and receive capabilities, cover-sheet editors, and viewers, you can send faxes from within other applications and poll remote fax machines. You can even use ProComm Plus to set up a fax-back service. This is by

far the most valuable communications utility around.

ProComm Plus 2.0
DataStorm Technologies
(800) 315-3282
$179

WinComm Pro 1.1

Long known for WinFax Pro, Delrina enhanced its modem management capabilities with WinComm Pro 1.1, a full-featured communications suite. Its Fax Broadcast feature lets you send and receive faxes via MCI even when you're on the road.

WinComm Pro 1.1
Delrina
(800) 268-6082
$129

E-Mail Connection 2.0

Too many of us have too many e-mail addresses. E-Mail Connection 2.0 cuts through it all by offering a way to integrate your mail systems. It picks up all your mail and funnels it into one in-box. If you spend time using e-mail, it's a must.

E-Mail Connection 2.0
ConnectSoft
(206) 827-6467
$50

THE REMOTE POSSIBILITIES ARE ENDLESS

LapLink 6.0 for Windows

It's Saturday night. You're at home, working on that all-important proposal due

Monday morning. Suddenly, you realize that the spreadsheet you need to generate a chart is on your hard disk at work. After a moment of panic, you realize that all is not lost. You have LapLink for Windows, and your office system is on with LapLink running there, too. (Aren't you smart for remembering all these details?) You dial in and download the file just in time to watch "Weekend Update." With LapLink 6.0 for Windows—the first Windows release, reviewed here in beta form—Traveling Software takes its staple file-transfer utility to the next level: remote access and control. You can now run programs on a remote system as if you were sitting at its keyboard. During our testing, LapLink handled standard DOS programs running in a DOS window on the remote system—a task other remote-access applications have trouble with.

With its file transfer and remote access, LapLink competes not just with DOS's own file exchange function and transfer programs like Grand Junction Networks's FastLink and SoftWorx's Interlink, but also with products like Ocean Isle's ReachOut, Symantec's pcAnywhere, and Triton Technologies's CoSession.

LapLink provides a number of methods for connecting two computers. In addition to the traditional serial or parallel cable connection (cables are included), you can connect systems over a modem or a NetWare network. The program also supports the AirShare wireless transmitter/receiver used in LapLink Wireless (it works over a range of about 30 feet).

To copy files from place to place, you can choose the specific files you want transferred or use the SmartXchange or Clone options for speedy batch-style operation. SmartXchange updates a directory with the most recent version of files from the source system. Clone is the most efficient way of duplicating systems—say, when you create a "master" PC configuration and want to make a dozen machines just like it.

For managing your own files in a timely manner, a SpeedSync feature sends only those portions of a file that have changed since the last update. A similar SmartXchange lets you synchronize two computers's operations by ensuring that only the

newest version of any file exists on each.

Installing LapLink is a breeze. The Setup program analyzes your hardware and configures itself automatically. Just specify a directory in which it should store its files and assign a name to your computer. A remote install option lets you add LapLink to a second computer through a serial cable.

LapLink's file management utilities are so versatile that they can stand in for File Manager. And the bonus of remote control makes LapLink 6.0 for Windows a communications utility every multimachine user needs.— Jack Nimersheim

LapLink 6.0 for Windows
Traveling Software
(800) 343-8080
$140

The Macintosh was based on a computer made by Apple called the Lisa, which introduced the graphical user interface that made the Macintosh famous. Unfortunately, Apple charged an extravagant $10,000 for the Lisa, forcing users to pay for seven expensive software programs when they purchased the computer. Believe it or not, Apple actually wondered why it couldn't sell any.

The Vision Thing

maybe they're whistling in the graveyard. Maybe they just don't get it. But they can't possibly be serious. Maximum industry leaders Louis Gerstner of IBM and Michael Spindler of Apple have come out firmly against the future. Or at least against playing leadership roles there. Gerstner started it off when he sniffed "The last thing that IBM needs right now is a vision." Spindler picked up the baton at a recent conference as he bashed Microsoft's Bill Gates and Intel's Andy Grove for having "too much vision."

Well, maybe Spindler isn't totally visionless. He did talk wistfully of one element that—who knows—could become a key strategy: "We still have to switch our computers on and off. We go to the rest room, and when we leave it flushes automatically." Perhaps a whole new metaphor for Apple is in store?

Spindler also dumped on the Information Superhighway, 500-channel TV, and electronic tools that organize our lives. But he saved his real venom for Gates and Grove, who were keynote speakers at Comdex/Fall: "They believe that just because of the technospeak it's going to happen, but it's not."

Technospeak? In his Comdex speech, Grove saw a future where the tenfold kick ISDN offers over modems will make desktop video common and blur the distinction between LAN and WAN, and where in 18 months the e-mail message volume in North America will eclipse first-class mail.

Grove's vision is of systems with communications and multimedia built in instead of slapped on. His proposed solution is Native Signal Processing (NSP), which steals unused CPU cycles to handle jobs normally done by separate DSP chips.

Gates's speech was predictably more ambitious. Noting the continuing "exponential improvement" from the 33 MIPS 8088 to the 100 MIPS Pentium, he painted a world where wallet PCs offer "books, catalogs, shopping approaches, professional advice, art, movies" on demand, where video phones supplant car phones, where TV is interactive and smart (well, at least the interface is), where a global net really does offer virtually any information at your fingertips, where ATMs are in hotel rooms, where even kids can do sophisticated multimedia programming, where teaching has "the production values of TV," where speech and natural language interfaces actually work, where you can buy a house or renew your driver's license remotely, and where a "social interface" will open up technology to the masses and supersede today's graphical interface. Whew. Where do I get one?

Spindler can keep knocking Gates and Grove all he wants. But here's the reality: This year at Comdex, those G-men were the keynotes. If the heads of Apple and IBM keep laughing at such visionaries, they each risk becoming just footnotes.—Paul Somerson ■

REFERENCE

Software Development: A Legal Guide, by Stephen Fishman

If you're in any way connected to the process of creating or marketing software, or if you're thinking about getting into the business, then you'll be extremely grateful for the considered counsel of *Software Development: A Legal Guide*. While the title may be straightforward enough, the intellectual-property arena is anything but. The usual rules for protecting books, inventions, and such don't always apply to software—or at least not in the same way. Attorney Fishman's book is a lifeboat of sorts for sailing through these turbulent waters.

Software Development: A Legal Guide is a logically organized, exceptionally thorough book for the nonlawyer. It introduces the concept of intellectual property, relating it to software and the need to have a plan of action. It proceeds with lengthier chapters

on software copyright issues, trade secrets, patents, and trademarks. It also spends several chapters dwelling on the relationships between employers, employees, and independent contractors in the software business, and how these arrangements can affect copyrights, patents, and secrets. In the process, there is plenty of detailed advice on drafting agreements that protect you, whether you are the employer or employee.

For a book on a topic that is changing so rapidly, *Software Development: A Legal Guide* seems surprisingly up to date. It includes a chapter on multimedia projects and the added questions they raise, such as obtaining permission to use copyrighted materials. There's even an appendix that provides an analysis of the highly controversial "multimedia search" patent granted to, and then revoked from, Compton's NewMedia.

Yet, for all of its breadth and the weighty topics it tackles, *Software Development: A Legal Guide* remains a very readable tome, even if you're a legal neophyte. Nolo Press has more than 20 years of experience in self-help legal books, and it shows. The tone is authoritative and fairly dry, but invariably clear and to the point.

And there's a bonus, too: All of the forms shown in the book are provided in file form on an included floppy disk.—
Christopher O'Malley

Software Development:
A Legal Guide
Nolo Press
950 Parker St.
Berkeley, CA 94710
(800) 992-6656; (510) 549-1976
$44.95

Essential Software for Writers, by Hy Bender

Essential Software for Writers is about specific PC products, but it's clearly more about the job they conspire to help you do than about the products themselves. The book is subtitled *A Complete Guide for Everyone Who Writes With a PC*, which, while probably a good example of promotional copywriting, overstates its scope. *Essential Software for Writers* is for writers in the more earnest sense of the word, not your average memo-and-report writer. But if 500-plus pages on writing tools doesn't scare you away, you qualify.

The books starts with the obligatory "choosing a word processor" chapter, but spends mercifully little time going over the options (DOS and Windows favorites, and some low-priced alternatives). Most people reading the book are likely to be using a word processor already and are unlikely to switch. After a second cursory chapter on the basics of what a word processor can and cannot do, author Bender moves on to what many writers will consider far meatier chapters on idea generators,

"collaborators" (story-telling aids), electronic dictionaries and thesauruses, grammar and style checkers, and a group of miscellaneous editing tools.

That's where many earlier "software for writers" books stopped. To his credit, Bender can see beyond the desktop and beyond his own occupation. There are three chapters on getting information for your writing efforts, including solid overviews of CD-ROM and online sources. And there are no less than nine chapters on tools for specialized writing tasks, spanning everything from poetry and scriptwriting to medical and legal writing. There's a chapter for multilingual writers in there, too.

Bender takes a hands-on approach to many of the products he mentions and is not afraid to inject some strong opinions and insightful commentary. But he also comes across as an earthy and evenhanded observer who tips his biases in advance.

If there's a serious omission in "Essential Software for Writers," it's the lack of discussion on corporate issues such as effective business communication, workgroup software, and document-management systems. It's not sexy, but corporate writing usually leaves plenty of room for improvement.—
Christopher O'Malley

Essential Software for Writers
Writer's Digest Books
F&W Publications Inc.
1507 Dana Ave.
Cincinnati, OH 45207
(800) 289-0963
$24.95

Troubleshooting Your PC, by Jim Aspinwell, Rory Burke, and Mike Todd

Troubleshooting Your PC, a hefty guide to solving basic problems from Jim Aspinwell, Rory Burke, and Mike Todd, is a good bookshelf addition for the user who knows a little about what happens when he flicks on the switch, but lacks an electrical engineering degree.

Troubleshooting starts with the basics. Early chapters attempt to remove the mystery of a PC's innards by giving an overview of the subsystems and a few basic tips on how to identify where a problem might lie. Reading the first three chapters should provide enough basic information to identify a problem.

Because the last thing you want to do when you have a

problem is read a 700-page book, each chapter ends with a set of symptoms, a list of "suspects," and possible solutions. Chapter summaries provide an explanation for why the problem may have occurred in the first place. The symptom list is duplicated at the beginning of the book for easier access.

Many of the offered solutions are probably too technical for a casual reader, however. For a user faced with a PC that refuses to turn on, for instance, Troubleshooting advises you to first reduce the clock speed, then to check CMOS setup parameters, lower ambient temperature, and finally, replace the CPU. This would be cold comfort for a novice weekend worker skimming to solve this problem.

The book does offer a reasonably logical map to where problems may arise, starting with configuration errors. It walks you through the arcana of CONFIG.SYS and AUTOEXEC.BAT files, hardware and operating system problems, and diagnostic software packages that can aid in detective work. Included with the book is DiagSoft Inc.'s QAPlus, a list of vendor BBS services, and a shareware communications program called COM-AND (so you can dial up for help).

While *Troubleshooting Your PC* won't get you to the point where you'll be commanding legions of tech-support workers, it's a good introduction to the basics for users irked at mysterious IRQ problems or

confounded by COM port conflicts.—Nate Zelnick

Troubleshooting Your PC,
By Jim Aspinwell, Rory Burke, and Mike Todd
MIS Press
(800) 628-9658
$32.95

NEED LEGAL AID? DON'T FEED THE SHARKS

LegalPoint

First the bad news: LegalPoint won't replace your lawyer any more than accounting software will eliminate your accountant. The rest is mostly good news. Teneron's LegalPoint gives business users a lawful head start by providing templates for 70 common contracts and legal documents. The program also includes context-sensitive help and useful advice from a team of lawyers.

When you ask lawyers to draw up traditional business documents, they don't start from scratch. They take existing text in templates and fill in the blanks. But who needs a law degree to fill in blanks? LegalPoint makes it easy for you to write in the details by highlighting parts of its boilerplate documents. When you place the cursor over this highlighted text, the program explains the clause in question.

Red highlights indicate where to make changes specific to the document. If you're creating a promissory note, clicking on the Borrower explains that LegalPoint assumes a bor-

rower is an individual, though it could be one of six other possibilities, including a corporation or general/limited partnership. Green text indicates subtext relating to the general topic.

Filling in these blanks ultimately creates a basic—though not final—legal document that you can then take to a lawyer for input. Naturally, no collection of computer code will eliminate the need for wise counsel, but this program can reduce the amount of time (and money) you must spend with folks who charge megabucks per hour.

LegalPoint is more than a time-saver. The information in its dialog boxes is written in clear, understandable English. If you're mystified by what you're reading, click on the icon labeled Business Law Topics, and a context-sensitive database of background information appears. In the six categories—business, employment, corporate, intellectual property, financial, and legal—you'll find 56 articles written by Teneron's staff of lawyers and laypeople.

LegalPoint's one failing relates to its linking abilities. The opening screen, with a background of a table in a law library, shows six simple choices. When you click on Create a Document, you can choose a document template by name, category, or keyword. Even though the titles of the documents are clear and helpful, Teneron needs to work on linking its keywords to documents. For instance, if you use such obvious terms as taxes, finance, default,

insurance, liability, and harassment as keywords, no document template comes up even though there are templates related to them.

Otherwise, LegalPoint features a briefcase full of nice touches. You can adjust the toolbar to resemble either Microsoft Word or Lotus's Ami Pro (but not Novell's WordPerfect). Its help icon is a life preserver, and the six choices on the opening screen are duplicated in a handy button bar.

Overall, it's an open-and-shut case in favor of LegalPoint. The program takes a process most people find fraught with anxiety and transforms it into a simple matter of filling in the blanks.—Howard Baldwin

LegalPoint
Teneron
(800) 529-5669; (913) 451-3663
$69

UNCLE SAM IS WIRED

The National Technical Information Service

When you think of the relationship between business and the U.S. government, you probably think of bureaucracy, regulations, and, of course, taxes. But don't overlook a key element: information. Government information amounts to more than 10 million documents, reports, studies, and databases—and the pile keeps growing. And the best way to navigate this sea of documents is with the

National Technical Information Service (NTIS).

The NTIS, an agency of the U.S. Department of Commerce, adds an average of 1,300 new titles to its collection each week, covering everything from management studies to oceanic technology. If it's unclassified government information, you can find it here.

NTIS includes FedWorld, which links to all government Web pages; the Bibliographic Database; Alerts, a customizable news service; Federal Research in Progress, which keeps you current on ongoing projects; Promotional Materials, including documents and software; and Foreign Broadcast Information, which includes political and economic briefings.

Considering a franchise purchase? Scan demographic information about the surrounding neighborhoods from the 1990 U.S. Census. Think you've developed the latest and greatest widget? Check the U.S. Patent and Trade Office first. Working on an import plan involving the Pacific Rim? NTIS offers a wealth of information on doing business in Japan.—Rich Schwerin

You'll need an Internet connection and World Wide Web access to get online, then to reach NTIS simply point your browser (for example, Netscape or Mosaic) to http://www.fedworld.gov/ntishome.html or call (703) 487-4608.

Lock, Stock, and Password

i f you handle sensitive or confidential data, you might as well just paint a target on your PC. An intruder can slither through a network cable and poke around in your hard drive without leaving a trace. Anyone who can get into your e-mail account can rifle your mailbox and even send messages under your name. If you're careless, a casual snoop can even come right through the front door and take a quick peek at what next year's payroll numbers really look like.

Maybe it's just a curious coworker who's having a bad ethics day. Maybe it's a disgruntled soon-to-be-ex-employee who wants to deliver a trophy to one of your competitors. Odds are there's something on your PC that someone else would like to look at, and you'd prefer they didn't. At the very least, if you're using a PC in a business environment you should have a basic security program that keeps out the casual intruder. If your data is truly sensitive, your security routine should be more sophisticated.

In the most basic terms, there are four techniques you can use to keep your data secure: Lock it up, hide it, scramble it, or take it with you.

Lock It Up

A good lock—the physical kind, with a key or a combination—is the first line of defense for all your worldly goods, at home and at the office. So, first make sure there's always at least one locked door between prying eyes and your data. For an extra level of protection, add a digital lock, too, in the form of a system-level password.

The Hardware Solution

If your PC offers the option, use its CMOS settings for password-protection. Anyone who wants to get in still can, but only if they're willing to pry off the cover of your PC, reset a jumper on the motherboard, and then reset all your CMOS values. That's enough hassle (and leaves enough evidence of intrusion) to keep out all but the most brazen thieves. The route to the password setup screen varies by manufacturer: On a system with an AMI BIOS, you access the setup routine by pressing F1 or Del at startup. On Toshiba notebooks and most Compaq desktop PCs, you use a separate utility program to write a system-level password in CMOS.

The Windows Way

Use a Windows screen saver with a password option. It's not exactly 007-class security, since anyone can bypass the password by rebooting and restarting Windows. But it will prevent a passing stranger from Alt-Tabbing through open windows to see any work in progress (another reason to make sure you save your work every time you walk away). The password option is located in the Screen Saver section of the Control Panel's Desktop applet. Your password can contain up to 20 characters, including punctuation, and it's not case-sensitive. One caveat is that the encrypted password is a line in the CONTROL.INI file, and anyone can remove it with any text editor.

The Network Lockout

A network password is the most secure and flexible of all. Store your data files on a server, protect your desktop with a Windows screen saver, and anyone who wants to get at your data will run straight into a catch-22. They can

reboot to get past the Windows screen saver, but they'll also lose the network connection and access to your confidential data. On a Novell NetWare network, you set the password by running the SYSCON utility from any prompt, choosing User Information, selecting the user's name (in this case, your own), and selecting Change Password, or by running SETPASS at any DOS prompt. Other networks provide similar facilities. Security, fortunately, is at the heart of a network.

Windows for Workgroups 3.11, which is a network operating environment, offers its own password options. They're generally less powerful than the Novell variety, but you can still lock some doors. If you've given other network users access to a directory or printer, for example, you can choose a read-only password, a full-access password, or both. (Or neither, for that matter, if you don't mind leaving the back door to your system wide open.)

Hide It

If they can't find it, they can't read it. That simple truth is the key to several effective security strategies.

Oops

The most embarrassing lapses are the accidents—you're working on a performance review, and the reviewee reads your first draft while you're away from your desk. The solution? Use a screen saver with a hotkey, like those found in After Dark and Norton Desktop for Windows. Or make your own screen saver by adding a program item to the StartUp group which has the command line filename.scr /s, and then assign a hotkey to it. Then, before you walk to the water cooler, you can save your work and also blank your screen instead of waiting for the screen saver's timer to kick in. Of course, one of the best screen savers is the power switch on your monitor.

One among Many

It's also possible to hide a sensitive file in plain sight, by giving it an innocuous name instead of a tempting one. A snoop will probably zero right in on 95SALARY.XLS, but the same file is less likely to jump out of a crowded directory if it's called WALDO.WK1.

Marked Hidden

Old DOS tricks, like hiding files and directories, are less effective than they used to be now that Windows file utilities routinely let you see hidden, read-only, system, and even deleted files. But you can slow down an unsophisticated intruder by using File Manager's File Properties dialog box or the DOS ATTRIB +H command to hide the files and the directories they're stored in. Make sure you uncheck File Manager's Show Hidden/System Files option (follow the View menu to the By File Type dialog box). This way, any busybodies will have to jump through an extra hoop before they can even find the directory your file is stored in.

The Null

Use Alt-255 as part of a file name. When naming a file or directory, use a null as the last character (hold down the Alt key and type 255 on the numeric keypad to create it). The result looks like a space but doesn't act like one. Anyone using a point-and-shoot navigator like the Windows File Manager can bypass this trick

in a hurry, but in combination with the DOS H attribute it will slow down a technically unsophisticated snoop.

Dollars to Doughnuts

You can do a similar quick-and-dirty trick with shared resource names under Windows for Workgroups 3.11 by adding a dollar sign ($) to the end of the share's name, and it won't show up when another network user browses network resources. That's a minor hassle for legitimate users, who'll have to know the exact name before they can make a connection. But it's a surprisingly effective roadblock for coworkers who are just too curious for their own good (or yours).

Scramble It

Even if someone can find a file and open it, there's not much they can do with it unless they can read the data inside. That's the theory behind encryption programs, which turn the data into a mess of characters that can be unscrambled only with a digital key. Encryption can be simple or sophisticated, depending on how closely you want your office to resemble the set of a Tom Clancy movie.

Password, Please

At a minimum, use your application's password option. Every leading word processor and spreadsheet, for example, includes a document-level password option that also encrypts the file. Is it truly secure? Not really. There's a thriving trade in password cracking programs, fueled mostly by frazzled MIS people who have to unlock crucial documents for users who forget their passwords.

Compress and Encrypt

To move up one rung on the security ladder, try compressing and encrypting your data in a single step. With PKzip Version 2.04g, add the -s (for scramble) option. This adds two levels of hassle—decompressing and decrypting—for a would-be snoop. Other compression programs offer similar options.

PGP

If your paranoia-meter is bouncing around at the top of the scale, don't settle for anything less than Pretty Good Privacy. Forget the ironic understatement in the name—even the nastiest hackers can't crack its public key/private key encryption scheme. There are bootleg versions of PGP floating around on various bulletin boards, but the real thing, Version 2.7, is available in single-user, network, Windows, and CompuServe Information Manager flavors from ViaCrypt.

Take It with You

A thief can't steal anything from an empty office, and a snoop can't nose around in data that isn't there. To be truly safe, take your secrets with you. Copy that file to a floppy, and then erase it from your hard disk. (Just make sure you put the floppy disk in your pocket or lock it up securely.)

Be aware that DOS doesn't really erase that file; it just marks its space as unused. So an amateur detective can reconstruct some or all of the data marked for deletion using simple tools such as the MS-DOS 5 UNDELETE, or Norton Utilities, PC Tools, or another third-party utility. To be safe, use a utility such as WipeInfo, which is part of the Norton Utilities, or Jeff Prosise's Shredder, described above, to scrub those sectors clean.—Ed Bott ∎

NO SIN IN SYNONYMS
Microsoft Bookshelf 1994

Your CEO has decided that a major section of the company's annual report has too much jargon. To translate it into plain English, you're going to have to employ your trusty thesaurus. But which one? The one built into your word processor, the dog-eared copy you used in college, or something else? While some of our testers found the thesaurus in Microsoft Bookshelf 1994 (Roget's Thesaurus) helpful, most—especially the WordPerfect users—preferred the ones already built into their word processors.

To add something from its thesaurus to your current document, Bookshelf uses a copy-and-paste procedure to insert new material. Many of our testers found this operation to be cumbersome and noted the need for smoother integration. And although Bookshelf can paste information directly into a Word document, bypassing the need to copy to the clipboard first, few of our testers discovered this feature on their own.

As a result, most people required more time to reword a document with Bookshelf than without it, and because of the awkward integration, the thesaurus proved to be more hassle than help for our testers from a usability standpoint. —Gordon Meyer

Microsoft Bookshelf 1994
Microsoft
(206) 882-8080
$70

MEMORIES OF COMPOSITION 101
Grammatik 6.0

"Proof this," comes the request from the legal department. The entire document must not only be precisely worded but grammatically perfect as well.

While our testers were reasonably satisfied with the grammar checkers built into their respective word processors, there was a definite preference for proofing the test document with Novell's Grammatik 6.0.

When it came to what Word and WordPerfect can do on their own (the latter incorporating an earlier version of Grammatik), many of our testers complained about the lack of suitable explanations for errors. Several Word users bemoaned its limited nature, and testers from both groups complained about the way in which the built-in grammar checkers seemed to be preoccupied with verbs in the passive tense (that is, sentences using some conjugated form of the verb is). The stylistic choices made by the built-in checkers were yet another bone of contention. Complained one of our testers about the suggestions made, "These were not my changes!"

The majority of both the Word and WordPerfect users saved time using Grammatik. Even those testers whose time savings were negligible praised Grammatik's ease of use and customizable proofing criteria. And since Grammatik is published by Novell, WordPerfect users can easily integrate a standalone version of it into their software.—Gordon Meyer

Grammatik 6.0
Novell
(801) 225-5000
$35

Select Phone

Want to look up a long-lost love? Or maybe a couple of thousand people you can sell salad spinners to over the phone? Either way, Select Phone will help you get the job done. This collection of five CD-ROMs is billed as a comprehensive business and residential phone book of the complete United States (in Windows, DOS, and Mac formats). Naturally, when you get something like this, the first reaction is instinctive—look up your own name. My ego is still shattered by the fact that I couldn't find my name despite the fact that I've lived in my current home for more than a year. But since 2.5 million phone numbers change weekly, and it takes about six months after a new local phone book appears for new numbers to make it into a quarterly update, that's to be expected. Select Phone gives you a nice interface to look up and sort numbers by name, address, and area code, and it performs searches quickly. There's even a stripped-down version of Map Linx that plots the location of all the phone numbers you find. I just haven't figured out why I'd want to.

Select Phone
Pro CD
(617) 631-9200
$149 with one free update,
$400 per annual subscription

RISKY BUSINESS
Risks Digest

Did you hear the one about the squirrel that shut down the NASDAQ computerized stock-trading system for 34 minutes in August? It's no joke, especially for the now-deceased rodent, who picked the wrong piece of cable to gnaw on while scampering about outside the stock market's computer center in Trumbull, Connecticut.

According to news reports, the sudden blackout caused trade reconciliation algorithms to fail, sending the system into overload. A supposedly fail-safe backup power supply didn't switch on, either. Oops.

This wasn't the first computer-related problem at NASDAQ in 1994; it was just the first to make the *Wall Street Journal* and *The New York Times*. But for anyone who subscribes to the Risks Digest, it was a familiar story. If you haven't heard of the Risks Digest, you're not alone. It's the by-product of one of thousands of Internet newsgroups. Its official name—the Forum on Risks to the Public in Computers and Related Systems—doesn't exactly roll off the tongue. And its sponsoring body, the Committee on Computers and Public Policy of the Association for Computing Machinery, isn't exactly a household word.

Most newsgroups provide a virtual soapbox to anyone with a modem and two brain cells to strike together. But the Risks Digest is a moderated newsgroup, which means that every word has to pass the editorial scrutiny of moderator Peter G. Neumann. Contributions that aren't "relevant, sound, in good taste, objective, cogent, coherent, concise, and nonrepetitious" are rejected. Everything else is subject to editing.

The result is an extremely witty virtual magazine with a simple message: Blind devotion to computer technology translates directly into risks to our daily lives. What constitutes a risk? For starters, there's public safety, such as our faith that a big enough CPU can keep high-speed trains from smacking head-first into one another or land a jumbo jet without human intervention.

If you prefer to attach a dollar value to your hazards, take your pick of economic risks. Like automated price-scanning systems, which routinely err in the grocer's favor as surely as a piece of buttered toast will hit the ground business-side down. Or automated securities-trading programs like the one that ruined the day for several thousand capitalists (and one unlucky squirrel) earlier this year.

The most frightening risk of all is the full-court press on privacy that computers make not just possible but inevitable. The Clipper Chip is the most heavily hyped risk to privacy, but the Risks Digest is full of chilling, matter-of-fact accounts of everyday assaults on our private lives that involve nothing more complicated than a database manager and an out-of-control bureaucracy.

How would you like it, for example, if you and your spouse were mistakenly listed as child abusers in a state-run database? That happened to a couple in suburban Washington, D.C., after a doctor mistakenly diagnosed their infant's rare bone infection as a fractured arm. The state acknowledges that the database entry is in error, but refuses to correct it. An appeals court upheld the state's decision, holding that there is no constitutional right to have records of an investigation destroyed. Meanwhile, the damning (and completely untrue) allegations have a digital life of their own.

More than anything else, though, the Risks Digest is a good read. I look forward to seeing it plop in my electron-

ic mailbox two or three times a week. If you missed the Risks Digest in the last six months, you missed some pretty good stories, like the following e-mail message one correspondent received last summer: "One of IBM's electronic mail distribution nodes [recently] experienced a problem routing mail…This may have resulted in your having received proprietary information that was not intended for you. If you have received such information, please return it to the Internet address: xxx@xxx.ibm.com without retaining any copies of it. If you have already destroyed or discarded the information, please confirm this by sending a note to this address stating that the information you received has been destroyed."

Kafka would have been proud. And I now think twice about trusting anything to e-mail.

Yes, there are unique risks to us all as a result of the widespread and sometimes unquestioned adoption of computer technology. You can stay in touch by reading the Risks Digest (look for the Usenet newsgroup comps.risk) or Peter G. Neumann's just-published compilation of material from the same source, Computer-Related Risks (ACM Press and Addison-Wesley, 1994). If you do, you just might discover two surprising facts. Internet newsgroups really can be literate and tasteful. And anyone who takes com-

puter technology for granted is living in a fantasy world.—Ed Bott

Risks Digest

Business Library Volume 1

In the business world, information is power. The person with the fastest draw on data wins the conference room shoot-out. Business Library Volume 1 is the Colt 45 around these office parts. This collection of 12 books puts hundreds of facts essential to running a business at your fingertips. What's the best tax advantage you can get on a real estate investment? What customs laws could affect your new export plans? What bright idea can you use as the basis for a direct-mail marketing campaign? The answers to questions like these are just a mouse click away.

Covering business communications, telemarketing, selling strategies, finance, real estate, and international business and travel, this CD includes essential books that every business can benefit from having. There's even one about climbing the corporate ladder. The latest version of Business Library also includes

three business videos, as well as a new Windows interface that makes the material easy to search and integrate into your reports, marketing plans, and business correspondence. This disc can mean never having to tell your boss or a client, "Sorry, I don't know that."—Ron White

Business Library Volume 1
Allegro New Media
(800) 424-1992; (201) 808-1992
$59.95

Multimedia Business 500

Wouldn't you love a corporate spy, someone who could give you the skinny on your competitors and potential clients? Forget wiretaps and hidden cameras—much of the information a spy would get for you is already available in Multimedia Business 500, a collection of detailed data on the 500 largest public and private companies in the country.

The multimedia referred to in the program's title consists mainly of Windows videos about the companies and their products. These videos make handy backgrounders—watch one and you'll be able to approach a company with what seems like firsthand knowledge of what it does. A decent search engine lets you find a particular company quickly, and handy onscreen buttons present preconfigured details, graphs, and financial facts so you can quickly see trends.

Multimedia Business 500 does the snooping for you. It

provides pertinent, sometimes juicy information on hundreds of companies, from the salaries of their executives to their sales and stock price histories.—Ron White

Multimedia Business 500
Allegro New Media
(800) 424-1992; (201) 808-1992
$49.95

SHHH! IT KNOWS WHERE YOU LIVE

Scan/US

If you can't target your customers with cross-hair accuracy, your marketing plans—no matter how creative—will fail. To distribute materials efficiently, plan branch office locations, and target direct mailings, you need accurate demographic information fast.

Your choices? Spend thousands (or tens of thousands) of dollars for a custom report from a demographer, or fork over just $695 for Scan/US's geomarket software for Windows and make an unlimited number of custom reports for yourself. Not a tough choice.

Scan/US is a serious data arsenal for marketers, sales professionals, or just about anyone who needs accurate customer demographics. Suppose your target market is college-educated 35-to 45-year-olds earning $60,000 or more per year, and you want to know where they live. Scan/US pinpoints this market down to county, city, zip code—even 1/16-square-mile accuracy.

The program comes with figures from the most recent census (1990) and projections based on it. In the base package, all the census variables you might need are covered, including population trends, race, age, and labor force data.

Beyond basic demographics, there are figures that include household and family income, school enrollment, and education by race. And if you need to know median house prices in a given area, you can get some idea of that, too—although fast-changing data like this isn't always correctly tracked by the census department.

Added to the demographics are geographical snippets that go beyond county and state lines. The U.S. Interstate road network, cities, and large shopping malls are covered in the program's various views.

You can also add data of your own to the program painlessly. If you have a database of clients with zip codes, you can import Excel, DBF, or ASCII data and have it recognized right away. And Scan/US sells packs of business-related data, such as shopping mall break downs and zip codes, separately.

It's just as easy to export data. We produced an information-dense report in minutes by exporting regional demographic information to a spreadsheet and formatting the data a little. For researching business proposals, it's a godsend.

You're new to demographics? Don't worry about it—the program's clear primer and the accompanying subscriptions to Business Geographics and American Demographics magazines get you started. And the easy map-based Windows layout, while a little fussy at first, is less overwhelming once you get used to it.—Matthew J. Lake

Scan/US
Scan/US
(800) 272-2687; (310) 820-1581
$695

Government Spending

Oh great, I thought, when I got Government Spending in the mail, more statistics for old men to complain about at family gatherings. But no, it's just the opposite. This is a CD for enterprising executives who want the feds to spend even more—in their direction.

A searchable database of all federal government contracts, Government Spending lets you find out just what your competitors are doing for the government, when their contracts come up for renewal, and exactly how much agencies are paying to whom. The CD is DOS based, and I've seen friendlier interfaces on a ticked-off gorilla. But the concentration required to devise complex searches is rewarded by the depth of material you can access quickly from the more than 425,000 records on the disc.

I can think of at least half a dozen old codgers I'm giving it to. Maybe they'll shut up if they get a first-class ticket to ride the gravy train, too.—Ron White

Government Spending
CD Publishing
(800) 460-2371
$99.95, $250 per year for quarterly updates

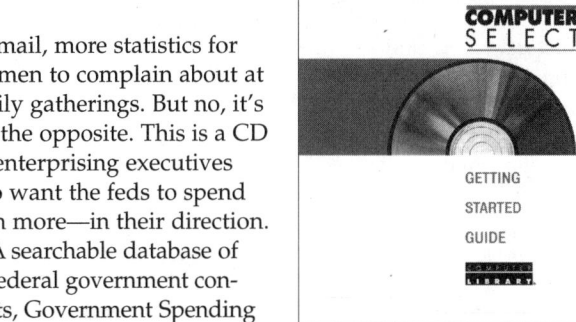

Computer Select

Want to gain a reputation as a computer guru? With Computer Select, you'll soon be spewing out specs for dozens of products and programs. The disk brings you a year's worth of articles from 150 computer publications, including *Macworld*, *PC Magazine*, *PC Week*, and *PC World*. It includes nearly 75,000 articles, 12,500 computer company profiles, 70,000 hardware and software product specifications, and a spiffy search engine.

Computer Select
Computer Library
(800) 827-7889
$1,250

Random House Unabridged Dictionary

If its 315,000 entries seem paltry next to the Oxford English Dictionary's 616,500, that's because the Random House Unabridged Dictionary, Second Edition, doesn't include obsolete terms and expressions. For some users, Random House will be the better choice because it's a dictionary of American English, and it's easier to use.

The definitions may be a bit terse, but Random House's operation is intuitive, and its price is wallet-friendly.

Random House Unabridged Dictionary
Random House Reference and Electronic Publishing
(800) 733-3000
$79

Infoactive

A new monthly bulletin on telecommunications issues for the nonprofit community, Infoactive reports on the latest Internet developments, explains communications technologies, and analyzes legislation in Congress, the White House, and the Federal Communications Commission. Published by the Center for Media Education in Washington, D.C., InfoActive also reports on how nonprofit organizations can take advantage of government-sponsored grants and pilot projects.

Infoactive
Annual subscription rates are $35 for individuals, nonprofit organizations, and the government; $100 for corporations.

Street Atlas USA

This is the program to show friends who are considering a CD-ROM drive. You can find locations by name, zip code, or phone number, but zooming in is the most fun. Start with a map of the U.S.A. and then, at magnification level 7, highway numbers will appear; at level 13, you'll see railroads, and at 15, you'll read street names. With 12 million street segments packed into the disc, we're talking about every street in the country, including those in that old neighborhood you haven't visited for years.

Street Atlas USA
DeLorme Mapping
(800) 452-5931
$169

PhoneDisc PowerFinder

Some businesses live and die by the phone. If you have a permanent crook in your neck from cradling a receiver on your shoulder, you need PhoneDisc PowerFinder. It won't help your neck, but it will help you find any person or business anywhere in the country.

The five-disc set has 91 million residential and business addresses and phone numbers, which can be updated quarterly. If the person you're trying to locate isn't on one of these discs, there's a good chance that he or she hasn't been born yet.

PhoneDisc PowerFinder's information is in the form of databases that you search by name, phone number, street, city, state, zip code, business type, or Standard Industrial Classification number. You can pick a street, for example, and take a cyberstroll down it, seeing which businesses and residences are located along the way. The new Windows interface makes it easier to use than previous versions, and you can export data to popular

contact managers and personal information managers. You can even print directly to popular label and envelope formats.

PhoneDisc PowerFinder
Digital Directory Assistance Inc.
(800) 284-8353; (617) 639-2900
$249

Government Giveaways for Entrepreneurs

The government taketh, but it can giveth as well. At least that's the gospel according to Matthew Lesko, an enthusiastic pitchman who wrote the CD Government Giveaways for Entrepreneurs as a guide for businesses that want to benefit from government programs. His theory is that if you need some information or advice, chances are someone in the federal government has already researched the topic and come up with an answer. And if what you need is money, the CD tells you how to put in for your share of the

grants and contracts lying around just waiting to be claimed by small-business start-ups.

Sound too good to be true? Just watch the video of Lesko admonishing you to take advantage of what your taxes have already paid for—he'll convince you. The CD won't make you rich quick, but it has some of the basic ingredients for people who dream of starting their own businesses. There's even information on how to create a good business plan—something a lot of would-be entrepreneurs can always use advice on.—Ron White

Government Giveaways for Entrepreneurs
Infobusiness Inc.
(800) 657-5300; (801) 221-1100
$59.95

Executive's Factomatic

Forget the fact that the name of this CD makes it sound like something you'd expect to find being hawked on cable TV at 1 a.m. Executive's Factomatic provides no-nonsense advice on topics that most people at the top will sooner or later have to confront, from management salary freezes and white-collar crime to restless managers and backlash from affirmative action and office affairs. Don't know which manager to fire first? This disc will advise you. It will even offer a number of suggestions for getting the accounting department and the warehouse in line.

Unfortunately, there's nothing that even resembles pizzazz in this disc. The Windows interface makes it easy to search through the hyperlinked text, but there are no videos, cute animations, or still graphics to sugarcoat the harsh realities that infringe on the executive suite. It's just text and more text, packed with everything you need to know as an executive. But if you've risen that far, hopefully you can take it.—Ron White

Executive's Factomatic
Compton's NewMedia
(800) 862-2206; (619) 929-2500
$39.95

Secrets of Executive Success

Programs such as Executive's Factomatic are fine if you've already made it to the top and are now trying to hang on. But if you're still climbing the corporate ladder, with others nipping at your heels, give yourself a boost with Secrets of Executive Success.

Do the powers that be say you're too young for a promotion? Did they promote someone less experienced over you? Are you feeling burned out? If you answer yes to any of these questions, then you need this CD. It focuses more on how to manage your own career than how to run the office.

Secrets of Executive Success tells you the things they don't teach in business school: how to better control your body language, the unwritten dress code, ener-

gizing yourself out of passive mode, how to stop worrying, even how to prevent your presentation from being interrupted by gas (no kidding). If you want an office with a view, or simply an office of your own, then this is the CD for you.—Ron White

Secrets of Executive Success
Compton's NewMedia
(800) 862-2206; (619) 929-2500
$39.95

OTHER USEFUL STUFF

AUTOMAP PRO SHOWS BUSINESS TRAVELERS THE WAY TO GO

Automap Pro

Automap Pro is a sophisticated Windows program that allows business travelers to map out long, complex journeys, establish the most efficient way to hit the greatest number of towns in the least amount of time, and figure out how much all those miles are going to cost. Using an Edit Journey window, you can list all the stops you need to make along the way, how long you're going to stay

(including overnights), and whether there are any additional stops you must make. An Optimizer feature then plans out the quickest (according to straight-line distances), fastest (according to actual road distance), or shortest methods of getting through your journey.

Automap Pro comes with a number of databases and overlays that you can add to the map—you can, for example, show all the tourist attractions in an area. But the most useful new feature is the ability to compile your own database (Automap Pro will import DBF and ASCII files) and have that information placed on the map, cross-referenced to such data as zip codes, area codes, or longitude/latitude. The process is not instinctive, but it is effective—after a bit of work and a call to tech support, we were able to import a list of names and zip codes, and have Automap automatically flag them on the map. You can also link your database entries to other file types, such as BMP or WAV files.

Automap Pro's level of detail gets as specific as local roads. But if you need a street-level view of, say, New York or Chicago, the company now offers Automap Streets, a CD-ROM product that lists for $49.95. In addition, users who don't need the more-sophisticated database features may want to try Automap Road Atlas for Windows 3.0, which lists for $79.95.

With the amount of data that the program has to pro-

Buying Smarter:
Macs and PCs—Can We Talk?

i t's top priority. You and your colleagues are working on an ad campaign layout or a competitive analysis that will sway a major decision. Your copywriters are at their PCs, typing up a storm, while your designers are creating illustrations on the Macs. You try to marry the two products and…nothing. You can't get the Mac files into your PC application. Nor will it work the other way around.

Trying to share data with a Macintosh can be like asking for directions in a foreign country: You ask questions and get answers and understand nothing. Fortunately, with a few pieces of knowledge and some software tools, you can read and write Macintosh files as if you were a native.

Dance Steps

Trading documents with Macs involves several steps. The first is to move the file from the Mac to your PC. You can do this with a simple floppy disk or over a network. Either way, you'll need an application that understands the file's format.

If floppy disks are the delivery medium of choice, either you or the Mac users will need a utility that enables your machine to read foreign disks, since Macs format disks differently from the way PCs do. Insignia Solutions and DataViz both have products that enable your PC to recognize a Mac floppy disk.

If your goal is moving editable text from one platform to another, the simplest format to use is pure ASCII text. Most DOS, Windows, and Mac applications can save a document as ASCII text. The first 128 ASCII characters—the lowercase and capital letters, as well as numbers and punctuation marks—are common to both PCs and Macs. Beware, however, of the so-called upper 128 ASCII characters, which differ on Macs and PCs. These include Greek letters and other symbols, and they don't convert with the ASCII format.

The limitation of ASCII text is that it is text only. All of a file's formatting information—such as bold, italic, fonts, and tables—will be lost or converted to meaningless text strings when a file is saved in pure text format.

Same App, Different Platform

One of the benefits of using the same applications for your Macs and PCs is that each version of the software can read files created with the other version and keep the formatting, including embedded graphics. This is true for WordPerfect 6.x for Windows and WordPerfect 3.x for Mac, as well as for the Mac

vide, it isn't surprising that there is an occasional error. For example, the neighborhood of Astoria in Queens, New York, was apparently located in the middle of the East River. However, despite these small flaws, Automap Pro succeeds in offering professional-level mapping

for everyday travelers.—Barbara Krasnoff

Automap Pro
Automap Inc.
1309 114th Ave. S.E.
Suite 110
Bellevue, WA 98004-6999
(800) 440-6277; (206) 455-3552
$399

REACH OUT AND GET HELP
QAPlus/Win

The new version of DiagSoft's diagnostic software package QAPlus/Win offers online access to technical support professionals. While most help-desk tools typically sell for thousands of

dollars and require a dedicated server, QAPlus/Win lists at $99.95 and includes one toll-free call to DiagSoft's new Electronic Technical Support Center (ETSC).

Normally, fixing a system malfunction can lead to hours on the phone, with time wasted not only in determining

the nature of the problem but in pinpointing which vendor is responsible. Whom do you call, for instance, if your word processor won't print—the system manufacturer, the printer maker, or the software vendor? ETSC is designed to solve such problems.

and Windows versions of Microsoft Word 6.0. Word for Mac users can also save in DOS format or rich text format (RTF), which can be read by most versions of Word for Windows. The graphics programs Painter, PowerPoint, and QuarkXPress come in Mac and PC versions that can read the other's files. Some applications, such as Adobe Photoshop and Microsoft Excel, are multilingual, and can read or write in the file formats of several applications.

However, there are still many Mac-only and Windows-only applications, as well as dozens of Mac and PC file formats that some applications can't read. The solution is to translate between file formats using a filtering application, also called a file translation program. These filters will convert formatting information as well as all 256 ASCII characters between a variety of Mac and PC programs.

The most versatile translators are Word for Word from Mastersoft and Conversions Plus from DataViz. Both are general-purpose file translators, digital Rosetta Stones containing thousands of conversion combinations between Mac and PC word processing, database, spreadsheet, page layout, and other formats.

One of the trickiest aspects of converting files is fonts. If you don't have the original font installed on your PC, the translator programs will try to substitute the closest one available. It helps to have the same type of fonts on both PCs and Macs. While Macs use both TrueType (the most common Windows font technology) and Adobe Type I fonts, the latter is far more common in Mac desktop publishing.

Universal Document Formats

If all you need to do is distribute a document that is to be read and not edited (the finished copy of an annual report, for example), you can convert it to a so-called universal document format before you send it on. In these cases, the authors create a document with the goal of broadcasting the information it contains, not its file format. However, readers can annotate the document.

The technical challenges of these read-and-comment situations can be solved by a new breed of software called a universal document reader. Some examples are Adobe's Acrobat, No Hands Software's Common Ground, WordPerfect's Envoy, and Farallon's Replica. Such products convert your documents into read-only images. Users can then read, annotate, highlight, and suggest changes using the product's markup tools.

The Paper Detour

As an absolute last resort, you may consider printing out the files on one platform, then scanning them in on the other. You'll keep all your formatting, but you won't be able to edit the content of the files very easily—they're now bitmapped images. If you run optical character recognition software, you'll gain access to the text, but lose the formatting—back to square one.

Some day, we will all be able to share information without worrying about the application and platform on which it was created. For now, however, we have to use innovative workarounds.—Robert L. Hummel and John Rizzo ■

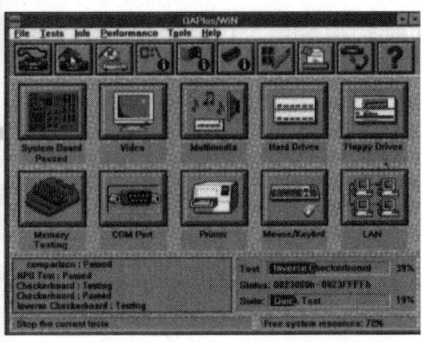

With QAPlus/Win, a simple keypress will run a battery of tests to determine the cause of a system glitch. If the tests are unsuccessful, another button click will automatically connect users to ETSC via modem, upload information about your PC, and prompt you to type in a brief description of the problem. ETSC's support professionals can then gain remote control of the computer to diagnose and fix the malfunction.

Annual ETSC support packages are available, as is support on a per-call basis. Support hours are currently 8 a.m. to 5 p.m. Monday through Friday PST, but queries can be uploaded 24 hours a day. DiagSoft plans to extend the service to 24-hour, seven-day-a-week operation.—Elaine X. Elliott

QAPlus/Win
DiagSoft
$99.95

TRANSLATING FROM ENGLISH TO SPANISH AND BACK AGAIN

Spanish Assistant for Windows

You can get by in spoken Spanish using simple objects and modifiers, but in business letters your Spanish must be idiomatic and grammatically above criticism. That's where Spanish Assistant for Windows enters the picture. It's a translation tool that can handle anything from a word to a book in Ami Pro, Microsoft Word, Microsoft Write, and WordPerfect formats.

At the core of Spanish Assistant is a 100,000-word bilingual dictionary that contains most forms of commonly used words and idiomatic expressions. Of course, Spanish Assistant's accuracy has its limits. There's no artificial intelligence, so it won't "learn" from repeated literary conventions. As a result, Spanish Assistant is far better at handling straightforward business correspondence than academic papers or special-interest articles.—Barry Brenesal

Spanish Assistant for Windows
Microtac Software
(619) 272-5700
$99.95

SQUEEZING YOUR CREATIVE JUICES

Inspiration 4.0

Inspiration is a powerful productivity tool, utilizing features and elements from outliners, flowcharters, and automated graphics and presentation applications. Uniquely, Inspiration seamlessly bridges all of these modes, letting you choose the one that works best for you: Brainstorm in one mode, polish your thoughts in another, and communicate your results to the rest of us in yet another.

Inspiration's diagramming helps you quickly visualize and record your thoughts and ideas (called symbols). For example, type software review as a Main Idea symbol, and then connect related symbols such as evaluate usability and weigh feature set. Inspiration automatically connects them to the Main Idea. Symbols can also be unconnected using Inspiration's Point and Type feature, and with the program's Rapid Fire, graphical symbols appear as quickly as you type them in—perfect for charting a group brainstorming session.

Inspiration is an ideal solution for visualizing, focusing, and organizing your ideas, especially at the start of a new business project when they should be given top priority. Its intelligent diagrams make for great business visuals and presentations, letting you communicate complex information with clarity. Inspiration is an indispensable tool for managers and other business professionals who, for strategic reasons, need an effective idea-mapping application.—Jon Zilber

Inspiration 4.0
Inspiration Software
(800) 877-4292; (503) 245-9011
$82

NETTING A NOTION

IdeaFisher

IdeaFisher tackles your mental block from a slightly different perspective, applying a highly structured methodology to help you discover creative solutions. After stating the problem or issue you want to explore, IdeaFisher walks you through one of several extensive batteries of canned (but customizable) questions. Along the way, it keeps track of your comments and responses in an online journal. If the process doesn't trigger a full solution, the journal should at least provide you with a number of helpful discussion points.

IdeaFisher is best suited for language-related creative challenges. Many of its question sets focus on linguistic tasks, such as product naming and the development of advertising and promotional materials. Separate business plan, presentation and grant proposal modules are also available.

IdeaFisher's best feature is its dictionary containing cross-referenced word associations. Pick any two words, and the program will find related words and the underlying connotations they have in common. Need a headline for a software review? Playing around with different options for the target words software and review or reviewer generated lots of not-so-obvious counterpoints, including air-traffic controller, fuzzy logic, H. Ross Perot, and Terminator 2: Judgment Day.—Jon Zilber

IdeaFisher
IdeaFisher Systems
(800) 289-4332; (714) 474-8111
$82

YOU WON'T GET LOST IF YOUR CAR GIVES YOU DIRECTIONS

Oldsmobile 88 LSS Special Edition

TripMaker

You have to travel; you have to compute. So take it with you and improve the quality of your journey. With Oldsmobile's four-wheeled global positioning system (GPS)—available with power steering—and a digital dictation device, you'll know you're on the right track.

This is not your father's GPS: Don't ask strangers for directions. Your car can tell you the way—and it won't miss an exit. The Oldsmobile Navigation/Information System (NIS) incorporates regional maps and databases with a GPS system right inside an 88 LSS Special Edition.

And while the valet is parking the Olds, you can plan your route from the restaurant with Rand McNally's handy TripMaker software and an IBM ThinkPad 510CS. This laptop displays the maps clearly, but don't leave it on the hood—a gust of wind will blow it away.—Matthew J. Lake

88 LSS Special Edition
Oldsmobile
(800) 535-6537
$23,295

TripMaker
Rand McNally
(800) 627-2897
$79.95

Flashback
Assist /PCvoice

You have a stray thought behind the wheel and want to remember it. Whisper your words into a digital dictation device. Flashback keeps 30 minutes in flash memory; Assist attaches to a PC and creates WAV files.—Matthew J. Lake

Flashback
Norris Communications
(619) 679-1504
$249

Assist /PCvoice
(404) 343-8201
$249

WORD PROCESSING FOR SCIENTIFIC MINDS

Scientific WorkPlace 2.0 for Windows

When TCI Software Research brought out Scientific Word a few years back, you could almost hear the collective sigh of relief in the academic world. Here at last was a Windows technical word processor that not only made it easy to create documents

mixing text and math, but provided a front end to the LaTeX computer typesetting system that most people consider the leader in scientific publishing.

Scientific WorkPlace 2.0 builds on these achievements. Like Scientific Word, it displays formulas and functions as they appear in books, and it spares users the need to insert hellishly complex LaTeX formatting codes into their documents manually. But the package does much more: It provides a fairly complete implementation of Waterloo Maple Software's highly regarded symbolic and numerical mathematics program Maple V release 3.

If you are familiar with Scientific Word, you will be right at home with Scientific WorkPlace. The two products offer the same word processing features. However, newcomers have a surprise in store for them. Although Scientific WorkPlace has the overall look and feel of a standard Windows word processor, it purposely has not been designed to be WYSIWYG. You can change the onscreen appearance of your documents to your heart's content—these changes just don't affect the appearance of the printed text. But what if you really need to modify an existing style or create a new one from scratch? You can—by running a separate Style Editor, which, however, does not let you interactively preview your changes. Whether or not TCI Software Research is right in claiming that this approach makes it easier to

concentrate on content will be a matter of personal taste.

In any event, it's impossible not to be impressed by Scientific WorkPlace's splendid array of easy-to-use tools for entering mathematical expressions into documents. Nearly a score of icons on the main toolbar provides access to different palettes and pick lists of mathematical symbols, functions, operators, and the like. In addition, the program provides a Find and Replace function that works as well with mathematics as with text. There's also a convenient table editor for placing tables in your documents. And more than 100 predefined styles make it easy to create documents that conform to the style requirements of a host of technical publishing houses and scores of academic journals.

Unfortunately, despite its many innovations and general ease of use, Scientific WorkPlace still suffers from some of the traditional aggravations of LaTeX and TeX systems. LaTeX is a dialect of TeX that adds support for such things as automatic table-of-content generation and cross-references. Like virtually every other TeX system, Scientific WorkPlace lacks any file-export function. The reason: Translating TeX codes for mathematics into anyone else's codes poses daunting technical challenges. You can import ANSI, ASCII, RTF, and WordPerfect text files into Scientific WorkPlace, but any mathematics in these files are stripped out. At least one oversight can't be blamed on

LaTeX and TeX's intrinsic complexity: The program lacks a macro function that would let users create their own keystroke shortcuts for common editing commands.

On the other hand, TCI Software Research has done a superb job of integrating the Maple kernel into the Scientific WorkPlace interface. Scientific WorkPlace provides a generous sampling of the heavy-duty graphic, numeric, and symbolic computational functions provided in the package. Many types of computations are easier to perform in Scientific WorkPlace than in the full version of Maple. One reason is that while Scientific WorkPlace displays mathematics the way you learned it, Maple V 3.0 for Windows still displays unsolved equations as complicated ASCII mnemonics and codes. Also, a single Scientific WorkPlace menu option, such as Factor, performs the same functions as several Maple commands (Factor, used with numbers, and Ifactor, used with equations). And Scientific WorkPlace is less picky about mathematical syntax than Maple is.

Still, there's no free lunch, even at the digital deli. For one thing, Scientific WorkPlace's generally excellent online help system provides not a whisper of assistance for Maple. Fortunately, TCI Software Research supplies a well-written manual that puts most of the documentation provided with the full version of Maple to shame. And Maple's programming function and its file

input/output functions are disabled in the Scientific WorkPlace version. This means that you can't, for example, write a short Maple program that reads data into a large matrix from a disk file, perform some calculations on the matrix, and then store the results in a new disk file.

A number of important Maple graphics capabilities are missing. Scientific WorkPlace lacks the marvelous interactive tools that let you instantly modify your view of a 3-D graph. In addition, you cannot create animations or manipulate the position of highlights and shadows in 3-D graphs. Nor can you place text anywhere you wish on a graph or use different types of lines (solid, dashed, and so forth) when displaying more than one data set on a graph. But these caveats are relatively minor. Scientific WorkPlace will not be for everyone—but then, neither is number theory, matrix algebra, or calculus. For technical users who need to move their ideas to paper in the shortest possible time, Scientific WorkPlace's seamless integration of mathematics with word processing makes it a pearl beyond price.—John Gliedman

Scientific WorkPlace 2.0
for Windows
TCI Software Research
1190 Foster Rd.
Las Cruces, NM
(800) 874-2383; (505) 522-4600
$595

Reap the Rewards of Easy File Sharing

Portable document software won't get you a van Gogh on your screen. But when you want to share files that include even unsophisticated formatting, and the person you want to share with has different software or is on a different platform altogether, it can serve well. And it's easy to build a business case for portable documents.

First, converting the original document to simple ASCII text is an inexpensive solution at less than $500. All you need is a little software conversion tool, a communications package, a modem, and an electronic mail service such as CompuServe. Unfortunately, ASCII file conversion is useless for most business applications.

The second method—scanning and optical character recognition—is labor intensive, slow, and prone to human screwups. However, you can equip yourself with an inexpensive laser or ink jet printer, a scanner, and OCR software for less than $1,500.

The third solution? Use portable document software (PDS) to translate files into the format of the receiving computer. Candidates are Adobe's Acrobat, No Hands Software's Common Ground, Farallon Computing's Replica, and WordPerfect Envoy. This alternative is the best one available today. The cost is palatable—less than $1,000 to equip you and a recipient with the proper software—and offers a substantial and continuing return on investment.

The Check Is Not in the Mail

Portable document success stories are easy to find among companies in insurance, financial services, and publishing. Insurance companies use it to cut down on forms, inventories, and mailing costs, and to provide quicker responses to customers. Easier document distribution means less overhead. (Witness my father, who is an insurance agent. After 30 years of hugging paper, PDS drives him crazy. PDS is reengineering him into retirement.)

Financial services use PDS to deliver timely and comprehensive information to clients. Newspapers use PDS to take print advertisements from customers. The advertising industry is also ripe for PDS. Buck & Pulleyn, Eastman Kodak's ad firm, cut costs by 30 percent and production time by 50 percent using Adobe Acrobat.

Closer to home, I have a special need for PDS. I'm working on a project that will tap PDS's ability for full-text indexing and retrieval. My company has more than 100 application manuals. They're printed on paper and distributed to remote sites. This tree assassination costs several hundred thousand dollars annually. The documents are created and maintained on a variety of hardware. And, of course, each application group uses different software. It's possible to turn these isolated manuals into PDS documents and create a CD-ROM collection. So what?

First, it ends the paper chase, which my users hate. It creates the ability to index and electronically retrieve information. Most important, the PDS format provides a workable way to update thousands of pages of text and graphics without scanning and editing them by hand. We save time, which saves money, and paves the way for new work opportunities.

Big Payoff

Tandem Computers uses a customized version of Acrobat to create CD-ROMs with catalogs, fact sheets, white papers, and presentation materials. Creating, editing, maintaining, and distributing paper documents would have cost them millions of dollars. They figure the PDS/Acrobat/CD-ROM combination costs one-tenth of that.

In the long run, portable document software improves communication among people so they can produce better widgets. That's the key to using PDS and that's the key to justifying it.—Marc Dodge ∎

TWO MAPPING PROGRAMS HELP YOU GET FROM HERE TO THERE

Streets On A Disk 6.0
Map 'n' Go 1.0

Streets On A Disk 6.0 and Map 'n' Go 1.0 are very different approaches to map-routing programs that complement each other. Either of the two will get you from here to there, but while Map 'n' Go is a flashy CD-ROM Windows routing program for long-distance travelers, Streets On A Disk provides a comprehensive set of tools for those whose business requires intimate knowledge of local roads.

With Map 'n' Go, you use a dialog box to establish the starting and ending cities for your journey and as many as 48 other cities to visit en route. You can search for specific cities on the basis of area code, zip code, or city name. Once your itinerary is established, Map 'n' Go will calculate either the shortest route, the fastest route, or the route that adheres to your preferences for roads, such as back roads. It then highlights the route on-screen and provides a travel plan. Because Map 'n' Go doesn't include lesser roads such as county highways, it probably won't please scenery buffs or those interested in traversing the roads less traveled. It does, however, include a sizable database of suggested stops, such as historical sites. While you can print descriptions of the sites, Map 'n' Go doesn't provide directions to them.

While Map 'n' Go is excellent for intercity travelers, Streets On A Disk is a powerful tool for those who use regional roads. Streets requires that you buy extra county maps that include every road. The interface is straightforward but is less intuitive than Map 'n' Go. Streets offers an exceptional level of detail and flexibility. For example, you can search for itinerary points on a number of criteria, including street addresses and even latitude and longitude. Itineraries can have as many stops as you want, making Streets ideal for the planning and dispatching of truck or car routes. Streets even supports the satellite-based Global Positioning System (GPS). If you buy third-party GPS modules for each vehicle in your fleet and link them to Streets, you can view the location of the vehicles on-screen as they move.

Even with its dated DOS interface, Streets On A Disk is a powerful tool for those who must master the roads in their region. However, if you need a tool for planning long-distance road trips, Map 'n' Go is fast, simple, and thorough. Map 'n' Go requires 4MB RAM, 3MB hard disk space, CD-ROM drive, Microsoft Windows 3.1 or later. Streets On A Disk requires 500K lower memory; 2MB extended memory, 3MB hard disk space, Klynas Engineering, DOS 5.0 or later, Microsoft Windows 3.1 or later. —David Haskin

Map 'n' Go
DeLorme Mapping
Lower Main St
Freeport, ME 04032
(207)865-9291
fax: (800) 452-5931
Estimated Price: $50

Streets On A Disk
P.O. Box 499
Simi Valley, CA 93062
(805) 583-1133; (805) 583-1133
fax: (805) 583-1457
$225 plus $95 per county

Taxi

Are you a business traveler who has trouble navigating strange cities? A traditional way of getting the scoop on a city is to interrogate those founts of urban wisdom, taxi drivers. A more dependable way is to interrogate Taxi, a CD packed with intelligent maps of most major U.S. cities, including New York, Chicago, Los Angeles, and San Francisco.

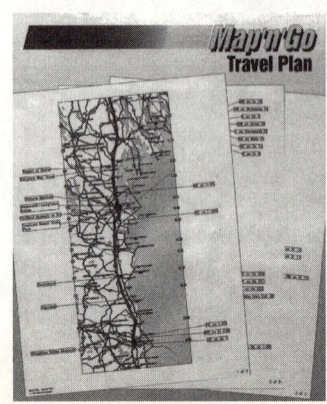

Taxi's maps are intelligent because they're linked to Zagat travel guides, which include detailed appraisals of many hotels and restaurants. Want to take one of your most important clients to a French restaurant with a good wine list and don't care what it costs? Taxi will provide you with a list of all the places that match this criteria—with details on their food, service, and pricing—and show you where they are on a map. It can even show you the best routes to the restaurants from your hotel or your client's address.

Taxi lets you print its maps or copy them to a hard disk so you don't have to carry a CD-ROM drive with your laptop when you're on the road. The only thing the program needs is a surefire way to hail a real taxi when it's raining.—Ron White

Taxi
News Electronic Data
(800) 439-8294; (908) 735-2555
$79.95

Let Taxi be your guide to New York, Chicago, Los Angeles, San Francisco & Washington D.C.

Taxi
CD ROM With Zagat Surveys

EASY SCRIPT FORMATTING
Final Draft

Final Draft offers screenwriters all the functions of a word-processing program while eliminating all the formatting hassles specific to screenwriting. Its built-in macros let you apply standard script styles or type common phrases (such as "CUT TO:") with just a couple of keystrokes. The program also lets you easily mark changes as a script goes through the revision process, showing revisions in red type on-screen and marking them with asterisks in the right margin if you choose. In addition, Final Draft takes care of page breaks (automatically inserting continued where required) and scene numbering or renumbering—unless you lock your file, which allows you to add text and scenes without changing scene numbers or page breaks.

Final Draft's word-processing features are quite complete. The program includes a spelling checker, a thesaurus, a print-preview mode, and even an annotations option. Although a few of the features are awkward to use—it's not as easy as it should be to reformat sections of text, for instance—most perform as smoothly as the features in mainstream word processors. Final Draft supports Microsoft's RTF (Rich Text Format), so you can exchange files easily with other word processors that support RTF.

Final Draft costs about as much as full-fledged word processors, but it saves you enough time that it's money well spent—especially if you sell your script.—Jason Snell

Final Draft
MacToolkit
Santa Monica, CA
$349

Ambassador

Ever wished you could write a letter in English and have it print in Japanese, or vice versa? Either scenario can come true with the Japanese version of Ambassador, a bilingual document program (soon to be available in European-language versions as well) that translates commonly needed business phrases involving movements of people, money, information, and merchandise.

The program includes 190 model letters and forms, 467 canned sentences (such as "Damage occurred in transit…"), and translations of 1,250 business words and place names (plus the option to add 250 more words in kanji).

Businesses that often need to communicate simple logistical information across the English/Japanese language barrier may find using Ambassador a cost-effective strategy. Even with the selection of hundreds of canned choices, however, you'll sometimes find that what you want to say is not there. If your communication is at all complicated, you may be better off reaching for the phone and an expert interpreter on AT&T's Language Line (at standard long-distance rates plus $3.50 per minute extra).—Marilyn Bancel

Ambassador
Language Engineering Corp.
385 Concord Avenue
Belmont, MA 02178
(617) 489-4000
Version 1.0. $295;
KanjiTalk, $250

Anti-Static Cleaning Towelettes

Work-at-home Macs are magnets for everything from cat hair to fingerprints. Clean up with Anti-Static Cleaning Towelettes, premoistened towelettes that clean your screen, remove dust-attracting static, and are guaranteed not to scratch or streak displays.

Anti-Static Cleaning Towelettes
Allsop
$6.95

Drive Tech Floppy Diagnostic

Drive Tech Floppy Diagnostic includes a drive-cleaning kit and diagnostic software that tests your floppy drive's health. The drive-cleaning kit is a must for anyone who works in a dusty environment.

Drive Tech Floppy Diagnostic
MicroMat Computer Systems
$59.95

Toner Tuner

Laser-printer owners who want to save money on toner cartridges will love Toner Tuner, a utility that lets you control just how much ink your printer puts down on paper. If you're printing just draft versions of documents, printing them with less toner makes the cartridge you have last a lot longer—it's kinder to the environment too.

Toner Tuner
Working Software
$24.95

CD Caddy

Keeping CD-ROMs in a caddy is the best way to eliminate scratches and dust, which can slow your drive's read mechanism. So for the CD-ROM freak who has everything, consider picking up a CD Caddy 5-pack.

CD Caddy
CD Technology
$24.95

CD-ROM Organizer

Anyone who has begun collecting CD-ROMs will appreciate the CD-ROM Organizer, which neatly stores 25 CD-ROMs. Organizers can be stacked as your collection grows.

CD-ROM Organizer
Allsop
$15.95

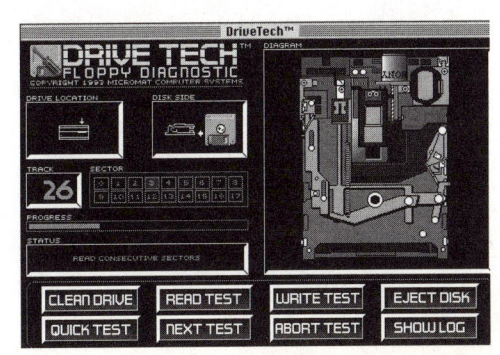

SIMM Remover

The SIMM Remover makes performing memory upgrades a little simpler by letting you easily lift out old SIMMs. It comes with easy-to-follow directions, but you have to provide your own grounding strap.

SIMM Remover
Stratos
$4.99

SECTIONS

ESSAYS

Fun

un. Work really hard, play really hard. That's the motto of most computer users I know. The biggest payoff of computers hasn't been increasing your productivity; it's been increasing your opportunity to play solitaire, DOOM, or some other completely unproductive pursuit. When I'm feeling defensive, I like to point out that many games, such as SimCity for instance, really do provide a great deal of educational benefit. But that's really beside the point, because I've got a gut feeling that having fun is actually good for you. So it's no surprise to me that the computer world is just chock full of fun stuff.

In *CyberSource:Fun*, we indulge ourselves by taking a merry jaunt through the wacky world of computer fun and games. We'll show you games, games, and more games: arcade, adventure, fantasy, role-playing, simulation, and strategy—it's all here. We'll also show you some amusing software that doesn't have anything to do with games, from silly screensavers to computer books that talk to your kids. And we'll also take a look at the serious side of fun, such as movies, art, and music.

ADD ONS

Bloopers

College wouldn't be college without a few pranks, right? With Bloopers, you can booby-trap any Mac in many ways. Make really disgusting sounds emanate from the speakers. Make your roommate's word processor type messages by itself. Or make the victim's cursor drift off the screen, even though the mouse isn't moving.

Bloopers
Binary Software
$25

LIVEN UP YOUR DESKTOP
Now Fun!

Any program with the word fun in its name has a lot to live up to. But Now Fun!, a collection of five control panels from Now Software, provides enough desktop-livening action that you're sure to find something worthy of the name. Fun Screen Savers, similar to After Dark, includes more than two dozen screen-saver modules, ranging from ho-hum to awesome, plus a game—Xeno Blaster—that we liked even better than More After Dark's Lunatic Fringe. Fun Screen Savers can also use most After Dark and More After Dark modules.

Fun Pictures lets you replace your desktop pattern with any PICT, EPS, GIF, MacPaint, or Wallpaper picture or pattern. Like Thought I Could's Wallpaper, it can display repeating patterns on your desktop. But unlike Wallpaper, Fun Pictures allows pictures of any size (not just 128 × 128 pixels) and lets you arrange multiple pictures on your desktop, although multiple-color pictures tend to slow your Mac appreciably.

Fun Sounds, like the shareware program SoundMaster or Nova's Kaboom!, lets you assign sounds to Mac events such as emptying the Trash or inserting or ejecting a disk. It includes more than 100 sounds of varying quality and usefulness. Fun Cursors is similar to the freeware control panel CursorAnimator. It lets you replace your cursors—the arrow, the beach ball, the cross hair, and so on—with colorful animated cursors.—Bob LeVitus

Now Fun!
Now Software
Portland, OR
(800) 938-8669; (503) 274-2800
$69

Screenies

For visual stimulation, try framing your monitor with a Screenie, a cardboard frame that comes in one of 100 variations, from a Baroque-style gilt picture frame to a politically correct rain-forest scene—there are even Screenies for kids. For the home office, try the corkboard or whiteboard models, onto which you can pin or scribble notes. In sizes to fit 9-inch or 13- to 15-inch monitors.

Screenies
$9.95 and $11.95

Zounds

Change your auditory environment with Zounds, a control panel/sound package that lets you set groups of sounds (farm noises, a tropical setting) to play through your Mac's speaker at random intervals. Just beware: Some people love this program, but others find it annoying.

Zounds
Digital Eclipse Software
$39.95

PowerBall

Getting sick of the granite-gray look of your PowerBook? Replace the trackball with a colorful PowerBall. The balls, colored orange, yellow, green, or pink, come in sizes to fit all PowerBooks, including the 100s and the Duos.

PowerBall
APS Technologies
$9.95; set of four, $19.95

Wallpaper The Zebra Edition
Wallpaper Light & Dark

For users of black-and-white PowerBooks—and other Macs without color or gray-scale displays—comes Wallpaper The Zebra Edition, a new version of the popular desktop-pattern utility. Now you don't need to keep staring at that plain old gray grid on your desktop. And if you have a color PowerBook (or desktop machine), Wallpaper Light & Dark gives you even more patterns and lets you run After Dark modules.

Wallpaper The Zebra Edition
Wallpaper Light & Dark
Thought I Could Software

Baseball Mousepad

True baseball fans can show their allegiance to the home team with a Baseball Mousepad featuring the official logo of their favorite major-league team.

Baseball Mousepad
MouseWares
$13.99

NiteCap

Dropping a NiteCap over the top of your Mac shields it from even the dustiest dorm room. And because NiteCaps have cool patterns, they liven up the room while they're protecting your Mac.

NiteCap
$18 to $22, depending on size

Bliss Saver

Bliss Saver is a design-it-yourself screen saver that decorates your monitor with animated paintings. The color synthesizer lets you add colors, shapes, and textures with a keystroke. Even with all the paintings loaded, this program takes up only 4MB of disk real estate.

Bliss Saver
Imaja
$49.95

Save your screen with a symphony of animation and color! Simply touch the keyboard for fabulous color effects!

imaja

"There is no reason anyone would want a computer in their home."—Ken Olson, president, chairman and founder of Digital Equipment Corp., 1977.

UnderWare

UnderWare is a control panel that animates After Dark modules (and its own modules) on your desktop so you can watch flying toasters while you're working in your favorite application. UnderWare also offers its own After Dark-compatible screen saver, although it doesn't run special After Dark modules such as the Star Trek or Disney screen savers.

UnderWare
Bit Jugglers
$59.95

MouseStick
GamePad

If you're used to the feel of a Nintendo or Sega game pad or like handling a joystick, the MouseStick II or the GamePad is what you need. The MouseStick is best suited for flight or driving simulators; the GamePad is good for

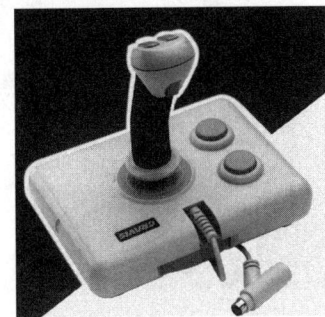

arcade-style games. These devices hook into the ADB port and have custom settings for various games (they're not compatible with all games).

MouseStick
Advanced Gravis Computer Technology
$99.95

GamePad
Advanced Gravis Computer Technology
$49.95

Flightstick Pro

One of the most popular products in this category is the Flightstick Pro from CH Products. This is a large unit with trim wheels for both axes, and smooth, fluid motion. To the left of the stick is a large wheel that serves as the throttle control for FS5.

The trigger on the stick activates the brakes—as with most joysticks—but there are three more buttons and a "coolie-hat" control on the large top surface of the stick. The three buttons control the

flap settings and landing gear (toggles up and down). The coolie hat is a four-position switch that selects different views: forward, sideways, and back. With a pair of rudders, you can do much of your flying without touching the keyboard.

Speaking of rudders, CH Products was scheduled to come out with a pair of rudder pedals after press time. The pedals will pivot for flight simulators, but can also move independently for car-driving games. CH Products is also slated to release a new version of its popular Virtual Pilot; the Pro model will add six buttons and a pair of four-way switches to the existing yoke and throttle controls, offering even more control than the Flightstick Pro.

Flightstick Pro
CH Products
970 Park Center Dr.
Vista, CA 92083
(800) 624-5804
$99.95

Pro FCS and Mark II WCS

In spite of the fact that they were created primarily to support combat sim programs, the Pro Flight Control System (FCS) and Mark II Weapons Control System (WCS) combine to make a winning pair for FS5 fans as well. The FCS is a large, solid joystick with a bunch of buttons; it also is one of the stiffest controllers in the bunch. The WCS is a potato-shaped handle on a stick that bristles with its own set of buttons. The FCS uses a standard game-port connector that plugs into the back of the WCS (as does your keyboard), and then the WCS plugs into your computer's game and keyboard ports.

You now have more than 16 switches and buttons that you can program to issue just about any keystroke or combination of keystrokes you need. These switch assignments are set up in text files that you then download to the controls before starting

up FS5. The units come with predefined files for a number of games, including FS5, so you can get started without having to learn the programming language.

Pro Flight Control System
ThrustMaster Inc.
10150 S.W. Nimbus
Portland, OR 97223-4337
(503) 639-3200
$149.95

Mark II Weapon Control System
ThrustMaster Inc.
10150 S.W. Nimbus
Portland, OR 97223-4337
(503) 639-3200
$149.95

buttons, even when assigning multiple keystrokes to a single button.

Thunderstick With OTC
MicroSpeed Inc.
5005 Brandin Ct.
Fremont, CA 94538
800 438-7733; (510) 490-1403
$90

Phoenix Flight and Weapons Control System

The new Phoenix Flight and Weapons Control System from Advanced Gravis looks like a spaceship from a "Star Trek: Deep Space Nine" episode, and is serious when it comes to flight-sim controls. It plugs into both your game and keyboard ports, and provides elevator and aileron control; rudder and throttle control; and 24 programmable buttons, each of which can be defined to have two different functions.

There is also an excellent configuration program that makes it easy to define a con-

figuration or explore one of the predefined ones that come with the unit. You can use the Windows-like menus, or simply click on the image of the Phoenix and its buttons to see what each button is defined to do. Then you download the configuration to the unit, and you're ready to fly.

Controlling the rudder with your left hand may take some adjustment, but the push/pull throttle control is easy and natural. The joystick itself has variable tension settings in four directions, so you can get just the touch you want. This one works as great as it looks.—Alfred Poor

Phoenix Flight and Weapons
Control System
Advanced Gravis Computer
Technology Ltd.
1790 Midway Ln.
Bellingham, WA 98226
(800) 663-8558; (604) 431-5020
$149.95

🖐 "There is no reason anyone would want a computer in their home."—Ken Olson, president, chairman and founder of Digital Equipment Corp., 1977.

NEW FUN TO YOUR DESKTOP

After Dark for Windows 3.0

While the odds of getting phosphor burn on your monitor are pretty slim, screen savers are still a lot of fun. True, they can prevent unauthorized people from accessing your machine without the password, but for After Dark fans, it's really all about flying toasters. They can become an obsession. And just when you think the obsession may pass, Berkeley Systems releases version 3.0 of After Dark for Windows.

Some 15 new modules have been added, along with updates of 13 from the original package. Bad Dog digs up your desktop, rips apart icons, and generally wreaks havoc. Draw Morph not only gives you various images that change and move smoothly across your screen, but lets you create your own line art for morphing. Rat Race has harnessed rodents running a circular track, though they spend more time preening and running the wrong way. You Bet Your Head is an interactive quiz show that is complete with cartoon violence.

Thunderstick With OTC

The new Thunderstick With OTC joystick from Microspeed also provides programmable buttons. It has a throttle slider along the left side of the housing and eight buttons on the front panel. The joystick action is on the stiff side, and perhaps a little more difficult to control than those with a lighter touch. The unit comes with software that makes it easy to program the

The ever-popular flying toasters have new behavior patterns—barrel rolls, toast that can pop from one toaster to another, and so forth. Perhaps the quirkiest addition is the flying-toaster anthem, "On Mighty Toaster Wings," complete with a karaoke feature that scrolls the lyrics on your screen. Sadly, you can only access these if you have a sound card, and the plaintive flapping noise on the PC speaker is gone. Several of the new modules will not run without a card that supports 256 colors, and some of those visible in 16 colors have additional features at higher resolutions.

The new After Dark control panel includes options to update custom modules, screen-saving during full-screen DOS sessions under Windows, and support for shutting down Eco-Logic-compliant monitors.—Jim Freund

Berkeley Systems Inc.
2095 Rose St.
Berkeley, CA 94709
(800) 344-5541; (510) 540-5535
$49.99

MICROSOFT SCENES SCREEN SAVERS BRING CULTURE TO YOUR DESKTOP

Microsoft Scenes

While most screen savers tend to go for the cute, funny, or downright scathing, Microsoft has chosen a somewhat different path. Its combination screen saver and wallpaper program, Scenes, is

to After Dark what PBS is to the Fox Network.

Scenes comes in three visually stunning collections, each made up of 48 different slides. Outer Space features photographed space vistas such as Earth from Apollo 17 and the Horsehead Nebula; Impressionists offers work from famous artists such as Cezanne, Degas, Gauguin, and Monet; and Sierra Club includes photographs from the Adirondack Mountains, Grand Canyon, and other natural wonders. A portion of the proceeds from the Sierra Club collection goes to that organization.

A small control window is your command center. On the left side, you preview the next slide that will appear on the screen saver; on the right, you see the current slide being used as wallpaper. You can select the collection you want to use as a screen saver (but not which specific slide); the kind of wipes you want between each slide; and the length of time each image remains onscreen. If you're using Scenes as wallpaper, you can have it switch slides

each time the screen saver changes, or have it remain as a more permanent background picture.

If customization is what you seek, you have the option of creating a personalized collection using your own BMP or DIB files. And proud parents can take advantage of a deal Microsoft has worked out with Genographics Corp., where they can have three photographs converted into Scenes format free of charge.

Lovers of After Dark can also join the cultural elite. Microsoft lets you run the Scenes screen saver, though not the wallpaper, directly from After Dark.

There is one unfortunate side effect to all this quality—performance. It took nearly 60 seconds to change slides on a 486DX2/66 with 16MB of RAM; on a slower machine, the wait is a lot longer. To its credit, the program doesn't hold you up if it's in the process of changing slides—as soon as you move your mouse, you're back in your application. In addition, Microsoft recommends that

you use at least 256 colors on your display; while the slides are certainly visible at 16 colors, they will not be at their best.—Barbara Krasnoff

Microsoft Scenes
Microsoft Corp.
One Microsoft Way
Redmond, WA 98052-6399
(800) 426-9400; (800) 563-9048
$29.95/each collection

DELIGHTING THE AUDIO-VISUAL SENSES

Imaginaria

In addition to safeguarding your CRT from phosphor burn-in and blanking your screen for security on demand, Claris Clear Choice's Imaginaria screen saver adds multimedia pizzazz to your rest breaks. Imaginaria features three types of screen modules. First, there are ten simple but eye-catching animations that parade across the desktop as you work in Windows applications. You'll see fanciful depictions of a winged monkey, a monarch butterfly, a rowboat, and more. These objects move in and out of view behind open windows.

Second, Imaginaria offers 11 dynamic transition screens that appear before the screen saver actually kicks

in. Some transitions are just special-effect wipes and dissolves; others are humorous animations like a tuxedoed, opera-singing bulldog or a finger-snapping, egg-tossing frog. Finally, 15 photo-realistic animated scenes strut their stuff (with MIDI sound effects and music) after a designated period of inactivity.

You can configure the program to run automatically when Windows starts up, or launch it manually by double-clicking on its desktop icon. You can specify how long Imaginaria waits before blanking the screen, whether moving the mouse to certain corners will disable the saver or activate it immediately, and whether the modules and animations appear in random or selected order. If you define a special hotkey combination, you can start the screen saver on demand from the keyboard.

You can stop Imaginaria's animations when your computer is busy or prevent modules from activating when a

istic pile of red pixels. You don't shoot a gun, you press a Ctrl key. It's not a bullet flying, just some white pixels moving on a small screen. Nobody thinks anything of the ersatz blood and guts, since that's too ludicrous to

for for for for for for for for for for for

serial or parallel port is active (as during modem communications or a printing session). There's even a Power Saver option for Energy Star-compliant systems—if activated, the screen goes black and all animation stops after a designated interval. Imaginaria's exotic scenes and surrealistic animations make it an audio-visual treat that entertains as it works.

—Carol S. Holzberg

Imaginaria
Claris Clear Choice
5201 Patrick Henry Dr.
Santa Clara, CA 95052-8168
(800) 325-2747; (408) 987-7000
$49

Altec Lansing ACS50 Personal Computer Speaker System

Back in 1992, when multimedia still meant SPEAKER.- DRV and some sound files for Windows startup, Altec Lansing was already anticipating the convergence of the PC and high-end audio. Its ACS300 speaker system ($285 at USA Flex) took the reviewers by storm with rich sound, a separate bass subwoofer for ambient effects, and controls that let you mix two sound sources at whatever level you like. While this set still remains the choice for the PC audiophile, the company's entry into the low-end market with its modestly priced ACS50 was the magic combo that won our readers' hearts and ears.

Longtime advertiser and reseller USA Flex sells the ACS50 for a mere $75, slightly higher than a plain set of Labtecs, but clearly a cost-effective solution, considering the convenience features and sound quality. Replete with an amplifier module that sits atop your monitor, the set is known for its wide tonal range and the stick-on Velcro setup that attaches the speakers to the monitor as quickly as donning a pair of earmuffs.

Sound on the multimedia PC is still light-years from the THX experience, but it only takes the ACS50 to rival your average Discman speakers. Unlike other speakers in their class, the ACS50s feature special circuitry in the amplifier to boost bass signals when the volume is low in order to ensure that the sound doesn't seem hollow.

You can even blend sound from two different sources like the ACS300, albeit without a special control on the speakers to mix it precisely. While most multimedia PCs still come with more run-of-the-mill speaker offerings, the ACS50 is clearly an inexpensive way to upgrade your existing PC with audio.

Maybe you mess around with MIDI files, or perhaps you just like Star Wars: Imperial Pursuit. Whatever your excuse, you can buy a pair of Altec Lansings through USA Flex.

—Jim O'Brien

ACS50
USA Flex
471 Brighton Dr.
Bloomingdale, IL 60108
(800) 944-5599
$75

Altec Lansing Multimedia ACS 100.1

Altec Lansing has been a leader in multimedia speakers ever since it introduced the innovative ACS 300 speaker system in 1992. At $350, however, that system is out of reach for many PC owners, so Altec has expanded its line with the ACS 100.1.

The ACS 100.1 system, a smaller version of the ACS 300 design, is a real value. Each of the two clamshell-style speakers contains two drivers, a dome tweeter for crystal-clear treble, and a 3-inch midrange and bass driver. Up front are controls for volume, bass, and treble. Although the internal power amplifier supplies 12 watts per channel, these speakers are not as efficient as others, so the maximum volume level—while enough to fill an office—is somewhat less than that of the Yamaha or Roland speakers reviewed here.

The ACS 100.1 includes a mini-headphone jack, which automatically mutes the speakers for private listening, as well as an on/off button and two audio inputs to accommodate additional sound sources, such as a portable CD player.

Front-mounted bass and treble controls enable you to adjust the sound to your taste, and the system can accommodate a subwoofer to improve bass response (the ACS 150, an additional $150). While the speakers are sharp on the high notes, there is some weakness in the low end, both with and without the subwoofer. Overall, though, the sound quality is excellent. Its low distortion and sonic accuracy are apparent on a variety of music, from classical to rock.—John R. Quain

Altec Lansing Multimedia
ACS 100.1
Altec Lansing Consumer Products
(800) 258-3288; (717) 296-4434
$100

Yamaha YST-M10

Yamaha has been building musical instruments and cutting-edge synthesizers for years. So it's no surprise that the company offers speakers for multimedia PCs. The Yamaha YST-M10s are simple well-rounded speakers, and their typical street price of

$80 makes them a particularly attractive choice for a home multimedia PC setup. The YST-M10s have power, volume, and presence controls located up front. The last dial boosts the treble range of the sound.

When it comes to strict audio fidelity, the YST-M10s don't outperform the ACS 100.1s, but they are well balanced and easy to listen to. They offer plenty of top-end sound, but lower bass notes suffer somewhat. On the other hand, there's lots of power, with a built-in 10-watt-per-channel amplifier proving ample enough for the efficient 3.5-inch speaker drivers.

The YST-M10s don't have the multiple inputs and controls that the Roland speakers offer or the sophisticated design of the Altec models. They're more like the powered speakers included with most mini-stereo systems. Consequently, they're easy to install (they come with nearly every kind of adapter included) and attractive enough to sit in the corner of a living room.

—John R. Quain

YST-M10
Yamaha Corp. of America
714-522-9240
$149

✍ The first multimedia development tool was developed by Macromedia (then called MacroMind) in 1985. It was called VideoWorks, and it enabled companies to write software programs that incorporated sound, animation, and interactivity. Today, Macromedia Director (as it is now called) has a 150,000-user installed base. Most multimedia software programs on the PC and the Macintosh are developed using Director.

Disney Wired—The Mouse That Snored

i t's fine to speculate about the future. It's even better to experience it yourself. So we were all (mouse) ears to hear about Walt Disney World's Innoventions—a new Epcot exhibit featuring technology leaders like Apple, AT&T, IBM, Microsoft, Oracle, and Silicon Graphics, and offering "a special sneak preview of products for the near future."

Maybe we should have been worried that the same Disney press blurb also hyped attractions like "Disney Presents Bill Nye the Science Guy….He'll…blow steam out of his nose…pound nails with a frozen banana…." But we couldn't pass up a chance to see the future firsthand.

Epcot was lush and green, the result of the daily tropical deluge that had turned the place into an ankle-deep lake. We slogged our way into the exhibit through the roiling mosh pit of water-logged future-seekers in cheap yellow Disney rain ponchos.

Some future. It was pretty much limited to a simulated home with fancy thermostats, a coffin-sized AT&T telephone with enormous buttons, a dated picture-phone, and a ton of video games and geeky educational software. Few actual products were on display. Instead, everywhere we saw printed signs that were short on devices and long on promises.

Tumbling 3-D images on rows of IBM displays caught my eye. As my finger pressed the screen where it said "Touch Here," the system instantly crashed. An omen?

Nearby was a chance to go behind the scenes to see previously secret workings in a laboratory as computer graphics "wizards" developed a virtual reality attraction. Silicon Graphics logos were plastered all over the place. But when we tried to enter, Disney goons spotted our press cameras and barred the door.

We explained that we had made previous arrangements with the PR department. We showed them the entrance passes the PR folks had left for us at the main gate. We flashed the Disney PR card the press representative had sent us. No joy.

These folks were mean. They're the kind who would shotgun Bambi, then tear out his heart and stomp on it. Only after hours of phone calls back to the mouse politburo did they grudgingly relent.

Once inside, we watched an unsuspecting victim struggle inside his insectlike virtual-reality helmet. A monitor above his head displayed what he was seeing. He obviously hadn't quite gotten the swing of things, and kept careening across the virtual city, smashing hopelessly into walls. Not much future here.

Near the exit were a few Apple workers toying with an inoperative global positioning tracker. We asked about other futuristic hand-held devices. They led us over to the Hammacher Schlemmer area beside theirs.

A pair of night-vision goggles sat on a shelf. "Could we take a photo of those?"

Panic. The word must have gotten around. "No! I'm not authorizing you to take a picture!" "But aren't those just the ones on sale in every Hammacher Schlemmer catalog in the country, and in the gift shop next door?"

"Yes, but I absolutely can't authorize you to take a picture." We turned the corner. A Disney cop materialized from out of the shadows and blocked our path.

So far, the whole visit had been a bust—and we were about to be busted. "I'd like to see some ID, boys." Clots of tourists all around us were strobing their Instamatics like groupies at a Metallica concert. "Are you going to stop those people from using their cameras, too?" "Yes, if we have to! Every single one!" He wandered off with our paperwork.

It's a tough mouse-eat-mouse world out there. What were they so intensely afraid of? "The Shocking Expose: COMPUTER MAGAZINE BLOWS LID OFF THEME PARK RACKET!"

The Disney cop returned. It was clear that even after making arrangements and flying 3,000 miles, we were not welcome. We quickly headed for the exits.

I turned to my photographer, a highly respected photojournalist who had spent some time in Iraq documenting the plight of the Kurds. He had told me how the police were everywhere over there, and how you had to really be on your toes to avoid getting into serious trouble. I asked him if he had been hassled more in Iraq or at Disney. "Disney."

Maybe this really was the future. Long lines. Video screens everywhere. Rampant commercialism. Everything overpriced. Lots of unfulfilled expectations. A consumer market expressed mostly as violent, expensive, kiddie games. Broken promises. Secret police popping out of the woodwork.

Walt must be spinning in his stainless steel cryotank time capsule.—Paul Somerson ∎

THE WIDE WORLD OF CYBERSPORTS

Baseball's Greatest Hits

If you want to hear Ty Cobb giving base-stealing advice, watch Bobby Thomson's miracle in 1951, or play the most arcane baseball-trivia game ever devised, get Baseball's Greatest Hits. This fan pleaser captures baseball's most memorable moments in a wealth of QuickTime movies, play-by-play recordings, photographs, interviews, and period writings.

Baseball's Greatest Hits
The Voyager Company
$79.95

Greg LeMond's Bicycle Adventure

Imagine hanging out with Greg LeMond and other cycling pros—traveling around the world, hearing their stories, getting tips on technique, and so on. That's what Greg LeMond's Bicycle Adventure CD-ROM lets you do—without making you leave your Mac.

Bicycle Adventure is easy to use. A globe lets you click on parts of the world to see items about cycling in those regions (each item includes a picture or a QuickTime movie plus a narrative vignette presented in a scrolling text window). A time line lets you learn about the history of cycling and envision cycling in the future. Click on a row of buttons to jump through

items by category, or use the directory to navigate by title. Online help and Balloon Help make the first half of the game's manual pretty unnecessary, but the second half is an interesting discussion of Greg LeMond's bicycle-sizing philosophy.—Louis E. Benjamin Jr.

Greg LeMond's Bicycle
Adventure
Eden Interactive
San Francisco, CA
(800) 743-3360; (415) 241-1450
$79.99

Microprose Ultimate Football

If you think you could have coached the Bills to Super Bowl victory, or you just want to play football without risking bumps and bruises, try Ultimate Football from MicroProse. It's a football fan's ultimate toy. The game flows like a real football game: Play starts from a hud-

dle, and you then watch as the players run to their positions, the substitutes come in from the sidelines, and everyone runs back to the huddle after the play is over. You can interact to varying degrees, from choosing plays as coach to directing a particular player. Combine this action with the sound support, and you have a very captivating presentation.

Ultimate Football is impressive in its presentation as well as its depth. Plays are run in 3-D and are amazingly realistic. However, the blockiness of the VGA resolution becomes more apparent on screens larger than 14 inches. You can watch the action from almost any camera angle and flip between different cameras just like on TV. There are also signals and commentary to listen to, and you can play against another person via modem.

The depth of Ultimate Football shows in the detail on individual players; the

ability to select game settings, such as whether the game simulation is for an indoor or outdoor field; and the completeness of the number of NFL teams covered. MicroProse makes good use of the CD-ROM to pack in all this information without cluttering up your hard drive.

Ultimate Football also comes bundled with Fantasy Football. Fantasy Football lets many people work together to run a football league. It is based on tracking stats rather than Ultimate Football's interactive game play. The two products can be used independently.

Now for the bad news. The main menus are easy to use, but the game interface is a bit cryptic and not well-documented. Worse, there is no online help. However, once you get used to the functions that can be done with the left and right mouse buttons, you'll find play easier. Like many DOS games, Ultimate Football may require a custom setup or boot disk.

This version of Ultimate Football had a number of operational quirks. A team's performance does not always follow its capabilities, and controlling an individual player is difficult. MicroProse has been making updates available to correct these deficiencies.

Ultimate Football needs a few more minor revisions to make it a really great product, but don't wait if you want to have some real football fun. You may wind up spending more time playing

on your computer than watching TV.—William Wong

MicroProse Inc.
180 Lakefront Dr.
Hunt Valley, MD 21030-2245
(800) 879-7529
$57.95

BRINGING THE GAME TO YOUR PC

ESPN Sports Shorts CD-ROM

Moon Valley Software's $39.95 ESPN Sports Shorts CD-ROM is a jam-packed multimedia collection of sports-related clip media, utilities, and screen savers. Sports Shorts includes hundreds of still images, video clips, and sound files culled from ESPN game coverage, Sports Center broadcasts, and miscellaneous programming. A viewer utility lets you browse through any of the disc's stills, videos, or sounds, while eight predefined slide shows display sequences of clips organized into categories such as football.

You also get a Speak Up Recorder utility, which duplicates most of the functionality of Windows' Sound Recorder, and a copy of Moon Valley's Icon Hear-It Too, a set of ten applications such as talking clocks, calculators, and games. Icon Hear-It also lets you install Sports Shorts graphics as Windows wallpaper, replace standard Windows icons with animated Sports Shorts icons, and create moving cursors that wander away.

You can also arrange the disc's graphics and videos into custom screen savers, complete with special effects such as fades or animated images that dart about the screen. Particularly effective are a pair of hockey players who plow back and forth at random. You can also attach humorous WAV files to common Windows events. Minimize a window, for instance, and the system cries, "Honey, I minimized the kids!"

Sports Shorts is relatively simple to install and use. Its main drawback is that it seems more like a hodge-podge of utilities than a coherent program—instead of a single integrated user interface, it presents you with 14 different icons. Even worse, running Icon Hear-It brings up a floating palette with yet another dozen-plus buttons. Still, ESPN Sports Shorts has the diversity to be a winner on any sports-lover's desktop. Hey, sports fans, are we having fun yet?—John Meyer

ESPN Sports Shorts CD-ROM
Moon Valley Software
$39.95

Empire Soccer '94

Empire Software's Empire Soccer '94 has features and options that let you advance from novice to world-class soccer, where you compete with teams with strengths and weaknesses based on actual 1994 World Cup participants.

Empire Soccer '94 uses smooth, clever animation to represent players and game officials. Most of the time you have a full-screen view of part of a soccer field, following the ball in play. Two can play at once (using keyboard, mouse, or joystick) or a single player can take on the computer. You manipulate a single player at a time (the rest are kept in motion by the computer), controlling direction; moves such as kicks, passes, tackles, or throw-ins; and a special move you select before the game begins, such as a banana kick. When a noteworthy event such as a scored goal occurs, close-ups of significant figures, such as the scorer, the goalie, and the referee, appear in separate windows, giving the game a bit of personality.

There are three modes of play: training, exhibition, and World Cup. You can choose national teams for both sides in all modes. Team skill levels can be tailored to either help or handicap you, and you also can select game duration.

In training mode, you play a single match with selected skill levels for each team. Exhibition mode lets you pit any two of 32 national teams against each other. And as many as eight players can select teams in World Cup mode, which starts with a first round of six groups of four teams that play 36 matches, before moving to round two with 16 teams and 15 matches.

Unfortunately, installing Empire Soccer '94 can be a challenge. The program requires 570K of conventional memory (it can't use extended RAM—you must have 583,680 bytes of lower RAM free) and a 3.5-inch floppy drive A:. If your 3.5-inch drive is drive B:, you have to change drive assignments, either by switching drive cables and resetting your CMOS setup, or by using the DOS ASSIGN command. You can call Empire Software for help if you're installing the game from drive B:.

Installation hassles aside, Empire Soccer '94 remains entertaining and challenging. If you're a soccer fan who follows World Cup play, the opportunity to pit teams against each other as you choose is appealing. As a conventional one- or two-player game, Soccer '94 is worth its purchase price—you can replay the World Cup until the 1998 games and never get bored.—Bruce Brown and Rich Brown

Empire Software
4 Professional Dr.
Suite 123
Gaithersburg, MD 20879
(800) 216-9706
$49.95

Microsoft Golf

Can't get to the golf course this evening? Tee up with Microsoft Golf and hook, slice, drive, and putt your way around 18 holes. It won't do much for your waistline, but it's sure a lot of fun.

The holes are spectacular. No artist's renderings of make-believe links here; instead, the disk offers digitized images of the real thing—either Torrey Pines in San Diego or Number Two at Pinehurst in North Carolina. SVGA graphics clearly show the undulations of the fairways and the textures of the trees with a photographic realism not found in other golf simulations.

The whoosh of a long drive, the clunk of a ball in the cup, and the splash of water are a few of the authentic sound effects. But the full-motion video is what really distinguishes this multimedia version from other golf games. Every hole has a full-motion fly-over to give you a bird's-eye view of the lay and location of the fairway, bunkers, traps, and green. More video is available in the pull-down window, where a pro gives tips on how each hole is best played. Access Links courses are compatible with Microsoft Golf, but you won't have the fly-overs and pro tips.

Microsoft Golf
Microsoft Corp
(800) 426-9400
$64.95

A Clean Desk

Yes, let's try to make computer interfaces light and fun, even humorous. I think it's okay for the computer to have a personality. Or even better, I think it would be great if the computer reflected the better parts of my personality.

Looking at my Mac desktop, it reminds me that certain parts of my life are unorganized. My desktop is littered with icons for utilities that I use sometimes, old e-mail messages, various versions of scripts, folders for lots of different projects. And one monster folder called Old Desktop Stuff. I never look in there. Every once in a while, usually when I return from a trip, I select all the icons on my desktop and drag them into that folder. A clean desk! I like it.—Dave Winer ■

Microsoft Complete Baseball

The thrill can last through the off-season thanks to this multimedia reference. Microsoft Complete Baseball has a full history of the game, player biographies, and an almanac laden with statistics, as well as multimedia clips. Fantasy-league aficionados can subscribe to Microsoft Baseball Daily ($1.25 an issue), a baseball newspaper delivered via modem.

Microsoft Complete Baseball
Microsoft Corp.
(206) 882-8080
$79.95

Sports Illustrated 1994 Multimedia Sports Almanac

You know what's really nice about the Sports Illustrated 1994 Multimedia Sports Almanac? You can do a search of the entire disc and find only one reference to Tonya Harding! But wait. How could a 1994 sports review miss the Tonya story and, for that matter, the entire 1994 Winter Olympics? The answer is that, despite the title, this CD covers 1993. Nonetheless, the almanac is a jaunty look back at 1993 sports, including video highlights from the big pro events, enough charts, statistics, and trivia to satisfy the most obsessed armchair athlete, and the full text of an entire year of Sports Illustrated. If you're the type who has three TVs in the same room tuned to three different games on Sunday, you'll love it. Our only disappointment was the bloopers video. Choppy editing combined with the choppy replay of Windows video meant that we had a hard time figuring out what many of the bloopers were about.

Sports Illustrated 1994
Multimedia Sports Almanac
StarPress Multimedia
(800) 782-7944
$59.95

ADVENTURE/FANTASY/ROLE PLAYING

Out of This World

Ready for a fantastic trip to another dimension? As its name implies, MacPlay's Out of This World can take you there. It's an action adventure game that's guaranteed to keep you glued to your Mac for hours.

In a nuclear experiment gone wrong, you find yourself transported through time and space to another dimension—a place where ferocious beasts and armed aliens are out for your blood. Your only ally is a friendly alien who helps you get out of tough spots from time to time.

This game requires a perfect balance of arcade-style hand/eye coordination (timing your jumps, firing at enemies, deflecting their hits) and problem-solving abilities—your surroundings are much like a maze, and the obvious ways of getting to the next level seldom work. Fortunately, the keyboard controls are simple. You can also use an Advanced Gravis MouseStick for maneuvering. If you happen to die during the course of the game (and you will—many times), you get a four-letter pass code that lets you return to life at the location of your demise instead of starting over.

The animation in Out of This World is first-rate. The game's best feature, though, is how it pulls you in: It reaches out and grabs you, and it won't let go.—Tony A. Bojorquez

Out of This World
MacPlay
17922 Fitch Avenue,
Irvine, CA 92714
(714) 553-3530
$59.95

Sam and Max Hit the Road

One of the most sophisticated adult CD games features a dog in a cheap suit and a wisecracking rabbit with a reckless disregard for life—others' lives anyway. They're Sam and Max, freelance police—a couple o' mugs stuck in a tongue-in-cheek film noir cartoon that rings of sixties underground comics.

The cartoon detectives are hot on the trail of a carnival's bigfoot. Your mission: guide them, solve visual riddles, ask the right questions, pick up objects to use later, and find a place for Sam to go to the bathroom. On the way, play games within the game. Unlike most other game characters, Sam and Max deliver a witty script in a perfect deadpan. It's like Naked Gun 33 1/3 on disc. I'm a sucker for it.—Ron White

Sam and Max
Hit the Road
LucasArts
Entertainment
(800) 782-7927
$55.95

The Magical Death

Ninety percent of murders in the United States are solved within six hours of taking place. Based on that premise, The Magical Death gives you six hours to figure out who killed a woman found surrounded by the trappings of Vodoun worship. To solve the case, you view videos of the suspects, click on objects in photographs of the murder scene for information, examine lab and autopsy reports, and rummage through the victim's desk and personal effects. All of this has an unglamorous ring of authenticity—the subject matter speaks for itself without the gimmicks of a "Murder, She Wrote." If you're a mystery buff, this is the CD you've been waiting for.—Ron White

The Magical Death
Creative Multimedia Corp.
(503) 241-4351
$29.95

How many CD-ROM titles come to market each month? 100? 200? 300? Guess the latter number and you're right. At least for now.

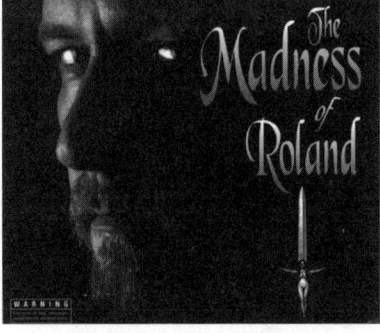

Outpost

Crave a thinking person's game that requires more than just hand-eye coordination to ensure survival? Forget Doom. Windows-based Outpost is the answer. Engage your mind and leadership skills as you lead a band of interstellar pioneers who escape Earth before it's destroyed by an asteroid. You have tough decisions to make now that you're in charge: How many people do you take? What type of supplies should they bring along? Where's the best place to land? How do you build an infrastructure that will ensure the species' survival? Outpost's high-resolution animations and realistic graphics draw you in completely. Before long, you're a cross between Moses and the mayor of SimCity.—Ron White

Outpost
Sierra On-Line
(800) 757-7707; (206) 649-9800
$59.95

Spaceship Warlock

The first of the high-concept graphical CD-ROM adventure games, Spaceship Warlock still sports impressively slick graphics—but be prepared to spend a fair amount of time waiting around.

Spaceship Warlock
Reactor, Inc.
445 W. Erie Avenue
Chicago, IL 60610
$95

Hell Cab

Hell Cab is yet another entry in the multimedia adventure-game genre—this time you're

at the mercy of a devilish cab driver who's out for more than just your fare. The ride is hip and stylish but, like the real thing, not particularly fast.

Hell Cab
Time-Warner Interactive Group
$99.99

Sherlock Holmes Consulting Detective

Sherlock Holmes Consulting Detective, Volume III, is the latest in the popular series that pits Holmes and Watson against the criminals of London. Use the hour of interactive video—sometimes comically overacted—to interview suspects and witnesses. Listen to the Baker Street Irregulars and scan The Times for clues. Once you're sure of your facts, present them to the judge. The disk contains three unrelated mys-

teries, all of which should satisfy any mystery buff.

Sherlock Holmes Consulting Detective, Volume III
Viacom New Media
(800) 877-4266
$70

Alice: An Interactive Museum

Finding your way through the gorgeously rendered 3-D Alice: An Interactive Museum is a surreal, sometimes maddening adventure. Your clicks animate objects and paintings (some sexually explicit, be warned), open doors, and uncap bottles of Perrier labeled "Drink Me" or "Don't Drink Me."

Alice: An Interactive Museum
East West Communications
1631 Woods Drive
Los Angeles, CA 90069
$99

The Madness of Roland

The Madness of Roland is based on medieval legend and it looks like an illuminated manuscript, but the strategy of this multimedia novel is purely modern. You move among five sometimes conflicting points of view, branching off into layers of witty or poetic commentary and startling QuickTime movies.

The Madness of Roland
HyperBole Studios
1756 114th Avenue S.E.
Suite 204
Bellevue, WA 98004
(800) 554-9696
$59.95

Star Trek 25th Anniversary

If you've always wanted to run the USS Enterprise, now's your chance. With Star Trek 25th Anniversary, you become Captain James T. Kirk, exploring new worlds in the company of Spock, Scotty, and the rest of the crew. Although we played with a prerelease version, the game (now available) was slated to come complete with voice-recognition commands

Barney the purple dinosaur, who sings "I love you, you love me" while hurling bombs at you), it's extremely well-coded, you can play it online with others over a modem, it's complex, and it's just plain fun. I find the violence

fun fun fun fun fun fun fun fun fun fun fun

for use on AV Macs, so you'll be able to say "Fire!" with the same melodramatics as Shatner himself. This program is optimized for 13-inch monitors, so the graphics are low-resolution and are slow on larger displays.

Star Trek 25th Anniversary
MacPlay
$59.95

Myst

Thousands of strangely beautiful 3-D scenes, video clips, eerie music, and authentic sound effects combine to make up a sensual if frustrating experience on the Island of Myst. It's frustrating because you are never sure of the plot or what you are seeking; about all you do know is that something has gone horribly wrong on the island and the inhabitants have vanished.

In a kind of sequential slide show, you visit one scene after another to investigate the planetarium, the space ship, the misty forest, the secret tunnels, and the strange mechanisms that dot the landscape. Eventually the rocky little island will give up

its secrets and you'll solve the mystery.

If you like a neat plot with defined goals, you will be disappointed. But if you are looking for an original and groundbreaking game, you need look no further than Myst.

Myst
Broderbund Software Inc.
(800) 521-6263
$60

Pathways into Darkness

In Pathways into Darkness, an alien god, buried under the earth eons ago, is ready to wake and rule the universe. You must bury it farther into the earth, but you're hampered by creatures from the god's dreams that have come to life and roam the caverns through which you must weave to fulfill your mission. Although each level is different, we found this game a little repetitious at times.

Pathways into Darkness
Bungie Software
$69.99

✋ Arnold Schwarzenegger Virus—Terminates and stays resident. It'll be back.

The Journeyman Project

In the world of The Journeyman Project, time travel and world peace have been achieved. But history has been disturbed, threatening the global tranquillity. You are sent back in time to correct what's gone wrong. This game can be glacially slow at times, but the graphics are awesome.

The Journeyman Project
Presto Studios
$99.95

Lunicus

In Lunicus, earthlings find an alien device that displays footage of the Jurassic period. The device also doubles as a way for the aliens to monitor life on Earth. Onboard the Lunicus, you must prevent

the aliens from attacking the motherland. If you don't like shoot-'em-ups, this CD-ROM adventure probably isn't for you, but it is one of the fastest games we've seen.

Lunicus
Cyberflix
$99.95

Superhero League of Hoboken

The title sounds like something out of a Mel Brooks film, and the spirit is the same. It's set in a futuristic United States overwhelmed by melting ice caps, radioactive fallout, and toxic waste. Deadly mutations roam the countryside: Junk Bond Amoebas, Steroid Men, and Aerobots that jazzercize their victims to death. Mutant McNuggets scream, "You deserve a break today!" as they deliver fatal karate chops.

Only one thing stands between what's left of civilization and its total collapse: your trusty League. Superheroes of the venerable

League of Hoboken include the likes of Tropical Oil Man, who can raise the cholesterol level in a villain's bloodstream, and RoboMop, a brawny android who can clean up any mess. As the game progresses, your heroes can buy better weapons and armor, and locate radioactive isotopes that grant newer, stranger abilities, like the power to cause root rot, or to vanquish baked goods. With effort, you may even rid the world of a few deadly menaces.

At League Headquarters, your devoted computer Matilda provides five missions at a time; complete them all, and you're ready for five more. Many are interrelated— succeed in one and you'll

receive objects that can be successfully applied in others.

Solving missions requires a little forethought and patience, but they're relatively easy compared to the mind-boggling efforts required in most graphics adventures. However, the missions involving the evil, ever-resourceful Dr. Entropy are tougher. Reviving a cryogenically frozen George Steinbrenner and making him ruler of the known world is only one of Entropy's nefarious schemes. You must stop him, time and again, in all seven levels of the game.

SLH's MCGA graphics are effective, and the musical score is excellent. The role-playing/battling elements are generally easy. You're supposed to enjoy the satirical monsters and amusing text in SLH—not die constantly.

Legend Entertainment Co.'s lack of experience in role-playing design, however, begins to show at the game's higher levels. Your characters' experience points and development max out; you've seen nearly all the monster types around; and few places remain to be explored. But until this point arrives, SLH remains one of the silliest and most delightful computer games on the current scene. Ignore it at your own peril—unless you're a dedicated George Steinbrenner fan.—Barry Brenesal

Legend Entertainment Co.
14200 Park Meadow Dr.
Chantilly, VA 22021
(800) 658-8891; (703) 222-8500
$59.95

Robinson's Requiem

Most of us like to think that we're survivors—that work, traffic, paying bills, and going to the gym are tough enough to prove our mettle. But when you're a crash sur-

vivor on a prison planet far from home, all this seems like a cakewalk. That's just where ReadySoft's Robinson's Requiem puts you: On a planet in the middle of nowhere, with little to go on but your ability to make the best of a bad situation.

You play an agent who's been double-crossed by the government and sent on a fake reconnaissance mission to an "unknown planet." Your ship crashes, and you have little on which to survive. To escape, you need to collect all the personal computers carried by the rest of the prisoners, plug them into the main computer, and deactivate the force field.

The planet you land on has a few other crash survivors and prisoners, one of whom communicates with you telepathically. Some of the other survivors are friendly and want to help, some are bitter and a bit crazy: You find out who your friends are fast.

You also have to deal with the planet's native inhabitants. There's nothing too surprising here—some of the more mundane inhabitants include an eagle, a tiger, some cave-dwelling apes, and some big spiders, while among the more esoteric are dinosaurs, robots, a buffalo-rabbit, a werewolf, and a centaur. Through all this, you need to stay healthy by purifying water, staying warm, taking antibiotics and other drugs, and even operating on yourself if necessary. There is a well-supplied medical kit to

help, and your personal computer can provide a diagnosis.

Robinson's Requiem tries to put a new spin on the traditional adventure game with now-popular continuously scrolling 3-D graphics, somewhat akin to Doom. Well, sort of. While the moving Voxel graphics add a more interesting element to the game with randomly generated landscapes, the resolution is average. At times, it is hard to spot navigable paths amid the flora and fauna, but, in general, the items that you need to see and collect for escape are readily apparent. Actual play is mostly icon-based with interaction both on and off the viewscreen. It's fairly intuitive, though it took me seven tries to get a match lit to light a torch, even when I was referring to the manual. The documentation could be more thorough, and some of the syntax is ambiguous.

Robinson's Requiem is a good choice if you want to experience adventure on a new level. There are quirks, but they don't make the game unplayable, just annoying at times. But, on the whole, Robinson's Requiem from ReadySoft will give you more vicarious entertainment than Daniel Dafoe could shake a stick at.—John Marrin

Robinson's Requiem
ReadySoft Inc.
3375 14th Ave.
Units 7 and 8
Markham, Ont.
L3R OH2 Canada
(905) 475-4801
$59.95

Return to Ringworld

Game software continues to showcase multimedia technologies. Return to Ringworld, Tsunami Media's CD-ROM adventure game and interactive novel, employs a variety of techniques that add to your involvement and the game's relative realism. With 3-D special effects, cinematic sequences, digitized speech, and the ability to change characters during play to take advantage of special knowledge and abilities, Return to Ringworld is both challenging and entertaining.

This game is based on the Ringworld book series by Larry Niven and is a sequel to Ringworld: Revenge of the Patriarch, an earlier interactive novel. In Return to Ringworld, three renegade characters, two humans and one member of the catlike Kzin species, are hiding from organized human and Kzin forces. While in hiding, they are trying to discover the secrets of the planet Ringworld. Their ultimate goal is to maintain a precarious peace between humans and Kzin.

As the game player, you can switch among the three

renegades and assume their personalities, strengths, and weaknesses. The characters are Quinn, a male human mercenary who values information above all else; Miranda, a female human engineer who excels at keeping systems working; and Seeker-of-Knowledge, a Kzin pilot and communications expert. In some cases, you must be in the role of a particular character in order for the story and the game to advance.

Cinematic sequences with 3-D effects appear in the game's opening scenes and at times when you make major progress. Usually, you look at a screen split between a view of the present character's location on top and that player's current inventory on the bottom. There are several other entertaining sub-games within Return to Ringworld that add to your enjoyment, but can distract from your main mission.

You can save up to eight games in progress, a vital capability if you want to try different strategies. The depth of features, cleverness, and complexity of the game assure that you won't finish this one in an afternoon. Plan on several hours to figure out the general scenario. Packed with features and sure to keep you entertained for a long time, Return to Ringworld gives you an excellent return on your investment.—Bruce Brown

Tsunami Media Inc.
(Distributed by Time Warner Interactive)
48677 Victoria Ln.
Suite 201
Oakhurst, CA 93644
(800) 482-3766; (209) 683-8266
$59.95

DARK, DEMENTED, AND DOOMED

DOOM!

Want to really make your favorite DOOM addicts happy for the holidays? Give 'em their own level. It's no secret that DOOM's incredible. 3-D graphics and playability have made it one of the most popular games of all time. But if you're only casually addicted to DOOM, you may not realize how flexible it really is. With this software hit, id Software has invented an extremely sophisticated action/adventure engine, one that works just as well with episodes designed with third-party DOOM editors as with the episodes that come as part of the game.

When you purchase the $40 registered version of DOOM, you're actually getting two things: the DOOM engine, and a much larger WAD file, which contains all the actual levels (also called the IWAD). This main file

contains a bunch of things: pictures of DOOM creatures, wall textures, music and sound effects, as well as detailed descriptions of the architecture.

A WAD file is big—larger than 10MB in the registered version of the game—because all this graphics and sound information takes up a lot of space. When you pay to register a copy of DOOM, you're actually paying for the artwork and music for three missions, with 27 impressive levels written by id Software. In the bargain, you're also getting the rights to use other WAD files designed by you or others.

If the DOOM engine acts like a projector, the WAD file is the film. The analogy isn't so far off; you'll see that these three utilities let you use the same cast of characters. Your enemies will still be the same—Troopers, Cyber Demons, Spider Bosses, for instance. Custom DOOM levels generally have the same inhabitants and textures as the originals. But the possibilities for combining and recombining these elements are endless, and there are thousands of available WAD files to prove it.

With the impending release of DOOM 2.0 (titled "Hell on Earth"), DOOM edi-

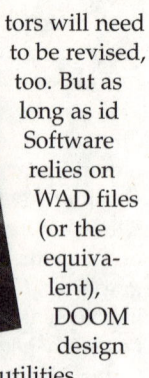

tors will need to be revised, too. But as long as id Software relies on WAD files (or the equivalent), DOOM design utilities should continue to thrive. Certainly, there's no indication id Software will change its open philosophy toward these utilities, which allow anyone, with a little work, to design and customize new levels.

After all, to use any custom level, you first need to obtain a registered version of DOOM. With registered copies, users get an almost unlimited supply of new WAD files. So DOOM editors add real value to every copy of the game that's sold, which is good news for those creative minds at id Software and for DOOM maniacs everywhere.—Rich Dragan

DOOM!
GT Interactive (distributor)
(800) 362-9400; (212) 951-3000
$40

Doom!

Doom is offered from ID Software, creators of the shareware favorite Wolfenstein 3-D. ID has made Doom an outrageously challenging and fun game, not just a rehash of Wolf.

While Doom uses the same stunning 3-D view and basic controls as Wolfenstein, it is more complex. There are puzzles, and you must take the time to solve them rather than merely blasting everything in sight. Not that there's no blasting involved: You face a variety of enemies ranging from fireball-spitting imps to soldiers armed with shotguns and rifles. No need to fret, because along the way, you pick up armor, first aid, and weapons—shotgun, rocket launcher, chainsaw (gulp!), plasma gun, and the ultimate in portable weaponry, the BFG-9000.

Doom consists of three episodes. While the first, Knee-Deep in the Dead, is widely distributed as shareware, the next two come as a retail combo. With full support for sound and multiple difficulty settings, even the free game alone can provide days of gore-soaked entertainment.

Each episode has nine levels of play, with plenty of secret rooms that you can miss if you're not thorough. That shouldn't be a problem because Doom also supports auto-mapping. Stumped or frightened Doomers can also seek relief online. Game players' forums are chock-full of Doom advice and undocumented commands.

Doom also has network multiplayer capability, though it currently runs only in broadcast mode, sending signals to every station on the network. This drags LAN efficiency down to

abysmal levels. The upside is that playing on the network is a blast. Players have the option of playing cooperatively or against each other.

The creativity and playability of Doom are second to none. Look for the first episode of Doom on ZiffNet's PBS Arcade Forum (GO ZNT:PBSARC).—Oliver Rist, Steve Baldwin, John Marrin

Doom
GT Interactive (distributor)
(800) 362-9400; (212) 951-3000
$40

Doom II: Hell on Earth

This commercially released DOS CD picks up the battle you started on another planet and moves the scene to the underworld, where you blow away assorted demon meanies. There are more levels, more baddies, and more weapons than ever before. Presented in a virtual-reality 3-D format that you've got to see to believe (and take dramamine to endure), this death fest turns political correctness on its head, provides enough violence to engender nightmares in most youngsters,

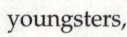

and keeps you away from the family all evening. What more could you ask for? .—Ron White

Doom II: Hell on Earth
GT Interactive
(800) 362-9400, (212) 951-3000
$49.95 est. street price

The C.H.A.O.S. Continuum

An alternative to bloodletting is The C.H.A.O.S. Continuum, an imaginative one-player science-fiction adventure. Here's the setup: You're working at a computer that's being tapped through another dimension by scientists in the year 2577. These scientists are being held prisoner by an all-powerful computer in orbit around one of Jupiter's moons. Your mission is to rescue the white coats by using your PC to steer a robot around the orbiting computer. The well-done graphics and animations, strong storytelling, and convincing interface make it darn good play.—Ron White

C.H.A.O.S. Continuum
Creative Multimedia
(800) 262-7668; (503) 241-4351
$39.95

Inca II

Once you get past its bizarre premise, Inca II is challenging on all levels. Imagine this: The lost Incan civilization is battling a number of evil galactic conquistadors in space while trying to stabilize its government and counter a threat from a mysterious meteor.

You're the offspring of the Incan ruler, and you spend half your time solving adventure-style riddles and the other half flying a stone— yes, stone—spaceship to battle the villains. Woven between these levels of gaming is a soap-opera mystery in which you're ticked off at your father. Better yet, this is one of the few CDs that successfully blends video and other multimedia effects into the action.—Ron White

Inca II
Sierra On-Line
(800) 757-7707; (206) 649-9800
$29.95

Ultima VIII: Pagan

Ultima VIII: Pagan continues the saga of the Avatar, a young man who periodically crosses from our world into Britannia, a land of Arthurian-based fantasy.

In Ultima VII: The Black Gate, the Avatar uncovered a plot by the malicious Guardian to take over Britannia. Now it's the Guardian's turn for revenge. He has captured the Avatar and dropped him into Pagan, an oppressive and sadistic medieval world, without his usual traveling companions, supplies, or information.

Pagan continues the Ultima series' shift away from exclusively strategic gaming to a faster-paced, action-oriented product. You control a more athletic Avatar, one who must scale walls and jump across chasms. Of course, he can also fall off walls and jump into chasms.

Pagan has no automatic, magical resurrection. You can only bring the Avatar back to life by loading a saved game.

A similar approach governs battle. In Pagan, you handle all of the Avatar's fighting yourself—directing weapon swings, all-out attacks, kicks, blocks, advances, and retreats.

The biggest problem confronting you may not be the Guardian or his representatives, but the interface. It's resolutely mouse-based, and having two buttons govern all movement and combat makes for redundancies. In battle, for instance, a quick left-click swings a sword, a double left-click initiates a sweeping attack, and a held left-click blocks an attack. Right-clicking moves your character or changes the direction of attack. Trying to keep the actions straight while foes gang up on you from several directions at once is difficult.

If the interface is somewhat unrealistic, the world of Pagan itself comes ever closer to a computer-generated reality. There are 10,000 unique VGA objects and 4,000 scrolling screens, with even greater detail at a closer-to-ground level than in Ultima VII. Pagan is a living, multi-level environment, one which goes about its ever-changing business whether the Avatar is present or not.

Animation is also smoother. As for sound, a four-channel mix lets you hear several effects simultaneously.

The Ultima series continues to excel in the variety of activities and situations that

confront you. You'll have to explore an enormous, colorful world and vanquish a variety of new and deadly enemies. There are complex subplots to unravel before you can find out how to break the Guardian's hold on Pagan. This is a far cry from standard cookie-cutter role-playing fare, which gives you a series of simple object quests and thousands of identical, slavering monsters along the way.

Pagan is certainly harder to play than any previous Ultima, and its mouse-based combat may frustrate fans of earlier releases. In addition, fans can no longer opt to make the Avatar a woman. But there's no denying the remarkable detail of Pagan's animated universe, nor its compelling mixture of complex plot, extended gameplay (more than 150 hours), and highly charged action.—Barry Brenesal

Ultima VIII: Pagan Origin
Systems Inc.
12940 Research Blvd.
Austin, TX 78750
(800) 245-4525
$79.95

Lord of the Rings

Although it's adapted from J.R.R. Tolkien's classic book and Ralph Bakshi's animated movie, you needn't be familiar with either to enjoy Interplay's Lord of the Rings Enhanced CD-ROM. This new CD version adds an improved interface and numerous multimedia features, including many clips

from the film, to the 1990 floppy-disk-based game. Even on CD-ROM, Middle Earth isn't as vast as it is in the book, but it's still big (and dangerous) enough to impress the most hardened adventurers.

At the start of the story, you are Frodo Baggins, nephew of Bilbo Baggins, the hero of The Hobbit. When he

retired from his adventuring days, Bilbo gave you his powerful but inherently evil ring of invisibility. You and the wizard Gandalf must destroy the ring before its original owner, the Dark Lord Sauron, gets it back. You assemble a small party and venture into the dangerous parts of Middle Earth. The real action starts as you try to build your party's strength and number and destroy the ring, while avoiding nasty barrow wights, trolls, and Dark Riders.

There are numerous quests and adventures en route, but not all of them are essential to finishing the game—it's up to you to figure out which are important. Quests grow progressively more challenging as your characters acquire more strength and skills.

The most striking feature of Lord of the Rings Enhanced is the use of clips from the movie. The film window is a generous 7 × 7 inches, and playback was smooth, with a minimum of pixeling, on a 486DX/33 system and a multispin CD-ROM. The scenes give life to the story's characters and should whet the appetites of fans still waiting for the film's release on video. A long clip at the beginning sets the plot in motion, and more are triggered when the party reaches certain points or when characters perform certain acts. The movies provide extra motivation to figure out parts of the game.

You control members of your party via the game's icon- and text-based menu. Talking to non-player characters consists of typing one or two key words at most, so there's no difficulty in finding correct phraseology. Trading items between characters, however, is complex: First you choose the trader, then the tradee, then select items from an inventory list. Since your party can contain up to ten characters, it's easy to forget who's carrying what. Additionally, you can only trade one item at a time. When characters become overencumbered, you may end up discarding items and regretting it later. Another complication is the fact that you can only save one at a time, although you do get to choose two start points.

Starting a new game erases everything by default.

Compared to the movie clips, the overhead view of the characters and their surroundings is not spectacular, but the spartan views do make it easy to move characters and see the layout of a room or area. A new Automap feature lets players concentrate on the game and not on drawing maps. The Automap view is limited to the general area you are in, however. If you're a purist, you can disable the feature and draw maps yourself.

While Lord of the Rings Enhanced CD-ROM has its quirks, the quests are challenging, and the inserted movie clips make play more exciting. Best of all is the tantalizing demo on the disc—it shows scenes from Interplay's forthcoming sequel.—John Marrin

Lord of the Rings Enhanced CD-ROM Interplay Productions Inc. 17922 Fitch Ave. Irvine, CA 92714 (800) 969-4263; (714) 553-6678 $79.95

King's Quest VI

King's Quest VI: Heir Today, Gone Tomorrow continues the saga of the Graham family, as young Alexander seeks the hand of the fair princess Cassima. Though darker and more ominous than earlier quests, the action and production values nevertheless demonstrate how good multi-

media adventure games have become.

A 50MB animated cartoon introduces the quest and ends with Alexander shipwrecked on one of the Green Islands. He quickly learns that Cassima is not only on this very island but betrothed to the wicked Vizier. Of course, adventure and mishap follow as Alex searches for a way to rescue his true love.

The story is full of the witty and bizarre characters that are hallmarks of King's Quest games. There's a participle dangling from a tree, a barking dogwood, a head of iceberg lettuce (you need it to cool a steaming pond), and a delightful group of five animated gnomes, each of which specializes in one of the five senses.

Sierra has developed a truly friendly user interface. There is nothing to read and nothing to type in the CD-ROM version; all dialog is spoken by professional actors. And by using the point-and-click interface, even a six-year-old can move through the program with ease.

King's Quest VI: Heir Today, Gone Tomorrow Sierra On-Line (800) 326-6654 $79.95

Dracula Unleashed

Dracula is stalking blood donors in turn-of-the-century London, and you, as the brother of a victim, must try to stop him. More than 90 minutes of video and 50 min-

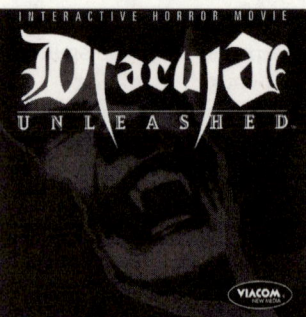

utes of sound lead you from one clue to another. Are you smart enough to put all the pieces of this dazzling multimedia puzzle together before it's too late?

Dracula Unleashed Viacom New Media (800) 877-4266 $70

Iron Helix

In Iron Helix, you control a robot aboard a crewless spacecraft on a collision course with a populated planet. Aboard is Iron Helix, the ultimate Doomsday weapon. Your objective is to find the DNA of an officer with high enough rank to allow you to fool the defender robots and reprogram the

spaceship's course. Iron Helix contains about an hour of detailed animation.

Iron Helix Spectrum HoloByte (800) 695-4263 $72.99 (estimated street price)

Return to Zork

Return to Zork combines an unusually friendly mouse interface with a host of live actors to draw you effortlessly into the action. You quickly forget that you are out to save yet another world (the Underground Empire of Zork) from yet another villain (the IT&L Corp.) and begin to enjoy Return to Zork for what it is: a first-class cinematic adventure.

Return to Zork Activision Inc. (800) 477-3650 $79.95

Nomad Faces Off Against the Aliens

The problem you're faced with in Nomad is a Master Control Robot that's reprogramming the Korakian robotic race for total aggression and replication. The other galactic races are outnumbered and outgunned.

As Earth's sole space-faring representative, the Nomad, it's up to you to stop the massacre. Along the way, you'll encounter 11 alien races, dozens of star systems, and hundreds of planets. Nomad's aliens themselves are a delightful mix. In the tradition of Microprose's Hyperspeed, they are an anthropomorphic mix of samurai rabbits, ursine merchants, and walrus-like warriors, among others. Each representative of an alien species also reveals personal traits governing character response, dialog, trading, and battle. There's much fun to be had in Nomad's universe.—Barry Brenesal

Nomad Faces Off Against
the Aliens
Gametek Inc.
(305) 935-3995
$39.95

action game Dragon's Lair. You fight your way from the drawbridge through the snake room, past the Lizard King and other monsters, to the ultimate goal—the Dragon's Lair. Only then can you slay the beast and rescue the fair princess, Daphne.

The CD-ROM incorporates the same laser disc scenes and sounds that made the original arcade version a megahit more than a decade ago. To guarantee great performance on home systems, the software can fine-tune itself to your video/sound/CD-ROM components, storing information in a small file on the hard disk about how much of each scene to prebuffer during playback. But be prepared; this process can take a while.

Dragon's Lair is a CD-ROM for those who love the challenge of truly fast-paced arcade action.

Dragon's Lair
ReadySoft Inc.
(905) 475-4801
$69.95

Guided Missile Cruiser and engage the enemy in a variety of military situations. With three skill levels and over 100 missions, there's work enough to keep you in command for months.

The layout of the ship, Combat Information Center, weapons systems, and radar is as accurate and realistic as security allows. A closed-circuit TV screen in the Combat Information Center shows missiles being launched, and several animated radar screens track hits, misses, and kills. The sound effects and dialog could be more plentiful, but the graphics are right on.

Aegis: Guardian of the Fleet
Time Warner Interactive
(800) 482-3766
$69.99

Flix that combines arcade action, crisp graphics, and an ecologically conscious plot to create a fast-paced, futuristic adventure. In a world reminiscent of the film Blade Runner, terrorists are capturing the valuable DNA of extinct species. As Jump Raven, a renegade hovercraft pilot, you must rescue the samples by battling the terrorists and searching the streets. The animation that pulls you into the story has a smooth, dark, futuristic feel, and the characters you encounter along the way add a comical touch to the arcade action.

The game's help function clues you in on how to proceed. You can select your weaponry, background music (grunge, hip-hop, techno, or metal), and copilot (the choices range from a wisecracking Eddie Murphy type to a Valley girl straight from Moon Zappa land).

Some players may be annoyed that Jump Raven requires about 10MB of hard-disk space (into which some of the game is offloaded to provide a faster data path) or that it's not particularly P.C. (attaining biodiversity through violence?). What Jump Raven lacks in political correctness, however, it makes up for in humor and pizzazz.—Roman Victor Loyola

Jump Raven
CyberFlix
Knoxville, TN
(615) 546-1157
$69.95

Spectre Supreme

Just like movies, computer games have sequels, and Spectre Supreme—one of the few games you can play with friends over a network—is one of the newest. Arm your tank with an awesome arsenal to destroy new as well old enemies as you struggle to survive and capture flags in an electronic arena. In network mode, six players can participate in several variations of tag, capture the flag, and tic-tac-toe. We liked this better than Spectre—there's a real feeling of progression.

Spectre Supreme
Velocity Development
$69.95

Cosmic Osmo and the Worlds Beyond the Mackerel

Cosmic Osmo and the Worlds Beyond the Mackerel transports you to some truly weird places. Climb aboard the Cosmic Osmo plane (which is equipped with the ultimate weapon: a cotton-swab shooter), and travel to planets where dinosaur skeletons play horns and cupboards

Politically Correct Virus—Prefers to call itself an "electronic microorganism."

Dragon's Lair

You are Dirk the Daring in Don Bluth's classic animation

Aegis: Guardian of the Fleet

For the latest in naval warfare, check out Aegis: Guardian of the Fleet. In it, you take command of the newest class of

Jump Raven

Eco-warriors who have CD-ROM drives will jump at the chance to play Jump Raven, a CD-ROM game from Cyber-

open to warp-zone hallways that take you to other planets where…well, see for yourself.

Cosmic Osmo and the Worlds Beyond the Mackerel
Cyan, Inc.
P.O. Box 28096
Spokane, WA 99228
(800) 235-3565
$59.95

Eight Ball Deluxe

Finally, a video pinball game that feels like a traditional pinball machine. Eight Ball Deluxe has the arcade sounds, realistic ball motion, and flipper finesse of the real thing—and the ability to tilt the machine. The only thing that's missing is the smoky arcade room.

Eight Ball Deluxe
Amtex Software
$49.95

Glider

Glider is a deceptively simple arcade game that pits you, as the pilot of a paper airplane, against a houseful of surprises. Your goal is to fly your plane across each room, from left to right, without crashing into furniture or encountering other hazards such as

tables, balloons, helicopters, electrical outlets, and candles. Your glider has no engines, of course, so it will drift to the ground after a few seconds unless you maneuver it near the heater vents in the floors. Because warm air rises, these vents lift your glider toward the ceiling. (**Hint:** Wiggling—by tapping the right and left keys in rapid succession—is key to mastering rising and falling motions.) But be careful: Many rooms also have vents in the ceiling that suck in your glider when you fly too close….

You can control your glider with the mouse, a joystick, or the keyboard. Although the game's manual implies otherwise, the user-definable keyboard controls—backward and forward (left and right)—seemed the most accurate to us.

My criterion for a great arcade game—minutes to learn, months to master—describes Glider to a T. You'll be up and running within minutes of installing it, but you won't become proficient for a long while.

Glider
Casady & Greene, Inc.
22734 Portola Drive
Salinas, CA 93908
(800) 359-4920; (408) 484-9228.
Version 4.06. $49.95;
More Glider, $19.95

ARCADE MADNESS TO THE MAX

Crystal Crazy

Crystal Quest fans will go crazy with all the fun new elements in the game's successor, Crystal Crazy. Building on Crystal Quest's familiar plot (stay alive, pick up crystals, rack up points, and shoot things), Crystal Crazy adds new bad guys (from peripatetic cuspidors to mutant Dumples with detachable, lethal eyes); special weapons; and handy shields, such as a

rubber hat that gives you bounce-ability. Plus, after every three levels, you now get a bonus round in which you can tear around and pick up points, extra lives, and weapons—as many as you can grab before the walls move in on you.—Louise Kohl Leahy

Crystal Crazy
Casady & Greene
Salinas, CA
(408) 484-9228
$49.95

Rebel Assault

Punctuated with video and original music from the Star Wars trilogy, Rebel Assault is an arcader's delight. Pilot

your skyhopper from training missions in Beggar's Canyon to an encounter with the Death Star. There's no better blend of action, music, sound effects, and dialog—but you may need some hardware tweaking to get it to work.

Rebel Assault
LucasArts Entertainment Co.
(415) 721-3300
$63.95 (estimated street price)

Microcosm

Journey through various body parts and shoot things. It's been done before, but the Rick Wakeman-scored sound track is original.

Microcosm
Psygnosis
(617) 497-5457
$69.00

Troubled Souls

Tetris fans have had their share of knockoffs, but nothing comes close to the invention and beauty of Troubled Souls. As in Tetris, the goal is

to arrange descending segments into whole units. Unlike the horizontal/vertical approach Tetris takes, however, Tortured Souls is all circles and loops. You put together closed loops with the quarter-circles, bars, and crosses you get; the more twisted they are, the more points you earn.

Segments plunge down into a tube, and you place them by clicking on the playing field. As you create a closed loop with the pieces, it disappears. At first you get generic pieces for easy-to-figure circular combinations, but then things get more engaging and bizarre as intricately depicted body parts start falling down the chute as well. Eyes and ears and hands and skulls don't mix: Only like (and generic) parts can come together to form closed objects. As putting together loops becomes harder, you run out of field space and the tube starts filling up with pieces that have no place to go. When the tube overflows with parts, you lose one of your three lives. When you lose your last life, the game ends.

What makes Troubled Souls unique is its darkly gothic look, its moody musical score, and its icy sound effects. The only trouble with it is that it's highly addictive—just try not to keep playing when it's time to get back to work.—Joe Hutsko

Troubled Souls
Varcon Systems
San Diego, CA
(800) 266-6700; (619) 563-6700
$49.95

MOVIES

It's a Wonderful Life

It's not enough that *It's a Wonderful Life* is shown 5,832 times on TV every December. Kinesoft's presentation of the Christmas favorite is still worth getting. In addition to the movie on two Windows discs, you get the final script linked to each scene in the movie, reviews, trailers, stills, and the short story it's based on. The best set of multimedia controls I've seen lets you change the volume and the size of the display—up to full screen (although that's a bit chunky). You can search for words in the script and jump to the scenes in which they're used. You can even click on a button for spoken commentary on what you're watching. It's a fun way to explore an old favorite.—Ron White

It's a Wonderful Life
Kinesoft Development
(708) 806-9562
$79.95

Movies on TV and Videocassette

Okay. We lied. A few issues back we vowed never to review another CD-ROM that translated the text of a book to digital form without taking advantage of the multimedia possibilities of CD-ROM. The reason we're making an exception this time is for the benefit of fellow couch potatoes for whom Steven H. Scheuer's paperback Movies on TV and Videocassette is a bible. It's the most complete listing of movies you'll find anywhere, and the terse descriptions and star ratings are right on the money.

Sure, this CD's search engine is not the best, and unlike Microsoft Cinemania and Mega Movie Guide, there are no video or sound clips—or even stills. But for fast recommendations—and warnings—it's still the authority to turn to.

Movies on TV and Videocassette
Compton's NewMedia
(800) 862-2206
$39.95

Multimedia Performance Artist

hat unites everyone in (my theatre group, which is composed of computer enginneers, musicians, actors, singers, and artists) are the common idiosyncracies that seem to affect many engineers and artists. These include the tendency to be inspired beyond the ability to plan for it; attitudes that are purely creative in nature and may be impractical and irrational to implement; and the tendency to stay up late in cafes talking about things you know nothing about with utmost authority.—George Coates ■

A Hard Day's Night

Little did Richard Lester realize in 1964 when he began filming *A Hard Day's Night* that it would influence rock videos 30 years later. In case you haven't seen the Fab Four's movie in a while, this Voyager disc shows what an impact the movie and the band have had on subsequent generations. Furthermore, this full-length digitized version of the Beatles movie is an excellent history lesson for kids who think Pearl Jam invented rock and roll.

Coupled with the movie (which plays best in a small, 2 × 2.75-inch window) are Beatles biographies, a lengthy commentary, a photo library, and the original script. Extras include the movie's original

trailer (replete with screaming prepubescent girls), two of Lester's early films (a short and a clip from a feature), and, of course, all the movie's songs.

A Hard Day's Night
The Voyager Company
(800) 446-2001
$39.95

Criterion Goes to the Movies

At first glance, Criterion Goes to the Movies looks like a promotional catalog for the Criterion Collection of video laser discs. But because that collection includes 150 of the best movies ever, this CD-ROM full of QuickTime clips becomes a joy for any movie fan. Click on *Five Easy Pieces*, and watch Jack Nicholson tell a waitress to hold some chicken between her knees. High-quality stills of all major cast

If DOOM is rated ZZZ (extremely violent), then that's what they'll want. 💻 But let's face reality. Computer games are nothing more than cartoons. And in my opinion, cartoons are not the problem.—John Dvorak

for for for for for for for for for for

members and a short essay are standard issue for each of the films on the disc.

Criterion Goes to the Movies
The Voyager Company
1351 Pacific Coast Highway
Santa Monica, CA 90401
(206) 441-9355
$24.95

Funny: The Movie in QuickTime

Funny: the Movie in Quick-Time doesn't have the greatest picture quality, but it more than makes up for that with its material: QuickTime clips of about 100 funny stories, anecdotes, and one-liners. And since Funny's interface lets you sort by categories, you can even choose to see only jokes told by

people with red hair or a strange accent—no kidding.

Funny: The Movie in QuickTime
Time-Warner Interactive Group
$39.99

MovieSelect

If you've ever wandered through a video store unsure of what to take home, you need MovieSelect, a CD-ROM containing information on hundreds of movies. Search by actor, director, or theme, or let MovieSelect do the work for you: Just pick three of your favorite movies, and the program will generate a list of compatible suggestions.

MovieSelect
Paramount Interactive
700 Hansen Way
Palo Alto, CA 94304
(415) 885-4080
$59.95

QUICKFLIX! PUTS AMATEUR QUICKTIME MOVIE BUFFS IN THE DIRECTOR'S CHAIR

QuickFLIX!

Billed as personal moviemaking software, VideoFusion's new, low-cost QuickFLIX! lets amateur film buffs edit their own QuickTime movies. QuickFLIX! skips the advanced digital-editing features of Adobe Premiere and Avid's VideoShop in favor of tools that are simpler to learn and use. QuickFLIX! is designed to take you through every step of the moviemaking process, from video and sound recording, editing, and

special effects to titling, layering, and motion control.

A QuickFLIX! strength is that the program works much like any standard Mac application. You can cut and paste clips from one storyboard to another, for example. And creating transitions between two clips is as simple as holding down the Shift key, selecting two clips, and selecting an effect in the Transition dialog box.

One of the best features of QuickFLIX! is its titling. With a little coaxing, you can get the program to create titles that fade in and out. It's also surprisingly easy to create flying logos with QuickFLIX!'s layer, motion, and opacity controls. However, creating eye-catching titling effects is a multistep process that can be tricky. If you're not careful, you may even inadvertently delete frames from your movie.

QuickFLIX! is designed for amateur moviemakers, but its storage requirements are major-league. QuickTime-movie files are large—even short movies that run for a few seconds can approach a megabyte in size. And because QuickFLIX! must process your movies when it creates transitions, plan to set aside some time as the program renders wipes and dissolves frame by frame.

For those who don't require the sophisticated fea-

tures of a high-end video-editing program, QuickFLIX! offers solid editing tools in a user-friendly package. It doesn't let you create complicated video effects or print your movie to tape, but if you're looking for a fairly simple way to assemble QuickTime clips for presentations or just for fun, QuickFLIX! is a good choice. At $149, it's the first affordable entry-level program for casual QuickTime-movie buffs.—Jason Snell

QuickFLIX!
VideoFusion
Maumee, OH
(419) 891-1090
$149

Cinemania '95

I've played around with plenty of CD-ROM encyclopedias, but I didn't fully grasp the delight of hyperlinked,

multimedia reference tools until I got my hands on Cinemania's 23,000 movie listings. It's like having Roger Ebert, Leonard Maltin, and Pauline Kael come to live with you.

Cinemania lets you ride endless trains of cinematic thought. You read Keanu Reeves' biography and then jump to the listing for one of his films, *River's Edge*. Read three different reviews, then read the filmography of the movie's co-star, Dennis Hopper. Click again to jump to the listing for *Easy Rider*, and click once more to learn about Peter Fonda, that movie's co-star. Also included, facts, figures, and plot synopses from *Blackwell's Film Guide*, 4,000 biographies, and hundreds of photos, audio clips, and video clips.

Anyone with cable TV or a VCR is living an incomplete life if this CD-ROM isn't spinning somewhere nearby.—Donald Willmott

Cinemania '95
Microsoft Corp.
One Microsoft Way
Redmond, WA 98052
(800) 426-9400; (206) 882-8800
$79.95

KIDS

Where in the World Is Carmen Sandiego? (Junior Detective Edition)

Once, only older kids could pursue red-hatted thieves. With Where in the World is Carmen Sandiego? Junior Detective Edition, even early readers can become gumshoes for the Acme Detective Agency.

In this junior version of the popular Carmen Sandiego series, the goal is the same as in the older kids' version: to stop Carmen. As usual, Carmen and her henchstaff are making trouble all over the world, and it's up to the Junior Detective to travel the globe to uncover the clues that will help him catch the crooks. Along the way, kids will learn facts about a variety of countries and see digitized photographs from many different nations.

What's different here is that the game's interface and mode of play have been simplified to make it more fun for early readers. Now detectives aged 5 to 8 can pursue Carmen and her gang as part of an Acme Action Team. The agency's Chief pops in from time to time with useful commentary, and a crime-stopping computer offers spoken help. All of the information and clues are presented online; there's no printed reference book to slow things down. What's most important about Carmen Junior, though, is that it gives younger detectives a shot at the fun that used to be reserved for their older siblings.

Where in the World Is Carmen Sandiego? (Junior Detective Edition)
Broderbund Software
(800) 521-6263
$40

Aesop's Fables

Discis pioneered the CD-ROM-stories-for-kids concept, and Aesop's Fables is an example of why its titles are among the best. The illustrations are excellent, and each fable's accompanying music is well chosen. Kids can have the fables read to them or can read them themselves.

Aesop's Fables
Discis Knowledge Research
45 Sheppard Avenue E.
Suite 410
Toronto, ON
M2N 5W9 Canada
(800) 567-4321
$29.95

Rodney's Wonder Window

Kids under ten will love the unusual Rodney's Wonder Window, which contains silly QuickTime-movie antics and cartoonlike action. Kids can't make their own movies, but the graphics and concepts may inspire them to create their own "wonder windows," using programs such as Broderbund's KidPix.

Rodney's Wonder Window
The Voyager Company
$39.95

A Silly Noisy House

A Silly Noisy House is an engaging CD-ROM for the under-five set that lets kids navigate through a magical house inhabited by a family of teddy bears. A click of the mouse sends household objects cavorting across the screen to the sound of familiar nursery rhymes and songs.

A Silly Noisy House
The Voyager Company
$59.95

Beauty and the Beast

Beauty and the Beast offers an interactive version of the favorite tale, with animated illustrations and definitions of difficult words. The program can be slow at times, but the illustrations are good.

Beauty and the Beast
New Media Schoolhouse
P.O. Box 390
Pound Ridge, NY 10576
(206) 882-8080
$69

Victor Vector & Yondo: The Vampire's Coffin

Some first-rate comic-book graphics enliven Victor Vector & Yondo: The Vampire's Coffin, an interactive time-travel adventure aimed at kids (although teenagers may find it fun too). Yondo's a talking Saint Bernard; Victor's an over-muscled eager beaver. More installments of their adventures are forthcoming.

Victor Vector & Yondo: The Vampire's Coffin
Sanctuary Woods Multimedia Corp.
1875 S. Grant Street
San Mateo, CA 94402
(619) 549-8285
$59.95

Creepy Crawlies

If you like bugs, slugs, and things that live in rugs, you'll love Creepy Crawlies. This CD-ROM encyclopedia contains facts and QuickTime movies about more than 70 of the strangest creatures alive. A guaranteed kid pleaser.

Creepy Crawlies
Sony Electronic Publishing
$69

✍ Of all multimedia PCs, 80 percent are going into homes, reports Dataquest. In a 1994 survey done by Odyssey, 27 percent of U.S. households have a PC—that's equivalent to almost 97 million American homes.

Computer Crayon

Small hands need a small mouse—or maybe a crayon that acts like a mouse. The Computer Crayon does just that, plus it's available in primary colors or as a dinosaur-green Jurassic Mouse.

Computer Crayon
Appoint
$49

EasyBook

Who says desktop publishing is just for adults? EasyBook lets kids write and illustrate their own books. Besides creating their own drawings, they can "stamp" graphics that come with the program. After the pages print, fold them in half, and you've got your young author's first book.

EasyBook
Chickadee Software
$59.95

My Own Stories

A great tool for creating storybooks—from design to content—is My Own Stories, from MECC. Youngsters aged eight through 14 can write, illustrate, and publish stories by filling pages with objects, text, color, sound, people, places, and pets. A Spell button helps them proofread, and the Preferences dialog box lets them choose fonts and printing formats.

My Own Stories
MECC
$49.95

LIVING BOOKS

Just Grandma and Me Arthur's Teacher Trouble

If you have kids, drop whatever you're doing, pick up your phone, and order Just Grandma and Me and Arthur's Teacher Trouble, the first two discs in Broderbund's animated, interactive Living Books series. If you don't have kids, buy Grandma and Arthur anyway, if only to see just how elegant and entertaining multimedia can be. Both multilingual discs, based on popular children's books, lead you through witty, whimsical worlds where—at the click of a mouse—starfish dance, cookies sing doo-wop, and the shy kid beats the class brain in the annual school spelling bee.

Just Grandma and Me
Arthur's Teacher Trouble
Living Books
Broderbund Software, Inc.
500 Redwood Blvd.
P.O. Box 6125
Novato, CA 94948
$59.95 each

Disney Screen Saver

After Dark, the venerable Mac screen saver from Berkeley Systems, now offers the Disney Screen Saver, a set of modules for kids—and for adults who have fond memories of Disney classics. They're all there—Mickey, Goofy, the Little Mermaid, even Beauty and the Beast.

Disney Screen Saver
Berkeley Systems
$49.95

Kid Cuts

Kids aged four through 12 can make everything from paper dolls to rainy-day projects with Kid Cuts (it even includes safety scissors!). Kid Cuts lets you make hats, masks, puppets, and more by clicking on various tools. Print the projects, cut them out, and then decorate them.

Kid Cuts
Broderbund Software
$29.95

Dinosaurs!

It's difficult to imagine a CD-ROM subject with more kid appeal than Dinosaurs! Maybe a disc that contained a complete set of X-Men trading cards? Although this might seem a little tame after seeing Spielberg's velociraptors stalk the silver screen, it contains a lot more real information about the creatures themselves. Unfortunately, the only animated QuickTime dinosaurs on hand are elderly paleontologists.

Dinosaurs!
Sony Electronic Publishing
2100 Colorado Avenue
3rd Floor
Santa Monica, CA 90404
$79

The Velveteen Rabbit and Other Children's Classics

The Velveteen Rabbit and other quaint English children's stories can now be enjoyed on CD-ROM. The Velveteen Rabbit and Other Children's Classics is an interactive storybook for children aged five and up—complete with sound, music, and illustrations. A question option makes it a great reading-comprehension tool.

The Velveteen Rabbit and Other Children's Classics
Queue
$49.95

Wallobee Jack: The Bingi Burra Stone

If your kids are tired of reading and writing and doing math problems, give them a treat with Wallobee Jack: The Bingi Burra Stone, an interactive cartoon on CD-ROM for kids aged five and up. Featuring sound, color, and fantastic animation, it's like watching a Saturday-morning cartoon, only better, because kids get to play along.

Wallobee Jack: The Bingi Burra Stone
Tune 1000
$29.95

Where in America Is Carmen Sandiego?

Where in America Is Carmen Sandiego? (Deluxe Edition) is aimed at kids aged 12 and above. Like the others in the series, Where in America has young detectives seeking Carmen and her band of evil cohorts, this time across the U.S. This version features music, beautiful four-color scenes of famous American sites, maps, and a new Chief.

Where in America Is Carmen Sandiego?
Broderbund Software
$49.95

Crayola Amazing Art Adventure
Crayola Art Studio

The collaboration between a leading manufacturer of graphics software—Micrografx—and the premier children's-art-supply company—Binney & Smith, maker of Crayola crayons—has produced two of the best art-for-kids programs on the market.

Crayola Amazing Art Adventure and Crayola Art Studio are two versions of the same product, each tailored to a specific age group. This is an important distinction because these products provide age-specific structured activities.

Comprising ten different games based on childhood favorites such as Connect-the-Dots, Amazing Art Adventure is geared at younger painters. Art Studio offers a variety of project templates that let users create things like notepaper, certificates, and badges, and it also offers many of the Art Adventure games, which have been revamped to appeal to more sophisticated older artists. So while tiny tots play the Monster Mix-Up game, older kids can use that mix-and-match technique to design clothing or vehicles. After playing the games, kids can color the pictures.

These packages share the same easy-to-use yet powerful painting tools. The watercolor and marker tools paint transparently, so children can mix new colors right on the page, and the fill tool produces smooth gradients. And where other children's art programs let users paint with simple pictures, these products offer brushes that look just like dinosaurs or gemstones. The best part is the interface, which incorporates the metaphor of a child's room, so even the youngest computer artist will feel right at home.

Crayola Amazing Art Adventure
Crayola Art Studio
Micrografx

Microsoft Fine Artist

Microsoft Fine Artist transports your children to Imaginopolis, an exciting new place where creativity is king. Once there, they will meet three cartoon characters: a gnomelike creature named McZee and two cool kids named Maggie and Max, who

Top Ten Signs You Bought a Bad Computer

10. Lower corner of screen has the words "Etch-a-Sketch" on it.

9. Its celebrity spokesman is that "Hey Vern!" guy.

8. In order to start it you need some jumper cables and a friend's car.

7. Its slogan is "Pentium: Redefining Mathematics."

6. The "quick reference" manual is 120 pages long.

5. Whenever you turn it on, all the dogs in your neighborhood start howling.

4. The screen often displays the message, "Ain't it break time yet?".

3. The manual contains only one sentence: "Good Luck!"

2. The only chip inside is a Dorito.

1. You've decided that your computer is an excellent addition to your fabulous paperweight collection. ■

act as guides. All of Microsoft Fine Artist's support is provided through these online characters. In the beginning, it's great to learn about things such as negative space by painting along with Maggie. But the constant pop-ups containing questions and instructions require users to read lots of text, and they can sometimes feel intrusive.

Microsoft Fine Artist uses the metaphor of a building to organize activities, and whether you travel via a goofy elevator, a fire pole, or surprise animations, getting to each of the floors is half the fun. Special animated stickers come to life when clicked with the magic wand, so birds can flap their wings and snakes can slither across the screen. With sound effects such as dinosaur roars, boinks, and animal squawks—which can be assigned to individual objects—and the ability to sequence paintings and transition effects into a screen show, Microsoft Fine Artist may be

the perfect gift for budding multimedia producers.

Microsoft Fine Artist
Microsoft

Kid Pix 2

Kid Pix, once the defining product in the children's art category, is beginning to show its age. But even though Kid Pix 2 is basically a repackaging of Kid Pix and Kid Pix Companion, it still has a lot of life in it. Unique features include the ability to switch from English to Spanish, which is a great learning tool when used in conjunction with such features as the talking alphabet, hidden pictures that can be revealed only with the mystery eraser, and an idea generator that produces a silly sentence for children to illustrate. Users can even expand Kid Pix's horizons with the more than 400 stamps, 32 ready-to-paint scenes, and 40 hidden pictures that come in The Kid Pix Fun Pack, a $19.95 add-on. Using Kid Pix 2's simple interface, which puts all of the tools on-screen at once, even the smallest painter will be making art in no time. Older children may outgrow the painting tools, but the ability to record sounds and the new support of AVI movies (which users can paste into paintings or create from a Kid Pix Slide Show) will keep even preteens interested in this classic program.

Kid Pix 2
Broderbund Software

2 AWARD-WINNING PROGRAMS IN 1: KID PIX, KID PIX COMPANION & M

The Original Paint & Picture Show Program Just for Kids!

KID PIX 2

Broderbund

Mario Is Missing CD-ROM Deluxe

The main trouble with giving a kid this title is that the tyke will think it's a run-and-jump action game like its Nintendo predecessor. Actually, it's much closer to Carmen Sandiego than anything in a video game arcade—though the DOS interface isn't as much fun. Mario is missing (as if you couldn't guess), and to find him you have to lead his brother, Luigi, to different landmarks around the world in order to return valuable artifacts to their rightful places. But if you're wondering why one of the Mario Brothers has Mario for a first name, don't expect any expla-

nations. He may be Mario Mario, but nobody's letting on.—Ron White

Mario Is Missing CD-ROM Deluxe
Mindscape
(800) 234-3088; (415) 883-3000
$35

Rallo Gump

Tom Hanks running at lightning speed? Wrong Gump. But there's plenty of running and jumping going on nonetheless. I don't understand the appeal of these Mario-style arcade games myself, but every kid under 12 seems to be hooked. They'll probably go ape over the more than 100 levels in

this game. Just don't look over their shoulders: The excellent blending of color and wild illustrations is enough to draw in adults, too.—Ron White

Rallo Gump
Just SoftWorks
(708) 257-7616
$30

Little Monster at School
Arthur's Birthday
Ruff's Bone
Harry and the Haunted House

Living Books CDs are supposed to be for small children, but like Sesame Street, they're for everybody. Of the four latest discs, two are based on well-known children's books: *Little Monster at School* by Mercer Mayer and *Arthur's Birthday* by Marc Brown. The other two are Living Books originals: *Ruff's Bone* by Colossal Pictures (which produces animations for MTV) and Harry and the Haunted House by Mark Schlichting (the mastermind behind Living Books).

Each disc carries on the winning formula behind the first Living Book, Just Grandma and Me. You page through an illustrated kid's story told in Spanish or English and click on everything in sight. Hilarious animations pop up at almost every click: A periscope pops out of a cereal bowl, a lunch box sings, a bird lays down a funky bass riff, or golf balls explode (my favorite). The surprises are funny even the twentieth time around. Get them for your kids and yourself.—Ron White

Little Monster at School
Arthur's Birthday
Ruff's Bone
Harry and the Haunted House
Living Books
(800) 521-6263; (415) 382-7818
$39 est. each

SHOW-AND-TELL GOES HIGH TECH
Magic Theatre

When telling a story with words and simple pictures ceases to amuse your young raconteurs, it's time to introduce them to Magic Theatre, a creativity program that lets kids create their own animated movies.

The Studio is the heart of the program; here kids

choose scenery, paint in props, and add moving objects, animated characters, and background music. To complete the storytelling process, kids can add their own narration using the included microphone. Magic Theatre records each of these actions (ignoring any undos) and then plays them back in real time as a movie scene. Movies may consist of single or multiple scenes.

Spoken help and large icons make it easy for even little filmmakers to get the hang of the program. Magic Theatre is a wonderful tool for helping kids develop their storytelling and creativity skills. Show-and-tell will never be the same again.— Gayle C. Ehrenman and Adam A. Hicks

Magic Theatre
Knowledge Adventure
(800) 542-4240; (818) 542-4200
$59.95

Busytown

Kids aged three through seven will feel at home in this familiar world, based on characters created by children's author Richard Scarry. All their favorite characters are here, encouraging them to participate in learning activities that range from pumping gas to controlling the wind. There are three levels of play to choose from, lots of delightful animations to explore, and an original musical score. If you don't have fun in Busytown, you just don't know how to have fun.

Busytown
Paramount Interactive
(415) 813-8040
$49.95

It's a Bird's Life

In Shelley Duvall's It's a Bird's Life, a group of exotic birds journeys from Los Angeles to the Amazon rain forest and back in a digital storybook that is ambitious in scope and modest in animation. The illustrations are beautiful and the story and games engaging for kids aged three and up.

It's a Bird's Life
Sanctuary Woods Multimedia
Corp.
(415) 578-6340
$39.95

The Cat Came Back

What if you had a cat you couldn't give away? Every time you thought you'd found him a home, he came right back to you. That's the premise behind this engaging program, part of Sanctuary Woods's I-Learn series.

The Cat Came Back helps children learn and explore in four different activity areas, all of which are tied to the cat theme. Children can listen, read, sing, or write along with the story line. Kids can even choose a male or female narrator and decide whether to hear the story in English, Spanish, or French.

In addition to the story, there are activities to keep the fun flowing. In the Sing-Along section, kids can hear the song played on a variety of instruments (including a guitar and a steel drum), have the song sung to them, or record their own voice singing the song. In the Write-Along section, young readers gather clues to solve the mystery of where Mr. Johnson sent his cat and then write diary entries about their detective work. Kids can use the program's art to create and print their own stories— pictures, words, and all.

In the Read-Along section, kids can explore the attractive hot-spot animations hidden

on the various pages, as well as learn new words and their definitions while reading the story. As in the Living Books, there's a hidden animation for kids to find on each page. The program also includes a printed activity book that tests kids' knowledge of what they've just read.

There may be no lesson to learn, but that's no drawback. The program is loads of fun and keeps kids interested for hours. One word of warning: The theme song can become addictive.

The Cat Came Back
Sanctuary Woods Multimedia
Corp.
(800) 245-4525; (415) 286-6100
$39.95

Somebody Catch My Homework

Somebody Catch My Homework is a 49-page electronic storybook that contains 19 poems written by David L. Harrison. These poems cover important moments in a child's life, such as reading a book alone for the first time, facing a schoolyard bully, or making up an excuse for not having done the assigned homework. Some poems explore a child's everyday problems. For example, "A Better Answer" muses on how to handle the class know-it-all. Other poems, such as "My Advice," are humorous romps through fantasy.

The poems flow well and are easy for children to read.

One particularly appealing option allows children to read the poems themselves before the program reads them aloud. Children can choose to have the program read to them in either a child's voice or in Harrison's own voice. The poems will delight children and will bring back many memories for parents; school tests and unidentifiable lunch foods seem to be timeless parts of growing up.

Although Somebody Catch My Homework may not include the high-impact animations and sounds of other electronic storybooks, it does have a focus on serious study that will appeal to many parents. The program guide that comes inside the jewel box suggests ways to help children relate the poems to their lives.

Somebody Catch My Homework
Discis Knowledge Research
(800) 567-4321
$29.95

Club KidSoft

If you've ever bought expensive software for your kids only to find they hated it, Club KidSoft CD-ROM might provide the answer you've been waiting for. This software club and magazine combination gives you more than 30 interactive demos of popular titles for kids, including a couple of titles reviewed here; if your little one spots a game that catches her fancy, you can help her download the complete ver-

sion or call a toll-free number to purchase it.

In addition to the demos, this latest issue of the CD-ROM includes a ClubRoom where kids can enter a contest, listen to a song, or browse through winning stories and illustrations by previous contest winners. There are no games or hands-on activities, however.

A $29.95 annual club membership gets you quarterly CDs and magazines; single issues are also available.—Gayle C. Ehrenman

Club KidSoft
KidSoft Inc.
(800) 354-6150
$29.95

GROW SOME DIGITAL FUNK OF YOUR OWN
Rock, Rap, and Roll

Most of the interactive music titles in today's spotlight have some grand gimmick along with sponsorship from a big name. Not here. Instead, this program has backing tracks set in a dozen different modern musical genres.

You create an integrated backing track by pulling musical objects into the "Song-a-lizer" and add different pre-recorded snippets using the mouse or the keyboard.

The results sound professional, in a generic way. In fact, Rock, Rap, and Roll is a complete catalogue of modern

musical clichés. You can toss the "all right," "get it on," and whatever other musical trill in at random. The results are—in their own way—unique. Like a man walking through a river, the particular clichés that you have assembled for this particular performance cannot be duplicated.

Cynics will say that rock and roll is nothing but a series of cliches anyway. This is, however, one way to reproduce the sound without the skill. Consequently, you can take it one step farther. A built-in recorder allows you to save sound files and use them in other formats. Or you can set the program on automatic and use it as a backdrop for your own original

musicianship.—Charlie Bermant

Rock, Rap, and Roll
Paramount Interactive
700 Hansen Way
Palo Alto CA 94504
(415) 812-8200
$79.95 (CD) $59.95 (floppy)

The Grammy Awards

This should be a great topic for a multimedia disc: music, TV, and high-gloss production values. But alas, this DOS-based CD-ROM delivers only the minimum. In other words, most of it is text. Although the Help file mentions that sound and pictures are not available for five of the 34 ceremonies the disc

covers, even when they are available, they're limited to a few still shots and the audio from the TV presentations. Something that claims to be a retrospective like this should at least include the complete version of each year's winning song. (Of course, when it comes to Perry Como singing his Grammy-winning "Catch a Falling Star," incompleteness can be a virtue.) If you're absolutely desperate for Grammy trivia, get it. Otherwise, spend your cash on music CDs.—Ron White

The Grammy Awards
Compton's NewMedia
(619) 929-2500
$49.95

Heart: 20 Years of Rock & Roll

This is what you get by combining rock and CD-ROM without adding a healthy dose of imagination. The disc is a tribute to Ann and Nancy Wilson, known collectively as Heart, with no game or gimmickry, just videos, photos, audio interviews, and songs—not exciting, just okay, even if you're a big Heart fan.

Some parts of the CD-ROM are downright irritating—such as the requirement for a display with 32,000 colors (without one, the photos on the disc don't display correctly). And some of the lyrics shown onscreen don't match what's being sung.

But the biggest disappointment comes from the CD-ROM trying to be a comprehensive look at a 20-year career and nearly a dozen albums. There's not enough room for a greatest hits compilation, so many songs get clipped to a just few seconds, leaving you wanting more. Such a tease.—Ron White

Heart: 20 Years of Rock & Roll
Compton's NewMedia
(619) 929-2500
$49.95

Interactive

He used to go by just one name, but was that short enough? Noooooo. Prince calls himself by a symbol now—a silliness we won't encourage here. We'll call him Glyph for the rest of the column.

This disc shows that weirdness can be fun. You wouldn't expect Glyph to do the obvious (take his new name…please), and this Windows and Mac title won't disappoint you. Instead of watching a bunch of music videos on disc, you explore Glyph's pleasure dome—sort of a Playboy Mansion designed by someone with even less taste than Hugh Hefner. Along the way you experience Glyph's videos and songs as you collect the parts of a key that eventually lets you access "a special treat" (less scary than it sounds).

Myst-like in its feel (a good thing), this is a more intellectually challenging and mystic CD-ROM game than Myst. Both are unrushed, nonviolent explorations, but Glyph Interactive has more rock and talk.

My only question is this: Are the people who enjoy watching videos of a guy who can't grow a decent mustache the same type of people who like to play mystery games? I hope so, because Prince—er, Glyph— deserves credit for doing it right.—Ron White

[Prince Symbol] Interactive
Compton's NewMedia and
Graphix Zone
(619) 929-2500
$59.95

World Beat

World Beat is a musical sojourn around the world. It's packed with music and video clips, articles, and interviews. The graphics are lively, and the music's never dull. There are three narrated guides and a discography with nearly 2,000 listings. From Afoxe to Zydeco, World Beat covers over 150 musical styles, explaining the history of each form and its influence on contemporary genres.

World Beat
Medio Multimedia Inc.
(800) 788-3866
$59.95

It's an even better trip on CD-ROM!

Woodstock 25th Anniversary CD-ROM

Like wow, man, it's three days of peace, love, and music on one disk. It's better this time around since you won't have to sleep in the mud just to hear "Suite: Judy Blue Eyes."

Woodstock 25th Anniversary
CD-ROM
Time Warner Interactive Group
(800) 482-3766
$39.95

Billy Graham-Virus—When you save a file, it prints, "I am saved!" to the screen.

Dolby Sound

i think the next chapter is beginning to unfold. I can see a vision of entertainment in the next century as something very, very different from what we've become accustomed to in the later part of this century. Obviously, the technological advances in communications are paving the way for that. Maybe just your mood will define the kind of music that you select, rather than going "let's see what the new U2 album is like." Instead, a new release will be selected for you, and even modified for you, by some unbelievably tiny personal entertainment control probably implanted behind your left ear. In any case, I think there will be a lot of music around and freely available to the public. I think the public will be involved in a far more interactive way in the way that music sounds. But the question is how to begin exploring this musical world without tripping yourself up in a horrible quagmire of backroom sweaty VR helmets and 3-D handcards and MIDI riffs flashing through themes…the Frankenstein part of it, which I find unappealing.

—THOMAS DOLBY, ELECTRONIC MUSICIAN, FOUNDER, HEADSPACE MULTIMEDIA STUDIO

INSIDE THE TODD POD
No World Order

Todd Rundgren's entry in the interactive musical sweepstakes has several unique aspects. It is the first program to be created expressly for the new musical frontier, incorporating original interactive music from a major artist. And while the standard passive musical CD will not go away any time soon, No World Order precedes how at least some people will make albums in the future.

The "album" contains the standard dozen-or-so songs, in a form to be disassembled and reassembled at will. It contains about 1500 musical snippets that become part of a "database." Once you become familiar with the contents, you can pick and choose the parts you like and play them over and over (and ignore the stuff that you hate). Or you can just set it

on autopilot, and let the program make the choices.

Rundgren has announced that he is now an interactive artist and his future "recordings" will consist of new additions to the musical data base. His albums, then, will refine and improve the style he has already established, with one musical phrase building from and connecting to the last. The only disadvantage of No World Order—as it stands today—is that the music isn't as rich or enjoyable as much of what Rundgren has done in the past. That, however, should change as this art form matures and the No World Order database deepens its scope.—Charlie Bermant

No World Order
Electronic Arts
P.O .Box 7578
San Mateo, CA 94403
$24.95

PLAY GUITAR
Virtual Music

So you want to be a rock-and-roll star, but you're stuck at your PC all day? Not to worry. Strap on your Virtual Guitar and enter the world of West Feedback, where anyone who can hit the beat can make it to the big time.

Virtual Music is an air guitarist's dream come true. The system includes the Welcome to West Feedback game CD-ROM and the aforementioned Virtual Guitar. The Virtual Guitar, which is roughly 95 percent the size of a standard electric guitar, serves as your game controller in the rock-and-roll fantasy game that is West Feedback. You use it as both a pointing device and as a musical-input device.

In the West Feedback adventure, you're a grungy guitar-playing kid who dreams of unseating Eric Clapton as this generation's rock god. To make it to the top, or in this case to the stage of the local club (The Dead Inn), you'll have to start practicing in your bedroom. Here you can strum along with a variety of songs, including selections from Cracker, Pantera, and Gin Blossoms, until you get the rhythm down. A handy visual aid called the Rhythm EKG (REKG) displays the proper rhythm scheme for a song as a series of spikes. Match those spikes as you strum along to the music, and you'll earn the points necessary for advancing to the next level of

musical success: playing with a local garage band. Click with the band and you'll pick up an agent who can guide you to the stage of the Dead Inn. Whether you win or lose will depend on how much the concert-goers appreciate your performance and how many credibility points you amass along the road to fame.

To make it to the end of this game, all you need is a sense of rhythm and some persistence. You don't need to know anything about music, since you won't actually be playing notes. The fretboard of the guitar is inactive, and the six strings are really just one guitar string artfully wound.

You'll want to hang on to your Virtual Guitar when you've made it to the top of West Feedback. Upcoming adventures will let you play along with Aerosmith, as well as other music notables. And you'll be able to start a virtual band before long, when Virtual Drums, Virtual Keyboard, and Virtual Bass are released.

Virtual Music won't help you learn to play guitar, but who needs lessons when you can star in your own rock-and-roll fantasy?—Gayle C. Ehrenman

Virtual Music
Ahead Inc.
(800) 872-7827
$99

🖑 Michael Jackson Virus—Hard to identify because it is constantly altering its appearance. This virus won't harm your PC, but it will trash your car.

21st Century Media PhotoDisc Series

21st Century Media PhotoDisc Series is a seven-volume (and counting) series that steers clear of clichés while offering images ranging from people at work and play to wildlife and the environment to world commerce and tourism. Its innovative image-cataloging software makes finding files a snap.

21st Century Media PhotoDisc Series
21st Century Media
2013 Fourth Avenue
Suite 403
Seattle, WA 98121
(800) 446-2001; (310) 451-1383
$299; starter kit, $69

BrushStrokes

The most recent entry to the budget-color-paint-program category more than holds its own against the competition. BrushStrokes is a 32-bit program that features an elegantly designed interface, a wide assortment of feature-rich tools, and surprising image-processing power—all for an affordable $139.

The BrushStrokes interface is intuitive and easy to use and provides lots of helpful feedback. Floating palettes let you customize brushes, patterns, and colors. Many of the program's dialog boxes allow you to experiment with brush settings. Preview windows let you view the effects of filters before you apply them. You can configure the Tools palette to display icons that represent currently selected foreground, background, and line colors, so you know at a glance what the results of using a particular tool will be.

Similarly, when you select a brush, the cursor shows you exactly what that brush will do when you apply it. If you've chosen a large square brush to apply a dark-red foreground color, for example, the cursor becomes a dark-red square. This helpful feedback takes a lot of the guesswork out of painting. Other pluses are five levels of undo and the program's ability to interrupt screen redraws as you make menu selections.

BrushStrokes offers an impressive array of features at a budget price. The program's well-designed interface lets you get your hands on its power quickly and intuitively, and its flexibility encourages experimentation. —Eric Taub

BrushStrokes
Claris
5201 Patrick Henry Drive
Santa Clara, CA 95052
(408) 727-8227
$139

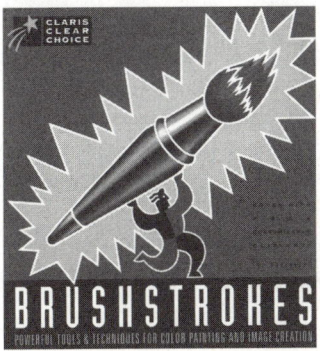

Stereolusions

Now you see it, now you don't. Take artwork you've created in a paint package, then render it into one of those vision-shattering hidden images. And let me know if you can find the hidden picture.

TURNING BACK THE PAGES
FlipBook

Moviemaking comes full circle with FlipBook. Now you can turn your QuickTime movies into paper flipbooks—tiny pages showing still images that appear animated when you riffle their edges with your thumb. After importing QuickTime or PICS files or Scrapbook frames into FlipBook, you step through the movie frame by frame and then open it as a FlipBook layout. You can set page size, right- and left-hand margins, and other options. FlipBook automatically determines how many pages are required. The product ships with special perforated paper for easy assembly into books, but you can manually cut up standard paper. Is it useful? Not really. Is it fun? You bet. FlipBook is from S.H. Pierce & Co., the same company that brings you large-scale printing with PosterWorks.—Pamela Pfiffner

FlipBook
S. H. Pierce & Co.
(617) 338-2222
$89

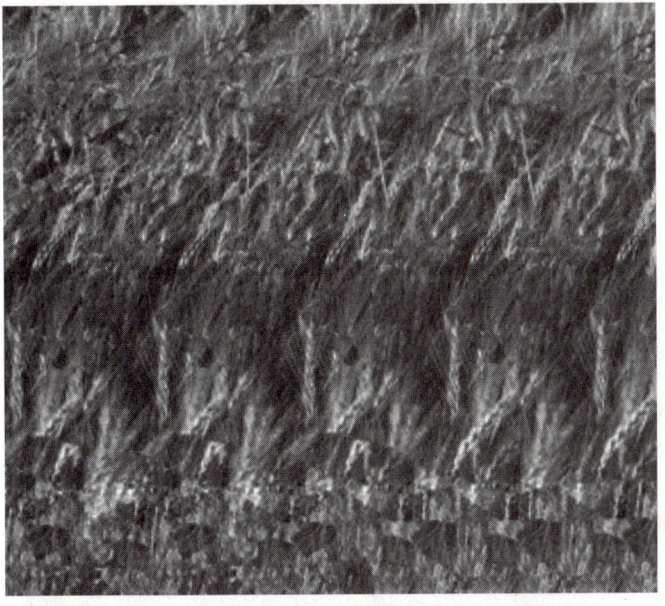

Stereolusions
I/O Software Inc.
(800) 800-7970; (909) 483-5700
$39

LEARNING TO PAINT WITH DABBLER
Dabbler

Fractal Design Dabbler isn't about instant art. There are no clip-art pictures, no wacky drawing tools, and no animated stamps here. Simply stated: Dabbler is about learning to paint. Like its older sibling Fractal Design Painter, Dabbler mimics traditional art media. So drawing with the pencil tool on one of the 20 different paper grains produces nubby, textured lines. Likewise, markers blend into the underlying colors, and crayons display waxy buildup. The program includes 12 different painting tools ranging from

Impressionist oil paint to chalk or spray paint.

Tools are stored in drawers, which makes the program easy to use for both children and novice artists. But Dabbler doesn't have any of the limitations inherent to children's art programs. It isn't restricted to one unchanging palette, for example, and it won't work with anything less than a 256-color adapter.

Dabbler knows that in order to make pretty pictures you have to know how to draw. Toward that end, the manual includes discussions on color theory, as well as a series of abridged drawing lessons by well-known art instructor Walter Foster. There are also prerecorded drawing sessions that can be played back stroke by stroke. You can record and play back your own sessions as well.

While you might buy Dabbler for your kids, you should also consider buying it for yourself. With practice, you'll be able to recapture your lost creative urges.— Luisa Simone

Dabbler
Fractal Design Corp.
(800) 647-7443; (408) 688-5300
$99

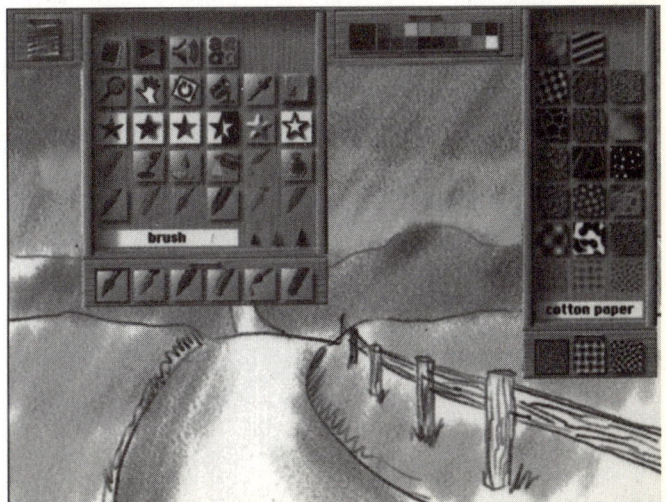

Microsoft Art Gallery

When it comes to art, most people subscribe to the "I don't know how to define it, but I know it when I see it" school of thought. Microsoft Art Gallery certainly enables you to see a lot of it—and may change how you think about painting.

Based on the National Gallery of London's collection of thirteenth- to twentieth-century paintings, Microsoft Art Gallery beautifully presents the lives of the painters, an historical atlas, and four narrated tours. It also has practical help, such as spoken pronunciations; there's no excuse for mispronouncing Ingres or *trompe l'oeil* anymore. Microsoft Art Gallery's paintings are hyperlinked to other related works—an advantage this medium has over typical museums. There are limitations, however.

Much of the material only scratches the surface. Microsoft Art Gallery won't tell you about the controversy surrounding Velasquez's "The Rokeby Venus," and because it's based on a single art collection, its coverage is limited. Also, the images don't match the detail of photographs in a good art book. Van Gogh's brush strokes look smudged, and the point in Seurat's pointillism is blotchy. But what this disc lacks in completeness and detail, it makes up in its elegant yet easily navigated presentation.—John R. Quain

Microsoft Art Gallery
Microsoft Corp.
(800) 426-9400; (206) 882-8080
$79.95

Exploring Ancient Architecture

Goethe once called architecture "frozen music." Exploring Ancient Architecture, from Medio Multimedia, sets that music in motion with impressive 3-D animation.

Covering four eras—the Neolithic, Egyptian, Greek, and Roman periods—this disc uses multimedia effects to recreate architecture none of us can ever visit. Each period is covered by an overview using slides and models, while the narrator delivers a thumbnail sketch of the era's crowning architectural achievements. The overviews can be tedious, but the real gems are the building tours.

The seven building tours allow you to become a virtual tourist. In the Neolithic period, for example, you can wander through Stonehenge, which actual tourists are no longer allowed to do. Furthermore, buildings long since destroyed (such as the Temple of Khons) are re-created for you to stroll through.

Other aspects of the disc suffer from a lack of creativity. The navigation controls are stifling, and search mechanisms are nonexistent. In addition, the narration sounds like a sixth-grade history film. As a reference tool, Exploring Ancient Architecture is merely a coffee-table book; still, it's a great coffee-table book.

Exploring Ancient Architecture
Medio Multimedia Inc.
(800) 788-3866
$59.95

I Photograph to Remember

I Photograph to Remember is Latin American photographer Pedro Meyer's exquisite black-and-white homage to his parents. Told in his own images and narration, this work brings into the home on a single disk what many museums can't achieve in an entire exhibit—more personalized contact with the artist.

I Photograph to Remember
The Voyager Co.
(800) 446-2001
$39.95

The Print Shop Deluxe CD Ensemble

Broderbund has thrown its entire set of cult-success desktop publishing utilities onto a single disc, The Print Shop Deluxe CD Ensemble. These are not corporate presentation tools, but for the kids, home use, quick-and-dirty business cards, and that all-important Happy Labor Day card for Grandma, there's nothing better around. The CD version brings together all of Print Shop's easy-to-use Windows programs, its vast collection of borders, clip art, and initial caps, and a utility (which, strangely enough, is DOS) for converting graphic formats. If you've liked any part of the original Print Shop programs, you'll love this ensemble.—Ron White

The Print Shop Deluxe CD Ensemble
Broderbund Software
(800) 521-6263
$80

SIMULATORS: ROCKETS, PLANES, CARS, BOATS, TANKS, SUBS

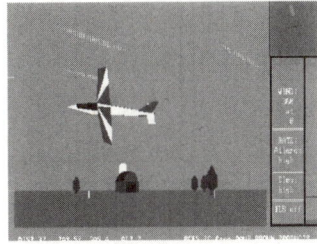

RCFS PC Release 4

There are thousands of aficionados of fixed-wing and rotary-wing (helicopter) RC aircraft. It can cost a couple of hundred dollars to start, and many RC pilots invest a small fortune.

A radio-control craft has the same controls as a real airplane: an elevator, ailerons, a rudder, and throttle. Instead of having a yoke and pedals, however, the RC pilot uses a pair of joysticks mounted on the transmitter box. The left joystick is self-centering in the horizontal axis for the rudder, with the vertical axis remaining free for the throttle control. The right joystick is self-centering in both directions, with the ailerons controlled by the horizontal axis and the elevator by the vertical axis.

This control arrangement presents a significant challenge because the pilot's point of view doesn't always match that of the aircraft. Therefore, the directional controls work backward when the plane is headed toward you, compared with

when it is heading away. There is a strong financial incentive for mastering these controls; auger into the ground with a $300 model airplane, and you've made an expensive mistake.

Dave Brown Products Inc. has an answer: RCFS PC Release 4, a radio-controlled flight simulator. The program lists for $79.95, but for $169.95, you also get a control box that plugs into your computer's joystick port. You could fly with two standard joysticks, but the control box makes a difficult task a bit easier.

You can pick among a variety of airplane designs: high wing, low wing, delta wing, biplane, nose wheel, and tail dragger. There is even an electric glider. In addition, you can alter the configuration of the flight model, including control sensitivity, stall speed for airplanes, weathervane tendency for the helicopter, and how many minutes of fuel the aircraft can carry. Both modules have trainer settings that provide fairly docile handling characteristics.

Another feature designed to help beginners is the ILS, which displays a gray box over the end of the runway. Fly your plane so that it stays in the box, and you're guaranteed a smooth arrival at the end of the runway. It's still hard to do, but the graphic guide is a big help.

The graphics are strictly 16-color EGA, so don't expect any FS5-style photo-realistic terrain here. You can have a

featureless landscape, or add some mountains in the distance and a pond, trees, and barn nearby. You can go whole hog with racing pylons and a limbo-style pole to fly under. The tip of a pylon changes from black to red as your plane nears it, then turns to green after you have cleared the pylon and can make your turn. The manual also suggests having competitions for flying under the limbo pole—in regular and inverted flight. I found upright flying difficult enough, and my every attempt at inverted flight resulted in an unscheduled landing. To add to the realism after you crash, the screen clears and offers an assessment of the damage and an estimate of repair costs.

So if you're looking for a way to practice RC flight, experiment before making a serious investment, or find a new flight sim challenge, check out RCFS PC—it's good for hours of fun.—Alfred Poor

RCFS PC Release 4
Dave Brown Products Inc.
4560 Layhigh Rd.
Hamilton, OH 45013
(513) 738-1576
$79.95; software with control box $169.95

SimLife

When it's time to take a break from studying for the biology final, why not try creating your own life-forms? With SimLife, you can create plants and animals and set

them loose on a planet of your making. Watch them evolve, take over the planet, and go extinct. The worst part of the whole experience is that when you're done playing God, you've got to go back to the real world—the one where your biology professor has the power over life, death, and grades.

SimLife
Maxis
$49.95

BLAST OFF TO NEW HEIGHTS

Strike Commander CD

If there's any game that deserves to be on CD-ROM, it's Origin Systems' Strike Commander. A graphically dazzling adventure game/flight simulator, Strike Commander came at a high price in its original floppy-disk-based format: You couldn't run it on anything slower than a 486DX2/50, it required 41MB of hard-disk space and lots of RAM, and game play was still choppy. This recently released CD-

ROM version is like a new lease on life. It makes fewer technical demands, improves overall performance, and adds some speech capabilities and missions that previously were sold separately.

Like Spectrum Holobyte's complex Falcon 3.0, Strike Commander places you behind the rudder of a F-16 jet fighter. Here, though, you're soaring through a near-future world where the global economy is teetering on disaster. Mercenary squadrons, flying late-twentieth-century fighter aircraft, have become the tools of the rich and famous; the IRS has its own squadron, making audits even scarier.

You play a rough-and-ready male pilot in the ranks of Stern's Wildcats—a mercenary squadron that prides itself on accepting only ethical missions, such as delivering supplies to besieged government forces. You must complete missions and survive confrontations with only minimal equipment damage and few casualties in order to maintain a profit margin that

allows you to continue operations. Each mission is followed by a cinematic sequence that advances the story and introduces new characters. You can talk to these characters to learn information or bargain for a new mission.

But the heart of Strike Commander is simulation—perhaps more playable than Falcon 3.0, but definitely simulation. Flying an F-16 is tricky business, and there is a steep learning curve. Still, Strike Commander is worth the effort. There's nothing like strafing a skyscraper and watching the windows get blown out! And the bubble canopy of the jet gives you such a wide field of vision that you actually get the feel of craning your neck to look for aircraft.

Strike Commander CD is quite a bargain. It's packed with hundreds of hours of gaming fun.—Bernard H. Yee

Strike Commander CD
Origin Systems Inc.
(800) 245-4525; (512) 335-0440
$79.95

Microsoft Space Simulator

Twenty-five years ago, residents of Earth set foot on the moon for the first time. If you haven't made the cut for NASA's next crop of astronauts, you might want to try your hand at Microsoft's new Space Simulator. We had the chance to evaluate a late beta of the program, and aside from a few display bugs, it promises to be an astounding package.

The program was developed by the Bruce Artwick Organization (BAO), using the same basic code as Microsoft's Flight Simulator 5. This provides 3-D graphics, the ability to map photorealistic images onto surfaces, and sophisticated shading of objects. There are also many commands and features in common with FS5, such as a full-screen display, stored situations, and still- and moving-image recording.

Also like FS5, Space Simulator chooses authentic performance over gameplaying. While many space programs let you point your craft and fly in that direction, this one forces you to cope with a universe governed by Newtonian physics. Your spacecraft has momentum, and in order to change direction, you must apply the correct force in the right direction. This means that when you

travel from the Earth to the moon, you have to turn your ship around and fire your rockets in order to slow down before you arrive. The principle is simple to grasp; learning how to execute it accurately is much more difficult.

Flying in space is far more difficult than in an airplane. An airplane has gravity acting more or less like a keel, providing a steady force against which you can work. In space, you not only move freely in all directions, but your craft can also rotate freely. Matching speeds with an orbiting space station, then maneuvering your ship to line up with the docking port takes skill, patience, and lots of practice.

There is a rich universe for you to explore. There are stored situations that can start you with familiar scenarios: launching in the space shuttle and returning to

Creating Online

i think there's a lot of amazing stuff that can happen over the network but I think in terms of the real meaning, it has to be a bit more intimate. Usually communities are communities because there is something they hold very deeply in common, usually shared adversity. I'm not sure if I fully have come to believe in that idea. I'll be delighted if it does happen. I'm more interested in the intimate things that will happen in virtual reality, such as people sharing worlds together, kids being able to create fantasy worlds. Collaborative creation is very exciting.

—JARON LANIER, VIRTUAL REALITY EXPERT

Earth, or recreating the lunar landing and departure, including the rendezvous with the Apollo module. There are near-future elements included, such as a space station in Earth's orbit. You get a number of familiar spacecraft, including the shuttle and a Manned Maneuvering Unit (MMU) for spacewalks. There are also futuristic craft, including a space fighter, freighter, explorer, ram-jet, and craft designed for space and atmospheric flight. There is even an alien craft found orbiting Jupiter. You can travel to either of two Earth-orbiting space stations, one at the moon, or one orbiting Mars. There is also a com-

plete colony on Mars that can serve as a base for explorations.

You can travel to all the planets and their moons; the manual has lots of suggestions for trips and challenging tasks for you to attempt. There are comets that move through the galaxy, and you can travel to other stars within the Milky Way—some of which have their own system of planets waiting to be discovered. The controls let you display the names of all objects in your field of view, or only certain classes of objects, if you want to limit them. You can view the skies from spacecraft, or choose to look from various observatories based on Earth that can serve as your private planetariums, since the movements of planets and other objects are accurately modeled.

Space travel takes a long time and requires some tricky navigation. The program addresses both these issues. You can accelerate the passage of time so that you can travel light-years in only a few moments, and an autopilot can be programmed to perform any task from a rendezvous to a landing.

The program places significant performance demands on your system, much like FS5. The minimum configuration is a 386DX/25 with 2MB of RAM, a hard drive with at least 15MB available, a VGA adapter and monitor, and DOS 5.0. A 486DX/33 system with a Super VGA display will give significantly better performance, and is the recommended configuration. Performance is a bit better than FS5 in general because the scenery in space is generally less complex. The program will support 800 × 600 by 256 colors with some SVGA adapters, resulting in absolutely stunning space images. Only a keyboard is required, but it is helpful to have both a mouse and joystick. There are digitized sound effects, or you can choose to play background music—these require an Ad Lib-compatible sound card.

So if you're tired of flying around the same old Earthbound places, light the burners and head for the stars.
—Alfred Poor

Microsoft Space Simulator
Microsoft Corp.
One Microsoft Way
Redmond, WA 98052-6399
(800) 426-9400; (206) 882-8080
$64.95

Detroit

Martha and the Vandellas once sang that you "can't forget the Motor City," and you may not be able to forget Motown, either, after you've played Detroit, a business simulation that places the player at the helm of an automobile company.

Players start out in 1908 with $60,000 in the bank, a factory, a single car model, a sales office, and a territory. From there, as president of the company, you open new factories and sales offices in different regions of the world; hire factory workers; and allocate advertising funds to the various media forms like magazines and billboards.

This can become an interesting balancing act. In keeping with actual historical performances, for example, some territories grow much faster than others. Starting up your company in the northeastern U.S., for example, is probably better than starting it up in China. And you should remember that factory workers have to be treated well as you control wage levels, benefits, and the hiring and firing of employees. Be careful, or the workers may strike.

The most fun part of the game is the automotive-design menu. There are

numerous components (engine, brakes, safety features, luxury features, coolant system) that make up each car. These components have a certain level of technological sophistication. You must allocate technicians to research advances in the different components if you want to have, say, a stronger engine or better road handling.

When designing a car, you get to choose what type of car (luxury, sedan, sports, van), its name, color, and the various systems. Once the car is complete, it can be tested on a track in order to find out its true performance.

As time goes by and your corporate empire grows, you build more car models of increasing sophistication and luxury. The game play is divided into months and lets you print out month-end reports. Actual world events and their impact on the auto industry are also factored into play. For example, during the Arab oil embargo in the 1970s, car sales drop.

Be forewarned: This game is not a no-brainer. Fortunately, it has excellent documentation, including a much-appreciated tutorial. The simulation's interface is

very easy to use, with many icons providing common-sense indications of what they activate. Though the game deals with a complicated subject, it is easy to play. Detroit's graphics are solid, and the background music is inoffensive enough. Up to four players can take part, and the game also supports modem play. If you are looking for something that challenges your business acumen with edge-of-your-seat competition, pick up a copy and get those assembly lines rolling.—John Terra

[Editor's Note: This product is no longer sold on it's own, but is bundled with other products.]

Detroit
Impressions Software Inc.
222 Third St.
Suite 0234
Cambridge, MA 02142
(800) 545-7677; (617) 225-0500
$69.95

Rally

Going around an oval track is monotonous, but adrenaline certainly pumps when you accelerate down narrow country roads and skid into curves filled with spectators.

That's the difference between Accolade's Rally and the rest of the competition. In Rally, you roar down reproductions of real—and rough—roads in Great Britain, not a digital duplication of a smooth asphalt circle. You'll have to pay closer attention to the terrain, use your brakes and gears with greater skill, and demonstrate more deft driving skills in Rally than in almost any other computerized automobile simulation.

Each segment of the road rally shows different characteristics. One segment may be heavily forested, while another may feature long stretches of straightaway, perfect for putting a heavy foot on the accelerator.

Other than that, the mechanics of Rally are familiar to anyone who's been behind a virtual wheel. You can choose from several cars, and you steer with either a set of keys or a joystick. A slew of options lets you customize Rally so that the car automatically brakes and shifts gears; shows you a map; becomes indestructible; or, if you have a supported sound board, tells you of upcoming curves and hazards. There's also a variety of weather conditions.

Road-rally racing sets you against the clock, not against other drivers. As you drive each of the stages, you're trying to climb up in the standings by getting to the next checkpoint as fast as possible. Whenever you complete a stage, you get the chance to repair damage to the car. Even here you often won't be able to finish all the repairs before you need to hit the road again.

Graphically, Rally keeps pace with most PC driving simulations, though it's not as slick-looking as something like Indycar. The scenery consists of bitmapped images that look blocky close up on a VGA screen. Nor does Rally snap on a slow system. Even on a 486DX/33 PC, for instance, the animation tends to be jerky. You can combat the problem to some extent by turning off the road texture.

Casual PC drivers can skip Rally, but the complete autophile won't be happy unless this driving-with-a-difference simulation is on the hard drive.—Gregg Keizer

Rally
Accolade Inc.
53 Stevens Creek Blvd.
San Jose, CA 95129
(800) 245-7744; (408) 985-1700
$59.95

Microsoft New York
Microsoft Paris

Microsoft Flight Simulator 5.0 comes with several basic scenery areas. Microsoft relies on the FS5 texture-mapping feature for the major portion of the scenery, instead of scanned photographs. The bulk of the effort goes into polygonal graphics objects, which take up less disc space and are

quicker to draw than scanned images. The end result is scenery that has the object density of some of the best FS4 scenery files, with texture-mapped backgrounds in place of the featureless green carpet of FS4.

Each of these two approaches has its benefits, but the differences demonstrate just how powerful a development environment FS5 is proving to be. As soon as we get scenery-creation tools for end users, I expect that we will see more scenery of greater variety than we had with FS4 (and that's saying a lot!).

Microsoft New York adds many new airports to the New York area, plus all ILS approaches. Local landmarks such as bridges and the Statue of Liberty are provided in enhanced detail. The terrain is more accurate, including the Palisades along the New Jersey side of the Hudson. Microsoft Paris also adds more airports and all ILS approaches, but the big story is the scenery itself. The Eiffel Tower is wonderful, especially at night, and you'll be amazed to see the

stained-glass windows in Notre Dame.

The scenery packages were developed for Microsoft by MicroScene, creators of some of Mallard Software's scenery collections, such as Tahiti and Japan. These new collections for FS5 continue to enhance MicroScene's reputation for creating vivid and detailed places to fly.—Alfred Poor

Microsoft New York
Microsoft Paris
Microsoft Corp.
One Microsoft Way
Redmond, WA 98052
(800) 426-9400; (206) 882-8080
$39.95 each

✋ Gallup Virus—60 percent of the PCs infected will lose 38 percent of their data 14 percent of the time (plus or minus a 3.5 percent margin of error)

"SimCity 2000 is one of the best programs I've ever seen."
— Todd Copilevitz, Dallas Morning News

Sim-City

Whether you're a man, woman, or child, how can you resist being the mayor of Sim-City? You plan, build, manage, and maintain a city from the ground up. If you do well, your city will prosper; if not, you'll end up with Sim-Slum.

In Sim-City you build houses, industrial areas, power plants, and roads. As the population grows, you need more utilities, a seaport, a stadium, new commercial districts, a park or two, and, of course, higher taxes. A cantankerous collection of city dwellers are always beating on your office door demanding more police officers, fire stations, and affordable housing. To keep you on your toes, the simulator throws in a few surprises—a fire here, a tor-

nado there. Before you know it, the budget is shot and you need money to build a new power plant.

Construction is easy: click an icon and drag it to the city map. The accompanying sound effects of jackhammers and bulldozers add to the realism. When disaster strikes, a video window opens and you are there. Meanwhile, the audio help feature is constantly nagging: "Put commercial zones near the residential areas…Build more affordable housing." Sounds a lot like a city council.

Sim-City is the Lincoln Logs and Lego blocks of the computer generation and splendid entertainment for the whole family.

Sim-City
Interplay Productions Inc.
(714) 553-6655
$50 (estimated price)

A CHOPPER FOR EVERYONE
Comanche CD

The RAH-66 Comanche attack helicopter was designed for speed and maneuverability at low altitudes, so you'd expect a simulation of it to provide lots of hot action over detailed terrain. Comanche CD delivers on all counts. This disk includes the entire Comanche trilogy, as well as ten bonus missions. The graphics are far more detailed than in other flight simulators, so you can clearly see boulders, rubble, and reflections as you fly through canyons and over water. The best part is that you can fly without spending much time studying the manual. The only controls you need are the collective (altitude) and the cyclic (direction).

Missions are the focus of Comanche, and there are 100 to choose from. In addition to a handful of training scenarios, there are a number of realistic operations from which to choose, with Maximum Overkill being the ultimate multibattle, theater-wide campaign. Each operation has a different objective and different complications to overcome; at times you may be low on fuel or shy on ammunition. Welcome to the military!

Great graphics, sound, and animation come at a price. For best performance, you'll need at least a 486-based PC and lots of memory. Even if you never shoot down an enemy gunship, the graphics alone are worth the ride.
—Don Trivette

Comanche CD
NovaLogic Inc.
(818) 774-0600
$74.95

SUBS AHOY!
SubWar 2050

Combine "SeaQuest DSV" and Star Wars, then stir in a volatile mix of high-tech weaponry and a setting that's as exotic as it is futuristic. What you end up with is SubWar 2050, an undersea combat simulation set in a near-future world. This isn't the kind of submarine warfare game players are used to: It's more like an air-combat game in slow motion.

Putting aside the questionable plot of private companies waging undersea warfare, SubWar 2050 is an entertaining shoot-'em-up. Its five campaigns offer different landscapes with different scenarios. One campaign is designed for rookie sub captains; the rest are full-bore combat missions.

Sub pilots must rely on their high-speed submersible's sonar to track the enemy, then use thermal layers (places where warm and cool water meet), which can block sonar, to hide from or sneak up on their adversaries. These strategic tactics are enhanced by the product's use of 3-D terrain, decent sound effects, and an interesting graphical representation of the thermal layers.

SubWar 2050 may appeal to computer combat warriors looking for a new experience, but it doesn't quite have its sea legs. The game doesn't have the panache of such futuristic space combat classics as Origin's Wing Commander. Nor does it reflect real-world strategic undersea warfare models such as Electronic Arts' SSN-21 Seawolf. A pedestrian story line and a focus on hard-hitting, quick-turning dog fights turn SubWar 2050 into an arcade-flavored fire fest.—Peter Scisco

SubWar 2050
MicroProse Software
(800) 879-7529; (410) 771-0440
$59.95

FLIGHT SIM BURNOUT CURE
Flight Sim Toolkit

Are you a little bored with your favorite flight simulator? Never fear: Domark Software's Flight Sim Toolkit (FST) includes everything you need to create your own worlds and planes, and then fly and fight in them when you're done.

FST consists of five Windows-based design utilities and a powerful flight simulator. The World Editor, which is very easy to use, lets you create and modify the physical setting for your flight. Choose from more than 100 3-D clip-art images to add targets to your landscape. To color these objects, turn to the Color Editor. For creating your own objects or modifying the clip-art images, turn to the Shape Editor, a powerful and complicated CAD utility.

You customize the aerodynamic qualities and engine power of your aircraft in the Model Editor. Despite thorough documentation, this utility can be somewhat intimidating to nonengineers. The Cockpit Editor lets you position your aircraft's instruments and displays over a .PCX representation of a real cockpit.

When you're finished crafting the ultimate flying machine, it's time to launch the DOS-based flight simulator. FST uses the same outstanding graphics engine as Domark's Super VGA Harrier and is one of the most realistic flight simulators on the market. While you can run the simulator under Windows, don't expect it to perform reliably.

If you like flight simulators, you'll want to get your hands on Flight Sim Toolkit. The ability to custom-design and fly through target-rich environments is a sure cure for flight-simulator boredom.—Michael Ryan

Flight Sim Toolkit
Domark Software Inc.
(415) 513-8929
$79.99

SHOOT 'EM UP

Raptor

If you're fed up with plodding along in role-playing games, and you've reached maximum system overload on Doom, then you'll be glad to find that no-holds-barred shoot-everything games are alive and well. Raptor, Apogee Software's latest release, puts you in the pilot seat of a high-tech jet. You play a mercenary paid to destroy the ships and ground targets of a vaguely defined enemy. There is essentially no plot beyond that—you're out to wreak as much havoc as possible.

Raptor is a bit reminiscent of the arcade hit Xevious: You pilot the jet via an overhead view, shooting both air and ground targets. But while

Raptor is simple, it's not easy. There are four levels of difficulty to choose from: training mode, rookie, veteran, and elite. Even on rookie level, Raptor is no milk run. At times, there are so many projectiles on the screen it's hard to see your jet. Various enemy ships come at you in waves, each with its own attack patterns. In addition, land-based guns fire at you with very sharp accuracy. Raptor toes the line between utter frustration and pure addiction very well.

To start, you enter your name and callsign, choose a sector to attack, and fire up the engines. Your ship is armed with a minigun (a rapid-fire machine gun) to begin with. The minigun handles both ground and air

targets fairly well, but you'll need extra firepower for tackling the higher levels.

Because you're a mercenary, you get paid by how many enemy ships and ground targets you destroy. With all the cash you collect (assuming you survive), you can buy better weapons and replenish your armor at Harold's Death Emporium. In addition, you can trade in any weapons you don't need for about half the price you paid for them. Careful selection of weapons and saving up to buy some of the more expensive—and more devastating—firepower definitely

The Computer Users' Grace

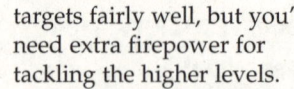

ur fileserver, who art on LAN
NETSERVER be thy name
Thy programmes come
Thy commands be done
In DOS, and sometimes in WINDOWS
Give us this day our daily login
And forgive us our hacking
As we forgive those who hack in our files
Lead us not into corrupt procedures
But deliver our e-mail
For thine is the CPU, the powersource and the monitor
For ever until obsolescence
Hey, man… ■

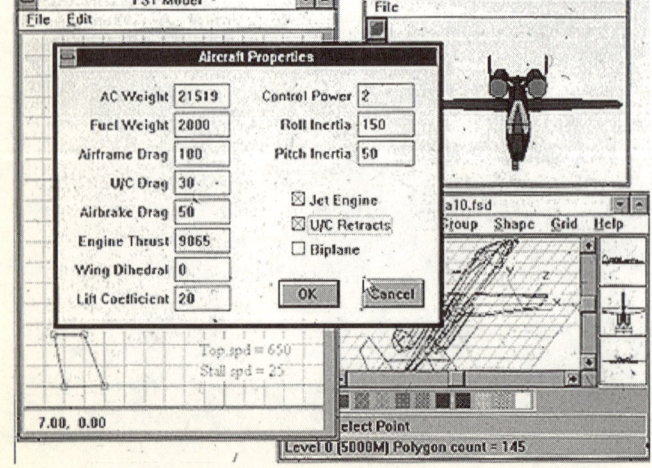

More CD-ROM drives were shipped in 1994 than in all the previous years combined. The figures are approximately 18 million in 1994 versus 10 million previously.

pays off. In addition, it helps to keep only about three weapons onboard at any one time, because you have to cycle through them to select which one you want to use. Weapons range from a $250,650 auto-targeting mini-gun to a $950,000 death ray. A laser turret that can be bought for a cool $512,850 is so efficient at destroying air targets that you may want to limit yourself to less-devastating munitions.

Raptor is pure shoot 'em up: Hold down the fire button and don't let go. It doesn't break any new ground in arcade-style games, but it's solid mindless entertainment.—John Marrin

Raptor
Apogee Software
P.O. Box 496389
Garland, TX 75049
(800) 426-3123; (214) 278-5655
$34.95

Corridor 7 Operation Body Count

Corridor 7 and its evil twin, Operation Body Count, both use the 3-D technology that was found in 1992's MVP finalist Wolfenstein 3-D and later improved on for Doom. That means the sense of reality is not as great as in Doom, but there's still plenty of shoot-'em-up action on more than 40 levels in each of the DOS games. The plots are ... well, who cares? The point is that you get to blow away a lot of bad-guy extraterrestrials. If the two Dooms on their

own didn't turn you into a natural-born killer, these should push you over the edge.—Ron White

Corridor 7, Operation Body Count
Capstone Entertainment Software
(800) 468-7226
$39 each

THINKING GAMES

BlackJack Tutor

Heading to Vegas? BlackJack Tutor will prepare you for the casino (or your weekly card came). You'll get the most out of this program if you already know the game; you can then use Tutor to drill you on strategies, including count values, surrender, splitting, and doubling.

BlackJack Tutor
ConJelCo
$75

Cogito

Cogito is the infamous Apple Puzzle DA on steroids. In it, you return a jumbled geometric figure to its original configuration. Things get complex as the levels get higher—controls get switched, and the configuration gets difficult. New Age music adds a soothing touch.

Cogito
Inline Software
$59.95

Heaven and Earth

If action-packed arcade-style games aren't your cup of tea, try Heaven and Earth. It comprises three parts: the Card Game, the Illusions Puzzle, and the Pendulum Toy. This game takes a while to master, which is part of its charm. Heaven and Earth

Heaven and Earth
Buena Vista Software
$59.95

Star Wars Chess

Playing chess on PCs carries the potential for a double whammy of nerdness. But adding Star Wars to the mix transforms the most cerebral of games into something even a Hulk Hogan fan can appreciate.

Star Wars Chess's animation makes the game as much fun as it is cerebral. The nicely drawn character pieces walk from one square to another, accompanied by their own theme songs. When a piece is captured, a battle takes place in which the piece is shot, skewered, incinerated, or squashed. All these frills can be turned off for a faster game. There's just one strange thing about Star Wars Chess: The Darth Vader piece is a queen. I, for one, would not like to tell him that to his face.—Ron White

Star Wars Chess
Mindscape (Software Toolworks)
(800) 883-3000
$69.95

Star Wars Chess

Whether you earned your varsity sweater in the chess club or hung out at the video arcade, you'll enjoy Star Wars Chess.

Star Wars Chess installs from Windows and launches from an icon, but doesn't have a standard Windows interface. An icon toolbar splits off into separate sub-toolbars with headings of Games, Play, Action, and Mentor. A QuickStart card helps you navigate, but standard Windows menus would be much more useful. However, don't let the awkward toolbar system scare you away.

You can match wits with the computer on five levels, with the option of playing other humans or watching the computer play itself. Captures have animated blast-and-die scenes. Each character kills any other character differently. Serious chess-heads can disable the music and animated sequences.

Setup mode allows you to pre-position pieces and play what-if scenarios. You can rotate your troops to the top or bottom of the board, but you can't move or rotate your basic vantage point. The game has a Hint button that demonstrates which move to make.

A booklet explains the movements of chess pieces in general. Star Wars Chess supports castling and en passant, and pawns reaching the end of the enemy side are promoted to queens.

The animated sequences and familiar sci-fi characters of Star Wars Chess gives players a needed break from the starched-collar environment that chess tradition often dictates.—Rebecca Rohan

Star Wars Chess
Mindscape (Software Toolworks Inc.)
60 Leveroni Ct.
Novato, CA 94949
(800) 283-8499; (415) 883-3000
$69.95

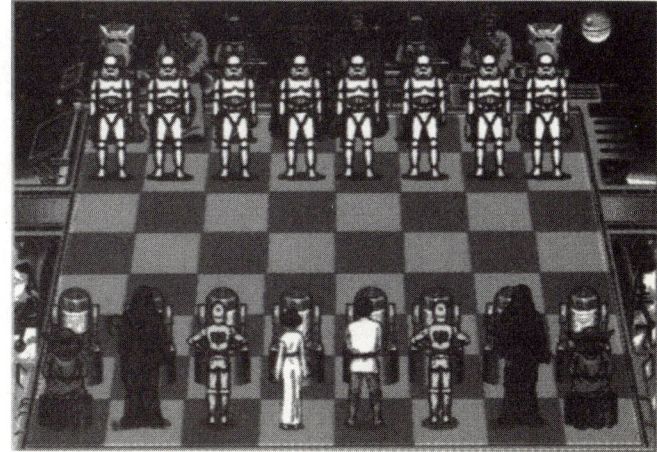

DOOM Excuses: What to Tell Your Boss When . . .

. . .You are suspected of playing DOOM:

1. "Oh, that must have been my screensaver you saw!"

2. "Those files are my Database program. DOOM stands for Database Online Operational Management. Yeah, you're right, 'WAD' is a pretty strange extension, isn't it?"

3. "Yeah, I've heard some strange noises around here, too. Rodents in the HVAC ducts, maybe?"

. . .You are overheard playing DOOM:

1. "Growling? Oh, that was probably my stomach you heard; I worked straight through lunch today."

2. "Chainsaw? No, I don't have a chainsaw in here. Mrs. Smith said something about pruning the plants at the reception desk this morning, though—you might ask her."

3. "I'm sorry, I didn't realize I was talking that loud. It was my wife on the phone, we're not getting along lately. Thorny Brown Bastard? Ha! It's a long story—she hates it when I call her that."

. . .You are caught red-handed playing DOOM:

1. "You know, this is a great screensaver but the damn thing keeps locking up or something and I can't get it to go off."

2. "It's the latest in CAD!"

3. "It's an assertiveness training program."

4. "It's supposed to be Barney's Jungle Adventure—I just picked it up for the kid, you know; but it looks pretty warped to me."

5. "I don't know what the hell it is—it said Lotus on the disk. Maybe we got some bad interference on the Net or something."

6. "I hate to say this, but I'm pretty sure it's the KillingGlee VGA virus. Don't know how I could have picked it up. Only way to get rid of it is to play it out." ■

Russian 6 Pak

Install these strategy games at your own risk: The six Russian-born beauties may look simple, but they're so addictive you'll never be able to get any work done.

Russian 6 Pak
Interplay Productions Inc.
(800) 969-4263; (714) 553-6655
$40

MISCELLANEOUS

Know Your Waterfowl

Like English people and grandmothers, bird fanciers are regarded by most of us as quaint and essentially harmless. This is also a pretty good description of Know Your Waterfowl.

The contents of this Windows CD aren't half bad—if you're into ducks and geese. The videos and stills of fowl in flight are fine, as are the audio samples. If you fancy yourself a waterfowl expert, take the dandy little quiz. But if mergansers aren't your thing, take heart: Now that waterfowl rate their own multimedia disc, your pet pastime can't be far behind.

Know Your Waterfowl
Axia Internationl
(403) 262-2942
$69.95

Loon Magic

Apparently, there are many lovers of that shy waterbird, the loon. Loon Magic is a perfect gift for anyone struck with this admittedly odd affection. This CD-ROM (which includes a special version for kids) contains facts (did you know the loon has red eyes so it can see fish better underwater?), stories, films, pictures, songs, and recorded loon cries. It's spectacular, if a little arcane.

Loon Magic
Wayzata Technology
$59

Space Shuttle

It's the ultimate in efficiency: On a single 4.75-inch CD-ROM, Space Shuttle squeezes a multibillion-dollar space program, a six-month astronaut-training course, and a detailed report on each shuttle flight—including dozens of QuickTime scenes depicting space walks, blastoffs, and landings.

Space Shuttle
The Software Toolworks
$49.95

TALES OF THE MACABRE
CD-ROM Ghosts

Are there ghosts in your machine? You might think so when you load Media Design Interactive's CD-ROM Ghosts. The horror-movie veteran Christopher Lee plays Dr. Marcus Grimalkin, who leads you on a tour of the world's most haunted house, Hobbs Manor. Here you'll discover an apparition in every room, listen to eyewitness accounts, view spooky photographs, and gawk at authentic ghostbusting equipment. Leave the hall light on ....—Kristin Balleisen

CD-ROM Ghosts
Psygnosis
(510)709-5755
$49

☞ There are 12 million multimedia home PCs in use in the U.S. as of 1994, according to a report by Business Week. Eight percent of all U.S. households own a multimedia computer.

Dream Vacations Hawaiian Style

Hawaii on your monitor is nothing like sand between your toes. Too little useful information.

Dream Vacations Hawaiian
Style
Advanced Software
(800) 441-9177
$79.95

Multimedia Kaleidosonics

Like wow! Nature scenes, an audio sound track, and endless ways to manipulate them. It's a hallucinogen for your PC.

Multimedia Kaleidosonics
Masque Publishing
(800) 765-4233; (303) 290-9853
$24.99

ALL THE NEWS THAT'S FIT TO ROM
NautilusCD

NautilusCD, a monthly CD-ROM "magazine," is helping to define how the new media fits into the scope of publishing. It contains familiar reference points such as regular departments, a table of contents and letters to the editor. At the same time, it provides a steady dosage of multimedia clips (still pictures, sound, and video) for use in a Windows or Macintosh environment. Ultimately, a NautilusCD reader does a lot more than just read: The format offers the opportunity to interact with and manipulate the information. And each issue is packed with software demos, shareware, and freeware tools.

NautilusCD also supports the arts, in a way that a conventional magazine cannot. It features multimedia performances from Windham Hill, the Celestial Navigations performance group, and Xanadu that are unavailable anywhere else. It also contains sound and video clips from various sources, which turns each issue into an exclusive, interactive digital snapshot of its time.—Charlie Bermant

NautilusCD Magazine
7001 Metatec Blvd.
Dublin, OH 43017
(800) 637-3472
$6.95 (per month) $79.95
(per year)

The *Playboy* Interview: Three Decades

You get *Playboy* only because it makes great reading? Sure. That's the same excuse every 15-year-old boy gives his mother for having the magazine ("I bought it to learn more about the philosophy of Buckminster Fuller"). Well, here's your chance to prove it. This Windows CD is a collection of 352 interviews from *Playboy*. The disc has the full text of all interviews from 1962 to 1992, plus selected sound bites. For all the fun you can poke at *Playboy*, the interviews offer a significant, wide-ranging look at three decades of popular culture as it was seen by Jimmy Carter, David Letterman, Miles Davis, Salvador Dali, Lee Iacocca, Robert Frost, and hundreds of others. Yes, there are photos as well, but you won't have to hide them under your mattress.

The Playboy *Interview: Three Decades*
IBM Multimedia Publishing Studio
(800) 898-8842
$40

UFO

Still waiting for aliens from Alpha Centauri to beam you up to their mothership? Maybe you've been trying to get picked up in the wrong places. You need UFO, a Windows CD that contains a complete database of UFO encounters organized by place, date, number of flying

saucers, and whether or not anyone was abducted. Based on the criteria you choose, a map pinpoints popular spots for the vacationing extraterrestrial. You can click on any of these spots to get details of past encounters, and many of the summaries include video or still photos. Don't leave Earth without it.

UFO
Software Marketing Corp.
(800) 545-6626; (602) 893-3377
$59.95

The People vs. O.J. Simpson: Interactive Companion to the O.J. Simpson Trial

Are you an O.J. junkie, too? "Hard Copy" and *The New York Times* don't provide enough dirt for you to wade through? The fix is in—The People vs. O.J. Simpson: Interactive Companion to the O.J. Simpson Trial.

With an hour of video drawn from CNN files, dozens of photos, and commentary by attorneys, this Windows CD lets you replay

testimony, get close-up views of blood spots 114 and 177, and study the autopsy sketches that pass by fleetingly on TV. A time line tracks events, and a cast of characters identifies the major players. For the latest developments, there's even a CompuServe membership so you can log on to a special O.J. forum.

The People vs. O.J. Simpson: Interactive Companion to the O.J. Simpson Trial
CNN Interactive and Turner Home Entertainment
(800) 294-0022
$20

Monty Python's Complete Waste of Time

And now for something completely insane, it's ... Monty Python's Complete Waste of Time, a Windows CD that brings total anarchy to computing. The disc is a compilation of the comedy troupe's animation and classic BBC skits—the cheese shop, the dead parrot, and the argument clinic, among others—all scattered willy-nilly through an interface that defies logic. Clicking anywhere onscreen can have just

about any result, from a game of Spot the Loony to the famous lumberjack song to a warning not to click on a given spot again. If you don't click at all, the CD proceeds in its own chaotic fashion.

For doing something wrong, you're occasionally sent to a penalty box where you have to listen to horrid music and vocalizations—and there's nothing you can do about it until the program decides to let you out. If you need help, press F1 for an endless stream of excuses for why you can't get any help. There's a collection of sounds, wallpaper, icons, and screen savers to totally Pythonize your PC. In addition, the disc has three arcade-style games. All are Pythonized, of course (try the flying pig shoot-'em-up for size), and one game has a bounty: Solve the puzzle, and you're eligible to win a multimedia PC or $5,000. But nothing tells you how to play this last game, or that it even exists.

If you're a Python fan, you have to have this CD. If you're not, why did you read all the way to the end of this piece?—Ron White

Monty Python's Complete Waste of Time
Seventh Level
(214) 437-4858
$59.95

How Did They Do It? Computer Illusion in Film & TV

How Did They Do It? Computer Illusion in Film & TV is more of a softbound coffee-table book than a traditional computer book. It's a big, bold, colorful peek inside the digitalization of Hollywood. More specifically, author Christopher W. Baker takes you into the increasingly computerized world of animation and special effects. The book doesn't take you far enough to give you practical tips for creating your own magic, but that's not the point. Intrigue is the point.

The first half of the book leads you through a word-and-picture history of computer graphics and a light primer on the hardware, software, and processes used to make magic on film. All of this would likely be classified as more than we need to know on another subject. But

Interactive Music

just as rock videos helped cable get going, interactive music will help interactive TV get off the ground. The biggest challenge is not to make compromises. I'm not adding interactivity for its own sake. I'm going to make sure that it adds to the music—every song and story will have a different form of interactivity, based on what the song is about. The Media Band is primarily about music and entertainment, not about technology.

—MARC CANTER, FOUNDER, MACROMEDIA, PRODUCER AND CREATOR OF MEET MEDIA BAND, AN INTERACTIVE MUSIC CD-ROM

these are movies and TV commercials we're talking about, which somehow makes rendering and reflecting techniques seem interesting. The second half of the book takes a closer look at some of these effects in action—or at least as much of a look as you can have in two dimensions—in movies, TV spots, and music videos. Never mind that it's a swinging Listerine bottle or a morphing Exxon tiger on the surface; the story lies in the making.

Indeed, the latter part of the book, while very interesting, points out some of its own inherent limitations. Even with big color pictures,

the printed page doesn't do justice to illustrating and explaining the techniques involved. If ever a book cried out for an accompanying CD-ROM disc or even a CD-ROM version, it's this one. Still, you need only be a fan of computer graphics or Hollywood to enjoy *How Did They Do It?* If you're a fan of both, it's a must for your collection.—Christopher O'Malley

How Did They Do It?
by Christopher W. Baker
Alpha Books
201 W. 103rd St.
Indianapolis, IN 46290
(800) 428-5331; (317) 581-3500
$20.00

Leisure Suit Larry 6: Shape Up or Slip Out

Not all games appeal to the brain or the trigger finger—there are other parts of the anatomy. The sixth Leisure Suit Larry game has perennial nebbish Larry still trying to make out in a world that considers him the score of last resort. Unlike previous Larry games, he speaks in this DOS and Windows CD (and sounds as dippy as you'd imagined). In all other respects, it's Larry as usual. The opening sequence—a satire of dating-game TV shows—is a riot. But I didn't make it much past that. The first puzzle of the game makes it too hard to pry Larry away from an attractive hotel clerk and into a room (by himself, as usual). My friends who have made it past first base, so to speak, tell me it's great fun. But they're probably just bragging.—Ron White

Leisure Suit Larry 6: Shape Up or Slip Out
Sierra On-Line
(800) 757-7707; (206) 649-9800
$59.95

SoftWear

People who want to show they've been with their Macs through thick and thin can do so by wearing hats and shirts from the SoftWear collection. What could be better than a bomb icon on your head? Simple—a bomb icon and the phrase "Sorry, a system error occurred" on your boxers.

These clothes will make you the talk of the campus.

SoftWear
Iconz
hat: $10
boxers: $15
t-shirt: $18
sweatshirt: $35
mug: $10

Axis: The GameCheater

Getting demolished by Slicers on Spectre Supreme? Need more Diggers on Lemmings? Axis: The GameCheater sifts through a game's memory allocations and fits the game with a patch. Getting ammo or adding extra Diggers is as easy as pressing a key combination. Axis works with most games, and Baseline plans to release modules to keep up with new ones.

Axis: The GameCheater
Baseline Publishing
$59.95

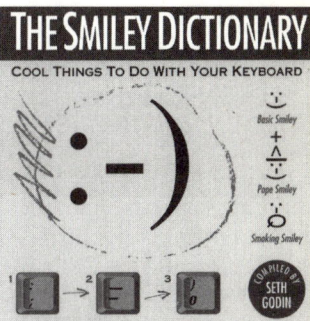

THE SMILEY DICTIONARY
COOL THINGS TO DO WITH YOUR KEYBOARD

Basic Smiley
Pope Smiley
Smoking Smiley

1 → 2 → 3
COMPILED BY SETH GODIN

The Smiley Dictionary

Spice up your online correspondence with *The Smiley Dictionary*. You can add expressions and personality to plain text with simple keystroke combinations, such as '-) (wink), :-t (pout), and :-" (whistle). This book contains hundreds of examples, from basic smiley faces to more-complex smiley characters.

The Smiley Dictionary
Peachpit Press
$6.95

Daily Tripper

If you're a Deadhead, this is the program for you. Daily Tripper is a FileMaker Pro-based personal scheduler and organizer that's loaded with features, including hundreds of photos and QuickTime movies starring the Grateful Dead. It's slow and takes up a lot of disk space, but Deadheads won't care.

Daily Tripper
BrainDance Development
$69

Digital Restaurant Guide

Need to know the closest place to eat in San Francisco? The best Thai food? Then check out Digital Restaurant Guide, a HyperCard stack containing information on just about every restaurant in the City by the Bay—nearly 3,000 entries. Digital Lantern plans to add other cities to the lineup soon.

Digital Restaurant Guide
Digital Lantern
$59.95; seasonal updates
$18.95 each

SECTIONS

ESSAYS

Self

Self

elf. Yeah, *you*. You're already reading this book, so you obviously understand that the most important thing about personal computers is the personal part. A major reason for having a computer—and reading this book, for that matter—is to make life simpler and better for yourself. And with the powers of personal computer technology at your disposal, you can take self-help into the cyberdimension. In CyberSource: Self, we don't forget that the most valuable part of your computer system is you, so we cover everything from ergonomics—which shows you how to stay healthy while using your computer—to cooking, drinking, and just about anything affecting your health. We've selected programs that serve as your personal dietitian and medical guides that can help you diagnose a problem before you take the trouble to see a doctor. And even if you're a healthy person who is using your computer in a healthy way, we haven't forgotten about keeping your finances healthy too, whether that means balancing your checkbook or finding a new job. Of course, all work and no play is definitely not what this book is about, so we also help you tune out by tuning in on your favorite hobby: genealogy software can help you track your family tree and gardening software can help you with trees of the green and leafy kind. And just to prove that even computers can be mystical, we've tossed in a taste of the occult with some mind-tickling programs on tarot.

NOW BOTTLED ON CD-ROM
Wines of the World

You'd like to know more about that delicious Merlot you drank last month in California. Or maybe you just want to learn how to open and serve a bottle of champagne. Before you pop the cork, pop Multicom's Wines of the World into your CD-ROM drive. This multimedia guide to the great wine-producing regions and the bottles they fill can enhance your appreciation of wine, especially if you're a novice wine connoisseur.

The disc is divided into four parts: Wine Quality, Wine Appreciation, Wine Regions, and Wine Browser. The first three categories tell the story of wine from the grape to the tasting. The Wine Appreciation section describes professional ratings and teaches novices to educate their own palates. The Wine Regions section uses maps to explore vineyards around the world.

The articles provided on each section of the disc are uniformly well-written and informative. Photographs and narrated video clips add multimedia flair and help you understand the process of making and selecting a wine.

Through the Browser, you can search a database of more than 20,000 wines according to producer, variety, vintage, price, and other attributes. This otherwise excellent database is somewhat marred by inconsistencies: The search categories are not hyperlinked to the program's glossary. You must use the scroll button to navigate the lengthy Producers list, with no typing allowed. And one window, called Browser's Controversy, is not explained except in the help file.

Despite these shortcomings, it's still possible to use the Browser to find, for example, a recent Merlot with a good rating and a price below $30. As an electronic guide, Wines of the World is pleasing to the palate. Demanding connoisseurs, however, may find the taste a bit short.—Peter Scisco

Wines of the World
Multicom Publishing Inc.
1100 Olive Way, Suite 1250
Seattle, WA 98101
(800) 850-7272; (206) 622-5530
$59.95

Mangia

In the past, there haven't been as many good recipe programs for the Mac as for the PC, but Mangia may change that. You can use Mangia to file your own

recipes and then search for dishes by ingredient, nationality, or course. Mangia also helps you manage your pantry and shopping by automatically creating shopping lists you can print and take to the store. One drawback is that you can't import or scan in recipes.

Mangia
Upstill Software
$49.95

Family Tree Maker Deluxe

If there were ever a job that cried out for a PC and a CD-ROM drive, digging up your family roots is it. Family Tree Maker Deluxe is the right program for the job, but there's a catch.

The good news is that this Windows CD is an attractively designed, specialized database that lets you connect all sorts of relatives hither and

yon. Nice touches include folder tabs that let you navigate generations and the extra notes you can use to add family yarns. The program even prints out a family tree suitable for framing or adding to the family album.

The catch is this: Although the CD supplies 150 million names taken from birth, death, marriage, Social Security, and census records,

you can't access detailed information on the names without buying additional CDs, which cost from $18.99 to $64.99. Oh, it's no scam. You couldn't get all the information you need on a single disc, and you wouldn't want to buy a jukebox full of discs you don't need.

If you're serious about genealogy, this is a great program—especially if you're willing to use your billfold to dig a little deeper into your family's past.—Ron White

Family Tree Maker Deluxe
Banner Blue Software
(510) 794-6850
$59.99

CD-ROM GUIDE TO YOUR OWN PRIVATE EDEN

The Exotic Garden

It's never too late to start planning your garden, and

The Exotic Garden CD-ROM from VT Productions can teach you all you need to know to do it. This MPC Level 1-compliant CD-ROM provides four search paths to botanical studies, whether you want specific details or simply a picture show. The disc contains 500 color photographs and a narrated time-lapse film called "Why Plants Flower". The photos are accompanied by the flowers' Latin names and their pronunciations, as well as information on such aspects as native habitats and plant care.—Adam A. Hicks

The Exotic Garden
VT Productions
511 Calle Serra
Aptos, CA 95003
(408) 464-1552
Fax: (408) 464-1554
$49.95

The Exotic Garden

The Exotic Garden is a fascinating catalog of common and exotic plants and flowers. Information includes Latin names, growing requirements, pests and dis-

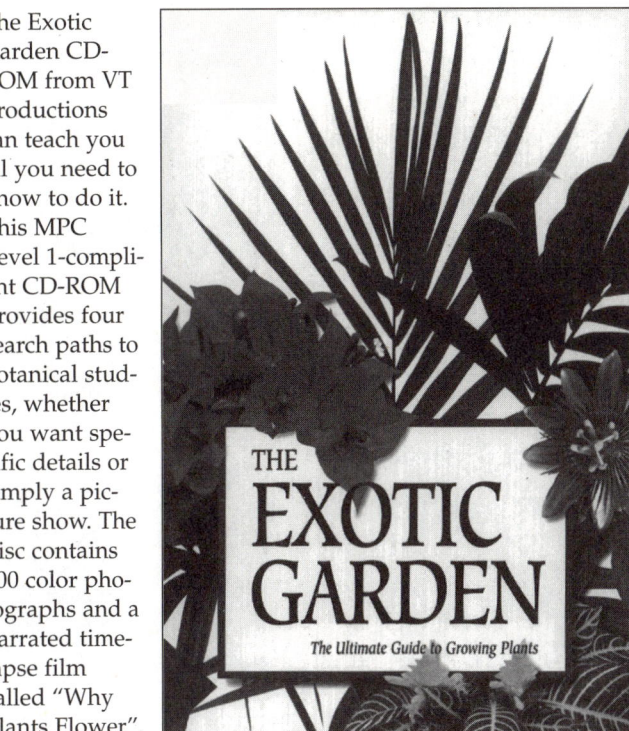

eases, propagation, and more than 500 full-color photographs. Nevertheless, this gardener yearns for more photos and more entries. The Exotic Garden includes an interesting time-lapse video called "Why Plants Flower."

The Exotic Garden
VT Productions
(408) 464-1552
$49.95

LandDesigner for Windows

How does Contrary Mary's garden grow these days? Quite well, if she used this design tool to plan it. Hundreds of landscaping symbols, plus drawing and drafting tools.

LandDesigner for Windows
Green Thumb Software
(800) 336-3127
$49.95

I Photograph to Remember

I Photograph to Remember is a series of almost 100 haunting black-and-white photographs that testify to the strength of photographer Pedro Meyer's family relationships. In a choice of English or Spanish, Meyer's spoken narrative movingly conveys his feelings toward his parents as they confront terminal illness.

I Photograph to Remember
The Voyager Company
$39.95

Personal Ancestral File 2.1

The mother of all genealogy programs, this program from the Mormon church lets you easily record, manage, and share genealogical information. It consists of three modules that record your personal data, add relatives, and help you transmit and receive files. Available for Mac and Dos.

Personal Ancestral File 2.1
Church of Jesus Christ of Latter-day Saints
(800) 537-5950; (801) 240-1174
$35

3-D Landscape

If you're planning to hire a landscape designer to spruce up your yard (or if you want to do it yourself), you'll profit from consulting this innovative program first. It lets you browse around your site electronically, adding design elements as you please. Its advanced features show the growth over time of trees and shrubs, shadows cast at different times of the year, the cost of plants and materials, and more.

3-D Landscape
Broderbund
(800) 521-6263; (415) 843-4400
$49.95

Less Is More: The IRS Gears Up to Slim Down

The Internal Revenue Service has begun the Herculean task of streamlining its antiquated system of manually processing income tax returns. And Herculean is no exaggeration: According to a U.S. General Accounting Office report, by September of 1994, the IRS had received 113.4 million individual income tax returns for the 1993 tax year. That's a lot of returns. With the population—and thus the volume of tax returns—continuing to grow, change was inevitable.

The passage of the North American Free Trade Agreement (NAFTA) in 1993 has also played a role in the IRS's decision to update its system. For the IRS to comply with NAFTA regulations, approximately 94 percent of tax remittances have to be collected via electronic funds transfer (EFT) by the year 2000. With only about a 3 percent EFT remittance rate this past year, the IRS has a long way to go.

To address these issues, the IRS has developed a three-pronged strategy for receiving and processing tax and payment information electronically. The plan is to receive about 50 percent of individual returns electronically, process 100 percent of payments through a third-party transmitter, and implement optical character recognition (OCR, or as the IRS calls it, "image character") technology for processing the remaining data. The target date for implementing this ambitious plan is 2001.

Parts of the IRS's new procedures are already in place. More than 15.4 million filers (both business and personal) posted returns electronically in 1994. And according to the GAO report, electronic filing and TeleFiling (submitting a 1040EX via touch-tone

LEARN THE TRICKS OF THE TRADE

Understanding Exposure

Despite its name, Understanding Exposure is not about surviving extreme weather conditions. Instead, it is an interactive course that helps you get a better grip on the complexities of your camera and teaches you how to take fantastic photos rather than simple snapshots. Your personal tutor is none other than Bryan Peterson, an award-winning photographer and author who specializes

phone) increased slightly in 1994. In addition, certain types of payments were handled using third-party payment processors for the 1993 tax year.

The next and possibly most important step in this ambitious automation process, however, is the introduction of a standardized, machine-readable tax form—the 1040S. It will be a hybrid of the current 1040A and 1040 with Schedules A and B and should roll out for experimental purposes in 1995. According to the IRS, this form (which will be fully available in 1997) could be used by the estimated 40 to 45 percent of the tax-paying public who don't file returns electronically.

As for OCR, Loral Federal Systems was awarded the contract to develop the new character recognition technology. At press time, Loral was hard at work, and representatives from the company indicated that bar code reader technology may be included in its systems. If Loral is able to develop this, computers at the IRS could recognize which software package was used to prepare each return and could therefore read the return accurately.

The IRS estimates that half of currently filed U.S. tax returns are prepared using a computer. And the IRS hopes that percentage will continue to increase. The two filing methods the IRS prefers are electronic filing and the abbreviated 1040PC, but handwritten returns will still be accepted.

So where does this leave tax preparation software? As it stands now, tax software companies are at a real advantage, because most of them already provide tools for two of the three filing options. And if the optical character readers being developed by Loral are indeed able to scan the returns generated by tax software accurately (a possibility that's still uncertain), tax software manufacturers can only benefit.

Overall, your income tax filing process will change little as the IRS streamlines. Perhaps the biggest difference will be that you may get any refund you're due a little faster.—Kathy Yakal ■

in available-light photography.

Peterson's lessons focus on the holy trinity of photography: film speed, aperture setting, and shutter speed. Using the full richness of multimedia, he demonstrates the interdependence of these three factors and explains how to use them to capture just the right effect. In the Photolab section you get to play with these variables and watch how each change affects the image displayed on-screen. I found these hands-on exercises more valuable than reams of text.

The Workshop section presents principles, techniques, and examples on scores of topics—from shooting the moon (no, not *that* moon) to intentional double exposures. For the "monkey-see-monkey-do" photographer, the Gallery section has 500 stunning photographs grouped by subject with detailed exposure information.

Some of the photographs in Understanding Exposure are annotated with spoken comments from Peterson about where, when, how, and why he shot what he did. I particularly enjoyed these intimate insights and wished they were available for every photo. I learned, for instance, that professional photographers leave nothing to chance—they take an avalanche of shots. Where I would be inclined to take two or three photos, Peterson exposes six or eight rolls. Make way paparazzi, here I come!—Don Trivette

Understanding Exposure
Diamar Interactive
(800) 234-2627; (206) 340-5975
$79.95

TAROT READING

CyberTarot

Perfect for those times when you'd rather be divining the future than toting up that spreadsheet. Good graphics, strong interpretations, and all the layouts a good fortune teller will ever need.

CyberTarot
Axis Mundi
(312) 866-8035
$39.95

Virtual Tarot

Virtual tarot is a CD-ROM that lets you explore the world of tarot-card readings through multimedia. This beautiful program has copious online notes on tarot philosophies, card significance, and reading interpretations.

Virtual Tarot is lots of fun, and it would probably work well for tarot aficionados as an adjunct to real-time card readings (you can buy a version that includes a deck of the superb Rider-Waite cards used on the CD-ROM). But the program has its drawbacks too. Because it was created with Macromedia Director, it's painfully slow. It's also a little unstable—the manual advises that you turn off all but crucial extensions when using Virtual Tarot, and that's good advice. We crashed repeatedly before discovering (in the Read Me notes) that the program is incompatible with ATM. What's more, we were unable to print any of the readings on either a Hewlett-Packard LaserJet 4Si or an Apple LaserWriter II.

Here's some advice the cards won't give you: Read the manual. It contains useful navigation tips as well as vital information on shortcuts that radically speed up the program.—Victoria von Biel

Virtual Tarot
Virtual Media Works
Sunnyvale, CA
(800) 292-3157; (408) 739-0301
$49.95;
with the Rider-Waite tarot deck,
$69.95

"Computers in the future may weigh no more than 1.5 tons." — Popular Mechanics, forecasting the relentless march of science in 1949

YOUR CAREER

JobHunt

If your approach to finding a job is to mail résumés in quantity and hope for a response, then JobHunt is the package for you. This is basically a mail/merge program with a 6,000-company database that you can search by region and type of job.

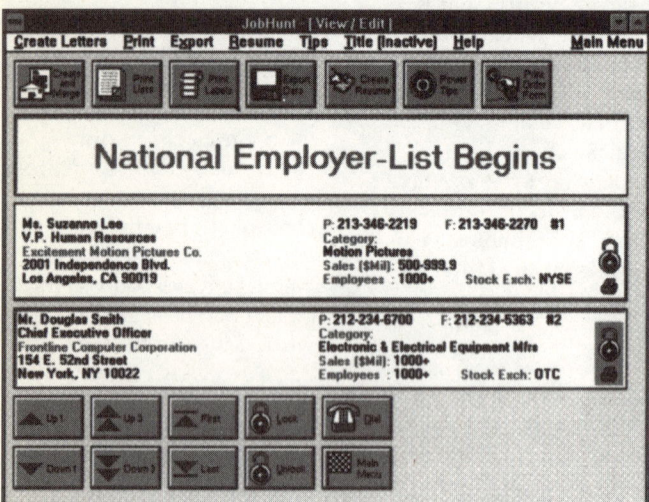

Companies are categorized by 200 SICs (standard industrial classifications), ranging from advertising to wire products. When searching, you can select multiple SICs and regions of the country. If you want to target financial and investment institutions in Texas, this is the way to do it. When your search is complete, you can display or print the results, which include contact data as well as statistical information such as annual sales and number of employees. The hits can also be easily merged with a

cover letter for assembly-line efficiency, although the included word processor is decidedly low tech. JobHunt is basically a one-trick pony, but it's not a bad trick.—Don Trivette

JobHunt
Scope International Inc.
(800) 843-5627
$50.00

Job Power Source

Job Power Source is the ultimate multimedia training course for finding a job. This CD-ROM contains the full text of 11 career books written by career experts Ron and Caryl Krannich, as well as the government's Occupational Outlook Handbook. Textual information is supplemented and enhanced by almost 2 hours of video from award-winning trainer Pat Sladey, who lectures on topics such as methods of finding jobs and getting contact names.

Scores of interactive worksheets focus on specific topics like discovering your work style and skills and setting career goals. Although there's no built-in word processor/résumé writer, the package does include 200 sample résumés. This is an excellent resource that should be in every high school and college.—Don Trivette

Job Power Source
InfoBusiness
(800) 657-5300
$59.95

Job Power Source

If you've tried every other way to make your job more enjoyable with no luck, maybe it's time to try Job

Power Source, a collection of 11 books and several videos designed to help you find a new job.

The books offer meat-and-potatoes facts and advice, such as which jobs have the most demand for new people, what you can expect to earn in a given job, how to get into an old-boy or old-girl network, and how to write a foolproof résumé. The videos tutor you in the essential job-hunting skills, such as successful interviews and letters.

If you haven't a clue what career you want to pursue, there's also a lengthy questionnaire. By working with it, you may find that you'd be happier driving a cab in Los Angeles than a BMW in the executive rat race. Sometimes

winning is knowing when to quit.—Ron White

Job Power Source
InfoBusiness
(800) 657-5300; (801) 221-1100
$49.95

Résumé Writer

Low price isn't always an indication of low quality. This inexpensive résumé and job-search system offers a straightforward, efficient approach. It comes with over 100 sample résumés for all kinds of jobs including executive, clerical, and trade positions, as well as a good selection of cover letters for everything from responding to a newspaper ad to working your contacts. The résumé templates also allow you to choose either chronological or functional format. There's also a contact manager and an appointment calendar for tracking dates, names, and addresses. You can use the built-in word processor to insert names and addresses from the contact manager to your cover letter. And because the word processor uses a multiple-document interface, you can edit several résumés and cover letters at the same time.

Creating a résumé is simply a matter of filling in the blanks in the templates. To be sure your résumé is accurate, there's a pop-up guide to action verbs and a built-in spell checker. When you're ready to print, you can fine-tune the fonts and formatting so that the output will be

When Your PC's Healthy, but You're Not

In the effort to protect your computer from its many adversaries, don't forget that you may need to protect yourself from it. Monitors, for example, are major causes of eyestrain and headaches when viewed in a flicker-prone interlaced mode or with a vertical refresh rate below 72Hz. More seriously, cathode-ray-tube monitors (CRTs) emit electromagnetic radiation, which some scientists blame for skin and eye irritations, fatigue, and respiratory problems as well as headaches. Many of today's monitors meet the Swedish government's MPR-II limits on extremely low frequency (ELF) and very low frequency (VLF) radiation, but yours may not.

Add-on screen filters, available from vendors such as NoRad (800-262-3260), Kantek Optical Drives (800-269-8801), and NEC (800-632-4636), divert electric radiation, but can reduce picture clarity and don't stop magnetic radiation. By contrast, Zenion Industries (707-584-3663) has taken an original approach to reducing monitor emissions: Its Screen ELF neutralizes some of the potentially harmful radiation generated by your CRT. According to Zenion, the $69.95 Screen ELF unit sits atop your monitor, using a silent, motor-free "pulsed plasma field" to "replenish" the air supply within a 6-foot radius.

If you're concerned about how much radiation your PC is generating, consider a radiation monitor such as the $149.50 RM-60 from Aware Electronics Corp. (302-655-3800). The RM-60 provides a Windows-based interface and feeds data on different radiation levels, including electromagnetic, through the serial port.

Repetitive-motion disorders, frequently caused by too many hours at the keyboard, are a more tangible computer-related health hazard than screen emissions. The most famous repetitive-motion disorder, carpal tunnel syndrome, is caused by continuous stress on the median nerve, which passes through a narrow channel in the underside of the wrist called the carpal tunnel. Damage to this nerve leads to tingling, numbness, and pain, and may eventually require surgery.

Wrist rests provide some relief by supporting your wrists, preventing you from flexing them painfully upward while you type. These are commodity items, but some companies add clever distinctions. Key Tronic (800-262-6006), for example, puts a miniature trackball in its TrakMate, while a keyboard-activity monitor in its PaceMate alerts you with LEDs and alarms if you've worked for too long without a break.

Bucky Products (800-692-8259) fills its $23 Polartec-covered Bucky Wristpillow with buckwheat hulls, a traditional Japanese stuffing material that adapts comfortably to your form. Its slight crunchiness has a stimulating and restorative effect, which some will find more pleasant than dull foam and rubber pads.

New ergonomic keyboards, which angle the keys to fit your natural hand position, keep wrists even straighter. The market for ergonomic keyboards is still evolving, and innovative and just plain weird designs are available. Apple's Adjustable Keyboard, for instance, splits in the center but angles only horizontally, missing part of the problem. Others, such as the $179 MiniErgo from Marquardt (315-655-8050) and the $390 Ergonomic from Kinesis (206-455-9220), fit the keys into an angled but fixed case.

Best are keyboards that are angled and adjustable both vertically and horizontally, such as Key Tronic's FlexPro and the Ergo Max from Maxi Switch (602-294-5450). In the FlexPro, the main QWERTY keypad splits, angling up and toward you on a hinge; adjustable wrist rests are built into the front. Another approach, used in the Kinesis and IBM's Quiet Touch, features special quick-response keys to relieve the stress that hard typing inflicts on your hands and wrists.

Even if you're not concerned about ELF emissions or plagued by repetitive stress injuries, it's important to have good lighting and back support, to keep your forearms and upper arms at a 90-degree angle, and to position your monitor about two feet from, and level with or a bit below, your eyes. All of these things can be done without spending a penny. ■

attractive and professional looking. No muss, no fuss, just good-looking résumés. Résumé Writer may not be the most full-featured program, but at $14.95, it's easy to like.—Don Trivette

Résumé Writer
Expert Software
(800) 759-2562
$14.95

WinWay Job Interview

Practice makes perfect. That's the idea behind WinWay Job Interview, which poses 200 typical interview-type questions for you to ponder and respond to. Questions are organized into topics such as experience, teamwork, education, and performance and can be timed to appear at set intervals.

If you have a sound card, you can hear interviewers ask questions like, "What makes you angry?" Or you can rely on your PC's built-in speaker. Along with each question, you'll receive a hint explaining the key elements of a successful answer, as well as an example of just such a response. Of course, you're encouraged to form and type your own answer before looking at the professional suggestions. Of particular interest are the sections on stressful and illegal questions and how to handle them. There's also a strategy section that covers all aspects of preparing for an interview, from what to wear to what questions to ask.

You can fill out an evaluation sheet for each answer, and the program will generate a summary with charts and graphs so you can track your strengths and weaknesses. Because no interview is complete without a follow-up, the program includes a handful of sample thank-you letters.

WinWay Job Interview has all the tools first-time interviewees and nervous applicants need to build confidence and nail that job —Don Trivette

WinWay Job Interview
WinWay Corp.
(800) 494-6929
$69.95

WinWay Résumé, Version 2.0.

When it comes to creating an attractive résumé, WinWay Résumé is the hands-down favorite. This package includes more than 100 sample résumés in areas such as administration, sales, management, technical, creative, and education, and using those samples is a snap.

Selecting the organization and style of your résumé is as simple as choosing from a series of dialog boxes. Once you've typed in your name and address, for example, you can choose any of 18 type and format styles. The same concept is used in other sections like education and job experience: You simply click on a section in the sample, and then enter your

information. If you don't like the appearance, click a button to reformat the data. To ensure grammatical accuracy, you can consult the online active-verb glossary and built-in spell checker.

To add graphic impact, you can choose from a selection of borders, bullets, and colors. The program will automatically adjust the spacing to accommodate your embellishments.

WinWay Résumé 2.0 doesn't offer the bells and whistles of career-guidance software, but it's got everything you need for creating powerful résumés.—Don Trivette

WinWay Résumé
WinWay Corp.
(800) 494-6929
$69.95

You're Hired

You're Hired combines a career counselor, résumé writer, contact manager, and interview adviser under one umbrella. The package can help you with every step of a job search, from choosing a career to following up on interviews.

For help in finding the right job, turn to the Career Counselor, which takes your answers to a series of question and produces a list of vocational choices.

When you're ready to write your résumé, you can choose from dozens of job descriptions and titles, which include statements of duties, skills, and job functions. If you need help choosing a

résumé style, Selection Assistant will recommend the most appropriate format based on your answers to 12 key questions. For writing cover letters, there's a complete word processor and a contact manager for storing names, addresses, and appointments.

If the interviewing process stumps you, the Interview Assistant should be your first stop. This section guides you through preinterview research on the company you're interviewing with and produces a checklist of information and interview tips. Landing the job is up to you.—Don Trivette

You're Hired
DataTech Software Inc.
(800) 556-7526
$59.95

THE MAC GOES TO COLLEGE
Achieving Your Career

Anyone looking for a new job or career, including college students preparing for life after graduation, will find loads of information and encouragement in Achieving Your Career. The software includes a list of big companies as well as helpful hints for job seeking. There's even a phone number you can call to get free advice from a real person.

Achieving Your Career
Up Software
$69

processing capability. It seems to me that you should be able to sample someone's voice with a tape recorder, feed the tape

Michael Dell, CEO of Dell Computer, is already a legendary American success story. Dell Computer didn't exist ten years ago, but it has already become one of the five largest personal computer manufacturers in the world. At the head of Dell Computer is Michael Dell, the 28-year-old whiz-kid who founded the company. Michael Dell dreamt of becoming an entrepreneur even as a young child. At the age of 13, he started his first company, a mail order business for stamp collectors. At 16, he took a job selling his local newspaper by telephone and rose to salesman of the month. These early jobs gave him the experience with mail order and telemarketing that would provide some of the foundations for his future computer empire.

As a teenager in the early 1980s, Dell spent time visiting his local computer stores to try out different systems and keep abreast of trends and new products. It didn't take him long to notice that something was wrong in many computer stores. First, both he and many of the customers knew quite a bit more about the technology than the salespeople working in the stores. Secondly, customers were paying a great deal of money for systems. Prices were high because computers were sold through several levels of distribution: The retail store would order from a distributor, who would in turn order from the manufacturer. These middlemen got in between the customer and the manufacturer. In the process, they also added significant costs to the products, but did not add much value or provide much service.

In 1984, Michael Dell started college at the University of Texas at Austin. While in his first year of college, he started selling computer systems from his dormitory room. After only three months of operation, his fledgling business had taken in over $180,000 in sales. At the end of his first year, Mr. Dell had grossed over $6 million. With sales accelerating at this pace, Dell realized that he would have to choose between college and his business. The choice was easy. According to Mr. Dell, "I was having more fun selling computers than going to school."

At the age of 19, Dell left the University of Texas to work full time on his company, which was then named PCs Limited. By 1988, sales were up to $159 million, and Dell Computer became a publicly owned company, trading shares on the stock exchange. Estimates are that Dell will sell more than $2 billion worth of products this year, making it one of the top computer companies in the world in its short, eight-year history.—Fred Davis. ■

ORGANIZE YOUR JOB SEARCH

RésuméMaker with Career Planning

The personnel offices of large companies process hundreds, if not thousands, of résumés every year. Even if your qualifications are excellent, you need to make your résumé and cover letter stand out. Individual Software's RésuméMaker With Career Planning gives you a competitive edge. It not only helps you write a great résumé and cover letter, it also manages the job-search process and offers career-planning advice. The package also comes with a copy of *The New Quick Job-Hunting Map* by Richard N. Bolles (author of *What Color is Your Parachute?*), a step-by-step guide that identifies the job setting that is best for you.

RésuméMaker helps you create high-impact résumés by taking a fill-in-the-blank approach. First, you select the résumé type best suited to your needs: chronological to list relevant experience, functional to highlight specific skills or accomplishments, or performance, a combination of the two. Then you choose a particular format for the selected résumé type (such as academic, management, pro-

fessional, or business). Each format contains sections addressing the specific accomplishments or experiences of that profession. Onscreen prompts guide you to include all relevant information.

After you've completed a rough résumé, you can adjust page margins; change font, type size, or type style; move sections around; alter a design; and more. You'll find extensive online help and an electronic guide to important program features, plus several helpful tips to make a résumé look as professional as possible.

RésuméMaker With Career Planning also includes a simple word processor with a spell checker and mail-merge capabilities; several templates for cover letters and thank-you notes; a database for tracking prospective companies; a calendar to remind you of appointments, follow-up calls, and scheduled meetings; and an address book. An activity log documents all contacts and activities for targeted companies. For cover letters, a Guided-Letter system enables you to compose letters incorporating paragraphs of text written by experts. You can use a prewritten paragraph as is, or customize it for your own needs. A glossary of action verbs lists powerful words to emphasize your skills.

More than one person can use the program. It associates the letters and résumés you write with a particular ID card, which contains name, address, phone number, and other information. While this ID card has fields for both home and work phone numbers, it does not ask for either a fax number or an e-mail address. The same holds true for any address-book card you fill out.

Your chances of landing a new job or making a career change depend in large part upon how good you look on paper. RésuméMaker With Career Planning has many helpful tools to get you through the front door for an interview.—Carol S. Holzberg

RésuméMaker With Career Planning
Individual Software Inc.
5870 Stoneridge Dr. #1
Pleasanton, CA 94588
(800) 822-3522
$49.95

Business Library, Volume 1

The Business Library, Volume 1 from Allegro New Media is perhaps the closest to the familiar reference-compilation approach found in many CD-ROM titles. This disc contains the text of 12 books which cover a wide range of business topics—selling and marketing techniques, persuasion skills, and direct marketing, to name some. There's even a book on how to make money in the real-estate market.

The Windows-based interface is well-designed, making it easy to browse through references using the keyboard or mouse. The files are displayed using Microsoft's Viewer program; a search feature allows you to locate relevant information in any of the reference works. There are lots of specific facts and pointed advice that business users will be able to put to use, such as tips designed to get better than 15 percent return rates on mailed questionnaires.

The Business Library is not without problems, however. Stray errors occur, such as spaces missing between words, unformatted lines, and references to page numbers from the printed books that no longer have meaning in a CD-ROM version. In some instances, scanned images have been left out, with only their file names appearing in the text.

Another problem is the uneven quality of the material. The career information is explicitly written for 15- to 25-year-olds who are seeking their first job. Veteran employees will be able to extract plenty of useful information, but they will have to read around sections with titles like "Gee, All I Ever Did Was Baby-Sit." And the book about making a killing in real estate with zero cash down, with its strong-sell motivational presentation, is oddly out of place.

Despite its shortcomings, the Business Library is a worthwhile value. It provides accurate and useful information, and the search engine makes it easy and quick to come up with lots of references for any problem you might encounter in a typical business setting. The disc contains a wealth of information that would be particularly helpful to nonprofit organizations, as well. Whether you run your own home office or small business or are part of a larger operation, there'll be plenty of occasions when you'll find reason to refer to this disc.—Alfred Poor

Business Library, Volume 1
Allegro New Media
387 Passaic Ave.
Fairfield, NJ 07004
(800) 424-1992; (201) 808-1992
$59.95

Multimedia Powertalk!

Nothing could be more different from the Business Library than Multimedia PowerTalk! This DOS-based multimedia package has all the zip of a television infomercial, which is not surprising since it is put together by Anthony Robbins and Paul Zane Pilzer. Robbins is well-known for his motivational TV ads, as well as his best-selling books, *Unlimited Power* and *Awaken the Giant Within*, and his seminars, which feature fire-walking. Pilzer also has a pair of best-sellers, *Unlimited Wealth* and *Other People's Money*. Both men are dynamic and accomplished presenters.

The core of the CD-ROM is a recording of Robbins interviewing Pilzer. The soundtrack is recorded in audio CD format, so you can play it on a standard audio CD player, but you'll want to run it from your PC to get the full effect. As the soundtrack plays, one section of the screen is filled with a printed transcript of the conversation, which switches to the next page in sync with the spoken words.

You can even turn off the sound and just read through the transcript if you want to save time.

The top right-hand portion of the screen has colorful still images that change in context with the conversation. In addition, three jump buttons take you directly to relevant portions of the two men's books—the disc includes the full text of all four books cited above. The choices on these jump buttons change as the interview progresses. You can also browse the books directly, or use a search engine that lets you locate sections based on a list of keywords or by entering your own search words.

The CD comes across as a slick promotion, but even the most jaded skeptic will have a hard time remaining unmoved by the content. There are some technical glitches, such as the fact that the software reinstalls itself on your hard disk each time you run the program and the keyboard navigation commands are disabled if you have a mouse, but these are merely annoying flaws. If you've ever watched a motivational infomercial and are curious to know more about the self-help tips offered by these two authors, this is an entertaining way to do so.—Alfred Poor

Multimedia PowerTalk!
ZCI Inc.
The Infomart
1950 Stemmons, Suite 6048
Dallas, TX 75207
(800) 460-4623; (214) 746-5555
$41.99

> "My father taught me binary code, set theory, symbolic logic, and as a result I became a budding young geek. One of my clearest childhood memories was sitting on the playground—all the other little girls had their Barbies and stuffed animals—but I was happily sitting there playing with my slide rule and logarithm tables."
>
> —CINDY BARON,
> MUSICIAN/MULTIMEDIA ARTIST, 1994

Executive's Factomatic

The disc, chock full of information and advice, is based on the contents of a single book of the same title by Jack Horn (published by Prentice-Hall). It is divided into many short sections, each one devoted to a specific set of circumstances. These settings are generally designed from a management point of view—such as what to do about an employee with a drug- or alcohol-abuse problem—but you can find out how to deal more effectively with your boss as well.

The content wastes little time on the abstract, getting straight to the point. You'll come across lots of specific tips and suggested responses for all sorts of situations. In addition to this "what to do and why" information, there are supplemental references, including a dictionary, a thesaurus, and a range of statistical and other reference data.

One interesting aspect of this title is the software that delivers the content. It is based on Compton's new M.O.S.T. (Multiple Operating System Technology) system, which makes the same disc ready to run under DOS, Windows 3.1, or even the Sony Multimedia CD Player.

The Windows interface has a number of attractive features of its own. You can use either a typical multiple document interface with many windows open at a time in the same workspace, or Compton's "virtual workspace," which lets you spread open windows over an area much larger than your screen. A small window provides a map of all the open windows; double-click on any one to bring it to the center of your screen. This lets you open windows on many different sections of the book at a time and navigate quickly and easily between them. Another aspect of the Windows interface is its "fuzzy" search facility that will find terms close to the one you asked it to find. Enter "fire" in the search box, and the program will return with references that include "fired" and "firing" as well as "fire."—Alfred Poor

Executive's Factomatic
Compton's NewMedia Inc.
2320 Camino Vida Roble
Carlsbad, CA 92009
(800) 862-2206; (619) 929-2500
$49.95

The On-Line Job Search Companion

Looking for a job is hard work. Why don't you put those newspaper want ads aside, clean your ink-stained fingers, and get online? After all, this is the age of electronic information, so let James C. Gonyea's The On-Line Job Search Companion help you find the thousands of up-to-date job openings that are listed online.—Rick Ayre

The On-Line Job Search
Companion
McGraw-Hill Inc.
(800) 227-0900
$14.95

HEALTH AND FITNESS

Dr. Ruth's Encyclopedia of Sex

Sooner or later you want to get down and dirty, and Dr. Ruth's Encyclopedia of Sex is the Windows CD-ROM to do it with. Ruth Westheimer, everyone's favorite cheery sex gnome, chats blithely about body parts, positions, and devices that don't get reviewed in computer magazines.

There are visuals on the disc, but don't get too excited: The videos are tasteful, while the grittier topics are reserved for animations, Victorian drawings, and art from the Kama Sutra. The closest this gets to one of those CD-ROMs is that it uses the same kind of cheesy music as porn films. It's easy to joke about a disc like this, but it's serious stuff, with enough clinical detail to be educational and enough design smarts to ease the route to the information you were too embarrassed to ask for.

Dr. Ruth's Encyclopedia of Sex
Creative Multimedia
(800) 262-7668; (503) 241-4351
$29.99

Family Medical Software

A TOP-NOTCH, INTERACTIVE MEDICAL REFERENCE

Medical HouseCall

While the practice of medicine is something best left to professionals, Medical HouseCall from Applied Medical Informatics provides users with medical information helpful in self-diagnosis. It analyzes symptoms, outlines drug side effects, and warns of potentially harmful interactions.

Medical HouseCall is divided into three interactive sections: Symptom Analysis, Drug Interactions, and Medical Record. The program also includes a medical encyclopedia.

The Symptom Analysis section gives you an idea of what disorders are most likely indicated by a specific combination of symptoms. You pick from a list of 215 symptoms, divided into categories like Heart/Chest and Mental Changes, answer follow-up questions, and get a list of possible disorders displayed in order of likelihood. Over 1,100 diseases and 6,000 medical findings are tracked, and hypertext help is used effectively throughout the program to further explain terms.

You can pick from the database of 2,890 drugs to get a description and a list of possible side effects, and cross-reference two or more drugs to check for potential harmful interactions. In the third interactive portion, you answer a series of questions to build your medical history.

The medical encyclopedia includes information on 394 poisons (and how to treat an ingestion), 515 medical tests, and 50 injuries.

Credible medical information and a fast, understandable interface add up to one of the best products of its kind.—Kathy Yakal

Medical HouseCall
Applied Medical Informatics
2681 Parley's Way, Suite 101
Salt Lake City, UT 84109
(800) 863-4666, Code A-11;
(801) 464-6200
$99.95

DIAGNOSIS AT YOUR FINGERTIPS
Medical HouseCall

For those who have ever lain awake at night puzzling over the origin of an ache, pain, or sniffle, HouseCall, from Applied Medical Informatics, brings sound medical advice to the Mac. And although the company is the first to assert that nothing can replace a doctor's diagnosis, the program is an excellent addition to anyone's home software library.

Developed in conjunction with 40 physicians, HouseCall is a powerful medical reference many users will find both useful and practical. Using plain English, the software provides in-depth information on more than 1,100 diseases, such as Alzheimer's and AIDS, as well as on more-common ailments, such as influenza and chicken pox. Each entry in its extensive, cross-referenced database provides clear definitions of the conditions as well as causes, symptoms, common treatments, and alternative names. HouseCall has an elegant, easy-to-use interface that includes a window with hints on using the program.

Additionally, HouseCall gives you details on common tests and on nearly 3,000 prescription and nonprescription drugs. The drug-interaction feature lists the possible side effects of a drug when used alone or with other medications and potential reactions

when used with caffeine or alcohol.

The symptom-analysis feature first asks which part of your body is ailing and then runs through a series of questions, with each question based on the answer to its predecessor. The program then provides a list of possible diagnoses, listed by percentage from most probable to least. For a common headache, for example, the software offers a variety of causes, ranging from the most likely (stress), to the least likely (a tumor). The symptom-analysis feature is helpful in diagnosing problems, but we wouldn't be surprised if it alarmed those with hypochondriacal tendencies.

Although HouseCall provides well-researched diagnoses for all kinds of problems, the manual always reminds users to consult with their doctor.

Updates to the program will be offered several times a year, keeping users current with the latest medical information. At present, the program consists of four disks and requires 11MB of hard-disk space; a CD-ROM version should be available soon. HouseCall is a great reference tool to have on call, especially when your doctor is hitting the links.—Steve Rubel

Medical HouseCall 1.0
Applied Medical Informatics
Salt Lake City, UT
(800) 584-3060; (801) 464-6200
$89.95

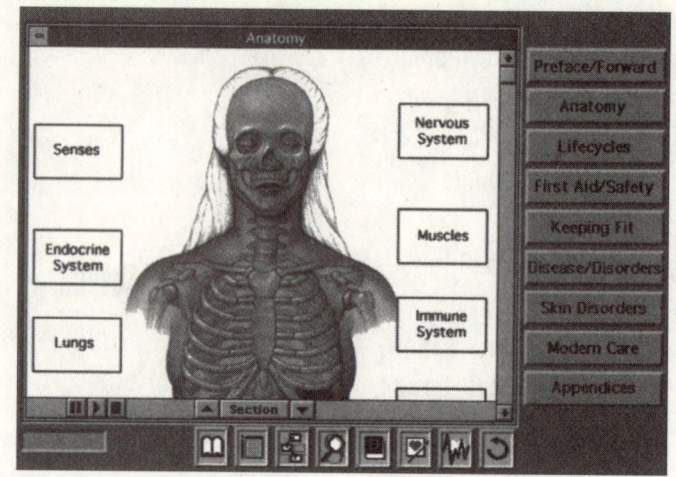

Mayo Clinic Family Health Book

This is hypochondriac heaven. Now you can find obscure causes for those pains and palpitations on one Windows-based CD. It took me no time at all to make several deadly diagnoses for the lump in my throat. (It was actually the beginnings of a common cold—not half as exciting as some of my own diagnoses.)

Okay, you don't have to be a hypochondriac to appreciate Family Health Book. Even for people with only a normal interest in their health, the collection of videos, animations, narration, and text is a treasure trove of advice and warnings. The animations in particular do a spectacular job of explaining subjects. My only complaint is the feature for searching text: It's pretty coarse, and you still have to do a lot of scrolling to find exactly what you want.—Ron White

Mayo Clinic Family Health Book
IVI Publishing
(800) 432-1332
$69.95

Mayo Clinic Family Health Book

Mayo Clinic Family Health Book includes several dozen animations, 500 illustrations, and 90 minutes of narration, but the most important element is the superb 1,400-page book. The pop-up dictionary, hyperlinks between articles, and text-search capabilities take this work far beyond a printed text. The disc also includes a color atlas of human anatomy.

Mayo Clinic Family Health Book
IVI Publishing Inc.
(800) 754-1484
$69.95

FAT-BURNING STAR KATHY SMITH ON CD-ROM
Kathy Smith's Fat Burning System

Fitness expert Kathy Smith and Xiphias have extracted material from Smith's exercise books, audio tapes, and videos to create a 10-week multimedia training course on diet and exercise. The $69.95 CD-ROM version, Kathy Smith's Fat Burning System, supports Windows and Mac systems.

Like other Xiphias titles, the disc uses a "matrix-interface" grid with seven boxes down and 10 across. Each box represents a segment of the multimedia presentation; rows represent categories such as Nutrition and Activities, while columns represent weeks in the regimen.

You can approach the data in four ways. Author mode runs through the segments in a preselected order; Point Of View mode lets you pick a category and run through it from left to right. The User mode lets you choose any series of segments, while Random mode plays single segments.

Most segments offer an Info button leading to detailed, printable text. You'll also find charts to record your diet and exercise results.

Smith's materials are solid. Her dietary recommendations are sound and up-to-date. Although the exercise and activity segments are too breezy and short to be of much use, the additional text fills them out.

Unfortunately, the disc's overall organization is poor. The interface defaults to playing a single topic across all 10 weeks, rather than all the topics for a single week. To see things properly, you must pick each of the categories for one week in User mode.

The CD-ROM also makes unwise use of its multimedia elements. Reminders and suggestions twirl distractingly toward you, pause, then go twirling off again. Key words appear and disappear while Smith speaks. Video excerpts are too brief, existing only as minor embellishments to the computer graphics and voiceovers.

If you go for the disc's motivational speaking, and for the subliminal reinforcement of words and slogans flying at you on the screen, you'll appreciate the other segments, too. But the overall product could be better. —Philip F. H. Rose

Kathy Smith's Fat Burning System
Xiphias
8758 Venice Blvd.
Los Angeles, CA 90034
(310) 841-2790
$69.95

FIND OUT WHAT AILS YOU
Home Medical Adviser Pro

Hypochondriacs will love Pixel Perfect's Home Medical Advisor Pro, but even healthy folk will appreciate the CD-ROM's wealth of

information and advice about aches and pains. When you have a medical question, the program's opening screen prompts you to highlight the appropriate region of a male or female body, then walks

you through a series of diagnostic questions and suggests possible diagnoses. Besides this help with specific symptoms, the disc provides a host of biological, medical, pharmaceutical, and dietary data.

A drug library lists information about the effects, side effects, and potential interaction problems of more than 2,400 prescription and over-the-counter drugs. A file of more than 100 video clips shows medical procedures, as well as instructional videos

about different body systems. You can block access to some images.

Another image library illustrates various anatomies, clinical symptoms, and X-rays. Several clips show first aid for traumas ranging from gunshot wounds to attacks from undersea creatures. There's also a module that maintains personal clinical histories, which can be printed in wallet-size versions and handed over to health-care workers in an emergency.

Developed by a physician specializing in emergency medicine, Home Medical Advisor Pro is the perfect electronic addition to your first-aid kit or medicine cabinet.—Mark Brownstein

Home Medical Advisor Pro
Pixel Perfect
10460 S. Tropical Trail
Merritt Island, FL 32952
(800) 788-2099; (407) 777-5353
$99.95

Dr. Schueler's Home Medical Advisor Pro 4.0

A while back I had some fun at the expense of Dr. Schueler's Home Medical Advisor Pro (HMAP) because it couldn't diagnose my obscure hypochondriac ailments. Now, after seeing how poorly several rival products did at this same task—and after seeing Version 4.0 of HMAP, which is packed with more information and a smoother interface—I owe it a higher rating.

Unlike other medical CDs, HMAP makes no distinction between generic and brand-name drugs. And it's more specific in detailing drug interactions. Even more importantly, HMAP lets you give your symptoms, then it

tries to come up with a diagnosis. And if you're not sure what the program means by asking if your skin is flaky or scaly, it shows you photos of the two conditions. (If you're squeamish, you might want to skip the photos and just guess.) Although this CD sometimes comes up blank, human doctors aren't always right either—nor are CD reviewers, for that matter.—Ron White

Dr. Schueler's Home Medical Advisor Pro 4.0
Pixel Perfect
(800) 788-2099; (407) 779-0310
$60

PharmAssist

PharmAssist is like having your own personal pharmacist. You'll find useful information on just about any aspect of prescription medicine, such as how to handle missed doses. PharmAssist also contains a section on commonly abused drugs and lists the phone numbers of substance-abuse agencies across the country.

PharmAssist
Software Marketing Corp.
(602) 893-3377
$69.95

PharmAssist

You have to give credit to a CD-ROM of drug information that includes a listing for Acapulco Gold. The interface for PharmAssist (say it fast) is a bit awkward, but with some practice you can check for drug interactions, side effects, first-aid advice, what to use for specific ailments, how to deal with drug abuse, and the federal penalties for illegal drugs. There are even illustrations of each pill. Only two complaints: For starters, drug names are classified as brand name or generic; if you don't know which is which, you wind up having to make two searches instead of one. And for some reason, the installation changed the volume setting for my sound card to zero without telling me. That's just stupid. But otherwise this is one smart title.—Ron White

PharmAssist
SoftKey Intl.
(800) 377-6567
$40

DIGITIZE FAMILY HEALTH RECORDS

Family HealthTracker

Great Bear Technology has created a program that will help you fine-tune your latest personal health goals, log long-term health data, and organize your personal medical records. Family HealthTracker has a section for tracking your daily exercise patterns, fat intake, body measurements, and vital

signs. A graphing feature can show you relationships among up to five variables— such as your workout patterns, your body weight, and your cholesterol levels—so you can track improvements or spot trends. The package also gives you a central location where you can track the medical history of family members, as well as the associated costs and insurance information.—Adam A. Hicks

Family HealthTracker
Great Bear Technology Inc.
1100 Moraga Way
Moraga, CA 94556
(800) 795-4325; (510) 631-1600
Fax: (510) 631-6735
$49

Wellness Checkpoint

Who wouldn't jump at the chance to find out how healthy we are? Wellness Checkpoint from HealthSoft forecasts your health through a series of yes-or-no and multiple-choice questions.

To get this prediction, you'll have to answer a detailed survey about your health history, habits, environment, and family diseases in order to evaluate your physical well-being. Compiled by a group of Canadian physicians, the questionnaire focuses on habits—generally things we can do something about. Questions include: Do you eat beans or lentils often? How many years since you

quit smoking? Do you exercise vigorously every day? Do you lay out in the sun on weekends? Do you always wear a seat belt? The program neglects to ask about illegal drug use and sexual activity, although these could be important factors.

Even as you answer the questions, you'll begin to see where you can improve your chances by making some simple lifestyle changes. Some of the questions are gender specific; out of about 160 total, men can expect to answer about 120, while women will be asked a few more, mostly regarding the reproductive system. The entire survey takes about 15 minutes.

After you've completed the survey, Wellness Checkpoint displays a vertical bar chart that shows your wellness risk score. That score comprises two factors: family risk and lifestyle risk. My own score was just 22 percent—low on the scale of Low-Moderate-High-Extreme. But what does this really mean? The program hedges, and a spokesman for HealthSoft was equally vague. All I know is that a 100 is bad but not terminal, and a 0 score is very good but impossible to attain.

Wellness Checkpoint provides powerful incentive for altering your habits. Set goals—eat more broccoli, drink less alcohol, always wear seat belts—and you get immediate feedback on how this decreases your risk. The

goals can be recorded and printed.

There are several things I like about Wellness Checkpoint and a few that I don't. On the positive side, it is easy to go back if you misunderstand a question. The program also lets each member of the family save and recall his or her own survey. On the negative side, the interface is labored. For example, after you start the program you have to press Enter twice after you type your name and twice more after your password. Navigation depends on cursor keys, even though it's a natural application for a mouse. In some places the text automatically advances every few seconds, instead of waiting for you to press Enter.

The second part of the program, the Wellness Game, is best described as lame. A series of flash cards gives a few facts about smoking, eating, relaxing, and exercising. The information presented is basic, and the presentation is boring. It reminds me of the overhead projection in a high school health class. Wellness Checkpoint gets raves for its health survey and boos for its tutorial.—Donald B. Trivette

Wellness Checkpoint
HealthSoft
1100 Moraga Way
Moraga, CA 94556
(800) 795-4325
$99

Birthday Virus—Keeps advancing your clock by another year.

B.A.B.Y.

B.A.B.Y. (Birth and Baby Years) is a graphical, computerized pregnancy guidebook that takes you on a tour of pregnancy, the growth and development of the fetus, and labor and birth. The software condenses the rather exhaustive information found in most books on the subject, and covers such topics as infertility, genetics, diet, exercise, and pregnancy tests.

Information is displayed in text boxes and with animated pictures and graphs. Most of the charts are for illustration only, but a few will track personal data—for example, an expectant mother's weight gain and ovulation. Enter the date of your last period and the program will calculate your due date and display how far you are into your pregnancy and how many days you have left. The B.A.B.Y. software will store this and other information, such as your daily appointments and your doctor's phone number, in a personal file.

The program includes checklists that help you organize the nursery and pack your hospital bag. If you haven't chosen a name yet, you can always refer to B.A.B.Y.'s extensive names dictionary. Once your baby comes home, you can use B.A.B.Y. to record milestones for the first year, such as your child's first words.—Janet Rubenking

B.A.B.Y.
Software Marketing Corp.
9830 South 51st St.
Building A-131
Phoenix, AZ 85044
(602) 893-3377
$69.95

Babydoc In A Disk

Babydoc In A Disk is a text-only family medical database chock full of useful information about your child's health. If your child is showing signs of illness, name the symptoms and narrow your search for the cause. If you are unsure about your child's medication, look it up in the drug database. Or if you are just curious about your child's physical growth, chart it with the developmental checklist and the percentile rankings for weight, height, and head size.

Babydoc doesn't come with a manual, but the online help system is adequate. The database of diseases is extensive, including more than most families will probably ever need. But that thoroughness doesn't always promise an accurate diagnosis. For instance, when I listed a group of symptoms of the common cold, the program turned up dozens of disorders but not cold or flu.

Babydoc exists to help prepare you for your child's well-baby visits to the pediatrician. It will call attention to unusual growth patterns, provide information about the risk of lead poisoning, and remind you which immunizations your child should receive at a particular checkup. This program isn't meant to replace the family doctor but to help you between visits. Used in this manner, Babydoc In A Disk can help you survive the first several months with your new child.—Janet Rubenking

Babydoc In A Disk
Babydoc Publishing Co.
P.O. Box 26180
Fresno, CA 93729-6180
(800)642-3543; (209) 725-2070
$49.95

THE DOCTOR IS IN

A.D.A.M. The Inside Story

Remember your high school biology book with its clear plastic pages that revealed a dissected frog in layers? Turn one page and the skin disappeared; turn another and…well, you remember. A.D.A.M. is that book made better. View the human skeleton, nerves, glands, and other innards, either in predefined views or by peeling away layers. But it's not just for ghouls: A.D.A.M.'s animations and narrations explain the complex functions of the body with gentle humor. For kids, you can install a PG version with strategically placed fig leaves. But wise up: They already know what's what. And by using interior cutaway views, they'll always have access to—you guessed it—a womb with a view.— Ron White

A.D.A.M. The Inside Story
A.D.A.M. Software
(800) 408-2326; (404) 980-0888
$49.95

The Magic School Bus Explores the Human Body

This Windows CD is what AnnaTommy should have been. This version is based on the Scholastic book series and popular PBS show "The Magic School Bus." It has full-screen, full-action animation. And while it has games to play, you can skip them if you want. Plus, it has endless "clickables," which are objects that do surprising things when you click on them. Click on some odd morsel in the stomach and it turns into what it used to be before it was ingested—a

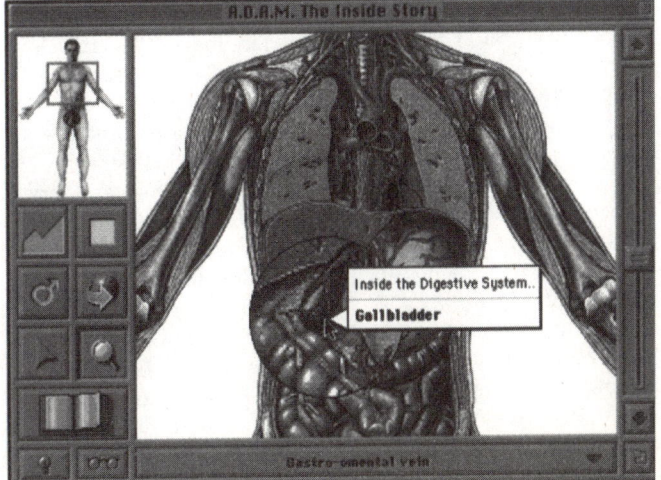

"I think one of the things that interests me is the change of the role of the artist in the sense that we have been the final arbiter of the work. With the increased role of interactivity, we are also going to be the supplier of information and collage material, which people will then either be able to receive as the author intended and/or use as material for their own variations and their own work. It's part of the shift from skill-based work to decision making, editing, and choice being as important the actual construction of the piece of work. That's very exciting."

—PETER GABRIEL,
MULTIMEDIA
COMPOSER/MUSICIAN,
1994

hamburger or a cheese puff. This approach really makes learning fun.—Ron White

The Magic School Bus Explores the Human Body
Microsoft Home
(800) 426-9400; (206) 882-8080
$49.95

LifeSaver

Preparing your household for medical emergencies is easier with LifeSaver, a CD-ROM containing a complete first-aid course. LifeSaver teaches you how to deal with everything from bee stings to poisoning, with a good dose of CPR on the side.

LifeSaver
Sony Electronic Publishing
$99

PERSONAL LAW

It's Legal

Parsons Technology may be the king of low-cost, home-use software. It's Legal, Version 4.0, often available for as little as $29.95, is designed for personal and small-business use, and it shows. This application is easy to use, with many interactive and dynamic prompts, and help suggestions given along the way.

It's Legal has evolved over the past few years, culminating in an easy-to-use Windows version of the DOS-based software. This program provides basic documents an attorney would draft for home users and small-business owners.

Estate instruments include a simple will, living trust, living will, and health-care power of attorney (all customized by state). Business forms include corporate minutes, notice documents, employment documents and consulting agreements, promissory notes, and equipment leases. For consumers, the program includes many expertly drafted letters, such as credit-rating challenges, debt demand letters, and complaints to companies, the Better Business Bureau, or the attorney general. Additional accessories include a notepad, a calculator, and an amortizer.

It's Legal lacks an online interview process, but online help provides a brief overview of each document's function. Although this overview does not require legal knowledge, you will need some business sophistication to know how to use a promissory note or get involved in an equipment lease. You would be well advised to consult a live attorney for handling such complex areas, even though the program provides the tools.

It's Legal provides more documents for the buck than any other package available. Couple that with a smooth interface and low price and this package becomes a no-lose proposition for PC users willing to take legal matters into their own hands.—Bernie Yee

It's Legal
Parsons Technology Inc
One Parsons Dr.
P.O. Box 0100
Hiawatha, IA 52233
(800) 223-6925; (319) 395-9626
$69

Home Lawyer

A good, solid product, Home Lawyer has lost some ground to newer packages like It's Legal but remains flexible and competent enough in its areas to be worthy of consideration. For the past few years, Home Lawyer has been a solid performer for personal legal services on a PC, with 16 common legal documents, including wills, powers of attorney, employment forms, credit and collection documents, leases, and bills of sale. The package even throws in a consumer complaint letter for good measure.

The most important part about drafting a legal document is getting the right information from the client. Home Lawyer's effective interface makes this crucial part easy. The program provides a Preventive Law Interview for first-time users to determine their legal needs. Simply answer a series of questions and Home Lawyer refers you to its general online information guide, entitled Personal Law Topics. Similarly, those seeking to make a will can fill out the Estate Planning Worksheet, which makes a client consider the factors of property division before making out a will. The Personal Law Topics section explains basic areas of law relevant to Home Lawyer's forms and, most important, advises you on when to consult a lawyer.

Each legal document is assembled after the user answers the questions in the interview. This process makes you consider your decisions in distributing your property under a will. You can then print out a completed document, or save the document as a text file and continue modifying it with your word processor.—Bernie Yee

Home Lawyer
MECA Software Inc.
55 Walls Dr.
P.O. Box 912
Fairfield, CT 06430-0912
(203) 256-5000
$89.95

Legal Partner

Legal Partner feels as if it was written by lawyers. Its bare-bones interface and proud use of "legalese" assume a degree of knowledge the other packages don't. Legal Partner features more than 150 forms, ranging from copyright licenses to limited powers of attorney, but doesn't cover such topics as wills and durable powers of attorney. The authors claim that these documents are too complex and important for a fill-in-the-form approach, a typically conservative legal attitude.

Legal Partner has a simple, context-sensitive help system but lacks a fancy interface. Nor will the documentation be of much help: The complexity of many of the documents will definitely prove to be intimidating to the layman. But the documents available are impressively complete for sophisticated businesspeople, and they even allow users to input commonly used documents for later fill-in usage.

The documentation adequately explains how to use the software, but it is sadly silent as to any basic legal discussion of the effect of each document. Documents such as trade-secret confidentiality agreements and indemnification agreements presuppose a good sense of their legal usage already; in other words, if you don't know what they're for and when they should be used, you should talk to a lawyer first.

Legal Partner may very well find its way onto your attorney's hard disk, since the documents are fairly sophisticated and the program allows users to enter their own commonly used documents into the program for automated filling out. Though the text entry feature is not particularly sophisticated, it's fine for entering shorter contracts, such as releases, verification pages for court documents, and other commonly used documents. This package is best saved for attorneys themselves.—Bernie Yee

WillMaker

If you want to draft a will, WillMaker, from Nolo Press, is a good option. In fact, many general-practice attorneys may be interested in Nolo's product.

WillMaker is an outstanding program, available in both DOS and Windows versions, and the documents it generates are top-notch. The program breaks down the entire will-drafting process into its component parts, so that any user with the desire to learn about the estate process will come away with an excellent basic knowledge.

To keep this process simple, WillMaker interviews the user before it assembles the will. Questions pop up, one at a time, on the screen, and each screen has hypertext and corresponding online help, with topics covered in even more depth in the manual. No fancy graphics here: The interface is text-based but perfectly adequate for the task at hand.

WillMaker comes with outstanding documentation. The manual explains in simple terms the legal effect of terms such as joint tenancy, residuary estates, and more. It explains the program's limits. For example, you won't be able to draft codicils,

amendments to a will, which are often challenged in court. If you insist on using them, you're left to consult a human attorney. Most practical, the documentation contains plenty of examples, using fictitious people with particular sets of estate goals and circumstances.

While it's no substitute for a real attorney and it's more expensive than its jack-of-all-trades rivals, WillMaker offers more flexibility in creating a specialized document, and it provides the best drafts to use.—Bernie Yee

NEED LEGAL AID? DON'T FEED THE SHARKS

LegalPoint

First the bad news: LegalPoint won't replace your lawyer any more than accounting software will eliminate your accountant. The rest is mostly good news. Teneron's LegalPoint gives business users a lawful head start by providing templates for 70 common contracts and legal documents. The program also includes context-sensitive help and useful advice from a team of lawyers.

When you ask lawyers to draw up traditional business documents, they don't start from scratch. They take existing text in templates and fill

in the blanks. But who needs a law degree to fill in blanks? LegalPoint makes it easy for you to write in the details by highlighting parts of its boilerplate documents. When you place the cursor over this highlighted text, the program explains the clause in question.

Red highlights indicate where to make changes specific to the document. If you're creating a promissory note, clicking on the Borrower explains that LegalPoint assumes a borrower is an individual, though it could be one of six other possibilities, including a corporation or general/limited partnership. Green text indicates subtext relating to the general topic.

Filling in these blanks ultimately creates a basic—though not final—legal document that you can then take to a lawyer for input. Naturally, no collection of computer code will eliminate the need for wise counsel, but this program can reduce the amount of time (and money) you must spend with folks who charge megabucks per hour.

LegalPoint is more than a time-saver. The information

in its dialog boxes is written in clear, understandable English. If you're mystified by what you're reading, click on the icon labeled Business Law Topics, and a context-sensitive database of background information appears. In the six categories—business, employment, corporate, intellectual property, financial, and legal—you'll find 56 articles written by Teneron's staff of lawyers and laypeople.

LegalPoint's one failing relates to its linking abilities. The opening screen, with a background of a table in a law library, shows six simple choices. When you click on Create a Document, you can choose a document template by name, category, or keyword. Even though the titles of the documents are clear and helpful, Teneron needs to work on linking its keywords to documents. For instance, if you use such obvious terms as taxes, finance, default, insurance, liability, and harassment as keywords, no document template comes up even though there are templates related to them.

Otherwise, LegalPoint features a briefcase full of nice touches. You can adjust the

toolbar to resemble either Microsoft Word or Lotus's Ami Pro (but not Novell's WordPerfect). Its help icon is a life preserver, and the six choices on the opening screen are duplicated in a handy button bar.

Overall, it's an open-and-shut case in favor of LegalPoint. The program takes a process most people find fraught with anxiety and transforms it into a simple matter of filling in the blanks.—Howard Baldwin

ERGONOMICS

ENTER THE COMFORT ZONE
Microsoft Natural Keyboard

Repetitive Stress Injuries (RSIs) are a significant concern for people who use keyboards a lot. Proper keyboard height, chair height and angle, and proper typing positioning of your arms and wrists can all help prevent fatigue and injury. The Microsoft Natural Keyboard

> "Because of multimedia, I think that instrumentalists are going to become more aware of visuals and will become more involved in visuals. They will start to want to paint using their instruments, whether it be a piano, or drums, or a saxophone. By the same token, I think that artists are going to want to do music, so that the paintbrush will become a musical instrument. The technology is almost there."
>
> **—HERBIE HANCOCK**

Self Self Self Self Self

trend created by computers and ignored by the sages and pundits: Computers take away people's jobs. All those science-

is designed for comfort and to provide a more natural typing posture, hopefully lessening the chance of injury, though Microsoft disclaims that the keyboard cures or prevents carpal tunnel syndrome or other RSIs.

The Microsoft Natural Keyboard is larger than most desktop-system keyboards. It measures 21 × 9.8 × 2.5 inches high with the Wrist Leveler extended; conventional keyboards are about 18 × 6.5 × 1.5 inches.

The keyboard's main alphabet-key grouping is separated in the middle with each half angled back a bit. You really can spread your wings with the Microsoft Natural Keyboard: Rather than tucking your arms in to keep your wrists straight, your elbows can rest comfortably on chair arms. The keyboard is all one piece, unlike an earlier Apple Macintosh keyboard with similarly rotated key groups that was physically split into two articulated pieces.

The three-position Wrist Leveler raises the front of the keyboard so your wrists and hands are straight. The keyboard curves away at the ends of the alpha section and slants just a bit to the back, which felt awkward at first, but didn't take long to get used to and appreciate. The cursor-control and numeric-keypad keys are located in the usual position, to the right of the right half of the keyboard, demanding a bit longer reach than usual.

Three extra keys adjacent to the Natural Keyboard's curved spacebar include two function keys and a programmable application key. The usual keyboard status-indicator lights for NumLock, Caps-Lock, and ScrollLock are located in the middle of the keyboard, between the two alpha-key groups.

The Intellipoint software adds utility, but the real reason to buy the Microsoft Natural Keyboard is comfort. If you're the type who will spend hundreds of dollars to upgrade a monitor, this

$99.95 keyboard upgrade can make the second-most-noticeable feature of your computer less stressful to use.
—Bruce Brown

Microsoft Natural Keyboard
Microsoft Corp.
One Microsoft Way
Redmond, WA 98052-6399
(800) 426-9400
$99.95

Microsoft Natural Keyboard

Sure it looks funny, and yes, it takes some getting used to, but we bet you'll love Microsoft's Natural Keyboard if you give it a chance. Aside from a unique ergonomic design that decreases strain on hands, wrists, and shoulders, the Natural Keyboard makes Windows easier to use through clever software and special Windows keys.

Microsoft Natural Keyboard
Microsoft
(800) 426-9400
$99 list

Classic Touch Keyboard

Okay, mouse haters, we have a keyboard for you. Lexmark, a spin-off of IBM, has taken one of those little eraserhead pointing devices found on IBM notebooks and put it on the home row of one of their Classic Touch keyboards. Here's another great feature: The company put a backspace/erase key right next to the space bar.

Classic Touch Keyboard
Lexmark Intl.
(800) 438-2468
$140

THEY'VE GOT THE LOOK... HAVE THEY GOT THE FEEL?

Microsoft Natural Keyboard Lexmark Select-Ease Keyboard

Ergonomic keyboards with odd shapes—irregular slopes and curves instead of the more traditional straight-line design of standard keyboards—used to be expensive oddities. Now, Microsoft's $99 Natural Keyboard and Lexmark's $179 Select-Ease Keyboard put full-size keyboards designed to fit your hands firmly in the mainstream. While both are viable alternatives to standard fare, the more expensive Lexmark Select-Ease keyboard grows on you the more you use it, while the Microsoft Natural keyboard seems more idiosyncratic as time goes on.

Microsoft's Natural Keyboard looks like a standard keyboard that melted in the back seat of your car. The left and right half of the main keyboard area are split into two regions for improved comfort. The beauty of the Natural keyboard is that you don't have to reach for the farthest keys. It also adds something no other keyboard does—shortcut keys. The layout key, which is between the Control and Alternate keys, brings up a new Windows task manager. An additional menu shortcut key will tied to Windows 95. Special software adds features such as mouse emulation. On the downside, the rubbery response of Microsoft's keys may disappoint some. In addition, the only physical adjustment available is one that raises or lowers the slope of the keyboard to improve wrist comfort. Microsoft's first attempt at a keyboard is quite a good effort at redefining what a keyboard is and does.

Lexmark's sturdy and responsive Select-Ease keyboard is a study in contrast compared with the Microsoft product. It also divides the main keyboard area in two halves, but with a twist. You can twist them, turn them, or even split them apart. The keyboard comes without software, but no other keyboard lets you adjust it so precisely for maximum comfort. Lexmark's layout is more compact, with smaller motions required to reach the arrow keys and keypad. The only major flaw is Ctrl and Alt keys that are the same size as letter keys, instead of the more generous size used on most other models.

For software enhancements and mouse emulation, consider Microsoft's keyboard. For the ultimate in responsiveness and comfort, choose Lexmark's. Both models make the standard keyboard seem as constraining as a corset.—Edward Mendelson

Select-Ease Keyboard
Lexmark International Inc.
740 New Circle Rd. NW
Lexington KY 40511
(800) 438-2468; (606) 232-3000
$179

Microsoft Natural Keyboard
Microsoft Corp.
One Microsoft Way
Redmond WA 98052
(800) 426-9400; (206) 882-8080
$99

BUILDING A BETTER KEYBOARD
MicroMachines TrackBoard

Ergonomic, colorful, and modular—that's the goal of the TrackBoard, a new keyboard from MicroMachines. Taking a cue from the PowerBook, the compact TrackBoard sports a built-in trackball, a thumb bar, and keys for drag and double-click. But like an extended keyboard, the TrackBoard has function, Escape, and reset keys. Desktop-space hogs,

such as a numeric keypad, are optional.

You can customize the TrackBoard according to function or whim. Flipping a DIP switch sets which key on the trackball unit is drag and which is double-click or lets you change the right-hand Command key to an Enter key. Dual-function arrow keys also serve as Page Up, Page Down, Home, or End keys. As for whimsy, the unit is sold in platinum and in charcoal gray and the provided key-cap puller lets you colorize your keyboard for easier recognition of critical keys.—Pamela Pfiffner

MicroMachines TrackBoard
MicroMachines
(800) 248-4001; (818) 901-1700
$100; numeric keyboard $49;
wrist rest $15

Take Five

Sitting in front of a computer all day can take its toll on your health—both physical

and mental. You can decompress a little with Take Five, a CD-ROM full of exercises, music, and psychic vacations designed to unkink your mind and body.

Take Five
The Voyager Company
$49.95

Total Health at the Computer: How to Be Pain Free

Did you know that you should blink every three to five seconds when you're staring at a computer display? You would if you'd read *Total Health at the Computer: How to Be Pain Free*, by Martin Sussman and Dr. Ernest Loewenstein, with Howard Sann. It's a practical guide to setting up your work space and using your computer in a way that minimizes health problems such as carpal tunnel syndrome,

repetitive-stress injuries, and eyestrain.

Total Health at the Computer:
How to Be Pain Free
Station Hill Press
$13.95

Nada Chair Back-Up

The Nada Chair Back-Up is an innovative ergonomic back support. It acts as a sling from your knees to your back, using reverse pressure from the knees to apply traction to the lower back. Okay, so it looks a little funny, but it packs up smaller than a Duo and is surprisingly comfortable.

Nada Chair Back-Up
Ergonomics
$39.95

PERSONAL FINANCE

FLEX YOUR FINANCE MUSCLE
Quicken 4 for Windows

When Quicken first hit the market more than a decade ago, it resembled nothing so much as a Volkswagen Bug—a cheap and friendly little program that did a couple of things really, really well. Quicken has grown a lot since then; the newest version is the Cadillac of personal finance. Yet it's even easier to drive and gets much better mileage.

The easiest program to use is the one you already know. Despite a number of budgeting, planning, and data-entry

enhancements, the interface of Quicken 4 for Windows (and the new DOS-based Quicken 8) will be comfortably familiar to all 6 million of Quicken's current users. New users are helped into the program in several new ways, the most significant being the optional HomeBase shell.

Click on one of the six activities on the left side of the HomeBase ledger and the appropriate menu choices scroll up on the right side. This early foray is eased by pop-up Q cards that offer specific instructions for each activity—and when you're tired of them, you can turn them off one by one. HomeBase is not as stylish as Managing Your Money, but it's just as usable.

Quicken groupies will be particularly happy that the new features don't require them to sacrifice old ways of working. They'll also appreciate the program's new conveniences. For example, you can now rearrange data fields in your registers to enter check numbers or amounts before dates, and a new scrollable ribbon of account names lets you jump to another account with just a click. It's easier than ever to schedule future transactions by dropping them on the Financial Calendar, and the Post-it-like notes you create there now appear in several other places, letting you use Quicken much as you would a PIM.

Quicken 4 also has new ways to help you find out where your finances stand today as well as where they're headed in the future. And the new SnapShots feature lets you set up quick views of your income, expenses, and investments to find just the information you need amid mounds of confusing data.

Similarly, new Super Categories help you cut through omnibus budgets to focus on your progress on certain discretionary items. You might group dining, travel, and entertainment categories into a Super Category called Discretionary Expenses to better track your spending against amounts budgeted. Tax planning is also easier now that the Quicken Tax Planner has been integrated into both of the new Quicken versions with improved links to Intuit's TurboTax. The luxo-cruiser edition of the program, called Quicken Deluxe 4, adds the Quicken Companion array of financial management and investment add-ins.

Despite the new features, the new Quicken should sell for about $10 less than its predecessor. And Quicken's ease of use puts competing products from Microsoft and Computer Associates to shame. Quicken 4 is one of the best values in software.— Mike Hogan

Quicken 4 for Windows
$39.99 floppy disk or CD-ROM
(Windows only);
Quicken Deluxe 4 for Windows
$59.99 on floppy disk or
CD-ROM
Intuit Software
(800) 624-8742, (415) 322-0573

Charles J. Givens Money Guide

This Windows CD is a bit like eating your vegetables. After a rich stew of *It's a Wonderful Life* and the chocolate-coated delight of Monty Python, listening to a talking head's financial advice is like so much cold broccoli—good for you, but *still* cold broccoli. The Charles J. Givens Money Guide is designed sensibly enough. You're guided through a series of questions about your financial status and goals, then given specific advice for meeting these goals. For example, I can retire a millionaire through the simple strategy of investing $98,000 a year at 15 percent interest. Now, why didn't I think of that?

The multimedia element of this disc comes in the form of Charles J. Givens himself offering advice. Throw in a

dozen or so simple programs for calculating finances, and you have a relatively decent program. Too bad getting rich isn't as much fun as Mr. Givens makes it sound.—Ron White

Charles J. Givens Money Guide
Friendly Software Corp.
(800) 968-4654; (419) 868-6090
$49.95

Charles J. Givens Money Guide

Charles J. Givens is the author of a number of national best-selling books on personal finance, and is a familiar face to channel-surfers who have seen his infomercials. Some of his ideas and advice are now packaged in a CD-ROM published by Friendly Software Corp.

One unusual aspect of this title is that it is linear. Most CD-ROMs are designed for random access; pick a topic of interest and jump to it. The Givens CD is designed to start at the beginning and be worked through step by step to the end.

The topics are divided into three sections: Wealth Management, The Ten Biggest Money Management Mistakes, and Ask Charles J. Givens. The first section is designed to help you develop a comprehensive financial statement for your current situation and a set of goals for the future. As a result, you need to fill out worksheets, record-keeping forms, and lists as you go along,

building a cumulative personal profile. The next section arms you with information to help you avoid expensive mistakes in areas such as credit cards, auto loans, or life insurance. The final section offers some specific questions and answers on a wide range of topics.

All this material is presented in a manner that is easy to use and understand. The interactive worksheets and documents are generally useful, making short work of calculations and providing graphic representations of the advantages of Givens's strategies. The question-and-answer section uses Windows Help, making it possible to search for key words. There are also 130 color video clips that provide additional information and encouragement for putting the plans into action.

Givens is a bit of a cheerleader for his concepts, but his highly motivated tone should help users keep up their enthusiasm as they work through the various steps.—Alfred Poor

Charles J. Givens Money Guide
Friendly Software Corp.
1627 Henthorne Dr.
Suite C
Maumee, OH 43537
(800) 968-4654; (419) 868-6090
$49.95

DO-IT-YOURSELF CAPITALISM

StreetSmart for Windows

Two hundred years ago, buying stock in the American dream was a matter of saun-

tering down to Wall Street and striking a bargain with an eager entrepreneur. Today, securities are bought and sold by specialists screaming at one another in 30 or 40 different exchanges around the country. You and I can't even get in to watch this process, much less directly participate. Instead, we pick up the phone and give our orders to a broker. Or we can pick up a copy of Charles Schwab & Co.'s StreetSmart for Windows, a software package that uses a modem to place buy/sell orders directly with Schwab's trading computer, eliminating the live Schwab middleperson from the transaction.

With StreetSmart, you can buy or sell stocks, bonds, mutual funds, or options directly from your PC screen. You still pay Schwab's commissions (competitive with other discount brokers), but receive 10 percent off the price paid by those who use the telephone to place orders with Schwab.

StreetSmart isn't the only PC trading program, nor even the first. Schwab still sells its $59.95 DOS product, Equalizer (first offered in 1986); another discount brokerage house—Fidelity— offers On-Line Express. Both are DOS-based products with online trading features similar to those of StreetSmart. However, neither product matches StreetSmart for intuitive ease of use, and StreetSmart's Windows interface is an attractive icon-based format, offering many portfolio-management features.

To use StreetSmart, you must have a Schwab account, but there is no charge for opening or maintaining it, nor does Schwab have any restrictions such as minimum income. (Some restrictions do apply for margin accounts.) The only requirement is that you pay your bills, including paying for securities you purchase, within five days, plus any online charges you incur while using the research services.

The StreetSmart opening screen is uncluttered, with only menu and icon bars. The menu/ icon choices fall roughly into three different groups: trading, research, and portfolio information. The trading icon leads to four radio buttons, one each for adding, editing, deleting, and submitting orders. Creating an order involves entering the action (buy or sell), the number (of shares, units, or whatever), and the name of the security. StreetSmart, unlike some of its competitors, allows placing a price limit (buy at a price no higher than 50 1/8, for example) or a stop limit (sell if the price drops to 48 or lower). You can also sell short, restrict the buy/sell order to one day, or choose options such as "good until canceled" or "fill or kill" (that is, if the order can't be filled as specified, it's canceled). For mutual funds, you can specify that dividends be reinvested, posted to your Schwab account, or sent to you.

Unlike market analyzers AIQ or WealthBuilder, StreetSmart doesn't provide personal financial guidance or advice on which securities to buy. It does give you (at an extra cost) access to research assistance and ample resources to do your homework. Standard & Poor's MarketScope Company Reports—summaries of a firm's financial position—are $4.50 each (the first one is free) plus connect-time charges. The Dow-Jones Market Monitor (which offers an after-hours flat fee) provides access to almost 20 financial databases for $29.95 per month. You can download realtime stock quotes from Schwab; the first 100 are free, and you receive 100 more free each time you make a trade. In addition to current price and volume, you can request "extended quotes," with price/earning ratio, dividend history, and other information on a company.

StreetSmart's portfolio management includes user-definable views of information about your securities. For instance, you might create a "position" view to summarize your mutual-fund holdings sorted by price, name, or ticker symbol, and including up to 18 columns of data selected from 26 options. The view options include data such as 52-week high, current yield, last stock split date, or your last trade. These customized views can be exported to Quicken, Lotus (or other spreadsheets com-

patible with WKS format), or CSV files. StreetSmart also exports gain/loss figures to tax programs such as TurboTax and others using TXF format for inclusion on Schedule D.

StreetSmart automatically dials Schwab or other services when you select a command—such as getting a price quote—requiring online access. Disconnect is automatic, though there is a disconnect option. The program uses the CompuServe network, and is set up so there is never a long-distance charge (but per-minute connect charges do apply for services such as Dow-Jones quotes). StreetSmart currently supports modem speeds up to 9,600 bps, although that may be at 14,400 bps by the time you read this.

Charles Schwab & Co. has an interest other than selling the software. As mentioned, you pay Schwab's regular commission (based on the size of the order) less 10 percent. However, for almost 300 of the 700 or so mutual funds in which Schwab trades, Schwab charges nothing, not even a transaction fee. For other no-load funds, a $25 transaction fee applies.

Documentation and on-screen support are excellent. Schwab provides a toll-free support number during business hours and a computerized question-answering service 24 hours per day.

StreetSmart adequately handles trading, research, and portfolio management. It's easy to learn and to use.

Don't expect much handholding—it's your money to make or lose, and you, not Schwab, are responsible for what StreetSmart does. But even if you never trade a share, StreetSmart can still help manage your portfolio and provide online information access for researching investment choices.—Steve Gilliland

StreetSmart 1.0c
Charles Schwab & Co. Inc.
101 Montgomery St.
San Francisco, CA 94104
(800) 334-4455
$59

Fidelity On-line Xpress, Version 2.1

Fidelity On-line Xpress, Version 2.1, is a workman-like DOS program that allows Fidelity customers to make trades electronically and update their portfolios online without paying a monthly fee. Developed by MECA Software, Fidelity On-line Xpress (FOX) does the job, but not spectacularly: Trading and portfolio management services are adequate, but FOX offers little investment analysis.

You'll need an established Fidelity account before installing FOX, since part of the startup procedure involves dialing into the database and defining your account. The program's installation routines are not rich in creature comforts. For example, you'll have to look up and enter the access net-

work's phone number manually, modem diagnostics aren't included, and the modem initialization string is hard-coded into the communication routines. Be sure to save the setup data before going online; if you crash, you must reboot your computer and re-enter all phone number and modem setup information. The online help is limited, so you may have to contact the FOX technical support crew if you have problems during setup.

Once you log on to the Fidelity database, your account information is automatically updated, and you can easily view reports showing what's in your portfolio. FOX doesn't link directly to any personal finance package, but the manual details how to send current securities pricing data to Managing Your Money.

Executing trades is at the heart of FOX. You prepare your order off-line and are given several opportunities to review and edit it before completing the transaction. Or you can trade in batch files and work online with the Turbo Trader feature.

FOX has easy access to Fidelity mutual funds, which are maintained in a Fidelity Mutual Fund Account. To trade in stocks, bonds, options, and non-Fidelity mutual funds, you can set up a Fidelity Ultra Service Account. FOX can track transactions by tax category, which should make your Schedule D a little easier come April.

If you don't have Managing Your Money but want some analysis, the software for a service called Telescan is included in the FOX box. You pay a monthly fee to use Telescan, and it's integrated with the FOX menu. You can also use FOX to launch S&P Market Scope and Dow Jones News/Retrieval.

Though it's not pretty, FOX does a decent job of keeping Fidelity accounts updated and gives you access to quite a bit of information about Fidelity mutual funds. If you've got a Fidelity account already, FOX is a good investment. Fidelity plans to release a Windows version in 1995.—Theresa W. Carey

Fidelity On-line Xpress 2.1
Fidelity Investments
82 Devonshire Street
Boston, MA 02109
(800) 544-9375
$59

"Personal computers have failed to dramatically increase personal productivity. The problem is that most PCs are used merely to replace standard office equipment, such as the typewriter (word processing), the adding machine (spreadsheets), and filing cabinets (databases). True, productivity has increased in a few niche areas, such as CAD and desktop publishing, but most office workers are still doing the same tasks."

—FRED DAVIS

TURNING TO THE EXPERTS
Clark Howard's Consumer Survival Kit

Clark Howard is a radio consumer talk-show host from Atlanta who has co-authored a consumer guide with author Mark Meltzer. The Mescon Group used the book as the basis for a multimedia CD-ROM, which is being marketed by the IBM Multimedia Publishing Studio.

The disc addresses a range of consumer issues, broken up into separate chapters such as Money, Cars, Real Estate, Insurance, Travel, and Rip-offs. Each chapter is divided into sections, in which you can view text, action items, and tips. The text is not lengthy, but it includes important general principles and plenty of examples.

The action items are simply Windows Write files that are copied to your Windows directory during program installation—a preferable alternative might have been to copy them to the program's own subdirectory. The items include sample letters, checklists, and record-keeping forms. Windows Write has some drawbacks as an interactive tool, but it does get the job done.

The tips often summarize the principles covered in the text. In many cases, you'll also find a video clip available. These small black-and-white clips (with poor audio quality) are all interview shots of Howard discussing the same topic as the text—often with different words, but essentially making the same points.

The program has some other tools as well, such as a phone directory and search engine. The phone directory is just a Windows Cardfile database, but you can employ it as a phone dialer. The search engine is easy to use and supports some Boolean logic operators.

The content is not as deep as some users might desire, but for people just starting out on their own, it provides an excellent overview of a range of financial issues. The multimedia aspects are more "Windows-dressing" than substantive, but the net result is an approachable and useful product.—Alfred Poor

Clark Howard's Consumer Survival Kit
IBM Multimedia Publishing Studio
1500 River Edge Pkwy.
Suite 200
Atlanta, GA 30328
(800) 898-8842; (615) 793-5090
$39.95

Government Giveaways for Entrepreneurs 2.0

Matthew Lesko is an expert on the U.S. government, and has tons of information about where to find just about any service the government provides. He has written a number of books, and has put much of the information into this CD-ROM.

The program uses the Folio VP presentation engine, which treats the disc contents as a single long stream of data divided into records. You can scroll through the records in sequence, or jump to the topic you want using the Table of Contents outline view. There is also a search feature that supports Boolean and proximity operators. Overall, however, the interface is a bit clumsy and slow compared with those of other reference CDs.

The CD includes 77 audio clips in fairly decent-sounding 8-bit, 22KHz files and 11 Video for Windows clips. The unfortunate part about these multimedia items is that they are tacked onto the end of the disk, without any links to the topics they cover. Furthermore, Lesko's narration gets so wildly enthusiastic that ultimately it gets a little hard to believe.

Still, the true value of this disc lies in its text material, not in the multimedia. The content is not limited to just federal government information, either; you'll also find data about state, local, and private programs. You can find details about government loan programs; projects that provide free or low-cost services to start-up businesses; sources of technical assistance; and special opportunities for businesses owned by women and minorities.

One of the best aspects of this disc is that you can learn about resources you never knew existed. Our government agencies have grown so large, so numerous, and so spread-out that there is no easy way for the average citizen to be aware of all that is available. This disc puts much of that information right on your screen.

By the time you read this, version 3.0 should be available. According to Infobusiness, this version will contain updates to over 12,000 sources of money, help, and information to start or expand your business. Other features will include a new interface; a special section on IRS secrets, shortcuts, and savings; and information on practically every government contract and who serviced them for the past year.—Alfred Poor

Government Giveaways for Entrepreneurs 2.0
Infobusiness Inc.
887 S. Orem Blvd.
Orem, UT 84058
(800) 657-5300; (801) 221-1100

Fax: (801) 221-1194
$59.95

MacInTax

The latest version of MacInTax has a simple interface that makes tax-preparation disarmingly easy. As with previous versions of the program, you can type information directly into the tax forms or have MacInTax lead you through the process, using its EasyStep method. EasyStep is primarily an interview—you answer questions about your employment, filing status, and financial data in a series of dialog boxes, and MacInTax puts this information into the appropriate forms.

This year, the main window for the EasyStep interview has a row of notebook-binder-like tabs that let you move forward or backward to any one of the seven main tax-preparation steps. In the interview section (where MacInTax does all of its fact gathering for your return), you can review any of the questions. For instance, if you want to look at how you answered the questions about your 1994 investment income, you can click on the Topics button and select the Investments topic.

You can also jump back and forth freely between the interview and the forms, which is useful if you're already fairly tax-savvy and find going through the interview too slow. When you come across a confusing line on a form, you can pop back into the interview and let MacInTax gently prompt you for the necessary information.

Intuit has actually taken out features that were in the 1993 version. You can no longer generate graphs that show your tax and income data. Neither can you annotate individual lines in the forms with notes or audio memos.

Instead, Intuit has put its energy into adding features and enhancements that more users will find practical. For example, you can now magnify a form in order to read all the fine print for which the IRS is famous. Fifteen new forms and worksheets help you figure out specialized tax issues, such as interest income and medical deductions. Furthermore, Intuit has added state versions for Indiana, Louisiana, Nebraska, New Mexico, Oklahoma, South Carolina, Utah, and Wisconsin—bringing the number of states MacInTax supports to 28.

For those who want help deciphering the forms and worksheets, MacInTax provides the full IRS instructions together with its own instructions for each form. Most of the help is quite good, but beware of gratuitous plugs for Intuit products. When you've finished your tax return, MacInTax scans it for problems. Unlike previous versions, which just gave you a list of any missing information, this year's MacInTax lets you jump directly to the line you need to fill in.

MacInTax 1994 Edition
Intuit
(619) 453-4446
$39.95

AM-Tax Personal 1040

Preparing taxes is a dreaded task for most people: The process can all too often be slow, complex, and confusing. But AM Software's AM-Tax Personal 1040 proves that the software supporting the process doesn't have to be. Now in its tenth season, this DOS-based title has built its reputation on speed, simplicity, and accuracy.

AM-Tax doesn't have numerous data entry options, detailed explanations and help files, or the navigational and functional ease of a graphical interface. But if all you really want is a reliable, few-frills electronic tax preparer, AM-Tax is a safe bet. It's also a good choice if your

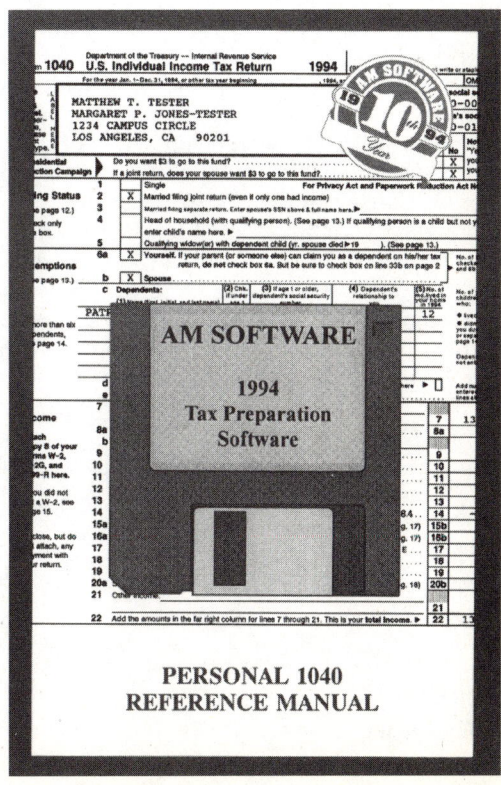

computer can't accommodate the hardware requirements of Windows-based tax software.

Entering your data is easy and straightforward: Just go to one of the program's 69 forms, schedules, and worksheets and start entering. Supported fields are marked with an asterisk, and calculated fields, a "C." Unlike packages such as TurboTax and TaxCut, AM-Tax Personal 1040 will not import data from other programs. But a new feature in this year's release will let you maintain a tax history for up to five years.

All navigational keystrokes are supported in AM-Tax. Scrolling is not, but the PgDn and PgUp keys move you around pretty efficiently. Use the function keys to jump to and from supporting documents, override and recalculate data, access the state return, get help or a list of forms and options (calculator, tax summary, and so on), save, and print. The Review Return feature displays a list of forms you've worked on, which saves time when revisiting screens. Another handy feature is that every screen keeps a running tally of your tax obligation and tax bracket.

When it comes to tax advice and money-saving tips, AM-Tax falls behind most of the pack. Program help is thorough, and IRS instructions are also available—although no interpretations of IRS-speak are provided. The program does let you create "what if" sce-

narios, and you can view a constantly evolving summary of your tax obligation (which is where your five-year data appears).

This year's edition of AM-Tax provides enhanced detail for working on more complicated tax returns. Other new features include three forms and one schedule, an option for joint reporting on Schedules C and F, and the option to handle more depreciable assets and rental properties. And as always, you can file your taxes by printing out and mailing in either the condensed, IRS-approved 1040PC form or the standard forms and schedules.

If you want or need step-by-step walk-throughs, Windows's easy navigation, or more than basic instructions, AM-Tax Personal 1040 clearly is not the best title. But for people with older PCs, AM-Tax is the tax preparation program of choice: It will even run off of floppy disks (minus the help and audit functions). And for those of you who just want to burn through your tax return with minimal intervention, there's nothing better than AM-Tax.

AM-Tax Personal 1040
AM Software Inc.
P.O. Box 25010
Kansas City, MO 64119
(800) 859-8537; (816) 741-7848
$39

Kiplinger's TaxCut

Block Financial Software has done it again with the 1994 versions of TaxCut for DOS and TaxCut for Windows. TaxCut has been one of *PC Magazine*'s top two tax packages for several years running, and this year's releases carry on the tradition. Block refined the new Windows version by toning down the colorful interface, tightening the operation to make it clearer and cleaner, and adding some snazzy new navigational options. These improvements widen the gap between this version and its DOS sister, but features remain similar in both.

Kiplinger's TaxCut, an enhanced version of Block's package, is also available. Now in its third year, this product incorporates expert tax advice from Kiplinger and is available for DOS and Windows. You can order the software only from Kiplinger; the federal edition is $39.95, and the state editions sell for $24.95 each. The head-start version sells for $11.95.

Like most packages, TaxCut allows you to import existing financial information—but it gives you greater flexibility than other packages. You can import data from last year's TaxCut or TurboTax, and you can also bring files in via .FOX, .TAX, or .TXF formats. As for entering current information, TaxCut gives you three options: interview (here called Q&A), shoebox, and direct data entry.

If Q&A is your preferred method, see the list box that displays 12 primary topics such as "If You Are Self-Employed." A separate box lists subtopics within that section. Clicking on Start Q&A will take you to a series of screens that offer background information and ask specific questions. The program will automatically enter your answers on the appropriate forms.

The opening Q&A screen also contains buttons marked Go to Form and Find Topic; the latter provides an alphabetical list of tax-related subjects. Select one and you can jump either to the actual form or to the matching section in the Q&A. You can also access IRS instructions and program help from Q&A.

The Shoebox, found in the Forms menu, lists miscellaneous topics. Here too, TaxCut will carry you to the appropriate area of your return.

If direct data entry is more your style, you may want to use a new feature in the Windows version: the "roving I," a graphical "I" that remains on-screen during the process. Clicking on this icon will bring up much of TaxCut's help (though you

can still use standard, searchable help), let you flag an entry as tentative for later review, or let you create a detail list.

When you start crunching numbers, you should bear in mind that clicking on Instructions will give you IRS instructions for the form you're using. And if you need a less formal reading than the IRS's, go to Explain Form. Ctrl-F4 takes you back to the form you were working in, but a glitch in the head-start edition caused the original form to shrink. This will be corrected in the final version, according to Block.

No matter which method you choose to complete your return, TaxCut offers a constantly updated progress report that has both summary and detail views. The summary displays both a graph and a breakdown of actual figures illustrating current income and tax tallies. The detail view lists all entries made on your return, with the option to jump directly to them.

Getting around is definitely easier in this year's TaxCut for Windows. Block abandoned the cartoon-strip Navigator for a simpler look: The opening screen now uses simple tabs that take you to the program's nine main areas.

In addition to cleaning up the interface, Block has streamlined navigation. For example, at any point in the Q&A or forms entry options, you can move back to the Navigator (or to other core features, such as the Auditor) by clicking the Return button. Find Topic is available in a pull-down menu if there's no on-screen button. And topics you've visited in the Q&A but not completed are marked with a different symbol than those you've finished.

The new "roving I" feature also offers navigational help. As you move through forms entry, clicking on the "I" opens a small box containing several buttons. The Related Entries button will take you to a list of forms and schedules linked to that line. You can either move there or revisit other forms listed in the box.

Accommodating different user styles is another of TaxCut's strengths. The pro-

gram designers have taken pains to offer more than one way to move through your return in both versions. For example, you can jump to related entries by hitting Ctrl-J or selecting Jump to Related from the Forms menu. Ctrl-V or Previous Form takes you back.

Many of us have anxiety about getting everything right on our tax return. This year's TaxCut offers more help than ever to make sure you do so. TaxCut's Auditor, for example, is always with you. If you've made an entry that seems unusual, a question box will pop up. Auditor also scrutinizes your completed return for errors, omissions, and inconsistencies; clicking on any line number box will move you to the relevant form for corrections. TaxCut's extensive tax-planning section helps you strategize, using tools such as "what if" worksheets, a five-year summary, and information on filing an amended return. Miniworksheets help document final totals on the 1040. And now, thanks to H&R Block's 1993 acquisition of MECA, TaxCut customers can call local H&R Block offices to ask tax-related questions. If you're audited, a Block representative will accompany you to the audit.

When you're ready to file your polished return, you can print out and mail in either the condensed, IRS-approved 1040PC form or the standard forms and schedules. Block thoughtfully includes an uninstall utility to remove the

program—but not your data—from your PC.

TaxCut didn't take the giant step it did with last year's Windows version, but the truth is that it didn't need to. By toning down some of the navigational elements that caused minor confusion last year, yet retaining its reliability, depth, and usability, TaxCut has proved once again why it's one of the top tax programs available.
—Kathy Yakal

TaxCut
Block Financial Software
55 Walls Dr.
Fairfield, CT 06430
(800) 288-6322; (203) 256-5000
$39.95

Kiplinger's TaxCut
Kiplinger
1729 H. St. N.W.
Washington D.C. 20006
(800) 235-4060
$24.95

Simply Tax for Windows

4Home Productions's mantra while reconstructing Simply Tax for Windows may well have been "If we rebuild it, they will come." After practically giving away the first version of Simply Tax last year, 4Home Productions started from scratch to produce this year's release. It combines previous content with a completely overhauled look and feel and a meatier guidance system. But these welcome cosmetic and substantive changes are offset by an overly busy, sometimes confusing interface and some

glitches in the head-start version. Still, there's a lot to like about this year's offering.

Many of the functional elements of the top tax titles are included in the new Simply Tax, although it's still a bit shorter on forms and schedules. Data can be imported directly from last year's version or from Simply Money. And like some other packages, Simply Tax lets you choose how you want to prepare your return: via direct data entry, the Interview feature, or the catch-all Shoebox.

A new feature is the Pathfinder, a pop-up box that contains tabs such as History (a list of documents you've visited during the current session but not necessarily opened), Forms, Shoebox (a list of miscellaneous tax topics), Interview Elements,

Active (a list of documents you've worked with during current session), and Bookmark (a list of places you've earmarked on forms and schedules).

Although Simply Tax has simplified navigation, it still has some interface problems. Moving through the Interview is not difficult, but keeping your eye on the right place in the rather cluttered screen is quite challenging.

We also discovered some irritating glitches in the head-start version. For example, jumping back and forth among topics and forms—and between forms and the Interview—is difficult. If you click on a program icon within a document, the form shrinks and does not resize when the requested dialog box opens. Also, newly

Telecommuting Aids Economy, Ecology, Firm, and Employee

Wouldn't it be great if we could discover a technology that could increase worker productivity, improve the quality of life, help strengthen the family, reduce pollution, diminish traffic congestion and even lower taxes through increased government productivity? According to its proponents, telecommuting—the use of telecommunications to perform work outside of the workplace—has the potential to do just that.

The development of computer technologies such as ISDN, LANs, groupware applications, and PC-based videoconferencing promises to broaden the applicability and appeal of telecommuting even further. Companies with LANs are best positioned to promote telecommuting, because much communication today—even gossip—already takes advantage of the line that ties computers, and potentially, telecommuters. —Fred Davis ■

opened forms or boxes do not replace the previous display. All of these are distracting, but 4Home says they will be fixed in the final version.

Even though Simply Tax is still quirky, 4Home need not apologize for its prolific help system. You have access to three levels of guidance—an explanation of the current element, verbatim IRS instructions, or insight from the Ernst & Young Tax Advisor—and program help. You're also provided with miniworksheets in the direct data entry option and right-mouse button support for overriding fields and jumping to required forms.

Other pluses include the Validate function, which scans your return for simple errors and omissions. Tax Savings, expected to be included in the 1994 final edition, will comb your entries for commonly overlooked deductions. And Audit Alert will compare your data to national averages. When you're done, you can file

your taxes by printing out and mailing in either the condensed, IRS-approved 1040PC form or the standard forms and schedules.

The overhauled Simply Tax is quite simply a diamond in the rough. The package has a long way to go before its stability, navigational ease, speed, and usability match the best of the bunch—but its new beginning shows promise.—Kathy Yakal

Simply Tax for Windows
4Home Productions (a division of Computer Associates International)
One Computer Associates Plaza
Islandia, NY 11788
(800) 773-5445; (516) 342-2000
$69.99

Personal Tax Edge TaxSaver

This tax roundup includes two nearly identical products with different names from different companies: Personal

Tax Edge for DOS or Windows from Parsons Technology and TaxSaver for DOS or Windows from WordPerfect, the Novell Applications Group. Now we'll try to explain. Parsons was forced to license PTE to WordPerfect, which now sells the package as TaxSaver. Intuit also now has the license to this product, because it purchased Parsons; it has not put a third version on the market, though. The two available programs are so similar that much of the time we'll refer to them together (as PTE/TaxSaver).

This year, PTE/TaxSaver is sporting a new help and navigational aid called Personal Tax Guide in PTE and Tax Coach in TaxSaver. Still, it continues to offer a comfortable balance of simplicity and tax-processing power. The Interview option, though

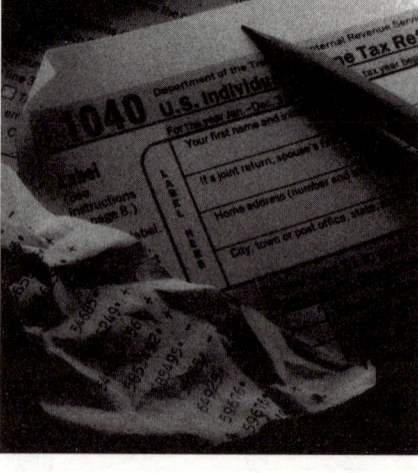

comprehensive, remains one of PTE/TaxSaver's cruder elements; the boilerplate Tax Organizer (similar to the shoebox feature in other products) isn't as all-encompassing as its competitors'. But slow, careful growth, a fine online help system, and the low price make PTE/TaxSaver an attractive, reliable tax product.

Parsons first released the graphical version of PTE two years ago, but the DOS and Windows products have maintained similar feature

sets. Both import financial data directly from MoneyCounts, PTE, and TaxMate (a "lite" version of Personal Tax Edge with fewer forms) and accept files in .TXF format. Their 63 forms, schedules, and worksheets can be filled out via the Interview option, direct data entry, or the Tax Organizer; the last requires extensive editing of the boilerplate list of built-in documents. The Tax Guide/Tax Coach is a dialog box that outlines the program's seven tax-preparation steps. Click on one and Tax Guide will walk you through each substep.

PTE/TaxSaver's Interview framework hasn't evolved much over the last two years. It leads you through every element of your return but asks only a couple of basic questions in each before dumping you into the form or schedule for direct data entry. On-screen directions tell you exactly which lines to fill in before returning to the Interview. If you exit

Interview without finishing, however, you won't be taken back to your stopping point when you resume. Completed topics are checked off in the list, but if you haven't fully completed a topic, it won't be checked.

The overall interface in PTE/TaxSaver is so clean and understandable it's almost spare. Pull-down menus are brief but adequate, and the toolbar contains the most critical, often-used icons.

PTE/TaxSaver offers numerous ways to document each entry and to get help. You can, for example, attach a generic note or a more specific Bookkeeper to most lines (the latter lets you enumerate details subsumed under an entry).

Whether you're using Interview or direct data entry, you have fast access to Tax Tips—context-sensitive explanations of the current line combined with advice on how best to handle a specific tax situation. Online IRS instructions explain points of tax law and direct you to related IRS publications. And program help is available through the Help menu.

Additional tools—a simple math calculator and a more complex depreciation calculator—assist with any computations your tax return may require. PTE (but not TaxSaver) also includes Interest Vision SE, a utility that calculates long-term interest and principle on loans, annuities, savings, and investments and can also generate amortization and accumulation schedules.

PTE/TaxSaver offers two audit options and a handful of tools designed to help you plan future tax strategies: Audit Report simply lists errors and omissions and flags possible problems; Review Audits takes you directly to the line in question for consideration. Tax at a Glance provides a snapshot of your completed return and allows "what if" musings. Review W-4 may point to wiser employer tax withholdings; Tax Savers offers personalized suggestions for more advantageous planning.

With PTE/TaxSaver, you can file your taxes by printing out and mailing in either the condensed, IRS-approved 1040PC form, the 1040X form, or the standard forms and schedules.

Though perhaps not as feature-packed or elegant as the premiere tax preparation products, PTE has long been a favorite of many users. PTE/TaxSaver is clean and simple yet thorough enough to meet many peoples' needs. If the products' current vendors ever complete its partially constructed Interview feature, PTE/TaxSaver might find itself head-to-head with the market leaders.
—Kathy Yakal

Personal Tax Edge
Parsons Technology Inc.
One Parsons Dr.
P.O. Box 100
Hiawatha, IA 52233
(800) 223-6925; (319) 395-9626
$19

TaxSaver
WordPerfect, the Novell
Applications Group
1555 N. Technology Way
Orem, UT 84057
(800) 451-5151
Free to registered users

TaxPerfect Personal 1040

TaxPerfect Personal 1040 has always lagged behind its competitors in interface design, online guidance, and data entry options. In an attempt to catch up, Financial Services Marketing Corp. completely revamped the interface in this year's version. The new look certainly enhances usability, but TaxPerfect still can't compete with other DOS-based tax preparation software—espe-

cially considering the bugs we encountered in the head-start edition. The program's speed and simplicity may, however, appeal to users who just want electronic tax forms and don't need help preparing their returns.

TaxPerfect can't import data from other tax programs or personal finance packages, but data entry has been improved in this year's version. In the past, you had to enter data on a special screen; now you can enter data directly on any of TaxPerfect's 91 forms, schedules, and worksheets. Numeric fields that contain a yellow zero require a supporting form or schedule, but you can easily override these. Pressing Alt-R pops up a box displaying the document required; unfortunately, TaxPerfect's automatic jump wasn't working in the Head-start edition we reviewed.

Interview and shoebox data entry options aren't offered in TaxPerfect, but pull-down menus and function key descriptions do provide instructions for program operation. This year's version is missing the on-screen running tally and the list of already processed forms, but a function key will display them. TaxPerfect now also supports limited mouse operations—not including navigation. Consult the program help for an explanation of navigational options.

Guidance for puzzled taxpayers has never been TaxPerfect's forte, though the 1994 head-start and final ver-

sions both contain IRS instructions. And some help can be found in the program's forms list. To see an explanation of the highlighted document, click F10; clicking F9 will display a tree diagram illustrating the forms and schedules related to each document.

TaxPerfect offers several features that will help you detail and thoroughly document your return before printing: DataChek briefly scans your entries for simple omissions and errors. The Notepad helps you keep track of detail lists and other offstage documentation, although you can't link notes to individual lines or forms. The standalone depreciation calculator can compute simple depreciation equations. Running TaxPerfect in tax-planning instead of tax-preparation mode lets you explore "what if" projections. And the Tax Calendar file lists important dates for tax reports and payments.

TaxPerfect's head-start edition suffered from many unexplained glitches. For example, we were unable to save without naming a data directory and could not print a return in IRS-approved format. The depreciation calculator locked up in one test, and in at least one form (2441) we had to supply information that should have automatically carried over.

Admittedly, TaxPerfect's new interface and additions are big steps forward for the product. But even if Financial Services Marketing patches

the program's holes by final release, recommending this title to anyone but former users and those who need only a bare-bones tax preparation program is tough.— Kathy Yakal

TaxPerfect Personal 1040
Financial Services Marketing Corp.
500 N. Dallas Bank Tower
12900 Preston Rd.
Dallas, TX 75230
(800) 525-5611; (214) 386-6320
$79.95

TurboTax for DOS and Windows

As it did two years ago, TurboTax for Windows has taken a giant step forward— this time by designing the cleanest, most understandable interface ever for a personal tax product. Intuit has also added numerous substantive features, among them Tax Advisor—an enhanced audit feature—and TaxLink, a dynamic connection between TurboTax and Quicken 4 for Windows (Intuit's popular personal finance product).

These careful, balanced cosmetic and functional enhancements make TurboTax for Windows the foremost personal tax preparation program for the 1994 tax year. And although the DOS version hasn't changed as significantly, it is also a solid product.

Quicken 4 for Windows users have an unprecedented import tool this year. Using

Tax experts answer your questions — in full-motion video!

the new TaxLink feature, you can pull Quicken data directly into TurboTax. TaxLink displays a list of transactions and where they went, and previously uncategorized transactions can be assigned to a tax document.

Because Quicken runs in the background when you use TaxLink, new or edited transactions are constantly updated. You can also import financial data from earlier versions of Quicken, last year's TurboTax, or any files in ASCII, .TAX, or .TXF formats into any of TurboTax's 100-plus forms and schedules.

It's taken a couple of years for TurboTax's developers to tame the new EasyStep (interview) navigation option introduced in 1992, but the pieces have finally fallen into place. Besides being attractive and uncluttered, the revamped interface makes

your options and next moves clear at every step.

File-folder tabs guide you through each major program section. Large, nonstandard buttons and icons on every screen let you move forward and backward, itemize, and connect to TaxLink. Chiseled buttons along the side offer help, a summary, and a calculator; they also let you jump to forms. Pull-down menus provide additional navigational help. One of the menus on the Interview screen outlines topics and subtopics.

Direct data entry fans have many new navigational and guidance tools, too. For example, if you're entering data directly and want to return to Interview, click the EasyStep icon and you'll be given a choice between resuming Interview where you left off or jumping to the section related to the open form.

In TurboTax for Windows, Intuit has introduced a new way to move quickly to supporting forms and schedules—QuickZoom. Double-click any line in any document (or select QuickZoom from the menu) and the appropriate form opens. If there are multiple layers, QuickZoom will keep drilling down; if no forms are linked, an itemization worksheet opens. (Alternatively, you can click the Cross-Reference icon to display a list of related forms.) A small box in the upper-left corner indicates whether the current line can use QuickZoom or whether it's a direct numeric or text field.

Integrated worksheets further detail your bottom-line figures. Forms can be viewed in various magnifications, from thumbnail to 200 percent. And you can run the Error Summary at any time— without waiting for the final

audit—to clean up oversights.

A third data entry option (available in both versions) is TurboTax's File Cabinet, which lists tax-related subjects and documents in alphabetical order. Click on one and you're carried to the appropriate form or schedule's line.

Though you probably won't encounter much trouble navigating through TurboTax, there may be places where you'll have questions or will want a sneak preview of how your tax picture is shaping up. TurboTax manages to accommodate all of this in both its DOS and Windows versions.

Tax help and program help are both available. Neither is searchable, though TurboTax Help makes good use of hypertext extensions for additional background in direct data entry. IRS instructions were not available in the head-start edition but should be present in the final release.

More abundant help is offered in the Interview than in direct data entry mode. Each question posed is brief, but again the hypertext help expounds on selected words and phrases for a more complete explanation. The new Tax Advisor (Windows only) offers guidance on selected screens, but visits from this virtual expert were few and far between in our tests.

The Tax Summary, accessible at any point in TurboTax, displays a constantly updated list of the most crucial bottom line figures, like Adjustments to Income and Refund or Balance Due. Four tax graphs—Where Your Money Goes, Tax Analysis, Deductions, and Income Sources—offer a visual view of your tax obligation. (Neither Tax Graphs nor the File Cabinet is available when using EasyStep in the Windows product, but both can be accessed via Forms. This glitch should be corrected in the final version.)

Unlike TaxCut, which does a good deal of error checking in the background as you're filling out your return, TurboTax saves much of this task for the end. Its Review function is divided into four areas. Errors and Omissions checks for missing or erroneous information (TurboTax displays a split screen so you can fix the problem immediately). The Audit Flags section answers common questions about IRS audits and alerts you to any flags it's found in your return. Tax Savings Ideas offers advice on ways you might reduce your tax debt. The Deduction Finder points out legitimate deductions that people sometimes miss.

You can file your taxes by printing out and mailing in either the condensed, IRS-approved 1040PC form or the standard forms and schedules. Though you may not want to think about taxes again for some time, TurboTax offers a 1995 tax planning option to help you prepare for next year's

ordeal. An uninstall utility is also included.

Intuit has taken the complex and decidedly nonlinear process of tax preparation and made it gratifyingly clear and linear in the 1994 edition of TurboTax—particularly in the Windows version. (DOS's EasyStep is still somewhat confusing.) So the battle between the big three—Personal Tax Edge, TaxCut, and TurboTax—continues. But this year, TurboTax comes out on top.—Kathy Yakal

TurboTax
Intuit Inc.
2650 E. Elvira Rd., #100
Tucson, AZ 85706
(800) 964-1040 ext. 6017;
(602) 295-3110
Fax: (800) 756-1040
$69.95

MASTER OF THE FINANCIAL UNIVERSE
Windows on WallStreet Pro

What sends a stock through the roof—fundamentals or fever? If you could get a PC to give you the answer, you could out-trade Warren Buffett. But while Buffett would be the first to tell you that fundamentals—such as earnings, assets, and revenues—are the best indicators of a stock's worth, consider Buffett's famous jab at stockbrokers: A guy walks into a fly-fishing store and grabs a hairy handful of flies. "Fish actually like these?" he says. The storekeeper's reply: "I don't sell to fish."

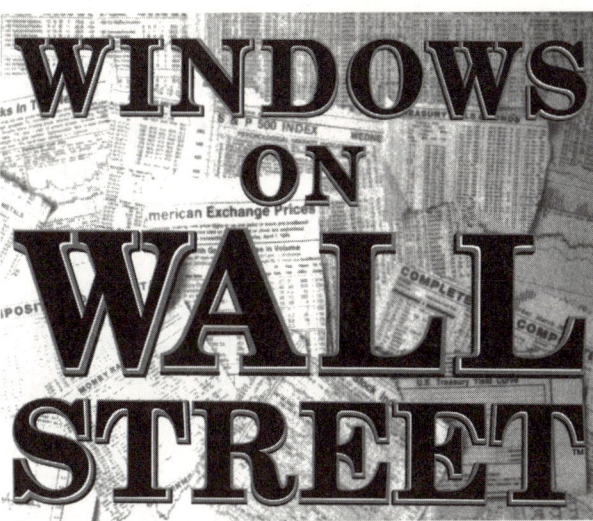

Fundamentals may be the long-term determinants of fair value, but a herd of crazed buyers can still shoot a stock price up faster than Michael Milken's courtroom blood pressure. Nonetheless, technical analysts ski up and down securities charts, slaloming around indicators like Chaikin Oscillators in their quest to predict stock performance. The new Windows on WallStreet Pro software brings their brand of analysis to your desktop.

Like its close competitor MetaStock, Windows on WallStreet Pro is an armchair technical-analyst's jewel. We found the program's price rate-of-change indicator particularly useful. This indicator points to securities that are overbought or oversold. We tested the indicator against the charts of a few hate stocks of the last few years. For example, had you invested $10,000 in Citicorp in 1991—when Windows on WallStreet Pro's indicators called it out

as extremely oversold—you'd have made nearly $30,000 by now. Not bad.

There are countless other indicators in Windows on WallStreet Pro, most of which are designed to point to extreme swings in price and volume. One of the more fascinating charts, Cycle Lines, includes the charted price of a security over time segmented by evenly spaced vertical lines. This view is useful when charting the performance of cyclical stocks. Chrysler has seen its stock price plummet by more than 25 percent since the beginning of the year, despite record earnings. Why? Chrysler is a classic cyclical stock. Using Cycle Lines, we found it easy to spot the fact that Chrysler's uptrend had already become long in the tooth by January.

Compared to the charting capabilities of other mainstream investment products, such as Reality Technologies's Reuters Money Network,

Windows on WallStreet Pro's charts are a graphical tour de force. Aside from all the indicators it plots, it puts an unlimited number of securities in one chart.

Reuters Money Network, on the other hand, can plot only four securities concurrently. If you're a comparison shopper, that difference is important.

We found Windows on WallStreet Pro's charts addictive, but we also think investors should offset its graphical approach with a product that lets you get at financial fundamentals such as price/earning ratios and dividend yields. For that data, Reuter's Money Network is the best bargain, and Value Line Publishing's Value Screen III has detailed company data. Remember: The well-prepared stock picker has done the reading, not just looked at the pictures.—Sebastian Rupley

Windows on WallStreet Pro
MarketArts
(800) 998-8439; (214) 235-9594
$295; $69.95 for Investor's
Power Pack including data on
200 top stocks

Windows on WallStreet

A powerful investment analysis tool that grows with you is what you get in MarketArts's Windows on WallStreet, Version 2.1. Although the package has no portfolio management capabilities—nor does it recommend investment strategies—WOW's analytical features can help you select what to include in your asset base. WOW also lets you set up a hypothetical portfolio to test the behavior of specific securities before you invest real money. If you don't find the usual market indexes helpful, WOW lets you create your own.

Beyond analysis of individual securities, WOW includes indicators to help you decide on buy and sell timing. WOW's manual and online help are excellent aids toward understanding how to develop personalized market-tracking indicators.

To keep those indicators current, securities price updates are available on-line via CompuServe, Dial Data, and Dow Jones News/Retrieval. (ZiffNet members, make sure your account can access CompuServe, and add a GO CIS line to the CompuServe log-on macro.) Each online service configuration includes ten user-modifiable buttons that execute commands such as logging on to an investment forum. These are handy if you want to do something online besides download quotes and news. If you need to enter securities data manually, you can; but if you want to track pricing on a daily basis, you'll spend lots of time typing.

Once a securities data file is set up, the graphic-intensive analysis functions come into play. WOW has more than a dozen predefined graphical templates, and you can easily create new

ones such as sophisticated pricing graphs with multiple securities and indexes displayed. Advanced graphical analysis options include moving averages, regression trendlines, Fibonacci and Gann studies, Andrews pitchforks, cycle lines, and others. Charts can be tiled to display several on one screen.

WOW's modem setup includes diagnostics, but you must supply the correct phone number for your online system. Although you can download securities prices from several different places within the program, you have to enter log-on information for each one. Once you develop a routine—for example, logging on to update stock prices, then calculating updated analytical tables and printing them out—WOW's Personal Investment Assistant will execute it at your command.

Windows on WallStreet is a highly sophisticated technical-analysis package, but it offers no management capabilities. So if you're happy with your portfolio management program and want a personalized market tracker, WOW is a good choice.
—Theresa W. Carey

Windows on WallStreet, Version 2.1
MarketArts Inc.
1810 North Glenville, #124
Richardson, TX 75081
(800) 998-8439; (214) 235-9594
$149.95

CASH OR CHARGE?
Jonathan Pond's Personal Financial Planner

Is all that money stuffed under the mattress disturbing your sleep? Do you think a CD belongs in a computer rather than a bank? If so, then you need Jonathan Pond's Personal Financial Planner.

Based on Pond's printed books, the disc has a few bonuses. Pond appears in videos to give additional advice—but like any talking head, that's no big deal. What you'll truly benefit from is the customized reading list: By answering a few questions at the outset, you get to skip the chapters you don't need. (Why couldn't we have had something like this in college?) And by answering other questions as you read, you get advice tailored to your age, goals, income, and family situation.

The disc doesn't tell you which stocks or mutual funds to buy, but it does suggest how to balance your investments and how much you should be saving to retire in style or send the kiddies to college. The interface needs a little fixing, though: If you enter conflicting information in different questionnaires, Personal Financial Planner is only smart enough to catch the mistake once—it doesn't locate the conflict in the second questionnaire. Once that's fixed, this disc will be hard to fault.

Jonathan Pond's Personal Financial Planner
Vertigo Development Group
(800) 688-475
$49.95

HAS QUICKEN FINALLY MET ITS MATCH?
Managing Your Money

"Easy to use" is the most overworked cliche in computing, but the interface in the first-ever Windows version of MECA Software's Managing Your Money is more than easy to use—it's a breakthrough for the personal finance category. More than just a work-alike of Intuit's market-leading Quicken, Managing Your Money provides you with an object-oriented simulation of your home office called SmartDesk.

SmartDesk isn't just cute; it truly adds functionality. Each object on the screen is the functional equivalent of a pull-down menu, but far more intuitive. Of course, Managing Your Money for Windows has the usual menu and quick-action buttons for those who prefer them, but

new users and even experienced veterans can save mouse clicks and mind time by using the checkbook, calculator, and other objects in and around SmartDesk.

Managing Your Money for Windows focuses on the four areas that define most people's finances—banking, investments, taxes, and planning.

The banking section is similar to Quicken's except that it lacks support for the online services IntelliCharge and CheckFree. On the other hand, Managing Your Money combines a scrollable check register and a blank check on a single screen—or on separate screens, if you wish.

Managing Your Money's tax planner is superior to Quicken's. You don't have to design a report or buy a separate add-on to get this functionality. Right out of the box, Managing Your Money gives you an up-to-date readout of your tax liability at the push of a button. The tax calculator dialog box instantly pops up with subtotals from the most commonly used tax forms so that you can perform what-if calculations and find out the tax consequences of any given financial move. At the year's end, you can easily export your data to MECA's TaxCut, ChipSoft's TurboTax, or any tax program that supports the TXF format.

Similarly, the investment analysis window gives you a quick look at the status of all your investments sliced in a variety of ways. Like Quicken, Managing Your Money lets you track the cost, price changes, annual and simple appreciation, and dividends on stocks, bonds, and mutual funds—even collectibles. But with Managing Your Money, you also can track puts and calls, strike prices, and expiration dates, as well as esoterica like beta coefficient and industry performance.

True to its name, Managing Your Money has a strong planning module. You can create budgets for up to three years at a time and compare those to actual budgets in ready-made and customizable reports and graphs. More important, the expert advice of Andrew Tobias is always just a right-mouse click away.

If you're a longtime Quicken user, you probably won't want to convert your data and work style to Managing Your Money. MECA made the import easy, but remember that the easiest interface is the one you already know. For new users, however, Managing Your Money for Windows is the first real competitor we've seen for Quicken. It's truly unique and definitely worth a try for the low $35-to-$40 street price.—Mike Hogan

Managing Your Money
MECA Software
(800) 820-7458
$79.

TaxCut

TaxCut lets you enter data directly into forms or takes you through an interview and it allows you to jump between the interview and the forms. It also uses notebook-binder-like tabs, each of which takes you to one of the program's tax-preparation steps. Once you've completed your tax return, TaxCut gives you quick access to a one-screen summary of your tax liability and an overview of your return. It can also give you a more detailed summary that lists all the entries you've made, or it can show you a pie-chart summary of your tax return.

Now that MECA Software has been acquired by H&R Block, the most noteworthy enhancement to TaxCut isn't the software but the support. When you buy TaxCut, you can get free advice on tax-related questions from any local H&R Block office. You don't even have to look in your phone book for the numbers, since TaxCut has a database in which you can find your local office by typing in your area code, state, and ZIP code. Furthermore, if you use TaxCut to file your final return and you subsequently get audited, H&R Block will help you prepare for the audit at no charge.

TaxCut's online help is strong as well. An entry-info icon, a tiny round button marked with an i, always appears next to the currently active field. When you click on the button, a dialog box pops up. From this box, you can choose to look at the IRS's or TaxCut's instructions for the form.

You don't have to sort your documents before you start preparing your return with TaxCut. In its Shoebox window, you select who sent you a form (for instance, your employer or a broker) and what it's about (for instance, your wages or dividends), and TaxCut automatically takes you to the appropriate form for the information.

Overall, TaxCut's interface is functional, but it's not as elegantly designed as

Signs That Computers Have Taken Over Your Life

- You think of the gadgets in your office as "friends," but you forget to send your mom a birthday card.

- You know Bill Gates's e-mail address, but you have to look up your own social security number.

- On vacation, you are reading a computer manual and turning the pages faster than everyone else who is reading John Grisham novels.

- You would rather get more dots per inch than miles per gallon.

- You own a set of little screwdrivers and you actually know where they are.

- You rotate your screen savers more frequently than your automobile tires.

- You are reading this book.

MacInTax's. For instance, the Q&A interview has tiny windows that require far too much scrolling in order to read everything. Additionally, when you reduce the size of certain windows in the program, such as in the Summary Reviews window, lines of text crash into each other.

Unfortunately, TaxCut's assistance for state forms is limited—it still has state editions only for California and New York. Unless you live in those states—or a state that doesn't make its residents pay income tax—you'll be back to using a pen and a calculator to figure out how much you owe.

TaxCut 1994 Edition
Block Financial Software
(203) 255-1441
$39.95

MetaStock for DOS

Do you want to perform complicated, in-depth technical analysis when making an investment decision? Do you have some cash to sink into the purchase of a program and some time to invest in setting it up and figuring it out? If so, MetaStock for DOS, Equis International's investment program, is the analytical partner for you.

You'll need the add-on Pulse program to manage and analyze your portfolio, since MetaStock's sole purpose is securities analysis. And for full bidirectional information exchange, you'll need The Downloader—an add-on that

grabs quotes online. These services aren't cheap: MetaStock comes in an "end-of-day" version for $195 and a "real-time" version for $495. Pulse is $195 and The Downloader, $99. If you need the power, though, this may be the right combination for you.

Why? For starters, MetaStock goes far beyond the analysis possible in the other programs. It has more than 80 predefined trading indicators, ranging from the Accumulation Swing Index to the ZigZag. If you don't know how a particular indicator is defined or how to use it, the program's documentation and online help tell you all about it. And if you want a customized indicator, MetaStock helps you develop the formula, letting you know if you've made an error and

suggesting ways to correct it. You can even incorporate some predefined indicators into your custom formula.

MetaStock by itself is ideal for investors who like to delve into available data to develop and optimize a trading system. You can set up the program to test combinations of securities automatically against groups of indicators. During installation, MetaStock provides you with data for roughly 50 securities so you can see how the program works right away. You can add your data manually or grab it online with Pulse or The Downloader.

The Downloader gives you access to five investment-data vendors and lets you collect end-of-day trading data. Still, you need an account with at least one ven-

dor to log on. You can analyze data in MetaStock, but the programs are not well integrated: You must quit The Downloader to use MetaStock, and vice versa.

The add-on portfolio management program, Pulse, has comprehensive reporting features, can manage up to 75 real or hypothetical portfolios, and can get you online—but it is somewhat dated. Released in 1991, the program has a maximum transmission rate of 2,400 bps, an outdated interface, and a difficult menu system. Equis released a Windows versions of both MetaStock and online in early 1995.

Equipped with powerful investment features and analysis tools, MetaStock and its add-ons are worth the price for the sophisticated investor who is well versed in the stock market. But the investment novice may find this suite overwhelming in terms of money, time, and resources.—Theresa W. Carey

MetaStock for DOS, Version 4.5
Equis International Inc.
3950 South 700 East, #100
Salt Lake City, UT 84107
(800) 882-3040; (801) 265-8886
$495

WealthBuilder for DOS and Windows

If you like the idea of a personal investment coach helping you handle your portfolio, WealthBuilder, from Reality Online, may be just the package for you. It pro-

vides investment advice based on your financial situation and goals—along with portfolio management.

Although WealthBuilder's financial advice focuses primarily on selecting mutual funds, the package provides information on topics from annuities to stocks. WealthBuilder also encompasses Reuters Money Network, an online financial information and trading.

During installation, WealthBuilder asks 12 questions that help its WealthAdvisor feature develop your investment strategies. You tell the program your age, feelings about risk, investment philosophy, and favorite types of investments. Sample questions include: "If you won $500 on a bet, would you: A) Pocket the money; or B) Go for double or nothing." It then develops a Financial Blueprint and assigns you to one of five possible risk levels.

The questionnaire's main weakness is that it assumes you are knowledgeable about the various sorts of investments. Fortunately, as your knowledge grows, you can go back and amend your profile.

The next step is entering data from your existing portfolio (if you have one), so WealthAdvisor knows what you're working with. This can be tricky unless you follow the setup steps carefully.

First you must define your accounts, keeping the taxable assets separate from tax-deferred to ensure correct reporting. You also need to

specify a costing method for each account, which cannot be changed once the setup is complete.

Once WealthBuilder is set up, you can invoke Wealth-Advisor's expert advice. Using your current holdings and Financial Blueprint, WealthAdvisor recommends specific transactions, which you can conduct through the Money Network.

The Windows version of WealthBuilder was introduced just too late for full coverage, but it does offer some enhancements. You can, for instance, group online requests and send them in a batch. This version also makes tweaking your financial profile easier by providing slider bars to adjust your preferred risk level and then automatically recalculate portfolio recommendations.

WealthBuilder is a well-rounded program for the beginning to intermediate investor. It doesn't offer sophisticated technical-analysis features, but it gives you a good look at your financial situation and helps you set realistic goals. If you're new to the investing game and don't want to deal with a broker's high-pressure sales techniques, WealthBuilder can educate you and guide you along the road to your financial goals.—Theresa W. Carey

WealthBuilder
Reality Online Inc.
2200 Renaissance Blvd.
King of Prussia, PA 19406-2755
(800) 521-2475; (610) 277-7600
$99.95

WealthBuilder 3.0

If you've always wanted a business newspaper devoted to your particular investments, you'll like WealthBuilder 3.0. This latest version of Reality Technologies's electronic financial planner features a "personal newspaper" interface, automatic downloads and alerts, and solid financial advice.

You begin by entering information about your income and expenses, assets and liabilities, and financial objectives—such as retirement with a specified annual income. You also specify the level of risk you're willing to accept. WealthBuilder then suggests general strategies for achieving your goals; that is, it recommends categories, such as bonds and equities, rather than specific securities. To research specific securities—and to get the most out of WealthBuilder—you need to connect via modem to the online service maintained by WealthBuilder's publisher.

The Reuters MONEY Network provides current quotes on stocks, bonds, mutual funds, and financial indexes as well as a library of articles from financial publications. You pay $9.95 a month for this service; for $17.95, you also get historical performance graphs for investments and complete monthly updates of roughly 18,000 stocks, bonds, and mutual funds. Once you have this data in WealthBuilder's database, you can display lists filtered by category as well as sorted alphabetically or by performance.

Version 3.0 adds some powerful online features. The personal news-clipping service ($6.95 per month extra) automatically downloads articles about industries and investments you've identified as important. Alerts keep you aware of events that affect your investments. Historical price graphs display daily statistics for stocks and indexes, helping you spot trends.

If you can't spend the time and money to go online frequently and monitor your investments, WealthBuilder 3.0 isn't for you. But if a personal investment newspaper sounds like your dream come true, Reality Technologies won't let you down.
—Darryl Lewis

WealthBuilder by Money
Magazine 3.0
Reality Technologies, Inc.
King of Prussia, PA
(800) 346-2024; (215) 277-7600
$109.95; access to the Reuters
MONEY Network, $9.95 to
$24.90 per month, depending on
the services requested.

Your Mutual Fund Selector

About the riskiest thing you can do with your money is invest it without knowing anything about the investment. Vertigo Development Group, creators of the ActiveBook products, offers Your Mutual Fund Selector, a $49.95 interactive multimedia tutorial and reference book that will help you get started with mutual-fund investments.

The program looks like a book, but provides much more than just text and graphics; many pages include video clips and interactive elements. One screen helps you to determine your investment needs by asking you to enter your age, the number of years before your retirement, and how much you have available to invest. Another screen asks about your retirement-income needs, and how much money you'll require for your children's college education. Your answers here will automatically adjust the totals on the first page. Other screens help you figure out additional important factors, such as your willingness to take risks with your investments.

Once the program knows enough about your needs, it will suggest a portfolio of mutual funds based on information provided by Morningstar Inc., a leader in fund research and analysis. You can then access the disc's large database to get more information about those or other funds.

A CD-ROM that professes to explain mutual funds must walk a fine line between being so oversimplified it becomes patronizing and so detailed it becomes incomprehensible. The program handles this balancing act with aplomb, though some users may find the video clips a bit contrived.

The product has more fundamental limitations, however. For one thing, it's inherent–

Star Trek Virus—Invades your system in places where no virus has gone before.

ly self-contradicting, because while you're encouraged to study prospective funds carefully, including reading the fund prospectus and other material, the program goes ahead and provides a list of recommended funds anyway. If you're tempted to simply accept those recommendations without any further research, don't.

On the whole, however, Your Mutual Fund Selector is an excellent and engaging introduction to mutual funds, and well worth the time if you are new to this form of investment.—Alfred Poor

Your Mutual Fund Selector
Vertigo Development Group
58 Charles St.
Cambridge, MA 02141
(617) 225-2065
$49.95

Mutual Funds OnDisc

If you're actually going to invest in mutual funds, you need more detailed information than the Vertigo title can provide. Morningstar, the same company that supplied the fund information for Vertigo's product, has a CD-ROM title of its own: Mutual Funds OnDisc. The disc is available under a number of different subscription and pricing plans, starting at $295 for a single copy.

The June 1994 disc I sampled includes extensive information on 4,371 funds, drawn from a wide range of sources. For every fund, you can call up a summary of its objectives, a graph of its performance over time, charts of total returns, and annual performance data, portfolio holdings, and other items. You can also see review statements by Morningstar analysts, which provide useful insights into the statistics.

The program lets you slice and dice the data almost any way you can imagine. You can select from the list of funds based on criteria that you specify, and combine criteria with Boolean operators. Want a list of the no-load growth funds with four-star or higher Morningstar ratings, sorted in ascending order of estimated risk? You can get an answer in seconds.

Mutual Funds OnDisc is a character-based DOS program, though it does use VGA graphics for its charts. Its speed is good in spite of its large database, thanks in part to the 4MB of files that it installs on your hard disk. Also included are more than 70 commentaries—text reports that explain topics ranging from mortgage derivatives (and why it's not such a hot idea for funds to use them) to how Morningstar computes its "duration" figures for bond funds.

Mutual Funds OnDisc is an invaluable tool for anyone working with mutual funds. The financial information and analysis tools can help you quickly settle on your top prospects.—Alfred Poor

Mutual Funds OnDisc
Morningstar Inc.
225 W. Wacker Dr.
Chicago, IL 60606
(800) 876-5005; (312) 696-6000

$295 (one disc); $495 (one year with quarterly updates); $795 (one year with monthly updates—multiuser and LAN licenses available)

Fortune 500 on Disk

The CD-ROM version of Fortune 500 on Disk is published by Disclosure Inc., a company well known for heavy-duty financial databases. While those products typically sell for thousands of dollars, Fortune 500 on Disk has a list price of $395, putting it within reach of individual investors.

The character-based program runs in DOS and puts less than 200K of material on your hard disk. There are some noticeable pauses when searching—even with a fast CD-ROM drive—but performance is satisfactory.

Fortune 500 on Disk provides information on 1,000 companies with publicly traded stocks, including the Fortune 500 Industrial and Fortune 500 Service companies. The data comes from a variety of sources such as annual reports, proxy statements, and 10-K filings. The disc also includes information from Fortune magazine, such as sales, profits, and return on investment.

You can search for companies according to different criteria—such as SIC code, state, or financial information—and sort the resulting list in different ways as well. One handy feature is the option to export the results as delimited files

for import into other programs, or to create mailing labels directly from within the program.

On the downside, the documentation fails to adequately explain some of the terms and data categories reported on the disc, and the explanations of some terms refer to the year ending in 1990, when in fact the data runs through 1993. Also, the on-screen help files give some incorrect information about a few of the function-key commands.

These are small blemishes that don't significantly diminish the value of this affordable and accessible collection of information about the nation's top companies. Fortune 500 on Disk is a valuable tool for any investor.
—Alfred Poor

Fortune 500 on Disk
Disclosure Inc.
5161 River Rd.
Bethesda, MD 20816
(800) 945-3647; (301) 961-2789
$395

CheckWriter Pro 6.0.

You don't have to be a CPA to use CheckWriter Pro 6.0, from Aatrix. Recently beefed up with investment features that bring it closer to its main competitor, Intuit's Quicken, Check Writer Pro also features a notably novice-friendly attitude.

With its newly added investment features (brought over from Aatrix's Hi! Finance), CheckWriter Pro goes further than Quicken in some ways. It lets you monitor

changing stock quotes and can automatically download quotes from online services. CheckWriter Pro offers an informal, friendly approach geared to novices. Its manual avoids accounting terms in favor of basic, concise explanations (three pages to explain check-register balancing, for example, versus Quicken's ten). Reminders of impending bills are another friendly feature, as is the program's exceptional variety of tools for budgeting tasks such as planning for college costs, calculating a loan, and buying insurance. CheckWriter Pro also makes it easy to quickly format output for personal checks. It took us only 15 minutes to create a template from scratch that worked perfectly with bank checks from a personal checkbook.

For small businesses, CheckWriter Pro offers such features as a simple but complete inventory system and a way to produce invoices. The latter even lets you attach a sound, a PICT file, or a QuickTime movie as part of an inventory item's description.

Although CheckWriter Pro lacks Quicken's efficient interface and snazzy charts, the program's novice-friendly approach, economical check printing, and unique billing and inventory features may make it the right financial program for you.—Thom Holmes

CheckWriter Pro 6.0
Aatrix Software, Inc.
Grand Forks, ND
(800) 426-0854; (701) 746-6801
$79

Community

Community

Community

No computer is an island. Or at least it doesn't have to be. Just plug a wire into the back of your computer, and you can become part of a global virtual community. Someday soon, you won't even need the wire. But for the time being, the miracle of communications technology lets us link our systems and create an amazing synergy that turns your computer into your personal cyberspace-ship. Your modem, ISDN link, or other network connection lets you blast off into cyberspace. But unlike outer space, cyberspace is not a lonely place. Instead, it's teeming with some of the smartest and brightest people in the world. And in cyberspace, it really is a small world after all, where people from all countries and all backgrounds are brought together in a land of tremendous freedom and equality.

In CyberSource:Community, we take you on a tour of cyberspace that begins with the simple yet powerful concept of e-mail, moves on to the land of commercial online services such as CompuServe, America Online, and Prodigy, and then helps you get started in exploring the vast reaches of the Internet. But you don't need a giant Internet server to set up your own shop in cyberspace; with a simple PC or Macintosh, you can start your own bulletin board system, or BBS, and in this way launch your own online adventure for peanuts. Thousands of other folks have done just that, and our list of BBSs shows you how to access this diverse online underground.

E-MAIL

ALL FOR ONE, ONE FOR ALL

E-Mail Connection 2.0

You've got the Internet, CompuServe, and MCI Mail: You could spend your life online. Because e-mail is so complicated and time-consuming, you need a single Windows application that integrates mail services and automates mail messaging. Try ConnectSoft's new E-Mail Connection 2.0.

E-Mail Connection provides postal, fax, and multiple e-mail addresses for all the contact names inside and outside your company. You can reach out directly to major online services and LAN-based e-mail products. If you send e-mail, E-Mail Connection 2.0 is not only a boon, it's the only all-in-one e-mail package out there.

What about the Internet, America Online, GEnie, AT&T EasyLink, MobileComm, and automated faxing? E-Mail Connection links you to all those services and others using your choice of CompuServe, MCI, or Prodigy as gateways. Since the routing for these gateway services is built in, you just kiss all those confusing e-mail strings good-bye.

E-Mail Connection isn't just for external e-mail services either. It provides a sin-

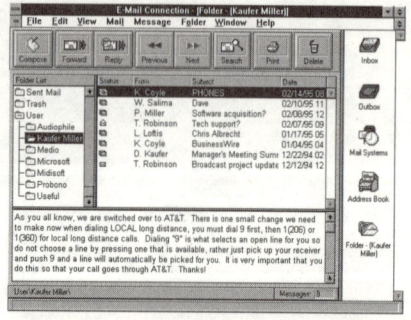

gle interface for all your e-mail, including LAN-based e-mail like cc:Mail, Lotus Notes, and Microsoft Mail, or any package that uses Novell's MHS messaging protocol. That means you can send and receive messages on your company's internal e-

mail system from E-Mail Connection, too. You can also send e-mail directly from mail-enabled applications, so the next time you're drafting a memo, you could send it to a colleague for comments without even leaving your word processor.

E-Mail Connection delivers on the largely unfulfilled promises of virtually every other e-mail front-end that has come before it. You can save money by taking advantage of the options for offline message reading, composition, and replying. And you can schedule automatic message sending and retrieval to all supported online services and LAN-based e-mail.

Version 2.0 improves on the previous version by adding integral support for

Prodigy, VIM (the messaging protocol for cc:Mail and Lotus Notes), 9,600-bit-per-second (bps) support for MCI Mail, 14,400-bps support for CompuServe and improved international access. Also new: the ability for one installation of the product to maintain databases and settings for multiple users with password protection, background uploads and downloads, and a long list of new destinations.

No other e-mail package comes close to the functionality and flexibility of E-Mail Connection 2.0. SWFTE's Wire provides similar services, but it offers a direct connection to only MCI. CompuServe's WinCim helps automate services on CompuServe only. There are

ityCommunityCommunityCommunityCommunityCom

HOME PHONEYS—You can never go home again, at least not if you want to make money. I don't know why computer companies, software companies, phone

no other packages that offer such complete integration with a wide range of online services. With this major new version, ConnectSoft has improved the usability of the product by reducing the number of mouse clicks it takes to complete many operations. If you juggle e-mail from two or more sources, this is a breakthrough product that automates the mail-management chores you put up with daily. Anyone who takes e-mail seriously should seriously consider E-Mail Connection 2.0.—Scot Finnie

E-Mail Connection 2.0
ConnectSoft
(800) 234-9497
$99.95

SITcomm 1.0

Aladdin Systems has brought a breath of fresh air to telecommunications software, with SITcomm. SITcomm gently nudges novice modem users into the mainstream with an extremely well written manual and a simple user interface while providing powerful features that stay out of the way until they're needed.

SITcomm's main window, which displays incoming and outgoing communications, has a handy floating tool bar with buttons for every major function in the program, including the useful address book. This lets you store all the information you need for smooth connection to remote com-

puters and your favorite online services and BBSs. If you want to change any of this information on the fly, you can do so directly from the tool bar. The tool bar also lets you access a notepad for general notes as well as one for each address-book entry.

SITcomm handles compression well. You can stuff or unstuff files within the program, which itself needs only 500K of RAM and 600K of disk space (roughly half of what its main competitors require).

Modem setup is another area that SITcomm aims to simplify. SITcomm's enhancement of version 1.5 of Apple's new Modem Tool (the software that lets you use your modem to make remote connections) adds support for the most-popular modems—so you don't need to enter arcane setup-string information. The company has even provided a cabling diagram for each supported modem. Plus, Aladdin's versions of the other standard telecommunications tools—terminal emulators, the text tool, and so on—are more

powerful, easier to use, and less memory-consuming than Apple's.—Ken Gruberman

SITcomm 1.0
Aladdin Systems
Watsonville CA
(408) 761-6200
$120

The Elements of E-mail Style by David Angell and Brent Heslop

Given the explosion of interest in electronic mail and online services, it was inevitable that someone would write a book like *The Elements of E-mail Style*. Fortunately, David Angell and Brent Heslop got there first, and their slim, witty paperback, which quite deliberately models itself on Strunk and White's classic *The Elements of Style*, has plenty of commonsensical advice for writing and managing e-mail effectively.

Like Strunk and White, Angell and Heslop provide some basic grammar lessons. In fact, grammar rules fill about half the book, but you can skip them. Let's face it: If you don't know how to use apostrophes and semicolons correctly by now, no single book is going to give you the help you need. Things like printed lists of commonly misspelled words are also of questionable value.

The book is much more valuable as a guide to e-mail style and etiquette (or "netiquette"). Since e-mail is conversational but not oral, the danger of being misinterpret-

---

The Elements of E-mail Style

Communicate Effectively via Electronic Mail

David Angell

Brent Heslop

---

ed is ever present. Jokes, sarcasm, and the like can easily cause trouble and lead to dreaded "flame" mail. Angell and Heslop point out the pitfalls and show you how to avoid them with careful, concise wording of your messages. They even tell you how to respond diplomatically when you get flamed. One amusing New Age piece of advice: "Acknowledge the person's need to flame."

Another fun chapter shows you how to use ASCII characters to create boxes, lines, and even rudimentary art for your e-mail messages, and the final chapter gives special advice for users of the Internet, that chaotic corner of cyberspace where good online behavior is especially important.

If you use e-mail with any frequency, you eventually learn what works and what doesn't when you write messages. *The Elements of E-mail Style* can help you eliminate some of the trial and error.

After all, no one likes to get flamed.—Don Willmott

The Elements of E-mail Style
by David Angell and Brent Heslop
Addison-Wesley Publishing
(617) 944-3700
$12.95

AN INTERNET ADDRESS ON THE CHEAP

MCI Mail

In this day and age of high-tech communications, some people might consider you a nonentity if you don't have at least some sort of an Internet address—that symbol of prestige that separates the computer-savvy from, well, everyone else. If you're not fortunate enough to already have such an address courtesy of, say, an employer, and you don't want to pay the higher charges of maintaining an America Online, CompuServe, or Prodigy account, MCI Mail may be just the ticket. For $35/year, you can receive e-mail from every major online service and Internet site around the world. Plus, if you're a DOS user, you get a free copy of MCI Mail Express Lite, an excellent piece of specialized communications software that makes it easy for even the least computer-literate to compose, send, receive, organize, and even schedule e-mail. What's the catch? Well, although you can receive all the e-mail you want for free, each message you send costs $.50 or more, depending on message length. (Volume discounts are available for the more verbose.) Nevertheless, if all you want is an Internet address to put on your business card or résumé, then look no further.—Christopher J. Benz

MCI Mail
MCI International, Inc.
Suite 700
1133 19th Street NW
Washington, DC 20036
(800) 444-6245
$35/year

PC Eudora

The most popular use for the Internet is still sending and receiving e-mail. Unfortunately, there are few good tools for sending, receiving, and managing e-mail. PC Eudora stands out because it handles Internet mail with ease and grace. The program basically provides everything that you need in an e-mail: an address book that uses "nicknames," an in-box and out-box, user-defined folders, an option to forward messages, and, of course, printing.

You can search the body text of messages if you can't remember who sent the e-mail to you, as well as sort messages by sender, priority, and status (such as "Read" or "Unread"). The budget-conscious will note that PC Eudora is also an offline reader. Even better, sending and receiving binary files is a snap, so you don't have to worry about encoding and decoding the file properly for transfer.

In short, if you're looking for an e-mail program for your Internet mail, this is a great bet.

Personal E-Mailbox

Do you feel deprived when you hear talk of e-mail and you're reminded that you're neither on a network nor online to get any? Well, take heart. AmerCom's Personal E-Mailbox offers in-house e-mail services, requiring no outside service or network. All that's required is a modem, a telephone connection, and a copy of the program—no special wiring, no expensive software, and no network.

Installation of this DOS application is simple, which is a good thing considering it's hard to find instructions, both in the mini-manual and in the README.DOC file. Personal E-Mailbox runs from the DOS prompt or in a DOS window in Microsoft Windows or OS/2. The program consists of a simple editor and communications package. A mail system is set up, including an in-box and out-box, and it's used to send and receive e-mail from other Personal E-Mailbox-equipped computers using a modem/phone line connection. All operations are menu-driven. You have many

options including reading, editing, forwarding, or printing E-mail messages.

Once installed, Personal E-Mailbox can run in one of a variety of modes. To avoid greeting a voice caller with a modem squeal, the Home mode lets you answer a ringing phone. If there's silence rather than a caller, you can quietly hang up. Personal E-Mailbox keeps the connection open, and after about 20 seconds, the modem handles the call. It also features an Away mode, which lets an answering machine take voice calls while the modem takes e-mail.

Incoming mail is password-protected and can be retrieved by dialing in using another copy of Personal E-Mailbox. Normal outgoing mail can be left in the out-box for later batch operation or sent immediately to another computer running Personal E-Mailbox. The only real hitch with our evaluation copy was that it didn't support pulse (rotary) dialing. AmerCom has promised that the next release will be able to do this.—Dennis Fowler

Personal E-Mailbox
AmerCom Inc.
P.O. Box 19868
Portland, OR 97280-0868
(800) 239-8295; (503) 531-2880
$49.95

🖐 It's estimated that the number of people who can use interactive services on the Internet is 13.5 million.

ROUND MAGAZINES

CompuServeCD

CompuServe is good for a lot of things: finding quick answers, chatting with people you'd never meet in person, and downloading shareware. But the service is not good to look at, and it's poor territory for multimedia—until now,

In the musical kingdom, either you play or you're prey. Now, Guitar World roars online with a virtual guitar lesson that combines expert instruction with the convenience of learning at home. These multimedia guitar exercises are truly interactive and we've included one below. Check it out, then visit the Guitar World library in the Music Industry Forum for other lessons. With practice, maybe you'll become king of the jungle.

Virtual Guitar Lesson

Recent Guitar World Covers

Venture into Guitar World

that is. CompuServeCD is a monthly disc that does offline all those things that CompuServe doesn't do well online.

The CD is like a monthly magazine with its own departments: home and leisure, entertainment, shopping, software tips, and so on. It's much of the same information you can get online, except that just about everything has Windows sound, photos, or video attached to it—from a track off Jimmy Buffet's new album to a catalog for ordering flowers. The best feature, howev-

er, is that you can use CompuServe's File Finder offline to select files for downloading, then have the CD call CompuServe to get the files you want.

The disc also comes with the latest version of CompuServe Information Manager for Windows (WinCIM) to access CompuServe through Windows, plus five bucks of connect time. If you're a CompuServe member, it's a no-brainer.—Ron White

CompuServeCD
CompuServe
(800) 848-8199
$7.95 per issue, including $5 usage credit

CompuServe Information Service

An old star in the online universe, CompuServe Information Service continues to bring together a wide range of resources and ser-

start with the idea of downloading home games to the family TV via an expensive, set-top box. This runs counter to the true long-term gaming trend: complex games

vices to address the needs of business and home users. Its news and financial information, research databases, and hundreds of discussion forums remain uncommonly strong. It doesn't have the great built-in interface of America Online, but most people use it with one of many other available interfaces. CompuServe could do with stronger Internet connectivity tools (ftp access was recently introduced), but it nevertheless remains the best choice for many users.

Connecting to Compu-Serve is relatively simple. But CompuServe's abundance of offerings can be daunting and may look disorganized despite front ends like CompuServe Information Manager for Windows (WinCIM), which we used in our review. The new Host Micro Interface (HMI), which replaces the outdated terminal emulation ASCII interface, is also your connection to the Internet.

The service's pricing will have undergone important changes by the time you read this (but at the time of our review, CompuServe's pricing plan was still full of additional charges). The service will be reasonably priced at a flat fee of $9.95 per month for the use of any of 100 basic services, including news and weather information, Eaasy Sabre, and the equivalent of 60 three-page CompuServe e-mail messages (or $9 free credit per month). Extended services, which include CNN Online, European railway schedules,

and AP Sports Wire, can cost up to $4.80 per hour.

CompuServe's e-mail service is the most full-featured among the competing services. You can send messages to 13 mail systems, including MCI Mail and the Internet. Files can be sent individually but not as attachments. Options such as return-receipt and an address book (offered through WinCIM) make this a complete service.

The news and financial sections are unmatched among the consumer-oriented services. AP Online offers extensive news and is updated throughout the hour; it includes international news wires. Although it doesn't have the number of periodical providers that America Online does, CompuServe does offer the Newspaper Archives, which provides the two-day delayed full text of more than 50 major U.S. newspapers.

CompuServe has unique strength in the quality and variety of its more than 700 forums, which cover everything from computer-vendor support to science fiction to pets. Moreover, CompuServe forums are distinguished by their thoughtful level of conversation.

Checking stock quotes is simple: You may download up to 20 current quotes for stocks, options, indexes, exchange rates, and mutual funds per session at a 15-minute-or-greater delay from the floor. Meanwhile, if you're doing research, you can head for a comprehensive

database or brokerage service, including *Money* magazine's FundWatch Online.

CompuServe's research databases for both the home and business user abound. They cover such areas as health, computers, and general-interest magazines. Full text and abstracts are available from hundreds of periodicals.

The CompuServe travel services are extensive, too, with support for Eaasy Sabre and Worldspan Travelshopper. Information databases, including Travel Britain Online and regional forums, provide perspectives for potential visitors.

Game addicts also have plenty to cheer about. Compu-Serve has an active Multi-players Games Forum, lots of shareware games to download, and the greatest number of game publishers' forums in any one location. You can download DOOM II at $29.95 plus connect-time fees.

Since its introduction of Usenet Newsgroups access last August, CompuServe has slowly been catching up with the Internet explosion. CompuServe recently introduced ftp access and plans for World-Wide Web access by early this year.

CompuServe is still the most well rounded of these online services, and the best choice for many business users. It is, however, relatively lacking in some areas.—Melissa Perenson

*CompuServe
CompuServe Inc.
5000 Arlington Centre Blvd.
Columbus, OH 43220*

*(800) 848-8199; (614) 457-8600
e-mail, 70006, 101@
compuserve.com.*

AN ONLINE WORLD FOR ALMOST EVERYONE
America Online

Not sure what you're looking for in an online service? Then try out America Online, the online service that tries to be everything to everyone—and does a reasonable job of it. This rapidly growing online service, originally formed as a Mac-only service and now serving over 1,000,000 Mac-, Windows-, and DOS-based members, offers a low-cost way to see what the online hoopla is all about. After your first free month of membership and ten free hours of online time, you pay only $9.95/month, which includes five hours of online time monthly. For this you get free, easy-to-use software; the ability to establish up to four America Online subaccounts for family members or very trustworthy friends; unlimited electronic mail; limited but growing access to the Internet; news, weather, and stock reports; online magazines and reference materials, including an encyclopedia; online games and shopping; and over 50,000 download-able files, including some of the best shareware available. Despite all these positives, America Online is far from perfect. Local access numbers can be a pain to locate, are often busy, and as of this writing only support up to

9,600 bps (although faster speeds are in the works). At peak usage periods (usually evenings and weekends), the system can slow to a crawl. And if you plan on letting your kids get online, watch out!

There are plenty of members out there spewing nasty and suggestive language at record rates. (Fortunately, you can electronically block your kids from much of this unpleasantness.) Nevertheless, America Online is a definite must-try, even if only for the first free month.—Christopher J. Benz

*America Online
America Online Incorporated
8619 Westwood Center Drive
Vienna, VA 22182
(800) 827-6364
$9.95/month*

America Online

Behind America Online's slick graphical interface is an online service that has a lot to boast about: a wide array of online resources, easy-to-use e-mail, a well-designed set of basic Internet tools, and simple installation. It's an especially good choice for home users, although it has the potential to be a lot more. People are noticing, too: AOL has grown from about 500,000 users to more than 1.25 million users in the past year.

AOL is one of the bargains here. Its basic rate is only $9.95 per month, which includes five hours of online time, with very few additional charges

($2.95 for each hour beyond five and some per-page charges for faxes and paper mail messages). And in a structure that challenges CompuServe's, AOL's flat monthly rate also includes unlimited e-mail messaging and Internet services.

Getting up and running is a breeze. We installed the AOL Windows software (software is also available for DOS and the Macintosh) and were online in less than ten minutes. Like Prodigy, AOL supports multiple aliases (or screen names)—in this case, up to five per account. This is a great feature for families.

The AOL interface, which was recently redesigned, is the best in the group. It's more graphical than ever and includes much-improved navigation tools. Nearly every feature is accessible through a graphical menu.

Similar ease of use extends to AOL's e-mail system. Although CompuServe offers the most completely integrated e-mail system in this roundup, AOL's is the most intuitive. You can send mail to AOL users as well as to Internet users and members of other services that are accessible on the Internet. Unlike CompuServe, AOL requires no complicated treatment of Internet addresses. A customizable address book is available.

AOL currently offers the best Internet connectivity (beyond e-mail) of the group—with the exception of Delphi. AOL's Internet Connection provides access to ftp, gopher, Usenet Newsgroups, and WAIS databases. AOL has done a tremendous job of incorporating ftp and gopher into the standard AOL interface, making these tools very user-friendly. Telnet and World-Wide Web services are planned for 1995.

In addition, AOL recently purchased three Internet software vendors—Advanced Network & Services, NaviSoft, and BookLink Technologies—to further expand its Internet offerings and presence.

All these access tools help you get at the considerable amount of content on AOL. Its numerous news services are kept current for the most part. Reuters provides the largest news coverage, although ABC, *Time* magazine, *The New York Times*, CNN, and UPI also maintain news services on AOL.

The quality and content of AOL's magazines vary widely. Time puts most of its stories online every week and even offers hourly updates for major events. *Consumer Reports* posts a major story only every month or so.

For weather, AOL offers and constantly updates plentiful five-day forecasts, colorful weather maps, and satellite images.

Many computer vendors also have homes on AOL, offering product information, software libraries, and well-monitored technical-support forums. Some vendors, such as Compaq Computer Corp., maintain rich, well-designed sections that provide a wealth of useful information. Others offer limited, text-only menus and slim, rarely updated software libraries.

AOL also includes some business resources, but not as many as CompuServe, Dow Jones, and GEnie. Still, you can track financial news and stock prices, and even make some purchases. For market novices, there's an online game called Bulls and Bears that lets you learn the ways of Wall Street by simulating stock trades with a fictional $100,000 credit line.

If you add up all of AOL's content services and throw in

New Software Bonds Local BBSs with the Global Internet

Electronic bulletin board systems—those grass-roots communities of cyberspace—are quickly gaining access to the Internet's global data highway, letting these communities interact with each other in new and more powerful ways. Part of the credit goes to BBS software vendors such as ResNova Software of Huntington Beach, California, which recently gave Mac users a direct Internet connection with its NovaLink Professional 3.0. In addition to supporting Internet e-mail (SMTP) and Usenet Newsgroups (NNTP), NovaLink Professional provides complete Telnet support.

This means that Nova-Link client users can Telnet out to other host systems on the Internet, and users of the Internet can Telnet in to NovaLink hosts. While this type of service has been available to Unix hosts for years, it's reportedly a first for Macintosh BBS software.

NovaLink Professional also supports a variety of graphic standards. By supporting multiple configuration files, system operators can offer various graphic interfaces to their callers.

Meanwhile, DOS BBS vendors, such as Mustang Software, are also building entrance ramps onto the Internet highway. Mustang has added wcUUCP as a feature for providing Internet mail, and Usenet Newsgroup support for BBSs running its WildCat software. Another vendor, Searchlight, plans to add Internet support to its BBS software before the end of the year.—Dennis Fowler ■

its low cost, easy-to-use e-mail, and basic Internet connectivity, you end up with a solid online service that is perfect for home use. With some other features, it could become a lot more attractive to the business user as well.—Michael Ryan

America Online

America Online Inc.
8619 Westwood Center Dr.
Vienna, VA 22182-2285
(800) 827-6364; (703) 448-8700
e-mail: postmaster@aol.com

America Online for Macintosh

The Macintosh version of AOL is similar to its Windows cousin, although one difference we noticed is that at the sign-on screen, you have the option of selecting Home (for dial-up operations) or TCP. The TCP option is used if you are connected to a TCP/IP-based network that is in turn connected to the Internet. The TCP option is typically faster than a standard dial-up connection if your network connects to the Internet over a Switched 56 or T1 line. In the Windows version, getting to the TCP/IP option is not as obvious. Macintosh-interface screens are interesting and colorful, but the first time you enter a new area you can expect to wait a couple of minutes while you download the graphics for that screen.

America Online for Macintosh
America Online Inc.
(800) 827-6364

GEnie

Though somewhat expensive, GEnie is an excellent source of business, technical, and general information for the professional user. Its interface and content are showing some dustiness, but GEnie now has a Windows front end, and significant Internet access is planned. All in all, this is an impressive but potentially costly online package.

Getting setup was not as easy as with some of the other online services: GEnie's graphical elements do not come into play until you have completed your sign-on. And you're assigned a cryptic user ID and password at sign-on, which you should be sure to write down and change at the first opportunity. To its credit, the GEnie package includes a complete visual road map of all the services available with jump words and page numbers. (You can also access GEnie using Aladdin, a DOS-based front end that has more advanced offline features.)

Once you're logged on, the primary method of moving around GEnie in Windows is the Menu Navigator, a graphical element that shows the options for the area you're in. In the Navigator, you view a pull-down menu history of your current session and move backward and forward by double-clicking on the page description. You can also jump to locations using key words or page numbers through an option on the menu bar.

Cost is a major consideration when you are accessing GEnie. The basic fee itself is not bad—$8.95 per month, which includes four hours of free connect time (additional connect time is $3 per hour). The real price shock comes with the surcharges for prime time—$9.50 per hour (8:00 a.m. to 6:00 p.m., Monday through Friday)—and 9.6-Kbps connections at $6 per hour. You can pay as much as $18.50 per hour while connected. These are among the most expensive timed charges of any online service, and above these charges are additional charges for premium services such as Charles Schwab Brokerage Services and the OAG for travel.

Yet GEnie's real strength is its ability to function as a research and information repository. In addition to Schwab, OAG, and many others, GEnie gives you access to Businesswire, Dialog, Peterson's College Database, and TRW corporate credit profiles, as well as a gateway to Dow Jones News/Retrieval. The high cost of actually using some of these services, however, sug-

gests they are for business users with well-directed searches only, not the casual browser.

GEnie's content comes in three formats: roundtables (the equivalent of discussion forums), information databases, and chat areas. Participating vendors in the computer section include Borland, IBM, Microsoft, and WordPerfect. Hardware vendors are not nearly as well represented.

In addition to visiting professional forums in areas such as law, medicine, and real estate, you can go to more than 80 areas devoted to hobbies, entertainment, and other special interests. Although we found the participation levels in the roundtables fairly active, some areas are not updated as often as others. Furthermore, GEnie offers some great multiplayer games. And people looking for travel services will find Eaasy Sabre, as well as a wide range of travel roundtables.

The creation of e-mail in GEnie is substantially easier thanks to the greatly improved interface. GE also has added an address book. Aside from

the per-hour charges, GEnie does not charge for e-mail or attachments. There's also an easy-to-use Internet mail option.

In keeping with the current rage, GE plans to add greater Internet access with ftp and Telnet features, as well as Usenet Newsgroup postings, gopher, and WAIS (Wide Area Information Server) services. As of this writing, though, e-mail was the only Internet service available.

GEnie maintains its content well enough to be a significant alternative to CompuServe as an information source for business users. The Windows interface and the soon-to-be-added Internet connectivity keep it in the race for your online dollars, but unless costs are reduced, its appeal seems limited to those doing serious research. There are better online choices for the home user.—Amarendra Singh

GEnie
GE Information Services Inc.
401 N. Washington St.
Rockville, MD 20850
(800) 638-9636; (301) 251-6475
e-mail: feedback @genie .geis.com

already set up a games "workstation" for the children someplace out of earshot in a far corner of the house where the kids can play games until they are bored

IS EWORLD A DIFFERENT WORLD?

eWorld

Taking an electronic stroll through Apple's new eWorld online service is like wandering the back lot of a Hollywood studio—it's visually intriguing, but there's not much behind the facade. Or, in eWorld's case, not much you haven't seen already on other online services.

But before I'm too hard on Apple's attempt to resurface the information highway in tie-dye colors, let me grant it this: If eWorld's primary mission is to make cyberspace a more inviting place, it's a big step in the right direction. It's only a first step, and Apple will need to beef up eWorld if it expects to keep the modem wanderers it manages to lure into its "community." Still, it's a user-friendly start.

On one level, eWorld is the successor to AppleLink—an early attempt to connect the Apple universe that never stretched very far beyond Apple itself and a few loyal customers. But eWorld is more than that. Apple wants to woo the computing masses away from the likes of America Online, CompuServe, and Prodigy, and into its eWorld. It also wants to bring understandably leery first-timers into the online fold. Mac users are getting a taste of eWorld first, and Newton users can tap into its e-mail system via NewtonMail. But Apple says it also intends to bring the service to Windows users eventually.

eWorld makes a great first impression. In place of a conventional menu and a screen full of text, you're greeted with a colorful, cartoon-like depiction of a downtown scene with buildings that represent different areas of interest. There's the Newsstand, the eMail Center, Marketplace, Business & Finance Plaza, and so forth. Click on a building, and you enter that portion of the service.

More charming still, you briefly hear the bustling sounds of a downtown area as you enter eWorld, and a pleasant, very lifelike female voice informs you if you have e-mail waiting. True to its name, logging on to eWorld feels like entering a little electronic community much like your own, rather than entering a cryptic place with unknown rules.

Unfortunately, this refreshing reorganization of the cyberworld melts away far too quickly. Once inside the buildings, metaphors yield to menus (albeit very nice-looking ones), and eventually to plain old text. You can summon news stories from Reuters or USA Today, for instance, but you'll simply get unadorned words—no newspaper-style layouts, no pictures, and certainly no video or sound bites.

The same goes in other parts of eWorld. You're invited to shop Mac Zone's catalog in the Marketplace building, but it looks and feels nothing like a catalog. It's simply a series of lists. Ditto for the encyclopedia in the Learning Center, the movie reviews in the Arts & Leisure Pavilion, and the discussion "forums" in the Community Center. In short, once you get to the information in eWorld, it looks and feels no better than it does in, say, CompuServe or America Online.

Invariably, that's disappointing, since eWorld's philosophy of reflecting the familiar world around us is trumpeted and trashed within your first ten minutes online. Apple has talked a lot about "publishing" online via eWorld. Apparently, none of the talk has yet prompted a serious effort—by Apple or third parties—to markedly enhance the presentation of online information the way desktop publishing has enhanced our documents.

One reason for the hesitancy may be speed. With a 2,400-bps modem, eWorld staggers a bit even with textual information. Downloading icons and files can be painfully slow at this speed. A 9,600-bps or 14,400-bps modem yields faster responses, naturally, but whether that's enough bandwidth to drive a truly graphical service remains to be seen. However, at this writing, eWorld operates no faster than 9,600 bps.

These visual limitations would be easier to accept if eWorld provided a host of information you could find nowhere else. Instead, Apple has mostly rounded up the usual online suspects: The news, sports, business, e-mail, shopping, travel, forums, education, entertainment, and computer-support features in eWorld are either the same as or similar to the basic features of America Online, CompuServe, and Prodigy. Indeed, eWorld has fewer options in many of these areas than the other major services.

The modest information package might be easier to accept if eWorld were less expensive than competing services. It's not. In fact, eWorld will likely cost you substantially more. The basic monthly charge is a modest-sounding $8.95, but that price includes only two hours of free evening and weekend use. Additional off-peak hours are $4.95 per hour, and weekday rates are $2.95 for the first two hours and a stiff $7.90 after that. (You don't even want to know about international rates.) The bottom line: For light use (two hours per week) your tab will range from $38.65 to $62.25 a month. Similar access on the other three major services would run you about $9 to $20.

There are bright spots, however. Apple doesn't charge extra for 9,600-bps service, and there are no charges for sending e-mail via Internet. E-mail, in fact, may be eWorld's most useful feature. Its Internet link enables you to send messages to almost anyone, and its address book feature is a convenient, point-and-click repository for your frequent correspondents.

For all its current shortcomings, eWorld does embody the kernel of a very good idea: an information service constructed around the visual and logical expectations of ordinary people, not computer geeks. That's a long-overdue notion in cyberspace.—Chris O'Malley

eWorld
Apple Computer Inc.
1 Infinite Loop
Cupertino, CA 95014
(800) 775-4556

Prodigy

This year's roundup finds Prodigy with the same cumbersome interface—but with the company preparing to release a dramatically improved version (promised in the first quarter of 1995). Even as is, Prodigy is a good choice for people who are new to personal computers, particularly children. It is well priced, at $9.95 per month, which includes five hours of connect time; after that, it's $2.95.

Installation wasn't as easy as it could have been. We were using a high-speed modem that supports ER/RC (extended result/response codes) and had difficulty connecting to Prodigy. Only after we used the ASSIST program and attempted to set up several times were we able to connect.

Prodigy's commitment to embrace new technologies overall is apparent. The company recently released its interfaces to Internet e-mail, Usenet Newsgroups, a WorldWide Web browser, and its separate Web service, AstraNet (http://www.astranet.com). The company is also commited to exploiting the wider bandwidth of cable technology in up-to-the-minute services. The new software that's coming is based on the same technology that's turning the Internet into a user-friendly environment. In 1995, Prodigy's interface could become the best that online services have to offer.

Although its Usenet Newsgroups' interface is better than America Online's, Prodigy's Internet services are not comparable. On Prodigy you cannot use gopher, WAIS, or ftp; and sending Internet mail requires using a separate dialog box if the address is longer than 40 characters. The recently announced—and heavily advertised—chat area is a bad copy of AOL's. Also, finding files on the system is easier on CompuServe.

Prodigy's sports coverage, bulletin boards, and online shopping area are second to none. Teaming up with ESPN, Prodigy offers up-to-the-minute information on games in progress. Using cable technology, Prodigy will be able to deliver, on-demand, video clips of an ongoing baseball game to your PC.

This service also has an extensive selection of more than 1,000 bulletin boards rich with useful, current information. And it's the place to meet celebrities in your fields of interest, from well-known financial advisors to actors.

Paying for online time and any premium services aren't the only ways to spend money while online. Prodigy's electronic shopping mall is remarkable. The service continues to use the lower portion of your screen to advertise its services and products you can purchase online.

Prodigy is now deploying 14.4-Kbps modem support, a welcome addition. In addition, Prodigy can update the software on your hard disk remotely and free of charge, but this can take over 15 minutes at 9.6 Kbps. New users may need updates to start using areas they haven't visited before.

You can download tools to perform tasks offline, to use Prodigy efficiently and reduce your online charges. The E-Mail Connection and the Bulletin Board Manager tools let you send, receive, and manage e-mail and bulletin board messages; no online tools compare with them.

Prodigy has put a lot of work into providing a safe environment for children. Users must authorize each household member's account before those members can use selected Prodigy areas, including all areas that are not under Prodigy's supervision (such as Usenet Newsgroups and Chat areas). Smaller children will enjoy the Sesame Street area as well as the online, interactive games (including Where in the World Is Carmen Sandiego?).

They can also access Homework Helper (a database of 35 periodicals and 700 reference books), the *Academic American Encyclopedia*, *National Geographic*, and many other reference materials. Prodigy's editorial staff says the available content is appropriate.

Prodigy has succeeded in building a very complete selection of online information and services, but its current interface has left much to be desired. The recent release of Newsweek InterActive, though, is a good preview of what is you can expect in the next release.—Sean Gonzalez

Prodigy
Prodigy Services Co.
445 Hamilton Ave.
White Plains, NY 10601
(800) 776-3449

Delphi Internet

The leader for Internet connectivity in this field, Delphi Internet is the only service here to offer a complete set of services and tools for seamlessly exploring the Internet. Even so, you'll need some knowledge of the Internet to get started. Delphi also offers its own services, including news, weather, sports, and travel. Its e-mail facility is outdated, however, and it is difficult to locate information. Perhaps the company will address these and other concerns in a new version of the software due out sometime this year. Right now, though, it's not the best choice as a balanced service.

Delphi's new front end will be similar to that of the graphical WorldWide Web browsers and will include hyperlinking and multimedia support. It will provide a standard interface across both Delphi and the Internet, as well as gopher and ftp for Internet documents.

We'll skip the expensive, set-top box altogether. ▫ **How about video on demand? Isn't that one of the hoped-for killer apps in this futuristic set-top-box world?**

Delphi's current interface—InterNav, Version 1.11—is a Windows-based, VT-100 terminal emulator. It is easy to install and allows you to automate logging in, but InterNav's menus are text-based even though it is a Windows front end. You can, however, point and double-click on a menu selection, and the number or word is passed through to the prompt.

Users can connect to Delphi through several options, including SprintNet, Xstream (formerly called Tymnet), the Internet, and a direct dial-up number for members in the Boston and Kansas City areas. Beware, though: SprintNet and Xstream each add a surcharge of $9 per hour during business hours. Delphi also offers

a free five-hour trial period. And for newcomers, Delphi provides useful services such as guided tours, online documentation, and tips.

The company offers two different pricing options. The 10/4 Plan costs $10 per month with the first four hours each month free, after which an hourly charge of $4 kicks in. The 20/20 Advantage Plan costs $20 per month, with the first 20 hours each month free; then it's $1.80 per hour for additional time (there's a one-time fee of $19). Internet access costs you another $3 per month for either plan—but that's very worthwhile.

The Delphi connection provides access to Internet services such as the Web, Usenet Newsgroups, gopher, and tools such as finger and

PING. The tools are text-based, however, and require some basic knowledge to be useful. The majority of the information accessible through Delphi is located on the Internet. The News Corporation, Delphi's parent company, also owns BIX, a specialized online service for computer professionals with Internet access.

It's not easy to get at information on Delphi. When you search for topics or information, you must wade through several layers before finding what you want. In many cases, the information is located on the Internet, and you are bound to the throughput of the service. We also found that some services were not available when we tried to access them because they were full.

You can connect to Internet sources via gopher for news, online shopping, sports, computer hardware and software support, and games. You can access stock quotes, which are updated every 20 minutes, but you cannot purchase stocks. One big drawback is that none of the major computer-industry players have a direct presence on Delphi, although you can access forums in which the participants seem well-versed in their areas.

News and sports sections provide reports from Reuters and UPI. Delphi's online shopping is particularly strong. Multiplayer games are available, and you use gopher to travel to related materials in newsgroups or directly onto a game vendor's home page.

Delphi's e-mail implementation is archaic. For example, although you can send binary file attachments, it's not as simple to do as it is with CompuServe's e-mail. In addition, you cannot request return receipts, and even though an address book is available, you need to create it in a separate ASCII file or use the InterNav address book.

Delphi can be a portal to vast amounts of information because of its superior Internet connections. But you'll need some basic Internet knowledge to make this service a worthwhile investment. The new front end, due out sometime this year, might help make Delphi a powerful online service

that is also easy to use.— Padraic Boyle

Delphi
Delphi/General Videotext Corp.
1030 Massachusetts Ave.
Cambridge, MA 02138
(800) 694-4005; (617) 491-3393

ONLINE FEVER

CompuServe
Prodigy
America Online

You know where you want to go, but the Internet's awesome diversity has you feeling like a doormat on the floor of Grand Central Station. Your business needs are simple—send e-mail, get the latest stock and news information. Sometimes the fastest way to get the information you need is to veer off the main thoroughfare and shop the surface streets— online services.

The three major online services—America Online, CompuServe, and Prodigy— can often be the fastest ways to get answers to your business questions. All three are either Windows-based or have Windows front ends designed to make navigating to the data you need easier. They've all recognized that merely offering megadata doesn't cut it any more. Folks need an easy way to get at that information—and fast.

To find out if the online services have turned the corner in putting information at hand, we delved into all three services online. Then we brought computer users—people just like you—into our Usability Labs and conducted tests with them at the wheel.

We found that the online world has come a long way since the days of text-based interfaces and obscure navigational commands. Now when you want to read a news story or get stock quotes, you can click on an easy-to-understand icon. That's not to say that the road signs are always well-lit on this particular stretch of the information highway. We found that even a task that should be simple—sending e-mail—can be surprisingly difficult at times.

Given that Prodigy and CompuServe claim almost 2 million members, and America Online has yet to hit the million mark, the results of our tests may surprise you. If you'd like to hit the data highway immediately, read on for the best possible road map. Because if you can't figure out how to get at the information, it doesn't matter how much data awaits you online.

America Online—Our usability testers rated America Online's clean interface much higher than CompuServe's and Prodigy's. Each service's interface changes daily based on news and other events.

CompuServe—When it comes to downloading patches and technical information, our usability testers gave the thumbs-up to CompuServe's extensive databases.

Prodigy—This service got the nod from our usability testers for providing the easiest access to trading news, shown here for Intel.

In a world of meetings, travel, and quality time for family, e-mail is sometimes the fastest and most convenient way to communicate. Subscribing to an online service is a simple way to tap into an e-mail network, but be sure to check out who you can talk to first.

For sheer elegance of design, as well as functionality, our testers gave America Online the thumbs-up for e-mail. A typical comment: America Online's mail handling is "well-designed . . . one of the best I've seen." It uses a simple screen and makes it clear where addresses, subject, and body text should go. To attach a file to a message, or detach it, you need only to click on an icon.

There's a great address book that lets you create groups of addresses, which makes it easy to do a mass mailing.

Although the methods are similar, our testers found CompuServe's mail to be less intuitive than America Online's. It also lets you create groups and attach binary files easily. But sending mail to other services can require a fairly complex addressing scheme that makes it more difficult to use than America Online.

For Prodigy, our testers also reported that the basic layout for mail is confusing, and the capabilities less than adequate. We can't recommend Prodigy if e-mail is your primary interest. As far as the testers were concerned, the less said, the better.

The information you seek is out there—it sits on an unknown server, waiting. For many, the lure of online services is indeed that buried treasure of magazine articles, shareware, freeware, and software drivers.

Our testers found it was easier to find and download files on America Online than it was on CompuServe or Prodigy. Keep in mind, though, that the tests covered only the ease of finding and downloading files, not the number of files available. This is where CompuServe surpasses the competition.

It's easier to find and download technical files on America Online because they can all be found under a single umbrella—the Computing and Software area. Once you get there, it can be confusing to figure out where to go next. But handy tools for searching by category, date, and keyword do help.

Downloading files using CompuServe is more complicated at first because there's

no central area in which to look—the files are in hundreds of forums across the entire sprawling service. While it may seem disorganized, this is also a strength—more and varied files are available than on the other services.

Our testers found Prodigy slightly more difficult to use than CompuServe. They liked that all of the files were in one location. But once they found the treasure chest they sought, they were a bit confused about how to find the jewels they wanted most.

Online services have an immediacy that no other medium for delivering information can match. Our testers again gave the nod to America Online, although it was close. Users found Prodigy's stock features more straightforward and easier to use than its competitors, but when it came to travel reservations and news, America Online and CompuServe made up the difference.

Each service has strengths and weaknesses in this area. For example, when you read a news story on Prodigy, you can click on a button that brings you to related articles or displays a photo. Graphics, such as maps, are often included in the stories. Similarly, when you get a stock quote, you can click on a button to get a list of financial news stories about that stock. What sets CompuServe apart from both its competitors is not simplicity so much as depth: There are multiple sources of financial, travel, and news information.

While testers gave America Online another thumbs-up overall, they complained about it occasionally forgoing the Windows interface for a text menu, as it does in its travel reservations area.

What gave America Online the boost was the clarity in its help section. We don't penalize a product when the testers need the help section—we penalize it when the testers don't get help when they go looking for it. Here, America Online's documentation gave the best assist, and as a result, got the highest overall productivity ratings from our testers.

So much ballyhoo surrounds the sudden accessibility of the Internet that an important subtlety gets lost. You can access the Internet—that is, get data from the multitude of servers and databases around the world—or you can use it simply as a medium for e-mail. As you get started in the online world, you're more likely to stick to the latter.

Prodigy and CompuServe only let you send and receive mail through the Internet (with varying degrees of pain). For the most part, our usability testers found sending mail through the Internet difficult because of its unique addressing conventions. Even then, finding an address—even for Bill Clinton—wasn't easy. America Online came out ahead because its internal addresses already resemble Internet addresses.

If you want to access Internet data from one of these services, go with America Online. It lets you access some of the popular Internet services: newsgroups, gopher and WAIS databases, as well as mail and easy-to-use mailing lists. At press time, there were plans to also provide access to ftp and Telnet services.

All this isn't to say that the access to Internet services couldn't use improvement. There should be a way to read and respond to newsgroups offline.

The idea behind working offline is simple—when you're not connected, the meter's not ticking, so you're not being charged for "think time." Not surprisingly, it's difficult to work offline with these services—they've been designed to generate income.

CompuServe and America Online let you create mail offline, and then upload it to the service—but our testers found the process wasn't always intuitive. As we were going to press, Prodigy announced it planned a summer release of a Windows-based Bulletin Board Note Manager that will let you work offline more easily.

America Online is the best of the three when it comes to working offline. To do it well in CompuServe, you'll pay extra for CompuServe Navigator for Windows, available for $30 (which includes a $10 usage credit). It works like this: You tell it which forums you like to visit, and the program then

downloads the headers—subject lines of messages—to your PC. You mark which messages you'd like to read, and Navigator then goes back online and downloads those messages, which you can read and respond to offline. Working this way, you can easily accomplish in five minutes what otherwise might take 30 minutes or more of online time. Translated into dollars, you could save as much as $4 every time you log on.

All the online services promise to let you send e-mail to just about everyone on the planet—and it's generally true. That's the good news. The bad news is that it can be an incredibly difficult and frustrating task—one often not worth the effort. But if you follow this primer, the job will be much easier. Note that you'll always have to know the specific e-mail address of the person you're sending mail to. In the examples below, we're assuming that our recipient's MCI Mail address is 123-4567; their CompuServe address is 12345,6789; their Prodigy address is ProdigyID; and their America Online address is AOLname.

Sending mail from America Online to another service is easy—you do it using the same kinds of naming conventions used on the Internet.

There are two parts to an Internet address. The first is the name or ID of the person to whom you're sending mail. The second part is the

Internet name of the system that person is on. The two parts are divided by an @ sign. For example, if you were sending mail to Joe Bigelow on the Othermail.com service, the address would be: JoeBigelow@othermail.com. In Internet parlance, each entity has a three-letter designation. For instance, .com stands for company, .edu for educational institution, .gov for government, and .org for non-profit organization. Service Address MCI Mail 123-4567@mcimail.com OR 123-4567@mci CompuServe 12345.6789@compuserve.com OR 12345.6789@cis Prodigy ProdigyID@prodigy.com OR ProdigyID@prodigy Internet name@entity.xxx CompuServe

Use these formats when you need to send mail from CompuServe to people on another online service: Service Address MCI Mail MCIMAIL:123-4567 America Online AOLname@aol.com Prodigy ProdigyID@prodigy.com Internet name@entity.xxx

There is no way to send mail to another service from directly within Prodigy. You'll need ConnectSoft's add-on program for Windows, E-Mail Connection for Prodigy, which costs $14.95. There's also a "universal" version that sells for $49.95 and lets you access other e-mail services such as AppleLink, GEnie, EMBARC, and NewsCard through MCI, Prodigy, CompuServe, or LAN-based mail systems. To

send mail to other services with it, you need only to know the user ID on the other service; there's no need for complex addressing schemes.

While our testers rated America Online the most usable online service, it's not necessarily the best service for everyone. For your particular needs, one of the other online services might be better.

Who delivers the best e-mail service? While any of the services will let you send e-mail to other members, testers found that America Online has the best mail-handling abilities.

Who has compiled the most complete collection of shareware and other downloadable files? The place to turn is CompuServe. Just about all of the scores of special interest forums on CompuServe are stocked full of downloadable files.

Where is the most complete collection of databases? Again, CompuServe is the place to go. You should be prepared to spend some serious money, though: Most of these databases carry surcharges for time spent on them, information retrieved, or a combination of the two—and you can quickly run up some steep bills.

What is the best source of tech support for hardware and software? CompuServe has become the de facto standard online service to use for technical support. Scores of companies—everyone from industry giants like Microsoft to small shareware firms—

movies. They get out of the house. The video store is just another excuse for social interaction. 🖳 You see, most people can stand only so much sitting at home.

ityCommunity CommunityCommunity Col

sponsor forums on Compu-Serve where you can ask technical questions and download the latest drivers and patches.

Who offers the simplest pricing structure? If the pricing information is confusing you, you're not alone. One month's charges for e-mail and downloading can stack up. We recommend America Online's simple setup.

Which online service offers the best access to current news, sports, travel, and stock quotes? Our usability testers rated America Online just a nose better, but all do well at presenting weather and current news stories.—Preston Gralla

America Online
Online Incorporated
8619 Westwood Center Drive
Vienna, VA 22182
(800) 827-6364
$9.95/month

CompuServe Inc.
5000 Arlington Centre Blvd.
Columbus, OH 43220
(800) 848-8199; (614) 457-8600
e-mail, 70006, 101@compu-serve.com.

Prodigy
Prodigy Services Co.
445 Hamilton Ave.
White Plains, NY 10601
(800) 776-3449

Dialing for Dollars

Theory: Online services are organized religions. Posits: (a) The role of religion is to liberate the human spirit in preparation for higher states of being. (b) 11 of the 17 most popular world faiths (and John Lennon too, but as I recall, he had an awful lot of hi-fi gear, so I'm not going to mention him) believe that material wealth exists as an anchor for the human spirit (source: *Oh, Boy! Religion!*, Li'l Golden Book Press, 1963). (c) The strongest link between a commercial online service and its users is its ability to siphon off their material wealth. (d) A commercial online service therefore relieves its users of a spiritual anchor, thus liberating human souls in preparation for higher states of being.

Conclusion: Your online service is an organized religion. Which slides us quite coolly into this month's topic, how to cut your online-service bills: Claim them all as legitimate tax-deductible donations to your place of worship. It'll work. I haven't tried it myself, but that's only because I haven't filed a return since Reagan was in office. And have I been caught? No! One of you will just have to step forward for the good of the group. But as for the rest of you—and don't think I can't see you, the one with the big hair, hiding way over there in Wisconsin—give these online money-savers a whirl:

The Totally Obvious

But I have to mention it nonetheless: Do as much work offline (and off the clock) as you can. CompuServe Navigator is legendary for its ability to allow you to do everything you'd normally do on CIS while the clock is running, offline and more easily. Navigator will cut your bill at least in half. Although there's no direct equivalent available for America Online, AppleLink, or GEnie, there's almost always a way to use the access software for those services so that you spend as little time as possible staring dumbly at the screen while dollar bills float eerily out the window.

While you're at it, make sure you're aware of all of your service's hidden costs for extra features. Most of you know that your service has certain areas that carry extra fees, but did you also know that CompuServe, for example, charges you 15 cents for each message received via the Internet?

Speed Kills

A bit less obvious is falling into the American trap of using all the technological muscle at your disposal simply because you have it. Before you unthinkingly log in to your online service's high-speed (9,600 or 14,400 bps) nodes, consider that the speed at which the service waits for you to do something is about as close to light speed as you can get in Einstein's universe.

Unless you are specifically planning to download files or are using an automated off-line Navigator-type program to read messages and reply to them for you, you'll almost certainly find that logging in to one of the service's less expensive 2,400-bps access numbers will save you a pile of dough, and the lower access rate probably won't be as big an inconvenience as you thought it would be.

While on the subject of choosing a different access number ... Ask Your Ma (Bell). An obscenely lame and inexcusable pun, but a nice segue. Chances are, you can access a service by using any of a dozen phone numbers within your area code. But instead of allowing the service to choose a number for you (based simply on zip code or your area code and exchange), get a complete list and ask your phone company which one will be cheapest to call. This can be a big money-saver if you wind up calling your service regularly. Several of those access numbers, although technically local calls, may lie outside your immediate calling area; you can stay online with 768-9283 all month and still be charged your basic monthly fee, but 776-9182 will steadily eat up billable message units like PEZ and wind up costing one of your children a college education.

Leave Them Gits Alone

Okay, it's balm for the soul to call someone a malodorous, cloth-eared, knee-biting, toffee-nosed heap of parrot droppings when he disagrees with your message promoting the merits of seaQuest DSV. But do keep in mind that at least one person on this planet has succeeded in suing the britches off someone for online slander. No kiddin'. All this happened in Australia, which makes it something of an impotent precedent here in the good old U.S., but it still ought to give one pause.

Seems an anthropologist at Western Australia University was fired for "lack of productivity." After his colleagues gave him overwhelming support on a BBS that has worldwide distribution, another anthropologist called him Something Quite Nasty (trust me here) and implied that the SQN had been the reason for his dismissal. The judge was

impressed and handed down a judgment of $40,000.

Choose Wisely

Just as The Right Service will enrich your life, The Wrong Service will bleed you dry. It's been a decade since we've been forced to use one online entity for all of our telecommunicating; nowadays, we can choose the cheapest online (or even offline) service for the problem at hand. For instance, why pay megabucks to download software from America Online, CompuServe, or GEnie when you can download the same software for free from a local BBS? Granted, their national scope means that big services generally get the best software first, but with few exceptions, anything of value will soon make its way to a good bulletin board, particularly if it's run by a user group (there are exceptions; for instance, ZiffNet/Mac, our own beloved online entity, regularly commissions unique free software that can be obtained only through the service). Or why go online at all? For about 50 bucks, the Boston Computer Society or BMUG (my two faves) or a dozen other groups will sell you a CD-ROM containing 600MB of quality shareware. BCS (617 864-1700) and BMUG (510 549-2684) update their discs at least twice a year, and I dare say that with both discs in your library, 90 percent of your shareware needs will be covered.

And, of course, the Internet can provide you with enough software to choke 11 medium-sized dogs. Unlike a free BBS,

though, the Internet can provide free (or almost free) analogues to some of CIS's and America Online's pricier added services. Telnet into public libraries and online bookstores, and search their databases for free instead of searching for books via Books in Print. If your Internet provider subscribes to the ClariNews newsgroup, you have access to the most useful parts of the Associated Press and Reuters news feeds, organized into dozens of handy topics, plus syndicated columns by Dave Barry and others. ClariNet also includes NewsBytes, comprehensive coverage of the computer scene. As a group, ClariNet is about a thousand times more useful than the lush opportunity to read half of next week's *Time* magazine on America Online as money goes down the drain.

Lack of space prevents me from talking in any real depth about the vast, free informational resources available via the Internet. Trust me; somewhere there's a gopher server or a World Wide Web page containing all the info you need. I refer you to Adam Engst's neat *Internet Starter's Kit* for Macintosh as well as any of the thick Internet users' directories currently blocking the fire exits at bookstores all across America.—Andy Ihnatko ∎

stores. 💻 (I don't know about you, but I've never even used the video-on-demand feature already available in most Class-A hotels. I'd rather surf the channels or

Keeping Things Friendly Online, CompuServe Goes 14.4, and Murdoch Buys Delphi

Increasing numbers of people are hopping aboard online services. This is a good thing; the more, the merrier. Still, I can't help but notice that certain bad habits keep cropping up. In an effort to maintain civility, here are some tips from Vaughan-Nichols' rules on online etiquette.

It all begins with respecting your fellow users. Too many people seem to think that just because they're online, they've been given a license to be rude—they couldn't be more mistaken. Insults sting just as hard when written on cathode-ray tubes as they do in person. Online arguments can get heated, but there's never any call to resort to personal insults.

If you've ever been "flamed," you know that your first powerful impulse is to immediately respond in kind. But usually a far better course is to file the flame, log off, and think long and hard about the consequences of adding fuel to the fire before responding. It's the equivalent of counting to ten. Although some charges might warrant an immediate shoot-from-the-hip response, it's more often the case that flamers discredit themselves by flaming. Anger is contagious, but so is patience. In the long run, thinking like Gandhi online will benefit

you more than acting like Wesley Snipes.

Another example of poor manners is found in how women are sometimes treated online. All too many female friends have recounted instances in which they've gotten lewd mail messages or online chat requests from jerks who know nothing about them except that their online name indicates they're women. This is completely unacceptable behavior that's just as destructive to open communication online as it is in the real world.

I'll get off my soapbox now, and move on to the latest news.

People who have kids have never really had enough choices in their online selections. But with the introduction of the online version of the Disney Adventures magazine (keyword: Disney), America Online (AOL) becomes a kid's delight.

Besides giving youngsters the text of each month's issue, Disney Adventures features message boards, real-time discussion groups, and a chance for kids to talk to the editors of the magazine. If I were ten again, I'd love this place, and I'm betting your kids will love it, too.

Internet-connected online services are springing up like mushrooms after an April shower, and America Online is also leaping to link up with the Internet.

AOL has long had a mail connection to the Internet. You can mail to AOL users with the address:

user_name@aol.com. Now, however, AOL's Internet Center brings other Internet features to its users.

AOL plans to phase in Internet services gradually to ensure that nothing goes haywire. I can't blame AOL one bit, because the initial plans are ambitious, including access to WAIS and gopher. These are Internet services that greatly reduce wear and tear on service- and file-hunting users. AOL will also bring Usenet's ever-popular news groups and online discussion groups to its users. As a longtime fan of AOL's interface, I'm looking forward to seeing how AOL tames the unruly Internet.

BIX also has big plans for the Internet and is redesigning its Windows interface program, BIXnav, and renaming it Internav.

This won't be just a cosmetic change. Internav makes it possible to work with BIX and the Internet almost transparently. For example, you'll download a file from a remote Internet site just as you would when copying a file with Windows' File Manager. That's it. You don't have to know about ftp or even Zmodem; Internav takes care of everything for you. Downloading files, much less ftping files, has never been easier.

Now, that's the theory. I haven't had the opportunity to see an actual beta, but if BIX makes good on its promises, this will be the Internet interface to beat.

The really hot news from CompuServe is that it has broken the online speed record by being the first major online service to offer 14,400-bps access. By the time you read this, CIS should have 14,400-bps lines active in most major cities.

Better still, CIS isn't adding extra fees for zooming your data long at the new speed limit. The 14,000-bps access will cost the same as 9,600-bps access. While that's not exactly cheap, and your tab will still run from $16 to $22.80 an hour, getting 50 percent more throughput for a 0 percent increase in charges is a great boon, and a healthy model for other online services upgrading their access rates to follow.

What's CRIS? CRIS, from Concentric Research Corp., is a new entry in the online races. CRIS offers the usual range of services, e-mail, tele-conferencing, news, online shopping, and so on, and while it's small in relation to giants like CompuServe and Prodigy, it's a friendly service with some unique attributes.

CRIS's basic service fee is $20 a month. Yes, that's higher than many other online services. But CRIS becomes affordable when you consider that this fee buys you ten hours of connect time at any connection speed from 1,200 to 14,400 bps. Every additional hour will cost you a mere $2 an hour, again regardless of how fast your connection is. CRIS will also be supporting 19,200-bps connections as

the next generation of modems begins to enter the market.

The other neat thing about CRIS is its BBS Direct service. Once you're in the CRIS system, you can head to a menu and pick out a BBS based on geographical location or content type. Once you've picked one out, CRIS takes care of connecting you to the BBS. This will run you an additional $2 an hour, but that's a lot cheaper then trying to dial into the BBS via long distance.

If you're interested in giving CRIS a look, the service can be reached on Sprintnet by entering C CRIS at the @ prompt. You also can call the service directly at (517) 895-0510. If you want to talk it over first with a CRIS representative, you can reach one at (800) 745-2747.

This month's big news from Delphi comes in two parts. First, General Videotext, Delphi's parent company, is changing its name to Delphi Internet Services. Second, Rupert Murdoch, millionaire and media mogul, has bought the company.

What does Murdoch's takeover mean to you? Well, for starters, the name change signifies a new direction for Delphi. While other online services are increasing their Internet capacities, it would appear that Delphi is going full-bore into the Internet.

Next, Murdoch (love him or hate him) is a mover and a shaker. I suspect Delphi will be changing from its current rather sleepy self to a major online player.

Transformations like this typically take a lot of cash, but Murdoch has deep pockets.

Is Delphi destined to become a "tabloid" online service? Right now, it's too soon to tell. Currently, the only concrete change wrought from Murdoch's purchase is that Murdoch's News Corp. plans to market a worldwide, PC-accessible online newspaper. Other online services have moved in this direction—witness the partnership between *The Chicago Tribune* and America Online. Even so, what News Corp. proposes is an entirely new level of online newspaper, so it's worth watching.

Virtual reality is the hottest topic around these days, and GEnie is on top of the situation. One of the service's newest roundtables is devoted to virtual reality, multimedia, and desktop video. This new service will look at everything from the high end of specialized virtual reality equipment to the more mundane issues of working with desktop video on the Amiga with Video Toaster. Type Cyberspace or Move 2000 at any major GEnie prompt to get to it.

Another cutting-edge area of computing to which GEnie is paying attention is the PowerPC. Two new roundtables devoted to Motorola's RISC chip are in place: the PowerPC RoundTable, devoted to general discussions for PowerPC users, and the PowerPC Developers RoundTable, for development support. Both forums can be

Cybercelebs Look Ahead

Prognosticating is dangerous business, but hey, we like to live a little dangerously. So, apparently, do a lot of other people. We asked a variety of technology watchers to gaze into their crystal balls and answer some questions about what the office of tomorrow will be like. Here's what they told us:

In the year 2000, what will be the one new technology everyone will have to have?

"A PCS phone—the ones that will be smaller and cheaper than cellular phones. And a pager so you don't have to take and pay for calls from Bozos. And you'll need a Batman utility belt to carry all this crap."

—SCOTT ADAMS, CREATOR OF THE CARTOON *DILBERT*

"I don't know the technology, but it will provide real-time interactive communications to everywhere (without wires). The killer app will be either Mosaic Version 8.0 (maybe under another name) or Lotus Notes Version 16."

—ESTHER DYSON, EDITOR OF RELEASE 1.0 NEWSLETTER

reached in GEnie's Computing RoundTables area.

Two or three times a week, I get a request from someone asking about how to connect with the Internet. Although connecting keeps getting easier every day, it's still not as easy as checking out CIS with the free trial membership that came with your modem. Even so, it just became easier than ever to connect to the Internet thanks to a book and a new Internet information service.

The book *Connecting to the Internet* by Susan Estrada (O'Reilly and Associates, ISBN 1-56592-061-9), gives you the tools to do exactly what its title promises. This 170-page volume tells you all you'll need to know about connecting to the Internet, whether you want just a dial-up asynchronous connection to read mail or an all-out 1.54-MB/sec net connection. If you've got Internet connection questions, this is the

book to go to. I only wish I had written it.

Of course, a book is bound in time, and some of the specific connection information will date quickly. Thanks to a service provided by Peter Kaminski, keeping up to date is no longer a problem. Kaminski compiles the Public Dialup Internet Access List (PDIAL). This list, which is updated regularly, contains listings for all public-access Internet sites. PDIAL includes full details on the kind of ser-

vices provided, their cost, and areas where the service is available. To get the most recent copy of PDIAL, all you need do is send a message to the Internet address: info-deli-server@netcom .com, and you'll automatically get a copy by return post.

Finally, Prodigy is also getting into the Internet act. By the time you read this, Prodigy will have introduced its own mail gateway to the Internet. To send mail to a Prodigy user, use the following address format: user_id@prodigy.com. For example, my Prodigy address is: VBKP51F@prodigy.com.

How much more this service will cost, if anything, was still to be determined at press time.

Even more is happening online than I can tell you about today, but come back next month for the latest and greatest in online news. In the meantime, let's all be a little bit polite, eh? —Steven J. Vaughan-Nichols

Coming Attractions

If you think it's difficult to choose between services now, just wait until more come on the scene next year. This next generation will be better graphically and easier to use, offer more information, cost less, and include advanced features.

You won't be able to ignore The Microsoft Network even if you want to. The service's front-end software is written into Windows

ple to stay home too much. Now the boneheads who are designing set-top boxes and hoping people will bite into video-on-demand schemes are trying to entice peo-

95—scheduled to ship sometime in 1995—and includes an option to sign up immediately after you install it. (Competitors already have complained about an online monopoly.)

The Microsoft Network will integrate seamlessly with Windows 95 applications. And it will include all the standard features of an online service. Microsoft hopes to lure content providers by promising them a strong online identity via an interactive publishing tool. Users will pay a flat monthly fee, and providers will have complete control over pricing and advertising. With its potential installed base of 10 to 15 million users, The Microsoft Network will attract all kinds of companies that are eager for a presence.

We had expected to review the Interchange Online Network this year (which at press time had just been purchased by AT&T), but it's scheduled to launch in early 1995. Interchange will provide comprehensive special interest areas built around the concept of linked information. Throughout the service, Lotus Notes-type links jump you to related topics and services; you'll be able to drag icons representing subjects of interest into your inbox to be updated each time you log on. Interchange automatically saves local copies of e-mail and archived documents for off-line reading. The underlying data is full-text indexed.

One principal area will be Interchange Computing, created by Ziff-Davis Interactive. Interchange Computing will add to the ZiffNet Information Service—which is now available on CompuServe and Prodigy. It will add editorial content, a three-year full-text archive of Ziff publications, and 75 PC vendor forums.

Users will pay for one or more specific content areas and will have access to a general news and reference section. Interchange is also developing special interest areas with *The Washington Post*, Starwave Corp., the *Minneapolis Star Tribune*, and Cowles Business Media.

Launched for Macintosh users in June 1994, cozy and

cute eWorld is the kind of online service you might expect from Apple Computer, which licenses its server software from America Online. Apple plans to make the service available later this year to Windows users. The company may need to add a PC Stadium with hardware and software vendors to its bucolic Town Square—eWorld's visual opening screen—to attract PC users.

From AT&T comes an online service that's designed to be smarter, more portable, and more personalized. First available last September on the Sony Magic Link PDA, AT&T PersonaLink Services should become available to desktops and portable PCs this year. PersonaLink

Services uses "intelligent agents," software that performs assigned tasks remotely. Finally, look for the USA Today Information Network from Gannett. The Network will expand the newspaper's online sports network to include information from Gannett and other providers.—Todd Spangler

OZCIS BRINGS OUT THE BEST IN COMPUSERVE

OzCIS 1.1 for Windows

If keeping track of your CompuServe forums, newsgroups, and e-mail seems like the impossible dream, Ozarks West Software's OzCIS for Windows (OzWin) may be an eye-opener. The first third-

party navigator that integrates CompuServe's Host Micro Interface, OzWin simplifies the online service.

Available on CompuServe or directly from Ozarks West, OzWin sits on top of WinCIM or CSNav. OzWin's interface is functional rather than glitzy. We found the multiplicity of parameters for mail and forum management daunting at first, but the online help module proved thorough and useful in the absence of an adequate manual.

Message management features include indexing, purging, and archiving of old mail. Since files are in ASCII format rather than a proprietary one (as in WinCIM and CSNav), you can either use the program's excellent tracking and message management, or move the messages into another program.

OzWin also offers a capable message editor that allows you to view multiple messages at once. A macro language is included to automate online access; built-in modules will obtain weather forecasts and stock quotations.

Though we found several minor bugs in this initial version, OzWin is a reliable performer that's a prime choice as a CompuServe navigator.—Earle Robinson

OzCIS for Windows, Version 1.1
Ozarks West Software Inc.
Colorado Springs, CO
CompuServe: 74774,417
$69

What will surprise us least about technology in the year 2000? What will surprise us most?

"It's a billion-way tie for least-surprising. I would expect religious objections to the proliferation of cool technology. It's too much fun to expect it to continue guilt-free."

—SCOTT ADAMS

"The least No. 1: Smaller, faster, cheaper. The song (and continued margin slide) stays the same. The least No. 2: Most people will still think Windows is 'good enough.' Agents will surprise us the most. I think agent technology will play an increasingly significant role in our lives in the future. There are agents today (real estate agents, travel agents, and so on….), but you have to pay these people quite a bit of money and they're painful to deal with."

—FRANK CASANOVA, EVANGELIST FOR APPLE COMPUTER'S ADVANCED TECHNOLOGY GROUP

Journalist for Prodigy

The toughest part about this interface was getting it up and running. After three attempts, we called Prodigy's technical support. We learned about the undocumented fact that the application can run only on Power Macs, Performa 475s and higher, and certain models of Macs built on the Motorola 68040. The statement AVMAC=1 needs to be placed in your Prodigy settings file for successful operation. Prodigy also informed us that depending on your system, you may need a different statement to get the application to run. Once you get the application running, you can expect to see the same interface as in the Windows version. (Prodigy is also preparing a front end for OS/2 users.)

Journalist for Prodigy
PED Software Corp.
(800) 548-2203
E-mail: info@ped.com
$29.95

Journalist for CompuServe

Journalist is not just another front end. It is a Windows-based hybrid between a desktop publishing package and a CompuServe interface. Just tell Journalist the type of information you would like to see every day (information about finance or the arts, for instance), and it will automatically download and paste this information into a colorful newsletter.

We would, however, like to see forums included in the options, and we did have some trouble using a special ZiffNet CompuServe account. Still, it is the most innovative package reviewed and is certainly worth a look. Journalist is also available for Prodigy.

Journalist for CompuServe
PED Software Corp.
(800) 548-2203
e-mail: info@ped.com
$79.95

NavCIS Pro 1.25

This CompuServe navigator is among the most highly developed of the front ends we looked at. It has the WinCIM-type interface with buttons for access to stock quotes and weather, and even a button to retrieve billing information. You can also create customized buttons.

Dvorak promises a future version that will support Usenet newsgroups. NavCIS Pro 1.25 is shareware, and the 30-day timed edition is available via a download. To upgrade to Version 1.25 from the timed edition costs $69.

NavCIS Pro 1.25
Dvorak Development and Publishing Corp.
(800) 861-0345
CompuServe e-mail: 71333,11

CompuServe Information Manager for Macintosh

This Mac-based front end has the same buttons and similar menus as its cousin, WinCIM. Taking advantage of the Macintosh GUI, the interface looks a bit better but provides the same functions as the Windows version.

CompuServe Information Manager for Macintosh
CompuServe Inc.
(800) 848-8199
Download at "Go CISSOFT"
Upgrade price: $10 (includes $10 usage credit)

Download at "Go DVORAK, Free Software library"
$69

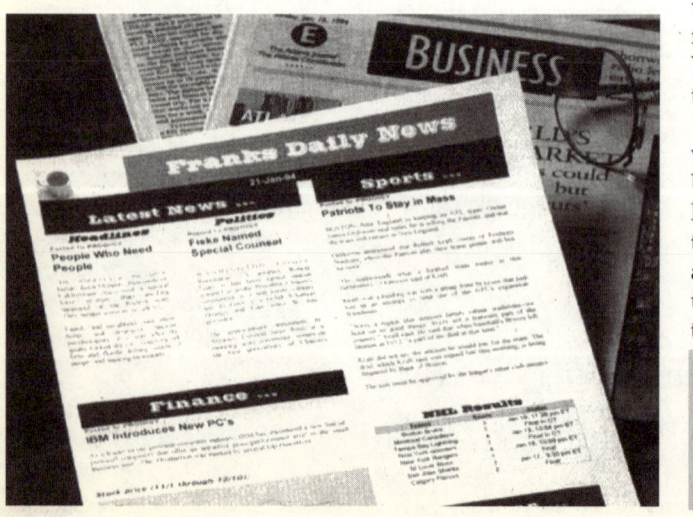

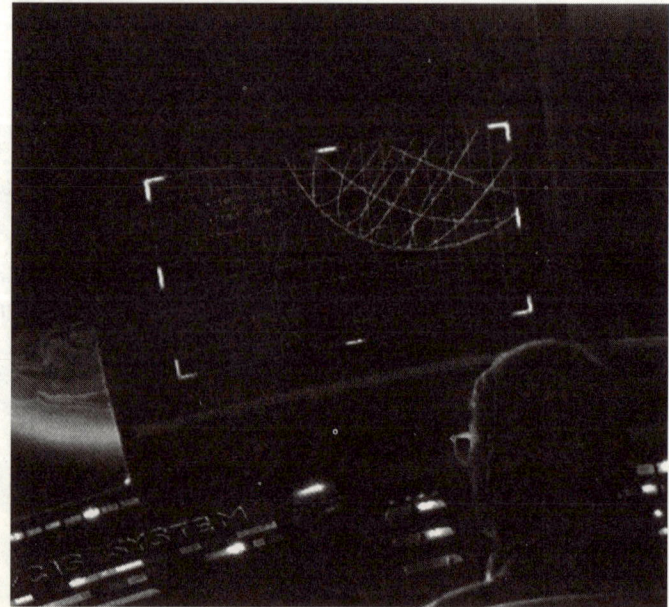

ving home in gridlock. Studies show that telecommuters consistently outproduce their office counterparts. So why doesn't every company encourage employees to

CompuServe Information Manager for DOS

If you're looking for a way to access CompuServe from DOS, you won't be intimidated by the straightforward interface. This front end is organized like its Windows and Macintosh CIM counterparts. The interface is well designed, considering the limitations inherent to a DOS text-based interface. One thing to keep in mind when you are using this interface: The Esc key is your friend. If you get buried deep within a menu structure, you can hit Esc to bring you back out one level at a time. (CompuServe is also preparing to release a version of CIM for OS/2 users.)

CompuServe Information Manager for DOS
CompuServe Inc.
(800) 848-8199
Upgrade price: $10 (includes $10 usage credit)
Download at "Go CISSOFT"

TapCIS 5.43b

Like Golden CommPass and the CompuServe Navigator, TapCIS is an offline mail and forum interface—but DOS-based. TapCIS is not for the beginner who might be intimidated by the interface. But if you're a CompuServe power user who's seeking a DOS-based offline product, TapCIS has proven itself over time. Once you get to know the DOS text-based interface, it's simple to navigate through the messages.

TapCIS 5.43b
Support Group Inc.
(800) 872-4768
CompuServe e-mail: 74020,10
Download at "Go TAPCIS"
$79

Golden CommPass 2.11

For OS/2 power users, Golden CommPass is an offline mail and forum interface that works off a similar premise as the CompuServe Navigator products. But unlike the single-page setup that the Navigator products employ, Golden CommPass requires you to go through several pages to set up each desired forum. Once setup is complete, however, you won't have any trouble monitoring the forums. Designed with OS/2 users in mind, each setup screen uses the traditional OS/2 Presentation Manager's notebook-tab style.

Golden CommPass 2.11
Creative Systems Programming Corp.
(609) 234-1500
CompuServe e-mail: 71511,151
Download demo version at "Go GCPSUPPORT"
$99

A CHANGE OF FACE
CompuServe Navigator for Windows

If you're looking for a way to use CompuServe without racking up those large connect charges, this product is for you. Mail and forum messages can be read offline, so that only a relatively short period of time must be spent online to post the messages.

To do this, you create scripts that indicate the appropriate forums as well as the message options. When you run the script, it dials CompuServe, sends and receives any new messages in the forums that you've selected, and disconnects. This is not a complete replacement for WinCIM, however: Interactive tasks are not possible.—Robert P. Lipschutz, Tim M. Crawford, John Garris, and Russ Iwanchuk

CompuServe Navigator for Windows
CompuServe Inc.
(800) 848-8199

CompuServe Navigator for Macintosh

The CompuServe Navigator for Macintosh has the same look and feel as the Windows version. When you're creating a script, you're forced to wade through many screens for even a simple change. It's a bit more cumbersome than its Windows counterpart, but once the scripts are created, it's a time-saving package.

CompuServe Navigator for Macintosh
CompuServe Inc.
(800) 848-8199
Download at "Go CISSOFT"
Upgrade price: $30 (includes $10 usage credit

FOR DELPHI INTERNET
Win-D 1.0

With Win-D, Windows users can automate many of the tasks performed in interactive Delphi sessions, such as sending and receiving mail and performing file transfers. For example, you can create scripts to have Win-D automatically log on to Delphi, upload e-mail you prepare using Win-D's e-mail editor, download new messages, transfer files, and then log out of Delphi—all in one action.

Win-D does not, however, completely shield you from Delphi's text-based interface.

What's the coolest product of the future you can buy today?

"Magic Cap PDAs like Sony's Magic Link."

—PAUL SAFFO, DIRECTOR, INSTITUTE FOR THE FUTURE

"Apple's QuickTake 100 digital camera. Go to a wedding in the morning, and you can digitally switch the heads of the bride and groom in the afternoon before they leave for the honeymoon. I always take my QT to parties…it's too cool."

—FRANK CASANOVA, APPLE'S (ADMITTEDLY BIASED) TECHNOLOGY EVANGELIST

"PDAs. They are in the Model T stages now, but we will look back on them and realize that they were the forerunners of wallet PCs and many other portable information devices that will be popular in the next decade."

—TIM BAJARIAN, PRESIDENT OF MARKET RESEARCH FIRM CREATIVE STRATEGIES

telecommute? The big argument against working at home is that you don't get to socialize as much as you should "for the team" and all that. ▢ Now I ask you,

You still see Delphi's text-based menus on-screen, with Win-D inserting the appropriate commands at various command prompts to automate routines. To navigate online, you can use Win-D's pull-down menus to jump to places within Delphi or across the Internet using ftp. Win-D also lets you click on any text on-screen to help you maneuver through Delphi's online menu structure.

Win-D 1.0
Circular Logic
(610) 584-0300
E-mail: perry@delphi.com
Download in the Computing
Groups Forum, in the D-LITE
Forum on Delphi
$39

OS/2 Delphi Navigator

OS/2 users should try the OS/2 Delphi Navigator (ODN) to interact with Delphi. Like Win-D, OS/2 Delphi Navigator manages your Delphi sessions for you; you let it talk directly with Delphi to perform all the actions you want, such as sending and receiving e-mail, downloading SIG messages, and transferring binary files. Then you use the slick user interface to view all your new messages. Messages are clearly sorted by thread, and responding to a message is as easy as clicking on a button. Furthermore, ODN's text editor is easy to use, and you can embed sound files in your messages that others can play automatically upon receipt.

OS/2 Delphi Navigator
E-mail: rollert@delphi.com
Download in OS/2 Custom
Forum on Delphi
(Custom Forum 41)
$35

FOR GENIE

Aladdin 1.72

This software combines a straightforward DOS interface with some time-saving canned scripts to make your online GEnie experience more productive. Among other things, Aladdin permits user-created menus that automate roundtable discussions. For example, a user may download all new RT messages or only download those messages that he or she has taken part in. GEnie's e-mail is automated in the same way.

Describe the desktop/office of the year 2000

"The organizations of 2000 and beyond will be nimble and shifting coalitions of smaller, networked teams who group and regroup for specific contracts. The desktop of the year 2000 goes anywhere and fits in your pocket."

—**HOWARD RHEINGOLD, AUTHOR AND INTERNET VISIONARY**

"It will be messy. It will be implemented in the communications cloud and displayed on screens ranging from a projector to a pen-pad to a watch. You will be able to talk to it, listen to it, write on it, and type into it. All these modes of input and output have their utility, and all will persist."

—**ESTHER DYSON**

Aladdin 1.72
GE Information Services Inc.
(800) 638-9636
Download by typing
"FRONTEND"
Free

AOL Job Resources

After the demise of the job-search service, *The New York Times*'s newspaper division took the online plunge in July, joining America Online in electronic form with a service called @Times (keyword: TIMES). At the service's core are the Gray Lady's Entertainment Guide, which includes reviews and information about local arts-and-leisure activities, and the current day's top stories from the News, Business, and Sports sections. @Times is uploaded each day, seven days a week. Eventually the paper plans to put writers online, so that you can converse with the staff about the articles that appear in print.

@Times also provides a valuable job-search tool for anyone in the New York metropolitan area, posting the Classifieds section with every Sunday feed. In addition to the want ads, the Classifieds section includes real-estate info and automobile ads.

A broader-reaching job-search resource is AOL's Help Wanted-USA, a listing of thousands of professional job openings around the country. This service is updated every Wednesday morning. In addition, you can post or browse business and job postings (as well as other classified ads) in AOL's Classified Bulletin Board.

Use the keyword JOBS to access both of these services.

You'll also want to check out AOL's Career Center (keyword: CAREER). Here, you'll find articles on career advancement, resume templates, and sample employment letters. You can also arrange for private counseling sessions (in real-time chat) with professional career counselors, or post public questions in the counselor bulletin board.

America Online
(800) 827-6364

CompuServe Newswires

CompuServe recently added three international newswires to its basic services, from the UK's Press Association (GO CIS: PAO), France's Associated Press France en Ligne (GO CIS: APFRANCE), and Australia's Associated Press Online (GO CIS: AAPONLINE). These wires provide business, financial, and governmental news, as well as details like television listings and weather reports. Note, however, that France's Associated Press en Ligne is not translated.

CompuServe's new Newspaper Archive (GO CIS: NEWS ARCHIVE) includes full-text articles from domestic and UK papers dating back five to ten years, searchable by keywords in the copy's headline, lead, or body. In addition to your standard connect rates, you pay $1.50 per article viewed or downloaded from the

how does this jibe with the idea of creating a home-shopping environment in which people can order groceries, movies, games, clothes, washing machines, and every-

database. Dialog Information Services Inc. is the first content provider to supply the Newspaper Archive with articles, and CompuServe is pursuing others.

In other news, CompuServe has reorganized and enlarged its Apple-oriented areas. To access your old favorites as well as the new forums, type GO CIS: MAUG. Also, IBM, which has long had multiple services on CompuServe, has now consolidated them under one area (GO CIS: IBM).

CompuServe Newswires
CompuServe
(800) 848-8199

WHAT'S NEW WITH DELPHI
Delphi

Delphi is now supporting 14.4-Kbps access via its direct lines for no additional fee. The service is also working in concert with Phoenix Technologies, best known for its PC BIOS, to build and distribute Delphi's Windows interface, due out late this year. The plan is to bundle Delphi's new GUI with computers, modems, and communications suites.

If you're an OS/2 user, you might want to consider OS/2 Delphi Navigator ($25), which features both online and offline e-mail, forum, and Usenet support. Head over to the OS/2 forum (keyword: CUS 41) for more info.

Delphi
(800) 695-4005

NEW PRODIGY RESOURCES
Prodigy

While Prodigy is not yet experimenting with want ads or job listings online, the service is working with a couple of regional Bell operating companies (RBOCs) to test the success of electronic yellow-page listings and classified ads. In November, Pacific Telesis and Times Mirror's *The Los Angeles Times* will introduce a service that includes yellow-page listings and classified advertising in the shopping section of the electronic version of *The Los Angeles Times* on Prodigy. Also scheduled for the fourth quarter is the rollout of an ad-supported online yellow pages sponsored by Nynex Information Resources, the yellow-page branch of Nynex Corp.

Prodigy is also the first online service to add over-the-wire sound capabilities. To access audio news summaries, sound bites, and music, you need Prodigy for Windows 1.1. To get your hands on 1.1, use the JUMPword PRODWIN. At press time, Prodigy planned to release a sound-capable Macintosh version in late August. For more information, use the JUMPword SOUND CLIPS.

Prodigy also continues to charge into the interactive arena with its connection to NBC's new America's Talking all-talk cable network. Each America's Talking set has a Prodigy connection, and the hosts have been instructed to read aloud and respond to select Prodigy postings. Subscribers can interact directly with hosts and guests on the network's dozen daily live shows, which feature real-time opinion polls on the day's subject, and participate in live, online discussion groups using Prodigy's new chat feature. Use the JUMPword AMERICA'S TALKING to tune in.—Steven J. Vaughan-Nichols

Prodigy
(800) 776-3449

INTERNET

GRAPHICAL INTERNET
NCSA Mosaic

Make the Internet more Mac-like with Mosaic, an interface to the World Wide Web (WWW) that puts a hypertext face on the navigation commands necessary to move around the Internet. Mosaic uses the metaphor of a home page for each WWW server. From the home page, you simply click on hypertext links that automatically connect you to Internet services throughout the world— there's no need to worry about trying to learn those cryptic Internet pathnames. Developed and distributed free by the National Center for Supercomputer Applications, Mosaic is available for the Macintosh and for Windows and X Windows machines via anonymous ftp from a variety of Internet sites and from ZiffNet/Mac (filename MOSAIC.SIT in Library 1 of the Download & Support Forum).

What technologies are we overlooking today that will play a big role tomorrow?

"Global Positioning System will be integrated into virtually all aspects of computing. We will be able to locate each other and resources with pinpoint accuracy anywhere on the globe."

—PATRICIA SEYBOLD, FOUNDER OF RESEARCH FIRM PATRICIA SEYBOLD GROUP

"Voice recognition, pattern recognition, encryption."

—ESTHER DYSON

"Bell's Theorem. It's more than I can explain here, but the gist of it is that experiments prove we can influence matter instantly from any distance. I wouldn't call it a technology yet, but a technology will develop around it. And it will change everything."

—SCOTT ADAMS

munityCommunityCommunityCommunityCommunit

thing else by using the computer or the TV? Talk about minimizing socialization! This dream world of the multimedia mavens and set-top-box promoters is incredibly

One of the WWW servers you can access with Mosaic is run by Novell to provide software updates, marketing information, and technical support to its customers. By clicking on one of the book-shaped icons on the Novell home page in Mosaic, you can burrow deeper into the company's customer-service system. You can reach Novell through Mosaic (or through any other WWW client), with a network connection to the Internet and MacTCP 2.02 or later, at http://www.novell.com/. —Shelly Brisbin

The Mac Internet Tour Guide

Most college students have access to the global Internet computer network. But whereas the majority of college Internet users are stuck typing commands into UNIX systems in order to access the network, *The Mac Internet Tour Guide* shows how Mac users can use Mac programs to connect with the Internet. Once you're connected, you can download the latest shareware and talk to far-off friends.

A KEY TO THE INTERNET KINGDOM
WinGopher

You've heard the complaint: The unmanaged Internet is such a vast labyrinth that it's sometimes impossible to find that one special piece of information you're looking for. True enough, and that's why savvy Internet users have long employed gopher servers and the menus they present to jump from one Internet site to another. gopher menus may not have the style that Mosaic and its World Wide Web servers have, but they're the gate-keepers to a seemingly limit-less wealth of information. WinGopher is a Windows user's key to that wealth. A gopher agent's assignment is to go out and find something: a library, a file, a database, or all three. Using gopher servers, Internet sites orga-nize the information they store in a hierarchical fashion and present menus that let users jump from place to place. There are over 1,400 gopher servers offering everything from the full text of the NAFTA treaty to all the back issues of *Wired* magazine.

The gopher protocol has been extended with links to search tools, like archie (which searches ftp indexes so that you can locate files to download) and veronica (which searches gopher menus for specific text strings). By linking all of these tools, gopher users can jump from site to site or search for files and text sim-ply by choosing various menu options. When you start a search from a gopher, the results are returned as a gopher menu. The interface is simple and intuitive.

To access gopher servers, you need a gopher client such as WinGopher. As the first Windows-based gopher client software, WinGopher reduces your searches to a series of point-and-click actions. It represents gopher menu items with icons: Another gopher menu is a file cabinet, a text file is a piece of paper, a binary file is a PC, and a search is an eye. Text next to each icon describes what it represents. By making Internet access so easy, WinGopher encourages exploration—and exploration on the Internet can be bound-less. Be warned: WinGopher can make the Internet addic-tive beyond belief. Requires: 2MB RAM, 4.5MB hard disk space, Microsoft Windows 3.1 or later.—Rick Ayre

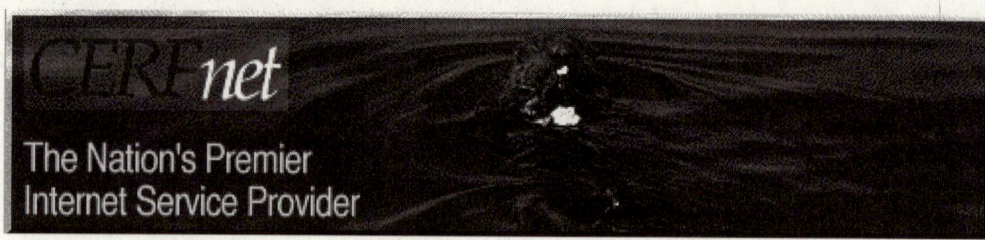
The Nation's Premier Internet Service Provider

CERFnet

Users of CERFnet will appre-ciate the Internet Compass, a help menu for navigating the system, and the gopher-based help system. By using the help system to access the very useful and well-orga-nized system information, you also will learn how to use the gopher tool itself.

The Internet Compass menus ask you for informa-tion needed to run the avail-able Internet tools, so getting to the tools is as simple as fol-lowing these well-organized menus. A lot of help screens are missing, though, so help is not always available through the menus.

DIGEX

The DIGEX help system gives you information about all the functions available online. There are documents that list interesting ftp, Telnet, gopher, and IRC sites, with instructions to help you access them. Accessing an Internet tool is as easy as typ-ing the tool name at the com-mand prompt (such as Telnet or gopher). Unfortunately, once you access the tool, you are limited to its help, and that is sometimes scarce. The printed manual we received from DIGEX was a great help. It contains the informa-tion you need to use the sys-tem utilities.

✇ The ARPANET was a research network that led to the creation of many networking innovations and ultimately evolved into the Internet.

NETCOM

This provider has a great help menu that serves as a gateway to many Internet tools available online, and provides useful system-related information. Help is always available, and—thanks to the included utilities—managing your account is easy as well. For example, deleting a file in a subdirectory is as simple as using the arrow keys to locate the file and pressing R(emove).

From the menu you can also access NETCOM's FAQs (frequently asked questions). The FAQs are complete and easy to search; it's like having technical support staff with you all the time. Furthermore, while all providers we reviewed offer technical support, NETCOM is the only one with a 24-hour help line. If help is not available online, it is always just a phone call away.

NETCOM
NETCOM On-Line
Communication Services Inc.
info@netcom.com
(800) 353-6600

PANIX

When you log on to PANIX, you see a menu with options to execute common system tasks such as accessing e-mail, news, and system help files, or managing your files. The menu also allows you to run Unix commands by pressing a single choice—you don't have to learn the commands. Experienced users can activate a Unix shell, then return

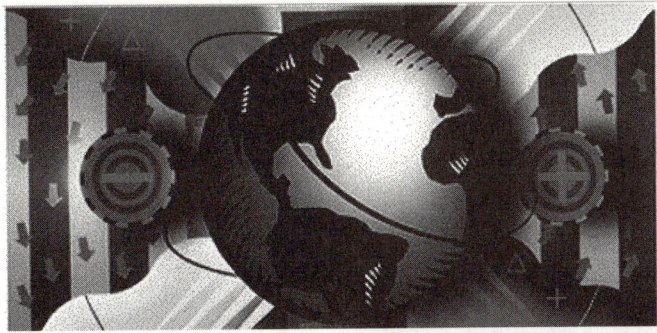

to the menu. PANIX offers online technical support.

PANIX Public Access Networks Corp.
info@panix.com
(212) 741-4400

The Pipeline

This provider takes NetCruiser's approach to easy Internet navigation a step further with its wealth of search tools, front ends to popular Internet resources, and value-added services. It's not just one of the best Internet gateways available, but a great personal-use and business-research tool. The Pipeline is freeware, so you can either download it or have it shipped to you.

On The Pipeline you can easily find virtually any information, from Amtrak's train schedules to book excerpts to weather maps to the latest from the AP. The

a gopher server, all at the same time. If you access The Pipeline from outside the New York area (area codes other than 212, 516, or 914), however, you will dial-in via SprintNet (and incur a surcharge of $5.00 per hour for primetime access and $2.50 during off-hours). Pink Slip

Pipeline is a hybrid of an online service and an Internet provider—a must-have gateway to electronic information resources.

Thanks to its proprietary, prioritized packet-transfer protocol, Pink Slip, you will never have to wait for your computer to "stop thinking." You can start a long file transfer and read News or browse

and The Pipeline's efficiency ensure that you get the most out of your connect-time charges.

The Pipeline has graphical interfaces for most Internet resources, but notoriously missing is a GUI World Wide Web browser. A text-based browser called lynx is available. The Pipeline will soon release its GUI Web browser, making it a complete GUI Internet access tool.

The Pipeline
Pipeline Network Inc.
info@pipeline.com
(212) 267-3636

The Pipeline

Although The Pipeline is best known for its superior GUI connectivity you can also use your account as a shell account. Upon log-on you are presented with The Pipeline menu, a help menu that resembles the GUI version of The Pipeline.

Like its GUI counterpart, using The Pipeline as a shell account is a breeze. The help menus are some of the best available. Using Internet services from the menus is as easy as answering a few simple questions. It is hard to believe The Pipeline could have done any better (short of figuring out how to make the shell accounts look as sharp as the GUI) with its shell-account interface.

The Pipeline
The Pipeline Network Inc.
info@pipeline.com
(212) 267-3636

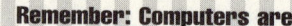

The WELL

Don't think of The WELL as just another Internet gateway. Rich in content, it has more than 200 conferences on nearly every topic imaginable. When you connect for the first time, you can take a very worthwhile automated tour of the system.

As with DIGEX, you access Internet tools by typing each tool name. From that point on, you're on your own with The WELL's Unix-like tools. Should you have any questions, however, refer to the online conferences. Answers to all your questions most likely are already posted and readily available in the conferences.

The WELL
info@well.com
(415) 332-4335

The World

Dropping into The World was a rude awakening. This is the type of system that non-computerphiles want to avoid. Fortunately, the help command reveals a wealth of useful information, and the Internet help section is well-organized and complete. So, as long as you can recover from the shock of running into a system prompt immediately after log-on, you should be ready to go after you read the help files. (Software Tool & Die plans to create a graphical interface.) Compared with all other service providers, The World is the least expensive one for occasional use.

The World
Software Tool & Die (The World)
info@world.std.com
(617) 739-0202

AlterNet

If you want a provider that specializes in reliable SLIP/PPP connectivity, consider AlterNet. UUNET's support staff keeps users well informed about system downtimes and network problems.

AlterNet
UUNET Technologies Inc.
info@uunet.uu.net
(800) 488-6384

The Mosaic Handbook for Microsoft Windows

The Mosaic Handbook for Microsoft Windows, by Dale Dougherty and Richard Koman, is clear, concise, direct, and just a little bit technical. The book comes with a Spyglass-enhanced version of Mosaic, giving it an advantage over its competition. It offers just the right mix of instructions on how to use Mosaic, the Web, and the Internet and does a nice job of describing the breadth of services available.

Since *The Mosaic Handbook* comes with a version of Mosaic, its directions can be very explicit. It also has the distinct advantage of having been written by Dougherty, who is the publisher of the Global Network Navigator—O'Reilly and Associates' venture into electronic publishing. The book is very specific both when giving directions to get you online and when telling you what to do once you get there.—Rick Ayre

The Mosaic Handbook for Microsoft Windows
By Dale Dougherty and Richard Koman
O'Reilly and Associates Inc.
(800) 998-9938
$29.95

Features Demo for *MAZE*, The World's Most Challenging Puzzle

MOSAIC

User's Guide

- Learn NCSA Mosaic for Windows, Macintosh, and X Window platforms
- Install and configure Mosaic, including SLIP and PPP
- Covers Hypertext, the World Wide Web, and navigation procedures
- Recipes for creating your own home page

BRYAN PFAFFENBERGER

Disk includes everything you need for a dial up SLIP or PPP connection on a Windows computer!

Mosaic User's Guide

Mosaic User's Guide, by Bryan Pfaffenberger, deals with using the original NCSA version of Mosaic, but because it covers the Windows, Macintosh, and X Window versions of the program, it tends to be less specific in many of its directions. Where it must be specific, it is, but since it describes how to use each version of Mosaic, only a third of the presented information is relevant—depending on which platform Mosaic is run.

Mosaic User's Guide also comes with bundled software. On the included disk is NetManage's Chameleon Sampler, a software bundle that enables SLIP/PPP connections to the Internet. Also included are programs that let you use e-mail, newsgroups, and ftp, as well as a preview of a really intriguing MAZE that's implemented using documents written in HTML, the format Mosaic can view. Mosaic itself is not included, unfortunately.

Mosaic User's Guide
By Bryan Pfaffenberger
MIS Press
(800) 628-9658
$24.95

Mosaic Quick Tour for Windows

Mosaic Quick Tour for Windows, by Gareth Branwyn, is the manual that should come with Mosaic. Just as Mosaic is fun to use, this book is fun to read, and it can get you up and running fast. For those of us in a real hurry, there's a section in the introduction called the Super-Duper Mosaic Quick Start, which tells you how to get started so quickly you can almost get there before you start.

For the most part, Branwyn sticks to the Mosaic essentials. He does, though, cover the cool stuff and manages to find the right level of detail to keep you interested and give you the guidance you need. The layout of the book helps in this regard, as information is made accessible in context. Also, Branwyn's suggestions for places to explore are more interesting than the ones found in the other books reviewed here.

Mosaic Quick Tour for Windows
By Gareth Branwyn
Ventana Press
(800) 743-5369
$12

The Internet via Mosaic and the World Wide Web

The Internet via Mosaic and the World Wide Web, by Steve Browne, is a very detailed and technical book. Its many tables and charts contain valuable information that the authors of other books might chose not to cover. Unfortunately, the book's layout is downright ugly. Browne's lists of places to visit are pretty good, though.

The Internet via Mosaic and the World Wide Web
By Steve Browne
Ziff-Davis Press
(800) 688-0448
$24.95

AIR Mosaic 1.1

Surfing the World Wide Web has never been easier, thanks to SPRY's AIR Mosaic, Version 1.1. Although its 16-bit architecture can slow things down, especially when grabbing large .GIFs, AIR Mosaic is a flexible, easy-to-use, easy-to-configure WWW front end. (A 32-bit version of AIR Mosaic is available but is not fully supported by SPRY.) This browser is available as a standalone over the Internet; you can download it via ftp (ftp.spry.com\Air Mosaic Demo\AMOS DEMO.exe) from SPRY to give it a trial run and then register it for $29.95. AIR Mosaic is also included in SPRY's Internet In A Box, available in retail outlets for $149.99, as well as in its popular AIR Series.

One of AIR Mosaic's strongest selling points is its ease of installation; you don't need to update any Windows drivers or add Win32s support. (This is important because of incompatibilities between Win32s and many systems.) But as with most of the browsers reviewed, AIR Mosaic requires a separate TCP/IP stack or PPP-compliant communications package with Winsock support. Fortunately, AIR Mosaic operates with all the popular TCP/IP and PPP packages on the market.

Once you are connected to the Internet, AIR Mosaic automatically retrieves SPRY's home page; from there you're introduced to the world of the Web. If an error occurs or you get lost, AIR Mosaic's context-sensitive online help gets you back on track.

AIR Mosaic is exceptionally easy to use and to customize. With the click of a button, you can add documents to a hotlist that can be quickly retrieved using a hotkey. A row of buttons at the top of the screen allows you to execute tasks without having to use the pull-down menus.

For a more manageable structure as you wend your way through the maze of resources, AIR Mosaic lets you categorize documents into folders, which can be added to the menu bar. You can create up to 15 hotlist folders, each of which can handle approximately 200 URLs.

A feature unique to AIR Mosaic is the Kiosk mode, which allows you to view the full screen without the obstruction of the menu. This is particularly handy if you wish to view a home page in its entirety, but the feature is

(plain old-fashioned, preprogrammed TV). It's too easy to be swayed into thinking all this high technology is an end in itself. Gee, with the computer, I can do every-

somewhat limiting. You can only travel forward using hyperlinks in Kiosk mode, and you can't use the menu selections. Also, you have to exit Kiosk mode to toggle between pages or navigate backwards.

AIR Mosaic's sluggishness when loading large .GIFs can cause some anguish, especially if you're dialing in to a service and paying by the minute. You can turn off the graphics to save time, but then you'll lose the beauty of the more creative home pages. Some of the other browsers handle this better. Netscape Navigator, for example, lets you navigate through a page while the .GIF is downloading.

As for other features: ftp and gopher utilities, a graphics viewer, Telnet, and 3270 emulation are all included in AIR Mosaic. The package also provides limited support for Usenet newsgroups and e-mail. Both Internet In A Box and AIR Series provide full newsgroup and e-mail capabilities.

If time is not of the essence and you need a good, utilitarian Web browser, AIR Mosaic is an excellent choice. Although a bit sluggish, AIR Mosaic is easy to use and configure, and its utilities more than make up the difference.—Padraic Boyle

AIR Mosaic
SPRY Inc.
Seattle WA
(800) 777-9638, ext. 26;
(206) 447-0300
info26@spry.com

Business Glossary to the Internet

Acceptable Use Policy (AUP)
The official policy statement of a network (for example, NSFNet) or a service provider (for example, Netcom) that defines which activities may occur on the network. Some AUPs have strict guidelines on which business applications are permitted.

Flame
A strong and inflammatory message delivered by e-mail or public posting on an electronic bulletin board. The most enthusiastic flames are typically reserved for businesses that violate AUPs.

ftp (File Transfer Protocol)
The original and most popular way to transfer files over the Internet. Networks that allow "anonymous ftp" enable anyone to log on to a system and retrieve files, while other ftp systems require that the user enter a password.

Gopher
A navigation tool for the Internet that provides local computers with access to files and services on remote servers that support gopher software, based on a menu system for easy browsing.

Mosaic
Software invented at the National Center for Supercomputing Applications (NCSA) at the University of Illinois at Urbana-Champaign to facilitate easy, graphical browsing of the World Wide Web. Mosaic is one of the primary means of "window-shopping" on the Web, but note that it also supports gopher, ftp, WAIS, and—if you have an additional program—Telnet. Mosaic presently supports Windows, Macintosh, and Unix platforms.

Telnet
The Internet protocol whereby users at local PCs can log on to remote systems and use their resources. Telnet systems can be private or public. For example, Digital Equipment Corp.'s home page includes a hypertext Telnet link to the company's direct-sales system, provided the user has a Telnet program installed.

SLIP or PPP (Serial Line Internet Protocol, Point-to-Point Protocol)
Two types of Internet connections (PPP is newer and on the rise) that allow the dialer to link to the Internet using standard Internet protocols (TCP/IP) on a normal phone line. As such, they are the best solutions for businesses exploring the possibilities of the Internet.

Usenet
A cooperative network reachable through the Internet that consists of several thousand discussion groups (called newsgroups), ranging from forums for computer programmers specializing in esoteric languages to people who avidly memorize each episode of "Star Trek." Advertising on the newsgroups is Usenet's hottest business topic.

Wide Area Information Servers (WAIS)

A program that allows relatively easy searching and retrieval from indexed text databases on remote computers. WAIS can be used to make your business' documents and databases available to customers or other businesses. WAIS supports simple keyword searches.

World Wide Web (WWW or W3)

A hypermedia system designed at the European Laboratory for Particle Physics in Geneva, Switzerland (CERN), that allows a user to search for related "pages" globally, from simple text to multimedia graphics, just by pointing and clicking with a mouse. Built on the concept of linking different types of information, the WWW is the fastest-growing segment of the Internet and the most useful for commerce. Note that some of the Web browsers, such as Lynx, are text-based. To view Web billboards, you'll need a graphical Web browser such as Mosaic or Cello.—Peter H. Lewis ■

InternetWorks

The phrase explosive growth is used a lot in the PC industry, but perhaps never more appropriately than for the current Web-browser market. In one startling example, 1.25 million America Online subscribers will soon have access to the World Wide Web through InternetWorks—a product so new it hadn't even shipped when AOL purchased it last November. I-Works didn't reach us in time for full review, but it should be available in final form by the time you read this. We were able to take a good look at all three packages. Here's our report:

InternetWorks doesn't come with its own TCP/IP stack, but it is Winsock 1.1-compliant. This means it will work with any TCP/IP package, through either a direct or a modem-based connection.

Like many other browsers, I-Works introduces you to the Web through its own home page; it then offers a variety of ways to navigate the Internet. The most innovative of these is by clicking the notebook-style divider "tabs" that the package provides for each Web page. Another cool I-Works navigation feature is the card catalog, which lets you create what are essentially hotlists. The advantage here is that InternetWorks supports multiple card catalogs, so you can sort your favorite Web sites in multiple dimensions.

Still other features set this package apart from the current crop of browsers: I-Works offers true multithreading so you can send an e-mail message, download a file, and visit your favorite home page—all at the same time. Another key feature is I-Works' OLE 2.0 support; presently, InterAp from California Software has the only browser to offer OLE functionality. I-Works also has newsgroups, file saving, and printing.

BookLink is offering another versions of I-Works: InternetWorks Lite is available for free at ftp: //ftp. booklink.com/lite, but it has only limited multithreading capabilities and doesn't offer OLE 2.0 support or e-mail. The full version of I-Works is scheduled to sell for $129 and will include the Internet Yellow Pages.—Sarah Roberts and Amarendra Singh

InternetWorks
$129

Enhanced NCSA Mosaic for Windows

Spyglass holds a big card—the official licensing agreement for commercial rights to the NCSA Mosaic graphical interface—and recently played it by unveiling Enhanced NCSA Mosaic for Windows (now in Version 1.02).

When Spyglass acquired the rights to Mosaic, it decided essentially to start over by streamlining and stabilizing the code and eliminating some features such as the hotlist and some task buttons. Several of these features will begin reappearing in the next release. Meanwhile, in Version 1.02, Spyglass has improved the original Mosaic by including printing, support for forms and multiple windows, a proxy gateway, and a newsreader (albeit a very limited one).

You can get Spyglass's Enhanced NCSA Mosaic by buying *The Mosaic Handbook for Microsoft Windows* ($29.95), published by O'Reilly and Associates. But the package is primarily shipped from OEMs to companies that then customize the package and ship their own integrated release.

Installing Spyglass's Enhanced NCSA Mosaic is pretty straightforward. Windows drivers are automatically installed and configured for Win32s operations; however, Win32s may cause problems in systems with high-end graphics cards or with less than 4MB of RAM. The package does not come with either a TCP/IP stack or an asynchronous package, but it does work with most TCP/IP stacks or PPP-compliant packages that support WINSOCK.DLL.

To configure Enhanced NCSA Mosaic you have to make selections in the Preferences dialog box or manually edit the .INI file, which can be cumbersome. (This is in contrast to SPRY's AIR Mosaic, for example, which handles configuration via pull-down menus.) Version 2.0 of Enhanced NCSA Mosaic, due out by the time you read this, should include a friendlier configuration menu.

Once you're connected, your first glimpse of the Web is through Spyglass's home page, which is stored on your local PC—not Spyglass's server. From there you can hyperlink to the Web.

One of Enhanced NCSA Mosaic's most useful features is support for multiple windows. This allows you to connect to multiple hosts and switch between windows to

view data. Navigating Enhanced NCSA Mosaic is similar to navigating most of its competitors, except that it has few of the one-click navigation aids provided by other packages (only backward and forward arrows are available).

Other minor inconveniences: When you retrieve a document or .GIF, the status bar at the bottom of the screen shows the source path and name but offers no information about the size of the file or the progress of downloads. Furthermore, the package includes no graphics viewer, although it supports third-party viewers.

Another of Enhanced NCSA Mosaic's strong points: If you're in the middle of

retrieving a document and the transmission is taking too long, you can abort the task by hitting the Esc key. Multiple windows support is still its biggest plus. Enhanced NCSA Mosaic is not as feature-rich as other products on the market, such as AIR Mosaic, but it does provide a no-frills steppingstone to the wonders of the Web.—Sarah Roberts and Amarendra Singh

Enhanced NCSA Mosaic for Windows
Spyglass Inc.
Naperville, IL
(708) 505-1010
info@spyglass.com

A ROSE BY ANY OTHER NAME
Enhanced NCSA Mosaic

One of the first companies to license Enhanced NCSA Mosaic from Spyglass was ftp Software, best known for its TCP/IP package (included in its Internet tool set, Explore OnNet). Ftp's version of Mosaic naturally has much the same functionality as the Spyglass, but ftp has made some welcome improvements to the basic package.

Explore OnNet Mosaic offers the basics—support for multiple windows, printing, forms, proxy gateway, the ability to create hotlists, and more. Perhaps the most exciting addition is that (as with Netscape Navigator) you can read and view your files as they are downloading instead of having to wait. Explore OnNet is designed for a modem-based connection but works with most TCP/IP stacks and PPP- and Winsock 1.1-compliant packages.

One area that still needs work is Web navigation. Explore OnNet Mosaic has only two simple navigation icons—one to move forward and one to move backward. You have to use the menu bar or hotkeys to access all commands, which can be irritating. Also, you can't modify the .INI file to customize your menu bar, which you can do in the original NCSA Mosaic. Overall, Explore OnNet has made a decent showing and is currently available for $149.—Sarah Roberts and Amarendra Singh

Enhanced NCSA Mosaic
ftp Software

SURFING SAFARI
WebSurfer

This package may have the easiest configuration and installation process yet. All you have to do is click on the "Instant Internet" icon and voilà—your software is configured for an Internet connection, ready for you to sign up for an Internet account through any one of several online services.

Netmanage's home page is the first place you'll go. Like IBM Web Explorer, WebSurfer includes some features seasoned Web veterans will appreciate, like support for simultaneous connections and the ability to import your old Mosaic .INI file so you can automatically retain all your favorite sites. In addition, WebSurfer keeps a "history" page that allows quick connections to previously visited sites, lets you create hotlists of your favorite locations, and supports printing.

To get WebSurfer, you must either buy Chameleon, which retails for $199, or download just the Web browser at ftp.netmanage.com. —Sarah Roberts and Amarendra Singh

WebSurfer
$199

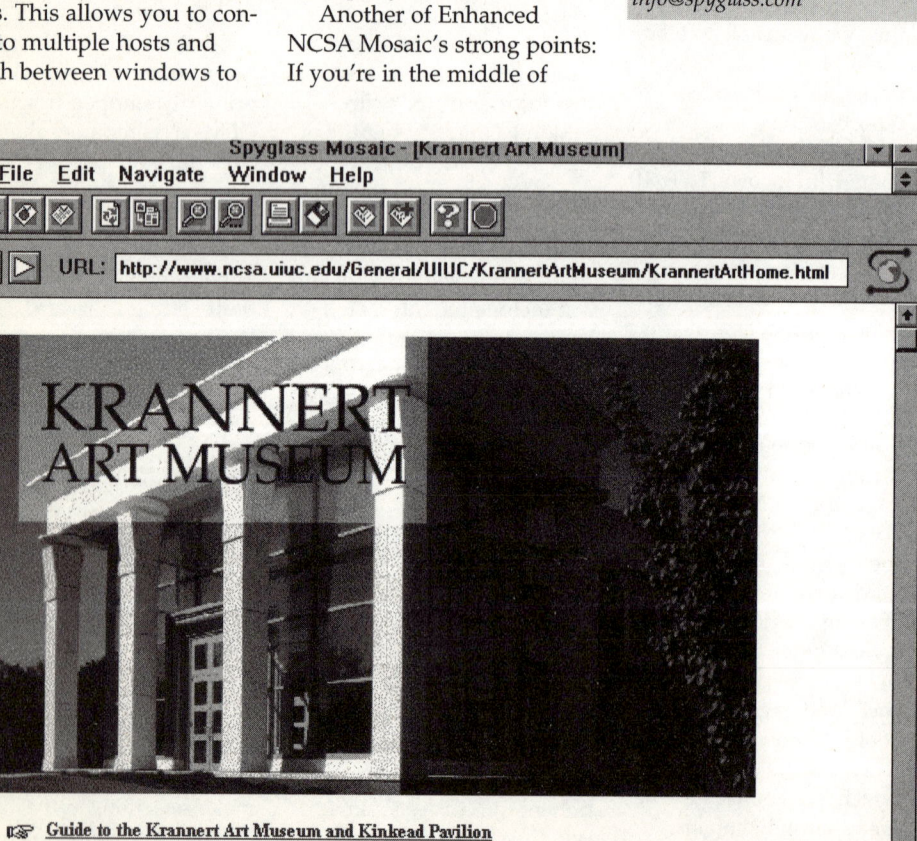

Spyglass Mosaic - [Krannert Art Museum]

File Edit Navigate Window Help

URL: http://www.ncsa.uiuc.edu/General/UIUC/KrannertArtMuseum/KrannertArtHome.html

KRANNERT ART MUSEUM

☞ **Guide to the Krannert Art Museum and Kinkead Pavilion**
An electronic sampler of the museum's permanent collection
☞ **Education Resource Center**

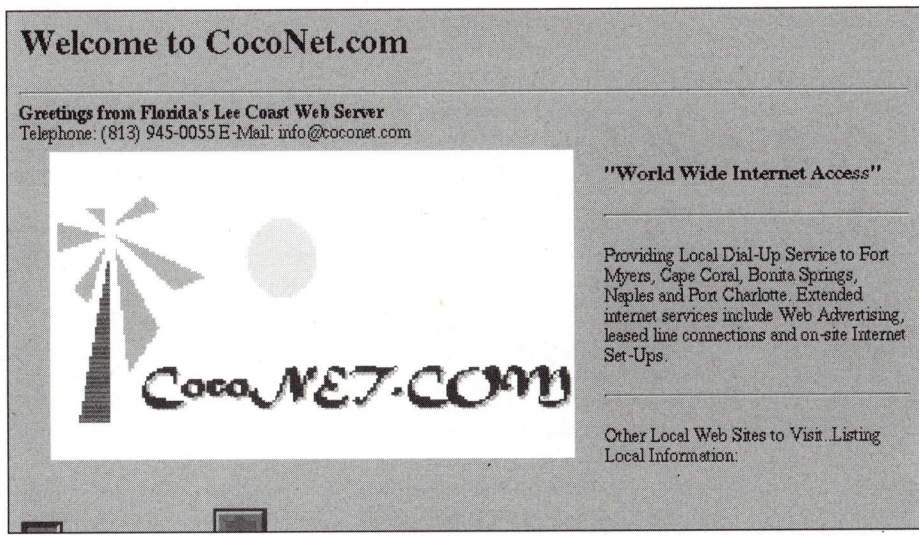

Welcome to CocoNet.com

Greetings from Florida's Lee Coast Web Server
Telephone: (813) 945-0055 E-Mail: info@coconet.com

"World Wide Internet Access"

Providing Local Dial-Up Service to Fort
Myers, Cape Coral, Bonita Springs,
Naples and Port Charlotte. Extended
internet services include Web Advertising,
leased line connections and on-site Internet
Set-Ups.

Other Local Web Sites to Visit..Listing
Local Information:

InterAp

If California Software comes through with all the goodies promised for InterAp, its Internet access package, this product should be a real presence in the rapidly evolving scene. And at press time, California Software seemed pretty close to delivering. This version of InterAp, Version 26 has a complete, highly functional set of Internet tools—Web Navigator (the Web browser we review here), a newsreader, plus full-featured e-mail, ftp, and Telnet utilities. But when we looked at InterAp in November, it was still prerelease software; as you might expect, there were a few rough spots.

Luckily, installation was smooth and simple. The comprehensive installation process automatically detects if an existing WINSOCK.DLL is running. If not, you can either install California Software's WINSOCK.DLL and TCP/IP stack with PPP support (which comes automatically with InterAp), or use another vendor's stack. All major TCP/IP stacks are supported. And as an installation bonus, InterAp provides handy information about rates, locations, and services offered by several Internet providers. The release we reviewed did not have a built-in dialer; according to California Software, one will be included in Version 1.0, due out by the time you read this.

Once InterAp is installed, configuration is a breeze: You use the pull-down menus to customize everything from font sizes and colors to your own Telnet and 3270 emulation packages.

Though it's a 16-bit application, InterAp is nonetheless quick. It makes up for any lost speed by transferring data in both asynchronous and block modes, an ability inherent to Cello-based applications. (In contrast, products based on NCSA Mosaic code, such as AIR Mosaic, can transfer data only asynchronously.)

Now you're ready to work the Web. Similar to Spyglass's Enhanced NCSA Mosaic, Web Navigator gives you speedy Internet access from its home page, which is stored on the local hard disk. Once you're there, Web Navigator's interface makes navigation easy. Hot buttons and pull-down menus smoothly guide you through the Web and its sundry services. Like most of the products in this roundup, Web Navigator lets you create a hotlist to store your favorite home pages. You can then categorize bookmarks into folders to organize your stockpile of home pages better—just as in AIR Mosaic.

Some peculiarities did surface, though. When navigating between several loaded documents, Web Navigator lets you jump backward only with a hot button. To jump forward, you have to use the menu. (This will be fixed in Version 1.0.) Accessing a hypertext link is also a little quirky—you have to double-click the mouse instead of single-clicking, as with other browsers. California Software assured us, however, that this too will be corrected with Version 1.0. Also, when receiving a document with multiple .GIFs, Web Navigator does not indicate the percentage received. This information can be crucial in determining whether your system is hung or if you're just connected to a slow host.

Web Navigator is among the few products in this category to offer OLE 2.0 support, which lets you link to documents with other OLE 2.0-compliant applications. You can drag a hyperlink from a Web site and drop it in a Microsoft Word 6.0 document, for example, or automate tasks such as gathering information and placing it in a document. And with Web Navigator's scheduler module, these tasks can take place after hours when Internet traffic is lighter.

With InterAp, California Software has rolled out an impressive suite of Internet tools—including an excellent Web browser. If the official release fulfills the promise of the prerelease version, InterAp should be a tough contender.—Padraic Boyle

InterAp
California Software Inc.
(714) 675-9906
support@calsoft.com
$295

NCSA Mosaic

If you have direct or dial-up TCP/IP Internet access and don't have NCSA Mosaic, Version 2.0, wait no longer to download this World Wide Web browser (ftp.ncsa.uiuc.edu). Mosaic 2.0, younger sibling of the browser that started it all, is available free of charge (though not yet officially released) over the Internet for noncommercial purposes. (Licensing for commercial use is possible through Spyglass, whose Mosaic product is also reviewed here.)

Mosaic 2.0 is a 32-bit application for Microsoft Windows 3.1, Windows for Workgroups, Windows NT, and OS/2. But unless you run Windows NT, you'll need your vendor's 32-bit extensions for Windows (Microsoft's 32-bit extensions for Windows—Win32s, Version 1.1.5a—are in the same directory as Mosaic 2.0). For those who can't run 32-bit applications, two old, unsupported 16-bit versions (Version 1.0 and Version 2.0 Alpha 2) are still available from NCSA.

Thanks to a great installation guide and FAQ document, installing Mosaic 2.0 is a snap. If you need more information, you can order it via the Mosaic support line or by e-mail (orders@ncsa.uiuc.edu).

Mosaic 2.0 will run as-is from the distribution package, but you may want to make some changes to MOSAIC.INI, such as adding your e-mail address and defining your SMTP and NNTP servers for Usenet News. If your system has sufficient RAM, increasing the setting for the number of automatically cached documents will speed access to recently viewed pages.

When you run Mosaic 2.0, the first thing you'll see is NCSA's home page, which includes links to Mosaic 2.0's online documentation and Web-server directories. The documentation contains such useful information as how to configure any necessary viewers. (NCSA's upcoming GUI configuration tool should make this a lot simpler.)

Mosaic 2.0 includes a couple of useful feedback tools: Tool Tips identifies each toolbar button's function, and the status bar displays URLs as you move the cursor over them and informs you of a page's download size and progress.

Mosaic 2.0 also provides three tools for managing URLs. You can annotate pages you've visited; each annotation is then displayed as a URL at the bottom of the page the next time you open it. You can create a hotlist of URLs—a good way to store those you access infrequently. And you can build cascaded menus of URLs using the Menu Editor. Both the hotlist and the Menu Editor let you open URLs from pull-down menus.

Although HTML standards are still being defined, Mosaic 2.0 is almost fully HTML, Version 2-compliant. This means you can use most

Internet resources, including forms, ftp, gopher, newsgroups, Telnet, and WAIS. Newsgroup support is limited to read-only, however; no tools to manage subscriptions to newsgroups are available. Mosaic 2.0 does not support MAILTO URLs (which allow you to send e-mail directly from the browser), but NCSA plans to implement this feature soon.

Mosaic 2.0 lets you view or save the HTML source of a page. You can also print the formatted page or even use a Print Preview feature, but these tools are still unreliable. NCSA hopes they'll be bug-free by the official Version 2.0 release.

Site administrators should be pleased with Mosaic 2.0's advanced features. Kiosk Mosaic disables configuration-editing options to prevent unauthorized changes. Mosaic 2.0 also supports proxy gateways, and, in a joint effort with Spyglass, NCSA plans to add data encryption and authentication and digital signature support.

Aside from a few quirks and bugs, Mosaic 2.0 is a stellar Web browser. Having paved the way for others, it remains at the leading edge of this new and exciting technology.—Sean Gonzalez

NCSA Mosaic
National Center for
Supercomputing Applications
University of Illinois
Champagne, IL
(217) 244-3473
orders@ncsa.uiuc.edu

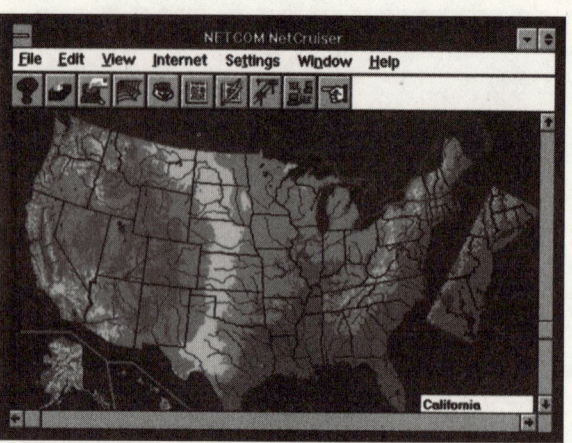

NetCruiser

Using Netcom On-Line Communication Services' NetCruiser, Version 1.50, means taking the bad with the good. Although there's much to like about NetCruiser and its Web browser, there's also much that may fail to please.

Part of NetCruiser's appeal is that it comes free with subscriber service to Netcom's Internet access service, which is $19.95 a month with a $25 startup fee. (Note that the software works only with this service.) NetCruiser offers a variety of Internet tools, including a separate Web browser. Connecting to the Internet in this manner is absolutely painless; NetCruiser handles all of the messy network-connection details.

The other side of the access equation, however, is that using Netcom's service limits you to the proprietary NetCruiser tools. So if you like NetCruiser's Web browser, you're sitting pretty; if you dislike it, this could be a problem.

Chances are you will like the NetCruiser browser, as it affords easy access to World Wide Web servers. A well-designed toolbar lets you navigate through previously chosen Web sites as well as add sites to a list of bookmarks. In a move that 14.4-Kbps modem users will love, the NetCruiser browser provides full information about the status of a page download, telling you how much of the page has been grabbed and how much is to come—including graphics files. Anyone who's sat through the interminable download of a massive .GIF—or of a .GIF-studded page—will appreciate this level of feedback.

NetCruiser and the Web browser seem clearly intended for Internet novices; unfortunately, the browser is configured with a minimum of interesting Web sites. Users are also expected to know a Web site's URL or its physical location. The only linked searching tool is the CERN Web-server listings, which tends to be more difficult to use than indexes such as

Carnegie-Mellon's Lycos. Netcom also provides its own home page and linked pages for NetCruiser users; though these are useful, they could be expanded to provide a larger view of the vast WWW.

The NetCruiser browser's performance was regrettably inconsistent. Out of 19 test connections, the browser failed to connect to a Web server five times. Twice it connected but then choked on the resulting home page, returning an error message. Additionally, we experienced two general system failures that may have been due to the network connection.

Part of the problem lies in the frequent NetCruiser upgrades released during the evaluation period (indeed, it sometimes seemed like upgrade *du jour*). It's clear that the code hasn't achieved an acceptable level of stability, as evidenced by the system crashes and errors. The flip side, of course, is that Netcom seems committed to bringing out new versions of NetCruiser as needed.

In the end, NetCruiser is an adequate tool for novices who want relatively painless exposure to the Internet and are willing to contend with some stability issues. More sophisticated Internet users who need a reliable, robust Web browser may find their needs better served elsewhere.—Kevin Reichard

NetCruiser
Netcom On-Line
Communication Services Inc.
San Jose, CA
(800) 501-8649; (408) 983-5970
info@netcom.com

wants to admit it, but the more anonymous and sexually explicit the service, the more successful it is. It's a dirty secret nobody wants to discuss. 🖥 Before I go on, let me say that I'm

Netscape Navigator

With all the media hype surrounding NCSA Mosaic, the question on everyone's mind is: Can the Web move beyond this alleged "killer app?" Judging from the early release of Netscape Navigator we downloaded in November, the answer seems to be yes. This sparkling new freeware browser from Netscape Communications Corp. is still under construction but is available via ftp from ftp.mcom.com/netscape/. The designers of Netscape were on the original NCSA Mosaic team, and from the looks of things, they've learned from that pioneer product's triumphs and shortcomings. Netscape is designed with a finer understanding of what people want from the Web: faster graphics and fewer configuration hassles.

Installation is simple: Download the file, unzip it, move the NETSCAPE.INI file to the Windows directory (if you've never used any other version of Mosaic before), and manually add the icon to a program group. Be warned that crucial configuration information isn't available in the beta .ZIP file; Version 1.0, however, will have the info. You have to connect to the home.mcom.com site to find out which TCP/IP stacks have been tested with the browser—an annoying Catch 22. (At press time, the freeware product Trumpet, Chameleon's NetManage, ftp Software's PCTCP, Microsoft Windows for Workgroups, and Microsoft NT had all been tested.)

Once the package is loaded and linking, you may never want to log off again. Netscape positively crackles compared with older browsers. Part of the speed may be attributable to psychology; Netscape keeps you so well informed about your transfer status (by byte count and status thermometer) that no time is spent fretting over it. This perception is enhanced by the "fade-in" effect: When Netscape links to a server using Netscape Communications' server software, you can view graphics before they've entirely arrived. Saving to disk and printing work as expected; however, a few of the more advanced Web pages, particularly those with forms, proved troublesome to access. (It's unclear whether the fault lay with Netscape or the server.)

To retrieve help information, you have to go online, but help and certain other pages linked to Netscape Communications' home page are well-chosen and are echoed on the main screen by a set of interface buttons. Netscape doesn't allow you to import old lists from NCSA Mosaic, but that's not a problem; designing a new hotlist is a treat. The program keeps track of the pages, when they were created, and any notes you care to make about them (a welcome throwback to the old Annotate function in NCSA Mosaic). You can also arrange pages into submenus and use the search engine to page through the list if it gets too long.

Two of Netscape's navigation aids can truly enhance your travels. First, you can keep track of your links for days, weeks, or even a year after you've first used them. Second, the history list (which is configurable to take up as much memory as you wish) makes it easy to generate bookmark items you've already seen without actually having to be in the page.

Netscape also graciously forgives bad habits. For example, if you start loading an image type you don't have a viewer for, Netscape reminds you that an application hasn't been chosen and asks if you want to try anyway, abort, or save to disk. And scrolling down mid-transfer doesn't faze the software; pages continue loading without incident. This is a real boon if you're impatient when grabbing graphics-heavy pages.

That Netscape was built to work with proprietary server software called Netsite doesn't really seem to matter. (Netscape Communications is giving away the browser to encourage sales of its server software to Web sites.) It's still a star, even as a solo act. The lack of configuration files may intimidate the novice user, but even slightly experienced Internet surfers should download Netscape and check out the future of World Wide Web browsers. What the heck—it's free.—Angela Gunn

Netscape Navigator
Netscape Communications Corp.
Mountain View, CA
(800) 638-7483
info@mcom.com

Web Explore

Some packages require you to change your TCP/IP stack, but IBM's Web Explorer actually asks you to change your operating system. Web Explorer is part of a package of Internet tools and services called Internet Connection for OS/2 that IBM is essentially giving away with the new OS/2 Warp, Version 3.

As of November, this product was freely available only as a prerelease version; upon completion it will be freely available to all OS/2 Warp users. To get Web Explorer, just click the Update Software icon in the Internet Access group of

WELCOME TO NETSCAPE

ESCAPES | COMPANY & PRODUCTS | NETSCAPE STORE | NEWS & REFERENCE | ASSISTANCE | COMMUNITY

munityCommunityCommunityCommunityCommunit

not necessarily objecting to any of this (I'm no prude). It's just interesting to me that the American public at large and the Information Highway-crazed news media don't have a clue as

OS/2 Warp's interface and the program will be downloaded from the Internet. Those with earlier versions of OS/2 can download the browser at ftpq1.ny.us.ibm.net.

As of this review—and as far as we or IBM knows—Web Explorer is the only native OS/2 Web browser on the market. Built from the ground up by the folks at Big Blue, it's neither a rehash of an existing Windows-based product nor a minimalist make-do. Web Explorer is a complete, full-featured browser designed to take specific advantage of the operating system.

IBM has done an excellent job of making connections to its Internet access service (the IBM Global Network, also called Advantis) transparent to users. Setup is no more complicated than filling in a couple of details about your system and location. Once it has the necessary info, the system dials out and registers you automatically.

You can, of course, use Web Explorer with other access providers, but you're on your own if problems crop up. Web Explorer's extensive online help doesn't deal with non-IBM connections. (Although IBM has clearly designed the product with modem-based connections in mind, Web Explorer can also be used with a direct LAN-based TCP/IP connection.)

OS/2 Warp's browser is easy to navigate: Buttons and pull-down menus guide you effortlessly through the Web

and its services. When navigating between several loaded documents, you can move backward and forward with the click of a button. Like most of the products we tested, Web Explorer lets you store your favorite home pages in an easily accessible hotlist. Web Explorer (like Frontier Technologies' WinTapestry) goes beyond standard capabilities to let you access multiple Web pages simultaneously, but OS/2 Warp's multitasking capabilities make the process smoother than with other products. You can even run multiple sessions of Web Explorer simultaneously.

The Web explorer is also easy to configure. A pull-down menu lets you customize everything from font sizes and colors to the use of your own applets for file viewing.

In addition to Web Explorer, IBM's Internet Connection for OS/2 provides a complete set of native OS/2 tools for accessing Internet services. The list of applications includes e-mail, ftp, a news reader, and Telnet.

Despite the fact that it is quite literally in a category by itself, Web Explorer is clearly going to be a major contender in the Web browser arena. It may be the only OS/2 game in town, but it's definitely one you'd want to play in. We strongly recommend that all OS/2 users check it out. Of course, you can't run it under Windows. But if IBM smiles and says "That's the

point," you can hardly blame them.—Amarendra Singh

> *Web Explorer*
> *IBM Corp.*
> *Armonk, NY*
> *(800) 342-6672*

WinTapestry

Frontier Technologies Corp.'s WinTapestry is a stellar tool for sampling the wares of the World Wide Web. Preconfigured to connect with an amazing 410 archie, ftp, gopher, veronica, WWW, and WAIS servers, WinTapestry is among the most fully prewired browsers in existence. Unfortunately, getting its parent program, the $149 SuperHighway Access for Windows, properly installed and configured can be a bit of a headache.

Before installing SuperHighway Access, you'll need to have either a preexisting dial-up account with an Internet service provider (Frontier provides none) or an existing TCP/IP connection. Frontier does, however, include scripts for 53 modems and log-in configurations for 44 service providers, subdivided by protocol (CSLIP, PPP, or SLIP).

For many Internet users, this configuration process will probably seem pretty arcane—after all, dial-up connections have a well-deserved reputation for being finicky. If your dial-up script doesn't work immediately—as was the case when we connected to the Minnesota

Regional Network, for example—you may find yourself experimenting with the underdocumented SuperHighway Access scripting language to work out the problem.

Telephone support from Frontier (which is available only to registered users of the company's SuperTCP product and requires a long-distance call to suburban Milwaukee) was adequate, if slow. In the end, problems were solved by the time-consuming process of trying several slightly different scripts over and over. We can't blame Frontier for the anarchy among dial-up service providers, but the product's documentation—both printed and online—should devote more attention to the daunting task of configuration.

Since SuperHighway Access is Winsock 1.1-compliant, you can use it with any other Winsock-compliant tools you fancy, such as Cello, NCSA Mosaic, or Netscape Navigator. You probably won't want to, though, as WinTapestry is (as we mentioned) preconfigured to take you effortlessly to an amazing number of sites on the Internet—perhaps as many as 1,000 if you count all the secondary (submenu) links.

The World Wide Web was envisioned as a vast supranational pool of universally accessible information. In theory, it shouldn't matter if the information is maintained on an ftp, gopher, or Web server; more importantly, the user

shouldn't need to make these distinctions, either.

WinTapestry fulfills this egalitarian promise by organizing sources by subject, such as politics, education, or science. Want to grab some position papers from your state government? Just click on Government Information under the Politics menu and you'll be presented with a list of states. You don't need to worry if the ultimate destination is an ftp, gopher, Telnet, Usenet newsgroup, or Web site. (There is explicit support for archie, gopher, veronica, and WAIS servers within WinTapestry, however, should you need them.)

Adding your personal favorite Web resource is delightfully easy; just select the Add button on the toolbar and attach the resource to the appropriate category—or create your own set of categories. Instead of placing an emphasis on the process of cruising the Internet, SuperHighway Access puts the emphasis on the content within the Internet—a crucial difference that most Web browsers fail to address.

Unfortunately, you'll need separate SuperHighway Access tools to access mail and newsgroups. With their varied interfaces, the SuperHighway tools are more a collection of disparate programs than a unified package for browsing the World Wide Web.

This doesn't diminish the ultimate worth of WinTapestry, however. If you're looking for a Web browser that points you in

WinWeb International

the direction of hundreds of useful resources, WinTapestry should be on your short list of contenders. Just walk in with your eyes wide open—and build in some frustration time when configuring your dial-up connection.—Kevin Reichard

WinTapestry
Frontier Technologies Corp.
Mequon, WI
(414) 241-4555
superhighway@Frontiertech.com

WinWeb

With the explosion of Web browsers on the market, more and more companies are trying to differentiate their products based on content. WinWeb, from EINet, certainly seems to be taking that route: Its browser offers no extraordinary features, but its integration with EINet's Galaxy site gives you access to some stellar information. And that alone sets WinWeb apart.

You can download WinWeb from ftp.einet.net as a .ZIP file containing the application and viewers for .GIF, text, and .WAV files. Setup is simple and well-described in the included README file. But as we said, WinWeb's access stands out in one important respect: its

integration with the EINet Galaxy site.

This terrific World Wide Web site offers a comprehensive and varied starting home page. In addition to a range of links—from amateur radio to societal law—the site provides a search engine that allows you to search the local galaxy server, other Web sites, or even gopher servers. Though the Galaxy page is your default home page, you can change this to a different Web page or local file if you like.

This package ranks right in the middle for ease of navigation. WinWeb supports history lists, pages you have traveled to during the current session, and hotlists—permanent lists of oft-visited pages. All are reliable and easy to access, but two important features are missing: a Move Forward button for when you're navigating through a range of pages (oddly, a Move Back button is provided) and the ability to keep multiple hotlists or to add pages to the hotlist with a single click, both of which would make your travels on the Web more efficient.

When you load a page, the browser keeps you informed of transfer status in a small pop-up window; it also shows details about the current page and URL links

defined in the document. One complaint: The page doesn't load until all its images have transferred, making it seem slow. Forms work as they should, and WinWeb's overall compliance with both HTML and Microsoft Windows is good. WinWeb's error messages are clear, to the point, and accurate. Print (with Print Preview) and Save to File features are provided.

Although customizing certain features (such as fonts and background colors) is easy, you'll find yourself editing the .INI file if you ever change or add viewers, since you can't do it within the program. The toolbar is limited and noncustomizable. Furthermore, WinWeb supports neither e-mail nor newsreaders.

Infoactive

Infoactive, a new bulletin on telecommunications issues for the nonprofit community, reports on the latest Internet developments, explains communications technologies, and analyzes legislation in Congress, the White House, and the Federal Communications Commission.

WinWeb has some great things to offer—its basic features, a well-thought-out guide to Internet resources, and a strikingly rich home page—making it a package to consider for most users. But it definitely has some strikes against it that may make you think twice: the inability to do newsgroups and e-mail and some navigational awkwardness.—Angela Gunn

WinWeb
EINet
Austin TX
(800) 844-4638
winweb@einet.net

Published by the Center for Media Education in Washington, D.C., InfoActive reports on how nonprofit organizations can take advantage of government-sponsored grants and pilot projects.—Carol Levin

Infoactive
Published by the Center for Media Education
cme@access .digex.net
(202) 628-2620
$35/yr for individuals, nonprofit organizations, and the government
$100 for corporations

Trumpet Winsock

In order to use sophisticated Windows Internet tools, you need a piece of software that provides a networking layer between Windows and the Internet. Trumpet Winsock will do that for you. Be forewarned, though, that due to the complex nature of the Internet, Winsock can be a chore to set up.

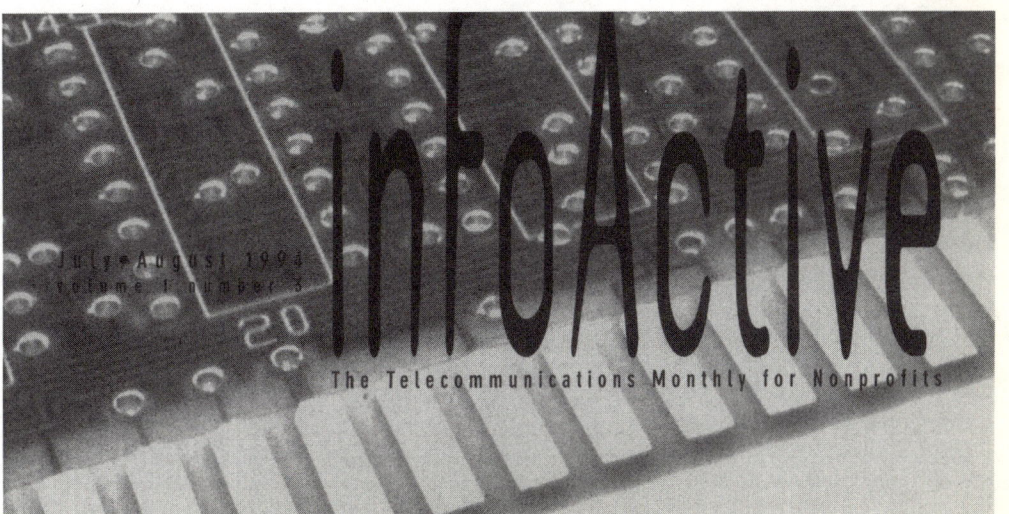

ers has been its CB chat sessions, in which you chat (type, actually) anonymously. You can join the CB Simulator and assume a name such as Don Juan or Mr. Big Stuff or Lois the

Winsock is going to ask you for a lot of very detailed and specific information about your Internet setup that you need to get from your Internet provider. That means that the most important thing you can do is pick the right provider, one that supplies this information, preferably in written form, supplemented by phone support.

The following is some of the vital information that you will need from your provider: your IP address (such as 199.7.128.112), your network mask (such as 255.255.0), your default Internet gateway (such as 199.0.65.1), your name server (such as 199.0.65.2192.94.207.66), and your domain suffix (such as tiac.net). Leave the Time Server information blank, as Trumpet doesn't require it. Also, note that when putting in your IP address, you will need to put it in numerical form (as above) rather than in an address format such as johndoe@tiac.net.

There are other details you'll need to know as well. For example, you should click on the Hardware Handshake option if you're dialing in at 9,600 bps or higher—and you should be connecting at high speed if you want to access graphical Internet tools like the World Wide Web. It's especially important to find out if you should click on the Compressed SLIP option, too. You'll also need to put in the phone number you're dialing and your name and password.

When you get all this information entered correctly,

you should be ready to go. Click on Internal SLIP when you're done with setup, then run the program, click on the Dialer menu, and choose Login. Winsock should dial your service, log you in, and establish a connection. —Preston Gralla

Trumpet Winsock
Trumpet Software International
GPO Box 1649
Hobart, Tasmania
7001 Australia

Cello

Mosaic gets all the press, but the truth is, it's not the only Windows-based Web browser. Cello, a little-known gem developed at Cornell, also enables you to browse through the Web. As with Mosaic, you can launch ftp, gopher, and Telnet sessions, but with Cello, you receive the added benefit of built-in Internet mail.

To use ftp, for example, you choose Launch FTP Session from the Jump menu, then type in the ftp location. The program displays the directory structure graphically, with folders representing directories, and document icons representing files. Double-clicking on files automatically brings up a dialog box for download. The same thing holds true for gopher: Type in the name of the gopher and you get a fully graphical screen.

Unlike Mosaic, which requires additional software to support Telnet, Telnet is built into Cello, which pops

up a terminal window for your session. Sending mail with Cello is also as simple as choosing a menu item, but you should realize that replies will be directed to the mailbox you entered into Cello as your main e-mail address; the program does not have an in-box.

Note that for the setup of the program, you'll need to know not just your own Internet address, but also the address of your mail server and your news server. If you don't put in the mail address, you won't be able to send mail, and if you don't put in the news server, you won't be able to access news documents linked to Web pages. Unlike Mosaic, which requires you to enter an INI file to configure the news server, it's just a menu item on Cello.

Like the latest version of Mosaic, Cello offers printing. It allows you not only to print the page you're viewing, but to save it as a text file, whereas Mosaic is still only capable of saving in HTML.

While some of Cello's non-Web tools are a step ahead of Mosaic, it doesn't measure up in look and feel for Web browsing. Cello doesn't have the handsome, sculpted look that Mosaic does, and it handles scrolling oddly: The program waits until you let go of the mouse button to show you how far you've scrolled. Other goodies, like internal sound support for AU files, are also missing. —Preston Gralla

WSGopher

Gopher servers organize text and files so that you can find what you want easily. Nevertheless, while Web browsers like Mosaic and Cello support gopher, they lack the convenience of WSGopher.

In the first place, WSGopher supports multiple gophers simultaneously. This way, you can keep several open at a time and switch between them. You can even set bookmarks for places that you visit frequently, including categories like Environment or Music. The program also includes categorical groupings for dozens of gophers for a quick look at the best of the Internet.

Especially useful is WSGopher's printing and file-saving options, so that you never lose the text articles you find combing the online circuits. Support for gopher file transfers rounds out the interface.—Preston Gralla

WinWAIS

One way to find information on the Internet is through a database tool called WAIS (Wide Area Information Servers). WAIS uses sophisticated search techniques to quickly sift through indexed articles and information on remote servers. And WAIS is one tool that's difficult to use through Web browsers like Mosaic and Cello.

WinWAIS puts a graphical, Windows layer on top of

WAIS's Unix-based search engine. With WinWAIS, you scroll through a list of resources that you want to search, type in your search request—which can be in the form of a sentence, a partial sentence, or a word—and then wait for the results. When you get your list of responses, notice the rating system of stars. The files on the list with the most number of stars are the most likely to match your search, while those with the least number of stars (or none at all) are the least likely candidates.

At this point, you can ask WinWAIS to "match" any document that you've selected from the list as an example of what you would like to see, narrowing the search to other similar documents and saving valuable search time.

When the program sends you a document that matches your request, you can browse through it, print it, and save it to file. WinWAIS also highlights the search term that you used for quick reference to pertinent portions of the article.—Preston Gralla

FTP Client for Windows

FTP (file transfer protocol) is the general method for obtaining files from the Internet, but command-line versions are generally clumsy, and Web browsers like Mosaic have limited support for ftp through what is known as "passive mode," which doesn't work with all servers.

Hooker (be you male or female) and chat with all sorts of people. It's all virtual and nobody is certain whom they're talking to. You can go into private virtual "rooms" and exchange

FTP Client for Windows maintains a simple list of ftp locations, then makes it easy to transfer files once you get where you want to go. The software splits your screen into two windows, displaying files on your local PC on the left and the files on the remote system on the right. To transfer files to your computer, you highlight a file on the right, click on the arrow button, and your file is transferred to the directory of your choice. It's that simple.

There are a lot of nice tools here: You can read text files from the ftp site while online or scroll back through your session to see what you've done. The program also comes prefigured with a large list of ftp sites on which you can build your own hot list.

Another nice touch is that as long as you set the file associations properly, you can launch files upon transfer. For example, if you set the association for a GIF file to a particular GIF graphics viewer, when you click on the Execute button, it will transfer the file, then launch your viewing application and display the image.—Preston Gralla

Trumpet News Reader

For many people, the Internet means one thing: participating in Usenet newsgroups. Usenet is a series of global discussion groups about every topic imaginable—and no doubt many topics that you've never imagined. Trumpet

News Reader lists all the newsgroups available to you, and it keeps you updated about new groups once you've subscribed to your favorites.

Note that you'll need to know the name of your Internet news host (the server that your Internet service provider has dedicated to handle the newsgroups feed) before you'll be able to use this program. Type the address in a form such as mydog@giallo.net, where "mydog" represents the news host and "gialo" represents the service provider.

Usenet vets also will like the threading feature, which organizes messages by topic rather than as one chronological list.—Preston Gralla

Trumpet News Reader
Trumpet Software International
G.P.O. Box 1649
Hobart, Tasmania
7001 Australi
Registration Fee: $40

HOW TO TAME A WILD PROTOCOL

Chameleon-TCP/IP 4.0 for Windows

TCP/IP is one of the most contrary network protocols known to man. It's also, however, the networking protocol of choice for minicomputers, workstations, and the Internet. NetManage's Chameleon-TCP/IP for Windows tames this savage protocol with numerous TCP/IP utilities, a small memory footprint, and relatively easy installation and configuration programs.

Compared to installing such popular TCP/IP programs as FTP Software's PC/TCP for DOS and Windows, Chameleon's installation is a snap. Chameleon also does well at coexisting with other network protocols such as NetWare's IPX. Since Chameleon's TCP/IP stack is implemented

as a Windows Dynamic Link Library (DLL), it takes up only 6K of conventional memory. This makes managing multiple protocols much easier since a shortage of base memory is often the straw that breaks the multiple networks on a single system camel's back.

Experienced TCP/IP administrators will also be happy to find that Chameleon can run multiple TCP/IP sessions. With this ability, you can concurrently connect with a local file server using Ethernet with TCP/IP, while also connecting with a remote mail server over a phone line with the Serial Line Internet Protocol (SLIP). In theory, Chameleon can support as many as 128 TCP/IP sessions.

For any of these connections, Chameleon supplies more than the usual assortment of DEC terminal emulations. The program also comes with a top-notch 3270 emulator, making it easy to connect with IBM mainframes. Best of all, Chameleon comes with a 5250 emulator, which lets you work with IBM AS/400 minicomputers—good 5250 emulators like Chameleon's are scarcer than hen's teeth. Any office using TCP/IP to connect with AS/400s should seriously consider Chameleon for this reason alone. Chameleon also supports PROFS, an IBM mainframe e-mail sys-

tem. Chameleon's support of IBM business protocols and programs, and its more commonplace TCP/IP support for workstations and VAX minicomputers, makes it uniquely qualified for offices that use everything from mainframes to PCs.

As good as it is, Chameleon TCP/IP for Windows doesn't support the Network File System (NFS) and X-Windows. These two standards of heavy-duty TCP/IP network work can be found in other Chameleon packages. If you discover after you've bought Chameleon that you need NFS and/or X-Windows support, NetManage will sell you the upgraded version for the price difference between vanilla Chameleon and the augmented Chameleon.

Most users will be delighted with Chameleon's suite of Internet applications. Chameleon comes with a Usenet newsreader and a simple mail-transfer protocol called SMTP; this is the Internet standard e-mail front end and mail gateway.

The Usenet reader lets you read, reply, and start Usenet news messages. The program also lets you sort messages by author, date, or subject. While this is not as strong as the threading capacities of native Internet newsreaders like trn or nn, it is superior to such PC newsreaders as the one provided in Spry's Internet in a Box.

The e-mail front end, however, is first-class all the way. The program supports not

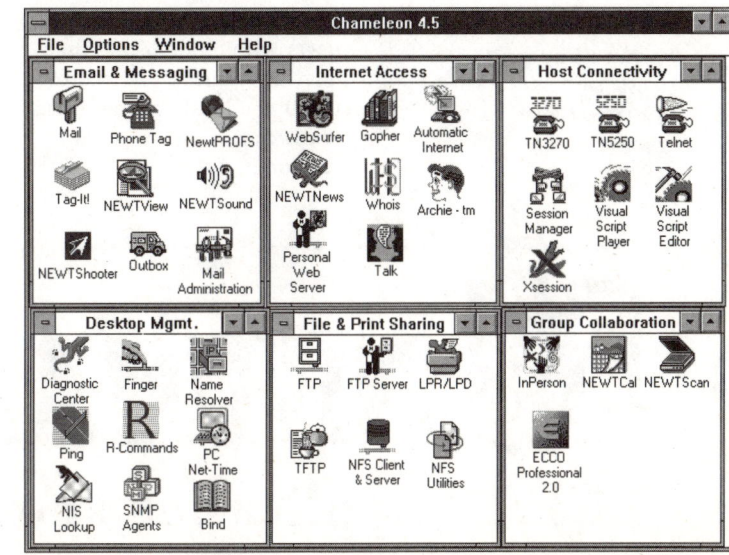

only normal ASCII mail, but supports binary and multimedia file transfers with the Multipurpose Mail Internet Extensions (MIME). The e-mail front end also comes with an address book, automatic mail checking, and user-adjustable mail filters a la Lotus's cc:Mail. In brief, this is simply the best Internet e-mail front end around.

To access Internet information resources, Chameleon comes with a gopher client. This is a real plus, since most TCP/IP products do not come with a gopher. The program, unlike some gopher clients, clearly illustrates whether the resource you're accessing is a directory of other resources or a resource in its own right. Chameleon's gopher integrates well with Windows. For example, when you access a text file, this gopher automatically brings the file up in your default word processor.

If gopher leads you to files, you can use Chameleon's file transfer protocol (ftp) to download them. While this is far easier to use than native ftp commands, there are better ftp implementations available. Spry's Internet in a Box version, for example, lets you ftp files using what appear to be merely Windows File Manager windows.

For other file and information searches, you'll need additional programs. For instance, Chameleon doesn't come with a World Wide Web (WWW) browser.

Chameleon's TCP/IP stack, however, does support Mosaic and Cello, the two most popular WWW browsers, should you wish to load these yourself. All of Chameleon's applications work well, but there is room for improvement. For example, you can't read a highlighted message in either the mail or newsreader programs by pressing the Return key. In these situations, you must still mouse-click on the highlighted item.—Steven J. Vaughan-Nichols

Chameleon-TCP/IP 4.0 for Windows
NetManage Inc.
10725 N. DeAnza Blvd.
Cupertino, CA 95014
(408) 973-7171
$400

NOTHING BUT THE NET
Internet Chameleon

According to the box, installing this scaled-down version of the $499 Chameleon 4.0 package should take five minutes. We took about an hour. After clicking through the last dialog box, we were smoothly running the NetManage Enhanced Windows TCP/IP (NEWT) stack and Chameleon's eight Internet utilities.

If you get Internet access from a major provider, scripts to automate the configuration process are prebuilt. On the other hand, setting up a PPP connection for a new provider can be overly complicated.

NEWTnews, Chameleon's News Reader, forces you to work with a single list of articles. Sorting by subject line helps organize articles but is a poor substitute for a true, threaded news reader.

Thanks to support for Multipurpose Internet Mail Extensions (MIME), the mail client can send and receive multimedia attachments. It can filter incoming mail using rules and user-defined folders and handle binary attachments. You can also hide address headers and build address book entries from incoming messages.

The tree-oriented gopher client works well (although we couldn't automatically view files using anything except Notepad). The ftp client is a mess as far as usability goes, with a slew of unintuitive buttons and nonstandard controls. But with the single exception of the ftp client, this is a solid package that really provides everything you need at a reasonable price.

Internet Chameleon
NetManage
(408) 973-7171
sales@netmanage.com
$199

UNTANGLE THE WEB WITH MOSAIC
Mosaic

The Internet is chaos in action. Bringing order to the chaos has been the goal of several Internet projects including gopher, archie, and veronica. The most interesting project right now is the World Wide Web, which uses hypertext- and image-filled rich-text-format documents to guide you through vast amounts of information. And the most popular way to navigate the World Wide Web is with Mosaic.

If that sounds too good to be true, it is. Mosaic can be difficult to get running. But it doesn't have to be. Here are simple, step-by-step instructions for getting your PC and modem talking to the Internet with Mosaic. In addition to these instructions, you'll find several zipped archives on PC Contact that contain everything you need to get started.

This article is for Windows users with modems. If you have an Internet connection through a local area network, know that your setup is a stallion of a slightly alternate

hue. See your systems administrator for details.

To get started, of course, you need a modem, and if you're serious about working with Mosaic don't even bother with anything less than 14.4Kbps (28.8Kbps is much better if your service provider supports it). Second, you need an Internet account with a Point-to-Point Protocol (PPP) or Serial Line Internet Protocol (SLIP, pronounced "slip") connection. Third, you need software that lets Windows communicate in TCP/IP (Transmission Control Protocol/Internet Protocol—the communications standard for the Net). And last but not least, you need Mosaic itself.

There are several other ways to connect to the Internet. Two of the most common are gateways and shell accounts. Gateways are usually limited to exchanging e-mail between an online service such as CompuServe and the Internet. With a shell account, you dial in to a computer that's on the Internet and use that computer to send e-mail and access various Internet utilities. Mosaic won't work with either of these types of access systems.

Mosaic requires your computer to actually be "on" the Internet—speaking the Internet Protocol.

Fortunately, Internet service providers are popping up all over. Check the ads in your local newspaper, phone your computer store, or download the file PDIAL.TXT from PC Contact's data library 3 (Utilities/Misc.). If none of these pans out, you can try two of the larger international service providers: UUNET Technologies at (800) 488-6384 and Performance Systems International (PSI) at (800) 827-7482.

When you call the service provider to set up your connection, specify that you need either a SLIP or PPP account—these are the types of connections that Mosaic can use over modem lines. Most providers offer both. With SLIP or PPP, your computer essentially becomes a node on the Internet. (There are lots of things you can do without SLIP or PPP—like reading e-mail and browsing newsgroups—but running Mosaic on your PC isn't one of them.)

Acquire the following details about your account from the service provider: Your IP (Internet Protocol) address, netmask, default gateway, e-mail address, and name server (sometimes called a domain naming system, or DNS). You'll need these when installing some of the networking software that runs under Mosaic (specifically, Trumpet Winsock).

Usually, you'll be provided with these details when you subscribe.

Let's say you have your account and its associated information in hand. Next, you'll need two bits of software to launch your Mosaic session. The first one is Trumpet Winsock, the best of the shareware packages for enabling TCP/IP in Windows. The other package is Mosaic itself. Both are available on the Internet, but we've bundled them together and placed them on PC Contact. If you have access to PC Contact, you need only download and unzip the appropriate bundle. Otherwise, contact Public Brand Software at (800) 426-3475 to get the files you want on disk (for a modest packaging and shipping fee). Or, if you already have some kind of access to the Internet (or know somebody who does), you can get the packages using the Internet's ftp procedure.

We're making six separate file archives available on PC Contact. Three contain the Trumpet Winsock package (if you don't already have TCP/IP and Winsock running under Windows) and various versions of Mosaic. The other three contain those versions of Mosaic, but cater to users who already have Winsock software installed. For the remainder of this article we'll assume that you need both Trumpet Winsock and Mosaic.

If you want to retrieve the files from the Internet, you'll need access to ftp. Any number of Internet books can

show you how ftp works; essentially, it lets you log in to a remote machine and download software. You'll find the Trumpet Winsock package at oak.oakland.edu, in the directory /pub/msdos/winsock. The filename is twsk10a.zip. Mosaic is available via ftp from ftp.ncsa.uiuc.edu, in the directory /PC/Mosaic. The 32-bit version is wmos20a7.zip, and the Win32 extensions are win32s.zip. If you want the 16-bit version, enter the directory /PC/Mosaic/old, and get the file called wmos20a2.zip.

Once you have the archives you need, create a directory called C:\WINSOCK and put them there. Then uncompress them. Next, create icons in Program Manager for your two new program files, TCP Manager (TCPMAN.EXE) and Mosaic (MOSAIC.EXE). You can do this by opening Program Manager, opening the Main program group, and selecting File, New, Program Item, then filling in the blanks in the resulting dialog box. After Command Line, enter the name of the program you're adding. Repeat the process for the other application.

There's a chance that your service provider offers Winsock software with easy installation instructions. If so, you won't need the Trumpet Winsock software we've provided. Some providers even have an automatic installation procedure for their Winsock package.

For now, however, let's assume that you're using Trumpet Winsock. To configure it, load the TCP Manager program. A setup screen will appear, asking for details such as IP address, domain suffix, gateways, and other information that your service provider should have sent. If you don't have that information, contact your provider. There's nothing you can do without it.

The Winsock data, when combined with your provider's SLIP or PPP service, makes it possible for your PC to become a full-fledged Internet node, at which point you can use Windows-based GUI software. Mosaic is one such program. **Note:** Configuring the socket software is the hardest part of the procedure. Once you've passed this stage, everything else should be easy. But until that happens, you can't go any further.

To get Mosaic running properly, you first need to copy the MOSAIC.INI file into your main Windows directory (typically C:\WINDOWS). If you want to run the latest version of Mosaic, 2.0alpha7, you'll need to install Microsoft's 32-bit Windows extensions. Since we're swell people, we included them with the PC Contact files. Unzip the files into a directory called WIN32TMP, then go to Program Manager, select File, Run and run C:\WIN32TMP\SETUP.EXE. (Actually, the name of the directory into which you

unzip your files isn't that important, but WIN32TMP is a good temporary resting place for the files.) You'll need roughly 1.5MB of free disk space.

The next step is to edit MOSAIC.INI very slightly, using any text editor (Notepad or Windows Write will do). In the first line, type your full e-mail address—your service provider should have provided you with one. Leave the other lines as they are, but eventually you might want to change them. In the PC Contact files, several of the other lines have been preset. The Home Page line, for example, automatically loads a document included with our files. You can change this if you want (although you'll be missing out on some very neat stuff). Also, the Grey Background feature has been set to "no," since white is more readable on Windows desktops. There are several other customization choices, letting you configure graphics viewers, and sound and video players. When you have Mosaic running, use File, Load Local File to call up MOSINI.HTM (included with the PC Contact files) which explains these options.

Close TCP Manager and your text editor, and then double-click on the Mosaic icon. A page titled "Welcome to Mosaic" will appear, and if you've ever used the Windows help system you'll immediately know what to do: Just click on one of the blue underlined hyperlinks, and you're off into the Web.

munityCommunityCommunityCommunityCommunit

online chatting. There are thousands and thousands of people doing it every minute. CompuServe has CB Simulator, GEnie has a chat system, and America Online (AOL) has something

Mosaic has two ways of letting you know what's going on. The first, the famous globe in the upper-right corner, spins when the program is retrieving data. The second, the status bar at the bottom, tells you precisely what is transpiring. If the globe keeps spinning but the status bar is still trying to get started, you have a bad connection somewhere. It might be your Winsock setup, but it might just as easily be a problem with the service provider or the remote computer. Generally, though, as long as Mosaic gets past the first status message, "Doing nameserver lookup," you can rest assured that you're up and running. After that, it's a matter of faith in telecommunications.

The "Welcome to Mosaic" page we've included with the PC Contact files connects you to some of the most useful sites on the Web. We've also added a PC Computing menu item in the menu bar with additional interesting sites. As you come to sites of your own, bookmark them by using the Navigate, Menu Editor feature. Once installed, Mosaic is a snap. And the World Wide Web is jammed with fascinating sites. Work or play, you'll find a great deal to do.—Neil Randall

The Net Connection

Now that the Internet's a reality and the shackles that hindered its business use have been removed, you may be wondering how it's going to translate promise into competitive advantage. It's true that the Net offers you global e-mail, constant updates to government information, an opportunity to expand customer support to the entire world, a huge reservoir of research resources, and new opportunities in marketing and advertising. But can it deliver? With a few caveats, yes.

The Problem
You want instant access to a broad spectrum of timely competitive data without having to subscribe to several expensive research services.

The Solution
Establish a high-speed Internet connection. This is the most expensive solution, although with integrated services digital network (ISDN) coming into play, high-speed connections are quickly becoming more realistic. You'll need a service provider and a high-speed switched-56Kbps line, or, if you have the funds to do it, a full T1 or even T3 line for maximum speed. An ISDN line will cost $30 to $100 per month, a leased line will run about $250 to $400 per month, and a T1/T3 line will be in the ballpark of $5,000 to $25,000 per month. You'll need high-quality hosts (usually Unix) and a full range of Internet software for every PC on your office network. Once it's all in place, you're ready to hit the ground racing. Sound daunting? It needn't. Internet access can be had inexpensively. As your needs increase, you'll find it cost effective to spend more on faster and higher-capacity access.

The Problem
You've got 20 users on the Internet, each working under his or her own name. If you're paying for the lines, you want to leverage the opportunity to establish a corporate presence amidst a potential audience.

The Solution
Register your own domain name. If your company's name is Fine Stuff, Inc., why should your e-mail address read joesmith@provider.net? Along with your initial connection, your service provider should be willing to help you register a unique name so that your e-mail, ftp, World Wide Web, and gopher addresses all share the finestuff.com label.

Make sure that employees dialing in can also have the finestuff.com domain name, whether or not they're working from a different type of account with the provider. This way, every time you go online you're building a corporate image—and the exposure is practically free, since you're paying for the service anyway. While some service providers will set up a domain name at no extra charge, others will bill you up to $50.

called the People Connection. There are hundreds of bulletin boards specializing in online chatting, and the Internet is totally out of control with its Internet Relay Chat (IRC) system.

The Problem

You're spending too much money on the time it takes several employees to peruse the Net in search of information.

The Solution

Establish your own gopher, World Wide Web, and ftp servers. The Net is flooded with information, but your employees don't have time to search for it. By establishing servers for ftp downloads, gopher directories, and World Wide Web pages on your company's host machines, you'll be able to offer continually updated information. The server plus the labor to install it will cost up to $5,000. But once you have it up and running, you can equip an information specialist with Internet access tools like NetCruiser from NetCom, or Spry's Internet in a Box. Or try InternetWorks from BookLinks Technologies, which was recently purchased by America Online. Frontier Technologies' SuperTCP for Windows offers an alternative product. The Pipeline, from the same-named company, is free software but you'll pay access fees.

The Problem

You want everyone to be fluent in Internet skills and your staff is eager to go. But simply sending them forth on their own risks wasting precious hours. What to do?

The Solution

Take advantage of the resources available offline. Mastering the Internet takes time, patience, and training. But while everything you need is on the Net itself, you can be much more efficient by making use of the increasing horde of offline materials available

to you. These include books, CD-ROMs, seminars—everything you could possibly want to know is out there in the bookstores, the computer shops, and the training rooms. Then get online, and watch productivity soar. To equip all of your employees, you may spend as little as a couple of hundred dollars or as much as a few thousand on books or CDs. Training seminars will cost more—often upwards of $2,000 to $3,000—but may be a more effective way to develop skills. You may want to train a few individuals and then slate time for them to share their new skills with their colleagues. The investment you make in training employees will pay off quickly and continuously as more vital information is exchanged and more business transactions are conducted online.—Neil Randall ◾

HTML ASSISTANT VERSUS HOTMETAL: INTERNET PUBLISHING MADE EASY

HTML Assistant Pro
HotMetal Pro

In the multimedia networking arena, very few services are even close to matching the hyperlink prowess of the Internet's World Wide Web. And if you've ever cruised the Web using the MVP Award-winning NCSA Mosaic, you can already appreciate the ease of use and diversity that the Web provides.

But after awhile, read-only lurking just isn't enough. In other words, you want to publish your own home page. If you have a restless urge to publish and give something back to the Web community, you need a HyperText Markup Language (HTML) editor such as HTML Assistant or HotMetal.

First, a little technical background: The World Wide Web and HTML are inexorably linked. All Web documents are formatted in HTML, and Web browsers like Mosaic are little more than HTML readers. In fact, this review was converted into a Web document using HTML Assistant and HotMetal. (If you want to check it out, point your Web browser in the direction of http://watarts.uwaterloo.ca/ENGL/nrandall/html—editors.html.)

HTML Assistant and HotMetal save you from the task of manually coding HTML into your documents by placing the necessary

Brooklyn North Software Works

codes in the document for you. Simply type what you want using any text editor (Windows' Notepad, for example), then highlight the text and use HTML Assistant or HotMetal to apply the desired format. These tools also help you build links to local files, remote files, and images, and they assist in the creation of fill-in forms.

Like many Internet-related applications, HTML Assistant and HotMetal are available as freeware (ftp.cs.dal.ca or ftp.ncsa.uiuc.edu, respectively) and as commercial products. Just like test-driving a car before you buy it, we recommend that you try the freebies first. Then if you need advanced features and technical support, buy one of the commercial versions.

If you're looking for the easiest route to Web publishing, HTML Assistant is your best choice thanks to its easy-to-use formatting and linking features. Programming purists and experienced Web publishers, on the other hand, will appreciate HotMetal's strict adherence to exact code language.

HTML Assistant is a pleasure to use. It's available as freeware, and recently Brooklyn North Software Works released a commercial version, HTML Assistant Pro. Download the freeware version to find out how deeply you want to get involved with HTML authoring, then upgrade to the commercial release if you need more power, a smoother interface, and technical support.

HTML Assistant makes it easy to apply formatting codes. To create a numbered list, for example, you need only type the listing, highlight it, then press the List button in the freeware version or the numbered-list icon in the Pro edition. The program's customizable User Tools feature establishes your most frequently used commands and includes additional commands for creating objects like forms and clickable maps.

For creating links to other documents, home pages, protocols, and sites on the Net, you won't find an editor that's easier to use than HTML Assistant. Its Link feature is useful, but it becomes indispensable when paired with the capability to import Uniform Resource Locators

(URLs) from your Cello bookmark file or your mosaic.ini file. (URLs are pointers to other Web documents.) When building a home page, this capability lets you include links to any of your favorite Web sites.

HTML Assistant Pro takes the idea one step further by offering the WWW Page Creator, a kind of HTML Wizard that automatically generates an HTML page by using the URL information in an existing document. A superb idea, this feature makes even the most complex HTML page creation nearly effortless.

HotMetal, which began life as a Unix package, is available via anonymous ftp from SoftQuad. (The company also offers a commercial version, HotMetal Pro.) While it offers much of the power of HTML Assistant, HotMetal is significantly less sensitive to the needs of novice users, burying many of its commands beneath somewhat unintuitive menu items. Also, it treats HTML as a rigidly structured language. As a result, it insists that documents be coded according to strict formatting rules. In

other words, HotMetal is designed precisely for the HTML standard, while HTML Assistant is a more free-form, forgiving editor.

With HotMetal, it's almost certain that you'll get your HTML document correct on the first try, mainly because the program won't let you include elements incorrectly (unless you turn off its rules checking feature, which more or less defeats the program's purpose). With HTML Assistant, on the other hand, you code a little, debug, then see what it looks like, then change what's wrong, then code some more.

HotMetal codes are shown as unusual 3-D tags. While they take some getting used to, these 3-D tags provide one major advantage for authors: Because they're shaped like labeled arrowheads, they make it immediately apparent that HTML codes must be paired. What this means is that HTML structures require both an opening tag and ending tag (a pair). HTML Assistant's 3-D tags make it almost impossible to forget this requirement.

HotMetal's contextual structure windows are designed to let you know precisely where you're currently working in the document. This can be invaluable for long HTML documents because it helps you determine whether or not current codes are complete. If you're creating shorter documents, however, this feature becomes less important.

HotMetal Pro includes a spelling checker, thesaurus, and macro creator, as well as support for tables, protocols, and other advanced HTML features. It even displays in-line graphics files within the editor itself—a nice visual feature and a smart nod to usability.

Both HotMetal and HTML Assistant are adequate solutions for homegrown publishing on the Web. You can try both programs as freeware, and upgrade to the one you like the best.

If you're familiar with programming and code—or you want to establish strict coding standards right from the start—take a good look at HotMetal. But if experimentation and free-flowing programming appeal to your novice instincts, you'll be better served by HTML Assistant.

Calling All World Wide Web Editors: To publish your own home page on the World Wide Web, you need a HyperText Markup Language (HTML) editor like HotMetal (above) or HTML Assistant.
—Neil Randall

HTML Assistant Pro
Brooklyn North Software Works
(902) 835-2600
Free, $99 for the commercial version

HotMetal Pro
SoftQuad Inc.
(800) 387-2777; (416) 239-4801
Free, $195 for the commercial version

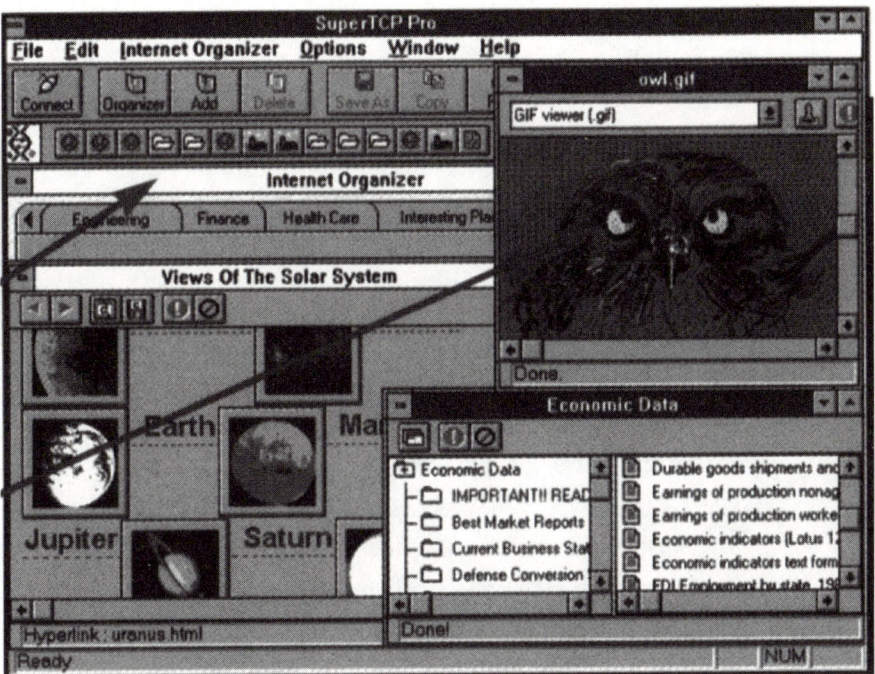

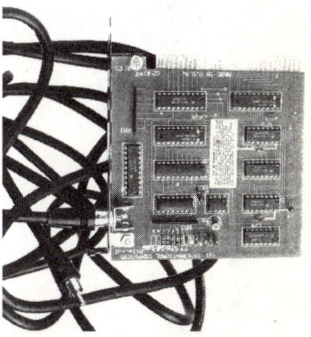

SuperTCP For Windows

Frontier Technologies gave us more than we bargained for: a full-featured networking product that's at home in big PC-Unix environments (and priced to match). Fortunately, the straightforward instructions walked us deliberately through the installation.

We had no trouble installing the TCP/IP stack, and the detailed online help made it easy to configure the PPP connection. Our main criticisms: sketchy documentation and too many nested dialog boxes.

SuperTCP's bundled Internet utilities range from serviceable to slick. The ftp utility is busy but not hard to figure out. The mail client goes beyond simple e-mail, supporting the MIME standard and processing messages through the use of simple rules.

On the downside, there's no gopher client, and the rudimentary news reader is both ugly and limited in strength. For example, it doesn't allow you to sort messages in any way.

By late summer, Frontier plans to release Superhighway Access, a $149 dial-up-only version. The stripped-down package drops high-end features such as servers (mail and ftp), but adds gopher and archie clients, plus a Web browser that's reportedly more advanced than Mosaic.

SuperTCP for Windows
Frontier Technologies
(414) 241-4555
tcp@frontiertech.com
$395

THE INTERNET FOR LESS
Trumpet Winsock
HGopher
WinVN
Eudora 1.4

We found a nearly complete suite of free and shareware tools that were a match for anything in shrink-wrap. (The free Mosaic World Wide Web reader is also a must.) All of the products mentioned below can be found in pub/pc/win3/winsock at ftp.cica.indiana.edu. We've included filenames that were accurate at press time. We've also posted them on PC Contact as NETUTL.ZIP in data library 3 (Utilities/Misc).

Trumpet Winsock Trumpet Winsock (WINSOC.ZIP) is a $20 shareware package that includes a TCP/IP stack, command-line ftp utility, and basic Telnet package. It turned out to be one of our easier SLIP installations. However, Trumpet Winsock also offers a news reader that's hard to recommend.

HGopher HGopher (HGPH24.ZIP) is a free Windows gopher client good enough to be a commercial product. Best of all, it supports the new Gopher+ protocol, unlike other gopher clients we saw.

WinVN WinVN (WNVN082S.ZIP) is a news reader that sorts messages by threads. For serious news users, it's a must—and it's free.

Eudora 1.4 Eudora 1.4 is the freely distributed version of QualComm's popular mail client. It supports MIME and sports an interface complete with icons and folders. To get it, anonymous ftp to qualcomm.com.

Trumpet Winsock
HGopher
WinVN
Eudora 1.4
pub/pc/win3/winsock
ftp.cica.indiana.edu

Newscast for Windows

All the News That Fits: Pick an infosource—Dow Jones, AP, CNN, whatever. Newscast for Windows' FM receiver (left) taps them all and sends out the facts via VIM or MAPI mail.

Newscast for Windows
Mainstream Data
(800) 299-2278
$495 receiver, $995 software; subscription costs vary

Closed Caption Decoder
WeatherBrief Plus

It's on TV: Fill your disk with stock reports, news updates, and more by installing the Closed Caption Decoder board in your PC. Then plug WeatherBrief hardware into your parallel port for a meteorological fix (center PC).
—Matthew J. Lake

Closed Caption Decoder
International Computers
(800) 992-9000
$89

WeatherBrief Plus
WeatherBank
(800) 201-4585
$295

SIMUNET: OFFLINE INTRODUCTION TO THE INTERNET

SimuNet

Have you been itching to get on the Internet but daunted by the sheer vastness of it all? Bridge Learning Systems may have the answer: the second edition of its Internet tutorial program called SimuNet. At $19.95, this program allows you to test-drive the Internet before you actually go online.

SimuNet is a DOS-based simulation of the Internet based on James Potter's book *Bridging the Internet Gap*. SimuNet is extremely easy to use: Just follow the prompts and you're on your way through the program's seven tutorials. The first, "Introduction to the Internet," explains what the Internet is and how it evolved. This section includes useful definitions of basic terms as well as an explanation of Internet addressing conventions.

SimuNet's second tutorial shows you how to create, send, and accept electronic mail over the Internet, and includes the useful tip of how

to take your name off a mailing list to stem the flow of unwanted junk mail. The remaining SimuNet tutorials cover topics such as how to print, download, and upload files; how to use indexes including archie and World Wide Web; and how to navigate your way around the Net using gopher. Each is easy to follow, and warns you ahead of time of any incompatibilities or differences in command protocols that you may encounter once you're actually online.

More than a static program, SimuNet offers updates from a gopher site at California State University, Hayward (instructions for accessing the site are included in the book).—Carol Venezia

SimuNet
Bridge Learning Systems
(800) 487-9868
$19.95

☞ During business hours, someone registers a new domain on the World Wide Web every two minutes.

Anarchy Won

The WWW was built on the sheer love, the sheer enthusiasm, and the sheer energy of the people who wanted to create it. I think that the corporations have fundamentally misunderstood what people love and what people want. They still think that people want to have something packaged for them; that people aren't really smart enough to create for themselves. What people actually want, and the WWW proves it—the first worldwide anarchy—that people want to express themselves, they want to create, they want to reach each other, and they also want the freedom

My overall impression is that this has been a miraculous year and half or so in which the Web has grown. I call it miraculous for several reasons. Just for the Web, you've had online services like America Online, CompuServe spending an enormous amount of money to promote themselves. These guys include free disks and magazines and they purchase television advertising time. So they were really pouring money into each new user they got. They were able to get actual online users in the million neighborhood apiece. I think that that might even be an inflated number. But for all that money they spent, then the Web came out of the blue with no money, no planning, no advertising, no marketing, no ownership, no intention and surpassed the commercial services in six months. So in this case, anarchy won.

So the question is, do people in the industry get the message or not? Just because anarchy won doesn't mean you can't make a lot of money within that framework. I think it's completely compatible with the free-market system and completely compatible with capitalism.

—JARON LANIER, MUSICIAN/FATHER OF VIRTUAL REALITY

ityCommunityCommunityCommunityCommunityCo

you're given a number out of a hat. You choose a "handle" when chatting——maximal anonymity. AOL encourages people to add extensive personal profiles accessible by keyword search-

BULLETIN BOARDS

Magic City BBS: (205) 664-9883
Sysop: Beverly Crider
2 lines—MS-DOS 486; 1,200MB running WildCat 4.0 with US Robotics at up to 168 bps. Estab. 11/92 with no fee. Your online source of information about Birmingham. Birmingham Post-Herald online.

Lid's Lounge: (205) 235-2660
Sysop: Jeff Liddle
1 line—MS-DOS 386; 120MB running MacroBBS (Commo) 3.01 with US Robotics at up to 14,400 bps. Estab. 05/93 with no fee. Shareware files, netmail, and pharmacy technician information for use by the general public (free).

Harvey's Home of the Lazy Dog: (205) 586-0216
Sysop: Seth Whetstone
1 line—MS-DOS 486; 2,300MB running PCBoard 15.1 with US Robotics at up to 57,600 bps. Estab. 07/93 with no fee. Never touch keyboard. Optional fee, not req. ANSI, RIP, EGA, SB doors. Free file conference.

The Old Fart's B.B.S.: (205) 230-6315
Sysop: Jack Maton
1 line—MS-DOS 286; 560MB running WildCat 4.0 with Supra at up to 2,400 bps. Estab. 09/13 with a fee of $3 monthly. Special BBS for retired and over 40. Classified ads, matchmaker doors. Files and other specials.

Warlord BBS: (205) 368-8079
Sysop: Wayne Braswell
1 line—MS-DOS 486; 498MB running WildCat 4.0 with US Robotics at up to 19,200 bps. Estab. 03/94 with no fee. Adult areas, Windows, DOS, archive, 5 CDs. Online games (TradeWars 2002 registered).

DFG Financial BBS: (205) 745-0579
Sysop: David Dorsey
1 line—MS-DOS 386; 90MB running TriBBS 5.10 with US Robotics at up to 14,400 bps. Estab. 07/93 with no fee. Helping individuals and small businesses manage their money. Software and messages. Member ASP. CD-ROM.

The Flip Side: (205) 798-3961
Sysop: Scott Dean
1 line—MS-DOS 486; 900MB running Renegade 05-31Exp. with US Robotics at up to 14,400 bps. Estab. 06/92 with no fee. Online CD-ROM, multiple message/file bases. Support for Renegade systems and much more.

The Neon Moon: (205) 477-5894
Sysop: Glenn Rollins
2 lines—MS-DOS 486; 2000MB running TriBBS 5.1 with Hayes at up to 19,200 bps. Estab. 07/92 with a fee of $35 annually. World headquarters for the new SeXXXnet. New nodes wanted.

The Computer Addict's BBS: (205) 933-5360
Sysop: Brad Beasley
1 line—MS-DOS 486; 540MB running RoboBoard/FX 1.04 with Intel at up to 14,400 bps. Estab. 07/94 with no fee.

Lumby's Palace BBS: (205) 520-0041
Sysop: Lumby
1 line—MS-DOS 486; 2,000MB running VBBS 6.14 with Zoom at up to 38,400 bps. Estab. 12/92 with no fee. Gaming BBS with 30+ online games. Apogee and Epic Megagames distribution sites. Fun.

The Computrion BBS: (205) 595-0183
Sysop: Efrem Stringer
2 lines—MS-DOS 486; 600MB running RemoteAccess PRO 2.02 with Zoom vfx at up to 14,400 bps. Estab. 06/92 with no fee. User-friendly BBS. Internet e-mail/newsgroups. Supporting Remote Access sysops and OS/2 users.

AJ's: (205) 593-0705
Sysop: Art Smith
1 line—MS-DOS 486; 250MB running WildCat 4.0 with Wang at up to 14,400 bps. Estab. 02/93 with a fee of $20 annually. Free new user access. 3 CD drives. Epic and Apogee release center. Friendly folks.

Mystery Island BBS: (205) 926-3943
Sysop: Larry Boyd
1 line—MS-DOS 486; 130MB running WildCat 3.91S with Practical Peripherals at up to 14,400 bps. Estab. 11/91 with no fee. Apogee hub #999. CD-ROM library. Internet conferences. Fax. 30+ online games. Local weather.

The Shareware Exchange: (205) 809-0270
Sysop: Russ Haag
1 line—MS-DOS 486; 1,300MB running SpitFire 3.5 with US Robotics at up to 19,200 bps. Estab. 07/93 with no fee. New users welcome. Apogee distribution site. CD-ROM online. Circuit-Net mail. Motivation files.

Dateline BBS: (205) 747-4194
Sysop: Jim Melvin
2 lines—MS-DOS 386; 1,500MB running WildCat 3.91 Multi with US Robotics at up to 38,400 bps. Estab. 02/90 with no fee. Multipurpose BBS. Popular features include: FidoNet echoes, door games, CD-A-Month, Faxing, and more.

ShadowVision BBS: (205) 306-0486
Sysop: David Stanton
2 lines—Amiga with 1000MB running Stasis BBS .03.650 with US Robotics at up to 21,600 bps. Estab. 02/89 with no fee. Adult files and messages. IBM/Amiga/Mac files and messages. Strange/bizarre msg. nets. Instant access.

Wiregrass Graphics: (205) 793-0978
Sysop: Michael Scott
1 line—MS-DOS 486; 10,600MB running WildCat 3.9 with US Robotics at up to 16,800 bps. Estab. 01/91 with a fee of $20 biannually. 75,000+ files, 12 CDs online at all times. Support BBS for great pricing on computer parts. Save.

Computer Works: (205) 671-0092
Sysop: Jim Lambert
1 line—MS-DOS 386; 4000MB running SpitFire 3.4 with US Robotics at up to 28,800 bps. Estab. 01/94 with no fee. Public BBS with 6 CD-ROMs online, Circuit-Net intl. mail, Genesis Daily News, online games, CD sales.

munityCommunityCommunityCommunityCommunit

es. You can do a search on just about any sexual habit or wacky orientation imaginable, and you'll find a slew of people——men and women——who list themselves as aficionados beg-

DataLink BBS: (205) 677-3086
Sysop: Ody Ramwey

2 lines—MS-DOS 386; 4,000MB running Gap 6.3/Multi with Twincom's 14.4k at up to 14,400 bps. Estab. 03/89 with no fee. Free access with pay areas available. $40.00 annually for special areas only. Visa/MC instant upgrade.

MetalShoppe BBS: (205) 767-3197
Sysop: Rocker/Babe

2 lines—MS-DOS 386; 1,240MB running VBBS 6.X with Intel/Boca V42.bis at up to 14,400 bps. Estab. 03/93 with no fee. Matrix system. 3 BBSs in one. Four networks, 2 CDs, 250+ national/international message conferences.

Access CoCo of L.A. (Lower Alabama): (205) 598-2100
Sysop: Dave Spicer

1 line—OS/2 2.1; 250MB running VBBS OS2 6.14 with Zoom at up to 14,400 bps. Estab. 06/94 with no fee. Supporting OS/2.

Thunder Mountain BBS: (205) 582-4719
Sysop: Tim Roberts

1 line—MS-DOS 386; 1,200MB running WildCat 3.91s with Twincom 14,400 at up to 57,600 bps. Estab. 12/93 with no fee. Fast-growing BBS in north Alabama, RIP graphics, HomeNet, LinkUSA, CDs. Full access first call.

Inferno BBS: (205) 837-7715/3990/9787
Sysop: Michael Konor

3 lines—A3,000T/040; 5,036MB running MebbsNet V1.0 with US Robotics at up to 28.8k bps. Estab. 05/91 with no fee. MS-DOS, Amiga, Windows, generic files, and newsgroups. Adult areas, games. Easy to use.

SFE Systems USA: (205) 650-0107
Sysop: Timothy Blake

1 line—MS-DOS 386; 2700MB running SFE Systems 4.0 with Hayes at up to 14,400 bps. Estab. 01/93 with no fee. Education, games, 70 file areas, CD-ROMs. Something for everyone, fun for the whole family.

Power Windows BBS: (205) 881-8619
Sysop: Cyrus Cathey

2 lines—MS-DOS 486; 4000MB running WildCat latest with Generic at up to 57,600 bps. Estab. 04/92 with no fee. Featuring Windows, DOS, OS/2, games, general MIDI, MT-32 MIDI, sound cards, RIME, ILink, FidoNet, QWK.

Terminal Velocity: (205) 883-6070
Sysop: Devin Carlen

1 line—MS-DOS 486; 425MB running Renegade 5-31 with US Robotics at up to 28,800 bps. Estab. 02/94 with no fee. Internet e-mail and Usenet, plus many other networks. Large file areas, many reg'd online games.

Razz-ma-Tazz: (205) 859-5459
Sysop: John Michael

2 lines—MS-DOS 486; 5,200MB running TriBBS 5.2 with US Robotics at up to 14,400 bps. Estab. 08/91 with no fee. 8 CD-ROM drives online with huge shareware selection. Uses EZROM CD-ROM door for easy access.

Plug into the Internet

Everybody's talking about the Internet. Once the exclusive domain of academics and hard-core UNIX nerds, the Internet has grown into a vast storehouse of information useful—and easily accessible—to even the most inexperienced traveler of the information superhighway.

Originally, the Internet was created to serve the needs of university researchers, government agencies, and the military. Large corporate sites were the next to see the advantages of an open community where information is shared and provided freely and where geographic boundaries can be traversed transparently.

Now just about every online dabbler has discovered—or at least heard about—the Net. Maybe you've heard jargon such as surfing the Net, flaming, or WWW (World Wide Web). Maybe you've received a few business cards with strange e-mail addresses such as john—paul@vatican.org. Now you're thinking that it's time to check out this new way of communicating.

Well, rest assured, you can connect to the Internet from your Mac. It's easy, but careful planning is essential. Here's our step-by-step guide to getting wired.

From the viewpoint of Joe or Jane User, the Internet is an information resource, a gathering place, and a message center all in one—but it's much bigger and far less structured than even the largest, most popular online service or bulletin-board system. The reason is simple: The Internet isn't a single, identifiable entity—it's a network of networks, a multitude of computers all around the world, communicating via phone lines, Ethernet, and any other media that can support IP (Internet Protocol), the Internet's special language. Each host computer (a remote Internet computer you log onto) is set up so information can move freely through it and, therefore, around the entire Internet. The Internet's e-mail and newsgroups

ging to be chatted with or sent mail. 💻 This is completely fascinating to anyone with any curiosity at all. So you might spend hours dreaming up odd keyword searches to see what you

Billster's World: (205) 435-7064
Sysop: Bill Wood
1 line—MS-DOS 386; 100MB running SpitFire 3.4 with Microcom at up to 28,800 bps. Estab. 08/93 with a fee of $15 one year. 600MB+ of files, 30+ door games (war games, AD&D games), Fido-Net, free one-month subscription.

The Crenshaw County BBS: (205) 335-3968
Sysop: Ed Welch
2 lines—MS-DOS 386; 1,500MB running PCBoard 15.1/5 with US Robotics at up to 28,800 bps. Estab. 04/93 with no fee. General interest board. Astronomy, gardening, hobbies, games, utilities, etc. Easy access. Free.

Calluses Dungeon (adult): (205) 460-4034
Sysop: Calluses
1 line—OS/2 486DX2/66; 1,000MB running Renegade v1-2 with Supra at up to 19,200 bps. Estab. 02/94 with a fee of $10 biannually. 1.2GB of adult files. 7,000+ general files. 60+ online games. Large message section. KinkNet.

The Unearthed Arcana II BBS: (205) 473-8989
Sysop: Slayer/Lady Morgan
1 line—MS-DOS 386; 6,050MB running Renegade 05.31 with Cardinal at up to 14,400 bps. Estab. 05/93 with no fee. Renegade/Sysop: support. Occult, adult, anarchy, RPG, more. 6+ GB online.

Montgomery PC Users' Group: (205) 277-3889
Sysop: Jerald Conway
1 line—MS-DOS 8088; 170MB running QuickBBS 2.66 with US Robotics at up to 14,400 bps. Estab. 01/93 with no fee. Eight general-interest and computer-related message bases. 1,500 program files.

Dave's BBS: (205) 275-0554
Sysop: David Smith
1 line—MS-DOS 486; 1,200MB running VBBS 6.1 with Hayes at up to 28,800 bps. Estab. 08/92 with no fee. VirtualNet @1205607, FidoNet 1:18/6, Internet @davesbbs.com. Family-oriented BBS. Fun for everyone.

The Forbidden Realm: (205) 270-8489
Sysop: The Boss
2 lines—MS-DOS 486; 2,790MB running VBBS 6.14 with US Robotics at up to 38,400 bps. Estab. 04/89 with no fee. 15,000+ files, 200+ worldwide netted message bases. Metaphysical/occult-related topics and support.

Knight's Castle: (205) 631-6668
Sysop: Sir Odie
1 line—MS-DOS 386; 230MB running WWIV 4.23 reg with Practical Peripherals at up to 14,400 bps. Estab. 12/93 with no fee. Based on life in the Middle Ages. All S.C.A. members are welcome. Several national nets.

Romulan Ship BBS: (205) 629-7266
Sysop: Romulus
1 line—dual Pentium; 1,000MB running WWIV 4.23 with US Robotics at up to 14,400 bps. Estab. 05/94 with no fee. Instant access first call, PC and Mac files, GIFs, lots of unique message bases (caters to new user).

depend on this free-flowing movement of information.

Some of these hosts also act like file servers—that is, they contain information Internet users can download to their own computers. In many cases, the information is contained in public directories, whose files anyone can access.

What You'll Find on the Internet
Although the Internet has a wealth of resources, a few of its features are more commonly used than others:

E-Mail
The most basic Internet service is electronic mail. Like e-mail within your company or on an online service, Internet e-mail lets you send messages to one or more other users, regardless of where they are located or what type of computer they use.

Newsgroups
Newsgroups are the Internet's town hall. Over 5,000 discussion groups, or newsgroups, cover a multitude of topics. Devotees of The Simpsons, bicycle repair, linguistics, the Newton, African-American culture, fax technology, and particle physics all have one or more newsgroups, with readers and contributors from around the world. In the true Internet spirit of information exchange, many newsgroups include regular postings of answers to frequently asked questions (FAQs). Newsgroups such as comp.sys.mac.comm, which focuses on telecommunications for Mac users, have extensive FAQs that are updated regularly.

Some newsgroups are sedate forums for researchers; some are the homes of novice computer users seeking help; and some are arenas for rabid conspiracy theorists, political activists, and troublemakers. The most vitriolic of the messages they send are called flames.

Mailing Lists
Like newsgroups, mailing lists bring together people with similar interests, through postings that can be read by the group. Mailing lists are managed by one person or through automated

munityCommunityCommunityCommunityCommunit

can find. Of course, this all takes time (especially on AOL, which is incredibly sluggish at peak hours) for which you're charged money. ⌨ The future for online chatting is rosy. During

Electronic Trader: (205) 774-5347
Sysop: Jerry L. Gearhart
1 line—MS-DOS 386; 600MB running VBBS 6.14 with Infotel at up to 19,200 bps. Estab. 02/94 with no fee. Offers online catalog ordering, 20,000+ products. BBSaleNet sysop sales program.

The Anchor Inn: (205) 675-8406
Sysop: Jim Wilson
1 line—MS-DOS 486; 600MB running PCBoard 15.2 with Practical Peripherals at up to 14,400 bps. Estab. 10/92 with no fee. RIPscrip, FidoNet, doors, many message bases, auto verification. Latest ver. of PCBoard. Downloads.

The Edge of Reality: (205) 249-8090
Sysop: Ray Vanderver
2 lines—MS-DOS 486; 650MB running RoboBoard 1.04 with US Robotics at up to 14,400 bps. Estab. 07/94 with a fee of $11 monthly. View GIFs online, get tech support on software/hardware 24 hrs. a day.

Airtech BBS: (907) 349-3421
Sysop: Bruce McWhorter
1 line—OS/2 486/66; 1,500MB running WildCat 3.9 with US Robotics at up to 14,400 bps. Estab. 11/92 with a fee of $35 annually. Aviation dedicated BBS. FlyNet, Aeronet, CapNet, FidoNet, Policenet, GWNnet, lots of aviation files.

Virtual Autobahn: (907) 563-3407
Sysop: Stephan Stevens
2 lines—MS-DOS 386; 1,000MB running Synchronet 2.0a with Hayes at up to 28,800 bps. Estab. 03/94 with no fee. Internet, business, entertainment, shareware. Internet is for demo and e-mail. PPP for fee.

The Play Room: (907) 338-7049
Sysop: Tracy Dreyer
4 lines—Novell network with 4500MB running WildCat 3.91m with US Robotics at up to 14,400 bps. Estab. 01/92 with a fee of $50 annually. 6 CDs always online. 500+ message conferences including Internet mail access. 50+ online games.

TSW OS/2 BBS and Information Service: (907) 372-1624
Sysop: Lori Martin
1 line—OS/2 LAN; 1,020MB running WildCat 4.0/RIP with PPI ProClass PC288SA at up to 28,800 bps. Estab. 01/91 with no fee. Fido 1:355/20, OS/2net 81:312/5, Wildnet, RIP Net, Team OS/2, 7 CD-ROMs, Beakware, OS/2, Win, DOS, Unix.

Bandit Connection: (907) 428-2649
Sysop: Gypsy Bandit
1 line—MS-DOS 386; 300MB running WWIV 4.23 with Supra at up to 14,400 bps. Estab. 07/92 with no fee. Military-oriented, CD-ROM, online games, WWIVnet, ICEnet, Sex-Net. A little bit for everyone.

The Trading Post (North): (907) 356-7632
Sysop: Dean S. Nash (Trader Jack)
2 lines—MS-DOS 386; 340MB running WWIV 4.23+ with Zoom Vfc at up to 28,800 bps. Estab. 02/91 with no fee. General BBS. Items for sale, rent, trade. FidoNet 1:355/22. Line 2: (907) 356-7649, NN: Guest.

---

mailing-list software and are distributed through e-mail to subscribers. You subscribe to a list about, say, folk music or Claris's FileMaker Pro by sending an e-mail message to the list's owner. You will soon receive daily, weekly, or occasional e-mail messages from people who submit them to the list. You can contribute your questions, comments, or information in the same way.

Some mailing lists receive many messages per day, and the owner sends periodic collections of posted material in digest form, keeping your e-mail traffic down considerably.

ftp
Like many other Internet terms, ftp (file transfer protocol) is often used as a verb, as in, "Where can I *ftp* the agenda of last year's International AIDS Conference from?" You use ftp to transfer files from an Internet host computer to your computer. Many Internet hosts support anonymous ftp (you don't need an account for the machine you are trying to reach), which lets you retrieve files from public directories.

Search Engines and Browsers
The Internet's vastness has given rise to software that helps you search for and retrieve information even when you don't know where it is stored. Using search engines with names such as archie, WAIS (Wide-Area Information Server), and gopher, you can learn the location of information on almost any topic. You can then ftp it to your Mac (getting the hang of the jargon?).

A WWW browser lets you take a virtual walk around the Internet or one of its sites, checking out what's available and deciding whether you'd like to see more, all via hypertext links. WWW is among the Internet's flashiest and fastest-growing services.

Telnet
Think of Telnet—another versatile noun/verb—as a transporter, ala Star Trek. Telnetting refers to logging on to one computer from another. For example, you can log on to the Internet host at your office and Telnet from there to an Internet-connected computer at your firm's European office. If you have an account for the remote computer, you have all of that computer's privileges available to you. If

The Outlands BBS: (907) 247-1219
Sysop: Mike Gates
3 lines—MS-DOS 486; 1,500MB running PCBoard 15.1 with Hayes at up to 14,400 bps. Estab. 09/92 with a fee of $2.50 monthly. Thirty days free access. Tons of online door games, online CD-ROM, ReadRoom door, new users welcome.

T.C.'s Byte Bank System: (907) 488-3751
Sysop: Tom Creek
1 line—MS-DOS 386; 1,200MB running QuickBBS 2.80 g-5 with Practical Peripherals at up to 14,400 bps. Estab. 12/91 with no fee. FidoNet echomail, MS-DOS files and info on Fairbanks, North Pole, and Alaska. Callback verifier.

NorthStar BBS: (907) 747-2601
Sysop: Jeff Parker
1 line—MS-DOS 386; 13,500MB running Excalibur Windows .70 with Zoom at up to 14,400 bps. Estab. 10/93 with no fee. S.E. Alaska's Windows BBS featuring int'l trade, computer bargain outlet, int'l gifts, pure Windows.

Valley Online: (907) 376-8257
Sysop: Kit Brady
1 line—MS-DOS 486; 1,000MB running SpitFire 3.4 with US Robotics at up to 14,400 bps. Estab. 05/93 with no fee. Full-access first call including uploads/downloads.

Alaska Information Cache: (907) 373-3205
Sysop: Bob Southwick
3 lines—MS-DOS 486; 700MB running Galacticomm 6.21f with US Robotics at up to 14,400 bps. Estab. 12/93 with no fee. Alaska travel information, list keeper of travel-related BBSs.

Identity Crisis BBS: (907) 376-2779
Sysop: Covert Spy
2 lines—MS-DOS 286; 80MB running Synchronet 2.0b with Supra at up to 14,400 bps. Estab. 05/92 with no fee. One CD-ROM online and 9 registered doors. We are the hub system for NDS and VBBC.

Scott's Spot BBS: (602) 982-6156
Sysop: Scott Sparks
1 line—MS-DOS 386; 1,100MB running GT Power 18.00 with AT&T Paradyne at up to 14,400 bps. Estab. 05/92 with no fee. 1,000s of files. Game doors, echoes, netmail, RIP graphics, official dist. SWC, and Apogee.

Rose Cross/1 BBS: (602) 982-3578
Sysop: Robert Jacobs
1 line—MS-DOS 386; 340MB running Galacticomm 6.21 with Zoom at up to 14,400 bps. Estab. 06/87 with no fee. Dedicated to the promulgation of Rosicrucian Christianity via multilingual textfile library.

The Warzone BBS: (602) 932-9243
Sysop: David Schepper
1 line—MS-DOS 386; 2,158MB running RemoteAccess 1.11 with Zoom at up to 28,800 bps. Estab. 06/91 with no fee. ISANet coordinator, filebone hub, 120+ online games, large message base, thousands of files.

---

you have Telnet access to an online service such as CompuServe or America Online, you can log on to the Internet without using a modem.

The Easy Part: Getting Connected
The basic requirements for Internet access are an account with an Internet service provider; communications software; and in most cases, a modem. Some corporations maintain their own Internet connections; if you work for one of them, you can usually log on to the net via AppleTalk networks in-house. For most, though, Internet access requires a dial-up connection—that is, through a modem and an account you pay for. The scope of your Internet

access will depend on the type of account you have and the software you use.

Internet service providers are connected directly to the Internet, usually through one or more UNIX-based computers. You pay for an account that allows you to log on to the provider's system, just as you would log on to an online service or corporate mainframe. Logging on puts you on the Internet. Service-provider lists, including nixpub and pdial (two of the most well-known lists of service providers), are available on the Internet and online services.

The other way to get onto the Internet is to go through a commercial online service such as CompuServe. Such services have gateways to the Internet, although you can

generally exchange only e-mail and occasionally news if you go through them.

The Hard Part: Choosing an Interface
The Rubicon of Internet connectivity is the choice between text-based access—terminal emulation and a graphical interface, like the one you're used to on the Mac. This may seem like a no-brainer, but applying a friendly face to an Internet connection takes a bit of work and forces you to confront the nuts and bolts of Internet networking. On the other hand, terminal emulation requires you to learn UNIX commands, something Mac users rarely relish.

The easiest way to log on to the Internet is to dial in to your service provider's system

chat-only BBSs such as the Garbage Dump are doing a great business. And the Internet has a phenomenal online chat audience with people discussing sex and politics more than any-

Access Arizona: (602) 763-4285
Sysop: Tim and Bonnie Chaplin
4 lines—MS-DOS 486; 800MB running Synchronet 2 with Zoom at up to 14,400 bps. Estab. 01/94 with a fee of $10 for two months. RIP graphics, teleconference, online games (LORD, BRE, SRE), thousands of files incl. CD-ROM.

Run-Time BBS: (602) 525-3711
Sysop: Dan Shearer
1 line—MS-DOS 486; 1,200MB running WildCat 3.91 with US Robotics at up to 38,400 bps. Estab. 10/90 with no fee. DOS, OS/2, and Amiga files. Fido echoes: Paul Revere Net, pro-gun echoes. CD-ROM, and many games.

The Silicone Silhouette: (602) 525-2238
Sysop: David Dewey
1 line—MS-DOS 486; 340MB running TriBBS 5.1 with Zoom at up to 57,600 bps. Estab. 04/94 with no fee. Business- and variety-oriented.

The Nucleus II BBS: (602) 459-3653
Sysop: Greg Thompson
1 line—MS-DOS 286; 75MB running SuperBBS 1.16B with Supra at up to 2,400 bps. Estab. 05/92 with no fee. Part of FidoNet, SUPERnet, and RBBSNet. Running online games as well as international echoes.

Dark Side BBS: (602) 692-7426
Sysop: Dark Side
1 line—Macintosh; 500MB running Hermies II 3.0.1 with Supra at up to 28,800 bps. Estab. 08/93 with no fee.

Pegasus II Software: (602) 491-0620
Sysop: Dave Sauer
1 line—MS-DOS 486; 1,200MB running WildCat 3.90 with Zoom at up to 38,400 bps. Estab. 02/93 with no fee. Doors, online games, national- and local-mail networks available. Internet access. Files, bulletins. Fun.

The Gallery: (602) 396-6556
Sysop: Bungee
2 lines—WFW 3.11 EtherNet; 460MB running Excalibur .65a with Microcom at up to 28,800 bps. Estab. 04/93 with no fee. U/l, d/l, read/write e-mail and messages, multiline chat, all at the same time. View GIFs before d/l.

Pinnacle Information Center: (602) 951-8379
Sysop: M. Hickman
4 lines—MS-DOS 486; 2,000MB running Galacticomm v6.21f with Hayes at up to 57,600 bps. Estab. 06/92 with no fee. Multipurpose information and game center. Nine CD-ROMs online, multiplayer games, Fido, Internet, and so on.

RaceBBS: (602) 669-9225
Sysop: Jim Wooddell
1 line—MS-DOS 386; 130MB running WildCat 3.6 with Supra at up to 28,800 bps. Estab. 01/94 with no fee. RaceNet region 500 hub. RiverNet, SupraSupportNet. Seeking QWK and FTN nodes.

---

with a Mac communications program such as the shareware ZTerm or Hayes' Smartcom II. Your Mac then becomes a terminal on the Internet host. Because the Internet host uses the UNIX operating system, you need to use UNIX commands to read news, send mail, and transfer files. Some UNIX applications running on an Internet host have rudimentary menus, but the menus are driven by your keyboard, not your mouse. Fortunately, you can use e-mail and access newsgroups without learning many commands. You can also read documentation for the application you're using while you're connected or after you have downloaded it.

The commands for transferring files and searching for information are trickier, and they vary with the telecommunications protocols your Internet host supports.

Terminal emulation's advantages are ease of configuration (all you need to get connected is to know your user ID, your password, and the phone number of the Internet host's modem), speed, and full functionality. Terminal emulation—sometimes called a shell account—is usually the cheapest kind of Internet account, although that is changing a bit. The UNIX-based software for reading news often has more features than the Mac alternatives. Since UNIX-based mail and news software is not burdened with a graphics interface, reading large volumes of news or mail often goes faster.

Internet Access: The Mac Way
If you find the Mac's point-and-click interface indispensable, you can apply it to the Internet, as long as you have two important items: Apple's MacTCP software and a SLIP or PPP account from your service provider. MacTCP is a control panel that lets your Mac communicate with an Internet host in its native language, IP. A SLIP (Serial Line Internet Protocol) or PPP (Point to Point Protocol) account puts your Mac on the Internet.

Getting MacTCP is easy—it's part of Apple's System 7.5 and is also included with several Internet software packages. You can't, however, just buy a copy of MacTCP alone. Setting up MacTCP can be a headache (fortunately, you have to set it up only once). It's

thing else. 💻 This is a sociological trend that needs closer study. Is there some secret need for this lurking in our collective unconscious? I think it's time some sociologists take a

THe GaRBaGe DuMP BBS: (602) 331-1112
Sysop: Dean Kerl
105 lines—MS-DOS 486; 10,300MB running Galacticomm v6.21 with Hayes at up to 2,400 bps. Estab. 12/90 with no fee. Huge system featuring chat, message forums, CD-ROM library, games, trivia.

Tyrell CompuSystem Enigma: (602) 849-0362
Sysop: Robert P. Reyes
1 line—Novell System 7; 900MB running Searchlight 2.25D with BIS Technology at up to 2,400 bps. Estab. 01/93 with a fee of $10 annually. Tech support, Apogee, CD-ROM sect., Internet tyrell@ramp.com. Sales online, much more.

Sunwise: (602) 584-7395
Sysop: Keith Slater
1 line—MS-DOS 386; 250MB running TBBS 2.2M with US Robotics at up to 14,400 bps. Estab. 06/86 with no fee. Internet, Fido, Finet echoes, arcade, genealogy, and investment.

Circle Of Fellowship: (602) 942-8921
Sysop: Terry Erickson
1 line—OS/2 386 33MHz; 1,700MB running PCBoard 15.1 with Hayes at up to 14,400 bps. Estab. 07/93 with a fee of $25 annually. Friendly atmosphere. Two local e-mail networks and INT-ELEC national network. Message-based board.

The Rock Garden: (602) 220-0001
Sysop: Jeff Moriarty
40 lines—MS-DOS 486; 1,000MB running Galacticomm 6.21 with Supra at up to 2400 bps. Estab. 06/88 with no fee. Chatting, games (including interactive TradeWars 2002), files, online pizza, and general chaos.

The Black Hole: (602) 849-9744
Sysop: The Hound
1 line—MS-DOS 486; 1,980MB running VBBS 6.14a with US Robotics at up to 14,400 bps. Estab. 9/93 with a fee of $5 optional. 10,000 shareware, freeware, and adult files. VirtualNet, AZ. AC for Magnet. CD-ROM, online games.

Cosmo's: (602) 468-0567
Sysop: Cosmo Magnus
1 line—MS-DOS 386; 500MB running Synchronet 2.0b with Supra at up to 14,400 bps. Estab. 12/93 with no fee. Small board new to the southwest. Many networks available, including FidoNet. Apogee and MVP distrib.

Bob's Westside: (602) 247-0405
Sysop: Bob Wilkens
2 lines—MS-DOS 386; 500MB running WildCat with Hayes at up to 14,400 bps. Estab. 01/78 with no fee. IBM/IBM compatibles. Also ASCII Club forum. Business, programming, and games. Ham radio forum.

The Sun State Fun BBS: (602) 971-4205
Sysop: Mark Gresin
2 lines—MS-DOS 386; 3,000MB running GTPower V-19 with US Robotics at up to 28,800 bps. Estab. 09/90 with no fee. 300+ message areas, games, and our own financial creative vision echo. Lots of fun and info.

---

best to have your service provider configure MacTCP for you to ensure that all settings are correct. If the provider won't do that, you need to find out several things, some of which will be needed when you configure SLIP or PPP: The service provider's modem phone number, an IP address (your unique Internet identifier), and an e-mail address for your use.

Whether your IP address is determined manually (you enter a permanent IP address) or dynamically (one is assigned by the host each time you log on). The name and IP address of your Domain Name Server (there might be more than one).

You may also need a gateway address for the server you're dialing in to. The name of your news server (the machine on which news-group information is stored). Now all you have to do is open the MacTCP control panel, click on the More button, and fill in the settings with the information you received from your service provider.

Once you have MacTCP configured, your next task is to configure SLIP or PPP software. SLIP tools such as Synergy Software's VersaTerm SLIP, part of VersaTilities, and InterCon Systems' InterSLIP, part of TCP/Connect II, come with commercial Internet software packages. InterSLIP is also distributed freely through the Internet. MacSLIP is available for $49.95 from TriSoft (800-531-5170). InterPPP is a separate product from InterCon Systems. MacPPP is available free on the Internet and from online services.

Be forewarned that not every Internet site supports SLIP and PPP. And, compared to terminal-emulation accounts, SLIP and PPP accounts are often more expensive. SLIP and PPP accounts are more likely to be billed on an hourly basis than are terminal-emulation accounts, so you may pay a higher monthly fee (more than $30 a month) plus a per-hour charge (as opposed to a flat fee of $20 a month for a terminal-emulation account).

SLIP is more common than PPP, primarily because it has been around longer. PPP, a more efficient protocol, is growing in acceptance. Since both kinds of access use the service provider's system in the same way, you shouldn't have to pay more for PPP. If you have a choice, pick PPP.

close look and tell us what it all means. I'd like to know!——John Dvorak

Saguaro Station BBS: (602) 846-2318
Sysop: Steve Thraen
2 lines—IBM 486/LAN; 1,300MB running WildCat 4.0 with US Robotics at up to 14,400 bps. Estab. 01/94 with no fee. Specializing in radio frequencies, Windows software. CD-ROM, QWKmail, fax door, games, files.

Phoenix PCUG BBS: (602) 222-5491
Sysop: MS-DOS 486; 1,500MB running PCBoard 15.1 with US Robotics at up to 38,400 bps. Estab. 07/84 with no fee. "Users helping users." Free 1/2 hr. access for nonmembers. Group news, conferences, files.

Terrestrial: (602) 945-8416
Sysop: David Ray
1 line—Novell network; 8,600MB running WildCat 3.9M with Zoom at up to 38,400 bps. Estab. 07/93 with a fee of $10 monthly. Thirteen online CDs, full Internet connection (Telnet, ftp), Internet e-mail/news, magazines, games.

BlackStar: (602) 459-6788
Sysop: Andrew Murphy
1 line—MS-DOS 486; 3,000MB running WildCat 4.00 with US Robotics at up to 38,400 bps. Estab. 09/91 with no fee. Messages, doors, thousands of file listings, and a place to meet nice people.

USA-Net Online: (602) 966-5155
Sysop: Dirk Hilbig
4 lines—MS-DOS 486; 1,500MB running WildCat 3.90 with Hayes at up to 14,400 bps. Estab. 08/91 with a fee of $12 monthly. Huge adults-only section. 20,000 files. Online games. Chat. PC Catalog. AdultNet and Internet.

Lightspeed Space Station BBS: (602) 325-6674
Sysop: Captain Donovan
1 line—MS-DOS 386; 130MB running Gap 6.4 with US Robotics at up to 14,400 bps. Estab. 03/93 with no fee. Star Trek/B5 news and info; Esterian Conquest, Ult. Universe, other space games; trivia, more.

Infoplus: (602) 623-7828
Sysop: Bill Rossmiller
20 lines—MS-DOS 486; 2,000MB running Galacticomm 6.2 with Boca at up to 14,400 bps. Estab. 01/94 with no fee. Online shopping, games, chat, fax, and databases. Full RIP support.

Utopian Gateway: (602) 628-9908
Sysop: Michael Elkanich
2 lines—MS-DOS 486; 2,000MB running Proboard 2.01 with Zoom at up to 14,400 bps. Estab. 06/94 with a fee of $50 annually. Run by 3 UofA medical students offering medical advice, info, and Q&A. 27,000 files, 30+ door games.

The Desert Reef: (602) 624-6386
Sysop: Eric Gray
1 line—486/40; 756MB running WildCat 3.91M with Boca at up to 14,400 bps. Estab. 01/94 with no fee. Artistic GIFs/aquarium-related files, tons of msg. bases, patriot issues and civil liberties, hobbies, lots more.

If you decide to go with a graphical Mac interface, you'll have several shareware Mac applications to choose from when assembling a software tool chest. Mail and news readers, FTP client software (the software used to transfer files to your Mac), information browsers, and clever utilities circulate freely from anonymous FTP sites. Most of this software is good and well supported. With these applications, you may miss some advanced features available in UNIX-based software on your Internet host—news readers don't yet support filtering of the kind you find on UNIX systems, for example—but using Mac software definitely beats learning UNIX.

Several telecommunications products take an integrated approach to the Internet.

Synergy Software's VersaTilities, Software Ventures' MicroPhone Pro II, and InterCon Systems' TCP/Connect II each combine e-mail, news, FTP, and Telnet into one software bundle. The integrated approach speeds configuration of your Internet account and provides a standard interface for several Internet services. You also gain the advantage of technical support.

Internet in the Office

Many companies, particularly in high technology, have joined the Internet, either through direct links (using their own UNIX-based systems) or through service providers. If your company has an Internet connection and allows its employees to access the Internet,

you may be able to reach the Internet directly from your Mac and the office network. Your system administrator should be able to provide what an Internet service provider would: MacTCP configuration and software. If your company is not on the Internet, it can purchase access from a service provider or buy equipment to make the connection.

Some businesses have integrated the net to the extent that Internet e-mail arrives on your Mac directly from your company's e-mail system. Several vendors, including StarNine, sell e-mail gateways. With one of the StarNine Mail*Link SMTP Internet e-mail gateways, a QuickMail, Microsoft Mail, or PowerTalk user can receive Internet e-mail. You can attach

Vulture Nest: (602) 684-3974
Sysop: Roy Reyer

1 line—MS-DOS 486; 500MB running PCBoard 15.1 with US Robotics at up to 19,200 bps. Estab. 09/91 with no fee. Community-based BBS. 10GB of files available on CD-ROM.

The Night-Line BBS: (602) 329-0691
Sysop: Leo P. Fisher

1 line—MS-DOS 386; 11,500MB running WildCat 4.00 with PPI PROClass Modem at up to 28,800 bps. Estab. 01/91 with a fee of $10 quarterly. Large collection of quality shareware and online doors.

The Batcave: (501) 632-4068
Sysop: Batman

1 line—MS-DOS 386; 300MB running WWIV 4.23 with Zoom at up to 38,400 bps. Estab. 12/93 with no fee. TradeWars/Usurper/BRE. Thousands of GIFs and games. CD-ROM online. BatNet, WWIVnet coming soon.

Starbase 13: (501) 898-4526
Sysop: Tracy Poole

1 line—Commodore with 30MB running Image 1.2a with Generic at up to 2,400 bps. Estab. 05/93 with no fee. Networked forums, online games, and PD/shareware files. Supporting Commodore, IBM, Mac.

Petit Jean BBS: (501) 493-2451
Sysop: Paul Wagner

4 lines—MS-DOS 486; 3,000MB running WildCat 4.0 with US Robotics at up to 57,600 bps. Estab. 05/89 with no fee. Generous UL/DL limits. Download first call. Amiga and IBM. Everyone welcome.

The Chicken Coop: (501) 273-2442
Sysop: Don Chick

4 lines—MS-DOS 386; 600MB running TBBS 2.2m16 with Hayes at up to 28,800 bps. Estab. 10/87 with a fee of $10 quarterly. Hayes Optima 288s online. Very popular, busy chat/message system, online games, large file library.

Black Fire BBS: (501) 545-3643
Sysop: Joey Fowler

1 line—MS-DOS 386; 1,100MB running Darkstar/QuickBBS 101.c/2.75 with Zoom at up to 19,200 bps. Estab. 04/94 with no fee. An extremely graphical program requiring the download of Commlink; otherwise use QBBS.

Wye Mtn. BBS: (501) 330-2845
Sysop: Paul Dolman

1 line—MS-DOS 386; 1,079MB running WildCat 3.9M with Boca/2 lines at up to 19,200 bps. Estab. 04/93 with no fee. Echoing Wildnet. 24,000+ files, games, Windows utils., and large TW 2002 file area. Access first call.

Redbeard's Place BBS: (501) 574-1124
Sysop: Redbeard

1 line—MS-DOS 386; 1,000MB running SpitFire 3.5 with Cardinal at up to 57,600 bps. Estab. 03/94 with no fee. Thousands of shareware and original files. Friendly users. SFNet.

---

files to e-mail messages, because StarNine gateways support MINE (Multipurpose Internet Mail Exchange), which lets you transfer non-text files such as spreadsheets and graphics via the Internet. These gateways must be installed on your local mail server, which must then be connected to the Internet.

Choosing a Good Service Provider

Whether you are seeking Internet access for yourself or for your organization, the choice of an Internet service provider is important. Since service providers offer connections to users with a wide variety of computers, it's important that the provider you select understands Mac connectivity. If the provider has never heard of MacTCP, it's probably a good idea to look elsewhere.

Service providers with Mac experience can help you configure a connection and can recommend software. Some standardize on e-mail, news readers, or other software, which they provide and/or support. You may even find newsgroups devoted to the provider's Internet services, where you can ask questions and get support.

Service providers' charges for Internet access vary, and you should shop around to find the best deal. Service providers with local phone numbers around the country make it possible for you to dial a local phone number for Internet access when you travel. On the other hand, these large service providers may charge more and offer less support than providers with fewer subscribers.

The explosive growth of the Internet has strained the resources of some service providers. Be sure that yours has enough phone lines to accommodate its users. Continual busy signals or a slow response from the host machine are warning signs.

Information, Please

The Internet's sheer vastness makes locating the service or information you seek a daunting prospect. Fortunately, information, both electronic and printed, is readily available to the curious. If you're looking for an Internet service provider, for example, have a friend who's

The Tower of High Sorcery: (501) 329-7508
Sysop: Chris Bates
2 lines—486DX2/66 OS/2; 4,000MB running RemoteAccess 2.02+ with Zoom at up to 28,800 bps. Estab. 02/93 with a fee of $1/30 days free. 30+ games, FidoNet via satellite, adult access, 6 CDs, BlueWave, and SX, new files daily.

The Gamma Quadrant: (501) 862-1560
Sysop: Paul Kuykendall
1 line—DESQView/X 386; 180MB running WWIV 4.23 with Boca at up to 19,200 bps. Estab. 05/94 with no fee. Featuring online games, message areas, and lots of files. Call for more great services.

The Serial Connection BBS: (501) 785-0477
Sysop: Russ K.
2 lines—MS-DOS 386; 3,600MB running WildCat 4.0 10M with Supra at up to 28,800 bps. Estab. 08/92 with a fee of $20 annually. 270 file areas, all on CD-ROM. Home of The Star Trek Log Book. Many Fido areas.

Hector Programmer's Forum: (501) 284-2086
Sysop: Chuck Poynter
1 line—MS-DOS 486; 1,200MB running TriBBS v5.1 with Dallas Fax at up to 14,400 bps. Estab. 10/91 with no fee. 175,000+ files. Lots of programmer's source code for Pascal, C, Assembler, BASIC, and others.

Camelot 2010: (501) 623-2010
Sysop: Robin Halbert
1 line—MS-DOS 386; 700MB running WildCat 3.91M with Intel at up to 57,600 bps. Estab. 12/94 with no fee. Door-oriented, TW 2002 v2, SRE, BRE. Utopia H.S. mail net w/Camelot and ISH. CD-ROM w/#2 soon.

The Moonman BBS: (501) 565-6868
Sysop: James Mooney
5 lines—MS-DOS 486; 20,000MB running WildCat 3.91M with US Robotics at up to 38,400 bps. Estab. 08/91 with a fee of $25 annually. 20GB, all interests. 20 CDs online. Games, IBM utils., Windows. 8GB adult ($25/year).

The Cutting Edge: (501) 663-3343
Sysop: William Billingsley
20 lines—DOS Pentium; 9,000MB running Galacticomm 6.21 with Generic at up to 28,800 bps. Estab. 10/92 with no fee. Chat, games, full Internet, Clinton-bashing, right-leaning free-speech system, health care, 663-Edge.

The Deserted Island: (501) 224-1605
Sysop: Mike Nestrud
1 line—Pentium/66; 500MB running Synchronet 2.0 with Hayes at up to 38,400 bps. Estab. 03/94 with no fee. CD-ROM, FidoNet echoes (1:3821/6).

The Gameroom: (501) 234-8128
Sysop: Bill Norris
1 line—MS-DOS 386; 90MB running RBBS 17.4 with Generic at up to 2,400 bps. Estab. 04/94 with no fee. Online games, messages, files, chat. Also boat/engine conf.

Backwoods Hideout: (501) 394-3076
Sysop: Blackheart
2 lines—MS-DOS 486; 550MB running Excaliber with US Robotics at up to 14,400 bps. Estab. 07/94 with a fee of $30 annually. 30,000+ files pertaining to computers and games w/adult area available.

The U.S.A. BBS: (501) 753-8575
Sysop: Jason Chandler/Robert Durham
16 lines—MS-DOS 486; 12,000MB running TBBS 2.2ML with AT&T at up to 19,200 bps. Estab. 02/93 with a monthly fee of $5. Varied user base. Truly a place where people from all walks of life can come live in peace.

RiverBend: (501) 563-6829
Sysop: Jim Tanner
2 lines—MS-DOS 486; 6,000MB running RemoteAccess 2.01 with US Robotics at up to 38,400 bps. Estab. 10/88 with a fee of $10 biannually. 40,000+ files of all descriptions. Graphics, database, MS-DOS utils. Home of GolfLog for Golfers.

already an Internetter provide you access to the Internet's nixpub or pdial lists.

Each of these directories, which are also posted on the Internet forums of such popular online services as America Online, CompuServe, and ZiffNet/Mac, provides listings of Internet service providers. Lists of FTP sites, mailing lists, and WWW servers can tell you where to find everything from Macintosh software to the lyrics of popular songs.

Internet books abound. At least two, accompanied by disks of shareware containing Internet utilities and tools, are specifically for Mac users. Adam Engst's *Internet Starter Kit for Macintosh* (Indianapolis: Hayden Books, 1993) comes with a copy of MacTCP, InterSLIP, the Eudora e-mail reader, and more. Michael Fraase's *The Macintosh Internet Tour Guide* (Chapel Hill, NC: Ventana Press, 1993) also comes with a disk of software. Each book includes lists of newsgroups, service providers, and ftp sites as well as detailed explanations of Internet services, conventions, and commands. If you're serious about exploring the Internet, these books will prove a valuable investment.

The Internet is a vast source of information, growing daily. Once you've started surfing the net, you won't regret the time it took you to get set up. In fact, the only regret you may have is that you have to log off and get back to work.—Joe Clark ∎

Absolute Zero: (501) 621-9047
Sysop: Anagoge
1 line—MS-DOS 486; 800MB running
RemoteAccess 2.01 with ZyXel U-1496-E at up to
14,400 bps. Estab. 04/92 with no fee. The source for
demos, intros, MOD, S3M, and the latest releases
from all demo groups.

The Power Station BBS: (501) 636-7974
Sysop: Thomas Morrow
1 line—MS-DOS 486; 1,500MB running Power
BBS/Windows 3.4 with US Robotics at up to 14,400
bps. Estab. 10/93 with no fee. Multiple online CD-
ROMs. Door games, echomail, and files for DOS,
Win, and OS/2.

Arkansas River Valley Online Services:
(501) 968-1931
Sysop: Michael Gray
2 lines—MS-DOS 486; 12,000MB running WildCat
WC 3.9M with Supra at up to 28,800 bps. Estab.
10/87 with a fee of $25 biannually. Home of
International Online Magazine and IOMag-Net. 9+
GB of files and fun. Also Internet access.

For God and Country BBS: (501) 843-2614
Sysop: Lynn and Gwen Sadler
1 line—MS-DOS 386; 240MB running Searchlight
v4.0 with US Robotics at up to 21,600 bps. Estab.
01/94 with no fee. Christian BBS. Pro-life, pro-
family, and pro-American. Many files for home
educators.

Back Door: (501) 469-5220
Sysop: Jeffery Goad/Jim Carter
1 line—MS-DOS 386; 345MB running SpitFire 3.4
with Generic at up to 14,400 bps. Estab. 05/94 with
a fee of $40 annually.

Shadow Lands BBS: (209) 452-1158
Sysop: Shadow Wing
1 line—MS-DOS 386; 700MB running Vision-X .99c
with Infotel at up to 28,800 bps. Estab. 03/93 with
no fee. VGA Planets game, Software Creation site,
Apogee, Epic. Lots of music files.

FresnoLink VFC BBS: (209) 225-8639
Sysop: Zoltan DeWitt
1 line—Macintosh; 40MB running TeleFinder 3.2
with Supra at up to 28,800 bps. Estab. 12/92 with
no fee. Graphic user interface for Macintosh. Just
like Finder. GIF, JPEG, PICT online previews.
600+MB.

CyberTown BBS: (209) 277-3008
Sysop: SharpShooter
32 lines—MS-DOS 486; 660MB running
Galacticomm 6.21f with Zoom V.FC at up to 28,800
bps. Estab. 06/93 with no fee. Chat, files, FidoNet,
interactive TradeWars. System is supported by
donations from happy users.

The Wizard's Palace VBBS: (209) 798-2092
Sysop: Mr. Wizard a.k.a./Glen Carter
1 line—MS-DOS 486; 2,000MB running VBBS 6.14a
with Hayes at up to 28,800 bps. Estab. 08/92 with
no fee. 5 CD-ROMs online. VirtualNet @1209006,
FidoNet @1:214/26, online games. Thousands of
message bases.

R&R BBS: (209) 998-7249
Sysop: Bill Quinn
1 line—MS-DOS 486; 410MB running WildCat 3.9S
with US Robotics at up to 14,400 bps. Estab. 09/92
with no fee. Massive registered doors. 1000+ of the
newest files. FidoNet 1:214/53, FlyNet 196:6010/6.

Hangar 7: (209) 675-3218
Sysop: Dennis E. Conner
1 line—MS-DOS 486; 700MB running
RemoteAccess 2.02+ with Zoom at up to 14,400 bps.
Estab. 01/89 with no fee. Christian and aviation.
FlyNet, Fido, RBBS.

The Punchline BBS: (209) 525-9985
Sysop: The Joker
1 line—MS-DOS 386; 350MB running WWIV 4.21
with US Robotics at up to 19,200 bps. Estab. 12/92
with no fee. Subs include jokes, debate, and technical
discussion. Games and file section also available.

The Golden Nugget: (209) 575-4405
Sysop: Diamond Lil
2 lines—MS-DOS 486; 680MB running Searchlight
4.0 with US Robotics at up to 38,400 bps. Estab.
07/87 with a fee of $20 annually. 4 CD-ROMs
online, RIP graphics, free access available.

The Tim Continuum: (209) 877-4921
Sysop: Tim Wisseman
1 line—MS-DOS 286; 245MB running WildCat 4.0
with US Robotics at up to 14,400 bps. Estab. 07/93
with no fee. Main support board for VGA Planets,
an e-mail-based 11-player space combat game.
Download it here.

The Gallows Pole: (209) 847-6656
Sysop: Trebor
1 line—MS-DOS 486; 340MB running RBBS 5-31
with Zoom at up to 14,400 bps. Estab. 06/94 with
no fee.

The Wrong Number Virtual Community:
(209) 943-1880
Sysop: Charles R. Hague, "kcuhC."
4 lines—MS-DOS 386; 1,000MB running PCBoard
15.1 /10 with Supra at up to 19,200 bps. Estab.
06/87 with no fee. Intelligent conversation and lots
of files (adult and regular). Next time, dial the
Wrong Number.

The Code-3 BBS: (209) 686-3575
Sysop: David Singleton
1 line—MS-DOS 286; 130MB running Renegade
5.31 with Generic at up to 14,400 bps. Estab. 10/93
with no fee. 2 CD-ROMs online, free access to
7,000+ files. Adult, shareware, IBM, and Mac files
and messages.

Mr. Wonderful's Lair: (213) 261-8055
Sysop: Daniel Barcenas (Mr. Wonderful)
4 lines—MS-DOS 486; 2,100MB running WildCat
4.0 with Hayes at up to 28,800 bps. Estab. 06/93
with a fee of $10 monthly. ASP-approved. Internet,
echomail, games (local and InterBBS), 12 CDs
online, adult files, and mail.

Connect Time

Increasing numbers of people are hopping aboard online services. This is a good thing; the more, the merrier. Still, I can't help but notice that certain bad habits keep cropping up. In an effort to maintain civility, here are some tips from Vaughan-Nichols's rules of online etiquette.

It all begins with respecting your fellow users. Too many people seem to think that just because they're online, they've been given a license to be rude—they couldn't be more mistaken. Insults sting just as hard when writ-ten on cathode-ray tubes as they do in person. Online arguments can get heated, but there's never any call to resort to personal insults.

If you've ever been "flamed," you know that your first powerful impulse is to immediately respond in kind. But usually a far better course is to file the flame, log off, and think long and hard about the consequences of adding fuel to the fire before responding. It's the equivalent of counting to ten. Although some charges might warrant an immediate shoot-from-the-hip response, it's more often the case that flamers discredit themselves by flaming. Anger is contagious, but so is patience. In the long run, thinking like Gandhi online will benefit you more than acting like Wesley Snipes.

Another example of poor manners is how women are sometimes treated online. All too many female friends have recounted instances in which they've gotten lewd mail messages or online chat requests from jerks who know nothing about them except that their online name indicates they're women. This is completely unacceptable behavior that's just as destructive to open communication online as it is in the real world.

I'll get off my soapbox now, and move on to the latest news. I know you share my hopes that 1995 will be a thoroughly courteous year online.

People who have kids have never really had enough choices in their online selections. But with the introduction of the online version

The Westside: (213) 954-4444
Sysop: HBFH 6, Bat 7
160 lines—Unix; 7,500MB running Metropolis 1.101b with AMT at up to 2,400 bps. Estab. 04/87 with a fee of $10 monthly. ASP-approved. Large shareware/GIF lib. Forums, games, chat, 10,000+ members, much more.

CyberKorea: (310) 926-1899
Sysop: J. Kim
3 lines—MS-DOS 486; 800MB running Galacticomm 6.21d with 14,400 at up to 14,400 bps. Estab. 01/94 with no fee. PC support, files, business, education, Korean software, Game Connection (modem-to-modem games).

Far East Asian Connection BBS: (310) 402-5213
Sysop: Denny Chuang
1 line—MS-DOS 486; 1,000MB running PCBoard 15.1 with Supra at up to 38,400 bps. Estab. 06/92 with no fee. Supports Big 5 Chinese characters. Carries Fido, RIME, CCNet,and Internet conferences.

Miller's Party Board: (310) 815-0117
Sysop: Jack Stern
32 lines—MS-DOS 486; 1,230MB running Galacticomm 6.2 with AT&T Paradyne at up to 14,400 bps. Estab. 06/93 with a fee of $10 monthly. 32 lines of chat, live games nightly, WorldLink, online games, TradeWars 2002 v2, pubs, and more.

LabsLine/ComputerTutor BBS: (310) 643-9566
Sysop: Doctor Science
1 line—Pentium 90; 2,000MB running PowerBBS Windows 3.4d with US Robotics at up to 57,600 bps. Estab. 12/91 with a fee of $10 annually. Full-featured BBS. Science/student topics, games: Doom, ID, Apogee, Epic, adult, and free Internet e-mail.

Upper Transylvania BBS: (310) 515-6843
Sysop: Ron Hoffman
2 lines—MS-DOS 486; 400MB running WildCat 4.00M with US Robotics at up to 28,800 bps. Estab. 03/93 with no fee. Approx. 4GB of files online. Western hub for Fishnet Christian network. For all PC users.

LabsLine: (310) 643-9566
Sysop: Doctor Science
3 lines—Pentium 90; 2,500MB running PowerBBS/Windows 3.1 3.5 with US Robotics at up to 38,400 bps. Estab. 01/92 with a fee of $10 biannually. Public Internet access and full-service BBS. DOOM. Games, public health info, local news, and adult.

The Bizopps Connection: (310) 677-7034
Sysop: Lawrence C. Toliver
1 line—MS-DOS 486; 250MB running The Major BBS 6.21-2 with Practical Peripherals at up to 14,400 bps. Estab. 07/92 with a fee of $10 monthly. Business and franchise opportunities, money-making opportunities, venture-capital sources, and more.

The Crypt BBS: (310) 690-1780
Sysop: Mortifier
3 lines—MS-DOS 486; 2,600MB running Synchronet 2.00b with ZyXel at up to 16,800 bps. Estab. 11/92 with no fee. Multinode, 20,000+ files, networked messages, online games, chat, CD-ROMs, more.

of the *Disney Adventures* magazine (keyword: Disney), America Online (AOL) becomes a kid's delight.

Besides giving youngsters the text of each month's issue, Disney Adventures features message boards, realtime discussion groups, and a chance for kids to talk to the editors of the magazine. If I were ten again, I'd love this place, and I'm betting your kids will love it, too.

Internet-connected online services are springing up like mushrooms after an April shower, and America Online is also leaping to link up with the Internet. AOL has long had a mail connection to the Internet. You can mail to AOL users with the address: user_name@aol.com. Now, however, AOL's

Internet Center brings other Internet features to its users.

AOL plans to phase in Internet services gradually to ensure that nothing goes haywire. I can't blame AOL one bit, because the initial plans are ambitious, including access to WAIS and gopher. These are Internet services that greatly reduce wear and tear on service- and file-hunting users. AOL will also bring Usenet's ever-popular news groups and online discussion groups to its users. As a longtime fan of AOL's interface, I'm looking forward to seeing how AOL tames the unruly Internet.

BIX also has big plans for the Internet and is redesigning its Windows interface program, BIXnav, and renaming it Internav.

This won't be just a cosmetic change. Internav makes it possible to work with BIX and the Internet almost transparently. For example, you'll download a file from a remote Internet site just as you would when copying a file with Windows' File Manager. That's it. You don't have to know about ftp or even Zmodem; Internav takes care of everything for you. Downloading files, much less ftping files, has never been easier.

Now, that's the theory. I haven't had the opportunity to see an actual beta, but if BIX makes good on its promises, this will be the Internet interface to beat. The really hot news from CompuServe is that it has broken the online speed record by being the first major online service to offer 14,400-bps access. By

Independent Filmmakers Forum: (310) 425-0012
Sysop: Philip Matuzic

8 lines—MS-DOS 486; 1,400MB running WildCat 4.0 with Practical Peripherals at up to 14,400 bps. Estab. 05/93 with a fee of $19.95 quarterly. Online networking for independents, forums, e-mail, chat, free screening passes, and movie promos.

Fantasia BBS: (310) 986-9705
Sysop: Brian Andrus

1 line—MS-DOS 486; 2,500MB running Maximus 2.01 with Zoom at up to 38,400 bps. Estab. 02/92 with a fee of $25 biannually. Free access to many items including Internet. Online games, FidoNet, CD-ROMs, ASP releases. Epic.

The French Flyer BBS: (310) 597-2235
Sysop: Greg French

4 lines—MS-DOS 486; 3,000MB running WildCat 3.9 with US Robotics at up to 38,400 bps. Estab. 06/92 with a fee of $25 annually. Free 1st call download access to 50,000+ files. Subscription includes unlimited files and Internet.

The Colossal Collection BBS: (310) 422-8599
Sysop: Mach 4

3 lines—MS-DOS 486; 6,000MB running WildCat 3.90m with Practical Peripherals at up to 38,400 bps. Estab. 07/93 with no fee. 6+ GB online, group chat, echomail, doors, 33,000+ files ,and growing.

The Home Office On-Line: (310) 422-0401
Sysop: Don Bearor

9 lines—MS-DOS 486; 2,800MB running PCBoard 15.1/10 with US Robotics at up to 14,400 bps. Estab. 03/94 with a fee of $25 annually. 4 boards on each line. Main board, Windows board, office board, network board. Free visiting!

Why Not: (310) 436-1311
Sysop: David A. Scott

5 lines—MS-DOS 486; 300MB running WildCat 4.0 with US Robotics at up to 14,400 bps. Estab. 03/89 with no fee. 4 CDs, adult areas, private chat, all major shareware, online games, TW 2002, great for beginners.

BBS Guide (type [tbgh] at login): (310) 477-0408
Sysop: Tom Hamilton

32 lines—MS-DOS 486; 500MB running Galacticomm Major BBS with Generic at up to 14,400 bps. Estab. 04/94 with a fee of $3.33 hourly. Online BBS yellow pages. Search by category/keyword/technical/networks. Sysops can advertise also.

The DragonsBane BBS: (310) 472-4484
Sysop: Warlock

1 line—MS-DOS 486; 1,000MB running WWIV 4.23 with Intel at up to 14,400 bps. Estab. 08/93 with no fee. Great message subs, online games, and 2 CD-ROMs online.

Manhattan Online: (310) 374-9994
Sysop: Paul Swanno

4 lines—MS-DOS 486; 2,000MB running WildCat 4.0 with Hayes at up to 28,800 bps. Estab. 06/93 with no fee. Latest in DOS, Windows, Mac, and OS/2 shareware. FidoNet, Internet, CD-ROMs, PC Catalog, much more.

the time you read this, CIS should have 14,400-bps lines active in most major cities.

Better still, CIS isn't adding extra fees for zooming your data long at the new speed limit. The 14,000-bps access will cost the same as 9,600-bps access. While that's not exactly cheap, and your tab will still run from $16 to $22.80 an hour, getting 50 percent more throughput for a zero percent increase in charges is a great boon, and a healthy model for other online services upgrading their access rates to follow.

What's CRIS? CRIS, from Concentric Research Corp., is a new entry in the online races. CRIS offers the usual range of services, e-mail, teleconferencing, news, online shopping, and so on, and while it's small in relation to giants like CompuServe and Prodigy, it's a friendly service with some unique attributes.

CRIS's basic service fee is $20 a month. Yes, that's higher than many other online services. But CRIS becomes affordable when you consider that this fee buys you 10 hours of connect time at any connection speed from 1,200 to 14,400 bps. Every additional hour will cost you a mere $2 an hour, again regardless of how fast your connection is. CRIS will also be supporting 19,200-bps connections as the next generation of modems begins to enter the market.

The other neat thing about CRIS is its BBS Direct service. Once you're in the CRIS system, you can head to a menu and pick out a BBS based on geographical location or content type. Once you've picked one out, CRIS takes care of connecting you to the BBS. This will run you an additional $2 an hour, but that's a lot cheaper then trying to dial into the BBS via long distance. If you're interested in giving CRIS a look, the service can be reached on Sprintnet by entering C CRIS at the @ prompt. You also can call the service directly at (517) 895-0510. If you want to talk it over first with a CRIS representative, you can reach one at (800) 745-2747.

The big news from Delphi comes in two parts. First, General Videotext, Delphi's parent company, is changing its name to Delphi Internet Services. Second, Rupert Murdoch, millionaire and media mogul, has bought the company. What does Murdoch's takeover mean to you? Well, for starters, the name change

LACS BBS: (310) 827-8171
Sysop: Frances Ames
2 lines—MS-DOS 486; running VBBS with Generic at up to 8 bps. Estab. 12/92 with no fee. For the members of the Los Angeles Computer Society.

The Gameman BBS: (310) 537-7534
Sysop: Derrick Wagner
1 line—MS-DOS 486; 840MB running WildCat 4.0 with Cal-Com at up to 14,400 bps. Estab. 08/94 with no fee. The best place to find the latest and greatest in shareware games. 3GB+ of the best.

Coastline File Exchange: (310) 396-6011
Sysop: Steve Sobka
2 lines—MS-DOS 486; 1,000MB running WildCat 4.0 with US Robotics at up to 19,200 bps. Estab. 11/92 with no fee. Dedicated to the community for file exchange, Net-Echo mail, Fido, Internet, online games, everything.

The Vortex: (310) 212-7666
Sysop: Michael Anders
1 line—MS-DOS 486; 540MB running VBBS 6.14 with Hayes at up to 14,400 bps. Estab. 04/94 with no fee. Door games and CD-ROM library. No upload/download library. VNet @1310011.

The Inner Circle BBS: (310) 532-7444
Sysop: Surfman
2 lines—MS-DOS 486; 200MB running Renegade 12.25 with Datacomm at up to 14,400 bps. Estab. 12/93 with no fee. West Coast RC, Los Angeles hub for PowerNet, 1.5GB files access. No DL/UL ratios. Quick validations.

Xchange-Net: (310) 452-3374
Sysop: RexBrains
2 lines—MS-DOS 486; 300MB running Custom with Intel at up to 9,600 bps. Estab. 12/92 with no fee. A swap meet of computer hardware/software and anything else this side of Saturn.

Compu-Net Online Services: (310) 822-0038
Sysop: Customer Service
20 lines—MS-DOS 486; 1,800MB running WildCat 3.9 with Hayes at up to 38,400 bps. Estab. 06/88 with a fee of $35 quarterly. SoCal's large file and message board. Internet, dating, IBM, Mac, Amiga, adult, stocks, news.

Garlique Graphics Image Center: (408) 847-0665
Sysop: Greg Leas
12 lines—MS-DOS 486; 7,000MB running WildCat 4.0 with US Robotics at up to 19,200 bps. Estab. 07/90 with no fee. World famous images.

The Ride BBS: (408) 399-4515
Sysop: Tex/Pandora
14 lines—MS-DOS 486; 3,000MB running Galacticomm 6.21F with US Robotics at up to 14,400 bps. Estab. 04/86 with a fee of $10/20 hours. Internet, Usenet, satellite, 10MB files a day, ladies free. Chat. Tons of games, MajorNet.

signifies a new direction for Delphi. While other online services are increasing their Internet capacities, it would appear that Delphi is going full-bore into the Internet. Next, Murdoch, love him or hate him, is a mover and a shaker. I suspect Delphi will be changing from its current rather sleepy self to a major online player. Transformations like this typically take a lot of cash, but Murdoch has deep pockets.

Is Delphi destined to become a "tabloid" online service? Right now, it's too soon to tell. Currently, the only concrete change wrought from Murdoch's purchase is that Murdoch's News Corp. plans to market a worldwide, PC-accessible online newspaper. Other online services have moved in this direction—witness the partnership between *The Chicago Tribune*

and America Online. Even so, what News Corp. proposes is an entirely new level of online newspaper, so it's worth watching.

Virtual reality is the hottest topic around these days, and GEnie is on top of the situation. One of the service's newest roundtables is devoted to virtual reality, multimedia, and desktop video. This new service will look at everything from the high end of specialized virtual reality equipment to the more mundane issues of working with desktop video on the Amiga with Video Toaster. Type Cyberspace or Move 2000 at any major GEnie prompt to get to it.

Another cutting-edge area of computing to which GEnie is paying attention is the PowerPC. Two new roundtables devoted to Motorola's RISC chip are in place: the

PowerPC RoundTable, devoted to general discussions for PowerPC users, and the PowerPC Developers RoundTable, for development support. Both forums can be reached in GEnie's Computing RoundTables area.

Two or three times a week, I get a request from someone asking about how to connect with the Internet. Although connecting keeps getting easier every day, it's still not as easy as checking out CIS with the free trial membership that came with your modem. Even so, it just became easier than ever to connect to the Internet thanks to a book and a new Internet information service.

Connecting to the Internet, by Susan Estrada (O'Reilly and Associates, ISBN 1-56592-061-9), gives you the tools to do exactly what

---

Monterey Gaming System: (408) 655-5555
Sysop: David and Lisa Janakes
32 lines—MS-DOS 486; 600MB running MGS Custom Software with Supra at up to 14,400 bps. Estab. 01/92 with no fee. 32 lines. Free Internet e-mail, live chat, monthly contests, custom games, Time-SlipI, and much more.

Nitelog BBS: (408) 655-1096
Sysop: Karl Van Lear
26 lines—MS-DOS 486; 8,400MB running PCBoard 15.1 with US Robotics at up to 28,800 bps. Estab. 02/89 with a fee of $28 quarterly. Internet e-mail/Usenet/FidoNet/RIME/ILink. Chat. DOS/Mac/OS/2/Windows/Unix, and adult. Nat'l weather update.

Breakwater BBS: (408) 899-3104
Sysop: Mark Herrick
2 lines—MS-DOS 486; 800MB running WildCat 4.0 with Supra at up to 14,400 bps. Estab. 08/93 with no fee. General files and utils. Ham radio and scanning areas. Wildnet and AR-Net echoes.

San Jose Connection: (408) 956-8819
Sysop: Earl Faneuf
2 lines—MS-DOS 486; 2,000MB running PCBoard 15.1 with US Robotics at up to 14,400 bps. Estab. 07/89 with no fee. Files, job listings, GIFs, messages, Internet, StudNet, FidoNet.

The Shuttle BBS: (408) 289-1911
Sysop: Michael S. Vedda
1 line—MS-DOS 486; 26,000MB running RemoteAccess Rapro 2.02 with Hayes at up to 28,800 bps. Estab. 06/91 with no fee. Full multimedia support BBS. Online doors. 28.8. ANSI/RIP/VGA. 2 CD-ROMs online.

Unofficial Software Support BBS (USSBBS): (408) 464-0350
Sysop: Roger Wegehoft
4 lines—MS-DOS 486; 350MB running Galacticomm 6.x with US Robotics at up to 9,600 bps. No fee. User-to-user software support. All products. Writer's workshops. Unique files and graphics. TeamB.

Borland On-line Automated Support: (408) 431-5250
Sysop: Roger Wegehoft
16 lines—MS-DOS 486; 1,000MB running Galacticomm 6.x with MICC at up to 9,600 bps. Estab. 12/91 with no fee. Guided access support, file libs (code, examples, patches), usr2usr msgs., Telecon, RIP graphics.

its title promises. This short publication tells you all you'll need to know about connecting to the Internet: whether you want just a dial-up asynchronous connection to read mail or an all-out 1.54-MB/sec net connection. If you've got Internet connection questions, this is the book to go to. I only wish I had written it.

Of course, a book is bound in time, and some of the specific connection information will date quickly. Thanks to a service provided by Peter Kaminski, keeping up to date is no longer a problem. Kaminski compiles the Public Dialup Internet Access List (PDIAL). This list, which is updated regularly, contains listings for all public-access Internet sites. PDIAL includes full details on the kind of services provided, their cost, and areas where

the service is available. To get the most recent copy of PDIAL, all you need do is send a message to the Internet address: info-deli-server@netcom.com, and you'll automatically get a copy by return post.

Finally, Prodigy is also getting into the Internet act. By the time you read this, Prodigy will have introduced its own mail gateway to the Internet. To send mail to a Prodigy user, use the following address format: user_id@prodigy.com. For example, my Prodigy address is: VBKP51F@prodigy.com.
—Steven J. Vaughan-Nichols ■

The OtherSide: (415) 802-9661
Sysop: Rob Glasener
1 line—MS-DOS 486; 500MB running Searchlight 4.0 with US Robotics at up to 14,400 bps. Estab. 05/93 with no fee. Great message bases including Usenet, Fido, RIME. 100 doors, 9 CD-ROMs. Growing all the time.

P.C. Hackers Nest BBS: (415) 755-2284
Sysop: Ben Gordon
1 line—MS-DOS 386; 600MB running WildCat 3.90s with Hayes at up to 2,400 bps. Estab. 03/94 with no fee. Tech. talk and more. Stupid computer tricks. Bikini babes. Sarcasm. Alien thought processes and stuff.

Flying High BBS: (415) 467-2303
Sysop: Jack Garner
1 line—MS-DOS 386; 1,700MB running WildCat 3.91M with Lightning 14.4 at up to 57,600 bps. Estab. 11/92 with no fee. Games, Windows files, gay/straight Asian XXX. Validation for adult access. New users always welcome.

Springboard: (415) 327-4591
Sysop: Wendie/Mike/Lisa/Bob/Scott
8 lines—MS-DOS 486; 850MB running Galacticomm 6.2 with AT&T Paradyne at up to 14,400 bps. Estab. 05/93 with a fee of $9.95 monthly. Great discussions of current events. Free Internet e-mail/forums, Reuters/AP news, free 30 days.

Window World BBS: (415) 931-0649
Sysop: Bob Cram
3 lines—MS-DOS 386; 300MB running WildCat 3.0 with US Robotics at up to 14,400 bps. Estab. 08/90 with no fee. Devoted mainly to Windows-type software. Hundreds of shareware programs for Windows.

NightShade Online Services: (415) 456-2126
Sysop: Sage Information Systems
5 lines—MS-DOS 486; 6,000MB running PCBoard PCB 15.1 with US Robotics at up to 14,400 bps. Estab. 06/92 with a fee of $30 quarterly. Internet e-mail, 1,000s of Internet conferences, huge XXX, DOS, Mac, IBM, virus, fonts, 1000+ new files.

California Online Internet Services: (415) 331-4081
Sysop: Chris Ward
72 lines—MS-DOS 486; 7,300MB running Galacticomm + Unix with Supra at up to 19,200 bps. Estab. 07/92 with a fee of $15 monthly. Internet provider. Shell accounts/SLIP/PPP/dedicated access. Full BBS services, California chat line.

StarPort Valhalla: (510) 522-3583
Sysop: Papa Bear (Tracy Baker)
1 line—DR-DOS 386SX-33; 2,152MB running WWIV 4.23 with Practical Peripherals at up to 19,200 bps. Estab. 10/90 with no fee. 9 networks, many online games, 25,000+ files for downloading, major WWIV support/programming.

KRIJAQ BBS: (510) 673-0103
Sysop: John Dulaney
1 line—MS-DOS 486; 170MB running PCBoard TD with Zoltrix at up to 14,400 bps. Estab. 06/94 with no fee. CD-ROM, floppy, hardware, deep discount catalogs; games; text; D/L first time.

The GIFt Shop: (510) 609-1123
Sysop: Waik Gan
20 lines—Pentium 90; 50,000MB running WildCat 4.0 with US Robotics at up to 28,800 bps. Estab. 09/90 with a fee of $20.35 quarterly. Reknowned images worldwide. To get the best images in town, you just need to push the right buttons.

Windows OnLine: (510) 736-8343
Sysop: Frank Mahaney
17 lines—MS-DOS 486; 13,000MB running PCBoard 15.1 with US Robotics at up to 38,400 bps. Estab. 11/90 with a fee of $69.95 annually. Largest Windows BBS (26,000 Win 3.x files). Internet e-mail. Publisher of the WinOnLine Review Mags.

Synergy: (510) 743-9314
Sysop: N. Alex Carr
3 lines—MS-DOS 486; 800MB running Searchlight 4.0 with Best Data at up to 14,400 bps. Estab. 10/88 with no fee. A forum for open discussion and free thought. Free access and instant validation first call.

Sonshine Express Christian BBS: (510) 797-8700
Sysop: Anton Johnson
1 line—MS-DOS 386; 119MB running TBBS 2.1m with US Robotics at up to 9,600 bps. Estab. 03/94 with no fee. Christianity, FidoNet, PC-Clubhouse PC User Group BBS.

Bay Area Mega Board: (510) 247-8300
Sysop: Sam Thompson
16 lines—MS-DOS 486; 38,800MB running TBBS 2.2 with Microcom at up to 57,600 bps. Estab. 11/93 with no fee. UltraChat, games, nets, and 35.16 GB including newest CDs, Planet Connect feeds, and VSysop.

Lost Worlds BBS: (510) 888-1714
Sysop: David Parks
3 lines—MS-DOS Pentium 90; 3,500MB running WildCat 4.0M with Infotel 14.4 at up to 57,600 bps. Estab. 04/91 with a fee of $9.95 quarterly. Hot BBS with 3.5GB online. Sizzling hot adult section. Full Internet, Fido, echo, and more.

The Clubhouse BBS, Hayward Chapter: (510) 785-1123
Sysop: Tim Wilcox
1 line—MS-DOS 486; 3,000MB running EZYcom 1.2 with Microcom at up to 38,400 bps. Estab. 06/89 with no fee. General-interest. Genealogy and naturist/nudist message areas. No adult areas.

ORiON: (510) 447-1060
Sysop: Shaun Coleman
2 lines—MS-DOS 486; 620MB running Renegade 1-2 Exp with Zoom Telephonics at up to 28,800 bps. Estab. 03/93 with no fee. Space/science-related BBS. Many msg. nets, tons of files, intelligent users, 28.8K. 600+MB online.

Eyes on the Skies: (510) 443-6146
Sysop: Mike Rushford
1 line—MS-DOS 386; 2,000MB running PCBoard 15/2d with AT&T Paradyne at up to 38,400 bps. Estab. 03/91 with no fee. Mature astronomy, FidoNet, Internet. Telescope to use via modem. View by GIFs live.

Great Mutant Valley BBS: (510) 294-9052
Sysop: Sysop (Dave)
4 lines—MS-DOS 386; 600MB running Galacticomm V6.21 with Practical Peripherals at up to 9,600 bps. Estab. 12/88 with a fee of $15 annually. Fun and files. Door, telecon, and flash games. Amiga, Mac, IBM support. Kid and adult access.

Fred Haney and Sons Computers: (510) 792-5119
Sysop: Fred Haney
2 lines—MS-DOS 386; 300MB running WildCat 3.90 M with Generic at up to 14,400 bps. Estab. 01/91 with no fee. To promote sale/service of PC components and systems. A national distributor. Dealers call.

The Access Network: (619) 247-1816
Sysop: Robert Parsons/Paul Reimche
2 lines—MS-DOS 386; 540MB running PCBoard 15.2 with US Robotics at up to 28,800 bps. Estab. 04/91 with no fee. Distribution site: MVP, Apogee, ID, Software Creations. Friendly message bases. AccessNet, RelayNet.

Public Access BBS: (619) 665-8028
Sysop: John Sayer
1 line—MS-DOS 386; 650MB running WildCat 3.9 with US Robotics at up to 19,200 bps. Estab. 03/93 with no fee. General/adult files. CD-ROM. 9,200 + programs. Netmail. Novices welcome. Dl 1st call.

Hi-Desert Amiga BBS: (619) 947-4856
Sysop: Victor Bobier
1 line—Amiga; 397MB running BaudBandit BBS v.7.4 with US Robotics at up to 14,400 bps. Estab. 06/94 with no fee.

The Rosicrucian Fellowship BBS: (619) 721-1828
Sysop: Marie-Jose Clerc
1 line—MS-DOS 486; 525MB running Galacticomm 6.21 with Practical Peripherals at up to 14,400 bps. Estab. 06/92 with no fee. Dedicated to the promulgation of Rosicrucian Christianity via multilingual text file download library.

Gray's Anatomy: (619) 778-1866
Sysop: Jeff Brewi
1 line—MS-DOS 386; 210MB running WildCat 2.5s with Boca Research at up to 14,400 bps. Estab. 10/92 with a fee of $36 annually. Dedicated to research and serious discussion on topics of UFOs, paranormal, and newsworthy events.

Ground Zero BBS: (619) 325-5038
Sysop: Scott "Conrad" Estes
1 line—MS-DOS 486; 840MB running Renegade 05-31 Exp. with Zoom FVX 28.8k at up to 38,400 bps. Estab. 01/94 with a fee of $30 optional. 1 CD-ROM online, 10 CDs total. BayDez discussion net, Renegade utils., adult areas w/proof of age.

Computing Technology BBS: (619) 371-1665
Sysop: Rod Kenly
1 line—MS-DOS 386; 7,000MB running PCBoard 15.1 with Intel at up to 14,400 bps. Estab. 01/86 with a fee of $25 annually. Large # files: CDs, nets: ILink, U'NI, INTELEC, MetroNet, Usenet, Internet e-mail. Sat. system.

Bare Bones BBS: (619) 384-2824
Sysop: Snow Dragon
1 line—MS-DOS 386; 420MB running WildCat 4.0 M10 with Supra at up to 28,800 bps. Estab. 06/92 with no fee. Node of JobNet career search network and Throb-Net adult network. Utilities, GIFs, text files.

BIZynet BBS: (619) 283-1721
Sysop: Chris Gunn
3 lines—MS-DOS 386; 160MB running QuickBBS 2.76 with ZyXel at up to 14,400 bps. Estab. 03/90 with no fee. Business-oriented BBS and network for small-business persons with a balance for the family side of life.

Deuce Bruce Exclusive Horseplayer's BBS: (619) 542-1662
Sysop: Kimberley Coulson
1 line—MS-DOS 486; 65,670MB running WildCat 3.9 with Hayes at up to 14,400 bps. Estab. 06/94 with a fee of $40 monthly. Exclusive horseplayer's BBS. Handicapping programs, horseracing games, daily tips, and best bets.

Sailing San Diego: (619) 792-2785
Sysop: Norman McPhail
1 line—MS-DOS 486; 210MB running RoboBoard 1.04 with Generic at up to 14,400 bps. Estab. 05/94 with a fee of $10 monthly. Sailing BBS with race results, crew lists, sailing tips, nautical shareware, sailing pictures, more.

Club->Infinity: (619) 728-8878
Sysop: Dennis Ditoro
100 lines—MS-DOS 486; 9,999MB running Galacticomm 6.21f with US Robotics at up to 38,400 bps. Estab. 07/92 with no fee. 60GB. Live chat/news/sports/100+ games/57 CDs.

PD-SIG Inc., "The TBBS": (619) 749-2741
Sysop: BJ Nash
5 lines—MS-DOS 8088;1,000MB running TBBS 2.2 16M with Zoom 28.8 at up to 28,800 bps. Estab. 10/86 with no fee. Multiple lines, multiple SIGs for various types of computers and interests.

The Philosopher's Stone BBS: (707) 464-8722
Sysop: Larry Simmons
1 line—Pentium; 540MB running WildCat 3.91 with Supra at up to 19,200 bps. Estab. 05/94 with no fee. Featuring unusual files. Individual creativity encouraged.

The Aerodrome BBS: (707) 464-1128
Sysop: Chuck Essex
1 line—MS-DOS 386; 230MB running WildCat 3.9 with US Robotics at up to 14,400 bps. Estab. 03/94 with a fee of $15 annually. CD-ROM file area, door games, a place for modem game players to meet and set up challenges.

The Study Group: (707) 441-1196
Sysop: William Maxwell
1 line—MS-DOS 386; 215MB running RBBS 17.4 with Supra at up to 14,400 bps. Estab. 03/94 with no fee. Education-oriented BBS. K-graduate school. Education and other related FidoNet echoes.

InfoSearch Research BBS: (707) 442-8984
Sysop: Jeffrey McDonald
1 line—MS-DOS 386; 200MB running PowerBBS 3.5 with Zoom at up to 19,200 bps. Estab. 03/12 with no fee. A free information and text BBS provided by InfoSearch Research Systems.

Internet for Profit; Businesses Rush to Capitalize on the Internet

In the Internet, Richard Bangs has discovered a high-tech tool that helps people get to low-tech places. Bangs, co-founder of Mountain Travel-Sobek, an adventure travel company in El Cerrito, California, that takes its customers to exotic and remote locations, says one of the biggest adventures his company has undertaken in its 25-year history was its decision earlier this year to explore the Internet as a new way of doing business.

"Someone signed up recently to get to the outback of Turkey," Bangs recalled. "He was out browsing the Internet and came across our travel resource center on the Net, and he signed up on the spot. He sent me an e-mail that day, saying, 'I'm outta here, I'm gone.'"

Across the United States and, indeed, across the world, thousands of businesses have set a course for the Internet, where they see a new frontier for doing business. From giant international corporations to tiny bookstores, businesses are opening up shop online, tapping into the global network's vast pools of information, or using its communications facilities in order to become active in the emerging global marketplace.

To support these businesses, scores of Internet service providers, entrepreneurs who portray themselves as online real-estate developers, and commercial consortia are being created. On the Internet today, you can buy a computer or shop for erotic lingerie; hold an international conference or send flowers to a customer; research current Securities and Exchange Commission filings or the latest headlines and foreign-currency quotes; hand out electronic

Clever Endeavor BBS: (707) 263-6612
Sysop: George Ramos

1 line—MS-DOS 486; 1,500MB running PC Board 15.1 with US Robotics at up to 38,400 bps. Estab. 08/89 with no fee. The fun place to call. Free access. No ratios. 1.5GB+, 2 lines, latest 1994 files.

The Spiders Web: (707) 937-2755
Sysop: SugerLips

1 line—Macintosh; 500MB running TeleFinder 3.1 with LineLink at up to 9,600 bps. Estab. 02/94 with no fee. CD-ROM online. Chat, files, 50+ conferences, all topics.

Executive Protection Products Inc.: (707) 257-3327
Sysop: Jeff Kaczor

3 lines—MS-DOS 386; 800MB running PCBoard 15.1 with US Robotics Dual at up to 57,600 bps. Estab. 07/94 with no fee. Specializing in security, surveillance, business control systems, and more.

Color Galaxy Milky Way: (707) 585-8246
Sysop: Eric Levinson

2 lines—MM/1 68K; 340MB running RCIS 2.3 with Digicomm Eagle at up to 57,600 bps. Estab. 01/87 with no fee. Usenet gateway, adult conferences, online games.

The Party Line BBS: (707) 588-8055
Sysop: Jami Chism

12 lines—MS-DOS 486; 5,000MB running Galacticomm 6.25 with Practical Peripherals at up to 14,400 bps. Estab. 12/85 with a fee of $10 monthly. Internet e-mail/newsgroups. Petaluma access: 707-792-5286. ChatLink nightly, PC Catalog, huge file area.

Xyzzy MIDI BBS: (707) 544-9661
Sysop: Bob

1 line—OS/2 386/40; 250MB running Maximus/2 2.01wb with Supra at up to 14,400 bps. Estab. 11/87 with no fee. MIDILink network. MIDI, Forth, OS/2 files.

The Information Exchange: (707) 542-7901
Sysop: Dan Johnston

1 line—MS-DOS 486; 1,000MB running PCBoard 15.1 with Supra at up to 14,400 bps. Estab. 02/94 with a fee of $50 annually. Extensive shareware, Internet e-mail, MetroLink and Omnilink mail. Adult area. Instant CC upgrades.

Atlantica: (707) 539-8361
Sysop: AquaMaestro

2 lines—MS-DOS Pentium; 900MB running WWIV 4.24 (m) with PPI at up to 28,800 bps. Estab. 06/92 with no fee. Happy-go-lucky electric cafe; WWIVnet/ICEnet/MicroNet/Internet. ANSI/RIP, interBBS BRE.

Dobbs Enterprises: (707) 427-0277
Sysop: Chuck Dobbs

10 lines—Novell; 9,400MB running Gap 6.49 M/99 with US Robotics at up to 14,400 bps. Estab. 11/91 with a fee of $48 annually. Large file BBS. Carrying 4 QWK nets: U'NI-net, UsNet, ProgNet and JobNet. Also Apogee dist. #419.

---

sales brochures; send e-mail from one home office in Montana to another home office in Washington, D.C. (that is, president@whitehouse.gov); broker unused manufacturing capacity, and even plan a business dinner.

Likewise, companies are using the Internet to link employees in remote offices; communicate with foreign customers and suppliers regardless of time zones; distribute sales information more swiftly and efficiently; speed product development; cut printing costs; make better use of resources; and, increasingly, advertise and market their services and products. New resources make it possible even for those who have little or no computer experience to benefit from online advertising, and computer-savvy businesses can push the envelope further—in some cases, as far as selling products through electronic transactions.

Although the businesses vary greatly, along with their depth of participation on the Net, the goals are often the same: to find new customers, new sources of profit, and new ways of doing business in a global marketplace that is suddenly as close as the computer screen.

An Electronic Fifth Avenue

Several factors have conspired to spur business interest in the Internet, among them the declining cost of PCs and modems; the proliferation and aggressiveness of Internet service providers; the influx of Internet-savvy college graduates into businesses; and the emergence of software tools for exploring the Internet.

The days when getting on the Internet meant typing cryptic Unix command lines are fading. Although it still has a long way to go in terms of ease of use, the Internet is emerging as a colorful, graphical web over which text, pictures, and sound can travel at high speed to users scattered on every continent, by using the basic tool every Windows user is familiar with: the mouse.

Traditional Internet tools like gopher, Telnet, and WAIS have been joined by the World Wide Web, an initiative started by CERN labs in Switzerland in 1989 that introduces hypertext links among areas known as "pages" on servers around the world.

4Next GT BBS: (714) 956-4698
Sysop: Jeff/Chris/Lonnie
72 lines—Pentium 60 ; 40,000MB running
Galacticomm 6.21 with 8-28.8bd. 64-16.8bd. at up to
57,600 bps. Estab. 12/93 with a fee of $13
hourly/monthly. 24 CD-ROMs of shareware,
Internet, FidoNet, 40+ online games, teleconference,
no age restrictions.

The Big Blue Mac: (714) 493-4779
Sysop: Todd Miller
6 lines—MS-DOS 486; 4,700MB running Gap
6.4b/M with US Robotics at up to 14,400 bps.
Estab. 09/91 with no fee. 16 e-mail networks, 25
online mags, 22 registered online games, Mac, PC,
OS/2, and Windows shareware.

Free Money Manager BBS: (714) 642-7627
Sysop: Jonathan Berry
3 lines—MS-DOS 386; 200MB running ProBoard
2.01 with Practical Peripherals at up to 14,400 bps.
Estab. 10/92 with no fee. Download unique and
free money manager.

CWI-BBS: The Alternate Route Adventure:
   (714) 870-1033
Sysop: Jimmy Chen
16 lines—MS-DOS 486; 5,900MB running PCBoard
15.1 with US Robotics at up to 14,400 bps. Estab.
04/94 with a fee of $52 annually. Entire CWI disc
catalog + 6 CD-ROMs. Free disk/file catalog. Chat
still free. Subscribe to download.

3 Systems in One: (714) 969-9624
Sysop: Doug Campbell
14 lines—Pentium 90; 4,100MB running
Galacticomm 6.21f with US Robotics at up to 57,600
bps. Estab. 07/93 with a fee of $50 annually.
Entertainment system, real-estate system, online
shopping mall. Check out all three for free.

Software Exchange BBS: (714) 552-3515
Sysop: John Coon
5 lines—MS-DOS 386; 2MB running WildCat 3.91P
with Supra at up to 14,400 bps. Estab. 07/86 with a
fee of $20 biannually. 29,000+ files online. Internet,
Throb-Net, 6,000+ users, 2 weeks free access.

Southern California OnLine: (714) 556-9667
Sysop: John Kelly
8 lines—MS-DOS 386; 1,200MB running
Galacticomm 6.21 with Practical Peripherals at up
to 14,400 bps. Estab. 01/94 with a fee of $10 month-
ly. Chat, dating, business, files, msg. base, classifieds, free graphical comm. prog. games, jobs.

TradeComm/DailyNet: (714) 581-9699
Sysop: David Revington
6 lines—MS-DOS 486; 1,600MB running
Galacticomm 6.12f with Hayes at up to 14,400 bps.
Estab. 08/88 with no fee. Usenet investment/finan-
cial forums, real estate, trade, Commerce Business
Daily, hist. stock data.

Sleepless Knights BBS: (714) 523-8838
Sysop: Enrique Diaz
1 line—MS-DOS 386; 1,360MB running WildCat
3.60 with US Robotics at up to 38,400 bps. Estab.
01/93 with a fee of $3 monthly. 2 high speed CD-
ROMs w/8500+ IBM- and Windows-based files.
Online games, ROCIE netmail, and adult files.

If the Internet is hot, the Web is positively molten. In January 1994, there were 750
Web servers in operation, according to the
newsletter Internet Letter. By June, that had
risen to 3,250. "These Web servers have gone
hyper," said Tony Rutkowski, president of the
Internet Society, the closest thing the Internet
has to an official organizing body. In response
to its popularity, CERN and the Laboratory for
Computer Science at MIT (www.lcs.mit.edu)
recently joined together to promote the standards for the Web.

The heart of the Web's appeal is that no
matter how powerful traditional tools like
Gopher can be to users familiar with the Net's
terrain, the Web hides the chaos of the Internet
behind an attractive, mouse-driven interface
when used in conjunction with popular client
software like Mosaic and Cello—granted that
you've got the right connection. This software
makes exploration on the Internet more a matter of navigational steering via graphical landmarks, versus the traditional hunt-and-peck,
trial-by-error typing routines that can take
months to master on your own.

Since setup can be tricky for the lone
user, Internet providers are making their services even easier to conceptualize.
Increasingly, they offer turnkey packages with
names like "Internet in a Box," not only to help
new users get online, but also to entice them.
Most of these comprehensive packages
include the Windows version of Mosaic, the
freeware version of which was developed by

the National Center for Supercomputing
Applications (www.ncsa.edu) at the University
of Illinois at Champaign-Urbana. When Mosaic
caught on in the spring of 1994, the Web
became the online equivalent of Rodeo Drive
or Fifth Avenue.

These days, a company does not even
have to operate its own computer to establish a
presence on the Internet. Mountain Travel-
Sobek, for example, has someone else manage
its colorful storefront on the Web (gnn.com).

Grant's Florists and Greenhouse in Ann
Arbor, Michigan, doesn't even own a PC, but
for $1,000 a year, it leases the electronic
equivalent of a billboard on the Web that draws
business from as far away as Japan

Cloud Lake BBS: (714) 768-3585
Sysop: Ed Barnes

1 line—MS-DOS 386; 12,500MB running WildCat 3.9M with US Robotics at up to 57,600 bps. Estab. 01/94 with no fee. Windows, DOS, games, programming, source code, astronomy, graphics, woodcarving + more. 40,000+ files.

The Solar System BBS: (714) 837-9677
Sysop: Peter Guethlein

6 lines—MS-DOS 486; 17,000MB running WildCat 4.0+ with US Robotics at up to 38,400 bps. Estab. 12/88 with no fee. Home of the Remote Power Switch, which reboots your computer over the phone.

The Safety Net BBS: (714) 457-8066
Sysop: John Heath

1 line—MS-DOS 486; 2,000MB running PCBoard 15.1 with US Robotics at up to 38,400 bps. Estab. 03/92 with a fee of $30 annually. 200+ echomail areas, 35 registered game doors, 40+ file areas and easy new user access.

Happy Trails BBS: (714) 547-0719
Sysop: Donald Inglehart

7 lines—MS-DOS 386; 540MB running TBBS 2.2 with Supra at up to 19,200 bps. Estab. 07/81 with a fee of $18 biannually. CD-ROM w/44 discs of PD shareware, SIGs, FidoNet, chat, Interchange, many online games, IBM only.

Old Codgers BBS: (714) 639-1139
Sysop: Old Codger

1 line—MS-DOS Pentium 120 with 9,000MB running Remote Access 3.2 Multi with US Robotics at up to 38,400 bps. Estab. 01/87 with no fee. Largest current filebase. Free. Graphics, games, utilities, Windows, DOS.

Dolphins' PlayGround BBS: (714) 858-5112
Sysop: SeaWitch

2 lines—MS-DOS 386; 420MB running Synchronet 2.0 with ViVa at up to 2,400 bps. Estab. 08/93 with no fee. Scuba-related files and messages, echo msg., environmental and water topics, game files, adult access.

The Interchange BBS: (714) 498-8123
Sysop: Doug Hunkele

2 lines—MS-DOS 486; 440MB running Synchronet 2.0 with TwinCom at up to 14,400 bps. Estab. 08/93 with no fee. Rotating 14 CDs for access to 50,000+ files. No file ratios, d/l first call. Fido 103/955.

Sherlocktron: (714) 492-0724
Sysop: Willis Frick

1 line—custom; running custom with generic at up to 2,400 bps. Estab. 01/94 with no fee. A Sherlock Holmes BBS.

AIDS Education General Information Sys: (714) 248-2836
Sysop: Sr. Mary Elizabeth

5 lines—MS-DOS 486; 2,000MB running TBBS 2.2[16] with Hayes at up to 38,400 bps. Estab. 09/90 with no fee. Dedicated AIDS information service and US hub for the Global Electronic Network for AIDS (GENA).

(branch.com). Orders are sent from the Internet to a fax machine in the back of the shop.

At the other end of the scale, some companies are spending hundreds of thousands of dollars a year to create new businesses and augment existing operations with Internet connections.

Rose Ann Giordano, vice president of the Internet Business Division of Digital Equipment Corp., one of the most active PC companies on the Net, said that her company has gleaned "substantial" financial opportunities in terms of new business as a direct result of its Internet presence.

"By providing our Internet expertise, packaged products, and services, we enable customers to capitalize on the Internet in a way that directly impacts their business," said Giordano. DEC's online offerings include an electronic link to its online direct-sales service, a "WebMall" (www.service.digital.com) for businesses that lease Web space from the company to advertise their products, and a commercial "demonstration" area (www.commerce.digital.com) for still other online stores.

Among the vendors hosted by DEC servers are the Vermont Teddy Bear Company, the Future Fantasy Bookstore, and the Palo Alto Chamber of Commerce. On top of that, the company offers consulting services to businesses with more complex endeavors in mind.

While some businesses are visionary, and others are bold, still others are rushing to the Internet simply out of a fear of being left behind. "In some cases, they won't have much choice about participating in some fashion," said Jerry Michalski, managing editor of Release 1.0, a computer-industry newsletter in New York. "An Internet e-mail address is quickly becoming a requirement for business communication, as a fax number did in the U.S. around 1988."

Decentralization and Opportunity
Although the decentralized nature of the Internet makes reliable census figures hard to come by, most observers agree that the Internet is at least doubling in size every year, or growing at a rate of 10 to 15 percent a month. In less than a decade, the Internet has

Digital Dollars: (714) 858-9444
Sysop: Rob Mapstead

1 line—MS-DOS 486; 780MB running PCBoard 15.1 with ViVa 14.4 at up to 14,400 bps. Estab. 04/94 with a fee of $15 annually. We provide you with ways to make money and save money. Business opportunities and money-making tips.

Vivid Image BBS: (714) 669-8823
Sysop: Veno DosSantos

1 line—MS-DOS 486; 15,000MB running WildCat 3.9 with Accex V.32bis/V.42bis at up to 19,200 bps. Estab. 04/94 with no fee. DOS/Windows/GIF/music. General file areas. Adult section to verified adults. Full access 1st call.

Mission Online: (714) 258-0707
Sysop: Kurt Steffien

3 lines—MS-DOS 486; 4,000MB running Galacticomm 6.2 with Practical Peripherals at up to 57,600 bps. Estab. 07/94 with no fee. Forum for programmers, data processing profs., and the computer enthusiast.

The Flight Deck II: (805) 541-3538
Sysop: Jon Godfrey

1 line—Amiga; 300MB running DLG Professional 1.0 with Supra at up to 14,400 bps. Estab. 08/90 with no fee. Amiga, Grfx., and mods. Fido, AmigaNet, ADS/SAN via Planet Connect. AmiNET CD-ROM. Online entertainment.

Message Center BBS: (805) 489-1966
Sysop: Jim Tinlin

2 lines—MS-DOS 386; 1,300MB running QuickBBS V2.76a with Zoom/Hayes at up to 14,400 bps. Estab. 04/84 with no fee. Games, files, FidoNet echoes, CoastNet echoes, 2 nodes. Online 10 years at the same location.

Desert Jewel On-Line Mall and BBS: (805) 397-2063
Sysop: Jerry Bransom

4 lines—MS-DOS 486; 1,024MB running Galacticomm 6.21 with US Robotics at up to 19,200 bps. Estab. 11/91 with no fee. Online mall, support, Internet e-mail, games, education, network, 1GB files, PC support.

Quality of Life-Mentor BBS: (805) 393-5332
Sysop: Jim Opperman

1 line—MS-DOS 386; 420MB running WildCat 3.9 with Practical Peripherals at up to 57,600 bps. Estab. 03/93 with no fee. Family board. 20 timely quality-of-life topics. Stamp/coin combos (PNC's), genealogy info exchange.

SoftCity BBS: (805) 325-8285
Sysop: John Campbell/Jim Coster

2 lines—MS-DOS 486; 340MB running WildCat 4.0 Multi with Practical Peripherals at up to 38,400 bps. Estab. 01/89 with no fee. Law-enforcement-related BBS open to the public. CD-ROM and national mail echoes. Internet online.

Beyond the Realm BBS: (805) 987-5506
Sysop: Musical

8 lines—MS-DOS 486; 7,000MB running VBBS v6.14/2 v6.14/2 with Intel at up to 14,400 bps. Estab. 03/93 with a fee of $25 annually. Internet, satellite, ASP-certified, chat, chat, and more chat, FidoNet, VNet and 100s of other services.

---

grown from 200 host computers to 3.1 million hosts and approximately 25 million users.

At the Pipeline, an Internet service provider in New York City (www.pipeline.com), company president James Gleick calculates business growth at 10 percent a week.

Although the Internet began in the conservative Department of Defense in 1969, like the Woodstock generation, the Internet scientists and academicians were initially wary of big business. There has always been some commercial presence on the Net, although in early years it was confined mainly to aerospace contractors and computer companies.

The National Science Foundation (NSF), which has long operated the network backbone of the Internet, discouraged the flow of commercial traffic over its portion of the Net. But those restrictions have been circumvented since the mid-1980s through the Commercial Internet Xchange (CIX), a group of service providers who agreed to pass commercial data through their networks without going over the backbone. In the next few months, the restrictions will be phased out completely, as the NSF prepares to give up control of the backbone.

Scott Williamson, program manager for InterNIC Registration Services based in Hearndon, Virginia (www.internic.net), a project partially funded by the NSF to provide a range of networking services to the Internet community, says that there are now more than 15,000 commercial domains—recognized by the .com designation in the node address—registered on the Internet. A year ago, there were only half that many.

More than 1,000 commercial domains are being added to the Internet every month, according to Internet Info, an unofficial monitoring service based in Falls Church, Virginia.

As one might expect, computer and telecommunications companies are embracing the Internet with great zeal. "Over 30 percent are in computer-related fields," said Michael Walsh, an analyst from Internet Info. However, big companies often lag behind newer ones in the race to stake out turf on the Internet.

"Most [70 percent] of the companies are small or very new," Walsh added. "This observation is based on the fact they do not show up in any of the standard directories of busi-

The FunZone: (805) 988-0549
Sysop: Crazy Al
14 lines—MS-DOS 486; 600MB running Galacticomm 6.21 with US Robotics at up to 14,400 bps. Estab. 06/93 with a fee of $10 monthly. Friendly chat system. Multiplayer TradeWars and Doom via Game Connection. CD-ROM files and much more.

Blowing Sands BBS: (805) 258-4576
Sysop: Tim Holman
1 line—MS-DOS 486; 470MB running WildCat 3.90 with US Robotics at up to 28,800 bps. Estab. 02/93 with no fee. Carry/hub Wildnet, MSI SupportNET and Cownet. Also FidoNet.

The Granola Board: (805) 735-3315
Sysop: Deborah Taylor
24 lines—MS-DOS Pentium; 2,100MB running Galacticomm 6.21d with Generic at up to 2,400 bps. Estab. 01/90 with no fee. IBM files/forums, games, chat, netmail, disability issues, and more. Santa Maria and HS access available.

The Landing Zone BBS: (805) 736-6609
Sysop: Russell Sechler
]2 lines—MS-DOS 486; 10,000MB running VBBS 6.14 with Practical Peripherals at up to 57,600 bps. Estab. 05/90 with no fee. Computer catalog ordering at discount prices! Apogee Games distribution site. IBM, Mac CD-ROMs.

TCA Blues: (805) 736-5031
Sysop: Mike Madrid
1 line—MS-DOS 386; 420MB running WildCat 3.91 with US Robotics at up to 14,400 bps. Estab. 03/94 with no fee. Aviation- and computer-related. Updating to WildCat 4.0 soon. Many swimsuit and plane GIF files.

VC Info Net: (805) 485-8982
Sysop: Bill Pearson
1 line—MS-DOS 486; 1,500MB running WildCat 4 with Cardinal at up to 14,400 bps. Estab. 11/93 with a fee of $20 annually. Apogee Dist. site #1627. Great BBS for both kids and adults. Good file section.

GraFX Haus BBS: (805) 683-1388
Sysop: Mike van der Sommen
1 line—MS-DOS 386; 2,000MB running WildCat v3.90m with US Robotics at up to 14,400 bps. Estab. 09/93 with no fee. Specializing in high-end graphics/animations and utilities. Support for DOS/Windows/Amiga platforms.

Santa Barbara On-Line: (805) 681-1600
Sysop: Jason Bennett
9 lines—MS-DOS 486; 1,000MB running Falken 7.0 with Hayes at up to 14,400 bps. Estab. 04/94 with no fee. Teleconferencing, huge file library, messages, publications, games, and a growing menu of items (RIP).

The Résumé File: (805) 581-6210
Sysop: Steve Hawley
1 line—MS-DOS 386; 345MB running WildCat 3.6 with Intel at up to 14,400 bps. Estab. 04/92 with a fee of $5 monthly. Job seekers upload their résumé for inclusion in an online résumé database. Online jobs database.

---

ness organizations or full-text databases of newspaper and trade articles."

Small companies interested in direct sales, for instance, are often attracted to the Net because they can fulfill online orders with low overhead. The Internet Shopping Network (ISN) (shop.internet.net) of Menlo Park, California, sells computer peripherals and software through a Web "storefront" with only a dozen employees.

Not that big companies haven't caught on. This past July, Dell Computer Corp. was out in force on the Web (www.dell.com), posting both its international phone directory and, more to the point, its Dell Direct product catalog. (The company is exploring options to sell its wares online.)

The proliferation of Internet connections in business over the past few years can be compared to the spread of PCs in the early 1980s. "In both cases, the driving force was innovative departments latching onto a useful new resource to meet an immediate need, rather than centralized planning by top-level management," said Mary J. Cronin, who is a university librarian at Boston College and the author of *Doing Business on the Internet* (Van Nostrand Reinhold).

Indeed, it's often the case that a small group of Internet-savvy employees take the initiative by experimenting with online on their own time. Warner Brothers Records, for example, has a six-person team responsible for setting up shop and running online

forums on America Online and CompuServe. At press time, Warner joined several other labels on the Web (www.iuma.com/Warner) through the auspices of the Internet Underground Music Archive.

Despite this decentralized approach, big companies are making the transition to the Internet. "Half of the Fortune 500 companies are on the Internet, and you can almost go department by department through a company and look at the things that are being done right now by many of them," said Rutkowski of the Internet Society, who is also a former executive with Sprint.

The Washington Towne Crier BBS: (805) 527-4502
Sysop: Dr. Kenneth Buchholz
4 lines—MS-DOS 486; 5,000MB running Galacticomm 6.21f with Intel at up to 57,600 bps. Estab. 10/86 with no fee. Windows and MS-DOS systems. 5+ GB, private e-mail/file transfers, SIGs/forums, teleconferences.

CD-ROM Multimedia Specialty: (805) 373-2965
Sysop: Robert Riley/Cheryl Yamamoto
10 lines—MS-DOS 486; 9,000MB running PCBoard 15.1 with US Robotics at up to 16,800 bps. Estab. 11/87 with a fee of $10 monthly. Shareware CD-ROMs, 2GB adult CD-ROM, 900+ CD-ROM titles, public/retail/wholesale, online shopping.

Shoreline Park BBS: (805) 373-6919
Sysop: Brian Waingrow
2 lines—MS-DOS 386; 500MB running TBBS 2.2M with Practical Peripherals at up to 28,800 bps. Estab. 07/94 with no fee. New Age, animal rights, ecology, current events, files, messaging, and more.

Ventura Coast BBS: (805) 653-1480
Sysop: Kirby Russell
1 line—MS-DOS 386; 1,200MB running WildCat 3.9m and 4.0 with Linelink at up to 57,600 bps. Estab. 11/85 with no fee. RIP support, Apogee games, and more, Windows 3.x and NT, network analysis forum, and more.

Impact Employment BBS: (818) 879-7405
Sysop: Ken Palmer
1 line—OS/2 486; 900MB running WildCat 3 with US Robotics at up to 14,400 bps. Estab. 01/92 with no fee. Computer-related jobs. Call for job listing or D/L resume. Have a job opening? D/L requirement.

Operation: Barbarossa: (818) 282-0410
Sysop: Blitzkrieg
1 line—MS-DOS 486; 300MB running Synchronet v2.0 with Practical Peripherals at up to 28,800 bps. Estab. 06/94 with no fee. 1,200-28.8k, 4 nets (250+ conferences), adult files/games, CD-ROM, online games, ANSI, RIP, more.

IntelNET: (818) 358-6538
Sysop: Fred Coles
1 line—MS-DOS 486; 245MB running VBBS 6.14A with Supra at up to 28,800 bps. Estab. 01/91 with a fee of $60 annually. International business networking. Criminal justice networking. Loss prevention networking.

Blue Thunder BBS: (818) 848-4101
Sysop: Cris McRae (JAFO)
2 lines—MS-DOS 486; 1,750MB running WWIV v4.24 with US Robotics at up to 16,800 bps. Estab. 10/91 with no fee. Home of Terranet. Official WWIV support board. Internet e-mail. Lots of WWIV files. 1.75GB online.

Bad-Boy's BBS: (818) 846-9304
Sysop: Brandon Hess
5 lines—MS-DOS 486; 6,400MB running Fido with US Robotics at up to 28,800 bps. Estab. 05/91 with no fee. 75+ online games, interBBS competition, 170+ int'l msg. echoes, tons of shareware, Apogee site, and so on.

Popularity Drives Applications

As a communications medium, the Internet has the potential to surpass any business system yet developed. By the end of the decade, some analysts suggest, the Internet will have more than 100 million users.

And as these millions flock to the Internet for communications, commerce will inevitably follow, not vice versa, says Marc Andreeson of Mosaic Communications Inc., based in Mountain View, California (mosaic.mcom.com), who, as a student, was one of the developers of Mosaic. "If everybody's connected, if everyone is on this thing, it makes so much sense," he said. "As people spend more and more of their time connected to the Net, they will find the allure of doing business on the Net more compelling."

E-mail is clearly one of the most commanding features of the Internet for most businesses, allowing virtually instant messaging, including complex files, to millions of other users. Heavy Internet users such as DEC measure e-mail traffic in the millions of messages each month.

Another popular application is file transfer and document delivery, which can be handled either manually or automatically. Companies can save thousands of dollars in printing and distribution costs just by posting office telephone directories electronically, for example.

Many companies envision a day when mundane business forms, ranging from purchase orders and invoices to paychecks, can be sent over the Internet electronically. Such a networked application, known as Electronic Data Interchange (EDI), is already working in such common areas as bank cash machines, but only on a limited basis. When EDI is widespread, as some analysts think it may be in several years, businesses may be able to slash procurement, ordering, and payment times to hours instead of weeks; cut the time it takes for product bidding, reduce inventories, and so on. In many cases, EDI over the Internet also will eliminate expensive proprietary hardware.

Right now, financial institutions like Bank of America (www.commerce.net/directories)

Barter Exchange: (818) 999-1829
Sysop: Richard
8 lines—MS-DOS 486; 1,200MB running Excalibur .70D Beta with AT&T Paradyne at up to 19,200 bps. Estab. 01/90 with no fee. True Windows GUI with full multitasking capabilities. Simultaneously download, upload, and chat online.

Sleuth BBS: (818) 727-7639
Sysop: Mark Valentine
3 lines—LAN; 4,000MB running Searchlight 4.0 with US Robotics at up to 14,400 bps. Estab. 11/93 with a fee of $5 monthly. USA Today, Boardwatch, extensive file area, conferences. Full FidoNet.

Tele-Link BBS: (818) 966-4420
Sysop: Bob De Forge
2 lines—MS-DOS 486; 4,200MB running VBBS 6.12 with US Robotics at up to 14,400 bps. Estab. 10/92 with no fee. Friendly sysops, VirtualNet, FidoNet online games, many mesage areas, 305,000+ IBM and adult files.

Panasia BBS: (818) 569-3740
Sysop: William Padilla
1 line—MS-DOS 486; 120MB running PCBoard 15.1 with US Robotics at up to 28,800 bps. Estab. 05/89 with no fee. Internet e-mail. Echomail nets: INT-ELEC, Throb-Net, PlanoNet, BasNet, JobNet, FSNet, MEGnet, ILink.

The Jungle II BBS: (818) 914-9010
Sysop: Watcher/Tarzan
11 lines—Pentium; 2,000MB running Galacticomm 6.21f with US Robotics at up to 19,200 bps. Estab. 07/94 with no fee. Your tropical computer hideaway. All ages welcome. Games, chat, files, Internet, free guest access.

The Ledge PCBoard: (818) 896-2007
Sysop: Joseph Sheppard
3 lines—MS-DOS 486; 2,500MB running PCBoard 15.2 with US Robotics at up to 21,600 bps. Estab. 01/87 with a fee of $40 annually. Home of U'NI-net. Internet e-mail. Usenet news. ASP-approved. $5/30-day trial subscription.

KBBS: (818) 886-1156
Sysop: Dale
68 lines—IBM/Novell; 10,000MB running Galacticomm 6.21f with Zoom at up to 57,600 bps. Estab. 09/88 with a fee of $10 monthly. 24-hour WorldLink chat, 10GB of files, Internet, match, games including trivia and TradeWars 2000.

Computer One: (818) 763-0678
Sysop: Ed Baker
3 lines—MS-DOS 486; 3,092MB running WildCat 4.0M with US Robotics at up to 14,400 bps. Estab. 07/93 with a fee of $35 annually. 20,000+ 1994 file, FidoNet, free Internet, and Usenet newsgroups. Live chat. 25 games. Free trial.

Merchants of Wonder: (818) 508-0214
Sysop: Teresa and John Lipski
12 lines—MS-DOS 486; 1,190MB running Galacticomm 6.2 with US Robotics at up to 14,400 bps. Estab. 10/92 with a fee of $20 quarterly. General-interest BBS with forums, file areas, chatting, online games, and more.

and Wells Fargo & Co. (www.wellsfargo.com) are establishing a presence on the Net in anticipation of a range of services that they can offer over time.

The Internet allows companies to use remote resources that otherwise would be prohibitively expensive, including access to supercomputers and expensive medical devices. The aerospace giant Lockheed, for example, is planning to use the Internet to broker time on its underutilized manufacturing facilities, thus creating business where none existed before.

With sufficient bandwidth, as in ISDN (Intergrated Services Digital Network) or switched 56-Kbps telephone connections, companies can use the Internet for video and audioconferencing. At IBM Corp. (www.ibm.com), Internet videoconferencing allows engineers to work from home either as a lifestyle choice or because of illness or injury.

Virtual workgroups can be formed to work on temporary projects, even if the workers are scattered in different offices. In many cases, the cost of the Internet conferencing facilities is more than offset by the savings in airline, hotel, and other travel costs, not to mention lost productivity.

The publishing industry is among the early proponents of the Internet, and you'll find magazines like Ziff's *PC Magazine* and *PC Week* (both on www.ziff.com) as well as *Wired* (www.wired.com) appearing on the Net with electronic products. Other publications, including *The New York Times* (which is experimenting with online versions of its classified ads), plan to have Internet offerings. At a minimum, these versions can augment their printed counterparts.

Along the same lines, Bangs of Mountain Travel-Sobek says the Internet will eventually allow his company to save thousands of dollars on the printing of its elaborate annual color catalog, which costs $2.60 per copy to print and more than $2.50 to mail, plus other distribution costs. By placing the electronic version of the catalog online through Global Network Navigator (gnn.com), a commercial Web service developed by the print publisher O'Reilly & Associates Inc. of Sebastopol,

The Hard Drive Cafe: (818) 993-5516
Sysop: Ira Goldstein
8 lines—MS-DOS 486; 500MB running Galacticomm 6.21D with Practical Peripherals at up to 28,800 bps. Estab. 08/83 with a fee of $8 monthly. 5 GB files, Internet, live chat, and interactive games, TradeWars 2002, MajorNet, RIP graphics.

Kinetic: (818) 830-8467
Sysop: Larry Hess
4 lines—MS-DOS 486; 3,000MB running Roboborad FX 1.04 with US Robotics at up to 9,600 bps. Estab. 08/93 with a fee of $5 monthly. Download FXT102.EXE and see graphics that will blow you away. Epic, Apogee, NASA photos, and Internet.

The Sports Club BBS: (818) 792-4752
Sysop: Tom Fota
1 line—MS-DOS 486; 1,660MB running WildCat 3.9M with Practical Peripherals at up to 14,400 bps. Estab. 07/93 with no fee. Sports-oriented board. Sports messaging, sports door games, trivia. Shareware files. Internet.

StarShine BBS: (818) 577-7827
Sysop: Didi Dey
5 lines—MS-DOS 386; 345MB running DLX 7 with Generic at up to 2,400 bps. Estab. 04/94 with a fee of $10 library access. Chat live, make friends. High-speed line and CD-ROM library. Weeknight chat. Join our community.

Night's Edge: (818) 908-1974
Sysop: Sean Stephens
1 line—MS-DOS 386; 110MB running RoboBoard Fx 1.04 with DigiCom Systems at up to 14,400 bps. Estab. 07/15 with no fee. 1024x768/256 SVGA 10-second GIF previews @2400. Real-time graphics. The cutting edge.

BlockBuster Bulletin Board: (818) 831-9942
Sysop: Sean Stephens
2 lines—MS-DOS 486; 13,000MB running WildCat 3.90M with Zoom at up to 14,400 bps. Estab. 12/92 with a fee of $5 monthly. 10GB of shareware and 3GB of adult. RIPscrip, chatting, free FidoNet.

The Sprawl: (818) 342-5127
Sysop: John Schofield
1 line—MS-DOS 486; 650MB running RemoteAccess 2.02+ with Zoom at up to 9,600 bps. Estab. 05/93 with no fee. Focus on civil liberties, data encryption, PGP. Home of Keep Out magazine. Free access, FidoNet.

Lasix BBS: (818) 892-5477
Sysop: Patrick Springer
1 line—MS-DOS 386; 800MB running WildCat 4.00 with US Robotics at up to 14,400 bps. Estab. 10/93 with a fee of $25 annually. Featuring only the best GIFs of beautiful women. Horse-racing areas and online door games. Fun.

Big Bear Online: (909) 866-2136
Sysop: Robert Rose
4 lines—MS-DOS 486; 600MB running TBBS 2.3 with AT&T Dataport at up to 14,400 bps. Estab. 01/94 with a fee of $1 monthly. Netmail/echoes, infobases, forums, chat, online store, trading post, local directory, and tourist info.

California, Bangs can deliver the catalog to potential customers at a fraction of the cost. Also, because the electronic catalog can be updated at any time, it offers more current information than the printed version.

The Bottom Line

Internet pricing is something of a black art, with prices varying significantly from provider to provider. The best analysis comes from Susan Estrada, a founder of CERFnet (www.cerf.net), an Internet service provider in San Diego that was among the first commercial Internet supporters in the nation: "High prices do not necessarily guarantee better service. Lower prices do not always mean you are getting a good deal."

In other words, shop around.

To link a small business or an individual, the basic requirements are typically a PC, a modem, access to a telephone line, some basic communications software, and an account with a local Internet service provider.

Internet service providers range in size from large, international companies, such as Performance Systems International of Herndon (www.psi.com), or Netcom Inc. of San Jose, California (www.netcom.com/netcom/home-page.html), which has tens of thousands of users and offers large-scale network connections, to small start-ups run by a teenager in a spare room, such as Cloud Nine Inc. (www.cloud9.net) of White Plains, New York.

For simple Internet access, many businesses discover that the services offered by the Cloud Nines and even local BBSs of the world are just as good, often less expensive, and typically more responsive than those of the big-name carriers.

Hardware and software aside, the Internet connection can cost as little as $20 a month. (Some cities have "FreeNets" that offer free Internet connections, but typically only for individuals.) On the other hand, any business that wants to set up mission-critical Internet applications will certainly want to start searching for established companies, which, in this business, can mean anyone around for two or more years. As might be expected, larger busi-

The After Hours BBS: (909) 597-3004

Sysop: Chuck Goss

2 lines—MS-DOS 386; 590MB running PCBoard 15.1 with US Robotics at up to 38,400 bps. Estab. 04/90 with a fee of $12 fee/no fee. U'NI-net intl. echonet, ASP-approved, Apogee dist., door games.

Easy Street: (909) 590-4307

Sysop: Galal

40 lines—MS-DOS 486; 13,000MB running Synchronet 2.0 with ZyXel at up to 57,600 bps. Estab. 12/88 with no fee. Netmail, usegroups, Fido, DOVE-NET, chat, files, games. Just about something for everyone.

Wild Weasel BBS: (909) 825-8450

Sysop: Matt Dietz

1 line—MS-DOS 486; 700MB running WildCat 3.9 with Practical Peripherals at up to 38,400 bps. Estab. 01/94 with no fee. Totally free. 2 hours 1st call. Doors, GIFs, games, and so on. No ratios.

The Well of Souls BBS: (909) 370-0980

Sysop: Bill Haworth

1 line—MS-DOS 486; 350MB running SpitFire 3.5 with Supra at up to 14,400 bps. Estab. 09/94 with no fee. 15 CDs available, 7 BRE leagues, 60+ game doors, 100+ message conferences available.

The Midnight Escape BBS: (909) 371-2247

Sysop: Keith Mangold

1 line—MS-DOS 486; 550MB running Searchlight 4.0 with Intel at up to 14,400 bps. Estab. 04/94 with no fee. Many netmail networks. CD-ROM online. No registration fee required.

Legend Graphics OnLine: (909) 689-9229

Sysop: Joey Marquez/Phil Long/Brian McGrew

16 lines—486 LAN with 12,000MB running PCBoard 15.2/100 with US Robotics at up to 28,800 bps. Estab. 08/91 with a fee of $10 monthly. Super VGA photo images, movie pics, 3-D animations, ray-tracing and renderings, large adults-only areas.

Nothin' But: (909) 338-6716

Sysop: David Castillo

3 lines—MS-DOS 486; 5800MB running SpitFire 3.4 with Practical Peripherals at up to 14,400 bps. Estab. 05/83 with a fee of $4.71 monthly. Several adult and multiuser games. Several adult and general message conferences. Free trial period.

NightPlayer BBS: (909) 860-9668

Sysop: Leon Lien

2 lines—MS-DOS 486; 1,500MB running PCBoard 15.1 with Practical Peripherals at up to 28,800 bps. Estab. 02/92 with a fee of $30 biannually. Adult motion pictures, AVI files, shareware.

Edge Of The Ledge: (909) 357-2119

Sysop: Roger Flowers

1 line—MS-DOS 286; 80MB running SpitFire with Digitian at up to 2,400 bps. Estab. 07/94 with a fee of $20 annually. Large Windows section. Copy unprotects and many graphic files. Also an adult section.

---

nesses can anticipate spending substantially more for reliable Internet access.

For a company that wishes to connect more than 20 users to the Internet, it often makes sense to secure a leased line from the telephone company. These dedicated lines can provide communications speeds of 56 Kbps to 1.5 Mbps or more. The variables include installation fees, monthly network charges, monthly line charges, and sometimes fees for use of the service company's routers and high-speed modems.

Installation fees can range from tens of dollars to thousands of dollars depending on the type of lines used and the eagerness of the phone company or service provider to hook them up. Be sure to inquire whether promo-tional or advertised rates are sustained, too. A home-office worker in Austin, Texas, recently was offered an ISDN phone line, with a theoretical speed of 128 Kbps, for a promotional installation fee of $59. A week later, the "regular" installation fee jumped back to more than $800.

The cost of connecting an existing office network to the Internet varies so widely that no meaningful estimates can be given. In general, though, counting hardware, software, service fees, maintenance, and other variables, a medium-sized business wishing to tap fully into the Internet can count on spending from $10,000 to $50,000 just to get themselves established, analysts say.

Nevertheless, out-of-the-box solutions designed for businesses, including hardware, customized software, and Net access are beginning to appear almost as quickly as the packages designed to entice end users online. NovX, a Seattle-based Internet provider, recently began selling Web servers with custom home pages tailored to individual business needs in addition to Internet access.

According to NovX's marketing manager, Marc Goodman, the basic cost of Web service (not including e-mail, ftp, and other tools) with a server and a 56-Kbps connection to the Internet starts under $20,000 per year. If you want to go beyond the first four pages that NovX throws in with the product, you need

The Library BBS: (909) 780-6365
Sysop: Kim Martin
1 line—MS-DOS 386; 1,200MB running WildCat 3.90M with US Robotics at up to 14,400 bps. Estab. 12/89 with no fee. Multi-interest, ASP-approved. Offline mail, Windows, business, graphic utilities, door games.

NightVision: (909) 369-6556
Sysop: John X. Williams
16 lines—MS-DOS 486; 8,000MB running WildCat 4.00I with US Robotics at up to 14,400 bps. Estab. 11/93 with a fee of $69 annually. Amateur GIF contests, Internet access, massive library of adult files, OS/2 utilities, other files.

EcTech BBS: (909) 780-5175
Sysop: Jim Pierce/Allan Huertas
15 lines—MS-DOS 386; 6,000MB running WildCat Pro 5.12 with V.32bis and HST 14.4K at up to 14,400 bps. Estab. 09/87 with no fee. Technical support. File distribution (Apogee and Epic Megagames). E-mail hub for RIME. Door games, adult.

GMS Support Online: (909) 688-3104
Sysop: G. Michael Short
1 line—MS-DOS 386; 250MB running WWIV 4.23 with Hayes at up to 2,400 bps. Estab. 11/93 with a fee of $10 annually. Games to play online, game files, game messages, game reviews, and more. CD-ROM now online.

Black Storm Rising: (909) 682-0409
Sysop: Nathan L. Henry
1 line—MS-DOS 386; 200MB running WildCat 3.9 with Boca at up to 14,400 bps. Estab. 05/94 with a fee of $40 annually. A homestyle BBS with doors and good local conference. A pretty good file base. Pagan and AD&D.

GameMaster BBS: (909) 889-3219
Sysop: George Kuhl
2 lines—MS-DOS 486; 1,000MB running SpitFire 3.5 with Supra at up to 28,800 bps. Estab. 03/84 with no fee. 24 hours reg. Usurper. 75 door games. West Coast Net, FidoNet and RIME netmail worldwide. 3 BRE leagues.

Empire BBS: (909) 946-1448
Sysop: Ken and Tina Podejko
9 lines—MS-DOS 486; 1,000MB running Galacticomm 6.12 with Hayes at up to 2,400 bps. Estab. 09/93 with a fee of $7.50 monthly. Chat, live games, adult access, pubs (SIGs), files, flower shop, matchmaker, personal ads.

CyberCulture: (909) 797-3135
Sysop: Todd Novak
2 lines—Macintosh; 520MB running FirstClass 2.5 with Hayes at up to 38,400 bps. Estab. 01/93 with a fee of $30 annually. Mac and PC files, 3 online CD-ROMs, OneNet, and FidoNet. Live chats.

The Firehouse BBS: (909) 790-0079
Sysop: Tom Clark
1 line—MS-DOS 486; 750MB running SpitFire 3.4 with US Robotics at up to 14,400 bps. Estab. 07/89 with no fee. File-oriented with a Pioneer 6 CD-ROM multichanger unit online. 20 recent CDs available.

Chico Online: (916) 898-1815
Sysop: Rich Graves/Paul Bracamonte
4 lines—MS-DOS 486; 16,000MB running Galacticomm 6.21 with Zoom at up to 28,800 bps. Estab. 02/94 with no fee. Thousands of files including online CD-ROM. Internet access. RIP graphics, adult areas, online games.

Dragon's Lair BBS: (916) 894-6146
Sysop: Max Smoke
1 line—MS-DOS 486; 600MB running WildCat 3 with Zoltrix at up to 19,200 bps. Estab. 06/94 with no fee. For Doom lovers and other game freaks. Help for 600+ games. Also lively political debates.

The Dixon Sub-Station BBS: (916) 678-8383
Sysop: Mark Morrison
1 line—MS-DOS 486; 250MB running WildCat 3.90 with Practical Peripherals at up to 14,400 bps. Estab. 09/93 with no fee. Designed for law enforcement and emergency services personnel. 100 networked LE msg. conferences.

your own experts at hand. However, Goodman notes that NovX supports the hardware setup.

In late-breaking news, commercial online service giant CompuServe announced its intentions not only to offer full Internet access—including the Web—to subscribers, but to help businesses set up Web servers and home pages through its own network services in conjunction with a startup called Network Publishing, Inc.

If you go through the trouble, the rewards can be great. At Synopsis Inc., a maker of custom electronic circuitry in Mountain View, California (www.synopsis.com), a $100,000 investment for an Internet server and software development allowed the company to double its customer-support capacity and offer round-the-clock service for a large international client base without hiring new engineers.
—Peter H. Lewis ■

Jonny Cat BBS: (916) 272-6737
Sysop: Government Cheese
11 lines—MS-DOS 486; 225MB running RemoteAccess 2.01 with US Robotics at up to 14,400 bps. Estab. 01/94 with no fee. General interest/punk/main site of PhishNet. Free CD-ROM access. Online door games.

The Break/West PCBoard BBS: (916) 727-3007
Sysop: Jim Thompson
4 lines—MS-DOS 486; 1,700MB running PCBoard 15.1 with Hayes at up to 57,600 bps. Estab. 10/87 with no fee. IBM general interests. Supports jewelry and movie business. Adult areas.

Indigo Software BBS: (916) 682-2294
Sysop: Mike Swindell/Zane Rathwick
1 line—MS-DOS 486; 400MB running Synchronet v2.0 with Microcom at up to 28,800 bps. Estab. 06/94 with no fee. Windows shareware games and utilities. Files, online registration, and support from Indigo Software.

Knight Owls: (916) 334-4934
Sysop: James Roe
1 line—MS-DOS 486; 360MB running Renegade 5-31 with Hayes at up to 57,600 bps. Estab. 11/93 with a fee of $10 annually. 30+ games, 20,000 files, CD-ROM, OS/2, IBM, e-mail, and more.

FAO BBS: (916) 962-3973
Sysop: Dale DeBord
14 lines—MS-DOS 486; 3,000MB running Oracomm-Plus 7.1 with Practical Peripherals at up to 14,400 bps. Estab. 01/88 with a fee of $6 monthly. Home of the FAO Friendship network. 3-hour free trial period. Download first logon.

Search-BBS: (916) 392-4640
Sysop: Seth Jacobs
3 lines—MS-DOS 386; 350MB running TBBS 2.2 with US Robotics at up to 14,400 bps. Estab. 09/89 with no fee. Focus on criminal justice shareware, databases, publications and forums for CJ professionals.

The Coconut Telegraph: (916) 366-3216
Sysop: Mike Sommer
1 line—MS-DOS 386; 1,200MB running TriBBS 5.1 with GVC at up to 14,400 bps. Estab. 07/94 with no fee. Anarchy, adult, door games, netmail (echoes). Current local weather. Fun stuff.

Data-Base: (916) 573-1100
Sysop: Sandy Bodnar
1 line—MS-DOS 486; 250MB running PCBoard 15.1 with Generic at up to 14,400 bps. Estab. 01/94 with a fee of $75 monthly. Contracts up for bid by small and large businesses to supply all types of parts to U.S. government/military.

The InterMountain Connection: (916) 623-2954
Sysop: Chris Forslund
1 line—MS-DOS 486; 420MB running Synchronet 2.0 with Practical Peripherals at up to 14,400 bps. Estab. 12/93 with no fee. Free public-service BBS. CD-ROM with 3,000+ files for downloading.

The Saturday Knights BBS: (303) 420-8927
Sysop: Don Johnson
1 line—MS-DOS 486; 700MB running Telegard 2.7 with US Robotics at up to 14,400 bps. Estab. 03/91 with no fee. Telegard beta site. Fishnet international HQ. 1 CD-ROM drive.

Digi-Comp Online Services: (303) 431-6796
Sysop: Chris Reed
1 line—MS-DOS 486; 50,050MB running RemoteAccess 2.01+ with Hayes at up to 9,600 bps. Estab. 09/93 with a fee of $10 monthly. FidoNet, online games, file areas, and much more. Call and receive a free listing in our BBS list.

Christian Family BBS: (303) 426-0407
Sysop: Jack Dean/Susie Rolstad
2 lines—MS-DOS 486; 5,000MB running TBBS 2.2M[16] with US Robotics at up to 19,200 bps. Estab. 08/94 with no fee. Home schooling, Bible study, serving the body of Christ.

RS Imagery BBS: (303) 940-8328
Sysop: Rob Henson
8 lines—MS-DOS 486; 1,000MB running Excalibur Beta .70 with Practical Peripherals at up to 14,400 bps. Estab. 06/94 with no fee. Full multitasking, CDs, Windows On the Rockies User Group. DTP+ more.

Sound Doctrine Institute's BBS: (303) 680-7209
Sysop: Tim
5 lines—MS-DOS 486; 7,000MB running TBBS 2.2 with Supra at up to 14,400 bps. Estab. 01/87 with no fee. Totally free (Luke 16:13). Files, Internet. Order free items while online. More.

Beyond Reality: (303) 690-4044
Sysop: Brian Heineman
1 line—MS-DOS 486; 3,100MB running RoboBoard/FX 1.04 with Supra at up to 14,400 bps. Estab. 03/94 with no fee. Colorado's fastest-growing BBS dedicated to C/C++ programming and file distribution.

Terra Main: (303) 344-4788
Sysop: Cappy Kirk
1 line—MS-DOS 8088; 40MB running WWIV 4.22++ with Comudyne at up to 2,400 bps. Estab. 11/89 with no fee. Lots of messages and games. 4 different networks.

North Street BBS: (303) 884-1391
Sysop: Jason Short
1 line—MS-DOS 486; 120MB running WildCat 3.9s with Zoom at up to 14,400 bps. Estab. 07/93 with no fee. Games, Chili-Net, MIDI and GIF, door games, recently upgraded.

Rolling Stone BBS: (303) 532-4911
Sysop: Dan Edwards
1 line—MS-DOS 486; 700MB running WildCat 4.0 with Hayes at up to 38,400 bps. Estab. 10/92 with no fee. 7GB+ of files available from 14 CD-ROMs (2 online at a time). Games, Fido network.

Deep Space Nine BBS: (303) 494-8447
Sysop: Admiral Picard
1 line—MS-DOS 386; 700MB running Renegade 06-03 with Boca at up to 19,200 bps. Estab. 07/15 with no fee. Really huge Star Trek BBS. Home of TrekkerNet. Looking for boards to join. Free access.

♨ The percentage of World Wide Web users who are single is estimated to be 53 percent. The male/female ratio is supposed to be around 80 to 20 percent.

Hi, This Is Ken

The 1994 Usenix Technical Conference in Boston was lousy with smart computer people, very smart people. I don't know what parasite got into their little ant brains but they had me, a guy who writes the only really noncomputer column in a major computer magazine, give the keynote address.

Speaking of being off the subject of computers—I would like to explain why I have ant brain parasites on my mind: Several years ago, *The New York Times* wrote about this groovy parasite whose life cycle circles through sheep guts and ant brains. We know how it gets from the sheep to the ant—ants aren't as fastidious as that grasshopper/ant hype leads us to believe—but how do they get from the ant into the sheep? Sheep don't eat ants. Ah ha, that's what you think. They don't eat ants on purpose. They don't eat ants unless the ants are climbing up to the top of blades of grass and sitting there like nutty monkeys. And they don't do that, no, they don't do that, unless they have this parasite in their little ant brains that makes them climb up to the top of blades of grass! Cool, huh? The quotation was something like "the parasite gets in their ant brain and makes them do things no sane ant would do." You just don't expect that much wisdom and poetry from the Science Section. Once I grasped the idea of parasites in our little ant brains making us do things that no sane ant would do, I was no longer puzzled by little things like Xerox's idea of letting you grab files from your hard drive with a fax machine. There are ideas no sane ant would have.

So, one goofy thing they did at Usenix was book a guy who rants about insect eccentricities in a computer mag, but the totally wacky thing was the last line of the whole conference, "Don't forget to change your password." They had this computer room set up for people to log on and even though these guys have privacy algorithms that make Wild Bill Clinton and the NSA trash the Constitution—they still have to change their passwords

Colorado Catacombs BBS: (303) 938-9654
Sysop: Mike Johnson
1 line—MS-DOS 386; 550MB running WildCat 3.90m with Microcom at up to 28,800 bps. Estab. 03/91 with no fee. Christianity; Bible search programs; cryptography and privacy, including PGP; general DOS downloads.

The Live Wire: (303) 833-2096
Sysop: Tad and Lisa Brooker
1 line—MS-DOS 486; 1,600MB running WildCat v4.0 with US Robotics at up to 14,400 bps. Estab. 06/93 with a fee of $29.95 annually. 13-CD-ROM library, Internet access, 50,000+ files.

The Garbage Dump: (303) 457-1111
Sysop: Dean Kerl
105 lines—MS-DOS 486; 10,300MB running Galacticomm v6.21 with Hayes at up to 14,400 bps. Estab. 12/90 with no fee. Huge system featuring chat, message forums, CD-ROM library, games, trivia.

The File Bank Inc: (303) 534-4646
Sysop: Brian Bartee/Girard Westerberg
22 lines—MS-DOS 486; 15,000MB running TBBS 2.2M[32] with USR D/S/Hayes V.FC at up to 28,800 bps. Estab. 01/93 with a fee of $10 monthly. Hundreds of thousands of files for your PC. Vast astronomy, ham radio, programming, and adult areas.

Denver Matchmaker: (303) 232-5523
Sysop: Steve Coker
22 lines—486/25; 8MB with 660MB running Custom Matchmaker 6.0 with USR/Hayes/Zyxel at up to 19,200 bps. Estab. 01/93 with no fee. Chat, e-mail, Internet mail access, Holodeck, pen pals, matching, X-referencing.

InfoPort: (303) 429-0291
Sysop: James Barry
6 lines—Macintosh; 1,600MB running NovaLink Pro 3.1 with Hayes at up to 57,600 bps. Estab. 11/93 with no fee. Internet access, Telnet, mail newsgroups, Mac and Windows shareware, political forums, files.

Some Assembly Required: (303) 252-1588
Sysop: Chris Farrow
1 line—MS-DOS 486; 15,000MB running WildCat 3.9 with PPI at up to 28,800 bps. Estab. 01/94 with no fee. The Sysop: support board. Supporting sysops of all BBS packages. 1GB+ online, FidoNet 1:104/786.

because someone might have looked over their goddamn shoulder and watched them type their personal "iluvuma!"

Kevin Mitnick is called by *The New York Times* "Cyberspace's Most Wanted." (Ant brains and cyberspace, what a paper.) How does he break into enough supersecure computers to make the FBI climb tall blades of grass and sit there? Well, on the continuation page they explain one of his wily techniques: "By masquerading as a company executive in a telephone call, he frequently talks an unsuspecting company employee into giving him passwords and other information that makes it possible for him to gain entry into computers illegally."

Get it? He calls them up and asks them for the password and how to use it, and they

tell him. Isn't that great? He just asks them. It saves a lot of random typing.

You would think AT&T Bell Labs computer network would be pretty safe. Ken Thompson and the kids have enough brain cells to remember passwords even harder than their spouses' birthday backwards, but about ten years ago a hacker got into one of the development systems at Bell Labs. They offed the intruder in a New York minute (by powering off the system), but were puzzled by how security was breached. They finally tracked it down to an operator in the machine room who got a phone call: "Hi, this is Ken. What's the root password?" We have to keep fighting the government to keep our privacy, we need better and better encryption, and we have to shoot

down and slide around any laws that weaken anyone's privacy.

We have to get bigger and bigger primes and multiply them together until we're blue in the face. We need digital cell phones and scrambled cordless. And when someone asks us what our password is—we have to remember not to tell them.

Privacy is important—keep those parasites out of your little ant brain and don't do things that no sane ant would do.
—Penn Jillette ■

Stoic Financial BBS: (303) 238-0588
Sysop: Richard Hiatt

1 line—MS-DOS 386; 300MB running WildCat 3.55 with ZyXel at up to 14,400 bps. Estab. 11/91 with a fee of $50 annually. Financial information, shareware. Also Internet, misc. invest newsgroups, and e-mail. info@stoicbbs.com.

Blue Sky, Green Fields: (303) 936-3837
Sysop: Bill Zipprich

1 line—MS-DOS 386; 120MB running TBBS 2.2 with Hayes at up to 38,400 bps. Estab. 06/94 with no fee. An open system for all types of people.

The Denver Chat: (303) 770-8832
Sysop: Pat Yeager

8 lines—MS-DOS 486; 16,000MB running Galacticomm 6.12 with US Robotics at up to 14,400 bps. Estab. 03/93 with no fee. Great games and chat. 7 CD-ROMs online.

Microwire BBS: (303) 752-2943
Sysop: Jim Kochmann

2 lines—MS-DOS 386; 90MB running TBBS 2 with US Robotics at up to 14,400 bps. Estab. 05/85 with no fee. The BBS of the Micro Computer Club in Denver. CD-ROM available to club members.

The Mars Hotel: (303) 360-6626
Sysop: Cap Bateman

1 line—MS-DOS 386; 500MB running VBBS 6.14a with US Robotics at up to 14,400 bps. Estab. 07/93 with no fee. Virtual support board, Internet e-mail, multinetworked, online games, 200+ msg. areas, files.

The Dart Board RBBS: (303) 882-2360
Sysop: Dart Nielson

1 line—MS-DOS 386; 1,200MB running RBBS 17.4/CDoor with MTI at up to 14,400 bps. Estab. 12/92 with no fee. Access to 22 CD-ROM discs, ASP-approved BBS, FidoNet/LDSnet, 50+ door games.

The Forum: (303) 226-4218
Sysop: Norm Bastian

3 lines—LANtastic network with 1,900MB running RemoteAccess 2.02 Pro with Practical Peripherals at up to 14,400 bps. Estab. 05/91 with no fee. Lots of online games, plenty of files. FidoNet, CFR-Net, RANet, Radist, NeverNet, Internet mail.

The Pentagon BBS: (303) 498-0864
Sysop: Adam Warbington

1 line—MS-DOS 286; 255MB running RemoteAccess 2.01 with AT&T at up to 14,400 bps. Estab. 10/92 with no fee. Home of The Five. Complete strangeness and other nonsense. Numerianism, Dobbs, and more. Messages.

The Hot Line BBS: (303) 245-1147
Sysop: Jason Franklin
3 lines—MS-DOS 486; 1,700MB running SuperBBS v1.173 with Hayes at up to 28,800 bps. Estab. 02/91 with no fee. Huge shareware file base, Internet access, online games, one of western Colorado's largest BBSs.

WRM and DBS BBS: (303) 245-6017
Sysop: Russell Wynne
1 line—MS-DOS 486; 900MB running SuperBBS with Supra at up to 14,400 bps. Estab. 11/93 with a fee of $5 annually. File collection center for DBS. Looking for latest shareware from indivs. and companies. 6000+ files.

The 9600 Club: (303) 351-0974
Sysop: Evan Barrett
1 line—MS-DOS 386; 1,000MB running TriBBS 5.1 with ViVa at up to 14,400 bps. Estab. 06/93 with no fee. FidoNet, Nineties' Net, CFR-Net, and SouthWest Net echomail networks. CD-ROM.

The Flaming Yawn BBS: (303) 494-3684
Sysop: Gnossos
1 line—MS-DOS 486; 420MB running Telegard 7.2 with Hayes at up to 2,400 bps. Estab. 06/08 with no fee. A fun, personal board. Sysop ichat. Good message base conversations.

Wizards Mansion: (303) 980-8486
Sysop: Master Wizard
2 lines—MS-DOS 486; 345MB running PCBoard 15.1/5 M with Supra at up to 57,600 bps. Estab. 10/92 with no fee. InterBBS games, many files, and conference areas. Lots of GIF files, SPELL'EM for WPxx and WPWINxx.

Keyhole BBS: (303) 477-6337
Sysop: Lou-Lou
3 lines—MS-DOS 486; 3,600MB running Renegade 1-02-94 with US Robotics at up to 38,400 bps. Estab. 09/93 with a fee of $25 biannually. Online chat, 500+MB of graphic, sound and support files, 3 CD-ROMs, and 45+ online games.

Bob's BS: (303) 914-0336
Sysop: Bob Pascarell
1 line—MS-DOS 386; 980MB running SpitFire 3.4 with Boca at up to 19,200 bps. Estab. 04/94 with no fee. Features CD-ROM areas, games, Windows, advice, tech help, software help, also baseball info.

DLS InfoNet: (303) 347-2921
Sysop: Jerry McCarthy
5 lines—MS-DOS 486; 8,000MB running WildCat 3.90 IM with Supra at up to 14,400 bps. Estab. 02/93 with no fee. Huge Windows file area, Internet news groups, and e-mail accounts. USA Today, online chat.

20 Miles North of Nowhere: (303) 932-1195
Sysop: TcP
1 line—MS-DOS 486; 1,200MB running VBBS 6.14a with Zoom at up to 28,800 bps. Estab. 12/86 with no fee. Free. Internet/FidoNet access, CD-ROM online, 2 dozen+ games, thousands of files, many nets.

LostSoles BBS: (303) 651-2988
Sysop: Glenn Scott
1 line—MS-DOS 386; 250MB running WildCat 3.51 with ATI at up to 9,600 bps. Estab. 11/91 with no fee. Public BBS open to all. No fees. No ratios. Only the latest and best downloads.

Colorado Catacombs of Longmont: (303) 772-1062
Sysop: Mike Johnson
2 lines—MS-DOS 386; 510MB running WildCat 3.90m with Microcom at up to 28,800 bps. Estab. 03/91 with no fee. Bible study software; cryptography and privacy (including PGP); general DOS downloads; programming.

The Conifer Connection: (303) 670-9118
Sysop: Kayak
1 line—OS/2 Pentium; 1,600MB running VBBS with Hayes at up to 28,800 bps. Estab. 03/94 with no fee. Supporting OS/2, DOS, and Windows. Connected to FidoNet and VirtualNet. Large message and file base.

Star One: (303) 429-0597
Sysop: Gary Carr
2 lines—MS-DOS 386; 1,200MB running GT Power 18.00 with US Robotics at up to 16,800 bps. Estab. 11/91 with no fee. Files available to first-time callers, free access line one. Additional access 2nd line (fee).

The Goblin's Reach BBS: (719) 597-7877
Sysop: Ed Williams
2 lines—MS-DOS 486; 515MB running SBBS 1.173 with Practical Peripherals at up to 14,400 bps. Estab. 05/93 with a fee of $5 annually. An AD&D-only BBS. Join the group of dedicated TSR fans worldwide. Maps, dungeons, and lots more.

Merlin's Realm BBS: (719) 481-9881
Sysop: Tim Peterson
2 lines—MS-DOS 486; 240MB running WildCat 4.0 with US Robotics at up to 14,400 bps. Estab. 04/94 with a fee of $5 monthly. 6 CDs online. 34,000+ files available for download. Online games, RIP graphics, Internet, and chat.

Electric Dreams: (719) 390-9457
Sysop: Michael and Suzi Boltz
10 lines—Amiga; 24,000MB running CNet Amiga 3.05c with Intel at up to 19,200 bps. Estab. 09/93 with a fee of $3.50 monthly. Low monthly membership fees. Supports adult, IBM, Amiga, EText, GIFs, source code, much more.

Center City BBS: (719) 579-9359
Sysop: Mark Farmer
2 lines—MS-DOS 486; 4,000MB running Robo/FX 1.04 with Hayes at up to 14,400 bps. Estab. 04/83 with a fee of $20 annually. Straight, gay, bi areas. Must be 18 years old. Fido 1:128/186, SMUTNET, VNet, FidoNet, more.

Telegraph Road BBS: (719) 390-8608
Sysop: John Pearson
1 line—OS/2; 680MB running Maximus 2.01wb with US Robotics at up to 21,600 bps. Estab. 08/93 with no fee. Lots of echomail areas from FidoNet and the US Political Net. Politics and household chat.

Glass Onion: (203) 732-5746
Sysop: Bob Dunn
1 line—MS-DOS 386; 470MB running SpitFire 3.5 with Zoom at up to 28,800 bps. Estab. 03/92 with no fee. RIP graphics. SFNet, FidoNet, and SoundTrax netmail systems. Internet e-mail, CD-ROM areas. Doors.

TEK World BBS: (203) 645-9246
Sysop: Manny Quinteiro
8 lines—MS-DOS 486; 10,000MB running Galacticomm 6.21e with US Robotics at up to 38,400 bps. Estab. 01/92 with a fee of $50 annually. CD-ROMs online, Internet, WorldLink, Net ACCESS, MajorNet, Fido. 5000+ message areas, online games.

OPAL Network: (203) 250-0938
Sysop: John McCaffrey
2 lines—MS-DOS 486; 800MB running Cheshire BBS 0.3 with US Robotics at up to 19,200 bps. Estab. 01/89 with no fee. Specializing in science, education, games, and graphics files. Adult section also available.

Alien Nation: (203) 290-8615
Sysop: Gary Willett (Gazoo)
2 lines—MS-DOS 486DX2-66; 3,000MB running Synchronet v. 2.0a with Zoom at up to 28,800 bps. Estab. 05/91 with a fee of $2.50 monthly. 7 NEC CD-ROMs online. OS/2, Windows, modems/BBSing, games. All the latest and greatest shareware.

The A-Zone BBS: (203) 468-2012
Sysop: Bruce Pantani
1 line—MS-DOS 486; 1,000MB running RoboBoard/FX 1.04 with Zoom at up to 14,400 bps. Estab. 01/94 with no fee. 2 CD-ROM drives. Internet newsgroups and e-mail. FidoNet, RoboNet, doors, weather, 8,000+ files.

The Medieval Tavern: (203) 253-9006
Sysop: Drahcir
1 line—MS-DOS; 800MB running Renegade with Zoom at up to 19,200 bps. Estab. 03/94 with no fee. 25+ online games, adult area, files, and more.

Fairfield Community Connection: (203) 335-4073
Sysop: R. Scott Perry
8 lines—MS-DOS 386; 1,200MB running Galacticomm Major 6.2 with Hayes at up to 14,400 bps. Estab. 01/94 with no fee. Community-oriented. Internet access, files, chat, ads, movie reviews, more added everyday.

The Download America BBS: (203) 676-1708
Sysop: Eric Knight
6 lines—MS-DOS 386; 6,000MB running RBBS 17.4 with Hayes at up to 19,200 bps. Estab. 09/88 with a fee of $10 one-time. 100,000 files. 6GB. Entire PC-SIG collection. Free international messaging. Chosen a "Top 5" BBS.

Chronicles InfoNet: (203) 445-0607
Sysop: John Luce
2 lines—MS-DOS 486; 1,200MB running PCBoard 15.1 with Hayes at up to 38,400 bps. Estab. 03/92 with no fee. 375+ message areas. Large file areas supported by various FDNs. 6 CD-ROMs. Online games and QWKmail.

The Outhouse: (203) 445-0190
Sysop: Mark Lovelace
1 line—MS-DOS 386; 1,000MB running Searchlight 4.0 with Microcom at up to 38,400 bps. Estab. 05/94 with no fee. Fantastic RIP graphics. Designed for new users. Door games, files, and message areas. A family BBS.

The Great Albion: (203) 230-2128
Sysop: Michael Pitchford
2 lines—Amiga; 1,100MB running DLG Professional 1.0 with Supra at up to 28,800 bps. Estab. 06/92 with no fee. All systems welcome. Areas for Amiga, IBM, Mac, special interests. Easy online registration.

Sherwood Forest of CT: (203) 645-1417
Sysop: Robin Hood (Cj)
1 line—MS-DOS 286; 212MB running Telegard 2.7 with Twincomm at up to 14,400 bps. Estab. 01/90 with no fee. Specializing in rare FidoNet echoes. Lots of files, few games. Helpful, friendly staff.

The Hour Glass: (203) 878-2367
Sysop: Michael Vignola
2 lines—MS-DOS 386; 750MB running VBBS 6.2 OS2 with US Robotics at up to 57,600 bps. Estab. 12/92 with no fee. Support OS/2/DOS files. CD-ROM. FidoNet/VirtualNet/Kineticnet.

Banglor BBS: (203) 564-0280
Sysop: Virus
1 line—MS-DOS 486; 320MB running PCBoard 15.1 with Hayes at up to 38,400 bps. Estab. 03/94 with no fee. Good board with balanced doors, files, and messages.

U.S.S. Nautilus BBS: (203) 827-0280
Sysop: Hector Cintron
1 line—MS-DOS 486; 250MB running RemoteAccess 2.02+ with Practical Peripherals at up to 14,400 bps. Estab. 02/93 with no fee. The electronic home of the USS Nautilus, the greater chapter of Starfleet, the Int. Star Trek fan assoc.

Computer Caddie: (203) 444-0731
Sysop: Gordy Duer
2 lines—MS-DOS 486; 1,300MB running Maximus 2.01wb with Intel 400i at up to 14,400 bps. Estab. 02/89 with no fee. FidoNet/StormNet/DoorNet system with online games, message bases, IBM files, callback validation.

Pleasure Net: (203) 831-0547
Sysop: Ronald Leighton
8 lines—MS-DOS 486; 100MB running Excalibur 67 with Supra at up to 14,400 bps. Estab. 06/93 with no fee. Nightly chat. Subjects range from computer-related to adult subjects. Files and games. Full-service BBS.

Sea of Noise: (203) 886-1441
Sysop: Robert Szarka
1 line—MS-DOS 486; 425MB running RemoteAccess 2.02+ with Zoom at up to 28,800 bps. Estab. 10/92 with no fee. Specializing in text files, obscure information, encryption, and viruses.

Connecticut Adult Connections: (203) 889-0735
Sysop: Daniel J. Cronister
5 lines—MS-DOS 486; 8,000MB running RemoteAccess 2.02/250 with Supra at up to 14,400 bps. Estab. 01/93 with a fee of $25 quarterly. Your one-stop BBS for files and message bases. Help for RADIST and OS/2. All Fido echoes.

Our House BBS: (203) 599-3970
Sysop: David and Kathy Murphy
2 lines—MS-DOS 486; 500MB running Tag 2.7 with Microcom at up to 28,800 bps. Estab. 04/91 with no fee. Files, games, messages. FidoNet, StormNet, DoorNet interBBS games.

The Handicap News BBS: (203) 926-6168
Sysop: Bill McGarry
1 line—MS-DOS 386; 250MB running Maximus 2.1 with US Robotics at up to 14,400 bps. Estab. 12/88 with no fee. One of the largest disability-related BBSs with 1000+ files/programs. Home of Handicap BBS List.

Dream Stages: (203) 875-2924
Sysop: Ahren Niles
1 line—MS-DOS 386; 420MB running Tag 2.7 with Supra at up to 14,400 bps. Estab. 03/92 with no fee. Multiple themes (selectable) with random menus for each. InterBBS Barren Realms Elite online game.

GameMaster's Refuge BBS: (203) 626-0473
Sysop: Dale Mottram
1 line—MS-DOS 386; 175MB running Renegade 01-02b with Zoom at up to 9,600 bps. Estab. 10/91 with no fee. CD-ROM online. No ratios. Amiga support. Net coordinator for CCSO. Fido, ITC member.

Phone Henge BBS: (203) 673-6247
Sysop: Scott Livingston
1 line—MS-DOS 486; 3,000MB running RemoteAccess 2.02+ with US Robotics at up to 16,800 bps. Estab. 05/88 with no fee. Huge variety. DOS, Windows, tons of OS/2. Many FidoNet file and message echoes: BBS, OS/2, WIN. 2 CD-ROMs.

The Continuum BBS: (203) 759-5853
Sysop: Scott Roncarti
1 line—MS-DOS 386; 1,200MB running SpitFire 3.5 with Hayes at up to 9,600 bps. Estab. 05/93 with no fee. Games and educational software for IBM comp. FidoNet.

AdamsCom BBS: (203) 442-3510
Sysop: Mark Adams
1 line—MS-DOS 386; 107MB running WildCat 3.91M with Practical at up to 14,400 bps. Estab. 05/94 with a fee of $8 monthly. Internet e-mail gateway, Internet newsgroups, matchmaker service for singles, electronic flea market.

The Fire House BBS: (302) 798-0924
Sysop: Arthur Burke (Fire Chief)
1 line—MS-DOS 386; 176MB running WWIV 4.23 with Zoom VFP 28.8 at up to 28,800 bps. Estab. 10/93 with no fee. The only WWIV-based emergency services-related BBS in Delaware. Dedicated to America's heros.

E-ffective Mail

I got an electronic message the other day from a guy whom I thought was my friend. "It has come to our attention you hvn't yet RSVP'd to yr invitation vis a vis the november 9 security analyst's meeting in petaluma at which you are scheduled to participate in a panel on outyear restructuring," read the missive. "Pls inform Donna on extension #4568 about your intentions/needs for transportation and hotel accommodations immediately. Bert." Man, was that terse.

I called him up. "Hey, Bert," I said. "You mad at me about something?"

"No, man!" he yelped. Bert always speaks like a man at one end of a wind tunnel. "I ain't mad! I just wanted to snap you a quick e-mail on it! Don't you just love your e-mail? Ain't it a real time-saver?"

"Sure, Bert," I said. "Here you've only spent time writing the message, I've spent time reading it, and we've had a nice phone call about it, too. That's what I call a real time-saver."

So it goes. To the time we spend on everything else in this life, we now must add the time we are forced to spend clarifying e-mails. The people who communicate the worst love e-mails the most. "Did you get my e-mail?!" they chortle. And you must answer,

"Yeah, Chuck, I got your e-mail. Now, what was it supposed to be about? And can we talk about whatever it is…right now? On the phone? Like we used to?" The tragic thing is, it doesn't have to be this way—e-mail doesn't have to stink as a communications vehicle. There are really only three elements to excellent e-mail: clarity, brevity, and extreme courtesy. It's a stone-cold medium, so put a smile in your voice when you write that puppy, will you, Bud? Thanks. Let's move on. Here are six essential templates to help the novice e-mailer craft e-messages while remaining somewhat human, if you believe that is indeed a virtue.

1. The "Please get back to me about something" message. Sure, you need a response. But don't be bombastic—be nice! For

Thunderbyte Support USA: (302) 732-6399
Sysop: Jeff Cook

1 line—386-25; 210MB running RemoteAccess 2.01+ with Intel at up to 14,400 bps. Estab. 10/91 with no fee. Thunderbyte USA antivirus support site. No ratios. First-time callers welcome here.

The Small Blunder: (302) 234-2792
Sysop: Chip Daiger

3 lines—OS/2 486; 1,500MB running VBBS 6.14 OS/2 with Zoom VFX 28.8 at up to 57,600 bps. Estab. 03/92 with no fee. OS/2 and VBBS support. Internet, RushNet, VirtualNet, FidoNet. Doors, active discussions.

The DVUG BBS: (302) 324-8091
Sysop: Barry Connolly

2 lines—MS-DOS 386; 102MB running SpitFire 3.5 with US Robotics at up to 57,600 bps. Estab. 06/90 with a fee of $25 annually. Online doors, e-mail, RIMENet, Circuit-Net, FidoNet, JF-Net. 2 CD-ROMs, 2GB+ files. Multinode.

The Krystal Palace BBS: (302) 292-1510
Sysop: Michael A. James

10 lines—MS-DOS 486; 10,000MB running PCBoard 15.1 with US Robotics at up to 38,400 bps. Estab. 11/91 with no fee. Huge shareware library, Internet access, 4,700 Internet newsgroups, large adult library, online games.

BaseLine BBS: (302) 834-1089
Sysop: Rick Reuling

3 lines—MS-DOS 486; 5,000MB running Galacticomm 6.21f with US Robotics at up to 38,400 bps. Estab. 07/91 with a fee of $25 quarterly. 40,000+ files available for download. FidoNet, ChatLink national teleconference, and online Doom.

Dark Tower BBS: (302) 629-4780
Sysop: Jake Devros/William Metzler

2 lines—Amiga; 4,500MB running C-Net 3.05c+ with Zoom at up to 28,800 bps. Estab. 05/93 with a fee of $10 annually. 6 CD-ROMs online. Amiga, IBM 60+ online games. First-time callers get instant access.

UnderGround BBS: (302) 436-6214
Sysop: Tony Paolillo

1 line—Generic; running WildCat 3.90 with Supra at up to 38,400 bps. Estab. 01/94 with a fee of $15 annually. 75,000+ files, 75+ conferences. Meet new friends.

Up's and Down's BBS: (305) 434-8403
Sysop: Steve Alves

1 line—MS-DOS 486; 700MB running WildCat 4.0 with Hayes at up to 28,800 bps. Estab. 06/92 with no fee. Free Internet e-Mail access. Wildnet echo hub, adult files, lots of games.

Sysop of the Phantasm BBS: (305) 344-2034
Sysop: Anthony G. La Forge

1 line—MS-DOS 486; 750MB running RoboBoard/FX 1.04 with Zoom 14.4 at up to 14,400 bps. Estab. 05/94 with no fee. Adult files, mass shareware, and ever-changing CD-ROM titles, including NightOwl 10.

---

example: Dear —————, I can't believe it's been so long since we traded e-mails! Let's ameliorate that situation real soon! Like now! And while you're at it, what's your response on the Forbisher proposal? I await your reply…like today! Time's a-wasting! Your associate, Larry. See? Friendly! Demonstrative! Affable! That's the ticket!

2. The "I will be attending the meeting on the 18th" message. Getting to someone with timely data on upcoming plans is important. But why make it perfunctory just because it's short? Do better. As in: Dear —————, Until this morning I had no reason to live. Yes! I will attend your seminar on the tax implications of limited partnerships in leveraged development scenarios! Wouldn't miss

it! Yours till the prime rate falls, Barry. For one second, the person receiving this may doubt your seriousness as a person. That's good, especially if you are an essentially serious person.

3. The "Here are my ideas on the Flabushnik situation" message. The purpose of any such communication is to make your recipient want to know more. To wit: Dear —————, The Flabushnik thing will work if we 1) pay him enough money, 2) make him go away by next Thursday. Send up a smoke signal if you agree. Thnx. Harry. Pithy? Yep! Cybernetic? No way!

4. The "Here's what I think of your idea on the marketing issue" message. Sometimes

you need to communicate something equivocal. All the more reason to be tender, warm, and loving. Dear —————, A free poached salmon with guacamole is waiting for you next Tuesday at 12:30 p.m. at Cafe Fauteuil. At that time, you may also hear the six things I think are wrong with your proposal of October 3rd. See ya there! Best, Gary. Who could resent that?

5. The "Here's what I plan to do in regard to Ms. Cromagnon" message. Most sensitive are human resource issues that pertain to individuals who need schooling of some sort. Beware! A whisper of an indication with a soupcon of deniability is all that's required: My dear —————, Ms. Cromagnon's obvious strengths as an employee must have

Pagan's Way: (305) 925-1620
Sysop: Ronald Thorp
2 lines—MS-DOS 486; 540MB running WildCat 3.91 with US Robotics at up to 14,400 bps. Estab. 06/93 with no fee. A place to meet the Pagan in all of us. Echoes in over 6 occult-based nets.

The Aguda/2 BBS: (305) 424-0465
Sysop: Albert Afonso
1 line—MS-DOS 486; 2,500MB running RemoteAccess 2.0 with Zoom V.FC at up to 57,600 bps. Estab. 01/85 with no fee. OS/2 support BBS.

The Picture Window: (305) 584-6270
Sysop: Chris Overstreet
1 line—MS-DOS 486; 1,200MB running WildCat 3.6 with Boca at up to 14,400 bps. Estab. 01/93 with no fee. Lots of pictures, lots for Windows. GIFs, Windows shareware/support, CD-ROM, adult section.

Photo Image BBS: (305) 792-3887
Sysop: M. R. Dolliver
2 lines—MS-DOS 386; 400MB running Searchlight 4.0a with Smartlink at up to 14,400 bps. Estab. 01/90 with no fee. Computer/Dayo business applications, custom CDs, digital imaging, photography, videography, more.

Sheer Fantasy: (305) 792-6325
Sysop: Camille
3 lines—MS-DOS 386; 400MB running Robo/FX 1.5 with Supra at up to 38,400 bps. Estab. 09/93 with no fee. DTP images, Robo computer graphics. Scanning. Pro photography. CD-ROM distrib. Computer trade/sell.

Acquired Knowledge BBS: (305) 720-3669
Sysop: Wieslaw Samek
6 lines—Unix; 60,000MB running Custom 2.1 with ATT at up to 14,400 bps. Estab. 11/90 with a fee of $10 signup. Internet access, e-mail, UUCP, ftp, IRC, free Unix software (LINUX, FreeBSD).

Infinite Darkness: (305) 792-8716
Sysop: Mitchel Waas
6 lines—MS-DOS 386; 3,500MB running Renegade with US Robotics at up to 16,800 bps. Estab. 09/89 with no fee. Specializing in freedom of speech and the interchange of information. Intelligence-oriented.

DJSA Bulletin Board: (305) 749-6458
Sysop: David Smith
3 lines—MS-DOS 486; 200MB running SpitFire 3.5 with Hayes at up to 14,400 bps. Estab. 04/89 with a fee of $25 quarterly. Publishing the National BBS Directory, which lists 2,000+ BBS numbers in the USA.

The Ashlin BBS: (305) 987-9003
Sysop: Ron K. Smith
1 line—MS-DOS 486; 1,000MB running Galacticomm 6.2f with Boca at up to 14,400 bps. Estab. 02/90 with no fee. The BBS dedicated to helping BBS users make money. Great computer buys and just plain fun.

Trade 80 BBS: (305) 764-2743
Sysop: Joe Agrella
2 lines—MS-DOS 386; 650MB running GT Power Comm 18 with Zytel at up to 57,600 bps. Estab. 03/88 with no fee. Graphics and sound files. Welcomes downloaders.

Wild Palms BBS: (305) 472-4431
Sysop: Dan Waldon
8 lines—MS-DOS 486; 2,500MB running GalacticommMBBS 6.2 with Boca 14.4 at up to 38,400 bps. Estab. 12/93 with a fee of $10 monthly. 24-hr. WorldLink chat, view photos online (DC Net), games, huge file libraries, custom RIP graphics. More.

Phoenix Software Library: (305) 791-9574
Sysop: Terry Windmiller
2 lines—MS-DOS 386; 5,000MB running Galacticomm 6.2 with Hayes at up to 9,600 bps. Estab. 01/86 with no fee. 65,000 files, huge adult section, desktop publishing, graphics, sound, games, technical topics, fun.

become obvious to someone at some point in her illustrious career. Please forward such evidence to me, as I must confess that her existing file is bulging with conflicting impressions. Looking forward to your reply, I remain yours very truly, Maury.

6. The "Here's what I really think about the chairman's plan to acquire Romania" message. Finally, various and sundry people will be stupid enough to call for dangerous opinions to be expressed in this forum. Resist. Call me, —————, There are some things that don't belong on e-mail and this here is one of them. Ten-four. Jerry.

And when you sit down to write your 23rd cryptic minimessage of the day—how about a really bright idea, Sparky?
Pick up a phone!—Gil Schwartz ■

The Dollhouse BBS: (305) 964-7111
Sysop: Ken Pollock

3 lines—MS-DOS 486; 2,000MB running WildCat 4.00M with Hayes at up to 28,800 bps. Estab. 09/93 with no fee. Wildnet. Internet access. Adult conferences, adult GIFs, CD-ROM, shareware, instant access via TABS.

Loreli BBS: (305) 985-0883
Sysop: Sean Puckett

5 lines—Unix; 650MB running custom software with US Robotics at up to 14,400 bps. Estab. 02/88 with no fee. Internet news and mail, games, friendly users. The BBS where everyone knows your name!

Cybertown BBS: (305) 242-1160
Sysop: Tom Merrick

8 lines—MS-DOS 486; 1,000MB running TBBS 2.2 with Boca Research at up to 28,800 bps. Estab. 05/94 with a fee of $10 monthly. Internet forum and graphics info exchange. Art, literature, design contests monthly. Huge adult GIF area.

Astro Cafe: (305) 245-6393
Sysop: David Allen

1 line—MS-DOS 386; 200MB running SpitFire 3.4 with Supra at up to 14,400 bps. Estab. 03/92 with no fee. Many online games, including TradeWars 2002, Legend of the Red Dragon, others. Many files, messages.

Au Naturel BBS: (305) 292-6373
Sysop: Ferret

1 line—MS-DOS 386; 320MB running Searchlight 4.0 with Zoom at up to 28,800 bps. Estab. 07/93 with no fee. Nudist-style BBS. JCS Distribution CD online. Various other topics covered.

The Genesis BBS: (305) 753-5033
Sysop: David Sosnin

1 line—MS-DOS 486; 1,600MB running RemoteAccess 2.02+ with US Robotics at up to 28,800 bps. Estab. 12/91 with no fee. FidoNet, FlyNet, Adult Links, Adult Connections, CD-ROM files.

The TechLands BBS: (305) 977-0098
Sysop: Bryan Branam

4 lines—MS-DOS 486; 16,000MB running WildCat 4.0 with Boca at up to 28,800 bps. Estab. 04/91 with no fee. 12 online CD-ROMs, 900+ message area. Usenet message areas, Internet e-mail, 70,000+ files!

Pro-Entropy: (305) 265-9073
Sysop: Eric A. Seiden

1 line—Apple IIgs; 127MB running Proline 3.0 with Practical Peripherals at up to 38,400 bps. Estab. 01/93 with no fee. Full Internet e-mail access. Many Usenet feeds (COMP.SYS.*, ALT.FAN.*, PRO.*, and so forth) and more.

Rock'n'Roll Harbour BBS: (305) 551-2526
Sysop: Joey Feghali

1 line—MS-DOS 486; 1,228MB running Synchronet 2.00b with US Robotics at up to 16,800 bps. Estab. 10/93 with no fee. BBS for FoxPro, dBASE and other database programmers. Lots of files/discussions.

The Software Cuisine: (305) 642-0754
Sysop: Peter Hebert

1 line—MS-DOS 386; 330MB running Maximus 2.01wb with Lightcom at up to 14,400 bps. Estab. 08/89 with no fee. General fun BBS. CD-ROM, FidoNet file and message areas. No UL/DL ratios. FidoNet node 1:135/57.

Crash and Burn BBS: (305) 238-0569
Sysop: Mr Fixit

3 lines—Amiga; 16,000MB running A3,000 C-Net 3.05 with Supra at up to 14,400 bps. Estab. 05/85 with no fee. CBM 8-bit, Amiga and IBM support. Usenet access. 2 CD-ROM drives. Multiuser online games.

RCR BBS and Computers: (305) 823-3852
Sysop: Richard Rossy

2 lines—OS/2 peer-to-peer with 6550MB running WildCat 4.0 with US Robotics at up to 21,600 bps. Estab. 12/90 with a fee of $30 annually. The best prices on computers and 30,000 programs online.

Cybertown BBS: (305) 242-1160
Sysop: Tom Merrick

10 lines—MS-DOS 486; 2,200MB running TBBS 2.2m with Generic at up to 38,400 bps. Estab. 05/94 with no fee. Miami-based multiline BBS featuring online conferencing, local artist exhibitions, always expanding.

The PowerBoard: (305) 271-6426
Sysop: Fast Eddy Felson

2 lines—MS-DOS 386; 100MB running Searchlight 4.0 with US Robotics at up to 14,400 bps. Estab. 12/93 with no fee. Miami's source for online shopping, GIFs, games, and chat! Out of state call toll-free 305-271-SHOP.

Whatnow BBS: (305) 559-9151
Sysop: Alex Rubio

1 line—MS-DOS 386; 690MB running WildCat 4.0 with Intel at up to 14,400 bps. Estab. 04/89 with no fee. Home of the MiamiBBS list, tons of files, online games, CD-ROM with 10,000+ files.

SunShine PCBoard: (305) 432-2223
Sysop: Michele Stewart

2 lines—MS-DOS 486; 1,024MB running PCBoard 15.2/5 with US Robotics at up to 38,400 bps. Estab. 05/89 with no fee. FidoNet and Adult Links message areas. Files/messages/games/CD-ROM. ANSI lovers' heaven. A great place!

Trek Land: (305) 370-0374
Sysop: Steven "Zapper" Rosbury

1 line—OS/2 2.1, 486DX/50; 1,002MB running WildCat 4.00MP with Practical Peripherals at up to 14,400 bps. Estab. 03/91 with no fee. Dedicated sci-fi BBS. 200MB+ of ST and sci-fi GIFs. Home of the USS Triumph on TrekNet.

DJSA Bulletin Board: (305) 749-6458
Sysop: Jonathan Smith

3 lines—MS-DOS 486; 200MB running SpitFire 3.5 with Hayes at up to 14,400 bps. Estab. 04/89 with a fee of $10 monthly. Shareware, national netmail, local telephone access, national BBS directory, Internet information.

Just the FAQs

Hi. My name's Ed, and I'm a newbie. (Hi, Ed!) Welcome to this month's meeting of Newbies Anonymous, an informal self-help group for those of us who feel lost, bewildered, and completely overwhelmed by the Internet. If you've ever traveled in an exotic foreign land—like Nepal or Tierra del Fuego or Southern California—you know the feeling. Connecting to the Internet offers more opportunities for public humiliation than a Friars Club roast or a high school prom. And there's nothing like a Usenet newsgroup—with 3 million people looking on—to show off our lack of technical knowledge and our underdeveloped social skills. Hey, we're all newbies once. Here's how to get over it.

For starters, learn the language. The folks at Berlitz pioneered the total immersion technique, and it works just as well with Netspeak as it does with Norwegian. Read a few hundred newsgroup postings. Pay attention to how the regulars talk. You don't download a file, you ftp it. It's not a forum, it's a newsgroup. Don't forget the acronyms, either. Like IMHO (in my humble opinion), RTFM (read the, uh, manual), and LJBF (let's just be friends—useful in the alt.sex hierarchy).

But total immersion doesn't mean full participation. Resist the urge to post until you're sure you know how a particular newsgroup works. If Mark Twain had had a modem, he might have said: "It's better to lurk quietly and be thought a fool than to post a stupid question to 30,000 newsgroup servers and remove all doubt." Besides, every stupid question has already been asked and answered. Anyone determined to become a Net expert reads the FAQs—the lists of Frequently Asked Questions designed to keep us newbies from gobbling up bandwidth by repeatedly asking the same questions. One of the best is Answers to Frequently Asked Questions about Usenet, found in news.announce.newusers. Like most FAQs, it's cross-posted in news.answers, which is a great place to look for Net wisdom. And every FAQ can be ftp'd from rtfm.mit.edu.

FAQs aren't the only source of wisdom on the Net. Some of the most entertaining and instructive reading in cyberspace can be found in documents written just for us newbies. Emily Postnews, for example, is the foremost authority on proper Net behavior. Check out her occasionally caustic advice on how not to act on the Net. ("Q: What does foobar stand for? A: It stands for you, dear.") For the latest edition of Emily Postnews Answers Your Questions on Netiquette, look in news.announce.newusers.

Mark and Joe's Just Put Us In Our Place: (407) 884-6470
Sysop: Mark Wilson
1 line—MS-DOS 286; 210MB running WWIV 4.23 with US Robotics at up to 14,400 bps. Estab. 07/92 with no fee. Orlando's official Q-Zar BBS. Entertainment-based, movies, TV shows, amusement parks, and IBM tech.

Dragon World: (407) 487-9355
Sysop: Blue Dragon (aka Mark Graham)
24 lines—MS-DOS 486; 600MB running Major BBS latest with US Robotics at up to 28,800 bps. Estab. 01/91 with a fee of $10 monthly. RPG discussions and games. SCA group. ANSI and RIP art. Magic-The Gathering HQ, e-mail, Usenet!

Static BBS: (407) 479-1063
Sysop: James Sammartino
1 line—MS-DOS 486; 850MB running WildCat 3.9 with US Robotics at up to 14,400 bps. Estab. 05/94 with no fee. A great BBS. Lots of files and many online games available. Very fun!

The Adult Information Exchange (AIE): (407) 451-1984
Sysop: Alex Barenboim
6 lines—Pentium 100MHz; 3,500MB running DLX 6.0 with Intel at up to 57,600 bps. Estab. 01/90 with a fee of $15 annually. Large adult GIFs. Matchmaker to find your ideal mate! OS/2 technical support!

The OutDoor Sportsman BBS: (407) 635-9590
Sysop: John Cornelius
1 line—MS-DOS 486; 1,200MB running PCBoard 15.1 with Hayes at up to 28,800 bps. Estab. 06/92 with no fee. Quality files, message areas, fishing, hunting, boating, and so on. Weather, tides, more. RIP. Two 24-hr. nodes.

Politically Incorrect BBS: (407) 632-7549
Sysop: The Pundit
2 lines—MS-DOS 486; 4,500MB running Synchronet Version 2 with Zoom at up to 14,400 bps. Estab. 12/92 with a fee of $20 lifetime. Massive conservative/high-tech BBS. 4 CD-ROMs, Novell files, games, 100s of message areas, 50% free.

With apologies to Robert Fulghum, everything we need to know about newsgroups we probably learned in kindergarten. Like these simple lessons:

Be nice. Newsgroups bring out the worst in some people. Faced with a rational argument, they respond with abuse and invective. In Netspeak, a posting that crosses the line into personal attack is called a flame. We newbies are often horrified the first time we see a flame, especially if it's directed at us. Relax. Get over it. That's what kill files are for.

Clean up after yourself. Every posting that goes out to a newsgroup gets routed through a few thousand servers (at least), and potentially stored on hundreds of thousands of hard drives. Some newsgroup readers let you attach complex signatures to the end of each posting. If your signature file is longer than four lines, you might as well hang a sign on your back saying, "Flame me!" Another band-width-wasting breach of netiquette: Littering a newsgroup with meaningless messages ("I agree." "This is a test.") and simple thank yous that are better sent by e-mail.

Don't be a bore. There are a few ancient stories that simply won't vanish from the Net. Like the one about the dying kid who wanted to set a record for receiving the most get well cards. Or the rumor that the FCC wants to impose a tax on modems. The kid set the record and doesn't want any more get well cards. The FCC doesn't raise taxes. Every so often some newbie resurrects one of these tired old yarns. But it won't be one of us.

And then there's semi-criminal behavior. Want to get lots of vicious, intensely personal mail aimed straight at you? Then try spamming the Net—sending identical copies of one posting to dozens, even hundreds of newsgroups. I won't name the two bozos who posted ads for their law firm's services on 6,000 Usenet newsgroups, because they don't deserve any more free publicity. They broke two cardinal rules of the Internet: Send advertising only to those who want it, and post only where it's appropriate. Sadly, they weren't even newbies—they knew exactly what they were doing.

Wanna be a good Net citizen? Just learn the basic ground rules. You'll dodge the wrath of the Net's elders. And maybe you'll get a chance to help some poor newbie.—Ed Bott ∎

Liberty BBS: (407) 243-3959
Sysop: William Zakreski
9 lines—MS-DOS 486; 6,000MB running PCBoard 5.1 with US Robotics at up to 57,600 bps. Estab. 11/92 with a fee of $30 annually. Technology and networking. Internet, online fax, 50+ doors, QWK/rep mail, 250 live chat areas.

The No-Name BBS: (407) 348-2006
Sysop: Brian Keck
3 lines—MS-DOS 486; 3,400MB running WildCat 3.9 with US Robotics at up to 19,200 bps. Estab. 09/91 with a fee of $10 annually. Apogee/Epic game site. Fido 1:3633/2. 4 CDs online. 30-day free trial. 2nd node 407-348-9551.

AmiTrek BBS: (407) 348-3365
Sysop: Locutus
1 line—Amiga; 213MB running CNet 3.05c with US Robotics at up to 28,800 bps. Estab. 05/93 with no fee. Devoted to Amigas and Star Trek. Many doors and files online. All Amiga/Trek Fido areas. 1:3633/1701.

Osceola Express BBS: (407) 348-5295
Sysop: Larry Charpiat
2 lines—MS-DOS 486; 20,000MB running WildCat 4.0 M with Practical Peripherals at up to 14,400 bps. Estab. 05/93 with no fee. Message bases, Florida Net, 150+ online games, 22 CD-ROMs with 6 online. RIP/ANSI. Node 2: 348-3188.

The Program Exchange: (407) 870-2735
Sysop: Fred Kushner
1 line—MS-DOS.386; 612MB running Maximus 2.01 with Zoom at up to 14,400 bps. Estab. 10/88 with no fee. Files, games, Fido echo, no UL/DL ratio.

The Eagle's Hideout BBS: (407) 547-4233
Sysop: Mark Miller
3 lines—MS-DOS 386; 900MB running PCBoard 3.9m with Hayes at up to 19,200 bps. Estab. 10/91 with no fee.

🐛 Federal Bureaucrat Virus—Divides your hard disk into hundreds of little units, each of which does practically nothing, but all of which claim to be the most important part of the computer.

Exec Talk BBS: (407) 729-1463

Sysop: Rob Taylor

16 lines—MS-DOS 486; 2,000MB running MPCBBC-Pro 1.80 with Boca at up to 14,400 bps. Estab. 03/93 with a fee of $6 monthly. Free basic limited accounts. Internet access. FidoNet. Planet Connect. Chat. Games. CD-ROMs.

The Eagle's Nest BBS: (407) 242-2431

Sysop: Bradley

16 lines—MS-DOS 486; 1,000MB running Galacticomm v6.2 with US Robotics at up to 14,400 bps. Estab. 06/93 with no fee. Chat system. CD-ROM, WorldLink, files, message bases, Internet, games!

Access America Online: (407) 723-4634

Sysop: Bob Morton

10 lines—MS-DOS 486; 6,000MB running PCBoard 15.1 with Supra at up to 14,400 bps. Estab. 01/91 with a fee of $20 quarterly. Local message bases and FidoNet 1:374/119; loads of fresh, high-quality files; doors; shop online.

Sci-Fi Spaceport Collectibles BBS: (407) 690-1808

Sysop: Charles Swartwout

1 line—MS-DOS 486; 300MB running Galacticomm 6.2 with Infotel at up to 19,200 bps. Estab. 03/94 with no fee. Collectibles for sale from Star Trek, Star Wars, Aliens, NASA, and so on.

CyberNexus: (407) 459-9100

Sysop: Steven Sheeley/David Beiger

15 lines—MS-DOS 486; 4,096MB running PCBoard 15.1 with US Robotics at up to 14,400 bps. Estab. 09/84 with a fee of $25 monthly. Extensive message bases covering all topics. MedievalNet ZC. Internet newsgroups and ftp mail.

Narcoossee BBS: (407) 892-8483

Sysop: Frank Walker

2 lines—MS-DOS 486; 2,200MB running PCBoard 15.1/10 with US Robotics at up to 28,800 bps. Estab. 09/89 with a fee of $15 annually. Member RIME network with 140+ conferences. 30 CD-ROM discs; 9 (5GB+) always online.

FAA ASO-FSDO-15: (407) 648-6963

Sysop: William Hoenstine/Obie Young

1 line—MS-DOS 386; 330MB running QuickBBS 2.76 G-3 with Microcom at up to 9,600 bps. Estab. 12/91 with no fee. First FAA southern region BBS dedicated to serving the needs of the North Florida District.

The Lair of the Wolverine BBS: (407) 294-9446

Sysop: Patch

1 line—MS-DOS 286; 960MB running WWIV 423+ with Practical Peripherals at up to 19,200 bps. Estab. 05/89 with no fee. Independent software author support board. Hi-res. ANSI graphics, CD-ROM.

Dirty Deeds: (407) 290-5189

Sysop: Michael Primavera

2 lines—MS-DOS 486; 12,000MB running RoboFX 1.04 with Zoom at up to 38,400 bps. Estab. 07/92 with a fee of $35 donation. All-adult BBS, registration required. 25 CDs, 12 CD-ROMs, Throb-Net Adult Net, donation not required!

Infinite Space Online: (407) 856-0021

Sysop: Charlie Scherker

32 lines—MS-DOS 486; 500MB running Galacticomm 6.12d with US Robotics at up to 19,200 bps. Estab. 04/93 with no fee. Live interactive games. Internet, WorldLink, USA Today, and PC Catalog. Much more.

The Computer Custodian: (407) 354-5304

Sysop: Morey J. Haber

1 line—MS-DOS 486; 1,200MB running WildCat 3.9 with Zoom VPXbis at up to 14,400 bps. Estab. 12/93 with no fee. Add ",,,,22" after the phone number to access BBS. Required for BBS access.

No Name Yet BBS: (407) 384-7166

Sysop: Brett

1 line—MS-DOS 386; 1,200MB running WWIV 4.23 with Hayes at up to 28,800 bps. Estab. 10/89 with no fee. Networked message bases, online games, downloadable files (many GIFs).

Custom Computers BBS: (407) 743-1112

Sysop: John Skakandy

2 lines—486 LAN/W/ROM server; 1,600MB running RoboBoard/FX 1.4 with Boca 28,800 at up to 57,600 bps. Estab. 04/89 with no fee. Multinode BBS. VGA graphics with mouse control. FidoNet. Node 2: 743-1500, 14,400. No 2,400 calls!

PC Access Online Information System: (407) 633-1015

Sysop: Elam Ashman

1 line—MS-DOS 486; 250MB running PCBoard 3.91s with Generic at up to 38,400 bps. Estab. 07/94 with no fee. 6,000+ files. Full access first call, no verification. Plenty for everyone!

JumpStart: (407) 337-2559

Sysop: Sandy Dykes

6 lines—MS-DOS 486; 1,100MB running PCBoard 15.1 with US Robotics at up to 14,400 bps. Estab. 03/92 with a fee of $45 annually. Internet access. Full Usenet newsgroups. 10GB+ online. Sound card conference.

FarPoint: (407) 631-9198

Sysop: Tim Tyler

1 line—OS/2 2.1 486; 1,024MB running RemoteAccess 2.1+ with US Robotics at up to 16,800 bps. Estab. 01/92 with no fee. Many OS/2-oriented files and message areas. Many conferences. CUD, CPD, and EFF archives. Lots more.

Black Orchid BBS: (407) 892-3970

Sysop: Chuck Carpenter

1 line—MS-DOS 386; 1,000MB running WildCat 3.90 with Practical Peripherals at up to 19,200 bps. Estab. 09/04 with a fee of $20 annually. Large message base. Wildnet and HotNet echomail. 100+ online doors/CD-ROM files.

Derringer's Realm: (407) 692-4857

Sysop: Derringer

10 lines—MS-DOS 486; 800MB running WildCat 3.91M with Digicomm at up to 38,400 bps. Estab. 01/89 with no fee. 10 lines for your enjoyment. 800MB of files, 100+ door games including Barren Realms online.

Travel/Tainment Today: (407) 747-4343
Sysop: Don/Sally

2 lines—MS-DOS 486; 300MB running Galacticomm 6.21 with Supra at up to 14,400 bps. Estab. 02/94 with no fee. Promotes tourism and activities in Florida. Provides a database of thousands of topics. Up to date.

The Ice Cave: (407) 793-8598
Sysop: Icer

1 line—MS-DOS 486; 625MB running Renegade 05-07 with Practical Peripherals at up to 28,800 bps. Estab. 10/92 with no fee. Message BBS. Multinode support! 407-793-1368. All speeds accepted on node 2!

Benjamin Computer Services BBS Node 1: (407) 687-1622
Sysop: John Benjamin

2 lines—MS-DOS 386; 500MB running WildCat 3.91M with US Robotics at up to 14,400 bps. Estab. 11/88 with a fee of $25 annually. Genealogy, Internet, Usenet, FidoNet, CD-ROM, live door games, buy or lease new car.

Round Table Software BBS: (407) 740-8353
Sysop: Allan Holtz

1 line—MS-DOS 386; 200MB running WildCat 3.90 with Infotel at up to 14,400 bps. Estab. 01/94 with no fee. Provides support for Round Table and Powerlinx software plus a great selection of shareware.

Southern City Central BBS: (813) 749-0664
Sysop: Phillip Benson

2 lines—MS-DOS 486; 500MB running Telegard 2.7 with Digicom at up to 19,200 bps. Estab. 05/92 with no fee. Messages, mail/file nets, online games, 2 CD-ROMs online. Line 2: 813-795-7705.

Manatee On Line: (813) 755-3748
Sysop: Farrel Tackett

1 line—MS-DOS 386; 15,000MB running WildCat 4 with Generic at up to 2,400 bps. Estab. 02/91 with no fee. Supports MS-DOS and members of not-for-profit computer club, to teach others and help one another.

Computer World BBS: (813) 748-7513
Sysop: James Smith

2 lines—MS-DOS 486; 30,000MB running WildCat 4.0 with Zoom 28.8 at up to 28,800 bps. Estab. 02/91 with no fee. Supporting MS-DOS and Commodore programs, the handicapped, and religious.

Family Circuit BBS: (813) 689-6937
Sysop: Chris Burroughs

1 line—MS-DOS 386; 100MB running TriBBS 4.2 with Nuvotel at up to 38,400 bps. Estab. 10/93 with no fee. Christian, files, CD-ROM with Christian files, doors, soon ChristNet.

Hard Facts Information Systems: (813) 786-9026
Sysop: Wayne Fusco

4 lines—MS-DOS 486; 1,024MB running WildCat 3.9 with Zoom at up to 57,600 bps. Estab. 12/93 with a fee of $20 annually. Files, FidoNet, GameNet, InfoNet, online games, CD-ROM areas, Internet newsgroups, e-mail.

J-Connection: (813) 791-0101
Sysop: Maryann Miller/David Gregory

2 lines—MS-DOS 486; 200MB running WildCat I-M with Hayes at up to 19,200 bps. Estab. 10/93 with no fee. Data-processing job listings. Jobs throughout the U.S.A. and foreign. No fee to job seekers.

Tampa Bay OS/2 Users' Group: (813) 562-2249
Sysop: Greg Dodge

5 lines—IBM PC-compatible; 5,000MB running Maximus with Hayes at up to 9,600 bps. Estab. 12/93 with a fee of $20 annually. Available to members of the Tampa Bay OS/2 Users' Group (TBOUG). News, freeware, and shareware.

CyberSpace DataBase: (813) 796-5627
Sysop: Steve Sanders, N4WAK

10 lines—MS-DOS 486; 2,000MB running PCBoard 15.1 with US Robotics at up to 57,600 bps. Estab. 09/82 with a fee of $50 annually. Windows, fonts, graphics, GIFs, adult area, SoundBlaster, 85,000 files. 12 CD-ROMs. V.FC modems.

Vern's Windows: (813) 473-2118
Sysop: Chris Takasawa/Vernon Fields

1 line—MS-DOS 486; 450MB running Super BBS 1.17-3 reg with Supra at up to 28,800 bps. Estab. 01/91 with a fee of $5 optional. 3 CD-ROMs at once (1.8GB+ compressed), many registered doors, friendly staff, FidoNet 1:137/409.

The Pegasus Project...the Next Generation: (813) 481-5575
Sysop: Chris Michaels

8 lines—MS-DOS 486; 10,000MB running PCBoard 15.2 with US Robotics at up to 14,400 bps. Estab. 05/84 with no fee. Voted No.64 of the Top 100 BBSs in the U.S.A. Largest in Florida. 40,000+ files, free access, adult areas.

The TandyTane BBS: (813) 574-2301
Sysop: Jay Wiggington

8 lines—MS-DOS 486; 2,000MB running Galacticomm 6.2F with US Robotics at up to 28,800 bps. Estab. 10/89 with no fee.

PD Playhouse BBS: (813) 422-7391
Sysop: Lorin Winchester

1 line—MS-DOS 486; 700MB running Renegade 5-31 Exp with Practical Peripherals at up to 14,400 bps. Estab. 01/94 with a fee of $5 quarterly. Renegade support site; RGSNet 50:270/501; ITCnet 85:881/518.

The Baywatch BBS: (813) 934-7881
Sysop: Dale Hutchinson

1 line—MS-DOS 386; 500MB running GT Power 18.00 with US Robotics at up to 57,600 bps. Estab. 09/91 with no fee. Messages, files, online games, NASA information, police/fire support BBS. Now with RIP graphics!

The River of Time BBS: (813) 688-2987
Sysop: John Dedeo

3 lines—MS-DOS 486; 790MB running WildCat 3.9 with US Robotics at up to 14,400 bps. Estab. 08/93 with a fee of $10 monthly. Florida's largest file server with 30 CDs using Romdoor, with 7 online. 25GB+ of files.

The V.Fast VP

Nowhere is the stunning paradigm shift away from substance and into communications for its own sake more dramatic than in the convergence between Vice President Al Gore and the electronic cause he so boldly champions. For those who don't, can't, or won't understand the beauty of the conceptual highway that lies ahead, the vice president is the clearest physical representation of the medium he is trying to create. In these ten important ways, he is the thing itself, and as we understand him, we understand it:

1. They're both very good looking and make a powerful first impression. Although the superhighway is significantly more wiry than the vice president, both are big and handsome, with attractive interfaces that draw you almost immediately into whatever hooey is transpiring. Even those who don't really want to like them end up shaking their heads in grudging admiration.

2. Both have a lot of information and aren't afraid to show it. Anyone who saw the VP take on Mr. Perot in the last election knows that he's capable of retaining gigabytes of data in his random access memory banks and core dumping the contents at will, amazing friends and influencing people all over the place.

3. They both represent a commitment to reinventing things. The vice president is on a mission to reinvent government. The electronic superhighway wants to reinvent the way we bank, shop, visit our imaginary neighbors, eat simulated breakfast, and make virtual love.

4. You have to be very smart to understand either of them. Like the superhighway, which will reward people who know how to access its many levels, the VP has a tendency to talk up—not down—to the public, assuming a certain level of technical sophistication on matters of great importance to us all. This can lead to some problems, since….

5. They both tend to wander off into unspeakable technobabble given half a chance. Getting backed into a corner at a party with Mr. Gore as he delves in to the arcana of telecommunications deregulation—or finding yourself in a digital data swamp alongside the I-Way after making an innocent query—is no fun for those with MTV attention spans.

6. They both make conservatives very angry. On the other side of society's spectrum from youngsters who find a 30-second commercial the intellectual equivalent of *War and Peace*, there are the tortoise-headed Luddites who hate anything new and reinventional. These individuals have a smarmy, condescending aversion both to the earnest, hardworking vice president and to the implications of the digital revolution, just as they despise all those laboring to replace existing institutions, technologies, jobs, belief systems, and people with theoretical ones.

7. They're both very clean and morally impeccable, though. The superhighway will be as G-rated as a bucketful of raw transactional data, jammed full of squeaky infotainment and jolly bitmaps of faraway places. Like the veep, the superhighway won't get one bit funky until way after hours, and even then only when we consent.

8. And yet, they're both perceived by some to be relatively nonessential. At the same time, Mr. Gore, as vice president, and the superhighway, as a fictional construct, both suffer from the public perception that, were they to drop from existence altogether, nothing substantial would change. This has to do with the functions both now serve. One is vice president, heretofore a largely ceremonial position that has had little day-to-day impact on the workings of the Republic. The other is an almost wholly fanciful creation of futurists, hopeful investment bankers, and the New York Times. That's not very many people, although they are influential. But all that will change! Because….

9. They each show far more potential for greatness than they've yet delivered. There's nowhere to go but up for Mr. Gore and his superhighway. Both have shown they can achieve the heights of publicity, are willing to put forth tremendous ideas that can be neither proved nor disproved with great passion, and can build on existing infrastructures to create air castles of daunting proportions—blueprints of a tomorrow yet to come.

10. The future belongs to them both! And what a place it will be, too! A networked festival of services where information hovers just a micron from our fingertips all the time; where movies, music, shopping, and other stimuli are always on the window ledge, cooling; where earnest folks with pinstriped headgear serve up a virtual reality that does battle with the real thing and wins. And in the middle of it all, presiding with vision and good humor, look! It's President Wonk at his computer, at play in the fields of the Internet, interacting with the people, by the people, and for the people. Huzzah!—Gil Schwartz ■

Hawks Nest BBS: (813) 425-1000
Sysop: Tom Parsons
1 line—OS/2 486; 2,000MB running WildCat 3.91 with US Robotics at up to 14,400 bps. Estab. 06/92 with no fee. Online games, graphics, FidoNet, utilities, OS/2, and more.

The Cat Box BBS: (813) 434-0911
Sysop: Tom McDonald
1 line—OS/2 486; 880MB running WWIV 4.21a+ with US Robotics at up to 57,600 bps. Estab. 04/91 with no fee. Message bases from four networks. Tons of files with CD-ROM online. 30+ online games, surprises.

The Metropolis BBS [ASV]: (813) 775-1776
Sysop: Dave Goldstein
1 line—MS-DOS 386; 460MB running WWIV 4.23 with Infotel at up to 14,400 bps. Estab. 09/92 with no fee. One of the hottest BBSs in town! Multinetworked: WWIVnet/ICEnet/Terranet /FidoNet. Give it a try!

Ground Zero: (813) 849-4034
Sysop: Dave Anderson/Sean Fleeman
4 lines—Amiga; 2,400MB running CNet Amiga 3.05c with Hayes/US Robotics at up to 28,800 bps. Estab. 04/87 with no fee. Supporting the Amiga, Macintosh, and Atari ST. Files, national message echoes, Internet, CNet support.

Board of Trade BBS: (813) 862-4772
Sysop: Richard Ziegler
1 line—MS-DOS 486; 670MB running PCBoard 15.1 with US Robotics at up to 14,400 bps. Estab. 06/92 with no fee. Home of the Pasco BBS Magazine, Shadoware, and the Westcoast 813 BBS Directory.

Excalibur BBS: (813) 426-8662
Sysop: Randolph Stover
1 line—MS-DOS 486; 540MB running WildCat 3.91 with Smart One 14.4 at up to 38,400 bps. Estab. 06/94 with no fee. 2 CDs/6,000+ files with 3,000+ online at one time. Adult area/28+ doors/local mail.

Supersonic BBS: (813) 467-9794
Sysop: Ryan Harris
1 line—MS-DOS 386; 1,024MB running WildCat 3.50S with Infotel at up to 57,600 bps. Estab. 01/89 with no fee. CD-ROM, files, online doors, message conferences, contests, more.

Starving ProgrammersD-BBS: (813) 763-4195
Sysop: Ty Byrn/Pat Cartner/Thomas Plant
1 line—MS-DOS 386; 300MB running WildCat 4.0SL with Generic at up to 14,400 bps. Estab. 06/93 with no fee. Many CDs. 100+ TW 2002 files on hard drive and 1600+ files total. Growing Doom base.

The NutHouse BBS: (813) 625-8233
Sysop: Doc Larkins/Edna Kelly
6 lines—MS-DOS 486; 1,000MB running WildCat 3.9 with Generic at up to 38,400 bps. Estab. 01/94 with a fee of $25 annually. Multiline chat, multi-CD drives, friendly sysops. Still growing.

The Brewing Company: (813) 764-9510
Sysop: Marlboro Man
1 line—MS-DOS 486; 2,000MB running Remote Access 2.02 with US Robotics at up to 28,800 bps. Estab. 01/94 with a fee of $50 annually. Latest files and utilities. 2 CD-ROMS, FidoNet/TurboNet/GameNet. InterBBS BRE door game beta site.

BBShare: (813) 758-3223
Sysop: Kevin Pulford
3 lines—MS-DOS 486; 1,000MB running WildCat 4.0MP with US Robotics at up to 16,800 bps. Estab. 07/92 with a fee of $10 monthly. Serving all computer interests including many file areas and networking info. of all types.

Clay's BBS: (813) 471-0451
Sysop: Clay Welsh
1 line—MS-DOS 286; 120MB running SpitFire 3.4 with Infotel at up to 14,400 bps. Estab. 05/92 with no fee. Amateur radio-oriented with 2,000MB of CD-ROM shareware available. No games or doors.

The 128th Parallel: (813) 397-5261
Sysop: Alex Brooks

2 lines—MS-DOS 486; 1,700MB running Searchlight 4.0 with Microcom at up to 28,800 bps. Estab. 04/90 with no fee. FidoNet, SL-Net, Usenet, RIP Net, and ISGNet, QWK door. DOS, OS/2, and Windows file areas.

Close Encounters: (813) 528-8294
Sysop: Liney and MsBehaven

38 lines—MS-DOS 486; 255MB running Galacticomm 6 with Supra at up to 28,800 bps. Estab. 10/85 with no fee. Adult, interactive chat, and games, PD and shareware, links to other systems, weekly get-togethers.

Mercury Opus: (813) 321-0734
Sysop: Emery Mandel

10 lines—MS-DOS 386; 12,000MB running PCBoard 15.1/10 with Hayes at up to 28,800 bps. Estab. 09/88 with a fee of $30 biannually. 2,000 conferences, 100,000 files, Fido, Usenet, Internet, RIME, ILink, DOS, Windows, OS/2, and adult.

C.R.S. BBS: (813) 327-8842
Sysop: David Mueller/Tom Downs

3 lines—MS-DOS 486; 90,000MB running SpitFire 3.4 with Zoom at up to 28,800 bps. Estab. 11/91 with a fee of $35 annually. 60,000+ files. No adult. Fido, Internet messages. RIP Net, Planet Connect.

The Alternative: (813) 882-3887
Sysop: Chris Fenton

4 lines—MS-DOS 486; 1,575MB running Searchlight 4.0 with Zoom at up to 28,800 bps. Estab. 09/86 with no fee. User-friendly BBS supporting shareware, message bases, SL-Net, Pridenet, and adult files. No ratios.

Weekend Warrior: (813) 961-6120
Sysop: Hugh

1 line—MS-DOS 386; 850MB running WWIV 4.23 with US Robotics at up to 14,400 bps. Estab. 10/91 with no fee. 7 CD-ROMs. 3GB+ of storage. Host system of InsanityNET. Free WWIV help.

Longbow BBS: (813) 961-3653
Sysop: Eric Neff

1 line—MS-DOS 486; 800MB running WildCat 3.91M with US Robotics at up to 21,600 bps. Estab. 09/90 with no fee. FidoNet 1:377/77 NEC. MedievalNet 180:107/1 NC. CD-ROM files area. 200+ Fido and MedievalNet echoes.

A KinKy World: (813) 671-4347
Sysop: The Enticer

2 lines—MS-DOS 486; 1,500MB running RoboFX V1.4 with Practical Peripherals at up to 14,400 bps. Estab. 10/87 with no fee. Online GIF viewing, 6 CDs always online. Shareware, celebrity, amateur, and original GIFs. GIF-oriented.

The Village: (813) 986-1945
Sysop: Number Six

1 line—MS-DOS 386; 1,000MB running WWIV v4.22 with US Robotics at up to 14,400 bps. Estab. 09/92 with no fee. British entertainment such as "The Prisoner" and "Doctor Who" messages and files. GIFs and games, nets.

The Inner Sanctum: (813) 848-6055
Sysop: Rob and Carolyn Marlowe

10 lines—MS-DOS 486; 14,000MB running TBBS 2.2M with Hayes at up to 14,400 bps. Estab. 03/85 with a fee of $53 annually. Pinellas: 813-934-5533. UltraChat with Australia and elsewhere. 18 CD-ROMs online. Great games.

The Upper Room BBS: (904) 689-2377
Sysop: Light Warrior

1 line—MS-DOS 386; 450MB running WWIV 4.23 with AT&T at up to 14,400 bps. Estab. 02/91 with no fee. A BBS of many games and message bases. WOLFnet @15003. 15 onliners and growing every day.

Jack's Review: (904) 563-0704
Sysop: Jack Davis

1 line—MS-DOS 486; 210MB running ProBoard 2.00 with Hayes at up to 14,400 bps. Estab. 03/87 with no fee. Online games (Barons Realms Internet), upload/download, mail, netmail, 3,000 files. Open to all.

Exotica's Pets and Stuff: (904) 563-0066
Sysop: Mark Davis

5 lines—MS-DOS 486; 4,200MB running WildCat 4.0 with Generic at up to 14,400 bps. Estab. 06/92 with no fee. One of area's fastest-growing BBSs. Chat, thousands of conferences, many networks, games galore, and more.

Oreos and Milk BBS: (904) 238-7829
Sysop: Council of Lords

1 line—MS-DOS 486; 340MB running Remote Access 2.02 with BestData at up to 14,400 bps. Estab. 07/94 with no fee. Shareware CD online. Dedicated to games, fun, and mayhem. No fee, but beware psychotic sysops.

Craig's Data Exchange: (904) 483-2498
Sysop: Craig Salmond

6 lines—MS-DOS 486; 5,000MB running PCBoard 15.2/M with US Robotics at up to 28,800 bps. Estab. 02/92 with a fee of $12 lifetime. Devoted to having fun and access to lots of files. INTELEC, CompuLink, FidoNet, and Internet.

Alternate Reality: (904) 862-6387
Sysop: Edward Thorne

1 line—MS-DOS 386; 200MB running RemoteAccess 2.02+ with Hayes at up to 28,800 bps. Estab. 06/92 with no fee. MS-DOS-based file areas, FidoNet echomail, official Outpost Trader beta site and dist. point.

Sailor's Choice BBS: (904) 651-2707
Sysop: Seadog

1 line—MS-DOS 386; 8MB running WildCat 3.9 with Hayes at up to 2,400 bps. Estab. 06/94 with no fee. Sail-related software, nudist forum, personal ads, Florida sailors' info, marinas.

Esoteric Oracle: (904) 332-9547
Sysop: Jason Cook

6 lines—Macintosh; 2,000MB running Precision Systems 1.0 B83 with Supra at up to 38,400 bps. Estab. 02/85 with no fee. FidoNet messages and mail, interactive chat, online text games, "The Homeboy System."

The Information Station: (904) 373-0645

Sysop: Ron Chartier

2 lines—MS-DOS 486; 1,300MB running SpitFire 3.5 with Boca at up to 14,400 bps. Estab. 12/89 with a fee of $10 annually. 100+ online doors, message base, low annual fee, 1.5GB+ storage, members-only second node.

Dragon Keep International: (904) 375-6431

Sysop: Dragon/Cerebus

50 lines—MS-DOS 486; 5,000MB running Galacticomm 6.2 with US Robotics at up to 38,400 bps. Estab. 01/87 with no fee. Live chat/games/5GB+ files. Full Internet access (telnet: dkeep.com). Instant access w/credit card.

Farthinghale Arms: (904) 378-4861

Sysop: Marshall Sutherland

1 line—MS-DOS 486; 640MB running Arms-PC 2.16 with US Robotics at up to 14,400 bps. Estab. 12/89 with no fee. UUCP node. Libernet, CuD, Caver's Digest.

The Virtual Gateway: (904) 376-6601

Sysop: Gateway Telecommunications

14 lines—MS-DOS 486; 3,000MB running Galacticomm 6.2Mod with Supra at up to 14,400 bps. Estab. 02/94 with a fee of $5 monthly. Information and entertainment. Free instant trial period. Internet access. Many message networks.

Prime Time BBS: (904) 637-3713

Sysop: Mark Beaubien

2 lines—MS-DOS 486; 1,200MB running Searchlight 4.0 with Hayes at up to 38,400 bps. Estab. 06/87 with a fee of $15 annually. Planet Connect, major FDNs, FidoNet mail, Internet mail. Huge file area. Weather maps updated daily.

The City Lights: (904) 786-9914

Sysop: Big Mo

1 line—MS-DOS 486; 1,044MB running WWIV 4.23+ with US Robotics at up to 14,400 bps. Estab. 05/90 with no fee. User-friendly, networked message bases, and special interests to hobby programmers (especially C++).

The Wall BBS: (904) 730-8659

Sysop: Zeus

1 line—SpartaDOS Atari 8-bit; 200MB running BBS Express Pro 2.1a with US Robotics at up to 14,400 bps. Estab. 09/88 with no fee. Supporting the Atari 8-bit and ST with message bases, file SIGs, library, and online games.

Achilles' BBS: (904) 886-2779

Sysop: FrontRunner

1 line—MS-DOS 386; 540MB running WWIV 4.23 with Practical Peripherals at up to 14,400 bps. Estab. 12/91 with no fee. Alternative lifestyle board. Games/subs/up-downloads/CD-ROM. A great place to be yourself.

Parados: (904) 260-3172

Sysop: Steven White

1 line—MS-DOS 386; 2,200MB running Maximus 201 wb with US Robotics at up to 14,400 bps. Estab. 12/92 with no fee. No U/D ratio. 2.2 GB of shareware files, FidoNet w/large message base. A user-dedicated BBS.

Whistlers Hollow: (904) 727-9289

Sysop: Whistler

1 line—MS-DOS 386; 2,000MB running WWIV 4.23 with Practical Peripherals at up to 38,400 bps. Estab. 11/91 with no fee. 2GB online. FidoNet and other networks. The best onliners. User-friendly software. Modified.

Danno's BBS: (904) 221-3634

Sysop: Dan Keller

2 lines—MS-DOS 486; 5,600MB running Tag 2.7 with Infotel V.FC at up to 28,800 bps. Estab. 11/91 with no fee. Dual-node LAN. Files, online games, message bases. FidoNet/TAGnet/ACCNET. Node 2 phone: 904-221-3632.

Victory Station: (904) 693-3147

Sysop: DarNaka

1 line—MS-DOS 386; 1,300MB running WWIV 4.23 with Best Data at up to 14,400 bps. Estab. 05/92 with no fee. 2 CD-ROMSs online and 100+ message bases. No cursing or adult material. The cleanest board in JAX.

Southern Accent: (904) 777-0694

Sysop: Ellen Bell (Kitty)

1 line—MS-DOS 386; 250MB running Tag 2.6e with US Robotics at up to 14,400 bps. Estab. 05/92 with no fee. 80+ online doors, calls up to 14,400, files and messages. A little southern hospitality.

Demo(plus): (904) 396-3064

Sysop: Ed Krayer

1 line—MS-DOS 386; 1,000MB running PCBoard 15.1 with Intel at up to 14,400 bps. Estab. 03/84 with a fee of $20 annually. Demos of commercial software packages; FoxPro/dBASE/xBase; large selection of PD/shareware biz-board.

Gateway To The World: (904) 730-7692

Sysop: sysop@jax.gate.com

8 lines—Unix; 2,000MB running GTTW BBS 1.0 with US Robotics at up to 19,200 bps. Estab. 06/94 with a fee of $30 monthly. Complete Internet access, must call 904-730-7692 (voice) to receive an account.

The Fishing Hole: (904) 260-9688

Sysop: Eddie Van

1 line—MS-DOS 486; 1,500MB running Tag 2.7 with Nuvotel at up to 14,400 bps. Estab. 02/94 with no fee. Family-oriented BBS with online games, files. FidoNet, StormNet, ACCNET, TAGnet. Active message areas.

Land of the Lounge Lizards: (904) 645-3846

Sysop: Gecko/Q

1 line—MS-DOS 486; 1,200MB running WWIV 4.23 with Zoom at up to 24,000 bps. Estab. 05/93 with no fee. A wide variety of information available. Shareware to TQM files. Online games. WWIVnet, WWIVLink.

SBG Online: (904) 757-7878

Sysop: Al Segura

1 line—MS-DOS 8088; 800MB running PCBoard 15.1 with Supra at up to 57,600 bps. Estab. 02/93 with no fee. Pier shareware CD online. PCBoard PPEs/source. Clip art, fonts. Home of FaxAnAd. No callback verify.

E-mail Bonding

The news just gets stranger every day. Someone sees a stain on a wall resembling a religious icon and the faithful swarm to worship it. Rush Limbaugh marries an aerobics instructor who once flamed him on CompuServe. And you can't get too much more bizarre than the nutso tales of Lorena, Tonya, Lyle and Eric, Gennifer, and others known by their first names, but whom you personally wouldn't want to know on a first-name basis.

However, here's some truly oddball news: One of the Great Problems of the Communications Universe is about to be solved by... IBM. If you recall, IBM's previous communications entry was Prodigy, a waddling gobbler they ought to deliver with cranberry sauce.

IBM's new effort, called Intelligent Communications, is an electronic Emancipation Proclamation that frees users from slavery to their phones, faxes, and e-mail. Due in early 1995, it's a universal mailbox complete with intelligent agents called Alter Egos that learn how you work and streamline all your voice, fax, paging, and private/public data needs.

Whoa...Hold on...If your eyes glaze over at the sound of this, it's understandable. Clanky patchwork solutions have been around for ages, but they've invariably fizzled. A few exceptions, like the slick Symmetry (formerly WordPerfect Office), AT&T's PersonalLink, and the fledgling Delrina/MobileComm venture, are impressive but deliver only pieces of the puzzle. IBM promises to do it all.

Intelligent Communications will handle any hardware from desktops to notebooks to phones to fax machines to PDAs, wireline to wireless. It'll deal with the insane multiplicity of maddeningly unintuitive online interfaces.

It can send someone an executable form-based "actor" that interviews the recipient interactively just as a human assistant would. And since all incoming information funnels through your Alter Ego, which filters, prioritizes, and forwards just the right stuff, you'll never miss an important message. Or log onto ten different services hourly to see if there's anything hot waiting for you. Or drown in the unsolicited electronic gorp of junk data.

These guys have really thought it out. They've constructed firewalls to protect sensitive data from aggressive outside agents. They've built in protection against chaotic "mailstroms" that could result when agents trigger each other to respond in mad exploding loops. They've even made it smart enough to "deconstruct" newspaper pages into columns that will be readable on tiny palmtop screens.

They insist that from beginning to end it will be a delightful experience. When's the last time you heard those words in the same breath with voice mail, fax, and e-mail?

This is a tall order, but with more than 200 top IBM engineers cranking to get it done, it has a real shot. Yeah, it's still vapor, but I want it. I need it. Sign me up.

—Paul Somerson ■

The Electric Post Office: (904) 473-7064
Sysop: Diamond Industries
1 line—MS-DOS 286; 119MB running SpitFire 3.4 with Zoom at up to 14,400 bps. Estab. 01/91 with no fee. Message base. Supports Geoworks Ensemble, Power BASIC, DR/Novell DOS, and Boca modems.

The Unknown BBS: (904) 581-4520
Sysop: Paul Silver
1 line—MS-DOS 486; 450MB running Excalibur Beta with Hayes at up to 28,800 bps. Estab. 01/94 with no fee. Beta site for Excalibur BBS software. Win 3.1-based BBS. Nine CD-ROMs on rotation.

Compu-Quest BBS: (904) 264-7462
Sysop: Don Koch
1 line—MS-DOS 486; 5,000MB running Robo-FX V 1.04 with Practical Peripherals at up to 57,600 bps. Estab. 01/94 with no fee. 8 CD-ROMs online, 4 nets, games, great graphics, latest files, Silver Xpress mail door, and more.

The Renegade: (904) 735-4461

Sysop: John Hopke

2 lines—MS-DOS 486; 2,048MB running WildCat 3.91M with Hayes at up to 28,800 bps. Estab. 05/93 with no fee. Internet, FidoNet, WeftNet, YankeeNet, MSInet, Adult Net. 10,000+ files, 50+ doors, 95,000+ msgs.

Last Days: (904) 735-0531

Sysop: Jeff Rose

2 lines—MS-DOS 486; 650MB running WildCat 4.0M-10 with Zoom 28.8k V.FC at up to 28,800 bps. Estab. 08/93 with no fee. FidoNet: 1:3669/10,15, PHILEOnet, Florida host for Cyber-ChurchNet. Doors, multiple CDs, fellowship.

Genius Loci BBS: (904) 383-0472

Sysop: Greg Braithwaite

1 line—MS-DOS 486; 1,000MB running WildCat 3.9M with Practical Peripherals at up to 14,400 bps. Estab. 02/93 with no fee. Specializing in architecture, CAD, construction, raytracing, and graphics. Echoes BRRAnet and UsNet.

The Gaia Hypothesis: (904) 383-0907

Sysop: Steve Burton

1 line—MS-DOS 286; 130MB running PCBoard 14.5 with US Robotics at up to 14,400 bps. Estab. 06/90 with no fee. Promotes Wicca, a nature-based Goddess-oriented religion, and Neo-Pagan philosophy. Large file base.

Terrapin Station BBS: (904) 939-8027

Sysop: Jeff Norton

2 lines—MS-DOS 386; 1,300MB running SpitFire v3.4 with US Robotics at up to 38,400 bps. Estab. 06/91 with no fee. NW FL business exchange. BizyNet, Internet, EchoNet, and FidoNet access. Files and online games.

Networking in the Improbability: (904) 465-4802

Sysop: Thomas Ayers

1 line—MS-DOS 486; 450MB running Robo/FX 1.04 with Infotel at up to 38,400 bps. Estab. 09/94 with no fee. 3-D animations, advertisement, CD-ROM shareware to download.

Nightmare Cafe: (904) 874-2296

Sysop: Brian Hendricks

1 line—MS-DOS 486; 700MB running Renegade 05-31-94 with Zoom at up to 28,800 bps. Estab. 11/92 with no fee. Fido, RGSN, LapTimes (NASCAR news and info.) several online games, file areas, and message bases.

Mystic Infinity: (904) 784-1294

Sysop: Brenda Carlson/Michael Smeby

1 line—MS-DOS 486; 208MB running RemoteAccess 2.01 with Hayes at up to 14,400 bps. Estab. 01/93 with no fee. Full service BBS. Formerly Mystique BBS of Albuquerque, NM. FidoNet, ITCnet, Home of MysticNet.

The Double Springs BBS: (904) 784-6336

Sysop: David A. Coleman

1 line—MS-DOS 486; 1,750MB running WildCat 3.91M with US Robotics at up to 28,800 bps. Estab. 11/91 with no fee. 100+ echoes, 8 CD-ROMs, 30+ games, 1.7GB HD, 30,000+ files, FidoNet 1:3608/250.

The Legacy: (904) 286-6429

Sysop: Dennis Joslin

1 line—MS-DOS 386; 430MB running Renegade Beta with Zoom at up to 14,400 bps. Estab. 05/91 with no fee. Well-rounded file areas, active message areas, Renegade support BBS, unique menu system.

Titan Software Solutions: (904) 476-1270

Sysop: Clayton Manson

10 lines—Novell NetWare; 10,000MB running DarkStar Stereo 1.02c with Generic at up to 19,200 bps. Estab. 08/88 with no fee. 100,000+ shareware and adult graphic files. Huge multiline system. Active group chat and database.

The Electronic Shopper: (904) 457-0280

Sysop: Ralph Hunter

1 line—MS-DOS 486; 500MB running WildCat 2.61 with Cardinal at up to 14,400 bps. Estab. 05/94 with no fee. Dedicated to placement of ads (for sales and so forth). No charge. Full access to new users.

Freddie's Nightmare: (904) 457-8929

Sysop: Fred Pope

3 lines—MS-DOS 486; 990MB running Synchronet 2.00b with Zoom 28.8 at up to 38,400 bps. Estab. 05/93 with a fee of $10 biannually. A little something for everyone.

The Land of Imagination: (904) 438-0890

Sysop: Carol Lee

10 lines—MS-DOS 486; 2,000MB running DarkStar 1.02a with Supra at up to 14,400 bps. Estab. 08/93 with a fee of $5 monthly. Multiuser system with lots of messages and files, using 4 CD drives.

Cool World BBS: (904) 788-1807

Sysop: Jason Palumbo

1 line—MS-DOS 386; 262MB running Renegade 5-31exp with DigiCom at up to 19,200 bps. Estab. 06/05 with no fee. New system, just recovered from HD crash. Specializing in messages, doors, MOD files, Barney Splat door.

The Digital Driveway: (904) 651-6811

Sysop: Zac Schinz

1 line—MS-DOS 486; 1,000MB running Excalibur .66 with Zoltrix at up to 14,400 bps. Estab. 06/94 with no fee. CD-ROM file area, running Excalibur Windows software. True multitasking. Super online graphics.

The Toy Shop-PC BBS: (904) 688-9124

Sysop: Chuck Curtis

1 line—MS-DOS 486; 2,100MB running RemoteAccess 2.02 with US Robotics at up to 38,400 bps. Estab. 10/85 with no fee. A family-oriented BBS with lots of files, messages, and games for all.

Thunder Struck BBS: (904) 666-8918

Sysop: James Arnold

4 lines—DESQView 486DX33; 3,250MB running WildCat 3.91m with Practical Peripherals at up to 57,600 bps. Estab. 08/93 with no fee. 4 CDs online, nets and conferences, door games, live chat system. A family-based BBS.

The Black Lodge: (904) 794-5263
Sysop: Ed Coyle
1 line—MS-DOS 486; 550MB running Renegade 05-31 with US Robotics at up to 14,400 bps. Estab. 12/93 with no fee. 200+ file areas, 350+ msg. echoes, 9+ nets. Dedicated to message bases. 1:3620/22 and 62:3812/15.

Chiphead's Place: (904) 797-4912
Sysop: Mike Tippit
1 line—MS-DOS 386; 60MB running WildCat Test drive with Supra at up to 14,400 bps. Estab. 02/94 with no fee. Free board with 600MB of files to download from CD-ROM. Message area. For sale area.

The Paisano Olive Oil Import/Export Co.: (904) 562-8708
Sysop: Vince Sbordone
1 line—MS-DOS 386; 245MB running WildCat 3.9 with Hayes Optima 288 at up to 57,600 bps. Estab. 06/93 with no fee. Trivia 24 hrs. a day. Home of Those Two Programming Guys. RIP active. HS.Link protocol. Local weather.

Club Torgy BBS: (404) 974-0460
Sysop: Jim Torgerson
4 lines—MS-DOS 486; 700MB running PCBoard 15.1 with Hayes at up to 14,400 bps. Estab. 02/93 with no fee. Open system with many files, doors, and active message bases.

Warp Factor BBS: (404) 773-7966
Sysop: Mark Stewart
2 lines—MS-DOS 486; 2,100MB running Searchlight 4.0 with Practical Peripherals at up to 19,200 bps. Estab. 05/90 with no fee. North Georgia's Doom headquarters with hundreds of add-ons, Star Trek, 2 CD-ROMs, several message areas.

411-Exchange: (404) 587-4071
Sysop: Wayne Wallace
2 lines—MS-DOS 486; 600MB running PCBoard 15.1 with ZyXel/Boca at up to 19,200 bps. Estab. 02/01 with no fee. Serving the AutoCAD and engineering community. Global AutoCAD Users Groups, third-party vendors, and so on.

Prime Time On-Line: (404) 667-1081
Sysop: Brent Cantrell
18 lines—MS-DOS 486; 5,500MB running PCBoard 15.2 with US Robotics at up to 19,200 bps. Estab. 11/92 with a fee of $29 annually. Full Internet access.ftp/Telnet/gopher, online games, family fun and entertainment, e-mail, Usenet.

TFDBBS—The Final Dimension BBS: (404) 876-0422
Sysop: The Wiz
1 line—MS-DOS 386; 2,000MB running WildCat 3.0 with Smart One at up to 14,400 bps. Estab. 07/91 with no fee. 24,000 files. Immediate access. 3 CD-ROMs. Home of ANSICHK9.ZIP (the ultimate ANSI bomb detector).

Paradise BBS: (404) 925-8980
Sysop: Travis Hancock
2 lines—MS-DOS 486; 6,000MB running TriBBS 5.1 with Intel at up to 14,400 bps. Estab. 05/93 with a fee of $20 annually. 10,000+ GIFs, shareware games, utils., communication, general, GIF downloads first call.

Serious Fun: (404) 433-8213
Sysop: Crash
1 line—MS-DOS 486; 5,000MB running WildCat 4.0 with Hayes at up to 57,600 bps. Estab. 10/93 with no fee. DOS, Windows, and OS/2 files, games (700MB+), sound, graphics, and text files. Many nets, doors, and so on.

Graffiti Online: (404) 972-4999
Sysop: Jim Maddox/Ric Helton
24 lines—Pentium 66MHz; 3,200MB running Oracomm Rel 8.4b with US Robotics at up to 14,400 bps. Estab. 06/86 with a fee of $60 annually. One of Atlanta's largest gay online services. IBM-compatible and Mac support, software, news, politics, more.

Global KAOS: (404) 489-4919
Sysop: David Greene
4 lines—MS-DOS 486; 2,190MB running PCBoard 15.1 with Hayes at up to 38,400 bps. Estab. 02/88 with no fee. Files galore.

The Clubhouse: (404) 509-0910
Sysop: Michael Reeves
1 line—MS-DOS 486; running WildCat 3.9 with US Robotics at up to 38,400 bps. Estab. 02/93 with no fee. Latest files via satellite filebone feed. Hundreds of message and file areas.

Game Room: (404) 723-9150
Sysop: Paul F. Mayberry
5 lines—MS-DOS 486; 2,000MB running PCBoard 15.2 with Hayes at up to 38,400 bps. Estab. 01/90 with a fee of $9.95 annually. Great files and doors. Get your Internet mail here. New users always welcome.

Radio Active: (404) 499-7795
Sysop: Phil West (N4NBL)
2 lines—MS-DOS 386; 2,200MB running WildCat 4 with Hayes at up to 14,400 bps. Estab. 09/90 with no fee. Engineering/ham radio/SWL conferences. Unix/Novell discussions. 2 CD-ROMs. Packet/Usenet mail.

The Quest BBS: (404) 732-9860
Sysop: Marlon Finley
1 line—MS-DOS 486; 700MB running PowerBBS 3.5 with GVC at up to 38,400 bps. Estab. 10/93 with no fee. Family-oriented BBS. Christian areas. Disabled users welcome. FidoNet, AC-Net, Internet.

AirComm Online: (404) 345-0284
Sysop: Matthew Giles
1 line—MS-DOS 486; 1,000MB running PCBoard v15.2 with ZyXel at up to 19,200 bps. Estab. 06/94 with a fee of $25 biannually. Providing the information resources you need today. Free trial access.

Pandius, City of the Immortals: (404) 667-6909
Sysop: Asterius, Master of Thought
1 line—MS-DOS 486; 854MB running WWIV 4.23+ with Hayes at up to 14,400 bps. Estab. 08/93 with no fee. Force Against Force Against Spam (FAFAS) South HQ, CD-ROM online, wide range of discussion topics.

Michael's Lair: (404) 735-6454
Sysop: Michael L. Waters

1 line—MS-DOS 486; 1,600MB running TriBBS 5.1 with Zoom at up to 28,800 bps. Estab. 10/93 with no fee. 32 door games, BRE interplanetary, WME, Dixie-Net, YankeeNet, VIP, BaseNet, Seeknet, Fido, Skynet.

Windows Online America: (404) 477-8942
Sysop: Talal Ghosheh

1 line—MS-DOS 386; 470MB running VBBS 6.20 with US Robotics at up to 14,400 bps. Estab. 12/92 with no fee. Windows-oriented BBS. Latest shareware and message echoes. FidoNet, Internet e-mail, RIME. CD-ROM.

The Ghost Town BBS: (404) 603-6700
Sysop: Lory Broadhead

4 lines—MS-DOS 386; 130MB running SpitFire 3.4 with Supra at up to 19,200 bps. Estab. 01/94 with a fee of $12 annually. Many online games, CD-ROM file areas, busy message bases, no-fee access available. Friendly sysops.

The Lookout: (404) 717-7430
Sysop: Austin Smith

1 line—MS-DOS 386; 720MB running RyBBS 8.0 with Zoom at up to 14,400 bps. Estab. 04/94 with no fee. InterBBS games, CD-ROM, RyBBS distribution site. Good ol' fun.

Robots R4U BBS: (404) 978-7300
Sysop: John W. Gutmann

1 line—MS-DOS 286; 425MB running RBBS 17.4 with Hayes at up to 14,400 bps. Estab. 01/90 with no fee. Detailed information. How to build hobby robots. Real robot experimenter amateur league.

The Vortex: (404) 971-7730
Sysop: Jim Azar

2 lines—MS-DOS 486; 2,000MB running VBBS 6.10 with Zoom at up to 28,800 bps. Estab. 05/93 with no fee. Shareware, programmer's tools, games. Internet and FidoNet. TradeWars 2002. Adult access. Free.

Atlanta On-line: (404) 426-7461
Sysop: Joseph Wheatley

1 line—MS-DOS 386; 685MB running WildCat 3.9 with US Robotics at up to 57,600 bps. Estab. 09/92 with no fee. All welcome. 39+ doors, U'NI-net, Internet, Usenet, Annex, Atl-Net, AFS, CNet echomail conferences.

Comet BBS: (404) 438-1758
Sysop: Robert Olsen

1 line—MS-DOS 486; 420MB running Renegade 1.0 with US Robotics at up to 14,400 bps. Estab. 05/92 with no fee. 4+ GB in CD-ROM shareware. 50+ doors online. Adult area.

The Clubhouse: (404) 509-0910
Sysop: Michael Reeves

1 line—MS-DOS 486; 1,700MB running WildCat 4.0 with US Robotics at up to 38,400 bps. Estab. 03/93 with no fee. The latest in files and messages direct via satellite. Quite a few online games including EGA graphs.

Twilite Time BBS: (404) 267-2191
Sysop: Ben Kelly

2 lines—MS-DOS 486; 650MB running WildCat 3.9 with Hayes at up to 14,400 bps. Estab. 08/93 with a fee of $30 annually. 12,000+ files. Astronomy, games GIFs. Shareware for every need. Free classifieds. NightNet, Visa/MC.

The Wizard's Castle: (404) 921-8900
Sysop: Ken Kirkland

1 line—MS-DOS 386; 799MB running GT Power 18.00 with US Robotics at up to 28,800 bps. Estab. 12/88 with a fee of $24 annually. AT&T files galore. 175+ international echoes and netmail. 4,000+ files online.

No Frills BBS: (404) 435-9608
Sysop: Keith Griffin

2 lines—MS-DOS 386; 460MB running PCBoard 15.1b with Cardinal at up to 14,400 bps. Estab. 07/91 with no fee. Atlanta's up-and-coming e-mail connection. Message areas for all interests. Internet coming soon.

Deep Space Nine: (404) 432-1262
Sysop: Frank Diacheysn (ShadowLord)

1 line—MS-DOS 486; 1,500MB running Renegade Beta with Hayes at up to 14,400 bps. Estab. 04/91 with no fee. Shareware BBS with a lot of programmer support. 13 CD-ROMs, 60,000+ files.

The Dining Room: (404) 292-5303
Sysop: Adam Zuckerman

1 line—MS-DOS 386; 1,200MB running TriBBS 5.0 with Microcom at up to 28,800 bps. Estab. 04/92 with a fee of $15 optional. Support board for TriBBS. Home of several TriBBS utilities. GA hub for WME and LobsterNet.

The Index System TBBS: (404) 924-8472
Sysop: Rodney Aloia

32 lines—MS-DOS 486; 10,000MB running TBBS 2.2M with Hayes at up to 28,800 bps. Estab. 04/83 with no fee. Internet, FidoNet, games, chat, and much more on one of the largest BBSs in Athens and Atlanta.

The Imperial Palace BBS: (706) 592-1344
Sysop: Tsar Nicholas

1 line—MS-DOS 386; 570MB running WildCat 3.91 with US Robotics at up to 14,400 bps. Estab. 09/91 with no fee. Fantasy, RPG, educational, assorted nets on a family-oriented BBS. Wide variety of games and files.

The LandFill: (706) 792-9838
Sysop: Andrew Phillips/Walter Basil

1 line—486DX/33MHz OS/2 2.1 with 500MB running WildCat 3.9 with US Robotics at up to 14,400 bps. Estab. 12/93 with no fee. Where one man's trash is another man's gold. Plenty of files, games, message bases, and much more.

Modern Vision BBS: (706) 771-9888
Sysop: Scott Burrows

2 lines—MS-DOS 486; 500MB running WildCat 3.91M with Reveal at up to 14,400 bps. Estab. 07/93 with no fee. General-topic BBS featuring 24,000+ files, 380 message conferences geared toward education.

CrossFire BBS: (706) 602-2281
Sysop: Tim Jacobsen
1 line—MS-DOS 386; 500MB running TriBBS 5.1B with Infodel at up to 14,400 bps. Estab. 03/93 with no fee. Support board for Seth Ables' Lord and Planets door games. Member of NwGaNet and more to come.

The Patriot BBS: (706) 695-8757
Sysop: Warren Davis
706 lines—MS-DOS 486; 1,000MB running ProBoard 2.01 with Zoom at up to 38,400 bps. Estab. 07/93 with a fee of $20 annually. ZarpNet echomail, shareware CDs, home of the Shiznit BBS Newsletter and much more. Free/30 days.

CompuData BBS: (706) 695-1655
Sysop: Josh Jones
1 line—MS-DOS 486; 120MB running ProBoard 2.01 with Zoom at up to 14,400 bps. Estab. 09/93 with a fee of $15 annually. Home of the "soon to be famous" ZarpNet echomail, growing file database, and CD-ROM coming soon.

Cross-N-Crown BBS: (706) 754-8492
Sysop: Tim McIntosh
1 line—MS-DOS 486; 1,320MB running PCBoard 14.5a with US Robotics at up to 14,400 bps. Estab. 04/94 with a fee of $10 biannually. Files, RIME, CD-ROM, online games, and more.

Populus: (706) 569-0773
Sysop: David McAfee/David Mackley
2 lines—MS-DOS 386; 600MB running Galacticomm 6.12 with TwinCom at up to 38,400 bps. Estab. 05/93 with no fee. Windows, programmers' support, C++, OOP, flash games, online chat, 6 CD-ROMs, programming available.

The Ridge Runner: (706) 682-1228
Sysop: Eric Alexander
1 line—OS/2-486; 1,005MB running QuickBBS 2.80 G5B17 with InfoTel 14.4 at up to 14,400 bps. Estab. 05/93 with no fee. 40 online games, 150 message conferences, specific OS/2 file areas. CD-ROM online. Join the fun.

The Potter's House BBS: (706) 637-9276
Sysop: Nancy Powers
2 lines—MS-DOS 386; 4MB running ProBoard 2.02 with Intel at up to 14,400 bps. Estab. 05/91 with a fee of $10 annually. Family board w/Christian flavor, files, doors, echoes, teen area. Specializing in the online Bible.

The PC Connection BBS: (706) 868-6474
Sysop: Mike McGahee
1 line—MS-DOS 386; 345MB running WildCat 4.00M with US Robotics at up to 28,800 bps. Estab. 11/93 with no fee. Help for the beginning user. Wildnet, AUG-Net. 4,000+ files and contests. Join the fun.

Madmen and Maniacs: (706) 860-5781
Sysop: Leonard Gray
1 line—OS/2 486; 1,700MB running WildCat 3.90M with US Robotics at up to 28,800 bps. Estab. 06/90 with no fee. Dedicated to data processing professionals with education and information to all as a primary goal.

E-mail Love and War Stories

This is the story of how one hapless e-mail user sent 100 copies of a love letter to 100 surprised recipients. What was intended to be a confidential e-mail sealed with a kiss for that special someone turned into a rather embarrassing situation. One simple mistake at the keyboard and the letter was sent via MCI Mail to an entire list of people at the company. Oooops!

After trying all sorts of ways to retrieve it, this person contacted MCI Mail to recall the love letter. No dice. It can't be done. Hitting the Send button is equivalent to dropping a letter in a mailbox. Nothing can stop its delivery, explained a spokesperson from MCI Mail; like regular mail delivered by the postal service, e-mail can't be unsent.

I take issue with this policy and find the argument specious, because this could never have happened with conventional, paper-based mail. Is anyone going to print out 100 extra copies of a letter by accident? Then, by accident, print 100 envelopes with 100 different people's names and lug the pile of envelopes to the mailbox and unknowingly mail all of them? Impossible.

If this message had been sent over America Online, which has an Unsend feature, the embarrassing situation could have been avoided. AOL also has a Save as New feature, which lets you read a message and then put it back in the queue as if it had never been seen.

I have a problem with the dishonesty of this feature. Let's say you send a message to someone who reads it and then places it back by clicking on Unread. When you scan your outbox for a status report, you're told the message was not read—when in fact it was. In real life, on the other hand, you can't unread anything.

OS/2Tower: (912) 439-4054

Sysop: Claud Cutler

1 line—OS/2 486; 1,536MB running Maximus/2 2.01wb with Hayes at up to 57,600 bps. Estab. 08/92 with no fee. Supporting IBM OS/2 v2.x. Offering applications, games, utilities. Member Fido 1:3617/12; RIME #5555.

DOS Connexion BBS: (912) 431-0836

Sysop: Lloyd Graham

1 line—MS-DOS 386; 200MB running ROS 4.5 with Zoom Fax/Modem at up to 14,400 bps. Estab. 06/87 with no fee. IBM/MS-DOS and compatibles. Free public access to files, messages, and doors. Voice validation req'd.

The Omega One BBS: (912) 888-0656

Sysop: Richard McDuffie

1 line—MS-DOS 486; 640MB running SpitFire 3.4 with US Robotics at up to 38,400 bps. Estab. 11/89 with a fee of $12 annually. Public access to missing children GIFs and a lot of files and areas. CD-ROMs online. SpitFire filebone.

The Comic Shoppe: (912) 432-2558

Sysop: Jerry Luckey

1 line—MS-DOS 386; 250MB running TriBBS 5.1 with Zoom at up to 14,400 bps. Estab. 08/94 with no fee. Dedicated to comic books. Also subscription service for collectors. 40 percent off.

The Crack of Dawn BBS: (912) 369-7023

Sysop: The Linkster

1 line—MS-DOS 486; 571MB running SpitFire 3.4 with Wang at up to 14,400 bps. Estab. 06/08 with no fee. Door games, FidoNet, adult message areas, and adult files. CD-ROM coming soon.

The Reef BBS: (912) 369-7289

Sysop: Jim McHenry

1 line—MS-DOS 486; 3,760MB running Excalibur v.71a with Zoom at up to 28,800 bps. Estab. 07/93 with no fee. A full-featured BBS specializing in the exploration and keeping of aquatic creatures.

Future World BBS: (912) 876-2453

Sysop: Gene Long

1 line—MS-DOS 486; 170MB running RoboBoard/FX with US Robotics at up to 14,400 bps. Estab. 03/93 with no fee. Up to 800MB online with CD-ROM. Silver Xpress dist site. RoboNet 90:1001/8. FidoNet 1:3659/3.

The Outhouse BBS: (912) 368-9626

Sysop: Jon Chrisman (Mr Klean)

2 lines—MS-DOS 486; 1,000MB running SpitFire 3.5 with Practical Peripherals at up to 28,800 bps. Estab. 01/93 with no fee. Fido, HealthCare, Circuit-Net confs. Many online games. 16 CDs in rotation. Huge.

Q and A BBS: (912) 729-4157

Sysop: Mr. Question/Mrs. Answer

2 lines—MS-DOS 486; 500MB running RemoteAccess 2.01 with GVC at up to 14,400 bps. Estab. 05/93 with no fee. Tech BBS for IBM PC-compatible hardware and software. Many games and files.

There's a way to do this in MCI Mail, too, but it's more of a bug than a feature. Here's how. You never know if your message was delivered by MCI Mail unless you request a receipt. When you get a receipt attachment from someone with whom you don't want to exchange e-mail and you don't want to let him know that you read his message, you can bypass the receipt system by deleting the message. The receipt notice is never delivered to the sender. Then all you have to do is scan the garbage can and read the message. The sender assumes that the message was never read. It's the electronic equivalent of steaming open a letter.

Though both these tricks defeat the reliable transmission of messages from desktop to desktop, other e-mail features could enhance it. Some bulletin board systems tell you how many times a message was read. Why not extend this feature to e-mail? Imagine getting a receipt from a memo you sent to the boss that says "Message was read twice, forwarded, and discarded."

Also, e-mail systems should hand off some sort of receipt to confirm delivery and to let the sender know for sure that the mail was received in its entirety. Often, I've received half a message with this note at the end: "Message too long for MHS. File truncated." And many messages, especially those I send to Europe, just disappear when they go through a gateway. This information is never communicated to the sender; as far as the sender knows, the e-mail server delivered the entire file.

It's also too easy to hack into e-mail systems. Years ago some industrious but misguided hacker sent me a message on MCI Mail using my own account and my own name. He just wanted to show me how easy it was (for him, maybe) to hack into an e-mail system.

I think it's time to stop pretending that e-mail is as secure or has the same legal protections as mail delivered by the postal service. We need electronic signatures implemented, along with a more reliable reporting trail. And an Unsend feature should be available on all the systems.—John C. Dvorak ■

African Peoples Electronic Xchange: (912) 741-7222
Sysop: Michael Nobles
1 line—MS-DOS 386; 540MB running PowerBBS 3.40 with US Robotics at up to 14,400 bps. Estab. 06/94 with a fee of $7.50 monthly. The latest shareware/freeware, Internet e-mail, Usenet newsgroups, doors, business reg.

Charlie's World: (912) 471-1705
Sysop: Charles Yearwood
1 line—MS-DOS 386; 880MB running Telegard v2.7 with Zoom at up to 2,400 bps. Estab. 07/94 with no fee. 640+MB online. No ratio. Downloading doors and more.

Baudville BBS: (912) 741-8722
Sysop: Fast Eddie
2 lines—MS-DOS 486; 1,000MB running TriBBS 5.1 with Zoom at up to 28,800 bps. Estab. 09/93 with a fee of $5 annually. RIP, personal services: singles' connection, job placement and tech support, event and concert data, more.

Ancient Egypt: (912) 882-7424
Sysop: Melvin Stevens
4 lines—MS-DOS 386; 2,000MB running Galacticomm 6.2d with US Robotics at up to 19,200 bps. Estab. 05/91 with no fee. FidoNet, Internet access, files, interactive online games and chat. 3 free hours to every caller.

Microcosm: (912) 882-1845
Sysop: Dan
2 lines—MS-DOS 486; 1,000MB running Galacticomm 6.21 with Supra at up to 14,400 bps. Estab. 07/94 with no fee. A communication and entertainment system for the whole family. No adult material. Lots of games/fun.

The Cannon BBS: (912) 764-8799
Sysop: Steve Sheldon
1 line—MS-DOS 386; 700MB running WWIV 4.23 with US Robotics at up to 21,600 bps. Estab. 08/89 with no fee. Netted message subs, loads of shareware, all online games registered. Best of all, it's free.

The Scratching Post: (912) 249-8622
Sysop: Bill The Cat
1 line—Amiga; 700MB running CNet Pro Amiga 3.05c with US Robotics at up to 16,800 bps. Estab. 06/23 with no fee. Almost exclusively Amiga. All platforms welcome. Unlimited file ratios to long-distance callers.

The Cornerstone BBS: (912) 538-7950
Sysop: Michael Brazell
1 line—MS-DOS 386; 420MB running WildCat 3.90 with Boca at up to 14,400 bps. Estab. 04/93 with a fee of $5 annually. General-purpose BBS with files, doors, online games, and Wildnet echo. File access with validation.

Code Plus BBS: (912) 953-1191
Sysop: Chuck Warren
3 lines—MS-DOS 386; 2,300MB running WildCat 4.0M(M10) with Microcom at up to 28,800 bps. Estab. 07/92 with no fee. Multiline system. 6 CDs. Message/file networks via satellite.

Islam On Line and Mini Mosque: (912) 929-1073
Sysop: Eugene Hassan Hazer
2 lines—MS-DOS 486; 400MB running SpitFire 3.4 with Zoom vfp 28.X at up to 28,800 bps. Estab. 12/92 with no fee. Dedicated to Al—islam and DOS. 2 CD-ROMs, conferences, games, mail, Islamic files.

Prophet's Place: (808) 625-3609
Sysop: Ryan Masaru Kawailani Ozawa
1 line—Macintosh; 240MB running Hermes II 3.0 with Supra at up to 14,400 bps. Estab. 10/92 with no fee. One of Oahu's premiere message boards. Discussion, debate, collaborative fiction. 100 percent net and echo free.

Hawaiian Oasis BBS: (808) 935-3148
Sysop: Donald Bowers
2 lines—MS-DOS 386; 10,000MB running FeatherNet Pro 1.10 with US Robotics at up to 14,400 bps. Estab. 07/93 with no fee. Games, graphics, utilities, educational. 19 CD-ROM drives. One of the largest BBSs on the Big Island.

The "In-Touch" BBS: (808) 521-2359
Sysop: Lei'd Flat
1 line—IBM 386/40 OS/2 2.1; 250MB running Maximus/2 for OS/2 with Supra at up to 14,400 bps. Estab. 08/91 with no fee. Electronic forum/support BBS for people who are curious about/active in the swinging lifestyle.

TBird's BBS: (808) 423-3152
Sysop: Tim (The TBird) Glore
1 line—MS-DOS 486; 35,000MB running PCBoard 15.1M/5 with Intel 144/144e at up to 19,200 bps. Estab. 10/92 with no fee. RIME/PCRelay message exchange. FidoNet. Usenet. Space games and more.

Rob's Wanna BBS: (808) 737-2665
Sysop: Rob Wehrli
2 lines—Pentium 90MHz; 6,000MB running Synchronet 2.00b with Microcom at up to 28,800 bps. Estab. 06/94 with no fee. Technical support dialogue encouraged. Advanced operating systems, Visual BASIC and NetWare areas.

The Color Computer Library: (808) 735-3776
Sysop: John Wight
2 lines—MS-DOS 486; 3,500MB running RemoteAccess v 2.01 Pro with Twincom at up to 57,600 bps. Estab. 11/89 with a fee of $10 annually. FidoNet: 1:345/200. MS-DOS, Windows, CoCo, OS9, multimedia, graphics, sound, friendly service.

Kerr's Digital Systems: (808) 624-1527
Sysop: Jim Kerr
2 lines—MS-DOS 486; 900MB running Excalibur 0.7 with Supra at up to 28,800 bps. Estab. 02/93 with no fee. C++ prgming., accepting photos, slides, artwork for exclusive image line. Royalties paid. Scan/hire.

Paradise BBS: (808) 625-5120
Sysop: Lou Steinritz
1 line—MS-DOS 486; 3,000MB running PCBoard 15.1 with US Robotics at up to 19,200 bps. Estab. 06/89 with no fee. Eight mail networks, 300 conferences, 86 online doors, 3GB of files, adult CDs, private mailboxes.

One Step Beyond BBS: (808) 695-8352
Sysop: Don Paul Jones
1 line—MS-DOS 486; 1,700MB running PCBoard 15.1/10M with US Robotics at up to 19,200 bps. Estab. 06/90 with no fee. 180+ registered online door games, latest file collection, RIME message echoes.

Idaho Interactive BBS: (208) 345-4987
Sysop: Bob Cooper
16 lines—MS-DOS 486; 400MB running Galacticomm 6.21c-20 with US Robotics at up to 14,400 bps. Estab. 05/92 with no fee. One of Idaho's biggest, fully featured entertainment and business BBSs. 3.5GB of files. Chat and more.

Idaho Central Interchange: (208) 677-2028
Sysop: John Ellis/Al Norris
3 lines—MS-DOS 386; 380MB running VBBS 6.14 with Zoom at up to 14,400 bps. Estab. 05/93 with a fee of $22 annually. Internet access to e-mail and Usenet. Featuring Chris Clark, media critic.

The Shuttle BBS: (208) 678-3242
Sysop: Scott and John Hellewell
1 line—MS-DOS 486; 212MB running VBBS 6.14a with Zoom at up to 24,000 bps. Estab. 08/93 with no fee. Internet @shuttle.win.net. Registered doors. CD-ROM with So Much Shareware 3.

Barnes' Graphics BBS: (208) 365-5223
Sysop: LeRoy Barnes
1 line—MS-DOS 286; 660MB running SpitFire 3.5 with Zoom at up to 14,400 bps. Estab. 02/92 with no fee. 660MB hard drive storage with 640MB+ in files from Monster Media #3 CD. Lots of Doom stuff.

Prairie BBS: (208) 983-0799
Sysop: Jeff Adkison
2 lines—MS-DOS 386; 4MB running WildCat 3.90m with ViVa/Zoom at up to 28,800 bps. Estab. 04/93 with a fee of $5 monthly. Good clean BBS connected to the world.

Night Flight: (208) 529-4248
Sysop: George Hayduke
2 lines—MS-DOS 386; 430MB running Searchlight 4.0 with Intel at up to 14,400 bps. Estab. 05/91 with a fee of $10 annually. Several GB of CD-ROM software for DOS, Windows, OS/2. Games, chat, RIP graphics support.

The Cat's Lair: (208) 887-4752
Sysop: Kim Gross (Cougar)
1 line—MS-DOS 486; 12,000MB running VBBS 6.14 (OS/2) with US Robotics at up to 28,800 bps. Estab. 01/93 with no fee. Dedicated to Fire/EMS and OS/2. VBBS support board. Networked to Internet, FidoNet, VirtualNet.

High Tech Playhouse: (208) 832-7867
Sysop: Techno Geek
1 line—MS-DOS 386; 500MB running Synchronet 2.0 with Cardinal at up to 14,400 bps. Estab. 04/94 with no fee. Message areas, files, CD. DOVE-NET and Magnet echoes. Internet e-mail and Usenet news.

Rocky Mountain HUB BBS: (208) 237-8557
Sysop: Matt McClung
1 line—MS-DOS 486; 1,750MB running Searchlight 3.5C with Zoom at up to 57,600 bps. Estab. 07/89 with a fee of $25 annually. FidoNet feed, InterBBS gaming, Doom add-ons galore. GIF. Something for everyone and then some.

D.R 1st BBS: (208) 265-2937
Sysop: Don Sleuth
2 lines—MS-DOS 486; 999MB running WWIV 2.23 with Hayes at up to 14,400 bps. Estab. 01/89 with no fee. Great online games, 1GB+ of shareware software. All the latest virus protection software.

Indigo Base: (208) 734-6592
Sysop: Gary Eyerly
1 line—MS-DOS 386; 685MB running WildCat 3.91M with US Robotics at up to 14,400 bps. Estab. 08/93 with no fee. Many confs. including adult. Several online doors. No file ratios. Multiple CDs online. Two nodes.

Starship CUCUG: (217) 356-8056
Sysop: Kevin Hisel
1 line—Amiga; 500MB running PCBoard 15.1 with Supra at up to 14,400 bps. Estab. 05/84 with no fee. Supporting Commodore Amiga and C-64/128 computers. Sponsored by C-U Commodore Users Group.

FBN BBS: (217) 359-2874
Sysop: Greg Smith
1 line—MS-DOS 386; 695MB running FBN 4.6 with Intel at up to 14,400 bps. Estab. 01/85 with no fee. Ham radio, weather information, conversation, 700MB+ file collection. No ratios or time limits.

Sonic Boom: (217) 352-1863
Sysop: Clint Smith
1 line—MS-DOS 486; 200MB running Renegade 1.1 with Macronix at up to 28,800 bps. Estab. 06/94 with no fee. Many files, games, online games, conference groups, e-mail, and so on.

Brian's Brainy System BBS: (217) 442-9818
Sysop: Brian Bridges
1 line—MS-DOS 486; 650MB running TriBBS 4.01 with Hayes at up to 2,400 bps. Estab. 12/93 with no fee. 650MB, CD-ROM with 9,000 programs. Programming, ham radio, electronics-oriented BBS.

Computer Corner BBS: (217) 422-2585
Sysop: Dennis Kreher
2 lines—MS-DOS 386; 4,200MB running PCBoard 15.1/10 with US Robotics at up to 21,600 bps. Estab. 06/89 with no fee. Software Creations site, U'NI-net node. Files: games, DTP, prod., draw, graphics, animation. 6 CD-ROMs.

The Ultimate Connection: (217) 792-3663
Sysop: John Faber
130 lines—Pentium; 9,000MB running Galacticomm 6.21x with ZyXel at up to 19,200 bps. Estab. 09/93 with no fee. Free megasystem with huge P-D, shareware file area. Awesome chat, Internet for free.

✶ Jerry Brown Virus—Blanks your screen and begins flashing an 800 number.

Information to Go, Please

If you need to move information wirelessly today, you can. But it won't be cheap, easy, or 100 percent reliable. Here's an overview of what you can do.

You can receive personal e-mail or broadcast messages to colleagues. You can get stock quotes, headline news, and news about the industry you work in. With some wireless technologies, you can also originate and respond to messages.

Here's how it might work if you're a pharmaceuticals rep on an out-of-town business trip. While you're asleep, your PCMCIA pager card receives updated price lists and inventory status on your most critical products. When you turn your notebook PC on in the morning, it automatically updates your price-list database. En route to your first appointment, you get headline news on the health-care industry that keeps you abreast of your competitors and gives you a good conversation starter. Throughout the day, the subject lines and the first sentences of all e-mail messages marked "urgent" or from your boss are forwarded as well.

With a two-way device, you could do all this and place your orders without the need of a telephone jack.

Wireless Technology

Paging, or one-way wireless messaging, is the simplest technology. The signal penetrates deep into buildings; it works nationwide and in many other countries. For portable PCs and PDAs, pagers take the form of Type II PCMCIA cards with reader software in the computer. Currently, they're one-way (receive only), but within the year some pagers will be able to issue short responses on the order of "got the message," "yes," and "no."

We're seeing the first PCMCIA pagers now with built-in LCD displays. Services include Embarc from Motorola International Networks Division (800 362-2724), MobileComm Nationwide Messaging from

---

ProfitMaker BBS: (217) 224-3203
Sysop: David Ayers
6 lines—MS-DOS 486; 500MB running Galacticomm 6.2 with Zy-Xel at up to 14,400 bps. Estab. 09/92 with a fee of $30 annually. Serving the successful entrepreneur with Internet e-mail and Usenet newsgroups, daily news, files.

The Ultimate Connection: (217) 792-3663
Sysop: Ted Glenwright
130 lines—Pentium; 9,000MB running Galacticomm 6.21 with ZyXel at up to 38,400 bps. Estab. 10/92 with no fee. Internet access/accounts, nationwide chat, bar listings across the USA, GIFs galore, latest shareware.

Derive BBS: (217) 337-0926
Sysop: Jerry Glynn
1 line—MS-DOS 286; 65MB running FBN 4.6 with Generic at up to 14,400 bps. Estab. 09/89 with no fee. Support for Derive math program. Math and science education discussions, mathematics files.

Deep Space BBS: (217) 384-0322
Sysop: Rawley Greene
1 line—MS-DOS 386; 130MB running Maximus 2.00 with US Robotics at up to 14,400 bps. Estab. 02/93 with no fee. Sound and music files. CD-ROM packed with 600MB of MODs and MIDIs. Expecting more soon.

Adventurer's Corner: (309) 664-0881
Sysop: Scott Kuntzelman
1 line—OS/2 486DX2/66; 1,765MB running Maximus/WWIV 2.01 /4.24 with US Robotics at up to 28,800 bps. Estab. 07/89 with no fee. Official WWIV support. Apogee distribution node #5. Large OS/2 2.0+ file section and support.

CyberHawg RBBS: (309) 852-2165
Sysop: Kevin Clarke
2 lines—MS-DOS 486; 340MB running RBBS 17.4 with Zoom at up to 14,400 bps. Estab. 03/93 with a fee of $24 optional. Lots of games, monthly USBBS and McAfee updates, no adult files or areas.

Le Roy Acres BBS: (309) 962-2273
Sysop: Jack and Jean Corzine
1 line—MS-DOS 386; 250MB running WildCat 3.91S with ZyXel U-1496E at up to 19,200 bps. Estab. 02/93 with a fee of $25 optional. Fully RIP customized. Religious and RIP files, 5 message nets, many online games and conferences.

Rod's Place BBS: (309) 836-1432
Sysop: Rod Rouse
1 line—MS-DOS 386; 340MB running WildCat 4.0 with Hayes at up to 14,400 bps. Estab. 08/93 with no fee. Files, messages, QWKmail, online games, RIP graphics.

Hacker's Haven: (309) 734-4675
Sysop: Jason and Paul Foreman
1 line—MS-DOS 486; 115MB running SpitFire v3.5 with US Robotics at up to 14,400 bps. Estab. 06/94 with a fee of $15/25 annually. Several online door games, CD-ROM online, two different access levels available.

BellSouth (800 685-5555), and SkyPage from SkyTel Corp. (800 759-9779).

Cellular data is a great concept that barely works. You need your cellular phone, a cellular-ready modem, and a $100 cable to connect the two. Expect 2.4-Kbps data throughput when you're standing still and nothing when you're moving. Look into modems with special cellular error-checking: Celeritas's TX-CEL from Toshiba America Information Systems, ETC from AT&T, and MNP 10 from Microcom.

In the few areas where it's available, CDPD (cellular digital packet data) piggybacks a digital signal onto unused cellular frequencies. It's great for short, bursty messages. CDPD modems cost $300 to $1,500 (they're not the same as digital cellular phones). CDPD is backed by McCaw Cellular Communications and AT&T, McCaw's new owner.

Two-way messaging uses RF (radio frequency) modem transceivers the size of your notebook PC's power transformer and plug into your notebook's serial port. You need one RF modem ($500 to $1,000) for each roaming computer, as well as one back in the office on a file server that transmits to the service provider (or you can use a phone link to the service provider). Service providers include Ardis (800 662-5328) and RAM Mobile Data USA LP (800 726-3210). To communicate via RAM Mobile's network, you can use e-mail programs such as cc:Mail or Microsoft Mail. If you're more interested in communicating outside your company, RadioMail (from RadioMail Corp., 800 597-6245) works atop Ardis or RAM.

In 1995, SkyTel's parent, Mobil Telecommunication Technologies Corp. (Mtel), hopes to have a two-way pagerlike system, Desitneer, with a fast outbound channel (to your remote device) and a slower, battery-conserving return channel. Metricom (800 556-6123) plans a two-way, peer-to-peer service using spread-spectrum technology. When several devices are close by—on the same corporate campus, for instance—they can talk among themselves without going through the Metricom network.

PCS, or personal communications services, will receive and send data, faxes, voice, and eventually video. Expect them around 1997 or 1998 at the earliest.

Arguenet: (309) 699-6070
Sysop: Argue Goddess
1 line—MS-DOS 386; 100MB running Turboard 2.0 with US Robotics at up to 14,400 bps. Estab. 03/93 with no fee.

The Round Table BBS: (312) 777-9480
Sysop: Kevin Keyser
2 lines—MS-DOS 386; 629MB running SLBBS 4.0 with Supra at up to 14,400 bps. Estab. 09/87 with no fee. Online magazines. CD-ROM. 8,000 great files just waiting do be downloaded. Online games.

OnLine ReSource BBS: (312) 631-7191
Sysop: Casey Drozd
8 lines—MS-DOS 486; 12,000MB running PCBoard 15.1 with Zoom 28.8 at up to 28,800 bps. Estab. 01/91 with a fee of $25 annually. One of the largest file libraries in the Chicagoland area. 800,000+ shareware, public domain, and message areas.

The New User BBS: (312) 283-3919
Sysop: Craig Pease
1 line—MS-DOS 486; 540MB running Renegade 5.31 with US Robotics at up to 14,400 bps. Estab. 07/93 with no fee. Home of InfoNet. A Chicagoland and surrounding suburbs message network.

Home Again: (312) 665-7319
Sysop: William Johnson
1 line—MS-DOS 486; 3,750MB running GT Power 19.00 B7 with US Robotics at up to 14,400 bps. Estab. 09/93 with no fee. CD-ROM changer, game doors, QWKmail, online verification, free access, download first call.

The Power Palace: (312) 594-0643
Sysop: Steven Hauswirth
1 line—MS-DOS 486; 3,200MB running PCBoard 15.1 with Hayes at up to 28,800 bps. Estab. 03/93 with no fee. 500+ conferences. Free Internet e-mail and Usenet mail. NightOwl 11 and 12 CDs online. 15,000+ files.

Stygian Abyss BBS: (312) 384-6250
Sysop: Sir Sammy
5 lines—Amiga; 4,000MB running CNet 3.05c with Supra at up to 14,400 bps. Estab. 04/93 with no fee. 110+ online games. CD-ROMs. IBM, Mac, Amiga. FidoNet: 1:115/384.0, C-Link: 911:6200/2.0. Usenet.

The Chicago Conservative: (312) 248-3809
Sysop: Jim Nicolalde
2 lines—MS-DOS 386; 940MB running WildCat 4.00 with Infotel at up to 14,400 bps. Estab. 05/93 with a fee of $4.95 quarterly. Conservative thought and Christian Deists, 3,600+ files and text, doors, baby holocaust files.

NiteBeats: (312) 769-1323
Sysop: Paul Montgomery
2 lines—MS-DOS 486; 750MB running TBBS 2.2-16 with Microcom at up to 57,600 bps. Estab. 12/93 with no fee. Supporting PCs w/ANSI. Internet gateway, CD-ROMs. Download first visit. Adults preferred. Free.

What It Costs and Who Sells It

Costs vary widely, and vendors are subsidizing early adopters to build interest. Here are some ballpark prices. Some two-way networks offer fixed-priced service for $75 to $150 a month. Paging with nationwide coverage might run about the same, escalating quickly if you send a lot of messages. Cellular service costs 50 cents to a dollar a minute, plus roaming charges outside your local area. Pagers cost $200 to $300, cellular modems are $200 to $500, and two-way RF transceivers are $500 to $1,000.

You can buy products and service from a variety of services, including paging companies, makers of PDAs and personal communicators, and regional phone companies.
—Bill Howard ■

The East Village BBS, Inc.: (312) 777-2574
Sysop: Peter Koski
2 lines—MS-DOS 486; 545MB running TriBBS 5.1 with Practical Peripherals at up to 14,400 bps. Estab. 09/91 with a fee of $25 annually. A TriBBS support board. WME, AccessNet, and LobsterNet. 4 CDs online. 25,000+ files.

N9CSA N.A.B.S.A. Bulletin Board System: (312) 776-9768
Sysop: John "Jay" Serafin, N9CSA
1 line—MS-DOS 486; 65,000MB running WildCat 4.00m-10 with US Robotics at up to 38,400 bps. Estab. 08/86 with no fee. 259,000+ files, Internet/Usenet, 60+ CD-ROMs, one of the Midwest's largest. Optional adult areas.

WorldWide Access: (312) 282-8605
Sysop: Gregory Gulik
20 lines—Unix; 5,000MB running BSDI 1.1 with AT&T Paradyne at up to 57,600 bps. Estab. 08/89 with a fee of $10 monthly. The highest quality Internet services: e-mail, netnews, WWW, Telnet, ftp, IRC, MUD, SLIP/PPP, more.

Lakefront Leisure: (312) 761-2077
Sysop: James Simonson
3 lines—MS-DOS 386; 1,000MB running Searchlight 4.0 Multi with US Robotics at up to 14,400 bps. Estab. 07/90 with no fee. Online games, SL support, utility programs, and updates.

The Flying High BBS: (312) 286-7870
Sysop: Gregory Zonsius
1 line—MS-DOS 486; 1400MB running RoboFX 1.02 with ViVa at up to 14,400 bps. Estab. 04/94 with no fee. SVGA graphical BBS with mouse control specializing in aviation and flight-simulator-related files.

National Islamic: (312) 274-8136
Sysop: Mohammad Khan
1 line—MS-DOS 486; 200MB running RemoteAccess 2.02 with US Robotics at up to 28,800 bps. Estab. 06/93 with no fee. Usenet/FidoNet/WMN, library of files on Islam, and other religious topics.

Starz Chicago: (312) 348-3508
Sysop: Mitch Arnstein
2 lines—MS-DOS 486; 10,000MB running Galacticomm 6.20 with US Robotics at up to 14,400 bps. Estab. 05/92 with a fee of $10 annually. WorldLink chat plus Internet/Usenet mail, multiplayer games, CD-ROM files, MajorNet.

PUB Desktop Publishing BBS: (312) 767-5787
Sysop: Steve Gjondla
2 lines—MS-DOS 486; 2,000MB running PCBoard 15.1/10 with US Robotics at up to 38,400 bps. Estab. 05/92 with a fee of $20 biannually. Dedicated to desktop publishing, writers, artists. 3 CD-ROMs, Internet, 10 e-mail nets, active sysop.

The Lunchbox BBS: (312) 637-0428
Sysop: Dan Novak
1 line—MS-DOS 486; 340MB running WildCat 3.9 with Hayes at up to 14,400 bps. Estab. 06/94 with a fee of $30 annually. GIFs, text, games, utilities. Adult access available. Free trial with downloads.

The Aircrash Bureau: (312) 327-0226
Sysop: Eric Schreiber
1 line—MS-DOS 386; 340MB running Telegard 2.7 with US Robotics at up to 28,800 bps. Estab. 03/93 with no fee. Open system featuring FidoNet and GhotiNet message areas and 250+ Doom files.

Lakeview Links: (312) 281-7018
Sysop: Greg Bates
1 line—MS-DOS 486; 424MB running SpitFire 3.5 with US Robotics at up to 19,200 bps. Estab. 04/94 with no fee. Linking you to files, doors, messages, sports, and more.

The Anarchy BBS: (618) 529-2760
Sysop: Teaseme2
2 lines—MS-DOS 486; 3,200MB running Excalibur .66 Beta with US Robotics at up to 28,800 bps. Estab. 08/93 with a fee of $15 annually. True Windows interface. Windows support. Write custom CDs. Adult, games, lots of fun.

Pooh's Corner: (618) 985-4747
Sysop: Gregory Chambers
1 line—MS-DOS 286; 170MB running WildCat 4 with Boca at up to 14,400 bps. Estab. 04/90 with no fee. Doors, QWKmail, Internet e-mail, and Usenet newsgroups.

The Garage BBS: (618) 344-8466
Sysop: Tom Guelker
1 line—386Dx40; 3,000MB running WildCat 4.0SL with US Robotics at up to 28.8K bps. Estab. 10/89 with no fee. 4 CD-ROMs online all the time. Free downloads first call. FidoNet. "Your One Stop BBS Shop."

The Darkroom BBS: (618) 345-3663
Sysop: Dave Davidson

2 lines—MS-DOS 486; 2,040MB running VBBS-VFido 6.12b with Zoom at up to 28,800 bps. Estab. 03/92 with no fee. Communications, desktop publishing, photography our speciality. Multi CD-ROMs.

Steve's MailDrop and BBS: (618) 281-8702
Sysop: Steve B

1 line—MS-DOS 486; 600MB running Maximus 2.01 with Microcom at up to 28,800 bps. Estab. 11/93 with no fee. FidoNet-based BBS with quality material. New and inexperienced users welcome. QWK-based messaging.

ChatLink BBS: (618) 452-3182
Sysop: Grizzley

8 lines—MS-DOS 386; 150MB running DLX 7.0 with various at up to 9,600 bps. Estab. 11/91 with no fee. Chat board. Also public message area. Database area. We like to talk.

Crimson Cross BBS: (618) 253-3608
Sysop: Kevin L. Cummins

1 line—MS-DOS 486; 845MB running SpitFire 3.5 with US Robotics at up to 57,600 bps. Estab. 12/89 with no fee. 28.8K VFC ChristNet hub, RIME international network. Bible programs and text. 4 CDs online.

The Lawrenceville Weather Wizard: (618) 943-6000
Sysop: George D Nuttall

1 line—MS-DOS 8088; 40MB running WildCat 3.6 with Zoom at up to 2400 bps. Estab. 10/93 with no fee. Local NMS weather data, local e-mail.

The Hard Disk Cafe: (618) 684-3990
Sysop: Marc Albrycht

2 lines—Gateway 2000 P5-90; 6,000MB running WildCat 4.00M with US Robotics at up to 28,800 bps. Estab. 03/89 with no fee. One of the largest free BBSs south of Rte. I-64 in southern Illinois. Friendly, too. Six CD-ROMs.

Business Opportunity BBS: (618) 423-2331
Sysop: Michael Reiss

1 line—MS-DOS 386; 80MB running WildCat 3.9 with Zoom at up to 14,400 bps. Estab. 01/94 with a fee of $30 annually. Business opportunity ads. Enter and read ads while online. Business files also available.

The...Engage BBS: (618) 735-2849
Sysop: Jerry Hook

1 line—MS-DOS 386; 1,500MB running GT Power 19.00 with US Robotics at up to 28,800 bps. Estab. 10/89 with no fee. GTNetwork node 011/000. 100 echomail/netmail msg. areas. 2 CD-ROMs online. RIP graphics. Door games.

Addison DOS Haus: (708) 832-7754
Sysop: Leroy Hein

1 line—MS-DOS 486; 600MB running WildCat 3.91 with Zoom 14.4 at up to 19,200 bps. Estab. 06/93 with no fee. T&J Software distribution site. No fees; Wildnet; CD-ROM; adult access available. Online games.

The Quest BBS: (708) 844-1469
Sysop: Jeff Moser

1 line—MS-DOS 486; 1,200MB running Roboboard/FX 1.04 with Generic at up to 14,400 bps. Estab. 10/92 with no fee. A board for the whole family. Classified ads, FidoNet, Internet access. E-mail. Featuring SVGA, GUI.

Creative Thoughts BBS: (708) 382-3904
Sysop: Paul Hildmann

2 lines—MS-DOS 486; 3,000MB running SpitFire 3.40 with US Robotics at up to 14,400 bps. Estab. 04/93 with no fee. Member ASP, RIME network. Creative thoughts for creative people.

Chicago Syslink: (708) 795-4442
Sysop: George Matyaszek

16 lines—MS-DOS 486; 1,000MB running TBBS 2.2M with Hayes at up to 14,400 bps. Estab. 06/81 with a fee of $30 annually. New CD-ROM every weekend. Internet/FidoNet, jobs database, 100+ games/chat, Virtual Sysop, Genesis News.

The Game Guild: (708) 749-7375
Sysop: Ed Rentka

1 line—MS-DOS 386; 300MB running Searchlight 4.0 with Hayes at up to 14,400 bps. Estab. 08/94 with no fee. Dedicated to game file transfers and game bulletin board.

The Rest of Us BBS: (708) 868-6013
Sysop: Andre Outlaw

2 lines—MS-DOS 486; 3,000MB running Excalibur Beta with US Robotics at up to 57,600 bps. Estab. 04/94 with a fee of $30 annually. Hardware, software, CD-ROM, Windows, and DOS support. Rush Limbaugh and Jay Marvin discussion forums.

American Archive Electro Mail BBS: (708) 426-8903
Sysop: John "Dr. Byte" Rosengarten

1 line—MS-DOS 486; 2,350MB running ProBoard Custom BBS 4.5 with US Robotics at up to 14,400 bps. Estab. 10/85 with no fee. Fifteen conferences include astronomy, technical, shortwave radio, Novell, PCBoard, MIDI, and sound.

Sportsman's Plus: (708) 516-8953
Sysop: Don Krenz

2 lines—Pentium 66; 10,000MB running PCBoard 15.1 with US Robotics at up to 14,400 bps. Estab. 04/94 with a fee of $25 annually. Member RIME, 2 CD-ROMs with offline discs available. The latest shareware.

Eye Resources Network: (708) 299-0687
Sysop: Tom Young

3 lines—MS-DOS 486; 3,000MB running Remote Access 2.02 Pro with US Robotics at up to 28,800 bps. Estab. 06/89 with no fee. Primary emphasis on eye care, medicine, and disabilities. Internet ocular.com, FidoNet 1:115/299.

Arte Graphics BBS: (708) 259-0215
Sysop: Mike Labellarte

10 lines—Mixed Network (DOS); 5,000MB running WildCat 3.9M with PPI at up to 38,400 bps. Estab. 06/85 with a fee of $25 biannually. Estab. system with all the standard features. Drop in for your free 10-day visit.

Zoot's Place BBS: (708) 299-5140
Sysop: Zoot and Firefly

4 lines—MS-DOS 486; running RoboBoard 2.1 with US Robotics at up to 14,400 bps. Estab. 05/94 with a fee of $25 annually. 6 CD-ROMs online, games, mail…you name it.

Cyber Information Services: (708) 697-9572
Sysop: Armor Robinson

10 lines—Amiga; 28,000MB running VBBS with Supra at up to 38,400 bps. Estab. 09/92 with a fee of $55 annually. Business, general, and adult, serving IBM, Mac, Amiga. Featuring online games, Fido/Internet topics.

The National PC and MIDI Databank: (708) 593-8703
Sysop: Duane Antor

2 lines—MS-DOS 386; 12,000MB running Spitfire 3.5 with US Robotics at up to 57,600 bps. Estab. 06/90 with no fee. 150,000+ files related to MIDI, multimedia, pro audio, audio and video recording.

Cue Ball Online: (708) 782-0948
Sysop: Paul Podgornik

2 lines—MS-DOS 486; 640MB running TBBS 2.2 with Hayes at up to 14,400 bps. Estab. 10/93 with a fee of $49.95 annually. The first online information service for pool and billiards. Member of the BCA.

Clockwork Orange: (708) 869-7978
Sysop: Jonathan Nowak

1 line—MS-DOS 486; 750MB running VBBS 6.14 Beta with Supra at up to 14,400 bps. Estab. 04/92 with no fee. 2GB+ CD-ROM, Internet clock.com, FidoNet, VirtualNet, RIP, QWK, 600+ MOD files, sound files, RushNet.

Grey Matter: (708) 208-0662
Sysop: Jim Karaganis

2 lines—MS-DOS 486; 3,500MB running WildCat 3.90M with US Robotics at up to 14,400 bps. Estab. 03/90 with a fee of $32 annually. 13,000+ files online, international e-mail (YankeeNet and ProgNet). Something for everyone.

SaveWare Computer Shopping BBS: (708) 724-2427
Sysop: Don Rieb

8 lines—MS-DOS 486; 18,000MB running Renegade 1.0 with US Robotics at up to 28,800 bps. Estab. 04/91 with no fee. 100,000 files in 18GB. Store: CD-ROM, hardware, and more. Adult area. 708-724-2449 hunt. Free Internet.

NixPix Person-To-Person: (708) 223-4802
Sysop: Doc Hunter

17 lines—MS-DOS 386; 60MB running Oracomm Plus 7.P with Generic at up to 2,400 bps. Estab. 02/92 with a fee of $25 biannually. An online social club featuring members from across the U.S. and around the world.

Cesspool BBS: (708) 352-9231
Sysop: Rick Gross

2 lines—MS-DOS 486; 860MB running SpitFire 3.5 with US Robotics at up to 38,400 bps. Estab. 10/92 with no fee. 60+ online games, 3 CD-ROMs, ASP approved BBS. 2.8MB+ of files. FidoNet 1:115/320. All ages.

Uncle Bob's BBS: (708) 265-0698
Sysop: Uncle Jerry

2 lines—Novell network; 4,800MB running SpitFire 3.5 with US Robotics at up to 14,400 bps. Estab. 01/91 with a fee of $20 optional. 6 online CDs. Request CDs. Fido Netmail. Large shareware collection, large adult section on CDs.

Arena: (708) 367-6890
Sysop: David Tisinai

4 lines—MS-DOS 386; 340MB running PCBoard 14.5a/e9 with Generic at up to 38,400 bps. Estab. 06/89 with no fee. The ultimate in online wargaming. Compete against other players for world domination.

The House of Games: (708) 918-8421
Sysop: Joe Walsh

1 line—MS-DOS 286; 528MB running WWIV 4.23 with Practical Peripherals at up to 14,400 bps. Estab. 02/94 with no fee. The home BBS of the TreasureQuest door game. Featuring online games and intelligent discussions.

Com One: (708) 717-9370
Sysop: Craig Wells

8 lines—MS-DOS 386; 6,000MB running Galacticomm 6.21 with US Robotics at up to 19,200 bps. Estab. 05/92 with a fee of $4 monthly. 60,000 files, 9 CDs online, Internet e-mail/newsgroups/mailing lists at no extra charge.

Zone BBS: (708) 637-0071
Sysop: Debbi Ayala

20 lines—MS-DOS 486; 5,000MB running Galacticomm 6.21 with US Robotics at up to 14,400 bps. Estab. 11/90 with a fee of $10 varied. Chat, files, online games, message bases. Technical support for Mac and PCs.

Easy Access: (708) 966-4372
Sysop: Rick Chiero

1 line—MS-DOS 486; 800MB running WildCat 3.90m with US Robotics at up to 57,600 bps. Estab. 07/93 with no fee. 800MB online and 10 CDs, 35+ doors with Wildnet and local echoes.

Fully Automatic: (708) 501-4851
Sysop: Cataclysm

4 lines—MS-DOS 486; 2,100MB running VBBS 6.14a with US Robotics at up to 28,800 bps. Estab. 03/94 with no fee. Connected to 20 networks, Planet Connect satellite, thousands of message areas.

Rick's Cafe Americain: (708) 423-1468
Sysop: Rich Petroskey

2 lines—MS-DOS 486; 4,000MB running WildCat 3.90IM with US Robotics at up to 14,400 bps. Estab. 10/92 with no fee. Friendly gen'l purpose BBS with an excellent selection of games and utils. Internet e-mail, newsfeeds.

The Village Oak BBS: (708) 430-7732
Sysop: Jim Boyce

2 lines—MS-DOS 486; 1,000MB running Galacticomm 6.21 with Hayes at up to 14,400 bps. Estab. 06/94 with a fee of $40 annually. Dedicated to network support and online entertainment. Internet voe.com, Usenet, ChatLink, and games.

PC Products and Services PCPS BBS: (708) 307-8596

Sysop: Steve Ekblad

2 lines—MS-DOS 486; 32,000MB running PCBoard 15.1/10M with US Robotics at up to 57,600 bps. Estab. 01/91 with no fee. Large file base. Audio/video related conferences. For sale area. Friendly to all users.

Castle KingSide: (708) 546-0301

Sysop: Don Martin

2 lines—MS-DOS 386; 750MB running PCBoard 15.1 with US Robotics at up to 14,400 bps. Estab. 06/94 with no fee. 2 CD-ROMS online, fanasty league baseball, chess, The Bookie Joint, adult access. More doors.

Crimson Gallows BBS: (708) 673-3256

Sysop: Patron

708 lines—MS-DOS 486; 420MB running WildCat 4.0 with Zoom at up to 14,400 bps. Estab. 07/94 with no fee. Net hub of Crimson Net. Home: Micro Professor Software. 11,000 files, 2 CDs.

B.A.S.E. BBS: (708) 741-8335

Sysop: Larry Rasmussen

1 line—MS-DOS 486; 1,300MB running TriBBS 5.1 with Infotel at up to 14,400 bps. Estab. 04/85 with a fee of $35 annually. Family-oriented BBS. Something for everyone. Doors, files, and message networks.

WorldWide Access: (708) 367-1871

Sysop: David Vrona

20 lines—Unix with 5,000MB running BSDI 1.1 with ZyXel at up to 57,600 bps. Estab. 08/89 with a fee of $10 monthly. The highest-quality Internet services: e-mail, netnews, WWW, Telnet, ftp, IRC, MUD, and more.

Mortgage Market Information Service: (708) 834-1450

Sysop: Dan Eaton

12 lines—MS-DOS 486; 1,000MB running TBBS 2.2m with US Robotics at up to 19,200 bps. Estab. 01/88 with no fee. Supporting fractal image format photos online, real estate for sale and finance.

FS Midwest: (708) 279-1647

Sysop: Don Shore

3 lines—MS-DOS 486; 2,000MB running TriBBS 5.10 with US Robotics at up to 14,400 bps. Estab. 11/93 with a fee of $40 annually. 2GB+ online. CD-ROMs, adult file sections, and much more.

Caer Tuatha: (708) 393-7750

Sysop: Gwydion

2 lines—MS-DOS 386; 120MB running Galacticomm 6.20 with Cardinal at up to 2,400 bps. Estab. 12/93 with a fee of $30 annually. Exploring the unknown. Message base and chat system, research and fun. Free trial memberships.

Black Hole: (708) 263-7221

Sysop: Wizard

1 line—MS-DOS 486; 35,000MB running Searchlight 4.0a with US Robotics at up to 14,400 bps. Estab. 08/93 with no fee. 3GB+ in online files on 5 CD-ROMs; general, games, Windows, sights and sounds, business files.

Electronic Businesses

With a PC, some Web server software, and lots of savvy, you too can tap into the millions of users on the Internet. We'll help you pick the software and avoid the potholes as you build your online presence.

Your customers are on it and so are your competitors. The World Wide Web (the Web), once the haven for academia and scholars around the world, has transformed in the past few years into one of the hottest sources of customer support and advertising. Today there are thousands of companies, ranging from bookstores to pizza shops, that offer a variety of services to millions of Internet users.

And the numbers continue to grow at a mind-boggling rate. Each week 200 sites are added to the thousands of sites that already exist. What was originally a small research project of the European Laboratory for Particle Physics (CERN), which in mid-1992 occupied a mere .02 percent of all Internet traffic, grew to 10 percent of all Internet traffic by October 1994.

Capturing a portion of this audience is a matter of establishing a home page on a Web server. The home page is like a billboard introducing the user to the site and its available content. Hyperlinked objects let the user click on a term or phrase and pull up information about that topic. Its rich graphics and increasingly interactive nature make the Web fine for advertising and customer support. And with the Web spanning the globe, any company can now easily and inexpensively sell its products across international boundaries

Establishing a Web server is simple if you're familiar with the Internet. But for the network manager looking to set up a Web server the decisions seem endless. What connections do you need? What kind of hardware do you have to buy? Who do you call to get an Internet address?

We'll tell you here the issues and the answers for setting up that Web presence. Along the way we look at the commercial Web

Info Expressway BBS: (708) 462-2572
Sysop: Nick Poulos
7 lines—MS-DOS 486; 13,600MB running Excalibur Windows 0.72d with Supra at up to 14,400 bps. Estab. 12/93 with a fee of $40 annually. An exciting new GUI interface using Windows; super-friendly to new users, but contains info for all.

Doom BBS: (708) 766-5326
Sysop: Testosterone (Mike Nelson)
1 line—MS-DOS 486; 340MB running Renegade 07-94 with Zoom at up to 28,800 bps. Estab. 04/94 with no fee. The shareware game Doom. 100 P-Wads, all editors, sounds, graphic editors, sound editors.

The Illustrious I.C.I.X. BBS: (815) 459-0825
Sysop: John Krone
3 lines—MS-DOS 286; 200MB running SpitFire 3.4 with US Robotics at up to 16,800 bps. Estab. 04/89 with no fee. A fine BBS with a friendly atmosphere. SFNet (node #A0815004). Node 2: 815-459-9201, 2,400 bps.

The File Depot: (815) 455-7279
Sysop: Bill Masella
1 line—MS-DOS 386; 2,000MB running WildCat 4.0M with Hayes at up to 14,400 bps. Estab. 11/88 with a fee of $28 annually. The family-run BBS with a little something for everyone. 31,000+ files, RIME, Wildnet, doors, etc.

JBIC BBS: (815) 359-7328
Sysop: David McLindsay
1 line—MS-DOS 486; 750MB running WildCat 4.0 with Supra at up to 28,800 bps. Estab. 04/94 with no fee. Just havin' fun. Call and let's chat. 2 CD-ROMs online and some door games. Also a local net.

The Squirrel's Nest: (815) 795-6371
Sysop: Neal Roberts
2 lines—MS-DOS 486; 1,850MB running WildCat 3.90 with Hayes at up to 19,200 bps. Estab. 09/91 with a fee of $30 annually. Free demo access. Online shopping, doors galore, Fido, Wildnet. New files daily. Adult access.

The Boomtown BBS: (815) 868-2422
Sysop: Kevin Zimmerman
1 line—OS/2 2.11 486DX2/66; 540MB running RemoteAccess 2.02 with US Robotics at up to 28,800 bps. Estab. 04/89 with no fee. FidoNet node 1:2270/868. Large OS/2 and game file library. QWK offline mail door.

Under The Influence: (815) 942-2930
Sysop: Bill Wolf
2 lines—MS-DOS 486; 750MB running RemoteAccess 2.x Beta with US Robotics at up to 38,400 bps. Estab. 10/87 with a fee of $10 donation. Full Planet Connect feed. FidoNet 1:2235/10. Internet uti.com. 28.8k USR Duals on all nodes.

American Digital Marketing Service: (815) 962-0885
Sysop: Mike Williams
1 line—MS-DOS 486; 425MB running RBBS 17.4b with Hayes at up to 14,400 bps. Estab. 09/91 with no fee. Flea market BBS. Buy, sell, trade items. Free access.

---

servers—SCO Computers Global Access for SCO Unix and Netscape Communication's Netsite Communications Server for Solaris 2.3—and beta, public domain versions of hypertext transfer protocol (HTTP) software from CERN and NCSA for Macintosh, Microsoft Windows NT, and Solaris platforms.

We selected these products for their availability and popularity. The public domain servers, along with less popular Web server implementations, are available free via the Internet from either CERN or the National Center for Supercomputing Applications (NCSA). If you want customer support and assurance that your Web server will continue to grow in functionality, consider one of the commercial versions of the Web server soft-ware from SCO or Netscape. With the growing popularity of these servers you will likely find in the near future an increase in the number of vendors offering commercial versions of Web server software. A number of vendors such as SPRY and Beame & Whiteside Software have announced products that should be available by the time you read this. Netmanage is currently shipping a Windows version of Web server software in its TCP/IP package.

What you'll learn here is that the Web server you buy will depend on the type of platform you select and the purpose of your server. Products for the Sun platform, or for PCs running Windows NT or SCO Unix, are best for sites with heavy traffic, while the Macintosh and Microsoft Windows 3.11 versions are suit-ed for sites with little traffic. For ease of use, none of the products can match MacHTTP. This product, while not suited for sites with heavy traffic, is perfect for experimental servers that are set up locally or even for elementary and primary schools that are teaching pupils about the Internet. None of the products, however, yet offer the security features necessary to pass around credit-card information, though those standards are in development.

Hook Me Up!
While setting up a Web server and publishing on the Internet can prove to be taxing, with the right information and solid preparation the process can be quite simple.

Multi-Link PC BBS: (815) 963-9717

Sysop: Rick Bergdahl

2 lines—MS-DOS 486; 3,500MB running Falken BBS 6.6 with US Robotics at up to 57,600 bps. Estab. 09/91 with a fee of $10 annually. 24,000+ files and games to play online. Large message base. TABS online to register easier.

Pay No Mind: (815) 654-9806

Sysop: Neko

1 line—MS-DOS 486; 300MB running Renegade 05-31 with Zoom at up to 28,800 bps. Estab. 06/94 with no fee. Text-file-oriented BBS. FidoNet, Wacky-Net, and EMSINet, with more nets coming soon.

Bloomford Network: (815) 633-6752

Sysop: Hubcap

23 lines—MS-DOS 486; 1,200MB running Galacticomm 6.2 with Multiple at up to 14,400 bps. Estab. 08/84 with a fee of $10 monthly. One of Rockford's oldest continually running BBSs. Doors, games, teleconference, online live trivia Sundays.

CorpSoft BBS: (815) 886-9388

Sysop: Robert Neal

3 lines—MS-DOS 486; 2,500MB running PCBoard 15.1 with Hayes at up to 28,800 bps. Estab. 10/87 with a fee of $30 annually. Carrying RIME/INT-ELEC/ProgNet/BasNet and Internet e-mail and Usenet. 3 CD-ROMs online.

The Resting Place: (815) 786-6240

Sysop: Lee Taylor

2 lines—MS-DOS 386; 680MB running WildCat 3.9 with US Robotics at up to 38,400 bps. Estab. 08/91 with a fee of $20 annually. Wildnet netmail, FidoNet netmail, doors, 4 CD-ROMs online with lots of files and fun.

Shadowgate BBS: (815) 622-9639

Sysop: Tony Harrison

3 lines—MS-DOS 486; 5,000MB running WildCat 4.00 M10 with Hayes at up to 28,800 bps. Estab. 10/93 with a fee of $25 annually. Features 200+ message areas, 5GB online. Files, doors, Internet e-mail access, Wildnet, FidoNet.

The Morgue BBS: (815) 625-6550

Sysop: Morgan Mcconnell

2 lines—MS-DOS 386; 1MB running TriBBS 5.1 with Supra at up to 14,400 bps. Estab. 10/92 with a fee of $25 annually. 2 CDs online. 40+ doors on one node. Netmail, WME, YankeeNet.

Wild Side: (219) 693-1714

Sysop: Bruce Witzenman

1 line—MS-DOS 486; 340MB running SpitFire 3.4 with Zoom at up to 57,600 bps. Estab. 11/93 with a fee of $10 annually. FidoNet:1:236/54. Apogee and Epic site. 2 CD-ROMs, lots of OS/2, Windows, DOS, and adult files.

The Labyrinth Underground: (219) 244-3251

Sysop: Eric Bockelman

1 line—MS-DOS 486; 520MB running Renegade 5-31 with Intel at up to 14,400 bps. Estab. 01/94 with no fee. A unique system with many online games, large message bases, FidoNet, and multimedia files.

Perhaps the easiest approach for many will be to go through an Internet Presence Provider (IPP). An IPP, such as the Uunet Technologies alliance with Interse, will publish your home page, freeing you from the responsibility and effort of installing and maintaining an Internet connection. Not surprisingly, it is best to use an IPP if you lack in-house expertise and are concerned about up-front costs.

Choosing an IPP also means that the amount of information you're offering is not much more than what appears on a home page. If you plan to offer a full-fledged service, with all the bells and whistles, consider setting up your own server, which is a bit more complicated.

To set up your own server, you'll need to consider four requirements: the link to the Internet, the IP address, the server hardware, and the HTTP server software. A link to the Internet should be your first priority. You can get such a connection through an access provider in your area such as Netcom On-Line Communications Services, Performance Systems International (PSI), or Uunet, or go through your local phone company. The link can range from a standard 14.4-Kbps modem line to a full 45-Mbps (T3) line, though in our testing we found 128 Kbps (ISDN speed) to be the minimum acceptable speed.

With the service provider's link, you have the physical connection, but you will still need an IP address. If you're lucky the service provider will also give you more than the one required IP address. If not you'll need to go to the InterNIC, the central authority, which manages the distribution of Internet addresses.

One note about IP addresses: If you really want to distinguish your company online consider a domain name like microsoft.com or novell.com. Domain names are particularly helpful since the general rule of thumb in accessing a company's home page is to use www followed by the company name and identifier. For example to access Silicon Graphics, your command would be http://www.sgi.com. The InterNIC will not only assign you a set of IP numbers but will also register your domain name on the Internet. If, however, you don't want to go through the hassle of applying for your own domain name from the InterNIC, you can ask your service provider to set up your

Midnight Escape BBS: (219) 456-4127
Sysop: Earl E. Gibson
2 lines—Novell DOS 7 386/40; 891MB running SpitFire 3.5 with Zoom at up to 28,800 bps. Estab. 07/92 with no fee. Apogee, Epic, site #730. Large Wolf/Spear/Doom area. CD-ROM. FidoNet 1:236/42, RIP Net. 154:700/200.

Summit City Computers BBS: (219) 432-7110
Sysop: Jim Becher (Wayne Murninghan—Mac)
1 line—MS-DOS 486; 2,900MB running WildCat 3.9 with US Robotics at up to 14,400 bps. Estab. 07/91 with no fee. Mac, Windows, DOS, OS/2. Totally free, no ratios. 8,000 files.

Cherry Bomb: (219) 463-8454
Sysop: Don Sabelhaus
1 line—MS-DOS 486; 212MB running PowerBoard ver 1.26 rd with Infotel 14.400 at up to 14,400 bps. Estab. 07/94 with no fee. Free access area, door games, discussions, shareware files, CD-ROM, online shopping, RIP graphics.

ArcadiaVision BBS: (219) 766-2378
Sysop: John C. Tabler
1 line—MS-DOS 486; 535MB running Telegard v2.7s with US Robotics at up to 28,800 bps. Estab. 04/92 with no fee. Member 7 nets. 1,950+ files, 368MB for download. Up-to-date filebase maintained. (1:230/41).

KA9FAW's Bulletin Board System: (219) 324-6386
Sysop: Chester Konopacki
1 line—MS-DOS 386; 130MB running Galacticomm 6.21f with Infotel at up to 14,400 bps. Estab. 06/93 with no fee. A free-access BBS with 13,000+ files for downloading, forums, and online games.

The Data Deli BBS: (219) 753-7910
Sysop: Mike Leonard
1 line—MS-DOS 486; 1,300MB running SpitFire 3.5 with US Robotics at up to 28,800 bps. Estab. 02/94 with a fee of $18 annually. Full-featured BBS. 4 CD-ROMs online, RIP support, 45,000+ files, 1.3GB of HD space.

Magicland BBS: (219) 879-7184
Sysop: Tim Downs
1 line—IBM; 440MB running Exechost with Practical Peripherals at up to 14,400 bps. Estab. 03/93 with no fee. 2 CD-ROMs. 10,000+ files. Doors, conf. Very user friendy.

Gary's Olde Towne BBS: (219) 258-9702
Sysop: Gary Barnard
1 line—MS-DOS 386; 900MB running TBBS 5.1 with Boca at up to 19,200 bps. Estab. 11/92 with no fee. Family board offering files, message nets, and doors.

Kodiak's Cavern BBS: (219) 288-2534
Sysop: Paul Chaffee
1 line—MS-DOS 486; 210MB running RemoteAccess 2.02 with Practical Peripherals at up to 28,800 bps. Estab. 08/93 with no fee. A growing system with games and a few mail networks.

home page with an alias that corresponds to your company name. An alias is an image of your domain name that is not officially registered but looks like a domain name to the outside world.

After you decide on a service provider and get an IP address, you will then need to choose your hardware and operating system. Currently the majority of Web servers that are on the Internet use Unix workstations or servers, such as Sun's SPARCstation 20 or the HP Apollo 900/735. But with the proliferation of multithreaded operating systems for PCs with products such as Microsoft Windows NT and IBM's OS/2, along with more powerful processors and faster bus speeds, your choices are no longer limited to Unix.

You can also choose an all-in-one server solution such as the Netra Internet Server from Sun Microsystems Computer Co. These solutions come preinstalled with Web server software; all that the user needs to do is plug the server into the digital link. The Netra Internet Server is designed to hide many of the complexities of Unix from the end user. In most cases you can actually set up the server without a monitor, since there are speech capabilities built into the server, which notify you of any problems.

Your platform choice depends on the amount of traffic you expect and the cost. What primarily dictates the type of hardware and operating system that you choose is the type of service that you provide. For example, if you

plan to provide technical support for a large number of users, you can expect hundreds of thousands of hits per day, which means you probably need to consider a powerful Unix server or workstation. Windows users shouldn't give up hope though. Windows NT, while still a fairly new platform, is starting to prove its muscle. At press time, one of the most popular Web and ftp sites was www.microsoft.com, which runs on—you guessed it—Microsoft Windows NT Server 3.5. Sites that plan for only a home page with little traffic have more options using Windows 3.11, OS/2, or even Macintosh platforms.

Another factor to consider regarding your choice of platform is cost. The cost of setting up a server goes beyond the price of hardware,

PC-Quest: (219) 223-7395
Sysop: Daniel Zellers
2 lines—MS-DOS 386; 104MB running TriBBS 5.10 with US Robotics at up to 14,400 bps. Estab. 03/92 with a fee of $20 annually. 2 CD-ROMs online. Good access first call. GIFs, Geos Ensemble files.

Simple Simon's BBS: (219) 289-0771
Sysop: Don Devlin
2 lines—LANtastic network; 3,000MB running SpitFire 3.5 with US Robotics at up to 28,800 bps. Estab. 08/92 with a fee of $15 annually. Doors, 1.5GB+ files. Apogee, Epic, MVP s/w, CNet, ModemNews, Moraff, PC Catalog, 1st call access.

The Rock Pile BBS: (219) 288-8950
Sysop: Randy Milliken
3 lines—MS-DOS 486; 2,600MB running TriBBS 5.1 with Zoom at up to 28,800 bps. Estab. 08/91 with a fee of $22 annually. General files with 700MB+ of adult files. 28.8 access on 2 nodes. Limited free access.

Computer Works Technical Support BBS: (219) 272-8129
Sysop: Les Turner
2 lines—MS-DOS 486; 4,000MB running RemoteAccess 2.01 Pro with Practical Peripherals at up to 14,400 bps. Estab. 02/92 with no fee. Hardware and software support, full FidoNet backbone online, full access first call.

KSI Public BBS: (219) 626-2150
Sysop: Joe McIntosh
1 line—MS-DOS 486; 1024MB running WildCat V3.9 with Supra at up to 14,400 bps. Estab. 11/93 with a fee of $35 annually. 57,000+ files, 14-day free trial. Easy immediate subscription via TABS.

Lake City BBS: (219) 269-1033
Sysop: Tom Wagoner
1 line—OS/2 386; 300MB running Renegade 5-31 Exp with US Robotics at up to 28,800 bps. Estab. 11/93 with no fee. RIP support. Hottest games, files, and messages. Unofficial Renegade support BBS.

The Gilwell Connection: (317) 643-7302
Sysop: Richard Bickel
1 line—MS-DOS 386; 500MB running PowerBBS 3.4 with Zoom at up to 14,400 bps. Estab. 01/94 with no fee. Promoting use of computers for Scouting. Scouting files and helps, online games, local activities.

The I.O. Board: (317) 644-3039
Sysop: Bert Happel
1 line—MS-DOS 386; 1,140MB running Maximus 2.01 with US Robotics at up to 14,400 bps. Estab. 08/86 with no fee. FidoNet 1:2255/10. 300+ echoes. K12Net, OptNet (optometrists), CIN, AEN, IGA, EFF, CDN, FamilyNet.

A.C.M.E. BBS: (317) 640-9295
Sysop: Bobby Kokinos
1 line—MS-DOS 386; 500MB running Remote Access 2.01+ with Supra at up to 14,400 bps. Estab. 04/93 with no fee. 2 CDs online. 15+ mail networks. One of the best ANSIs in area. Plenty of doors. Very user friendly.

---

which can range from a $2,000 PC to a $25,000 SPARCstation 20 and higher. Fully configured Web server hardware can easily cost $75,000 to $100,000. Naturally, the exact hardware configuration for your server will depend on the site. For example, Microsoft's heavily used Web server runs on a Compaq ProLiant 2000 with two Pentium/90 processors, 128MB of RAM, and five 2GB hard disks; we estimate the price at over $30,000.

Cost also refers to the level of expertise that you have in-house. For instance, choosing a SPARCstation 20—which offers excellent features and performance—without the required expertise would mean expensive consultant time. You might be able to perform the same task by choosing Windows NT or OS/2 as your platform and investing in a high-end multiprocessor server.

Once you decide on your platform, you need to pick the type of software that best fits your needs. There are versions of HTTP server software available for a number of operating systems and platforms. If you are enterprising, you can even write the software yourself, since the source code and a set of instructions are publicly available on the Internet at http://info.cern.ch/hypertext/WWW/Daemon/JanetAndJohn.html.

Home Pages

The best way to decide on the appropriate platform and software is to decide the purpose of your server. In our testing, we found that there are currently two ways you can utilize a Web server. You can include basic documents that convey information and provide links to other sites. Or you can set up a more complicated Web server that integrates search engines and forms. In the future expect—perhaps most impressive—a third alternative, which will add security to Web servers so they can conduct financial transactions on the Internet.

The most basic way to utilize the Web is to provide company information and links to other sites via a home page. The content can include text, graphics, and sound, and it can be accessed with any Web browser on the network. These pages are created using HTML, a simple but powerful scripting language offered

The Mail Room BBS: (317) 644-5029

Sysop: Scott McPheeters

1 line—MS-DOS 386; 2,200MB running WildCat 4.0 with US Robotics at up to 14,400 bps. Estab. 10/93 with a fee of $25 annually. 9,000+ files, 200+ message areas. Genealogy, OS/2, Christian files/messages.

Classified Connection BBS: (317) 827-1376

Sysop: John Friend

1 line—MS-DOS 386; 250MB running WildCat 3.91 with VTech at up to 14,400 bps. Estab. 03/93 with a fee of $20 extra access. Cownet and Boondock echomail. PC-SIG 12th online (registered callers only). Many TradeWars games.

CCS-BBS: (317) 781-5799

Sysop: Dan Voils

15 lines—MS-DOS 486; 5,000MB running PCBoard 15.1 with Arch Tech/Smart Link at up to 57,600 bps. Estab. 07/92 with a fee of $20 annually. 4 CDs online. Free downloads first call. Multinode chat, adult area, FidoNet, and much more.

Barbarian Kingdom: (317) 546-4513

Sysop: Blackrose, The Circle City Madman

1 line—Novell DOS 486SX; 940MB running PCBoard 14.5 with Infotel at up to 9,600 bps. Estab. 09/92 with a fee of $15 optional. Indy hub for RushNet. Debate, files, DR-DOS, writers, adult, and doors. WME node, more.

The Wheel: (317) 298-0798

Sysop: Ken Heda

2 lines—MS-DOS 486; 2,000MB running TBBS 2.2m with Hayes at up to 14,400 bps. Estab. 07/92 with no fee. Supports all PC systems. 5GB+ of DOS files, online games. FidoNet 1:231/855, Internet e-mail.

The Shuttle Bus: (317) 839-1333

Sysop: Guy Damlovac

1 line—MS-DOS 486; 1,500MB running WildCat 4.0 with US Robotics at up to 28,800 bps. Estab. 10/92 with no fee. Incognet, Indiana-Net. Always the latest shareware programs online. Your one-stop file source.

CD Roma BBS: (317) 454-9766

Sysop: Andrew Barlow

1 line—MS-DOS 486; 210MB running WildCat 4.0 with Zoom Fax at up to 14,400 bps. Estab. 05/94 with no fee. To help new online users. 6 CD-ROM drives.

Bill and Ted's Excellent BBS: (317) 883-4510

Sysop: Cale Hollingsworth

7 lines—MS-DOS 486; 3,000MB running WildCat 4.0 with Boca at up to 38,400 bps. Estab. 12/89 with a fee of $7 monthly. 12 CD-ROMs. Internet, Usenet, Fido. USA Today. Satellite.

Sudden Impact: (317) 457-5957

Sysop: Randy and Michelle Martin

4 lines—MS-DOS 486; 6,000MB running PCBoard 15.2 with US Robotics at up to 28,800 bps. Estab. 09/91 with a fee of $25 annually. 50,000+ files. RIME, Fido, IN-Net. 1200+ PCboard PPE files. 5 CD-ROMs. No adult.

---

by a number of HTML editors available online. (If you want a wealth of information on writing a home page see http://mosa ic.mcom.com /home/how-to-create-web-services.html.)

Any of the Web server products checked out are fine for publishing basic home pages. The decision on the product and platform, however, again depends on your expected traffic. For example neither the Macintosh running Mac HTTP nor a PC running NCSA HTTPd for Windows offer the operating system to service many Web requests.

Of the products here, Netsite Communications Server, from Netscape Communications Corp., offered the best combination of features and functionality. Netscape covers the majority of Unix platforms on the market today with offerings for HP, IBM, Sun, and Silicon Graphics workstations, along with a BSD-compliant version for Intel-based Unix platforms, with the Netsite Communication Server. We tested the Netsite Communications Server on a SPARCstation 10. In our testing we found that the Netsite Communications Server was the easiest to install and configure and offered the richest set of features, such as a graphical installation routine and full remote management of the server. The rest of the Unix products in the group, which include SCO Global Access and the CERN HTTPd for Sun, proved to be more difficult to install and configure. The other shareware versions of the HTTP server that we looked at—MacHTTP for the Macintosh, and a version of the CERN server that runs on Windows NT—were also easy to install and configure. Neither lets you manage the Web server remotely.

We found little difference among the products in functionality. SCO Global Access was the only product here that did not offer forms support. We also found that MacHTTP does not support CGI Shell Scripts, a necessary feature if you want to add extra Internet functionality such as ftp and gopher within your documents. When setting up a server, you should also consider the memory requirements of each product. While none of these products define a preset requirement for memory, that amount is dependent on the traffic of your server. The more memory you have, regardless

Workplace Connection: (317) 742-2680
Sysop: Craig Morrison
1 line—OS/2 2.1 486; 600MB running Maximus/2 2.01 with Intel at up to 14,400 bps. Estab. 10/93 with no fee. Files and message areas for OS/2, DOS, Windows, and Macintosh users. RIP callers welcome. Many doors.

Graffiti on the BBS Wall: (317) 448-2842
Sysop: The Gitzman
2 lines—OS/2 486; 575MB running Maximus 2.01 with US Robotics at up to 14,400 bps. Estab. 01/92 with no fee. Friendly conversation, FidoNet message echoes, PC and OS/2 help and discussions, science talk, files.

The Cannibal's Buffet BBS: (317) 747-1039
Sysop: Brian Clevenger
1 line—MS-DOS 486; 800MB running RemoteAccess 2.01 with Generic at up to 14,400 bps. Estab. 09/92 with no fee. Free access to Forbidden Subjects CD. Anti-Barney files and door game, and more. Not your average BBS.

Delaware Online Services: (317) 741-8631
Sysop: Jerry Harvey
1 line—MS-DOS 486; 10,000MB running Search-Light 4.0 with Generic at up to 19,200 bps. Estab. 08/93 with no fee. Free board. Verifed users receive 50 minutes per day, free. Games. Shareware. Mail.

In Through The Out Door BBS: (317) 282-6862
Sysop: Gregory and Lori Smith
2 lines—MS-DOS 386; 2,600MB running Remote-Access 2.02Pro with Practical Peripherals at up to 28,800 bps. Estab. 10/89 with no fee. Offering: Planet Connect satellite; Apogee and Epic distribution site; adult areas; BW 100 BBS.

New Ross BBS: (317) 723-1510
Sysop: Jean White
2 lines—MS-DOS 486; 1,000MB running PowerBBS v3.5 with Infotel at up to 14,400 bps. Estab. 09/93 with a fee of $25 annually. Game doors, local forums, classified ads, and more.

Optima BBS: (317) 867-0903
Sysop: Jason C. Wendling
1 line—MS-DOS 486; 280MB running WildCat 3.91S with Codex at up to 19,200 bps. Estab. 05/94 with no fee. Free system loaded with features. 14 CDs (ROM/week). Fun doors. Huge message base. Tons of GIFs and zips.

The Tradin' Place: (812) 334-0442
Sysop: Bennie Sexton
2 lines—OS/2 2.11 486; 2,181MB running Maximus/2 2.01wb with US Robotics at up to 28,800 bps. Estab. 05/91 with no fee. OS/2 and MS-DOS files. FidoNet/Usenet message areas. Three CD-ROMs. Free Internet mail access.

Interstellar War BBS: (812) 339-8563
Sysop: Jim and Julia Day
2 lines—MS-DOS 486; 1,000MB running Robo-board/FX 1.4 with US Robotics at up to 28,800 bps. Estab. 08/93 with no fee. VGA Planets and Global War played here. Specializing in games with online CD-ROM file areas.

---

of the platform, the better your performance and the server's response time will be.

Home Page + Forms + Gateway Services

The second and more complex level of service on the Internet involves not only setting up home pages, but also providing gateway services to other Internet resources such as ftp, gopher, and Wide Area Information Service (WAIS), along with forms support. These servers are best suited for sites that want to provide a multitude of services from product information to technical support. The way to provide other services via the Web is with CGI Shell Scripts. These simple scripts, which you can write or acquire over the Internet, allow your Web server to act as a gateway to other Internet services such as gopher and news. All the products here, except MacHTTP, support CGI Shell Scripts.

Form support is another important factor to consider. If you want to gather user information, conduct surveys, or even provide interactive services, then forms support is a must. Forms must be supported by both the client and the server for successful implementation. Forms makes Web browsing an interactive process for the user and the provider. Of the products we looked at, only SCO Global Access and MacHTTP did not support forms.

What good is the information if you can't find it! Search tools are another way to enhance your home page offering. You can provide either local or wide area searches. There are number of search tools currently available on the Internet: Veronica, for instance, searches gopher servers. The most popular search tool for the World Wide Web is WAIS, a distributed text-searching system. WAIS is a subset of Z39.50—a spec that provides a common language for clients and servers to retrieve information and conduct queries for documents across the Internet.

Financial Transactions

The most difficult of the services is conducting financial transactions over the Internet. That means doing banking and buying products using the Internet. While it holds a lot of

Indiana On-Line: (812) 332-7227
Sysop: Greg Rumple/John Taylor.
5 lines—OS/2 486; 5,500MB running Magnum OS/2 BBS v8.01B with US Robotics at up to 28,800 bps. Estab. 07/84 with no fee. OS/2-based system supporting MS-DOS, OS/2, Unix, Novell, adult, and many other areas.

The Black Hole BBS: (812) 323-0301
Sysop: Stephan Tai
1 line—MS-DOS 486; 0MB running WWIV 4.23 with US Robotics at up to 14,400 bps. Estab. 04/93 with no fee. Several message bases. Free downloads (no ratios), lots of externals, validation first logon.

Dude's Bait Shop and Sushi Bar: (812) 332-8159
Sysop: Dave Ferguson
1 line—MS-DOS 386; 320MB running WWIV 4.23 with Intel at up to 57,600 bps. Estab. 10/91 with no fee. WWIV board running 3 TradeWars games and chess. Downloads feature OS/2 files. 60+ discussion subs.

The Data Connection BBS: (812) 897-8757
Sysop: Billy Sargent
1 line—MS-DOS 486; running PCBoard 15.1 /2 M with ViVa at up to 38,400 bps. Estab. 06/90 with no fee. Tons of GIFs and great files. 6.0GB online. Visa/MasterCard accepted.

The Last Outpost BBS: (812) 836-4343
Sysop: Toby Davis
1 line—MS-DOS 386; 400MB running SpitFire 3.5 with US Robotics at up to 38,400 bps. Estab. 01/94 with no fee. Online files, SFNet, and Circuit-Net node. Member 812 BRE league.

Homer's Place: (812) 479-6505
Sysop: Yoda
2 lines—MS-DOS 486; 4,000MB running WildCat 3.9 with Infotel at up to 14,400 bps. Estab. 12/92 with a fee of $20 annually. Languages, travel, fun.

The Windows Source: (812) 476-4534
Sysop: Craig Kohler
2 lines—MS-DOS 486; 1,000MB running RemoteAccess 2.01+ with Zoom at up to 19,200 bps. Estab. 10/93 with no fee. Windows CD-ROM, Fido 1:2310/2, BRE InterBBS, great ANSI/RIP, lots of different forums, all free.

Courier On-Line: (812) 424-1099
Sysop: Mark Blanchard
12 lines—Pentium; 4,000MB running Galacticomm Major 6.2 with US Robotics at up to 19,200 bps. Estab. 07/94 with no fee. The Evansville Courier's BBS. Education files, shareware, games, graphics.

The Top of the Hill BBS: (812) 824-8682
Sysop: Steve Fichtner
1 line—MS-DOS 486; 877MB running WildCat 4.0 with US Robotics at up to 38,400 bps. Estab. 02/92 with no fee. General-purpose BBS, shareware and public-domain, 8 CD-ROMs, V.34 and V.FC 28.8K modem.

promise for the future, this type of service is not yet feasible, because there are no viable security measures. At present, critical information such as credit-card numbers and financial records is not encrypted and can be intercepted by any savvy Internet hacker. This poses a problem for anyone planning to perform commerce over the net. There are, however, two solutions on the horizon that promise to rectify this situation.

The first is called secure HTTP (S-HTTP) and is being undertaken by a consortium that includes Enterprise Integration Technologies, NCSA, and RSA Data Security. S-HTTP is a revision of HTTP that will enable the incorporation of various different cryptographic message formats, such as DSA and RSA standards into both the Web client and the server; most of the security implementation will take place at the protocol.

The second measure—called security socket layer (SSL)—which is under consideration by Netscape, plans to use RSA security to wrap security information around HTTP. This implementation, while different from S-HTTP, accomplishes the same task. The benefit of SSL over S-HTTP is that SSL is not restricted to HTTP, but can also be used for security for ftp and Telnet among other Internet services.

To implement security correctly we need a standard. Thus security would be provided for the client as well as the server. As both security camps are currently working with the World-Wide Web Organization (W3O), it is likely that in the near future they will collaborate to develop a single standard.

While you might not want to perform financial transactions over the Internet, the Web remains an invaluable tool for customer support and advertising. So join your customers and get a head start on your competitors. What are you waiting for?
—Ryan O. Tabibian ■

Datastream BBS: (812) 481-1216
Sysop: Paul Steltenpohl

2 lines—MS-DOS 486; 250MB running Synchronet 2.0 with VFP at up to 14,400 bps. Estab. 04/94 with a fee of $9 optional. Local information on tourism in southern IN and prompt responses from sysop.

DownTown: (812) 273-4422
Sysop: Kevin Mefford

2 lines—MS-DOS 486; 580MB running SpitFire 3.5 with Infotel at up to 38,400 bps. Estab. 04/93 with no fee. 17 CDs online. Circuit-Net host. Supporting emergency services, scuba, Amiga/Mac. 2 BRE IP leagues.

DataCom USA: (812) 949-4904
Sysop: Frank Fendley

2 lines—MS-DOS 486; 2,300MB running Renegade 5-31 with Infotel at up to 28,800 bps. Estab. 12/91 with a fee of $29.95 annually. 100,000+ files available. Well-maintained, friendly staff, information services, and more.

SpellSinger II: (812) 232-1821
Sysop: Strange Brew

1 line—MS-DOS 486; 800MB running WWIV 4.23 with Supra at up to 57,600 bps. Estab. 07/93 with no fee. 700MB+ in the files section. Member 4 networks. Lots of message bases. You'll like it.

Blarty-Toot BBS [GSA]: (812) 466-4222
Sysop: Calvin/gUs/Coffin Man

1 line—MS-DOS 286; 100MB running WWIV 4.23 mod with US Robotics at up to 57,600 bps. Estab. 08/92 with no fee. Home of Platypus Programming, Encyclopedia Absurdia, VGA Planets Players' Pub. Consider themselves "spleen-like."

Media Prism: (812) 234-0460
Sysop: Money Man/Oops

1 line—MS-DOS 386; 600MB running VBBS 6.14a with Practical Peripherals at up to 14,400 bps. Estab. 06/89 with no fee. Apogee, Epic Megagames, id Software, Lucida Group official site. Quality instead of quantity. Internet.

The Lion's Den BBS: (812) 232-7853
Sysop: Aslan

1 line—MS-DOS 386; 120MB running WWIV 4.23 with Supra at up to 14,400 bps. Estab. 05/93 with no fee. BBS for users over 18. Many different topic areas of interest to adult users. Multi-issue forum.

The Short's BBS: (319) 381-1591
Sysop: John Albrecht

1 line—MS-DOS 386; 900MB running GT Power 18 with US Robotics at up to 38,400 bps. Estab. 07/90 with no fee. General BBS with worldwide messaging system through GT-Power network.

Eternal Flame BBS: (319) 752-3656
Sysop: Theron Smith

1 line—MS-DOS 486; 1,000MB running Renegade 4.0 with ZyXel V.32b/V.42b at up to 19,200 bps. Estab. 06/01 with no fee. Several CDs. High speed modems. The latest shareware. One of the best boards in town.

Purgatory: (319) 266-4310
Sysop: Tim McGraw

1 line—Pentium with 510MB running SpitFire 3.5 with Best Data at up to 57,600 bps. Estab. 09/93 with a fee of $5 annually. Free limited access. Registered door games, adult files, and games avail. SFNet msg. confs.

The Magic Man BBS: (319) 243-7685
Sysop: Dave Hereid Sr.

2 lines—MS-DOS 386; 120MB running RBBS 17.4 with Zoom at up to 14,400 bps. Estab. 12/92 with no fee. Free to all verified except CD-ROM access ($5 per year). 20+ door games.

Predator's Domain BBS: (319) 582-8085
Sysop: Jeremy Herrig (Predator)

1 line—MS-DOS 486; 570MB running SpitFire V3.5 with Hayes at up to 28,800 bps. Estab. 05/94 with a fee of $8-15 annually. 6GB+ of files. 6 CD-ROMs. Member SFNet mail network. SFNet and CD-ROMs subscription only.

The Missing Link: (319) 235-0772
Sysop: Aahz/Desiree

2 lines—MS-DOS 386; 425MB running WildCat 3.90M with Hayes at up to 28,800 bps. Estab. 06/89 with a fee of $10 annually. Relaxed atmosphere, online games, and some of the latest files. Wildnet, DREAMnet, HomeNet.

Sammy's Litter Box: (319) 232-5627
Sysop: Larry Edler

2 lines—MS-DOS 486; 2,400MB running WildCat 3.9M with Hayes at up to 28,800 bps. Estab. 12/91 with a fee of $20 annually. Home of Sammy Software. 100+ online games. 80,000+ files.

Epstein's Mother: (319) 266-2955
Sysop: Billy Badass

1 line—OS/2 2.1 486DX/2 66; 4,000MB running SpitFire 3.5 with Infotel V.32/V.32bis at up to 14,400 bps. Estab. 01/94 with no fee. Online tape and CD-ROM. Wildnet, UN'I and several other net echoes. Dozen of the hottest door games.

CLU Puternet: (515) 232-7631
Sysop: M. Hannibal Toal

1 line—MS-DOS 286; 80MB running Waffle 1.65 with Infotel at up to 19,200 bps. Estab. 10/93 with no fee. All text. No ratios. No hassles. Usenet news. Internet e-mail.

The Robot Fun Club: (515) 472-8027
Sysop: Robert Chapin

1 line—MS-DOS 386; 100MB running Sapphire BBS 4.09D with Intel Faxmodem at up to 19,200 bps. Estab. 08/94 with a fee of $2 monthly. Pyroto Mountain is what makes this board fun. This cool game will be played by up to 350 users.

The Blue Collar BBS: (515) 423-7905
Sysop: Jeremy Hovland

1 line—MS-DOS 486; 1,150MB running WildCat 4.0 M with Practical Peripherals at up to 14,400 bps. Estab. 04/92 with no fee. 50,000+ CD-ROM files. Games, adult files, more.

Up All Night: (515) 732-4555
Sysop: Tracy Anderson
1 line—MS-DOS 386; 1,500MB running WildCat 4.00 with Zoom at up to 28,800 bps. Estab. 08/92 with no fee. Complete access first call. NightOwl 11 online, thousands of files. Help for the PC novice.

The Main Street BBS: (515) 628-3101
Sysop: Steve Jansen
2 lines—MS-DOS 486; 600MB running SpitFire 3.4 with US Robotics at up to 14,400 bps. Estab. 12/92 with no fee. 7 CD-ROMs online with many special interest files (ham, MIDI, programming), FidoNet address: 1:290/108.

Bananna League BBS: (515) 627-5606
Sysop: John Kroes
1 line—MS-DOS 386; 600MB running SpitFire 3.5 with US Robotics at up to 14,400 bps. Estab. 05/94 with a fee of $10 annually. 6 CD-ROM changer online. Many SpitFire support files. Fun door games.

Exegete's Haven RBBS: (712) 758-3483
Sysop: Richard Jordan
1 line—MS-DOS 386; 2,000MB running RBBS 17.5 with Microcom at up to 28,800 bps. Estab. 06/89 with no fee. General BBS specializing in biblical studies, DTP, and RBBS support.

The Virtual Reality BBS: (712) 737-3960
Sysop: Travis Noteboom
1 line—MS-DOS 386; 340MB running Renegade 05-31 Exp with Supra at up to 14,400 bps. Estab. 05/91 with no fee. 100+ Seeknet and YankeeNet mail conferences. Great Renegade support file area.

Mega Modem BBS: (712) 277-3208
Sysop: Bruce Johnson
1 line—MS-DOS 486; 800MB running ProBoard 2.01 with Telepath II at up to 57,600 bps. Estab. 04/94 with no fee. Specializes in games/graphics/FAO. 3 CDs online. Message bases, large file base, RIP graphics.

Midwest Connection BBS: (712) 276-6534
Sysop: Hunter/Deputy Dan
2 lines—MS-DOS 486; 2,500MB running Searchlight 4.0 with US Robotics at up to 38,400 bps. Estab. 07/93 with a fee of $15 annually. 16 CD-ROMs online ready for download. Large adult.

Trans Plus BBS: (712) 255-0784
Sysop: Craig Staggs
4 lines—MS-DOS 486; 2,500MB running WildCat 3.90 with Telepath II at up to 19,200 bps. Estab. 12/27 with a fee of $25 annually. One of Sioux land's largest BBSs. 50,000+ plus, very large mature file area, online games. Free eval. period.

The MotherLode: (316) 441-0047
Sysop: George Stockton
1 line—MS-DOS 386; 2,812MB running RYBBS 7.6 with Best Data at up to 19,200 bps. Estab. 01/93 with no fee. Full access first call. Short registration. 27,000 files avail., online games, active message base.

The Firehouse BBS: (316) 442-3702
Sysop: Randy Leach
1 line—MS-DOS 386; 2,000MB running WildCat 3.9 with US Robotics at up to 19,200 bps. Estab. 04/93 with no fee. Home of the Firewire QWKmail echo for fire and emergency medical services.

Phone Cops Donut Shop BBS: (316) 364-8584
Sysop: Kevin Bailey
1 line—MS-DOS 486; 420MB running Celerity 2.01 with Lightcomm at up to 14,400 bps. Estab. 02/93 with a fee of $30 annually. ASP distribution site with Epic, Apogee, and other programs/games.

The Loading Zone: (316) 431-9502
Sysop: Rod March
1 line—MS-DOS 486; 6,000MB running Excalibur v .67a with Hayes at up to 14,400 bps. Estab. 10/93 with no fee. Full multitasking thru Windows, lots of games, Windowsware, shareware, and much more.

The ACS BBS: (316) 251-2761
Sysop: Ken Collins
2 lines—MS-DOS 486; 2,048MB running WildCat v 3.91 with Practical Peripherals at up to 14,400 bps. Estab. 11/90 with no fee. Supports MS/PC-DOS. Download 1st call, short registration. RIP graphics. 24,000+ files.

Hanger 18: (316) 251-7460
Sysop: Paul Head
1 line—MS-DOS 286; 500MB running Remote-Access 2.01 with Practical Peripherals at up to 19,200 bps. Estab. 01/90 with a fee of $20 annually. Downloads first call. Various echoes.

The Digital Connection: (316) 792-3314
Sysop: Tom Shorock
1 line—MS-DOS 386; 215.2/5 with US Robotics at up to 38,400 bps. Estab. 05/89 with no fee. FidoNet and Adult Links message areas. Files/messages/games/CD-ROM.

USER GROUP LISTS

United States User Groups

ALABAMA

Brindlee Mountain Computer Club
Contact: Michael Wisenant, (205) 753-2538.
Supporting PC-based computers with meetings held the second and fourth Tuesday of every month. Membership fee is $10. Group of novice through expert users getting together to share knowledge and experience with others. Education about computers and their ability to help us become more productive.

Castle Rock Crusaders
Contact: Michael Lonbardo, (205) 934-6928.
Supporting IBM and Apple, VBBS sysops, with meetings held Thursdays, monthly. Easygoing group that likes to talk about computers and debug any problems that deal specifically with VBBS boards and more.

☞ Analysts predict that by 1996, 43 percent of all American households—that's 42 million homes—will have an office at home or someone who telecommutes. This sudden growth in virtual offices will fuel an $18 billion online market by 1998.

398   C Y B E R S O U R C E

Educational Software for IBM

Contact: Timothy Blake, (205) 650-0901.
Supporting IBM, educational shareware, modeming, for parents/students. Meetings held monthly, at a school in Huntsville, evenings. Membership fee is $10. Dedicated to education, with all types of support available, including a BBS (205-650-0107, 24 hours a day). Promotes modeming and the use of educational software from preschool-12th grade.

Auburn/Opelika PC Users' Group

Contact: Tony Ledbetter, (205) 749-3684.
Supporting IBM/MS-DOS computers. Meetings held the second Monday of every month. Membership fee is $15. General-interest users' group. Monthly newsletter for members.

Computer Users of the Shoals

Contact: Birgit U. Longcrier, (205) 383-6189.
Supporting IBM compatibles, DOS, Windows, and multimedia. Meetings held the fourth Monday of every month. Membership fee is $15. Computer users with different levels of experience assisting each other and learning together. Contact address: 316 N. Montgomery Ave., Sheffield, AL 35660.

ALASKA

Alaska Computer Widows Societ

Contact: Paul Davis, (907) 278-3303.
Supporting Lotus (Ami Pro), MS (Works), BBSing. Meetings held every other Sunday. Special interest: dealing with spouses of modemers. Contact address: 518 Denali, Anchorage, AK 99501.

Adak Computer Users Group

Contact: Marvin Heilesen, (907) 592-2145.
Supporting all types of computers. Meetings held the third Monday of every month, 19:00 hours, at the base chapel. Membership fee is $10. Local and remote memberships, interesting presentations at the meetings. SIGs provide additional machine-specific help.

A Billion Websites

It seems that the Web should be a finite thing—that someday all the Websites will be done, and we can do something else! But that's just an illusion too. The breadth of the Web is limited only by the available space on hard disks, and the availability of human thoughts and feelings to fill that space. There's no shortage of either!

Every writer can participate in the Web. Someday, very soon, I believe, every writer will. That's the next big opportunity in the online world.—Dave Winer ∎

ARIZONA

The Electronic Alliance.

Contact: Jacob Bailly/Scott Fell, (602) 526-5745.
Supporting IBM, Amiga, Mac, and "oddballs", with meetings held the second and fourth Wednesday of every month. Membership fee is $10. All computer users or those interested in any aspect of computing are welcome. Bimonthly newsletter lets members know of the latest in the northern Arizona computing scene. Help available on all platforms from experienced users. Contact address: , P.O. Box 22362, Flagstaff, AZ 86002-2362.

Phoenix PC Users Group

Contact: Ray Moore, President, Phoenix PC Users Group, (602) 222-8511.
Supporting Windows- and DOS-based computers. Meetings held the third Tuesday (west side) and the Wednesday following (east side) of every month. Membership fee is $40. Devoted to IBM-type computers, with nearly 1,000 members. We have a monthly newsletter, 20 SIGs, and activities to interest both the beginner and experienced computer user. Visitors welcome. Contact address: P.O. Box 35637, Phoenix, AZ 85069-5637.

Bisbee User's Group (BUG)

Contact: Millie Galliher, (602) 432-5087.
Supporting DOS, Mac, other platforms. Meetings held the fourth Thursday (DOS) and Tuesday (Mac) of every month. Membership fee is $20. Dedicated to promotion of computer use through help, support, training, and education of members and the community. Source of legal shareware exchange for all. Also fun.

Sierra Vista IBM PC User Group

Contact: Sarah Pepper, (602) 378-3415.
Supporting IBM compatibles. Meetings held the first and third Tuesday of every month. Membership fee is $20. Nonprofit organization. Member Association of PC Users Groups. Meetings offer discussion on PCs and PC compatibles, and software and hardware demonstrations.

ARKANSAS

Arkansas Sysops Association

Contact: John Shores, (501) 982-5748.
Supporting all BBS operators/systems. Meetings held the last Saturday of every month, Little Rock Public Library. Membership fee is $12. Supports responsible operation of online systems in the Arkansas area by holding seminars and monthly training on equipment, software, and issues facing today's system operator.

Central Arkansas PC User Association (CAPCUA)

Contact: Wendell Brown, (501) 225-9304.
Supporting IBM PCs. Meetings held the first and third Monday of every month, 6 p.m. Membership fee is $24. Member of APCUG. BBS with 1.5GB online and 2.4GB requestable (501-225-7902). Non-members welcome. Contact address: P.O. Box 24064, Little Rock, AR 72221.

Conway PC Users Group Inc

Contact: Tim Stone, (501) 329-7239.
Supporting DOS/Windows-based systems. Meetings held the second Thursday of every month, 7 p.m., Holiday Inn in Conway. Membership fee is $25. If you live in the Central Arkansas area and are interested in computers, we're interested in you. Member Assoc. of PC Users Groups. Members have access to shareware library, club BBS (501-329-7227), SIGs, and more. Contact address: Toadsuck Station, Conway, AR 72032.

Digital Equipment Computer User's Society (DECUS)/ARKLUG

Contact: Michael Smith, (501) 569-8713.
Supporting Digital computing (PC/VAX/Alpha AXP/Pathworks/networks). Meetings held the first Thursday of every month. The Arkansas chapter of DECUS was formed to further the use of DEC hardware and software. Contact address: 2801 S. University Ave., Little Rock, AR 72204-1099.

ARK/OK PC Users Group

Contact: James W. Stevens, (501) 784-8406.
Supporting MS-DOS, OS/2. Meetings held the second Thursday of every month, 7 p.m. Membership fee is $20. Support DOS, Windows, and OS/2 users of PCs. SIG meetings every Thursday night. Contact address: P.O. Box 853, Ft. Smith, AR 72902-0853.

CALIFORNIA

Merced Amiga Group (MAGI)

Contact: Jim Crawford, President, MAGI, (209) 383-1047.
Supporting Amiga. Meetings held the first and third Thursday of every month at Merced Sun Star Building, 3033 N. G St., Merced, 7 p.m. to 9 p.m. Operates MAGI BBS, Sysop: Brian Finley, supporting Amiga/IBM/C-64/C-128 computers with access to FidoNet; Internet e-mail; RIP graphics; and local sysops, programmers, and repair people to help you with your needs. MAGI members get higher access. Contact address: P.O. Box 341, Atwater, CA 95301-2903.

South Bay All Computers Users

Contact: Mary Creech.
Supporting Atari, IBM, Mac, hardware, and software. Meetings held the second Tuesday of every month at VFW Hall, 1865 Lomita Blvd., Lomita (one block west of Western Ave.). Membership fee is $25. Dues entitle users to attend the meetings, receive a monthly newsletter, and attend SIGs. Family membership is $30 annually. Meetings include Q&A from members with various software

It's Show Time!

The first personal computer show I attended was in 1977. Dubbed the West Coast Computer Faire, it attracted a huge crowd and marked the beginning of the personal computer scene. It was a show for users. Over the years the shows grew, then suddenly started to fade until the whole scene was taken over by business geeks, and users were left with some Mac shows and swap meets. But now it looks like we're going to see a reemergence of computer shows for users. And the Comdex folks may be plotting to take over the entire show phenomenon.

Winning Formula?

Comdex, for those of you who don't follow the industry, is a bunch of dealer and reseller shows highlighted by a monster show in Las Vegas every year called Comdex/Fall. The Interface Group, which sponsors the shows, has them all over the world and now sports unusual regional shows such as Comdex/PacRim in Vancouver. The company has wanted to go into user shows ever since it bought the West Coast Computer Faire a few years back. But it hasn't found the winning formula. I now suspect that it will turn Comdex itself into a massive be-all and end-all show for everyone from corner dealers to gawking newcomers. There soon will be a Comdex coming to your hometown.

The strongest indicator of this has been the annual Comdex show guides and the changing claims they've made. I've followed these since the show's inception. Comdex was originally what its acronym spelled out: a Computer Dealers Exposition. But the percentage of actual computer dealers who now attend is small.

What's taking place becomes obvious when you look at the annual greeting penned

and hardware problems, demos, and new computer happenings. Contact address: South Bay All Computers Users, 21320 Hawthorne Blvd., Suite 208, Torrance, CA 90745.

Long Beach IBM Users Group

Contact: Orasio Robles, (310) 420-3670.
Supporting IBM and compatibles. Meetings held the third Wednesday of every month. Membership fee is $25. Monthly meetings at Monte Vista Masonic Temple Association, 1120 E. Market St., Long Beach. Attended by computer-industry vendors that demonstrate their new releases to members. SIGs: DOS, Windows, OS/2, hardware, database.

Los Angeles Computer Society

Contact: Los Angeles Computer Society, (310) 476-2726.
Supporting PCs. Meetings held the second Tuesday of every month at Culver City High Auditorium. Membership fee is $36. Benefits of membership include: monthly newsletter, public-domain and shareware library, SIGs, BBS, quick consultant's resource, drawings for prizes at meetings, group purchase discounts, and special seminars.

SMAUG

Contact: Tetsuo Shima, (408) 626-4425..
Supporting Amiga computers. Meetings held the second and third (varies) Wednesday of every month. Membership fee is $20. Supports the Amiga family of computers, focusing on specific user concerns and interests. We welcome visitors.

SD OS-9/OS-K/OS-9000 Users Group

Contact: Shaun Marolf, (619) 447-9721.
Supporting OS-9, OS-K, OS-9000. Meetings held twice monthly, on the first Saturday and the third Thursday. Membership fee is $20. Real-time multitasking users' group for support of systems using the OS.

Software Gallery Support Board

Contact: Joe Engebretson, (714) 991-4019.
Supporting IBM compatibles, MS-DOS. Meetings held monthly. We are a group of BBS users. Contact address: 1775 W. Castle Ave., Anaheim, CA 92804.

Peachtree User Group

Contact: George Schaefer, (714) 239-4308.
Supporting Peachtree Accounting. Meetings held the first Wednesday of every month, in Orange, second Tuesday in L.A. Membership fee is $40. First meeting, no dues.

Classic Computer Society

Contact: Andy Shapiro, (805) 684-8838.
Supporting MS-DOS. Meetings held the second Tuesday of every month. We cater to solving the problems of all who walk through our doors. We talk about the newest topics as well as how to get the most out of our older machines. Contact address: P.O. Box 2007, Santa Barbara, CA 93120.

AVACE

Contact: Marlene Brandom, (805) 943-1559.
Supporting Atari computers. Meetings held the third Wednesday of every month. Membership fee is $20. Interested in all aspects of computing. Contact address: P.O. Box 900512, Palmdale, CA 93590-0512.

---

by show promoter Sheldon Adelson in the first few pages of each year's massive show guide. Study the subtle changes in the message over the years and you begin to see the show's evolution and understand its future direction. According to these letters, until 1984 the show was for independent sales organizations (ISOs)—and the show guide clearly said so on the inside cover. When Comdex shrank after the big 1983 show, the ISO moniker was dropped and Adelson sometimes mentioned resellers in his letter but mostly talked about the size of the show. In 1989 he started looking for a new theme. In 1990 he changed his photos and began to change the theme every

year until now. Here are some direct quotes from the Adelson letters:

1988: Comdex is "big, really big" and "for resellers." This was the last "old theme" show.

1989: Comdex is dubbed "the gateway to the global marketplace."

1990: Comdex is called the "trade show for computer distribution professionals."

1991: Comdex is now the "world's leading international trade show and conference for computer professionals."

1992: Suddenly the show becomes the "world's #1 computer and communications marketplace."

1993: Now Comdex is "the world's #1 information technology event for resellers and corporate decision makers."

1994: The message is almost stable with one interesting word change. Comdex/Fall is "the world's #1 information technology marketplace for resellers and corporate decision makers."

Note the word *marketplace*. Because Comdex, until now, was not a selling show (vendors were not allowed to sell products on the floor), it's interesting to see this change. In

Crestline CUG

Contact: Brad Ashforth, (909) 338-2949.
Supporting Windows, BBSing, programming, desktop publishing, beginners, advanced. Meetings held the first Wednesday of every month, 7:45 p.m. to 9:30 p.m. To support all computer users in the San Bernardino mountains. Meetings held in the offices of Mountain Area Computer Services Computer School in Crestline. Contact address: P.O. Box 400, Crestline, CA 92325.

MUGIE

Contact: Kim Martin, (909) 780-6365.
Supporting modeming/BBS/general chat. Meetings held the fourth Tuesday of every month. No membership fee. Meets at: Carlos O'Briens, 3667 Central Ave., Riverside, at 6:30 p.m., Fireplace room. If you or someone you know owns a modem and would like to meet with other modem users, please come on down and join us.

COLORADO

Rocky Mountain OS/2 User's Group

Contact: Ronald Van Iwaarden, (303) 744-1834.
Supporting OS/2. Meetings held the first Thursday of every month. If you're running OS/2 in the Denver area, this is the place to come for information, support, demos, giveaways, help, and fun. Call the OS/2 Source at (303) 744-0373 or the OS/2 BBS at (303) 755-6859 for specifics of each meeting.

Computer Users Group of Greeley

Contact: Jim Gossman, (303) 356-4171.
Supporting MS-DOS/Windows/telecommunications/beginners. Meetings held the second Saturday of every month. Membership fee is $20. Nonprofit group featuring vendor demos, shareware, monthly newsletter, BBS access, SIG classes for beginners.

Fort Collins Commodore Computer Club

Contact: Kevin Dunn, (303) 221-4894.
Supporting Commodore 64s and 128s, and Amigas. Meetings held the first Tuesday of every month. Membership fee is $15. Monthly newsletter and extensive public-domain library. Our group is growing, with members from coast to coast.

Windows on the Rockies Users

Contact: William R. Trowbridge, (303) 331-2695.
Supporting Windows and Windows applications. Meetings held the third Wednesday of every month, 7 p.m. Membership fee is $30. Our SIGs include the programmers' information exchange, the database users' exchange, and the beginners' forum. Visitors are always welcome. We have numerous benefits.

P*PCOMPAS

Contact: Bermoe Herpin, (719) 596-3921.
Supporting Pcs. Meetings held the first Saturday of every month. Membership fee is $20. Provides a forum for beginning to advanced users to share problems and get assistance with all PCs and software. Meetings feature a talk on PC-related hardware/software items. Newsletter and BBS. Contact address: 1011 N. Murray Blvd., Colorado Springs, CO 80915.

NUI of the Pikes Peak Region

Contact: Peter Van Vuren, (719) 473-6783.
Supporting Novell NetWare and related topics. Meetings held the second Thursday of every month at 2 N. Nevada. No membership fee. A local meeting place for users of and consultants and professionals for Novell NetWare and related topics. Anyone with an interest in Novell, from beginner to expert, is encouraged to participate. Contact address: 2 N. Nevada Ave., Colorado Springs, CO 80904.

---

fact, many CD-ROM makers were selling discs on the show floor this year, something unheard of in the past. There was even a booth where they would clean your gold ring for free and you could buy some monitor screen window wash. Will encyclopedias, fake horoscope readings, and guys selling food choppers be next?

Hit the Ceiling

Somebody finally saw that Comdex *per se* has reached its growth limit, that a number of competitors have appeared, and that the swap meet business is booming. At the latter shows (usually dubbed computer shows) the selling of computers, books, and boards is incredible.

The folks who run Comdex know its days as a pure trade show are numbered. It has already lost big clients, such as Compaq, and can expect an exodus of vendors because of the high costs and the lack of focus. By replacing the Compaqs with companies that can make money on the show floor selling computers, and by opening it to the public, Comdex suddenly becomes competition for CompUSA. The foreign attendees alone would flock to such a show. Most of them just want to buy products and haul them back home.

And here's the clincher: I suspect the Comdex management itself will have one of the largest booths and begin selling computers. I've always thought Comdex or even Comdexx would be a good brand name for a fast computer. Look for it soon.

—John C. Dvorak ∎

CONNECTICUT

Fairfield County Computer Users' Group

Contact: Marvin Hayes, (203) 838-6786.
Supporting IBM PCs and compatibles, beginner to expert. Meetings held the first Tuesday of every month. Membership fee is $30. Active group of computer users with a wide range of interests and knowledge; programs have sections for the beginner and the more expert. Contact address: 238 Rowayton Ave., Rowayton, CT 06853.

Business/Professional Micro Users Group

Contact: Steve Langford, (203) 644-9069.
Supporting IBM compatibles. Meetings held the third Monday of every month, except August. Membership fee is $15. Monthly meetings include general Q&A period, vendor demonstrations, shareware, member applications, and refreshments. Monthly SIG meetings explore specific topics at all levels, from novice up.

AppleShare

Contact: Joan Z. Hoffman, (203) 259-8513.
Supporting Apple II family only. Meetings held the last Tuesday of every month except December. Membership fee is $20. Meets at Westport Nature Center, 10 Woodside Ave., Westport, 7:30 p.m. Demos, large public-domain library, 24-hr. BBS. SIGs: Appleworks, IIgs, communications.

Hartford Amiga Users Group

Contact: Rich Hetherman, (203) 956-7677.
Supporting Amiga. Meetings held the third Thursday of every month, 7 p.m. Membership fee is $15. Large Amiga user group; one of the largest in New England. Aims to support all levels of members, from novices to the highly proficient.

FLORIDA

Miami PC User Group

Contact: Ernest Tornabell III, (305) 687-1184.
Supporting PCs, WordPerfect, comm., Windows, DOS, CorelDraw, Alpha4, Lotus. Meetings held the second Wednesday of every month at 7:30 p.m., St. Thomas Univ. Law School, Moot Court Rm., N. Miami. Membership fee is $24. Amiable group wanting to help others with PC problems. Help desk, computer literacy (BootCamp) classes, numerous SIGs. Monthly program with major software/hardware vendors.

DJSA BBS-Financial Services Computer Users Group

Contact: David J. Smith, (305) 749-6458.
Supporting insurance and investments. Meetings held the first Monday of every quarter. No membership fee. Meetings held to provide computer users with information about online financial services through south Florida.

Apple Tree of Central Florida

Contact: Ann Bennett, (407) 843-0545.
Supporting Apple II computers. Meetings held the first Monday of every month. Membership fee is $25. Meets 7 p.m. at Winter Park Adult Vocational Center, 901 Webster Ave., Winter Park. Pro-Magic BBS at (407) 366-0156. Contact address: 795 32nd St., Orlando, FL 32805.

Central Florida Computer Society

Contact: Conrad Gosheff, (407) 332-2883.
Supporting IBM and clones. Meetings held the first and third Sunday of every month. Membership fee is $25. APCUG member user group in Orlando area. Meetings 2 p.m. at Edgewater High School. SIGs: Windows, DTP, Corel, financial, spreadsheets, BBS/modem, WordPerfect, C, OS/2, advanced technical, etc. Newsletter, shareware library, courses. Contact address: P.O. Box 948019, Maitland, FL 32794-8019.

Lakeland Users Group

Contact: Jeff Topol, (813) 858-0679.
Supporting BBS users. Meetings held weekly, Fridays, 7 p.m. at the North Side Lakeland International House of Pancakes, off I-4, Exit 18. Local sysops and repair people/programmers to help with all your needs. Shareware/public-domain software available at reasonable prices. Contact address: 1912 Ridge Meadow Dr., Lakeland, FL 33809.

Manatee Personal Computer Users Group

Contact: James Smith, (813) 795-0063.
Supporting IBM, Macintosh, and Commodore computers. Meetings held monthly. Membership fee is $20. A nice place to learn, get door prizes, and listen to top companies show off their upcoming or already available products. Also mini trade shows and SIGs. Covering all types of problems. Contact address: P.O. Box 14190, Bradenton, FL 34280-4190.

Pinellas Atari Computer Enthusiasts (PACE)

Contact: Alan Frazer, (813) 791-0912.
Supporting Atari 8-bit computers: 400/800/XL/XE. Meetings held the second Saturday of every month at the Largo Public Library. Membership fee is $10. Members demo hardware and software at each meeting to get the most out of these older, inexpensive computers. Great opportunities to network for help and accessories.

Supersonic Users Group

Contact: Ryan Harris, (813) 763-2506.
Supporting IBM-compatible hardware and software. Meetings held at varied times. Run through Supersonic BBS, (813) 467-9794. Specializing in software review and new developments in hardware. Contact address: 7815 N.W. 89th Ct., Okeechobee, FL 34972-7331.

CNET Help

Contact: James Sumner, (813) 372-1558.
Supporting Amiga/CNET BBS. Meetings held the second Tuesday of every month. Membership fee is $10. Here, we get it all together and help you. Contact address: 12501 Walton Ave., New Pt. Richey, FL 34654.

Komputer Association of Professionals

Contact: Richard Walker, (904) 477-7136. Supporting CP/M and MS-DOS applications for all levels, beginner to experienced. Meetings held the fourth Thursday of every month. Membership fee is $24. A computer group that gets together for a program once a month and for a Saturday workshop whenever the interest level on a topic rises. Contact address: P.O. Box 1563, Gulf Breeze, FL 32561.

North FL MUG

Contact: Doug Rowe, (904) 771-8363. Supporting Macintosh. Meetings held the second Tuesday and fourth Saturday of every month. Membership fee is $25. Dedicated to serving Florida's first coast. Helping new users and old to get the most out of their Macs. BBS: (904) 388-5275.

PC Users' Group of Jacksonville

Contact: Jerry Gitchel, (904) 221-5628. Supporting IBM compatibles/DOS, database, word processing, desktop publishing. M eetings held the third Monday of every month. Membership fee is $35. Approximately 300 active members with approximately 150 attending monthly meetings. SIGs meet on an average of once a month. General meetings are held on the campus of the University of North Florida. Frog Pond BBS.

Suwannee County Computer Group

Contact: Duwane Higgenbotham, (904) 362-7176. Supporting new software and hardware, DOS-related problems, Windows. Meetings held the first Saturday of every month, 2 to 4 p.m. Looking for new members in Suwannee County or surrounding areas.

Computer People's Underground (CPU)

Contact: Darrell Fox, (904) 763-2991. Supporting BBS usage and computers in general. Meetings held Saturdays. No membership fee. BBS users who meet once a week to exchange ideas and see the person on the other side of the modem. Looking for chapters nationwide. Expecting national Fido echo soon.

Pensacola Amigans

Contact: John Adams, (904) 492-3705. Supporting Amiga hardware and software. Meetings held the first Friday of every month. Membership fee is $18. Pensacola's Amiga support group. Friendly laid-back group supporting the novice to the expert of the Amiga enthusiasts. Monthly newsletter available. Contact address: 5136 Choctaw Ave., Pensacola, FL 32507.

Tallahassee NetWare User Group

Contact: Steve Cullifer, (904) 386-1115. Supporting Novell NetWare. Meetings held the third Thursday of every month. Anyone interested in networking with Novell NetWare and using related hardware and software should attend the monthly meetings. Product demonstrations and company representatives are usually on hand. Contact Address: 1545 Raymond Diehl Rd., Tallahassee, FL 32308.

GEORGIA

Metro Atlanta Computer Klub

Contact: Todd Daniel, (404) 621-7990. Supporting all computers, family-oriented. Meetings held the second Saturday and fourth Tuesday of every month. Membership fee is $20. Full-service group offering library, BBS, technical support, classes, door prizes, refreshments, more.

Online Graphics User Group

Contact: Shawn Rhoads, (404) 395-6525. Supporting online information services. Meetings held the first Tuesday of every month. An online users' group committed to furthering online graphics and making the online community available to the average computer user. Contact address: Software @ Work, P.O. Box 566491, Atlanta, GA 31156-6491.

Online Atlanta Society

Contact: Nick Nicholson, (404) 627-2662. Supporting sysops and modem users. Meetings held the first Wednesday of every month. Membership fee is $25. Group BBS is Oasis (404-27-2662), with 1GB of files online. Meetings feature guest speakers from the modem and software industry.

The Mountain Computer Club (MCC)

Contact: Ken Ashworth, (706) 896-4774. Supporting IBM compatibles, MS-DOS, Windows. Meetings held the second Tuesday of every month. Membership fee is $15. Established as a common ground for PC users in the N. GA mountains. Our membership ranges from novice to expert, and our meetings are open to everyone. Our focus is the interests of our members. MCC is a member of APCUG.

ContryNet Users Group

Contact: Mark Stewart, (706) 629-8516. Supporting MS-DOS, Windows, graphics, and sound. Meetings held the third Tuesday of every month. Membership fee is $25. Local BBSs formed group to exchange information users would not get otherwise. New-product demos and various information classes. For more information, contact Warp Factor BBS: (706) 773-7966.

North Georgia PC Users Group

Contact: Kent Whitmire, (706) 384-4824. Supporting all computer types. Meetings held the second Tuesday of every month. Membership fee is $20. A friendly group of users with a wide range of interests and experience. Demonstrations of new items presented frequently.

Supporting the Stephens/Franklin county area. Open to all interested in furthering PC knowledge.

Albany Professional Sysops Association

Contact: Joe Recker, (912) 439-1934. Supporting BBS sysops. Meetings held yearly, January. Membership fee is $20. Local group of sysops interested in promoting BBSing in the area. Membership dues go into the Lightening Fund, which ensures our BBSs stay online in the event of equipment failure. We monitor questionable activities on local BBSs. Contact address: 1790 Alabama Ave., Albany, GA 31705-1070.

Coastal Georgia Computer Users

Contact: Chris Dubay, (912) 368-6365.
Supporting personal computers, all types. Meetings held the first Thursday of every month. Membership fee is $2. A group of all types of computer users getting together to share information and support the community by conducting special projects to help others. Contact address: Coastal Georgia Computer Users, P.O. Box 3866, Ft. Stewart, GA 31314.

BBS Users of South Georgia

Contact: Aulton White, (912) 242-6881.
Supporting BBS users. Meetings held the second Tuesday of every month. No membership fee. Social meetings to meet and enjoy others with similar interests. Information on BBS systems in the area. Software and hardware announcements. A place to bring the whole family. Contact address: South Georgia Counseling, P.O. Box 3511, Valdosta, GA 31604-3511.

HAWAII

East Hawaii Computer Club

Contact: Aaron Honea, (808) 965-8201.
Supporting IBM and compatibles. Meetings held the fourth Monday of every month. Membership fee is $15. Friendly group; all welcome. Database to put members in touch with others having similar hardware and software. Contact address: RR 2, Box 2228, Pahoa, HI 96778.

IDAHO

Sandpoint PC Users Group

Contact: Bill Rushmore, (208) 263-9764.
Supporting IBM PC compatibles. Meetings held the first Wednesday of every month. Membership fee is $34. Promoting the exchange of shareware (PC-SIG) and the support of computers.

ILLINOIS

Champaign-Urbana ST User's Group/CUSTUG

Contact: Lee Johnson, (217) 356-7916.
Supporting Atari ST/STE/TT/Falcon computers. Meetings held the second Wednesday of every month. Membership fee is $16. Come learn more about the computers. See demonstrations, commiserate. Questions welcome via phone, too. Contact address: CUSTUG, P.O. Box 3442, Champaign, IL 61826-3442.

Central Illinois BBS Association

Contact: Scott Sweitzer, (217) 352-1618.
Supporting all interests, concentrating on telecommunications via modem. Meetings held the first Monday of every month, 7 p.m. Formed to promote the use of free BBSs in the area. The assoc. charges a small fee to participating sysops, but users join for free. Publishes a newsletter/has social events.

Champaign-Urbana Commodore User Group (CUCUG)

Contact: Kevin Hisel, (217) 352-1002.
Supporting Amiga, C-64 and C-128. Meetings held the third Thursday of every month. Membership fee is $20. Since 1983, the Champaign-Urbana Commodore Users Group has been providing support for all users of Commodore machines in central Illinois. CUCUG is one of the most active and successful Amiga/C-64/-128 groups in the country. Contact address: Champaign-Urbana User Group, P.O. Box 716, Champaign, IL 61824.

Common People Using Computers

Contact: Karl Witsman, (217) 431-8979.
Supporting MS-DOS, GeoWorks, WordPerfect. Meetings held the second Thursday of every month. Membership fee is $20. Mostly IBM compatibles, but all users welcome. We have an educational discussion each month on topics suggested by membership.

Illinois. IL Heartland AutoCAD User Group

Contact: Gary W. Sutton, (309) 274-8104.
Supporting AutoCAD. Meetings held the third Monday of every month, 7 p.m. Membership fee is $24. Professionals who use AutoCAD. Meet at Rm. 206, Turner Hall, Illinois State University, Normal. Members from all types of businesses who all use AutoCAD.

Shawnee Amiga User Group (SHAUG)

Contact: Jim Dutton, (618) 453-6235.
Supporting all Amiga models. Meetings held the last Tuesday of every month. Membership fee is $5. Providing short product/hardware demonstrations; general discussions; new-user and general assistance; a growing public-domain software library; and fun.

S.E. Illinois Commodore Klub

Contact: Andrew Schwartz, (618) 392-7238.
Supporting Amiga, Commodore 64, Commodore 128. Meetings held irregularly. A group to help owners and users get the most from their machines. All are welcome.

North Sub. Chicago OS/2 User Group

Contact: James R. Schmidt, (708) 317-7405.
Supporting OS/2. Meetings held the last Tuesday of every month. Provides a platform for the exchange of any information related to OS/2. Contact address:. 1417 Lake Cook Rd., Deerfield, IL 60015.

Western Suburban Chicago OS/2

Contact: Dwight M. Cannon, (708) 742-0700.
Supporting IBM and compatibles using OS/2. Meetings held Wednesdays prior to the last Tuesday of every month (evenings). Devoted to exchange of information between users of OS/2, novice to expert. New users and those considering moving up to OS/2 are welcome. Call for meeting details. Contact address: 888 N. State St., Elgin, IL 60123.

Lake County Area

Contact: **Michael G. Brown, (708) 623-3815.**
Supporting Atari 8/ST, IBM-PC, Mac. Meetings held the second Saturday of every month. Membership fee is $12. Multiplatform user group offering PD library, BBS, publication library. Monthly developer/manufacturer demos, bimonthly MS-DOS SIG meetings. MIDI music SIG, yearly swap meet. Contact address: P.O. Box 8788, Waukegan, IL 60079-8788.

Sandwich Computer Users Group

Contact: **Tom Grimm, (815) 786-9223.**
Supporting Amiga; IBM and compatibles; Commodore. Meetings held the third Thursday of every month. Membership fee is $20. Contact address: P.O. Box 345, Sandwich, IL 60548.

Northern IL PC Users Group

Contact: **Bob Neal, (815) 886-6552.**
Supporting IBM PC and compatibles. Meetings held the first Sunday of every month. Membership fee is $25. Group for novices and experts alike.

McHenry County IBM Users Group

Contact: **John Katkus, (815) 455-3942.**
Supporting IBM PCs and clones. Meetings held the second Wednesday of every month. Membership fee is $24. Informal group. We help each other with problems, and arrange special presentations by members or outside suppliers about six times/yr. Contact address: 227 Terra Cotta Ave., Crystal Lake, IL 60014.

Sterling Computer Users Group

Contact: **Greg Adams, (815) 438-3253.**
Supporting IBM PC compatibles, most other formats. Meetings held the second Saturday of every month. Membership fee is $15. Member of APCUG; hosts demonstrations and presentations; programming SIG; special offers; welcomes everyone to the meetings.

Network of the Future

I'm part of a test that Pacific Bell is conducting, which will be eventually offered to the public. It's a high-speed communications link using a T1 network line. There are about 28 companies involved in the test now, and it's called Media Park. We first got involved in the project in the fall of 1994.

I have a recording studio in my facility that is networked—I'll be able to send files through my LAN and do music projects. If someone needs music for something short, like a television commercial, for example, they could actually send me the video over the network, I could work on it, and then send it back to them with the music on it. That's one of the main uses for this network. In fact, the network is fast enough so that they could play the movie over the network, and I could use Timbuktu Pro software to look at the movie playing on their computer, and then take my notes and create some music. Then, I could send the music down the network to them, or just store it in my computer, in my outbox, and they can pull it off the network whenever they want.—Herbie Hancock/keyboardist/composer ■

INDIANA

Michiana Area Sysops Association

Contact: **Les Turner, (219) 272-8129.**
Supporting sysops in northern Indiana and southern Michigan. Meetings held the first Saturday of every month, St. Joseph Public Library. No membership fee. Providing support and network coordination for BBS system operators. Membership is no charge for full- or part-time BBS operators. Support for most platforms and software.

MCCUG

Contact: **James Hunt, (317) 472-4587.**
Supporting all computers. Meetings held Sundays. Membership fee is $15. A group willing to help all computer users. Contact address: P.O. Box 1171, Peru, IN 46970.

The Evansville Area Unix User's Group

Contact: **Brian Fahrlander, (812) 424-8387.**
Supporting electronic mail and/or Unix computing. Meetings held monthly. Dedicated to creating electronic infrastructure in the Evansville area. Unix e-mail, cc:mail, and WordPerfect mail as well as local newsgroups available.

IOWA

Mahaska Computer User's Group
Contact: Paul Falck, (515) 673-0448.
Supporting Mac, Apple, IBM, and Commodore. Mahaska Computer User's Group, with meetings held the second Saturday of every month, 10 a.m. Membership fee is $24. Our goal is to enhance the computing experience, regardless of machine type, and facilitate learning about hardware, software, and industry trends.

Ft. Dodge Commodore Users Group
Contact: Patrick King, (712) 469-2463.
Supporting Commodore Amiga, 64, 128, MS-DOS, Mac, Apple, Unix, OS/2, with meetings held Sundays. Membership fee is $20. Dedicated to promoting computer use and its understanding. To help in intial purchase and setup of a computer. Group-sponsored BBS is provided for 24-hour support.

KANSAS

Topeka PC Users Club
Contact: Dean Jennings, (913) 273-0425.
Supporting new users, DOS, Windows, technical, word processing. Meetings held the second Thursday of every month. Membership fee is $15. Sponsored in part by Washburn University. Has over 225 family memberships. We offer a learning forum for the professional, corporate, or amatuer/beginner computer user. We have a variety of SIGs and monthly activities.

KENTUCKY

Kentucky-Indiana PC Users Group (KIPCUG)
Contact: Mike Robinson, (502) 458-8972.
Supporting IBM PC compatibles. Meetings held the first Tuesday of every month. Membership fee is $35. 1,000 members, with around 400 attending monthly meetings, which feature presentations by major vendors, along with information for novices and power users. About 18 SIGs, a 32-page newsletter, and a three-node BBS.

Computer Information Systems Association
Contact: Kevin L. Bruner, (502) 926-2567.
Supporting all computers and operating systems. Meetings held the third Monday of every month, September to May. Membership fee is $30. A professional association of information-management professionals and interested people meeting to promote information-management education and professions. We have announced our first scholarship for area college students.

Somerset Computer Users Group
Contact: Joe Burton, (606) 382-5371.
Supporting IBM PC, Atari ST. Meetings held the second Monday of every month, 7 p.m. Membership fee is $10. Assorted demos, shareware exchange. Occasional programming classes. After-hours BBSF.

LOUISIANA

Miss-Lou Computer User Support (C.U.S.S)
Contact: Howard Young, (318) 757-8300.
Supporting IBM compatibles. Meetings held the first Thursday of every month, 7 p.m. Just a local group. Mostly new computer users and some professionals. Interested in expanding microcomputer communications in the area.

MaClan
Contact: Claude Baines, (318) 929-4605.
Supporting Macintosh/beginner/comm./DTP/graphics/multimedia/ business/sound. Meetings held the second Saturday of every month, Vo-Tech, Bldg. E. Membership fee is $22. People interested in getting the most from their Macintoshes, both at work and at home. Shareware library, industry guest speakers, software raffles.

AppleMax
Contact: Curtis J. Garrison (318) 343-9400.
Supporting Apple/Macintosh-related products. Meetings held Wednesdays, 6-7 p.m. and monthly presentation meetings. Membership fee is $4.95. Apple-authorized MacUser group. Membership includes monthly disk, newsletter, meetings, and PowerLink BBS account.

PowerWindows
Contact: Curtis J. Garrison, (318) 343-9400.
Supporting IBM OS/2, DOS and Windows users. Meetings held Wednesdays, 6-7 p.m., and monthly presentation meetings. Membership fee is $4.95. We support all operating systems and related topics dealing with the IBM-compatible computers.

New Orleans P.C. Club
Contact: Langstom Goldfinch, (504) 482-5066.
Supporting IBM and compatibles, professional-level, mostly. Meetings held the first Wednesday of every month. Monthly meetings consist of two presentations, new users' group, vendor tables, auction for members. SIGs meet during the month. About 600 members from all professions. Club supports a bulletin board with four phone lines.

MARYLAND

Chesapeake Sysop Association
Contact: Howard Michalski, (410) 242-4226.
Supporting topics related to operating a BBS. Meetings held monthly, whenever we can all get together. All people operating a BBS in the MD/DC/VA area are welcome to join.

Computer Users of Baltimore
Contact: James Disharoon, (410) 235-7075.
Supporting CUB/PCUG/FoxPro. Meetings held the second and fourth Wednesday of every month. Membership fee is $15. Tackles the gammut of computer-related topics.

Econo-RBBS Users Group
Contact: Mike Miller, (410) 747-3619.
Supporting new BBS users. Meetings held not yet established, contact Econo-RBBS for details: 747-3619. Try a new alternative. If you are new to the world of BBSing, try a users' group.

Baltimore DTP Users Group

Contact: Valerie Styles, (410) 669-4552.
Supporting desktop publishing on PCs (including graphics and word processing). Meetings held the third Monday of every month. Membership fee is $35. Provides information on the latest desktop publishing software on the market. Demonstrations and product evaluations are major elements of the meetings. Provides technical support and assistance on all DTP packages.

ABCUG

Contact: Joe Korczynski, (410) 760-9764.
Supporting Commodore 64/128, Amiga, hardware/software. Meetings held the fourth Tuesday of every month, North County Library 7 p.m. to 9 p.m. Membership fee is $25. Monthly print newsletter, disk, access to public-domain software, Commodore 64/128 magazine, and Amiga videotape library. Interests include desktop publishing, graphics, animation, MIDI, multimedia, telecommunications, hardware projects.

MASSACHUSETTS

Pioneer Valley Computer Club

Contact: David D. Orcutt, (413) 562-1027.
Supporting MS-DOS, Amiga, Commodore. Meetings held the second, third, and last Thursday of every month. Membership fee is $25. One of the oldest clubs in the nation, and a member of the Association of PC User Groups. A friendly, informal club with helpful members.

Programmers and Developers Job Search

Contact: Programmers and Developers, (413) 592-4069.
Supporting Unix, RDBMS, IBM mainframe, AS400. Meetings held monthly. Nationwide networking/job search for programmers and developers in the Unix, IBM mainframe, and IBM midrange platforms. No charge. Free job listings by modem at: 592-9208.

Massachusetts. GroupNet

Contact: Larry Houbre, (508) 991-6055.
Supporting BBS system operators. Meetings held the third Saturday of every month. Membership fee is $35. An association of BBS system operators to provide support and promote the hobby, especially the distribution of conference mail using advanced groupmail technology.

MIT OS/2 Users Group

Contact: Kent Lundberg, (617) 453-1938.
Supporting 32-bit IBM OS/2. Meetings held the third Thursday of every month, 5 p.m. Emphasizing tech issues, software development, and advanced-user presentations, this group is committed to finding practical solutions using OS/2. All levels of users are welcome, from the just curious to the power programmer.

MICHIGAN

Southeastern Michigan Computer Org.

Contact: Thomas E. Callow, (313) 398-7560.
Supporting IBM, Macintosh, Timex Sinclair, AutoCAD, programming, new users. Meetings held the second Sunday of every month. Membership fee is $20. Serves the needs of all computer enthusiasts, from the professional to the new user. One of the oldest user groups in the country. Meetings open to the general public. Location: Dodge Hall, Oakland University.

The Detroit Area Clipper Users Group

Contact: Mark Kothe, 37895 Willowmere, Mt. Clemens, MI 48045.
Supporting Clipper programming. Meetings held the last Tuesday of each month except December. Membership fee is $45. BBS support for Clipper programmers. New programmers welcome.

Metro Detroit Sysop Association

Contact: Gary Gilmore, (313) 582-8607.
Supporting the fun side of sysopping. Meetings held the second Saturday of every month. Assistance in setting up and running a BBS. Not stuffy, no heavy rules and regulations; just fun.

Flint Apple Club Inc.

Contact: John R. Moore, (313) 235-6515.
Supporting Apple computers, education, telecomm. Meetings held the third Tuesday of every month. Membership fee is $20. Support for all Apple computers and clones.

Midland Computer Club

Contact: Rick Rosinski, (517) 631-7162.
Supporting MS-DOS, Amiga, Commodore, telecommunications, Windows. Meetings held 4th Wed. (DOS), 4th Mon. (Amiga), 3rd Thurs. (Commodore), 3rd Wed. (telecomm.). Membership fee is $20. Free copies from all disk libraries. IBM has 2,000+ disks, Amiga has 1,000+ disks, Commodore has 400+ disks. Monthly door prizes and newsletter. Guest speakers. Special group purchases and discounts. Fun and informal meetings.

Saginaw Valley Computer Association

Contact: Lynn Kauer, P.O. Box 5827, Saginaw, MI 48604.
Supporting IBM and compatible microcomputers. Meetings held the second Thursday of every month. Large, active computer user group.

Delta DOS User's Group (DDUG)

Contact: Ben Shaver, Librarian (906) 428-3210.
Supporting MS/PC-DOS or compatibles. Meetings held the last Thursday of every month. Membership fee is $20. Discussion of most any topics as they relate to the use of PCs. Including other operating systems such as OS/2 and Windows. A short business meeting followed by group discussion.

MINNESOTA

Dragnet Irregulars

Contact: Gordon Gillesby, (612) 753-1577.
Supporting accessible computing technology for people with disabilities. Meetings held by arrangement according to needs (generally monthly). People with disabilities (all ages, all types) and service providers who work to make personal computing technology more accessible to new computer users.

Waiting for the Great Leap Forward

Most personal computers are used primarily to author paper. Whether it's a word processor, a page layout program, a spreadsheet or a financial analysis program, a graphics program, or a presentation package, people are primarily generating the same media that society has used for hundreds of years. They're really composing pages on their computers and printing pages on the printer.

People do not use computers effectively to communicate. They use fax machines to communicate. They use telephones to communicate. They use mail systems to communicate very simple technically oriented messages. But when it comes to really fulfilling the requirement of systematically moving away from a paper-based to a computer-based information flow, computers have failed miserably.
—John Warnock, president, Adobe Corp. ■

CMACE
Contact: Daniel Dillman, (612) 259-4119.
Supporting IBM, Amiga, Mac, etc. Meetings held the second Wednesday of every month. Membership fee is $15. Devoted to assisting the growing computer-user community of central Minnesota. Monthly meetings include demonstrations and discussions of current and new technology, including the local BBS scene. CMACE is a nonprofit corporation.

MISSISSIPPI

Columbus Computer Users Group
Contact: Ben Groover, (601) 327-7493.
Supporting power users, new users, MS-DOS, Atari. Meetings held the second Thursday of every month. Membership fee is $15. Purpose is to freely share information and knowledge concerning computers. All computer enthusiasts are welcome. BBS running RBBS 17.4 on Boca 14.4 modem at 356-9032.

National Sysops Association
Contact: Jason James, (601) 483-4785.
Supporting PCs, Commodore. Meetings held Saturdays, 7 p.m., Westley Methodist Church, 1500 Eighth Ave. A Sysop: alliance group. We discuss current computer topics, hold fundraisers each month, have several support boards in the Meridian area.

Columbus Computer Users Group
Contact: Ken Foster, (601) 356-4167.
Supporting all computer types. Meetings held the second Thursday every month. Membership fee is $15. Formed to educate and provide a place to learn about all types of computer-related subjects. All new users are granted a 90-day trial subscription.

MISSOURI

Data Bytes User's Group of St. Louis
Contact: Bob Rosenfeld, (314) 727-2418.
Supporting MS-DOS and CP/M computers. Meetings held the second Saturday of every month (about noon), October through June. Membership fee is $20. Users' group supports MS-DOS and CP/M users with educational programs and volunteer helpers available for phone consultation. BBS provides lots of software for download and message base for helping members.

Data Bytes User's Group (DBUG)
Contact: Lance Morgan, (314) 652-7463.
Supporting MS-DOS, CP/M, NZ-COM computer systems. Meetings held the second Saturday of every month, 12:30 p.m., Oct.-Jan. Membership fee is $20. Formerly a Kaypro users' group, now IBM-compatible MS-DOS systems with CP/M as a subgroup. Programs organized for new and experienced users. Special programs conducted by software sales reps or club members. BBS: 821-0638, 24 hours.

St. Louis MIDI Users Group
Contact: Rik Brown, (314) 625-4052.
Supporting MIDI, mainly IBM-based, but also any type of computer system. Meetings held quarterly, per announcement. Dedicated to discussion of MIDI and music topics. Member of the national MIDIlink network.

ICON
Contact: (417) 882-3866.
Supporting IBM clones, software/hardware education. Meetings held the third Saturday of every month. Membership fee is $20. An IBM clone club in the Springfield area. Six SIG meetings each month. Specializes in helping new and old users alike. Shareware library has well over 1,200 disks. A friendly club.

Bushwhacker User Group
Contact: Steve Moyer, (417) 667-9256.
Supporting all types of computers, IBM and Mac, mostly. Meetings held the second Saturday of every month. Membership fee is $18. Friendly, close group with good mix of novices and knowledgeable computer users.

Knights of the Round Table

Contact: Charles Nance, (417) 886-9473.
Supporting telecommunications concerns for sysops and users. Meetings held the first Friday of every month, 7 p.m. Membership fee is $25. A nationally affiliated users' group for the support of BBS sysops and users. Call Alathea's Castle BBS at 886-9478 for more information.

PC-Lynx/Cameron Computer Club

Contact: Bob and Melony Schmidt, (816) 632-4192.
Supporting modems, educational, programming, spreadsheets, helping new users. Meetings held the second Friday of every month. No membership fee. Interested in helping people use their computers to the fullest extent. Use of commercial and shareware software. Special-access bulletin 44. No-ratio support BBS: 632-3297. Download on first call. Online help and e-mail.

NEVADA

Las Vegas PC Users Group

Contact: Bonna Savarise, (702) 452-9642.
Supporting IBM compatibles. Meetings held the second Thursday of every month. Membership fee is $30. Numerous SIGs including WordPerfect for DOS and Windows, accounting, desktop publishing, beginners. Info-packed news magazine. WildCat BBS. Shareware library. Beginners to power users. Visitors welcome at all meetings.

Las Vegas PC Users Group

Contact: Arno Seegers, (702) 431-4333.
Supporting beginners, Windows, OS/2, DTP, WP, acctng., dBASE, Paradox, C++, more. Meetings held the second Thursday of every month, 6:15 p.m. Membership fee is $30. 600 members and growing with the community. All user-group events are smoke-free. We present computer fundamentals from 6:15 to 6:45 p.m., followed by a guest speaker.

NEW JERSEY

Computer Connections

Contact: Ed Mecka, (201) 420-0398.
Supporting DOS, Unix, WP, Lotus. Meetings held monthly, announced via BBS/newsletter/phone. Group-mission statement: to facilitate the exchange of technical information.

Jersey Atari Computer Group (JACG)

Contact: Bill Bingham, (201) 666-2951.
Supporting Atari 8-/16-/32-bit computers. Meetings held the second Saturday of every month. Membership fee is $25. Dedicated people pushing support for a great system. Sample newsletter is available at no charge. JACG BBS: 690-5224, 9,600 and lower.

PC Users Group of South Jersey

Contact: Michael McConnell, (609) 678-3598.
Supporting PC compatibles: MS-DOS, OS/2, Windows. Meetings held the second Monday of every month. Membership fee is $25. Meetings feature vendor presentations on software/hardware products, then they separate into SIGs: Windows, new users, databases, Lotus, WordPerfect, graphics, telecomm., OS/2, genealogy.

South Jersey IBM Users Group

Contact: Dave Schubert, (609) 399-4111.
Supporting IBM PCs & compatibles. Meetings held the second Wednesday of every month, Ocean City High School, 7 p.m. Membership fee is $15. General membership meeting on second Wednesday with guest speaker; SIGs meet at various times and locations. Everyone welcome.

The Sysops Group

Contact: Ted Kraus, (609) 587-6200.
Helping sysops make a profit or lose less on their BBSs. Meetings held the last Saturday of every month. Sysops meet to discuss better methods to market their BBSs to the public and make the boards more profitable.

Somerset Hills PC Users Group

Contact: Mike Cipriano, (908) 766-4139.
Supporting legal matters. Meetings held the last week of every month. This group is dedicated to the free exchange of information regarding small business computer systems. We invite vendors and other suppliers of products and services to address our group or submit literature for review in our newsletter.

Shore PC Users Group (SHUG)

Contact: Blake Berning, (908) 531-5142.
Supporting hobbyists, many who built their own Pcs. Meetings held the second Wednesday of every month. Membership fee is $12. Amateur-radio enthusiasts, engineers, teachers, and homemakers who share an interest in the way a computer (software/hardware) works. Beginners are always welcome and gurus are always challenged.

Central Jersey PC Users Group

Contact: Judith Swit, (908) 364-8226.
Supporting IBM compatibles, novice to advanced. Meetings held the second Monday of every month. Membership fee is $25. Novices to advanced users. Telecommunications, multimedia, databases, strong support, DOS classes, and various SIGs and support.

United Regional Sysops Association

Contact: Stephen Reinen, (908) 206-1129.
Supporting MS-DOS and OS/2 BBS programs, IBM computers in general. Meetings held Fridays, 10 p.m. Mainly for system operators of small and large BBSs. Users of modems and people wanting to use bulletin boards are also welcome. Topics include e-mail, echomail, networking, and innovations in the field.

NEW YORK

Creative Computing Club

Contact: Douglas P. Margolis, (212) 888-3953.
Supporting nontechnical computer users (MS-DOS and CP/M, all Kaypro users). Meetings held the first Monday of every month. Membership fee is $15. Helps non-technical computer users to get the most out of their computing. Meetings feature an extended period of low-key discussions in which everyone is encouraged to participate.

☞ Only 25 percent of all PC owners are connected to an information service.

410   C Y B E R S O U R C E

Sysops Making Money Together

Contact: Richard C. Batka, (516) 488-5520.
Supporting all MS-DOS-based systems, new and old sysops welcome. Meetings held at the headquarters of The World of Greyhawk BBS, 488-5520. No membership fee. We like to get together every other weekend to talk about new trends in telecommunications. We help each other with all areas of BBSing, such as subscription rates, net/echo, Internet links, effective RIP.

Long Island Computer Association (LICA)

Contact: Gary Fishkin, (516) 586-3294.
Supporting all computers/SIGs for beginners, IBM advanced, MIDI, more. Meetings held the third Friday of every month at 8 p.m. (general meeting), at NYIT, Old Westbury. Membership fee is $25. LICA is a nonprofit organization for the benefit of its members. The $25 annual dues include a subscription to the Stack, the newsletter of LICA. LICA runs a club BBS at 561-6590.

The Sysop Association Network (TSAN)

Contact: Jim Marcheschi, (516) 931-6026.
Supporting buying and selling used PCs and equip., Sysop: interests and discussion. Meetings held quarterly, starting at 3 p.m. Membership fee is $25. TSAN publishes Sysop: help files and a bad-user list; helps in operating a BBS and Fido mail systems. Also an ANSI club, helping trade/buy/sell equipment. Barbeques held frequently in Plainview for all members and prospectives.

New York Bulletin Board Society

Contact: Martin Winter, (518) 436-0581.
Supporting the free exchange of information via BBS. Meetings held monthly. A watchdog and educational group dedicated to keeping its members informed of potential threats to their ability to operate and use computer BBSs.

Twin Tiers Computer User's Group (TTUG)

Contact: Jim Kreisler, (607) 732-4275.
Supporting MS-DOS, though all users welcome. Meetings held the first and third Tuesday of every month. Presentations.

The Dungeon User Group

Contact: Raoul Paquin, (716) 662-9238.
Supporting IBM PCs, fantasy role-playing, OS/2, telecommuncations, sales/training. Meetings held the third Tuesday of every month, 7:30 p.m. Established as the user group for The Dungeon BBS, the group has expanded to all types of computer-related fields and interests. Located centrally in the Buffalo area. Call any time for info.

Jewish Computer Software Users Group

Contact: Rabbi Reuven Blau, (718) 774-3997.
Supporting Jewish and Hebrew hardware and software support. Meetings held monthly. Primarily for the IBM. Online Jewish databases. Online search of Tanach, Talmud, Shulchan Aruch, Rambam, Medrashim, Zohar, and Responsa. Set up e-mail with Jewish oganizations and individuals worldwide.

Bronx User Group (BUG)

Contact: Bronx User Group, (718) 328-7544 (BBS).
Supporting Commodore 8-bit, Amiga, MS-DOS. with meetings held the second Thursday of every month. Membership fee is $30. Supporting the Commodore/Amiga world for over 10 years. We have an award-winning newsletter and a Disk of the Month for all SIGs every month. Also a 24-hour BBS just for members.

Catskill Power Users

Contact: James Oppenheim, P.O. Box #29, Monticello, NY 12701.
Supporting IBM Pcs. Meetings held the first Thursday of every month. Membership fee is $30. Monthly meeting to discuss current topics. Any skill level.

Rockland PC Users Group

Contact: H. Stanley Smith, (718) 634-6618.
Supporting IBM PCs and compatibles. Meetings held generally the second Tuesday of every month, verify schedule by phone. Membership fee is $25. General-purpose users group. Supported by monthly presentations by hardware/software/services/supplies vendors. Monthly newsletter. Active product-review program. Public welcome.

CPU:ADVDOS

Contact: Scott Waschitz and Paul Paradiso, c/o Monticello High School, Rte. #42, Monticello, NY 12701; (718) 794-8904.
Supporting advanced DOS techniques. Meetings held the second Thursday of every month at S.C.C.C. in room #F-110. Membership fee is $30. A user group focusing solely on instruction and help in the area of DOS. We explore all aspects of DOS from the most basic to advanced batch-file programming. Call MHS:BBS for details. Phone number is the BBS, not voice.

Westchester PC Users' Group

Contact: Joseph Blum (718) 962-7196.
Supporting IBM PCs and compatibles. Meetings held the first Thursday of every month. Membership fee is $30. Almost 500 members; 150 at monthly meetings: five SIGs: WordPerfect, Windows, DTP, investment, novice and beginners classes; supports conf. on Exec. Network BBS, discounted for WPCUG members.

Hudson Valley PC Club

Contact: Donald A. Peck, (718) 338-5184.
Supporting new users, Windows, Access, CorelDraw. Meetings held the third Thursday of every month. Membership fee is $20. Monthly newsletter. Major vendors make presentations and give door prizes. There is a conference available on a local BBS.

NORTH CAROLINA

Charlotte County PC User Group

Contact: John D. Skinner, (813) 627-5231.
Supporting computer literacy/education with classes and online help. Meetings held the second Monday of every month. Membership fee is $25. IBM and Mac user group. Concentrating on computer literacy through meetings, classes, and SIGS; i.e., DTP, word processing, Windows, OS/2, GEOWorks, modems, finance, etc. Call PC-Florida BBS for info (625-0775) or leave e-mail for John Skinner, UG president.

Greensboro PC Users' Group

Contact: George Hopkins, (910) 333-0276.
Supporting IBM PC's, clones, workalikes, hardware, and software. Meetings held the second Tuesday of every month. Membership fee is $24. We are a group for people at all levels of expertise. Our meetings feature speakers from major software and hardware companies.

North Carolina. Blue Ridge Computer Users Group

Contact: Alan Blevins, (919) 372-4195.
Supporting IBM compatibles, beginner to expert. Meetings held the second Friday of every month. Membership fee is $10. A friendly, informal group that focuses mainly on the beginner/intermediate user.

Triangle OS/2 Users Group

Contact: Steve Gallagher, (919) 254-2238.
Supporting IBM OS/2.0 and 2.1. Meetings held the fourth Tuesday of every month. Membership fee is $5. The premier OS/2 users group, established to help out North Carolina's large OS/2 user community. Q&A, demos, book library, and shareware library. Meetings held at 4800 Falls of the Neuse Rd., north Raleigh.

Chen's User Meeting

Contact: Tony Majors, (919) 765-7963.
Supporting all interests, computers, programs, BBSs, life. Meetings held Saturdays, 7:15. No membership fee. A user/Sysop: gathering for local members of the BBS community. We eat, we talk, we get to know one another. Getting out of the house is good for the soul and mind. Costs $10 if you eat from the wonderful buffet.

Norca Telecommunications User Group

Contact: Charles Smith, (919) 487-9995.
Supporting universal/graphics art, multimedia, CD-ROM creations. Meetings held the last Saturday of every month. Supporting all computers, specializing in computer animation and graphics, multimedia, C++, Cobol, ADA, Visual C, Visual Basic, telecommunications, comic-book artwork, Japanimation.

BBS Managers

Contact: Ty Carter, (919) 946-0351.
Supporting BBS management, new products, user wants. Meetings held the last Thursday of every month. No membership fee. How sysops can improve systems. Joint effort for community involvement in computer BBSing.

NORTH DAKOTA

PC Users Association (PCUSA)

Contact: John Lundell, (701) 775-5601.
Supporting IBM and compatible computers emphasizing electronic communications. Meetings held the first Thursday of every month. Beginner to advanced topics with emphasis on the latest in hardware and software. BBS supported with seminars covering all aspects of computers and software use. Newsletters, software library, guest speakers, and field trips provided.

Flight Simulation Squadron

Contact: James C. Hall, (701) 772-7323.
Supporting flight simulation on the IBM computer. Meetings to be announced. Membership fee is $3. Interests include flight simulation, MS Flight Sim. 5.0, Falcon 3.0, Mig 29.

OHIO

Basic Bits Commodore Group

Contact: Jerry Swartz, (216) 243-0887.
Supporting Commodore 64 and 128, new-user SIGs, Geos SIGs, special workshops. Meetings held the third Thursday of every month. Membership fee is $20. PD library; monthly newsletter; online presence on QuantumLink, GEnie, and other BBSs. Group buys and discounts.

Greater Cleveland PC Users

Contact: Paul Stork, (216) 781-4132.
Supporting IBM/Mac. Meetings held the first Saturday of every month, SIGs held various times monthly. Membership fee is $25. Meetings are presented by industry representatives, and SIG meetings focus on different topics like Windows, databases, WordPerfect, Unix, programming, telecommunications, etc.

North Coast Amiga User Group

Contact: North Coast Amiga User Group, (216) 256-8980.
Supporting all Amigas: 500-4000, video, new users, DTP. Meetings held the second Saturday of every month, 10 a.m. Membership fee is $20. Contact the Harbor BBS at (216) 352-6039 for more info. Contact address: 8323 Eagle #21, Kirtland, OH 44094.

Stark County PC Users Group

Contact: Thom Davis, (216) 477-7254.
Supporting all interests. Meetings held the first and third Saturday of every month. Membership fee is $3. To better enjoy and further understand computers and the online community.

Miami Valley Atari Computer Enthusiasts

Contact: Thomas Tolman, (513) 429-4677.
Supporting Atari classic, ST, TT, Falcon. Meetings held the second and third Saturday of every month. Membership fee is $20. Support for both novice and expert. Business and demo meeting 2nd Sat. Support meeting 3rd Sat. BBS: (513) 233-9500.

Dayton Microcomputer Association

Contact: John Hart.
Supporting all personal computers. Meetings held the fourth Tuesday of every month. Membership fee is $12. Meets at University of Dayton, Miriam Hall, at 7:30. Discusses new software and other computer products, enhances computer awareness in the community. Contact address: 2629 Ridge Ave., Dayton, OH 45410.

D.M.A. OS/2 SIG
Contact: Anthony Cogan, (513) 254-3811.
Supporting OS/2. Meetings held the first Thursday of every month. Membership fee is $12. Out to help with and promote OS/2. Lots of technical help available and can reach members just about any time through the week for help.

Revelation and Pick Users
Contact: Al Kender, (614) 766-3218.
Supporting Revelation and PICK/Prime. Meetings held the first Tuesday of every month. Share ideas with other Revelation and PICK users, download demos of applications written in advanced Revelation, message bases, bulletins for novices to learn more. Reveals some hidden stuff, which is not in the manuals. Contact address: 3370 Cranston Dr., Dublin, OH 43017.

Central Ohio Bulletin Board Association
Contact: James L. Powers, (614) 899-2980.
Supporting users and sysops of BBS systems throughout central Ohio. Meetings held the third Saturday of every month, 1 p.m. Membership fee is $25. Consists of local users and BBS sysops. Topics of interest to modem users.

OKLAHOMA

Green Country Computer Association
Contact: Robert Morton, (918) 251-4105.
Supporting MS-DOS laptops. Meetings held Saturdays. Membership fee is $12. Group dedicated to exploring the various uses of computers in our lives. Members like to meet to discuss computers and have fun. Contact address: P.O. Box 54543, Tulsa, OK 74155-4543.

OKC-PC User's Group
Contact: David McDuff.
Supporting Windows, DOS, DTP, genealogy, word processing, financial, spreadsheets, networks. Meetings held the third Thursday of every month, MetroTech Springlake Campus, 7 p.m. Membership fee is $25. Regional 24-page tabloid newspaper, The Monitor. SIGs evenings throughout the month. National speakers at general session. 1,100+ members, annual computer trade show (one of the largest in area). Contact address: OKC-PC User's Group, P.O. Box 12027, Oklahoma City, OK 73157-2027.

Stephens County Computer Association
Contact: Douglas Bell, (405) 252-5889.
Supporting C programming and general information. Meetings held the last Thursday of every month. Membership fee is $12. A growing club with interests in all areas with special interest in virus protection and education in computers. Door prize given away at meetings with a raffle. Contact address: P.O. Box 750382, Duncan, OK 73575.

OREGON

TBBBS
Contact: Mike Gholson, (503) 754-0433.
Supporting third-party programming for Galacticomm MajorBBS 6.xx. Meetings held various days and times. Galacticomm MajorBBS 6.xx add-ons. Contact address; P.O. Box 1798, Corvallis, OR 97339-1798.

Salem Area Computer Club
Contact: Salem Area Computer Club sysop and newsletter editor John Storme, (503) 364-6621.
Supporting free exchange of shareware and public-domain software. Meetings held monthly. Membership fee is $20, including SACC Spotlight monthly newsletter, access to group's RBBS BBS. Meetings include presentations from leading software/hardware companies. Contact address: 4537 Boulder Dr. S.E., Salem, OR 97301-5905.

PENNSYLVANIA

Philadelphia Area Computer (PAC) Society Inc.
Contact: Kenneth A. Sipos, (215) 951-1255.
Supporting IBM, Mac, Unix, Atari, Commodore, OS/2, MIDI, BBS, Tandy, telecomm. Meetings held the third Saturday of every month. Membership fee is $25. Complete range from A-Z with how-to, demonstrations, BBS, monthly publication. From novice to professional, with hands-on expertise, previews of new technology, and support of present technology with member participation invited.

Amateur Berks Users Group (ABUG)
Contact: Tony Talarigo, (215) 488-7629.
Supporting all computers. Meetings held the second Thursday of every month, 7:30 p.m., UGI Flame Room, Rte. 10. Open to public. Donations accepted. Monthly seminars for new users. MS-DOS crash courses. Monthly shareware disk highlighted. Contact address: Tony's Electronics, 984 N. Garfield Rd., Bernville, PA 19506.

Greene County PC User's Group
Contact: Joe Sadlek, (412) 627-7368.
Supporting IBM, Apple, Commodore, Windows, DOS, WordPerfect, DTP, Flight Sim. Meetings held the second Wednesday of every month, 7 p.m., Greene County Vo-Tech. Membership fee is $20. A forum for computer users in the Greene County area to share information and to help each other. Contact address: 95 Center Ave., Waynesburg, PA 15370.

Pittsburgh Area Computer Club
Contact: Phillip R. Cutrara, (412) 766-8790.
Supporting MS-DOS, CP/M, Windows, MIDI, OS/2, Geos, AI, MPC, CD-ROM, CAD, BBS. Meetings held the third Sunday of every month, 1 p.m., Point Park College, Room 311. Membership fee is $20. Members bring computers to the meetings and set up at 11 a.m. to work on new demos and computer hardware, magazines, free used books. Presentations follow.

Hershey Apple Core
Contact: Gene Bangert, (717) 564-1109.
Supporting Apple II, Macintosh. Meetings held the second Wednesday of every month. Membership fee is $10. Primarily Macintosh, but also the largest Apple II group in the Harrisburg area.

N.E.P.C.O.

Contact: John Owens, (717) 696-3336.
Supporting North East PA BBS users. Meetings held monthly, scheduled on BBS. For BBS users in the Wyoming Valley area of PA. Group mainly meets as a person-to-person recreational event to try to humanize the BBS community.

Consortium of Realities BBS Users Group (CORE BUG)

Contact: John Sergott, (717) 541-0510.
Supporting IBM and clones, GIF collectors. Meetings held the first Tuesday of every month. Membership fee is $15. Call via modem for more info. We support IBM and clone systems. At the meetings, we have open discussions, play games, review new software, and chat about sci-fi and fantasy books and videos. Contact address: 387 Aspen St., Middletown, PA 17057.

Harrisburg PC User Group

Contact: Harrisburg PC User Group, (717) 652-9097.
Supporting DOS and OS/2 computers. Meetings held the second Tuesday of every month. Membership fee is $15. SIGs, demonstrations, raffles, door prizes, auctions. Huge BBS, monthly newsletter.

FCBA Computer Users Group

Contact: Adam Viener, (717) 840-0139.
Supporting computers, telecommunications. Meetings held every other Thursday night, 7 p.m., call for dates. Friendly and diversified group of computer users. The meetings are social and informative. We meet to discuss using all types of computers at work and in the home. The wide range of topics vary each meeting. Contact address: FCBA Computer Users Group, 1604 Mt. Zion Rd., York, PA 17402.

Lancaster Computer Users Group

Contact: William Holz, (717) 392-7893.
Supporting MS-DOS, OS/2, CP/M, Windows, business and application software, LANs. Meetings held the last Wednesday of every month. Membership fee is $15. Q&A SIG (second Tuesday of month), tech SIG (Wednesday prior to last Wednesday of month), Windows and investment SIGs (dates vary). Meeting topics include hardware and software presentations by local and national vendors. Contact address: 177 River Dr., Lancaster, PA 17603-4747.

Computer Users of Erie (CUE)

Contact: Ray Hric, president, (814) 838-7316.
Supporting MS-DOS, Windows, OS/2, Tandy CoCo. Meetings held the second Thursday of every month. Membership fee is $25. Member APCUG. For more information, contact BBS: (814) 866-5315. Contact address: CUE, P.O. Box 1975, Erie, PA 16507-0975.

CompuClub

Contact: Gordon Lincoln, (814) 333-4513.
Supporting DOS. Meetings held the third Saturday of every month. A solid group of veteran DOS users dedicated to sharing their experience and knowledge. Contact address: 894 Alden St., Meadville, PA 16335.

RHODE ISLAND

South County Computer Users Group

Contact: Chuck Jacques, (401) 783-6469.
Supporting MS-DOS-based computers. Meetings held the third Tuesday of every month. Membership fee is $10. Catering to MS-DOS-based computers and assisting new owners with hardware- and software-related problems. Contact address: South County Computer Users Group, P.O. Box 493, Wakefield, RI 02880-0493.

SOUTH CAROLINA

Orangeburg Computer Club

Contact: Clarence B. Alston, (803) 534-6066.
Supporting IBMs and compatibles. Meetings held the fourth Tuesday of every month. Membership fee is $25. Includes novice and experienced users. Presentations and refreshments. Contact address: 751 Patriots Way, Orangeburg, SC 29115.

Sumter/Shaw Computer Club

Contact: Joe Carnes, (803) 773-7345.
Supporting MS-DOS. Meetings held the first Tuesday of every month. Membership fee is $25. Provides user support for IBM and compatible systems. BBS with shareware programs and information areas. Contact address: 109 Benton Dr., Sumter, SC 29150.

Southeast Sysops Association

Contact: Les Kirk, (803) 292-8602.
Supporting all brands and interests, including engineering support. Meetings held monthly, Saturdays, 2 p.m. Membership fee is $15. Designed to give sysops and users a collective voice against laws affecting BBS operations at the local, state, and federal levels. Also offers support to schools and PC user groups as well as the business community.

TriBBS Alliance

Contact: Patrick Driscoll, (803) 875-0847.
Supporting TriBBS BBS software, DOS. Meetings held Sundays at 2 p.m., monthly. Membership fee is $5. TriBBS user and sysop support located in Charleston, SC. DOS-based system support and advice. Dedicated to the modem-using community. Events to be planned. Fee applies only to BBSs that want to carry TribNET. Free to all general users. Contact address: P.O. Box 3241, Summerville, SC 29484-3241.

D.E.B.U.G.

Contact: Jennifer Credle, (803) 871-1268.
Supporting all platforms. Meetings held the second Sunday of every month, 1 p.m. For computer users of all levels/interests. A place to ask questions, offer suggestions, and just have a good time. Contact address: 4499 Kindlewood Dr., Ladson, SC 29456.

Hilton Head Island Computer Club

Contact: Harry Skevington, (803) 671-2250.
Supporting IBM and compatibles, DOS, Windows, financial, communications, WP. Meetings held the second Wednesday of every month, 7:30 p.m. Membership fee is $18. A group dedicated to educating members and the public on the use of computers and software. SIGs, software library, and national speakers help this nonprofit group to learn together. All ages and abilities welcome.

TENNESSEE

Modem User Pizza Thingy (MUPT)

Contact: Robb Fladry.
Supporting local-area BBSs and users. Meetings held monthly, Fridays or Saturdays. General get-together. Meet at Mr. Gatti's. Eat pizza, talk with other modem users. Only cost is what you eat! Call the X-Factor, (615) 358-3581. All times posted there. Contact address: 702 River Bend Dr., Clarksville, TN 37043-5359.

TEXAS

Alamo PC Organization Inc.

Contact: Vade Forrester, (210) 491-0036.
Supporting IBM Pcs/compatibles. Meetings held the second Thursday of every month. Membership fee is $25. 1,600-member group; 25 SIGs, award-winning monthly newsletter, magazine, four-node BBS with messages and files/QWK offline reader, shareware library, help committees, blank-disk sales. Plus lots of fun.

An Interview with John Walker, Founder, Autodesk

QUESTION

So do you think eventually the whole world will dissolve into communes or become one big federation?

WALKER

There are people who are not considered as crazy as I who believe that. I think we may find different ways of organizing things. The institutions we have were inevitable from the 1890s to 1950s perspective. The whole idea of representative government came out of the fact that there wasn't any physical way for everybody to vote on everything. We both know that with the Information Superhighway or whatever you call it, the technology will exist for everybody to vote on everything they care about. At least, theoretically. Look at corporations…the buzz-word is virtual corporation, downsizing, out-sourcing, and this is really the corporate equivalent of government saying at some level, why do we need to decide all these things centrally? Why do the people in Alabama have to follow exactly the same rules as the people in Oregon? People in those two states generally believe very different things.

Technology is changing more than the way we use computers. It is changing the incentive that drove us to build huge monolithic corporations, empires, and countries. Back when it a primary industry was the extraction of minerals, who was powerful might depend on who had more minerals, who had the best navy—those are things that economies of scale make very, very important. Today, those things have very little to do with economic power and perhaps political power, but rapid adoption of technology does. If you can imagine a world where there are maybe two and a quarter billion on the Internet, you can imagine many very different architectures for the way things are put together and the way things are divided.

Another thing that is happening is what the financial world is called disintermediation. We've all lived in a world where the media filters things. Most people get their news based on what the top three U.S. networks that are all headquartered within a couple of blocks within another in Manhattan choose to put on the TV news. Even mainstream political columnists—I would name Safire as an example—have now turned into the fact that there is this whole unmedia that has developed, where people get on America Online and they get on Delphi and they get on CompuServe and they talk to one another directly and there's nobody filtering it anymore. Of course, when nobody's filtering it, there's a lot more garbage. But I think we're developing the tools to cut through that. Just imagine, could the Cold War have existed if all Americans and Soviets could have talked to one another freely in the decades of the 1950s and 1960s? ■

Beware: Little Brother May Be Reading Your E-Mail

Computers have introduced a Brave New World of electronic communications. Never before has it been so quick and easy to send messages electronically…either across the hall or across the country. Delivery is almost instantaneous. Fees are miniscule compared with overnight letter services.

The dark side to this technology is that electronic mail opens the door to invasion of privacy—a right Americans have come to expect when they send a letter via the U.S. mail. If I were to open your mailbox, take a letter of yours, steam it open and read the contents, I'd be guilty of a Federal offense: tampering with the U.S. mail. But if I intercepted and opened your electronic mail, I might be violating a moral code…not necessarily a legal one. The courts are still deciding.
—Fred Davis ■

RGV Mid Valley C.A.T.S.
Contact: Doug Couch, (210) 412-5261.
Supporting all computers. Meetings held the third Tuesday of every month. Free support from Harlingen area sysops, local users, and some local computer shop owners/technicians. Meetings held at Computerworks on 77 S. Sunshine Strip. All are invited to attend. Software demos, etc.

DFW Modem Users Group
Contact: Garry Grosse, (214) 690-9295.
Supporting modems, telecommunications, BBSs, online community, shareware files. Meetings held the last Saturday of every month. Membership fee is $5. Discussions regarding modems, online services, BBSs, downloads, online community activities, BBS reviews, etc. Call our BBS at (214) 690-9295 or (817) 540-5565. Contact address: P.O. Box 867461, Plano, TX 75086.

CHUG
Contact: Allan Hall, (409) 291-6162.
Supporting BBSing/communications. Meetings held the second Sunday of every month. General computer knowledge, communications skills, and shareware trading. Lots of fun, tips, and help from sysops. Established primarily as support for local participating BBSs. Info by voice or from Pawn To King's Four BBS: (409) 291-3322.

South Texas Computer User Group
Contact: Mickey Whittle, (409) 244-3990.
Supporting IBM hardware and software. Meetings held the first Tuesday of every month. Membership fee is $20. Good discussions. Hardware and software reviews and presentations.

Coastal Area Users' Group
Contact: Rudy Reyes Jr., (512) 993-3522.
Supporting SIGs by/for the membership at its request. Meetings held the second Thursday of every month. Membership fee is $25. BBS, user journal, library, technical support, voice and onsite support. Contact address: Compu-Doc Computers, P.O. Box 270711, Corpus Christi, TX 78427-0711.

Houston Area League of PC Users (HAL-PC)
Contact: Ray Morris, President, HAL-PC, (713) 447-1616.
Supporting computer education through CEU units. Monthly meetings held generally the first Tuesday of every month. Membership fee is $25. Meetings with national presenters. Over 60 SIGs meeting week nights and weekends, offering support for beginning users, dBASE, DOS, Revelation, Windows, programming disciplines, stock market, WordPerfect, Word for Windows, communications, and offline readers. Over 10,000 members. Contact address: 1200 Post Oak #106, Houston, TX 77056.

NASA Area Macintosh Users
Contact: See address below.
Supporting active Macintosh users, all models. Meetings held the first Monday of every month. Membership fee is $20. Monthly newsletter, 24-hour BBS, public-domain/shareware library. Speakers from major hardware and software companies every month. Contact address: NASA Area Macintosh Users, 403 NASA Rd. One E. #384, Webster, TX 77598.

General User Group
Contact: Jerry Moon, (806) 274-6235.
Supporting all computers. Meetings held the first and third Saturday of every month.

AVNet
Contact: Jerry Gearhart, (817) 690-0891.
Supporting IBM/clones/Clipper and dBASE programming for business applications. Meetings held the second Tuesday of every month. Membership fee is $25. To promote the development and understanding of dBASE/Clipper/programming within business applications. Especially aviation management. BBS is online 24 hours, 7 days to support users' group: (817) 690-0890. National group network. Contact address: P.O. Box 10725, Killeen, TX 76543.

Red River PC Club

Contact: Jerry Simpson, (817) 851-1570.
Supporting DOS, Windows, GeoWorks, OS/2, more. Meetings held the third Thursday of every month, Region IX Educational Center. Membership fee is $25. We put on programs and presentations by various vendors and manufacturers. We also have many SIGs for those interested. Computer-skill group for new computer users. Two computer trade fairs each year. Contact address: P.O. Box 1611, Wichita Falls, TX 76307-1611.

Anderson County Computer Club

Contact: Chuck Yaunk, (903) 723-8096.
Supporting all computer types, modem users. Metings held the fourth Thursday of every month. Membership fee is $15. Interests of all types. Setting up several SIGs. Contact address: P.O. Box 124, Palestine, TX 75802-0124.

Marshall Computer User's Group

Contact: Roger Creasy, (903) 938-7157.
Supporting IBM-compatible computers, various software. Meetings held the third Tuesday of every month, 7 p.m. Membership fee is $25. Geared to all from novice to advanced. Group discusses and demonstrates new software/hardware and has a Q&A period at each meeting.

Control C

Contact: James Rich, (903) 872-8087.
Supporting IBM compatibles to Tandy. Meetings held the second and fourth Thursday of every month. No membership fee. Group of people trying to learn something. MS-DOS, word processors, games, programming. If it goes on a computer, we deal with it. Contact address: James Rich Computers, 117 Mall Dr., Corsicana, TX 75110.

Historical Computer Society

Contact: David A. Greelish.
Supporting all beloved "classic" computers. Meetings held by mail for now. Membership fee is $20. Establishing extensive database for use by members. Newsletter. Send SASE for an information packet. Contact address: 9550 Dyer #1106, El Paso, TX 79924.

Abilene Amiga Users Group

Contact: Kevin Palivec, (915) 690-0150.
Supporting Amiga computers. Meetings held the last Saturday of every month, 1 p.m. Membership fee is $12. Supports all Amiga users with information, software library for the full line of Amiga computers.

UTAH

Cedar Valley Computer Users

Contact: Ken Rhodes, (801) 586-6938.
Supporting IBM and clones. Meetings held the third Thursday of every month. Membership fee is $15. Computer users who like to meet for pizza and share information and ideas on computer-related topics. Contact address: 3870 N. Minersville Hwy. #22, Enoch, UT 84720.

ST Users Network (STUN)

Contact: James Hepworth, (801) 272-9203.
Supporting Atari ST/TT/Falcon computers. Meetings held the third Wednesday of every month. Membership fee is $20. Meeting every month to see new hardware/software for the Atari line of computers. Extensive disk library. Club-owned BBS. Bimonthly newsletter.

VERMONT

Champlain Valley PC Users

Contact: Ken Mahren, (802) 860-7198.
Supporting IBM PC compatibles. Meetings held the second Tuesday of every month. Membership fee is $15. New users to experienced. Different topics of interest each month. Membership includes monthly newsletter. Large group serving northern Vermont.

✌ Tipper Gore Virus—When you attempt to play any sound file, it pops up a warning window stating that some lyrics may be unsuitable for children.

VIRGINIA

Computer User's Group (CUG)

Contact: Jim Gandorf, (703) 768-4724.
Supporting New PC users and Doom enthusiasts. Meetings and game competitions scheduled by members. Membership fee is $15. Each month, members receive a newsletter and free shareware. Special help is available for new PC users. Modem and network game competitions run monthly. Limited adult access available. Free trial membership when you call. Contact address: CUG, 7221 Stover Ct., Alexandria, VA 22306.

Northern VA Apple Users Group

Contact: Dave Harvey, (703) 578-4621.
Supporting Apple II and clones. Meetings held the first Saturday of every month. Membership fee is $25. Monthly newsletter, public-domain library, paper library, and BBS with e-mail connections to Internet. Meet at Fairlington Community Center in Arlington.

Pentagon PC User Group

Contact: Fred Kolbrener, (703) 696-6060.
Supporting IBM PC/clones; Windows SIG. Meetings held the first Tuesday of every month, December membership meeting. Membership fee is $12. A user group of personnel who work in or have access to the Pentagon. Contact address: P.O. Box 47046, Washington, DC 20050-7046.

Macintosh User Group of Roanoke

Contact: Hal Welch, treasurer, (703) 387-1647.
Supporting Macintosh. Meetings held the second Thursday of every month. Membership fee is $20. An informal group of professionals, teachers, and hobbyists. Contact address: 722 Paragon Ave., Salem, VA 24153.

Troglobytes

Contact: Harry Winter, (804) 464-0943.
Supporting TRS-80 Models I/II/III/4/12/16/6000 and MS-DOS. Meetings held the third Thursday of every month. No membership fee. Shareware and public-domain exchange; demos of word processing, databases, spreadsheets, telecommunications, utilities, etc.; beginners welcome. Contact address: Troglobytes, P.O. Box 5021, Virginia Beach, VA 23455-0021.

Internet for the Mac

For years the Internet was a barren, elitist, members-only camp for techno-geeks, computer hackers, and university researchers. Now, thanks to the amazing work of this strange breed of computer scientist, the Internet is becoming a reality for the average user. The recent introduction of graphical interfaces for the legendary, yet cryptic, Internet tools allows any user to tap into the power of the Internet.

Now that anyone can use the Internet, how do you access it? What you need is a new type of utility company—an Internet provider. Such services are smaller in reach and range than the large commercial services in our main roundup, but they could be just the service you need.

An Internet provider is a company that maintains hardware and software to connect a network of computers to the Internet. Its role is to ensure that the end user—you, a company, a university, or even other Internet providers—has a reliable connection to the Internet.Because it is relatively easy to become an Internet provider, differentiating between large and small providers is not obvious.

Armed with a few telephone lines and modems, a PC with networking hardware and software, and a connection to the Internet, anyone can become an Internet provider. Many have done just that.

Whether it's large or small, the absolute minimum you should expect from your Internet provider is that your connection to the Internet is a phone call away. Beyond supplying the physical link to the Internet, some Internet providers offer different connection options: They have value-added services that may be what you're looking for.

Best of the Breed

The most important qualities of an Internet provider are the speed and reliability of the link, any value-added services (help menus, tutorials, GUIs), pricing, and accessibility. All the providers reviewed here offer fast and reliable links to the Internet, and most of them have good value-added services that facilitate access. Thus, pricing and accessibility most likely will be the influential factors in your selection.

Expect to pay an average monthly fee of $17.50 for your connection, plus $3.00 per hour of connect time. Accessibility also affects pricing. If your Internet provider cannot be reached via a local phone call, you may end up

incurring long-distance surcharges. To address this problem many providers use third-party network-access companies (such as SprintNet and CompuServe's Packet Network) to offer cost-effective access options.

Although good technical support will be most important to businesses and individuals who absolutely depend on their Internet connectivity, it is good to know there is a helping hand a phone call or an e-mail away. All the providers here offer good technical support, but the best are AlterNet and NETCOM.

Where Online Services Fit

Although online services have done a good job of bringing Internet access to the average computer user, many have done a bad job of implementing their Internet-access tools. It is probably the competitive nature of the business that has caused online services to stampede to have a presence on the Internet. Unfortunately, many have done so by stampeding their own customers.

Online-service customers get frustrated by the overwhelming amount of information that is presented to them, and Internet users get frustrated by online service customers's improper use of News. This is a transition that both sides will go through for some time.

Shell-Account Providers

Of all the Internet connectivity options, shell accounts are the simplest but the least user-friendly. You can access your shell account from any type of terminal, however, including public ones and PCs.

Unless the Internet provider offers help menus, you will need to learn Unix commands to use shell accounts and run Internet tools. If you're not a moderately sophisticated computer user, consider other connectivity options to spare yourself a lot of frustration.

All Internet providers we reviewed offer online manuals for helping you figure out how to use their systems to access the Internet. Some have innovative help systems or online tours to show you how to use the available system tools and resources. The easiest systems to use are those that offer robust help menus.—Sean Gonzalez ■

Virginia BBS Association

Contact: Jim Deal, (804) 496-0156.
Supporting modem users. Meetings held the first Tuesday of every month, 7 p.m. Membership fee is $5. A nonprofit organization formed to advocate for modem users. Contact address: P.O. Box 8306, Virginia Beach, VA 23464.

Tidewater Amiga Users Group (TAUG)

Contact: Tidewater Amiga Users Group, (804) 471-4642.
Supporting Amiga and all video work, image generation, and fun. Meetings held the first and third Tuesday of every month. To promote and expand the Amiga, for all ages and experience levels. Image generation, video and multimedia production and experimentation. A1000, A2000, A3000, A4000 and the Video Toaster for starters. If you want to learn the Amiga, stop here.

Tidewater Unix Users Group (TWUUG)

Contact: Buddy Cook, (804) 488-9310.
Supporting Unix/Linux, Usenet news, Internet. Meetings held the first Tuesday of every month, 7:30 p.m. Sharing of Unix tips and software. Group has Internet connection with Usenet news and e-mail. Linux splinter group.

Mid-Atlantic OS/2 User Group

Contact: Steven Grim, (804) 422-6692.
Supporting OS/2 and applications. Meetings held the third Saturday of every month, 10 a.m. at Egghead Software. Membership fee is $20. New newsletter coming online. New BBS for the user group for latest info and some shareware. Everyone interested is invited to attend. Contact address: Mid-Atlantic OS/2 User Group, 1478 Petite Ct., Virginia Beach, VA 23451-6013.

WASHINGTON

SPSCUG

Contact: Thomas Hood, (206) 866-3623.
Supporting C/C++ and related programming and system-engineering interests. Meetings held monthly. A group of programmers who wish to share resources. Contact address: 3138 Overhulse Rd. N.W., Suite 59, Olympia, WA 98502.

Computer Users of Grant County

Contact: Computer Users of Grant County, (509) 762-1127.
Supporting all IBMs and compatibles, BBSs. Meetings held every other Friday, 8 p.m. Have fun BSing about BBSs and computers in general. We offer nationwide support for anyone who needs help free. Call The Free BBS online (509-762-1129). Contact address: P.O. Box 1778, Moses Lake, WA 98837-1778.

WEST VIRGINIA

Associate Networks

Contact: Travis King, (304) 636-5493.
Supporting all PCs. Meetings held yearly. Membership fee is $10. Provides support to all local-area member sysops. Helps new users get online. Contact address: Rte. 1, Box 63, Montrose, WV 26283.

Personal Computer-Huntington Users Group

Contact: Edward H. King, (304) 736-7031.
Supporting IBM and clones. Meetings held the third Thursday of every month. Membership fee is $15. Contact address: P.O. Box 2173, Huntington, WV 25722-2173.

WYOMING

SMUG

Contact: Ray Kopczynski, (307) 672-5902.
Supporting IBM PCs and clones. Meetings held the third Tuesday of every month, September through May. Membership fee is $15. 400+ members. Large user group in northern Rocky Mtn. region. Monthly newsletter. 2,700-disk shareware library for members. Scholarship at local college. Our goal is to educate and help newer users of PC systems.

PUERTO RICO

EDP Marques Del Pepino

Contact: Leonardo Perez, (809) 896-0262.
Supporting Spanish shareware programming with art, music, etc. Meetings held as posted in the EDP college of San Sebastian, Puerto Rico. New and still undergoing many changes. Put together by interested students who wish to attend special need for Spanish-oriented shareware programs. Charges may be added later as the group forms. Good place to get advice.

Canada

ALBERTA

Northern Alberta OS/2

Contact: Robert Goshko, (403) 474-4557.
Supporting OS/2. Meetings held the first Wednesday of every month. Membership fee is $25. Established in the interest of promoting OS/2, and being a general support group for OS/2 users. Currently working toward being an IBM-recognized support group. Contact address: 3408-105 Ave., Edmonton, AL T5W 0B4.

MANITOBA

Winnipeg PC User Group

Contact: Hartley Macklin, (204) 488-9796.
Supporting Intel-based (MS-DOS). Meetings held the third Thursday of every month. Membership fee is $45. 1,000+ members. Great meetings. Six-line BBS. 32-page monthly newsletter. Contact address: P.O. Box 3149, Winnipeg, MB R3J 1T1.

Muddy Waters Computer Society Inc.

Contact: Jay Davidow, (204) 888-2586.
Supporting multiplatform. Meetings held the last Tuesday of every month, September through June. We support the user rather than just the platform. Monthly newsletter. Contact address: 47 Gomez St., Winnipeg, MB R3J 1T1.

NEW BRUNSWICK

The Moncton Users Group

Contact: Robert Manship or Dave Quinn, (506) 383-9664.
Supporting C-64 and IBM users, all others welcome. Meetings held the first Tuesday of every month. Membership fee is $20. Established in 1983. Expanded to MS-DOS-based machines, along with Amiga; Amiga users now have their own group. All welcome.

SASKATCHEWAN

Commodore Users Group of Saskatchewan

Contact: Tristan Miller, (306) 584-1736.
Supporting Commodore 8-bit computers. Meetings held the first Wednesday of every month. Membership fee is $15. Demonstrations, software and programming demos at every meeting. We publish a large newsletter every month. Mail members welcome.

Switzerland

Informatik Club der Telekurs

Contact: Mustafa Yurtbil, (411) 279-3308.
Supporting IBM and compatibles, DOS, Windows, and Unix. No membership fee. We look forward to making contact with other clubs and/or individuals in the world (mainly North America). Contact address: Informatik Club der Telekurs, Hardturmstrasse 201, 8005 Zurich.

On the Internet

With the growth of electronic messaging and the information highway, typing skills will replace facial expressions as a means of identifying people, characteristics and emotions. We will ultimately be able to separate what we are from what we say, and spelling accuracy will be important once again. —Richard K. Oppenheim ■

Sprint Virus—Periodically runs sound file of a pin dropping.